A CYCLOPÆDIC

DICTIONARY

OF MUSIC

(Curwen's Edition, 5620).

COMPRISING 14,000 MUSICAL TERMS AND PHRASES
6,000 BIOGRAPHICAL NOTICES OF MUSICIANS
AND 500 ARTICLES ON MUSICAL TOPICS

WITH AN APPENDIX

Containing an English-Italian Vocabulary, a List of Notable
Quotations, Hints on Italian and German Pronunciation, Notes
on Russian Musical Terms, a List of Spanish Musical Terms, a
Musical Bibliography, and Several Useful Charts and Tables.

By

RALPH DUNSTAN

Mus.Doc. Cantab., L. Mus.T.C.L., &c.
Prof. of Music, Westminster and Southlands Colleges.

SECOND EDITION
With 4,000 Additional References.

British Library Cataloguing-in-Publication Data
A catalogue record for this book is available from
the British Library

A Short History of Musical Notation

Musical Notation is any system used to visually represent aurally perceived music through the use of written symbols – including ancient or modern musical symbols. Although many ancient cultures used symbols to represent melodies, none of these systems are nearly as comprehensive as written language, limiting knowledge of ancient music to a few fragments. Although it has incredibly old roots, comprehensive music notation only began to be developed in Europe in the **Middle Ages** but has since been adapted to many kinds of music worldwide.

The earliest form of musical notation can be found in a cuneiform tablet that was created at Nippur, in today's Iraq around 2000 BC. The tablet represents fragmentary instructions for performing music, that the music was composed in harmonies of thirds, and that it was written in a diatonic scale. A tablet from about 1250 BC shows a more developed form of notation, and though the interpretation of the system is still controversial, it is clear that the notation indicates the names of strings on a lyre. Although fragmentary, these tablets represent the earliest notated melodies found anywhere in the world.

The ancient Greeks used musical notation from at least the sixth century BC until approximately the fourth century AD, and several complete compositions and fragments using this notation survive. This system consisted of symbols placed above text syllables, and the Delphic Hyms, dated to the second century BC use this notation – but are not completely preserved. Such methods appear to have fallen out of use around the time of the Decline of the Roman Empire. The Byzantine Empire was the other major civilisation to use musical notation, and theirs was remarkably similar to subsequent Western notation, in that it was ordered left to right, and separated into measures. The main difference is that the Byzantine notation symbols were *differential* rather than absolute, i.e. they indicate pitch *change* (rise or fall), and the musician had to deduce correctly, from the score and the note they were singing, which note came next.

In early Europe, a rough form of notation for remembering Gregorian chants was established, but the problem with this system was that it only showed melodic contours – and consequently the music could not be read by someone who did not know the tune. To address the issue of exact pitch, a staff was introduced consisting originally of a single horizontal line, but this was progressively extended until a system of four parallel, horizontal lines was standardized. This is traditionally attributed to **Guido of Arezzo**, who set out his thoughts on the changes in his first musical treatise, *Micrologus* (1026). The modern five-line staff was first adopted in France and became almost universal by the sixteenth century (although the use of staves with other numbers of lines was still widespread well into the seventeenth century).

As is evident from this incredibly short and potted history, musical notation has differed vastly over time – but has been adopted all over the globe. The modern musical notation we use today originated in European classical music, but is now used by musicians of many different genres throughout the world. The system, like that developed in France uses a five-line staff, and pitch is shown by placement of **notes** on the staff (sometimes modified by **accidentals**), and duration is shown with different **note values** and additional symbols such as **dots** and **ties**. There are also some specialised notation conventions, for example for percussion instruments or chord charts which contain little or no melodic information at all but provide detailed harmonic and rhythmic information, using slash notation and rhythmic notation. This is the most common kind of written music used by professional session musicians playing **jazz** or other forms of **popular music** and is intended primarily for the **rhythm section** (usually containing **piano, guitar, bass** and **drums**). We hope the reader is inspired by this book to find out more about this fascinating subject.

Preface to the First Edition.

THIS Dictionary, the only work of its kind published in England, has occupied nearly four years in preparation, and embodies the results of over thirty years' study and experience.

It aims at providing, in compact form, a reliable, comprehensive, and up-to-date compendium of musical information—a condensed musical library for the musician of limited means, and for the general reader. It is also hoped that it will prove a valuable supplement to more expensive works of reference.

"Everything about something, and something about everything" was the motto adopted by the author and publishers. Thus, the collection of Musical Terms and Phrases in this volume (nearly 14,000) is, as far as it is possible to discover, the most complete and accurate yet published; while the 6,000 Biographical Notices, the numerous short Articles, the Charts and Tables, and the miscellaneous items of musical interest cover an unusually wide field, and embrace every variety of musical topic.

The compiler of a work of this nature must, of necessity, make free use of the materials accumulated by others; and the author begs to acknowledge his indebtedness to the following standard treatises and text-books :—

Martini's *Storia della Musica.*
Burney's *History of Music.*
Hawkins' *History of Music.*
Sainsbury's *Dictionary of Musicians* (1824).
Naumann's *History of Music.*
Ricordi's *Dizinario dei Musicisti.*
Grove's *Dictionary of Music and Musicians* (1st and 2nd editions).
Riemann's *Dictionary of Music* (German and English editions).
Rockstro's *History of Music.*
Mathew's *History of Music.*
Davey's *History of English Music.*
Bonavia Hunt's *History of Music.*
Brown's *Biographical Dictionary of Musicians.*
Stratton and Brown's *British Musical Biography.*
Parry's *Great Composers.*
Lavignac's *Music and Musicians.*
Ella's *Musical Sketches.*
Goodworth's *Musicians of all Times.*
Warriner's *Gallery of British Musicians.*
Moore's *Encyclopædia of Music.*
The *Dictionary of National Biography.*
Butler's *Principles of Musick.*
Rousseau's *Musical Dictionary.*
Grassineau's *Musical Dictionary.*
Busby's *Dictionary of Music.*
A. Galli's *Teoria della Musica.*
Hamilton's *Dictionary of Musical Terms.*
Stainer and Barrett's *Dictionary of Musical Terms.*
Niecks' *Dictionary of Musical Terms.*
Hughes' *Musical Guide.*
Elson's *Music Dictionary.*

Briggs' *Elements of Plain Song.*
Helmholtz' *Sensations of Tone.*
Rameau's *Principles of Composition.*
G. Weber's *Musical Composition.*
Chevé's *Theory of Music.*
Gevaert's *Instrumentation and Orchestration.*
Berlioz's *Instrumentation.*
Prout's *Instrumentation, Harmony, Counterpoint,* etc.
Hopkins and Rimbault's *The Organ.*
Hinton's *Organ Construction.*
Ellis' *Pronunciation for Singers.*
Ellis' *Musical Scales of all Nations.*
Lussy's *Expression.*
Christiani's *Expression in Pianoforte Playing.*
David and Lussy's *Histoire de la Notation Musicale.*
Cherubini's *Counterpoint and Fugue.*
Richter's *Counterpoint and Fugue.*
Albrechtsberger's *Theoretical Works.*
Hiles' *Catechism of Harmony.*
Macfarren's *Harmony, Lectures on Harmony, Musical History,* etc.
Bussler-Cornell's *Musical Form.*
Stainer's *Composition.*
Callcott's *Grammar of Music.*
Mathews' *Wild Birds and their Music.*
Sir F. Bridge's *Shakespeare Birthday Book of Musicians.*
The *Encyclopædia Britannica.*
Murray's *Oxford Dictionary.*
The *Century Dictionary.*
Lloyd's *Encyclopædic Dictionary.*
Liddell and Scott's *Greek Lexicon.*
Smith's *Latin-English Dictionary.*
Cassell's *German Dictionary.*
Muret-Sander's *German Wörterbuch.*
Littré's *French Dictionary.*
Rosa's *Italian-Latin-English Dictionary.*
Baretti's *Italian Dictionary.*

And, especially, those excellent and carefully-edited books, Dr. Th. Baker's *Dictionary of Musical Terms* and *Biographical Dictionary of Musicians,* and Wotton's *Dictionary of Foreign Musical Terms.*

Terms and expressions peculiar to the Tonic Sol-fa system have been taken from Curwen's *Musical Theory;* and biographical notices of the chief writers of Hymns have been selected from Julian's *Hymnology* and other reliable sources. Many interesting details have also been gathered from the *Musical Times, Musical Herald, Musical News, Musical World,* etc., and from Daily Papers, Musical Programmes, and Contemporary Magazines; while some hundreds of musical terms and phrases which now appear for the first time in a Musical Dictionary have been collected from the works of Beethoven, Chopin, Schumann, Liszt, and numerous other composers.

About 500 articles of varying length have been specially written for this work. Many of these, though necessarily condensed in treatment, are complete and adequate expositions of the subjects discussed; while others are suggestive of the lines of study necessary for their more detailed investigation. They include *Accent, Accompaniment, Acoustics, Anthem, Appoggiatura, Aria, Arpeggio, Birthdays of Musicians, Cadence, Canon, Chant, Chronology of Music, Clef, Counterpoint, Criticism, Diatonic, Dictionaries of Music, Dynamics, Egyptian Music, English Music, Enharmonic, Expression, False Relation, Consecutive Fifths, Figure,*

Figured Bass, Fixed Do, Flute, Form, French Music, Fugue, Fundamental Discords, German Music, Greek Music, Harmony, Histories of Music, Hymn, Imitation, Instrument, Interval, Inversion, Irish Music, Italian Music, Japanese Music, Jewish Music, Key, Leitmotiv, Melody, Metrical Form, Mode, Modulation, Music, Notation, Opera, Oratorio, Orchestra, Organ, Ornaments, Overture, Phrasing, Pianoforte, Pronunciation of 250 Musicians' Names, Recitative, Rondo, Russian Music, Scale, Score, Sequence, Shake, Signature, Signs and Symbols, Sonata, Song, Suite, Suspension, Syncopation, Temperament, Thematic Development, Time, Tonality, Tonic Sol-fa, Turn, Unison, Valve, Variation, Viol, Violin, Voice, Welsh Music, and *Word-painting.*

The curious reader, or musical antiquarian, will also find the results of explorations into various " nooks and corners " under such headings as *Bird Music, Colour and Music, Imitative Music, Music of Insects, Key-Colour, Melody in Speech, Miraculous Effects of Music, Nature's Music, Shivaree,* etc.

Rigid economy of space, the free use of small type, and the grouping of terms of analogous meaning, have enabled the publishers to offer the work at a price which brings it within the reach of every student of music, while retaining everything essential to make it complete and authoritative.

The Musical Terms and Phrases have been selected chiefly from the English, Italian, French, and German languages, but numerous important Greek, Latin, Spanish, Danish, and other terms are also given. With the exception of French words, the principal accents of all foreign words are indicated, and the titles of important foreign theoretical works are generally rendered in English.

The author begs to acknowledge his great indebtedness to the well-known historian and critic, HENRY DAVEY, Esq., of Brighton, who has revised the whole of the proof-sheets, and suggested numerous valuable corrections and emendations, which have been incorporated in this volume. Thanks are also due to FRAU F. BERTIN, late of Vienna, and HERR FELIX BERTIN, for the correct accentuation and varied shades of meaning of many of the German words and phrases ; to A. BARRIBALL, Esq., B.A., M.Ph.S., vice-Principal and Professor of Languages, Westminster Training College, and LEIGH SMITH Esq., M.A., Fellow of Durham University, for much kindly help in the definition of Greek, Latin, and French terms ; to J. SPENCER CURWEN, Esq., who has throughout taken a keen interest in the preparation of this work, and has freely placed the whole of his extensive reference library at the author's disposal ; and to a large number of contemporary musicians who have generously supplied dates and details of their musical career.

Although the greatest care has been taken to ensure accuracy, and all the proofs have been carefully revised at least a dozen times, it is too much to hope that in a work of this kind (involving so many thousands of dates,* references, and quotations) there are no typographical or other errors. The author and publishers would be grateful for the correction of any slips which the reader may discover.

RALPH DUNSTAN.

August, 1908.

---

* Where authorities differ as to dates, or other particulars, the most probable statements have been selected.

Preface to the Second Edition.

THE rapid sale of the First Edition of this Dictionary is a gratifying proof of the need
for such a work. A book of this kind, covering so much ground and embodying so
many new features, must be to some extent tentative and experimental ; and it is not until
it has passed through the " fierce fires of criticism " and been carefully tested by competent
authorities that it is possible to ascertain and determine its proper limits and proportions,
and to amend, modify, and extend it to the best advantage.

In the Second Edition, over 1,500 fresh entries have been incorporated into the body
of the work, including about 750 Biographical Notices of contemporary musicians, and
numerous Musical Terms used by present-day composers. Among the articles amended,
lengthened, or specially written for this edition, are *Ornamental Appoggiatura (Verzierende
Vorschlag), Blind Octaves, Broken Pedal, Bye-tone, Cadence, Chromatic Harp, Chronology,
Congregational Singing, Disguised Intervals, Gramophone, Harmonic, Histories of Music,
Key, Lancashire Sol-fa, Mass, Military Band, Musical Periodicals, Mute, Objective Music,
Opera, Organ Builders in England, Peregrine Tone, Pitch, Rag-time, Scottish Music, Theory
of the Sharpest Note, Subjective Music, Te Deum Laudamus, Tuning of Bells,* and the *Supplementary List of German Technical Terms ;* while the Appendix has been extended by
the addition of *The Tonic Sol-fa Modulator, Charts of Note Names, Key Names,* etc., a short
article on the *Pronunciation of Latin, Notes on Russian Musical Terms* (with a *Key to the
four Russian Alphabets*), a list of 600 *Spanish Musical Terms,* a *Bibliography of* 1,250 *Works
on Music,* together with 125 *Terms and Phrases* included in the Addenda. In all, about
4,000 new references have been added.

The Author is greatly indebted to the numerous kind and disinterested friends who
have generously assisted him in the preparation of the Second Edition ; especially to
DR. HENRY FISHER, of Blackpool, for several emendations of Definitions of Musical Terms,
a list of Composers' *noms-de-plume,* etc. ; to DR. W. H. GRATTAN FLOOD, of Enniscorthy,
Ireland, for contributions concerning Irish Music and Musicians, Catholic Music, etc., and
for numerous historico-critical notes ; to CLEMENT A. HARRIS, Esq., of Ellangowan, for
Biographical details of noteworthy Yorkshire musicians ; to E. BRUNDRIT MEADOWS,
Esq., of Poulton-le-Fylde, Lancs., for much accurate information regarding Orchestral
Instruments, modern Organ Stops, Musical Terms found in modern full scores, etc. ;
to S. NICHOLL, Esq., of Halifax, and Thornton (Bradford), for a thorough revision of
Dates, Biographical Notices of a large number of living British Composers, and valuable
suggestions on other topics ; to DR. CHAS. WM. PEARCE, Director of Examinations, Trinity
College, London, for authoritative references on Organ Matters, Church Music, Plain
Song, Theory, Harmony, Counterpoint, etc., and for much help in preparing the List of
British Organ Builders, the Musical Bibliography (in the Appendix), and other articles ;
to W. R. PHILLIPS, Esq., of London, for kindly placing the whole of his MS. Dictionary
of Sol-fa Musical Terms at the author's disposal ; to PROF. EBENEZER PROUT, B.A.,
Mus.Doc., etc., for a careful and scholarly revision of the Notes on Russian Musical Terms
(in the Appendix) ; to DONALD ROSS, Esq., of Edinburgh, for the revised article on Scottish
Music, and for details concerning Scottish Musicians ; and to W. W. STARMER, Esq.,
of Tunbridge Wells, the well-known authority on Carillons, Bells, and Bell-Ringing, for
correcting all the definitions and articles relating to these subjects, for the article on the
Tuning of Bells, and for several other important contributions and suggestions.

Thanks to these able and experienced authorities, every department of the Dictionary
has been revised with an accuracy and completeness which would otherwise have been
impossible ; while those details of expert knowledge have been added which so considerably enhance the value of a work of reference.

Helpful advice, assistance, and information have also been received from MADAME SZIGETI; J. PERCY BAKER, Esq., Editor, *Musical News;* THOS. J. CRAWFORD, Esq., Mus.B., Organist, St. Michael's, Chester Square; DR. W. H. CUMMINGS, F.S.A., Principal of the Guildhall School of Music; DR. THOS. KEIGHLEY, of Manchester; JAMES L. KEITH, Esq., of West Hampstead; FRANK KIDSON, Esq., of Leeds; DR. JAS. LYON, of Liverpool; DR. CHAS. D. MACLEAN, English Editor of the Journal of the International Musical Society; WILSON MANHIRE, Esq., A.R.C.M., L.R.A.M.; DR. M. J. MONK, Organist of Truro Cathedral; ERNEST NEWMAN, Esq., of King's Norton; and Dr. CHAS. VINCENT. Thanks are also due to Messrs. BREITKOPF AND HÄRTEL for kindly placing their stock of Russian Music at the author's disposal when preparing the Notes on Russian Musical Terms.

The Author and Publishers are grateful for the many appreciative criticisms of the First Edition which have appeared in the Press, and for the numerous thoughtful suggestions forwarded by correspondents. Every suggestion has been carefully considered, and where possible acted upon; in some cases, however, the required information has not been obtainable, while in others the necessary matter could not be introduced without materially increasing the size and cost of the work.

In connection with the additional Musical Terms and References, several standard Russian, Spanish, French, and German Dictionaries have been consulted, together with a number of recently-published musical works, including Wedgwood's *Dictionary of Organ Stops,* and Fowles' *Studies in Musical Graces.*

The whole of the German Terms and Phrases have been carefully revised, and about 600 additional ones inserted in their proper alphabetical order.

It remains to add that Messrs. Curwen and Sons have spared no pains in the endeavour to make this edition as complete and useful as possible. The whole of the type has been re-set or carried on, and the book has been extended by 43 pages.

It is hoped that the Dictionary in its revised form will prove of increased value as a Work of General Musical Reference.

MAY, 1909.   RALPH DUNSTAN.

CONTENTS.

CYCLOPÆDIC MUSICAL DICTIONARY.

[*E.*, English; *I.*, Italian; *G.*, German; *F.*, French; *L.*, Latin; *Gk.*, Greek; *S.*, Spanish; *Cons.*, Conservatoire; *Pf.*, Pianoforte; *Org.*, Organ; *Vn.*, Violin; *Inst.*, Instrument; *Prof.*, Professor; *Orch.*, Orchestra; *b.*, born; *d.*, died.]

A

A (1) The 6th note of the major scale of C.

(2) The key-note, or tonic, of the standard minor scale (A minor); and of the major scale requiring three sharps (A major).

(3) The note sounded by the oboe, organ, or piano to which the instruments of a band or orchestra are tuned.

The exact pitch of this "tuning" note depends upon the standard used:—

French "Diapason Normal" = 435 vibrations per second.
Society of Arts' pitch = 440 vibrations per second.
"Concert" pitch (so-called) = about 455 vibrations per second. (See *Acoustics*.)
"New Philharmonic" = 439.

(4) The *Proslambanomenos* of the Greeks.

(5) The first note of the Hypo-Dorian and Eolian Church modes. (See **Modes**.)

(6) The name given to the second string of the violin, and to the first string of the viola and violoncello.

(7) In organ nomenclature:

(8) In Tonic Sol-fa nomenclature of absolute pitch:

(9) The "letter"-name of LAH in the keys of C major and A minor.

A (*pron.* AA *or* AH). The standard vowel-sound used in voice-production.

"A" position. A chord which has its root for the bass or lowest note of the harmony; the "*b*" position has the 3rd of the chord in the bass; the "*c*" position the 5th, &c.:

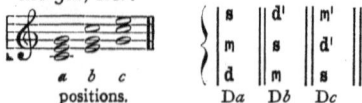

a   b   c
positions.

In Tonic Sol-fa, and in the Text-books issued by Trinity College, London, the "*a*" position is understood if no small letter follows the capital letter standing for the name of the chord.

A (*I.*). At, in, by, for, with, in the style of, &c.; as *a tempo*, in time; *a prima vista*, at first sight. When followed by a figure, it is sometimes used to indicate the number of voices or parts; as *canon a 3*, a canon for three voices.

A (*F.*). At, in, by, for, &c.; as *à deux mains*, for two hands.

AARON (or **ARON**), **Pietro.** Celebrated Florentine contrapuntist and writer on music; *b.* about 1480; *d.* before 1545. Chief work, *Il Toscanello della Musica*.

Ab (*G.*). "Off" (as an organ stop).

Ab'acus (*L.*). An ancient instrument for dividing the intervals of the octave.

A balla'ta (*I.*). (1) In the style of a ballad. (2) A song with a chorus at the end of each verse. Thus, "Rule, Britannia" is a song *a ballata*. (3) A vocal piece that may be danced to.

A battu'ta (*I.*). By the beat; *i.e.*, in strict time. Used after any break in the time, such as a *Recitative*, *Cadenza*, or *ad lib.*

Abbachia'to (*I.*). In a dejected style.

Abbada're (*I.*). Take care.

Abbandonamen'te (*I.*), **Abandon** (*F.*).
Abbando'ne (*I.*), or **Con abbando'no** (*I.*). With self-abandonment; unrestrainedly; wildly.

Abbandona're (*I.*). To quit, to leave.

Abbassamen'to (*I.*). A falling or lowering. *Abbassamen'to di ma'no*, a lowering of the hand; or the passing of one hand over or under the other. *Abbassamen'to di vo'ce*, a lowering of the voice.

Abbassan'do (*I.*). *Diminuendo* (*q.v.*).

Abbatimen'to (*I.*). The down-beat.

Abbella're (*I.*).
Abbelli're (*I.*). To embellish; to overload with ornament.

Abbellimen'ti (*I.*). Ornaments, embellishments; as the traditional florid passages in Allegri's *Miserere*.

2

Abbellitu′ra *(I.)*. Ornament, embellishment.

Ab′betont *(G.)*. With a *final* accent.

ABBEY, John. A famous organ-builder; *b.* Northamptonshire, 1785; *d.* Versailles, 1859. Built several celebrated organs in France, and initiated the modern French School of Organ-building.

Abbla′sen *(G.)*. To blow (a trumpet, horn, &c.).

ABBOTT, Bessie (Pickens). American Soprano; *début*, Paris Opera, 1902.

ABBOTT, Thomas M. Accomplished violinist. *B.* Bilston, Staffordshire, 1843.

Abbrevia′re *(I.)*. To abbreviate.

Abbrevia′tions *(E.)*, **Abbreviatu′re** *(I.)*, **Abbreviatu′ren** *(G.)*, **Abbrevia′zio′ni** *(I.)*.

(1) Abbreviations of words.
The meaning of each word is given in its proper place.

A.   *Altus* or *Alto.*
A.   *Associate;* as A.R.A.M.
Accel.   *Accelerando.*
Acct., Accomp.   *Accompaniment.*
Adgo. *or* Ado.   *Adagio.*
Ad lib.   *Ad libitum.*
Aevia.   *Alleluia.*
Affetto.   *Affettuoso.*
Affretto.   *Affrettando.*
Allo.   *Allegro.*
All′ ott.   } *All′ ottava.*
All′ 8va
Al seg.   *Al segno.*
Andno.   *Andantino.*
And.   *Andante.*
Animo.   *Animato.*
Arc.   *Arcato,* or *Coll′ arco.*
Arpo.   *Arpeggio.*
A t., *or* A temp.   *A tempo.*
Aug.   *By augmentation.*
B.   *Bass Voice. Contra-basso.*
Bn.   *Bassoon.*
B.C., *or* Bass. cont.   *Basso continuo.*
Bl.   *Bläser.*
Br.   *Bratschen.*
Brill.   *Brillante.*
C. a.   *Coll′ arco.*
Cad.   *Cadenza.*
Cal.   *Calando.*
Calm.   *Calmato.*
Can.   *Cantoris.*
Cant.   *Canto,* or *Cantabile.*
Cantuar.   *Canterbury.*
Cantab.   { *Cantabile. Cambridge.*
C.B.   { *Col Basso,* or *Contra Basso.*
Cb.   *Contrabässe.*
C.D.   *Colla destra.*
Cello.   *Violoncello.*
Cemb.   *Cembalo.*
C.F.   *Canto Fermo. Cantus Firmus.*
Ch.   *Choir Organ.*
Chal.   *Chalumeau.*
Cl. or Clar. or   } *Clarinet.*
Clartto.   *Clarinetto.*

Claro.   *Clarino.*
C.M.   *Choirmaster. Common Metre.*
Col C.   *Col Canto.*
Coll′ otta.   } *Coll′ ottava.*
C. 8va.
Col. Vo., C.V., or C. Voc.   *Colla Voce.*
Con. esp.   *Con espressione.*
Cont.   *Contano.*
Cor.   *Cornet, Corno, Corni.*
C.P.   *Colla Parte.*
Cres.   )
Cresc.   } *Crescendo.*
Creso.   )
C.S.   *Colla sinistra.*
C.S. or Co. So.   *Come sopra.*
Co. 1mo.   *Canto Primo.*
Cto.   *Concerto.*
D.   *Destra, droite.* *(Right Hand.)*
D.C.   *Da Capo.*
Dec.   *Decani.*
Decres., Decresc.   *Decrescendo.*
Delic.   *Delicatamente.*
Dest.   *Destra.*
Diap.   *Diapasons.*
Dim.   *Diminuendo,* or *By diminution.*
Div.   *Divisi.*
Dol.   *Dolce.*
Dolcis.   *Dolcissimo.*
Dopp. Ped.   *Doppio Pedale.*
D.S.   *Dal Segno.*
Dunelm.   *Durham.*
Esp. or Espress.   *Espressivo.*
F.   *Fine.*
F.   *Fellow,* as F.R.C.O.
f or For.   *Forte.*
Fag.   *Fagotto.*
Falset.   *Falsetto.*
ff, or *fff.*   *Fortissimo.*
Fl.   *Flute (Flauto).*
F.O.   } *Full Organ.*
F. Org.
fz. or forz.   *Forzato (Forzando).*
G.   *Gauche.*
Ged.   *Gedämpft.*
Geth.   *Getheilt.*
G. Org., G.O. or Gt.   *Great Organ.*
G.P.   (See *Pause.*)
Grando.   *Grandioso.*
Grazo.   *Grazioso.*
Gr.   *Grand.*
G.S.M.   *Guildhall School of Music.*
Hauptw., Hptw., or Hk.   *Hauptwerk.*
Haut.   *Hautboy (Hautbois).*
H.C.   *Haute-contre.*
Hlzbl.   *Holzbläser.*
Hr. or Hrn.   *Hörner.*
Intro.   *Introduction.*
Inv.   *Inversion.*
I.S.C.   *Incorporated Staff Sight-Singing College.*
I.S.M.   *Incorporated Society of Musicians.*
K.F.   *Kleine Flöte.*
L.   *Left.*
L.   *Licentiate:* as *L.T.C.L.*
Leg.   *Legato.* Leggo.   *Leggiero.*

L.H. *Left Hand.* L.M. *Long Metre.*
Lo. *Loco.*
Luo. *Luogo.*
Lusing. *Lusingando.*
M. ⎫
Main. ⎬ *Hand. Manual.*
Mano. ⎭
Maesto. *Maestoso.*
Magg. *Maggiore.*
Man. *Manual*(s).
Manco. *Mancando.*
Marc. *Marcato.*
M.D. *Mano destra,* or *Main droite.*
M.G. *Main gauche.*
Men. *Meno.*
Mez. *Mezzo.*
mf Mezzo forte.
M. *Metronome.*
M.M. *Maelzel's Metronome.*
Mod., or Modto. *Moderato.*
Mor. *Morendo.*
mp Mezzo piano.
MS. *Manuscript.*
M.S. *Mano sinistra.*
Mus.Bac. ⎫
Mus.B. ⎬ *Bachelor of Music.*
B.Mus. ⎭
Mus.Doc. ⎫
Mus.D. ⎬ *Doctor of Music.*
D.Mus. ⎭
M.V. *Mezza voce.*
Ob. *Oboe (Hautbois).*
Obb. *Obbligato.*
Oberst. *Oberstimme.*
Oberw., Obw. *Oberwerk.*
Oh. Ped. *Ohne Pedal.*
Op. *Opus,* or *Opera.*
Org. *Organ.* Orgt. *Organist.*
Ott., Ova., or 8va. *Ottava.*
8va alta. *Ottava alta.*
8va bas. *Ottava bassa.*
Oxon. *Oxford.*
p Piano.
Ped. *Pedal.*
Perd., or Perden. *Perdendosi.*
P.F. or Pf. *Pianoforte.*
P.F. ⎰ *Più forte.*
      ⎱ *Poco forte.*
Piang. *Piangendo.*
Pianiss. *Pianissimo.*
Picc. *Piccolo.*
Pizz. *Pizzicato.*
pp or *ppp Pianissimo.*
Prin. *Principal.*
1ma. *Prima.*
1mo. *Primo.*
Ps. *Psalm.*
4tte. *Quartet.*
5tte. *Quintet.*
Raddol. *Raddolcendo.*
Rall. *Rallentando.*
R.A.M. *Royal Academy of Music.*
R.C.M. *Royal College of Music.*
R.C.O. *Royal College of Organists.*
Recit. *Recitative.*

rf or *rfz. Rinforzando.*
R.H. *Right Hand.*
Rip. *Ripieno.*
Rit.   ⎫ *Ritenuto.*
Riten. ⎭
Rit.   ⎫ *Ritardando.*
Ritard. ⎭
S. *Senza ;* or *Sinistra (Left Hand).*
𝄋. *Segno.*
Scherz. *Scherzando.*
2da. *Seconda.*
2do. *Secondo.*
Seg. *Segue.*
Sem. or Semp. *Sempre.*
Sen. *Senza.*
7tt. *Septet.*
6tt. *Sestet.*
sfz, or *sf. Sforzando.*
Sim. *Simile.*
Sin. *Sinistra.*
Sinf. *Sinfonia.* S.M. *Short Metre.*
Smorz. *Smorzando.*
Sost.   ⎫ *Sostenuto.*
Sosten. ⎭
S.P. *Senza Pedale.*
Spir.   ⎫ *Spiritoso.*
Spirit. ⎭
S.S.   ⎫ *Senza Sordini.*
S. Sord. ⎭
S.T. *Senza Tempo.*
Stac., Stacc. *Staccato.*
St. Diap. *Stopped Diapason.*
String. *Stringendo.*
S.V. *Sotto voce.*
Sw. *Swell Organ.*
Sym. *Symphony.*
T. *Tenor, tempo,* or *tutti.*
T.C. *Tre corde.*
T.C.D. *Trinity College, Dublin.*
T.C.L. *Trinity College, London.*
Tem. ⎫ *Tempo.*
Temp. ⎭
Temp. prim. ⎫ *Tempo primo.*
Tem. 1o.   ⎭
Ten. *Tenuto.*
Timb. *Timballes.* Timp. *Timpani.*
T.P. *Tempo primo.*
tr. *Trillo.*
Trem. *Tremolando.*
3o. *Trio.*
Tromb. *Trombone.* Tbi. *Tromboni.*
Tromp. *Trompete.*
T. S. *Tasto Solo.*
T.S.C. *Tonic Sol-fa College.*
U.C. *Una corda.*
Unis. *Unison.*
V. *Voce* or *Volti.*
Va. *Viola.*
Var. *Variation.*
Vn., Vno., or Viol. *Violin (Violino).*
Vc., Vllo., or Vcllo. *Violoncello.*
Viv. *Vivace.*
V.S. *Volti subito.*
Vv., V.V., or Vni. *Violini.*
Zus. *Zusammen.*

(2) Abbreviated notation : " Musical Shorthand," chiefly used in manuscript music.

N.B.—The method of performance is shown *below* each example. (Quavers, *one* stroke ; Semiquavers, *two* strokes ; Demisemiquavers, *three* strokes.)

The following methods of abbreviation, once extensively used, are now practically obsolete:

segue (or simile).   *arpeggio.*

arpeggio.

(For other abbreviations see **Ornaments** and **Signs**.)

Abbrum'men *(G.)*. To hum over a tune.
A-B-C-di'ren, or **Abcidi'ren** *(G.)*. A method of sight-singing by using letter-names.
Abdämp'fen *(G.)*. To damp, to mute.
ABD el KA'DIR. Arabian writer on music, 14th cent.
ABEL, Carl Friedrich. *B.* Koethen, 1725; *d.* London, 1787. Renowned player of the viol-da-gamba. Chamber musician to Queen Charlotte, 1765.
    Composed overtures, concertos, sonatas, &c. In "form," one of the precursors of Haydn.
A'BELL, John. *B.* about 1660; *d.* Cambridge, 1724. "Counter-tenor" or Alto singer.
    Published several collections of songs, including some of his own compositions.
A'bendglocke *(G.)*. Curfew; evening bell.
    A'bendlied (G.). Evening song or hymn.
    A'bendständchen (G.). A Serenade.
A be'ne pla'cito *(I.)*. At pleasure.
    The performer is at liberty to alter the time or melody by introducing ornaments, &c., according to fancy.
A'benteuerlich *(G.)*. Adventurous; an epithet sometimes applied to the modern neo-German style of music.
A'ber *(G.)*. But; at the same time.
    A'ber im'mer noch nicht so schnell wie zu An'fang. But yet not so quick as at the beginning.
A'BERT, J. J. Bohemian composer; *b.* 1832. Has composed a symphonic poem and several operas.
Ab'gerundetes Spiel *(G.)*. A neat finished style (execution).
Ab'gesang *(G.)*. Aftersong; last section of a *Meisterlied.*
Ab'gestossen *(G.)*. *Staccato (q.v.).*
Ab ini'tio *(L.)*. From the beginning (Da Capo).
Ab'klang *(G.)*. Dissonance; echo.
Ab'kürzungen *(G.)*. Abbreviations.
Ab'nehmend, Ab'nehmung *(G.)*. *Decrescendo (q.v.).*
ABRAHAM, Dr. Max. *B.* Danzig, 1831; *d.* 1900.
    Started the famous "Edition Peters."
ABRAMS, Harriet. 1760-1825. Soprano vocalist and composer. Sang, "Handel Commemoration," 1784. Composer of the once-popular song "Crazy Jane."
Abrégé *(F.)*. Shortened. **Abréger** *(F.)*. To shorten.

Ab'reissung *(G.)*. A sudden pause.
Abrupt Cadence. An interrupted cadence.
Abrupt Modulation. An unexpected and abrupt change of key. (See **Modulation** and **Transition.**)
Ab'satz *(G.)*. A cadence, pause, phrase.
Ab'schleifer *(G.)*. A staccato mark.
Ab'schnitt *(G.)*. A Section *(q.v.)*.
Ab'schwellen *(G.)*. Diminuendo *(q.v.)*.'
Ab'setzen *(G.)*. } To play or sing staccato.
Ab'stossen *(G.)*. }
    Abstos'sungszeichen. Staccato mark.
Absolute, or Abstract, Music.
    "Music which depends solely on itself for its effects, and is in no wise dependent on words, scenery, acting, or any other extraneous condition."—*Sir F. A. G. Ouseley.*
    Absolute music is the opposite of program music.
Ab'stand *(G.)*. An interval.
Abstrak'ten *(G)*. Organ trackers. (See **Organ.**)
Ab'stufung *(G.)*. Shading (of expression).
ABT, Franz Wilhelm. *B.* Eilenburg, near Leipzig, 1819; *d.* Wiesbaden, 1885. Capellmeister successively at Bernberg, Zurich, and the Brunswick Hof-theater.
    A voluminous and melodious composer of songs, part-songs (especially for male voices), and cantatas. Most famous song: "When the swallows homeward fly." Cantatas: *Cinderella, Little Red Ridinghood, Water Fairies, Wishing Stone,* &c. He also wrote some pf. pieces &c.
Ab't(h)eilung *(G.)*. Part, movement, division.
ABU HASSAN. Comic operetta: music by Weber; composed 1810-11.
Ab'wärtsschrei'ten *(G.)*. To descend (in melody).
Ab'wechselnd *(G.)*. Alternating: changing organ manuals; changing fingers.
ABYNGDON, Henry. English composer, organist, and singer; 15th century. Succentor, Wells Cathedral, 1447. Mus.Bac., Cambridge, 1463: the first University musical degree on record. *D.* 1497.
Académie de Musique *(F.)*. Academy of Music.
Académie Nationale *(F.)*. "l'Opéra," or principal opera house of Paris.
Académie Spirituelle *(F.)*. A sacred concert.

Academy, Musical.
    The first English musical academy was instituted at the "Crown and Anchor" Tavern in 1710.

Academy of Music. Originally applied to the Royal Academy of Music, founded 1824.

A cappel'la, or **Al'la cappel'la** *(I.).* (1) In the Church style. (2) Unaccompanied vocal music: or with accompaniment simply doubling the voice parts in unison or octaves. (3) Church music in $\frac{2}{4}$ or $\frac{4}{4}$ time (same as **Alla Breve**).

A cappric'cio (capric'cio) *(I.).* At the fancy, or caprice, of the performer.

Acathis'tus *(L. from Gk.).* A special Greek Church hymn to the Virgin Mary.

Accablement *(F.).* Depression, dejection.

Accade'mia de'gli Arca'di *(I.).*
    A society of poets and musicians founded at Rome, 1690, "for promoting the progress of science, literature, and art."

Accarezze'vole, Accarezzevolmen'te *(I.).* In a tender, caressing manner.

Acceleran'do, Accelera'to *(I.).* Gradually quickening the pace. (Abbn. *Accel.*)
    Acceleran'do sin' al fi'no. ccelerating until the end.

Accent. The stress, or emphasis, laid on certain notes in a musical composition.
    Accent does not necessarily imply special loudness; it is often *felt*, rather than interpreted as force.

M. Lussy has classified accents under three heads: Metrical, Rhythmical, Expressive.

(A.) Metrical, or Grammatical, Accents.

The regularly recurring accents falling on the various beats of every measure, or bar.
    These accents are almost always in groups of *two* or *three* (a quadruple measure being formed of two duple measures).*

(1) *The Accents of Beats.*

Beat-accents are Strong, Weak, or Medium.
    In Tonic Sol-fa, a Strong accent follows a barline, a Weak accent follows a colon, and a Medium accent follows a thin short line.

N.B.—Weak beats are often called *unaccented* beats.

Binary, or Duple, Time.

Strong : Weak

Ternary, or Triple, Time.

Strong : Weak : Weak

* For the rare Quintuple and Septuple measures, see *Time.*

Quaternary, or Quadruple, Time.

Strong : Weak | Medium : Weak

All Simple Times are accented like $\frac{2}{4}$, $\frac{3}{4}$, or $\frac{4}{4}$;
all Compound Times like $\frac{6}{8}$, $\frac{9}{8}$, or $\frac{12}{8}$.

(2) *The Accents of Divided Beats.*

A Beat, like a Measure, naturally divides into *two* or *three* equal parts.
    Any one of these parts may be again sub-divided into two or three equal parts; and so on, at pleasure.

In all *Simple* Times the beat is a simple note (♩ or ♪ or ♫, &c.), with a tendency to divide into *two* equal parts.

In all *Compound* Times the beat is a dotted note (♩. or ♪. or ♫, &c.), with a tendency to divide into *three* equal parts.
    A simple note may be divided into three equal parts—or a Triplet. Thus:—

is identical with

A compound beat may be divided into two equal parts—or a Duplet. Thus:—

is identical with

By the laws of metrical accent, a divided beat (or pulse) is accented in the same way as a whole measure similarly divided.
    As Mr. Curwen puts it, "A pulse may be so accented as to become a miniature two-pulse measure, a miniature four-pulse measure, a miniature three-pulse measure, or even a miniature six-pulse measure."

The same principle applies to all subsequent subdivisions. But when a *weak* beat is divided it is obvious that its accents are of less value than those of a divided strong beat.

Binary Divisions.

$\frac{2}{4}$ time.

S   W

S   W   M   W

S   w   m   w   S   w   m   w

S w m w S w m w S w m w S w m w

Binary and Ternary Divisions.

$\frac{2}{4}$ time.

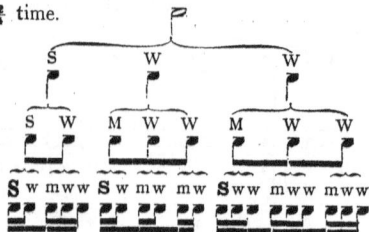

$\frac{6}{8}$ time.

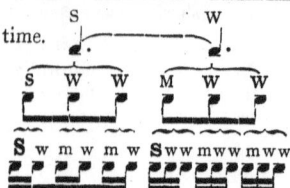

Theoretically, no two successive notes have the same metrical accent-values. In *slow* triple measures and divisions, therefore, one of the weak accents, generally the first, may be regarded as a little stronger than the other. But in *quick* music this distinction is practically impossible.

N.B.—In the Sol-fa notation of 6-pulse measure, the 4th pulse follows the *medium* accent sign; and in slow music this is the correct indication. In *quick* 6-pulse, there are, however, only two beats to the measure, and the accents are STRONG, *weak*, as in 2-pulse measure. Similarly, the primary accents of quick 9-pulse measure are the same as those of 3-pulse measure; and the primary accents of 12-pulse the same as those of 4-pulse.

(3) *The Accents of Groups of Measures.*

In quick pieces, such as waltzes, scherzos, &c., two, three, or four measures are grouped together and accented as if they formed one measure. In a quick waltz the "bar accents" are alternately STRONG and medium (or STRONG and *weak*); two bars of $\frac{3}{4}$ time being compressed into one bar of $\frac{6}{4}$ time. Thus:—

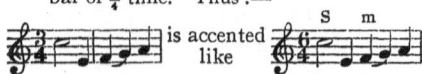

is accented   like

Part of the Scherzo of Beethoven's 9th Symphony stands thus:—

Ritmo di tre battute. *

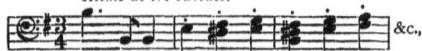

which is equivalent to:—

three bars compressed into one.

And a little further on:—

* See also Beethoven's Quartet No. 12, Op. 127, 3rd movement.

Ritmo di quattro battute.

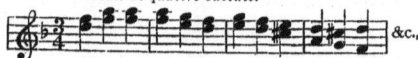

which is equivalent to:—

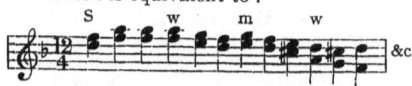

four bars compressed into one.

(4) *Cumulative Accent.* Some modern German theorists contend that metrical accent increases from point to point—each successive strong accent being stronger than the preceding—until a cadence is reached. This growth of stress is called "increased cadential power."

(B.) RHYTHMICAL ACCENT.

Metre (*G. Metrum*) is the "measuring out" of equal bars (or measures) in precise mathematical order; it may be said to be *instinctive*.

Rhythm is the arrangement of short and long notes or rests within measures at the composer's discretion; it may be said to be *intellectual*.

A "Rhythm" may be a *figure, phrase, section,* or *period*; it may commence at any part of a bar; and its length may be anything from *two notes* to four or more bars. (See *Rhythm, Figure, Phrase, Section, Period,* and *Motif*.)

The following are the usual rules for rhythmical accentuation or "punctuation":—

(1) "The energy of beginning" generally gives an accent to the *initial note* of a rhythm:—

SCHUBERT. "Adieu."

COWEN. "The Promise of Life."

CHOPIN. Op. 15, Op. 2.

If, however, the initial note is *low in pitch*, and of *short duration*, it is more frequently unaccented, being regarded merely as a *preparatory note*:—

The "*leap*" in such cases gives a special importance and emphasis to the high note.

(2) When the second note in a triple measure is longer than the first it takes a rhythmical accent:—

CHOPIN. Op. 71, No. 11.

(3) The note after a rest usually takes a rhythmical accent; especially when the note is the second beat of a triple measure:—

Even in a merely staccato passage, a slight accent is given to the weak beats:—

(4) All short notes of an anticipatory character are usually *unaccented*:—

BEETHOVEN. Op. 10, No. 1.

The "anticipation," however, in the *portamento* ending of a song is generally prolonged and accented; but this is more properly an *expressive* accent:—

HANDEL. *Messiah.*

un - to   your souls.

(5) Unless a mere preparatory note, the first of two or more slurred notes is accented:—

CHOPIN. Op. 9, No. 2.

(C.) EXPRESSIVE ACCENTS. A term specially applied to those *poetic* or *emotional* accents suggested by *sentiment*. Expressive accents may coincide with and reinforce metrical or rhythmical accents; or they may fall otherwise. Expressive accents are the accents given to *exceptional* and *unexpected* notes; they are often in the form of a swell, $<$ $>$

(1) All Syncopated notes are accented:— (See **Syncopation.**)

(2) Unexpected long notes after several short ones:—

(3) The highest note, or "point," of a phrase; or a high note approached by a skip:—

(4) Ornamented notes.
If an appoggiatura, the "grace" note is accented; in most other cases the "principal" note.

(5) Unexpected chromatics:—

Mozart. "Qui s'degno."

(6) Unexpected chords, especially *discords;* and the "transmutation chord" at a sudden change of key. (See also **Expression.**)

In performance, metrical accents give way to rhythmical, and these in turn to expressive accents, but the underlying metrical form must not be forgotten. In pianoforte music, the Left-hand accompaniment generally proceeds steadily with the metrical accents.[*]

CHARACTERISTIC ACCENTS. The special accentuation of certain musical forms. Characteristic accents of a *Mazurka*:—

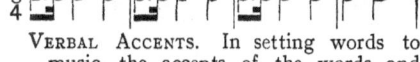

VERBAL ACCENTS. In setting words to music, the accents of the words and syllables should generally coincide with the metrical accents of the music.

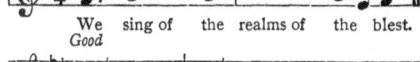

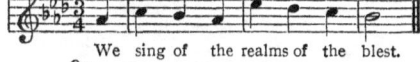

Bad

We sing of the realms of the blest.
Good

We sing of the realms of the blest.
Or

We sing of the realms of the blest.

Accent *(F.).* An obsolete ornament similar to an *Appoggiatura* or a *Nachschlag.*

Accenta′to *(I.).* Accented.

Accen′tor. Leading singer of a choir, &c.

Accentua′re, Accenta′re *(I.).* To accent.
Accentua′te e tenu′te (I.). The notes to be well-accented and sustained.

Accentui(e)′ren *(G.).* To accentuate, emphasize.

Accen′tus *(L.).* That part of the Roman Catholic ritual chanted or intoned by the priest and his assistants. The *Concentus* is the part taken by the choir.

[*] As in Chopin's *Nocturnes.*

Accen'tus Ecclesias'tici *(L.).* The inflection of the voice, made at certain marks of punctuation, in intoning the Gospels, Epistles, &c.

> Walther enumerates seven varieties (1) *immuta'bilis*, neither rising nor falling ; (2) *me'dius*, falling a third ; (3) *gra'vis*, falling a fourth ; (4) *acu'tus*, falling a third, then rising again to the reciting note ; (5) *modera'tus*, rising a second then falling to the reciting note ; (6) *interrogati'vus* (at a question), falling a second and rising again to the reciting note ; (7) *fina'lis*, falling diatonically by a fourth at the end of a sentence.

Accessis'ten *(G.).* Unpaid choir‑singers ; supernumeraries.

Acces'sory note. The higher note in a trill, &c.

Accessory tones. Harmonics. (See **Acoustics**.)

Acciacca're *(I.).* A broken and unexpected way of striking a chord.

Acciacca'to, Acciacca'ta *(I.).* Vehemently.

Acciaccatu'ra *(I.)* Pron. *Aht-chahk-kaa-too'-rah.* (1) A short *appoggiatura.* (See p. 28). (2) *(G., Zusam'menschlag ; F., Pincé étouffé).* An obsolete ornament once in great favour with organists and cembalists.

> The note a semitone below a principal note was struck with it, and immediately quitted, leaving the chief note to sustain the sound.

ACCIAJUO'LI, Filippo. Roman composer and dramatist ; *b.* 1637 ; *d.* 1700. Said to have been the first composer of *comic* opera.

Accident *(F.).* An accidental.

Accidental Notes. A name formerly applied to suspensions, anticipations, and "auxiliary" notes generally.

Accidentals. (1) *Sharps, double-sharps, flats, double-flats,* or *naturals* occurring accidentally in a piece of music ; *i.e.,* not in the key-signature.* (2) The term is now frequently applied without exception to all such signs, whether in the signature or occurring during the piece. (See **Chromatic Signs.**)

Accidentals, Cautionary. Accidentals not required by strict rule, but added by way of "caution :"—

Accolade *(F.).* The Brace, or Bracket, connecting two or more staves :

Accommoda're *(I.).* To repair, to put in order. To tune one instrument with another.

Accompagna'to *(I.).* Accompanied. (See **Recitative.**)

Accompaniment *(G. Beglei'tung ; F. Accompagnement ; I. Accompagnamen'to.).* The *accessory* part (or parts) added to support or intensify the *principal* part (or parts).

> The music to be accompanied may be a vocal or instrumental solo ; or it may consist of two or more voices or instruments (or both), in various combinations. The accompaniment may be either one or more instruments, or a vocal chorus, &c.

An *ad libitum* accompaniment is one which may be omitted at pleasure ; an *obbliga'to* accompaniment is of essential importance, and partakes of the character of a principal part.

Owing to its universal use, the pianoforte accompaniment to a vocal or instrumental solo is often spoken of as "*the accompaniment.*" Although no *set* form can be prescribed, six chief classes or styles of pianoforte accompaniment may be distinguished :—

(1) A simple harmonised setting of the melody :—

"The Soldier's Bride." SCHUMANN.

If on‑ly the Em‑per‑or knew

(2) Detached chords :—

"Where the bee sucks." Dr. ARNE.

On a bat's back do I fly, do I fly,

* Purcell, Handel, and Bach, marked them at every occurrence ; subsequently they were marked only once in a bar, the present practice.

(3) Chords in re-iterated notes, or in various forms of arpeggio, generally with a steady bass :—

"To Music." SCHUBERT.

Thou ho - ly art, how oft in hours of sad - ness,

"On wings of song." MENDELSSOHN.

On wings of song I'll bear thee To

(4) A characteristic melodic or rhythmical figure repeated through several bars :—

"The Linden Tree." SCHUBERT.

Now far I've left be- hind me The place I hold so dear,

"The Imprisoned Huntsman." SCHUBERT.

My hawk is tir'd of perch and hood, My

(5) A "counter-melody" forming a kind of duet with the solo part, or even becoming itself the chief melody :—

Redemption. GOUNOD.

Shall rise to light su - per - - nal

"The Lost Chord." SULLIVAN.

It flood-ed the crim-son twi - light, Like the close of an an - gel's psalm,

(6) A descriptive or dramatic accompaniment equal in importance to the solo part, and sometimes even the chief feature of the composition; as in Schubert's "Erl King," "The Young Nun," Henschel's "Young Dietrich," and many other modern descriptive songs. (See also **Leit Motiv.**)

> In a song of any length several of these styles may be used in turn, but it is not good to be constantly changing the form of accompaniment without definite purpose. "The more beautiful the melody, the less it needs in the way of embellishment."

Accompanist (*G. Beglei'ter; F. Accompagna teur, m., -trice, f.; I. Accompagnato're, m., -tri'ce, f.*). One who plays an accompaniment. Formerly specially applied to the performer on the harpsichord or organ who filled in the harmonies from a figured bass.

Accompany. To play an accompaniment.

> "The person who undertakes to play an accompaniment should be a skilful musician, and ought perfectly to understand the music; he must possess a quick ear and good taste, or he will mar the beauties of the music. As he will have the pitch to sustain, he must restrike firmly any notes where the voice falters. There should never be any attempt at display, except in the symphony."—*Moore.*

Accoppia'to (*I.*). Coupled, tied, joined.

Accord (*F.*). (1) A chord. (2) Agreement in pitch; being in tune; concord. (3) Same as *Accordatura* (*q.v.*).

> *Accord à l'ouvert.* A chord played on *open* strings (as by sweeping the bow over the open strings of a violin).
> *Accord arpégé, brisé,* or *figuré.* A broken chord (*q.v.*).

Accordable (*F.* and *E.*). Tunable; capable of being tuned.

Accordamen'to (*I.*). } Agreement; consonance.
Accordan'za (*I.*). }

Accord'ance. Sometimes used as an English word for *Accordatura* (*q.v.*).

Accordan'do (*I.*). Agreeing; being in tune; accordant.

> "Applied also to comic scenes in which the tuning of an instrument or instruments is imitated by the orchestra."—*Baker.*

Accordant (*F.* and *E.*). Consonant.

Accorda're (*I.*). To tune together; to be in tune.

Accordato'io (*I.*). A tuning-key, or hammer.

Accordatu'ra (*I.*). The series of notes to which the strings of an instrument are tuned. Thus ; the *Accordatu'ra* of the violin.

Accord de sixte Ajoutée (*F.*). The chord of the added sixth.

Accorder (*F.*). To tune.

S'accorder (*F.*). To get the pitch; the preliminary "tuning-up" of an orchestra.

Accordeur (*F.*). (1) A tuner. (2) The monochord. (3) A small instrument sometimes used by tuners, consisting of twelve tuning-forks tuned by equal semitones.

Accord'ion (*G. Accor'deon, Akkor'deon, Zich'harmonica; F. Accordéon; I. Accor'deon.*). A portable free-reed instrument—the smallest kind of organ—invented by Damian, of Vienna, in 1829. It is analogous in principle to the mouthharmonica, the metallic tongues being set in vibration by expanding the bellows to draw the air in, or compressing them to force it out. (See **Concertina.**)

Accor'do (*I.*). (1) A chord. (2) An old Italian instrument of the Lyre or Viol family, with from 12 to 24 strings—sometimes called the *Barbary Lyre*. It was played with a bow so that several strings sounded at once : hence *Accordo.* (See **Lyre.**)

Accordoir (*F.*). Tuning-key, tuning-hammer; tuning-fork ; tuning-cone (for organ).

ACCORIMBA'NI, Agostino. Italian composer; 1754-1818. Produced several operas, and poor sacred music.

Accoupler (*F.*). To couple. *Tirant à accoupler,* "Draw the coupler." *Tous les claviers accouplés.* All the manuals coupled.

Accrescen'do (*I.*). Crescendo (*q.v.*).

Accrescimen'to (*I.*). (1) Augmentation of a Fugal Subject. (See **Fugue.**) (2) *Pun'to d'accr.*, the dot after a note (♩•).

Accresciu'to (*I.*). Augmented, increased.

Accuratez'za (*I.*). Care, accuracy.

A cem'balo, or **A cemb.** (*I.*). For the harpsichord. A term found in old scores.

Aceta'bulum (*L.*). Ancient Greek instrument of percussion.

A chaque accord (*F.*). Press down the loud pf. pedal at each fresh chord.

ACHARD, Leon. Eminent French operatic Tenor singer, *b.* Lyons, 1831.

ACHENBACH. (See **Alvary.**)

Achromatic (*F.,Achromatique*). Not chromatic.

Acht (*G.*). Eight.
Ach'tel. A quaver, or eighth note (♪).
Ach'telnote. Quaver note ; *Ach'telpause,* Quaver rest.
Acht'füssig. Of 8ft. pitch (as an organ pipe).
Acht'klang. Octave.
Acht'stimmig. For eight parts.

A cinque (*F.*). For five parts.

ACK'ERMANN, Madame. Sang some of the principal parts in Mozart's operas at Königsberg (1796).

ACLAND, A. H. D. Author of "Letters on Musical Notation," 1841.

ACLAND, T. G. Author of "Chanting Simplified," 1843.

Ao'ocotl. Aboriginal Mexican wind-instrument. The dried stalk of a plant—from eight to ten feet long—played by inhaling the air through it.

Agœm'etæ (From a Gk. word meaning "not to sleep in bed ").
An order of ancient Eastern monks, who performed their religious offices—chiefly singing—both night and day. They divided themselves into three bodies, who "vociferized alternately.' '

Acolyth'ia (*Gk.*). The order of service in the Greek Church. Also applied to the hymns, psalms, &c., of the service.

Acoustic colour. The timbre, character, or quality of a sound.

Acoustics (*G. Aku'stik ; F. Acoustique; I. Acu'stica*). The science of the properties and relations of sounds. Sound is caused by sound-waves, or *vibrations* of the air— the more frequent the vibrations, the *higher* the pitch, and *vice versa.* Audible vibrations range in rapidity from 16 to 36,500 per second ; but the upward limit of *musical* sounds is 4,224 vibrations per second. Beyond this they become shrill, piercing, hissing, and painful to hear. Sound travels through the air (Temperature, 60° Fahrenheit) at about 1,120 ft. per second, and the length of the sound-wave corresponding to any sound is equal to $\dfrac{1120 \text{ ft.}}{\text{Number of Vibrations per second.}}$

(A) THE VIBRATIONS OF A STRETCHED STRING.
(*a*) The number of vibrations is (1) inversely proportional to the length ; (2) inversely proportional to the diameter ; (3) inversely proportional to the square root of the density ; (4) directly proportional to the square root of the stretching force (or weight).

Hence, the longer, thicker, heavier, and slacker a string is, the *slower* are its vibrations, and the *deeper* its pitch.
And the shorter, thinner, lighter, and more tightly stretched it is, the *quicker* are its vibrations and the *higher* its pitch.

(5) Loudness, or intensity, depends upon the *amplitude* (or extent) of the vibrations.

(*b*) The tone given by a stretched string is a *composite* (or *compound*) one. The *fundamental* tone, or *generator*, is accompanied by a number of higher sounds called *harmonics*, *over-tones* (*G. Obertöne*), *concomitant sounds*, or *upper " partials."* (The fundamental or lowest sound is regarded as the "*first partial.*") The higher upper partials are so relatively feeble in intensity that they cannot be individually detected by the ear without the aid of *Resonators* (but the first four or five can be easily heard on the pianoforte). Theoretically, the series of partials may be regarded as infinite, but only the first 16 partials are of any practical importance. The partials of a string whose fundamental note is : (produced by 64 vibrations per second, Philosophical Pitch), are as follows :—

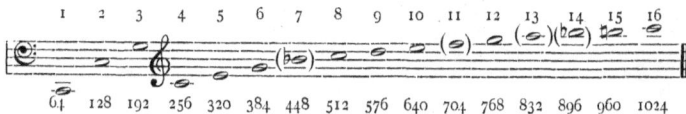

(N.B.—The notes in brackets are not quite in tune with those in ordinary musical scales.)

This is called the *Harmonic Series*, the *Harmonic Chord*, or the "Chord of Nature."

If the fundamental is [musical notation] the series becomes [musical notation] &c.

If [musical notation] it is [musical notation] &c.

From the Harmonic Series we deduce the following :—

(1) The partials approach nearer and nearer in pitch from the lowest to the highest, the successive intervals being an 8ve, Perfect 5th, Perfect 4th, Major 3rd, Minor 3rd, &c. From 8 to 9 is a Major Tone, from 9 to 10 a Minor Tone, from 15 to 16 a Diatonic Semitone. (For *musical* purposes the other successive intervals may be disregarded.)

(2) The octave above any note is produced by *twice as many* vibrations per second ; and every *even* partial is an octave higher than its half-number (*cf.* 6 with 3, 10 with 5, 14 with 7, &c.).

(3) The vibration-fraction (or ratio of vibrations) of any interval is that of the "partials" giving the two notes ; thus— an octave, $\frac{2}{1}$; Perfect 5th, $\frac{3}{2}$; Perfect 4th, $\frac{4}{3}$; Major 6th, $\frac{5}{3}$ [musical notation] ; Minor 6th, $\frac{8}{5}$ [musical notation] ; Major 3rd, $\frac{5}{4}$; Minor 3rd, $\frac{6}{5}$; Major tone, $\frac{9}{8}$; Minor tone, $\frac{10}{9}$; Diatonic Semitone, $\frac{16}{15}$; Major 7th, $\frac{15}{8}$ [musical notation] .

(4) The number of vibrations per second of any upper partial is found by multiplying the number of vibrations of the fundamental by the number of the partial. Similarly, if the vibration number of the *lower* note of any interval be known, the vibration number of the *upper* note is found by multiplying by the vibration-fraction of the interval.

(5) The vibration-fractions of the successive intervals of the major scale are :—

$$\mathbf{r}) \frac{9}{8} ; \ \mathbf{m}) \frac{10}{9} ; \ \mathbf{f}) \frac{16}{15} ; \ \mathbf{s}) \frac{9}{8} ; \ \mathbf{l}) \frac{10}{9} ; \ \mathbf{t}) \frac{9}{8} ; \ \mathbf{d'}) \frac{16}{15}$$
$$\mathbf{d}) \quad \ \ \mathbf{r}) \quad \ \ \mathbf{m}) \quad \ \ \mathbf{f}) \quad \ \mathbf{s}) \quad \ \mathbf{l}) \quad \ \mathbf{t}\langle$$

From these the vibration numbers of the notes of any scale can be calculated, at any standard of pitch. Thus, taking the French "Diapason Normal" A, 435 vibrations per sec., B = 435 × $\frac{9}{8}$; C♯ = 435 × $\frac{5}{4}$ × $\frac{10}{9}$ (or 435 × $\frac{5}{4}$) ; D = 435 × $\frac{4}{3}$; E = 435 × $\frac{3}{2}$; F♯ = 435 × $\frac{3}{2}$ × $\frac{10}{9}$ (or 435 × $\frac{5}{3}$) ; G♯ = 435 × $\frac{5}{3}$ × $\frac{9}{8}$ (or 435 × $\frac{15}{8}$). (These are the "scientific" numbers ; for the equally-tempered scale, see *Temperament*.)

(6) The first six partials give a major common chord, with the root occurring three times, the 5th twice, and the 3rd only once.

Thus, the rule of harmony, "Double the root or fifth rather than the third of a chord," is in conformity with physical law.

(7) *Inverting* the vibration-fraction shows the length of string necessary to produce any interval.

For example, one-half the length of the G string of the violin— [musical notation]

gives its octave, [musical notation] ; 2-3rds the Perf. 5th, [musical notation]

; 3-4ths the Perf. 4th, [musical notation]

(B) VIBRATION IN PIPES (as organ-pipes, flutes, clarinets, &c.).

Open pipes give sound-waves *double* the length of the pipe.

Stopped pipes give sound-waves *four times* the length of the pipe.

The number of sound-waves or vibrations per second is equal to $\frac{1120 \text{ ft.}}{\text{length of wave.}}$

Thus an open pipe 8 ft. in length, or a stopped pipe 4 ft. in length, gives $\frac{1120}{16} = 70$ waves, or vibrations, per second, which is equivalent to the note [musical notation] at a rather sharp pitch.*

(a) *Open pipes.*

(1) As an organ pipe 8 ft. in length gives the note [musical notation] , this is called "8 ft. C."

A 4 ft. length gives "4 ft. C," [musical notation]

a 2 ft. length gives "2 ft. C," [musical notation]

and so on—"1 ft. C," [musical notation] ; and "6 in. C," [musical notation] .

(2) Upper partials accompany the fundamental tone in the same order as those of a stretched string, but do not usually extend very far in the series.

(3) The length of pipe necessary to produce any given note may be found by comparison with 8 ft. C, by inverting the vibration fraction of the interval between them, and multiplying (as in (7) above).

(b) *Stopped pipes.* Though a stopped pipe gives the same fundamental note as an open one *of twice its length* (a stopped 4 ft. pipe giving 8 ft. C, &c.), only the "odd" partials are present in the constitution of its tone. Thus a Bourdon or Stopped Diapason whose fundamental

---

* The so-called 8 ft. pipe is really a little longer, giving from 64 to 68 vibrations per second according to the pitch-standard.

note is is not accompanied by its octave, nor its double octave ; but the 12th (G), the 3rd partial, comes out —often quite prominently ; and the 17th (E), the 5th partial, can also be easily detected :—

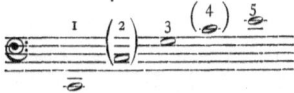

(C) TONE-QUALITY. Tone-colour, character, or *timbre*, depends upon the *order, number*, and *intensity* of the upper partials.

(1) Stringed instruments of all kinds are rich in partials, giving the regular series (*i.e.*, both odd and even), often to the 12th or 16th.

    Bowing, striking, or plucking, near the end of a string, favours the production of the high dissonant partials, and gives a keen, cutting quality of tone.

(2) Brass instruments—especially the trumpet and trombone—owe the brightness of their tone (which may by coarse blowing become a " blare") to their regular and extensive series of partials. *Loud* playing brings out the high, dissonant harmonics.

(3) Open organ pipes of wide scale favour the lower consonant partials, and the tone is full and majestic, but lacking in brightness.

Open pipes of narrow scale give more of the higher harmonics, and therefore a brighter and more characteristic tone-quality.

    "Mixtures" are used in the organ to supply some of the upper partials lacking in the tone of the large-scale pipes.

(4) Stopped organ pipes—giving only the *odd* series of partials—are of a soft, pleasing quality ; but the tone soon becomes monotonous, or even *dull*.

    Some organ pipes of this class, *e.g.* the Quinta-tön, are constructed so as to bring out certain partials, and produce a particular tone-quality.

(5) Reed instruments with a *conical* tube (as the oboe and bassoon) produce a rich, regular series of upper partials analogous to those of a string or narrow open pipe. But reed instruments with a *cylindrical* tube (as the clarinet) give only the *odd* series ; *i.e.*, they act as if the pipes were " stopped." In our present state of knowledge there is no adequate explanation of this peculiar phenomenon.

(*See also each instrument under its own name.*)

(D) SYMPATHETIC VIBRATION, OR RESONANCE.

(1) If two strings be tuned to the same pitch, and one set in vibration, the other will vibrate also. And if a string be set in vibration it will cause any other string to vibrate which has been tuned to the pitch of any one of the *upper*

partials of the first (up to, say, the eighth or tenth partial, according to the intensity of the original sound).

(2) If a " C " tuning-fork be struck and held in the hand it emits but a feeble tone. But if it be held, while still vibrating, near the end of a hollow cylinder, or tube, a foot in length, its tone is considerably re-inforced, because a pipe of that length is in unison with the " C " of the fork.

(3) A string stretched between two rigid stone walls, in the open air, can hardly be heard. The same string on a violoncello communicates its vibrations through the bridge to the body of the instrument, which in turn communicates them to the air, and a full powerful tone is produced.

This phenomenon of *Resonance* is of the utmost importance in the construction of every musical instrument, and also in the production of the human voice. It is hardly too much to say that " without it a good *musical tone* would be impossible ! "

(E) SIMULTANEOUS SOUNDS.

(*a*) *Interference : Beats.* Physical consonance is the result of coincidence of vibration. If the vibrations—or soundwaves—of two sounds synchronize in the order of 2 : 1 we get a perfect octave ; if 3 : 2, a perfect 5th ; if 4 : 3, a perfect 4th. In addition to these "perfect" consonances we have the major and minor 3rd, and the major and minor 6th. (See (A) above.)

If, however, the vibrations of two sounds coincide but rarely—say, in the ratio 101 : 100—the sound-waves *interfere* with one another and *beats* are produced, which distress the ear and cause *dissonance*.

Two sounds whose vibration-numbers are respectively 501 and 500 per second, give *one beat per second ;* if 502 and 500, *two beats per second*, &c.

When the beats become very rapid they cease to cause dissonance ; and Professor Helmholtz has explained that in such a case as that, for example, of a minor 9th, the upper note beats with the *2nd partial* of the lower note : ...2nd Partial.

It is also held that interference may be caused by *Resultants* (see below).

This is the scientific theory of dissonance ; but it cannot be said to be entirely satisfactory.

    "In reality, there is no absolute limit between consonance and dissonance ; it varies with the degree of sensibility of each individual, and also according to the habit resulting from education ; it is a question of the ear's tolerance, what appears harsh to one often seeming most agreeable to another."—*A Lavignac.*

(b) *Resultant Tones.* When two concordant tones are sounded together they produce a third sound whose vibration-number is equal to the sum of the vibration-numbers of the two original tones ; and also a fourth sound whose vibration number is equal to the difference.
One is called the *Summational*-tone, the other the *Difference*-tone. Difference-tones are also known as *Tartini's* tones. (See **Tartini.**)

Acoustic Bass ; Resultant Bass.
> Use is sometimes made of difference-tones in organ construction. An 8ft. pipe and its "quint" (a 5th higher) produce a 16ft. "C." A 16ft. pipe and its "quint" produce a 32ft. "C." But the "acoustical" notes so obtained are only effective on very large organs ; and it is doubtful whether they are ever heard to much advantage.

Act *(G. Akt, Aufzug; F. Acte,; I. At'to).* A division of a play or opera ; subdivided into *scenes* or *tableaux.*

Acte de Cadence *(F.).* Two or more chords forming a cadence.

Action *(G. Mecha'nik; F. Mecanique; I. Meca'nica).* The mechanical, or connective parts of an instrument.

Action-Song. A song with pantomimic or suggestive accompanying actions.

Act-tune *(Old E.).* (Curtain-tune). An entr'act. Music played between the acts of a play.

Acu'stica *(I.);* **Acu'stik** *(G.).* Acoustics.

Acu'ta *(L.* "Sharp, shrill"). (1) A high-pitched Mixture stop on the organ. (2) A Greek accent mark.
> *Vo'ce acu'ta.* A high voice.

Acute *(G. Scharf, Hoch; F. Aigu; I. Acu'to).* High in pitch ; sharp ; opposite to *Grave.*

Acutez'za *(I.).* Sharpness of pitch.

Acu'tus *(L.).* (1) Acute. (2) The name of one of the ecclesiastical accents.

A cylindres *(F.).* With valves *(q.v.).*

Ad *(L.).* At, to, &c., as *Ad libitum,* at pleasure. (Abbn. *ad lib.*).

Adagiet'to *(I.).* (1) Rather faster than *Ada'gio.* (2) A short *Adagio* movement or piece.

Ada'gio *(I.).* (1) Slow, but not so slow as *Largo.* (2) A movement, or piece, in *Adagio* tempo.
> The *Adagio* of a sonata or symphony is generally the second movement.

Ada'gio-Ada'gio *(I.).* Very slow.

Ada'gio assa'i *(I.).* } Very slow.
Ada'gio di mol'to *(I.).* }

Ada'gio canta'bile e sostenu'to *(I.).* Slow, and in a singing, sustained manner.

Ada'gio con molt' espressio'ne *(I.).* Slow, and with much expression.

Ada'gio non tan'to *(I.).* } Not too slow.
Ada'gio non mol'to *(I.).* }

Ada'gio pesan'te *(I.).* Slow and weighty.

Adagis'simo *(I.).* Very slow. Superlative of *Ada'gio.*

ADAM, Adolphe Charles. Melodious French operatic composer : " Successor and imitator of Boieldieu ; " *b.* Paris, July 24,

1803 ; *d.* May 3, 1856. Studied under Reicha and Boieldieu at the Paris Conservatoire.
> Made his mark in 1836 with *Le Postillon de Longjumeau,* still considered his best work. Appointed Professor of Composition at the Conservatoire in 1848. Wrote fifty-three stage pieces, including the operas *Richard Cœur de Lion, Le Fidèle Berger, Le Brasseur de Preston, La Rose de Péronne, Le Roi d'Yvetot, Giralda,* and *La Poupée de Nuremberg,* and the ballets *Giselle* and *Le Corsaire.* Also composed and arranged many pf. pieces. Adam's music is showy, clever, and effective ; but marred by triviality and flimsiness.

ADAM, J. Louis. Father of the above. *B.* Alsace, 1758 ; *d.* Paris, 1848. Prof. Paris Conservatoire, 1797-1843. Taught Kalkbrenner and Hérold. Pub. two works on pf. playing, and some pf. music.

A'DAM, Karl F. German composer of popular male-voice part-songs ; 1806-1868.

ADAM de la HALE (Le Bossu d'Arras). *B.* Arras ; *d.* Naples. A gifted French troubadour, about 1240-1287.
> Chief works : *Jeu de Robin et de Marion,* a sort of comic operetta, of which the words and music have been preserved ; *Jeu d'Adam, Jeu du Pélerin,* rondeaux, chansons, and motets. A collection of his works was published by Coussemaker, 1872. They are of great historical value.

A'DAM von [de] FULDA. *B.* 1450. Monk of Franconia. One of the earliest German composers ; highly esteemed in his day. Author of a treatise on the "Theory of Music" printed in Gerbert's "Scriptores."

A'DAMBERGER, Valentin. Renowned tenor singer and teacher of singing. *B.* Munich, 1743 ; *d.* Vienna, 1804. Great friend of Mozart's, who wrote some of his best music especially for him, including the part of Belmonte in *Il Seraglio.* His Italianised name was **Adamonti.**

ADA'MI da Bolsena, Andrea. *B.* Bolsena, 1663 ; *d.* Rome, 1742. Papal maestro. Wrote a valuable book on the music of the Pontifical Chapel, 1711.

ADAMOW'SKI, Mad. J. (See **Szumowska.**)

ADAMOW'SKI, Timothée. Violinist and composer ; *b.* Warsaw, 1858.
> Organised the Adamowski Quartet, 1888.

AD'AMS, Abraham. English organist and composer, end of 18th and beginning of 19th century. Compiled " The Psalmist's New Companion."

AD'AMS, John S. Author of " Five Thousand Musical Terms," London, 1861.

AD'AMS, Mrs. Sarah, 1805-1848. Daughter of a Cambridge editor named Flower. Author of the hymn, " Nearer, my God, to Thee."

AD'AMS, Stephen. (See **Maybrick, Michael.**)

ADAMS, Suzanne. Vocalist ; *b.* 18—. *Début,* 1894.

AD'AMS, Thomas. One of the most distinguished of English organists. Pupil of Dr. Busby. *B.* London, Sept. 5, 1785 ;

d. Sept. 15, 1858. Excelled in extempore playing. Works : organ fugues, fantasias, interludes, voluntaries, variations, &c. ; also some pianoforte and sacred music.

Adaptation. (See **Arrangement.**)

Adaptation of Hymns and Tunes.
"The haphazard way in which tunes are often adapted to hymns at the last moment before going in to the service is very distressing to all earnest-minded people. . . . A Bold and Spirited tune set to a hymn of penitence and submission jars upon the feelings. . . . A Solemn or merely Neutral tune adapted to a hymn of praise destroys joyfulness and injures worship."—*Curwen, "Musical Theory."*

Mr. Curwen classifies hymns as (1) Bold and spirited, (2) Grand, (3) Cheerful, (4) Solemn, and (5) Neutral and variable. Every organist, choirmaster, and precentor should study these distinctions, in order to select suitable tunes.

Ada'sio *(I.).* Old form of *Adagio.*

AD'COCK, James. *B.* Eton, 1778 ; *d.* Cambridge, 1860. Chorister and lay-clerk, St. George's, Windsor, and afterwards member of various church choirs. Published "The Rudiments of Singing," and a number of glees.

Added Lines. Leger lines.

Added Sixth. The chord of the Sub-dominant with a 6th added : . When the 5th from the bass is *prepared,* and *resolved* (by falling a step), this chord is regarded as the 1st inversion of a Supertonic (secondary) 7th. But when the 5th from the bass is unprepared, the chord is regarded as a Dominant 11th, with the 7th in the bass. In Sol-fa harmony-analysis the chord of the added sixth is ^7Rb. Another form of the chord has a *minor 3rd* with the bass :—

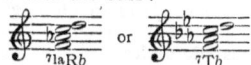

or

Two noted instances of the "added sixth" as the first chord of a composition are appended :—

BEETHOVEN. Op. 31, No. 3.

MENDELSSOHN. "Wedding March."

N.B.—Rameau (*q.v.*) regarded the subdominant as the root of this chord.

AD'DISON, John. *B.* about 1770 ; *d.* London, 1844. Composer of popular operettas, double-bass player, conductor, cotton manufacturer, music-seller, and teacher.
His wife, Miss Williams, was a "favourite singer at Vauxhall Gardens and other places in London."

AD'DISON, Joseph. Statesman and writer, 1672 - 1719. His hymns in the *Spectator* include "The spacious firmament on high " and " When all Thy mercies."

Addita'to *(I.).* With marks for fingering added.

Addition. Obsolete term for the dot after a note (♩·).

Additional Accompaniments. Parts added to those of the original score. They may be added for the following reasons :— (1) The original accidentally left incomplete ; *e.g.,* Schubert's *Unfinished Symphony* in E. (2) To supply parts for instruments unknown or unavailable at the composition of the work ; *e.g.,* Mozart's additions to Handel's *Messiah.* (3) The adaptation of parts written for obsolete instruments ; *e.g.,* the re-arrangement of Bach's Trumpet parts.
The subject of *additional accompaniments* is one of considerable controversy. It is certain that Handel and Bach would have written for all the instruments of the modern orchestra if they had known of them ; and they had often to score for a limited band conditioned by circumstances. There seems, therefore, little to urge against "reverent" additions to their works—such, for example, as those added by Robert Franz to some of Bach's compositions. They were usual in the 19th century, but there is now a reaction against them.

Additional Keys. Keys added to increase the compass of an instrument.

Addolcen'do *(I.).* Gradually softer.

Addolora'to *(I.).* Sorrowfully ; plaintively.

A défaut de *(F.).* In the absence of.

A'del *(G.).* Majesty, nobility.

À demi jeu *(F.).* With half the power of the instrument.

À demi voix *(F.).* Mezza voce. With half the power of the voice.

À deux *(F.),* A *du'e* (*I.*) (A2). For two voices or instruments.
"A2" is used in two precisely opposite ways. "If placed over a part (such as the violas) in which all the instruments usually play in unison, it is equivalent to *divisi,*" *i.e.,* divide into two parts ; "but if written over a line in which there are two parts (*e.g.,* the flutes or oboes), it indicates that the two instruments are to play in unison."—*Prout.*

À deux cordes *(F.).* On two strings.

À deux huit *(F.).* In $\frac{2}{8}$ time ; *À deux quatre* *(F.),* in $\frac{2}{4}$ time ; *À deux temps (F.),* in $\frac{2}{2}$ or $\frac{2}{2}$ time.

À deux mains *(F.).* For two hands.

Adi'aphon, Adi'aphonon, Adi'aphone.
An instrument of the pianoforte class with tuning-forks instead of strings. Invented by Schuster, Vienna, 1819. It is not liable to get out of tune, but the tone is lacking in character.

Adira'to *(I.)*. Irritated; angry.

Ad'junct. (1) Related; as adjunct keys or scales. (2) Notes not essential to the harmony occurring on unaccented parts of the bar.

Ad'ler *(G.)*. An obsolete organ stop.

AD'LER, Georg. Hungarian composer, violinist, teacher, &c. *B.* Ofen, 1806.

AD'LER, Dr. Guido. Distinguished theorist. *B.*Eibenschütz(Moravia),1855. Studied at Vienna; founded Univ. Wagner Society, 1874. With Chrysander and Spitta founded the *Vierteljahrsschrift für Musikwissenschaft*, 1884. Prof. Vienna Univ., 1898.

AD'LER, Vincent. French pianist and composer. *B.* 1828; *d.* Geneva, 1871.

A'DLGASSER, Anton C. Organist and composer; pupil of Eberlin. *B.* 1728; *d.* Salzburg, 1777.

Ad li'bitum *(L.)*. At pleasure, especially as to time. (1) The style of rendering is left to the performer's discretion. (2) The part so marked may be performed or omitted. (3) *Cadenza ad lib.* (*a*) The performer provides a Cadenza himself; or (*b*) performs the one given, if any; or (*c*) omits the Cadenza altogether.

AD'LINGTON, William. Pianist, writer, teacher, and publisher. *B.* Southwell, near Nottingham, 1838.

Ad lon'gam *(L.)*. In equal notes—"longs." Old church music.

AD'LUNG (ADELUNG), Jakob. German theorist and musical historian. *B.* near Erfurt, 1699; *d.* 1762. His "Musica Mechanica Organoedi" is a valuable treatise on organ construction, &c.

Adᵒ. Abbn. of *Adagio.*

ADOLFA'TI, Andrea. Italian Maestro; pupil of Galuppi. *B.* Venice, 1711; *d.* about 1760. His opera *Arianna* is said to contain an air in quintuple time.

Adornamen'to *(I.)*. A grace, or ornament.

Adoucir *(F.)*. (1) To soften. (2) To flatten.

Ad pla'citum *(L.)*. (1) At pleasure. (2) A *free* part added to a strict canon.

ADRAS'TOS. Greek philosopher and writer on music; 4th century B.C.

ADRIEN (ANDRIEN), Martin Jos. Belgian bass singer and composer, 1767 - 1822.

A'DRIENSEN, E. Distinguished lutenist, Antwerp, 16th century.

A du'e *(I.)*. Also *a duoi*, and *a doi*. (See **À deux**.)

A du'e cor'de *(I.)*. On two strings.

A du'e ma'ni *(I.)*. For two hands.

A du'e vo'ci *(I.)*. For two voices.

Adu'fe. A Spanish tambourine.

A dur *(G.)*. The key of A major.

Ad viven'dum *(L.)*. Counterpoint written down instead of improvised *(alla men'te)*.

AEGI'DIUS (1). Spanish friar; author of a work on musical theory; 13th century.

AEGI'DIUS (2). 15th century; wrote a treatise on "Measured" Music.

AELSTERS, Georges J. Belgian composer and carilloneur, 1770-1849. His *Miserere* is still performed.

Aengst'lich, Aehn'lich *(G.)*. Anxiously.

Æo'lian, or Eo'lian. The 9th ecclesiastical mode (5th authentic):

(See **Modes**.)

Æo'lian, or Eo'lian Harp. An anciently-invented instrument consisting of a box on which are stretched a number of long thin strings tuned in unison. They are set in vibration by the air passing over them, and the effect of the various "harmonics" is very pleasing.

Æo'lian Piano *(G. Ae'olsklavier')*. (1) An obsolete piano with wooden bars instead of strings. (2) A kind of harmonium with wooden reeds.

Æoli'na, Æoline. (1) A "mouth-organ" invented by Wheatstone, 1829. (2) A soft free-reed, echo gamba, or *voix céleste*, organ stop.

Æolod'icon, Æolid'ian, Æo'lomelod'icon, Chora'leon. Precursors of the harmonium.

Æolopan'talon. A combination of the Æo'lomelod'icon and piano, invented about 1830 by Dlugosz, Warsaw.

Aequal', Äqual' *(G.)*. Of "8 ft." pitch. Applied to organ stops; as *Aequal'-prinzipal.*

Æquiso'nus *(L.)*. In unison (or octaves); also **Æquiso'nant.**

Æquiva'gans *(L.)*. All the parts syncopated.

Ae'rophon. A harmonium.

AERTS, Egidius. Belgian flautist: 1822-53.

AERTS, Felix. Belgian violinist, conductor, and writer, 1827-1888.

Æsthet'ics (Esthetics). "The science of the beautiful in art" *(Niecks).*

Aeus'serst *(G.)*. Very, extreme(ly).

Äus'serst rasch. Extremely quick.
Aeus'serste Stim'men. The extreme parts.

AEVIA, aeuia. An abbreviation formed of the vowels of "Alleluia;" much used in old MS. music. (Compare **EVOVÆ**.)

Affa'bile *(I.)*. Sweetly, gently.

Affanna'to *(I.)*. Uneasily, distressfully.

Affannosamen'te *(I.)*. Anxiously, restlessly.

Affanno'so *(I.)*. Anxious, restless; mournfully.

Affectirt' *(G.)*, **Affetta'to***(I.)*. With affectation.

Affekt'voll *(G.)*. With fervour, passion.

Affet'to *(I.)*. Passion, tenderness, emotion; as *con affetto*, with much emotion or expression.

Affettuosamen'te, Affettuo'so *(I.)*.⎫
Con affezio'ne *(I.)*.   ⎭ With passionate or tender feeling; affectionately. "Affecting and sweet."—*Rousseau.*

3

Affi'lar (fi'lar) il tuo'no *(I.).* To sustain or "draw out" a tone steadily.

AFFILARD, Michael d'. French tenor singer and writer : end of 17th and beginning of 18th centuries. Wrote a once-popular work on Sight-singing.

Affinité *(F.).* Relationship ; affinity (especially of keys).

Afflocamen'to *(I.).* Hoarseness.

Afflit'to, Con afflizio'ne *(I.).* Sadly, mournfully.

Affrettan'do, Affretto'so, Affretta'to *(I.).* Hurrying the pace.

Ab. (1) The "flat" of A. (2) The major key requiring four flats in its signature.

AFRA'NIO degli ALBONE'SE (Ferrara). Reputed inventor of the bassoon, 1525. *B.* at Pavia, end of 15th century.

AFRICAINE, L'. Opera, Meyerbeer (1865).

After-beat. Last two notes of a *Trill* (*q.v.*).

After-note. The unaccented note of a pair.

After-striking. *(G. Nach'schlagen.)* A retardation in the bass. (See **Retardation.**)

After-stroke. The name given by Mr. Curwen to a dissonance on a weak pulse, or on the "after" part of a divided pulse.

Included by Macfarren among "Passing notes," by Ouseley among "Auxiliary notes," and by Richter among "Changing notes."

AFZE'LIUS, A. A. Pastor of Enköping ; published collections of Swedish Folksongs. *B.* 1785 ; *d.* 1871.

AGABEG, Madame E. (See **Wynne, Edith.**)

AGAZZA'RI, Agostino. Italian Maestro, and esteemed composer of madrigals and church music ; 1578-1640.

One of the first musicians to give rules for playing from a "figured" bass.

Agen'de *(G.).* "Things to be done."

The prescribed order of service of the German Lutheran Church.

Age'vole *(I.),* **Con agevolez'za** *(I.).* Lightly, easily.

Agg. Abbn. of *Aggiu'ngi*, "add."

Aggiun'to-(a) *(I.).* Added.

Aggiustatamen'te *(I.).* In strict time.

Aggrade'vole *(I.).* Pleasing, agreeable.

Aggravar la fugue *(F.).* To lengthen the notes of a fugue subject. (See **Augmentation.**)

Agiatamen'te *(I.).* Indolently, lazily.

Agilità' *(I.),* **Agilité** *(F.).* Sprightliness, vivacity ; *Con agilità'*, in a light, nimble style.

Agilmen'te. Nimbly, vivaciously.

Agitamen'to *(I.).* Agitation, excitement.

Agitatamen'te, Con agitazio'ne, Agita'to, Agitazio'ne. In an agitated, restless manner.

Agita'to con pian'to. Agitated, and with grief (pain).

Agité *(F.);* **Agiti(e)'rt** *(G.).* Agitated.

A'gli *(I.).* Same as **Alla.**

AGNEL'LI, Salvatore. *B.* Palermo, 1817.

Chief works : operas, *La Jacquerie, Lénore de Médicis, Les deux Avares.*

AGNE'SI, Luigi ; or Agniez. Renowned bass ; famed in London as a Handelian singer. *B.* near Namur, 1833 ; *d.* London, 1875.

AGNE'SI, Maria Theresia d'. Composer and excellent pianist. *B.* Milan, 1724 ; *d.* about 1780.

Ag'nus De'i *(L.* "Lamb of God"). Last movement of a Mass (Roman Service).

Ago'ge *(Gk.).* (1) Rules of melodic motion. (2) *Ago'ge rhyth'mica;* tempo, accent, and rhythm.

Ago'gics. The rules for the proper rendering of *Tempo rubato* (*q.v.*).

AGOSTI'NI, Ludivico. Italian maestro and church composer, 1534-1590.

AGOSTI'NI, Paolo. Papal maestro ; distinguished Italian contrapuntist and composer ; 1593-1629.

AGOSTI'NI, Pietro S. Operatic composer. *B.* Rome, 1650.

Agraffé *(F.).* A contrivance in some pianos to check vibration.

AGRAMON'TE, Emilio. Noted singing-teacher ; *b.* Cuba, 1844. Settled in New York, 1868.

A grand chœur *(F.).* For the full choir or chorus.

A grand orchestre *(F.).* For the full orchestra.

AGRELL', Johann. Capellmeister, harpsichord player, and composer ; 1701-1769.

Agrémens (Agréments) *(F.).* Ornaments, graces, &c., in harpsichord music. (See **Ornaments.**)

Agreste *(F.).* Rustic, rural.

AGRI'COLA, Alexander. Celebrated Belgian composer of the 15th century. Wrote songs, motets, and masses.

AGRI'COLA, Joh. Friedrich ; 1720-1774. German composer, organist, and writer on music. Studied under Bach.

Chief works : *Il Filosofo* and *La Ricamatrice.* His wife (Emilia Molteni) was a distinguished operatic singer ; 1722-1780.

AGRI'COLA, Martin. *B.* Sorau, 1486 ; *d.* 1556. Prolific and important writer on music and musical instruments.

AG'THE, Wilhelm J. A. 1790-1873. German composer of pf. pieces of some merit.

AGUA'DO, Dionisio. Celebrated Spanish guitar player ; 1784-1849.

A'GUILAR, Emanuel. Composer, pianist, and teacher. *B.* Clapham, 1824 ; *d.* 190(?). Son of a Spanish West Indian.

AGUJA'RI, Lucrezia (La Bastardella); *B.* Ferrara, 1743; *d.* 1783. Phenomenal soprano singer. Mozart heard her in 1770, when she sang passages extending in range from

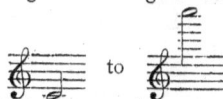

AGUTTER, Benj. Orgt. and composer ; *b.* St. Albans, 1844. Mus.Doc. Cantuar, 1891.

AH'LE, Joh. Rudolph. Cantor, organist, composer, and writer on theory. *B.* Mühlhausen, 1625 ; *d.* 1673.

AH'LE, Joh. Georg. Son of the above. Organist, composer, and writer ; 1650-1706.

AHL'STRÖM, Olof. Swedish organist, composer, and editor. 1756-1835.

AH'NA, Heinrich K. H. de. Violinist; *b.* Vienna, 1835 ; *d.* 1892. Chiefly known as 2nd violin in the "Joachim Quartet." His sister, Eleonore, was an excellent opera singer (mezzo-soprano) ; 1838-1865.

Ähn'lich *(G.).* Like, similar.

Ai *(I.).* To the, &c. Same as **Al.**

AI'BL, Jos. Music publishing firm, Munich, founded 1824. Now Spitzweg & Sons.

AI'BLINGER, Joh. Kaspar. Bavarian composer, and capellmeister ; 1779-1867. His compositions for the Catholic Church are highly esteemed in South Germany.

AI'CHINGER, G. German organist and composer of sacred music ; 1565(?) - 1628. One of the best musicians of his time. His "Sacræ Cantiones" (Venice, 1590), show many marks of real genius.

AÏDA. Grand opera by Verdi ; 1871.

AÏDÉ, Hamilton. Greek poet, novelist, and composer. *B.* Paris, 1830 ; *d.* 1907.

AIG'NER, E. Viennese ballet-director and composer ; 1798-1852(?).

Aigre *(F.).* Harsh ; sharp.

Aigu, Aiguë *(F.).* Acute ; high in pitch.

AIKIN, John. English writer on music and poetry ; 1747-1822.

AIMON, Esprit. French 'cellist and composer ; 1754-1828.

A in Alt.   **A in Altis'simo.**

AINSWORTH, Henry. English theologian and musician. Published a collection of Psalms, 1612.

Air. *(G., Melodie', Wei'se, Sing'weise; F., Air, Mélodie; I., A'ria.)* Tune, melody, song, ballad, &c. (See **Aria.**)
"The name of Air is given to all the measured chants, to distinguish them from the recitative."—*Rousseau.*

Air varié (F.). Theme with variations.

AIRD, James. Glasgow music-seller. Published, in 18th century, 6 vols. of national airs.

AIRETON, Ed. Renowned English violin maker ; 1727-1807.

A'is *(G.).* A♯.
A'is dur. A sharp major.
A'is moll. A sharp minor.
Ai'sis. Ax.

Aisé *(F).* (1) Easy. (2) Glad, cheerful.

Ajahli Keman. A Turkish stringed instrument of the 'cello kind.

Ajoutez *(F.).* Add (abbn. *Aj.*).

AK'EROYDE, Samuel. Popular and prolific song-composer, mentioned by Hawkins. *B.* Yorkshire, end of 17th century. Contributed to most of the collections of English songs from 1685 to 1696.

Akkord' *(G.).* (1) A chord. (2) A set of instruments, of different sizes, but of the same family, as viols.
Akkordie'ren. To tune.
Akkord' in Dur. Major chord.
Akkord' in Moll. Minor chord.
Akkord'-passage. An arpeggio.
Akkord'-zither. The auto-harp.
Dissoni(e)r'ender Akkord'. A discord.

Akt *(G.).* Act (of an opera, play, &c.).

Aku'stik *(G.).* Acoustics.

Al *(I.).* To the, up to the, at the, in the.
Cresc. al ff. Gradually louder up to *ff.*

A'LA, Giovanni Battista. Italian composer of madrigals, motets, &c. *B.* near Milan, latter part of 16th century.

ALABIEV, Alexander N. Song-composer ; Moscow, 1802-1852. Best-known song, "The Nightingale."

ALADÁR, Tisza. Pen-name of **V. Langer** (*q.v.*).

A la même *(F.).* ⎱ In the original time. *A*
A la mesure *(F.).* ⎰ *tempo.*

A la pointe d'archet *(F.).* With the point of the bow.

ALARD, Jean Delphin. One of the most famous of French violinists. *B.* Bayonne, 1815 ; *d.* Paris, 1888. Teacher of Sarasate. Composed and arranged much violin music, and published an excellent "Violin School."

Alargan'do *(I.).* (See **Allargando.**)

Alar'um. A call to arms (Shakespeare).

ALA'RY, Giulio E. A. Flautist, accompanist, and music-director. Made a name as composer of light opera. *B.* Mantua, 1814, *d.* Paris, 1891.

ALBANE'SE. 1729-1800. Singer, and composer of Romances.

ALBA'NI, Matthias. Two celebrated German violin makers, father and son ; 17th and 18th centuries : constructed their violins after the methods of Stainer and Amati.

ALBA'NI, Madame (Marie Louise C. E. La Jeunesse). Renowned soprano vocalist ; famous alike in opera and oratorio. *B.* near Montreal, 1852(50?).
First public appearance at *Albany*, hence her assumed name. (This is, however, denied.) First sang in London in 1872. Married Ernest Gye, 1878.
"Her voice is a rich soprano of remarkably sympathetic quality, and of great power. The higher registers are of exceptional beauty, and she possesses in perfection the art of singing *mezza voce*."—*Grove's Dictionary.*

ALBE'NIZ, Isaac. Pianist and composer ; *b.* Comprodon, Spain, 1861.

ALBE'NIZ, Don Pedro. Spanish monk, composer, and theorist ; 1755-1821.

ALBE'NIZ, Pedro. 1795-1855. Exponent of modern pianoforte playing in Spain. His "Method" (Madrid, 1840), was adopted by the Madrid Conservatoire.

ALBERGA'TI, Pirro C. Conte d'. Highly esteemed amateur Italian composer ; 1663-1735.

ALBERT, Charles D'. Musician and dancing-master. *B.* near Altona, 1809 ; *d.* 1866.

ALBERT, Eugène Francis Charles D'. Son of the above. Distinguished pianist and gifted composer. *B.* Glasgow, 1864. "Newcastle Scholar" under Pauer, Stainer, Prout, and Sullivan; "Mendelssohn Scholar" under Richter and Liszt.

ALBERT, Emile. French composer and pianist; 1823-1865.

ALBERT, Heinrich. Celebrated German composer, poet, and organist; 1604-1651. His songs and chorales are still sung in Germany. He has been called the "Father of the German *Lied.*"

ALBERT, H.R.H. Prince of Saxe-Coburg-Gotha. Patron of music and amateur composer; 1819-1861. Married Queen Victoria, 1840.

ALBERTAZ'ZI, Emma. Renowned English contralto singer; 1814-1847.

ALBER'TI, Domenico. Italian composer, abt. 1717-40. (See **Alberti Bass.**)

ALBER'TI, J. Friedrich. Learned German contrapuntist and composer; 1642-1710.

Alberti Bass *(G., Alber'tischen Bass).* A bass in broken harmony, common in pianoforte music; said to have been invented by Domenico Alberti.

BEETHOVEN. Op. 10.

ALBERTI'NI, G. Polish capellmeister and operatic composer; 1751-1811.

ALBER'TUS MAGNUS. Bishop of Ratisbon; wrote treatises on music; *d.* 1280.

ALBINO'NI, Thommaso. Violinist and prolific composer of operas; wrote some interesting instrumental works. *B.* Venice, 1674; *d.* 1745. Bach utilised some of Albinoni's themes.

ALBO'NI, Mariètta. Eminent Italian contralto singer; pupil of Bertolotti and Rossini. *B.* Cesena, 1823; *d.* 1894. "Esteemed the greatest contralto of the 19th century."

AL'BRECHT, Eugen M. *B.* St. Petersburg, 1842. Excellent violinist and teacher. Appointed music inspector of Imperial Theatres, St. Petersburg, 1877. *D.* 1894.

AL'BRECHT, J. Lorenz. German poet and composer. 1732-1773.

AL'BRECHTSBERGER, J. G. German composer and distinguished theorist. Teacher of Beethoven, Hummel, Weigl, Seyfried, and Eybler. *B.* near Vienna, 1736; *d.* 1809. His great work on "Composition" (Leipzig, 1790) is still highly valued.

ALBRI'CI, Vincenzo. *B.* Rome, 1631; *d.* 1696. Composer of church music.

Al'bumblatt *(G.).* (*F., Feuillet d'album.*) "Album leaf." A short instrumental piece. Schumann's *Albumblätter,* Op. 124, is a collection of twenty short pieces.

ALCAROT'TI, G. F. Composer of madrigals, 16th century.

ALCES'TE. Opera by Gluck; Vienna, 1767.

AL'COCK, Dr. John. Composer and orgt., *B.* London,1715; *d.* 1806. Pupil of Stanley, the blind organist. Organist Lichfield Cathedral, 1749; Mus.Bac. Oxon, 1755; Mus.Doc. 1761. Published anthems, psalms, glees, and harpsichord pieces.

ALCOCK, Walter G. *B.* Edenbridge, 1861; Mus.Doc. Dunelm, 1905; Organist, Chapel Royal, St. James's Palace, 1902.

Alcu'no,-a *(I.).* Some, certain. *Con alcu'na licen'za,* with some licence (as to tempo).

ALDAY. French musical family of mandolinists and violinists; 18th century.

ALDEN, J. Carver. Pianist and composer; *b.* Boston, Mass., 1852.

ALDOVRANDI'NI (Aldrovandini), G. A. V. Italian composer of operas, oratorios, motets, &c. *B.* 1665. Best opera, *Amor torna in cinque et cinquanta.*

ALDRICH, Henry (D.D.). Theologian, historian, and composer of anthems, glees, &c.; *b.* London,1647; *d.* 1710. Wrote treatises on "Organ-building" and other musical subjects. His church music—including two services and about fifty anthems—is still in general use.

ALDRICH, Rd. Critic and writer; *b.* Providence (U.S.), 1863.

A l'écossaise *(F.).* In the Scotch style.

ALEMBERT, Jean le Rond d'. French mathematician and acoustician. 1717 - 83. Exponent of Rameau's system of music.

Alerte *(F.).* Nimble, active, alert.

ALESSAN'DRI, Felice. Italian operatic composer and conductor; 1742-1811.

ALEXANDER BA'LUS. Oratorio by Handel; composed 1747.

ALEXANDER, Cecil Frances (Miss Humphreys), 1823 - 1895. Wife of Dr. Alexander, Archbishop of Armagh. Wrote nearly 400 hymns, including "There is a green hill," "The golden gates," "Jesus calls us," and "Once in Royal David's city."

ALEXANDER'S FEAST. Ode by Dryden. Set by Jer. Clarke (1697), and Handel (1736).

ALEXANDRE et Fils. Celebrated French harmonium makers; established 1829.

ALFARA'BI. Famous Arabian musical theorist; about 900-950.

ALFIE'RI, Pietro. Italian monk, professor of singing, musical writer and editor; 1801 - 1863. Issued a selection of Palestrina's works in seven volumes.

Al Fi'ne *(I.).* "To the end." Repeat the first part from the beginning *(Da capo),* or from the Sign 𝄋 *(Dal segno),* to the place marked *Fine* or

Al fi'ne, e poi la Co'da. After playing to the *Fine,* go on to the *Coda.*
Cres. al fi'ne. Continually louder to the end.
Dim. al fi'ne. Continually softer to the end.
Rall. al fi'ne. Continually slower to the end.

ALFON'SO und ESTREL'LA. Opera by Schubert; composed 1821-23.

ALFORD, Henry (D.D.). 1810-1871. Dean of Canterbury 1857-71. Wrote " Come, ye thankful people," and other hymns.

ALFORD, John. English lutenist; 16th century.

ALGAROTTI, Count Francesco. B. Venice, 1712; d. 1764. Wrote a famous treatise, on the " Opera," published 1755.

ALIPRAN'DI, Bernardo. Italian composer and 'cellist, 18th century. Four of his operas were produced at Munich, 1737-1740.

A'liquotflügel (G.). A grand piano, invented by Blüthner of Leipzig, with extra strings tuned an octave above each of the ordinary ones, to reinforce the tone by sympathetic vibration. (See **Acoustics**.)

Al'iquot tones. (G., *A'liquottö'ne*). Harmonics, overtones. (See **Acoustics**.)

A livre ouvert (*F.*). At sight.

ALKAN, Charles H. V. (**C. H. V. Morhange**.) Gifted composer and pianist; Paris, 1813-1888.

His pf. compositions are of great technical value, and he had exceptional descriptive power.

All', Al'la (*I.*). To the, at the, in the ; in the style of.

Al'la bre've (*I.*). With a *minim* to each beat. (See **A cappella**.)

Al'la bur'la, ma pompo'so (*I.*). In burlesque style, but pompously.

Al'la cac'cia (*I.*). In the hunting style.

Al'la ca'mera (*I.*). In the style of chamber music.

Al'la cappel'la (*I.*). (See **A cappel'la**.)

ALLAC'CI (ALLA'TIUS), Leo. Learned musical archæologist ; 1586-1669. Custodian of the Vatican library, Rome, 1661. Compiled a catalogue of Italian musical dramas to 1666.

Al'la co'da (*I.*). Go on to the Coda.

Al'la dirit'ta (*I.*). Ascending or descending by degrees.

Al'la France'se (I.). In the French style.
Al'la hanac'ca (I.). In the style of a *hanacca*, a Moravian dance resembling a quick polonaise.
Al'la Ma'dre (I.). "To the Mother;" *i.e.*, to the Virgin Mary.
Al'la mar'cia (I.). In the style of a march.
Al'la men'te (I.). Improvised. Originally, improvised counterpoint in 3rds and 5ths.
Alla milita're (I.). In the military style.
Al'la moder'na (I.). In the modern style.

ALLAN, Jas. The "celebrated Northumberland piper." A strolling vagrant whose performance on the pipes is said to have been extraordinary ; 1734-1810.

ALLAN, Jas. Scotch baritone singer and conductor ; 1842-1885. Conductor of the Glasgow Select Choir (1880-1885).

All' anti'co (*I.*). In the ancient style.

Al'la Palestri'na (*I.*). (1) In the style of Palestrina. (2) Unaccompanied.

Al'la polac'ca (*I.*). In the style of a polonaise.

Al'la quin'ta (*I.*). At the 5th.

Allargan'do, Allarga'te (*I.*). Same as **Largando**. Slower and broader.

Allargan'do al fi'ne. Slower until the end.

Al'la rove'scio (*I.*). By contrary motion.

Al'la Rus'se (*I.*). In the Russian style.

Al'la Scozze'se (*I.*). In the Scottish style.

Al'la Sicilia'na (*I.*). In the style of a *Siciliano*; *e.g.*, Handel's " He shall feed His flock."

Al'la stret'ta (*I.*). In the style of a *Stretto*. Bringing closer and closer ; hurrying the pace.

Al'la Tur'ca (I.). In the Turkish style.
Al'la Venezia'na (I.). In the Venetian style.
Al'la zin'gara (I.). In gipsy style.
Al'la zop'pa (I.). In a lame, halting style. Syncopation.

ALLCHIN, Wm. T. H. English organist and composer ; 1843-1883.

Al'le (*G.*). All, every.

Mit al'ler Kraft. Tutta forza (*q.v.*).

Allegramen'te (*I.*). Rather quick ; gaily.

Allegretti'no (*I.*). (1) A short *allegretto* movement. (2) Not so fast as *allegretto*.

Allegret'to (*I.*). Dim. of *alle'gro*. Moderately quick.

Allegretto da ca'po sin' al Maggio're, e poi la Co'da. Repeat the *Allegretto* up to the place marked *Maggiore*, and then go on to the Coda.
Allegret'to qua'si andanti'no. A rather slow *allegretto* —almost an *andantino*.
Allegret'to scherzan'do. Animated and playfully.
Allegret'to villerec'cio. Rather quick, and in rura style.

Allegrez'za, Allegri'a (*I.*). Joyfulness.

Con allegrez'za. Joyously, vivaciously.

ALLE'GRI, Domenico. 17th century Italian composer.

One of the first composers who wrote a real instrumental accompaniment.

ALLE'GRI, Gregorio. Rome, 1584-1662.

Composer of the famous *Miserere* (for 9 voices in two choirs) sung during Holy Week in the Papal Chapel at Rome, which was not allowed to be copied. Moz irt, on hearing it, wrote it out –partly while it was being sung, and partly from memory. It owes much of its effect to the traditional "abbellimenti." (See *Abbellimenti*.)

Allegris'simo (*I.*). Very quick.

Alle'gro (*I.*). (1) Gay, lively, quick. (2) An *Alle'gro* movement.

The *Allegro* is the first movement of a symphony, sonata, concerto, &c. ; it is sometimes preceded by an *Introduction* in slower time.

Allegro agita'to. Quick and agitated.
Alle'gro agita'to e appassiona'to assa'i. Quick and agitated, and very impassioned.
Alle'gro assa'i. ⎱
Alle'gro di mol'to. ⎰ Very quick.
Alle'gro viva'ce.
Alle'gro assa'i vi'vo. A very quick *allegro*.
Alle'gro ben modera'to. Quick, but only very moderately so.
Alle'gro con allegrez'za. Quick, and with joyousness.
Alle'gro con bri'o. Quick and with spirit.
Alle'gro con fuo'co. With " fire " and animation.
Alle'gro deci'so. Quick and with well-marked rhythm.
Alle'gro di bravu'ra. A quick "show" piece; *i.e.*, in bravu'ra style.
Alle'gro furio'so. Quick and impetuous.
Alle'gro modera'to. Moderately quick.

Alle'gro risolu'to. Quickly and energetically.

Alle'gro viva'ce. Quick and full of life.

Allegro is qualified by the addition of many other words; as *com'modo (com'odo), con mo'to, con spi'rito, giu'sto, ma grazio'so, ma non pres'to, ma non tan'to, ma non trop'po, velo'ce, vi'vo,* &c. (See under each word).

Allein' *(G.).* Alone, solo.

Allelu'ia, Allelu'iah, Allelu'jah, Hallelu'jah. "Praise ye Jehovah." (See **AEVIA.**)

Allemande *(F.). (I., Alleman'da.)* Also spelt *Alemain, Allemaigne, Almain, Almand, Almayne.* (1) A lively German dance in $\frac{2}{4}$ time. (2) A Swiss dance in $\frac{3}{4}$ time. (3) One of the chief movements in a *Suite.* (See **Suite.**)

The *Allemande* of a *Suite* is in moderate tempo, 4-4 time, and generally commences with a short unaccented note. Examples from Handel :—

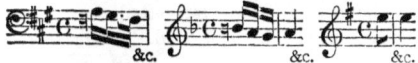

&c. &c. &c.

The *Allemande* consisted of two parts—each repeated—and the length of any one of these repeated portions varied from 6 to 27 bars. Handel specially favoured 11 bars (or 7, 9, 13) ; he occasionally used 8 or 16. Both with Bach and Handel the *Allemande* is written in imitative contrapuntal style. The *Allemande, Prelude,* and *Air* are the only movements in a Suite not taken from dance forms.

ALLEN, Alfred B. English pianist ; composer of songs and pf. music. *B.* 1850.

ALLEN, Ed. Heron. *B.* London, 1861. Noted authority on violins.

Author of *De Fidiculis Bibliographia,* &c. Contributor to Grove's Dictionary.

ALLEN, George B. Vocalist, and composer of operas, cantatas, anthems, songs, &c. *B.* London, 1822 ; *d.* 1897.

ALLEN, Maud Perceval. Soprano vocalist ; *b.* Ripley, 18—.

ALLEN, Henry Robinson. Esteemed bass singer. *B.* Cork, 1809 ; *d.* 1876.

ALLEN, Hugh Percy. Mus.D.Oxon, 1898 ; Orgt. New Coll., Oxford, 1901. Condr. Oxford Bach Choir, &c.

ALLEN, Richard. English writer on Psalmsinging, 17th century.

Allentamen'to, Allentan'do, Allenta'to *(I.).* Slackening the time ; same as **Rallentando.**

Al'le Sai'ten *(G.). Tutte corde (q.v.).*

All'gemeiner Bass *(G.).* Thorough - bass. *General'bass (q.v.).*

ALLIHN', A. Max. Writer on organ-building ; *b.* Halle-on-Saale, 1841.

All'improvi'sta *(I.).* Improvised ; extemporised.

ALLISON, Dr. Horton C. Composer, organist, and pianist. *B.* London, 1846.

ALLISON, Richard. Elizabethan composer. One of the ten contributors to Este's Psalter, 1592. Some of his tunes are still in use.

ALLITSEN, Frances. Contemporary vocalist. Composer of *A Song of Thanksgiving,* &c.

Allmäh'lich, Allmäh'lig, Allmä'lig *(G.).* Gradually ; by easy degrees.

Allmäh'lich bele'bend | Gradually quicker.
Allmäh'lich beweg'ter |

Allmäh'lich beweg'ter, ins Tem'po I. ü'bergehend. Gradually quicker until the original tempo is reached.

Almäh'lich et'was zurück'haltend. Gradually somewhat slower (slackening).

Allmäh'lich leb'hafter. Gradually faster.

Allmäh'lich nach'lassend. Gradually slackening.

Al lo'co, or **Lo'co** *(I.).* Play the notes as written ; used after 8va, 8ve, &c.

All°. Abbreviation of *Allegro.*

ALLON, Rev. Henry, D.D. Congregational minister and musical editor ; 1818-1892.

ALLON, H. Erskine. Son of the above. Composer. *B.* London, 1864 ; *d.* 1897.

Allonger l'archet *(F.).* To prolong the stroke of the bow in violin playing.

Allongez *(F.).* Slacken the time.

Allo'ra *(I.).* Then.

All' otta'va *(I.).,* **all' 8va,** or **8va.** At the octave ; an octave higher or lower.

All' otta'va al'ta. An 8ve higher.

All' otta'va bas'sa. An 8ve lower.

A l'otta'va per i Cem'bali á 7 otta'vi. An octave higher on pianos with 7 octaves.

All' uni'sono *(I.).* At the unison ; in unison (or octaves).

All'zugleich, All'zumal *(G.).* Altogether.

ALME'IDA, Fernando. Spanish monk, scholar, and writer on music ; about 1618-1660.

Al me'no *(I.).* Becoming as soft as possible.

AL'MENRÄDER, Karl. 1786-1843. Self-taught German musician and bassoon player. He greatly improved that instrument, and wrote a "Method" and several compositions for it.

ALOY'SIUS, John B. Composer of Italian church music ; middle of 17th century.

Alphabetical Notation. (See **Musical Notation.**)

Alphabet of Tune. The proximate mental effects of the notes of the scale. Mr. Curwen describes them as follows:—DOH, STRONG or *firm* ; RAY, ROUSING or *hopeful* ; ME, STEADY or *calm* ; FAH, DESOLATE or *awe-inspiring* ; SOH, GRAND or *bright* ; LAH, SAD or *weeping* ; TE, PIERCING or *sensitive.*

Al'penhorn, Alp'horn *(G.).* The Swiss shepherd's horn. It gives the natural series of harmonics (see *Acoustics*), and is used to play the *Ranz des vaches* and other simple melodies.

Al piace're *(I.).* At pleasure ; *ad lib.*

AL'QUEN, Peter C. German popular song writer ; 1795-1863.

Al rigo're di [del] tem'po *(I.).* In strict time.

Al river'so, Al rove'scio *(I.).* By contrary motion ; as the subject of a fugue or canon.

Als *(G.).* As, like ; than ; but ; when.

Al Seg'no *(I.).* At, or to the sign. (See **Dal Segno.**)

Al'so *(G.).* Thus, so ; therefore.

Al'so sprach Zarathu'stra. Thus spake Zoroaster.

Al'so nicht we'niger geschwind'. Not less quick.

ALS'LEBEN, Julius. 1832-1894. German pf. player, teacher, and musical editor.

AL'STEDT, J. H. German theologian, philologist, and writer on music ; 1588-1638.

Alt. *(G.).* The alto voice or part. The alto instrument of any family, as *Alt'horn, Alt'viole,* &c.

Notes "in Alt." The following names of notes were in use for many generations, and are still frequently referred to :—

Al'ta (Alto) *(I.)*. *(L. Altus.)* High. *Otta'va al'ta*, an octave higher.

Alt'clarinette *(G.)*. The alto clarinet; a 5th lower than the ordinary clarinet.

ALTENBURG, J. Ernst. Famous trumpet player. *B.* Weissenfels, 1736; *d.* 1801.

ALTENBURG, Michael. Prolific and esteemed German church composer; 1584-1640.

Altera're *(I.)*. To change, alter.

Altera'tio *(L.)*, **Altera'tion** *(G.* and *Eng.)*, **Altération** *(F.)*. (1) Doubling the length of a note in the old "mensural" music. (2) Raising or lowering the pitch of a note by a semitone: chromatic alteration.

Altera'to *(I.)*, **Altéré** *(F.)*. (1) Chromatically changed. (2) Weakened, altered.

Altered Chords. Chords formed by chromatic alteration of one or more of the notes of a major or minor triad. (See **Harmony.**) The following are examples of altered chords, the original triad being given first in each case :—

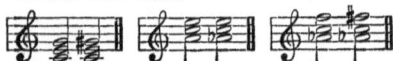

Alterez'za *(I.)*. Loftiness; pride. *Con alterez'za.* In a dignified style.

Alternamen'te *(I.)*. Alternatively.

Alternan'do *(I.)*. Alternating.

Alternations. Changes rung on bells.

Alternati'vo *(I.)*. Alternate. A part of a composition to be used in alternation with another, as the *Trio* of a *Minuet*.

ALTÈS, J. Henri. Celebrated French flautist; 1826-1895.

Alt'geige *(G.)*. The viola.

Alt'hoboe *(G.)*. The *cor anglais* *(q.v.)*.

Alt'horn, Alt'kornett *(F. Saxhorn alto.)* The Alto of the family of Saxhorns.
In England, the tenor-horn in E♭ or F.

Altieramen'te *(I.)*. Haughtily.

Al'ti natur'ali *(I.)*. Natural male altos, or counter-tenors.

Altiso'no *(I.)*. Ringing, sonorous.

Altis'simo *(I.)*. Very high, highest. (See **Alt.**)

Alti'sta *(I.)*. An alto or contralto singer.

Al'to *(I.)*, pl. **Al'ti** *(I.)*, or **Al'tos** *(Eng.)*. *(F., Haute-contre; G., Alt, Alt'stimme.)*
(1) One of the chief divisions of the human voice. Female altos are more properly called *Contraltos*. Male altos — more common in England than elsewhere— were formerly called *Counter-tenors*.

The average compass of the male alto

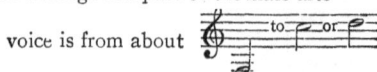

voice is from about

(2) The Viola, or Tenor Violin. *(G., Bra'tsche, Alt'viole; F., Alto, Quinte, Basse de Violon; I., Al'to, Vio'la.)*

Al'to Bas'so. An obsolete variety of Italian dulcimer.

Al'to Clarinet. (See **Alt'clarinette.**)

Al'to Clef. The "C" clef on the middle line: ; equal in pitch to
It is now chiefly used for the viola.

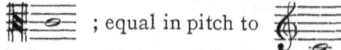

Al'to octa'vo *(I.)*. An octave higher.

Alt'posaune *(G.)*. Alto trombone.

Al'tra (Al'tro) *(I.)*. Other, another; as *Al'tra vol'ta*, "encore."

Al'tus *(L.* "High.")*. Alto.
Alt'sänger (G.). Alto singer.
Alt'schlüssel (G.). ⎫ The alto clef.
Alt'zeichen (G.). ⎭

Alt'viole *(G.)*. The Viola.

ALVAREZ. Pseudonym of **A. R. Gourron** *(q.v.)*.

ALVA'RY, Max (real name **Achenbach**). Fine Wagnerian Tenor; *b.* Düsseldorf, 1858; *d.* 1898.

ALY'PIUS. Greek writer, abt. 360 A.D. Gave rules for translating the musical characters of the ancient Greeks into modern notation.

Alzamen'to *(I.)*. A raising or lifting. *Alzamen'to di ma'no*, raising the hand. The opposite of *Abassamento*.

Am *(G.)*. On the, at the, near the. *Am Steg(e).* (Bow) near the bridge (vn., &c.).

Ama'bile *(I.)*., **Con amabil'ità** *(I.)*. Sweetly, tenderly.

AMADÉ, Baron L. Hungarian poet and composer of folk-songs; 1703-1764.

AMADÉ, Thaddäus, Graf. von. Friend and patron of Liszt. *B.* Pressburg, 1783; *d.* 1845.

A major. (1) The major key requiring three sharps. (2) The chord

A ma'n(o) drit'ta *(I.)*. For the right hand.
A ma'n(o) man'ca ⎫ For the left hand.
A ma'n(o) sinis'tra ⎭

Amare'vole *(I.)*., **Con amarez'za** *(I.)*. Sadly, bitterly, mournfully. Often confounded with *Amore'vole* *(q.v.)*.

Amateur *(F.)*. *(I., Dilettan'te.)* A lover of art who does not pursue it as a profession.

AMA'TI. A celebrated family of violin makers living at Cremona in the 16th and 17th centuries. The most famous was **Nicola Amati**, 1596-1684, among whose pupils were Andrea Guarneri and Antonio Stradivari.

Am'bitus *(L.).* The compass or range of an ecclesiastical mode or tone. (See **Mode**.)

Am'bo, or **Am'bon** *(Gk.).* A desk or pulpit.
"The raised platform in Eastern churches, on which the singers mounted when they sang."
—*Stainer and Barrett.*

AMBROS, August W. Bohemian composer and renowned musical historian ; 1816-1876.

AMBROSE, St. (Ambrosius). Bishop of Milan, 374-397. (*B.* 333.) Arranged the ritual of church music, and is the reputed writer of a number of hymns, including "Once more the sun is beaming bright." (See **Plain Song**.)

Ambrosian Chant. (See **Plain Song**.)

Ambrosian Hymn. (See **Te Deum laudamus**.)

Âme *(F.).* "Soul." The sound-post of a violin, 'cello, &c.

AM'ERBACH (Ammerbach), E. N. German 16th century organist. Wrote an historically valuable treatise on "Tablature."
Bach's copy is in the British Museum.

American Organ. An instrument of the harmonium class, but with the reeds more curved.
The tone is produced by drawing the air inwards instead of forcing it outwards as in the harmonium.

AMES, J. Carlowitz. Composer ; *b.* Bristol, 1860.

A mesure *(F.).* By the beat ; in strict time.

A mez'za for'za *(I.)* ⎫ With half the force of the
A mez'za vo'ce *(I.)* ⎭ voice (or instrument).
A mez'za ma'nico. (Bow) at the middle of the finger-board.

A minor. (1) The relative minor of key C, requiring no flats or sharps in the signature. (2) The chord

AMIOT, Père. Jesuit missionary and writer on Chinese music. *B.* Toulon, 1718.

AMMON, Blasius. Tyrolese contrapuntist and church composer ; *d.* Vienna, 1590.

AMNER, John. Church composer. Organist Ely Cathedral, 1610-1641.

A moll *(G.).* The key of A minor.

A'MON, John A. German composer and French-horn player ; 1763-1825.

A monocorde *(F.).* On one string.

Amo're *(I.).* Love, affection.
Con amo're. With tenderness ; lovingly.

A Mores'co *(I.).* In the Moorish style.

Amore'vole *(I.).*

Amorevolmen'te *(I.).* ⎫ Fondly, lovingly, af-
Amorosamen'te *(I.).* ⎭ fectionately, tenderly.
Amoro'so *(I.).*

A'morschall, A'morsklang *(G.).* A French horn with valves ; invented by Kölbel, 1760.

AMOTT, John. English composer ; organist Gloucester Cathedral, 1832-1865 ; *d.* 1865.

Am'phibrach. A metrical foot of three syllables—short, long, short (ᴗ — ᴗ), as *delightful, domestic.*

Amphim'acer. A metrical foot of three syllables — long, short, long (— ᴗ —) ; the opposite of *Am'phibrach.*

Amplitude. The extent of a musical vibration. (See **Acoustics**.)

Ampollosamen'te *(I.).,* **Ampollo'so** *(I.).,* **Ampoulé***(F.).* In an inflated, bombastic style.

Amt *(G.).* Office, ecclesiastical duty ; mass.
Hoch'amt. High mass.

Amusement*(F.).* Same as *Divertissement (q.v.).*

Amu'sia. Loss of musical faculty.

An *(G.).* On ; add ; at, against, to ; from.
An der Spit'ze. At the point (of the bow).

Anab'asis *(Gk.).* A series of ascending sounds.

A'NACKER, A. F. Conductor and composer ; *b.* Freiberg, 1790 ; *d.* 1854. Conducted the "miners' wind band," Freiberg, 1827 ; and also did much to promote the study of vocal music.

ANACREON. Opera-ballet by Cherubini ; produced 1803.

Anaka'ra *(Gk.).* The ancient kettledrum.

Anakru'sis *(G. from Gk.). (F., Anacrouse.)* The up-beat preceding the first accented note of a phrase (or rhythm). (See **Auftakt**.)

Anal'ysis. (1) Of sound: the resolution of a sound into its constituent partials, (See **Acoustics**.) (2) Of harmony: an explanation of the construction (roots, inversions, suspensions, auxiliary notes, &c.) and progressions of chords. (3) Of musical compositions : an enquiry into their form, style, harmony, modulations, &c. ; and the development of their principal themes.

Analytical Programmes. (See **Ella**.)

An'apest (An'apaest). A metrical foot of three syllables — two short and one long — (ᴗ ᴗ —) ; as

The *Anapest* is the reverse of the *Dactyl.*
In setting Anapestic verse to music the long accent need not necessarily fall on a *longer note* than the others, but it must be on a *stronger accent;* and this principle is universal in setting words to music.

ANATO'LIUS (St.). 8th and 9th centuries. Author of the hymn "The day is past and over" (translated by Dr. Neale).

An'blasen *(G.).* To blow, to sound.
Stark an'blasen. To blow loudly ; to blare.

Anche *(F.). (I., An'cia.)* The reed or mouth-piece of an instrument. A reed of an harmonium.
Anche d'orgue. Reed stop of an organ.
Anche libre. A free reed. *Jeu d'anche,* a reed stop.

An'che *(I.).* Also, too, likewise ; even.

Ancient Modes. The modes or scales of the Greeks, Romans, Egyptians, &c,

Ancient Signatures. *(See* **Signatures.***)*

Anco'ra *(I.).* Again ; *Da capo;* yet ; encore.

Ancor' più mos'so *(I.).* Still faster. Yet more motion.

ANCOT, Jean. Belgian pianist and composer; 1799-1829. Professor, Athenæum, London, 1823. Composed over 200 works, including sonatas, variations, fantasias, etudes, violin concertos, overtures, and vocal music.

ANCOT, Louis. Pianist, composer, and teacher. Brother of Jean ; 1803-1836.

An'dacht *(G.).* Devotion.

An'dächtig, or **Mit An'dacht** *(G.). (I., Devo'to, Con devozio'ne.)* Devotionally, devoutly.

Andamen'to *(I.).* (1) Movement or tempo in the style of an *Andante.* (2) An accessory passage, as an episode in a fugue. (3) Specially, an extended fugal theme consisting of two distinct and (rhythmically) contrasted portions, each of which is capable of separate development.

HANDEL. *Jephtha.*

Andan'te, Andan'do *(I.).* ("Walking, going, moving.") (1) Moderately slow time ; somewhat slow. (2) A movement in *Andan'te* time ; as an *Andante* for the organ, or the *Andante* of a symphony.

Andan'te affettuo'so (I.). Slow and with tenderness.

Andan'te canta'bile (I.). Rather slow, and in a singing, melodious style.

Andan'te con mo'to (I.). With energy or emotion. Not so slow as *Andante.*

Andan'te con variazio'ne (I.). An *Andante* with variations.

Andan'te grazio'so (I.). Slow and graceful.

Andan'te lar'go (I.). Slow, distinct, and exact : broad in treatment.

Andan'te maesto'so (I.). Slow and majestic.

Andan'te (ma) non trop'po (I.). Slow, but not too much so.

Andan'te pastora'le (I.). Rather slow, and in simple pastoral style.

Andan'te qua'si ada'gio. Slow, almost *adagio.*

Andan'te sostenu'to (I.). Slow and sustained.

Andantemen'te *(I.).* Like an *Andante.* Flowing easily.

Andanti'no *(I.).* A diminutive of *Andante.*
Authorities are not agreed as to whether it is quicker or slower than *Andante.* "The balance of opinion is in favour of regarding it as *quicker* than *Andante.*"—Dr. C. W. Pearce.

Andantin'o sostenu'te e semplicemen'te, il can'to un po'co più for'te. In a sustained and simple style, the melody a little louder than the rest.

Andar' dirit'to *(I.).* Go straight on.

Anda're *(I.).* To go ; to move on.

Anda're in tem'po *(I.).* Keep to the strict time.

AN'DER, Aloys. Famous Bohemian operatic tenor ; 1821-1864.

AN'DERS, G. E. Archæologist and writer on music ; *b.* Bonn, 1795 ; *d.* Paris, 1866.

AN'DERSEN, Carl Joachim. Conductor and composer ; *b.* Copenhagen, 1847.

ANDERSON, G. F. English violinist; 1793-1876. Hon. Treasurer to the Philharmonic Society, and to the Royal Society of Musicians.

ANDERSON, Lucy. Distinguished English pianist; wife of the above ; *b.* Bath, 1790 ; *d.* 1878. Teacher of Queen Victoria.

ANDERSON, Josephine. Famous English vocalist ; 1808-1848.

ANDERTON, Thos. Birmingham, 1836-1903.
One of the most successful of English amateur composers, especially of tuneful cantatas and operettas. *The Wreck of the Hesperus* is his most popular work.

An'derungsabsatz *(G.).* A half-close, or cadence on the dominant triad.

AN'DING, J. M. 1810-1879. German teacher ; composer of school and church music.

ANDRA'DE, F. d'. Operatic baritone ; *b.* Lisbon, 1859.

ANDRÉ, Johann. Offenbach, 1741-1799. Composer of operas, operettas, songs, &c.
Founder of the well-known music publishing house at Offenbach.

ANDRÉ, Johann Anton. 1775-1842. Composer, violinist, and theorist.
Third son of Johann. Established the prestige of the " house " by acquiring the whole of the musical remains of Mozart (from Mozart's widow) in 1796. Introduced several improvements in music printing.

ANDRÉ, Julius. 1808-1880. Organist and pianist. Son of J. Anton. Composed some good organ music.

ANDRÉ, Jean Baptiste. Frankfort pianist and composer ; 1823-1882.

ANDREO'LI, Giuseppe. Noted Italian player and teacher of the double-bass and harp ; 1757-1832.

ANDREO'LI, Guglielmo. 1835-1860. Accomplished Italian pianist; played in London, 1856-1859.

ANDREOZ'ZI, G. 1763-1826. Prolific Italian composer of operas ; wrote also three oratorios.

ANDRE'VI, Francesco. Distinguished Spanish composer and theorist ; 1786-1853.
Chief works : *Last Judgment* (an oratorio) *Requiem* for Ferdinand VII, and a *Stabat Mater.*

ANDREWS, Richard H. English writer and composer ; 1803-1891.

ANDRIEN. (See **Adrien.**)

ANDRIES, Jean. 1798-1872. Director of Ghent Conservatoire from 1851. Solo violinist and historical writer on music.

Anelantemen'te *(I.).* Ardently, eagerly.

Anem'ochord. *(F., Anémocorde, Anim'ocorde.)* A development of the Æolian harp, invented by Schnell, a German, 1789.
It was a keyboard instrument in which the tone was produced by small bellows forcing a current of air against strings. Herz' *Piano éolienne,* 1851, was a similar instrument.

ANE'RIO, Felice. 1560-1630. Famous Roman composer. Succeeded Palestrina as composer to the Papal Chapel. Wrote madrigals, hymns, motets, canzonets, *concerti spirituali*, litanies, &c., and a *Stabat Mater* for three choirs.

ANE'RIO, Giovanni Francesco. About 1567-1620. Roman composer; probably brother of F. Arranged Palestrina's *Missa Papæ Marcelli* for four voices.

ANET, Baptiste. (See **Baptiste**.)

An'fang *(G.).* The beginning. *Vom An'fang*, same as *Da capo*.
An'fangsgründe. Elements, principles.
An'fangs noch sehr ruh'ig. At the beginning very tranquilly.
An'fangstempo. The original *tempo* (speed).

AN'FORGE, Konrad. Pianist ; *b.* nr. Liebau, 1862.

ANFOS'SI, Pasquale. 1737-1797. Italian composer ; pupil of Piccini. Wrote 54 operas (including *l'Incognita Perseguitata* and *L'Avaro*), and some sacred music.

An'führer *(G.).* Conductor ; instructor.

An'geben *(G.).* To give, give out, announce.
An'geben die Melodie'. To start a tune.
Den Ton an'geben. To give the note for "tuning up."

ANGELET, Ch. F. 1797-1832. Belgian pianist.

Angelic Hymn. The hymn sung by the angels at Christ's birth, *Gloria in excelsis*.

Ange'lica, or **Vox Ange'lica** (" Angel's voice "). An organ stop. Formerly with free reeds and short tubes ; now, more frequently a *Voix Célestes (q.v.).*

Angélique *(F.).* (1) A keyboard instrument invented in the 17th century having seventeen strings tuned by semitones. (2) A kind of guitar.

ANGELO'NI, Luigi. 1758-1842. Italian author of a work on Guido d'Arezzo.

Angel'ophone. Early name for harmonium.

An'gemessen *(G.).* Appropriate, suitable.

An'genehm *(G.).* Pleasing, agreeable.

Anglaise *(F.). (I., Angli'co.)* A dance in " English " style ; generally of a lively character, and in ⅔ or ¾ time. (Country-dance, ballad, hornpipe.)

ANGLEBERT, Jean Henri d'. French composer for the clavier ; chamber musician to Louis XIV.

Anglican chant. (See **Chant**.)

Ango're *(I.)*
Ango'scia *(I.)* } Anguish, grief, distress.
Angosce'vole
Angosciamen'te } With anguish ; fearfully, plaintively.
Angoscio'so

Ängst'lich *(G.). (I. Timidamen'te.)* Timidly, anxiously, restlessly.

An'halten *(G.).* Prolonged ; *sostenuto*.
An'haltende Kadenz'. An organ-point (pedal).

An'hang *(G.).* Coda, codetta ; appendix.

A'nima, A'nimo *(I.).* Soul ; spirit ; mind.
Con a'nima. With soul ; with life ; with warmth ; with imagination.

Animan'do *(I.).* ⎫ With increasing animation ;
Anima'to *(I.).* ⎬ quicker.
Animez peu a peu jusqu'a la fin *(F.).* Quicker and quicker to the end.

Animo'so *(I.).* Spirited, animated, eager.
Animosis'simo. Very spirited.

ANIMUC'CIA, Giovanni. *B.* Florence, abt. 1500. *d.* 1570. Distinguished church composer; Preceded Palestrina as Papal *maestro*, and initiated the style of composition which Palestrina perfected. He has been called—perhaps without adequate reason—" The Father of the Oratorio."
Works : masses, madrigals, motets, &c., and a famous volume of " Laudi " (hymns).

ANKERTS, d'. (See **Dankers**.)

An'klang *(G.).* Harmony, tune, accord.
An'klingen. To ring, to sound, to accord.

An'lage *(G.).* (1) Plan or outline of a work. (2) Talent, capacity.

An'leitung *(G.).* An introduction ; guidance.

An'muth (An'mut) *(G.).* Sweetness, charm, grace, sauvity.
An'muthig, An'mutig. Sweetly, gracefully.

ANNIBA'LE. Italian 16th century contrapuntist ; born at Padua, and sometimes called Padovino or Patavinus.

Anom'alous Chords. Same as **Altered Chords**.

Anonner *(F.).* To perform or read music in a lame, halting manner.

An'pfeifen *(G.).* To whistle (or hiss) at.

An'satz *(G.).* (1) The adjustment of the lip, or *embouchure*, in wind instrument playing. (2) The method of attacking a phrase in singing.

An'schlag *(G.).* (1) Touch. (2) A kind of double appoggiatura now nearly obsolete.

Written   Played

An'schlagen *(G.).* To strike, touch, sound.
Den Ton an'schlagen. To give the key-note.

An'schmiegend *(G.).* Insinuating, yielding.

AN'SCHÜTZ, J. A. German musician and composer. *B.* 1772 ; *d.* 1856.

AN'SCHÜTZ, Karl. *B.* Coblenz, 1815 ; *d.* 1870. Son of the above. For many years opera conductor at New York, under Ullman.

An'schwellen *(G.).* *Crescendo ;* to swell.

AN'SELM of Parma. Learned 15th century writer on harmony.

Ansiosamen'te *(I.).* Anxiously ; hesitatingly.

An'spielen *(G.).* To play over, begin to play.

An'sprache *(G.).* (1) The "speech" of an organ pipe or orchestral inst. (2) Intonation.
An'sprechen. To sound, to emit a sound.

An'spruchslos *(G.).* Modest, unpretending.

Anstatt' *(G.).* Instead (of).

An'stimmen *(G.).* To announce, intone, strike up, tune, lead off.

Answer. *(L., Co'mes ; G., Gefähr'te, Ant'wort ; F., Réponse, Réplique ; I., Ripo'sta, Conseguen'te.)* In a fugue, the reply given by the 2nd voice to the *subject*, or *antecedent*, given by the 1st voice. (See **Fugue**.)

Antece'dent. *(L., Dux; G., Füh'rer; F., Thème; I., Anteceden'te, Propo'sta, Gui'da.)* The *subject* of a fugue or canon ; or any theme used in imitation.

ANTEGNA'TI. About 1550 - 1620. Italian organist, organ-builder, and composer. Published works in Organ *Tablature.*

Antelu'dium *(L.).* Introduction, prelude.

Anthem. (Probably derived from Anti-hymn or Antiphon, and originally implying antiphonal or "alternate" singing.) A peculiarly English form, developed by the requirements of the English Protestant church service. It is analogous to the German church-cantata and the Italian motet. The words are generally from the Bible ; but of recent years *Hymn-Anthems* have been largely used, especially in Nonconformist churches.

(1) FULL ANTHEM : consisting entirely of chorus. (2) VERSE ANTHEM : *beginning* with a portion to be sung by a single voice to each part. (See **Verse.**) (3) SOLO ANTHEM : containing one or more portions of solo. Most modern anthems are a combination of SOLO, VERSE, and FULL.

Typical anthems, with composer, and proximate date of production :—"I will exalt Thee," Tye ; 1530. "I call and cry," Tallis ; 1550. "Bow Thine ear," Byrd (Byrde) ; 1570. "Lord, for Thy tender mercies' sake," Farrant ; 1570. "Hosanna," Gibbons ; 1620. "Hear, O heavens," Humphreys ; 1660. "Awake up my Glory," Wise ; 1670. "I was in the spirit," Blow ; 1680. "O give thanks," Purcell ; 1694. "O praise the Lord," Aldrich ; 1694. "God is gone up," Croft ; 1694. "Hear my crying," Weldon ; 1715 (?). "I will love Thee," Clarke ; 1715. "O clap your hands," Greene ; 1720. "O give thanks," Boyce ; 1730. "Praise the Lord, O Jerusalem," Hayes ; 1730. "Call to remembrance," Battis-hill ; 1750. "Grant, we beseech Thee," Attwood ; 1800. "In Exitu Israel," Wesley ; 1800. "Me-thinks I hear," Crotch ; 1800. "The Wilder-ness," Goss ; 1840. Of later composers, Elvey, G. A. Macfarren, Sullivan, Barnby, and Stainer may be mentioned.

Anthol'ogy. *(L., Antholo'gium ; F. and G., Anthologie.)* "A collection of flowers." A choice selection of compositions, as anthems, hymns, &c.

An'thropoglossa *(Gk.).* A name sometimes given to the *Vox Humana* organ stop.

Antibac'chius, Antibacchy. A metrical foot of two long syllables followed by one short (— — ᴜ).

Anticipation. (See also **Hanging-note.**) "Striking beforehand a note or notes of the next chord."—*Curwen.*

* HANDEL.

The anticipation is often an 8ve. lower (or higher) than the anticipated note :—

MENDELSSOHN.

Anti'co *(I.).* Ancient, antique.

Antienne *(F.).* } Antiphon ; anthem.
Anti'fona *(I.).* }

An'tiphon, An'tiphone. *(Gk., Anti'phona, Anti'phonon ; G., Antiphonie' ; F., Antienne ; I., Anti'fona.)* (1) Alternate or responsive singing between two choirs, as practised in churches. (2) A short anthem, in response, &c. (3) A verse, or short sentence, sung before or after the Psalms or Canticles.

Antiph'onal. (1) Alternating, responsive. (2) A collection of antiphons or anthems.

Antiph'onary, Antiph'oner. *(L., Antiphona'rium ; G., Antiphonar' ; F., Antiphonaire ; I., Antifona'rio.)* A collection of antiphons, responses, &c., used in the ritual of the Roman Church.

Antiph'ony. Responsive singing by two choirs or a divided choir.

ANTI'POFF, Constantin. Composer ; *b.* Russia, 1859.

ANTI'QUIS, J. de. Italian composer of madrigals, *villanelle,* and *canzone ;* 16th cent.

ANTI'QUUS, A. (Antigo). Published a collection of the most famous *Masses* (Rome, 1516, and other vols. later).

An'tispast. A metrical foot of four syllables —short, long, long, short (ᴜ — — ᴜ).

Antis'trophe. The second of the three divisions of the Greek Ode : *stro'phe, antis'trophe, ep'ode ; c.f.* Mendelssohn's *Antigone.*

Antith'esis. Contrast.

AN'TON, K. G. German writer on Hebrew musical notation. *D.* 1814.

An'tonen *(G.).* To strike up ; to intone.

ANTO'NY, Franz J. 1790-1837. Westphalian organist, comp., and mus. archæologist.

Ant'wort *(G.).* Answer (of a fugue, &c.).

An'wachsend *(G.).* Crescendo.

Ä'olsharfe, Æ'olsharfe *(G.).* Æolian harp.

Ä'olsklavier *(G.).* "Æolian pianoforte."

A par'te *(I.).* Aside ; *Sotto voce.*

A pas'so a pas'so *(I.).* Step by step.

A'PEL, Dr. J. A. 1771-1816. German writer on rhythm and metre.

APELL', J. D. von. 1754-1833. German composer of sacred music, operas, &c.

Aper'to *(I.).* Open ; clear, distinct, broad. In pf. music, "with the loud pedal."

Aper'tus *(L.).* Open ; specially used to distinguish "open" from "stopped" pipes.

Ap'felregal *(G.).* An obsolete organ reed-stop.

Apho'nia *(L.),* **Aph'ony** *(Gk.).* Loss of voice, due to a variety of causes.
<small>Complete rest of the vocal cords will sometimes effect a cure, but medical treatment is generally advisable.</small>

A piace're *(I.).* ⎫ At pleasure ; *ad libitum ;*
A piacimen'to *(I.).* ⎰ not strictly in time.

A pie'na orche'stra *(I.).* For full orchestra.

A piene entendu *(F.).* Very soft ; scarcely heard.

A pistons *(F.).* With pistons (valves).

Aplomb *(F.).* Self-posession, coolness.

A po'co a po'co *(I.).* By degrees ; as *cres. poco a poco al ff* (increase by degrees to *ff*).
A po'co più len'to. A little slower.
A po'co più mos'so. A little quicker.

Apoggiatu'ra, Apogiatu'ra. Same as **Appoggiatu'ra.**

APOL'LO (Apollon). (1) The Greek god of poetry and music. (2) An obsolete lute with 20 strings.

Apollon'icon.
<small>A combined orchestrion and five-manual organ, with drums and other special mechanical effects, built by Flight & Robson, London, 1812-1816. It was taken to pieces in 1840.</small>

Apology. A term used by Mr. Curwen to explain, or justify, any unusual chord-position, dissonance, "incidental," &c.

APOSTLES, The. Oratorio, Elgar, 1903.

Apos'trophe. The sign ' often used as a breathing mark, or to indicate the beginning of a musical phrase.

Apo'tome. The Greek "chromatic semitone," ratio 2187 : 2048.

Appassionamen'te *(I.).* Ardently, passionately.

Appassionamen'to *(I.).* Passion, ardour.

Appassion'ato *(I.).* *(Fem. Appassiona'ta).* In an agitated, expressive manner ; "with passion and strong emotion."
<small>Beethoven's *Sonata Appassionata* (Op. 57) was not so named by himself, but probably by Cranz the publisher.</small>

Appeau *(F.).* Bird-like tone.

Appell' *(G.).* A bugle call. "Fall in."

Appe'na *(I.).* A little, somewhat.

Appena'to *(I.).* Distressed, sorrowful. With bitterness.

Applica'tio *(I.)* ⎫ Fingering ; also *(G.),*
Applikatur' *(G.)* ⎰   *Fing'ersatz.*

Appoggian'do *(I.)* ⎫ "Leaning." A note gliding without a break on
Appoggia'to *(I.)* ⎰ to the next ; as in the *portamento, appoggiatura,* and *suspension.*

Appoggiatu'ra *(I.).* *(F., Appoggiàture ; G., Vor'schlag.)* A grace note preceding the principal note, and generally a tone or semitone above or below it.

(1) *The Long Appoggiatura.*—In modern music the true length of this appoggiatura is always indicated. In old music the following rules apply. *(a)* When the principal note is naturally divisible into two equal parts (see **Accent**), the appoggiatura is *one-half the time-value* :—

Written.

Performed.

(b) When the principal note is naturally divisible into *three* equal parts, the appoggiatura is *two-thirds the time-value* :—

Written.

Performed.

(2) *The Short Stroked Appoggiatura or Acciaccatura.*—A small quaver or semi-quaver preceding the principal note, with a slanting stroke drawn through its "crook" :

Written.

Played.

Or, frequently, thus

(3) *The Nach'schlag (G.).*—A small single (or double) grace note *following* the principal note:—

Written.

Played.

(4) *Double Appoggiatura.* (See **Anschlag** and **Slide**.)

(5) *Ornamental Appoggiatura.* (See **Verzierende Vorschlag**.)

Appog'gio *(I.).* Strength, support; breath-resistance.

Appresta're *(I.). (G.,Appretie'ren.)* To regulate and adjust an instrument; to set it up.

APPUN', Georg A. I. 1816-85. German musician and renowned acoustical investigator.

Âpre *(F.).* Harsh.

À première vue *(F.).* } **A pri'ma vi'sta** *(I.).* At first sight.

A pri'mo tem'po *(I.).* At the first speed.

Appuyer *(F.).* To sustain.

APRI'LE, Giuseppe. 1738-1814. An eminent Italian alto singer and teacher of singing. Published an "Italian Method of Singing." Teacher of Cimarosa and Manuel Garcia (Junr.).

APTHORP, Wm. F. Distinguished American writer and critic. *B.* Boston, 1848.

APTOM'MAS (THOMAS), Thomas. Harpist; *b.* Bridgend, 1829.

A pun'ta d'ar'co, or *Col'la pun'ta dell' ar'co (I.).* With the point of the bow.

A pun'to *(I.).* In strict time.

À quatre mains *(F.).* } **A quat'tro ma'ni** *(I.).* For 4 hands: piano-forte duets, &c.

A quat'tro par'ti *(I.).* In 4 parts.

A quat'tro so'li *(I.).* For 4 solo voices.

À quatre voix *(F.).* } **A quat'tro voci** *(I.).* For 4 voices.

AQUILA. *Nom de plume* of **E. Ransford** (*q.v.*)

Arabes'ken *(G.* plural*).* Ornamental variations.

Arabesque. *(G., Arabes'ke.)* In Arab, or Moorish style. A showy or brilliant piece, generally in Rondo form.

Arab Music. The chief features of Arab music are most typically represented in Felicien David's work *Le Desert* (English translation, Novello & Co.)

ARA'JA, F. 1700-1770. Italian opera composer. Resided for some time in Russia, and wrote the oldest Russian opera, *Cephalos and Prokris,* 1755.

ARAN'DA, Del Sessa d'. Italian composer, 16th century. A collection of his madrigals was published at Venice in 1571.

ARAN'DA, Matheus d'. Portuguese writer on counterpoint, &c. (1533).

ARAU'JO (Arau'xo), Francisco. Spanish Bishop and writer on music; *d.* 1663.

ARBEAU, Thoinot. Jean Tabourot published under this pseudonym a curious book entitled "Orchésographie," in which drum and fife playing and dancing are taught by means of dialogue (1589).

Arbi'trio *(I.),* **A su'o arbi'trio** *(I.),* Arbitrarily; at one's will or pleasure. Same as **Ad lib.**

AR'BOS, E. Fernandez. Violinist; *b.* Madrid, 1863.

ARBUCKLE, Matthew. American writer and bandmaster; 1828-1883. Author of a Cornet Method.

AR'BUTHNOT, John. Physician; warm friend of Handel; wrote anthems. *D.* 1735.

Arc. Abbr. of *Arco.*

AR'CADELT (Arkadelt, Archadet, Harchadelt), Jacob. Celebrated Netherland composer of madrigals, &c., about 1514-1575. Teacher of the choir boys, Papal Chapel, Rome, 1539; member of the choir, 1540-55. King's Musician, Paris, 1557. Chief known compositions: Six books of madrigals for five voices; a volume of masses; motets, canzoni, &c.

Arcadia. (See **Accademia degli Arcadi**.)

ARCA'IS, Francesco, Marchese d'. 1830-1890. Italian writer; musical critic of the *Opinio'ne.* Upheld the pure Italian style of opera, and denounced Wagner and all other innovators.

Arca'to *(I.)* Played with the bow; opposite to *pizzica'to,* plucked with the fingers.

AR'CHADET. (See **Arcadelt**.)

ARCHAMBEAU, Jean Michel d'. Belgian composer and organist; *b.* 1823. Works: masses, motets, romances, &c.

Archchanter. *(F., Archichantre.)* Precentor.

Ar'che *(G.).* Soundboard.

Archeggia're *(I.).* To play with the bow.

ARCHER, Frederick. Organist; *b.* Oxford, 1838; *d.* 1901. From 1881, organist at Brooklyn (New York). His works and compositions for organ are well known.

Archet *(F.).* The bow (of a vn., &c.).

Ar'chi *(L.),* **Ar'ci** *(I.),* **Arch** *(Eng.),* **Erz** *(G.).* A prefix meaning "chief."

Ar'chi *(I.* plu. of *Arco).* Bows; the "strings." *Gli Archi,* the "bowed" instruments.

Arch'ilute, Archlute. *(I., Arciliu'to; F., Archiluth; G., Erz'laute.)* A large, or bass lute.

ARCHY'TAS. Greek mathematician, about 400-365 B.C. Probably fixed the ratio of the major third at 5 : 4. (See **Acoustics**.)

Arcicem'balo *(I.). (F., Archicembalo; G., Archicym'bal.)* An instrument with six keyboards, and strings to give all the tones of the ancient Greek modes, invented in the 16th century by Vincentino.

Arcivio'la di li'ra *(I.).* The largest kind of lyre; same as **Liro'ne** (*q.v.*).

Ar'co *(I.).* The bow: *coll' arco*, with the bow. Used after *pizzicato*, to show that the bow must be resumed.

Ar'co in giù. The down-bow.
Ar'co in sù. The up-bow.
Ar'co saltan'do. With skipping bow. (See *Saltare.*)

Ardemment *(F.).* Fervently, ardently.

Arden'te *(I.).* }
Arditamen'te *(I.).* } Ardent, fiery; with fervour.

Arditez'za, Con *(I.).* With spirit and boldness.

ARDI'TI, Marchese. 1745-1838. Italian archæologist. Composed the opera *Olimpiade*, several cantatas, &c.

ARDI'TI, Luigi. *B.* Crescentino, 1822; *d.* 1903. Violinist and composer. Conductor, Italian Opera, London, for several years.
The vocal dance "Il Bacio" is his most popular composition. He also wrote other vocal pieces, three operas, a number of pianoforte fantasias, &c.

Ardi'to *(I.).* Bold, spirited, daring.

Ardo're, Con *(I.).* With warmth, ardour.

AREN'SKY, A. S. Russian composer and pianist; *b.* 1862; *d.* 1906. Composed much music for orchestra, pianoforte, &c.

Aretin'ian or **Guido'nian Syllables.** The names *ut*, *re*, *mi*, &c., first used by Guido Aretinus. (See **Guido**.)

Arghool. An Egyptian "reed" wind instrument. The primitive type of the clarinet.

AR'GINE, Constantine dall'. 1842-1877. Italian composer of operas and ballets.

A'ria *(I.).* *(G. A'rie.)* (1) An air. (2) A vocal solo with instrumental accompaniment, generally three-fold in form. The words consist most frequently of *two* sentences.
The first part of the Aria is mainly in the principal key; and set to the first sentence of the words; the second part is in some contrasted key (or keys), and is set to the second sentence; the third part is a repetition, or modified repetition, of the first part. In modern Arias a coda is frequently added. "O rest in the Lord" (*Elijah*) is a typical example of a concise Aria in this form.
A'ria Buf'fa (I.). A comic air in Italian opera.
A'ria Concertan'te (I.). An aria with obbligato accompaniment for an instrument or instruments.
A'ria Concerta'ta (or *da Concer'to*) *(I.).* An aria not taken from an oratorio, opera, &c., but an independent composition (with orchestral accompt.) for the concert-hall.

A'ria da Ca'po, or **Grand Aria** *(A'ria Gran'de).* Introduced by Cavalli and A. Scarlatti, and one of the chief forms of Aria used by Bach and Handel.
GENERAL PLAN:—A. First part: (1) Instrumental prelude (or *ritornel'lo*) announcing the principal melody; (2) principal melody (vocal); (3) short modulations into closely related keys; (4) return to principal key; (5) instrumental postlude.
B. Second part: shorter than the first part, and contrasted in key and style.
C. Third part: repetition—*da capo*—of the first part (generally omitting the instrumental prelude).

"He was despised" *(Messiah)* is a fine example of the *Aria da Capo;* though, on account of its length, the second part

and the repetition of the first part are generally omitted. Practically all Handel's opera solos are examples.

A'ria da Chie'sa *(I.).* *(Church aria.)* An elaborated sacred song with orchestral accompaniment.

A'ria di Bravu'ra (or **Coloratu'ra**) *(I.).* }
A'ria d' Abil'ita, Aria d' Agilità' *(I.).* } An aria abounding in difficult passages, runs, &c., to exhibit the singer's skill, and the compass and flexibility of the voice; as "Why do the nations?" and "Rejoice greatly" *(Messiah).* The favourite form of aria in Italian opera.

A'ria di Canta'bile *(I.).* A smooth, flowing, "singing" aria.

A'ria Fuga'ta *(I.).* With the accompaniment in fugal or imitative style; as "But hark!" (Handel's *Semele*).

A'ria Parlan'te, or **Ario'so** *(I.).* An aria lying midway between recitative and song; a kind of spoken melody, as in "Comfort ye" *(Messiah).*

A'ria Tedes'ca *(I.).* An air in German style.

ARI'BO, Scholas'ticus. Author of a commentary on Guido's works (about 1078).

A'rie *(I.);* **A'rien** *(G.).* Airs, songs.

ARIEN'ZO, Nicola d'. *B.* 1842. Neapolitan operatic composer; pupil of Mercadente. Author of an important theoretical work on Temperament and Scales.

Ariet'ta *(I.),* **Ariette** *(F.).* A short aria.

A rigo're del tem'po *(I.).* In very strict time.

Arigot *(F.).* A fife.

Ario'so *(I.).* Used in four senses: (1) An *aria parlante.* (2) A short aria. Mendelssohn employs the term twice in *Elijah :* "Woe unto them." "For the mountains." (3) A short portion of melody interrupting or concluding a recitative. (4) Same as *cantabile* in instrumental music.
Ario'so dolen'te. In a singing plaintive style.

ARIOS'TI, Attilio. *B.* Bologna, 1660; *d.* 1740. Opera composer.
In his first opera, *Dafne*, he followed the style of Lully; afterwards he imitated A. Scarlatti. Came to London, 1716, and with Buononcini acquired fame until Handel eclipsed both. Published a volume of cantatas, 1728.

ARISTI'DES. Greek writer on music; 1st and 2nd centuries, A.D.

AR'ISTOTLE. (1) Greek philosopher, 384-322 B.C. His writings on music are considered valuable by antiquarians. (2) Assumed name of a writer on "Measured" music, 12th and 13th centuries.

ARISTOX'ENUS. Pupil of Aristotle, abt. 354 B.C. One of the most important of Greek writers on music. His book on "Harmonic Elements" has been preserved.

ARKWRIGHT, Godfrey E. B. Musical amateur; lives at Newbury.
Edited an important collection of English music, "The Old English Edition."

ARM'BRUST, Karl F. 1849-1896. German musician; organist St. Peter's, Hamburg, 1869; teacher and musical critic.

ARM'BRUSTER, Carl. *B.* Andernach, 1846. Settled in London, 1863. Esteemed Wagnerian conductor.

Armer la clef *(F.).* To indicate the key by means of the signature.

ARMES, Philip. *B.* Norwich, 1836; *d.* 1908. Mus.Doc.Oxon. Orgt. Durham Cathedral, 1862-1907. University Prof. of Music.
Works: Oratorio, *Hezekiah*; church music, &c.

Arm'geige *(G.).* (See **Viola da Braccio.**)

ARMIDE (ARMI'DA). One of Gluck's greatest operas; produced 1777.

ARMINGAUD, Jules. 1820-1900. Renowned French violinist. Leader of a celebrated string quartet (with L. Lacquard, E. Lalo, and Masq), which, by adding other instruments, became the *Société Classique.*

Armoni'a *(I.).* Harmony.

Armoni'a Milita're *(I.).* Military band.

Armo'nica *(I.).* (1) The Harmonica. (2) Harmonic.

Armonie *(F.).* An old instrument—12th and 13th centuries. Probably the *Vielle.*

Armoniosamen'te *(I.)* } Harmoniously.
Armonio'so *(I.).*

ARMSTRONG, Mrs. C. (See **Melba.**)

Armure *(F.).* (1) The key-signature. (2) The action or mechanism of an instrument.

ARNAUD, Abbé Francois. 1721-1784. French ecclesiastic, scholar, and writer on music. Specially noted for his zealous defence of Gluck's innovations in opera.

ARNAUD, Jean E. G. 1807-1863. French composer of favourite songs (Romances).

ARNE, Thomas Augustine. Mus. D. Oxon. *B.* London, March 12, 1710; *d.* March 5, 1778. Distinguished English musician; composer of "Rule, Britannia" and other well-known songs. Married Cecilia, daughter of Young the organist. (She was a pupil of Geminiani, and a renowned opera singer.) Arne's compositions include Oratorios: *Abel,* 1744; *Judith,* 1764. Operas: *Dido and Æneas,* 1734; *Eliza,* 1755; *Artaxerxes,* 1762; and several others. Music to *Love in a Village, As You Like It, Twelfth Night, Merchant of Venice, The Tempest, Romeo and Juliet,* and many other plays. He also published several collections of songs, and music for orchestra, organ, harpsichord, violin, &c.

ARNE, Michael. Son of the above. 1741-1786. Produced operas, and other theatrical music; wasted his fortune in an attempt to discover the Philosopher's Stone. Introduced Handel's *Messiah* to Germany, 1772.

ARNIE'RO, José A. F. V. Vicomte d'. Eminent Portuguese composer. *B.* 1838. Chief works: *Te Deum* (Lisbon, 1871); operas, *L'Elisire di Giovinezza* and *La Derelitta.*

ARNOLD, Georg. *B.* 17th century (Tyrol). Organist; composed motets, masses, &c.

ARNOLD, Ignaz E. F. Erfurt, 1774-1812. Published biographies of Mozart, Haydn, and other composers.

ARNOLD, Johann G. 'Cellist and composer; *b.* Niedernhall, 1773; *d.* 1806.

ARNOLD, Carl. 1794-1873. Son of Johann G. Conductor Christiania Philharmonic Society, 1849. Composed an opera, *Irene* (Berlin, 1832), chamber music, &c.

ARNOLD, Maurice. Composer; *b.* St. Louis, 1865.

ARNOLD, Samuel. London, 1740-1802. Chorister, Chapel Royal. Mus.Doc. Oxon, 1773. Organist, Westminster Abbey, 1793. Wrote over 40 works for the stage, including *The Maid of the Mill* (1765), and five oratorios. Chief works: "Cathedral Music" (4 vols., 1790)—a continuation of Boyce's three volumes—and an edition of Handel in 36 volumes.

ARNOLD, Yourij von. Composer and musical critic. *B.* Petersburg, 1811; *d.* 1898. Composed Russian operas, *The Gipsy* (1853) and *Swätlana* (1854), besides overtures, songs, &c. Professor of singing, Moscow Conservatoire, 1870.

AR'NOLDSON, Sigrid. Brilliant dramatic soprano. *B.* Stockholm, 1863.

ARNOTT, A. Davidson. Mus.Doc. Dunelm. *B.* Glasgow, 1870. Has composed *Young Lochinvar, The Ballad of Carmilhan,* &c.

A rove'scio *(I.).* Same as **Al rove'scio** *(q.v.).*

Ar'pa *(I.).* The harp. *Ar'pa dop'pia:* a double harp. (See **Spitzharfe.**)

Arpanet'ta, Arpanel'la *(I.).* A small harp.

Arpége *(F.).* Arpeggio.

Arpégement *(F.).* In arpeggio style.

Arpéger *(F.).* To arpeggio.

Arpeggian'do *(I.).* } In harp style, or arpeg-
Arpeggia'to *(I.).* } giated chords (called also *broken chords*).

Arpeggia're *(I.).* To play on the harp.

Arpeggiatu'ra *(I.).* A series of arpeggios.

Arpeg'gio *(I.).* (Plural *Arpeg'gi,* Eng. plural *Arpeg'gios.*) In harp style; *i.e.,* playing the notes of a chord in succession (generally beginning with the *lowest*) instead of striking them together. The chord is said to be "broken" or "spread." There is no hard and fast rule for the treatment of arpeggios, either as to the speed at which the successive notes should follow one another or as to what notes should be *held* after being struck.

(1) If the chord is so written that *all its notes could be struck together*, it is usual to strike each note rapidly and evenly in succession from the lowest to the highest, and to sustain each note from its percussion to the end of the whole time allotted to the chord :—

Written.   or   Played.

On the pianoforte the *pedal* may be used to sustain the notes, either *with* or *instead of* the fingers.

When the Arpeggios are separate for each hand they are written thus :

(2) In extended positions of chords, **or** when it is necessary to "bring-out" the melody of an arpeggiated passage, one or more of the lower notes must be quitted immediately, and sustained (when desirable) by means of the *pedal* only :—

{ L.H.
{ R.H.
{ L.H.

SCHUMANN. Nachtstücke 4.

p PED.   &c.

(3) Arpeggiando effects are often indicated by small notes, which are touched lightly and rapidly before the principal note :—

MENDELSSOHN "Songs without Words," No. 30.

&c.

(4) Organ arpeggios are now usually written out in full, exactly as they should be played :—

MENDELSSOHN. Organ Sonata, No. 1.
R.H.
L.H.
Ped.

(See also **Abbreviations** and **Ornaments**.)

Arpeggio'ne. An instrument like a viol da gamba, or small 'cello, with frets on the fingerboard. Invented by Stauffer, Vienna, 1823. Schubert wrote a sonata for it. Its six strings were tuned as follows :—

Arpicor'do *(I.),* or *Ar'pichord.* The harpsichord.

Arpo'ne *(I.).* A kind of harp with the strings horizontal instead of vertical. Invented by Barbieri, Palermo, 18th century.

ARQUIER, Joseph. French opera composer and conductor ; 1763-1816.

Arraché *(F.).* "Torn ;" strongly *pizzicato.*

Arrangement *(Eng., G.* and *F. I., Riduzio'ne).* (1) The adaptation of a piece for an instrument or voice (or any combination of instruments and voices), for which it was not originally intended ; *e.g.,* Liszt's pf. arrangements of Schubert's songs, and Gounod's arrangement of Bach's prelude as a song *(Ave Maria)* with violin and piano accompaniment. (2) A pf. (or org.) arrangement of orchestral accompts.

Arranger *(F.),* **Arrangi(e)'ren** *(G.).* To arrange.

ARRIA'GA, Jean C. de. *B.* Bilbao, 1808 ; *d.* 1826. Precocious violinist and composer, once highly esteemed.

ARRIE'TA, Don Juan E. 1823-1894. Director, Madrid Conservatorio. Composed *Ilde-gonde* and about 40 other operas, &c.

ARRIGO'NI, Carlo. Florentine lutenist. Visited London, 1732, and (with others) vainly endeavoured to supersede Handel in popular favour.

Ars Canen'di *(L.).* The art of singing.

Ars Com'ponendi *(L.).* The art of composing·

Ar'sis *(Gk.).* The up-beat ; the lifting of the hand. (The opposite of *Thesis.*)

ARTCHI'BOUSHEFF, N. V. (See **Artschibousheff.**)

Art de l'archet *(F.).* The art of bowing.

Ar'te *(I.).* Art.

ARTEA'GA, Stefano. Spanish Jesuit ; *d.* Paris, 1799. Friend of Padre Martini. Author of a celebrated "History of the Opera in Italy" (1783 and 1785).

ARTHUR, Alfred. American tenor singer, and composer of operas, *Water-Carrier, Adaline,* &c. B. 1844.

Articola're *(I.),* **Articuler** *(F.),* **Artikuli(e)'ren** *(G.).* To articulate distinctly.

Articola'to *(I.).* Pronounced distinctly.

Articulation. *(I., Articolazio'ne.)* (1) In speaking and singing, distinct utterance, especially of consonants. (2) In playing, proper observance of *staccato* and *legato;* and generally, clear and distinct performance of notes and rests.

Artificial Harmonic. (See **Harmonic.**)

Ar'tiglich *(G.).* Gracefully, neatly.

ART OF FUGUE, THE. A work written by J. S. Bach in 1749—the last year of his life—consisting of various fugues and canons on one theme.

ARTÔT, Maurice Montagney. 1772 - 1829. French bandmaster, conductor, and performer on the horn, guitar, and violin.

ARTÔT, Jean D. Montagney. 1803-1887. Son of the former. Celebrated horn player.
Published several compositions for horn.

ARTÔT, Alexandre Joseph Montagney. Brother of Jean D. ; 1815-1845. Studied at the Paris Conservatoire. Excellent violinist.

ARTÔT, Marguerite Josephine D. Montagney. Daughter of Jean D. ; *b.* Paris, 1835. Renowned dramatic soprano singer. Studied under Madame Viardot-Garcia. Engaged at the Paris Grand Opera, 1857, on Meyerbeer's recommendation. Toured through Europe with extraordinary success ; sang mostly at Berlin. *D.* 1907.
"As late as 1886 she was a star of the first magnitude."—*Riemann.*

Arts, Fine. Music, painting, sculpture, &c.
"Of all the fine arts," wrote Napoleon, 1797, "music is that which has most influence on the passions, and which the legislator ought the most to encourage."

ARTSCHI'BOUSHEFF, N. V. Pianist and composer ; *b.* Tsarskoje-Sielo, Russia, 1858.

ARTU'SI, Giovanni M. Italian ecclesiastic and contrapuntist (Bologna) ; *d.* 1613.
Chiefly remembered for his opposition to the "modern style" of music introduced by Monteverde. (See *Monteverde.*)

Arzil'lo *(I.).* Lively, sprightly.

As *(G.).* A♭.

A-Sai'te *(G.).* The A string.

ASANTSCHEW'SKY, Michael P. von. Composer ; Moscow, 1838-81.

As'as (or **As'es**) *(G.).* A♭♭.

A scel'ta del cantan'te *(I.).* At the singer's discretion.

Ascenden'te *(I.).* Ascending.

ASCH'ENBRENNER, Christian H. *B.* Alstettin, 1645 ; *d.* 1732. Excellent violinist ; musical director to the Duke of Sachsen-Reitz, 1695-1713 ; capellmeister, Duke of Sachsen-Merseburg, 1713-1719.

ASCH'ER, Joseph. *B.* London, 1831 ; *d.* 1869. Settled in Paris, 1849 ; Court pianist to the Empress Eugenie.
Known as a composer of light drawing-room pieces, and the song "Alice, where art thou ?"

As dur *(G.).* A♭ major.

As moll *(G.).* A♭ minor.

ASHE, Andrew. A celebrated flute-player. *B.* Lisburn, Ireland, about 1759 ; *d.* Dublin, 1838.

ASHLEY, John. English bassoon player, and conductor ; *b.* early in 18th century ; *d.* about beginning of 19th.
Assistant conductor, under Joah Bates, Handel Commemoration, 1784.

ASHTON, Algernon. *B.* Durham, 1859. Composer and pianist. Studied at Leipzig, and afterwards with Raff. Pianoforte teacher, R.C.M., 1885.

ASIO'LI, Bonifacio. Prolific Italian composer ; *b.* Correggio, 1769 ; *d.* 1832. When eight years of age is said to have already written three masses and several other works. First president of the new Milan Conservatorio, 1808-1813.
Wrote an oratorio, *Jacob,* seven operas, and many masses, cantatas, songs, instrumental pieces, &c. Author of "Elements of Music," "Piano Method," "Vocal Method," "A Treatise on Harmony," and several other theoretical works.

ASO'LA (Asula) Giovanni M. Italian composer ; *b.* Verona ; *d.* 1609. One of the first composers to write a *basso continuo* for organ accompaniment.

A so'la vo'ce *(I.).* For voice alone.

ASPA, Mario. Italian composer ; *b.* Messina, 1806 ; *d.* abt. 1868. *Il muratore di Napoli* was the most popular of his 42 operas.

Aspira're *(I.).* (1) To take breath. (2) In singing "to quaver a vowel by audibly interpolating successive *h's*" *(Baker).* (3) To aspirate ; *i.e.,* to observe the "h" in speaking or singing.
Aspiratamen'te. Aspiringly, longingly.

Aspiration *(F.).* An obsolete musical ornament :—

Written.	Played.

Aspiri(e)'ren *(G.).* To aspirate.

Asprez'za *(I.).* Asperity, harshness, roughness.
Aspramen'te. Harshly.
A'spro,-a. Harsh, rough.

ASPULL, George. *B.* Manchester, 1813 ; *d.* 1832. Precocious pianist, and composer of "exceptional brilliancy." During his brief career he gave concerts in England, Ireland, and Paris.

Assa'i *(I.).* Enough, very ; as *Allegro assai,* very quick.
Assa'i più *(I.).* Much more.

Assat. Corruption of **Nassat** *(q.v.).*

Assaying. "A flourishing before one begins to play, to try if the instrument be in tune ; or to run divisions to lead one into the piece before us."—*Grassineau.*

Assemblage *(F.).* A turn *(q.v.)*

Assembly. A drum or bugle signal to assemble soldiers.

Assez *(F.).* Enough, rather.
Assez lent. Rather slow.
Assez retenu. Somewhat slackened.

4

Assie'me *(I.).* *Ensemble,* concerted.

ASS'MAYER, Ignaz. Austrian organist and composer ; 1790-1862. Studied under M. Haydn. Imperial organist, Vienna, 1825; second Court-capellmeister, 1846. Wrote the oratorios *Saul's Tod, David and Saul,* and several masses and other church works.

Assolu'to,-a *(I.).* Absolute, chief. *Teno're assolu'to,* principal tenor.

Assonance *(F.* and *Eng.).* *(G.,* Assonanz', *I.,* Assonan'za.*)* Agreement or resemblance in vowel sound ; as *rest, bless, men.*

Assourdir *(F.).* To muffle.

ASTARITTA, Gennaro. Italian composer. Wrote *Circe ed Ulisse* (1777) and about 20 other operas.

ASTON, Hugh. *B.* Lancashire abt. 1480 ; *d.* 1522. Wrote vocal and important instl. music.

ASTOR'GA, Emanuele d'. *B.* Palermo, 1681 ; *d.* Prague, 1736. Trained in the Spanish Monastery of Astorga. Made Baron d'Astorga, 1704. By his songs and singing became a general favourite. Visited Portugal, Italy, England, Vienna, and Prague (where he spent his last years in a monastery). Wrote a celebrated *Stabat Mater* for four voices and orchestra, an opera (*Dafne*), and several songs and duets.

A su'o arbit'rio *(I.).* } At one's will, or
A su'o be'ne pla'cito *(I.).* } pleasure ; *ad lib.*

A su'o com'(m)odo *(I.).* At the performer's convenience.

A tem'po *(I.).* In strict time ; used after a *rallentando, accelerando,* &c., to show that the original speed must be resumed.

A tem'po com'(m)odo *(I.).* At a moderate, convenient speed.

A tem'po di gavot'ta *(I.).* In the time of a gavotte.

A tem'po di minuet'to *(I.).* In the time of a minuet.

A tem'po giu'sto *(I.).* In just, *i.e.* strict, accurate time. (In Handel, 4-4 time.)

A tem'po ordina'rio *(I.).* In ordinary time. At a moderate speed.

A tem'po pri'mo *(I.).* Return to the first, or original time.

A tem'po ruba'to *(I.).* Irregular, robbed time. (See **Tempo ruba'to.**)

ATHALI'A. Oratorio by Handel ; 1733.

A't(h)em *(G.).* Breath.
A't(h)em ho'len. To take breath.
A'themlos. Breathlessly.
Ath'men. To blow softly, to breathe.

ATKINS, Ivor A. *B.* Cardiff, 1869. Orgt. Worcester Cath., 1897.

A tre *(I.).* For three voices or instruments.
A tre cor'de. Release the soft pedal.
A tre ma'ni. For three hands.
A tre par'ti. In three parts.
A tre vo'ci. For three voices.

À trois *(F.).* For three voices or instruments.
À trois mains. For three hands.
À trois parties. In three parts.
À trois voix. For three voices.

Attac'ca *(I.).* Attack or begin the next movement or piece at once, or with a very short pause.
Attac'ca su'bito } Go on immediately.
Attacca'te su'bito }
Attac'ca su'bito il seguen'te. Go on at once with the next (movement).
Attac'ca su'bito l'Allegro. Go on at once with the Allegro.

Attacca're *(I.),* **Attaquer** *(F.).* To begin at once.

Attac'co *(I.),* **Attaque** *(F.).* (1) A short fugue-theme. (2) A short theme, or *motiv,* for imitation.

SULLIVAN. "Lost Chord."

The *Attac'co* is a characteristic feature of motets, madrigals, and many anthems.

Attack *(E.),* **Attaque** *(F.).* (1) The act or style of beginning either a solo or *ensemble* passage. (2) The clear and distinct commencement of a vowel sound in singing.
Chef d'attaque *(F.).* The leading 1st violin of an orchestra.
Chaque attaque 'assez en dehors *(F.).* Each entry (attack) to be made prominent.

ATTAIGNANT, Pierre (also **Attaingnant, Atteignant**). Music printer, first half of 16th cent. ; first, in Paris, to employ movable types. Printed 20 books of motets (1525-50), &c., now very rare.

Attasta're *(I.).* To touch ; to strike.

Attendant keys. (1) OF A MAJOR KEY.—The maj. keys with Tonic a perf. 5th higher and a perf. 5th lower ; and the 3 rel. minors (including that of the prin. key). Thus the attendant keys of C major are (1) G major, (2) F major, (3) A minor, (4) E minor, and (5) D minor.

(2) OF A MINOR KEY.—The min. keys with Tonic a perf. 5th higher and a perf. 5th lower ; and the 3 rel. *majors.* Thus the 5 attendant keys of C minor are (1) G min., (2) F min., (3) Eb maj., (4) Bb maj., and (5) Ab maj.

ATTENHOFER, Karl. *B.* Wettingen, Switzerland, 1837. Studied Leipzig Cons., 1857-8. Conductor of Rapperswyl Men's Choral Union, 1863. Settled in Zurich, 1867. Has also held various positions as organist, teacher of singing, &c. Well-known as a composer of men's-voice music. Cantatas : *Hegelingenfahrt,* 1890, and *Frühlingsfeier;* also masses, songs, violin-etudes, &c.

ATTERBURY, George L. Celebrated English glee composer. *B.* about 1735 ; *d.* 1796. Composed an oratorio, *Goliah.*

At'to *(I.).* An act (of an opera).

Atto're, Attri'ce *(I.).* An actor ; an actress.

AT'TRUP, Karl. *B.* Copenhagen, 1848. Succeeded Gade, 1869, as organ teacher at the Copenhagen Cons.; organist at several churches. His studies for organ are of educational value. *D.* 1892.

ATTWOOD, Thomas. *B.* London, 1765; *d.* Chelsea, 1838. Chorister, Chapel Royal, and pupil of Nares and Ayrton, from 1776-81; sent by the Prince of Wales (afterwards George IV) to Naples, 1783-5. Pupil of Mozart, Vienna, until 1787. Appointed organist of St. George the Martyr, London, and a member of the Prince's private band; teacher of the Duchess of York (1791), of the Princess of Wales (1795); orgt. of St. Paul's Cathedral (1795); composer to the King's Chapel Royal (1796); orgt. of the King's private chapel, Brighton (1821), and orgt. of the Chapel Royal (1836).

Works: 19 operas; anthems, services, glees, songs, pf.-sonatas, &c. He occupies a distinguished place among English composers, and was on friendly terms with both Mozart and Mendelssohn.

Au *(F.).* To the, with the, in the, &c.
Au mouvement. In time (tempo).

Aubade *(F.).* (1) A short instrumental piece in song-style. (2) A morning-piece corresponding to the old English "Hunt's up," the opposite of a Serenade. (3) A morning military band concert.

AUBER, Daniel-François-Esprit. A prolific composer of French operas. *B.* Caen, Normandy, Jan. 29, 1782; *d.* Paris, May 14, 1871. His father sent him to London to acquire a knowledge of his own business—that of an art-printer. Auber's inclination for music, however, proved irresistible, and he returned to Paris, 1804. His first opera, *Julie*, was produced in 1812, "with an orchestra of six stringed instruments." Cherubini, who was present, recognised Auber's talent, and undertook his further instruction. *Le Séjour militaire* (1813), and *Le Testament et les Billets-doux* (1819), were indifferently received; but *La Bergère Châtelaine* (1820) was a success. "From that date until 1869, scarcely a year passed without the production of one or several operas"—in all over 40. *Masaniello, ou la Muette de Portici* (1828), considered a masterpiece by Wagner, with Meyerbeer's *Robert le Diable* and Rossini's *Guillaume Tell*, "laid the foundations of French grand opera." Except *Masaniello*, all Auber's operas are *comic*, and in this style he stands first among French composers; his music is fresh and sparkling, "and has the true Parisian *chic* and polish." In 1842 he succeeded Cherubini as Director of the Conservatoire; in 1857, Napoleon III made him imperial *maître de chapelle.*

His last opera, *Rêves d'amour*, was produced when he was 87 years of age. Auber, a thorough Parisian, never set foot outside the city boundaries during the latter years of his life.

Operas: *Julie* (1812), *Le Séjour militaire* (1813), *Le Testament et les Billets-doux* (1819), *La Bergère châtelaine* (1820), *Emma* (1821), *Leicester* (1822), *La Neige* (1823), *Vendôme en Espagne* (1823, with Hérold), *Les Trois Genres* (1824, with Boieldieu), *Le Concert à la Cour* (1824), *Léocadie* (1824), *Le Maçon* (1825), *Le Timide* (1826), *Fiorella* (1826), *La Muette de Portici* (1828), *La Fiancée* (1829), *Fra Diavolo* (1830), *Le Dieu et la Bayadère* (1830), *La Marquise de Brinvilliers* (1831, with eight other composers), *Le Philtre* (1831), *Le Serment* (1832), *Gustave III* (*Le Ball masqué*, 1833), *Lestocq* (1834), *Le Cheval de bronze* (1835), *Actéon* (1836), *Les Chaperons blancs* (1836), *L' Ambassadrice* (1836), *Le Domino noir* (1837), *Le Lac des Fées* (1839), *Zanetta* (1840), *Les Diamants de la couronne* (1841), *Le Duc d' Olonne* (1842), *La Part du Diable* (1843), *La Sirène* (1844), *La Barcarolle* (1845), *Haydée* (1847), *L' Enfant prodigue* (1850), *Zerline* (1851), *Marco-Spada* (1852), *Jenny Bell* (1855), *Manon Lescaut* (1856), *Magenta* (1859), *La Circassienne* (1861), *La Fiancée du Roi de Garbe* (1864), *Le premier jour de bonheur* (1868), *Revés d' amour* (1869).

AUBER, Harriet. *B.* London, 1773; *d.* 1862. Author of hymn, "Our blest Redeemer."

AUBERT, Jacques ("le vieux"). Eminent French violinist (1668-1753). Leader in orch. of the Gr. Opéra and the Concerts Spirituels (1728). Wrote an opera, several ballets, and much violin music, &c.

AUBÉRY du BOULLEY, Prudent-Louis. French composer (1796-1870). Author of a method for guitar, and a "Grammaire Musicale" (Paris, 1830).

Auch *(G.).* But, also, so, likewise.
Auch in Zeit'mass. But in time.

Audace *(F.).* Bold, audacious, daring.

Au'diphone. A recent American invention for conveying vibrations to the teeth; said to be of great assistance in deafness.

AUDRAN, Marius-Pierre. Operatic tenor and song composer; *b.* Aix, Provence, 1816; *d.* Marseilles, 1887. Pupil of Arnaud. 1st tenor at the Opéra-Comique, Paris. Settled in Marseilles as Director of the Conservatoire, and professor of singing (1863).

AUDRAN, Edmond. Son of Marius. *B.* Lyons. 1842; *d.* 1901.

Composed 37 operas, operettas, &c., chiefly of a light character, a mass, a funeral march for Meyerbeer's death, &c. His most popular works are *Olivette* (1879), and *La Mascotte* (1880; given 1,700 times up to August, 1897).

AU'ER, Carl. (See **Frotzler.**)

AU'ER, Leopold. Distinguished Hungarian violinist. *B.* 1845. Pupil of Joachim. Since 1868, soloist to the Tsar, and leader of the Imperial Orchestra at St. Petersburg, and Professor at the Conservatoire. He is one of the finest of living performers.

Auf *(G.).* On, in, at, upon, near, &c.
Auf'blasen. To sound a wind inst.
Auf der Flö'te spiel'en. To play on the flute.
Auf der Mit'te der Sai'te. (Bow) at the middle of the string.
Auf ein'er Sai'te. On one string.

Auf'fassung. The general conception, or *reading* of a piece.

Auf'führung. Performance.

Auf'geregt. In an excited, agitated manner.

Auf'geweckt. Lively, brisk, animated.

Auf'halten. To suspend, to retard.

Auf'haltung. A suspension, a retardation.

Auf'lage. Edition, impression.

Auf'lösen. To resolve.

Auf'lösung. (1) The resolution of a discord. (2) Arpeggiating a chord.

Auf'lösungszeichen. The natural (♮), or other cancelling sign.

Auf'pfeifen. To play on a pipe.

Auf'satz. The tube of an organ-reed.

Auf'schlag. The up-beat.

Auf'schlagende Zung'e. A "beating" reed.

Auf'schnitt. The mouth of an organ pipe.

Auf'schwingend } In a lofty, impassioned style.
Auf'schwung, Mit }

Auf'schwung. Soaring, exaltation, rapture.

Auf'singen. To sing to; to arouse to singing.

Auf'spielen. To play to; to strike up.

Auf'steigende. Ascending.

Auf'strich. The up-bow.

Auf'takt. (1) The up-beat. (2) The initial part of a theme (if any) which comes before the first down-beat.

Auf'tritt. A scene (in an opera or drama).

Auf'wärts. Upwards.

Auf'zug. An Act (of an opera or drama).

AU'GENER & CO. Music-sellers and publishers. Founded 1853.

Augmentation. *(G., Vergrö'sserung, Verläng'-erung.)* (1) Doubling, or otherwise increasing the time-value of the notes of a fugue-subject, or of a theme used in imitative counterpoint.

Augmenté,-ée *(F.).* Augmented.

Augmented Interval. (See **Interval.**)

Augmented 6th Chord. (See **Extreme 6th.**)

Augmenter *(F.).* } To increase in loud-
En augmentant *(F.)* } ness; crescendo.

AUGUS'TINE (Augusti'nus), Aure'lius. Known as St. Augustine. *B.* Tagaste, Numidia, 354; *d.* Hippo, Algeria, 430. Called the "Father of the Church." His works contain important information concerning Ambrosian song.

AULETTA, Domenico. Produced the opera, *La Locandiera di Spirito,* Naples, 1760.

AULETTA, Pietro. Between 1728-1752 produced 11 ops. at Rome, Venice, Paris, &c.

AULIN, Tor. Violinist and composer; *b.* Stockholm, 1866.

Au'los *(Gk.).* A flute. *Di-aulos,* a double flute. *Aule'tes,* a flute player.

Aumentan'do *(I.).* } Increased, crescendo; aug-
Aumenta'to *(I.).* } mented.

A u'na cor'da *(I.).* On one string. Using the "soft" pedal in pianoforte playing.

AURELIA'NUS REOMEN'SIS. Monk at Réomé, 9th century. Wrote a treatise, "Musica Disciplina," published by Gerbert.

L'Aurore *(F.).* The dawn.

Aus *(G.).* From; out of; by, in, for.

Aus'arbeitung. Working out; development of a theme or composition.

Aus'bilden. To build up (the voice, &c.).

Aus'blasen. To blow out; to improve by blowing.

Aus'druck. Expression.

Aus'drucksvoll. With much expression.

Aus'führung. Performance, rendering, exposition, execution; working-out.

Aus'gabe. Arrangement, edition, setting.

Ers'te Aus'gabe. First setting, arrangement.

Aus'gehalten. Sustained, held out.

Aus'gelassen. Omitted, left out.

Aus'halten. Sustain. (Or, to sustain.)

Aus'haltung. Sustaining a note.

Aus'haltungszeichen. A hold, or pause, ⌒.

Aus'lauten. To cease to sound.

Aus'schlagen. To beat (time).

Aus'stattung. The staging, or "mounting" of an opera, &c.

Aus'tönen. To die away.

Aus'weichung. Change of key. (Modulation, transition.)

AU'SPITZ-KOLAR, Auguste. *B.* Prague, abt. 1843; *d.* 1878. Excellent pianist, pupil of Smetana and Proksch. Published a few pianoforte pieces.

AUSSENAC, Mlle. Young Portuguese pianist. First London appearance, 1907.

Äu'sserst *(G.).* Extreme; extremely.

Äu'sserst bewegt'. Extremely quick; *Presto.*

Äu'sserst rasch. Extremely fast.

Äu'sserst ru'hig. Extremely tranquil.

Äu'sserste Stim'men. The extreme or outer parts.

Aussi *(F.).* Also. *Aussi ... que.* As ... as.

Aussi calme que possible. As tranquil as possible.

AUTE'RI - MANZOC'CHI, Salvatore. Italian composer of operas and songs. *B.* 1845. Operas: *Dolores,* 1875; *Il Negriero,* 1878; *Stella,* 1880; *Il Conte di Gleichen,* 1887; and *Graziella,* 1894.

Authen'tic. *(G., Authen'tisch; F., Authentique; I., Auten'tico.)* A Mode, or melody, whose notes lie wholly (or principally) between the Tonic (or *Final*) and its higher octave. (See **Mode.**) It is opposed to *Plagal*—a Plagal Mode, or melody lying wholly (or principally) between the lower Dominant and its higher octave.

Authentic Melody.

Plagal Melody.

Authentic Part of the Scale.—From the Tonic to the Fifth above.

Plagal Part of the Scale.—From the Tonic to the Fourth below.

Authentic Cadence.—A final cadence, consisting of the Tonic chord preceded by the Dominant chord.

Au'to-Harp. A kind of zither.

It is so arranged that chords can be struck by means of mechanical compound dampers. The plectrum, swept across the strings, sounds the notes of the chord in arpeggio; and the melody is brought out by special stress on the highest (or some other) note of the chord.

Au′tophon. A form of barrel - organ. The notes to be sounded are determined by holes cut in a sheet of stout paper.

Auto′re *(I.).* Author, composer.

Autre *(F.).* Other, different.

AUVERGNE, Antonio d'. French violinist and composer. *B.* 1713 ; *d.* 1797. Conductor of the Paris Opéra Orchestra, 1751-1755 ; director until 1790.

In 1753 he made a sensation with *Les Troqueurs,* the first genuine *opéra comique;* "it resembled the Italian *intermezzi,* with spoken dialogue instead of recitative, and soon superseded the *comédie à ariette* (vaudeville with incidental music)." He wrote several other stage-pieces.

Auxiliary Note. *(G., Hilfs′note.)* A grace note : a note not essential to the harmony.

In Sol-fa, any " incidental " other than a passing-note used in the weak part of a pulse.

Auxiliary Scales. The scales of the five attendant keys.

Avec *(F.).* With. *Avec âme.* With soul.

Avec le chant. Same as *Col canto (q.v.).*
Avec plus d'accent. With more accent.
Avec un grand sentiment. With deep feeling.
Avec un peu plus mouvement. A little quicker.

A′ve Maria *(Lat.).* " Hail, Mary ! " " A favourite subject of sacred composition since the 7th century."

A′ve Ma′ris Stel′la *(L.).* " Hail, Star of the Sea ! " A famous Latin hymn.

AVENTI′NUS, Johannes (real name **Thurnmayer** or **Turmair**). Bavarian historiographer, 1477-1534.

Author of "Annales Boiorum" (1554), containing much information about musical matters ; editor of Faber's " Musicæ rudimenta," &c.

AVERY, John. 18th century English organ-builder. Erected organs at Carlisle, Winchester, Cambridge, &c.

Avici′nium *(L.).* An organ-stop imitating the warbling of birds.

A vide *(F.).* Open (as a string).

AVISON, Charles. Composer, organist, and writer. *B.* Newcastle-on-Tyne, 1710 ; *d.* 1770. Studied in Italy ; then in London under Geminiani.

Wrote some violin and harpischord music, and "An Essay on Musical Expression " (London, 1752, '53, '75); also publis ed with J. Garth, Marcello's "Psalm-Paraphrases," with English wo ds (1757). " Sound the loud Timbrel " is from a concerto.

A vis′ta, A pri′ma vis′ta *(I).* At first sight.

A vo′ce so′la *(I.).* (1) For a solo voice. (2) For voice alone (without acct.).

A voix sombre *(F.).* In a sombre tone.

A volonté *(F.).* At will ; *a piacere.*

A vue *(F.).* At sight.

AYLWARD, Florence. Song composer ; *b.* Brede, Sussex, 1862.

AYLWARD, Theodore. *B.* Salisbury, 1731 ; *d.* 1801. Mus.D. Oxon.

Orgt. St. George's, Windsor ; Gresham Prof. of Music from 1771.

AYLWARD, Theodore Ed. *B.* Salisbury, 1844. Orgt. Llandaff Cath., 1870-76 ; Chichester Cath. to 1886.

AYLWARD, Wm. Price. Salisbury, 1810-90. Excellent flautist and conductor.

AYRTON, Edmund. English composer and organist. *B.* Ripon, 1734 ; *d.* 1808.

Pupil of Nares. Master of Children of the Chapel Royal, 1780-1805. Wrote two full services and some anthems.

AYRTON, William. Son of E ; 1777-1858. Critic *Morning Chronicle,* 1813-26 ; *Examiner,* 1837-51. Editor *Harmonicon,* 1823-33 ; "Knight's Musical Library," 1834 ; &c.

AYTON, Fanny. Soprano vocalist. *B.* Macclesfield, 1806. Date of death uncertain.

AZEVE′DO, Alexis-Jacob. French writer and critic. *B.* 1813 ; *d.* 1875.

Author of a valuable life of Rossini (1864) ; contributor to *La France Musicale, Le Siècle, La Presse,* &c. A zealous but biassed partisan of the Italian school.

Azio′ne Sa′cra *(I.).* " A sacred action, or drama." Passion-music, or an oratorio.

B

B. (1) The leading-note (7th) of the scales of C major and C minor. (2) *Si (pron. see)* in "fixed-Do" systems. (3) The German name for B♭. (4) The highest "unmarked Doh" in Tonic Sol-fa.

In Germany, B♮ is called *H;* thus the numerous fugues on the name BACH are written on the notes

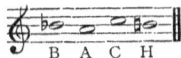

B A C H

B♭ *(G.).* Same as English B♭♭.

B cancella'tum *(L.).* The ♯; or B♭ *cancelled* by ♮ or ♯ in old music; therefore B♮.

B dur *(G.).* The key of B♭ major.

B du'rum *(L.).* B♮.

B major. The key requiring five sharps in the signature.

B minor. The relative minor of D major (2 sharps).

B moll *(G.).* B♭ minor.

B quadra'tum *(L.)* ⎫ *(I.,B quad'ro; F., B quarre).*
B quad'rum *(L.)* ⎭ "Square B,"*i.e.,* B♮.

B rotun'dum *(L.).* "Round B," *i.e.,* B♭.

B sharp. The old name of the ♯.

Ba, or **Bah.** (Pron. *Bay.*) The "occasional" (major) 6th in the Sol-fa minor scale.

BAB'BI, Ch. Violinist; 1748-1814. Wrote symphonies, vn. concertos, and fl. pieces.

BABELL, Wm. Eng. violinist and composer; 1690-1723. Member of the Royal Band. Made popular transcriptions from Handel's operas.

BABI'NI, Matteo. Renowned Italian tenor; 1754-1816. Sang in London, St. Petersburg, Vienna, Berlin, and Paris.

Baboracka (Baborak). Bohemian dances, with alternating or changing rhythm.

Baccalau'reus Mu'sicæ *(L.).* Bachelor of Music.

Bacchet'ta *(I.).* A drumstick.
Bacchet'te di le'gno. Wooden drumsticks.
Bacchet'te di spu'gno. Sponge-headed drumsticks.

Bac'chius *(Bacchy).* A metrical foot of one short and two long syllables (∪ — —).

BAC'CHIUS SENIOR. Greek writer,abt. 150 A.D. Two of his works are still extant.

Baccioco'lo *(I.).* A Tuscan guitar.

BACCU'SI, Ippolito. Italian comp., 16th cent.

BACFART (BACFARRE), V. (real name **Graew).** Transylvanian lutenist; 1515-1576.
Lived principally at Vienna and in Poland. Published works on lute tablature (1564-5).

BACH. An illustrious *family of musicians* and composers whose genius culminated in the great Johann Sebastian.
The family has been traced to HANS BACH, born nr. Gotha, abt. 1561. His presumed son, VEIT BACH (*d.* 1619), was a baker who played the zither. HANS, son of VEIT (abt. 1580-1626), was a travelling violinist popular throughout Thuringia, and known as "The Player" *(Der Spielmann).* Another son of VEIT was LIPS BACH (*d.* 1620); "from Hans and Lips, the two sons of Veit,sprang the main branches of the Bach family, whose male members filled so many positions as organists, cantors, &c. . . . that . . . even after there had

ceased to be any member of the family among them, the town musicians of Erfurt were known as 'The Bachs.'" When the families became dispersed they arranged to meet annually for mutual criticism and performance of the works they had composed during the year. In the middle of the 18th century as many as 120 Bachs attended this meeting, and eventually a collection of their compositions was formed, known as the "Bach Archives." The chief members of the family are given below. Johann (John) was quite a distinctive family name.

(1) BACH, Johann. 1604-1673. Eldest son of Hans; Organist at Schweinfurt, Suhl, and Erfurt.

(2) BACH, Christoph. 1613-1661. 2nd son of Hans; grandfather of J. Sebastian. Court musician, Eisenach. Wrote organ pieces.

(3) BACH, Heinrich. 1615-1692. 3rd son of Hans. Organist for 51 years at Arnstadt. Wrote organ music and hymns.

(4) BACH, Johann E. 1645-1717. 2nd son of J. (1). Music-director and organist at Erfurt. Chief work: a 9-part motet for double choir.

(5) BACH, Georg Ch. 1641-1697. Eldest son of Ch. (2). Cantor at Schweinfurt. Wrote a motet for two tenors and bass with an acct. for vn., 3 'celli, and basso.

(6) BACH, Joh. Ch. 1642-1703. Eldest son of H. (3). Organist and composer of great ability. Court organist, Eisenach, 1665-1703. Wrote motets (up to 22 parts), a wedding hymn (12 parts), and pieces for the clavecin (or harpsichord).

(7) BACH, Joh. M. 1648-1694. Brother of Joh. Ch.(6). Organist at Gehren. Wrote motets, preludes and fugues, &c.

(8) BACH, Joh. A. 1645-1695. Fine organist; 2nd son of Ch. (2). Father of J. Seb.

(9) BACH, Joh. Ch. 1645-1694. Court violinist, Arnstadt. Twin-brother of Joh. A. (8).
"There was such a remarkable resemblance between the brothers, in every particular, voice, gestures, moods, and style of music, that even their respective wives could distinguish them only by the colour of their clothes."

(10) BACH, Joh. B. 1676-1749. Son of J. E. (4). Organist at Erfurt, Magdeburg, and Eisenach. One of the best composers of organ music of his time. Wrote also pieces for orchestra and for harpsichord.

(11) BACH, Joh. N. 1669-1753. Eldest son of J. C. (6). Organist at Jena. Founded a harpsichord factory, and did much to establish equal temperament. Wrote suites, motets, &c., and a comic operetta.

(12) BACH, Joh. L. 1677-1730. Son of J. M. (7). Capellmeister at Saxe-Meiningen. Wrote a Requiem for two choirs.

(13) BACH, Joh. E. 1722-abt. 1780. Son of J. B. (10). Organist, St. George's Church, Eisenach. Wrote sonatas for violin and harpsichord.

(14) BACH, Joh. Ch. 1671-1721. Brother of J. S., eldest son of J. A. (8). Organist at Ohrdruff. Taught his distinguished brother the clavichord.

(15) BACH, Johann Sebastian. Most famous of the Bachs, and one of the greatest composers of all time. *B.* Eisenach, March 21, 1685; *d.* Leipzig, July 28, 1750. His father Joh. A. taught him the violin, but dying when J. S. was in his tenth year, the boy went to live with his brother J. Ch. (14), who gave him instruction on the clavichord. He was admitted chorister at St. Michael's, Lüneburg, 1700. Here he worked hard at the violin, clavichord, organ, and composition, often studying the whole night through. In 1703 he was appointed organist at Arnstadt, and in 1705 became acquainted with Buxtehude, who greatly influenced the style of Bach's later organ compositions. Appointed organist at Mühlhausen, 1707; court organist at Weimar, 1708; *Concertmeister,* 1714; *Kapellmeister* at Coethen, 1717. Visited Halle, 1719, to meet Handel, who, however, had just left for England. In 1723 he was appointed *Cantor* at the Thomasschule, Leipzig, and director at the two principal churches (Thomaskirche and Nicolaikirche). Here he remained for 27 years, and composed most of his sacred music. In 1747 he made his memorable visit to Frederick II of Prussia, and improvised on the various pianos in the palace. He also played on the chief organs in Potsdam, one of his feats being the improvisation of a six-part fugue on a theme set by the king.

Bach was near-sighted from childhood, and in 1749 an operation resulted in total blindness. His health declined, and he died the following year. He dictated a *choral* a few days before his death. Among his pupils were Krebs, Kirnberger, Goldberg, Marpurg, Vogler, and his own talented sons.

He promoted the adoption of equal temperament, and initiated the style of fingering still in general use.

Bach's mastery of counterpoint and fugue was supreme, and his music was in the highest degree intellectual. Schumann says that the "48 Preludes and Fugues" *(Wohltemperirtes Klavier)* should be every musician's "daily bread." His compositions mark an epoch—the fusion of the old and new styles, viz., the polyphonic (or contrapuntal) and the tonal (or harmonic).

"His originality and fecundity of thematic invention are astounding; moulded with his consummate contrapuntal art, and the freedom born of full mastery, polyphonic structures were reared which will be the admiration of ages."—*Th. Baker.*

After his death Bach's vocal works were little known, and it was not until Mendelssohn drew attention to their great value that they became appreciated.

Works: (1) Vocal: Five sets of cantatas for every Sunday and feast-day in the year, and many others, sacred and secular; five Passions including the famous *St. Matthew* and *St. John; Christmas* oratorio; Mass in B minor; two Magnificats; several fine eight-part motets, &c. (2) Instrumental: six French suites, six English suites, inventions, preludes and fugues (including the "48"—*Wohltemperirtes Klavier),* and many other works, all for clavier, harpsichord, or pf.; six sonatas for pf. and violin; solo sonatas for violin and 'cello; trios, &c., for various instruments in combination; concertos for from one to four pfs.; violin concertos; overtures and suites for orchestra; and a whole library of magnificent organ pieces—fugues, preludes, toccatas, &c.

The best biography of Bach is by P. Spitta (English trans. pub. by Novello & Co.).

(16) BACH, Wilhelm F. 1710-1784. Eldest son of J. S. Distinguished mathematician, and, next to his father, the cleverest German musician of his time. Unfortunately he gave way to dissipation, and died in misery.

(17) BACH, Karl Philipp Emanuel. 1714-1788. Third son of J. S. Chamber musician to Frederick the Great (1746-57). Succeeded Telemann, 1767, as music director of a church at Hamburg. A brilliant performer, he has been called "the father of modern pf. playing." He did much to originate the form of the sonata and symphony afterwards perfected by Haydn, Mozart, and Beethoven. He wrote a work on clavichord playing, showing his father's method of fingering.

Works: 210 solo pieces for clavier, 52 concertos, quartets, trios, &c., sonatas, 18 symphonies, and miscellaneous pieces of all kinds. Also two oratorios, 22 Passions, several cantatas, &c.

(18) BACH, Joh. Ch. F. 1732-1795. Ninth son of J. S. Capellmeister at Bückeburg. Wrote an oratorio, *The Resurrection of Lazarus,* a scena, *Die Amerikanerin,* cantatas, symphonies, concertos, &c.

(19) BACH, Johann Christian. Called the *English* Bach; 11th son of J. S. *B.* Leipzig, 1735; *d.* London, 1782. Studied with his brother, K. P. E. Organist, Milan Cathedral, 1754. Concert-director, London, and music-master to the Queen and Royal Family, 1759. Wrote several successful operas, including *Orione,* 1763.

(20) BACH, Wilh. Fr. E. 1759-1845. Son of J. C. F. (18); grandson and last male descendant of J. S.

Resided for some years in London as pianist, organist, and teacher. Capellmeister to King Frederick Wm. II, 1789. Wrote cantatas, songs, pf. pieces, &c.

Bach Choir. Founded, London, 1876.

Jenny Lind led the sopranos for some years.

Bach-Gesellschaft.

A Society formed in Germany, 1850, for publishing a complete critical edition of J. S. Bach's works. The idea originated with Schumann and others, and was taken up by the firm of Breitkopf & Härtel. (Publication completed, 1899.)

Bach Society. Founded, London, Oct. 27, 1849

BACH, Albert B. Singer and teacher. *B.* Hungary, 1844. Lives in Edinburgh. Author of "Musical Education and Vocal Culture," and other works on singing.

BACH, August W. Organist, teacher, and "Professor." *B.* Berlin, 1796; *d.* 1869. Wrote an oratorio, *Bonifacius*, and a sacred drama, *Iphigenia in Delphi.* His most famous org. pupil was Mendelssohn.

BACH, Leonhard Emil. Pianist and composer; *b.* Posen, 1849; *d.* 1902. Court pianist to Prince George of Prussia, 1874. Afterwards came to London.
Wrote some operas (*Irmengard, The Lady of Longford,* &c.), and pf. drawing-room pieces.

BACH, Dr. Otto. *B.* Vienna, 1833; *d.* 1893. Capellmeister at various German theatres, and afterwards at Salzburg Cathedral.
Wrote 5 operas, 4 symphonies, an overture, a requiem, chamber-music, &c.

BACHE, Francis E. *B.* Birmingham, 1833; *d.* 1858. Gifted and promising composer.
Wrote 2 operas, a pf. concerto, a trio (often played), songs, &c.

BACHE, Walter. Fine pianist, brother of F. E. *B.* 1842; *d.* 1888. Pupil of Plaidy, Moscheles, and Liszt. He did much to popularize Liszt's works in England.

BACHE, Constance. Sister of the above. 1846-1903. Studied under Walter, and also under Klindworth. Translator of *libretti: St. Elizabeth* (Liszt), *Pilgrimage of the Rose* (Schumann), *Hänsel and Gretel,* &c. Also translated Heintz's analyses of several of Wagner's operas, &c.

Bachelor of Music. Mus.Bac.; B.Mus. (See **Degrees.**)

BACH'MANN, Anton. 1716-1800. Instrument maker, Berlin. Invented the "machinehead" for tuning double basses.

BACH'MANN, Georg C. Belgian clarinettist and clarinet maker. 1804-1842.

BACH'MANN, Georges. *B.* about 1848; *d.* Paris, 1894.
Wrote numerous pf. pieces.

BACH'MANN, Gottlob. Saxon organist, 1763-1840.
Wrote 3 operas, 3 symphonies, a cantata, chamber music, songs, pf. pieces.

BACH'MANN, Pater Sixtus. 1754-1818. Brilliant Bavarian organist and pianist. His precocity and memory were wonderful. At 9 he is said to have played over 200 pieces by heart! In 1766 he held his own in an organ contest with Mozart (who was then 10 years of age). He afterwards became a monk.
Works: masses, cantatas, sonatas, symphonies, organ fugues, &c.

BACH'OFEN, Joh. K. *B.* Zurich, 1692; *d.* 1755. Wrote several sacred pieces once very popular in Switzerland.

BACH'RICH, Sigismund. Hungarian violinist and composer. *B.* 1841. Pupil of Böhm, Vienna. For 12 years member of the

"Hellmesberger Quartet." Now prof. at the Conservatoire.
Works: comic operas and operettas, a ballet, &c.

Back. *(G., Bo'den; F., Dos; I., Schie'na.)* Part of a violin, or other stringed inst.

BACK'ER-GRÖN'DAHL, Agathe. Norwegian pianist. *B.* 1847. Pupil of Kjerulf, Bülow, and Liszt. Married Gröndahl, the teacher of singing, 1875.
Works: pf. pieces and studies, songs, &c.

Backfall. (1) A piece of organ mechanism. (2) An obsolete ornament in harpsichord and lute music:

Written ∷ or ∷ ; played ∷

BACK'HAUS, Wilhelm. Pianist; *b.* Leipzig, 1884.

BACK'OFEN, Joh. G. H. 1768-1839. Talented performer on the harp, clarinet, flute, and horn. Established a wind-instrument factory, Darmstadt, 1815.
Wrote various compositions for the above instruments, and "methods" for harp, clar., and horn.

BACON, Richard M. Teacher and writer. *B.* Norwich, 1776; *d.* 1844. Founded the Norwich Triennial Festivals.
Wrote "Elements of Vocal Science" (1824).

BADARCZEW'SKA, Thekla. Warsaw, 1838-62.
Wrote the well-known "Maiden's Prayer" *(La prière d'une vierge),* and other pf. pieces.

BA'DER, Karl A. *B.* Bamberg, 1789; *d.* 1870. Organist Bamberg Cathedral, 1807. First tenor, Berlin court opera, 1820-45.
He was a fine actor and singer, being most successful in Spontini's operas.

BADI'A, Carlo A. *B.* Venice, 1672; *d.* 1738. Court composer, Vienna. Wrote 16 operas, 15 oratorios, and 45 "cantatas."

BADI'A, Luigi. *B.* near Naples, 1822; *d.* 1899. Wrote 4 operas and several songs.

BADIA'LI, Cesare. Distinguished Italian basso cantante. Specially good in Rossini's *Semiramide.* D. 1865.

Badinage *(F.).* Playfulness, trifling.

Bad'inerie, Badinage. An old vivacious dance form in 2-4 time. (Bach's *Orch. Suite in B minor*.)

BAER'MANN, K. (See **Bärmann.**)

Bagana. Abyssinian 10-stringed lyre.

Bagatelle *(F.).* A trifle; a short piece or sketch.
Many examples by Beethoven, Dvorak, &c.

BAG'GE, Selmar. *B.* Coburg, 1823; *d.* 1896. Journalist, composer, and critic. Editor, *Allgemeine Musikalische Zeitung,* Leipzig, 1863-6. Director, Basle Music School, 1868. Wrote "Lehrbuch der Tonkunst," 1873; composed a symphony, chamber music, songs, pf. pieces, &c.

Bagpipe (or **Bagpipes**). An ancient wind instrument of Eastern origin.
It was known to the Greeks and Romans, and formerly common throughout Europe, but is now only found in Italy, Sicily, Brittany, Calabria, Poland, Ireland, and Scotland. It

consists of a leathern bag, filled with wind either by the mouth or by bellows, two or three pipes of fixed pitch called *drones*, and a *chanter*, or *melody pipe*, which has 6 or 8 holes for the fingers. The scale differs very much from that in ordinary use. *Approximately*, it is as follows : —

Baguette *(F.).* A drumstick ; a fiddlestick.
Baguettes d'éponge. Sponge-headed drumsticks.
Baguettes de bois. Wooden drumsticks.
Baguettes ordinaires. Ordinary drumsticks.

BAHN, M. (See **Trautwein.**)

BAÏ (pron. *Bah'ee*), or **BAJ, Tomasso.** *B.* nr. Bologna, abt. 1650 ; *d.* Rome, 1714.
Famed for his *Miserere*, sung alternately with Allegri's and Baini's at the Papal Chapel during Holy Week.

BAIF, Jean A. de. *B.* Venice, 1532 ; *d.* Paris, 1589. Published works in lute tablature and some songs, &c.

BAILDON, Joseph. 1727-1774.
Composer of glees, &c. Gentleman of the Chapel Royal ; Lay Vicar at Westminster Abbey.

BAILEY, Lillian. (See **Henschel.**)

BAILEY, Marie Louise. Pianist. *B.* Nashville, U.S., 1876. Pupil of Reinecke and Leschetizky.
Played with success at Leipzig ; afterwards returned to America and toured through the United States and Canada. Has published pf. music.

BAILLIE, Peter. 1774-1841 (?). Famous itinerary Scotch violinist ; popular at "penny weddings," &c.

BAILLOT, Pierre M. F. de Sales. Celebrated French violinist. *B.* Passy, 1771 ; *d.* Paris, 1842.
In 1795 his reputation as a concert-violinist procured him a Professorship of vn. at the Paris Cons. Studied theory under Cherubini, Reicha, and Catel. He toured through Russia (1805-1808) ; Belgium, Holland, and England (1815-16) ; Switzerland and Italy (1833). Leader at the Grand Opéra, Paris, 1821 ; solo violinist, Royal Orch., 1825. Works : "L'Art du Violon" (1834) ; "Methode du Violon" (with Rode and Kreutzer) ; Essays on Viotti and Grétry ; violin concertos ; string quartets, trios, duos ; *airs variés*, &c., for violin.

BAILLOT, René-Paul. Son of preceding ; 1813-1889. Prof. at Paris Con.

BAÏNI, Abbate Giuseppe. Writer and composer ; *b.* Rome, 1775 ; *d.* 1844. Maestro of St. Peter's, Rome, 1817. Wrote a celebrated but not very trustworthy book on the "Life and Works of Palestrina" (Rome, 1828).
His chief composition is a *Miserere* which was given alternately with Allegri's and Baï's during Holy Week at the Papal Chapel. (See *Baï.*)

BAIRSTOW, Ed. C. Mus.Doc. Durham, 1900. Orgt. Leeds Parish Church, 1905.

Baisser *(F.).* To lower a note (as by a ♭).
Baissez vite le mi en ré. Lower quickly the E to D.

BAJ. (See **Baï.**)

BAJETTI, Gio. Italian composer ; 1815-1876. Leader of the orchestra, La Scala, Milan.
Wrote *Gonzalvo, L'Assedio di Brescia*, and other successful operas.

Ba'jo *(S.).* Bass.
Bajoncillo. (See *Baxoncillo.*)

BAKER, Benjamin Franklin. *B.* Wenham, Massachusetts, 1811. Succeeded Lowell Mason as teacher of music in the public schools, Boston, 1841. Established the Boston Music School, 1851.
Works : Cantatas, vocal quartets, songs, &c., and "Thorough-bass and Harmony."

BAKER, George. *B.* Exeter, 1773 ; *d.* 1847. Pupil of W. Jackson, Dussek, and Cramer. Organist successively at Stafford, Derby, and Rugeley. Mus. B. Oxon., 1797. Wrote anthems, glees, songs, organ pieces, and pf. pieces.

BAKER, Sir H. W. 1821-1877. Vicar of Monkland. One of the editors of "Hymns Ancient and Modern." Wrote "The King of Love" and other hymns.

BAKER, J. Percy. Orgt. and musical litterateur ; *b.* London, 1859. Educated R.A.M. ; A.R.A.M., 1888 ; Mus.Bac., Dunelm, 1896 ; editor *Musical News*, 1904.

BAKER-GRÓNDAHL. (See **Backer-Gróndahl.**)

BAKEWELL, John. 1721-1819. A Greenwich schoolmaster. Wrote the fine hymn, "Hail, Thou once despisèd Jesus."

BALAKI'REV, Mily Alex. *B.* Nishni-Novgorod, 1836. Opera conductor, Prague, 1866. Conducted classical concerts at St. Petersburg, 1867-70.
Works : A collection of Russian folk-songs, 1866 ; music to *King Lear ;* a symphonic poem, pf. pieces, &c.

Balala'ika. The common Russian guitar.

Balancement *(F.).* Tremolo. (See also **Bebung.**)

BALART, Gabriel. Spanish composer of "zarzuelas" (operettas). *B.* Barcelona, 1824 ; *d.* 1893. Director, Barcelona Cons.

BALATKA, Hans. *B.* Moravia, 1827 ; *d.* Chicago, 1899. Went to America, 1841 ; founded the Milwaukee *Musikverein*, 1851. Conductor Chicago Phil. Society, 1860 ; organised the *Liederkranz* and the Mozart Club, and conducted the Symphony Society from 1873.
Works : *The Power of Song, Festival Cantata*, choruses, quartets, songs, fantasias, &c.

BAL'BI, Ludovico. Italian Maestro from abt. 1600 at Padua and Venice. Wrote masses, motets, &c. Published (with Gabrielli and Vecchi) a collection of Graduals and Antiphones (Venice, 1591).

BAL'BI, M. Composer and theorist. *B.* Venice, 1796 ; *d.* Padua, 1879. Leader at the two Paduan theatres, 1818-53.
Works : Three operas, a miserere, masses, psalms, &c. Also edited and wrote important theoretical treatises.

Baldamen'te *(I.).* Boldly.

BALDASSAR'RI, Benedetto. Celebrated 18th cent. Italian tenor ; sang in Handel's and Bononcini's works.

BALFE, Michael Wm. Singer and composer. *B.* Dublin, May 15, 1808 ; *d.* Hertfordshire, Oct. 20, 1870. Violinist, Drury

Lane, 1824. Visited Italy, 1825, and studied at Rome and Milan. First baritone, Paris Italian Opera, 1828. Sang in Italian theatres until 1835; and produced some Italian operas. His first English opera was *The Siege of Rochelle*, 1835. *The Bohemian Girl*, his most popular work, was produced in 1843. He visited Vienna (1846), Berlin (1848), St. Petersburg and Trieste (1852-6), and retired to Rowney Abbey, Hertfordshire, 1864. (In 1857, his daughter, Victoire, made her *début* in Italian opera at the Lyceum.) Balfe's fame rests on his English operas and his songs.

English operas: *The Siege of Rochelle*, 1835 ; *The Maid of Artois*, 1836 ; *Catherine Grey, Joan of Arc*, 1837 ; *Diadeste, Falstaff*, 1838 ; *Keolanthe*, 1840 ; *The Bohemian Girl* (Drury Lane), 1843 ; *Daughter of St. Mark*, 1844 ; *The Enchantress*, 1845 ; *The Bondman*, 1846 ; *The Maid of Honour*, 1847 ; *The Sicilian Bride*, 1852 ; *The Devil's in it*, 1852 ; *The Rose of Castile*, 1857 ; *Satanella*, 1858 ; *Bianca*, 1860 ; *The Puritan's Daughter*, 1861 ; *The Armourer of Nantes, Blanche de Nevers*, 1863 ; *Il Talismano*, 1874. He also composed cantatas, ballads, part-songs, &c. "Come into the garden, Maud," is one of his most popular songs.

"Balfe ; His Life and Work," W. A. Barrett, is his best biography.

BALFOUR, Henry L. Organist ; *b*. Battersea, 1859. Orgt. Royal Choral Society.

Balg, Bäl'ge *(G.).* Wind chest ; bellows.
Bal'genregis'ter. Wind indicator.
Bal'gentreter \ The "bellows-treader," who. in old
Bälg'treter / organs, worked the bellows by standing or walking on them.

Bal'ken *(G.).* The bass-bar of a violin, &c.

Ballabi'le *(I.).* (1) A piece of dance music· (2) Ballet-music accompanied by dancing·

Ballad. *(I., Balla'ta.)* (1) A popular song· (2) A simple *narrative* song, or one which may also be used as a dance-tune.
"Formerly a little history, told in lyric verses, and sung to the harp or viol, either by the author himself, or the *jongleur*, whose profession it was to follow the bard, and sing his works." *Moore.*

Ballad-opera. Consisting chiefly of ballads, folk-songs, &c. (See **Beggar's Opera.**)

Ballad-Tune. The common tune of a ballad.

Balla'de *(G. & F.).* (1) A ballad ; a dance· (2) A descriptive setting of a poem in cantata form. (3) An instrumental piece "supposed to embody the idea of a narrative."
Balla'denartig \ In ballad style.
Balla'denmässig /
Balla'dendichtung. Ballad poetry.
Balla'denmässig, sehr rasch. In ballad style and very quick.

BALLARD. A French family of music-printers ; the first to use movable types. Robert Ballard had a patent from Henri II making him "sole music-printer to the King, &c.," 1552.

Balla're *(I.).* To dance.

Balla'ta *(I.).* (See **Ballad.**)

Balleri'na *(I., fem.).* \ A ballet-dancer.
Balleri'no *I., mas.).* /

Bal'let *(Eng.).* A kind of madrigal with a *fa la* refrain. (See **A ballata.**)

Ballet *(F.). (G., Ballett' ; I., Bal'lo, ballet'to.)* (1) A pantomimic representation of some story by means of dancing, gesticulation, &c., with accompanying music, but without words. (2) A spectacular stage dance.
Elaborate ballets are still danced at foreign opera houses ; formerly one was given after the opera at Covent Garden.

Ballet'to *(I.).* (1) A dance ; a ballet. (2) An *allegretto* in $\frac{4}{4}$ time *(Bach).*

Bal'li *(I., plu.).* Dances ; as *Balli Ingle'si*, English dances.

Ball'mässig *(G.).* In.dance time (or style).

Bal'lo *(I.).* A dance ; a ball. Any dance tune. *Da ballo*, in dance style.

BAL'LO IN MASCHE'RA. Opera by Verdi.

Ballon'chio *(I.).* An Italian country dance like the French *Passepied (Paspy).*

Ballonza're *(I.).* \ To dance recklessly ; to
Ballonzola're *(I.).* / skip about.

BALTAZARI'NI (Baltagerine). 18th century Italian musician. One of the best violinists of his day. Wrote several ballets.

BALTHAZAR (— Florence), Henri M. Belgian composer ; *b*. 1844. Pupil of Fétis.
Wrote operas, symphonies, cantatas, &c.

BALTZAR, Thos. *B*. Lubeck ; came to England, 1658. "The finest violinist of his time." Buried, Westminster Abbey, 1663.

BALY, William. Conductor and teacher. *B*. Warwick, 1825 ; *d*. 1891. Conducted the Exeter Madrigal Society for 15 years.

BANCHIE'RI, Don Adriano. *B*. Bologna, abt. 1567 ; *d*. 1634. Poet, composer, and organist.
Wrote masses, madrigals, motets, &c., and treatises on counterpoint and harmony. He opposed Guido's hexachordal system, and named the 7th note of the scale *ba*.

BANCK, Karl. *B*. Magdeburg, 1809 ; *d*. 1889. Pupil of Klein, Berger, and Zelter.
Friend of Schumann, and wrote for his *Zeitschrift*. Settled in Dresden as a teacher and critic, 1840. He edited a series of ancient works—vocal and instrumental—and wrote some part-songs and pf. pieces.

Band *(G.).* A volume.

Band. (1) An orchestra. (2) Any company of instrumentalists, as *brass band, military band*. (3) A section of an orchestra, as *wood-wind* band, *string* band, &c.

Ban'da *(I.).* (1) A band. (2) Specially, the brass and percussion instruments of an orchestra. (3) A band "on the stage."

Bande *(F.).* A band.
Une bande de musique militaire \
Une musique militaire \ A military band.
Une Harmonie /

BANDERA'LI, Davide. *B.* Lodi, 1789; *d.* 1849. Esteemed teacher of singing; well-known by his vocal exercises.

BANDI'NI, Primo. *B.* Parma, 1857. Has written the operas *Eufemio di Messina*, *Fausta*, and *Janko*.

BANDI'NI, Uberto. Composer; *b.* Rieti, 1860.

Bando'la *(S.).* A kind of lute.

Bando'nion. A kind of concertina, invented about 1830, by C. F. Uhlig, Chemnitz.

Bando'ra, Bando're, Bandalo're, Bandelo're. Spanish instruments of the lute family played with a plectrum, and essentially identical with the mandoline. Similar instruments are the *Bandolon, Bandura, Pandora, Pandura, Mandola, Mandura*, &c.

BANDROW'SKI, Alex. von. Tenor; *b.* Galicia, 1860.

Bandur'ria *(S.).* A kind of guitar or mandoline with wire strings.

BANÈS, Antoine A. *B.* Paris, 1856. Composer of a number of light operettas, ballets, &c., including *Toto, Madame Rose*, and *Le Bonhomme de neige*.

BANESTRE, Gilbert. Musician and poet, 15th century. Received 40 marks as "Master of the Song, assigned to teach the children of the King's Chapel," 1482 (1478?).

BAN'ISTER, Chas. Wm. 1768-1831. Published a "Collection of Vocal Music," London, 1803. Also wrote hymn-tunes, &c.

BAN'ISTER, Henry Ch. Son of Henry J. *B.* London, 1831; *d.* 1897. Pupil at R.A.M. of C. Potter; afterwards prof. of harmony and composition there. Prof. of harmony G.S.M. 1880, and at the Normal College for the Blind, 1881. He was a fine pianist. Wrote symphonies, overtures, chamber music, songs, &c. Also published some valuable educational works, &c., including "Text-book of Music,"1872; "Lectures on Musical Analysis," 1887; and a "Life of G. A. Macfarren," 1892.

BAN'ISTER, Henry J. *B.* London, 1803; *d.* 1847. Fine 'cellist; son of Chas. W. Wrote instruction books for 'cello.

BAN'ISTER, John. *B.* London, 1630; *d.* 1679. Violinist, member of the band of Charles II. Instituted regular concerts, 1672. Wrote music to *Circe* (Davenant) and *The Tempest*, 1676; "New Ayres and Dialogues for voices and viols," 1678; and some songs.

BAN'ISTER, John (Junr.). *D.* 1735. Violinist; son of the preceding. Member of the bands of Charles II, James II, and Queen Anne. Leader at the Italian opera.

Banja, or Banjo. A kind of guitar supposed to be of African origin. It has 5, 6, 7, or 9 catgut strings, variously tuned.

Bänk'elsänger*(G.).* Ballad singer; wandering minstrel.

BANNELIER, Ch. *B.* Paris, 1840; *d.* 1899. Translated Bach's *St. Matthew* Passion into French; arranged Berlioz's *Symphonie Fantastique* as a pf. duet.

BANNISTER, Ch. Bass vocalist and actor. 1741 (?)-1804.

BAN'TI (-GIOR'GI), Brigida. *B.* Lombardy, 1759; *d.* Bologna, 1806. A famous dramatic soprano. De Vismes, director of the Paris Académie, heard her singing in a Paris café. He engaged her for the Grand Opéra, and she afterwards sang in London, Milan, &c., with distinguished success. She had a lovely voice and wonderful natural ability, but would never take the trouble to learn to read at sight. Her success exemplified the old adage that "there are a hundred requisites of good singing, and whoever is gifted with a fine voice already possesses ninety-nine!"

BANTOCK, Granville. *B.* London, 1868. Entered R.A.M. 1889, and took the 1st Macfarren prize for composition. His first work was *The Fire Worshippers*, 1889. He has since written cantatas, much instrumental music, the operas *Caedmar*, *Rameses II*, *The Pearl of Iran*, &c. He was appointed Prof. of Music, Birmingham Univ., 1908.

BAPTIE, David. *B.* Edinburgh, 1822; *d.* 1906. Wrote anthems, glees, part-songs, &c. Author of "A Handbook of Musical Biography." and "Musicians of all Times" (1889; revised by Goodworth, 1907).

BAPTISTE (Baptiste Anet). Violinist; pupil of Corelli. Visited Paris about 1700, and introduced his master's works and style of playing. Died in Poland. Works: 3 sets of violin sonatas, 2 suites, 6 duos for two musettes, &c.

Bar. (1) A line drawn through the staff to divide the time into measures; the strong accent immediately follows the bar. (2) A measure; as "a few bars of music." N.B.—The line itself is now often called a *bar-line*. (3) The *Beard* of an organ-pipe.

BARBADETTE, Henri. French writer. *B.* 1828; *d.* 1901. Author of works on Beethoven, Chopin, Weber, Schubert, Mendelssohn, and Heller.

BARBA'JA, Domenico. *B.* Milan, 1778; *d.* 1841. Celebrated as manager of the opera houses at Vienna, Milan, and Naples, at all of which he introduced important operatic works.

BARBAR'INI, M. Lupi. 16th century motet composer. Also known as Lupi.

Bar'baro *(I.).* Barbarous, uncouth, wild, vehement.

BARBER, Abraham. Published "Barber's Psalm Tunes," Wakefield, 1686.

BARBER, Robert. Published various collections of psalmody, 1723 to 1753.

BARBER OF SEVILLE. Op. by Rossini, 1816.

BARBEREAU, M. A. B. *B.* Paris, 1799; *d.* 1879. Pupil of Reicha. Conductor, Th. Français. Professor of composition and musical history at the Conservatoire. Published two works on these subjects.

BARBI, Alice. *B.* Bologna, abt. 1860. Celebrated vocalist. Said to have revived the long-lost *Italian* method of singing.

BARBIER, Frédéric E. *B.* Metz, 1829; *d.* Paris, 1889. Wrote over 30 operas, including *Le Mariage de Columbine*, 1889.

BARBIER, Jules P. Dramatist. Paris, 1825-1901. Wrote, with Carré, several opera libretti, including *Faust* (Gounod), *Roméo et Juliette* (Gounod), *Hamlet* (A. Thomas), and *Françoise de Rimini* (A. Thomas).

BARBIE'RI, Carlo E. di. *B.* Genoa, 1822; *d.* 1867. Conductor at various theatres; finally director, National Theatre, Pesth.
Wrote the popular opera *Perdita* (Leipzig, 1865), and others; church music, songs, pf. pieces, &c.

BARBIE'RI, Francisco A. Famous Spanish composer. *B.* Madrid, 1823; *d.* 1894.
Wrote over 60 operettas, including *Gloria y peluca*, 1850, and *Jugar con fuego;* also orchestral works, motets, songs, &c.

BARBIREAU (also spelt **Barbarieu, Barberau,** &c.). Celebrated 15th cent. contrapuntist, Antwerp. Wrote masses, kyries, &c.

Bar'biton. An ancient Greek lyre.

BARBOT, Joseph T. D. Operatic tenor singer; *b.* Tolouse, 1824; *d.* 1897. Pupil of Garcia. Sang for many years in Italy. Created the *rôle* of "Faust" (Gounod).

Barcaro'la *(I.).*
Barcarole *(E. & G.).*
Barcarolle *(F.).*
A boatman's song; an imitation of the Venetian gondoliers' songs.
"These melodies possess a simple and artless beauty, equally delightful to the unpractised and to the most cultivated ear."—*Hamilton.*

BARCROFTE, Thos. English composer. Organist of Ely Cathedral, 1579. Wrote anthems, &c.

Bard. An ancient Celtic poet or singer.
"A kind of men, very singular, and to this time much respected among the Gauls, which were at the same time prophets, poets, and musicians."—*Rousseau* (1768).

Bar'de *(G.).* Bard, minstrel.
Bar'dengesänge. Songs of the bards.

BAR'DI, Giovanni. Count of Vernio. A Florentine nobleman, end of 16th century.
The attempt to revive the ancient lyric Greek drama by the artists and musicians who assembled at his house led to the birth of modern opera, 1600. (See *Peri.*)

Bardo'ne *(I.).* A baritone. A *Bourdon* (*q.v.*).

Ba'rem, Ba'ren *(G.).* A soft-toned organ stop with closed flue-pipes.
Bä'renpfeife. A bourdon (org. stop).

BAR'GE, Joh. H. W. Celebrated Hanoverian flute player; *b.* 1836. From 1867-95 1st flute Gewandhaus orchestra, Leipzig.
Works: "Method" for flute; flute studies; arrangements for flute, &c.

BAR'GHEER, Karl L. Violinist; pupil of Spohr, David, and Joachim. *B.* Bückeburg, 1833; *d.* 1902. Made several successful concert tours. Leader, Hamburg Philharmonic Society, 1876-89.

BAR'GHEER, Adolph. Brother of K. 1840-1901. Spohr's last pupil. From 1866, leader and professor Basle Music School.

BAR'GIEL, Woldemar. *B.* Berlin, 1828; *d.* 1897. Pupil of Moscheles and Gade. Director of a school of music, Amsterdam, 1865. Professor at the Royal Hochschule, Berlin, 1874.
His works, which were highly esteemed, comprise 3 overtures, a symphony in C, 3 danses brillantes, Psalm 96 for double choir, an octet, chamber music, part-songs, and pf. pieces.

Barginet (**Berginet, Bargaret, Bergaret**). A rustic or pastoral song or dance.

Baribas'so. A deep bass voice. (Also used for a *bass-baritone*).

BARING-GOULD, S. *B.* 1834. Rector of Lew Trenchard, Devon. Author of "Onward, Christian soldiers," &c.

Bariolage *(F.).* A medley.
"A cadenza, or series of cadenzas, whose appearance forms a design upon the music paper, 'a waistcoat pattern,' as it is called by performers."—*Stainer and Barrett.*

Bariteno're *(I.).* A second, or low, tenor.

Bar'iton(e) Clarinet. A clarinet whose tone and compass are between those of the clarinet and bassoon.

Bar'itone. (1) A brass instrument similar to the euphonium, but of narrower bore and lighter tone. (2) The baritone voice.

Baritone Clef. The F clef on the 3rd line :

Baritone Voice. (*G., Ba'riton; F., Bariton; I., Barito'ne.*) (See **Barytone.**)

Barkaro'le *(G.).* A barcarole.

BARKER, Chas. Spackman. Organ builder; *b.* Bath, 1806; *d.* 1879.
He invented the pneumatic lever, which, after being offered to several English builders, was adopted by Cavaillé-Col, Paris, 1837. He also invented an electric action.

BARKER, George A. 1812-1876. Wrote several songs, including "The Irish Emigrant," and "The White Squall."

BARLEY, Alf. Henry. Composer; *b.* London, 1872.

BARLOW, Arthur. Baritone; *b.* Cheshire, 1868.

BÄR'MANN, Heinrich J. Distinguished clarinettist; *b.* Potsdam, 1784; *d.* 1847. Weber and Mendelssohn wrote pieces specially for him.
Works: concertos, fantasias, quartets, variations, sonatas, &c.

BÄR'MANN, Karl. 1782-1842. Brother of H. J. Fine bassoon player.

BÄRMANN, Karl. 1820-1885. Son of H. J. Succeeded his father as 1st Clarinet in the Munich Court Orchestra. Wrote an excellent "Method" for clarinet.

BARNARD, Mrs. Ch. (*née* **Alington**). *B.* London, 1830; *d.* Dover, 1869.
Wrote many popular songs under the name of "Claribel." Some of them are still sung (especially "Come back to Erin").

BARNARD, D'Auvergne Henry. Song Composer; *b.* London, 1867.

BARNARD, Rev. John. Published the first collection of " Cathedral Music," 1641. He was a Minor Canon of St. Paul's.

BARNBY, Henry. 1826-1885. Lay-clerk, St. George's, Windsor. A fine bass singer.

BARNBY, Sir Joseph. Conductor and composer ; *b.* York, 1838 ; *d.* London, 1896. Entered York Minster choir at 7, and the R.A.M. in 1854. Studied under C. Lucas and C. Potter. Organist successively at St. Michael's, St. James the Less, to the Sacred Harmonic Society, and at St. Andrew's, 1862. Founded " Barnby's Choir," 1864. Organist St. Anne's, Soho, 1871, and succeeded Gounod as conductor of the Albert Hall Choir. Precentor at Eton, 1875. Principal, G. S. M., 1892. Knighted, 1892.

> Works: oratorio, *Rebekah*, 1870; Psalm 97; Service in E; Magnificat and Nunc Dimittis in E♭; Motet," King all-glorious ; " and many anthems, part-songs, hymn-tunes, carols, songs, &c. " Sweet and low " is probably his most widely-known composition.

BARNBY, Robert. 1821-1875. Brother of J. Alto singer, Westminster Abbey and Chapel Royal.

BAR'NETT, John. *B.* Bedford, 1802 ; *d.* 1890. Pupil of C. E. Horn. His first operetta, *Before Breakfast*, was produced at the Lyceum, 1825. Then followed other small pieces and the operas *The Mountain Sylph*, 1834, *Fair Rosamond*, 1837, and *Farinelli*, 1838. He settled in Cheltenham, 1841, as a teacher of singing.

> Other works: 2 unfinished oratorios, 2 string quartets, part-songs, &c., and many songs.

BAR'NETT, John Francis. Pianist and composer ; nephew of John. *B.* London, 1837. Won Queen's scholarships, R.A.M., 1850 and 1852. Studied also at Leipzig under Moscheles, Plaidy,and Hauptmann, 1856-9, and played at the Gewandhaus, 1860. Prof. R.C.M. 1883.

> Works: oratorio, *The Raising of Lazarus;* cantatas, *The Ancient Mariner, Paradise and the Peri, The Good Shepherd, The Building of the Ship, The Wishing Bell;* a symphony in A min., overtures, orchestral pieces, part-songs, songs, pf. pieces, &c.

BAR'NETT, Jos. A. Tenor singer ; brother of John. 1810-1898. Wrote songs, &c., and some sacred music.

BARNS, Ethel (Mrs. C. Phillips). Violinist and composer ; *b.* London, 1875.

Baroc'co (Baro'co) *(I.)*⎫ Singular, whimsical,
Barock' *(G.)* ⎬ eccentric.
Baroque *(F.)* ⎭ "Applied to music having a confused harmony, an unnatural melody, and full of modulations and discords."*—Hamilton.*

BARON', Ernst G. 1696-1760. Famous lutenist at the court of Gotha. Wrote important works on the lute and theorbo and several unpublished compositions.

Barox'yton. A deep-toned brass instrument invented by Červeny, Königgrätz, 1853.

Bär'pfeife, Bär'pipe, Baar'pyp (lit. a bear's pipe). A reed stop found in some old organs.

Barquarde *(F.).* An old term for Barcarolle.

BARR, Samuel. Glasgow composer, teacher, and writer ; 1807-1866.

Bar'ra *(I.).* A bar-line.

Barré *(F.).* " In guitar playing, a temporary nut,formed by placing the forefinger of the left hand across the strings."*—Hamilton.*

Barre *(F.),* **Barre de Mesure** *(F.).* A bar-line.

Barre d'harmonie *(F.).* The bass bar (of a violin, &c.).

Barre de luth *(F.).* The bridge of a lute.

Barre de répétition *(F.).* A dotted double-bar.

BARRÉ, Antonio. French composer of madrigals, &c., 16th century.

BARRE (or BARRA), Léonard. Pupil of Willaert. *B.* Limoges, 16th century. Singer in the Papal Chapel ; member of the musical commission, Council of Trent, 1545. Wrote madrigals and motets.

Barred C. The sign ₵, used for ₂ or ₄ time.

Barrel organ. A hand organ.

> An organ containing a cylinder turned by a crank, and fitted with pins or pegs which open valves to admit a current of air to a set of pipes. The bellows are filled by turning the handle, or (occasionally) by using the foot.

BARRET, Apollon M. R. Oboist; Paris, 1804-1879. Wrote a " Complete Method for the Oboe."

BARRETT, John. English composer ; 1674-1735. Pupil of Dr. Blow. Wrote theatrical music, popular songs, &c.

BARRETT, William Alex. Singer and writer. *B.* Hackney, 1836 ; *d.* 1891. Musical critic, *Morning Post*, 1869; *Globe*, 1874-5. Editor, *Monthly Musical Record*, 1877; *Orchestra and Choir*, 1881 ; *Musical Times*, 1887.

> Compiled with Sir J. Stainer a " Dictionary of Musical Terms," 1875. Wrote " English Glee and Madrigal Writers," 1877 ; " Balfe, His Life and Work," 1882, &c.

BARRETT, William L. Excellent flautist. *B.* London, 1847.

BARRI, Odoardo (Ed. Slater). Song composer ; *b.* 1844.

BARRIEN'TOS, Maria. Singer and violinist ; *b.* Barcelona, abt. 1884.

BARRINGTON, Daines. *B.* London, 1727 ; *d.* 1800. Wrote essays on Crotch, the Wesleys, and Mozart ; and " Experiments and Observations on the Singing of Birds." (See **Bird music**.)

BARRINGTON, Rutland. Contemporary actor and vocalist.

BARROW, J. Pub. a Book of Psalmody, 1730.

BARRY, Charles A. *B.* London, 1830. Studied at Leipzig, 1856-7. Editor, *Monthly Musical Record*, 1875-7. Sec. of the Liszt

Scholarship, 1886. Has written songs, hymns, pf. pieces, &c.

BARSANTI, F. *B.* Lucca about 1690; *d.* about 1760. Flautist, oboist, and viola player in London.
Published "A Collection of Old Scots Tunes," 1742. Also wrote violin concertos, flute solos, sonatas, &c.

BARSOTTI, Tommaso G. F. *B.* Florence, 1786; *d.* 1868. Founded the Free School of Music, Marseilles, 1821. Pub. "Méthode de Musique," 1828.

Bart *(G.).* Beard; ear of an organ pipe. *Bär'tig.* Bearded.

BAR'TAY, Andreas. Hungarian composer. 1798-1856.
Works: Operas, *Aurelia, Csel, The Hungarians in Naples;* an oratorio, masses, ballets, &c.

BAR'TAY, Ede. Son of A. 1825-1901. For several years director of the Pesth National Music Academy; founded the Hungarian pension fund for musicians.

BARTH (pron. *Bart*), **Christian S.** Famous oboe player. *B.* Saxony, 1735; *d.* 1809. Choir-boy under J. S. Bach. Played at Weimar, Hanover, Cassel, and Copenhagen.
Wrote concertos and other pieces for oboe.

BARTH, F. P. K. A. Son of C. S.; *b.* about 1773. Published collections of Danish and German songs.

BARTH, Gustav. *B.* Vienna, 1811; *d.* 1897. Cond., Vienna Male Choral Union, 1843. Court Capellmeister, Wiesbaden, 1858. Wrote male-voice pieces, songs, &c.

BARTH, Karl H. *B.* Pillau, Prussia, 1847. Able pianist. Pupil of Bülow, whom he succeeded as conductor of the Hamburg Philharmonic Concerts.
The Barth, De Ahna, and Hausmann Trio have toured through Europe with great success.

BARTH, Richard. Left-handed violin virtuoso. Director of Hamburg Phil. Concerts since 1894.

BAR'THE, Grat-Norbert. French composer; *B.* 1828. Pupil Paris Cons.; won *Grand Prix de Rome,* 1854.
Works: Operas, *Don Carlos, La Fiancée d'Abydos;* oratorio, *Judith;* cantatas, &c.

BAR'THEL (-Tel), J. C. 1776-1831. Saxon composer of church music, waltzes, &c.

BARTHE'LEMON (BARTLEMAN) François Hippolyte. Violinist and composer; *b.* Bordeaux, 1741; *d.* London, 1808. Leader at Vauxhall Gardens, 1770, and in Dublin, 1784.
Works: operas, *Pélopidas, Le Fleuve Scamandre, Le Jugement de Pâris, The Maid of the Oaks,* &c.; concertos, chamber music, vn. studies, &c.

BARTHOLOMEW, Mrs. A. S. *(née* Mounsey). Composer, organist, and pianist; *b.* London, 1811; *d.* 1905.

BARTHOL'OMEW, Wm. Violinist and writer. *B.* London, 1793; *d.* 1867. Friend of Mendelssohn. Translated into English the words of *Antigone, Athalie, Œdipus,*

Elijah, Lauda Sion, &c., of Spohr's *Jessonda,* Costa's *Eli* and *Naaman,* &c.

BARTLEMAN, Jas. London, 1769-1821. Celebrated bass singer, pupil of Dr. Cooke. Member of the choirs of Westminster Abbey and the Chapel Royal. He revived an interest in the music of Purcell.

BARTLETT, Homer Newton. Organist and composer; *b.* Olive (U.S.), 1845.
His published works include a sextet for strings and flute; a cantata, *The Last Chieftain;* quartets, anthems, glees, and several songs and pf. pieces.

BARTLETT, John. Mus. Bac. Oxon, 1610. Published "A Book of Ayres, with a Triplicitie of Musicke," &c., 1606.

BARTNAN'SKY. (See **Bortniansky.**)

BAR'TOLI, Padre E. ("Padre Raimo"). Italian composer; 1606-1656. Wrote masses, motets, psalms, &c.

BAR'TOLO, Padre D. Italian Jesuit; 1608-1685. Wrote a learned work on "Sound," 1679.

BARTON, Rev. W. *B.* abt. 1598; *d.* Leicester, 1678. Published a popular "Book of Psalms, with Tunes," &c.

Bar'ytenor. A deep tenor.

Bar'yton, Bar'ytone. The viola di bordone *(q.v.).* *Bar'ytonhorn (G.).* The euphonium. *Bar'ytonschlüssel (G.).* Baritone clef *(q.v.).* *Bar'ytonstimme (G.).* Barytone voice or part.

Bar'ytone, or **Baritone, Voice** (from *Gk. Barutonos,* deep-toned). A voice between a tenor and a bass. Compass from about
N. B.—The prefix "Bary" or "Bari" is from *Gk. Barus,* heavy. *Barytone* is perhaps the preferable spelling; but *Baritone* is much more usual.

Bas, Basse *(F.).* Low. *Bas-dessus.* The Mezzo-soprano voice.

Base *(Eng.).* The old spelling of Bass.

BA'SELT, Fritz. *B.* Oels, Silesia, 1863. Music-dealer, teacher, and composer. Since 1894 director of the Phil.-Verein, Frankfort-on-Main, and conductor of the "Sängervereinigung."
Works: *Der Fürst von Sevilla, Don Alvaro, René und Gaston,* and many other operettas and short operas; about 100 male choruses, songs, pieces for orchestra, violin, pf., &c.

BASE'VI, Abramo. *B.* Leghorn, 1818; *d.* 1885. Failing as opera composer he turned to writing. Founded *Armonia,* a musical journal, at Florence; instituted the Beethoven Matinées, 1859.
Published works on "Verdi's Operas," harmony, musical history, &c.

Basflicor'no *(I.).* A baritone **Flügelhorn** *(q.v.).*

BASIL (St.) the Great. Bishop of Cæsarea, 329-379. Said to have introduced antiphonal singing into the Eastern Church.

BASI'LI, Francesco. Italian composer, 1766-1850. Maestro St. Peter's, Rome, 1837.
Produced several operas and "dramatic oratorios" in Rome, Naples, &c. Wrote also motets, psalms, litanies, symphonies, songs, pf. sonatas, &c.

Bask'ische Trom'mel *(G.).* A tambourine.

Bass. *(G., Bass; F., Basse; I., Bas'so.)*
(1) The lowest note of a chord; the lowest part in any composition.
(2) The lowest male voice; average compass—
(3) The lowest of a family of instruments; as Bass trombone, Bass clarinet.
(4) The Double-bass, 'Cello (or both).

Bass Clarinet. A clarinet an octave lower than the ordinary clarinet.
   Notable instances of its use are by Meyerbeer in *The Huguenots*, and Wagner in *Tristan*, &c.
Bass Clau'sel (G.). The bass proceeding a fifth downwards, or a fourth upwards.
Bass Drum. (See **Drum**.)
Bass Flute. An 8 ft. pedal stop of the flute family.

Bass Horn (Cornobasso). (1) The precursor of the ophicleide. Compass from—
(2) The French horn in low B♭ or A. (See **Horn.**)

Bass Lute. (See **Theorbo.**)

Bass Trumpet. An old instrument now superseded by the trombone.

Bass Tuba. A kind of bombardon, with a full tone and extensive compass, much used by Wagner, notably in *Die Walküre*.

Bass Viol. (1) Old familiar name of the 'cello. (2) (See **Viol**).

Bas'sa *(I.).* Fem. of *bas'so*, "low."
Otta'va bas'sa. An octave lower.

BASSA'NI, Giovanni. Venetian composer, about 1600. Published 2 vols. of "Concerti Ecclesiastici," and some canzonette.

BASSA'NI (or BASSIA'NI), Giovanni B. Violinist; *b.* Padua about 1637; *d.* 1716. Maestro, Accademia della Morte, Ferrara, 1703. Teacher of Corelli.
   Works : 6 operas, motets, masses, violin sonatas, &c

BASSA'NI, Geronimo. 18th century. Contrapuntist and teacher. Pupil of Lotti.
   Works : 2 operas produced at Venice, *Bertoldi* (1718), *Amor per forza* (1721), masses, motets, &c.

Bass-bar. *(G., Bal'ken; F., Barre d'harmonie.)* A strip of wood in violins, &c., to support the pressure of the bridge and equalise the vibration.

Bass clef. The F clef on the 4th line. (See **Clef.**)

Basse *(F.).* Bass. The 'cello or other bass inst.
Basse chantante. (1) The vocal bass. (2) A *singing* bass (a baritone).
Basse chiffrée } A figured or continued bass.
Basse continue }
Basse contrainte. A ground bass. *Basso ostinato.*
Basse contre. (1) A deep bass. (2) The double bass.
Basse danse. A stately dance for two persons (15th and 16th centuries).
Basse de cremorne. The bassoon or its precursors.
Basse d'harmonie. The ophicleide.
Basse de hautbois. The corno inglese, or bassoon.
Basse de viole. The 'cello.
Basse de violon. The double-bass.
Basse double. Double-bass.
Basse figurée. Figured bass.
Basse fondamentale. The root or the generator of a chord.
Basse obstinée. A ground bass (*q.v.*).
Basse récitante. A *reciting* bass; same as *basse chantante.*
Basse taille. The baritone voice.

Basses. The 'cellos and double-basses of an orchestra.

Bas'set-horn. *(G., Bassett'horn; F., Cor de Basset; I., Cor'no di basset'to.)* An instrument of soft rich quality shaped like a clarinet, with a curved bell-shaped end.
   It is a transposing instrument, standing in F, *i.e.* all the notes sound a fifth lower than they appear on paper. Its compass is very extensive—real pitch. It is often confused with the *Cor anglais*, which is however, a *tenor oboe* while the basset-horn is a tenor *clarinet.*
   Mozart employed two basset-horns instead of clarinets in his *Requiem;* the opening of the *Recordare* is especially fine.

Corni di Bassetto.   *Recordare,* MOZART'S *Requiem.*

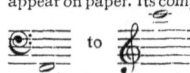

Basset'pommer *(G.).* A precursor of the bassoon.
Bassett' *(G.).* An old name for the 'cello.
Basset'to *(I.).* (1) A little bass. A viola. (2) An organ reed-stop; 8ft. or 16ft. tone.
BASSE'VI. (See **Cervetto.**)
Bass'flöte *(G.).* (See **Bass flute.**)
Bass'geige *(G.).* Violoncello, or double-bass.
Bas'si *(I.).* Plural of *Basso.*

BAS'SI, Luigi. Italian basso cantante; 1766-1825. Theatrical singer in Italy, Prague, and Vienna. Afterwards director of the Dresden opera. Mozart wrote the part of *Don Giovanni* for him.

BASSIRON, P. Contrapuntist, Netherlands. 15th century. Some of his masses were printed by Petrucci (Venice, 1508).

Bas'so *(I.).* Bass. (1) The bass part, or bass of the harmony. (2) A bass singer. (3) The double bass, or other bass inst.
Bas'so bas'so. A very deep bass.
Bas'so buf'fo. A comic bass.
Bas'so cantan'te. Same as *basse chantante*, a voice between baritone and bass.
Bas'so cifra'to. A figured bass.
Bas'so concertan'te. The principal bass instrument; that which accompanies solos and recitatives.
Bas'so conti'nuo. Continued, or figured bass.
Bas'so figura'to. (1) A figured bass. (2) A bass with runs, &c.
Bas'so fondamenta'le. The fundamental bass: root or generator of a chord.
Bas'so numera'to. Figured bass.
Bas'so ostina'to. Ground bass.
Bas'so profon'do. A deep heavy bass.
Bas'so ripie'no. (See **Ripieno**.)

Bas'so da ca'mera *(I.).* A small double-bass often used for solo playing.

Basson *(F.).* The bassoon.

Basson Quinte *(F.).* A tenor bassoon (tenoroon) a 5th higher than the ordinary bassoon.

Basson Russe *(F.).* A variety of the bass horn. Compass

Bassoon. *(G., Fagott'; F., Basson; I., Fagot'to).* The natural bass of the oboe, and the orchestral bass of the wood-wind family.
   It has a double reed, and gives the complete series of partials. (See *Acoustics*.) Its effective

compass is from [musical notation] to [musical notation] (with [musical notation] all the semitones on modern instruments). Solo players can extend the upward compass nearly an octave. The upper notes—like those for the 'cello—are often written with the tenor clef ; very high notes with treble clef.

Bass'posaune *(G.).* Bass trombone.
Bass'schlüssel. Bass clef.
Bass'stimme. Bass voice.
Bass'zeichen. Bass clef.

Ba'sta, Bastan'te *(I.).* Enough, sufficient.

BASTARDEL'LA. (See **Agujari**.)

BASTIAANS', J. G. Dutch composer, teacher, and organist ; 1812-1875. Pupil of Schneider and Mendelssohn. Organist of the great organ at St. Bavo's, Haarlem, 1868. Published chorals, songs, &c.

BASTIEN et BASTIENNE. Operetta by Mozart, written in his 12th year, 1768.

BASTON, Josquin. Netherland composer, 16th cent. His motets and chansons were very popular.

BATES, Frank. *B.* March, Cambridge, 1856. Mus.Doc. Dublin, 1884. Orgt. Norwich Cathedral since 1885.

BATES, James. Noted trainer of boys' voices ; *b.* London, 1856.

BATES, Joah. *B.* Halifax, 1740 ; *d.* London, 1799. Conducted the Handel Commemoration Festivals, 1784-91.

BATES, Wm. Abt. 1720-1790. Wrote and arranged much music for the popular concerts at Marylebone and Vauxhall.
Works : *The Jovial Crew* (1760), *Pharnaces*, (1765), *The Theatrical Candidates* (1775), and *Flora, or Hob in the Well* (1768) ; also glees, catches, violin sonatas, &c.

BATESON, Thos. Mus.Bac. Famous madrigalist ; *b.* abt. 1575 ; *d.* 1630. Orgt. Chester Cath. (1599-1611), then Dublin.
Works : "First Set of Madrigals for 3, 4, 5, and 6 Voices," 1604 ; "Second Set of Madrigals. Apt for Viols and Voyces," 1618.

BATHE, Wm. *B.* Ireland. 1564 ; *d.* 1614. Published a "Brief Introduction to the True Art of Musicke," 1584.

BATISTE, Antoine Édouard. Paris, '1820-76. Prof. Paris Cons. Organist of St. Eustache.
Composed much popular organ music. Edited "Solfèges du Conservatoire" (12 vols.).

BATISTIN. (See **Struck**.)

BATKA, Dr. Rd. *B.* Prague, 1868. Co-founder *New Musical Review*, 1896.
Works : Lives of Schumann and Bach, historical treatises, &c.

Bâton. *(F., Bâton de Mesure.)* The conductor's stick.
"The roll of paper or other material with which the conductor of an orchestra marks the time."—*Hamilton.*
"The baton first came into general use in England in 1832-33 ; one of the earliest instances of its employment was by Spohr at the Philharmonic, 1820."—*Grove.*
It was not used at Leipzig till 1835.

BATTA, Alex. Renowned 'cellist ; *b.* Maestricht, 1816 ; *d.* 1902.
Pub. pieces and transcriptions for 'cello and pf.

BATTA, Jos. 'Cellist and composer ; *b.* Maestricht, 1824. Brother of Alex. 'Cellist Paris Opéra Comique from 1846.
Works : symphonies, overtures, &c.

BATTAILLE, Chas. A. Bass singer ; *b.* Nantes, 1822 ; *d.* 1872. Sang Paris Opéra Comique, 1848-57. Pub. a "Singing Method."

BATTANCHON, Félix. Eminent French 'cellist ; 1814-1893.
Invented the "Baryton," a small 'cello, 1846.

Battante *(F.).* Beating.

Battement *(F.).* An obsolete ornament in singing, somewhat like the modern *tremolo* or *vibrato.*

BATTEN, Adrian. About 1585-1637. Vicar-Choral Westminster Abbey, 1614 ; St. Paul's, 1624 ; later organist of St. Paul's.
Wrote services and anthems, some of which are given in "Boyce's Cathedral Music."

BATTEN, Robt. (**H. J. L. Wilson**.) Baritone vocalist ; *b.* Gloucester, 18—.

Bat'tere, Il *(I.).* The down beat.
Bat'tere il tem'po }
Bat'tere la misu'ra } To beat time.

Batterie *(F.).* (1) A roll on a side drum. (2) Striking the strings of a guitar instead of plucking them. (3) Broken chords. (4) The percussion instruments of an orchestra.

Battery. An effect in harpsichord music.
Written [musical notation] Played [musical notation]

Battez à 2 temps *(F.).* Beat 2 in each bar.
Battez à 4 temps. Beat four in each bar.

Battimen'to *(I.).* Same as **Battement** (*q.v.*).

BATTISHILL, Jonathan. London, 1738-1801. Chorister, St. Paul's ; deputy organist Chapel Royal, under Boyce ; conductor, Covent Garden ; organist, several London churches.
Wrote many popular anthems, glees, songs, &c., and some operatic music.

BATTISTA, V. *B.* Naples, 1823 ; *d.* 1873. Wrote 13 operas, now forgotten.

BATTISTINI, M. Italian baritone ; *b.* 1857. Has sung in Buenos Ayres, Italy, Spain, London, Berlin, &c.

Battito're di mu'sica *(I.).* Time-beater ; conductor.

BATTMANN, Jacques L. Organist. *B.* Alsace, 1818 ; *d.* Dijon, 1886.
Works : masses, motets, a harmonium method, a pf. method, a work on plain-song, harmonium pieces, &c.

BATTON, Désiré A. *B.* Paris, 1797 ; *d.* 1855. Pupil of Cherubini ; won *Grand Prix de Rome*, 1816. Inspector of Branch Schools of the Cons., 1842.
His operas—except *La Marquise de Brinvilliers* (with Auber and others, 1832)—had little success.

Battre la Mesure *(F.).* To beat time.

Battu'ta *(I.).* (1) A measure. (2) A beat. (See **A battuta** and **Accent**, p. 7.)

Bau *(G.).* The *structure* of mus. insts., &c.

BAUDIOT, Ch. N. *B.* Nancy, 1773 ; *d.* Paris, 1849. Prof. of 'cello, Paris Cons., 1820.
Published much 'cello music and important instruction books for the instrument. Wrote, with Levasseur and Baillot, the 'cello method used at the Conservatoire.

BAUGHAN, E. A. Contemp. writer on music. Mus. critic, London *Daily News.*

BAU′ER, C. 18th century organ builder, Wurtemburg.
Introduced the single large bellows in place of the small ones previously used.

BAU′ER, Harold. Pianist ; *b.* London, 1873. *Début*, 1883.

Bau′ernflöte *(G.),* **Bau′ernpfeife** *(G.),* **Bäu′erlein** *(G.).* (1) A rustic flute. (2) An old-fashioned organ stop.
Bau′erlied. A rustic song.
Bau′ernleyer. A hurdy-gurdy.

BAU′MANN. (See **Paumann**.)

BAUM′BACH, F. A. German compr.; 1753-1813.
Wrote songs, pieces for harpsichord, pf., 'cello, guitar, &c., and various articles on music.

BAUM′FELDER, Fr. *B.* Dresden, 1836.
Composer of favourite drawing-room pf. pieces —" Confidence," " Rondo Mignon," &c.

BAUM′GART, E. F. 1817-1871. Music-director Breslau University. Edited K. P. E. Bach's " Clavier Sonaten."

BAUM′GARTEN, Cotthilf von. *B.* Berlin, 1741 ; *d.* 1813.
Wrote the operas *Zemire und Azor, Andromeda,* and *Das Grab des Mufti.*

BAUM′GARTEN, Karl F. *B.* Germany, 1754 (44?) ; *d.* London, 1824. Leader Covent Garden orchestra, 1780-1794.
Wrote *Robin Hood* (1786), *Blue Beard* (1792), and other stage pieces.

BAUM′GÄRTNER, A. Munich, 1814-1862. Published several papers, &c., on " Musical Shorthand."
Works : a *Requiem*, psalms, choruses, pf. pieces.

BÄUM′KER, Wilhelm. *B.* Elberfeld, 1842. School inspector and chaplain.
Has written much and well on musical subjects (including the Lives of Palestrina and Lassus) ; and has published several important collections of Dutch and German Lieder (from 15th cent.).

BAUSZ′NERN, Waldemar von. Composer ; *b.* Berlin, 1866.

BAX, A. E. Trevor. Composer ; *b.* London, 1883.

Baxoncil′lo *(S.).* (1) Spanish organ stop like an open diapason. (2) A small bassoon.

BAXTER, Richard. 1615-1691. Author of "The Saints' Everlasting Rest." Wrote the hymn "Lord, it belongs not to my care."

Bayadere, Bayadeer. Dancing girl in Hindu temples.

BAY′ER, Jos. Violinist ; *b.* Vienna, 1852. Prolific composer of ballets, operettas, &c. Ballet director, Vienna Court Opera, 1882.
Chief works : *Der schöne Kaspar* (1889), *Rouge et noir* (1892), *Die Welt in Bild und Tanz* (1892), *Columbia* (1893), *Rund um Wien* (1894), *Olga* (1896), *Die Braut von Korea* (1897).

Bay′la, Bay′le *(S.).* A dance ; a comic dancing song.

BAYLY, Barré Dalton. Violinist ; *b.* Jersey, 1850.

Bayreuth (Baireuth).
Franconian town celebrated for containing Wagner's " ideal theatre," and for its performances of Wagner's operas (1876, 1882, and since), attended by musicians from all parts of the world.

BAZIN, F. E. J. *B.* Marseilles, 1816 ; *d.* 1878. *Prix de Rome*, Paris Cons., 1840 ; Prof. of Composition, 1871 ; member of the Académie, 1872.
Works : nine operas, and a " Cours d'harmonie."

Bazuin *(Dutch).* Trombone.

BAZZI′NI, Antonio. Famous violinist ; *b.* Brescia, 1818 ; *d.* Milan, 1897. Maestro of the Church of S. Filippo, at 17, and wrote oratorios, masses, &c. On Paganini's advice toured successfully through Europe. Returned to Brescia, 1864, and devoted himself to composition. Director Milan Cons., 1882.
Works : Symphonic Poem, *Francesca da Rimini* ; overtures, *Saül* and *Lear* ; cantatas, *Senacheribbo* and *La Risurrezione* ; psalms, concertos, a string quintet (his finest work), and miscellaneous pieces of all kinds.

BAZZI′NO, F. M. 1593-1660. Italian virtuoso on the theorbo.

BAZZI′NO, N. *D.* 1639. Wrote masses, &c.,

bb *(G.).* Double-flat (♭♭).

BB♭ Bass. Contrabass Bombardon (in B♭).

Be *(G.).* The flat (♭).
Be-Ton′arten. Flat keys.

BEACH, Mrs. H. H. A. (**Amy M. Cheney**). Gifted American composer and concert pianist ; *b.* 1867.
Her numerous compositions include a Mass in E♭ ; a ballade in D♭ ; *The Minstrel and the King*, for soli, choir, and orchestra ; " Gaelic " symphony in E minor ; and many anthems, songs, pf. pieces, &c.

BEALE, Geo. G. *B.* London, 1868. Orgt. Llandaff Cath. since 1894.

BEALE, Thos. Willert. (" **Walter Maynard**.") London, 1828-94. One of the founders of the New Philharmonic Society.
Works : two operas, *An Easter Egg* and *Matrimonial News* ; some part-songs, &c.

BEALE, Thurley. *B.* Hertfordshire, 1849. Baritone vocalist.

BEALE, Wm. *B.* Cornwall, 1784 ; *d.* London, 1854. Famous composer of glees and madrigals. Pupil of Dr. Arnold.
Works : Collections of Glees and Madrigals, 1815 and 1820 ; prize madrigal, " Awake, sweet Muse,"1813 ; and many others.

Bear′beitet *(G.).* Revised, adapted, arranged.

Bear′beitung *(G.).* A revision, adaptation, &c.

BEARD, John. 1716-91. Leading English tenor of his time ; much of Handel's music was specially written for him.

Beards. Small projections in front of or across the mouth of an organ pipe to aid quicker speech.

Bearings. The notes first tuned (in tuning the organ, pf., &c.), from which all the others are regulated.

5

Beat. (1) A single motion of the hand, or bâton, in beating time.

(2) A division of a bar, or measure. (See **Accent.**)

(3) The "throb" caused by interference of vibrations. (See **Acoustics.**)

(4) An old "grace" or ornament :—

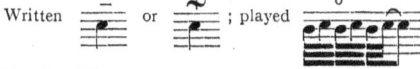

Written   [notation]   or   [notation] ; played   [notation]

Beating Time.

(1) Duple Measure : $\frac{2}{2}$, $\frac{2}{4}$,. Quick $\frac{6}{8}$ (or $\frac{6}{4}$) ; 2 - pulse, Quick 6-pulse.

| Down : Up ||

(2) Triple Measure : $\frac{3}{2}$, $\frac{3}{4}$, $\frac{3}{8}$, Quick $\frac{9}{8}$ (or $\frac{9}{4}$) ; 3-pulse, Quick 9-pulse.

| Down : Right : Up || *or* | Down : Left : Up ||

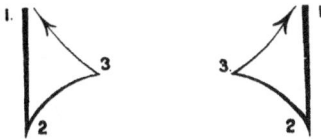

(3) Quadruple Measure : $\frac{4}{2}$, $\frac{4}{4}$ (**C**), $\frac{4}{8}$, Quick $\frac{12}{8}$ (or $\frac{12}{4}$) ; 4-pulse, Quick 12-pulse.

| Down : Left | Right : Up ||

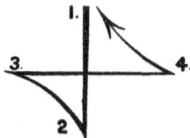

There are various methods of beating *Slow* Compound Times. Among the best are the following :

(4) Slow Compound Duple : $\frac{6}{4}$, $\frac{6}{8}$; 6-pulse.

| Down : Left : Left | Right : Up : Up ||

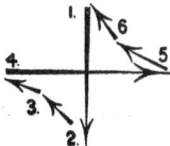

(5) Slow Compound Triple : $\frac{9}{4}$, $\frac{9}{8}$; 9-pulse.

| Down :dn. :dn. |Right :rt. :rt. |Up :up :up ||

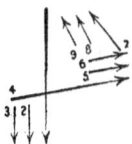

(6) Slow Compound Quadruple : $\frac{12}{8}$; 12-pulse.

| Dn :dn :dn |Lt :lt :lt |Rt :rt :rt |Up :up :up ||

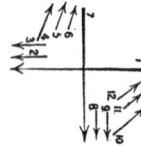

(7) Octuple Time.

In Slow Quadruple Time the beat is often divided into two : *e.g.* "Father of Heav'n," Handel, *Judas;* "See what love," Mendelssohn, *St. Paul.* Each of these is in $\frac{4}{4}$ time, with a beat to each ♪, and should be beaten thus :—

| Down .down :Left .left |Right .right :Up .up ||

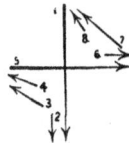

The great point in beating time is to give a firm, decided stroke, especially on the STRONG and medium beats.

"The ancient time-beaters beat time not only with the foot, but also with the right hand. . . Besides this beating of hands and noise of slippers they had still for striking the time, that of cockell-shells, oyster-shells, and the small bones of animals."—*Rousseau.*

Beaucoup *(F.).* Many ; much.
Beaucoup de son. Much sound ; very sonorous.
En élargissant beaucoup. Broadening a great deal.

BEAULIEU, Marie Désiré. *B.* Paris, 1791 ; *d.* 1863. Active promoter of the "Association Musicale de l'Ouest" and of the Parisian "Society for Classical Music."
His numerous works include the operas *Anacréon* and *Philadelphie,* 3 oratorios, masses, songs, orchestral and violin pieces, &c. He also wrote treatises on Rhythm, Ancient Greek and Gregorian Melodies, The Origin of Music, &c.

BEAUMARCHAIS, Pierre A. C. de. *B.* Paris, 1732 ; *d.* 1799. Poet and dramatist.
The libretti of Rossini's *Le Barbiere* and Mozart's *Figaro* were taken from his works.

BEAUMONT, Henry. Tenor ; *b.* Huddersfield, 1858.

BEAUMONT, Paul. Pen-name of **Sydney Smith** (*q.v.*).

BEAUQUIER, Ch. French writer ; *b.* abt. 1830. Author of "Philosophie de Musique," 1865, and many musical articles.

Beautiful in Music, The.
Pauer enumerates Formal beauty, Characteristic beauty, and Ideal beauty as the essentials of a real work of art.

Be'ben *(G.).* To shake, to tremble ; tremolo.
Be'ber, Be'bezug. Tremolo stop ; tremulant.

Bebisa'tion (Labeceda'tion). The syllables *La, Be, Ce, De, Me, Fe, Ge,* used by Hitzler, 1630, in teaching sight-singing.

Be'bung *(G.).* (*F., Balancement ; I., Tre'molo.*) Trembling ; vibrato. The *tremolo* stop.

Bécarre *(F.).* The natural, ♮.

Bec *(F.),* **Bec'co** *(I.).* A beak. The mouthpiece of a clarinet, flageolet, &c. (See **Flute à bec.**)

Bec'co Polac'ca *(I.).* A large kind of bagpipe.

Bech'er *(G.).* (1) The "bell" of an instrument. (2) The tube of an organ reed pipe.

BECHER, Alfred J. *B.* Manchester, 1803. Prof. of harmony, R.A.M., 1840. Went to Vienna, edited a revolutionary paper, and was shot for sedition, 1848.
Wrote a symphony, string quartets, songs, &c.; also pamphlets on "Jenny Lind," &c.

BECHER, Jos. B. *B.* 1821. Bavarian composer of sacred music. Wrote over 60 masses.

BECHSTEIN, F. W. K. Pf. maker. *B.* Gotha, 1826; *d.* 1900. Started in Berlin, 1856.
The firm has now an annual output of some 3,000 pianos.

BECK, C. F. Published concertos, sonatas, &c., for pf., 1789-1794.

BECK, David. Celebrated 16th century organ builder at Halberstadt, Germany.

BECK, Franz. Violinist and concert-director. *B.* Mannheim, 1730; *d.* 1809.
Wrote symphonies, quartets, pf. sonatas, &c.

BECK, Gottfried J. Bohemian orgt.; 1723-87.
Wrote church music, &c.

BECK, Johann H. Violinist and composer. *B.* Cleveland, Ohio, 1856. Founded the Schubert Quartet, Cleveland.
Works: overtures, chamber music, songs, &c.

BECK, Johann N. Fine baritone singer and actor. *B.* Pesth, 1828; *d.* 1893. Sang at Vienna, Frankfort, Hamburg, Cologne, &c. Died insane.

BECK, Karl. 1814-1879. Created the *rôle* of *Lohengrin*, Weimar, 1850.

BECK, R. K. Pub. a book of dance music for 2 violins and harp, Strasburg, 1654.

BECKÉ, J. B. Renowned flautist. *B.* Nuremburg, 1743. Court musician at Munich.
Published Flute concertos.

Beck'en, Schall'becken *(G.).* Cymbals.
Beck'enschläger. Cymbal beater (player).

BECKER, Albert E. A. Esteemed composer. *B.* Quedlinburg, 1834; *d.* Berlin, 1899. Teacher of composition at Scharwenka's Conservatoire, and conductor of the Berlin cathedral choir, 1881.
His best works are a Symphony in G minor, a Grand Mass in B flat minor, and the oratorio *Selig aus Gnade.* He also wrote a setting of the 147th Psalm for double choir *a cappella*, a pf. quintet, a concertstück for violin and orchestra, an opera *Loreley*, cantatas, and many songs, pf. pieces, &c.

BECKER, D. Pub. "Sonatas for Violin, Viola da Gamba, &c.," Hamburg, 1668.

BECKER, Georg. *B.* Frankenthal, 1824.
Works: "Swiss Music," "Old French Chansons," "Rousseau's *Pygmalion*," "Musical Notation," &c.; also pf. pieces and songs.

BECKER, Jean. Violinist; *b.* Mannheim, 1833; *d.* 1884. After several highly successful tours settled in Florence, 1866, and established the Florentine Quartet.
His son **Hugo**—a fine 'cellist—has been prof. of the 'cello since 1894 at the Hoch Conservatory, Frankfort. *B.* 1864.

BECKER, Karl F. *B.* Leipzig, 1804; *d.* 1877. Organ prof. at the Cons. 1843. Revised Forkel's "Systematic Chronology of

Musical Literature," and wrote important works on musical history. Pub. choral books, organ and pf. pieces, &c. Left his valuable library to the city of Leipzig.

BECKER, Konstantin J. *B.* Freiburg, Saxony, 1811; *d.* 1859. Edited the *Neue Zeitschrift f. Musik*, 1837-46.
Wrote an opera, a symphony, duets, songs, &c., and some theoretical treatises.

BECKER, Rheinhold. Saxon violinist and composer; *b.* 1842.
Works: two operas, *Frauenlob* and *Ratbold*, a symphonic poem, a violin concerto, songs, &c.

BECKER, Valentin E. *B.* Würzburg, 1814; *d.* Vienna, 1890. Works: 2 operas, masses, popular choruses for male voices, &c.

BECKMANN, Joh. F. G. German musician; 1737-1792. One of the finest organ and harpsichord players of his time.
Wrote an opera, *Lukas und Hannchen;* sonatas, &c.

BECKWITH, John Christmas. Mus.D. Oxon. *B.* Norwich, Dec. 25th, 1750; *d.* 1809. Organist of Norwich Cathedral.
Wrote many anthems, glees, &c., and a work entitled "The First Verse of Every Psalm of David, with an Ancient or Modern Chant in Score, adapted as much as possible to the Sentiment of each Psalm," with a preface on "Chanting."

BECQUIÉ, J. M. *B.* Toulouse, about 1800; *d.* 1825. Principal flautist, Opéra Comique, Paris. Composed and arranged some valued pieces for flute.

BECQUIÉ, J. M. Violinist; brother of the above. *B.* 1797; *d.* 1876. Member of the Théâtre Italien orchestra, Paris.
Wrote fantasias, &c., for violin.

Bedäch'tig *(G.).* Thoughtful, deliberate.

Bedeckt' *(G.).* Muffled; covered.
Bedech'te Stim'me. A husky voice.

Bedeu'tend *(G.).* Important, considerable.
Bedeu'tend lang'samer. Considerably slower.
Bedeu'tungsvoll. Very significant(ly); impressively.

BEDFORD, Herbert. Composer; *b.* London, 1867. Married Miss Liza Lehmann, 1894.

BEDFORD, Mrs. H. (See **Lehmann, Liza**.)

Bedon *(F.).* Old name for a tambour or drum.

Bedon de Biscaye. A tambourine.

BEDOS (de Celles), Dom François. 1706-1779. Known as Dom Bedos. Benedictine monk.
Wrote a valuable work on organ construction, on which later works were based, "L'art du facteur d'orgues" (Paris, 1766).

Bedroh'lich *(G.).* Menacing, threatening.

BEECHAM, Thos. Condr.; founded a new Symphony Orch., 1908.

BEECH'GARD (or Beehgard), Julius. *B.* Copenhagen, 1843. Pupil of Gade.
Wrote the operas *Frode* and *Frau Inge;* song cycles, an overture, part-songs, pf. pieces, &c.

BEE'CKE, Ignaz von. *B.* abt. 1730; *d.* 1803. After serving in the army became "Music-intendant" to the Prince of Ötting-Wallenstein. He was a friend of Gluck and Mozart. His works include an oratorio, 7 operas, symphonies, songs, &c.

BEER. The family name of Meyerbeer.

BEER, Jos. 1744-1811. Bohemian clarinettist. Added a "fifth key" to the instrument. Wrote clar. concertos, &c.

BEER, Max J. Viennese composer ; b. 1851.
Works: operas, *Friedel mit der leeren Tasche, Der Streik der Schmiede,* and others ; pf. pieces, songs, cantatas, &c.

BEETH (pron. *Bayt*), **Lola.** Dramatic soprano ; b. Cracow, 1862. Made her *début* as "Elsa" in *Lohengrin,* Berlin, 1882. Has sung at Vienna, Paris, New York, &c.

BEETHOVEN (pron. *Bayt'-hō-vn*), **Ludwig van.** Called the "Prince of Composers," was born at Bonn-on-Rhine, Dec. 16, 1770 ; d. Vienna, Mar. 26, 1827. His grandfather, Ludwig, was Capellmeister at Bonn, and his father, Johann, was a tenor singer in the Electoral Choir. Beethoven's father commenced to teach him music in his 4th year. At 8 he was a good violinist, and at 11 could play Bach's pf. fugues (" Wohltemperirtes Clavier"). He was next taught by Pfeiffer, Van der Eeden, and Neefe. In 1782 he was appointed Neefe's deputy at the organ, and in 1783, cembalist of the opera orchestra, where he also played 2nd viola under Reicha. His ability at extemporising on the piano was already remarkable ; and Mozart who heard him at Vienna, 1787, exclaimed "He will give the world something worth listening to." About this time he became acquainted with his lifelong friend and patron, Count Waldstein. In 1792, the Elector, influenced no doubt by Haydn's commendation, sent Beethoven to Vienna, where he had a few lessons from Haydn, and, in 1794, took a course of counterpoint under Albrechtsberger. He played his C major concerto for the pf. at a public concert in 1795, and in 1796 visited Nuremberg, Prague, and Berlin. Revisited Prague, 1798, his playing "making a profound impression." About 1800 a disease, which afterwards resulted in total deafness, began to seriously trouble him. With the increase of this malady his character, which, though "original" was genuine, honest, and sturdily independent, gradually changed, and he became taciturn and morose. He was totally deaf from about 1822 ; and the ingratitude of a worthless nephew still further saddened his later years. Beethoven's music is of unsurpassable nobility and greatness ; and probably no other composer has so justly and admirably blended the emotional and intellectual qualities. He stands supreme in "absolute" instrumental music ; and he brought the symphony and the sonata —forms moulded by Haydn and Mozart —to their highest point of development. His works have been divided into three styles, or "periods"—not strictly chrono-

logical, but roughly as follows : 1st period to 1800, including Ops. 1 to 18 (Symphonies 1 and 2,* nine pf. sonatas, &c.), Beethoven being still largely an imitator of Haydn and Mozart. 2nd period to 1815—Beethoven *individualised* and at his prime. The chief works of this period are Symphonies 3 to 8, the opera *Fidelio,* Mass in C, pf. Concertos in G and E♭, the Violin Concerto, 14 pf. sonatas, including the "Pastorale," "Waldstein," and "Appassionata," &c. The 3rd period to 1827 includes the later pf. sonatas, from Op. 101, the great Mass in D, the 9th Symphony, and the later string quartets. This last period, which was regarded as a "striving after the infinite and unattainable," was not generally appreciated even among musicians until half a century after Beethoven's death.

Chief works: *(a)* Instrumental—Nine symphonies, including No. 3, "The Eroica," in E♭ ; No. 5, in C minor ; No. 6, "The Pastoral," in F ; and No. 9, "The Choral," in D minor ; "The Battle of Vittoria ;" music to *Prometheus,* and to *Egmont.* Nine overtures, including *Leonora,* Nos. 1, 2, and 3. and *Fidelio.* Violin Concerto in D, Op. 61. Five pf. concertos (No. 5, "The Emperor," in E♭). Choral fantasia ; 2 octets for wind ; the septet for strings and wind, in E♭ ; 3 quintets for strings ; 5 string trios ; 8 pf trios ; 10 sonatas for violin and pf. ("Kreutzer," in A, Op. 47) ; 5 sonatas for 'cello and pf. ; 38 sonatas for pf. ; 21 sets of variations for pf. ; and many detached pieces of various kinds.
(b) Vocal: The opera *Fidelio* (1st production, 1805) ; Two masses—in C and D ; the oratorio, *Christus am Oelberg* (Eng. trans. as "Mount of Olives") ; cantata, *Der glorreiche Augenblick ;* several scenas, arias, vocal canons, songs, &c., including the fine tenor song "Adelaide." Thayer's chronological and Nottebohm's thematic lists of Beethoven's compositions are of great value.

BEFFARA, Louis F. 1751-1838. *Commissaire de Police,* Paris, 1792-1816.
Wrote a Dictionary of " l'Académie Royale de Musique," and several other historical works on the *Grand Opéra.*

BEFFROY de Reigny. (Cousin-Jacques). B. Laon, 1757 ; d. 1811.
Wrote several farcical pieces, of which *Nicodème dans la lune* was performed 191 times.

Befil'zen *(G.).* To put felt on pf. hammers.

Befing'ern *(G.).* To finger.

Begei'sterung *(G.).* Enthusiasm, spirit, exaltation, rapture, inspiration.

Beggar's Opera.
A celebrated "ballad" opera, words by John Gay, 1727, music arranged from popular tunes by Pepusch. Its success led to the foundation of En lish ballad opera.

Beglei'(t)stimmen *(G.).* Accompanying voices (or parts).

Beglei'ten *(G.).* To accompany.
Beglei'tende Stim'men. Accompanying parts.
Beglei'ter. An accompanist.
Beglei'tung. Accompaniment.
Oh'ne Beglei'tung. Without accompaniment.

Behag'lich *(G.).* Easy, agreeable.

* Some authorities place the 2nd Sym. in the 2nd period.

Behand'lung *(G.).* Management, treatment, manipulation.

Behend'ig *(G.).* Dexterous, agile, nimble.

Beherzt' *(G.).* Resolute, determined; spirited.

BEHM, Eduard. Pianist and composer; *b.* Stettin, 1862.

BEHN'KE, Emil. Voice specialist. *B.* Stettin, 1836; *d.* 1892. Lived several years in London as a teacher of voice production.
His published works include "The Mechanism of the Human Voice" (1880) "Voice, Song, and Speech," with Dr. Lennox Browne (1883), "Voice-training Exercises" (with Dr. C. W. Pearce,) &c.

BEHR, Franz. *B.* Mechlenburg, 1837; *d.* 1898.
Published popular pf. pieces under the names "Wm. Cooper," "Charles Morley," and "Francesco d'Orso."

BEHR, Therese. Contralto; *b.* Stuttgart, 1876.

BEHR'END, Arthur H. Composer; *b.* Danzig, 1853.

Bei *(G.).* At, with, for, by.
Bei Wie'derholung. To be repeated.

Bei'de *(G.).* Both.
Bei'de Peda'le. Both (pf.) pedals.

Bei'nah(e) *(G.).* Almost, nearly.
Bei'nah dop'pelt so lang'sam. Almost twice as slow.
Bei'nah dop'pelt so rasch. Almost twice as fast.

Bei'spiel *(G.).* Example; precedent.

Bei'sser *(G.).* A mordent *(q.v.).*

Bei'töne *(G.).* Harmonics, partials, undertones. (See **Acoustics.**)

Bei'zeichen *(G.).* An accidental.

Beklemmt' *(G.).* Oppressed, anxious.

Bel bel'lo *(I.).* Gently, softly, sweetly.

Bel can'to *(I.).* "Beautiful song." The (so-called) *Italian* (*cantabile*) method of singing.

BELCHER, William T. *B.* Birmingham, 1827. Mus.D. Oxon, 1872. *D.* 1905.
Wrote church music, cantatas, &c.

BEL'CKE, F. A. *B.* Lucka, 1795; *d.* 1874. Famed as "the first concert virtuoso" on the trombone. He was a member of the Gewandhaus orchestra, Leipzig.

BEL'CKE, C. G. Brother of F. A. 1796-1875. Brilliant flautist in the Gewandhaus orchestra. Wrote flute concertos, &c.

BELDOMAN'DIS (Beldemandis, or Beldemando). Wrote treatises on Mensural Music, 15th century.

Bele'bend, Belebt' *(G.).* Animated; lively.
Bele'bung. Liveliness; animation.
Belebt', nicht zu rasch. Animated, but not too fast.

Belegt' *(G.).* Hoarse, veiled, covered.

BELIA'IEV (BELJAJEW), M. P. St. Petersburg, 1836-1904.
Published abt. 2,500 works of young Russian composers.

BE'LICZAY, Julius von. Hungarian composer. *B.* 1835; *d.* Pesth, 1893. Pupil of Joachim.
Wrote numerous orchestral, vocal, and chamber works, including a symphony, a mass, a string quartet, songs, pf. pieces, &c.

Belie'ben *(G.).* Pleasure. *Nach Belie'ben; ad lib.*

Beliebt' *(G.).* Beloved, popular.

BELIN (Bellin), G. Parisian tenor singer, 16th century. Wrote cantiques and chansons.

BELIN, J. French lutenist; *b.* about 1530.
Published a collection of motets, chansons, &c. in lute tablature, Paris, 1556.

BELL, W. H. Contemp. Eng. Composer.
Works: *Arcadian Suite* for orch., &c.

Bell. (1) The enlarged bell-shaped end of an instrument. (2) *(G., Glock'e; F., Cloche; I., Campa'na.)* A hollow metallic instrument which gives a predominating musical note of definite pitch when struck.
Bell-diapa'son. An organ stop with bell-mouthed open metal pipes.
Bell-gamba. An organ stop with the pipes terminating in a bell.
Bell-harp. Usually known as "Fairy Bells." A small box strung with 8 or more strings of fine wire. "The player swings the instrument as he strikes, producing the effect of the sound of a peal of bells borne on the wind."—*Stainer and Barrett.*
Bellman. A town, or parish, crier.
Bell metal. An alloy of about 13 parts of copper to 4 of tin.
Bell metronome. A metronome with a bell which can be set to mark the beats.
Bell piano. (See *Glockenspiel.*)

BEL'LA, J. L. Hungarian priest; *b.* 1843.
Works: church music, orchestral works, pf. pieces, &c., and, especially, national songs for men's voices.

BELLAIGUE, Camille. *B.* Paris, 1858. Mus. critic *Revue des deux Mondes*, since 1885. Author of works on French music, &c.

BELLAMY, Richard. Mus.B.Cantab. *B.* 1738; *d.* 1813. Vicar choral, St. Paul's, 1777.

BELLAMY, Thos. Ludford. Son of Rd. 1770-1843. Renowned English bass singer; sang in all the chief concerts for nearly half-a-century.

BELLA'SIO, P. Venetian composer, 16th cent. Published madrigals, *villanelle*, &c.

BELLASIS, Ed. *B.* 1852. Has written "Memorials of Cherubini," songs, &c.

BELLAZ'ZI, F. Venetian 17th cent. composer. Published a mass, motets, &c.

BELLERBY, Edward J. *B.* Yorkshire, 1858. Mus.Doc. Oxon, 1895. Orgt., Margate.

BEL'LERMANN, Johann F. 1795-1874. Director of a gymnasium at Berlin. Wrote treatises on Greek music and notation.

BEL'LERMANN, J. G. Son of J. F. *B.* Berlin, 1832; *d.* 1903. Prof. at the Univ., 1866. His valuable treatises include an historical exposition of "Mensural Music."

BELLET'TI, G. B. Renowned Italian baritone. *B.* 1815. Sang with Jenny Lind in London, Paris, United States, &c.

Bellez'za *(I.).* Beauty, grace, style.

BEL'LI, Girolamo. Venetian composer, 16th cent. Published motets, madrigals, &c., some of them in 10 parts.

BEL'LI, Giulio. Maestro Imola Cath., abt. 1620.
Published masses, madrigals, canzonettes, psalms &c., mostly in 8 parts.

Bellicosamen'te *(I.)* } Bellicose, martial, war-
Bellico'so *(I.)* } like.

BELLINCIO'NI, Gemma. Soprano; *b.* Como, 1866.

BELLI'NI, Vincenzo. Gifted opera composer. *B.* Catania, Sicily, 1801 ; *d.* near Paris, 1835. Pupil for some time at a Naples Conservatorio, but learnt more by diligent private study of the works of Pergolesi, Haydn, and Mozart.

Operas : *Adelson e Salvini*, 1825; *Bianca e Fernando*, 1826; *Il Pirata*, 1827 ; *La Straniera*, 1829; *Zaira*, 182 ; *I Capuletti e Montecchi*, 1830 ; *La Sonnambula*, Milan, 1831 ; *Norma*, 1831 ; *Beatrice di Tenda*, 1833 ; *I Puritani*, 1834. *Norma* is his finest work.

" In his best moments Bellini surpasses his brilliant contemporary, Rossini, in the grace and sensuous warmth and charm of his melodies ; in other respects he is the latter's inferior."— Th. Baker.

BELL'MAN, Carl M. Swedish poet ; 1740-1795. Set many of his own lyrics to music.

BELL'MANN, Karl G. *B.* Muskau, 1772 ; *d.* 1862. Composed the German national song *Schleswig-Holstein meerumschlungen*.

Bello,-a, *(I.).* Beautiful, agreeable.

BELLOC, Teresa. Renowned mezzo-soprano, *B.* 1784 ; *d.* 1855. Sang at La Scala, Milan, 1804-24, also in Paris, London. &c., taking leading parts in over 80 operas.

BELLO'LI, Luigi. *B.* nr. Bologna, 1770 ; *d.* 1817.

Prof. of horn at Milan Cons., and horn player in La Scala orchestra. Wrote operas, ballets, &c., and a Horn Method.

BELLO'LI, A. Horn player, La Scala, 1819-29. Wrote ballets, operas, and horn pieces.

Belly. *(G., Deck'e; F., Table; I., Tav'ola, Pan'cia.)* The upper part of a violin, &c., over which the strings are stretched.

Bel metal'lo di vo'ce *(I.).* A clear, brilliant soprano voice.

BELSHAZZAR. Oratorio by Handel, 1745.

Belu'stigend *(G.).* Gay, joyful.

BEMBERG, Henri. *B.* Buenos Ayres, 1861. Has written the operas *Le baiser de Suzon* and *Elaine ;* also several songs.

BEMBERG, Hermann. Opera composer ; *b.* Paris, 1861.

Bemerk'bar *(G.).* Marked, prominent.

Bemes (Beemes). Old English horns or trumpets.

BE'METZRIEDER, T. Alsatian monk ; *b.* 1743. Lived several years in London. Wrote text-books of little value on harmony, &c.

Be'mol *(F.)* ⎫ The flat, ♭.
Bemol'le *(I.)* ⎭

Bemoliser (F.). ⎫ To flatten a note (or notes).
Bemollizza're (I.) ⎭

Ben, or Be'ne *(I.).* Well, good ; as *ben sostenu'to*, well sustained ; *a be'ne pla'cito*, at (one's) good pleasure *(i.e., ad lib.).*

BEN'DA, Franz. Famous Bohemian violinist ; 1709-1786. Pupil of J. S. Graun.

As leader of the orchestra of Frederick II he accompanied some 50,000 of his royal master's flute solos. Wrote violin pieces, symphonies, concertos, &c.

BEN'DA, F. L. Conductor and composer ; son of Georg Benda. *B.* Gotha, 1746 ; *d.* 1793. Wrote an opera, 3 violin concertos, cantatas, &c.

BEN'DA, F. W. H. Violinist and composer ; *b.* Potsdam, 1745 ; *d.* 1814. Eldest son of Franz. Wrote the operas *Alceste* and *Orpheus*, 2 oratorios, concertos, &c.

BEN'DA, Georg. Brother of Franz. 1722-1795. Capellmeister at Gotha, 1748.

Wrote successful melodramas, also operas operettas, concertos, &c.

BEN'DA, Karl H. H. Youngest son of Georg. 1748-1836. Excellent violinist ; taught King Fr. Wilhelm III.

BEN'DALL, Wilfred E, *B.* London. 1850.

Works : *The Lady of Shalott* and other cantatas operettas, songs, &c.

BEN'DEL, Franz. Accomplished Bohemian pianist ; 1833-1874. Pupil of Liszt.

Wrote several meritorious pieces and studies for pf., also symphonies, masses, songs, &c.

BENDER, J. Valentin. 1801-1873. Belgian clarinettist ; music-dir. to the royal house. Wrote clarinet pieces and some military music.

BEN'DER, Jakob. Brother of J. V. 1798-1844. Clarinet player and director of the Antwerp Wind-band.

Wrote some military music.

BEN'DIX, Victor E. Violinist, pianist, and composer. *B.* Copenhagen, 1851. Works : meritorious pf. pieces, 3 symphonies, &c.

BEN'DIX, Otto. *B.* Copenhagen, 1845. Pupil of Gade, Kullak, and Liszt. Settled in Boston, U.S., 1880. He is an excellent pf. teacher and concert director. Has published pf. pieces, &c.

BEN'DL, Karl. *B.* Prague, 1838 ; *d.* 1897. Chorusmaster, Amsterdam German Opera, 1864. Conductor of a male choral society, Prague, 1865.

His Czech national operas, *Lejla*, *Bretislaw*, *Karel Skreta*, and others, are on the standing répertoire of the Prague National Theatre. He also wrote 3 masses, several cantatas, a "Slavonic Rhapsody," some 200 Czech songs, &c.

Benedi'cite *(L.).* " The Song of the Three Children."

A very ancient canticle now used in Anglican churches, especially in Lent, as an alternative to the *Te Deum*.

BENEDICT, Sir Julius. *B.* Stuttgart, 1804 ; *d.* London, 1885. Son of a Jewish banker ; pupil of Weber. First opera given at Naples, 1829. Settled in London, 1835. Conductor, Drury Lane, 1837 ; produced his first *English* opera, *The Gypsy's Warning*, 1838. Went with Jenny Lind on her American tours, 1850-51. Conductor, Covent Garden, 1859. Knighted, 1871.

Chief operas : *The Brides of Venice* (1844), *The Crusaders* (1846), *The Lake of Glenaston* (1862), *The Lily of Killarney* (1862), *The Pride of Song* (1864). He also wrote 2 oratorios (*St. Cecilia*, 1866, and *St. Peter*, 1870), 4 cantatas, symphonies, pf. concertos, songs, &c.

Benedic'tus *(L.).* (1) A part, or movement, of the Roman Mass. (2) " The song of Zacharias," an alternative to the *Jubilate* in the Anglican Morning Service ; sung in Holy Week before the *Miserere* in R. C. Services.

BENEDIC'TUS AP'PENZELDERS. *B.* Appenzell, Switzerland. Master of the Brussels Boys' Choir, 1539-55. Pub. a collection of motets, Antwerp, 1553.

BÉNÉDIT, Pierre G. French composer and writer ; 1802-1870.

BENEL'LI, A. (See **Bottrigari.**)

Be'nepla'cito *(I.).* At pleasure ; *ad lib.*

BENE'VOLI, Orazio. Profound contrapuntist; *b.* Rome, 1602 ; *d.* 1672. Maestro at the Vatican, 1646.

Wrote masses in 12, 16, 24, and 48 parts. Also motets, psalms, &c., up to 30 parts. He was also a pioneer in adding independent instrumental accompaniment.

BENINCO'RI, Angelo M. *B.* Brescia, 1779 ; *d.* Paris, 1821. Wrote several operas. Only one, *Aladin,* was successful, and this was produced a few weeks after his death.

Ben marca'to la melodi'a *(I.).* The melody (to be) well marked.

Ben misura'to *(I.).* In exact rhythm and time.

BEN'NET, John. Famous English madrigal composer ; abt. 1570-1615.

BENNET, Th. (See **Th. Ritter.**)

BENNETT, George John. *B.* Andover, 1863. Mus.Doc. Cantab., 1893. Organist, Lincoln Cathedral, 1895.

BENNETT, Joseph. *B.* Gloucestershire, 1831. Musical critic of the *Sunday Times, Pall Mall Gazette, Graphic,* and *Daily Telegraph.* Has contributed largely to the musical magazines, especially the *Musical World, Musical Standard,* and *Musical Times.*

For some years he wrote the analytical programs for the Saturday and Monday Popular Concerts at St. James's Hall. His many publications include " Letters from Bayreuth," 1877.

BENNETT, Sir William Sterndale. One of England's most distinguished composers. *B.* Sheffield, April 13, 1816 ; *d.* London, Feb. 1, 1875. His father dying when Bennett was 3 years of age, his education was supervised by his grandfather. He became a chorister at King's College Chapel at 8, and at 10 entered the R.A.M., studying under Ch. Lucas, Dr. Crotch, C. Potter, and W. H. Holmes. In 1833 he played his pf. concerto in D minor at an R.A.M. concert. Messrs. Broadwood sent him to Leipzig for further study in 1837, and again in 1841-2. Here he became intimate with Schumann and Mendelssohn, the latter so influencing the style of his later works that he was called the " English Mendelssohn."

Bennett founded the Bach Society, London, 1849 ; was conductor of the Philharmonic Society, 1856-1866, and the Leeds Festival, 1858. Appointed Cambridge Professor of Music, 1856, receiving the Degree of Mus. Doc. Principal of the R.A.M., 1866 ; M.A. Cambridge, 1867 ;

D.C.L. Oxford, 1870 ; Knighted, 1871. He handed over the proceeds of a testimonial, 1872, to found the Sterndale-Bennett Scholarship at the R.A.M. He was buried in Westminster Abbey.

His works are not numerous, but in refinement " they vie with the best in musical art."

Works : Pf. concertos in D minor, E♭, C minor, and F minor ; overtures, *Parisina, The Naiads, The Wood Nymphs, Paradise and the Peri, The Merry Wives of Windsor;* symphony in G minor ; oratorio, *The Woman of Samaria* (Birmingham, 1867) ; pastoral, *The May Queen* (Leeds, 1858) ; odes, pf. sonatas, songs and duets, capriccios, rondos, sketches, studies, romances, fantasias, &c., for pf. ; sextet for pf and strings, &c.

BEN'NEWITZ, Anton. Bohemian violinist ; *b.* 1833. Director, Prague Cons. since 1882.

BEN'NEWITZ, Wm. *B.* Berlin, 1832 ; *d.* 1871. Wrote a successful opera, *Die Rose von Woodstock,* 1876.

BENOIS, Marie. Pianist ; *b.* St. Petersburg, 1861.

BENOIST, François. *B.* Nantes, 1794 ; *d.* 1878. Prof. at the Paris Cons., 1820. *Chef du chant* at the Opéra, 1840.

Wrote two operas, *Léonore et Félix* (1821), and *l'Apparition* (1848) ; four ballets, a requiem mass, &c. ; and a fine collection of organ music —" Bibliothèque de l'organiste "—in 12 vols.

BENOIT, Camille. French writer and composer ; pupil of César Franck.

Works : an overture (1880), "Souvenirs" (1884), &c.

BENOÎT, Pierre L. L. (Known as **Peter Benoît**). Distinguished Flemish composer ; *b.* Harlebeck, 1834. Studied at the Brussels Cons., 1851-55, and won the *Prix de Rome,* 1857. Appointed Director of the Antwerp Cons., 1867. *D.* 1901.

His numerous works include the fine oratorio *Lucifer* (and another oratorio, *De Schelde*) ; two operas ; a sacred drama, *Drama Christi;* a choral symphony ; music to *Charlotte Corday;* a mass, several successful cantatas, motets, &c., a pf. concerto, a fl. concerto, songs, &c.

He also wrote important treatises and articles on a variety of musical topics, and in 1882 was elected a member of the Berlin Royal Academy.

Ben pronunzia'to *(I.).* Distinctly pronounced ; emphatically.

BENVENU'TI, T. Venetian operatic composer ; *b.* 1832. His operas include *Guglielmo Shakespeare,* 1861 ; *La Stella di Toledo,* 1864 ; and *Il Falconiere,* 1878.

Bequad'ro *(I.)* **Béquarre** *(F.)* The natural, ♮.

Bequem *(G.).* Convenient, easy ; *comodo.*

BÉRANGER, Pierre J. de. French poet ; 1780-1857. His songs have been set to music by various celebrated composers.

BERAR'DI, Angelo. *B.* Bologna, 17th cent. Eminent musical theorist.

Wrote a requiem mass, motets, psalms, &c.

BÉRAT, F. 1801-1855. French composer of popular *romances* and *chansonettes—Ma Normandie, A la frontiére, Bibi,* &c.

BERBER, Felix. Violinist ; *b.* Jena, 1871.

BERBIGUIER, B. T. *B.* Vaucluse, 1782 ; *d.* 1838. Studied at Paris Cons.
Wrote several fine works for flute, including 15 books of duos, 6 grand solos, 10 concertos, 7 books of sonatas, 6 books of trios, fantasias, suites, arrangements, &c.

Berceuse *(F.).* A lullaby or cradle song.

BERCHEM (BERGHEM), J. de. *B.* nr. Antwerp, abt. 1500 ; *d.* 1580. Maestro at Mantua. Famous contrapuntist.
Wrote masses, madrigals, motets, &c.

BE'RENS, Hermann. *B.* Hamburg, 1826 ; *d.* 1880. Celebrated pianist ; pupil of Reissiger and Czerny. Royal music-director, Örebro, 1849. Conductor " Mindre " Theatre, Stockholm, 1860, and, later, Prof. at the Academy.
Works : Greek drama *Kodros;* opera *Violetta ;* 3 operettas, overtures, chamber music, songs, pf. pieces, &c.

BERETTA, G. B. *B.* Verona, 1819 ; *d.* Milan, 1876. Director for several years of the Cons., Bologna.
Devoted the later part of his life to the completion of an " Artistic, Scientific, Historical, and Technological Dictionary of Music " which had been commenced by A. Barbieri. Also wrote treatises on harmony, orchestration, &c.

BERG, Adam. Celebrated music printer, Munich, 1540-99. Publ. " Patrocinium musicum," a collection of 10 volumes of masses, cantiones, magnificats, &c., by Lasso, Francesco de Sale, Blasius Amon, and other noted contrapuntists.

BERG, Konrad M. Alsatian pianist and composer ; 1785-1852. Settled in Strasburg, 1808, as a pf. teacher.
Wrote chamber music, concertos, sonatas, variations, &c., for pf., and some excellent essays on pf. teaching and other subjects.

Bergamas'ca *(I.)* ⎫
Ber'gomask *(E.)* ⎬ A dance in imitation of the clownish rustics
Bergamasque *(F.)* ⎭ of Bergamo.

BER'GER, Francesco. *B.* London, 1834. Studied at Vienna and Leipzig. Prof. of piano at R.A.M. and G.S.M. For a time director, now hon. sec. of the Philharmonic Society. Has written a mass, an opera, songs, pf. pieces, &c., and a primer on pf. playing.

BER'GER, Ludwig. *B.* Berlin, 1777 ; *d.* 1839. Studied under Clementi. From 1815 pf. teacher at Berlin. Among his most famous pupils were Mendelssohn, Henselt, Taubert, and Fanny Hensel. Of his pf. works a toccata, a rondo, and a set of studies are highly esteemed.
He also wrote cantatas, songs, male-voice quartets, &c.

BER'GER, Wm. *B.* Boston, U.S., 1861. Studied at Berlin, and has since lived there as composer and pf. teacher.
Works : a Fantasy in overture form, part-songs, songs, and many compositions for pf., pf. and violin, &c. In 1898 won a prize of 2,000 marks for his setting of Goethe's " Meine Göttin."

Bergeret'. A rustic or pastoral dance or song.

BERG'GREEN, A. P. *B.* Copenhagen, 1801 ; *d.* 1880. Inspector of singing in the Copenhagen public schools, 1859. Wrote an opera and several collections of songs.

BER'GHEM. (See Berchem.)

BERG'MANN, Karl. Conductor, pianist, and 'cellist. *B.* Saxony, 1821 ; *d.* New York, 1876. Went to America, 1850 ; conducted the New York Philharmonic orchestral concerts from 1862 until his death.
" He was an ardent admirer of Wagner, Liszt, &c., and rendered important service to the cause of music in America by introducing their works."—*Th.* Baker.

BERG'NER, W. *B.* Riga, 1837. Organist of Riga Cathedral, 1868. Has founded a Bach Society, promoted the production of Rubinstein's *Moses* (1894), and the completion of the fine new cath. organ.

BERGON'ZI, Carlo. 1716-55. Violin maker, Cremona. Best pupil of Stradivarius.

Berg'reihen *(G.).* Alpine melody, miners' song, &c.

BERG'SON, Michael. Pianist and composer ; *b.* Warsaw, 1820. His opera *Louisa di Montfort* was produced at Florence, 1847. For some years he was director of Geneva Cons. ; afterwards came to London as a private teacher. Wrote orchestral, chamber, and pf. music. *D.* 1898.

BERGT, Christian G. A. Composer, organist, and teacher. *B.* Saxony, 1772 ; *d.* 1837.
His sacred music, including a Passion oratorio, a Te Deum, hymns, canticles, &c., is known throughout Germany. He also wrote operas, symphonies, &c., and some very popular *lieder*.

BE'RINGER, Oscar. Pianist ; *b.* Fürtwangen, 1844. Studied at Leipzig and Berlin. Established in London, 1873, an "Academy for the Higher Development of Pf. Playing." Prof. of pf. R.A.M. since 1894. He has published some pf. pieces and a book of technical exercises.

BÉRIOT, Charles Auguste de. Famous French violinist ; largely self-taught. *B.* Louvain, Feb. 20, 1802 ; *d.* Brussels, April 8, 1870. Played in public at the age of 9. Visited Paris, 1821 ; played with great success, and was appointed chamber-violinist to the French king. Solo violinist 1826-30 to the King of the Netherlands. Toured through Europe 1830-5. Married Mdme. Garcia-Malibran, 1836. Professor Brussels Cons., 1843-52 ; had to resign through failure of eyesight and paralysis of the left arm.
Works : 7 violin concertos, 4 pf. trios, *duos brillants* for pf. and violin, 11 sets of variations, many studies, &c., and an excellent "Methode de Violon"—published 1858.

BÉRIOT, Chas. V. de. Pianist ; son of the preceding ; *b.* 1835. Pupil of Thalberg. Prof. of pf., Paris Cons.
Works : a symphonic poem, overtures, a septet, pf. concertos, many pf. pieces, songs, &c.

BERLIJN' (Berlyn), Anton. Amsterdam, 1817-70. For several years condr. Royal Th., Amsterdam. Wrote an oratorio, 9 operas, 7 ballets, symphonies, overtures, &c.

BERLIOZ, Hector Louis. Famous French composer ; has been called the " Father of ultra-modern orchestration." *B.* near Grenoble, Dec. 11, 1803 ; *d.* Paris, March 9, 1869. His father sent him to Paris to study medicine, but yielding to his passion for music he forfeited his allowance and entered the Conservatoire, managing to earn a bare pittance by singing in the chorus of the Gymnase Dramatique. Original to the verge of eccentricity, he was, from the first, opposed to authority and established usage. He soon grew impatient of Reicha's instruction, and left the Cons. to join the new "romantic" school of composers. His first composition, a mass, was a ludicrous failure ; but two overtures, and the Symphonie Phantastique, " Épisode de la vie d'un artiste," later, showed unmistakable power. He now gave himself up without restraint to " program music." A piece entitled " Concerts des Sylphes," 1829, was accompanied by the following printed program :—

"Mephistopheles, to excite in Faust's soul the love of pleasure, convokes the spirits of the air, and bids them sing ; after preluding on their magic instruments, they describe an enchanted land, whose happy inhabitants are intoxicated with ever-renewed voluptuous delights ; little by little the charm takes effect, the voices of the sylphs die away, and Faust falls asleep to dream delicious dreams."

In 1826 he had re-entered the Cons., and in 1830 gained the *Grand Prix de Rome* for his cantata *Sardanapale.* After spending 18 months in Rome and Naples, he returned to Paris with an overture to *King Lear,* and a continuation of his Symphonie Fantastique, " Lélio, ou le retour à la vie." He now added journalism to composition, and by his brilliant, incisive —and generally controversial—writings, became widely known ; while the active friendship of Liszt extended his reputation throughout Europe. A successful concert tour in Germany, 1843, was followed by others through Austria, Hungary, Bohemia, and Russia. In 1853 he conducted his *Benevenuto Cellini* at Covent Garden, and *Béatrice et Bénédict* at Baden-Baden, 1862. He also visited St. Petersburg to bring out his *Damnation de Faust.* This peculiar but very popular oratorio marks, perhaps, the culminating point in Berlioz's artistic career. A distinguishing feature of all his works is his extremely original and masterly orchestration.

His works—in addition to those mentioned above—include a symphony, *Harold en Italie,* 1834 ; a grand *messe des morts,* 1837 ; dramatic symphony, *Roméo et Juliette,* 1839 ; *Carnaval romain;* opera, *Les Troyens à Carthage,* 1863 ; sacred trilogy, *l'Enfance du Christ;* Te Deum for 3 choirs, orchestra, and organ ; *Grande symphonie funèbre et triomphale;* overture, *Le Corsaire;* songs, &c.

His treatise on Instrumentation (English trans.

Novello), is a fine work ; but it is now practically superseded by Gevaert's more modern and complete treatises.

BERLYN. (See **Berlijn.**)

BERMU'DO, Juan. Spanish writer. Published one vol. of a work on Musical Instruments, 1545.

BERNABE'Ï, G. E. Papal Maestro, 1672. Court Capellmeister, Munich, 1674 ; Wrote 3 operas, 2 books of madrigals, motets, psalms, &c.

BERNABE'Ï, G. A. Son of the preceding ; *b.* Rome, 1659 ; *d.* 1732. Succeeded his father as Capellmeister, Munich, 1688. Wrote 15 operas ; also masses, motets, &c.

BERNAC'CHI, Antonio. Celebrated male soprano ; *b.* Bologna, abt. 1690 ; *d.* 1756. Engaged by Handel, 1729, for the Italian Opera, London. He was then regarded as the finest living dramatic singer. He founded a singing school, Bologna, 1736.

BERNARD, Émery. *B.* Orleans. Wrote a capital " Method of Singing " (16th cent.).

BERNARD, Émile. *B.* Marseilles, 1845. Org. Notre-Dame-les-Champs, Paris. *D.* 1902. Works : Violin concerto ; concertstück, pf. and orchestra ; suites, overtures, chamber music, cantatas, &c.

BER'NARD, Moritz. *B.* 1794 ; *d.* St. Petersburg, 1871. Pupil of Field. Music teacher, St. Petersburg, 1822. Wrote an opera, *Olga,* 1845.

BERNARD, Paul. Pianist, composer, and writer. *B.* Poitiers, 1827 ; *d.* 1879.

BERNARD, St., of Clairvaux; 1091-1153. Preached the 2nd Crusade. Author of some celebrated Latin hymns. *Jesu, dulcis Memoria* (Eng. trans. by E. Caswall—" Jesu, the very thought of Thee ") is one of the finest hymns in existence.

BERNARD, St., of Cluny. 12th cent. Born at Morlaix. Wrote fine Latin hymns. Dr. Neale trans. the two most famous— " Brief life is here our portion," and " Jerusalem, the golden."

BERNAR'DI, Enrico. Milan, 1838-1900. Composed light popular dance music.

BERNAR'DI, Steffano. Canon at Salzburg. Published motets, madrigals, &c., and a work on counterpoint (1634).

BERNARDI'NI, Marcello (Marcello di Capua). *B.* Capua, abt. 1762. Wrote words and music of over 20 successful stage pieces.

BERNASCO'NI, A. *B.* Marseilles, 1712 ; *d.* 1784. Court Capellmeister, Munich, 1755. Wrote sacred music and operas.

BERNASCO'NI, P. Built the organs in Como Cathedral, San Lorenzo Church (Milan), &c. *D.* 1895.

BERNELI'NUS. Wrote on " The Division of the Monochord " (Paris, 1000, A.D.).

BERN'HARD, Christoph. Son of a poor sailor. *B.* Danzig, 1612 ; *d.* 1692. Succeeded

Schütz, his teacher, as Capellmeister at Dresden. He was a very remarkable contrapuntist.

Works : hymns in triple counterpoint, &c. ; and treatises on Harmony, Counterpoint, and Composition.

BERN'HARD der Deutsche. Organist of St. Mark's, Venice, 1445-59. He is said to have invented organ pedals.

BER'NO (called **Augien'sis**). Abbot, Reichenau Monastery, 1008-1048. Wrote some learned treatises on music.

BERNOUILLI, Johann (Basel, 1667-1747), and **Daniel,** his son (1700-1782), wrote valuable works on acoustics.

BERNS'DORF, Ed. Writer and composer ; *b.* Dessau, 1825. Completed Schladebach's " Universal - Lexikon der Tonkunst " (1885-6). *D.* 1901.

BER'NUTH, Julius von. *B.* Rees, 1830. Studied at Leipzig Conservatoire, 1854-7. Founded the " Aufschwung " Society for chamber music, 1857, and the " Dilletantes' Orchestral Society," 1859. He also conducted the " Singakademie," and the Male Choral Society. Became conductor of the Hamburg Philharmonic, and in 1873 director of a Cons. there. His efforts gave a great impulse to music at Hamburg. *D.* 1902.

BERR, Friedrich. Celebrated clarinet and bassoon player ; *b.* Mannheim, 1794 ; *d.* Paris, 1838. Prof. of clarinet, Paris Cons., 1831 ; director of the School of Military Music, 1836. Wrote a " Traité complet de la clarinette," over 500 pieces of military music, and much music of every kind for clarinet and bassoon.

BERRÉ, F. *B.* nr. Brussels, 1843. Has composed some operas and over 50 songs.

BERTA'LI, Antonio. *B.* Verona, 1605 ; *d.* Vienna, 1669. Viennese Court Capellmeister, 1649. Works : 3 oratorios, 8 operas, and several cantatas.

BER'TELMANN, Jan Georg. *B.* Amsterdam, 1782 ; *d.* 1854. Professor at the Royal School of Music. He was an excellent teacher, and published some meritorious compositions.

BER'TELSMANN, Karl A. *B.* Westphalia, 1811 ; *d.* 1861. Director, " Eutonia " Society, Amsterdam, 1839.

Works : choruses for men's voices and for mixed choir ; songs, organ and pf. pieces, &c.

BERTENSHAW, Thos. Handel. *B.* Manchester, 1859 ; Mus.B. Lond., 1887.

Author of " Elements of Music ; Harmony and Counterpoint ; Rhythm, Analysis, and Musical Form."

BERTHAUME, Isidore. *B.* Paris, 1752 ; *d.* St. Petersburg, 1802. Conductor, " Concerts Spirituels," Paris, 1783 ; afterwards solo violin in the Imperial Orchestra, St. Petersburg. Wrote a violin concerto, a symphonie concertante for two violins, and other violin and pf. music.

BERT'HOLD, Karl F. T. *B.* Dresden, 1815 ; *d.* 1882. Court Organist, 1864.

Works : oratorio, *Petrus,* a symphony, overtures, church music, &c.

BERTIN, Louise A. Singer, pianist, and composer. *B.* nr. Paris, 1805 ; *d.* 1877. Pupil of Fétis.

Works : operas, *Loupgarou, Faust, Notre-Dame de Paris;* 6 ballades, and other compositions.

BERTI'NI, Abbate G. 1756-1849 (?). Published " Dizionario storico-critico degli scrittori di Musica," Palermo, 1814.

BERTI'NI, Benoît A. *B.* Lyons, 1780. Pupil of Clementi ; pf. teacher in London, abt. 1800.

Wrote pamphlets on a new method of writing music, &c.

BERTI'NI, Domenico. *B.* Lucca, 1829 ; *d.* 1890. Director of the " Cherubini Society," Florence.

Works : two operas, masses, chamber music, &c. Published " A New System of Music," 1866.

BERTI'NI, Henri J. Pianist and composer ; brother of B. A. *B.* London, 1798 ; *d.* 1876. Toured through Germany at 12 ; and throughout Europe, 1821-59. He was a talented player in the " classic " style, and did his utmost to oppose the " flashy virtuosity " then prevalent.

Works : many pf. pieces, much chamber music, and a valuable set of technical studies for pf.

BERTINOTTI, Teresa. *B.* Piedmont, 1776 ; *d.* 1854. Renowned singer and teacher of singing. Sang in London abt. 1810.

BERTON, Henri. M. Son of P. M. (below). *B.* Paris, 1767 ; *d.* 1844. Pupil of Sacchini. Prof. of Harmony, Paris Cons., 1795 ; conducted the Opera Buffa, 1807 ; member of the Academy, 1815.

Works : 47 operas *(Montano and Stéphanie,* 1799 ; *Le Délire,* 1799 ; *Aline, reine de Golconde,* 1803 ; &c.) ; 5 oratorios, 5 cantatas, songs, &c.

BERTON, Pierre M. *B.* Paris, 1727 ; *d.* 1780. Conducted the Royal Orchestra and the Grand Opéra. His fine conducting greatly improved French opera. He also composed operatic works.

BERTO'NI, F. G. *B.* nr. Venice, 1725 ; *d.* 1813. Pupil of Padre Martini. Organist, St. Mark's, Venice, 1752.

Works : 5 oratorios, 34 operas, church music, harpsichord sonatas, &c.

BERTRAM, Madam T. (See **Moran-Olden.**)

BERTRAM, Th. Baritone ; *b.* Stuttgart, 1869.

BERTRAND, Jean G. Esteemed writer and critic ; *b.* nr. Paris, 1834 ; *d.* 1880. Wrote an " Ecclesiastical History of the Organ," essays on " The Music of Antiquity," " The Origins of Harmony," &c.

Beruh'igend *(G.).* Becoming more tranquil ; *calando.*

Beruh'igung. Quieting down.

BER'WALD, Franz. Nephew of J. F. ; Stockholm, 1796-1868. Dir, Stockholm Cons.

Works : opera *Estrella di Soria,* 1862 ; symphonies, chamber music, &c.

BER'WALD, Johann F. Precocious violinist ; *b.* Stockholm, 1788 ; *d.* 1861.
Pupil of Abbé Vogler. Played in public at 5 ; wrote a symphony at 9. Chamber musician to the King, 1816 ; conductor Royal Orchestra, 1819.

BER'WIN, A. *B.* nr. Posen, 1847. Director, Royal Library and Cecilian Academy, Rome, 1882. *D.* 1900.
Wrote theoretical works.

Bes *(G.).* B♭♭.

Besai'ten *(G.).* To string an instrument.

BESARD, Jean B. Lutenist ; *b.* Besançon, abt. 1576.
Wrote learned treatises on the lute, and published collections of lute music.

Beschleu'nigen *(G.).* Accelerate (the speed).

BESCHNITT', Joh. *B.* Silesia, 1825 ; *d.* 1880. Teacher, Catholic School, Stettin, 1848.
Wrote easy choruses for men's voices.

Beschrei'bung *(G.).* A description.

Beschwingt' *(G.).* Hurried, hastened.

Beseelt' *(G.).* Animated, spirited.

BESEKIR'SKY, Vasil V. Contemporary Russian violinist ; *b.* Moscow, 1836.
Has published much music for violin.

Besing'en *(G.).* To sing ; to praise in song.

BES'LER, Samuel. 1574-1625. Rector of a Breslau Gymnasium. Many of his church compositions are extant.

BES'LER, Simon. Cantor at Breslau, 1615-28. Wrote part-songs, &c.

BESOZ'ZI, Louis D. *B.* Versailles, 1814 ; *d.* 1879. Won *Grand Prix de Rome*, Paris Cons., 1837. Composed pf. pieces, &c.

Bespan'nen *(G.).* To string an inst.

Bespon'nene Sai'ten *(G.).* Wire-covered strings.

BES'SEMS, Antoine. Composer and violinist ; pupil of Baillot. *B.* Antwerp, 1809 ; *d.* 1868. Conducted the " Société Royale d' Harmonie."
Works : masses, motets, graduals, &c., violin concertos, fantasias, études, duos, &c., for violin, chamber music, &c.

BESSON, G. A. Paris, 1820-1875. Noted for his improvements in the construction of brass instruments.

BEST, William Thos. Distinguished organist ; *b.* Carlisle, 1826 ; *d.* Liverpool, 1897. Held numerous organ appointments, including— Panopticon, London, 1852 ; Lincoln's Inn, 1854 ; St. George's Hall, Liverpool, 1855-94 ; was also organist to the Philharmonic Society. Received a Civil List pension of £100 per annum, 1880.
His fine playing made him in great request for public recitals, &c. Opened the Sydney Grand Organ, 1890. Played concertos at the Handel Festivals for many years.
Works : church services, anthems, &c. ; sonatas, preludes and fugues, fantasias, &c., for organ ; " The Art of Organ Playing " and " Modern School for the Organ." Also many arrangements and transcriptions for organ.

Bestimmt' *(G.).* With decision ; distinctly.

BETHISY. French composer ; published (1752) " An Explanation of the Theory and Practice of Music."

BETJEMANN, Gilbert J. Violinist and conductor. *B.* London, 1840(?) ; *d.* 1896.

Beto'nen *(G.).* To accent or emphasize.

Betont' *(G.).* Accented, emphasized.

Beto'nung *(G.).* Accent, stress, emphasis.

Betrübt' *(G.).* Grieved, perturbed, sad.

BETTINI. " Trebelli-Bettini." (See **Trebelli.**)

BETZ, Franz. Dramatic baritone ; *b.* Mayence, 1835. Especially eminent as a Wagnerian singer. Created the part of " Wotan," Bayreuth, 1876. *D.* 1900.

BEVAN, Frederick Ch. *B.* London, 1856. Composer of popular songs, " The Flight of Ages," &c.

BEVIGNA'NI, Cavaliere Enrico. Eminent conductor ; *b.* Naples, 1841 ; *d.* 1903. Condr. at Her Majesty's Theatre, 1864-70, then at Covent Garden ; alternating these with engagements at St. Petersburg, Moscow, and New York. Composed an opera, *Caterina Bloom*, Naples, 1863.

BEVIN, Elway. Abt. 1565-1640. Pupil of Tallis. Org. Bristol Cathedral, 1589.
Works : " A Briefe and Short Introduction to the Art of Musicke," 1631 ; services and anthems (in Boyce's Cathedral Music, &c.).

Bewegt' *(G.).* Moved, stirred, animated.
Froh bewegt'. Gaily animated.

Bewe'gter *(G.).* Quicker.
Bewe'gter und im'mer mehr zu beschleu'nigen. Quicker, and continually *accelerando.*
Bewe'gter wer'dend. Becoming more animated.

Bewe'gung *(G.).* Motion, emotion.
In dersel'ben Bewe'gung. At the same speed (as before).

BEXFIELD, Wm. R. *B.* Norwich, 1824 ; *d.* 1853. Mus.Doc. Cantab., 1849.
Works : oratorio, *Israel Restored* ; cantata, *Hector's Death* ; anthems, songs, organ pieces, &c.

BEY'ER, Ferdinand. *B.* Querfurt, 1805 ; *d.* 1863. Composed drawing-room pf. pieces.

BEY'ER, Joh. S. *B.* Gotha, 1669 ; *d.* 1744. Cantor, Freiberg, 1697 ; director, 1728. Published collns. of chorals, concert arias, &c.

BEY'ER, Rudolf. *B.* nr. Bautzen, 1828 ; *d.* 1853. Wrote songs, chamber music, &c.

Bey'speil, or **Bei'spiel** *(G.).* An example.

Bezeich'neten *(G.).* Sharply detached ; very *staccato.*

Bezeich'nung *(G.).* Accentuation.

Bezif'fert *(G.).* Figured (as a bass part).
Der bezif'ferte Bass. The figured bass.

Bhat. A Hindoo bard.

Bi *(S.).* B♮.

BIAG'GI, G. A. *B.* Milan, 1819 ; *d.* 1897.
Wrote an opera, *Martino della Scala*. Chiefly known as Editor of *l'Italia Musicale*, Milan, and writer of numerous essays on musical subjects.

BI'AL, Karl. Brother of R. (below) ; 1833-1892. Wrote pf. pieces and songs.

BI'AL, Rudolf. Violinist ; *b.* Silesia, 1834 ; *d.* New York, 1881. Capellmeister, Wallner Theatre, Berlin, 1864, where his numerous farces, &c., were produced.
Afterwards conductor, Berlin Italian Opera, and concert-agent, New York.

Bian'ca *(I.).* "White." A minim (♩).

BIANCHETTA. A celebrated female singer for whom Haydn is said to have written *Ariadne*.

BIAN'CHI, Bianca. Celebrated high soprano singer ; *b.* in a village on the Neckar, 1858. Pupil of Madame Viardot-Garcia.
Made her *début* in *Figaro*, Karlsruhe, 1873. Has also sung in Vienna and London.

BIAN'CHI, Eliodoro. Has composed operas, *Gara d' Amore* (Bari, 1873), *Sarah*, *Almanzor*, &c.

BIAN'CHI, Francesco. *B.* Cremona, 1752 ; *d.* 1810. Organist, St. Mark's, Venice, 1785. Conductor, King's Theatre, London, 1793. Teacher of Sir H. Bishop.
Wrote 47 operas, including *La Réduction de Paris* (Paris, 1775).

BIANCHI'NI, Pietro. *B.* Venice, 1828. Began as an orchestral violinist ; afterwards director, *Padri Armeni* music school, Venice.
Works: symphonies, chamber music, masses, songs, pf. pieces, &c.

Bi'belregal *(G.).* A regal shaped like a Bible.

BI'BER, Aloys. 1804-1858. Esteemed Bavarian pf. maker.

BI'BER, H. J. F. von. *B.* Bohemia, 1644 ; *d.* Salzburg, 1704.
One of the founders of the German school of violin playing. Published violin sonatas, &c.

Bibi *(F.).* A pianette.

Bi'chord. Two strings to each note.

Bicor'do *(I.).* A double-string (vn., &c.).

Bici'nium *(L.).* A duet.

BIE'DERMANN. Tax-gatherer, Thuringia, abt. 1786.
"A real virtuoso on the hurdy-gurdy, which he considerably improved."— *Th. Baker.*

BIE'DERMANN, Ed. Julius. *B.* Milwaukee, 1849. Organist successively of several New York churches.
Works: masses, anthems, and vocal music.

BIEHL, Albert. *B.* Rudolstadt, 1833. Has published several works on pf. technique.

Bien *(F.).* Well ; good.
Bien chanté. Molto cantabile.
Bien rhythmé. The rhythm (to be) well marked.

BIENE. (See Van Biene.)

Bier'bass *(G.).* A rough bass voice.

BIER'EY, G. B. *B.* Dresden, 1772 ; *d.* 1840. Capellmeister at Breslau.
Works: 26 operas, including *Wladimir* (Vienna, 1807), *The Swiss Shepherdess*, &c.; cantatas, orchestral music, &c.

Bi'fara *(L.).* An organ stop with two pipes to each note, tuned at slightly different pitches, producing an undulating effect, as the *Vox Angelica*, *Celeste*, &c.

BIGA'GLIA, Padre Diogenio. Venetian monk. Published 12 sonatas for vn. or fl., 1725.

BIGNA'MI, Carlo. *B.* Cremona, 1808 ; *d.* 1848. Director and 1st violin, Cremona orchestra, 1837. Paganini called him "the first Italian violinist."
Wrote a violin concerto, several fantasias, &c.

BIGNA'MI, Ernico. *B.* abt. 1842. Wrote a successful opera, *Anna Rosa*, Genoa, 1892.

BIGNIO, Louis von. Noted baritone ; *b.* Pesth, 1839. *Début*, 1858. Sang in London, &c.

BIGOT, Marie *(née* **Kiene).** *B.* Colmar, Alsace, 1786 ; *d.* Paris, 1820. Fine pianist ; lived for some years in Vienna, where she was an esteemed friend of Beethoven's.

BIL'LETER, Agathon. Popular composer of men's voice music. *B.* Lake Zurich, 1834. Organist, Burgdorf, Switzerland.

BILLINGS, Wm. *B.* Boston, U.S.A., 1746 ; *d.* 1800. Published several collections of hymn-tunes, anthems, &c. ("The New England Psalm-Singer," "The Suffolk Harmony," &c.).
"Billings was, in his rough way, a pioneer of good church music in America ; he first used the pitch pipe, introduced the 'cello into church choirs, and is said to have originated concerts in New England."—*Th. Baker.*

BIL'LINGTON, Elizabeth *(née* **Weichsel).** *B.* London, 1765 ; *d.* 1818. Pupil of Joh. C. Bach. A soprano singer of marvellous range :— Married Billington, a double-bass player, 1784. Made her *début* in opera in Dublin. First sang in London as "Rosetta" in *Love in a Village*, Covent Garden, 1786. Sang in Naples, 1794, and Venice, 1796. Returned to London and became a great favourite at Drury Lane, Covent Garden, &c. In 1818 she retired to her estate near Venice.

BIL'LINGTON, Thos. Harpist, pianist, and composer. *B.* Exeter, 1754 (?) ; *d.* 1832.

BILL'ROTH, Joh. G. F. *B.* nr. Lubeck, 1808 ; *d.* 1836. Published, with K. F. Becke, a collection of chorales of the 16th and 17th cents.

BIL'SE, Benjamin. Renowned orchestral conductor ; *b.* Liegnitz, 1816. Conducted at Liegnitz and at the "Concerthaus," Berlin, 1868-84. *D.* 1902.
"His concerts and concert tours were social events."

Bimol'le *(I.).* B♭.

Bi'na. (See Vina.)

B in Alt. The note

Bi'nary. Dual ; naturally divisible into two parts.

Bi'nary Form. (1) Founded on two principal themes or subjects. (2) Divisible into two parts.

BINCHOIS (Gilles de Binche). *B.* Belgium, abt. 1400 ; *d.* 1460. One of the most famous early Netherland composers.
Wrote masses, chansons, rondeaux, &c. Most of his compositions are in 3 parts.

Bind. *(G. Bin'de.)* (1) A tie *(q.v.).* (2) A brace or bracket.

Bin'debogen *(G.)* A tie, or a slur.

Bin'den *(G.).* To tie; to connect; to render smoothly *(legato).*

BIN'DER, K. W. F. Celebrated harp maker; *b.* Dresden, 1764.

BIN'DER, Karl. Vienna, 1816-1860.
Works: opera, *Die 3 Wittfrauen*, 1841; overture and choruses to *Elmar;* psalms, songs, &c.

Bin'dung *(G.).* ⎫ (1) A syncopation. (2)
Bin'dungsbogen *(G.)* ⎬ A suspension. (3) A
Bin'dungszeichen *(G.)* ⎭ *legato* sign. (4) A
slur, or a tie.

BINGHAM, Clifton. *B.* Bristol, 1859.
Author of words of songs, &c.

Biniou, Bignou. A Brittany bagpipe.

BIO'NI, Antonio. *B.* Venice, 1698. Wrote 26 operas, mostly given at Breslau.

Biquad'ro *(I.).* The natural, ♮.

BIRCH, Charlotte A. English soprano singer, 1815-1857.

BIRCH, Frederick. Composer; *b.* S. Ockenden, 1851.

BIRCH'ALL, Robert. *D.* London, 1819. Founded one of the first circulating musical libraries.

BIRD, Arthur. Contemporary American organist and composer. *B.* Cambridge, Mass., 1856.
Has written suites for orchestra, an opera *(Daphne,* 1897), a ballet, pf. music, &c.

BIRD, Henry Rd. *B.* Walthamstow, 1842. Excellent pf. accompanist. Accompanied regularly at the St. James's Hall Popular Concerts from 1891.

BIRD, William. (See **Byrde.**)

Bird Music. The following interesting table of the relative merits of British songbirds was compiled by Daines Barrington; 20 is supposed to represent absolute perfection :—

	Mellowness of Tone.	Sprightly Notes.	Plaintive Notes.	Compass.	Execution
Nightingale ...	19	14	19	19	19
Skylark	4	19	4	18	18
Woodlark	18	4	17	12	8
Titlark	12	12	12	12	12
Linnet	12	16	12	16	18
Goldfinch	4	19	4	12	12
Chaffinch	4	12	4	8	8
Greenfinch ...	4	4	4	4	6
Hedge Sparrow	6	0	6	4	4
Siskin	2	4	0	4	4
Red Poll	0	4	0	4	4
Thrush	4	4	4	4	4
Blackbird	4	4	0	2	2
Robin...	6	16	12	12	12
Wren	0	12	0	4	4
Reed Sparrow...	0	4	0	2	2
Blackcap	14	12	12	14	14

BIR'KENSTOCK, Joh. A. Violinist. *B.* Alsfeld, 1687; *d.* Eisenach, 1733. Capellmeister at Cassel and Eisenach (1730).
Works: 24 violin sonatas with basso continuo, 12 concertos for 4 violins, viola,'cello, and basso.

Birmingham Festivals. Instituted 1768.

Birn, Bir'ne *(G.).* A socket (as of a clarinet).

BIRN'BACH, Karl J. *B.* Silesia, 1751; *d.* 1805. Capellmeister, German Theatre, Warsaw.
Works: oratorios, 2 operas, masses, 10 symphonies, 16 pf. concertos, 10 violin concertos, &c.

BIRN'BACH, Jos. B. Son of K. J. *B.* Breslau, 1795; *d.* 1879. Founded a musical institute in Berlin. Taught Nicolai and Kücken.
Works: 2 symphonies, 2 overtures, concertos, sonatas and other pf. music, &c.

Birthdays of Musicians.

JANUARY.
1 C. y Cavedo, 1810. J. P. Goldberg, 1825.
2 F. W. Jähns, 1809. Hostinsky, 1847.
3 Pergolesi, 1710. Sontag, 1806. J. F. Schneider, 1786.
4 Storace, 1763. Heuschkel, 1773.
5 Ett, 1788. Rockstro, 1823.   [wenka, 1850.
6 H. Herz, 1806. Max Bruch, 1838. X. Schar-
7 Thalberg, 1812. Constantin, 1835.   [1812.
8 Von Bülow, 1830. A. Piatti, 1822. W. H. Holmes,
9 W. Jackson (Masham), 1816. Draud (Draudius),
10 Mächtig, 1836. Perger, 1854.   [1573.
11 O. Dienel, 1839. Ellerton, 1807(1?). Sinding,1856.
12 A. Jensen, 1837. Arabella Goddard, 1836.
13 K. T. H. Hofmann, 1842. F. Clément, 1822.
14 L. Köchel, 1800. J. De Reszke, 1852.
15 Lesueur, 1763. J. B. Faure, 1830.
16 K. Krebs, 1804. Piccinni, 1728.
17 Gossec, 1734. Kempter, 1819.
18 E. Rudorff, 1840. A. E. Chabrier, 1842.
19 F. Laub, 1832. Kretzschmar, 1848.
20 J. T. Carrodus, 1836. F. B. Conti, 1681.
21 A. Goria, 1823. T. A. Walmisley, 1814.
22 V. Righini, 1756. Karajan, 1810.   [berg, 1843.
23 H. Wrist Hill, 1828. F. Commer, 1813. Hoch-
24 Frederick II of Prussia, 1712. E. T. Hoffmann,
25 Hernandez, 1834. Steingräber, 1830.   [1776.
26 G. Gunz, 1831. E. A. Kellner, 1792. Corder,1852.
27 Mozart, 1756. A. Klengel, 1783. Lalo, 1823.
28 Herold, 1791. V. Nessler, 1841.
29 Auber, 1782. F. Cowen, 1852.
30 Quantz, 1697. Lessmann, 1844.
31 Schubert, 1797. C. G. Reissiger, 1798.

FEBRUARY.   [1851.
1 A. C. Schloesser 1830. Cl. Butt, 1873. Essipoff,
2 Crescentini, 1766. L. Marchand, 1669.   [1845.
3 Mendelssohn,1809. Albrechtsberger,1736. F.Niecks,
4 Sir M. Costa, 1808 (7). d'Ivry, 1829.
5 Ole Bull, 1810. Mancinelli, 1848. Franklin Tay-
6 H. Litolff, 1820. Damcke, 1812.   [lor, 1843.
7 R. Genée, 1823. Frank, 1847. V. Gabriel, 1825.
8 Grétry, 1741. Logier, 1780. N. Burgmüller, 1810.
9 Dussek, 1761. S. Weekes, 1843. A. von Dommer,
10 C. Gurlitt, 1820. Sir W. Parratt, 1841.   [1828.
11 J. N. Götze, 1791. Heise, 1830.
12 F. J. Rochlitz, 1769. B. Roth, 1855.
13 Cambini, 1746. A. Mees, 1850.
14 Hanns Seeling, 1828. H. J. Bärmann, 1784.
15 Prætorius, 1571. F. E. Fesca, 1789.
16 L.Achard,1831. L. P.Scharwenka,1847. Rode,1774.
17 E. German, 1862. Fritze, 1842.
18 Paganini, 1784. Rink, 1770. G. Henschel, 1850.
19 Adelina Patti, 1843. L. Boccherini, 1743.
20 De Bériot, 1802. Guénin, 1744. Vieuxtemps, 1820.
21 Czerny, 1791. Délibes, 1836.
22 N. Gade, 1817. Forkel, 1749. Chopin, 1810.
23 Handel, 1685. Mara, 1749.   [Widor, 1845.
24 S. Wesley, 1766. J. B. Cramer, 1771. Boito, 1842.
25 S. W. Dehn, 1799. Caruso, 1873. F. Westlake, 1840.
26 A. Holländer, 1840. L. Borwick, 1868.   [1848.
27 A. Reicha, 1770. E. G. Baron, 1696. Sir H. Parry,
28 C. Santley, 1834. Parish-Alvars, 1808.
29 Rossini, 1792. Hirschbach, 1812.

MARCH.
1 E. Prout, 1835. G. Weber, 1779.
2 G. A. Macfarren, 1813. F. Smetana, 1824.
3 C. Salaman, 1814. Nourrit, 1802. A. Page, 1846.
4 C. Oberthür, 1819. R. Lindley, 1776. J. P. Baker,
5 J. Gungl, 1828. A. Jaell, 1832.   [1859.

MARCH.

6 B. Klein, 1793. Schad, 1812. A. Williams, 1864.
7 Ed. Lloyd, 1845. V. Massé, 1822. G. W. Fink, 1783.
8 Alard, 1815. Bellermann, 1795. C. P. E. Bach, 1714.
9 J. J. Bott, 1826. J. G. Kastner, 1810. [stone.
10 Sarasate, 1844. J. B. Coninck, 1827. Lucie John-
11 F. Lamperti, 1813. Bazzini, 1818.
12 Sir A. Manns, 1825. Guilmant, 1837.
13 J. Kent, 1700. Ecker, 1813.
14 J. Strauss, 1804. A. Bungert, 1846.
15 Durante, 1684. Dibdin, 1745. N. Vaccaj, 1790.
16 E. Tamberlik, 1820. J. B. Calkin, 1827. R. O. Morgan, 1865.
17 M. Garcia, 1805. J. Rheinberger, 1839.
18 J. Staudigl, junr,, 1850. C. E. Stephens, 1821.
19 J. J. H. Verhulst, 1816. Joah Bates, 1740. Melba,—
20 L. Dulcken, 1811. Florence Lancia, 1840.
21 J. S. Bach, 1685. Kalliwoda, 1800. A. Brodsky,
22 Carl Rosa, 1842. T. Lemaire, 1820. [1851.
23 Taubert, 1811. J. S. Kruse, 1859.
24 Mdme. Malibran, 1808. Fricke, 1829.
25 Hasse, 1699. Fétis, 1784.
26 Mdme. Marchesi, 1826. Jenny Meyer, 1834.
27 Eberlin, 1702. G. J. Elvey, 1816.
28 A. E. Batiste, 1820. Weigl, 1766.
29 J. W. Hassler, 1747. E. Kastner, 1847. Lady Hallé (Norman-Neruda), 1839.
30 Sir John Hawkins, 1719. A. Catelani, 1811. H. Watson, 1846.
31 Haydn, 1732. J. A. P. Schulz, 1747.

APRIL.

1 F. B. Busoni, 1866. Demelius, 1643.
2 F. Lachner, 1803. Mabellini, 1817.
3 E. Prudent, 1817. Krigar, 1819.
4 N. Zingarelli, 1752. Dr. H. Richter, 1843.
5 Spohr, 1784. V. Fioravanti, 1799. Erard, 1572.
6 R. Volkmann, 1815. J. Mettenleiter, 1812.
7 Dr. Burney, 1726. Dragonetti, 1763. Fr. Ries, 1846. H. Berens, 1826.
8 C. Merulo, 1533. K. Evers, 1819. Hamerik, 1843.
9 T. Böhm, 1794. F.P.Tosti, 1846. Mdme. Pasta, 1798.
10 Franchomme, 1808. E. D'Albert, 1864.
11 Sir Chas. Hallé, 1819. Beaulieu, 1791.
12 Tartini, 1692. H. H. Pierson, 1816. Haberl, 1840.
13 Félicien David, 1810. Sterndale Bennett, 1816. Randegger, 1832.
14 J. Staudigl, 1807. Coccia, 1782. Huberti, 1843.
15 Euler, 1707. Fenaroli, 1730.
16 Ludwig Berger, 1777. Caffarelli, 1703.
17 Tomaschek, 1774. Heinichen, 1683.
18 B. A. Weber, 1766. Suppé, 1820.
19 Coussemaker, 1805. G. Catrufo, 1771.
20 T. Döhler, 1814. Krempelsetzer, 1827.
21 P. Hertel, 1817. F. Gumbert, 1818.
22 Wilfred Bendall, 1850. Mehrkens, 1840.
23 L. A. Julien, 1812. P. Dupont, 1821.
24 Kirnberger, 1721. Egghard, 1834.
25 Padre Martini, 1706. Tschaikowsky, 1840.
26 Panseron, 1796. J. A. Eyken, 1822.
27 Niedermeyer, 1802. Flotow, 1812. Romberg, 1767.
28 Dreszer, 1845. Titoff, 1801. H. Bauer. 1873.
29 Hey, 1829. Kopecky, 1850.
30 Kammerlander, 1828. Piutti, 1846.

MAY.

1 Hurel de Lemare, 1772. T. Krause, 1833.
2 Kircher, 1602. R. Kündinger, 1832.
3 T. Harper, 1787. Odenwald, 1838.
4 Gassmann, 1729. Cristofori, 1653. Turpin, 1835.
5 S. Moniuszko, 1820. K. Attenhofer, 1837.
6 Ernst, 1814. K. C. Krause, 1781.
7 T. Helmore, 1811. Brahms, 1833. Graun, 1701.
8 Gänsbacher, 1778. Parepa-Rosa, 1836.
9 G. Paisiello, 1741. C. Pinsuti, 1829.
10 I. De L'Isle, 1760. Sir G. Smart, 1776.
11 I. Fiorillo, 1715. Capocci, 1840.
12 A. Henselt, 1814. Massenet, 1842.
13 Sullivan, 1842. G. U. Fauré, 1845. Visetti, 1846.
14 J. P. F örtsch, 1652. J. P. Hartmann, 1805.
15 A. B. Marx, 1799. Balfe, 1808. S. Heller, 1815.
16 G. Nava, 1802. E. Hille, 1822. A. H. Mann. 1850.
17 Sainton-Dolby, 1821. Dalberg, 1752.
18 C. Goldmark, 1830. Deprosse, 1838.
19 Müller-Hartung, 1834. Alice M. Smith, 1839.
20 Eaton Faning, 1851. Gervinus, 1805.

MAY.

21 Amy Fay, 1844. Lotze, 1817. G F. Gear, 1857.
22 Rd. Wagner, 1813. Fesca, 1820. E. Sauret, 1852.
23 G. B. Viotti, 1753. J. Wieniawski, 1837.
24 T. Mattei, 1841. Dauprat, 1781.
25 A. Lwoff, 1799. Goovaerts, 1847.
26 P. Gaviniès, 1726. J. Drechsler, 1782.
27 Halévy, 1799. Raff, 1822.
28 Thos. Moore, 1780. Dessauer, 1798.
29 E. Breslaur, 1836. H. Káan, 1852.
30 Moscheles, 1794. J. C. Lobe, 1797.
31 Deldevez, 1817. Hartvigson, 1841.

JUNE.

1 I. Pleyel, 1757. F. Paër, 1771. Glinka, 1803.
2 N. Rubinstein, 1835. Führer, 1807. Elgar, 1857.
3 A. C. Lecocq, 1832. C. Steggall, 1826. Vilbac, 1829.
4 J. Janssen, 1852. Sittard, 1846.
5 P. Sainton, 1813. Hallström, 1826. Desvignes, 1805.
6 Sir J. Stainer, 1840. A. F. Servais, 1807.
7 Mertke, 1833. L. Ronald, 1873. Auer, 1845.
8 Schumann, 1810. G. M. Garrett, 1834. Janotha, 1856.
9 Nicolai, 1810. Braga, 1829.
10 Clara Novello, 1818. Catel, 1773.
11 R. Strauss, 1864. Pressel, 1827.
12 Puppo, 1749. Spengel, 1853. Plançon, 1854. [1753.
13 E. F. Rimbault, 1816. A. Eberl, 1766. Dalayrac,
14 Morlacchi, 1784. S. Mayr, 1763. A. J. Ellis, 1814.
15 Abbé Vogler, 1749. E. Grieg, 1843. C. Wood, 1866.
16 O. Jahn, 1813. W. Shakespeare, 1849.
17 Gounod, 1818. Pfundt, 1806. Hipkins, 1826.
18 H. Leslie, 1822. D. Popper, 1845.
19 Ferd. David, 1810. W. Bache, 1842. Sawyer, 1857.
20 Salvator Rosa, 1615. Schreyer, 1856.
21 Offenbach, 1819. Curschmann, 1805. [1763.
22 H. K. De Ahna, 1835. J. Handrock, 1830. Méhul,
23 C. H. C. Reinecke, 1824. E. Guiraud, 1837.
24 Farinelli, 1705. Plunket Greene, 1865.
25 F. A. Jakob, 1803. Landgraf, 1816.
26 Mercadente, 1797. Dr. Bunnett. 1834.
27 Fanny Davies, 1861. J. Hullah, 1812. Deiters, 1833.
28 Rousseau, 1712. R. Franz, 1815. Joachim, 1831.
29 Alfieri, 1801. Dettmer, 1808. Campanini, 1846.
30 E. J. Hopkins, 1818. Hervé, 1825.

JULY.

1 V. Wallace, 1814. A. Sighicelli, 1802.
2 Glück, 1714. G. Flügel, 1812.
3 Lampert, 1818. A. Morsch, 1841. Lecocq, 1832,
4 J. Labitzky, 1802. K. H. Döring, 1834.
5 Crotch, 1775. A. Zimmermann, 1847. Kubelik, 1880.
6 V. Adamberger, 1743. K. Engel, 1818.
7 G. Cooper, 1820. S. Pacini, 1778.
8 F. Chrysander, 1826. R. H. Thomas, 1834.
9 Opelt, 1794. W. M. Vogel, 1846. C. Sternberg, 1852.
10 Neukomm, 1778. H. Wieniawski, 1835.
11 A. Mehlig, 1846. P. Lacombe, 1837.
12 C. Barth, 1847. Molitor, 1817.
13 C. W. Corfe, 1814. Armbruster, 1846.
14 J. Steiner, 1621. P. Humphrey, 1647.
15 H. Esser, 1818. Genast, 1797. J. Barnett, 1802.
16 H. Viotta, 1848. Ysaye, 1858. Arditi, 1822.
17 I. Leybach, 1817. Tietjens, 1831. Gernsheim, 1839.
18 H. Riemann, 1849. Viardot-Garcia, 1821.
19 Lord Mornington, 1735. V. Lachner, 1811.
20 F. Chiaromonte, 1809. E. Hodges, 1796.
21 Saint F. Neri, 1515. Gouvy, 1819.
22 Proch, 1809. Sir H. S. Oakeley, 1830.
23 Sacchini, 1734. Colonne, 1838. Hol, 1825.
24 A. Adam, 1803. Lauterbach, 1832.
25 G. Cordella, 1786. Liebig, 1808.
26 J. Field, 1782. M. Fürstenau, 1824.
27 Onslow, 1784. V. de Pachmann, 1848.
28 C. Lucas, 1808. G. Grisi, 1811.
29 Sophie Menter, 1848. Lubrich, 1862.
30 E. Eggeling, 1813. Hrimaly, 1842.
31 F. A. Gevaert, 1828. Candeille, 1767.

AUGUST.

1 Marcello, 1686. Ladurner, 1766. Papini, 1847.
2 J. Schulhoff, 1825.
3 F. Clay, 1840. F. A. Barbieri, 1823.
4 J. Proksch, 1794. E. Kossak, 1814.
5 Ambroise Thomas, 1811. F. A. Kummer, 1797.
6 H. Mendel, 1834. Heintzsch, 1787.
7 Abbé Stadler, 1748. Hopffer, 1840. Foli, 1835. [1861.
8 H. A. Gelinek. 1709. Wieprecht, 1802. Chaminade,
9 N. H. Bochsa, 1789. M. Umlauf, 1781.

AUGUST.

10 S. Arnold, 1740. Coccon, 1826. Glazounow, 1865.
11 Schuster, 1748. E. C. Phelps, 1827.
12 Gerbert, 1720. Sir F. Ouseley, 1825. J. Barnby, 1838. Nicodé, 1853.
13 Sir G. Grove, 1820. R. Hausmann, 1852. Best, 1826.
14 Dulon, 1769. S. S. Wesley, 1810. [Gastinel, 1823.
15 Maelzel, 1772. P. Armes, 1836. E. Hartog, 1828.
16 H. Marschner, 1795. M. Drobisch, 1802.
17 P. L. Benoit, 1834. Pönitz, 1850.
18 B. L. P. Godard, 1849. F. Wieck, 1785. P. Lichthenthal, 1780.
19 Porpora, 1866. Salieri, 1750.
20 Frankenberger, 1824. Christine Nilsson, 1843.
21 O. Goldschmidt, 1829. Hirn, 1815. [E. Silas, 1827.
22 A. C. Mackenzie, 1847. W. H. Cummings, 1831.
23 M. Moszkowski, 1854. Beffara, 1751.
24 E. Lübeck, 1829. Dubois, 1837. F. Mottl, 1856.
25 A. L. Ritter, 1811. Haupt, 1810. D J. Wood, 1849.
26 A. Schmitt, 1788. J. C. Kessler, 1800.
27 H. Kipper, 1826. H. Urban, 1837.
28 W. Macfarren, 1826. F. Listemann, 1841.
29 Kiesewetter, 1773. J. H. Lambert, 1728.
30 A. Hesse, 1809. B. Asioli, 1769.
31 Helmholtz, 1821. T. Gautier, 1811.

SEPTEMBER. [1854.

1 C. G. Lickl, 1803. A. Horn, 1825. Humperdinck,
2 K. F. Hering, 1819. Petersen, 1761.
3 N. Amati, 1596. Pasqué, 1821. [1831.
4 M. F. Pleyel, 1811. A. Bruckner, 1824. D. Godfrey,
5 Meyerbeer, 1791. C. L. H. Köhler, 1820.
6 Diabelli, 1781. C. F. Pohl, 1819. V. Novello, 1781.
7 A. Philidor, 1726. Mad. Dorus-Gras, 1805.
8 E. Naumann, 1827. Dvorák, 1841.
9 Z. Buck, 1798. Kleeman, 1842.
10 Jomelli, 1714. Benoist, 1794.
11 E. Hanslick, 1825. G. C. Martin, 1844.
12 T. Kullak, 1818. J. L. Tolou, 1786. R. Pohl, 1826.
13 Gillet, 1856. Madame Schumann, 1819.
14 M. Haydn, 1737. Cherubini, 1760.
15 Pasdeloup, 1819. E. Wolff, 1816.
16 Gährich, 1794. A. Parsons, 1847. [1841.
17 Mercadente, 1795. H. Kjerulf, 1818. E. J. Crow,
18 Hans Müller, 1854. Ronchetti-Monteviti, 1814.
19 V. Bender, 1801. Croes, 1705. J. Bartleman, 1769.
20 C. B. Uber, 1746. C. Voss, 1815.
21 A. Wilhelmj, 1845. L. E. Jadin, 1768.
22 C. Kalkbrenner, 1755. Karasowski, 1823.
23 C. L. Kreutzer, 1817. Zellner, 1823.
24 G. A. Osborne, 1806. J. Klengel, 1859.
25 Pinto, 1786. Rameau, 1683. C. Klindworth, 1830.
26 M. P. Audran, 1816. Mühling, 1786. Reeves, 1818.
27 H. Wollenhaupt, 1827. A. Köttlitz, 1820.
28 J. Mattheson, 1681. Gobbaerts, 1835.
29 Gerber, 1746. A. Hahn, 1828. J. G. Schicht, 1753.
30 J. S. Svendsen, 1840. C. V. Stanford, 1852.

OCTOBER.

1 P. M. Baillot, 1771. G. M. Asola, 1609.
2 H. Panofker, 1807. Cip. Pottér, 1792.
3 W. Bargiel, 1828. W. Blodek, 1834.
4 J. Blumenthal, 1829. Lemmens-Sherrington, 1834.
5 H. Schütz, 1585. J. W. Davison, 1813.
6 Jenny Lind, 1820. J. A. André, 1775.
7 B. Molique, 1802. Dräseke, 1835. F. Kiel, 1821.
8 K. L. Mangold, 1813. Seydelmann, 1748. Sauer, 1862.
9 Verdi, 1813. Saint-Saëns, 1835.
10 J. L. Krebs, 1713. B. Hamma, 1831. [1835.
11 S. Sechter, 1788. F. Hegar, 1841. Theo. Thomas,
12 J. L. Hatton, 1809. Florimo, 1800. Friedländer, 1852.
13 M. Hauptmann, 1792. H. Rosellen, 1811. Faisst, 1823.
14 W. G. Cusins, 1833. V. Langer, 1842.
15 G. F. Cobb, 1838. W. A. Barrett, 1836.
16 J. Hollmann, 1852. J. F. Barnett, 1837.
17 A. W. Thayer, 1817. Monsigny, 1729.
18 Del Valle de Paz, 1861. Galuppi, 1706.
19 Louis Lee, 1819. A. Fumagalli, 1828.
20 H. Blagrove, 1811. J. A. Bach, 1766.
21 H. Lemoine, 1786. Choron, 1772. Sapellnikoff, 1868.
22 Liszt, 1811. L. Damrosch, 1832.
23 A. Lortzing, 1803. Meister, 1818.
24 E. F. Richter, 1808. F. Hiller, 1811.
25 Bizet, 1838. J. Strauss, 1825. Sivori, 1815.
26 J. Mayseder, 1789. H. Smart, 1813.
27 An. Kontski, 1817. J. Jenkins, 1592. Gibson, 1849.
28 H. Bertini, 1798. W. Spark, 1823. H. L. Balfour, 1859.

OCTOBER.

29 G. Aprile, 1738. E. C. May, 1806.
30 S. Arteaga, 1799. Gustav Weber, 1845.
31 R. Willmers, 1821. Max Pauer, 1866.

NOVEMBER.

1 Bellini, 1801. Jos. von Blumenthal, 1782.
2 A. Vianesi, 1837. Dittersdorf, 1739.
3 Heckmann, 1848. V. Dourlen, 1780.
4 C. Tausig, 1841. E. Dannreuther, 1844.
5 H. Sachs, 1494. Faminzin, 1841.
6 W. Schröder-Devrient, 1804. Paderewski, 1860.
7 I. Brüll, 1846. P. Demol, 1825. Deppe, 1828.
8 Gura, 1842. W. J. Krug, 1858. Komzak, 1850.
9 J. B. T. Weckerlin, 1821. A. Krause, 1834.
10 M. Luther, 1483. L. Kufferath, 1811.
11 B. Romberg, 1767. J. H. Scheibler, 1777.
12 Borodin, 1834. Nottebohm, 1817. Merkel, 1827.
13 B. Richards, 1819. G. W. Chadwick, 1854. [1816.
14 G. Spontini, 1774. Hummel, 1778. John Curwen,
15 W. Horsley, 1774. E. H. Richter, 1805.
16 F. W. Kücken, 1810. d'Alembert, 1717.
17 A. W. Ambros, 1816. Naue, 1787. W. Coenen, 1837.
18 Sir H. Bishop, 1786. Elwart, 1808.
19 S. Champein, 1753. Hainl, 1807. Zachau, 1663.
20 J. W. Callcott, 1766. W. Chappell, 1809. Himmel, 1765.
21 M. Blumner, 1827. Goring Thomas, 1851,
22 W. F. Bach, 1710. C. Kreutzer, 1780. Arneiro, 1838.
23 T. Attwood, 1765. E. Haddock, 1859.
24 B. Stavenhagen, 1862. K. A. Heymann, 1852.
25 J. F. Reichardt, 1752. J. L. Hopkins, 1819.
26 Bussler, 1838. L. T. Lacombe, 1818.
27 J. P. Duport, 1741. J. Benedict, 1804. Mailly, 1833.
28 Ferd. Ries, 1784. Plaidy, 1810.
29 Donizetti, 1797. Samara, 1861. [1830.
30 C. V. Alkan, 1813. Chladni, 1756. A. Rubinstein,

DECEMBER.

1 J. Gung'l, 1810. Castil-Blaze, 1784. Cellier, 1844.
2 J. Rosenheim, 1813. A. Agazzari, 1578.
3 J. Sterkel, 1750. Abbé Gelinek, 1758.
4 J. Töpfer, 1791. Bonawitz, 1839. Campra, 1660.
5 Nohl, 1831. Sir F. J. Bridge, 1844. C. W. Pearce,
6 L. Lablache, 1794. Duprez, 1806. [1856.
7 P. Mascagni, 1863. Eckert, 1820.
8 P. Lindpaintner, 1791. Liliencron, 1820.
9 Algernon Ashton, 1859. B. Ferri, 1610.
10 E. Petrella, 1813. W. Kuhe, 1822. Drieberg, 1780.
11 C. Zelter, 1758. Berlioz, 1803. C. Wesley, 1757.
12 Debillemont, 1824. Lebert, 1822.
13 E. G. Monk, 1819. Clarke (Whitfeld), 1770.
14 Leopold Mozart, 1719. Gamucci, 1822.
15 H. Gadsby, 1842. H. F. Chorley, 1808.
16 Beethoven, 1770. C. E. Horsley, 1822.
17 Cimarosa, 1749. H. Goetz, 1840. Tours, 1838.
18 Weber, 1786. Kazynski, 1812. MacDowell, 1861.
19 J. Ella, 1802. Dancla, 1818. S. Stratton, 1840.
20 L. Meyer, 1816. Kühnstedt, 1809. Perosi, 1872.
21 B. Berbiguier, 1782. E. Pauer, 1826. H. Fisher, 1845.
22 F. Abt, 1819. Carreno, 1853.
23 E. De Reszke, 1855. Rolle, 1718. [1812(?).
24 Bottesini, 1821(3). Cornelius, 1824. H. Russell,
25 Mazzinghi, 1765. Beckwith, 1750. E. T. Chipp, 1823.
26 Hünten, 1793. Grisar, 1808. F. Coenen, 1826.
27 Sir J. Goss, 1800. Kepler, 1571.
28 J. Reitz, 1812. Gallenberg, 1783.
29 C. H. Aschenbrenner, 1654. Hermstedt, 1778.
30 H. K. Ebell, 1775. Germer, 1837.
31 J. Herz, 1794. H. Hiles, 1826.

Bis *(L.)*. Twice. (1) The passage so marked to be repeated. (2) Again ; used in France for *encore*.

Bis *(G.)*. Up to, until, as far as.
Immer schwä'ker bis zum ppp. Continually softer to *ppp*.

BISAC'CIA, Geo. Naples, 1815-1897. Wrote an opera buffa, farces, &c.

BISCACCIAN'TI, Eliza (*née* **Ostinelli**). Brilliant singer in opera and concert ; b. Boston, U.S.A., abt. 1824 ; d. 1896. Sang in Boston, Philadelphia, and Europe.

Biscan'to *(I.)*. A duet.

Bische'ro *(I.)*. The peg of a violin, &c.

BISCH'OFF, Georg F. 1780-1841. Founder of the German musical festivals, 1810.

BISCH'OFF, Dr. Hans. Pianist, teacher, and writer. *B.* Berlin, 1852 ; *d.* 1889. Assisted in conducting the Monday concerts at the Berlin " Singakademie." Edited important works on pf. playing, &c.

BISCH'OFF, Kaspar J. *B.* Ansbach, 1823 ; *d.* 1893. Founded a " Lutheran Sacred Choral Society," Frankfort, 1850.
Works: an opera, 3 symphonies, overture to *Hamlet*, chamber music, &c., and a "Manual of Harmony."

Biscro'ma *(I.)*
Biscrome *(F)* } A semiquaver (♪).
Bis Un'ca *(L.)*

Bisdiapason. A double-octave, or 15th.

BISHOP (*née* **Rivière**) **Ann.** *B.* London, 1814 ; *d.* 1884. Soprano singer. Married to Sir H. Bishop, 1831. Eloped with Bochsa.

BISHOP, Sir H. Rowley. *B.* London, Nov. 18, 1786 ; *d.* Apl. 30, 1855. Pupil of F. Bianchi. First opera, *The Circassian Bride*, Drury Lane, 1809. From 1810 to 1830 conductor and composer at Covent Garden, Drury Lane, and the Philharmonic concerts. Director at Vauxhall, 1830. Mus.B. Oxon, 1839. Professor of Music, Edinburgh, 1841-43. Knighted, 1842. Professor of Music, Oxford, 1848 ; Mus.Doc., 1853. He was a prolific composer, and wrote over 80 operas, operettas, ballets, farces, &c., in addition to a large number of popular songs, and glees.
Among his best operas are *Cortez*, *The Fall of Algiers*, *The Knight of Snowdoun*, and *Oberon*. He also wrote an oratorio, *The Fallen Angel*, and published four vols. of national melodies.

BISHOP, John (of Cheltenham). *B.* 1817 ; *d.* 1890. Organist. Translated and edited many works on musical theory, &c., and compositions by the great masters.

BISP'HAM, David Scull. Dramatic baritone and favourite stage and concert singer. *B.* Philadelphia, 1857.

Bissa're *(I.).* *(F., Bisser.)* To encore.

Bit. A short piece of tube to lengthen the crook of a trumpet, cornet, &c., to slightly lower the pitch.

Bit'tend *(G.).* Supplicating, entreating.

BITTER, Karl H. 1813-1885. Prussian Minister of Finance, 1879-82.
Wrote a "Life of J. S. Bach," and valuable treatises on works by Mozart, Gluck, Handel, Wagner, &c. Also edited Karl Löwe's Autobiography, 1870.

Bit'terkeit *(G.).* Bitterness.

Bizzarramen'te *(I.).* Whimsically, fantastically.

Bizzarri'a *(I.).* Affectation, singularity, extravagance.

Bizzar'ro *(I.)* ; *(G. Bizarr').* Bizarre, odd, fantastic.

BIZET, Georges (Alex. C. L.). *B.* Paris, Oct. 25, 1838 ; *d.* June 3, 1875. Entered Paris Cons. at 9. Won the prize offered by

Offenbach for the best opera buffa, 1857, and also the *Grand Prix de Rome*. Most of his early operas were unsuccessful, as he leaned strongly towards Wagnerism ; but the ultimate striking success of *Carmen* (1875) shows what he might have accomplished had he lived longer. He died 3 months after ! Next in popularity ranks the music to *l'Arlésienne*, 1872. Besides operas he wrote some 150 pf. pieces, songs, &c.

BLACK, Andrew. Esteemed contemporary baritone singer. *B.* Glasgow, 1859 (60?).

BLACKBURN, Geo. A. Composer ; *b.* Manchester, 1853.

Black Keys. The " sharps and flats " of a manual.

Black note. A note with a " filled up " head ; as

♩ ♪ ♫

BLAES, Arnold J. 1814-1892. Succeeded Bachmann as solo clarinet and Professor at the Brussels Cons., 1842.

BLAGROVE, Henry G. Violinist ; *b.* Nottingham, 1811 ; *d.* London, 1872. Played in public at the age of 5. Studied under Spohr. Afterwards played at the chief London and provincial festivals, &c.

BLAGROVE, Richard M. 1827(?)-1895. Brother of H. G. Fine viola player. Pupil and many years Professor at the R.A.M.

BLA'HAG (BLAHAK), Jos. Hungarian tenor singer and composer ; 1779-1846. Capellmeister, St. Peter's, Vienna, 1842.
Works : many masses, graduals, Te Deums, &c.

BLAHET'KA (or Plahetka), Marie L. Composer and brilliant pianist. *B.* nr. Vienna, 1811 ; *d.* 1887. Pupil of Czerny, Kalkbrenner, and Moscheles. Wrote an opera, and several pf. pieces and songs.

BLAIKLEY, D. J. Contemp. authority on the construction of instruments. Contributor to Grove's Dictionary, &c.

BLAINVILLE, Chas. H. *B.* nr. Tours, 1711 ; *d.* 1769. Composed a symphony in the Phrygian (or *Me*) Mode, which was praised by Rousseau.

BLAIR, Hugh. Orgt., condr., and composer ; *b.* Worcester, 1864 ; Mus.Doc. Cambridge, 1906.

BLAKE, Rev. Dr. Ed. *B.* Salisbury, 1708 ; *d.* 1765. Wrote the anthem, "I have set God always before me."

BLAMONT, F. C. de. *B.* Versailles, 1690 ; *d.* 1760. Superintendent of the King's music.
Works : ballets, fêtes, operas, motets, songs, &c.

BLANC, Adolphe. French composer ; 1828-85. Pupil of Halévy. Won *Prix Chartier*, 1882. Conducted at the Theâtre Lyrique.
Works : opera, *Une aventure sous la Ligue;* two operettas, chamber music, pf. pieces, &c.

BLANCHARD, Henri L. *B.* Bordeaux, 1778 ; *d.* Paris, 1858. Violinist, composer, conductor, and distinguished musical critic.
Works : two operas and some chamber music.

Blanche (*F.*, " white "). A minim ($\wp$).

Blanche pointée (*F.*). A dotted minim.

BLANCKS, Ed. One of the ten contributors to Este's Psalter, 1592.

BLAND, Maria Theresa (*née* **Romanzini**). 1769-1838. Favourite ballad singer at Drury Lane, Vauxhall Gardens, &c.
> She excelled in "beauty of voice, simplicity of manner, and neatness of style."

BLANGI'NI, G. M. M. F. *B.* Turin, 1781 ; *d.* Paris, 1841. Played the Turin Cathedral organ at 12. Went to Paris, 1799 ; gave concerts and singing lessons and wrote *Romances.* Court Capellmeister, Munich, 1806 ; general music director, Cassel, 1809. Superintendent King's music and court composer, Paris, 1814.
> Works : 30 operas, 4 masses, 170 notturnos, 175 romances, &c.

BLA'RAMBERG, Paul I. *B.* Orenburg, Russia, 1841. Editor, *Moscow Russian Gazette.* Has composed operas (including the successful *Tuschinsky,* 1895), a cantata, and other works.

Bla'sebalg (*G.*). Bellows.

Bla'sen (*G.*). To blow ; to sound.
Bla'sebass. Bassoon.
Bla'ser. "Blower." A wind inst. player.
Blas'instrumeut. Wind instrument.
Blas'musik. Wind instrument music.

BLASER'NA, Pietro. *B.* nr. Aquileja, 1836. Prof. of Physics, Palermo Univ. Advocate of pure intonation.
> Chief work : "Theory of Sound."

BLASIUS, Matthieu F. *B.* Alsace, 1758 ; *d.* Versailles, 1829. Violinist, clarinettist, flautist, and bassoonist. Conductor, Paris Opéra Comique, 1791-1816. Prof. of wind insts. at the Cons., 1795-1802.
> Besides many popular pieces for flute, clarinet, and bassoon in various combinations, he wrote 3 operas, 3 melodramas, string quartets, violin concertos, &c.

BLASS'MANN, Adolf. J. M. Pianist and composer ; *b.* Dresden, 1823 ; *d.* 1891.

Blatt (*G.*). A leaf, sheet of music, reed of an inst.

BLATT, Franz T. *B.* Prague, 1793. Wrote a " Complete Method for Clarinet," and many pieces and studies for that inst.

BLAUVELT, Lillian E. *B.* Brooklyn, 1873.
> Sang in the *Golden Legend* at the Albert Hall with remarkable success, 1899 ; and as "Marguerite" in *Faust,* Covent Garden, 1903. Her voice is an exquisite soprano.

BLAU'WAERT, Emiel. Basso cantante ; *b.* St. Nicholas, Belgium, 1845 ; *d.* 1891.
> Sang with much success in Benoît's *Lucifer,* 1865, and as "Gurnemanz" in *Parsifal* (Bayreuth).

BLAZE, François H. J. (known as **Castil-Blaze**). " Father of modern French musical criticism." *B.* Vaucluse, 1784 ; *d.* Paris, 1857. Began as a law student, but devoted himself to music, 1820.
> He composed three operas, several " pastiches," chamber-music, &c. ; but his fame rests on his critical writings (*Journal des Débats,* &c.), and his many works on music. Works : "L'Opéra en France" (1820), "Dictionnaire de musique moderne" (1821), "Chapelle

musique des Rois de France" (1832) ; "La Danse et les Ballets depuis Bacchus jusqu'a Mademoiselle Taglioni" (1832) ; "Mémorial du Grand Opéra" (from 1669). "Le Piano : hist. de son invention, etc," "Molière musicien" (1852), "Théâtres lyriques de Paris ;" translations of the libretti of *Der Freischütz, Don Giovanni, Figaro, Il Barbiere, Fidelio,* &c.

BLAZE, Henri, Baron de Bury. Son of F. H. J. *B.* Avignon, 1813 ; *d.* Paris, 1888.
> Wrote " Etudes littera:res sur Beethoven," "Musique des drames de Shakespeare," &c., and critical essays for the *Revue des deux Mondes.*

BLECH, Leo. Composer ; *b.* Aachen, 1871.

Blech'instrument (*G.*). A brass (or other metal) wind instrument.
Blech'bande. Brass band.
Blech'musik. Brass band ; its music.

BLEW'ITT, Jonathan. *B.* London, 1782 ; *d.* 1853. Organist in various London churches, and at St. Andrew's, Dublin, 1811. Music-director at Sadler's Wells Theatre, 1826.
> Wrote and arranged much stage-music produced at Drury Lane, &c., and several popular songs. He also published " The Vocal Assistant," a work on singing.

Blind Octaves. A pf. passage in octaves for alternate hands ; sounding almost like double octaves.
> N.B.—Germer calls these " interlocking octaves,' and gives the name "blind octaves " to passages like the following :—
> BEETHOVEN, Op. 78.

Bloch'flöte, Block'flöte (*G.*). An organ (flute) stop with pyramidal or stopped pipes.

BLOCKX, Jan. Pianist and composer ; *b.* Antwerp, 1851. Professor of harmony, Antwerp Cons., 1886 ; director, 1901.
> Of his numerous vocal and orchestral works the operas *De Herbergprinses* (1896) and *La Fiancée de la Mer* (1902) are the most widely known.

BLODEK, Pierre A. L. Parisian composer and violin player ; 1784-1856.
> Works : opera, *Alla fontana ;* 3 overtures, a mass, Te Deums, chamber music, pf. pieces, songs, &c.

BLODEK, Wilhelm. *B.* Prague, 1834 ; *d.* 1874. Prof. Prague Cons., 1860. Died insane.
> Works : a very successful opera in the Czech language, *V Studni* (1867), a mass, quartets for male voices, songs, pf. music, &c.

BLONDEL. Minstrel to Richard I. Abt. 1190.
> By wandering through Germany singing a song known to both he discovered the castle where the king was imprisoned.

BLOOMFIELD - ZEIS'LER, Fanny. Brilliant pianist. *B.* Silesia, 1866. Parents settled in Chicago, 1868. Played in public at the age of 10. Studied with Leschetizky, Vienna, for 5 years (from 1878).
> Played with all the chief orchestras in the U.S., 1888-93. Toured through Berlin, Vienna, Leipzig, Dresden, &c., and the U.S., 1893-6 ; and has since played in England and France with great success.

BLOW, Dr. John. *B.* Nottingham, 1648 ; *d.* Westminster, 1708. Chorister, Chapel

Royal, 1660. Orgt. Westmr. Abbey, 1669. Retired in favour of Purcell, 1680. Reappointed on Purcell's death, 1695. Composer to the Chapel Royal, 1699.

Blow wrote much church music (including well-known anthems and services), also odes, organ music, harpsichord pieces, songs, &c.

BLUM (pron. *Bloom*), **Karl L.** Berlin, 1786-1844. Composer, organist, conductor, actor, poet, singer, &c. Chamber musician to the Prussian Court, 1820. Stage manager, Berlin Opera, 1822.

He wrote some 30 operas, vaudevilles, &c., being the "first to bring the vaudeville on the German stage."

BLU'MENFELD, Felix. Pianist; *b.* Kovaleska, 1863.

BLU'MENTHAL, Jacob (Jacques). *B.* Hamburg, 1829. Settled London in 1848; *d.* 1908.

His popular songs include "The Message," "My Queen," &c., and he has also written melodious pieces for pf., violin, &c.

BLU'MENTHAL, Joseph von. Violinist, &c.; *b.* Brussels, 1782; *d.* Vienna, 1850. Pupil of Abbé Vogler.

Works: opera, *Don Sylvio de Rosalba* (1805), a ballet, symphonies, chamber music, violin music, &c., and a violin method.

Blu'micht, Blu'mig *(G.)*. Flowery.

BLUM'NER, Dr. M. *B.* nr. Mecklenburg, 1827. Cond. Berlin Singakademie, 1876; *d.* 1901.

Works: oratorios, *Abraham* (1860), and *Der Fall Jerusalems* (1881), a Te Deum in 8 parts, cantata, *Columbus;* motets, lieder, &c.

BLÜTH'NER, Julius F. *B.* 1824. Founded his piano factory at Leipzig, 1853, with 3 workmen. Now employs over 500, turning out some 3,000 pianos per year.

B moll *(G.)*. The key of B♭ minor.

B mol'le *(L.)*. The note B♭.

Bob. (1) A term used to express the sets of "changes" in bell-ringing. *Bob minor*, 6 bells; *bob major*, 8 bells; *bob royal*, 10 bells; *bob maximus*, 12 bells. (2) A word of command in bell-ringing.

Bobiba'tion, or **Bocedisa'tion.** A method of Solfeggi used by Waelraent in the 16th and 17th centuries. The scale names were *bo, ce, di, ga, la, mi, ni.*

Bocal *(F.)*. The mouthpiece or cup of the horn, trombone, &c.

Boc'ca *(I.)*. The mouth. *Con boc'ca chiu'sa*, with closed mouth; humming.

Boc'ca riden'te *(I.)*. Smiling mouth; to produce pleasing tone.

BOCCHERI'NI, Luigi. Prolific composer; *b.* Lucca, 1743; *d.* Madrid, 1805. He undertook concert tours, and held some lucrative positions from time to time; but the patronage of "the great" failed him, and he died in extreme poverty.

Works: 20 symphonies, an opera, a suite for orchestra, a 'cello concerto, 2 octets, 16 sextets, 125 string quintets, 12 pf. quintets, 18 quintets for strings and flute, 91 string quartets, 54 string trios; 42 trios, sonatas, and duets for violin, &c.

Bocchi'no *(I.)*. Mouthpiece of a wind inst.

BOCH'SA, Karl. Oboist, composer, and music seller; *b.* Bohemia; *d.* Paris, 1821.

Works: 18 quartets for clarinet and strings, oboe and strings, &c., clarinet concerto, six duos for two oboes, and Methods for flute and clarinet.

BOCH'SA, Robert N. C. Renowned harpist; son of Karl. *B.* France, 1789; *d.* Sydney, Australia, 1856. "Played in public at 7, wrote a symphony at 9, and an opera at 16." He devised novel effects in harp playing, and was harpist to Napoleon and Louis XVIII. Came to London, 1817. Inaugurated the Lenten oratorios with Sir G. Smart, 1822. Conducted Italian opera, King's Theatre, 1826-32. Eloped with Sir H. Bishop's wife, 1839, and went to Australia.

His "Method for the Harp" is a standard work. He also wrote 9 French operas, 4 ballets, an oratorio, orchestral pieces, and compositions of all kinds for the harp.

BOCK, Frau von. (See **Schröder-Devrient.**)

BÖCK'ELER, Heinrich. *B.* Cologne, 1836. Conductor, cathedral choir, Aix-la-Chapelle, 1862. Editor, *Gregorious-Blatt*, since 1876.

BOCK'LET, Karl Maria von. Violinist and pianist. *B.* Prague, 1801; *d.* Vienna, 1881. Taught Louis Köhler and Jacob Blumenthal.

Bock'pfeife (or **Bock**) *(G.)*. The bagpipe.

BOCKQUILLON-WILHEM. (See **Wilhem.**)

BOCKS'HORN ("Capricornus"), **Samuel.** 1629-1665. Capellmeister, Würtemberg, 1657. Published masses, motets, lieder, &c., and pieces for klavier.

Bocks'triller *(G.)*. "Goat's trill." A shake like the bleat of a goat; repeating one note clumsily.

BODDA, Mrs. F. (See **Louisa F. Pyne.**)

BO'DE, Joh. J. C. *B.* nr. Brunswick, 1730; *d.* Weimar, 1793. Oboist, teacher, editor, and publisher.

Published concertos for 'cello, bassoon, and violin, symphonies, &c.

Bo'den *(G.)*. The back (of a violin, &c.).

BO'DENSCHATZ, E. Saxon pastor and writer; 1570-1638. Published valuable collections of motets and hymns.

Body. *(L., Corpus; G., Schall'kasten; F., Coffre, Corps; I., Cor'po.)* (1) The resonance-box of an instrument. (2) The part of a wind instrument remaining after mouth-piece, bell, &c., have been removed. (3) Fulness and sonority of tone.

BOE'DECKER, Louis. Pianist and critic; Hamburg, 1845-99. Published pf. pieces and songs.

BOEHM, BOEHME. (See **Böhm, Böhme.**)

BOE'KELMAN, Bernardus. *B.* Utrecht, 1838; has lived in New York since 1866.

"His analytical edition of Bach's 'Well-tempered Clavichord,' in colours, is unique."—*Baker.*

BOËLLMANN, Léon. *B.* Alsace, 1862; *d.* Paris, 1897. Pupil of Gigout.
Works: a symphony, variations symphoniques, &c., for orchestra and organ, and many other organ compositions, &c.

BOËLY, Alex. P. F. *B.* Versailles, 1785; *d.* 1858. Pianist and organist.
Works: a mass; four offertoires, and many other well-known organ pieces; pf. pieces, &c.

BOERS, Jos. K. Holland, 1812-1896. Conductor of theatres, &c., at the Hague, Paris, Metz, and Delft.
Wrote a "History of Musical Instruments in the Middle Ages," and a bibliography of Netherlandish works (ancient and modern), also a symphony, overtures, songs, &c.

BOESSET, Antoine (Sieur de Villedieu). Intendant of music to Louis XIII, abt. 1585-1643. Composed "Airs de Cour," and ballets.

BOETIUS (or BOETHIUS), Amicius M. T. S. *B.* Rome, abt. 475; executed abt. 524 by Theodoric.
Wrote the famous "De Musica," a Latin treatise in 5 books on Ancient Greek Music, which was for centuries regarded as a standard authority and text-book, hindering the development of harmony.

Bo'gen *(G.).* (1) A bow. (2) A tie, or a slur.

Bo'genclavier, Bo'genflügel *(G.).* A pianoviolin.

Bo'genführung *(G.).* The art of bowing.

Bo'geninstrument *(G.).* A bowed instrument.

Bo'genstrich *(G.).* The stroke of the bow.

BOHÈME, La. Opera by Puccini, 1896.

BOHEMIAN GIRL. Balfe's most famous opera; produced 1843.

BOHL'MANN, Th. H. F. German concert pianist; *b.* 1865. Since 1890, Professor of pf. at the Cincinatti Conservatoire.

BÖHM, G. *B.* Thuringia, 1661; *d.* 1734. Wrote fine organ preludes and clavichord suites.

BÖHM, Jos. *B.* Pesth, 1795; *d.* Vienna, 1876. Renowned violinist and teacher. Studied under Rode, St. Petersburg. Violin professor, Vienna Cons., 1819-48. His distinguished pupils include Joachim, Ernst, Auer, Hellmesberger, Ludwig Strauss, Rappoldi, and Hauser.

BÖHM, Karl. *B.* Berlin, 1844. Composer of *Salon* pf. pieces, songs, violin music, &c.

BÖHM, Theobald. Munich, 1794-1881. Inventor of the "Böhm flute."
His system of construction (with all holes covered by keys, a modified bore, &c.), has been applied to nearly all kinds of wind instruments. There has been considerable gain in accuracy of intonation and volume of tone, but much of the characteristic *timbre* of the older instruments has been lost (*e.g.* the older flutes, with their soft velvety quality, are quite distinct from the modern full-toned but less characteristic instrument). Many wood-wind instruments are now constructed partly on the Böhm and partly on the older method.

BÖH'ME, August J. *B.* nr. Brunswick, 1815; *d.* 1883. Pupil of Spohr. Composed orchestral music, songs, chamber music, &c.

BÖH'ME, Franz M. *B.* nr. Weimar, 1827; *d.* 1898. Teacher at Dresden for 20 years. Professor of counterpoint and musical history, Hoch Cons., Frankfort, to 1885.
Published a collection of German Folk-songs (12th to 17th centuries), several collections of part-songs and male choruses, besides theoretical and historical works.

BÖH'ME, Joh. A. Founder of a music publishing business, Hamburg, 1794.

BÖH'MER, Karl H. E. Violinist; *b.* The Hague, 1799; *d.* 1884. Member of Berlin Royal Orchestra, 1835.
Works: operas, including *Meerkönig und sein Liebchen;* violin music, &c.

BOHN, Dr. Emil. *B.* nr. Neisse, 1839. Founded the Bohn Choral Society. Director Breslau University Choral Society, and professor, 1884. Critic, *Breslauer Zeitung.*
Has composed songs, &c., edited the pf. works of Mendelssohn and Chopin, and written bibliographical and historical treatises on music.

BÖH'NER, Joh. L. *B.* nr. Gotha, 1787; *d.* 1860. A talented composer of weak character. Led a roving life, and finally gave way to drink.
Works: opera, *Der Dreiherrnstein;* overtures, marches, dances, pf. sonatas, &c.

BOH'RER, Anton. Violinist; *b.* Munich, 1783; *d.* Hanover, 1852. Toured successfully through Europe with his brother Max.

BOH'RER, Max. 1785-1867. After touring with Anton, settled in Stuttgart as 1st 'cellist in the orchestra, 1832.

BOIELDIEU, François Adrien. Operatic composer; *b.* Rouen, Dec. 16, 1775; *d.* nr. Grosbois, Oct. 8, 1834. First taught by Broche, a pupil of Padre Martini. Produced his first opera, *La Fille coupable,* Rouen, 1793, with some success. Went to Paris, 1795, and made the acquaintance of Cherubini, Méhul, and Garat the tenor singer, who sang some of his songs in public and thus made his name known. Professor of pf. Paris Cons., 1800. Conductor, Imperial Opera, St. Petersburg, 1803-1811. Succeeded Méhul as Professor of Composition at Paris Cons., 1817. Boieldieu ranks as the best composer of French opéra-comique of his time. Among his pupils were P. Zimmerman, Fétis, and A. C. Adam.
Operas: *La fille coupable* (1793), *Rosalie et Myrza* (1795), *La Dot de Suzette* (1796), *La Famille Suisse* (1797), *Zoraime et Zulnare* (1798), *Beniowski* and *Le Calife de Bagdad* (1800), *Ma tante Aurore* (1803), *Jean de Paris* (1812), *Le petit chaperon rouge* (1818), *La Dame Blanche* (1825), *Les deux nuits* (1829).
La Dame Blanche is his chief work. The overture to *Le Calife* is also very popular.

BOIELDIEU, Adrien L. V. Son of F.; 1816-83.
Wrote operas, operettas, cantatas, masses, &c.

Bois *(F.).* Wood.
Les Bois. The wind-wood insts.

BOISDEFFRE, Ch. H. French composer ; *b.* 1838. Works: church music, chamber music, songs, &c.

BOISSELOT, Xavier. Dramatic composer ; *b.* Montpellier, 1811 ; *d.* 1893.
Operas : *Ne touchez pas à la reine* (1847), *Mosquita la Sorcière* (1851) ; also a cantata, &c.

Boîte *(F.).* Box.
Botte d'expression } The swell box.
Botte expressive   }

BOITO, Arrigo. *B.* Padua, Feb. 24, 1842. Pupil Milan Cons., 1853-62. A passionate admirer and advocate of Wagner's music. Boito is a striking illustration of a composer whose fame rests, almost solely, on one work—the opera *Mefistofele*. His other compositions have been comparative failures, while some of them have not even been publicly performed. The product of several years' labour, *Mefistofele* was produced at Milan, 1868. It was almost a total failure ; but Boito re-wrote it, and in its new form it proved an immediate and immense success.
Boito is greatly esteemed in Italy as a *poet.* He wrote the words of his own *Mefistofele,* of Verdi's *Otello* and *Falstaff,* and of several other modern Italian operas.

BOLCK, Oscar. *B.* Prussia, 1837 ; *d.* 1888.
His opera *Pierre und Robin* was produced at Riga, 1876. He wrote two other operas, songs, pf. pieces, &c.

Bole'ro *(S.).* A Spanish dance in ¾ time, with castanets. Also called a *Cachu'cha.* The characteristic rhythm is

| 3/4 ♫♫ ♫♫♩ | or | ♫♫♫ ♩♩ |

Bom'bard, Bom'hart, Bom'mert, Pom'mer *(G.).*
Bombarde *(F.).*
Bombar'do *(I.).*
(1) The precursor of the bassoon. (2) A powerful organ reed-stop.

Bombar'don. The largest and deepest-toned instrument in a brass band. The most frequently used are the bombardon in E♭, and the contra in B♭ (BB♭).

Bom'byx *(Gk.).* An ancient Greek reed-flute.

BOMTEM'PO, J. Domingos. Pianist ; Lisbon, 1775-1842. Studied and resided in Paris and London till 1820. Director, Lisbon Cons., 1833.
Works : concertos, sonatas, and variations for pf.; an opera, masses, &c., and a pf. Method.

Bon *(F.).* Good.

Bon temps de la Mesure *(F.).* The strong beat.

BO'NA, Cardinal Giovanni. *B.* 1609 ; *d.* Rome, 1674. Wrote a treatise on ancient church music.

BONAR, Horatius, D.D. 1808-89. Scotch minister. Wrote many hymns, including "I heard the voice of Jesus say," and "A few more years shall roll."

BO'NAWITZ (or Bonewitz), Joh. H. *B.* Dürkheim, 1839. Conducted the New York "Popular Symphony Concerts," 1872-3. Produced 2 operas in Philadelphia, *The*

Bride of Messina, 1874 ; *Ostrolenka,* 1875. Has since lived in Vienna and London, and published pf. pieces.

BONCI, Signor. Contemp. operatic tenor. Choir-boy at Cesena, nr. Bologna. At 17 joined the Loreto Choir ; afterwards chief tenor. Then went into opera. Resides at Bologna.

Bonding of Chords.
(1) *Direct* Bond : when a note of one chord remains in the next chord *in the same part.*
(2) *Indirect* Bond : when a note of one chord is continued in the next, but in another part.
(3) *Implied* Bond : when two chords which have no direct bond are both directly bonded to a third chord.—*Curwen.*

BONHEUR, Theo. (Alfred Rawlings). Song composer ; *b.* London, 1857.

BONIVEN'TI (Boneventi), Giuseppe. *B.* Vienna, abt. 1660. Wrote 12 operas.

BONNET, Jacques. Paris, 1644-1724. Published historical works on music.

BONNET, Jean B. *B.* Montauban, 1763.
Works : two violin concertos, two *symphonies concertantes* for two violins, and much other violin music.

BON'NO (or Bono), Jos. Vienna, 1710-1788. Court capellmeister, 1774.
Works : 20 operas and serenades, 3 oratorios, Psalms, &c.

BONONCI'NI, G. M. Modena, 1640-78.
Published 12 volumes of symphonies, gigues, sonatas, madrigals, &c. ; and a work on counterpoint and song composition.

BONONCI'NI (or Buononci'ni), Giovanni Battista. Son of G. M. *B.* Modena, 1660 ; *d.* abt. 1750. Studied at Bologna, where he published 7 vols. of vocal and instrumental music (1685-91). Court 'cellist, Vienna, 1690. Produced his first opera at Rome, 1694. Court composer, Berlin, 1703-5. Produced several other operas, Vienna, 1705-10, and also in various Italian cities. Invited to London, 1720, to conduct the opera at the new King's Theatre, as the rival of Handel. The Duchess of Marlborough patronised Bononcini, and the operatic warfare was carried on with varying success till 1731, when it was found out that he had some years before passed off a madrigal by Lotti as his own. Through this, and Handel's supremacy, he lost position and friends, and was also swindled out of his fortune by an alchemist. He now wandered from place to place, and we find him, at the age of 90, in the capacity of theatre composer at Venice, "after which all traces of him are lost."
Bononcini wrote a large number of operas and incidental music of all kinds. He was a talented composer, and but for his unfortunate attempt to compete with the genius of Handel would have achieved enduring fame.

BONONCI'NI, M. A. Brother of G. B. 1675(?)-1726. Maestro to the Duke of Medina from 1721. His operas were praised by Martini for their "lofty style." They are now practically forgotten, as is also his oratorio, *La Decollazione di S. Giovanni Battista.*

BONTEM'PI (Angeli'ni), Giov. A. *B.* Perugia, abt. 1624; *d.* 1705. Maestro at Rome, Venice, Berlin, and Dresden.

Works : 3 operas, an oratorio, and several treatises on musical subjects.

BONVIN, Ludwig. *B.* Switzerland, 1850. Chiefly self-taught. Since 1887, director of chorus and orchestra at Canisius College, Buffalo.

Works : 3 masses, scenas and cantatas, orchestral pieces, organ pieces, songs, &c.

Book. Specially, the *libretto* (words) of an opera, oratorio, &c.

BOOM, Jan E. G. Flautist and composer ; *b.* Rotterdam, 1783.

BOOM, Jan van. Distinguished Pianist ; son of preceding. *B.* Utrecht, 1807 ; *d.* Stockholm, 1872. Professor, Royal Academy, Stockholm, 1849-65.

Wrote operas, symphonies, chamber music, much pf. music, &c.

BOOM, H. M. van. Fine flautist ; Utrecht, 1809-33. Brother of Jan van.

BOORN, Ed. van den. Belgian pianist and critic ; *b.* 1831 (?) ; *d.* Liége, 1898. Wrote many interesting articles on music.

BOOSEY, Thos. Founded the publishing-house of Boosey & Co., 1825.

Boot. The foot of a reed-pipe.

BOOTH, Josiah. Orgt. and composer ; *b.* Coventry, 1852.

BORDE, De la. (See **Laborde.**)

BORDES, Ch. *B.* Vouvray-sur-Loire, 1863. Renowned for his efforts to revive the best church music in France.

Founded "Association des Chanteurs de Saint-Gervais," 1892, and "Schola Cantorum," 1894, " for the restoration of church music in France."

BORDE'SE, Luigi. *B.* Naples, 1815 ; *d.* Paris, 1886. Settled in Paris as a successful singing teacher, 1834.

Works : 8 operas, 3 masses, &c., and hundreds of songs. His excellent vocal exercises are very popular. He also wrote two Vocal Methods.

BORDIER, Jules. *B.* 1846 ; *d.* 1896. Early French champion of Wagner's music.

Works : symphonic poems, two operas, violin music, dances, &c.

BORDIER, Louis C. Paris, 1700-64.

Published " Méthode de musique pratique," 1760, and a Treatise on Composition, 1770.

BORDO'GNI, G. M. Renowned tenor and teacher of singing ; *b.* nr. Bergamo, 1788 ; *d.* Paris, 1856. Made a brilliant *début* as "Tancredi," La Scala, Milan, 1813. From 1833 devoted himself to teaching.

Was for several years professor at the Paris Cons. Sontag was his most famous pupil. His " Vocalises " are in general use.

Bordo'ne (I.). A bourdon (*q.v.*).

BORDO'NI, Faustina. (See **Hasse, Faustina.**)

BOR'GHI, Luigi. Violinist and composer ; settled in London abt. 1780.

Led the 2nd violins, Handel Commemoration, 1784. Published much good violin music.

BOR'GHI-MAMO, Adelaide. Mezzo-soprano ; *b.* Bologna, 1829 ; *d.* 1901. Sang with great success in London, 1860. Her daughter **Erminia**—a fine soprano—appeared in Boito's *Mefistofele*, Bologna, 1875.

BORLAND, John E. *B.* London, 1866 ; Mus. Doc. Oxon, 1906. Ed. *Musical News,* 1895-1902.

BO'RODIN, Alex. P. St. Petersburg, 1834-1887. Surgeon. Friend of Liszt. Studied music and became a renowned exponent of the Russian school.

Works : 4-act opera, *Prince Igor,* 3 symphonies and a symphonic poem, 2 string quartets, songs, suite for pf., &c.

BOROIHME'S Harp.

Historically-celebrated Irish harp of King Brian Boroihme, killed at the battle of Clontarf, 1014. After being taken to Rome, it was sent by the Pope to Henry VIII, who gave it to the first Earl of Clanricarde. It is now in the Museum of Trinity College, Dublin.

BORO'NI (or Buroni), Antonio. Rome, 1738-97. Pupil of Martini. Court Capellmeister, Stuttgart, 1770-80 ; afterwards Maestro at St. Peter's, Rome.

Wrote 16 operas, produced at Venice, Prague, Dresden, and Stuttgart.

BOROW'SKI, Felix. *B.* Westmoreland, 18—. Studied under Dr. Pearce. Now Prof. of violin and composition, Chicago Cons.

BÖRERSEN, Hakon. Composer ; *b.* Copenhagen, 1876.

Borrowed Chords. Chords temporarily " borrowed " from other keys and not inducing modulation (or transition). Macfarren classified them as (1) Chromatic Concords, and (2) Fundamental Discords on the Supertonic and Tonic. (See **Chromatic Concords,** and **Fundamental Discords.**)

With the extension of harmony the number of admissible "borrowed" chords is constantly increasing.

Borrowed Harmony.

A name formerly given to the dominant 9th ; the 7th and 9th of the chord were said to be "borrowed " from the Sub-dominant triad.

BORTHWICK, Jane. 1813-97. Wrote the hymn " Thou knowest, Lord."

BORTNIAN'SKI (Bartnansky), Dimitri S. *B.* 1752 ; *d.* St. Petersburg, 1825. Director, Imperial Choir, St. Petersburg, 1799.

Works : opera *Quinto Fabio* (Modena, 1778), a Greek mass, 45 Psalms (several in 8 parts), 10 concertos for double choir, &c.

BORWICK, W. Leonard. Fine concert pianist. *B.* Walthamstow, 1868. Has played at many of the chief concerts in London and elsewhere.

BOS'CHI, Giuseppe. " Most celebrated basso of the 18th century " (*Grove*). Sang in Handel's operas, London, 1711-1728.

BOS'SI, Marco E. *B.* nr. Brescia, 1861. Maestro and organist Como Cathedral, 1881-91. Professor of Composition, Liceo B. Marcello, Venice, 1896.

Works : operas, *Paquita* (1881), *Il Veggente* (1890),

L'Angelo della notte; cantatas, a symphonic poem, masses and requiems, organ music, chamber music, orchestral pieces, &c. Also, with Tebaldini, "Metodo di Studio per l'Organo Moderno."

BOTE und BOCK. Berlin Firm of music publishers, founded 1838.

BÖTEL, Heinrich. *B.* Hamburg, 1858. Formerly a cab-driver; afterwards leading lyric tenor, Hamburg City Theatre.

BOTT, Jean Jos. *B.* Cassel, 1826; *d.* New York, 1895. Eminent violinist; pupil of Spohr; Capellmeister various German cities; went to New York, 1885.
Works: two operas, symphonies, violin concertos, songs, &c.

BOTTÉE de Toulmon, Auguste. Paris, 1797-1850. Published theoretical works.

BOTTESI'NI, Giovanni. Celebrated double-bass player. *B.* Lombardy, 1823; *d.* 1889.
Works: oratorio, *The Garden of Olivet* (Norwich Festival, 1887), several operas, including *Ali Baba* (London, 1871), symphonies, overtures, &c.

BOTTING, Herbert. Orgt., composer, and writer; *b.* Brighton, 1869. Mus. Doc. Dunelm, 1897.

BOTTRIGA'RI, Ercole. *B.* Bologna, 1531; *d.* 1612. Wrote learned musical treatises.

Bouché(e) *(F.).* Muted; stopped (of organ pipes).

Bouche fermée *(F.).* With closed mouth; humming.

BOUCHER, Alex. J. Paris, 1778-1861. Remarkable violin player. Called himself "l'Alexandre des violons." Wrote two violin concertos.

Bouffe *(F.).* Buffo *(q.v.).*

BOUGHTON, Rutland. Contemp. composer and writer.
Works: Critical essays, a "Life of Bach," &c.

BOUHY, Jacques. Baritone singer, teacher, and song writer; *b.* Belgium, 1848.

BOULANGER, Ernest H. A. Opera composer; Paris, 1815-1900.

Bourdon *(F.).* (1) A drone bass. (2) An organ stop with stopped wooden pipes.
In England it is generally of 16 ft. tone; in France of 4 ft., 8 ft., 16 ft., &c.
Bourdonnement (F.) Humm ng.

BOURGAULT-DUCOUDRAY, Louis A. *B.* Nantes, 1840. Pupil of Amb. Thomas.
Works: several important treatises on Modern Greek Music; two operas (including *Thamara*, Paris, 1891); orchestral music, songs, &c.

BOURGEOIS, L. *B.* Paris, abt. 1510.
He wrote a treatise on Musical Nomenclature, and was "one of the first to harmonize the melodies to the French version of the Psalms," some of which were his own.

BOURGES, Jean M. Composer and critic. *B.* Bordeaux, 1812; *d.* Paris, 1881.
Works: opera, *Sultana;* a Stabat Mater, &c.

Bourrée, Boree, Burre, Bouree *(F.).* A dance tune in ¾ time, said by Rousseau to come from Auvergne.
The *Bourrée* is similar in style and construction to the *Gavotte;* but while the *Gavotte* always

commences on the third crotchet of the measure, the *Bourrée* commences on the *last* crotchet (or quaver). A syncopated minim is very common in old *Bourrées :—*

BOUSQUET, Georges. French composer and critic; 1818-1854. Leading violin, Paris Opéra, 1847.
Works: 3 operas, 2 masses, a Miserere, &c.

Boutade *(F.).* (1) An impromptu dance or ballet. (2) A caprice; an extemporised solo.

Bout de l'archet *(F.).* The point of the bow.

Bouts. The curves at the "waist" of a vn., &c.

BOVY, Ch. S. Geneva, 1821-73. Wrote under the name of Lysberg.
Works: an opera, and many *salon* pieces for pf.

Bow. The bow of a violin was originally curved like a bow; hence its name.

Bowing. (1) The art of managing the bow. (2) *Legato, staccato,* and other signs to indicate the "bowing."

BOWDLER, Cyril Wm. *B.* Yorkshire, 1839. LL.D., Dublin, 1896.
Has composed church services, anthems, &c.

BOWEN, Edwin York. Pianist and composer; *b.* London, 1884.

BOWMAN, Ed. M. American organist, conductor, and teacher. *B.* 1848.
First President of the American College of Musicians, 1884. Conducts the Temple Choir, Brooklyn.
Has written and translated theoretical works, &c.

Boyau *(F.).* Catgut strings.

BOYCE, Ethel Mary. *B.* Chertsey, 1863.
Works: cantatas, songs, &c.

BOYCE, Dr. Wm. London, 1710-1779. Pupil of Greene and Pepusch. Organist St. Michael's, Cornhill, 1736, and composer to the Chapel Royal and the King. Conducted the Three Choirs Festival. 1737. Master of the Royal Band, 1775.
Boyce wrote an oratorio *(Noah),* masques, odes, symphonies, anthems, services, songs, &c., but his greatest work is an edition of *Cathedral Music,* in 3 vols. (1760-78).

Bozzet'to *(I.).* A sketch.

Br. Abbn. of *Bratsche (q.v.).*

Brabançonne, La. The Belgian National Song, dating from 1830.
It commences thus:—

Brac'cio *(I.).* The arm. (See **Viola da Braccio.**)

Brace. *(G.,Klam'mer; F.,Accolade; I.,Grap'pa.)* (1) The bracket connecting two or more staves. (2) A leather slide on the cords of a drum.
In a full score, a brace is used to connect all the instruments of the same family, *e.g.* the woodwind, the 3 trombones, the strings, &c.

BRADBURY, Wm. B. American composer and editor of popular music; 1816-68.
Some of his numerous collections had an immense sale, *e.g.* "Fresh Laurels" (1867) 1,200,000. He wrote the cantatas *Daniel* (with G. F. Root) and *Esther.*

BRADLEY, Chas. Orgt. and composer; *b.* Wakefield. 1846.

BRAD'SKY, W. T. Bohemian composer; 1833-81.
Works: opera, *Iolanthe* (1872), and several others; part-songs and songs.

BRADY, Nicholas. 1659-1726. *B.* Bandon. Issued with Nahum Tate the *New Version of the Psalms of David,* 1696.

BRA'GA, Gaetano. *B.* nr. Abruzzi, 1829; *d.* 1907. Fine 'cellist.
Works: a "Metodo de Violoncello;" the successful opera, *La Reginella,* and several others; chamber music, &c.

BRAHAM (Abraham), John. London, 1774-1856. Fine tenor singer with a compass of three octaves! Sang at Covent Garden, Drury Lane, and the Italian Opera with triumphant success. He created the part of "Hüon" in Weber's *Oberon,* London, 1826.
He was also renowned as a composer and singer of ballads. His "Death of Nelson" is essentially a "national" song.

BRAHMS, Johannes. *B.* Hamburg, May 7, 1833; *d.* Vienna, Apl. 3, 1897. Has been called "the last of the classic composers." As a young man his pf. playing and compositions excited the admiration and encouragement of Joachim, Schumann, and Liszt, and they hailed him as a "Romantic" composer of the greatest promise. He, however, turned his attention to classic models, leaving his mark on every branch of composition except opera. His music is noble, dignified, and truly great, but it is often heavy and lacking in charm. His most popular works are his beautiful songs—especially "Wie bist du, meine Königin"—his part-songs and chamber music, the *Deutsches Requiem,* and *The Song of Destiny.*
Works: sets of songs with pf. accompaniment; sonatas, ballads, variations, waltzes, &c., for pf.; trios, quartets, pf. quartets, pf. quintets and sextets for strings, and other excellent chamber music; pf. concertos in D min. and B flat; violin concerto in D; concerto in C for violin and 'cello; four songs for female voices, two horns, and harp; Deutsches Requiem for soli, chorus, and orchestra; cantatas, *Rinaldo, Song of Destiny, Nänie, Triumphlied* (Rev. chap. 19), for 8-part chorus and orchestra, *Gesang der Parzen* for 6-part chorus and orch., "Zigeunerlieder" for four voices and pf.; four symphonies (No. 1, C min., No. 2, D, No. 3. F, No. 4, E min.), serenades, variations, &c., for orchestra; Academic overture, Tragic overture; scenas, duets, trios, part-songs, motets, rhapsodies, and numerous other vocal compositions. In all, about 130 opus numbers.

BRAH-MÜLLER (or Müller), Karl F. G. *B.* Silesia, 1839; *d.* Berlin, 1878.
Works: operetta, *Deutschland in Urwald;* "Singspiel," *Ein Matrose von der Nymphe;* Te Deum; violin quartets, pf. music, songs, &c.

BRAM'BACH, Kaspar J. *B.* Bonn, 1833. Music-director, Bonn, 1861-9. *D.* 1902.
Works: several noteworthy secular cantatas—*Alcestis, Prometheus, Columbus,* &c.; opera, *Ariadne;* concert overture, pf. concerto, chamber music, vocal music, &c.

BRAM'BACH, Wilhelm. Philologist; *b.* Bonn, 1841. Head librarian, Karlsruhe, 1872.
Has written several theoretical music treatises.

BRAMBIL'LA, Marietta. 1807-75. Famous Italian contralto singer.
Made her *début* in Rossini's *Semiramide,* London, 1827, and afterwards sang with great success in Italy, Vienna, Paris, &c.

BRAMBIL'LA, Teresa. 1813-95. Sister of M.
Acquired great fame as a singer at La Scala, Milan, and afterwards at Paris and Venice.

BRAN'CA, G. *B.* Bologna, 1849.
Works: operas, *La Catalana* (1876), *Hermosa* (1883), *La Figlia di Jorio* (1897).

BRANCAC'CIO, Antonio. Naples, 1813-1846. Wrote several operas, produced at Naples and Venice.

BRAN'DEIS, Fred. *B.* Vienna, 1835. Went to United States, 1849. Organist from 1886 at Brooklyn, U.S. *D.* 1899.
Wrote works for orchestra, chamber music, pf. pieces, songs, &c.

BRAN'DES, Emma. Pianist; *b.* nr. Schwerin, 1854.

BRAN'DL, Joh. *B.* nr. Ratisbon, 1760; *d.* 1837. Music-director at Baden.
Works: oratorios, masses, two operas *(Germania* and *Hermann),* chamber music, &c.

BRAN'DL, Joh. *B.* Vienna, 1835. Has written about 20 operettas *(Die Kosakin,* 1892).

BRANDT, Marianne. Excellent contralto singer. *B.* Vienna, 1842. Sang as "Kundry" in *Parsifal,* Bayreuth, 1882.

BRANDT, Michael ("Mosonyi"). Hungarian composer; 1814-70.

Bransle, Branle *(F.).* (See **Brawl.**)

Brass; The Brass. The brass wind insts. (collectively) of an orchestra.

Brass Band. The favourite English band.
In 1895 there were upwards of 40,000 brass bands in the United Kingdom. Also four brass band associations, over fifty brass instrument makers and dealers, about twenty band-music publishers, and over twenty brass band journals. In 1908, 150 bands took part in the Crystal Palace competition.

BRASSIN, Gerhard. Violinist. *B.* Aix-la-Chapelle, 1844. Conductor, St. Petersburg, since 1880.

BRASSIN, Leopold. Brother of G. *B.* Strasburg, 1843; *d.* 1890. Court pianist at Coburg.
Composed concertos and solo pieces for pf.

BRASSIN, Louis. Brother of the two preceding. *B.* Aix-la-Chapelle, 1840; *d.* 1884. Prof. of pf. at St. Petersburg Cons.
Works: a valuable "Ecole moderne du Piano," two operettas, pf. pieces, songs, &c.

Brat'sche *(G.).* The Viola *(q.v.).*
Brat'schenspie'ler. Viola player.
Brat'schestimme. Viola part.

BRAU'ER, Max. *B.* Mannheim, 1855. Music-director, Karlsruhe, since 1888.
Works: sonatas, suites for orchestra, two operas, pf. and violin pieces, &c.

Braut'lied *(G.).* A bridal song.

Brav'a, Brav'o *(I.).* "Well done."

Bravour' *(G.).* \ Brilliancy ; a "showing off."
Bravu'ra *(I.).* ∫ (See **Aria di bravura.**)

Brawl. (1) An old French dance in $\frac{4}{4}$ time, the dancers joining hands in a circle. (2) A country dance.

> "To brawl is to outdo the natural extent of the voice, and singing with all our possible violence, as the churchwardens in the villages of Latrine, and several musicians elsewhere."— *Rousseau.*

BRAYTON, Coulthart. Pen-name of **C. H. Moody** *(q.v.).*

Break. (1) The point at which one "register" of a voice ends and another begins.

The "great break" is most noticeable in contralto and tenor voices, and usually occurs about [music notation] ([music notation] as now written for tenor.)

In high or "counter" tenor voices the break appears to be much higher, but these voices are becoming more and more rare.

(2) In the clarinet, between [music notation] and [music notation]

(3) In an organ stop, the sudden return in going up the scale to a lower octave (common in "mixtures").

Breakdown. A lively, noisy American "nigger" dance.

Breast. Old English for voice.

Breath marks. Signs to show where breath should be taken in singing ; as **Ν ٨ ,**

BREBOS, Gilles. (See **Gilles.**)

Brech'ung ein'es Akkor'des *(G.).* An arpeggio.

BREE, J. B. van. Amsterdam, 1801-1857. Wrote *Cecilia's Day,* operas, masses, &c.

BREI'DENSTEIN, H. K. *B.* near Hesse, 1796 ; *d.* 1876. Mus.-director, Bonn Univ., 1823. Wrote a Method of singing.

Breit *(G.).* Broad, slow, stately.
Breit und getra'gen. Broad and sustained.
Breit und wuch'tig. Broad and weighty (impressive).

BREIT'KOPF & HÄR'TEL. Renowned Leipzig firm of music publishers. Founded 1719. Have published complete editions of Palestrina, Mozart, Beethoven, Schubert, Mendelssohn, &c.

BREITN'ER, Ludovic. Pianist and composer ; *b.* Trieste, 1855.

BREMA, Marie. (Minny Fehrman). *B.* Liverpool, 1856. Distinguished dramatic mezzo-soprano.

BREN'DEL, Karl F. Distinguished German writer and critic ; 1811-68.

Edited Schumann's *Neue Zeitschrift* from 1844. Prof. Musical History, Leipzig Cons. President "Allgemeiner deutscher Musikverein." Wrote several important treatises and articles on music, advocating modern views.

BRENET, Michel. (Marie Bobillier). French writer on music ; *b.* 1858. Chief work, a sketch of *Jean de Ockeghem,* 1893.

BREN'NER, Ludwig. *B.* Leipzig, 1833 ; *d.* 1902. Works: Masses, Te Deums, symphonic poems, overtures, &c.

BRENNING, Frau. (See **Marie Krebs.**)

BRENT, Charlotte. Sang with much success in the works of Handel and Arne ; *d.* 1802.

BRERETON, William H. Bass vocalist ; *b.* Bedford, 1860.

BRES'LAUR, Emil. *B.* 1836. Founder of a Piano-Teachers' Seminary, Berlin. Author of several books on pf. playing. *D.* 1899.

BRETON (Breton y Hernandez), Tomas. Noted composer of Zarzuelas. *B.* Salamanca, 1846.

Brett'geige *(G.).* A pocket fiddle ; a kit.

BREU'ER, Hans. Dramatic tenor ; *b.* Cologne, 1869.

BREVAL, J. B. French 'cellist ; 1765-1825. Wrote a Method for 'Cello, 2 operas, 7 'cello concertos, 8 symphonies, &c.

BRÉVAL, Lucienne. Soprano ; *b.* Berlin, 1869.

Breve. *(L., Brev'is ; I., Bre've,* "short".) In mediæval music a note written thus, ◼ ; equal to $\frac{1}{2}$ the *long,* and $\frac{1}{4}$ the *double-long* or *maxima.* It is now written | ⊘ |, or. ⊘, or ◼.

Brev'iary. A Roman Catholic or Greek Church service book, with Table of Lessons.

BREVILLE, Pierre O. de. Composer ; *b.* Bar-le-Duc, 1861.

BREWER, Alf. Herbert. *B.* Gloucester, 1865. Orgt. Gloucester Cath., 1897 ; Mus. D. Cantuar, 1905.

BREWER, John H. American organist and composer ; *b.* Brooklyn, 1856.

BRIARD, Étienne. Founder of music-types, Avignon, early in 16th cent.

"His types had *round* heads instead of angular ones, and separate notes in place of ligatures."

BRICCIAL'DI, G. Celebrated flautist ; *b.* Papal States, 1818 ; *d.* 1881. Maestro to the Prince of Syracuse, 1834. Wrote an opera, *Leonora de' Medici;* a Flute Method, and many flute solos, &c.

Bridge. The piece of wood which on the violin, &c., raises the strings above the resonance box, determines the length of the vibrating portion, and communicates the vibrations to the whole instrument.

Bridge, or Transition. In Sonata Form *(q.v.),* the portion leading from the 1st Principal Subject to the 2nd Principal Subject.

BRIDGE, Frank. Contemp. Eng. composer. Author of Symphony-poem *Isabella, Phantasies,* &c.

BRIDGE, Mrs. F. A. (See **Eliz. Stirling.**)

BRIDGE, Sir John Frederick. *B.* Oldbury, Dec. 5th, 1844. Chorister Rochester Cathedral, 1850. Organist Manchester Cathedral, 1869 ; and of Westminster Abbey, 1882. Mus. Doc. Oxon, 1874. Gresham Professor, 1890. Conductor Royal Choral Society, 1902. Knighted, 1897. M.V.O., 1902.

Works: oratorios, *Mount Moriah, Nineveh ;* cantatas, *Boadicea, Callirhoë;* motets, *Rock of Ages, Hymn to the Creator, The Lord's Prayer, The Cradle of Christ ;* choral ballads; four of Novello's Primers ; anthems, services, glees, carols, &c. Also a "Harmony Course" and a work on Pepys.

BRIDGE, Jos. Cox. Brother of preceding. *B.* Rochester, 1853. Mus. Doc. Oxon, 1884. Organist Chester Cathedral, 1877. Prof. of Mus., Durham Univ., 1908.
Works : oratorios, *Daniel, Rudel;* chamber music part-songs, &c.

Bridge-note. The double note used in Tonic Sol-fa for changing the key; as **ˢd ʳl**₁₁ The tone represented by the bridge-note is called the " transmutation tone."

Brief. Old name for *Breve.*

BRIE'GEL, Wolfgang K. German composer ; 1626-1712. Wrote highly-esteemed church music.

BRIGHT, Dora. (See **Knatchbull.**)

Brillan'te *(I.). (F., Brillant,-e.)* Brilliant, showy, sparkling.

Brillan'te assa'i *(I.).* Very brilliant.

Brillantis'simo *(I.).* As brilliant as possible.

Bril'lenbässe *(G.).* "Spectacle basses;" music of the following character, resembling a pair of spectacles :—

Bril'lo *(I.).* Joy, delight.

Brin'disi *(I.).* A drinking song; "a toast."

BRINK, Jules ten. *B.* Amsterdam, 1838 ; *d.* 1889. Music-director, Lyons, 1860-8.
Works : opera, *Calonice,* 1870 (and others), orchestral music, a violin concerto, &c.

BRINSMEAD, John. *B.* North Devon, 1814 ; *d.* 1908. Founded his piano factory, London, 1835. His son Edgar wrote a " History of the Pianoforte," 1868.

Bri'o *(I.).* Spirit, fire, vivacity. *Con bri'o,* with fire, &c.

Brio'so *(I.).* Same as **Con brio.**

Brisé *(F.).* "Sprinkled." (1) Broken chords, arpeggios. (2) Short, detached bow-strokes.

BRISSAC. Jules. (See **Mrs. J. Macfarren.**)

BRISSON, F. French pianist and teacher ; *b.* 1821; *d.* 1900.
Works : *salon* pieces for pf., an " Ecole d'Orgue," an operetta, &c.

BRISTOW, George F. American violinist, conductor, and composer. *B.* Brooklyn, 1825 ; *d.* New York, 1898.
Wrote oratorios, operas, symphonies, chamber and pf. music, songs, &c.

BRITTON, Thomas. (Called the "Musical Small Coal Man "); *b.* Nottinghamshire, abt. 1651; *d.* London, 1714). Established weekly concerts over his shop, 1678, which attracted even the " nobility and gentry" of the period.

BRI'XI, Franz X. Prague, 1732-71. Capell-meister at the Cathedral, 1756.
Wrote 7 masses, several oratorios, &c.

BROADWOOD & Sons. Established by B. Schudi, 1730.

BROCKWAY, Howard A. American composer and teacher ; *b.* Brooklyn, 1870.

Broderies *(F.).* Ornaments used to embellish a simple melody. Graces.

BROD'SKY, Adolf. Distinguished Russian violinist ; *b.* Taganrog, 1851. Member of the " Hellmesberger Quartet." Violin Professor Leipzig Cons., 1883. Professor of violin, 1895, and afterwards director Royal Manchester College of Music.

Broken cadence. An interrupted cadence.

Broken chords. Arpeggios.

Broken music. Old Eng. name for "consorts" of wind and stringed insts. together.

Broken octaves.

Broken Pedal. A pedal (see **Pedal-point**) alternating with other notes, as C in the following :—

SULLIVAN.

BRON'SART, Hans von. Pianist. *B.* Berlin, 1830. Pupil of Kullak and Liszt. "Hofmusikintendant," Berlin, 1887.
Works : opera, *Der Corsar,* cantata, *Christnacht;* a symphony and other orchestral works, pf. concerto, chamber music, pf. pieces, &c.

BRONSART, J. von (*née* **Starck**). Wife of preceding. *B.* St. Petersburg, 1840.
She is a talented composer, and has written 3 operas and several pf. pieces.

BROOKS, Walter W. Critic and composer ; *b.* Egbaston, 1861.

BROS, Juan. Famous Spanish composer of church music ; 1776-1852.

BROS'CHI, C. (See **Farinelli.**)

BROSIG, Moritz. *B.* Silesia, 1815; *d,* 1887. Music-director, Breslau Cathedral, 1842.
Works : 7 masses, 7 books of Graduals, &c., 20 books of organ pieces, a " Choralbuch," and works on Theory, &c.

BROSSARD, Sébastien de. French composer ; 1660-1730. Capellmeister Strasburg Cathedral, 1689 ; *Maitre de Musique,* Meaux Cathedral, 1700-30. Wrote one of the earliest dictionaries of musical terms (Paris, 1703).

BROUGHTON, Alfred. 1853-95. Esteemed Leeds Festival choir-trainer.

BROUSTET, Ed. Pianist ; *b.* Toulouse, 1836.
Works : orchestral, chamber, and pf. pieces.

BROWN, Arthur Henry. Organist and Gre-gorianist. *B.* Brentwood, Essex, 1830.

BROWN, Colin. 1818-96. Published valuable works on Acoustics and Tuning. Constructed an harmonium on the principles of perfect intonation.

BROWN, Herbert. Bass ; *b.* Keighley, 1876.

BROWN, Jas. D. *B.* Edinburgh, 1862. Author of " Biog. Dict. of Musicians," 1886 ; " Brit. Mus. Biography " (with Stratton), 1897), &c.

BROWN, Rev. Dr. John. *B.* Northumberland, 1715; *d.* 1766.
Wrote a "Dissertation on the Rise, Union, and Power, the Progressions, Separations, and Corruptions of Poetry and Music, &c.," 1763.

BROWN, Lennox. Surgeon. *B.* London, 1841. Collaborated with Behnke in "Voice, Song, and Speech."

BROWN, Obadiah B. American teacher and composer ; *b.* Washington, 1829.
Has pub. several collections of school songs, &c.

BROWNING, Robt. English poet ; 1812-89. Many of his works have been set to music.

BROZEL', Philip. Dramatic tenor ; *b.* Russia. *Début* Covent Garden, 1896.

BRUCH, Max. *B.* Cologne, 1838. Won the Mozart Scholarship, Frankfort, 1853. Studied under Ferd. Hiller, Reinecke, and Breunig. At 14 wrote a symphony. His *epic* cantatas are distinguished for their flowing melodies and beautiful harmonies.
Works : cantatas, *Odysseus, Arminius, Lied von der Glocke, Achilleus, Frithjof, Salamis, Normannenzug, Leonidas ;* oratorio, *Moses ;* opera, *Hermione ;* 3 symphonies, 3 violin concertos, and smaller works.

BRUCK (Brouck), Arnold von. 16th century. Celebrated composer of motets, hymns, and German part-songs.

BRÜCK'LER, Hugo. Dresden, 1845-71. Highly gifted composer of songs and ballads.

BRUCK'NER, Dr. Anton. Famous organist and composer ; *b.* Upper Austria, 1824 ; *d.* Vienna, 1896. Son of a village schoolmaster ; chiefly self-taught. Cathedral organist, Linz-on-Danube, 1855. Court organist, Vienna, 1867. "Lektor" of Music, Vienna University, 1875.
Works : 9 symphonies, Te Deum, 3 Grand Masses, a Requiem, several works for men's voices, chamber music, &c.

BRUCK'NER, Oscar. *B.* Erfurt, 1857. 1st 'cello, Royal Theatre, Wiesbaden, and prof. at the Cons. since 1889.
Works : 'cello solos, songs, pf. music.

Bruit *(F.).* Noise, rattle, clatter.

BRÜLL, Ignaz. Celebrated Moravian pianist and composer ; *b.* Prossnitz, 1846 ; *d.* 1907.
Works : several operas, including *Das goldene Kreuz* (Berlin, 1875), and *Der Husar* (Vienna, 1898) ; overtures, serenades, and suites for orchestra, pf. and violin concertos, chamber music, songs, pf. music, &c.

BRUMEL, A. Flemish contrapuntist and writer of masses ; abt. 1480-1520.

Brumm'bass *(G.).* Bourdon ; drone ; double-bass.

Brumm'eisen *(G.).* A Jew's-harp.

Brum'mer *(G.).* A drone.

Brumm'stimmen *(G.).* Voices "humming" an accompaniment.

Brumm'ton *(G.).* A drone ; a humming tone.

BRUNEAU, L. C. B. Alfred. *B.* Paris, 1857. Composer and critic.
Works : operas, *Kerim* (1887), *Le Rêve* (1892), *l'Attaque du Moulin* (1893), &c. ; overture, légende, chamber music, several fine songs, &c.

BRUNEL'LI, Antonio. Maestro at Florence. Pub. motets, canzonette, madrigals, &c., and a curious work on Double Counterpoint and Canon (1610).

Brunette *(F.).* A little tender, delicate, and simple air ; a love song.

BRUNETTI, Gaetano. *B.* Pisa, 1753 ; *d.* 1808. Court musician to Charles IV of Spain.
Works : 37 symphonies, 6 sextets, 32 quintets, &c.

BRU'NI, Antonio B. Violinist and conductor, Piedmont, 1759-1823.
Works : Methods for Violin and Viola, 18 operas, violin music, &c.

Bruscamen'te *(I.),* **Brusquement** *(F.).* Brusquely; violently accented.

Brus'co *(I.).* Coarse, rough, brusque.

Brust *(G.).* The breast ; chest.

Brust'stimme *(G.).* The chest voice.

Brust'ton *(G.).* Chest tone.

Brust'werk *(G.).* The pipes set up in the middle part of the organ ; usually the *choir* or *swell.*

BRYEN'NIUS (Bryenne, Briennius), M. Abt. 1320. Last Greek writer on music. Described the early Byzantine scales. (See **Byzantine music.**)

Bu'ca *(I.).* The sound-hole of a lute, &c.

BUCALOS'SI Ernest. Composer ; *b.* London, 1867.

Bucci'na *(I.)* ⎫ An ancient Roman crooked
Buci'na *(L.)* ⎭ horn or trumpet.

Bucco'lica *(I.)* ⎫ Rustic, bucolic, pastoral. *A la*
Bucolique *(F.)* ⎭ *bucolique,* in a rustic style.

BUCHANAN, Mrs. R. (See **J. McLachlan.**)

BÜCH'NER, Emil. *B.* nr. Naumburg, 1826. Court Capellmeister, Meiningen, 1865.
Works : operas, *Dame Kobold* and *Launcelot ;* a cantata, symphonies, overtures, &c.

Büch'se *(G.).* The boot or foot of an organ reed-pipe.

BUCK, Dudley. One of the most widely-known of American composers. *B.* Hartford, Connecticut, 1839. Studied at Leipzig, Dresden, and Paris. Orgt. successively in various American churches, and of Holy Trinity, Brooklyn, from 1875.
Works : opera, *Deseret* (1880), orchestral music, organ music, pf. music, church music, several popular cantatas, *King Olaf's Christmas, Voyage of Columbus, Hymn to Music, The Light of Asia, The Christian Year* (a cycle of five cantatas), &c. Also a Dictionary of Musical Terms, and a work on the organ, &c.

BUCK, Dr. Percy C. *B.* West Ham, 1871.

BUCK, Zechariah. Mus.Doc.Cantuar. Organist and teacher ; *b.* Norwich, 1798 ; *d.* 1879. Organist Norwich Cathedral, 1819-77.

Bu'co, *pl.* **Bu'chi** *(I.).* Finger-hole of an inst.

Buf'fa *(fem.)* ⎫ *(I.).* Comic, humorous. (See **Aria**
Buf'fo *(mas.)* ⎭ **Buffa** and **Opera Buffa.**)

Buffet *(F.).* An organ or keyboard case.

Buffo'ne *(I.).* Comic singer in an opera.
Buffonescamen'te. In a droll, humorous style.

Bugle, Bugle-horn. (1) A hunting horn. (2) The instrument used for military calls and signals. (3) A precursor of the cornet.

The *Royal Kent Bugle* was furnished with six keys. It was the smallest instrument of the *Ophicleide* family. Compass from—

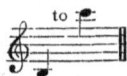

BÜHL, Jos. D. French trumpeter ; *b.* 1781. Pub. a Method for Trumpet.

BUHLIG, Rd. Pianist ; *b.* Chicago, 1880.

Büh'ne *(G.).* Stage ; scene, theatre.

Büh'nenweihfest'spiel *(G.).* "Stage-consecrating festival play." The term used by Wagner to describe his *Parsifal.*

Bund *(G.).* (1) A space between frets. (2) A fret. *Bund'frei.* Bichord *(q.v.).*

BULL, Dr. John. *B.* Somersetshire, 1563 ; *d.* Antwerp, 1628. Org. Hereford Cathedral, 1582. Mus. Doc. Oxon, 1592. Gresham Professor, 1596. Organist Notre Dame Cathedral, Antwerp, 1617.

He is said to have composed about 200 works. The melody of "God save the King" was long attributed to him. Many of his virginal and organ pieces are remarkably difficult.

BULL, Ole B. Famous Norwegian violinist ; Bergen, 1810-80. Travelled through Europe, and five times through N. America. Founded a National Theatre at Bergen.

He wrote 2 concertos and several other pieces for violin.

Ole Bull was not reckoned a classic musician, but he had a wonderful technique, and played his own compositions with remarkable expression and effect.

BÜLOW, Hans G. von. One of the most famous of modern pianists ; *b.* Dresden, 1830 ; *d.* Cairo, 1894. Court Capellmeister, and Director of the School of Music, Munich, 1867-9. Court Capellmeister, Hanover, 1878. Hofmusikintendant, Saxe-Meiningen, 1880-1885. Founded the Hamburg "Subscription Concerts," 1888. He was equally famous as conductor and pianist.

Works : orchestral pieces, masterly transcriptions for pf., critical editions of Beethoven's Sonatas and Cramer's Studies.

Bung'e *(G.).* A kettledrum.

BUNG'ERT, August. *B.* Mülheim-on-Ruhr, 1846. Studied at Paris, Berlin, &c.

Works : two opera cycles, *Die Ilias* and *Die Odyssee;* a comic opera, orchestral pieces, a pf. quartet, pf. pieces, songs, &c.

BUNNETT, Dr. Ed. Organist and composer. *B.* Norfolk, 1834.

BUNNING, Herbert. *B.* London, 1863.

Works : Italian scena, *Ludovico il Moro;* two symphonic poems, overtures, suites, songs, &c.

BUNTING, Edward. *B.* Armagh, 1773 ; *d.* Dublin, 1843. Published 3 volumes of Irish music, 1796 to 1840, the finest and most complete collection extant.

Bu'on, Buo'no,-a, Bô'no *(I.).* Good.

Buonaccor'do *(I.).* A small spinet for children.

Buo'na ma'no *(I.).* A good hand. Facility of execution.

Buonamen'te *(I.).* In just, accurate style.

BUONAMI'CI, Guiseppe. Pianist ; *b.* Florence, 1846. Pupil of Bülow and Rheinberger.

Has published and edited studies, preludes and fugues, and other pf. pieces, an overture, songs, &c.

Buo'na no'ta *(I.).* The accented note of a bar.

Bu'on gu'sto *(I.).* In good taste.

BUONONCI'NI. (See **Bononcini.**)

BURANEL'LO. (See **Galuppi.**)

BUR'CI. (See **Burtius.**)

BÜR'DE-NEY, Jenny. *B.* Gratz, 1826 ; *d.* 1886. Esteemed dramatic soprano. Sang at Olmütz, Prague, Vienna, Dresden, London, Berlin, &c.

Burden. (1) The refrain or chorus of a song. (2) A drone. (3) A tune sung to accompany dancing.

BURETTE, Pierre J. Scholarly Parisian writer on ancient Greek music ; 1665-1747.

BURG'MÜLLER, Norbert. *B.* Dusseldorf, 1810 ; *d.* 1836. Pianist, and composer of great promise. Pupil of Spohr and Hauptmann.

Works : two symphonies, pf. Concerto in F♯ min., sonatas for pf., chamber music, &c.

Burgomask. (See **Bergamask.**)

BURGON, Wm. H. Bass vocalist ; *b.* Croydon, 1858.

BURG'STALLER, Alois. Tenor ; *b.* Holzkirchen, 1871.

BURGUN'ZIO, Mad. (See **Hastreiter.**)

Bur'la *(I.).* A jest ; a joke.

Burlan'do *(I.)* }
Burlescamen'te *(I.)* } In a jesting, comic manner ; playfully.
Burles'co *(I.)* }

Burles'ca *(I.)* } An extravaganza. A travesty
Burlesque } of some serious work.

Burlet'ta *(I.).* A comic operetta or musical farce.

BUR'MEISTER, Rd. *B.* Hamburg, 1860. For several years music teacher in Baltimore and New York. Has written songs, a pf. concerto, and other pieces for pf.

BUR'MESTER, Willy. Contemporary popular violinist ; *b.* Hamburg, 1869.

BURNAND. (See **Strelezki.**)

BURNEY, Dr. Ch. *B.* Shrewsbury, 1726 ; *d.* London, 1814. Organist Lynn-Regis, Norfolk, 1751. Mus. Doc. Oxon, 1769. F.R.S., 1773. He wrote several compositions—now forgotten—"A General History of Music" (4 vols., 1776-89), his most celebrated work, and an account of the Handel Commemoration, 1784.

He ranks among the greatest musical historians.

BURO'NI. (See **Boroni.**) *(q.v.).*

BURR, Willard. American composer ; *b.* Ohio, 1877. Lives in Boston.

Works : chamber music, pf. pieces, violin pieces, songs, &c.

BURROWES, John F. London, 1787-1852. Wrote a "Thorough-Bass Primer," 1818.

BURSTALL, F. H. *B.* Liverpool, 1851. Orgt. Liverpool Cath. since 1880.

Burthen. Same as **Burden** *(q.v.).*

BUR'TIUS (Bur'ci, Bur'zio), Nicolaus. Parma, 1450- abt. 1520. His *Musices opusculum* (1487) contains the earliest specimen of printed "Mensural" music.

BURTON, Robt. S. *B.* Dewsbury, Yorks, 1820; *d.* 1892. Orgt. Leeds Parish Ch., 1849-1880(?). Chorusmaster first Leeds Festival, 1858. Conducted and trained more choral societies than any other Yorkshireman of his day.

Busain, Busaun, Buzain. An organ reed-stop, generally 16 ft. tone on the pedal.

BUSBY, Dr. Thos. *B.* Westminster, 1755; *d.* 1838. Mus.Doc. Cantab., 1800.
Wrote an oratorio, *The Prophecy*, a "General History of Music." a "Grammar of Music," &c.

BU'SI, Alessandro. Bologna, 1833-1895. Director, School of Singing, 1884.
Works : a Requiem, a symphony, several *Romanze* and pf. pieces, &c.

Bu'sna *(I.).* A kind of trumpet.

BUSNOIS, Antoine. Netherland contrapuntist; *d.* 1481. A few of his chansons, motets, and masses are still extant.

BUSO'NI, F. B. Fine pianist and promising composer ; *b.* nr. Florence, 1866. Has made several successful concert tours.
Works : an excellent edition of Bach's "48 Preludes and Fugues," a violin concerto, songs, chamber music, pf. sonatas, variations, transcriptions, &c., suites for orchestra, &c.

Bussan'do *(I.).* Thumping on the pf., &c.

BÜSSER, Henri P. Organist and composer ; *b.* Toulouse, 1872. Won *Grand Prix de Rome*, Paris Cons., 1893.
Works : *Antigone* and other cantatas, an orchestral suite, &c.

BUSSHOP, Jules A. G. Self-taught composer ; *b.* Paris, 1810 ; *d.* Bruges, 1896.
Works : prize cantata, *Le drapeau Belge* (1834) ; Te Deum, overtures, much military music, &c.

BUSS'LER, Ludwig. Musical theorist; *b.* Berlin, 1838; *d.* 1900. Musical critic, *National Zeitung*, Berlin, 1883.
Works : "Musical Form" (1878), "Elements of Music," "Text-book of Harmony," "Counterpoint and Fugue," "Practical Composition," "Instrumentation and Orchestration," &c.

BUSS'MEYER, Hans. Pianist ; *b.* Brunswick, 1853. Founded Munich Choral Society, 1879.

BUSS'MEYER, Hugo. Bro. of above ; pianist and composer ; *b.* Brunswick, 1842.

Buss'psalmen *(G.).* Penitential psalms.

BUTHS (pron. *Boots*), **Julius.** Excellent pianist ; *b.* Wiesbaden, 1851. Conducts the Musical Society at Elberfeld. Has written several pf. pieces.

BUTLER, Chas. *B.* Wycombe, 1559 ; *d.* 1647.
Pub. "The Principles of Music" (1636), a work praised by Burney, and highly prized by collectors.

BUTT, Clara (Mrs. R. H. Kennerley-Rumford). Highly - esteemed contralto singer. *B.* Southwick, Sussex, 1873. 4½

BUTT'STEDT, Joh. H. Distinguished organist ; *b.* nr. Erfurt, 1666 ; *d.* 1727. Wrote a famous "Defence of Solmization."
Published clavichord music and church pieces.

Bux'us *(L.).* } An ancient boxwood flute
Buc'ca tib'ia } with 3 finger holes.

BUXTEHU'DE, Dietrich. Famous organist ; *b.* Denmark, 1639 ; *d.* 1707. Organist, Marienkirche, Lübeck, 1668-1707. J. S. Bach walked 50 miles* to hear him play, and his own organ compositions were greatly influenced by Buxtehude's works. A complete edition of his organ compositions has been pub. by Ph. Spitta.

Buzzing. A drone *(Rousseau).*

BUZ'ZOLA, A. Italian operatic comp. ; 1815-71. Maestro St. Mark's, Venice, 1855.
Works : several successful operas and some good church music, &c.

Bye-tone. "A tone of the same chord, but different from that just struck in the same part."—*Curwen.*
Thus **r** (G) in the following example is a byetone. There may be two or even three byetones struck together. The term is an excellent one, and worthy of general adoption.

KEY **F.**

BYFIELD, John, senr., and **John, junr.** Eminent 18th century English organ builders ; afterwards Byfield, Jordan & Bridge.

BYRD (Byrde, Bird, Byred), William. *B.* 1543 ; *d.* 1623. Pupil of Tallis. Orgt. Lincoln Cath., 1563. Gentleman Chapel Royal, 1569. Remained a Catholic. A patent for the "exclusive privilege of printing music and selling music-paper" was granted to Byrd and Tallis, 1575, which became Byrd's at the death of Tallis, 1585. Byrd was one of the chief composers of his time, both vocal and instrumental.
Works : "Cantiones Sacræ," "Psalms, Sonets, and Songs," graduals, madrigals, services and anthems, music for the "virginals," a Mass in D min., &c.

BYROM, John, M.A., F.R.S. 1692-1763. Cambridge scholar ; friend of the Wesleys. Wrote the hymn, "Christians, awake!"

Byssinge Songes *(old Eng.).* Cradle songs.

Byzantine Music. The music of the Greek Christian Church. The Byzantine scales in early use were described by Bryennius.
They consisted of four authentic and four plagal modes, somewhat similar to those introduced by St. Ambrose and St. Gregory into the Western Church.

* 250 English miles.

C. (*G., C.; F., ut; I., do.*) (1) The key-note of the "Standard," or "Pattern," major scale.

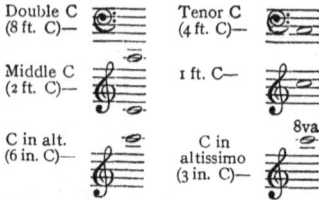

Double C (8 ft. C)—	*[musical notation]*	Tenor C (4 ft. C)—	*[musical notation]*
Middle C (2 ft. C)—	*[musical notation]*	1 ft. C—	*[musical notation]*
C in alt. (6 in. C)—	*[musical notation]*	C in altissimo (3 in. C)—	*[musical notation]* 8va

Instruments are "in C" when they produce the exact pitch (or an 8ve lower or higher) of notes "as written:" as Trumpet in C, Horn in C, &c. Otherwise they are "transposing instruments:" *e.g.* Clarinet in B♭, producing sounds a major 2nd lower than those written; Horn in F, producing sounds a perfect 5th lower than written.

(2) The letter which became the **C** clef.
(3) The lowest "unmarked doh" in Tonic Sol-fa.

C. ⁴/₄ time.

C. Canto, Cantus; the treble or soprano

C. (See Circa.)

C. A. Abbr. of *Col arco.*

C barré (*F.*). "Barred" C ; ₵.

C clef. The clef giving the pitch of "middle C" to the line of the staff on which it is placed. (See **Clef.**)

C dur (*G.*). C major.

C. F. Canto Fermo.

C major. (1) The major key or scale requiring no sharps or flats. (2) The chord *[musical notation]*

C minor. (1) The relative minor of E♭ major. The key or scale requiring 3 flats. (2) The chord *[musical notation]*

C moll (*G.*). C minor.

C-Schlüs'sel (*G.*). C clef.

Cabalet'ta (*I.*). A short, simple melody.

Cabalet'ta (*S.*). A piece in Rondo form, with variations; a simple air.
It has frequently a tripletted accompaniment to imitate a trotting horse.

CABALLE'RO, Manuel F. Writer of popular Spanish "zarzuelas" (operettas); *b.* Murcia, 1835.
La Rueda de la Fortuna (1896) is one of his best works.

CABEL, Marie J. (*née* **Dreulette**). Celebrated French singer and actress; *b.* Liége, 1827; *d.* 1885.

CABEZON, Felix A. de. "The Spanish Bach;" Madrid, 1510-1566. Eminent organist and harpsichord player. Blind from birth.

Cabinet d'orgue (*F.*). An organ case.

Cabinet organ. Reed organ; American organ.

Cabinet pianoforte. An old-fashioned "upright" pianoforte.

Cabis'cola (*L.*). Choir precentor.

CACCAMI'SI, Baronne. Blanche Marchesi (*q.v.*).

Cac'cia (*I.*). The chase; hunting. *Al'la cac'cia,* in hunting style (generally accompanied by horns).

CACCI'NI, Giulio. *B.* Rome, 1558; *d.* abt. 1615. Singer, lute player, and composer; known as "**Roma'no.**" With Peri, Bardi, and others, initiated the new *Musica in stila rappresentativo,* which led to the birth of oratorio and opera, and the "modern style" of composition. Caccini wrote the first Recitatives, which he sang to his own accompaniment. He has therefore been called "the father of the new style." With Peri he wrote the first "Pastoral Drama," *Dafne,* 1594, and *Euridice,* the first opera, 1600. He also wrote many excellent madrigals.

Cachée (*F.*). Hidden; as hidden fifths.

Cachu'cha (*S.*). A Spanish dance like the *Bolero* (in triple time, and *moderato*).

Cacofoni'a (*I.*). ⎫
Cacophonie (*F.*). ⎬ Harsh discordant sounds. Musical chaos.
Cacoph'ony (*E.*). ⎭

CADAUX, Justin. French composer; 1813-1874. Wrote six comic operas.

CADEAC. French 16th century composer of masses, motets, &c.

Cadence. (*G., Kadenz'; F.,Cadence; I.,Caden'za.*) (1) A cadenza. (2) A fall; the end of a phrase, section, &c.; the final chords of any piece of music.
In general, a cadence answers to a punctuation mark, and marks a *point of repose,* either momentary or complete. The chief cadences are—
(1) *Perfect* or *Authentic* cadence, or *Full Close*; Dominant chord (or Dominant 7th) followed by Tonic chord (S D, or ⁷S D).
(2) *Plagal* cadence; Subdominant chord followed by Tonic (F D).
(3) *Interrupted, Avoided, Surprise, Broken,* or *False* cadence; Dominant or Dominant 7th chord followed by some other chord than that of the Tonic.
(4) *Dominant* cadence, or *Half-close;* the Dominant chord preceded by any other chord.
(5) *Inverted* or *Incomplete* cadence ; a cadence on any inversion of a chord (see below).

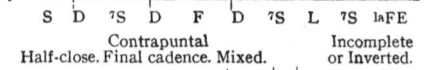

[musical notation]

Perfect.   Plagal.   Interrupted.

S D ⁷S D   F D ⁷S L ⁷S laFE
Contrapuntal   Incomplete
Half-close. Final cadence. Mixed.   or Inverted.

[musical notation]

D♭ S T♭ D   F S ⁷Sd D♭

Cadences are also named after their *final chord,* without special reference to the chords preceding :—

Tonic Super- Sub- Sub-
cadence. tonic. dominant. Dominant. mediant.

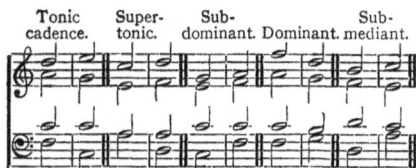

A *masculine* cadence ends on a strong accent ; a *feminine* cadence on a weak accent, or on a weaker accent than the preceding chord :—

Feminine cadences.   Ornamented.

Abrupt cadence. Interrupted.
Amen cadence. Plagal.
Complete cadence. Perfect.
Deceptive cadence. Interrupted.
Irregular cadence. Interrupted.
Mixed cadence. (See illustration.)
Phrygian cadence. (See *Phrygian*.)
Whole cadence. Perfect.

Cadence *(F.).* (1) A cadence (as above). (2) A trill.
Cadence brillante. A brilliant trilled cadence, or cadenza.
Cadence brisée
A trilled cadence :

Cadence évitée. Interrupted ; avoided.
Cadence imparfaite. Imperfect.
Cadence interrompue. Interrupted.
Cadence irrégulière. Half-close.
Cadence parfaite. Perfect.
Cadence perlée. Same as *Cadence brillante.*
Cadence rompue. Interrupted.

Cadent. An obsolete ornament. (See **Ornaments.**)

Cadenz' *(G.).* Cadence ; cadenza. (See **Kadenz.**)

Caden'za. (1) A passage—formerly extempore —introduced near the close of a solo to exhibit the singer's flexibility and compass of voice, &c. (generally sung to the vowel *aa*).
The following is one of the cadenzas sung by Jenny Lind :—

(2) A similar passage in a concerto or other instrumental piece.
BEST wrote cadenzas for Handel's organ concertos; Beethoven for Mozart's and his own pf. concertos.
In modern music the cadenza is generally added by the composer, and printed in small notes.

Caden'za *(I.).* A cadence.
Caden'za d'ingan'no. Interrupted cadence (in a fugue).
Caden'za fioritu'ra. A cadence embellished with runs, &c.
Caden'za sfuggi'ta. Interrupted cadence.
Caden'za sospe'sa. Suspended cadence.

CÆCIL'IA. (See **Cecilia.**)

Cæsu'ra *(L.).* A slight pause at or near the middle of a line of poetry.

CAFA'RO, Pasquale. (**Caffariel'lo**). Neapolitan composer ; 1706 - 1797. Succeeded Leo, Naples Cons., 1745.
Works : a fine *Stabat Mater;* operas, oratorios, cantatas, &c.

CAFFAREL'LI (or **Gaetano Majora'no**). Celebrated male soprano ; *b.* Bari, 1703 ; *d.* Naples, 1783.
A peasant boy taught by Porpora, who after five years' study said to him, "Go, my son, I have nothing more to teach you ; you are the greatest singer in Italy and in the world." He made little impression when he sang in London, 1738, but in Italy, Paris, Spain, and Vienna he was brilliantly successful.

CAF'FI, Francesco. *B.* Venice, 1786 ; *d.* 1874. Wrote a " History of the Sacred Music in the Ducal Chapel, St. Mark's, Venice, from 1318 to 1797," and other works.

CAGNO'NI, A. Opera composer ; *b.* nr. Voghera, 1828 ; *d.* Bergamo, 1896. Maestro in the cathedrals at Vigevano and Novarra— later at Bergamo.
Operas : *Don Bucefalo* (his finest work), 1847 ; and about 20 others.

CAHEN, Albert. Paris, 1846-1903.
Works : Biblical poem, *Jean le Précurseur ;* operas, *Le Bois, La Belle au bois dormant, Le Vénitien* (1890), &c.

CAHEN, Ernest. Paris, 1828-93. Pupil and afterwards teacher at the Cons.
Works : operettas, *Le Calfat* and *Le souper de Mezzetin.*

Cahier *(L.).* A book ; a part.

CAH'SE. Same as **Carse** *(q.v.).*

CA'IMO, Jos. *B.* abt. 1540(?). Published sets of madrigals, &c., Milan. 1571-84.

ÇA IRA. "That will do." The earliest of the revolutionary songs in France (abt. 1789). The tune commences thus :—

Caisse *(F.).* A drum. *Grosse caisse,* bass drum.
Caisse claire. Snare drum.
Caisse plate. Shallow side-drum.
Caisse roulante. Tenor drum.

Cal. Abbn. of *Calando.*

Calamaulos *(Gk.).* A flute made of a reed.

Ca'lamus *(L.).* A reed flute ; either like our oaten-pipe or like the *syrinx* (pan-pipes). *c.f. Chalameau* and *Shawm.*

Ca'lamus pastora'lis (or **tibia'lis**). An ancient flute with three or four finger-holes.

Calan'do *(I.).* Decreasing in loudness and speed. Dying away.

Calandro'ne *(I.).* A kind of small clarinet or chalameau with two finger-holes.

Calascio'ne, Coloscio'ne *(I.).* A two-stringed Italian guitar.

Cala'ta *(I.).* A sprightly Italian dance in $\frac{2}{4}$ time.

Calcan'do *(I.).* Hurrying the pace. Pressing on.

Calcant *(G.).* Treading. (See **Bäl'gentreter.**)

Calcantenglock'e *(G.).* Bells sounded by means of pedals.

Caldamen'te *(I.).* Warmly, ardently.

CALDA'RA, Antonio. *B.* Venice, 1670; *d.* Vienna, 1736. Chamber composer, Vienna, 1714.
Works: 66 operas ; much fine church music, including 36 oratorios, numerous masses, motets, &c. ; also chamber music.

CALDICOTT, Alfred Jas. *B.* Worcester, 1842 ; *d.* 1897. Organist St. Stephen's, Worcester. 1864. Mus. B. Cantab., 1878. Music Director, Albert Palace, Battersea, 1885. Principal, London College of Music, 1892.
Works : cantatas, *The Widow of Nain,* &c. ; operettas ; humorous glees ("Humpty Dumpty"), &c.

CALEGA'RI, Antonio. Padua, 1758-1828.
Works : operas, *Le sorelle rivali, L'Amor soldato, Il matrimonio scoperto ;* treatises on harmony, composition, &c.

CALETTI-BRU'NI. (See **Cavalli.**)

Calichon *(F.)* }
Calisonci'no *(I.).* } *Calascione (q.v.).*

CALKIN, John B. London, 1827-1905. Pianist, organist, and composer.
Works : services, anthems, part-songs, pf. pieces, organ pieces, &c.

Call. A military signal given on the bugle, fife, or drum.

CALL, Leonard von. German composer of popular male-voice part-songs ; 1779-1815.

CAL'LAERTS, Jos. J. *B.* Antwerp, 1838. Organist, and composer of organ music, &c. Pupil of Lemmens. *D.* 1901.

CALLCOTT, John Wall. Mus. Doc. Oxon. Distinguished composer of glees, catches, and canons ; *b.* Kensington, 1766 ; *d.* 1821.
Wrote a popular "Grammar of Music," 1806 ; also songs and church music.

CALLCOTT, Wm. H. Son of J. W. London, 1807-1882. Orgt., pianist, and composer.
Wrote songs, anthems, and pf. music.

Calli'ope (**Kalli'ope**). (1) "The beautiful-voiced." Greek *Muse* of eloquence and poetry : mother of Orpheus. (2) A harsh steam-organ ; a set of whistles blown by steam. (3) An organ stop ; 8-ft. or 4-ft. pitch.

Callithum'pian Concert. (*G., Katz'enmusik ; F., Charivari ; I., Chias'so, Scampana'ta.*)
"A boisterous serenade . . characterised by the blowing of horns, beating of tin pans, derisive cries, groans, hoots, cat-calls, &c."— *Th. Baker.*

Cal'ma *(I.).* Calm, repose, tranquillity.

Calman'do *(I.).* } With tranquillity ; be-
Calma'ta *(I.).* } coming more calm.

Calme et placide *(F.).* Calm(ly) and serene(ly).

CALMOND, Mark. A *nom-de-plume* of **J. Williams** *(q.v.).*

Calo're *(I.).* Warmth, passion. *Con calo're,* with much warmth and animation.

Caloro'so *(I.).* Same as **Con calo're.**

CALVÉ, Emma. (**Emma Roquer.**) *B.* South France, 1864(?). Fine operatic soprano ; specially good in the part of *Carmen.*

CALVIS'IUS (Kall'witz), Sethus. Distinguished writer and composer ; son of a poor Thuringian peasant. *B.* 1556 ; *d.* Leipzig, 1615. Maintained himself while studying by street-singing and teaching. Music-director, Paulinerkirche, Leipzig, 1581 ; cantor at the Thomasschule, and music-director at the Thomaskirche and Nicolaikirche, 1594.
Works : valuable theoretical Latin treatises ; Lieder, Psalms (up to 12 parts), the hymns of Luther, motets, &c.

CAMBERT, Robert. *B.* Paris, abt. 1628 ; *d.* London, as Master of the Music to Charles II, 1677. After several stage ventures, wrote the first real French opera, *Pomone,* 1671. The success of Lully drove Cambert to London.

Cambia're *(I.).* To change.
Cambia'no in do. Change to key C.
Nota cambia'ta. Changing note *(q.v.).*

CAMBI'NI, Giovanni G. Italian composer, 1746-1825 (?). Pupil of Martini.
Prolific composer of ballets, symphonies, operas string quartets, &c., of little permanent value

Cambridge Quarter Chimes.
These clock-chimes (made famous by being adopted for "Big Ben," Westminster) were taken from the oft-repeated phrase in Handel's "I know that my Redeemer :"—

Cam'era *(I.).* A chamber, a room.
Al'la cam'era. In the style of chamber music.
Mu'sica di cam'era. Chamber music.
Sona'ta di cam'era. Chamber sonata.

CAMERA'NA, Luigi. *B.* Piedmont, 1846. Maestro at the Savona Theatre.
Works : the successful opera, *Il conte di Mirabello* (1892), *Peterkin* (London, 1893), and others.

CAMIDGE, John. York, 1735-1803. Organist York Minster for 43 years, from 1756.
Pub. harpsichord music, church music, &c.

CAMIDGE, Matthew. York, 1758-1844. Son of preceding ; organist York Minster, 1799-1842.
Works : sonatas, &c., for pf. ; hymn-tunes ; "A Method of Instruction in Music by Questions and Answers," &c.

CAMIDGE, Dr. John. Son of Matthew ; 1790-1859. Mus. Doc. Cantab., 1819. Organist York Minster, 1842.
Works : a vol. of cathedral music ; anthems, chants, &c.

Camminan'do. Walking, flowing ; hurrying.

CAMPAGNO'LI, Bartolomeo. Celebrated violinist ; *b.* Cento, 1751 ; *d.* Neustrelitz, 1827. After successful tours, &c., became Court Capellmeister, Neustrelitz.
Works : chamber music, flute concertos, violin concerto, divertissements for violin, caprices for viola, a Violin Method, &c.

Campagnuo'lo,-a *(I.).* Rustic, pastoral.

CAMPA'NA, Fabio. Popular singing teacher and composer ; *b.* Leghorn, 1819 ; *d.* London, 1882.
Works : hundreds of songs, and several operas (including *Almina,* London, 1860)

Campa'na *(I.)* ⎫ (1) A bell; a church bell. (2)
Campane *(F.).* ⎭ A " high-pitch" org. stop.
Campanel'la *(I.).* ⎫ A small bell.
Campanel'lo *(I.).* ⎭
Campanelli'no *(I.).* A very small bell.
Campan'ile *(I.).* A belfry.
Campanis'ta *(I.).* A bell-ringer.

CAMPANA'RI, Leandro. Italian violinist; *b.* Rovigo, 1857. Organised the Campanari String Quartet, Boston, U.S.A. Director of the orchestral concerts, La Scala, Milan, since 1897.
Works: songs; text-books for violin.

Campanet'ta *(I.).* A set of tuned bells. (See **Glockenspiel.**)

CAMPANI'NI, Italo. Fine operatic tenor; Parma, 1845-1896. Sang in *Lohengrin, Mefistofele, Faust, Carmen, Don Giovanni, Les Huguenots,* &c., in Italy, London, and America, with great success.

Campanol'ogy. The art of bell-ringing; knowledge of the construction of bells.

CAMPBELL, Alexander. Scottish musician and writer; 1764-1824. Tried in vain to teach music to Sir W. Scott.
Pub. collections of Scottish songs, poetry, &c.

CAMPBELL, Jane Montgomery. 1817-1878. Translated " We plough the fields," from the German.

CAMPENHOUT, François van. Brussels, 1779-1848. Tenor singer.
Composed "La Brabançonne," the Belgian national air. Wrote 17 operas.

Campes'tre *(I.).* Rustic, pastoral.

CAMPION, François. Theorbist at the Grand Opéra, Paris, 1703-19. Published several works on theorbo playing, &c.

CAMPION (or **Campian**), **Thomas.** Physician and composer. *B.* 1575; *d.* London, 1619.
Works: "Books of Ayres," (1610 and 1612), "Ayres for the Masque of Flowers" (1613), "Songs of Mourning" (1613), and "A New Way of Making Foure Parts in Counterpoint."

CAMPORE'SE, Violante. Celebrated soprano; *b.* Rome, 1785; *d.* 1839.
Engaged King's Theatre, London, 1817. After a visit to Milan, she was re-engaged in London, 1821, "with a salary for the season of £1,550, paid in advance, with extra allowance for costumes, and permission to sing at concerts." Her voice was of exquisite quality and purity, and particularly beautiful in its highest notes.

CAM'PRA, André. *B.* Provence, 1660; *d.* Versailles, 1744. *Maitre de Musique,* Toulon Cathedral, 1680; Conductor. Royal Orchestra, Paris, 1722. His operas were good, but overshadowed by those of Lully, who preceded, and Rameau, who followed him.
Operas: *L'Europe galante, Le Carnaval de Venise, Hésione,Aréthuse, Tancrède. Les Muses, Iphigénie, Télémaque,* and several others. He also wrote some very fine motets and 3 books of cantatas.

CAMPS Y SOLER, Oscar. Spanish composer and pianist; *b.* Alexandria, 1837. Settled in Madrid after successful concert tours.
Works: songs, pf. pieces, theoretical treatises; a Spanish trans. of Berlioz's "Instrumentation."

Canarie *(F.)* ⎫ A sort of lively jig, of French
Canaries *(E.).* ⎭ or English origin, in $\frac{6}{8}, \frac{3}{8},$ or $\frac{4}{4}$ time. It consisted of two short phrases, each repeated.

Cancan *(F.).* A boisterous dance.

Cancrizans *(L.).* "Crab-like." (See **Canon.**)

CANDEILLE, Pierre J. French operatic composer; 1744-1827. His best work was *Castor et Pollux,* 1791.

CANDEILLE, Amélie Julie. Paris, 1767-1834. Soprano singer, actress, and composer. Sang in Gluck's *Iphigénie en Aulide,* 1782.
She wrote the words and music of a successful operetta, *La Belle Fermière* (1792); also pf. pieces, songs, &c.

Can'na *(I.).* "A cane." A reed or pipe.
Can'ne d' a'nima. Flue pipes.
Can'ne a lin'gua. Reed pipes.

CAN'NABICH, Christian. Violinist and famous conductor; *b.* Mannheim, 1731; *d.* 1798. Leader Electoral Orchestra, Mannheim, 1765; conductor, 1775.
Works: popular operas, ballets, symphonies, violin concertos, &c.

Canon. *(G., Ka'non; F., Canon; I., Ca'none.)* (1) A rule, a regulation; a system of rules. (2) Specially, a composition in which a theme or "subject" started in one part is strictly repeated (after a rest) in another part, or parts. The leading part is called the *Antecedent,* the repetition the *Consequent.*
The imitation may be at the unison, or any interval above or below, as canon at the 5th, 8ve, &c. There may be any number of parts and more than one theme: thus *Canon 3 in 1* means 3 parts, 1 theme; *Canon 4 in 2* means 4 parts, 2 themes, &c.
Canon Infinite, or *Perpetual.* A canon which may be repeated *ad lib.* Rounds and catches are examples of Infinite Canons *at the unison:*—
Round for 2 voices, or infinite Canon 2 in 1 at the unison.

Byrde's "Non Nobis Domine" is a well-known example of an Infinite Canon, 3 in 1 at the under 4th and 8ve; it begins thus:—

Canon, Accompanied, or *with free parts.* "Tallis's Canon" is an illustration of an Infinite Canon 2 in 1 at the 8ve between treble and tenor, with *free* accompanying parts in alto and bass. The Credo in Haydn's *Imperial Mass in D* is a fine example of an accompanied Canon 2 in 1 at the under 5th (the treble in 8ves with tenor and the alto in 8ves with bass):—

Free parts are said to be *ad placitum*.

Canon, Finite. One not constructed to be repeated.

Finite Canon 4 in 2 at the 4th and 5th.   BACH.

Canon by Augmentation. A canon in which the notes of the *consequent* are double (or triple, quadruple, &c.) those of the *antecedent*.

Canon by Diminution. One in which the notes of the *consequent* are shorter (one-half, one-third, &c.) than those of the *antecedent*.

In the following, by Cooke, the antecedent in the bass is given in the tenor by *Augmentation*, and at the same time, in the treble by *Diminution*:—

Circular Canon. A canon which modulates from key to key until it completes the "circle of keys."

Canon Cancrizans.
Canon, Recte et Retro (or Retrograde). A canon that may be sung *forwards* and *backwards* at the same time, producing two parts in one.

Example from SIMPSON.

Enigmatical, or Puzzle Canon. The performer has to discover the point and interval at which the *consequent* enters.

Canon. Tres in unum. MARTINI.

7

Canon, Strict. When the intervals of the *antecedent* are exactly imitated by the *consequent*.

Canon, Free. (1) When the intervals are not all exactly imitated. (2) Canonic imitation. (See also **Imitation**.)

Ca'none (*I.*). A canon.
Ca'none al sospi'ro. The parts coming in at a beat's interval.
Ca'none aper'to. Open. Written out in full.
Ca'none cancrizzan'te. Cancrizans (see above).
Ca'none chiu'so. A close canon; only a short rest between *antecedent* and *consequent*.
Ca'none enigma'tico. Enigmatical.
Ca'none infini'to. | Infinite.
Ca'none perpe'tuo. |
Ca'none sciol'to. A free canon. (See *Canon, free*.)

Canonical Hours. The seven established times for daily prayer in the Roman Church.

Canonic Imitation. Imitation in canonic style.

Cano'nico (*I.*). In the form of a canon.

Canta'bile (*I.*). In a singing, melodious, flowing style.

Cantacchia're (*I.*). To hum, to sing softly.

Cantamen'to (*I.*). The air, melody, or *Canto*.

Cantan'do (*I.*). Same as *Canta'bile*.

Cantan'te (*I.*). (1) A singer. (2) Singing. (3) Gay, sprightly.

Canta're (*I.*). To sing.
Canta're a a'ria. More or less improvised, as Welsh *Penillion* singing.
Canta're a ore'chio. To sing by ear.
Canta're di manie'ra. | To sing in a florid, embel-
Canta're di maniera'ta. | lished style.

Canta'ta (*I.*). (1) A piece to be *sung;* as opposed to *Sonata*, a piece to be sounded or played. (2) Originally a mixture of *recitative* and *melody* for a solo voice with accompaniment. (See **Caccini**.) (3) A short oratorio, sacred or secular.
Canta'ta da Chie'sa. A church cantata.

Cantate (*F. & G.*). A cantata.

CANTA'TE DOM'INO. The 98th Psalm.

Cantatil'la (*I.*), **Cantatille** (*F.*), **Cantati'na** (*I.*). A short cantata.

Canta'to,-a (*I.*). Sung.
Mes'sa canta'ta. High Mass.

Cantato're (*I.*). A male singer.

Cantato'rium (*I.*). A book to sing from; a service book, &c.

Cantatri'ce (*I.*). A female singer.

Canterellan'do (*I.*). | Singing softly; warbling,
Canticchian'do (*I.*). | trilling, humming.

Canteri'no,-a (*I.*). A singer; a chanter.

Canti'ci (*I.*). The *Laudi Spirituali* of the Roman Catholic Church.

Can'ticle. (*L.*, *Can'ticum;* *G.*, *Lob'gesang;* *F.*, *Cantique;* *I.*, *Can'tico*.) (1) A hymn; a song of praise. (2) A sacred chant.
The Evangelical Canticles are the *Magnificat*, *Benedictus*, and *Nunc dimittis*.

Can'tico (*I.*), **Can'ticum** (*L.*). A canticle.
Can'ticum cantico'rum. Solomon's Song.
Can'tica gra'duum. The Gradual.

Cantile'na. (*I.*, "A little song." *G.*, *Cantile'ne;* *F.*, *Cantilène*.) (1) A ballad. (2) Same as **Canto fermo**. (3) The *Canto* or highest part in a madrigal. (4) Same as **Cantabile**; in a flowing, singing style.

Cantilenac'cia *(I.).* Coarse, bad singing.

Cantilena're *(I.).* To sing in a low voice, or without accompaniment.

Cantilla'tio *(L.).* Declamatory singing.

Cantillation. An irregular form of chanting ; probably the earliest method of psalm-singing.

Canti'no *(I.).* The E string of a violin.

Can'tio *(L.).* An air or song.

Cantio'nes Sa'cræ (L.). Sacred songs.

Cantique *(F.).* (1) A canticle. (2) A hymn-tune, or choral.

Can'to *(I.).* (1) The melody ; the highest part ; the solo part. *Col canto,* same as **Colla voce** or **Colla parte.** (2) Same as **Cantino.** (3) A song, a melody.

Can'to a cappel'la. Same as *A cappella.*
Can'to Ambrosia'no. Ambrosian chant.
Can'to armo'nico. A part-song.
Can'to croma'tico. A chromatic melody or song.
Can'to fer'mo. (See *Cantus firmus.*)
Can'to figura'to. Florid melody.
Can'to Gregoria'no. Gregorian chant.
Can'to pla'no. Plain-song.
Can'to pri'mo. The 1st soprano.
Can'to recitati'vo. Recitative or declamation.
Can'to ripie'no. (See *Ripieno.*)
Can'to secon'do. The 2nd soprano.
Can'to sempli'ce. (Same as *Canto fermo.*)

Cantola'no *(S.).* Plain-song.

CAN'TOR, Otto. Composer ; *b.* Kreuznach, 1857.

Can'tor *(L.).* (1) Precentor. (2) (See **Kantor.**)

Can'tor chora'lis. Chorus-master.

Canto're *(I.).* A singer ; a chorister.

Canto're di capel'la. Precentor.

Canto'ris *(L.).* (" Of the Cantor.") The side of a choir (usually the north) on which the cantor or precentor sits ; also the choristers on that side. (See **Decani.**)

Cantri'ce *(I.).* A female singer.

Can'tus *(L.).* (1) A song, chant, melody. (2) The treble, or air.

Can'tus Ambrosia'nus. Ambrosian chant.
Can'tus corona'tus. A broken melody, accompanied by a *Fauxbourdon.*
Can'tus du'rus. Old music which modulated into a key with one or more sharps.
Can'tus ecclesias'ticus. (1) Plain-song. (2) Church music in general.
Can'tus figura'lis. Mensurable music.
Can'tus figura'tus. Florid or figured counterpoint added to a melody.
Can'tus fir'mus. (1) The tenor, originally the chief melody. (2) Any fragment of plain-song to which counterpoint has been added. (3) Any theme for contrapuntal treatment. (See *Counterpoint.*)
Can'tus frac'tus. A broken irregular melody.
Can'tus Gregoria'nus. Gregorian chant.
Can'tus mensura'bilis. (See *Mensurable music.*)
Can'tus pla'nus. Plain-song.
Can'tus Roma'nus. Roman chant. Gregorian chant.

Canun', Kanun'. A Turkish dulcimer with gut strings.

Canzo'na, Canzo'ne *(I.).* (1) A folk-song *(Chanson).* (2) A popular secular part-song. (3) An instrumental piece in madrigal style.

Canzonac'cia *(I.).* A commonplace, vulgar song.

Canzonci'no,-a *(I.).* A short melody or poem.

Canzo'ne sa'cra *(I.).* A sacred song.

Canzonet } A little *canzo'na ;* a short
Canzonet'ta *(I.)* } song. A madrigal.

Canzonie're *(I.).* A collection of lyrical songs or poems.

Caoinan. The Irish funeral song.

Capel'le *(G.).* (See **Kapel'le.**)

Capell'meister *(or Kapell'meister, G.).* "Chapel-master." (1) Conductor of an orchestra. (2) Choirmaster. (See also **Kapelle.**)

Capell'meistermusik (G.). Music without inspiration.

Capi'strum *(L.).* A kind of muzzle round the heads of ancient trumpeters "to prevent their cheeks from bursting."

Ca'po *(I.).* The head ; the beginning.

Da ca'po. From the beginning.
Capoco'mico,-a. Leading comic singer.
Ca'po d'opera. The finest song ; the masterpiece.
Capolavo'ro. A master-work.
Capo mu'sica. Conductor.
Capo-orche'stra. The conductor, or leader.

CAPOC'CI, Gaetano. Rome, 1811 - 1898. Organist, composer, and teacher.

Works : oratorios, *Battista* and *Assalonne ;* masses, motets, Psalms, &c.

CAPOC'CI, Filippo. Son of G. *B.* Rome, 1840. Said to be the finest living Italian organist. Has written numerous organ pieces.

Capodastre *(F.)* } Also *Capo di tasto,* and *Capo*
Capoda'stro *(I.)* } *d'astro.* (1) The nut of a
Capota'sto *(I.)* } violin, &c. (2) A piece of wood or ivory fastened over the strings of a guitar, &c., as a temporary nut.

CAPOUL, Jos. A. V. Celebrated tenor ; *b.* Toulouse, 1839.

Sang, French Opéra-Comique, 1861-72 ; afterwards in London, New York, &c.

Cap'pella, A (or **Alla**). (See **A cappella.**)

Capricciet'to *(I.).* A little capriccio.

Capric'cio *(I.).* A composition of irregular or unconventional form and style. A whim, a caprice.

A capric'cio }
Capriccio'so } *Ad lib.,* whimsical, fantastic.
Capricciosamen'te }

Caprice *(F.).* *Capriccio (q.v.).*

Capriciös' *(G.).* Capricious.

Cap'ut Scho'læ *(L.).* Precentor.

CARAC'CIO (or **CARAVAC'CIO**), **Giovanni.** Roman composer ; 1550(?)-1626.

Works : 2 vols. of Magnificats and 5 of madrigals ; a Requiem, Psalms, &c.

CARACCIO'LI, Luigi. Singing teacher ; *b.* Adria, 1849 ; *d.* London, 1887.

Works : opera, *Maso il Montanaro* (1874), and many songs.

Caractères de musique *(F.).* Musical characters—notes, rests, &c.

CARADO'RI - ALLAN, Maria C. R. *(née de Munck).* B. Milan, 1800 ; *d.* 1865. Gifted singer ; sang the soprano part at the first performance of *Elijah,* Birmingham, 1846.

CARA'FA de Colobra'no, Michele E. *B.* Naples, 1787 ; *d.* Paris, 1872. Professor of Composition, Paris Cons., 1840.

Works : 35 operas, including *Le Solitaire* (1822), *Masaniello* (1827), and *La Violette* (1828); popular pf. music ; cantatas, church music, &c.

Carat'tere *(I.).* Character, style, dignity.

Caratteris'tico. Characteristic.
Mez'zo carat'tere. Of moderate difficulty.

CARBONEL, Mad. (See **Chaminade.**)

CARBONEL'LI, Steffano. Violinist.
Came to England from Rome abt. 1720, and attached himself to Handel. Was a great favourite. *D.* London, 1772.

Caressant *(F.)* ⎫ In a soothing, caressing
Carezzan'do *(I.)* ⎬ manner.
Carezze'vole *(I.)* ⎭

CARESTI'NI, Giovanni. (Sang as **Cusanino.**) *B.* nr. Ancona, 1705; *d.* 1763. Famous male alto. Sang, under Handel, London, 1733-5 as the rival of Farinelli.

CAREY, Henry. *B.* abt. 1690; *d.* London, 1743. Music teacher and theatrical composer; chiefly self-taught.
Wrote 9 successful ballad operas (including " The most Tragical Tragedy that ever was Trage-dized by any company of Tragedians, called *Chrononhotonthologos* "), and pub. 100 ballads (1737). His " Sally in our Alley " is still popular. "God save the King" is claimed for him.

Carica'to *(I.).* " Caricatured." Overloaded with ornaments, graces, &c.

Carillon *(F.).* (1) A set of bells. (2) A piano with bells instead of strings. (3) A melody to be played on a set of bells ; or any instrumental imitation thereof. (4) An organ stop (mixture, tuned bells, metal bars, &c.).

Carillonneur *(F.).* A player on a carillon.

CARIS'SIMI, Giacomo. *B.* nr. Rome, abt. 1604 ; *d.* 1674. Maestro from 1628, Church of St. Apollinare, Rome. One of the most distinguished of early composers in the *new style* initiated by Caccini and Peri.
Works : 5 oratorios (including *Jephtha*, his finest work) ; motets, masses, *Arie da Camera*, &c.

Carità *(I.).* Charity, affection. *Con carità,* with tenderness.

CARL, William C. American concert organist ; *b.* Bloomfield, New Jersey, 1865.

CARLEZ, Jules A. Composer ; *b.* Caen, 1836.

CARLYLE, Thos. 1795-1881. " The Sage of Chelsea." Translated Luther's " Ein' Feste Burg " (" A safe stronghold ").

Carmagnole *(F.).* A dance and song dating from about 1792, very popular in Paris during the Reign of Terror.

Car'men *(L. & G.).* A tune, song, or poem.

CARMEN. Opera by Bizet, 1875.

CARMICHAEL, Mary Grant. Contemporary pianist and composer ; *b.* Birkenhead.
She has written an operetta and several songs, &c.

CARNABY, Dr. Wm. London, 1772-1839.
Wrote anthems, songs, glees, a Singing Primer, &c.

CARNICER, Ramon. *B.* Catalonia, 1789 ; *d.* 1855. Conductor Royal Opera, Madrid, 1828-30 ; Professor at the Cons. 1830-54.
Carnicer was one of the creators of the *Zarzuela*, or Spanish national opera. He also wrote symphonies, church music, songs, &c.

Carol. (1) To sing, to warble. (2) A joyous song celebrating Christmas or Easter.

Caro'la *(I.).* A circle-dance, with song.

Carola're *(I.).* To carol, to warble.

CARON, Rose Lucille *(née* **Meuniez).** Famous French operatic soprano ; *b.* 1857. Professor Paris Cons., 1902.

CARPA'NI, Giuseppe A. 1752-1825. Court poet at Vienna.
Wrote *La Haydine* (a eulogy on the works of Haydn), and several opera libretti.

CARPENTER, Nettie. Violinist ; *b.* New York, 1865.

CARPENTIER. (See **Le Carpentier.**)

CARPENTRAS' (Il Carpentras'so). Real name **Eleazar Genet.** Abt. 1475-1532. Maestro in the Pontifical Chapel, Rome.
Works : Masses, lamentations, hymns, motets, &c.

CAR'PI, Fernando. Tenor ; *b.* Florence, 1878.

CARR, Frank Osmond. *B.* nr. Bradford, 1858. Mus. Doc. Oxon, 1891.
Works : comic operas, *His Excellency, My Girl*, &c.

Carrée *(F.).* A breve.

CARRE'ÑO, Teresa. One of the foremost living lady pianists ; *b.* Caracas, Venezuela, 1853. She composed the Venezuelan National Anthem.

CARRO'DUS, John Tiplady. Fine violinist and orchestral " leader." *B.* nr. Keighley, Yorks, 1836 ; *d.* London, 1895.

CARROLL, Walter. *B.* Higher Broughton, Manchester, 1869. Mus. Doc. Manchester, 1900. Lecturer, Training Coll. Dept., Manchester Univ., 1892. Examiner for Mus. Degrees, Vict. Univ., 1904, &c.

CARSE, Adam von Ahn. Composer ; *b.* Newcastle, 1878.

Cartelle *(F.).* A sheet, a leaf.
" A large sheet of ass's-skin prepared for the purpose, on which are drawn the lines of the scale, for the benefit of marking thereon everything necessary for composition, and rubbing it out at pleasure with a spunge. . . With a cartel, a diligent composer may be supplied for ever, and spare many quires of ruled paper."
—*Rousseau.*

CARTER, Henry. *B.* London, 1837. Went to Canada (abt. 1854), where he has gained much distinction as an organist and composer.

CARTER, Thomas. *B.* Dublin, 1734 ; *d.* London, 1804. Settled in London, 1772.
Works : many popular songs (sung at Vauxhall and elsewhere), and " musical comedies " (*The Rival Candidates, The Constant Maid*, &c.).
On his ballad "Guardian Angels" was founded the hymn-tune *Helmsley.*

CARTER, Wm. *B.* London, 1838. Founded " Carter's Choir," 1871.
Works : Cantata *(Placida)*, anthems, songs, &c.

CARTIER, Jean B. Violinist ; pupil of Viotti. *B.* Avignon, 1765 ; *d.* 1841.
Works : " L'Art du Violon " (1801) ; operas, sonatas, violin pieces, &c.

CARUL'LI, Ferdinando. *B.* Naples, 1770 ; *d.* Paris, 1841. Self-taught guitar player. " His original method is the basis of modern guitar playing."
Wrote about 400 concertos, fantasias, solos, &c., and a Guitar Method, &c.

CARUL'LI, Gustavo. Son of F. ; *b.* Leghorn, 1800 ; *d.* 1877. Teacher of singing.
Wrote a "Méthode de Chant," an opera, vocal exercises, &c.

CARU'SO, Enrico. Eminent tenor ; *b.* Naples, 1873.

CARU'SO, Luigi. *B.* Naples, 1754 ; *d.* 1821.
Wrote 69 operas ; 5 oratorios, and much other church music.

CARVAL'HO (CARVAILLE), Léon. *B.* 1825 ; *d.* Paris, 1897. Renowned Parisian opera manager ; Vaudeville (1872-4), Opéra Comique (from 1885), &c. In 1853 he married Mlle. Miolan, known as

CARVAL'HO-MIOLAN, Caroline M. F. Famous dramatic soprano ; *b.* Marseilles, 1827 ; *d.* 1895. Pupil Paris Cons. at the age of 12.
She was an immense favourite at the French opera houses.

CARY, Annie Louise. Celebrated American contralto ; *b.* Wayne (U.S.), 1842.
Has sung in Brussels, London, St. Petersburg, and all the leading cities of America.

CARY-ELWES, Gervase H. Tenor vocalist ; *b.* Billing, Nth. Hants, 1866.

CARYLL, Ivan (real name Felix Tilkins). Composer ; *b.* Liége, 1861.

CASALS, Pablo. 'Cellist ; *b.* Vendrell, 1876.

CASE, Geo. Tinkler. Wrote instruction books, &c., for English concertina, from 1848-60.

CASEL'LA, Pietro. 1769-1843. Italian composer ; wrote several operas, produced at Naples and Rome.

Cas'sa, or Cas'sa gran'de *(I.).* The bass drum.

Cas'sa armo'nica *(I.).* The body (of a violin, &c.).

Cassation', Kassation' *(G.)* ⎱ A serenade com-
Cassazio'ne *(I.)* ⎰ prising several movements.

Castanets. *(I., Castagnet'te ; F., Castagnettes ; S., Castanue'las ; G., Kastagnel'ten.)*
A pair of small concave pieces of wood or ivory used to give a " clicking " accompaniment to a dance or song.

CASTEL, Louis B. Jesuit priest ; *b.* Montpellier, 1688 ; *d.* 1757.
Attempted to construct a " Clavecin Oculaire " to represent colour harmonies, &c. (See *Colour and Music.*)

CASTELLAN, Jeanne Anaïs. Distinguished French soprano singer ; *b.* Beaujeu, 1819.

CASTELMA'RY (Comte Armand de Castan). Baritone singer ; *b.* Toulouse, 1834 ; *d.* New York, 1897.
His *Mephistopheles* in *Faust* was particularly good.

CASTIL-BLAZE. (See *Blaze.*)

CASTLES, Amy. Celebrated Australian soprano. *B.* abt. 1884.
Début in London, 1902.

Castrat' *(G.),* **Castra'to** *(I.).* A eunuch.

CASTRUC'CI, Pietro. *B.* Rome, 1689 ; *d.* Dublin, 1752. Leading violin in Handel's opera orchestra, London, 1715.
He had a great reputation as player on the *violetta marina*, a kind of *viol d' amore* of his own invention. His brother, *Prospero*, published 6 violin sonatas, 1739.

Cäsur' *(G.).* Caesura *(q.v.).*

CATALA'NI, Alfredo. *B.* Lucca, 1854 ; *d.* Milan, 1893. Pupil Paris Cons., 1868. Prof. of composition, Milan Cons., 1886.
Works : operas, *Dejanire* (1883), *Loreley* (1890), *La Wally* (1892), and others ; orch. pieces ; songs, chamber-music, &c.

CATALA'NI, Angelica. Brilliant soprano singer ; *b.* Sinigaglia, 1780 ; *d.* Paris, 1849. After singing at Venice, Florence, Milan, Lisbon, Paris, &c., she came to London, 1806, where a single year's engagements brought her £16,700. She sang for the last time in England at the York Festival, 1828 ; and at Belfast, June, 1829.
She excelled in *bravura* singing, having a voice of marvellous flexibility, and compass up to—

Catch. A humorous round.
The catch is so contrived that ludicrous effects are produced by the singers *catching* at each other's words.

Catch Club. Founded 1761.
Many celebrated glees, &c., have been composed for this club.

CATEL, Charles S. *B.* L'Aigle, 1773 ; *d.* Paris, 1830. Prof. of harm., Paris Cons., 1795.
Works : "Traité d'Harmonie" (1802) ; 11 operas ; festival cantatas, &c.

CATELA'NI, Angelo. *B.* Guastalla, 1811 ; *d.* 1866. Town Maestro Correggio, 1837. Maestro Modena Court and Cathedral, 1838.
Works : several valuable books on mus. history.

Cate'na di tril'li *(I.).* A chain of shakes.

CA'TENHAUSEN, Ernst. Condr. and composer ; *b.* Ratzeburg, 1841.

Catgut. The material—from the intestines of sheep and horses—of which strings for the violin, &c., are made.

Cathedral Music. Music specially composed for the services of the Church of England since the Reformation.
The most important collections of cathedral music are those of Arnold, Barnard, Boyce, and Tudway (MS).

CATLEY, Anne. *B.* nr. Tower Hill, 1745 ; *d.* 1789. Favourite singer at Vauxhall and Marylebone Gardens, and Covent Garden Theatre.

Catlings. The smallest size lute strings.

CATRU'FO, Guiseppe. *B.* Naples, 1771 ; *d.* London, 1851.
Works : 14 operas ; a Méthode de Vocalisation ; church music ; songs, pf. pieces, &c.

Catti'vo *(I.).* Bad. *Catti'vo tem'po,* a weak beat of a bar.

Cau'da *(L.).* The tail or stem of a note.

CAVAILLÉ-COLL, Aristide. Celebrated French organ builder ; 1811-99. Invented the harmonic flutes, and made many other improvements in organ construction.

CAVALIE'RI, Emilio del. Roman nobleman, abt. 1550-99. One of the inventors of the new style of composition (See **Bardi, Caccini,** and **Peri**) called the *tilo rappresentativo,* which in attempting to revive the ancient Greek system led to the birth of modern music. His chief work, *La Rappresentazione di Anima e di Corpo* (Rome, 1600), is regarded as the " first oratorio." The "orchestra" used to accompany this work consisted of a lira doppia, a harpsichord, a chittarone, and two flutes.

The new *homophonic* music—a melody with accompanying harmonies—was necessarily crude when compared with the *polyphonic* music of the "Golden Age of counterpoint" which immediately preceded it (1500 - 1600). Bach was the first really great composer who successfully fused the two styles.

CAVALIE'RI, Katherina. *B.* nr. Vienna, 1761 ; *d.* 1801. Mozart thought very highly of her singing, and wrote much music especially for her.

Cavallet'ta *(I.).* (See **Cabalet'ta.**)

Cavalet'to *(I.).* "A little horse." (1) A little bridge. (2) The break in the voice. (See **Break.**)

CAVAL'LI, Francesco (real name **P. F. Caletti-Bruni**). *B.* Crema, abt. 1600 ; *d.* Venice, 1676. Pupil of Monteverde ; distinguished composer of the new school. (See **Cavalieri.**) Maestro St. Mark's, Venice, 1668.

Works : 41 operas, including *Giasone* (Venice, 1649), *Serse* (Venice, 1654), and *Ercole amante* (1662) ; a fine Requiem, church music, &c.

CAVALLI'NI, Ernesto. Milan, 1807-73. Called the "Paganini of the clarinet."

CAVAL'LO, Peter. Parisian organist. *B.* Munich, 1819 ; *d.* Paris, 1892.

Cavalquet *(F.).* A cavalry trumpet signal.

Cava'ta *(I.).* (1) Production of tone. (2) A cavatina.

Cavati'na *(I.).* (1) A short simple song. (2) Specially, a melody of one movement only (occasionally preceded by a recitative) without a 2nd strain and *Da Capo*. (3) Name given by Beethoven to the 2nd movement of his B♭ string quartet. (No. 13, Op. 130.)

CAVENDISH, Michael. One of the ten contributors to Este's Psalter, 1592. Published a set of "Ayres for 4 voices," 1599.

Cavi'glia *(I.).* Peg of a vn., &c.

CAVOS, Catterino. *B.* Venice, 1775. Went to St. Petersburg, 1798 ; Court Conductor, 1799 ; *d.* there, 1840.

Works : *Ivan Sussanina* (1799), and 12 other Russian operas ; 2 Italian operas ; ballets, &c.

C barré *(F.).* "Barred **C**," 𝄵.

Cebell. (1) A theme in $\frac{4}{4}$ time, characterized by the alternation of high and low notes, formerly used for "variations" on the lute or violin. (2) A gavotte.

CECI'LIA, St. A Christian martyr, Rome, 230. She is regarded as the patron saint of music, and is the legendary inventor of the organ.

Cécilium *(F.).* A free-reed keyboard instrument of the melodeon kind.

C clef. (See **Clef.**)

CEDERSTRÖM, Baroness. (See **Adelina Patti.**)

Cédez *(F.).* *Diminuendo* (or *rallentando*).

Ce'lere *(I.).* Swift, rapid, nimble.

Celerità, Con *(I.)* ⎱ With speed. Quickly and
Celeramen'te *(I.)* ⎰ easily.

Celesta. (1) A characteristic stop in the "Mustel" organ. (2) A keyboard instrument in which steel plates are struck by hammers.

Céleste *(F.).* "Celestial." An organ stop with a sweet veiled tone.

Pedale Céleste. A special "soft" pedal on some pianos.

Voix Céleste. Vox Angelica. Org. or harm. stop.

CELESTI'NO, Eligio. *B.* Rome, 1739 ; *d.* 1812. Fine violinist.

Lived in London abt. 1790. Pub. sonatas for violin and bass, &c.

'Cel'li *(I.).* Violoncelli.

CELLIER, Alfred. *B.* Hackney, 1844 ; *d.* 1891. Conductor Opera Comique, London, 1877-9 ; joint conductor with Sir A. Sullivan, Covent Garden Promenade Concerts, 1878-9.

Works : *Nell Gwynne, Dorothy* (1886), *The Mountebanks* (1892), *The Sultan of Mocha,* and several other popular operettas ; a symphonic suite ; songs, &c.

'Cel'lo *(I.).* Violoncello.

Cem'balist. *(I., Cembalis'ta.)* A player on the cembalo, harpsichord, or piano.

Cem'balo *(I.).* (1) A dulcimer. (2) A harpsichord, clavier, clavichord, &c. (3) A pianoforte.

A cem'balo. For harpsichord, &c. (see above)
Tut'to il cem'balo. Same as *Tutte corde.*

Cembanel'la, Cennamel'la *(I.).* A pipe or flute.

Cen'to *(I.)* ⎱ *(F., Centon).* "Patchwork."
Cento'ne *(I.)* ⎰ A medley, or *pasticcio,* made up of extracts from another work, or another composer.

CENTO'LA, Ernesto. Violinist ; *b.* Salerno, 1862.

Cercar' la no'ta *(I.).* "To seek the note." To feel for a note by slurring up to it in the style of a *portamento.*

CERO'NE, Domenico P. *B.* Bergamo, abt. 1566.

Pub. "Regole per il Canto Fermo" (1609), and other treatises.

CERRE'TO, Scipione. Lutenist and composer ; Naples, 1551-1632 (?).

Pub. works on musical theory, &c.

Certo,-a *(I.).* Certain, sure.

CERTON, Pierre. 16th century Parisian contrapuntist.

Works : masses, motets, psalms, chansons, and magnificats.

Cervalet', Cervelet'. An old reed wind instrument, similar in tone to the bassoon.

CERVENY, V. F. Bohemian inventor and improver of brass instruments, 1819-96.

His celebrated instruments are used in the Russian, German, and Austrian military bands.

CERVETTI. (See **Gelinek.**)

CERVETTO, Giacamo (real name **Bassevi**). Celebrated 'cellist ; *b.* Italy, 1682. Came to London, 1728 ; *d.* there, 1783. Manager of Drury Lane Theatre.

CERVETTO, James. Son of G. *B.* London, abt. 1749 ; *d.* 1837. Fine 'cellist.

Pub. pieces for violin and 'cello.

Ces *(G.).* The note C♭.

CESBRON, Suzanne C, Soprano ; *b.* Paris, 1879.

Ces dur *(G.)*. The key of C♭ major.

Ces'es *(G.)*. C♭♭.

CE'SI, Beniamino. Contemporary pianist ; *b.* Naples, 1845. Professor at the Cons. since 1866.

CES'TI, Marc Antonio. Franciscan monk ; *b.* Arezzo, 1620 ; *d.* Venice, 1669. Pupil of Carissimi. Did much to advance dramatic music in Italy.
Works : several successful operas, *Orontea* (Venice, 1649), *La Dori* (1663), *Il pomo d'oro* (Vienna, 1666), &c. ; cantatas, madrigals, songs.

Cesu'ra *(L.)*. (See **Cæsura**.)

Ce'tera, Ce'tra *(I.)*. A Cither or guitar.

Ch. Choir organ.

CHABRIER, Alexis E. *B.* Auvergne, 1842 ; *d.* Paris, 1894. Chorusmaster under Lamoureux, 1881.
Works : operas, *Gwendoline* (1886), *Le Roi malgré lui* (1887) ; operettas, scenas, pf. pieces, &c

Chacone. *(F., Chaconne ; S., Chaco'na ; I., Ciacco'na.)* (1) A slow dance in ¾ time. (2) A set of variations on a ground bass (8 measures in length) in rather slow ¾ time ; similar to the *Passacaglia.*

CHADFIELD, Ed. *B.* Derby, 1827. Secretary I.S.M., 1885-1907. *D.* 1908.

CHADWICK, George Whitfield. American composer ; *b.* Lowell, Mass., 1854. Dir. New England Cons. of Music, Boston.
Works : comic opera, *Tabasco* ; 3 symphonies ; overtures, chamber music, songs, several choral ballads, pf. music, &c.

Chair Organ. Choir organ, or Prestant.

Chalameau *(E.)*. *(F., Chalumeau ; G., Chalümau, Chalamaus ; I., Scialumò, Salmò.)* From Latin *calamus,* a reed. (1) Any reed pipe—as *Shawm, Pan's-pipe, Chanter* (of a bag-pipe). (2) The lower register of the clarinet and basset-horn.

Chal., or **Chalameau.** In clarinet playing, " an octave lower." *Clar.* or *Clarinet,* " play as written." (See **Clarinet.**)

Chaleur *(F.)*. Warmth, fervour.
Chaleureusement. Warmly, fervently.

CHALLINOR, Fredk. A. Composer ; *b.* Longton, Staffs., 1866. Mus.D. Durham, 1903.

CHAMBERLAIN, Houston S. *B.* Portsmouth, 1855. Author of "Richard Wagner" (1892), &c.

Chamber Music. Instrumental quartets, quintets, sextets, &c., suitable for performance in a chamber or small hall—as opposed to concert music, operatic music, &c.
Also applied to vocal music of similar character. Originally applied to all music not for the church or theatre.

Chamber Organ. (1) A cabinet organ. (2) Any organ for "chamber" use (as opposed to "Church" and "Concert" organs.

CHAMBONNIÈRES, Jacques C. (Known as **Champion de Chamb**). Celebrated cembalist and teacher ; 17th cent. Chamber cembalist to Louis XIV.

CHAMINADE, Cécile L. S. Composer of songs and pf. pieces ; *b.* Paris, 1861.
She is also a fine pianist, and has composed some orchestral and chamber music.

CHAMPEIN, Stanislas. Operatic composer ; *b.* Marseilles, 1753 ; *d.* Paris, 1830.
Works : 22 operas (*La Mélomanie, Les Dettes,* &c.) ; operettas ; sacred music, &c.

Champêtre *(F.)*. Rustic, pastoral.

Chang. A Persian harp.

Change. (1) A change of key—diatonic, chromatic, or enharmonic. (2) The mutation or breaking of the voice at puberty. (3) A variation in ringing a peal of bells.
Changeable Chant. A chant which by changing the key-signature may be sung in either the major or minor mode.
Changer de jeu (F.). To change the stops (organ or harmonium).

Change ringing. ⎱ The number of possible changes
Changes. ⎰ on a peal of 5 bells is 1 × 2 × 3 × 4 × 5 = 120 ; on 7 bells, 1 × 2 × 3 × 4 × 5 × 6 × 7 = 5,040, &c.

Changing Note. *(G., Wech'selnote, Durch'ganston, Durch'gehende No'te ; F., No'te d'appoggiature ; I., Nota Cambia'ta.)* (1) A dissonant passing-note on a strong (or medium) beat. (2) The 3rd note in the passages

&c., allowed by Macfarren and others in strict counterpoint. Many theorists, however, forbid changing-notes.

CHANOT, François. French naval engineer ; 1787-1823. Invented a new shape violin which for some time was claimed to be equal to a "Strad."

Chanson *(F.)*. (1) A simple ballad song. (2) A *lied* (solo with pf. accompaniment). (3) A part-song.

Chansonette *(F.)*. A little chanson ; a canzonet.

Chansonnier *(F.)*. (1) A composer of chansons. (2) A collection of songs.

Chant. (1) (See **Gregorian**.) (2) Cantus firmus. (3) *Anglican* chant ; a short composition used in chanting the Psalms and Canticles.
The first note of each phrase is called the *reciting note,* which is continued *ad lib.* to suit the words, and followed by a *cadence* in strict time. The arrangement of the words and syllables is called *pointing.*

Single Chant :

Double Chant :

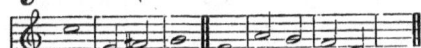

Triple Chant : 3 times the length of a single chant.
Quadruple Chant : 4 times the length of a single chant.

Chant *(F.)*. (1) A song or tune. (2) The principal melody. (3) Singing.
Chant composé. Plain-song.
Chant d'Eglise, or *Grégorien.* Gregorian chant.
Chant de Noel. A Christmas carol.

Chant du soir. An evening song.
Chant en ison, or *chant égal.* An old form of chant restricted to 2 tones (as F and G).
Chant figuré. Florid counterpoint.
Chant pastoral. A shepherd's song, or an imitation of one.
Chant royal. The mode or tone in which the prayer for the Sovereign is chanted.
Chant sur le livre. "A barbarous kind of improvised counterpoint"—or descant—sung by one body of singers to accompany the plain-song sung by the others.
Chantant *(F.).* In a singing, melodious style; *c.f., Café chantant,* a concert restaurant.
Chanter. (1) A singer. (2) A lay vicar. (3) The melody pipe of the bagpipes.
Chanter *(F.).* To sing.
Chanter à livre ouvert. To sing at sight.
Chanterelle. The soprano or highest string. Especially the E string of the violin.
Chanteur. A male singer.
Chanteuse. A female singer.
Chantre. A chanter; a precentor.
Chantey, Chanty. A sailors' song.
Chapeau *(F.).* "A hat." Name sometimes given to a " tie."
Chapel. *(F., Chapelle; I., Cappel'la; G., Kapel'le, Capel'le.)* The choir or orchestra (or both) of a church or other musical establishment.
The *Maître de Chapelle, Maestro di Cappella, Kapell'meister,* or *Capell'meister,* is the director (and generally the conductor) of the music. *Cap'pella pontifica'le :* the whole body of singers, &c., in the Pope's service.
CHAPPELL, Wm. *B.* London, 1809; *d.* 1888. Compiled a valuable collection of old English melodies—"Popular Music of the Olden Time," &c.
CHAPPELL & CO. Music publishers; founded 1812.
CHAPPLE, Samuel. *B.* Crediton, 1775; *d.* 1833. Organist and pianist; blind from infancy.
Works: 3 sonatas for violin and pf.; 18 anthems in score; psalm-tunes, songs, &c.
CHAPUIS, Auguste P. J. B. *B.* France, 1862. Pupil Paris Cons.; Professor of Harmony, 1894; Inspector-general of music in the Paris schools, 1895.
Works: operas and lyric dramas; oratorio, *Les sept paroles du Christ;* masses; suites, fantasias, &c., for orchestra; songs, choruses, &c.
Chaque *(F.).* Each, every.
Chaque attaque assez en dehors. Each attack (entry) well-emphasized.
CHAR, F. E. *B.* Cleve-on-Rhein, 1865; Opera conductor, Ulm, 1899.
Works: successful opera, *Der Schelm von Bergen* (1895); a pf. concerto and other pieces for pf.; choral works, &c.
Character of Keys. (See **Key Colour.**)
Characteristic piece. A piece characterised by some particular rhythm, style, or mood.
Characteristic tone } (1) The leading-
Characteris'tischer Ton *(G.)* } note. (2) Especially the new leading-note at a change of key. (3) Also used by Mr. Curwen for the new *fah* in flat removes.
Characters. General name for musical signs—notes, rests, &c.
Charak'terstimme (G.) A solo stop (organ).
Charak'terstück (G.). A characteristic piece.

CHARD, Dr. Geo. Wm. *B.* London, 1795; *d.* 1849. Mus.Doc. Cantab., 1812. Composed anthems, glees, &c.
Char'freitag *(G.).* Good Friday.
Charivari *(F.).* Mock music. (See **Callithumpian.**)
CHARKE, Rd. *B.* abt. 1695(?); *d.* Jamaica, abt. 1740. Said to be the first who wrote "Medley" overtures.
CHARPENTIER, Gustave. *B.* Lorraine, 1860. Studied Paris Cons.
Works: orchestral suite, *Impressions d'Italie; Louise,* musical romance in 4 acts, 1900—his most important work; and several other orchestral and dramatic pieces.
CHARPENTIER, Marc Antoine. Paris, 1634-1702. Pupil of Carissimi. Though considered superior in learning to Lully, he was overshadowed by the latter's position and influence.
Works: 16 operas (*Médée,* 1693, &c.); "tragédies spirituelles;" masses, motets, &c.
Chasse *(F.).* The chase. *À la chasse,* same as *alla caccia* (*q.v.*).
CHATTERTON, John B. Eminent harpist; *b.* abt. 1802; *d.* London, 1871.
CHAUMET, Wm. *B.* Bordeaux, 1842; *d.* 1903.
Works: comic operas, dramatic poems, orch. music, pf. pieces, &c.
Chaunter. (See **Chanter.**)
CHAUSSON, Ernest. Paris, 1855-1899.
Works: 3 symphonic poems, symphony in B♭, and other orch. pieces; chamber music, org. and pf. solos; some charming songs, &c.
CHAUVET, Chas. A. *B.* Marnes, 1837; *d.* 1871. Orgt. Église de la Ste.-Trinité, Paris, 1869. Renowned for his org. improvisations; pub. several org. pieces.
CHAVAN'NE, Irene von. Contralto; *b.* Gratz, abt. 1867.
Che *(I.).* Than; that, which, who.
Chef *(F.).* Chief.
Chef-d'attaque. The leader of an orchestra, chorus, &c.
Chef-d'œuvre. The masterpiece; chief work.
Chef-d'orchestre. (1) The leading 1st violin; or (2) The conductor.
Chef du chant. Trainer or conductor of an opera chorus.
CHELARD, Hippolyte A. J. B. *B.* Paris, 1789; *d.* Weimar, 1861. Took *Grand Prix de Rome,* Paris Cons., 1811. Court Capellmeister, Munich, 1828; conducted the German Opera, London, 1832-3; Court Capellmeister, Weimar, 1836-50.
Works: operas, *Macbeth* (1827), *Der Student, Mitternacht, Die Hermannsschlacht* (Munich, 1835—his best), and others.
Chelys *(Gk.* "Tortoise"). (1) The fabled lyre of Mercury. (2) Old name for the bass-viol and division-viol.
Cheng. The Chinese mouth-organ. Said to be the parent of the accordion and harmonium.
CHERRY, John Wm. London, 1824-89. Composed "Will-o'-the-Wisp" and other songs.
Cherubical Hymn. The *ter sanctus,* or *trisagion* in the Communion Service, "Holy, holy, holy," &c.

CHERUBI'NI, Maria Luigi C. Z. S. Distinguished composer and theorist; *b.* Florence, Sep. 14, 1760; *d.* Paris, Mar. 15, 1842. Pupil of Sarti, Milan, 1779. Visited London, 1784 and 1815. Professor of composition, Paris Cons., 1816. Director, 1821-41.
Cherubini was a master of counterpoint, and in his opera *Lodoïska* he initiated a fresh, vigorous, rich style of composition which revolutionized French opera.
Works: *Ifigenia in Aulide* (1788), *Lodoïska* (1791), *Médée* (1797), *Les deux journées* (1800), *Anacréon* (1803), *Faniska* (1806), and 23 other operas; 17 cantatas; 11 solemn masses; 2 requiems; much other sacred music of all kinds; orch. music; chamber music; pf. music; songs, romances, &c. His "Treatise on Counterpoint" is a standard work.

CHESHIRE, John. Distinguished harpist; *b.* Birmingham, 1839.

Chest of viols. A set of 6 viols—2 trebles, 2 tenors, 2 basses—necessary for a "consort of viols" (17th century).

Chest register } The lower register of a male
Chest voice } or female voice. (See
Chest tone } **Register.**)

CHETHAM (or CHEETHAM), Rev. John. 1700(?)-1763. Published "Chetham's Psalmody," 1718.

Chevalet *(F.).* The bridge (of a violin, &c.).

CHEVALIER, Albert Onesime Britannicus Gwathveoyd Louis. "The Coster's Laureate," "The Kipling of the music-hall;" *b.* Notting Hill, 1862. His brother **Auguste** writes most of his music (under the *nom de plume* of Chas. Ingle).

CHEVÉ, Emile Jos. M. Physician; *b.* Douarnenez, Finistère, 1804; *d.* 1864.

CHEVÉ, or Galin - Paris - Chevé System. A method of teaching sight-singing by means of figures, much used in France.
The idea was advocated by Rousseau (1712-1778). It was developed practically by Pierre Galin (1786-1821), and zealously promulgated by Aimé Paris (1799-1866). Chevé wrote a complete exposition of the system. The figures are used on a "Tonic basis," 1 always representing the key note, 5 the dominant, &c. Lower octaves are shown by a dot beneath the figure—as 6̲—higher octaves by a dot above—as i̇. Time-duration is shown by dashes and dots as below.

Example of the Chevé Notation, with the corresponding staff notes:

Mr. Curwen adapted the *Taatai* names (and several other features) from the Chevé method in developing the Tonic Sol-fa notation.

CHEVILLARD, Camille. Paris, 1859-1903. Assistant conductor, and afterwards (1897) conductor of the Lamoureux Concerts.
Works: symphonic ballades and poems; chamber music; pf. pieces, &c.

Cheville *(F.).* A peg (for violin, &c.).

Chevrotement *(F.).* Same as **Bockstriller** *(q.v.).*

Chia'ra, Chia'ro *(I.).* Clear, distinct.
Chia'ra vo'ce. A clear pure voice.
Chia'ra quar'ta. A perfect fourth.

Chiaramen'te *(I.).* Clearly, distinctly.

Chiarez'za *(I.).* Clearness, brightness.

Chiari'na *(I).* A trumpet or clarion.

CHIAROMO'NTE, Francesco. *B.* Sicily, 1809; *d.* Brussels, 1886. Professor of singing, Royal Cons., Naples, 1844. Settled in Brussels, 1871; Professor at the Cons.
Works: operas, *Fenicia, Caterina di Cleves,* and 5 others; an oratorio; and a Méthode de Chant.

Chia'roscu'ro *(I.).* Light and shade.

Chia've *(I.).* (1) A clef. (2) A key of an instrument. (3) A tuning-key.
Chia've di Bas'so. Bass clef.
Chia've di Violi'no. Treble (or vn.) clef.

Chi'ca. Ancient Spanish dance; precursor of the *Fandango, Bolero,* and perhaps the *Jig.*

CHICKERING & Sons. Celebrated American pf. makers. Established at Boston, 1823.

Chie'sa *(I.).* A church.
Concer'to da chie'sa. A sacred concert.
Sona'ta da chie'sa. A sacred sonata.
Da chie'sa. In church style.

Chiffre *(F.).* A figure. *Basse chiffrée,* figured bass.

Chi'fla *(S.).* A whistle.

Chifonie *(F.).* Old name for hurdy-gurdy.

Chi'kara. A Hindoo fiddle with 4 or 5 strings.

CHILD, Dr. Wm. *B.* Bristol, 1606; *d.* 1697. Mus.Doc. Oxon, 1663. Chanter, Chapel Royal, 1660; member of the King's band.
Works: a fine Service in D; "Choise Musick to the Psalmes of Dauid," "Divine Anthems;" catches, ayres, &c. Many of his services and anthems are given by Boyce, Arnold, &c.

CHILESOTTI, Oscare. Musical historian. *B.* Bassano, 1848. Writes regularly for the Milan *Gazzetta Musicale.*
Works: "A Collection of Musical Rarities" (4 vols.); Biographical Notes on great Italian musicians from Palestrina to Bellini; Popular Melodies of the 16th century, &c.

CHILLEY, Chas. Tenor; *b.* London, 1857.

Chime. (1) A carillon. (2) To play bells by swinging them only the smallest distance necessary to ensure the striking of the clappers. (3) The bells so played.

Chiming Machine. A machine with a revolving cylinder used for playing chimes.

CHIPP, Edmund Thos. *b.* London, 1823; *d.* Nice, 1886. Mus.Doc. Cantab., 1860. Organist, Ely Cathedral, 1866.
Works: oratorio, *Job;* church music; organ pieces, &c.

Chirogym'nast. A mechanical "finger-trainer;" "a set of rings attached by springs to a cross-bar."

Chi'roplast. An apparatus designed by Logier, abt. 1814, to form the hand by holding it in position at the keyboard. Liszt called it an "ass's guide," and it has long been discarded.

Chitar'ra *(I.).* A guitar.
Chitar'ra col ar'co. A "bowed" guitar.
Chitarra'ta. Pf. piece imitating a guitar.
Chitarri'na. Small Neapolitan guitar.
Chitarro'ne. A large guitar. (See *Theorbo.*)

Chiuden'do *(I.).* Closing ; ending with.

Chiu'so,-a *(I.).* Closed ; hidden, concealed.
Cano'ne chiu'so. Enigmatical canon.
Con boc'ca chiu'so. With closed lips; humming.

CHLAD'NI, E. F. F. Physicist; *b.* Wittenberg, 1756 ; *d.* 1827.
He was a renowned acoustician, and discovered the "Tonfiguren," or patterns produced by sand on a vibrating plate.

Chœur *(F.).* Chorus ; choir. À *grand chœur,* for full chorus.

Choice Notes. Optional notes *(q.v.).*

Choir. *(Old E., Quire ; G., Chor ; F., Chœur; I., Co'ro.)* (1) A company of singers. (2) The part of a church set apart for the choir. (3) A choral society. (4) The choristers and officiating singing priests—divided into *Decani* and *Cantoris.*

Choir organ *(Chair organ).* That part of a large organ containing the quieter stops suitable to accompany the choir, or a solo, &c.

CHOPIN, François Frédéric. *B.* nr. Warsaw, Feb. 22, 1810 ; *d.* Paris, Oct. 17, 1849. Played the pf. in public at the age of 9. In 1829 he played in Vienna, where he was described as a "player of the first rank." Settled in Paris, 1831. Visited London, 1848-9. His playing was of the utmost delicacy and refinement, with perhaps an excess of *tempo rubato,* and a certain "melancholy tint in his shading." His pf. solo compositions are world-renowned for their exquisite charm and wonderful "incarnation of the soul of the piano." His pf. concertos, pieces for pf. with other instruments, songs, &c., were comparative failures.
Works for pf. solo : *Allegro de Concert* (Op, 46), 4 Ballades, Barcarolle (Op. 60), Berceuse (Op. 57), Boléro (Op. 19), 3 Écossaises, 27 Études, 4 Fantasies, 3 Impromptus, *Marche Funèbre* (Op. 72), 52 Mazurkas, 19 Nocturnes, 11 Polonaises, 25 Preludes, 13 Valses, Variations, Rondos, Scherzos, Sonatas, &c.

Chor *(G.).* (1) Chorus ; choir. (2) A family of instruments of the same tone, as *Trompetenchor.*
Chor'-amt. Choral; choral service.

Chora'gus, Chore'gus *(L. from Gk.).* (1) The chorus leader in ancient Greek drama. (2) A musical official, Oxford University.

Chor'al. (1) Pertaining to a choir. (2) Anything sung in chorus.
Choral Service. A church service mainly musical.

Chor'al. *(G., Choral*—plu. *Chorä'le; F., Cantique, Plain-chant; I., Can'tico, Canzo'ne Sa'cra.)* A hymn-tune ; especially the Protestant hymn-tunes of the Reformation period.
In Germany it is also used for the Catholic plain-song.

Chora'leon. (See **Æolodicon.**)

Chora'liter *(L.)* } In the style of a choral.
Choral'mässig *(G.)* }

Choral music. Vocal part-music.

CHORAL SYMPHONY. Beethoven's 9th Symphony ; produced 1824.

Chord. (1) A combination of two or more sounds, consonant or dissonant. (See **Harmony.**) (2) A string.
Triad. A chord consisting of any note with its 3rd and 5th, as C, E, and G *(d, m,* and *s).*
Common chord. A triad with a *perfect* 5th (and a major or minor 3rd).
Major chord. A common chord with its 3rd major.
Minor chord. A common chord with its 3rd minor.
Altered chord. (See under *A.*)
Anomalous chord. (See under *A.*)
Augmented chord. A triad with an augmented 5th as C, E, G♯ *(d, m, se).*
Broken chord. (See under B.)
Chromatic chord. A chord with one or more notes altered chromatically.
Derivative chord. An inversion of a chord.
Diatonic chord. (See *Diatonic.*)
Diminished chord. A triad with a diminished 5th.
Doubtful or equivocal chord. A chord susceptible of various resolutions, as the chord of the dim. 7th.
Fundamental chord. (See under *F.*)
Imperfect, or *incomplete chord.* A chord with one of its notes omitted.
Inverted chord. (See *Inversion.*)
Transmutation chord. (See under *T.*)

Chord of Nature. A fundamental tone and its series of upper partials. (See **Acoustics.**)

Chor'da *(L.).* A chord, string, or tone.

Chor'da Characteris'tica *(L.).* A chord containing the leading-note ; especially the dominant 7th.

Chor'dæ essentia'les. The tonic triad.

Chordom'eter. A gauge for measuring the thickness of strings.

Chör'e *(G.).* Plural of *Chor*—choirs, choruses.

Chor'ee, Chore'us. Same as **Trochee** *(q.v.).*

Choriam'bus (Cho'riamb). A metrical foot : long, short, short, long (— ∪ ∪ —).

Chorist' *(G.)* } A singer in a choir. *(Old E., Quirister,* or *Choirister.)*
Choriste *(F.)* }
Chorister *(E.)* }

CHORLEY, Henry F. *B.* Lancashire, 1808 ; *d.* 1872. Musical critic, *Athenæum,* 1833-71.
Wrote "Thirty Years' Musical Recollections," "Music in France and Germany." Bitter opponent of Schumann and Wagner.

CHORON, Alexandre Étienne. *B.* Caen, 1772 ; *d.* Paris, 1834. Distinguished theorist and compiler. Director Grand Opéra, 1816-17. Established the "Institution Royale de Musique Classique et Religieuse," 1824. Versatile, but unstable.
Works : "Principes d'accompagnement" of the Italian schools, "Principes de Composition," ditto, "Encylopédie Musicale" (8 vols.), "Méthode de plain-chant," trans. of Albrechtsberger's works, &c. His writings "exercised a very useful influence on musical education in France."—*Grove's Dict.*

Chor'sänger *(G.).* Chorister ; vicar choral.

Chor'schüler *(G.).* Choir scholar ; choir boy.

Chor'stimmen *(G.).* Chorus parts.

Cho'rus. *(G., Chor ; F., Chœur; I., Co'ro.)* (1) A company of singers. (2) The choir, as distinct from the soloists and players. (3) A composition—or a part of one—to be sung by a choir. (4) A refrain—as the chorus of a song or ballad. (5) The "mixture" and other compound stops on the organ.

Double chorus. A chorus for two choirs, either singing together or in alternation.

Chorus-master. Leading singer ; precentor.

CHOUDENS, Antony. Paris, 1849-1902.
Works: 2 operas, songs, pf. pieces, &c.

CHOUQUET, Adolphe G. *B.* Havre, 1819 ; *d.* 1886. Music teacher in America, 1840-60 ; afterwards in Paris.
Wrote a "History of Music in France from its origin to the present time " (1873).

Chris'te ele'ison *(Gk.).* Part of the *Kyrie.* (See **Mass.**)

CHRISTIA'NI, Adolf F. Pianist ; pupil of Liszt ; 1836-1885.
Wrote "Expression in Pianoforte Playing."

CHRISTMANN, Joh. F. *B.* Ludwigsburg, 1752 ; *d.* 1817.
Works: "A Collection of Hymns and Chorals," pieces for pf., violin, &c.

Christmas Carols. Joyous songs for Christmas-tide.
"The Puritans, finding the festive carols of earlier times too joyous, endeavoured to introduce *religious* songs. About the middle of the 17th cent. a vol. appeared, under the title of 'Psalms or Songs of Zion, turned unto the Language, and set to the Tunes of a Strange Land, by W. S. Wm. Slatyr, intended for Christmas carols, and fitted to divers of the most noted and common but solemne Tunes, everywhere familiarly used and knowne.'"—*Moore.*

CHRISTMAS ORATORIO. " A sequence of 6 church cantatas" composed by Bach, 1734.

Chro'ma *(Gk.).* " Colour." (1) A modification of the ancient Greek tetrachord. (2) " A graceful way of singing or playing with quavers and trilloes."—*Grassineau.*

Chroma simplex (L.). A quaver (♪) or a ♯.
Chroma duplex (L.). A semiquaver (♫) or a x.

Chromat'ic. *(G., Chroma'tisch ; F., Chromatique ; I., Croma'tico.)* (1) " Semitonic," from the semitone being marked by a coloured string in some ancient Greek lyres. (2) Any melody or chord containing notes not included in the diatonic scale of the prevalent key. (3) Any note altered chromatically. (See also **Diatonic.**)

Chromatic alteration. Raising or lowering a note by a ♯, ♮, ♭, &c.
Chromatic harmony. Harmony comprising many chromatic chords.
Chromatic Harp. (See *Harp.*)
Chromatic interval. (See *Intervals.*)

Chromatic Chord. A chord containing one or more chromatic notes. When the chords preceding and following a chromatic chord are both in the same key, the chromatic chord is held to be also in that key ; and the chord is said to be " borrowed."

Chromatic Concords.
Macfarren gives the following for key C major:—

(a) Major chord on the minor 2nd of the scale (or key).
(b) 1st inversion : known as the " Neapolitan Sixth."
(c) Major chord on the major 2nd.
(d) Minor chord on the subdominant.
(e) 1st inversion of a diminished triad on the super-tonic.
(f) Major chord on the flattened 6th.
(g) Available in sequences.
To these Prout adds :— and the list is constantly being extended by composers. (See *Harmony.*)

Chromatic Discords. (See **Fundamental Discords.**)

Chromatic Form of the Minor Scale. (See remarks under **Diatonic.**)

Chromatic Scale. A scale proceeding by semitones. (See also **Scale.**)

Harmonic Chromatic Scale.

d r a r ma m f fe s la l ta t d'
Descending by the same notes. (See *Scale.*)

Chromatic Semitone. (See **Interval.**)

Chromatic Signs, or **Chromatics.** General name for the ♮, ♯, ♭, X, ♭♭, &c.
A chromatic sign affects the note before which it is written and every note of the same name *in the same bar ;* thus :—

Here the natural affects *(a), (b),* and *(c),* but not *(d).* If, however, the *last note* of a bar is chromatic and the *next* bar *begins* with the same note, this is also affected ; thus :—

Here the flat affects *(a). (b),* and *(c),* but not *(d).* "Cautionary" accidentals are, however, frequently used in such cases :—

Formerly the accidental was written every time it occurred. (See also *Accidentals.*)

Chromatics, Sol-fa. Sharps : de, re, my, fe, se, le, ty. Flats : du (or da), ra, ma, fu, sa, la, ta. **BAH, BAY** (or ba), major 6th of the minor scale ; be is the sharp of ba.

Chronology of Music. (Early dates are traditional or approximate).

3892 B.C. The " 7 sacred sounds " prescribed in Egyptian music.
3001   Date claimed by Hindus for the composition of the *Rig Veda* (Vedic Hymns).
2300   Invention of the Chinese *King.*
2000   Lyre said to have been invented by Mercury.
1500   Egyptian 11-holed flute.
1500-1100 *Rig Veda* compiled *(Max Müller).*
1450   Oldest extant Egyptian hymns.
1400   Zoroaster writes Persian Gâthas.
1284   Egyptian harp perfected.
1150   Olympus invents Greek Enharmonic system.
1122   Chinese giant drum invented.
1100   Date of the " Lady Maket " Egyptian flutes.
1100-1000 Homeric hymns written.
1055   David wrote Psalms.
1000   Oldest known Chinese book on music.
676   Tyrtaeus, Greek warrior and bard.
640-556 Tisias divided Greek chorus into *Strophe' Antistrophe,* and *Epode,*

638-634 Terpander founded Lesbian School of musicians and poets. [Dithyrambic.
620 Arion is said to have written the first Greek
620 Thaletes appeases the gods by his hymns.
610 Alcman imported the flute into Sparta.
590 Lasos arranged Dithyrambic contests.
584-504 Pythagoras wrote on philosophy and music. Originated the idea of the "Music of the
580 Alcæus, Greek poet and bard. [Spheres."
560 Sappho, "Queen of Greek love-songs."
559 Anacreon, celebrated Greek poet and singer.
550-478 *She King* (Chinese Book of Odes) arranged
535 First Greek tragedy by Thespis. [by Confucius.
527-521 Egyptian music begins to degenerate.
525-456 Æschylus, first of the three great Greek tragic poets.
518-439 Pindar, greatest Greek lyric poet.
495-406 Sophocles, second of the three great Greek tragic poets. [tragic poets.
480-406 Euripides, third of the three great Greek
456 Phrynis, famous Greek lyre player.
446-357 Timotheus added 4 strings to the Greek lyre (making 11).
427-347 Plato wrote treatises on music.
384-322 Aristotle wrote on music.
318 Aristoxenus wrote "Elements of Harmonics."
300 Euclid wrote "Sectio Canonis."
290 Cleanthes wrote the "Hymn to Zeus" quoted by Aratus (270 B.C.), and mentioned by St. Paul, Acts xvii. 28. [organ.
222 Ctesibus said to have invented the hydraulic
50 Diodorus wrote on Egyptian and Greek music.
16-13 Vitruvius wrote on architecture and music.
50 A.D. Aristides Quintilianus wrote "De Musica."
60-139 Ptolemy wrote three books on harmony *(Harmonics)*.
100 Plutarch wrote valuable works on music.
150 Nicomachus wrote "Introduction to Harmony" *(Harmonics)*.
330 Pope Silvester founded music school in Rome.
350 (abt.) St. Basil introduced antiphonal singing, Eastern Church.
360 Alypius translated Greek musical notation.
364 Chinese Emperor, Ngai-Ti, published a decree against effeminate music.
390 St. Ambrose arranged the Authentic Modes.
470 Boethius b.
570 Cassiodorus d.
590-600 Pope Gregory added Plagal modes.
657-672 Organ introduced into churches by Pope Vitalianus.
768-814 Gregory's system propagated by Charlemagne.
790 (abt.) Antiphonarium of St. Gall.
900 (abt.) Discant introduced by Hucbald. Red line used for F. Birth of the staff.
930 Hucbald d.
1020-1030 (abt.) Guido invents his Hexachordal system.
1050 Guido d.
1090 Franco of Cologne invented signs for mensural music *(Forkel)*. Other authorities give 1200.
1100 (onwards). Gradual growth of musical notation.
1150 Crude harmony added to folk-songs and church
1200 Minnesingers in Germany. [music.
1230 "Sumer is a cumen in."
1240-87 Adam de la Hale.
1260 Mehren on Musical Theory.
1290 W. Odington's Treatise on Music. [sonances.
1300 Marchettus of Padua on Consonances and Dis-
1326 (abt.) Robt. de Handlo on Mensural Music.
1330 J. de Meurs (Muris) wrote Florid Counterpoint.
1380 (abt.) Dunstable b.; d. 1453. Introduced passing-notes and suspensions.
1400 Dufay b.
1440 Josquin des Pres b.
1450 Development of Imitative Counterpoint.
1483 Luther b.
1490 Organ Pedals; Bernhardt, Venice.
1500 (abt.) Jean Mouton (Lorraine, 1475-1522) uses the first unprepared Dominant 7th.
1500 Invention of music type.
1500-1600 "Golden Age" of Counterpoint.
1510 (abt.) Tallis b.
1526 Palestrina b.
1530 Chorals in German tongue.
1532 Lassus b.
1539 Bassoon invented.

1550 Birth of the madrigal.
1556 Dawnings of oratorio.
1565 Palestrina's *Missa Papæ Marcelli*.
1567 Monteverde b.; d. 1643. Employed Dominant 7th and many new discords; *established* opera.
1577 (abt.) Violin in England.
1580 Invention of Recitative. Dawnings of Opera.
1594 or 1597. Peri and Caccini's *Dafne*, 1st lyrical drama.
1600 First oratorio, Rome: Cavaliere's *Rappresentazione dell' Anima e del Corpo.* [dice. First opera, Florence: Peri and Caccini's *Euri-*
1604 Musicians' Company founded.
1610 Harpsichord music published.
1627 *Daphne*: first German opera.
1633 Lully b.
1645 (abt.) Rise of French opera.
1658 Purcell b.
1659 A. Scarlatti b.; d. 1725. Developed the *Aria*.
1659 Cambert's French opera, *La Pastorale*.
1660 Carissimi introduced the *Arioso.* [England.
1670 (abt.) Copper plates for music engraving in
1673 Lock's *Psyche*, first English opera.
1677 Purcell's *Dido and Eneas*.
1680 Kang-Hi invented new Chinese melodies.
1683 Rameau b.; d. 1764. Founded modern scientific
1685 Bach and Handel b. [harmony.
1700 (abt.) Clarinet invented.
1710 Pergolesi b.
1710 (abt.) Hammer-clavier invented; leading to pf.
1712 Jordan invents swell organ. Rousseau b.; d. 1778
1714 Gluck b.
1729 Bach's *St. Matthew Passion*.
1730 (abt.) Harp pedals invented.
1732 Haydn b.
1738 Royal Society of Musicians founded.
1739 Handel's *Israel in Egypt*.
1741 Handel's *Messiah*.
1750 Bach d.
1756 Mozart b.
1759 Handel d.
1760 (abt.) Pf. gradually supersedes harpsichord.
1760 Cherubini b.
1770 Beethoven b.
1784 Spohr b. Paganini b. Fétis b.
1786 Weber b.
1787 Mozart's *Don Giovanni*.
1791 Mozart d.
1792 Rossini b.
1797 Schubert b.
1798 Haydn's *Creation*, Vienna.
1803 Berlioz b. Beethoven's *Mount of Olives*.
1804 Glinka b.; d. 1857.
1805 Beethoven's *Fidelio*, Vienna.
1809 Haydn d. Mendelssohn b.
1810 Schumann b. Chopin b.
1811 Liszt b.
1813 Wagner b.
1814 Verdi b.
1816 John Curwen b. Rossini's *Il Barbiere*, Rome
1818 Gounod b.
1821 Weber's *Der Freischütz*. Helmholtz b.
1822 R.A.M. founded. Raff b.
1824 Beethoven's Choral Symphony.
1827 Beethoven d.
1828 Schubert d. Gevaert b.
1829 A. Rubinstein b.; d. 1894. Rossini's *William Tell*.
1830 Bülow b. Auber's *Fra Diavolo*.
1831 Joachim b.; d. 1907.
1833 Brahms b.
1836 Mendelssohn's *St. Paul*, Düsseldorf.
1838 Bizet b.; d. 1875.
1840 P. Tschaïkowsky b. Mendelssohn's *Lobgesang*.
1841 Dvořák b. Schumann's 1st Sym., Leipzig.
1842 Sullivan b.; d. 1900.
1843 Grieg b.; d. 1907. Wagner's *Flying Dutchman*.
1845 Wagner's *Tannhaüser*, Dresden.
1846 Mendelssohn's *Elijah*, Birmingham.
1847 Mendelssohn d. Flotow's *Martha*.
1850 Wagner's *Lohengrin*, Weimar. Schumann's *Genoveva*, Leipzig.
1854 Humperdinck b.
1856 Schumann d.
1857 Elgar b.
1859 Paderewski b.
1864 R.C.O. founded. Richard Strauss b.
1865 Wagner's *Tristan*, Munich.

1868 Wagner's *Meistersinger*, Munich.
1869 Wagner's *Rheingold*, Munich.
1870 T.C.L. founded. Wagner's *Walküre*, Munich.
1875 T. S. College incorporated. Bizet's *Carmen*.
1876 Wagner's *Nibelungen*, Bayreuth.
1880 G.S.M. founded. John Curwen *d*.
1882 Gounod's *Redemption*. Wagner's *Parsifal*.
1883 R.C.M. opened. Wagner *d*.
1886 Sullivan's *Golden Legend*.
1893 Tschaïkowsky *d*. Verdi's *Falstaff*, Rome.
1897 Brahms *d*. I.S.C. incorporated.
1905 Rd. Strauss's *Salome*, Dresden.
1908 Elgar's 1st Symphony.

Chrot'ta. (See **Crowd.**)

CHRYSANDER, Dr. Friedrich. Noted musical historian ; *b*. Mecklenburg, 1826 ; *d*. 1901.
He is specially famous for his editions of the complete works of Handel, and for a Handel biography, unfortunately not completed. Three vols. have, however, been published.

CHURCH, H. Pen-name of **T. Crampton** (*q.v.*).

CHURCH, John. *B*. Windsor, 1675 ; *d*. 1741. Master of the choristers, Westminster Abbey, 1704.
Wrote anthems, services, and songs.

CHURCH & Co. Cincinnati music publishing firm ; established 1844.

Church Cadence. A Plagal Cadence *(q.v.)*.

Church Modes. (See **Mode.**)

Chute *(F.)*. An appoggiatura, or a slide.

CHWATAL, Franz X. *B*. Bohemia, 1808 ; *d*. 1879.
Wrote over 200 *salon* pieces for pf., male quartets, and two pf. methods.

Ciacco'na *(I.)*. A chaconne.

Cicu'ta *(L.)*. A kind of flute or pan-pipes.

CIBBER, Mrs. Susanna Maria. Renowned actress and singer ; sister of Dr. Arne. *B*. 1714 ; *d*. 1766.
"The contralto songs in the *Messiah*, and the part of Micah in *Samson*, were composed by Handel expressly for her."--*Grove's Dict.*

CI'FRA, Antonio. *B*. Rome, abt. 1575 ; *d*. abt. 1636. Pupil of Palestrina ; a noted composer of the Roman school.
Works : 5 books of motets ; over 200 *concerti ecclesiastici ;* 5 books of masses ; Psalms, madrigals, litanies, &c.

Cifra'to *(I.)*. Figured (as a figured bass).

Cigo'gna *(I.)*. "A stork." The mouth-piece of a wind instrument.

CILÈA, Francesco. Operatic composer ; *b*. Palmi, Italy, 1867.

CIMARO'SA, Domenico. Famous operatic composer ; son of a poor mason ; *b*. nr. Naples, 1749; *d*. Venice, 1801. Free pupil, Cons. di S. Maria di Loreto, 1761 - 72. Court composer, Petersburg, 1789-92. Court Capellmeister, Vienna, 1792. He was a most prolific composer, and wrote about 70 operas in 29 years. His finest work, *Il Matrimonio Segreto* (Vienna, 1792) eclipsed all contemporary operas ; even, for a time, those of Mozart !
Chief works : operas, *La finta paragina, Il Fanatico per gli antichi Romani* (1777), *Artaserse, La Ballerina amante, Il Matrimonio Segreto,* &c. ; 2 oratorios ; 7 symphonies ; cantatas, masses, Psalms, arias, &c.

Cim'bal. (See **Cymbal.**)

Cim'balo *(I.)*. (1) A cymbal. (2) A harpsichord. (3) A tambourine. (4) A dulcimer.

Cim'balon *(I.)*. A Hungarian dulcimer. (See **Zimbalon.**)

Cim'bel *(G.)*. A high-pitch *mixture* stop.

Cim'belstern *(G.)*. (See **Zimbelstern.**)

Cinel'li *(I.)*. *(F., Cimbales ; G., Cinel'len.)* Cymbals.

C in alt ⎫
C in altissimo ⎭ (See **Alt.**)

Cink *(G.)*. A small reed stop.

Cinq *(F.)* ⎫ A fifth part in concerted music.
Cin'que *(I.)* ⎭ A *cin'que*, in five parts.

Cinque-pace. An old 5-step dance.

CINTI-DAMOREAU. (See **Damoreau.**)

Cipher. The persistent sounding of an organ-pipe owing to some defect.

Cir'ca *(L.)*. Abbn. *Circ.* or *c*. About.
Circa M. 80. About Metronome 80.
c. 1900. About the year 1900.

Circle-canon, or **Circular canon.** (See **Canon.**)

Circle of fifths. (See **Fifths.**)

Cir'colo *(I.)*. "A circle." ○ or ℃ ; the old character for "perfect" or triple time. Imperfect or duple time was shown by a ⊙, which became "barred C."

Cir'colo mez'zo *(I.)*. A turn, or *gruppetto*.

Cir'culus *(L.)*. "A circle." An ancient time-signature.

Cis *(G.)*. The note C♯.
Cis dur. The key of C♯ major.
Cis moll. The key of C♯ minor.

Cis'is (Cis'cis) *(G.)*. C✕ (C double-sharp.)

Cistel'la *(L.)*. A dulcimer.

Cistole ⎫
Cistre *(F.)* ⎬ Forms of the zither.
Citole ⎭

Cistrum. (See **Sistrum.**)

Ci'tara *(I.)*. A guitar, cither, or cittern.

Ci'thara *(L. from Gk.)*. The ancient lute.

Ci'thara biju'ga *(L.)*. A double-necked guitar or lute.

Cith'er, Cithern, Cittern. *(I., Ce'tera, Ce'tra.)* A kind of lute or guitar, 16th and 17th centuries.

CIUMME'I, Alfredo ("Alfredo Donizetti"). Operatic composer ; *b*. Smyrna, 1867.

Civetteri'a *(I.)*. Coquetry. *Civettan'do, Con civetteri'a,* in a trifling, coquettish manner.

CLAAS'SEN, Arthur. *B*. Stargard, Prussia, 1859. Since 1890, conductor of the United Singing Societies, Brooklyn.
Works : *Festival Hymn* for soli, chorus, and orch.; an orchestral idyll ; songs, choruses, &c.

CLAGGET, Chas. Violinist ; *b*. Waterford, 1740 ; *d*. abt. 1820. Invented a chromatic trumpet, a chromatic French horn, and made many improvements in other instruments.
Wrote songs, violin duets, &c.

Clair *(F.)*. Clear, shrill, loud.

Clairon *(F.).* (1) A trumpet. (2) An organ stop. (3) An infantry bugle. (4) The clarinet register from (See also **Clarion**.)

Clang ⎫ (1) Tone colour. (See **Acoustics**.)
Clangor *(L.)* ⎰ (2) Clangour; the din caused by the clash of metals, or the overblowing of brass instruments.

Clang-colour, Clang-tint. Tone colour. (See **Acoustics**.)

CLAPISSON, Antoine L. *B.* Naples, 1808; *d.* Paris, 1866. Violinist and composer. Professor of harmony, Paris Cons., and custodian of its collection of musical instruments, 1861.
Wrote 21 operas *(La Promise, La Fanchonette,* &c.); over 200 songs. &c.

Clapper. The tongue of a bell.

Claque *(F.).* "A body of hired applause-makers."—*Stainer & Barrett.*

Claque-bois *(F.).* A xylophone *(q.v.).*

Clarabel'la. An organ stop invented by Bishop. It has open wooden pipes (8 ft. pitch) and the tone is soft and mellow.

Cla'ra vo'ce *(I.).* A clear voice.

CLA'RI, Giovanni C. M. *B.* Pisa, 1669; *d.* abt. 1745. Maestro, Pistoia, abt. 1712; Bologna, 1720; Pisa, 1736.
Best-known works: opera, *Il savio delirante* (1695); collection of madrigals for 2 and 3 voices (1720); masses, a requiem, &c.

CLARIBEL. (See **Barnard, Mrs. C.**)

Claribel flute. An organ stop—generally of 4 ft. pitch—similar to the *Clarabella.*

Clar'ichord, Clarico'lo, Clar'igold. Old names for clavichord.

Clarin *(G.).* (1) A clarion; a high-pitch trumpet. (2) A 4 ft. organ reed stop.
Clarin-blasen. The sound of the trumpet (especially its soft tones).

Clarinet (Clarionet) ⎫ "A little clarion." A
Clarinette *(F.)* ⎪ wood-wind instru-
Clarinet'to *(I.)* ⎬ ment of cylindrical
Klarinet'te *(G.)* ⎭ bore, played by a "single" reed. It gives only the "odd" series of partials (see **Acoustics**), hence its characteristic tone.
The clarinet is a modification of the ancient *shawm* or *chalumeau,* which was so greatly improved by J. C. Denner of Nuremburg (abt. 1659-1700) that he is frequently spoken of as its inventor. Its compass is very extensive:—

Chalumeau register. Medium. "Clarinetto" or high register. Super-acute.

Orchestral clarinets are made in C, B♭, and A. The first produces the notes "as written;" that in B♭ produces tones a major 2nd lower than the written notes, and that in A a minor 3rd lower. (See *Transposing Instruments*.)
In military bands the favourite clarinet is the one in B♭, but smaller ones are also used, especially the E♭ soprano, a perfect 4th higher than the B♭. There are also alto, tenor, and bass clarinets. (See *Alt-clarinette, Basset-horn,* and *Bass clarinet*.)

Clarinetti'sta *(I.)* ⎫
Clarinettiste *(F.)* ⎰ A clarinet player.

Clari'no *(I.).* (1) A clarion. (2) A trumpet or bugle; especially the small high-pitch trumpet used by Bach and Handel.
Clarino is now often used for *Clarinet* in Italian scores.

Clarion. (1) A trumpet. (2) An organ reed stop of 4 ft. pitch.

Clarionet. (1) A clarinet. (2) An organ reed stop of round mellow quality; same as **Krummhorn** or **Cremona.**

CLARK, Rev. F. Scotson. London, 1840-83. Founded the London Organ School, 1873.
Wrote several organ pieces, including 15 popular marches.

CLARK, J. Moir. Composer; *b.* Aberdeen, abt. 1863.

CLARK, Rd. *B.* Datchet, 1780; *d.* 1856. Vicar-choral, St. Paul's; Gentleman of the Chapel Royal.
Wrote glees, anthems, &c., and essays on musical topics.

CLARKE, Hugh Archibald. American composer and organist. *B.* nr. Toronto, 1839.
Works: oratorio, *Jerusalem;* songs, pf. music, and a treatise on harmony.

CLARKE, James Hamilton Smee. *B.* Birmingham, 1840. Organist Queen's College, Oxford, 1866; St. Peter's, Kensington, 1872. Music-director, Lyceum, 1878. Conductor Victorian National Orchestra (Australia), 1889.
Works: 2 symphonies, 6 overtures, pf. music, incidental dramatic music; school cantatas, operettas, &c.

CLARKE, Jeremiah. London, 1670-1707. Succeeded Dr. Blow as Master of the Children, St. Paul's, 1693. Joint organist with Croft, Chapel Royal, 1704.
Works: incidental music to several plays; a cantata; anthems, songs, &c.; and the first setting of Dryden's *Alexander's Feast* (1697).

CLARKE, Dr. John (Clarke-Whitfeld). *B.* Gloucester, 1770; *d.* 1836. Organist of Trinity and St. John's, Cambridge, 1798-1820; Hereford Cathedral, 1820-33. Mus. Doc. Cantab., 1799, and Oxon, 1810. Cambridge Professor of Music, 1821.
Works: oratorio, *The Crucifixion and the Resurrection;* 4 vols. of services and anthems; 52 glees; songs, chants, &c. Also edited "The Vocal Works of Handel."

CLARKE, Wm. Horatio. American organist and teacher; *b.* Newtown, Mass., 1840.
Has published several instruction books, &c., for reed and pipe organs.

Clarseach, Clairshach, Clarscat, Clarseth. The ancient Irish harp.

Clarté de voix *(F.).* Clearness of voice.

CLA'RUS, Max. *B.* Mühlberg-on-Elbe, 1852. Kapellmeister in various theatres, &c.
Works; operas, *Ilse,* &c.; ballets; "Festgesang;" dramatic cantatas; choruses, &c.

CLA'SING, Joh. H. Hamburg, 1779-1829.
Works: 2 operas, 2 oratorios, pf. pieces, &c.

Classic (Classical). (1) Music of the highest class. (2) The opposite of *Romantic* music.

CLAUDIN Le Jeune. (See **Le Jeune.**)

CLAU'DIUS, Otto. Saxony, 1793-1877. Works: operas *(Der Gang nach dem Eisenhammer, &c.),* church music, songs, &c.

Clau'sel *(G.).* **Clau'sula** *(L.).* A cadence.
Clau'sula fal'sa. A false, or interrupted cadence.
Clau'sula fina'lis. A final cadence.
Clau'sula ve'ra. A perfect cadence.

CLAUSZ-SZARVA'DY, Wilhelmine. Distinguished pianist; *b.* Prague, 1834; *d.* 1907.

Clavechord. (See **Clavichord.**)

Clavecimbalo. (See **Clavicembalo.**)

Clavecin *(F.).* (1) A harpsichord. (2) The keyboard of a carillon.

Claviatur' *(G.).* (1) A keyboard. (2) Fingering. (Also *Klaviatur'.*)

Clavicem'balo *(I.)* } A harpsichord; lit. "A
Clavicem'balum *(L.)* } keyed dulcimer."

Clavichord. *(G., Klav'ichord, Klavier'; F., Clavicorde; I., Clavicor'do.)* A precursor of the pianoforte, having metal wedges (called tangents) instead of hammers.

Clavicor *(F.).* A kind of horn with keys or pistons.

Clavicylinder. A keyboard instrument, constructed by Chladni (abt. 1800), with a revolving glass cylinder and steel bars instead of strings.

Clavicythe'rium. A clavichord.

Clavier. *(G., Klavier'.)* (1) The pianoforte, harpsichord, or clavichord. (2) An organ keyboard. *Clavier de récit.,* or *Récit. expressif (F).* The swell manual.

Clavier'auszug *(G.).* A pianoforte score. *Partitur (G.),* a full score.
Clavier'schule. A pf. instruction book.
Clavier'stück. A pianoforte piece.

Claviglissan'do. A keyboard instrument combining the effects of an harmonium and a violin.

Cla'vis *(L.).* A key (of an instrument); a clef; a note.

Cla'vis signa'ta *(L.).* A signed clef. (See **Clef.**)

Clavycymbal. (1) Clavichord. (2) Harpsichord.

CLAY, Frederic Emes. English composer; *b.* Paris, 1838; *d.* Great Marlow, 1889. Works: stage operettas, *Court and Cottage, Constance, Ages ago, Princess Toto, The Merry Duchess, The Golden Ring,* &c.; incidental music to the *Twelfth Night,* &c.; 2 cantatas; many fine songs ("I'll sing thee songs of Araby," "She wandered down the mountain side," "The Sands of Dee," &c.).

CLEAVER, Mrs. Eleanor (*née* **Beebe**). Contralto; *b.* Detroit (U.S.). London *début,* 1900.

Clé, Clef *(F.).* (1) Key (of a wind inst.). (2) Clef. *Armer la clef.* To add the key-signature to the clef.

Clef d'accordeur *(F.).* A tuning-key.

Clef, also **Cleff, Cliff, Clief.** *(L., Cla'vis; G., Schlüs'sel; F., Clé, Clef; I., Chia've.)* A sign placed on the staff to determine the name and absolute pitch of any note

written thereon. A clef assigned to a particular position on the staff was formerly called a "signed clef."

The clefs are merely modifications or developments of letters placed on the staff lines to indicate pitch. Only 3 are now employed, viz., G, C, and F.

(1) Some forms of the G clef:—

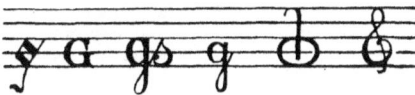

(2) Some forms of the C clef:—

(Also called the "mean cliff" as it is exactly midway in pitch between the G and F clefs.)

(3) Some forms of the F clef:—

The following table shows 9 different ways of writing the same identical phrase of 4 notes, the first note in each case being "Middle C:"

G Clef.	Ordinary Treble, or G Clef.
	French Violin Clef (obsolete).
	Tenor or Mean Clef.
C Clef.	Alto or Counter-tenor Clef.
	Mezzo-soprano Clef (rare).
	Soprano Clef.
	Low Bass Clef (obsolete).
F Clef.	Ordinary Bass Clef.
	Half-Bass, or Baritone Clef (rare).

Clef de Fa (F.). The F clef.
Clef de Sol (F.). The G clef.
Clef d'ut (F.). The C clef.

CLE'MENS (or **CLEMENT**), **Jacob.** (Known as "Clemens non Papa," to distinguish him from Pope Clement VII.) 16th century Netherland composer. Capellmeister, Vienna, to Chas. V.
Works: 11 masses; motets and chansons; 4 books of Psalms to Netherland tunes, &c.

CLÉMENT, Félix. Paris, 1822-85. Organist and musical historiographer.
Works: "Méthode complète du Plain-chant" (1854), "Méthode de musique vocale et concertante," "Histoire générale de la musique religieuse" (1861), "Les musiciens célèbres" (1868), &c.

CLÉMENT, Franz. Fine violinist; Vienna, 1784-1842. Capellmeister, Vienna, 1802-1811; and afterwards leader, under Weber, at Prague. Toured for some years with Catalani. Beethoven wrote for him his violin concerto.
Works: opera, Le Trompeur Trompé; 6 violin concertos; overtures, quartets, &c.

CLEMENT Y CAVEDO. Spanish composer; b. 1810.
Works: A magic opera, a farce, romances, &c.

CLEMENTI, Muzio. Composer and distinguished pianist; b. Rome, 1752; d. England, 1832. At the age of 14 he showed such promise that Mr. Peter Beckford, an English gentleman, brought him to England and defrayed the cost of his studies for some years. From 1777-80 he was conductor and cembalist of the Italian opera. He commenced a series of tours in 1781, and being in Vienna at the end of that year engaged in a "friendly" contest in piano playing with Mozart. He afterwards established a pianoforte factory (later Collard & Collard), and settled down in England as a "man of business." Clementi has been called "the originator of modern pianoforte playing, as distinguished from harpsichord playing." Among his most distinguished pupils were Field, Cramer, Moscheles, and Kalkbrenner.
Works: symphonies and overtures; 106 pf. sonatas; a celebrated book of études for pf. (Gradus ad Parnassum), 1817; and many other works now forgotten.

CLEMENZA DI TITO. Mozart's 23rd opera; 1791.

CLÉRICE, Justin. B. Buenos Ayres, 1863. Pupil Paris Cons. Resides in Paris.
Works: operas, Figarella, &c.; pantomime, Léda; &c.

CLEVE, Halfdan. Composer; b. Kongsberg, Norway, 1879.

CLICQUOT, François H. Paris, 1728-91. Fétis calls him "the most skilful organ builder of the 18th century."

CLIFFE, Frederick. B. Low Moor, nr. Bradford, 1857.
Has written a fine Symphony in C minor, and other works.

CLIFFORD, Rev. Jas. B. Oxford, 1622; d. London, 1698. "Senior Cardinal," St. Paul's, 1682.
Pub. "A Collection of Divine Services and Anthems," 1664.

CLIFTON, John Chas. London, 1781-1841. An exponent of Logier's system.
Works: opera, Edwin (1815); glees, songs; a "Selection of British Melodies," and a "Theory of Harmony."

CLINTON, John. Flautist; London, 1810-64. Published many instruction books, &c., for flute, which are "among the best ever produced in England."

Cliquette (F.). The bones.

CLIVE, Catherine ("Kitty Clive"). Favourite singer and actress; London, 1711-1785. Handel selected her for "Dalila" in Samson, 1743.

Cloc'ca (L.) ⎱ A bell.
Cloche (F.) ⎰

Clochette (F.). A hand-bell.

Clog dance. A dance with clogs.

Clog hornpipe. A hornpipe with clogs.

Close. Full close, half close. (See Cadence.)

Close harmony; Close position. Harmony with the upper parts written near each other in pitch.

It is opposed to extended, dispersed, or open harmony:—

Close play. In lute-playing, the fingers kept as much as possible on the strings.
Close score. Short score.
Close shake. Vibrato (q.v.), or Bebung (q.v.).

CLOTZ. (See Klotz.)

CLUER, John. D. London, 1729. Reputed inventor of engraving on tin plates.
He engraved and pub. several of Handel's works.

CLUTSAM, Geo. H. Song composer; b. Sydney, 1866.

Clynke-bell. A chime.

COATES, John. Tenor; b. nr. Bradford, 1870(?). 1st London appearance, 1894.

COBB, Gerard F. B. Kent, 1838; d. 1904. President, Cambridge University Board of Musical Studies, 1877-92.
Works: services, glees, pf. music, several songs, &c.

COBBOLD, Wm. B. Norwich, 1559 (-60); d. 1639.
One of the 10 contributors to Este's Psalter, 1592.

COC'CHI, Gioacchino. B. Padua, 1720; d. 1804. Composer of opera buffa.
Operas: Adelaide, Bajasette, Il pazzo glorioso, Zenobia, and several others.

COC'CIA, Carlo. B. Naples, 1782; d. 1873.
Works: opera, Maria Stuarda, and nearly 40 others; masses, arias, &c.

COCCON', Nicolò. Venice, 1826-1903. Esteemed composer. Maestro, S. Mark's, 1873.
Works: oratorio, Saül; 8 requiems; 30 other masses; 2 operas (Zaira, 1884), &c.

COCKS & Co. Founded by Robt. Cocks, 1827. Lasted till 1898.

Co'da (I., "a tail"). (1) The stem of a note (L., Cauda). (2) A passage added at the end of a composition to form an impressive conclusion.
In the modern sonata and symphony, the Coda often assumes important proportions.

Codet'ta. (1) A short coda. (2) A short passage in a fugue between the subject and the entry of the answer. (See Fugue.)

COE'NEN (pron. *Koo'nen*), **Cornelius.** Violinist. *B.* The Hague, 1838. Bandmaster, Garde Nationale, Utrecht, 1860. Has written overtures, choral works, &c.

COE'NEN, Franz. Concert violinist; *b.* Rotterdam, 1826. Director of the Amsterdam Cons. to 1895. *D.* 1904.
Works: a symphony, cantatas, quartets, &c.

COE'NEN, Joh. M. Distinguished bassoonist. *B.* The Hague, 1824; *d.* 1899. Municipal music-director, Amsterdam.
Works: cantatas; ballet and incidental music; 2 symphonies; concertos; a quintet; orchestral fantasias, &c.

COE'NEN, Willem. Pianist; brother of F. *B.* Rotterdam, 1837. Settled in London, 1862.
Works: oratorio, *Lazarus*; pf. music, songs, &c.

COFFIN, Chas. Hayden. Baritone vocalist; *b.* Manchester, 1862.

Coffre *(F.).* "A chest." The case of a pf.; body of a violin, &c.

Co'gli *(I.).* "With the;" as *co'gli stromen'ti*, with the instruments.

Cognoscen'ti *(I.).* Connoisseurs; experts.

COHEN, Jules E. D. *B.* Marseilles, 1835; *d.* 1901. Chef du chant, Paris Grand Opéra from 1877.
Works: 4 operas; choruses to *Athalie*, &c.; oratorios, symphonies, masses; 200 songs; pf. pieces, &c.

Coi *(I.).* With; as *coi violini*, with the vns.

Col, Coll', Col'la, Col'le, Col'lo *(I.).* "With."
Col bas'so. With the bass.
Col can'to. With the melody, or voice.
Col le'gno. Strike the strings (of a violin, &c.) with the "wood" (back) of the bow.
Coll' ar'co. With the bow.
Coll' otta'va. With the octave (*i.e.* in octaves).
Col'la de'stra. With the right hand.
Col'la par'te. With the principal part (or solo).
Colla più gran for'za e prestez'za. As loud and as quick as possible.
Col'la pun'ta d'ar'co. With the point of the bow.
Col'la sini'stra. With the left hand.
Col'la vo'ce. With the (solo) voice.

Colachon *(F.),* **Colascio'ne, Coloscio'ne** *(I.).* A kind of guitar. (See **Calascione.**)

COLASSE, Pascal. *B.* Rheims (?), 1639; *d.* 1709. Pupil of Lully. Favourite of Louis XIV. Master of the Music, 1683. Royal chamber-musician, 1696.
Works: 10 operas (*Les noces de Thétys et Pélée*, 1689); songs, &c.

COLBRAN, Isabella Angela. Famous operatic singer. *B.* Madrid, 1785; *d.* 1845. Was married to Rossini, 1822, and sang the principal part in his *Zelmira*, London, 1824.

COLE, Belle. Contralto; *b.* Chatauqua, abt. 1845; *d.* 1905.

COLE, Blanche. (See **Mrs. S. Naylor.**)

COLERIDGE-TAYLOR, Samuel. *B.* London, 1875. Father, a native of Sierra Leone; mother, English.
Works: *Hiawatha, African Suite, Dream Lovers*; songs, orchestral pieces, &c.

Collet de violin *(F.)* The neck of a violin.

Collinet *(F).* A flageolet.

COLLINSON, Thos. H. *B.* Alnwick, 1858. Mus.Bac. Oxon, 1877. Orgt. Edinburgh Cath. since 1878.

COLON'NA, Giovanni Paolo. *B.* Bologna (or Brescia) abt. 1640; *d.* 1695. Distinguished church composer; pupil of Carissimi. He taught the famous Bononcini.
Works: opera, *Amilcare*; oratorio, *La Profezia d'Eliseo* (1688); masses, psalms, motets, litanies, lamentations, vespers, &c.

COLONNE, Judas (known as **Édouard**). Distinguished conductor; *b.* Bordeaux, 1838. Founded the famous "Concerts du Châtelet," Paris, 1874. Visited London, 1896.

Col'ophony. *(G., Kolophon'; F., Colophane; I., Colofo'nia.)* Resin (rosin) for vn. bows, &c.

Colora'to *(I.).* "Coloured," florid, embellished.

Coloratu'ra *(I.). (G., Coloratur'.)* Runs, divisions, trills, &c., in a vocal or instrumental solo.

Colour. *(L., Color.)* (1) Tone colour or *timbre.* (See **Acoustics.**) (2) The characteristic features of a composition.
Orchestral colour. The effect of massing, blending, contrasting. &c., the tone-qualities of the instruments of the orchestra. Orchestration.

Colour and Music.
The analogy between the 7 notes of the diatonic scale and the 7 colours of the spectrum (or rainbow) has attracted the attention of scientists and musicians from the time of Newton, and there have been many attempts to construct an instrument to illustrate colour-harmonies, &c. (one of which was exhibited in London a few years ago). Sir John Herschell calculated tables of the vibrations of coloured light, which, when compared with those of the notes of a major scale, show a wonderful approximation of ratios. (As the vibrations of light are about 1,000,000,000,000 times as rapid as those of sound, the *comparative ratios* only are shown in the following table.)
Comparison of Colour and Sound Vibrations, taking 450 to represent Doh:—

Colour.	Relative Number of Vibrations.	Scale notes.	Relative Number of Vibrations.
Violet ...	727	Te ...	844
Indigo ...	672	Lah ...	750
Blue ...	632	Soh ...	675
Green ...	590	Fah ...	600
Yellow...	545	Me ...	562
Orange	506	Ray ...	506
Red ...	457	Doh ...	450

It will be seen from the above table that Red, Yellow, and Blue correspond approximately to *d, m*, and *s*, and form, so to speak, the "Tonic Triad" or "Key-chord" of colour, Also Green and Blue—always more or less discordant in combination—correspond to the discord *f s*, &c.

It is also interesting to note that the greatest classic painters, *e.g.* Leonardo da Vinci, Rubens, Titian, Guido, Veronese, &c., planned out their colour-harmonies in remarkable accordance with the analogous musical harmonies! It has also been pointed out that paintings in which this principle is disregarded are often weak and ineffective in colouring.

Of course the analogy must not be pushed too far, as the blending of all the colours of the spectrum gives beautiful, harmonious, *white* light, while the simultaneous sounding of the 7 notes of the scale gives anything but musical harmony!—(See "Sound and Colour," by J. D. Macdonald; Longmans & Co., 1869.)

Colour of Keys. (See **Key-colour.**)

Colour of the Tones of Instruments.
By analogy the tones of various instruments have been likened to colours: Violins, green; trombones, crimson; trumpets, scarlet; flutes, light blue; oboes, yellow-green; clarinets, red-brown; bassoons, dark-brown; drums, black, &c.

Col'po (*I.*). "A blow." *Di col'po*, suddenly, immediately.
Col'po di campanel'lo. Stroke of a bell.

COMBARIÉU, Jules. Writer on Musical Æsthetics, &c.; *b.* Cahors, 1859. Prof. Paris Lyceum.
Works: " Relation of Poetry to Music; " "Influence of German upon French Music; " " Rhythm; " " Musical Archæology," &c.

Combination Tones. (See **Acoustics.**)

Co'me (*I.*). As, like.
Co'me pri'mo. As at first.
Co'me re'tro. As before.
Co'me so'pra. As above.
Co'me sta. As it stands; as written.
Co'me tem'po del Te'ma. In the same time as that of the theme.
Co'me u'na fantasi'a, ma in tem'po. Like a fantasia, but in strict time.

Co'mes (*L.*). "A companion." The answer in a fugue; the consequent in a canon.

COMETTANT, J. P. Oscar. Composer and writer. *B.* Bordeaux, 1819; *d.* 1898.
Works: fantasias, caprices, &c., for pf.; songs; violin pieces, &c.; "Life of Adolphe Sax," "Music, Musicians, and Musical Instruments of the Different Peoples of the World; " important articles on Gounod, A. Thomas, &c.

Comma (Komma). The small interval between a major and minor tone; ratio 81:80.
This little interval—roughly about one-fifth of a semitone—is the source of all the difficulties in tuning! (See *Temperament.*)
Pythagorean Comma. The difference between an octave and 6 major tones; ratio 524288 : 531441; about one-fourth of a semitone.

Commençant (*F.*). A beginner (in music, &c.).

COM'MER, Franz. *B.* Cologne, 1813; *d.* 1887. Composer and musical historiographer. Arranged the library of the Royal Institute for Church Music, Berlin.
Works: music to *The Frogs* (Aristophanes) and *Elektra* (Sophocles); masses, cantatas, &c. Edited " Collectio operum musicorum Batavorum" (12 vols.); " Musica Sacra XVI, XVII," &c. (26 vols.); " Collection of Organ Pieces, 16th to 18th centuries" (6 parts), &c.

Comme un murmure (*F.*). Like a murmur; very soft.

Com'modo (Co'modo) (*I.*). At a convenient speed; easily.
Commodamen'te
Commodet'to } In an easy manner; leisurely.

Common Chord. A note with its major or minor 3rd and perfect 5th.
Common Metre. An Iambic 4-lined stanza of 8 and 6 syllables alternately; so-called because it was the "common" form of metre in the old metrical versions of the Psalms.
The man is blest that hath not bent
To wicked rede his eare :
Nor led his life as sinners doe,
Nor sate in scorners chaire.—*Psalme I.*
Common Scale. Name sometimes given to the Major Scale.
Common Time. Specially, $\frac{4}{4}$ time (**C**). Any duple or quadruple time.

Companion. A part which accompanies an imitative phrase in 3rds or 6ths.—*Curwen.*

Compass. (*G., Um'fang; F., Diapason; I., Estensio'ne.*) The range of a voice or inst.

Compass of Voices. Average compass of the voices of a choir :—

COMPÈRE, Loyset. Noted Netherland composer of motets, &c.; *d.* 1518.

Compiace'vole (*I.*). Pleasing, attractive.

Complement. The interval which, added to another interval, makes a complete 8ve: thus a 4th is the complement of a 5th, &c.

Compline. The last of the 7 canonical hours of the Roman Church. A short evening service.

Componi(e)ren (*G.*). (See **Komponieren.**)

Componiert' (*G.*) (See **Komponiert**).

Conponist' (*G.*)
Componi'sta (*I.*). } Composer; author.

Composer. (*F., Compositeur; I., Composito're.*) One who composes music.

Composition. (*I., Composizio'ne.*) (1) A piece of music. (2) The art of composing music. (3) The constitution of an organ *mixture*.
The Art of Composition includes (1) Melody, (2) Time, Metre, Rhythm, and Accent, (3) Harmony, Modulation, and Cadence, (4) Counterpoint, Imitation, Canon, and Fugue, (5) Form, Design, or Plan, (6) Thematic development, (7) Expression, (8) Knowledge of the Compass, &c., of Voices and Instruments, (9) Accompaniment and Orchestration, (10) Style, Character, &c. (See each of these under its own heading.)

Composition Pedal. A pedal on the organ which acts upon a group of stops.
Sometimes it acts only on one "special" stop.

Composizio'ne di tavoli'no (*I.*). Music for the table. Convivial music.

Compos'to (*I.*). In a composed manner; quietly.

Compound Interval. An interval greater than an octave.

Compound Stop. An organ-stop with more than one set of pipes; as mixtures, &c.

Compound Times. Measures divisible into groups of 3.
Compound Duple : $\frac{6}{8}$, $\frac{6}{4}$, &c. *Compound Triple :* $\frac{9}{8}$, $\frac{9}{4}$, &c. *Compound Quadruple :* $\frac{12}{8}$, $\frac{12}{4}$, &c.

Compressed Score. A short score.

Comprima'ria. (*I.*). "An assistant *prima donna.*" —*Stainer and Barrett.*

Con (*I.*). With.
Con is used with a great number of Italian nouns, as *Con amo're, Con mo'to, Con sordi'ni,* &c.

8

Concen'to *(I.).* (1) Harmony; concord. (2) A selection of musical pieces. (3) The opposite of *arpeggio*.

Concentran'do *(I.).* Concentrating; intense.

Concen'tus *(L.).* (1) Concord; harmony. (2) Part music. (3) (See **Accentus**.)

Concert. (1) A set of similar instruments; also *Consort*, and *Chest*. (2) A concerto. (3) A musical performance. Sacred concert, Ballad concert, &c.
Concert spirituel (F.). A sacred concert.

Concertan'te *(I.).* "Concordant." (1) A piece for a concert. (2) A display piece for 2 or more solo voices or instruments, with accompaniment. (3) A duo, trio, &c., for solo voices or instruments.

Concerta'to *(I.).* Concerted; in 2 or more parts.

Concerted Music. For 2 or more voices, instruments, &c. Music in several parts.

Concert-grand. The largest kind of grand pf.

Concerti'na. (1) English: a concertina with a compass of 3½ octaves, invented by Wheatstone, 1829. It can play in any key, and is capable of some fine effects. (2) German : the common concertina. It can only play in 2 keys, and its harmonic resources are limited to about 2 chords in each key.

Concerti'no. (1) A small concerto. (2) The leading or principal player : as *Violi'no concerti'no*, principal violin. (See **Ripieno**.)

Concerti'ren *(G.).* To accord.

Concert'meister *(Konzert'meister, G.).* The leading 1st violin ("leader") of an orchestra.

Concer'to *(I.). (G., Konzert'.)* (1) A concert. (2) An extended composition in sonata form for a solo instrument with orchestral acct. Violin concerto, pf. concerto, &c.
Concer'to gros'so. Early name for a composition for several instruments.
Concer'to spritua'le. A sacred concert.

Concert-spieler *(G.).* A solo player.

Concert'stück *(G.).* (1) A concerted piece. (2) A concerto in short and irregular form.

Concin'nous. Harmonious; coinciding.

Concita'to *(I.).* Perturbed, agitated.

CONCO'NE, Giuseppe. *B.* Turin, abt. 1810; *d.* 1861. Singing teacher, Paris, 1832-48.
Wrote 2 operas, songs, &c., but is specially known for his famous vocal exercises (50 Lessons, 30 Exercises, 25 Lessons, 15 Vocalises, 40 Lessons for Bass Voice).

Con'cord. (1) Agreement; consonance; the opposite of discord. (2) A consonant chord. (See **Consonant Chords**.)
Concords, perfect. (See *Perfect Concords*.)

Concor'dant. Consonant; agreeable.

Concordant *(F).* A baritone voice.

Conducting. (See **Beating time**.)

Conductor. *(G., Kapell'meister; F., Chef d'orchestre; I., Mae'stro di cappel'la, or Ca'po d'orchestra.)* The director, or "wielder of the *bâton*," of a chorus, band, &c.

Conductor's copy. A two-stave score with the "entries" of the instruments marked: as *vn., fl., ob., cl., fag.,* &c.
The 1st violin part is often marked in the same way, and for pieces of no great complexity forms a very useful conductor's copy.

Cone-gamba. (See **Bell-gamba**.)

Con esaltazio'ne *(I.).* With exaltation, sublimity.

Congenial tones.
"The characteristic tones in a melody, or those most *congenial* with its general spirit."—*Curwen.* (See *Mental Effect*.)

Con giustez'za *(I.).* With accuracy.

Congregational singing.
The "Injunctions" of Q. Elizabeth, 1559, provided for a "hymn or song" at the beginning or end of morning or evening prayer, to encourage congregational worship. Then came into being the crowds of *Metrical Psalters* (see *Hymn*). Bishop Jewell, writing in 1560, says that "you may now see at St. Paul's Cross after the service 6,000 people of both sexes all singing and praising God."
The Assembly of Divines, Westminster, 1644, decided that it was "the duty of Christians to praise God publicly by the singing of Psalms together in the congregation ; the whole congregation may join, and all who can read shall have a Psalm-book. But for the present, where many in the congregation cannot read, the minister may read the Psalm, line by line, before the singing thereof."

CONINCK, J. F. de. *B.* Antwerp, 1791 ; *d.* 1866. Founded and conducted the Antwerp "Société d' Harmonie."

Conjunct. *(F., Conjoint; I., Congiun'to.)* Proceeding by step : as **d-r, m-f** ; opposite of disjunct.

Connoisseur *(F.).* An expert, or critic.

CONRA'DI, August. Berlin, 1821-73. Friend of Liszt. Capellmeister successively of several theatres at Stettin and Berlin.
Works : operas, *Rubezähl, Musa der letzte Maurenfürst*, and half-a-dozen others ; 5 symphonies; overtures, quartets, vaudevilles, &c.

CONRA'DI, Johann Georg. Bavarian capellmeister, 17th cent. Wrote some of the earliest German operas.
Operas : *Ariane, Diogenes, Jerusalem* (1692), *Sigismund* (1693), *Pygmalion* (1693), &c.

Consecutives. Two or more intervals of the same kind in succession.
Consecutive 3rds or 6ths are pleasing, unless continued so long as to become monotonous; consecutive 4ths and 8ths are allowed under certain circumstances ; consecutive 2nds and 7ths are generally forbidden, but may be occasionally allowed ; consecutive 5ths are forbidden in strict harmony (and counterpoint), but there are certain exceptions to the rule. (See any standard work on *Harmony*.)

Consequent. ⎱ (1) The answer to a fugue
Consequen'za *(I.).* ⎰ subject. (See **Fugue**.)
(2) The "reply" in a canon (see **Canon**), or to a subject for imitation (see **Imitation**).

Conser'vatory *(E.).* ⎫
Conservatoire *(F.).* ⎪
Conservato'rio *(I.).* ⎬ A public school of music.
Conservato'rium *(L.).* ⎪
Konservato'rium *(G.).* ⎭

Consolan'te *(I.).* In a soothing, consoling manner.

Con'sole.
The part of an organ under the immediate control of the player—manuals, pedals, stops, &c. Sometimes at a distance from the rest of the organ.

Con'sonance. *(G., Konsonanz'; F., Consonance ; I., Consonan'za.)* (1) Agreement ; harmony. (2) Two or more notes which blend perfectly together, *i.e.* without dissonance. (3) An interval satisfactory in itself, and which does not require to be resolved.
Perfect consonances. The 8ve, perfect 5th, perfect 4th and unison.
Imperfect consonances. Major and minor 3rds, and major and minor 6ths.

Consonant chords. All major and minor common chords and their inversions and the 1st inversion of diminished triads.

Consonant interval. (See **Consonance,** 3.)
For the scientific explanation of consonance and dissonance see *Acoustics.*

Con sordi'ni *(I.).* (1) With mutes on (as a violin). (2) In pf. playing, with the left (or soft) pedal held down. (3) See **Sordino.**

Con'sort. (1) A set. Consort of viols, same as Chest of viols. (2) Agreement. (3) A company of musicians.

CONSTANTIN, Titus Ch. B. Marseilles, 1835.
Works : operas, violin music, songs, &c.

Constitution of Chords. Term applied in Sol-fa theory to the doubling or omission of notes of a chord.

Con stromen'ti *(I.).* With the instruments.

Construction. The plan, design, or form of a composition. (See **Form.**)

Conta'no *(I.).* The parts so marked to rest.

CON'TI, Carlo. B. nr. Naples, 1797 ; d. 1868. Prof. of counterpoint, Naples Cons., 1846; Vice-director, 1862. Teacher of Bellini, Buonamici, and Marchetti.
Works : 11 operas (*L' Olimpia,* 1829, &c.) ; church music, songs, &c.

CON'TI, Francesco B. B. Florence, 1681 ; d. 1732. Court composer, Vienna, 1713.
Works : 16 operas (*Don Chisciotte in Sierra Morena,* 1719, &c.) ; 9 oratorios, 13 serenades, 50 cantatas, &c.

CON'TI, G. (See **Gizziello.**)

Continua'to *(I.).* Sustained, continued.

Continued Bass. } *Basso continuo (I.).*
Conti'nuo *(I.).* } Thorough Bass *(E.).*
" The bass which continues or goes through the whole piece, from which, with the aid of figures, the accompt. used to be played."— *Grove's Dict.*

Conteurs *(F.).* Troubadours.

Contra *(L.). (F., Contre.)* Against. In compound words, " an octave lower."
Contrabass. } The double-bass.
Contrabas'so (I.). }
Contrabas'sist. A double-bass player.
Contra-dance. } (See *Country-dance.*)
Contraddan'za (I.). }

Contra fagot'to (I.). A double bassoon ; an 8ve lower than the ordinary bassoon.
Contra-gamba. A 16 ft. gamba.
Contra Posau'ne (G.). "Double trombone." A 16 ft. (or 32 ft.) pedal "reed" on the organ.
Contr'arco (I.). "Against the bow." Incorrect bowing on the violin, &c.
Contrassogget'to (I.). Countersubject (of a fugue).
Contra Tempo (I.). " Against the time." (1) Syncopation. (2) One part in long notes, another in short notes, &c.
Contra-tenor. The alto voice.
Contratö'ne (G.). Very deep bass voice tones.
Contra violo'ne (I.). The double-bass.

Contralto *(I.).* (1) The lowest female voice ;

compass from about

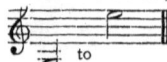

often with a marked " break " at about—
(See **Break.**)

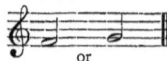

or

(2) Also used for **Alto** (*i.e.* the Male Alto).
The male alto has a smaller compass and less richness of tone.

Contrappunti'sta *(I.).* A contrapuntist *(q.v.).*

Contrappun'to *(I.).* Counterpoint.
Contrappun'to al'la men'te. Improvised counterpoint.
Contrappun'to al'la zop'pa. "Lame, halting," syncopated counterpoint.
Contrappun'to dop'pio. Double counterpoint.
Contrappun'to syncopa'to. Syncopated counterpoint.
Contrappun'to so'pra il sogget'to. Counterpoint above the subject.
Contrappun'to sot'to il sogget'to. Counterpoint below the subject.

Contrapunc'tus *(L.).* Counterpoint.
Contrapunc'tus ad viden'dum. Written counterpoint.
Contrapunc'tus flor'idus. Florid counterpoint.

Con'trapunkt (Kon'trapunkt) *(G.).* Counterpoint.

Contrapun'tal. (1) In the style of counterpoint. (2) Pertaining to its theory or practice.

Contrapun'tist. One skilled in the theory or practice of counterpoint.

Contrary Motion. Parts proceeding in opposite directions, *e.g.* :—

Contre *(F.).* Same as *L.* **Contra.** (See above.)
Contrebasse. Double-bass.
Contredanse. So called from the dancers being opposite each other.
Contrepartie. An *opposed* part in counterpoint ; especially either of the two parts in a duet.
Contrepoint. Counterpoint.
Contrepointiste. Contrapuntist.
Contre-sujet. Countersubject.
Contretemps. Same as *Contra Tempo* (see above).

Contrast.
If introduced with judgment, contrast of tone, style, loudness, accompaniment, &c., is one of the chief means of producing musical variety. It is, however, " very common for composers who are barren in invention to make a wrong use of the contrast, and to seek in that, for the sake of preserving the attention, those resources with which their genius is incapable of furnishing them."—*Rousseau.*

Con'tro *(I.).* Counter ; low.

CON'VERSE, Chas. C. (*nom de plume*, **Karl Redan**). American composer ; *B.* Warren, Mass., 1832.
Works: concert-overture on "Hail Columbia;" songs, hymns, quartets, &c.

Conver'sio (*L.*). Inversion.

COOKE, Benjamin. Famous glee writer; London, 1734-93. Conductor "Academy of Ancient Music," 1752 ; Organist Westminster Abbey, 1762. Mus.Doc.Cantab., 1775, and Oxon, 1782.
Works: "Collection of 20 Glees, &c.," 1775; "Nine Glees and 2 Duets," 1795; a fine Service in G, anthems, odes, organ pieces, &c.

COOKE, Thos. Simpson ("**Tom Cooke**"). *B.* Dublin, 1782 ; *d.* London, 1848. Tenor singer, and afterwards assistant conductor at Drury Lane. Professor of singing, R.A.M. ; teacher of Sims Reeves.
Works: about 20 operas, several glees, &c., and a treatise on "Singing."

COOMBS, Chas. W. American composer; *b.* 1859. Several of his songs are very popular.

COOPER, George. London, 1820-76. Noted organist. Organist Chapel Royal, 1856.
Works: "The Organist's Assistant," "Organ Arrangements," 3 vols., &c.

COOPER, Henry Christopher. Able solo-violinist and orchestral leader ; *b.* Bath, 1819 ; *d.* 1881.

COOTE, Chas. London, 1809-80.
Composed much light popular dance music.

COPERA'RIO. Name assumed by **John Cooper**, a famous lutenist and player on the viol-da-gamba ; London, abt. 1570-1627. Teacher of Henry and William Lawes.
Works: 2 Masques, sets of "Fancies," songs, &c.

Coper'to (*I.*). Covered, hidden.
Quin'ti coper'ti. Hidden fifths.
Tim'pani coper'ti. Muffled kettledrums.

COPLAND, Chas. Baritone vocalist ; *b.* Brightlingsea, 1861.

COP'POLA P. A. Sicilian opera composer ; 1793-1877. Conductor Lisbon Royal Opera, abt. 1839.
Works: opera, *Nina pazza per amore* (1835), and about 14 others ; masses, church music, &c.

Cop'ula. (*L. & I. ; F., Copule.*) A coupler.

COQUARD, Arthur. Distinguished composer ; *b.* Paris, 1846.
Works: oratorio, *Jeanne d'Arc;* operas, *L'Epée du roi, La Jacquerie, Jahel,* &c. ; ballades, &c.

Cor (*F.*). A horn.
Cor-alt. (See *Corno alto.*)
Cor-basse. (See *Corno basso.*)
Cor de basset. Basset horn.
Cor de chasse. A hunting horn.
Cor de signal. A bugle or signal horn.
Cor de vaches. A "cow-horn." Used by the Swiss herdsmen. (See *Ranz des vaches.*)
Cor omnitonique. A semitonic valve-horn.

Cor Anglais. "English horn." A tenor oboe, a fifth lower than the ordinary oboe.

Compass— (actual pitch)

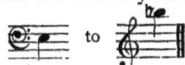

It is used with great effect in the opening of Wagner's *Tristan,* Act III.

Cora'le (*I.*). A choral, or hymn-tune.

Cor'anach (**Cor'anich, Cor'onach**). A Scottish funeral dirge.

Coran'to (*I.*). (1) A country dance. (2) A *Courante* (*q.v.*).

CORBETT, Samuel. Orgt. and composer ; *b.* Wellington, Shropshire, 1852. Blind from infancy. Mus.Doc. Cantab, 1879.

CORBETT, Wm. Violinist ; 1669(?)-1748. Member of the Royal Band. Bequeathed his collection of musical instruments to Gresham College.
Wrote music to *Love Betrayed, Henry IV,* &c. ; concertos and songs.

Cor'da (*I.*). A string.
So'pra u'na cor'da. On one string.
U'na cor'da. In pf. playing, "use the soft pedal."
Tut'te le cor'de, or *Tut'te cor'de,* or *Du'e cor'de.* Release the soft pedal.

Cordatu'ra. Same as *Accordatu'ra* (*q.v.*).

Corde (*F.*). A string.
Corde à boyau. Catgut.
Corde à jour. { An open string.
Corde à vide. {
Corde fausse. A false string.
Corde filée. A covered string.
Corde sourde. A muted string.
Une corde. Same as *una corda.* (See *Corda.*)

CORDEL'LA, Giacomo. Naples, 1786-1846. Pupil of Paisiello.
Wrote 19 operas, masses, &c.

CORDER, Frederick. *B.* London, 1852 ; Mendelssohn Scholar, R.A.M., 1875. Studied at Cologne. Curator, R.A.M., 1889.
Works: operas, *Nordisa* (1886), *Morte d'Arthur, Philomel;* overtures, orchestral idylls, &c.; cantatas, *The Bridal of Triermain* (1886), &c. ; operettas, trios, songs, &c.

Cordia'le (*I.*). Cordially ; with heartiness.

Cordier (*F.*) } Tail-piece (of a violin), &c.
Cordie'ra (*I.*) }

Cordome'tro (*I.*). A string-gauge.

COREL'LI, Arcangelo. Famous violinist ; *b.* nr. Imola, 1653 ; *d.* Rome, 1713. Settled in Rome at the house of Cardinal Ottoboni, 1681, as teacher and concert giver. Among his pupils were Baptiste Anet, Geminiani, and Locatelli. Corelli laid the foundation of modern violin technique, and his compositions are still looked upon as classics.
Works: 48 "sonatas" (or trios) for 2 violins and 'cello, &c., with a "continued bass;" 12 sonatas for violin and bass; "Concerti grossi" for 2 violins and 'cello *obbligati,* with 2 other violins, a viola, and a bass, &c. (See *Concerto grosso.*)
These celebrated "sonatas" are not like the modern highly-developed compositions called by the same name. The First Sonata, for example, consists of the following :—(1) *Grave,* C time, 14 bars. (2) *Allegro,* C time, 38 bars. (3) *Adagio,* 3-4 time, 37 bars. (4) *Allegro,* 3-4 time, 98 bars.

CORFE, Jos. *B.* Salisbury, 1740 ; *d.* 1820. Organist Salisbury Cathedral, 1792.
Works: a vol. of church music, glees, treatises on Singing and Thorough-bass, &c.

CORFE, Arthur T. Salisbury, 1773-1863. Son of Jos. Orgt. Salisbury Cathedral, 1804. Wrote anthems, glees, songs, &c.

Corife'o *(I.).* (See **Coryphæus**.)

Cori'sta *(I.).* A chorus-singer.

Cornamu'sa *(I.).*
Cornemuse *(F.).* } A bagpipe.

CORNE'LIUS, Peter. Mayence, 1824-74. Friend of Liszt and Wagner.
Works: operas, *Der Barbier von Bagdad, Der Cid, Gunlöd;* vocal duets, choruses for men's voices, songs, &c.

CORNELL', John H. American organist and writer. *B.* New York, 1828; *d.* 1894.

Cornet. (1) An obsolete wind instrument, similar to the Serpent, with a cup mouthpiece and holes for the fingers. (2) A mixture stop in the organ. (3) A pedal reed, 4 ft. or 2 ft., on some organs. (4) The *Cornet-à-pistons.* (*F.,* usually *Piston* only.)
Echo Cornet. A soft-toned cornet (2) placed in a box to produce "echo" effects.
Mounted Cornet. A cornet stop "mounted" on a special soundboard.

Cornet-à-pistons, or simply **Cornet.** The treble instrument of the modern brass band.

Its compass is from—
(or a few notes higher with specially talented players).
The ordinary cornet is in B♭, and it produces sounds "a tone lower" than the written notes. (See *Transposing Instruments.*)
A "soprano" cornet in E♭ is also much used in large bands.
On account of the facility with which it can be played, the cornet is often employed in orchestras instead of the trumpet.

Cornet'ta *(I.).* The *Cornet-à-pistons.*

Cornet'to *(I.).* A small horn; a cornet.

Cor'ni *(I.).* Horns.

CORNISH (CORNYSHE), Wm. Composer to the Chapel Royal in the reigns of Henry VII and Henry VIII; *d.* 1524.

Cor'no *(I.).* A horn. (See **Horn.**)
Cor'no al'to. The high horn in B♭ (or B♮).
Cor'no bas'so. The low horn in B♭.
Cor'no di basset'to. (See **Basset-horn.**)
Cor'no da cac'cia. Hunting horn.
Cor'no Ingle'se. (See **Cor Anglais.**)

Corno'pean. (1) Old name for a *Cornet-à-pistons.* (2) An 8-ft. org. reed-stop.

Cornophone *(F.).* A tenor saxhorn played with a horn mouthpiece (as a substitute for the horn).

Co'ro *(I.).* A chorus; a choir.
Co'ro del'la chie'sa. A church choir; a sacred chorus.
Co'ro favori'to. A select choir.
Co'ro pri'mo. The 1st chorus (or choir) in a double chorus.
Co'ro secon'do. The 2nd ditto. [chorus.

Coro'na *(I.).* "A crown." The hold or pause, ⌢.

Cor'onach. (See **Cor'anach.**)

CORONA'RO, Gaetano. *B.* Vicenza, 1852. Pupil (afterwards professor) Milan Cons.
Works: operas, *Un Tramonto, La Creola, Il Malacarne.*

Corps *(F.).* "Body." Fulness and quality of tone.
Corps de rechange. Crook (of a horn, &c.).
Corps d' harmonie. A fundamental chord.
Corps de voix. The range, volume, and quality of a voice.

Correcto'rium *(L.).* A tuning-cone.

CORREGGIO. (See **Merulo**.)

Corren'te *(I.).* A *Courante* (*q.v.*).

COR'RI, Domenico. *B.* Rome, 1746; *d.* London, 1825. Pupil of Porpora.
Works: operas, *Alessandro nelle Indie,* and *The Travellers;* arias, sonatas, &c.; a "Musical Dictionary," "The Singer's Preceptor," &c.

COR'SI, Jacobo. Florentine nobleman; *b.* abt. 1560.
He and his friend Bardi patronized the group of musicians and poets who initiated the "modern style" of music. (See *Peri, Caccini, Cavaliere, Galilei.*)

Cor'to,-a *(I.).* Short.

CORTOT, Alfred Noted French pianist. Pf. Prof., Paris Cons.; formerly Chorusmaster at Bayreuth. First London appearance, 1907.

Coryphæ'us *(L.).* (*G.,Koryphä'e; F.,Coryphée; I., Corife'o.*) (1) The leader of the chorus in ancient Greek drama. (2) The leader of an opera chorus. (3) The leader of a group of dancers.

COSS'MANN, Bernhard. Distinguished 'cellist; *b.* Dessau, 1822.
Played at the Paris Grand Opéra, and Opera-Comique, 1840-6; solo 'cellist at Leipzig Gewandhaus, 1847-48. Prof. of 'Cello at Frankfort Cons., 1878.

COS'TA, Sir Michael. *B.* Naples, 1808; *d.* Brighton, 1884. Studied Naples Cons. Came to England, 1829. Music-director, King's Theatre, London, 1832. Conductor, Philharmonic, 1846; New Italian Opera, 1846; Sacred Harmonic Society, 1848; Birmingham Festivals, 1849; Handel Festivals, 1869. Knighted, 1869.
Works: oratorios, *La Passione* (1825), *Eli* (Birmingham, 1855), *Naaman* (1864); 5 operas; 2 cantatas, 3 symphonies, &c.

COS'TA, P. Mario. Nephew of Sir M. *B.* Taranto, 1858.
Works: 2 pantomimes and several light popular songs (*Oje Caruli, A Frangesa,* &c.).

Costret'to *(I.).* Constrained, forced.
Bas'so costret'to. A ground bass (*q.v.*).

Cotillon *(F.).* A lively French dance, similar to the Quadrille.

COT'TA, Joh. *B.* Thuringia, 1794; *d.* 1868. Composed the German patriotic song, "Was ist des Deutschen Vaterland," 1813.

Cottage Piano. The ordinary small upright piano—as opposed to the grand.

COTTON, John. Probably an Englishman. Wrote a noteworthy treatise on music about the beginning of the 12th century.

Couac *(F.).* The quacking or "goose" sound produced by bad blowing (clarinet, &c.).

Couched Harp. The spinet.

COUCY, Regnault de. Troubadour ; *d.* in Palestine, 1192.

Several of Regnault's songs have been published in Paris, "with the old music."

Coulé *(F.).* (1) *Legato.* (2) A slur ; especially a group of two slurred notes. (3) A grace in harpsichord music ; a slide :—

Written   Played

Coulisse *(F.).* The slide of a trumpet or trombone.

Count. To count time.

In the orchestra a player has sometimes to count 100 bars or more. To be sure of entering correctly he counts mentally—ONE, two, three, four ; Two, two, three, four ; THREE, two, three, four, &c.

Counter. Same as *L.* Contra, and *F.* Contre.

Counter exposition. A second, contrasted exposition in a fugue.

Counter-subject. A counterpoint to accompany the subject of a fugue, and contrasted with it in rhythm, &c.

Counter Tenor. A high tenor, or alto voice. The natural counter-tenor voice was formerly common in England, but is now becoming quite rare.

Counter Tenor Clef. The Alto clef.

Counterpoint. *(G., Kon'trapunkt ; F., Contre-*

point ; I., Contrappun'to.) (1) The art of combining melodies. (2) An artificial system of composition supposed to be based on the works of the contrapuntists of the 16th century. (3) Any melody added to a Canto-Fermo.

Counterpoint had its origin in attempts to add accompanying parts to the Plain-song of the early Church. The word is derived from the Latin *punctus contra punctum* (point against point), the setting of "points" (*i.e.*, notes) in one part against those in another.

The *essence* of counterpoint is the writing of beautiful —or, at any rate, *singable* melodies. Unfortunately modern theorists have obscured the subject by a multitude of hair-splitting, confusing, and often contradictory rules, which have never been observed in the works of any great composers. The study of counterpoint is, nevertheless, interesting, and often valuable. Counterpoint—which includes Canon and Fugue—may be written in any number of parts ; but compositions in more than eight distinct parts are generally useless and ineffective.

The following 2-part examples are from Cherubini, the first really great composer who wrote a treatise on the subject. He claims that they are "conformable to the rules of *Strict* Counterpoint."

N.B.—The melody, or subject, to which the counterpoint is added, is also called the *theme, Canto-Fermo (cantus firmus)*, plain-song, plain-chant, &c. It is marked C.F. in the examples.

1st Species : note against note.

2nd Species : 2 notes against 1.

3rd Species : 4 notes against 1.

4th Species : Syncopation.

5th Species : Florid.

Combined Counterpoint. The combination of two or more different species.

4th Species.   ALBRECHTSBERGER.

C.F.
3rd Species.

It is only right to add that—in this country especially—we have wandered so far from the precepts laid down by Cherubini and Albrechtsberger that probably none of the above examples would be accepted without reserve by a Board of English examiners.

Invertible Counterpoint.

(*a*) DOUBLE COUNTERPOINT. A counterpoint added to a Canto Fermo—or two melodies composed simultaneously—so that either may serve as a higher or lower part to the other. Double Counterpoint may be constructed to "invert" at any interval, as 8th, 10th, 11th, 12th, &c. Counterpoint invertible at the 8ve (or 15th) is the most usual and useful. It is constantly employed in fugal writing.

Example of Double Counterpoint in the 12th.—and also in the 12th—from MOZART'S *Requiem.*

&c.

Inversion in the 8ve.

&c.

Inversion in the 12th (Relative Major).

&c.

(*b*) TRIPLE COUNTERPOINT. Three melodies, either of which may be bass, middle part, or upper part. It admits of 6 different arrangements :—

Overture, Messiah, HANDEL.

&c.

(*c*) QUADRUPLE COUNTERPOINT. Four melodies mutually interchangeable, admitting of 24 arrangements.

Adapted from ZIMMERMANN.

(d) QUINTUPLE COUNTERPOINT. Five interchangeable melodies—120 possible arrangements !

Finale, Jupiter Symphony, MOZART.

Counterpoint, *Strict* or *Pure.* With all the rules rigidly observed.

Counterpoint, *Free.* Contrapuntal part-writing allowing all the chords, progressions, and freedoms of modern harmony. Bach, Beethoven, and Wagner excelled in this style.

Counterpoint, *Florid.* The 5th species (Cherubini), or, according to other theorists, any other species than the 1st.

Counterpoint, Golden Age of. The 16th cent.; especially from about 1540 to 1600.

Chief composers : Palestrina (1526-94), Lassus (Lasso), (1532-94), Vittoria (abt. 1540-1608), Marenzio (1556(?)-99), A. Gabrieli (1510-86), G. Gabrieli (1557-1613), Croce (1560-1609), C. di Rore (1516-65), Leo Hasler (1564-1612), Tallis (1510-85), Byrd (1543-1623), Douland (Dowland) (1562-1626).

Country dance. A rustic dance, generally in $\frac{2}{4}$, $\frac{4}{4}$, or $\frac{6}{8}$ time, and in strains or sections of 4 or 8 measures.

As the partners in this dance are arranged in two opposing lines, it has long been natural to suppose that it is derived from *contra*-dance *(I., contra-danza ; F., contredanse).* This is denied in Grove's Dictionary, but Prof. Niecks (Dictionary of Musical Terms) says that it is "still a matter of controversy," and he adds that, whatever the derivation may be, "a country dance is a contra-dance."

Coup *(F.).* A stroke.

Coup d' archet. The stroke of the bow.

Coup de fouet. "The sudden application of brilliance at the termination of a passage or movement."

Coup de la glotte. "Shock of the glottis ;" a distinct, sudden attack (of a tone, &c.).

Coup de langue. "Tonguing" in wind inst. playing.

Double coup de langue. Double-tonguing.

Couper le sujet *(F.).* To shorten a theme or subject.

COUPERIN, François. The chief representative of a family of distinguished French musicians. *B.* Paris, 1668 ; *d.* 1733. Claveciniste de la Chambre du Roi, 1701. Chrysander describes him as "the first great composer for the harpsichord known in the history of music. . . He stands at the commencement of the modern period, and must be regarded as clearing the way for a new art." J. S. Bach was greatly influenced in his clavier music by Couperin's works. His compositions are specially valued for the great care and accuracy with which the numerous and characteristic *agrémens* (graces, embellishments, &c.), are indicated.

Works : 4 sets of pieces for clavecin ; a Clavecin Method ; trios for 2 violins and bass ; "Pièces de Viole," &c.

Coupler. A piece of organ mechanism to connect different manuals, manuals and pedals, &c.

Couplet. (1) A pair of rhymed lines (in poetry). (2) A duplet occurring in a tripletted time :—

COUPPEY. (See Le Couppey.)

Coupure *(F.).* A "cut."

Courante. *(F.,* from *Courir,* "to run ;" *I., Corren'te.)* (1) An old French dance in $\frac{3}{2}$ time. (2) A movement of a *Suite,* generally following the *Allemande.*

The *courante* was usually in 3-4 or 3-8 time ; there were 2 or 3 varieties, the Italian *corrente* being very quick and abounding in runs, &c., as its name implies.

Vivace ($\flat$. = 76).   BACH, *Suite II.*

Couronne *(F.).* A corona, or pause ⌢.

Court *(F.).* Short.

Courtal, Courtel. Ancient names for bassoon. (See *Curtal.*)

COURTEVILLE, Ralph (or Raphael). English song writer ; *d.* abt. 1735.

Wrote the hymn-tune "St. James's."

COURTOIS, Jean. 16th century French composer. Wrote motets, masses, &c.

COURVOISIER, Karl. Violinist ; *b.* Basle, 1846. Pupil of David and Joachim. Lived in Liverpool from 1885 ; *d.* 1908.

Works : "The Technics of Violin Playing," a Violin Method, &c.

COUSINS, Chas. *B.* nr. Portsmouth, 1830 ; *d.* 1890. Music-director, Kneller Hall, from 1874.

COUSSEMAKER, Chas. E. H. de. Eminent French musical historian ; 1805-1876.

Published works : "Memoir of Hucbald" (1841), "The Musical Instruments of the Middle Ages," "History of Harmony in the Middle Ages" (1852), "'Drames Liturgiques' of the Middle Ages" (1861), "The Harmonists of the 12th and 13th centuries" (1864), "Medieval Musical Compositions" (4 vols., 1864-76), "Complete Works of Adam de la Hale" (1872), &c. He also composed several songs, &c.

COUSSER. (See **Kusser.**)

COVE, Kate. Soprano ; *b.* London, 1871.

Covered Consecutives. (See **Hidden Consecutives.**)

Macfarren calls them "exposed" consecutives.

Covered strings. Strings covered with fine wire to increase the density and produce lower, deeper tones.

Covent Garden Theatre. Opened 1732.

COV'ERLY, Robt. *B.* Oporto, 1863. Lived in New York ; afterwards in London.

Works : numerous pf. pieces, and several songs widely popular in America.

COWARD, Henry. *B.* Liverpool, 1849. Mus.D. Oxon, 1894. Chorus-master Sheffield Festival Choir, 1896. "Has brought this choir into the front rank."—*Grove's Dict.*

Works : *Magna Charta* (1882), *Queen Victoria* (1885), *The Story of Bethany* (1891), *The King's Error* (1894), *The Fairy Mirror*, &c.; also anthems, songs, part-songs, &c.

COWARD, Jas. London, 1824-80. Organist Crystal Palace, 1857-80.

Wrote several glees and some songs, &c.

COWEN, Frederic Hymen. *B.* Kingston, Jamaica, Jan. 29, 1852. Brought to England for musical study at the age of 4 ; studied under Benedict and Goss, and later at Leipzig and Berlin. Director Edinburgh Academy of Music, 1882 ; conductor Philharmonic (succeeding Sullivan) 1887.

Works : 4 operas, *Pauline* (1876), *Thorgrim* (1890), *Signa* (1893), *Harold* (1895) ; 2 oratorios, *The Deluge* (1878), *Ruth* (1887) ; 7 cantatas, *The Rose Maiden* (1870), *The Corsair* (1876), *St. Ursula* (1881), *The Sleeping Beauty* (1885), *St. John's Eve* (1889), *The Water-Lily* (1893), *The Transfiguration* (1895) ; 6 symphonies ; orchestral suites, chamber music, &c. ; and over 250 songs (" The Better Land," "The Children's Home," "The Promise of Life," &c.).

COWPER, Wm. 1731 - 1800. English poet. Wrote the hymns "There is a fountain," "Hark, my soul, it is the Lord," "God moves in a mysterious way," &c.

Crackle. To "break" or arpeggiate the chords in lute playing.

Craco'viak } A Polish dance in $\frac{2}{4}$ time,
Cracovienne *(F.)* } with frequent syncopations :

&c.

CRAMENT, Jn. Maude. Orgt., composer. and conductor : *b.* Bolton Percy, 1845. Mus.Bac. Oxon, 1880.

CRA'MER (pron. *Crah'mer*), **Karl Fr.** *B.* Quedlinburg, 1752 ; *d.* 1807. Professor at Kiel.

Works : pf. pieces, songs, hymns, &c.

CRA'MER, Wilhelm. *B.* Mannheim, abt. 1745 ; *d.* London, 1799. Conductor of the King's band, and 1st violin at the leading concerts, London, 1761-72. Conducted the Handel Festivals, 1784 and 87.

Wrote 8 violin concertos, trios, violin solos, &c.

CRA'MER, Joh. Baptist. Eldest son of W. *B.* Mannheim, 1771 ; [*d.* London, 1858. Toured as concert pianist from 1788. Established (with Addison and Beale) the music publishing house of Cramer & Co., 1828.

Of his numerous compositions for the piano, all are now practically forgotten except the well-known " Cramer's Studies," all of which are still regarded as " excellent practice," and some as " really beautiful music."

CRAMPTON, Thos. *B.* Sheerness, 1817 ; *d.* 1885. Editor *Pitman's Musical Monthly.* Wrote several popular school songs, &c.

CRANZ. Hamburg music publishing firm ; founded 1813, by A. H. Cranz.

CRAWFORD, Major G. A. *B.* Dublin, 1827 ; *d.* 1903. Contributor to Grove's *Dict.*, *Musical Times*, Julian's *Hymnology*, &c.

CRECQUILLON (Crécquillon), Thos. J. Eminent 16th century contrapuntist ; *d.* 1557.

Works : masses, motets, chansons, &c.

CREATION, The. Haydn's 1st oratorio. Produced Vienna, 1798.

Crécelle *(F.).* A rattle.

Cre'do (*L.* "I believe"). The 3rd main portion of the Mass—the Nicene Creed.

Creed. The three Creeds used in the English Church are the Apostles' Creed, the Nicene Creed, and the Athanasian Creed. Musical settings of the Nicene Creed are very numerous.

Crem'balum. A Jew's-harp.

Cremo'na. (1) A violin made by any of the old " Cremona " makers. (See **Amati, Stradivarius,** and **Guarnerius.**) (2) An organ reed-stop. (See **Krummhorn.**)

Cremorne *(F.).* (See **Krummhorn.**)

CRERAR, Mrs. A. Evangeline Florence *(q.v.).*

Crescen'do *(I.).* Gradually increasing in loudness. The sign $\prec$.

Crescen'do e poi diminuen'do. Crescendo and then diminuendo.
Crescen'do po'co a po'co al ff. Increase gradually to *ff*.
Crescen'do po'co a po'co al for'te, ed un pochetti'no acceleran'do. Gradually louder up to the *forte*, and a very little *acceleran'do.*

Crescen'do Pedal. (1) The ordinary swell pedal of the organ. (2) A contrivance for bringing on the stops, in order, or diminishing them.

Crescen'do Zug *(G.).* (1) A crescendo pedal. (2) The swell-box.

Crescent, Chinese Crescent, Jingling Johnny, or **Pavilion.** A Turkish inst. used in military bands.

It has several crescent-shaped metal plates hung with little bells, mounted on a staff, and "jingled" in time with the music.

CRESCENTI'NI, Girolamo. Male mezzo-soprano ; *b.* nr. Urbino, 1766 ; *d.* 1846.

His success at Rome, Venice, London, Naples, and other European cities earned him the title of the "Italian Orpheus." Prof. of singing, Naples Royal Cons., 1816. Published a work on "Vocalization."

"Nothing could exceed the suavity of his tones, the force of his expression, the taste of his ornaments, or the broad style of his phrasing." —*Fétis.*

CRESER, Dr. Wm. *B.* York, 1844. Mus.Doc. Oxon, 1880. Organist Chapel Royal, St. James's, 1891-1902.

Has written *Eudora* (Leeds, 1882), and other works.

Cre'ticus *(L.).* A metrical foot ; one short syllable between two long ones (— ∪ —).

CREYGHTON (or Creighton), **Robert, D.D.** *B.* abt. 1639 ; *d.* Wells, 1733 (4). Precentor Wells Cathedral, 1674.

Wrote services and anthems. Best-known work, "I will arise."

Creyghtonian Seventh. A dominant 7th followed by a 7th on the sub-dominant ; said to have been first used by Creyghton.

Handel employs the progression with fine effect in "Envy, eldest born," *Saul.*—

CRISTOFO'RI, Bartolommeo (also known as **Cristofali** and **Cristofani**). *B.* Padua 1653 ; *d.* Florence, 1731. Invented the "hammer-action" which is the essential distinction between the pf. and the harpsichord.

The principle was adopted by G. Silbermann (Freiberg) and Broadwood (London).

Criticism. An estimate of, or judgment upon, the merits and demerits of a work.

Criticisms are necessary to guide and form the public taste. An ideal musical critic should be perfectly unbiassed, and should have a profound knowledge of every style of musical composition ; he should also be acquainted with current musical ideas and ideals, and gifted with sufficient prescience to be able to gauge the trend of general musical appreciation and progress. As no individual has ever possessed all these qualifications in due proportion, it follows that criticisms of new works should always be received with reserve. No great composer has ever endeavoured to explore a new region of musical composition without encountering a storm of adverse criticism for violating rules, introducing inartistic innovations, removing the ancient landmarks, &c.! Haydn and Mozart were savagely attacked ; Beethoven's later works were regarded by multitudes of critics as the "effusions of a madman," while later, no denunciatory adjectives were considered too strong to describe the music of Richard Wagner ! In 1855, after Wagner's visit to London, the

Musical World (then the leading London musical journal) devoted three full pages to a violent attack on Wagner and his music.

"We hold that Herr Richard Wagner is *not a musician at all*, but a simple theorist who has aimed a blow at the very existence of music. . . . It is clear that he wants to upset both opera and drama. . . . He can build up nothing himself. He can destroy, but not re-construct. . . . Look at *Lohengrin!* . . . it is poison, *rank poison.* . . . This man, this Wagner, this author of *Tannhauser,* of *Lohengrin,* and so many other hideous things— and, above all, the overture to *Der Fliegende Holländer,* the most hideous and detestable of the whole—this preacher of the 'Future,' was born to feed spiders with flies, not to make happy the heart of man with beautiful melody and harmony. What is music to him, or he to music ? . . . Who are the men that go about as his apostles ? Men like Liszt—madmen, enemies to music to the knife, who, not born for music, and conscious of their impotence, revenge themselves by trying to annihilate it. . . . The indignation we feel at the revelation of his impious theories is so great, that to give a tongue to it in ordinary language is beyond our means. . . . There is as much difference between *Guillaume Tell* and *Lohengrin* as between the sun and *ashes*."—(June 30th, 1855.)

"We regard Herr Wagner as the Arch-enemy of music. . . . He . is incapable of writing a tune." —(Feb. 2nd, 1856.)

This adverse criticism was extended to Schumann, Brahms, and Robt. Franz :—"*Lohengrin* is a bad thing, *Paradise and the Peri* is a bad thing, and the sonata of Brahms is a (very) bad thing ; but . . they have nothing in common but this badness."—(Aug. 23rd, 1856.) And again, "If this is music we do not know what music is, and by this we stand or fall !" Compare with all this the following sentence from Baker's "Dictionary of Musicians" (1900) :—"Richard Wagner was the grandest and most original dramatic composer of all times !" (See *Wagner.*)

M. Lavignac ("Music and Musicians," p. 376-7) makes some excellent remarks on criticism :—

"Usually, opinions are too hastily formed, in respect to any great musical production. I do not think there lives the musician capable of determining on a single hearing the exact value of a work in whose production months, or even years have been spent.

"Newspaper critics are forced . . . to perform constantly this presumptuous *tour de force.* . . Hence we often see these critics obliged . . . either to modify an opinion expressed until it is almost unrecognizable, or else to persist obstinately in an error of judgment. . . . Before forming an opinion of a work it is indispensable to feel sure that one has completely understood it. . . . It is unjust to say, 'This is poor, for I do not understand it at all ; I don't know what it means ; consequently, it is worthless.'"

CRIVEL'LI, Gaetano. Celebrated tenor ; *b.* Bergamo, 1774 ; *d.* 1836. Sang at all the chief Italian theatres, in Paris (1811-17), and in London (1817-18).

CRIVEL'LI, G. B. Renowned composer of motets and madrigals ; *b.* Modena ; *d.* there, 1682.

CRIVEL'LI, Domenico. Son of Gaetano ; *b.* Brescia, 1793 ; *d.* London, 1857.

Pub. a treatise on "The Art of Singing."

CRO'CE, Giovanni della. Eminent composer ; *b.* Chioggia, abt. 1560 ; *d.* Venice, 1609. Maestro, St. Mark's, Venice, 1603.

Works : motets, several volumes of madrigals, a collection of humorous songs in the Venetian dialect (his most famous work), "Cantiones Sacræ" for 8 voices, masses, Lamentations, Vespers for 8 voices, &c.

Croche *(F.).* A quaver, ♪

Croche, Double *(F.).* A semiquaver, ♫

Croche, Triple *(F.).* A Demisemiquaver, ♬

Croches liées *(F.).* Quavers with the stems joined, ♫♫

Croche'ta *(L.). (F., Crochet.)* A crotchet.

CROFT (or **Crofts**), **Dr. Wm.** *B.* Warwickshire, 1678 ; *d.* Bath, 1727. Gentleman Chapel Royal, 1700; organist, 1707. Organist Westminster Abbey, 1708 (succeeding **Blow**). Mus.Doc. Oxon, 1713. Buried in Westminster Abbey.

Works : *Divine Harmony* (anthems) ; 30 anthems and a Burial Service, *in score* (1724), " the first English church music engraved in score on plates ; " odes, overtures, vn. sonatas, songs, &c. The fine tunes " Hanover," " St. Ann's," and " St. Matthew's " are attributed to him.

Croisement *(F.).* Crossing of parts.
Croisez les mains. Cross the hands.

Cro'ma *(I.).* A quaver, ♪

Croma'tico *(I.).* Chromatic.

Crom-horn, Cromor'na. (See **Krummhorn.**)

CRON'THAL, W. Pen-name of **P. Gross** *(q.v.).*

Crook. *(G. Ton, Bo'gen ; F., Corps de réchange ; I., Pez'zo di reser'va.)* (1) An accessory tube which can be fitted to an instrument to lower the pitch.

The French horn, *e.g.*, is furnished with some 12 to 15 crooks, by which its fundamental pitch can be altered from B♮ alto, to A (or A♭) basso. (See **Horn.**)

(2) The metal tube connecting the body of a bassoon, saxophone, bass-clarinet, &c., with the reed (or mouthpiece).

Croque Note.
" A name given in derision to those silly musicians, who, versed in the combinations of notes, and capable of performing the most difficult compositions at sight, execute in general without sentiment, without expression, and without taste."— *Rousseau.*

CROSDILL, John. *B.* London, 1751 ; *d.* 1825. Fine 'cellist; played at all the principal English festivals, concerts, &c., from 1769 to 1788.

CROSS, Michael H. Philadelphia, 1833-1897. Organist, conductor, &c.
" For 30 years his name was connected with musical progress in Philadelphia."—*Th. Baker.*

Cross-fingering. (See **Fingering.**)

CROSSLEY, Ada (**Mrs. F. G. F. Muecke**). Favourite contralto singer ; *b.* Gippsland, Australia, 1874. Gave her first London concert in 1895.

Cross-relation. Same as **False-relation** *(q.v.).*

Cro'talo. (1) A Turkish cymbal. (2) Small bells hung on the necks of cattle.
They were sometimes attached to weapons of war, &c.

Cro'talum *(L.).* A kind of rattle or clapper used by the ancient Greeks.

CROTCH, Dr. Wm. *B.* Norwich, 1775 ; *d.* Taunton, 1847. Played in public at the age of 4. Assistant organist Trinity and King's Colleges, Cambridge, at the age of 11. Mus.Bac. Oxon, 1794 ; University Professor of Music, 1797 ; Mus.Doc., 1799. Principal, R.A.M., 1822.

Works : 2 oratorios, *Palestine* (1812), *The Captivity of Judah* (1834) ; 10 anthems ; glees, fugues, org. concertos, pf. sonatas ; odes ; a fine motet, " Methinks I hear the full celestial choir ; " " Elements of Musical Composition," " Practical Thorough-Bass," &c.

Crotchet. A note equal to ¼th of a semibreve (♩) ; called also a " quarter-note."

CROUCH, Frederick Nicholls. *B.* London, 1808 ; *d.* Portland, Maine, 1896. 'Cellist; member of Queen Adelaide's private band till 1832. Went to New York, 1849. Played the 'cello at various American theatres, conducted concerts, served in the Confederate army, and afterwards settled in Baltimore as a teacher of singing.
Of his compositions " Kathleen Mavourneen " is the only one that has become popular.

CROW, Dr. Edwin J. *B.* Sittingbourne, 1841 ; *d.* 1907. Orgt. Ripon Cathedral, 1874-1902. Mus.Doc. Cantab, 1882.

Crowd, Croud, Crouth. *(Irish, Crut ; Welsh, Crwth ; L. Chrot'ta.)* An ancient instrument—probably the oldest of its class— with six strings, four for the bow and two to be plucked with the thumb. It is regarded as a precursor of the violin *(q.v.).*

CROWE, Alf. Gwyllim. Composer ; *b.* Bermuda, 1835 ; *d.* 1894.

CROWE, Fred. Jos. W. *B.* Weston-super-Mare, 1862. Orgt. Chichester Cath., since 1902.

CROWEST, Frederick J. *B.* London, 1850.
Works : " The Great Tone-Poets" (1874), " Dict. of British Musicians " (1895) ; &c.

Crowning of Chords. The " crown " of a chord is its highest note (*i.e.*, the note used in the melody or highest part).
" When the root is in the highest part the chord has its 1st crowning ; when the 3rd, its 3rd crowning, &c."—*Curwen.*

Crucifix'us *(L.).* A portion of the Credo.

CRÜGER, Joh. *B.* 1598 ; *d.* Berlin, 1662. Wrote and edited several collections of Lutheran chorals, many of which are still in common use. His " Nun danket alle Gott " may be called the " North German National Hymn."
For a fine setting of this melody see Mendelssohn's *Hymn of Praise.*

CRUVEL'LI, Jeanne Sophie C. Celebrated soprano ; *b.* Westphalia, 1826 ; *d.* 1907.
Sang in Venice, London, Paris, &c. Retired on her marriage to Count Vigier, 1856.

Crush-note. An acciaccatura.

Crystal Palace Concerts. Started under August Manns, 1855.

C-Schlüssel *(G.).* The C clef.

Cuckoo's song.

When the cuckoo first comes to us (about the end of April) its cry is the interval of a *minor 3rd.* As time passes the upper note sharpens, and it becomes a *major 3rd.* Later the interval changes to a 4th or even a 5th. These intervals have all been used in imitative music:—

(1) *Minor 3rd.*

&c.

We love to hear thy song. Cuckoo!

(2) *Major 3rd.*
BEETHOVEN. *Pastoral Sym.*
"Kukuk."   *Popular American Song.*

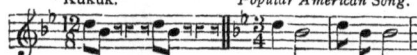

Cuckoo! cherry-tree, &c.

(3) *Perfect 4th.*
Mus. Magazine (1835).   Dr. ARNE.

Cuckoo!   Cuckoo! cuckoo!

Cue. "A hint."

The last notes (or words) of another part inserted (in smaller type) just before the re-entry of a voice or instrument after a long rest.

CUI, César Antonovitch. *B.* Vilna (Russia), 1835. A distinguished composer of the modern Russian school.

Works: 8 operas, *William Ratcliff* (1861), *Le Filibustier* (1894), *The Saracens* (1899), &c.; over 50 songs, several choruses, 4 orchestral suites, chamber and vn. music, pf. pieces, &c.

Cuivre *(F.).* Brass (lit. *Copper*). *Les cuivres,* the brass wind insts. (of an orch.).

Cuivré. Forced "brassy" notes (horn, &c.).
Cuivrez; Faites cuivrier. Make the tone brassy.

CULWICK, Jas. C. Orgt., composer, and writer; *b.* West Bromwich, 1845.

Cum can'tu *(L.).* With song.

CUMMINGS, Wm. Hayman. *B.* Sidbury, Devon, 1831. Chorister, St. Paul's and Temple Church; afterwards a leading tenor vocalist. Professor of Singing, R.A.M., 1879-96; Chorus-master, Sacred Harmonic Society, 1882 (afterwards conductor); Precentor, St. Anne's Soho, 1886-8; Principal G.S.M., 1896; Mus.Doc. Dublin, 1900. His splendid musical library includes some 5,000 vols., autographs, &c.

Works: cantata, *The Fairy Ring;* several prize glees, sacred music, songs, &c. Also a "Life of Purcell," a "Primer of the Rudiments of Music," a Biographical Dict., &c.

Cum Sanc'to Spi'ritu *(L.).* Part of the Gloria (in a Mass).

Cup. Mouthpiece of a brass inst.

Cu'po *(I.).* Dark, mysterious, close; sombre.

CUR'CI, Giuseppe. Italian composer, 1808-77.

Works: operas, sacred music, &c., and a book on singing, *Il Bel Canto.*

CURSCH'MANN, Karl F. *B.* Berlin, 1805; *d.* 1841.

Works: an opera, 83 songs (many of which were extremely popular), duets, trios, &c.

Curtal, or **Curtail.** An obsolete instrument of the bassoon type.

CUR'TI, Franz. *B.* Cassel, 1854; *d.* Dresden, 1898.

Wrote several operas given at Dresden, New York, &c.

CURWEN, John. *B.* Heckmondwike, Yorks., Nov. 14, 1816; *d.* nr. Manchester, May 26, 1880. Ordained minister; Pastor at Plaistow, Essex, 1844. Adopted Miss Glover's method of teaching singing, and developed the "Tonic Sol-fa" system and notation. (See **Tonic Sol-fa.**) Established the *Tonic Sol-fa Reporter* (now the *Musical Herald*), 1851. Founded the Tonic Sol-fa Association, 1853; Tonic Sol-fa College, 1863 (incorporated 1875). In addition to a large number of smaller books, he published the following:—

"The Standard Course" (1861), "The New Standard Course" (1872), "How to Observe Harmony" (1861, new ed. 1872), "The Commonplaces of Music" (1871-3), "Musical Statics" (1874), "The Teacher's Manual" (1875), "Musical Theory" (1879). He also edited and pub. many classical works, and collections of part-songs, choruses, hymn-tunes, school songs, &c. A biography, "Memorials of John Curwen," was published by his son, J. S. Curwen (see below), in 1882.

CURWEN, John Spencer. Son of the preceding; *b.* Plaistow, Sep. 30th, 1847. A.R.A.M., 1879; F.R.A.M., 1885. President, Tonic Sol-fa College, 1880. Active promoter of the Stratford Musical Festivals (est. 1883). Director of J. Curwen & Sons Ltd., 24 Berners Street, London. Editor of the *Musical Herald.* Has composed and arranged much music, but his life has been devoted to the Tonic Sol-fa movement and the promotion of music in schools. Towards this end he has visited and inspected the chief Continental schools, and has instituted conferences of music teachers throughout Great Britain.

Works: "Studies in Worship Music" (1880; 2nd series, 1885), "Memorials of John Curwen" (1882), "School Music Abroad" (1901).

CURWEN, Mrs. J. S. (*née* Annie Jessy Gregg). *B.* Dublin, 1845. Has published an educational method of teaching the pf., "The Child Pianist," 1886.

CURZON, Emmanuel H. P. de. Noted critic and writer on music; *b.* Havre, 1861.

Cushion-dance. An old English round dance in which each dancer selected a partner by dropping a cushion before him (or her).

CUS'INS, Sir Wm. Geo. *B.* London, 1833; *d.* 1893. Chorister Chapel Royal, 1843. Studied, Brussels Cons., and afterwards at the R.A.M. Conductor, Philharmonic, 1867-83. Conductor, Royal Band, 1870. Knighted, 1892.

Wrote an oratorio, *Gideon* (1871); cantatas, songs, &c.

CUSTARD, Reginald Goss. *B.* St. Leonards-on-Sea, March 29, 1877. Orgt. St. Margaret's, Westminster, since 1902. To Jan., 1909, has given 136 Recitals at this church, and many others in various parts of Great Britain.

CUSTARD, Walter Goss. Organist; father of above; nephew of Sir John Goss. *B.* 1841; *d.* Dec. 1907.

Cus′tos *(L.).* A direct *(q.v.).*

Cuvette *(F.).* The pedestal of a harp.

CUZZO′NI, Francesca. Celebrated soprano; *b.* Parma, 1700; *d.* 1770. Sang in Handel's operas, under his direction, London, 1722-6. She then joined the Bononcini side. (See **Bononcini.**) She is said to have died at Bologna in abject poverty.

Cyclical Forms. Compositions comprising a series of complete movements: suite, sonata, symphony, &c.

Cylinder   }   A rotary valve (for brass
Cylindre *(F.)* }   insts.) mostly used in Germany and Italy.

Cymbals. *(G. Beck′en; F., Cymbales; I., Piat′ti, Cinel′li.)* Percussion instruments, consisting of a pair of concave brass (or other metal) plates.

They are used in the orchestra by being clashed together, or struck with a drumstick.
Cymbale avec la mailloche (*F.*). Cymbal (struck) with a bass-drumstick.
Cymbale frappée avec une baguette de timbale (*F.*). Cymbal struck with a kettle-drumstick.

Cymbalis′ta. A player on cymbals.

Cym′bel. An organ mixture stop of high pitch.

Czakan. A Bohemian cane or bamboo flute.

CZAPEK. *Nom de plume* of **J. L. Hatton** *(q.v.).*

Czardas. A Hungarian national dance with constantly changing *tempo.*

CZER′NY (pron. *Chair′-nee*), **Karl.** Vienna, 1791-1857. Taught by Beethoven; celebrated as a pianist and teacher. Among his most famous pupils were Liszt, Döhler, Thalberg, and Jaell.

He published over 1,000 compositions, and left many more in MS., but his most important works were his pf. studies and exercises. His "School of Practical Composition," and a collection of his most useful pf. works—"Complete Theoretical and Practical Pf. School"—were published by Cocks & Co.

CZERSKY, Alex. *Nom de plume* of **F. W. Tschirch** *(q.v.).*

CZIBUL′KA, Alphons. 1842-94. Hungarian composer of dance music, operettas, &c.

Czimbal *(Hungarian).* A dulcimer.

Czimken. A Polish "country dance."

D

D *(G., D ; F., Ré ; I., Re).*
(1) The 2nd note, or Supertonic, of the standard scale of C.
(2) The 3rd string of the violin ; the 2nd string of the viola and violoncello.

D. Abbreviation of *Da* or *Dal; as* D.C. *(Da capo),* D.S. *(Dal segno).*

D dur *(G.).* D major.

D major. (1) The major key or scale requiring two sharps (F♯ and C♯).

(2) The chord

D minor. (1) The relative minor of F major. The harmonic scale of D minor requires B♭ and C♯. (See *Scales.*)

(2) The chord

D moll *(G.).* D minor.

Da *(I.).* From, by, of, for, in the style of, &c.
Da bal'lo. In the style of a dance.
Da ca'mera. (See *Chamber-music.*)
Da ca'po or *D.C.* Repeat from the beginning.
D.C. al Fi'ne. From the beginning to the *Fine,* or ⌒.
D.C. al Se'gno. From the beginning to the sign (⑤⸮, ⊕, or ⌒).
Da ca'po e poi la Co'da. Repeat 1st part, then go on to the Coda.
D.C. sen'za repetizio'ne (or *sen'za re'plica*). From the beginning, playing *only once* the parts which are marked with repeats (:‖:).
Da ca'po sen'za repitizio'ne, e poi la co'da. Da capo without repeats, and then the coda.
Da cappel'la. ⎫ In church style.
Da chie'sa. ⎭
Da lonta'no. (As if) from a distance ; an echo.
Da tea'tro. In theatrical style.

D'abord *(F.).* At first.

D'accord *(F.),* **D'accor'do** *(I.).* In tune.

Dach *(G.).* "A roof or deck." Also **Decke.**
(1) Soundboard. (2) Belly of a vn., &c.

DACHS, Jos. *B.* Ratisbon, 1825 ; *d.* 1896. Esteemed pianist and teacher.

Dach'schweller *(G.).* A swell-box.

Dac'tyl. A metrical foot of 3 syllables ; long, short, short (— ‿ ‿).

Dactyl'ion. A contrivance for finger gymnastics, invented by H. Herz, 1835.

Da'gli *(I.).* ⎫ From the, of the, to the, &c.
Dai *(I.).* ⎭

Daire. A Turkish tambourine.

Dal *(I.).* From the, &c.

DALAYRAC (or **D'ALAYRAC**), **Nicolas.** *B.* Muret, 1753 ; *d.* Paris, 1809.
Prolific composer of operas and operettas, of which he wrote about 80. They were very popular in Paris, but unknown elsewhere.

DAL'BERG, Joh. F. H. von. Aschaffenburg, 1752-1812.
Wrote cantatas, chamber music, pf. sonatas, songs, &c., and several theoretical works (including a translation of Sir Wm. Jones's treatise on "The Music of the Hindus").

D'ALBERT, Eugéne. (See **Albert.**)

DALCROZE, É. Jaques. *B.* Vienna, 1865.
Works : compositions for soli, chorus, and orch. ; and a number of popular Swiss chansons.

DALE, Alf. S. Orgt. and composer ; *b.* Rochester, 1868. Mus.Doc.Oxon, 1894.

DALE, Benj. D. Composer ; *b.* London, 1885.

D'ALEMBERT. (See **Alembert.**)

Dall', dal'la, dal'le, or **dal'lo** *(I.).* Same as *dagli,* or *dal.*

DALL, Roderick. The last of the Scotch wandering minstrels. He was "still living at Athol in 1740" *(Riemann).*

Dal se'gno *(I.),* or D.S. Repeat from the sign, ⑤. (Also *al segno.*)
Dal tea'tro (*I.*). In theatrical style.

DALVIMA'RE (or **d'Alvimare**), **M. P.** *B.* Dreux, 1772 ; *d.* Paris, 1839. Famous harpist, and composer of harp music.
Harpist at the Opéra, 1800 ; to Napoleon, 1806 ; and to the Empress Josephine, 1807.

DAMAN (or **DAMON**), **Wm.** Elizabethan composer of motets, &c. Harmonized collections of Psalm tunes, pub. 1579 and 1591.

DAM'CKE, Berthold. *B.* Hanover, 1812 ; *d.* Paris, 1875. Friend of Berlioz.
Conductor Potsdam Philharmonic Society, 1837, and Choral Union, 1839-40. Esteemed teacher in St. Petersburg (1845), Brussels (1855), and Paris (1859).
Works : oratorios, pf. pieces, part-songs, &c.

Damenisa'tion. A system of sol-faing used by Graun, on the syllables *Da, Me, Ni, Po, Tu, La, Be.*

DAMM, Friedrich. *B.* Dresden, 1831.
Has pub. a number of popular *salon* pf. pieces.

DAMOREAU, Laure Cinthie M. (sang first as "Mlle. Cinti"). Famous operatic soprano. *B.* Paris, 1801 ; *d.* 1863. Studied Paris Cons. Made her *début* as "Cherubin" in Mozart's *Figaro,* Théâtre Italien, 1819.
Sang in London (Italian Opera), 1822 ; at the Paris Grand Opéra, 1826-35 ; and at the Opéra-Comique, 1835-43. Created leading parts in operas by Rossini and Auber. Prof. of singing, Paris Cons., 1834-56.
Fétis described her as "one of the best singers the world has ever known."

Da MOT'TA, José V. Pianist ; *b.* Isle S. Thomas, Portuguese Africa, 1868.

Damp, To. To check the vibrations of a string (1) by means of the hand or finger, as on the harp, guitar, &c. ; or (2) by means of mechanical appliances, as on the pf.

Damper. (1) *(G., Däm'pfer; F., Etouffoir; I., Sordi'no, plur. Sordi'ni.)* A small piece of wood covered with felt used to check the vibration of a pf. string.
By pressing down the right (or loud) pedal all the dampers are raised from the strings. Notes struck while the dampers are thus raised continue sounding until the strings cease vibrating. If the right pedal be not used, the damper checks the vibration of the string the moment the corresponding key is released by the finger. (See *Pedal, Con sordini,* and *Senza sordini.*)
(2) The *mute* or *echo attachment* of a cornet, or other brass instrument.

Damper Pedal. The right or "loud" pf. pedal.

Däm'pfer *(G.).* A damper ; a mute (as for vn.).
Däm'pfer auf. Put on the mute (mutes).
Däm'pfer ab, fort, or *weg.* Take off the mute(s).

Däm'pfung *(G.).* (1) Damping, or muffling.
(2) The "damper" mechanism of a pf.

DAM'ROSCH, Frank H. Son of Dr. L. (below). *B.* Breslau, 1859. Went to New York, 1871, and has since held several important posts as conductor, &c., in America. Supervisor of music, New York public schools, 1897.
Has pub. a "Popular Method of Sight-Singing" (1894); songs, choruses, &c.

DAM'ROSCH, Dr. Leopold. Violinist, composer, and conductor. *B.* Posen, 1832; *d.* New York, 1885. Intimate friend of Liszt and Wagner. Solo violinist, Grand Ducal Orchestra, Weimar, 1855; conductor Breslau Philharmonic, 1859-60. Founded Breslau Orchestral Society, 1862. Conductor "Arion" Society, New York, 1871; founded New York Oratorio Society, 1873, and Symphony Society, 1878. Conducted first New York great Music Festival, 1881, and a season of German opera, 1884.
Works: Symphony in A, 7 cantatas, 3 vn. concertos, orch. pieces, pf. pieces, choruses, part-songs, songs, &c.

DAM'ROSCH, Walter Joh. Son of Dr. L. *B.* Breslau, 1862. Conductor New York Oratorio and Symphony Societies since 1885. Organised the Damrosch Opera Company, 1894.
Works: operas, *The Scarlet Letter* (1896), *Cyrano* (1904); songs, &c.

DANA, Chas. H. American pianist and composer; *b.* 1883.

DA'NA, Wm. Henry. American composer; *b.* Warren, Ohio, 1846. Studied in Berlin, and at the R.A.M., London. Director of Dana's Musical Institute, Warren, Ohio.
Works: a *De Profundis*, motets, songs, pf. pieces, &c.; also Text-books on Harmony, &c.

DANBE, Jules. *B.* Caen, 1840. Conductor Paris Opéra-Comique, 1895.
Works: violin pieces and transcriptions.

DANBY, John. 1757-98. Composed "Awake, Æolian lyre!" and other fine glees, &c.

Dance, Daunce, Daunse, Dawnce. *(G., Tanz; F., Danse; I., Dan'za; Sp., Dan'za.)*
(1) "A graceful movement of the feet or body, . . with or without the accompaniment of music to regulate its rhythm."
(2) "A tune by which the movements in dancing are regulated."—*Lloyd's Encylopædia.* .
Among old dances are the following: Gavotte, Tambourin, Jig (Gigue), Sicilienne, Bourrée, Rigadoon, Allemande, Minuet, Galliard, Polonaise, Chaconne, Saraband, Courante, Paspy, Passacaille, Pavan, and Musette. (See each under its heading.)

Dance of Death. *(F., Danse Macabre.)*
"An allegorical representation of the power of death over all ages and ranks. It is frequently met with in old MSS. books and decorations."—*Lloyd.*

Dancing was common in the early Christian Church. Odo, Bishop of Paris, forbade dancing in his diocese, 12th century.
It is still practised at Seville during Easter, and at Echternach.

DANCK'ERTS. (See **Dankers.**)

DANCLA, Arnaud. *B.* Bagnères-de-Bigorre, 1820; *d.* 1862. 'Cellist.
Works: études, melodies, &c., for 'cello, and a 'Cello Method.

DANCLA, Jean Baptiste Chas. Elder brother of A.; 1818-1907. Fine violinist. Prof. of violin playing, Paris Cons., 1857.
Works: about 130 violin pieces, including 6 concertos; 4 symphonies; pf. trios and quartets; a Violin Method; études, &c. His smaller works are graceful, melodious, and popular; his more ambitious pieces are of less value.

DANDO, Joseph H. B. Violinist; *b.* Somers Town, 1806; *d.* 1894. Noted orchl. leader; "the first to introduce public performances of instl. quartets."

D'ANGELI. (See **De-Angelis.**)

DANHAUSER, Adolphe L. Paris, 1835-96 Inspector of Singing, Communal Schools.
Wrote a "Thèorie de la Musique."

DANICAN. (See **Philidor.**)

DANK'ERS (DANKERTS, or DANCKERTS), Ghiselin. A noted 16th century contrapuntist. *B.* Tholen, in Zeeland. Chorister, Papal Chapel, 1538-65.
Works: motets, madrigals, &c.

Dank'lied *(G.).* A hymn of thanksgiving.

Dann *(G.).* Then, immediately.
Dann sogleich' im'mer lang'samer. Immediately gradually slower.

DANNELEY, John F. *B.* Oakingham, Berkshire, 1786; *d.* London, 1836.
Wrote "Thorough Bass" (1820), "Encyclopædia of Music" (1825), "Musical Grammar" (1826).

DANN'REUTHER, Edward Geo. *B.* Strasburg, 1844; *d.* 1905. Settled in London as pf. teacher, 1863; founded the London Wagner Society, 1872. Prof. of pf. R.C.M., 1895.
Works: Richard Wagner: His Tendencies and Theories" (1873), "Musical Ornamentation" (Novello's Primers); songs and pf. pieces.

DANN'REUTHER, Gustav. Brother of E. G. *B.* Cincinnati, 1853. Violinist. Director, Buffalo Philharmonic Society (N.Y.), 1882-4; founded the "Beethoven String Quartet," New York, 1884.

Danseur *(Fem. Danseuse) (F.).* A dancer.

Dans une exaltation croissante *(F.).* With increasing exaltation.

DAN'ZI, Francesca. (See **Lebrun.**)

DAN'ZI, Franz. Excellent singing teacher. *B.* Mannheim, 1763; *d.* 1826. Capellmeister, Stuttgart, 1807-8; then at Carlsruhe.
Works: 11 operas (*Cleopatra, Turandot, &c.*); an oratorio; cantatas, masses, symphonies, chamber music, &c.; and some good Singing Exercises.

DA PON'TE, Lorenzo. *B.* nr. Venice, 1749; *d.* 1838. Wrote the libretti of Mozart's *Figaro, Don Giovanni*, and *Cosi fan tutte.*

Da pri'ma *(I.).* (1) At first. (2) *Da capo (q.v.).*

DAQUIN, Louis Claude. Famous clavecinist; Paris, 1694-1772. Organist, St. Antoine, at the age of 12, his playing "attracting enormous crowds."
Works: "Pièces de Clavecin" (containing the celebrated "coucou"), a book of "Noëls," a cantata, organ pieces, &c.

DARCOURS, Ch. (See **Rety.**)

DARD-JANIN, Alf. Composer; *b.* Dijon, 1833.

DARGOMIJ'SKY, Alex. S. Pianist. *B.* Toula, Russia, 1813; *d.* St. Petersburg, 1869.
Works: operas, *Esmeralda*, *Russalka* (his greatest work, 1856), *The Triumph of Bacchus*, *Kamennoï Göst (The Marble Guest)*; orch. pieces (dances, fantasias, &c.); and over 100 romances, ballads, songs, waltzes, &c.

Darm *(G.).* Catgut.

Darm'saiten *(G.).* Catgut strings.

Das *(G.).* The, which; that; it.
Das dop'pelt lang'samer. Twice as slow.
Das zwei'te Mal. The second time.
Das Le'bewohl. (The) Farewell.
Das sel'be Tem'po. Same as *L'istesso tempo (q.v.).*
Das Wie'dersehn. The return.

Da Scher'zo *(I.).* In scherzo style.

Dash. (1) The sign for *staccatissimo:—*
Written. Played.

It was originally the only sign for *Staccato.*
(2) In figured bass, a line drawn through a figure to raise a note a *semitone:—*

(3) In harpsichord music the same as a *coulé:—*
Written. Played.

DAU'BE, Joh. F. 1730-97. Chamber musician at Wurtemburg.
Wrote a "General Bass" *(i.e.,* a *Thorough-Bass),* founded on three chords—the Tonic Triad, the "added 6th" on the Subdominant, and the Dominant 7th.

DAUDET, Alphonse. Novelist and dramatist. *B.* Nismes, 1840; *d.* Paris, 1897.
Wrote the libretti of *l'Arlésienne* (Bizet), and other modern operas.

Dau'er *(G.).* Duration (of a note, &c.).

Dau'men *(G.).* The thumb.

Dau'menaufsatz *(G.).* A thumb position (in 'cello playing).

DAUPRAT, Louis F. Celebrated horn player; Paris, 1781-1868. Member of the bands of the Garde Nationale and the Garde des Consuls. First horn, Bordeaux Theatre (1806) and the Opéra Orch. (1808). Chamber musician to Napoleon and Louis XVIII. Prof. Paris Cons., 1816.
Works: "Méthode for cor alto et cor basse," horn concertos, &c.

DAVENPORT, Francis Wm. *B.* Wilderslowe, nr. Derby, 1847. Pupil of Sir G. A. Macfarren (whose only daughter he married). Prof. R.A.M. (1879) and G.S.M. (1882).
Works: 2 symphonies, an overture, 10 pieces for piano and 'cello, a trio in B♭, part-songs; "Elements of Music" (1884), "Elements of Harmony and Counterpoint" (1886), &c.

DAVEY, Henry. *B.* Brighton, 1853.
Works: "The Student's Musical Hist." (1891), "Hist. of English Music" (1895), many articles in the "Dict. of National Biog.," important

essays on English music in German periodicals, &c. Corrector (for England) of Eitner's *Quellenlexikon*; wrote the Memoir of Shakespeare in the Stratford Town *Edition de luxe.*

DAVID, Adolphe I. *B.* Nantes, 1842; *d.* 1897. Wrote successful pantomimes and a comic opera; also popular pf. pieces.

DAVID, Félicien César. *B.* Vaucluse, 1810; *d.* 1876. Entered Paris Cons., 1830. Went on a concert tour with a number of brethren of the *Saint-Simonists* through Constantinople, Smyrna, and Egypt, returning to Paris in 1835.
His numerous compositions met with small success until 1844, when *Le Désert* (a descriptive cantata typical of Arab life) was received with "delirious applause."
Of his later works the most successful were the operas *La Perle du Brésil* (1851), *Herculaneum* (1859), and *Lalla Rookh* (1862).

DA'VID (pron. *Dah'veed),* **Ferdinand.** *B.* Hamburg, 1810; *d.* 1873. Eminent violinist; pupil of Spohr and Hauptmann. On Mendelssohn becoming conductor of the Gewandhaus Orch., Leipzig, 1835, he obtained the post of leader for David; and at the foundation of the Leipzig Cons., 1843, he was appointed Violin Professor. Both as leader and professor he was greatly celebrated, among his most distinguished pupils being Wilhelmj and Joachim. When Mendelssohn was writing his Violin Concerto he frequently consulted David, submitting passages for his approval, and accepting his practical suggestions, &c. It was first played in public by David at the Gewandhaus, 1845.
Works: an opera, 2 symphonies, 5 violin concertos, chamber music, violin pieces, &c.; also a very fine "Violin School," and a "Collection of Standard Works for the Violin."

DAVID, Marie L. (See **Dulcken.**)

DA'VID, Peter Paul. Son of Ferdinand; *b.* Leipzig, 1840. Music master at Uppingham School.

DAVID, Samuel. Paris, 1838-95. Won *Grand Prix de Rome,* Paris Cons., 1858.
Works: several operas (given in Paris), an "ode-symphonie" *(Le Triomphe de la Paix),* 4 symphonies, songs, &c.

DAVI'DE, Giacomo. Distinguished Italian tenor. *B.* nr. Bergamo, 1750; *d.* 1830.
Lord Mount-Edgcumbe says that "He was undoubtedly the first tenor of his time." He sang at the last of the Handel Commemoration Festivals, Westminster Abbey, 1791.

DA'VIDOFF, Karl J. Renowned 'cellist. *B.* Goldingen, Kurland, 1838; *d.* Moscow, 1889. First 'cello, Gewandhaus, 1859; also 'cello teacher at Leipzig Cons. Solo 'cellist to the Czar, 1862. Director, St. Petersburg Cons., 1876-86.
Works: a symphonic poem, concertos, pf. pieces, chamber music, songs, &c.

Davidsbündler.
"An imaginary association of Schumann and his friends, banded together against old-fashioned pedantry and stupidity in music, like David and his men against the Philistines."—*Grove.* Their names appear in Schumann's writings and compositions.

DAVIES, Benjamin Grey (" Ben Davies "). Favourite tenor singer ; *b.* Pontardawe, nr. Swansea, 1858. Studied R.A.M., 1878-80. Stage *début* in *The Bohemian Girl*, Birmingham, 1881.

DAVIES, David Thomas Ffrangcon. Fine stage and concert baritone. *B.* Bethesda, Carnarvon, 1860.

DAVIES, Fanny. Distinguished pianist ; *b.* Guernsey, 1861. Studied Leipzig (1882-1883), and with Madame Schumann (1883-5) at Frankfort. Made her London *début* at the Crystal Palace, 1885.

DAVIES, Henry Walford. *B.* Oswestry, 1869. Chorister, St. George's, Windsor, 1882. Mus.Doc. Cantab., 1898. Organist, Temple Church, 1898. Conductor, Bach Choir, 1903.
Chief work : cantata, *Everyman* (Leeds Festival, 1904).

DAVIES, Llewela. Pianist and composer ; *b.* Brecon, 1872.

DAVIES, Marianne. 1744-1792. Performer on the flute and "musical glasses."

DAVIES, Cecilia. 1750 (abt.)-1836. Vocalist.
These two sisters achieved considerable renown in London, Paris, Vienna, and Milan.

DAVIES, Mary. Distinguished soprano vocalist ; *b.* London (of Welsh parents), 1855. Retired from public life, 1900.
An excellent singer both in oratorio and ballad.

DAVIS, J. D. Composer and pianist ; *b.* Edgbaston, 1867.
Works : an opera, orchestral music, songs, &c.

DAVIS, Rev. Thos. H. *B.* Birmingham, 1867. Mus.Doc. London, 1900. Orgt. Wells Cath., 1899.

DAVISON, Arabella. (See **Goddard.**)

DAVISON, James Wm. *B.* London, 1815 ; *d.* 1885. Musical critic. Editor, *Musical Examiner* (1842-4), *Musical World* (1844-1885) ; *Times* musical critic (1846-79).
Wrote the analytical programs for the "Popular Concerts " to the time of his death. Married the pianist, Arabella Goddard, 1860.
Davison undoubtedly did much for the cause of classical music in England—especially during his earlier years ; but his uncompromising hostility to Schumann, Gounod, Liszt, Wagner, and Brahms greatly weakened the permanent value of his criticisms.

DAVISON, Munro. Orgt. and composer ; *b.* Stroud Green, 1865.

DAVY, John. *B.* nr. Exeter, 1765 ; *d.* London, 1824. Pupil of Jackson of Exeter.
Wrote music to several plays, but is now only remembered by his songs "The Bay of Biscay," and " Just like love."

DAWSON, Frederick H. Pianist ; *b.* Leeds, 1868.

DAY, Dr. Alfred. Physician ; London, 1810-49. Author of a "Treatise on Harmony " (1845) which was adopted, systematized, and promulgated by (Sir) G. A. Macfarren.

DAY, Major Chas. Russell. Great authority on Hindu music. *B.* nr. Norwich, 1860 ; killed, 1900.
Pub. "The Music and Musical Instruments of Southern India and the Deccan " (1891).

DAY (or **DAYE**), **John.** 1522-84. One of the earliest of English printers from "types."
Pub. "The Whole Booke of Psalmes" *(Day's Psalter),* 1563.

DAYAS, W. Humphries. Orgt., pianist, and composer ; *b.* New York, 1864.

DEACON, Harry C. London, 1822-90. Teacher of singing.
Wrote the article on "Singing" in Grove's Dict.

De AH'NA, Heinrich K. H. (See **Ahna.**)

De AH'NA, Eleonore. (See **Ahna.**)

De-AN'GELIS, Girolamo. *B.* Civita Vecchia, 1858. Prof. of Violin and Viola, Milan Cons., 1881. Solo violinist, La Scala, 1878-97. Violin Professor, Royal Irish Academy of Music, Dublin, 1897.
Has written a successful opera, *L'Innocente* (1896).

DEBAIN, Alexandre François. Paris, 1809-77. Inventor of the harmonium; patented 1840.

De'bile, De'bole *(I.).* Weak, feeble.

DEBOIS, Ferdinand. Brünn (Austria), 1834-93. Composer of popular male-voice choruses.

DEBORAH. Oratorio by Handel ; 1733.

DEBUSSY, Achille C. Noted composer; *b.* St. Germain, 1862. Won *Prix de Rome*, Paris Cons., 1884.
His works are specially interesting for the new chords produced by employment of the higher overtones to enrich the harmony (a method foreshadowed by Berlioz).

Début *(F.).* A first appearance.

Débutant *(mas.),* **Débutante** *(fem.).* An artist (singer, &c.) appearing for the first time.

Dec'achord. *(Gk., Decachordon; F., Décacorde.)* An obsolete guitar, or lyre, with 10 strings.

Deca'ni *(L.).* "Of the Dean." The choristers on the Dean's side of the choir (generally the south). (See **Cantoris.**)

De'cem *(G.).* An organ stop. (See **Decima.**)

Deceptive Cadence. (See **Cadence.**)

Déchant *(F.).* Discant.

Décidé *(F.).* With decision, energy, firmness.

De'cima *(L. and I.).* (1) The interval of a 10th. (2) An organ stop a 10th higher than the 8 ft. stops. Also called a 10th, *Tierce*, or *Double tierce.*

De'cime. A 10th.

Decimo'le *(G.).* (See **Decuplet.**)

Deci'so *(I.).* Same as **Décidé.**
Con decisio'ne. With decision and firmness.
Deci'so ed energe'tico assa'i. Very decided and energetic.

Deck'e *(G.).* A cover ; a deck. (1) Same as **Dach.** (2) The cover of a stopped metal organ pipe. (See **Gedacht, Gedeckt.**)

DECK'ER, Konstantin. *B.* Fürstenau, 1810 ; *d.* 1878. Pianist, teacher, and composer.
Works : 3 operas, 2 pf. sonatas, songs, &c.

Declaman'do *(I.).* } In a declamatory, rhetori-
Declama'to *(I.).* } cal style.

Declamation *(G., Deklamation').* The art of rendering words set to music in a distinct, impressive, and rhetorical style.
" What the Italians call *Recitativo.*"—*Grassineau.*

Décomposé *(F.)*. Disconnected, vague, incoherent.

Décompter *(F.)*. To sing *portamento (q.v.)*.

Découplez *(F.)*. In organ music, " uncouple," " push in the coupler."

Décousu(e) *(F.)*. Disconnected; lacking in form, or unity.

Decrescen'do, Decresciu'to *(I.)., decresc., decres., dec.,* or ⇒. Gradually decreasing in loudness; same as *Diminuendo.*

Dec'uplet. A group of 10 notes to be performed in the time usually allotted to 8 of the same kind :—

DE'DEKIND, Henning. Thuringian cantor and pastor ; abt. 1570 to 1628.

Pub. several text-books, &c., on music.

DE'DEKIND, Konstantin Ch. *B.* in Anhalt-Cöthen, 1628 ; *d.* 1697 (?). Poet-laureate to the Elector of Saxony.

Popular and prolific composer. Wrote often under the name " Concord." — Works : chamber music, sacred music, and several collections of excellent songs, sacred and secular. A list of his works, extending to 17 vols., is given in Grove's Dict.

Dedica'to *(I.)*. ⎫
Dédiée *(F.)*. ⎭ Dedicated.

DE'DLER, Rochus. *B.* Oberammergau, 1779 ; *d.* Vienna, 1822. " Composed the music of the famous Oberammergau Passion-Play " *(Riemann)*. (See **Passion-Play**.)

DEERING (or **DERING**), **Rd.** *B.* in Kent abt. 1575 ; *d.* 1630. Mus.B.Oxon, 1610.

Published, according to Hawkins, the oldest known compositions with *basso continuo* (Antwerp, 1597), but this is probably a mistake.

Defective. Old name for *diminished ;* as " defective 5th."

DEFERRA'RI. (See **Ferrari**.)

DEFFÈS, Louis P. Operatic composer. *B.* Toulouse, 1819 ; *d.* 1900.

Most successful opera, *Jessica* (Toulouse, 1898).

Deficien'do *(I.)*. Gradually dying away.

DE GIO'SA, Nicola. Bari, 1820-1885.

Wrote the successful opera *Don Checco* (Naples, 1850), and abt. 20 others ; also some 400 songs.

Degree. *(G., Stu'fe, Ton'stufe ; F., Degré ; I., Gra'do.)* (1) A line or space (of the staff). (2) A " step " in a scale.

A step may be a semitone, a tone, or (in the harmonic minor scale) an augmented 2nd *(f-se).* The steps of the scientific major scale are major tones, minor tones, and diatonic semitones. (See *Acoustics.*) Mr. Curwen called them "great" steps *(d-r, f-s, l-t)* ; "small" steps *(r-m, s-l)* ; and " little " steps *(m-f, t-d').*

Degrees, Musical. Regulations as to Degrees in Music granted by British Universities may be obtained on application as follows :—

OXFORD : "The Manager, Clarendon Press Depôt 116 High Street, Oxford."
CAMBRIDGE : " Cambridge University Press, Cambridge ;" or " C. J. Clay, Cambridge University Press Warehouse, Ave Maria Lane, London, E.C."
DUBLIN : "The Registrar of the School of Music, Trinity College, Dublin."
LONDON : "The Registrar, University of London, South Kensington, S.W."
DURHAM : "Rev. H. Ellershaw, M.A., Univ. Offices, Nth. Bailey, Durham."
VICTORIA UNIVERSITY (Manchester) : "The Registrar, Victoria University, Manchester."
ROYAL UNIVERSITY OF IRELAND : "The Secretaries, Royal University of Ireland, Dublin."
EDINBURGH : Regulations of the Faculty of Music (price 1d.) ; "Mr. J. Thin, Publisher, 55 South Bridge, Edinburgh."
UNIVERSITY OF WALES : "The Registrar, University of Wales, Cardiff."
(See also *Diplomas.)*

DEHN, Siegfried Wilhelm. *B.* Altona, 1796 ; *d.* Berlin, 1858. Theorist, teacher, and writer. Musical librarian, Royal Library, Berlin, 1842. Editor of *Cæcilia*, 1842-48.

Works : A Treatise on Harmony, An Analysis of the Fugues of Bach and C. M. Buononcini, A Collection of Vocal Compositions of the 16th and 17th Centuries, a work on Counterpoint, Canon, and Fugue, &c.

Deh'nen *(G.)*. To prolong, extend, expand. (See **Gedehnt'**.)

Deh'nung *(G.)*. Extension, prolongation.

Deh'nungstrich *(G.)*. A long stroke with a bow.

Dei *(I., plur.)*. Of the ; from the.

DEI'TERS, Dr. Hermann. *B.* Bonn, 1833. Director Bonn Gymnasium, 1883 ; Assistant in the Ministry of Public Worship, Berlin, 1890. *D.* 1907.

Works : articles on Beethoven, Schumann, Max Bruch, Brahms, &c., for the *Deutsche Musikzeitung ;* musical biographies ; German trans. of Thayer's "Life of Beethoven," &c.

Deklamation' *(G.)*. (See **Declamation**.)

De KO'VEN, H. L. Reginald. American composer ; *b.* Middletown, Conn., 1859.

Works : several operettas *(Robin Hood, The Highwayman, The Three Dragoons,* &c.) ; and over 130 songs and incidental pieces.

Del, dell', del'la, del'le, del'lo *(I.)*. Of the.

DELABORDE, E. M. Distinguished French pianist ; *b.* 1839. Pupil of Liszt and Moscheles. Prof. of Pf. Paris Cons., 1873.

DELACOUR, Victor. Pen-name of **Sydney Smith** *(q.v.)*.

Délassement *(F.)*. A trifle ; a light piece or entertainment.

De LATTRE. (See **Lasso, Orlando di**.)

DELDEVEZ, Edouard M. E. Paris, 1817-97. Pupil Paris Cons. Conductor Grand Opéra, 1873-77 ; Cons. Prof. from 1872.

Works : ballets *(Eucharis, Paquita,* &c.) ; operas *(Mazarina, Samson, Le Violon Enchanté) ;* 3 symphonies, chamber music, songs, &c. ; "Curiosités musicales ;" a work on the execution of grace-notes ; "L'art du chef d'orchestre ;" an "Anthology of Violinists" (4 vols.), &c.

De **LE'VA, Enrico.** Composer of popular Neapolitan songs ; *b.* Naples, 1867.

Deliberatamen'te *(I.).* ⎫
Delibera'to *(I.).* ⎬ Deliberately.

DELIBES, C. P., Léo. *B.* Sarthe, 1836 ; *d.* Paris, 1891. Entered Paris Cons., 1848. Orgt. St. Jean et St. Francois (1853), and accompanist Théâtre-Lyrique. Prof. of Composition, Paris Cons., 1881. His music is melodious, sparkling, and charmingly orchestrated.

> Works : ballets, *La Source* (1866), *Coppélia* (1870), *Sylvia* (1876) ; comic operas, *Le Roi l'a dit* (1873), *Jean de Nivelle* (1880), *Lakmé* (1883) ; cantata, *Alger* (1865) ; choruses, melodies, &c.

Delicatamen'te *(I.).* ⎫
Con delicatez'za *(I.).* ⎬ With delicacy and re-
Delica'to *(I.).* ⎭ finement.

Delicatis'simo *(I.).* Very delicate.

Délié *(F.).* Light, easy.

DELIOUX de SAVIGNAC, Chas. Pianist and composer ; *b.* Lorient, 1830.

Deliran'te *(I.).* Excited ; frenzied.

Deli'rio *(I.).* Frenzy ; delirium.

> *Con deli'rio.* With frenzied excitement, or passion.

DE'LIUS, Frederick ("Fritz "). *B.* Bradford, 1863.

> Works : "Appalachia," "Sea Drift," "Brigg Fair," music dramas, songs, orchl. pieces, a pf. concerto, &c.

Delivery. The management of the voice in singing with regard to tone and enunciation.

Deliziosamen'te, Delizio'so *(I.).* Sweetly, deliciously.

DEL'LA MARI'A, P. A. Dominique. *B.* Marseilles, 1769 ; *d.* Paris, 1800. Precocious musician and composer.

> Most famous works : operas, *Il Maestro di Cappella* (1792), and *Le Prisonnier* (1798). The latter was composed in eight days!

DEL'LE SE'DIE, Enrico. *B.* Leghorn, 1826 ; *d.* 1907. Baritone vocalist. *Début* in Verdi's *Nabucodonosor*, Florence, 1851. From 1861 Prof. of Singing Paris Cons., and one of the most esteemed of modern singing teachers.

> His valuable works on singing are published in one vol. as "A Complete Method of Singing" (New York).

DEL'LINGER, Rudolf. Condr. and operatic composer ; *b.* Graslitz, Bohemia, 1857.

DELMAS, Jean F. Dramatic bass ; *b.* Lyons, 1861.

DEL ME'LA, Don Domenico. Italian priest. Said to have invented the first "upright " piano, 1730.

DELMOTTE, Henri F. Mons, 1799-1836.

> Wrote a valuable "Biography of Roland de Lattre" (1836). (See *Lasso*.)

DEL'NA, Marie. Vocalist ; *b.* 1875. *Début*, 1892.

DELSARTE, François A. N. C. *B.* Solesmes, 1811 ; *d.* 1871. Singing teacher.

> Published a Method of Singing, and invented "an apparatus to facilitate the tuning of pianos" (*Baker*).

DEL VALLE de PAZ, Edgardo. *B.* Alexandria, 1861. Studied Naples Cons. Established the *Circolo del Valle*, Florence, 1893. Prof. Florence Cons.

> Works : a valuable "Scuola Pratica del Pianoforte," orchestral suites, chamber music, pf. pieces, vocal music, &c.

Dem *(G.).* To the.

Démanché *(F.).* ⎫ To shift ; changing the
Démanchement *(F.).* ⎬ "position" (as on a violin, lute, &c.).

Demancher *(F.).* To cross hands in pf. playing ; to shift in vn. playing.

Demande *(F.,* "a question "). The subject of a fugue, as opposed to the answer.

DEMAN'TIUS, Christoph. *B.* Reichenberg, 1567 ; *d.* 1643. Cantor, Freyburg (Saxony).

> Works : songs (sacred and secular), dances, funeral laments, 8-part motets, &c. ; and 2 text-books.

DEME'LIUS, Christian. Saxon composer, 1643-1711.

> Works : a "Gesangbuch" (1688), motets, &c.

DEMEUR, Anne Arsène (*née* **Charton**). *B.* Saujon (Charente), 1827 ; *d.* 1892. Distinguished soprano singer. Sang with great success at Drury Lane, 1846 ; also at Vienna, Paris, &c., and in America.

Demi *(F.).* Half.

> *Demi-bâton.* (1) A semibreve rest. (2) A rest extending over two bars.
> *Demi-cadence.* A half-cadence (or Dominant Cadence).
> *Demi-croche.* A semiquaver.
> *Demi-jeu.* *Mezzo forte;* with half the power of the instrument.
> *Demi-mesure* ⎫ A minim or half-bar rest.
> *Demi-pause* ⎭
> *Demi-quart de soupir.* A demisemiquaver rest.
> *Demi-soupir.* A quaver rest.
> *Demi-temps.* A half-beat.
> *Demi-ton.* A semitone.

Demiquaver. Another name for *semiquaver*.

Demisemiquaver. A 32nd note, ♪ ; equal to ¼th of a quaver.

Demoiselle *(F.).* An organ tracker.

Dem Säng'er fol'gend *(G.).* *Colla voce (q.v.).*

De MUNCK (or DEMUNCK), Ernest. (Son of **François De Munck,** a Belgian 'cellist, 1815-54). *B.* Brussels, 1840. Eminent 'cellist ; 1st 'cellist, Weimar Court Orch., 1870. Married Carlotta Patti, 1879. 'Cello Prof. R.A.M., 1893.

De MURIS. (See **Muris.**)

DENEFVE, Jules. 'Cellist ; *b.* Chimay, 1814 ; *d.* 1877. Distinguished as a performer, conductor, and composer.

DENGREMONT, Maurice. French-Brazilian ; *b.* 1866. Violinist ; juvenile prodigy. Gave way to dissipation, and *d.* 1893, cutting short a promising career.

Denis d'or. An inst. invented by a Moravian in 1762, "with a fingerboard like a piano and pedals like an organ."

DENNÉE, Chas. F. Composer ; *b.* Oswego (U.S.), 1863.

DEN'NER, Joh. Christoph. *B.* Leipzig, 1655; *d.* Nuremburg, 1707. Gave the clarinet its modern form, and so improved it as to be styled·"its inventor" (1690 to 1700). (See **Clarinet.**)

DEN'ZA, Luigi. *B.* Castellammare di Stabbia (Italy), 1846. Came to London, 1879. Prof. of Singing, R.A.M., 1898.
Works: over 500 songs, of which "Funiculì Funiculà" has had a phenomenal success.

Départ, Chant du. Celebrated French song; music by Méhul. The only French patriotic song "actually written during the Terror" *(Grove).* The opening phrases are identical with those of Braham's "Death of Nelson:"—

Dependent Chord, Triad, or Harmony. A dissonant chord; one requiring resolution.

De plus en plus vite *(F.).* Gradually quicker.

DEP'PE, Ludwig. *B.* nr. Lippe, 1828; *d.* 1890. Court Capellmeister, Berlin, 1886-88; afterwards conductor Court concerts.
Invented a system of pf. technique, of which a minute description is given in Amy Fay's "Music Study in Germany."

DEPRÈS (DESPRES, or DES PRÉS), Josquin. *B.* Hainault (Burgundy) abt. 1450; *d.* Condé, 1521. "The greatest of the early Netherland contrapuntists." Probably a pupil of Okeghem. Singer in the Papal Chapel, 1471-84.
Works: masses, motets, chansons, &c. Luther, and other contemporaries of Josquin, thought very highly of these works, and they are still valued by antiquarians.

DE PROFUN'DIS *(L.).* One of the seven penitential Psalms.

Derb *(G.).* Firm, vigorous, heavy, hearty.
Mit der'bem Humor'. With hearty humour.

DE'RENBURG, Mad. (See **I. Eibenschütz.**)

DE RESZKÉ, Édouard. Celebrated bass singer; *b.* Warsaw, 1855. Has sung with great success in Paris, Turin, Milan, London, and America.

DE RESZKÉ, Jean. Elder brother (and teacher) of Edouard. Fine dramatic tenor; *b.* Warsaw, 1852. First appearance in England, 1887, at Drury Lane.
He is a renowned interpreter of Wagner's music.

DERING. (See **Deering.**)

Derivative. (1) An inversion of a chord. (2) Also used (incorrectly) for the Root or Generator of a chord.

Dérivé(e) *(F.).* Derived; derivative.
Accord dérivé. An inversion of a chord.

Der Melodie' fol'gend *(G.).* *Colla parte (q.v.).*

Dernière fois *(F.).* The last time.

De SANC'TIS. Composer and writer; *b.* Albano, 1830.

Des *(G.).* D♭.

DÉSAUGIERS, Marc A. 1742-93. French composer of popular operettas.

Descant, or **Discant.** *(L., Discantus; G., Diskant'; F., Déchant.)* (1) The earliest attempts at written counterpoint (about the 12th cent.). (2) The highest vocal part. (Same as **Dessus.**)
Descant clef. Soprano (or Treble) clef.

Des'des or **Des'es** *(G.).* D double-flat (D♭♭).

Des dur *(G.).* The key of D♭ major.

DESHAYES, Prosper Didier. French composer.
Works: oratorios, *Les Machabées* (1780), and *Le Sacrifice de Jefte;* operettas, ballets, &c.

Deside'rio *(I.).* Desire.
Con deside'rio. In a longing, yearning manner.

Design *(F., Dessin).* The plan, or form, of a composition. (See **Form.**)

DESMARETS, Henri. *B.* Paris, 1662; *d.* 1741. Maestro to Philip V of Spain, and later, Music-intendant to the Duke of Lorraine.
Works: several once-famous operas *(Didon, Circe, Vénus et Adonis,* &c.).

Des moll *(G.).* D♭ minor.

DESPRÉS. (See **Deprès.**)

DES'SAU, Bernhard. Violinist; *b.* Hamburg, 1861.

DES'SAUER, Joseph. *B.* Prague, 1798; *d.* 1876.
Works: operas *(Lidwinna, Paquita, Oberon,* &c.); many songs; chamber music, pf. sonatas.

Des'sauer Marsch. A national German march.

Dessin *(F.).* (See **Design.**)

DES'SOFF, Felix Otto. *B.* Leipzig, 1835; *d.* 1892.
Capellmeister at various German theatres, 1854-60; Vienna, 1860-75; Carlsruhe, 1875; Frankfort, 1881.

Dessus *(F.).* "Above." Old name for the highest vocal part (treble).

Deste'rita *(I.).* Dexterity.

DESTINN, Emmy (E. Kittl). Soprano; *b.* Prague, 1878. *Début,* 1898.

De'sto *(I.).* Dexterous; sprightly.

DESTOUCHES, André C. Paris, 1672-1749. Superintendent, King's Music, and Inspector-General at the Opéra, 1713.
Works: several operas, of which the first, *Issé,* was the only one that achieved great success.

DESTOUCHES, Franz S. von. Munich, 1772-1844. Pupil of Haydn, 1787-91. Capellmeister, Homburg, 1826-42.
Works: an opera *(Die Thomasnacht,* 1792), an operetta, a comic opera, incidental music to several plays, pf. music, &c.

De'stra *(I.).* Right.
De'stra ma'no. ⎫
Ma'no de'stra. ⎬ The right hand. Abbr. *m.d.,* or *d.m.*
Col'la de'stra. ⎭

DESTRANGES, Louis A. E. R. Noted critic and writer; champion of Wagner; *b.* Nantes, 1863.

DESVIGNES, Victor F. *B.* Trier, 1805; *d.* Metz, 1853. Violinist and theatrical conductor. Founded a Cons. at Metz, 1835 (later a branch of Paris Cons.)
Works: choruses, songs, chamber music, a *Stabat Mater,* &c.

De SWERT (or DESWERT), Jules. Distinguished 'cellist; *b.* Louvain, 1843; *d.* Ostend, 1891. Played in public at 9. Concertmeister, Düsseldorf, 1865; 1st 'cello, Weimar Orch., 1868 ; Royal Concertmeister, solo 'cellist, and Prof. at Berlin Hochschule, 1869-73. Director, Ostend Music School, 1888.

Works : operas, *Die Albigenser* (1878), *Graf Hammerstein* (1884) ; a symphony ; 3 concertos, and several other compositions for 'cello.

De SWERT, Jean G. I. 'Cellist ; brother of Jules. *B.* 1830 (?) ; *d.* 1896. Prof. of 'Cello, Brussels Cons.

Détaché *(F.).* Detached, but not staccato (in violin playing).

Determina'to *(I.).* In a resolute, determined manner.

Détonation, Détonnation *(F.).* Bad, or false intonation.

Detoni(e)'ren *(G.).* ⎫ To sing out of tune ; to
Détonner *(F.).* ⎭ flatten.

DETTINGEN TE DEUM. Composed by Handel, 1743, to celebrate the victory of Dettingen.

DETTMER, Wilhelm. *B.* nr. Hildesheim, 1808. Bass singer ; son of a peasant.

Joined a wandering troupe of players, singing at various minor theatres. Afterwards took chief parts at Dresden and Frankfort (1842-74).

Det'to *(I.).* " Ditto." The same ; as before.

Il det'to vo'ce (I.). The same voice as before.

DE'US MISEREA'TUR. The 67th Psalm.

Used as an alternative to the *Nunc Dimittis* in the Evening Service of the Church of England.

Deut'lich *(G.).* Distinctly.

Deut'licher und stets gut hervor'tretend. More distinctly, and always well-defined (emphasized).

Deutsch *(G.).* German.

Deu'tsche Flöte. German, or orchestral flute.
Deu'tscher Bass. An obsolete inst. (between a 'cello and double bass) with 5 or 6 strings.
Deu'tsche Tän'ze. " German dances." Slow waltzes. (See *Valse* and *Waltz.*)

DEUTZ. (See **Magnus.**)

Deux *(F.).* Two.

À deux. (See under *A.*)
À deux mains. For two hands.
Deux-quatre. Two-four time.
Deux-temps (Valse à deux temps). A quick waltz (See *Valse* and *Waltz.*)

Deuxième *(F.).* Second.

Deuxième position. The 2nd position, or half-shift, on the violin.

Development. *(G.,Durch'führung.)* The organic working-out of a composition, movement, theme, or idea, according to artistic rules. (See **Form** and **Thematic development.**)

Development of Emotional Expression.

" A progressive development of emotion—carrying the mind through the various phases of expectation, discovery, and satisfaction—by means of (1) emphasis given to particular tones of the scale; (2) rhythm and style of movement ; (3) skilful use of key and mode ; (4) combinations of force and speed ; and (5) the nature and style of the harmony."—*Curwen.*

Development Portion. That part of a sonata, &c., which commences the 2nd part of the 1st movement. (See **Sonata.**)

DEVIENNE, François. *B.* Joinville (France), 1759 ; *d.* (insane), 1803. Flautist and bassoonist ; Prof. Paris Cons. Largely

influential in promoting the technique of wind instruments.

Works : 10 operas ; overtures, concertos, &c., for wind insts. ; a valuable Flute Method (1795) ; songs, romances, &c.

Devil's Sonata. A posthumous work for vn., " Il Trillo del Diavolo," by Tartini (*q.v.*), said to have been played to him by Satan while he slept.

Devo'to *(I.).* ⎫ In a devotional, or
Con devozio'ne *(I.).* ⎭ affectionate style.

DEVRIENT. (See **Schröder-Devrient.**)

Dex'tra *(L.).* Right. (Compare **Destra.**)

Dex'tra ma'nu. With the right hand.
Ma'nus dex'tra. The right hand.

DEZÈDE (or **DEZAIDES**). Composer of popular operas and operettas. *B.* abt. 1740 ; *d.* Paris, 1792. *Blaise et Babet* (1783) was his most successful work.

De'zem *(G.).* (Same as **Decima.**)

De'zime *(G.).* The interval of a 10th.

Di *(I.).* Of, for, with, by, as, from, &c.

Di bravu'ra. In *bravura* style; containing *bravura* passages.
Di chie'sa. For the church.
Di col'ta. At once ; suddenly.
Di ga'la. In gala style ; merrily.
Di gra'do. By degrees, or steps.
Di mol'to. Very much. (See *Allegro di molto.*)
Di nuo'vo. Anew, afresh, again.
Di sal'to. By leap or skip (as a melody).
Di so'pra. As above.

Di'a *(Gk.).* Through.

DIABEL'LI, Antonio. *B.* nr. Salzburg, 1781 ; *d.* 1858. Composer and music publisher. Pub. much of Schubert's music.

His numerous compositions are now forgotten, except some easy pieces and duets for pf.

" Diabolus in Musica." The name given by medieval musicians to the tritone.

Dia'logo *(I.).* ⎫ (1) A duet. (2) A vocal or in-
Di'alogue. ⎭ strumental piece in dialogue style.

Diapa'son *(Gk.)* An octave.

Diapa'son cum diapen'te. " Octave with 5th ;" *i.e.,* a 12th.
Diapa'son cum diates'saron. " Octave with 4th ;" *i.e.,* an 11th.

Diapa'son *(E.).* (1) An octave. (2) An organ stop (register).

Diapasons are either "open" or "stopped." (See *Acoustics.*) They are the chief "foundation" stops of an organ.

(3) Used poetically for the compass of a voice or instrument.

Diapason Phonon. Name originally applied by Hope-Jones to the diapason with " leathered " lips. Now used also for various other types of diapason.

Diapason *(F.).* (1) Range or compass of a voice or inst. (2) A " scale " used in the construction of an organ or other inst. (3) The " diapason " organ stop. (4) A pitch-pipe or tuning-fork.

Diapason normal *(F.).* The note A, produced by 435 vibrations per second. (See **Acoustics.**)

This standard was fixed by the French Academy (1859), and regulates what is called " French " pitch, or " International " pitch.

Diapen'te *(Gk.).* The interval of a 5th.

Diapenter *(F.).* ⎫ To proceed by skips of a
Diapentisa're *(I.).* ⎭ 5th.

Di'aphone. An org. stop of powerful tone. invented by Hope-Jones (1893-5).

Diaphoni'a *(Gk.).* ⎫ Discord ; dissonance.
Diaph'ony. ⎭

Diaph'ony, or **Or'ganum.** The early attempts at improvised counterpoint. (See **Organum.**) "Diaphony preceded Descant."—*Macfarren.*

Diaschis'ma *(Gk.).* (See **Interval.**)

Diaste'ma *(Gk.).* An interval.

Diates'saron *(Gk.).* Interval of a 4th.

Diaton'ic. ⎫ From the Greek, *diato'nos,*
Diato'nico *(I.).* ⎭ *diaton'ikos.*

(1) One of the 3 ancient Greek *genera;* diatonic, chromatic, enharmonic.

(2) Any chord, interval, note, or progression confined to the notes of *one* major (or minor) key or scale. (See also **Chromatic.**)

The exact meaning of the Greek is not quite clear. It is customary to say that it means "through" tones" (a diatonic scale proceeding mostly in tones, as opposed to a "chromatic" scale in semitones) ; but authorities derive *diatonos* from *diateino,* to stretch.

Diatonic chord. A chord with all its notes belonging to *one* major (or minor) scale or key.

Diatonic instrument. An instrument set to play in one key only, as the harp, which can only change the key by means of one or more of its pedals.

Diatonic interval. (See *Interval.*)

Diatonic harmony. ⎫ Employing only the notes of one
Diatonic melody. ⎭ scale or key, without chromatic notes.

Diatonic modulation. A modulation to a closely related key by means of a chord common to both.

Diatonic progression. Diatonic melody or harmony.

Diatonic scale. Any modern major or minor scale.

Diatonic semitone. (See *Interval.*)

N.B.—Many theorists include the Augmented 2nd (and its inversion, the Diminished 7th) among chromatic intervals. The harmonic minor scale was therefore called (by Hullah and others) the "chromatic form" of the minor scale. The present tendency is to regard it as "diatonic." Sir Hubert Parry includes both forms of the 6th and 7th in minor scales among diatonic notes *(Grove's Dict.).*

A passage containing "accidentals" is not necessarily chromatic. Thus, of the following, *(a)* is diatonic because all its notes belong to B minor ; *(b)* is diatonic because all its notes belong to E♭ major ; but *(c),* also in E♭ major, has 3 chromatic notes :—

Diau'los *(Gk.).* Ancient Greek double flute. (See **Aulos.**)

Diazeuc'tic *(Gk.).* Disjunct,

Diazeu'xis *(Gk.).* In ancient Greek music, two tetrachords separated by the interval of a tone. Also the interval itself.

DIBDIN, Chas. *B.* nr. Southampton, 1745 ; *d.* London, 1814. Author, singer, and composer ; chiefly self-taught. Engaged at 15 as singing-actor, Covent Garden. His first stage piece, *The Shepherd's Artifice,* was produced 1763. After engagements at Birmingham, Covent Garden, and Drury Lane, and "the failure of certain theatrical enterprises," he started (1789) a series of "table entertainments," at which he appeared as "author, composer, narrator, singer, and accompanist."

These became very popular, and were continued till 1805, when Dibdin retired on a Civil List pension of £200 per annum. Most of his seasongs were written for the "table entertainments ;" many of them have become standard national songs.

Works : abt. 70 stage pieces and 30 "table entertainments." About 20 of his songs are given in Boosey's "Songs of England," including "Tom Bowling," "The lass that loves a sailor," "The jolly young waterman," "Blow high, blow low," and "Farewell, my trim-built wherry."

Di'brach, Di'brachys (or **Pyrrhic**). A metrical foot of two short syllables (◡ ◡).

Di chia'ro *(I.).* Clearly.

Di'chord. (1) An instrument with 2 strings. (2) Same as **Bichord,** with 2 strings to each note.

Dich'ter *(G.).* Poet ; minstrel.

DICK, C. G. Cotsford. London, 1846-95. Works : operettas, songs, and pf. pieces.

DICKSON, Rev. W. E. *B.* Richmond, Yorks, 1823. Precentor, Ely Cath., 1858. Author of "Fifty Years of Church Music," 1895.

Dictée musicale *(F.).* Musical dictation as applied to musical training.

Dictionaries of Music, Chief.

Terminorum musicæ Diffinitorium ; Tinctor, 1474.
Dictionnaire étymologique ; Ménage, 1650.
Dictionnaire Universel ; Furetière, 1690.
Clavis ad thesaurum magnæ artis musicæ ; Janowka (Prague), 1701.
Dictionnaire de Musique ; Brossard (Paris), 1703.
Alte und neue musikalische Bibliothek ; Walther (2nd edition, 1732).
Musical Dictionary ; Grassineau (London), 1740.
Dictionnaire de Musique ; Rousseau (Geneva), 1767.
Musikalisches Lexikon ; Koch (Frankfort), 1802.
Neues historisch-biographisches Lexicon ; Gerber (Leipzig), 1790-2 and 1812-14.
Dictionnaire historique ; Choron and Fayolle (Paris), 1810-11.
Dizionario e Bibliografia della Musica ; Lichtenthal (French edition, Paris, 1821).
Biographie universelle des Musiciens ; Fétis, 1835-44.
Universal Lexikon der Tonkunst ; Schilling (Stuttgart), 1835-8.
Moore's Encyclopædia (Boston), 1850.
Musikalisches Conversations-Lexikon ; Mendel (Berlin), 1870.
Stainer and Barrett's Dict. of Musical Terms, 1876.
Grove's Dictionary of Music and Musicians, 1878-89 ; revised edition, 1905.
Musik-Lexikon ; Riemann (Leipzig), 1882.
Brown's Biographical Dictionary, 1886.
Brown and Stratton's British Musical Biography, 1897.
Quellen-Lexikon ; Eitner, 1900-4.
Cyclopædia of Music and Musicians ; Champlin and Apthorp (New York), 1889-91.
Baker's Biographical Dictionary (New York), 1900,

DID'YMUS of Alexandria. *B.* 63 B.C. Wrote a treatise on harmony (or harmonics).

Die Abwe'senheit *(G.).* Absence.

Die Akkor'de mög'lichst gebund'en *(G.).* The chords (played) as smoothly as possible.

Die Bäs'se durch'aus leicht und frei *(G.).* The bass (to be) light *(leggiero)* throughout.

Diecet'to *(I.).* A piece for 10 instruments.

Die Ferma'ten sehr lang und bedeut'ungsvoll *(G.).* The pauses (to be) very long and impressive.

DIEHL (pron. *Deal),* **Louis.** *B.* Mannheim, 1838. Resides in London ; married Miss Alice Mangold, 1863.
Works : several popular songs.

DIEM (pron. *Deem),* **Joseph.** Fine 'cellist ; *b.* Kellmünz, 1836 ; *d.* 1894. Son of a poor peasant ; taught himself the flute and violin ; took up the 'cello, Munich Cons., at 25. Prof. Moscow Cons., 1866. Toured through Europe and America.

DIEMER, Louis. *B.* Paris, 1843. Distinguished pianist ; Pf. Prof. Paris Cons., 1887.
Of his numerous compositions the following are the most important: Concertstück (Op. 31), and Concerto in C minor for Pf. and Orch.; Concertstück for Violin and Orch.; chamber music, songs, pf. solos, &c.

DIE'NEL, Otto. *B.* Silesia, 1839. Organist, Marienkirche, Berlin.
His organ pieces are well known.

Diesa're *(I.);* **Diéser** *(F.).* To sharpen.

DI'ES I'RÆ. A fine medieval Latin hymn sung in requiems, or masses for the dead.

Dièse, or **Diésis** *(F.);* **Die'sis** *(I.).* The sharp, ♯.

Diesel'be Bewe'gung *(G.).* The same speed.

Di'esis *(Gk.).* (1) The Pythagorean semitone ; 256 : 243.
(2) The modern *enharmonic diesis,* or the difference between 3 major 3rds and an octave ; ratio, 128 : 125. (See **Interval.**)

DIET, Edmond M. Parisian composer; *b.* 1854.
Works : operas, ballets, pantomimes, operettas, songs, and church music.

DIE'TRICH, Albert Hermann. *B.* nr. Meissen, 1829. Studied under Schumann, Dusseldorf, 1851-4. Court Capellmeister, Oldenburg, 1861. Settled in Berlin, 1890.
Works : opera, *Robin Hood* (1879) ; Symphony in D ; an orchestral overture ; cantatas, concertos, chamber music, pf. pieces, songs, choruses, &c. Also " Recollections of Brahms " (1899).

DIE'TRICH (or DIETERICH), Sixtus. *B.* Augsburg abt. 1490-2 ; *d.* Switzerland, 1548.
Works : Magnificats, antiphones, motets, songs, &c., of historical value.

DIETZ, Joh. Ch. *B.* Darmstadt, 1788 ; *d.* Holland, abt. 1845. Instrument maker ; invented the *Melodeon* (1805), *Claviharpe* (1814), and *Trochléon* (1812).

DIEUPART, Chas. French violinist and cembalist. Was for several years, from 1707, *maestro al cembalo* to Handel in London, where he died in great poverty abt. 1740.
Works : 6 suites for clavecin, violin, flute, bass, and archlute (the model for Bach's English suites) ; 6 overtures for clavecin and violin, with a continued bass,

Dièze *(F.).* A sharp, ♯.

Difference Tones. (See **Acoustics.**)

Difficile *(F.).* Difficult.

Dig'ital. " A finger," or " pertaining to a finger." Hence, a key of the pf., organ, &c., as opposed to Pedal, for the foot.

Digitorium. An instrument resembling a small piano, having 5 keys with very strong springs to exercise the fingers.
It is also called a *dumb piano.*

Dignitá *(I.).* Dignity.

Di gra'do *(I.).* (See **Di.**)

Dilettan'te *(I.).* An amateur.

Diligen'za *(I.).* Care, diligence.

DIL'LIGER, Joh. *B.* Eisfeld, 1590 ; *d.* 1647.
Pub. several collections of sacred and secular music (Psalms in 6 parts, &c.), 1612-40.

Dilu'dium *(L.).* An interlude ; specially, the instrumental interlude between the lines of *chorals.*

Diluen'do *(I.).* Dying away ; decreasing in loudness (and speed).

Dilungan'do *(I.).* Prolonging ; *rallentando.*

Dim'eter. (1) Divisible into 2 feet (poetry). (2) Consisting of 2 measures (music).

Diminished. *(G., Verklei'nert; F., Diminué(e); I., Diminu'to.)* Made less.
Diminished Interval. (See *Interval.*)
Diminished Subject, or Theme. (See *Diminution.*)
Diminished Triad. A triad with a diminished 5th, as—

Diminished Seventh, Chord of the. A chord consisting of 3 minor 3rds ; the supposed " root " is a *major* 3rd below the lowest note of the chord :—

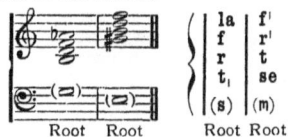

Root Root   Root Root

In the inversions of this chord one of the intervals becomes an augmented 2nd ; and as in equal temperament this is enharmonically equivalent to a minor 3rd, the chord is susceptible of several enharmonic forms. Thus, on the pianoforte, the following are all identical (the " roots " of the various presentations being given below) :—

There are only 3 *essentially different* diminished 7ths on the piano—one on C, one on C♯, and one on D. The diminished 7th on D♯ (or E♭) comprises the same pf. notes as that on C, and so on. As, however, each of these may be written in at least 4 ways (as above), it is possible to modulate by means of a diminished 7th into *any major or minor key.* (See *Modulation.*) In addition to the usual progressions of a dim. 7th (given in ordinary text books of harmony), a semitonic chain or sequence of diminished 7ths may be used either in ascending or descending ; *and any diminished 7th may be*

followed by any other diminished 7th (provided the separate parts be artistically written):—

&c.

Diminuen'do *(I.).* Decreasing in loudness.

Diminuer *(F.).* To diminish in loudness.

Diminution. *(G., Verklei'nerung; F., Diminution; I., Diminuzio'ne.)* The repetition of a theme in shorter notes. (See **Canon.**)

D in Alt ; D in Altis'simo. (See **Alt.**)

D'ingan'no *(I.).* Unexpected.

DING'ELSTEDT, Jenny (*née* **Lutzer**). Brilliant operatic singer. *B.* Prague, 1816 ; *d.* 1877. Sang chiefly at Prague and Vienna.

Diplo'mas and Certificates, Musical.

The following—in order of inauguration—are the chief colleges and societies which grant musical diplomas and certificates :—
Royal Society of Arts, 18 John Street, Adelphi, London, W.C. *Secretary,* Sir Henry Trueman Wood.
Royal Academy of Music, Tenterden Street, Hanover Square, London, W. *Sec.*. Mr. F. W. Renaut.
The Tonic Sol-fa College, 27 Finsbury Square, London, E.C. *Sec.,* Mr. Walter Harrison, M.A., Mus.B.Oxon.
The Royal College of Organists, Kensington Gore, London, S.W. *Registrar,* Mr. T. Shindler, M.A., LL.B.
Trinity College of Music, London, Mandeville Place, London, W. *Sec.,* Mr. Shelley Fisher.
The Guildhall School of Music, Victoria Embankment, London, E.C. *Sec.,* Mr. H. Saxe Wyndham.
The Royal College of Music, Prince Consort Rd., South Kensington, London, S.W. *Registrar,* Mr. Frank Pownall, M.A.
The Incorporated Society of Musicians, 19 Berners Street, London, W. *Sec.,* Mr. Hugo Chadfield.
The Incorporated Guild of Musicians, 11 Queen Victoria Street, London, E.C. *Sec.,* Mr. F. B. Townend.
Associated Board of the R.A.M. and R.C.M., 15 Bedford Square, London, W.C. *Sec.,* Mr. Jas. Muir.
The Incorporated Staff Sight-Singing College, 60 Berners Street, London, W. *Sec.,* Dr. Hamilton Robinson.
(See also *Degrees.*)

DIPPEL, Andreas. Tenor; *b.* Cassel, 1866.

Direct. *(L., Cus'tos ; F., Guidon ; I., Gui'da, Mo'stra.)* A sign, ᙡ, placed at the end of a line of music to show the position of the 1st note of the following line; now unfortunately obsolete.

Direct Motion. Similar motion. (See **Motion.**)

Directeur *(F.).* ⎱ The director, or conductor, of
Diretto're *(I.)* ⎰ an orchestra, choir, &c.

Diret'ta *(I.).* Direct, straight.
Al'la diret'ta. In direct motion.

Dirge. A solemn, funereal piece of music.

Dirigent' *(G.).* Director, conductor.

Dirit'to,-a *(I.).* (See **Diretta.**)

DIRU'TA, Girolamo. Organist. *B.* Perugia, abt. 1560 ; *d.* abt. 1639.
Pub. a very important treatise on "Organ-playing, Counterpoint, the Church Modes, &c."

Dis *(G.).* D♯.

Disarmo'nico *(I.).* Discordant.

Dis'cant. *(L., Discan'tus; G., Diskant'.)* (1) (See **Descant.**) (2) The principal melody.

Discant'geige *(G.).* Old name for the violin.

Discant'schlüssel *(G.).* The soprano clef.

Discenden'te *(I.).* Descending.

Discord. (1) Dissonance ; cacophony. (2) A chord requiring resolution by being followed by some other chord.
Discord, Fundamental. (See *Fundamental Discords.*)

Discre'to *(I.).* Discreet, prudent.
Con discretez'za ⎱ With reserve and discretion ; sub-
Con discrezio'ne ⎰ dued.

Disdiapa'son *(Gk.).* A double-octave or 15th.

Disguised Intervals, Consecutives, &c. (See **Interval.**)

Disharmo'nisch *(G.).* Discordant, dissonant.

Disinvo'lto *(I.).* Easy, free, natural.
Con disinvoltu'ra. Flowingly, with ease, gracefully.

Dis'is (or **Dis'dis**) *(G.).* D✗.

Disjunct Motion. (See **Motion.**)

Diskant *(G.).* (See **Discant.**)

Dis moll *(G.).* The key of D sharp minor.

Dispa'ri *(I.).* Unequal.

Dispera'bile *(I.)* ⎱ Hopeless ; despairing.
Dispera'to *(I.)* ⎰
Con disperazio'ne. In a despairing style.

Dispersed Harmony. With the notes of the chords at wide intervals from each other ; the opposite of close harmony *(q.v.).*

Disposition. *(G., Disposition'.)* (1) A specification of an organ. (2) The arrangement of the notes of a chord *(open* or *dispersed).* (3) The order of placing the parts in a full score. (4) The positions allotted to choir, soloists, orch., &c., for a musical performance.

Disposition *(F.).* Natural gifts, genius, talent, &c.

Dis'sonance. *(G., Dissonanz' ; F., Dissonance ; I., Dissonan'za.)* Discord.
The words *dissonance* and *discord* are generally used with the same meaning. Strictly speaking, however, *dissonance* is the unpleasant effect caused by the interference of sound-waves (see *Acoustics*), while a *discord* is any combination of sounds which produces dissonance. There is a similar distinction between *consonance* and *concord.*
Dissonant Interval. Any two sounds which produce dissonance. The dissonant intervals used in music are (1) all 2nds and 7ths, and their compounds, and (2) all diminished and augmented intervals.
Dissonant Chord. All chords except those given under *Consonant Chord (q.v.).*
Degrees of Dissonance. The closer 2 dissonating tones are in pitch the greater the dissonance. Thus, "*m* against *f* we call a *Primary* dissonance ; *m* against *f¹* a *Secondary* dissonance ; *m₁* against *f¹* a *Tertiary* dissonance."—Curwen.

Dissona're *(I.).* To be dissonant ; to jar.

Distance. Another name for *interval.*

Distan'za *(I.).* An interval ; distance.

Distich. A couplet ; two lines of poetry forming a complete group, or stanza.

DIS'TIN, John. English trumpeter ; 1793-1863. Member of George IV's private band. Invented the key-bugle.

DIS'TIN, Theodore. Son of J. B. Brighton, 1823 ; *d.* 1893. Singer, teacher, and French horn player.

Distinguishing tone. The tone which in a change of key "distinguishes" the new key from the old; **t** in a "one sharp" remove, and **f** in a "one flat" remove. (See **Characteristic tone.**)

Distin'to *(I.).* Distinct, clear.

Distintamen'te *(I.).* Clearly, distinctly.

Distona're *(I.).* To play or sing out of tune.

Distribution of Chords. (See **Disposition** (2).)

Diteggiatu'ra *(I.).* Fingering. (See **Dito.**)

Dithyram'bus *(Gk.).* A song or ode in praise of Bacchus.

Di'to *(I.).* A finger.
Di'to gros'so. The thumb.

Di'tone. *(L., Ditonus; F., Diton; I., Dito'no.)* A Pythagorean third consisting of two major tones. Ratio 81 : 64. Greater by a *comma* than a true major 3rd (5 : 4).

DITSON, Oliver. 1811-1888. Founded the Boston music firm of O. Ditson & Co.

DIT'TERS (von DITTERSDORF), Karl. *B.* Vienna, 1739; *d.* 1799. Celebrated violinist. Accompanied Gluck through Italy, 1761. Capellmeister to the Bishop of Gross-Wardein, Hungary, 1764-9; afterwards to the Prince-Bishop of Breslau (to 1795). Ennobled by the Emperor, 1773. "Ditters may be regarded as a worthy precursor of Mozart in national dramatic composition" *(Baker).*
Works: 28 operas *(Doctor und Apotheker, 1786);* oratorios and cantatas; 12 symphonies for orch., which are regarded as "remarkable examples of early program music;" 12 violin concertos; much chamber music; sonatas and other pf. pieces, &c.

Ditty. A short simple air, or song.

Di'va *(I.).* "A goddess." A specially gifted female singer.

Divagazio'ne *(I.).* A wandering; a digression.

Divertimen'to *(I.)* ⎱ (1) A light composition
Divertissement *(F.)* ⎰ intended for diversion or amusement, as opposed to a classical or serious piece. (2) A *pot-pourri*, or medley of well-known themes. (3) An *entr'acte.*

Dividing-place of the (Major) Scale. Between *soh* and *fah (Curwen).*

Divi'si *(I.). (G., Getheilt'.)* "Divided." A direction for vns., violas, &c., to divide and play two separate parts from the same staff instead of double stopping. It is contradicted by the word *unis.* (or *a due, a 2).* (See **A due.**)

VIOLAS. MOZART. *Sym. in G min.*
divisi.

Division. (1) A variation, especially an elaborate variation *(coloratura)* for a solo voice or instrument; so-called from the "dividing" of the simple notes of the theme into groups of shorter ones. (2) A series of vocal runs, brilliant passages, &c.

Division *(F.).* A double-bar.

Division viol. (1) A violin with frets. (2) The *Viola da Gamba.*

DI'VITIS, Antonius (or **Antoine le Riche**). 16th cent. French contrapuntist.
Wrote masses, motets, chansons, &c.

Divotamen'te *(I.).* ⎱ Devotedly; devoutly;
Divo'to,-a *(I.).* ⎬ with devotion.
Con divozio'ne *(I.).* ⎰ (See also **Devoto.**)

D'IVRY. (See **Ivry.**)

DIX, Wm. Chatterton. 1837-98. *B.* Bristol. Some 40 of his hymns are in common use, including "Come unto Me, ye weary."

Dixième *(F.).* Interval of a 10th.

DIZI, François Jos. Famous harpist; self-taught. *B.* Namur, 1780; *d.* 1847. Concert-player in London and Paris.
Pub. "A Complete Treatise on the Harp;" also harp sonatas, studies, variations, &c.

Do. (1) The Italian name of C. (2) The sol-fa name of C in "fixed *do*" systems. (3) The sol-fa name of the key-note in "movable *doh*" systems. (See **Doh,** and **Tonic Sol-fa Syllables.**)

DOANE, Geo. Washington, D.D. 1799-1859. Bishop of New Jersey. Author of the hymn, "Thou art the Way."

Doch *(G.).* Still, nevertheless, but.
Doch im'mer noch sehr leb'haft. But still very quick (animated).
Doch nicht all'zu sehr. But not so very much.

Doctor of Music. The highest musical degree conferred by a University. (See **Degrees.**)

DÖB'BER. (See **Doebber.**)

DOBRZYN'SKI, Ignacy Félix. *B.* Romanoff, 1807; *d.* 1867. Pianist; friend of Chopin. Conducted the Opera at Warsaw.
Works: 2 operas, chamber music, pf. music, and several successful songs.

DODDRIDGE, Philip, D.D. 1702-51. Nonconformist minister. Wrote "O God of Bethel," and other favourite hymns.

DODDS, Tom Wm. *B.* Leeds, 1852. Mus.Doc. Oxon, 1887. Orgt. Queen's Coll., Oxford, since 1872.

Dodecachor'don *(Gk.).* (1) An inst. with 12 strings. (2) A work on the 12 keys (or modes) by Glareanus (1547).

Dodec'upla di cro'me *(I.).* 12-8 time.

Dodec'uplet. A group of 12 notes to be performed in the time allotted to 8 of the same kind:—

Dodinette *(F.).* A lullaby.

DOEB'BER, Johannes. *B.* Berlin, 1866. Capellmeister Coburg-Gotha Theatre, 1895.
Works: operas, *Die Strassensängerin* (1809), *Die Rose von Genzano* (1895), *Die Grille* (1897), and others; pf. pieces; over 60 songs, &c.

Do'glia *(I.).* Grief, sadness, pain.

Doh. The Tonic Sol-fa spelling of *Do.*
In the Tonic Sol-fa system, *Doh* is the Tonic of all major keys; *Lah* the Tonic of all minor keys.

DÖH'LER, Theodor. *B.* Naples, 1814; *d.* 1856. Pianist; pupil of Benedict and Czerny. Toured as concert-pianist throughout Europe with great success (1836-48).
Works: opera, *Tancreda;* concertos, nocturnes, études, variations, transcriptions, &c., for pf. His music is showy, but without depth.

DOHNÁN'YI, Ernst von. *B.* Pressburg, Hungary, 1877. Distinguished pianist; first appearance in England, 1898. His compositions are original and interesting.
Works: Symphony in D minor, prize overture (1897), and some fine chamber and pf. music.

Doi *(I.).* Two.

Doigt *(F.).* Finger.
Doigt effleurant la corde. The finger lightly touching the string (in vn. playing).
Doigté. (1) Fingered; *i.e.,* with figures, &c., to show the proper fingering. (2) As a noun, "fingering."
Doigtés fourchus. Cross-fingerings.

DOLBY, Charlotte. (See **Sainton-Dolby.**)

Dol'can. (See **Dulciana.**)

Dol'ce. A sweet, soft-toned organ stop.

Dol'ce *(I.).* Sweet, soft, gentle, pleasant.
Dol'ce con gu'sto. Sweetly and with taste.
Dol'ce e lusingan'do. In a delicate insinuating style.
Dolce e piacevolmen'te espressi'vo. Sweetly, and with very pleasing expression.
Dol'ce manie'ra. In a sweet, soothing, delicate manner.
Dolcemen'te } Sweetly, softly.
Con dolcez'za }

Dolcian' *(G.)* } (1) An obsolete form
Dolcia'no, Dolci'no *(I.)* } of the bassoon.
(2) Dulciana. (3) An organ reed-stop.

Dolcis'simo *(I.).* Very sweetly and softly. With the greatest delicacy and sweetness.

Dolen'do *(I.)* } Sad, plaintive, doleful.
Dolen'te *(I.)* }
Dolentemen'te. Dolefully, sadly, &c.
Dolentis'simo. Very sadly, &c.

DO'LES, Joh. Friedrich. *B.* Saxe-Meiningen, 1715; *d.* 1797. Pupil of J. S. Bach. Cantor, Freiburg, Saxony, 1744. Mus. Director Thomasschule, Leipzig, 1756-89.
Works: much easy and popular church music, and an "Elementary Instruction in Singing."

DOL'METSCH, Arnold. *B.* Le Mans, 1858. Performer on the lute and other mediæval insts.

Dolo're *(I.).* Grief, dolour, sadness.
Con Dolo're
Dolorosamen'te } In a plaintive, sorrowful style.
Doloro'so

Dolz'flöte. *(G.).* (*F.,* *Flûte douce; I., Fla'uto dol'ce.*) (1) The old German flute. (2) A sweet-toned organ-stop of the flute family; often 8 ft. on the pedal.

DOM BE'DOS. (See **Bedos de Celles.**)

Dom'chor *(G.).* A cathedral choir.

Dominant. *(G. & I., Dominan'te; F., Dominante.)* (1) The 5th note of any major or minor scale. (2) The reciting-note of a church mode. (See **Mode.**)

Dominant Chord. (See **Dominant Triad.**)

Dominant Section. That part of the 1st movement of a sonata introducing the 2nd principal subject (which is usually in the key of the Dominant). (See **Sonata.**)

Dominant Seventh. The dominant triad with a minor 7th added.

DOMINANT TRIADS.		DOMINANT SEVENTHS.	
C major.	C minor.	C major.	C minor.

The dominant 7th is one of the most important chords in harmony, and was first used, as an unprepared discord, by Jean de Mouton, abt. 1500. (See also *Monteverde.*) The major or minor 9th, the 11th, and the major or minor 13th, may be added to the dominant 7th; but the *complete* chords of the 11th and 13th are very rarely used.

9ths.   11ths.   13ths.

The following, however, may be regarded as a complete chord of the 13th, root A; (or the C♯, E, G, and B♭ may be regarded as appoggiaturas):—

BEETHOVEN. *9th Sym.*

&c.

(See also *Fundamental Discords.*)
N.B.—All dominant discords are of great value in modulation. (See *Modulation.*)

Dominant Triad. The dominant with its *major* 3rd and perfect 5th.

DOMINICETI, Cesare. Italian opera composer; 1821-88.
Six of his operas were produced at Milan, 1841-81.

DOMINO NOIR, Le. Opera by Auber; produced, 1837.

DOM'MER, Arrey von. Critic and writer; *b.* Danzig, 1828. Secretary, Hamburg City Library, 1873-89.
Works: "Elements of Music" (1862), a revised edition of Koch's "Lexikon," a "Handbuch der Musikgeschichte," &c.

DONAJOW'SKI, Ernst. *B.* Calais, 1845.

Do'na no'bis pa'cem *(L.).* The last movement of a mass.

DONA'TI, Baldassaro. Composer of madrigals, motets, &c.; Venice, 1530-1603. Maestro St. Mark's, Venice, 1590.

DONA'TI, Ignatio. *B.* nr. Cremona, 1612; *d.* 1638. Maestro Milan Cathedral, 1631-8.
Works: motets, psalms, masses, madrigals, &c.

DONE, Dr. Wm. Worcester, 1815-95. Assist. orgt. Worcester Cath., 1825; cath. orgt. and conductor of the Worcester Musical Festivals, 1844. Mus.Doc. Cantab., 1894.

DON GIOVAN'NI, or IL DISSOLU'TO PUNI'TO. Mozart's finest opera; Prague, 1787.

DO'NI, Giovanni Battista. Florentine nobleman; 1593-1647. Learned writer on ancient music.
Works: a valuable treatise on "Ancient Greek Music" (1635-40), "De præstantia musicæ veteris" (1647), &c.

DONIZETTI, Alfredo (A. Ciummei). *B.* Smyrna. 1867. Pupil Milan Cons. 1883-9.

Works: operas (*Dopo l'Ave Maria*, 1897, &c.); orchestral works, pf. pieces, songs, &c.

DONIZETTI, Gaetano. Celebrated opera composer ; *b.* Bergamo, 1797 ; *d.* Apr. 8, 1848. Son of a weaver. Studied at the Bergamo School of Music, and (1815) at the Bologna Liceo Filarmonico. To avoid being a teacher he joined the army, and while stationed at Venice composed his first opera, *Enrico di Borgogna* (1819). The success of this and 3 other works procured his release from military service in 1822 ; and up to 1830 he composed 27 other operas, all, however, superficial and flimsy in character. *Anna Bolena* (1830) inaugurated a much finer and richer style of composition. From this time to his death he enjoyed European celebrity, and, travelling from place to place, produced a series of masterpieces.

In addition to 67 operas he wrote 7 masses, 12 string quartets, pf. music, cantatas, &c., and numerous songs.

Chief operas : *Anna Bolena* (1830), *L'Elisir d'amore* (1832), *Torquato Tasso* (1833) ; *Lucrezia Borgia* (1833), *Marino Faliero* (1835), *Lucia di Lammermoor* (his finest work, 1835), *La Fille du Régiment* (1840), *La Favorite* (1840), *Linda di Chamounix* (1842), *Don Pasquale* (1843).

Don'na, Pri'ma. The principal lady singer in an opera.

DONT, Jacob. Vienna, 1815-88. Violin Prof. Vienna Cons., 1873.

Works: an excellent "Gradus ad Parnassum" for vn., and some 50 other works.

DONZEL'LI, Domenico. Tenor singer ; *b.* Bergamo, 1790 ; *d.* 1873. Sang in London, 1829.

Rossini wrote for him the part of *Torvaldo*.

DOOR, Anton. *B.* Vienna, 1833. Accomplished pianist. Prof. Moscow Cons., 1864. Prof. Vienna Cons., 1869.

Door is noted as a fine teacher ; and he has edited several "classical and instructive works."

DOORLY, Martin Edward. Orgt. and composer. *B.* Demerara, British Guiana, 1847 ; *d.* Barbadoes, 1895.

Do'po *(I.)*. After.

Dop'pel *(G.)*. Double. *Dop'pelt*, doubled.

Dop'pel B. } The double-flat, ♭♭.
Dop'pelbee }
Dop'pelblatt. A double reed.
Dop'pelces. C double flat, C♭♭.
Dop'pelchor. A double chorus.
Dop'pelcis. C double-sharp, Cx.
Dop'pelfagott. Double bassoon.
Dop'pelflöte. (*I.*, *Fla'uto dop'pio*). An organ stop consisting of stopped wood pipes, each pipe having two mouths.
Dop'pelfuge. A double-fugue. (See *Fugue.*)
Dop'pelgeige. Another name for the *Viola d'amore.*
Dop'pelgesang. Duet.
Dop'pelgriffe. (1) Notes in pairs: as 3rds, 6ths, &c. (2) Double-stopping (on the violin).
Dop'pelkreuz. A double sharp, x.
Dop'peloktave. A double octave or 15th.
Dop'pelpunkt. A double dot (𝅗𝅥).
Dop'pelschlag. (1) A turn. (2) A double beat. (See *Beat.*)

Dop'peltriller. A double shake. (See *Shake.*)
Dop'pelvorschlag. A double appoggiatura.
Dop'pelzunge. Double-tonguing.

Dop'pio *(I.)*. Double.

Cano'ne dop'pio. A double canon.
Dop'pio movimen'to. At double the speed ; *i.e.*, twice as fast.
Dop'pio no'te } Each note doubled in time-value ;
Dop'pio valo're } *i.e.*, twice as slow.
Dop'pio peda'le. The pedal part in octaves (in organ playing).
Dop'pio più len'to. Twice as slow.

DOP'PLER, Albert F. *B.* Lemberg, 1821 ; *d.* 1883. Fine flautist ; 1st flute at Pesth Theatre, and Vienna Court Opera.

Works: 8 successful operas, ballet-music, overtures, flute concertos, &c.

DOP'PLER, Karl. Brother of A. F. *B.* Lemberg, 1826 ; *d.* 1900. Flautist ; conductor and mus. director Pesth Theatre.

Works: operas, ballet-music, flute music, &c.

DOP'PLER, Arpad. Son of Karl. *B.* Pesth, 1857. Since 1889 chorusmaster Court Theatre, Stuttgart.

Works: opera, *Viel Lärm um Nichts* (1896) ; orch. works, choruses for female voices, songs, pf. music, &c.

DÖRF'FEL, Alfred. Esteemed critic and editor ; *b.* Waldenburg, Saxony, 1821 ; *d.* 1905. Musical Librarian Leipzig City Library.

DO'RIA. (See **Clara K. Rogers.**)

Dorian, or Doric Mode. The Gregorian mode commencing on D. (See **Mode.**)

Do'rico *(I.)*. Dorian.

DÖ'RING, Karl Heinrich. *B.* Dresden, 1834. Esteemed pf. teacher and composer.

Works: several instructive pf. studies and pieces, male choruses, a mass, motets, orch. pieces, &c.

DORN, Alexander J. P. Son of H. L. E. (below). *B.* Riga, 1833 ; *d.* 1901. Pianist, "Royal Professor," Berlin R. Hochschule.

His works—over 400—include masses, cantatas, songs, and several brilliant pf. pieces.

DORN, Edouard. Pseudonym of **J. L. Roeckel.**

DORN, Heinrich Ludwig E. *B.* Königsberg, 1804 ; *d.* 1892. Mus.-director Leipzig, 1829 (taught Schumann) ; mus.-director St. Peter's Cath., Riga, 1831-42 ; capellmeister Cologne Theatre, 1843. Founded the Rheinische Musikschule (1845), which became the Cologne Cons., 1850. Court capellmeister, Berlin Royal Op., 1849-69.

Works: opera, *Die Nibelungen* (1854), and about a dozen others ; church music, symphonies, cantatas, songs, pf. music, &c. Musical editor, *Berliner Post*, bitterly opposing Wagner.

DORN, Julius P. Pianist and composer ; son of H. L. E. ; *b.* Riga, 1833.

DORN, Otto. Son of H.L.E. *B.* Cologne, 1848. Has written a successful opera, *Afraja* (1891) ; a symphony, overtures, songs, and pf. pieces.

DÖR'NER, Armin W. American pianist and teacher. *B.* Marietta, Ohio, 1852. Pf. prof. Cincinnati College of Music.

DORRELL, Wm. London, 1810-96. Pianist. Prof. R.A.M. for over 40 years. One of the founders of the Bach Society, 1849. Edited Mozart's pf. sonatas, &c.

DORUS-GRAS, Julie A. J. (stage name **Dorus**)· Brilliant soprano singer; *b.* Valenciennes, 1805; *d.* Paris, 1896. Studied Paris Cons. Sang at the Grand Opéra, 1830-45; visited London, 1847-48. Married M. Gras, 1843.

DOSS, Adolf von. Jesuit priest; *b.* Lower Bavaria, 1825; *d.* Rome, 1886.

He composed some 350 works, including 8 operas and operettas, 11 oratorios and cantatas, 3 symphonies, and 3 collections of church music.

Dossolo'gia *(I.).* Doxology.

Dot. *(G., Punkt; F., Point; I., Pun'to.)* (1) A dot after a note increases its time-value by *one-half;* and each successive dot is *one-half* the time-value of the preceding:

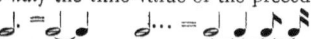

(2) A dot above or below a note indicates *staccato* • Slurred dots indicate *mezzo-staccato.* (See **Staccato.**) (3) Several dots over a note indicate that it has to be divided into a number of shorter ones:

(See **Abbreviations.**) (4) Dots are also used to show *repeats.* (See **Abbreviations.**)

In old music the dot of prolongation was often written in the next bar :—

Now written :—

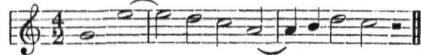

DOTZ'AUER, Justus J. F. Distinguished 'cellist; *b.* nr. Hildburghausen, 1783; *d.* 1860. Played in the Leipzig Orch. 1806-11, and in the Dresden Orch. 1811-52. He was also celebrated as a teacher.

Works: an opera; 'cello concertos, sonatas, exercises, &c.; a Method for 'Cello; orchestral and chamber music, &c.

DOTZ'AUER, Karl Ludwig (known as **Louis Dotzauer**). Son of the preceding. *B.* Dresden, 1811. First 'cello, Cassel Court Orch., 1830.

Double(*F.*). (1) Double. (2) Old name for a turn.

Double. (1) A variation. (See **Variations.**) (2) A repetition of words. (3) To give the same passage to different voices or insts., *e.g.* a violin may *double* a voice part at the unison or octave; the tenor may *double* the bass at the 8ve. or unison, &c. (4) In a chord, to use the same note or interval twice (as to *double* the 3rd, &c.). (5) With insts., an octave lower; as double bass, double bassoon, &c.

Double backfall. An obsolete ornament. (See *Ornaments.*)

Double bar. The sign ‖ used at the end of a piece of music, or at the end ‖ of some important division of it.

Double barre (F.). Double bar.

Double bassoon. A 16 ft. bassoon, an octave lower than the ordinary bassoon, and producing all its notes an octave lower than those written.

Double beat. (See *Beat,* and *Ornaments.*)

Double bémol (F.). The double flat, ♭♭.

Double bourdon. An organ stop of 32 ft. tone ; *i.e.,* an octave lower than the ordinary bourdon of 16 ft.

Double chant. (See *Chant.*)

Double chorus. A chorus for two choirs, either together or in alternation.

Double concerto. A concerto for two solo insts. and orch.

Double counterpoint. (See *Counterpoint.*)

Double coup de langue (F.). Double-tongueing.

Double croche (F.). A semiquaver, ♪

Double demisemiquaver. Half a demisemiquaver, ♪

Double diapason. A 16ft. diapason on an org. manual. (Also used for a 32 ft. diapason on the Pedals.)

Double dièse (F.). The double sharp, x.

Double dot. (See *Dot.*)

Double drum. A drum beaten at both ends.

Double flageolet. A flageolet with one mouthpiece and two tubes.

Double flat. The sign ♭♭.

Double fugue. A fugue on two subjects. (See *Fugue.*)

Double note. Name sometimes employed for the breve, ‖O‖.

Double octave. The interval of a 15th.

Double pedal (or *Pedal-point*). Two notes (generally the Tonic and Dominant) sustained together. (See *Pedal.*)

Double reed. (1) The reed of insts. of the oboe and bassoon type, as opposed to the single reed of the clarinet. (2) Also used to describe 16 ft. organ reed stops on manuals, and 32 ft. on pedals.

Double relish. (See *Ornaments.*)

Double shake. A shake on two notes at the same time.

Double sharp. The sign x or ✗; formerly 𝄪, or ♯♯.

Double sonata. A sonata for two solo instruments.

Double stopping. Stopping two (or more) strings at once (on the violin, &c.), so as to play 2 (or more) notes together.

Double time. Duple time.

Double travale. An effect produced on the tambourine by drawing the wetted thumb across the parchment.

Double-triple (F.). 3-2 time.

Double trumpet. A 16 ft. Trumpet stop on the organ.

Double-action Pedal Harp. (See **Harp.**)

Double After-note.

Written. Played.

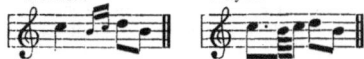

Double-bass (Contra-basso, Contrebasse, or Violone). The largest "bowed" string-inst. Two varieties are in common use: (1) the 3-stringed bass, generally tuned thus:—

(2) the 4-stringed bass, generally tuned thus:—

All the tones produced on the double-bass are an octave lower than the written notes.

Double C. CC. The note

Double-tonguing. The rapid reiteration of notes on wind insts. by using the tip of the tongue as if articulating *tootle-tootle, tikataka,* &c., while blowing.

Double touch. An arrangement on some modern organs by which a light pressure of the key brings on certain stops while a heavy pressure brings on others.

Doublette *(F.).* (1) An organ stop of 2 ft. tone. (2) A mixture of 2 ranks,

Douce, Doux *(F.).* Soft, sweet, gentle.
Doux mais très soutenu. Soft, but very much sustained.

Douced. Old name for dulcimer.

Doucement *(F.).* Sweetly, gently, softly.

Douleur *(F.).* Sadness, pathos.

Douleureusement *(F.).* Sadly, sorrowfully.

DOURLEN, Victor C. P. French composer; 1780-1864. Prof. Paris Cons.
Works: 9 operas, and some chamber music. Pub. a " Treatise on Harmony."

DOUSTE, Jeanne. Pianist and soprano vocalist; *b.* London, 1870.

Douzième *(F.).* The interval of a 12th.

DOW, Daniel. *B.* Perthshire, 1732; *d.* 1783. Compiled several valuable collections of ancient Scottish music.

DOWLAND (or **DOULAND**), **John.** *B.* Westminster, 1562(3); *d.* 1626. Famous lute player and composer. Travelled in France, Germany, and Italy, 1584. Mus.B.Oxon. 1588. Lutenist to Christian IV of Denmark, 1598-1605. Returned to England, 1606. Lutenist to the King, 1612.
Works: 3 "Bookes of Songes or Ayres of Foure Parts, with Tablature for the Lute," and compositions for lute and viols. His settings of psalm-tunes are in both Este and Ravenscroft

Down-beat. The 1st beat of a bar.

Down-bow. *(G., Herun'terstrich; F., Tirez; I., Ar'co in giù.)* The stroke of a bow from nut to point.

DOWNTON, Henry, M.A. 1818-85. Rector of Hopton-by-Thetford. Wrote the hymn, "Lord, her watch Thy Church is keeping."

Doxolo'gia *(L. from Gk.).* Doxology.

Doxolo'gia mag'na *(L.).* The greater doxology, "Gloria in excelsis Deo," sung in the Communion Service.

Doxolo'gia par'va *(L.).* The lesser doxology, "Gloria Patri," at the end of each Psalm.

Doxol'ogy. "A hymn or song of praise to God." The "Gloria in excelsis," or the "Gloria Patri," or any translation or metrical version of either of them.

DRAE'SEKE, Felix A. B. *B.* Coburg, 1835. Studied Leipzig Cons.; friend of Liszt and Bülow. Prof. Dresden Cons., 1884.
Works: 4 operas (*Herrat*, 1892); 3 symphonies, a grand mass, overtures, concertos, a requiem in B minor, chamber music, pf. music, songs, &c. Also treatises on theory.

Drag. (1) A *rallentando.* (2) A descending *portamento* or *glissando* in lute-playing.

DRA'GHI, Antonio. *B.* Ferrara, 1635; *d.* 1700. Settled in Vienna abt. 1660.
Works: 87 operas, 87 "festival plays" and serenades, 32 oratorios.

DRA'GHI, Giovanni Battista. Harpsichord player; lived in London 1667-1706.
Works: music to Dryden's ode, "From Harmony," several songs, Harpsichord Lessons, &c.

DRAGONETTI, Domenico. *B.* Venice, 1763; *d.* London, 1846. Celebrated double-bass player; called "the Paganini of the contra-basso."
Played with Lindley the 'cellist for 52 years at the

King's Theatre, the Philharmonic and Antient Concerts, &c. He left a fine collection of scores, old insts., &c., to the British Museum.

Draht'saite *(G.).* A wire string.

DRAKE, Mrs. F. (See **Edna Thornton.**)

Dra'matis perso'næ *(L.).* The characters of a play or opera.

Dram'ma *(I.).* A drama.
Dram'ma li'rica. A lyrical drama.
Dram'ma per mu'sica. A musical drama, or opera.

Drammaticamen'te *(I.)* ⎱ In a dramatic man-
Dramma'tico *(I.)* ⎰ ner; dramatically.

Dräng'end *(G.).* Hurrying; pressing on.
Dräng'end und im'mer hef'tiger. Hurrying, and with increasing impetuosity.

DRÁSEKE. (See **Draeseke.**)

DRAUD (DRAUDIUS), Georg. German bibliographer and antiquarian, 1573-1635.
"His works are one of the chief sources for the musical literature of the 15th, 16th, and 17th centuries."—*Baker.*

Drawing-room music. (See **Salon-music**).

DREAM OF GERONTIUS. Oratorio by Elgar; Birmingham Festival, 1900.

DRECH'SLER, Joseph. Bohemian composer, 1782 - 1852. Capellmeister University. Church and Hofpfarrkirche, Vienna, 1823. Capellmeister Leopoldstadt Th., 1822-30.
Works: 36 operas, operettas, pantomimes, &c.; church music, chamber music, organ music, pf. music, songs, &c. Also an Organ Method and a Treatise on Harmony.

DRECH'SLER, Karl. 1800-1873. 'Cellist and teacher at Dessau and Dresden.

Dreh'er *(G.).* A Bohemian waltz-like dance.

Dreh'leier *(G.).* A hurdy-gurdy.

Dreh'orgel *(G.).* A barrel-organ.

Drei *(G.).* Three.
Drei'achteltakt. 3-8 time.
Drei'chörig. (1) Trichord (as of a pf.). (2) For 3 choirs.
Drei'gestrichene Okta've. The "thrice-accented" octave, reckoned from C in alt. (See *Alt.*)
Drei'klang. A triad.
Drei'sang, Drei'spiel. A trio.
Drei'stimmig. In 3 parts, for 3 voices, &c.
Drei'zweiteltakt. 3-2 time.

Dreist *(G.).* Bold, confident, brave.

DRE'SEL, Otto. *B.* Andernach, 1826; *d.* Beverly, Mass., 1890. Settled in Boston, 1852, "where for some 15 years he was the foremost pianist" *(Baker).* He introduced some of the best German music to the American public.

DRES'ZER, Anastasius W. Brilliant Polish pianist; *b.* 1845. Director of a music school at Halle, which he founded, 1868.
Works: 2 symphonies, pf. pieces, songs, &c.

DREY'SCHOCK, Alexander. *B.* Zack, Bohemia, 1818; *d.* 1869. Fine pianist; played in public at 8. Toured through North Germany (1838), and afterwards through Russia; also visiting Brussels, Paris, London, and Vienna. Prof. Petersburg Cons. and Court Pianist 1862.
Works: an opera, orchestral pieces, and 140 pf. pieces (mostly *salon* music). His variations on "God save the Queen" were at one time much admired.

DREY'SCHOCK, Felix. Son of A.; pianist; b. Leipzig, 1860.

DRIE'BERG, Friedrich Joh. von. Charlottenburg, 1780-1856; Royal Chamberlain. Works: 2 operas, and a number of treatises on Ancient Greek Music.

Dring'ender *(G.).* Hurrying; pressing on.

Drit'ta *(I.).* Same as *diritta* *(q.v.).*

Driving notes. Old name for syncopated notes — notes "driven" through the following accent.

DRO'BISCH, Karl L. *B.* Leipzig, 1803; *d.* 1854. Capellmeister at Augsburg, 1837. Works: 3 oratorios, 18 masses, 3 requiems, motets, &c.

DRO'BISCH, Moritz W. Elder brother of K. L. *B.* Leipzig, 1802. Prof. of Mathematics (1826) and Philosophy (1842) at Leipzig University. *D.* 1896. Works: several valuable mathematical treatises on Temperament, Intervals, Scales, &c.

Droh'end *(G.).* Threatening(ly).

Droite *(F.).* Right. *Main droite* (or *M.D.).* The right hand.

Drone. *(G., Stim'mer, Bordun'; F., Bourdon; I., Bordo'ne.)* (1) A sustained monotone, as given by the *drone* of a bagpipe. (2) The *burden* or refrain of a song.

Drone-bass. A persistent Tonic or Dominant (or both) used throughout a piece or movement (as in some *Musettes*).

Drone-pipe. A pipe which gives only one note.

DROUET, Louis F. P. *B.* Amsterdam, 1792; *d.* 1873. Celebrated flautist; pupil Paris Cons.; played in public at the age of 7. Solo flautist to Napoleon, 1811, and afterwards to Louis XVIII. Played at the London Philharmonic, 1816. Works: over 150 concertos, fantasias, variations, sonatas, &c., for flute.

Drück'balg *(G.).* A wind-reservoir in an org.

Druck'er *(G.).* A very brilliant climax, or special effect.

Drü'cker *(G.).* An organ "sticker."

Druck'werk *(G.).* The whole "sticker"-action of an organ.

Drum. An inst. of percussion, consisting of a hollow cylinder with a vellum or parchment *head* stretched across one or both ends.

(1) *Side-drum.* (*G., Trom'mel; F., Tambour; I., Tambu'ra.*) A small drum with two heads; one head is beaten with the two drumsticks, and across the other catgut strings (called *snares*) are tightly stretched to produce a rattling sound. The side-drum is used for rhythmic effects, or for a continuous roll.

(2) *Tenor-drum.* A larger kind of side-drum, without snares.

(3) *Bass-drum*, or *Big drum.* (*G., Gros'se trom'mel; F., Grosse caisse; I., Gran cas'sa, Gran tambu'ra.*) A large drum with two heads, used chiefly to mark the principal accents in marching-music, &c., or for special effects in the orchestra. The cymbals are often attached to the big drum, so that one player can manipulate both instruments.

(4) *The Kettle-drum.* (See *Kettle-drum.*)

Drum Bass. A bass on a reiterated note :

&c.

Drum Major. The instructor of the drummers of a regiment.

DRYDEN, John. 1631-1700. Poet Laureate. Wrote " Creator Spirit! by whose aid," a trans. of the Latin hymn *Veni, Creator spiritus.* His Odes for St. Cecilia's Day have been set to music by several composers, including Handel.

DRYSDALE, F. Learmont. Composer; *b.* Edinburgh, 1866.

DUBOIS, C. F. Theodore. *B.* Rosnay, Marne, 1837. Entered Paris Cons., 1853; won *Grand Prix de Rome*, 1861. Prof. of Harmony Paris Cons., 1871; of Composition, 1891; Director, 1896. Works: operas and ballets, 3 oratorios, masses, orchestral and chamber pieces, pf. pieces, and several organ compositions.

DUBOIS, Leon. *B.* Brussels, 1849. *Grand Prix de Rome*, Brussels Cons., 1885. Has composed 3 operas, a symphonic poem, &c.

DUBOURG, Matthew. London, 1703-1767. Celebrated violinist. Master of the King's Band, 1752.

Du bout de l'archet *(F.).* With the point of the bow.

DUCHEMIN, Chas. J. P. Pianist and composer; *b.* Birmingham, 1827.

DUCIS, Benoît (or **Benedictus**). 16th century contrapuntist; pupil of Josquin. Orgt. Notre Dame, Antwerp. He is said to have visited England in 1515.

Du'delsack *(G.).* The bagpipe.

Du'e *(I.).* Two.

A du'e. (See under *A*.)

A du'e vo'ci. For 2 voices.

Du'e cor'de. (1) See *Corde.* (2) The same note to be played simultaneously on two strings (of a violin, &c.).

Du'e vol'te Twice.

I du'e peda'li. Both pf. pedals together.

Duet'. (*G., Duett'; F., Duo; I., Duet'to.*) A composition (1) for two voices or insts.; (2) for two performers on one inst. (as a pf., &c.); (3) to be played on 2 separate organ manuals.

Duetti'no *(I.).* A short duet. Dim. of *Duetto.*

Duet'to *(I.).* A duet.

DUFAY, Guillaume. Distinguished Flemish contrapuntist; *b.* Hainault abt. 1400; *d.* 1474. Chorister Papal Chapel, 1428. Finally Canon at Cambrai. He is said to have made many improvements in musical notation, including the invention of white or open notes. Works: a large number of masses, motets, magnificats, chansons, &c.

DUFFIELD, Geo., D.D. 1818-88. American Presbyterian minister. Wrote the hymn "Stand up! stand up for Jesus!"

DUGAZON, Louise Rosalie (*née* **Lefèvre**). Charming actress and singer; *b.* Berlin, 1753; *d.* Paris, 1821. *Début* in Grétry's *Sylvain*, Paris, 1774. Retired, 1806. Her impersonations were so original and striking that actresses of her class are still called " Dugazons."

DUG'GAN, Joseph F. *B.* Dublin, 1817; *d.* 1900. Pianist and teacher. Taught in America, Paris, Edinburgh, and London. Works: 2 operas, chamber music, pf. pieces; "The Singing-Master's Assistant," a translation of Albrechtsberger's "Science of Music," &c.

DU'IFFOPRUGGAR (or **Tieffenbrücker**), **Caspar.** *B.* Bavaria, 1514; *d.* Lyons, 1572.
He was long thought to be the first maker of violins, but this has been recently disputed. He is known to have constructed a fine type of *Viola da gamba.*

DUKAS, Paul. Noted composer; *b.* Paris, 1865.

Dulçaynas *(S.).* } A variety of small
Dulcian, Dulci'no *(I.).* } bassoon.

Dulcian'a. (1) A small bassoon. (2) An org. stop of sweet, delicate, soft tone.
Various other spellings are found, generally commencing with *dolc,* or *dulc,* all derived from *I. dolce,* or *L. dulcis,* sweet.

Dul'cimer. An instrument of very ancient origin, consisting of a number of wires stretched over a resonance box, and struck with hammers held in the hands of the player. It is regarded as the prototype of the pf. (See **Pianoforte.**)

DUL'CKEN, Luise. Sister of Ferdinand David. *B.* Hamburg, 1811; *d.* London, 1850. Fine pianist; played in public at 11. Queen Victoria was one of her pupils.

DUL'CKEN, Ferdinand Quentin. Son of the preceding. *B.* London, 1837. Pianist; pupil of Mendelssohn, Moscheles, Gade, and F. Hiller. Made many concert tours in Europe and America (where he lived several years). *D.* 1902.
Works: an opera, *Wieslav;* a mass, cantatas, songs, pf. pieces, &c.

DULON (DULONG), Fr. Ludwig. Blind flautist; *b.* nr. Potsdam, 1769; *d.* 1826. Toured through Europe from 1783. Chamber musician, St. Petersburg, 1796-1800.
Works: a flute concerto, flute duets, duets and variations for flute and violin, &c., and an interesting autobiography.

DULONG, Franz H. von. Tenor; *b.* Hamm, 1861.

Dulzaginas *(S.).* A dulciana.

Dumb Piano. (See **Digitorium.**)

Dum'ka. A Bohemian lament or dirge.

Dump, Dumpe. An old dance in slow 4-4 time. "A melancholy tune."—*Moore.*

Dumpf *(G.).* Dull, hollow.

DUN, Finlay. *B.* Aberdeen, 1795; *d.* 1853. Viola player; compiled and edited several collections of Scottish melodies, &c. (See **Scottish Music.**)

DUNCAN, Wm. Edmundstoune. Composer; *b.* Sale, Cheshire, 1866.

DUNHAM, Henry M. American musician and teacher; *b.* Brockton, Mass., 1853.
Works: an Organ School (4 vols.), 2 organ sonatas and other organ music; a "System of Technique" for pf., pf. pieces, &c.

DUNHILL, Thos. F. Composer; *b.* London, 1877.

DU'NI, Egidio R. *B.* nr. Naples, 1709; *d.* Paris, 1775. Pupil of Durante. The success of his early operas led him to settle in Paris, 1755. "He is regarded as the founder of French *operá-bouffe.*"
His 13 Italian and 20 French operas include *Nerone* (Rome, 1735), and *Ninette à la cour* (Paris, 1755).

DUNKLEY, Ferdinand L. Organist and composer; *b.* London, 1869.

DUNN, John. Violinist; *b.* Hull, 1866.

DUNN, M. Sinclair. Tenor vocalist, composer, and writer; *b.* Glasgow, 1846.

DUNSTABLE, John (of). *B.* Dunstable, Beds., abt. 1380; *d.* 1453. Tinctor called him "The chief of the English, by whom the new art of counterpoint had been invented." Dunstable, Binchois, and Dufay were "the three greatest contrapuntists of that period." He is said to have invented passing-notes and suspensions, and to have introduced progressions of 3rds and 6ths in place of the earlier 4ths and 5ths.
Some of his works are still extant in the libraries of the Vatican, British Museum, Bologna, Vienna, &c.

DUNSTAN, Ralph. *B.* nr. Truro, Nov. 17th, 1857. Mus.Doc. Cantab., 1892.
Works: services, anthems, school cantatas, school songs, &c.; "A Manual of Music" (18th edition, 1904), Novello's Primer, "Basses and Melodies," "First Steps in Harmony," "A B C of Musical Theory," "Voice Production Exercises," "The Organist's First Book," &c.

Du'o *(I).* A duet.

Duode'cima *(I.).* The interval of a 12th.

Duodecimo'le *(I.).* A dodecuplet *(q.v.).*

Duodram'ma *(I.).* (1) A drama for two performers. (2) A spoken dialogue with musical accompaniment.

Duo'i *(I).* Same as *Due (q.v..)*

Duo'le *(G.).* A duplet. Two notes in the time of three in tripletted times:—

Duo'lo, Con *(I.).* With sadness, grief, melancholy.

DUPARC, Henri. *B.* Paris, 1848.
Works: some beautiful songs, &c.

Duple Time. Any time with 2 beats to a measure; 2-pulse measure and quick 6-pulse measure.
Simple duple time: $\frac{2}{4}$, $\frac{2}{2}$, ¢.
Compound duple time: $\frac{6}{16}$, $\frac{6}{8}$, $\frac{6}{4}$.

Du'plet. (See **Duole.**)

Duplicazio'ne *(I.).* Doubling (a note, part, &c.).

DUPONT, Auguste. *B.* nr. Liége, 1828; *d.* 1890. Fine pianist and successful teacher. Toured in England and Germany. Prof. Brussels Cons. 1852.
Works: concertos, characteristic pieces, and études for pf.; and an excellent historical "Ecole de Piano."

DUPONT, Jean F. *B.* Rotterdam, 1822 ; *d.* 1875. Pupil, Leipzig Cons., of Mendelssohn and David. Capellmeister at Linz and Nuremburg.
Works : opera, *Bianca Siffredi* (1855) ; orchestral and choral works, &c.

DUPONT, Joseph (the elder). Liége, 1821-61. Violinist ; appointed Prof. at the Cons. when only 17.
Works : 2 operas, church music, chamber music, violin pieces, &c.

DUPONT, Joseph (the younger). Brother of A. *B.* nr. Liége, 1838 ; *d.* 1899. Conductor Warsaw, 1867 ; Imperial Theatre, Moscow, 1871. Prof. of Harmony Brussels Cons., 1872, and conductor of the popular concerts.

DUPONT, Pierre. *B.* nr. Lyons, 1821 ; *d.* 1870. Uneducated son of a labourer. His clever political songs caused such a sensation that he was banished, 1851. He was, however, pardoned in 1852 after the *Coup d'état*.

DUPORT, Jean Pierre. *B.* Paris, 1741 ; *d.* Berlin, 1818. First 'cello Court Orch., Berlin, from 1773 ; superintendent of the Court concerts, 1787-1806.

DUPORT, Jean Louis. Brother of J. P. Paris, 1749-1819. Played the 'cello in public in 1768, and from 1812 was considered " the foremost French 'cellist."
Works : 6 'cello concertos ; several nocturnes, sonatas, airs variés, &c., for 'cello ; and a standard text-book on 'Cello-playing.

DUPRATO, Jules L. *B.* Nîmes, 1827 ; *d.* 1892. Pupil (afterwards Prof. of Harmony), Paris Cons.
Works : 12 *opéras comiques*, 4 cantatas, songs, &c.

DUPREZ, Louis G. Paris, 1806-96. Distinguished tenor ; sang at the Grand Opéra, &c., 1836-55. Prof. of Lyrical Declamation Paris Cons., 1842-50.
Wrote an excellent vocal method, " L'art du Chant " (1845), and a set of supplementary " Studies " (1846).

DUPUIS, Sylvain. *B.* Liége, 1856. Pupil (and afterwards teacher of Counterpoint) Liége Cons.
Has produced the opera *l'Idylle* (1896), and others ; 3 cantatas, a symphonic poem, &c.

DUPUIS, Thos. Sanders. *B.* London, 1733 ; *d.* 1796. " One of the best organists of his time." Orgt. Chapel Royal, 1779. Mus.Doc. Oxon, 1790.
Wrote organ pieces, anthems, glees, chants, and pf. pieces.

Dur *(G.).* Major ; as G *dur*, G major.
Dur'tonart. A major key.
Durch'tonleiter. Major scale.

Dur *(F.).* Hard, harsh, coarse.

Duramen'te *(I.).* With harshness ; sternly, roughly.

DURAND (DURANOWSKI), Auguste F. *B.* Warsaw, 1770 ; *d.* abt. 1840 (?). Violinist, celebrated for his brilliant and original style of playing.

DURAND, Marie Auguste. *B.* Paris, 1830. Organist ; head of the music-publishing firm of " Durand et Fils."

DURAN'TE, Francesco. *B.* nr. Naples, 1684 ; *d.* 1755. Distinguished composer of sacred music ; one of the founders (with Scarlatti and Leo) of the " Neapolitan School " of composition. Also a very fine teacher, counting among his pupils Duni, Jommelli, Piccinni, Sacchini, Pergolesi, and Paisiello.
His works include 13 masses, 16 psalms, 16 motets, 12 madrigals, "The Lamentations of Jeremiah," a grand magnificat, &c.

Dura'te *(I.)* ⎱ Hard, harsh, disagreeable.
Du'ro,-a *(I.)* ⎰

Durch'aus *(G.).* Throughout.

Durch'aus fantas'tich und lei'denschaftlich vor'zutragen *(G.).* To be performed throughout fantastically and with passionate emotion.

Durch'blasen *(G.).* To play (a piece) through.

Durch'componi(e)rt *(G.).* ⎱ " Through - com -
Durch'komponi(e)rt *(G.).* ⎰ posed." Used to describe a song with different music for each stanza. *Old E.*, " set through."

Durch'dringend *(G.).* Shrill, penetrating.

Durch'führung *(G.).* " Through - leading." (1) The working-out or development of a theme or movement. (2) The development portion of a sonata, &c.

Durch'gang *(G.).* " Going-through."
Durch'gangsnote ⎱ A passing-note, appoggiatura,
Durch'gangston ⎰ changing-note, &c.

Durch'gehend *(G.).* Passing, transient. Also used in the sense of complete, or " going right through," as *Durch'gehende Stim'men*, complete organ stops.

Durch'spielen *(G.).* To play - through a composition.

Durch'weg lei'se zu hal'ten *(G.).* (To be) generally soft.

Durée *(F.).* Duration, length, time-value.

Dureté *(F.)* ⎱ Harshness, severity, sternness.
Durez'za *(I.)* ⎰

D'URFEY, Thomas. *B.* Exeter, 1653 ; *d.* 1723. Wrote several plays and songs which have considerable historic interest.

Du'ro *(I.).* Hard, firm, strong.

DÜRR'NER, R. J. J. *B.* Ansbach, 1810 ; *d.* Edinburgh, 1859.
Wrote several pleasing pieces for men's voices.

Du'rus,-a,-um *(L.).* Hard. Used in the sense of *major*.

DUS'SEK (pron. *Doo'shek*), **Johann L.** *B.* Tschaslau, Bohemia, 1761 ; *d.* 1812. Celebrated pianist and composer of pf. music. He led a wandering life, teaching and giving concerts in most of the European capitals. For some years he resided in London, where he married the singer, Sofia Corri (1792), and became a partner in a music business. The business failed, and in 1800 he retired to Hamburg to avoid his creditors. He afterwards served under Prince Louis Ferdinand of Prussia, the Prince of Isenberg, and Talleyrand (in Paris). His playing was characterised by a remarkable "singing-touch," and his compositions have a distinct Bohemian "national flavour."

His pf. works include 12 concertos, 80 sonatas (with vn.), 53 solo sonatas, 9 sonatas for 4 hands, waltzes, variations, rondos, fugues, &c.

Düster *(G.).* Gloomy, mournful, sombre.

DUSTMANN, Marie L. *(née* **Meyer**). *B.* Aix-la-Chapelle, 1831 ; *d.* 1899. Operatic soprano. Sang in the chief German cities, and in London.

Du talon *(F.).* At (with) the nut (of the bow).

Dutch Concert.

"An aggregation of inconsonant melodies ; a *concert* in which every man plays simultaneously his own tune."—*Moore.*

DUVAL, Edmond. *B.* Enghien, Hainault, 1809. Wrote several works on Gregorian music and its accompaniment.

DUVERNOY, Henry L. C. *B.* Paris, 1820. Prof. of Solfeggio Paris Cons., 1848 ; a very successful teacher.

Works : Psaumes et Cantiques ; several "Solfège" works, and numerous light pf. pieces.

DUVERNOY, Jean Baptiste. Parisian composer and pf. teacher. Pub. a large number of easy pf. pieces (from abt. 1825), and some useful pf. studies.

DUVERNOY, Victor Alphonse. Paris, 1842-1907. Pupil (afterwards Prof.) Paris Cons.; won 1st prize for pf. playing, 1855. Founded a series of chamber concerts, 1869. Musical critic *République Française.*

Works : operas, *Sardanapale* (1892), *Hellé* (1896), &c. ; symphonic poem, *Le tempête*, and other orch. pieces ; pf. music, &c.

Dux *(L.).* *(G., Füh'rer.)* The "leading" theme or subject of a fugue ; the answer being the *Co'mes*, or companion.

DVOŘÁK *(*pron. *Dvor-shahk'),* **Antonin.** *B.* Mühlhausen, Bohemia, Sept. 8th, 1841 ; *d.* Prague, May 1st, 1904. Son of an innkeeper ; taught the violin by the village schoolmaster ; entered the Prague Org. School at 16, maintaining himself by playing the violin in a small orch. Viola player Prague National Theatre, 1862. Came before the public in his 32nd year, with a patriotic cantata, *The Heirs of the White Mountain.* His "Slavische Tänze" for pf. duet, 1878, established his reputation as a composer. They were arranged for orch., and played at the

Crystal Palace, 1879. In 1883 his fine *Stabat Mater* (composed 1876) was performed by the London Musical Society. *The Spectre's Bride* was written for the Birmingham Festival, 1885. *St. Ludmila* (Leeds Festival, 1886) was not particularly successful. From 1892 to 1895 Dvorák was director of the New York National Cons. He then returned to Prague, and was appointed head of the Cons., 1901.

Works : 6 Bohemian operas ; oratorio, *St. Ludmila ;* Requiem Mass ; cantatas, *The Spectre's Bride* and *The American Flag ; Stabat Mater ;* psalms and hymns ; 5 symphonies, and several other orch. pieces ; 'cello concerto, vn. concerto, pf. concerto ; *Slavische Tänze ;* chamber music, pf. music, duets, songs, part-songs, &c.

DWIGHT, John Sullivan. *B.* Boston, Mass., 1813 ; *d.* 1893. Founded *Dwight's Journal of Music,* Boston, 1852 (discontinued, 1881). Valuable historical essays by A. W. Thayer formed a prominent feature of the journal.

Dwight deserves great credit for discerning merit in the works of Wagner, Schumann, and Brahms at a time when many influential critics utterly contemned them. (See *Criticism.*)

Dy'ad. A concord of two notes.

DYKES, Rev. John Bacchus. *B.* Kingston-upon-Hull, 1823 ; *d.* 1876. Educated at Cambridge ; minor canon and precentor Durham Cath., 1849. Mus. Doc. Durham, 1861. Vicar of St. Oswald, Durham, 1862.

Works : a service, anthems, part-songs, and a large number of very popular hymn-tunes.

DYKES, John Oswald. Son of preceding ; pianist and composer ; *b.* 1863.

Dynam'ics, Musical. The scientific theory of the relative force, intensity, or loudness of musical notes.

There are five principal dynamic degrees : *pianissimo, piano, mezzo, forte, fortissimo.*

"The effect of *fortissimo* is one of strength, massiveness, dignity. . . . The *pianissimo* resembles a glance at nature through a microscope, . . . it is the essence of spectral music. *Forte,* like major, is an image of day ; *piano,* like minor, an image of night."—*Riemann.*

"There are six dynamic tones : (1) The *organ tone,* $\sf{Z}$, which is commenced, continued, and ended with an equal degree of power. (2) The *crescendo,* $<$. (3) The *diminuendo,* $>$. (4) The *swell,* $<>$, which is, in one sense, applicable to all music. There is something of it upon every note played, and every syllable sung ; and it is numbered among the most refined and delicate beauties of melody. (5) The *pressure tone,* $<$, a very sudden *crescendo.* (6) The *explosive tone,* $>$, an instantaneous *diminuendo.*"—*Moore.*

(See also *Accent* and *Expression.*)

DYNE, John. Alto vocalist and glee composer. Gentleman Chapel Royal, 1772 ; Lay Vicar Westminster Abbey, 1779 ; sang at the Handel Commemoration, 1784. Committed suicide, 1788.

E

E. *(F. and I., Mi.)* (1) The 3rd note of the standard scale of C major. (2) The *final*, or lowest note of the Phrygian (or *Me*) Mode. (See **Mode.**) (3) The highest string (or *Chanterelle*) of the violin.

E *(I.).* And; as *'cello e basso,* 'cello and bass.

E dur *(G.).* The key of E major.

E major. The key or scale requiring 4 sharps;

signature [music] The chord [music]

E minor. The relative minor of G major;

signature [music] The chord [music]

E moll *(G.).* The key of E minor.

EAGER, John. *B.* Norwich, 1782; *d.* 1853. Organist and violinist. "An enthusiastic advocate and teacher of Logier's system."

EAMES (pron. *Aims*), **Emma** (Madame **Eames-Story**). Soprano singer; *b.* of American parents, Shanghai, 1867.
> *Début,* Paris Grand Opéra, 1889. First appearance in London as "Marguerite" in Gounod's *Faust,* Covent Garden, 1891. Sang in New York, same year.

Ear. A projecting piece of metal on each side of the mouth of some organ pipes.

Ear, Musical.
> An ear "impressionable to musical tones, affording to its possessor the capability of appreciating and analyzing compositions performed by others," but not always combined with musical memory or ability to play or sing.

EASTCOTT, Richard. *B.* Exeter, 1740; *d.* 1828.
> Pub. "Sketches of the Origin, Progress, and Effects of Musick," "The Harmony of the Muses," and some pf. sonatas.

EBDON, Thomas. Durham, 1738-1811; Cathedral organist from 1763.
> Works: anthems, glees, harpsichord sonatas, &c.

E'BELING, Christoph Daniel. *B.* nr. Hildesheim, 1741; *d.* Hamburg, 1817, where he was custodian of the City Library.
> Pub. translation of musical treatises, &c.

E'BELING, Johann G. *B.* Lüneburg, abt. 1620; *d.* 1676. Professor of Music, Gymnasium Carolinum, Stettin, 1668.
> Works: "120 sacred songs with 2 violins and continued bass," an "Archæology of Ancient Music," &c.

E'benfalls *(G.).* Likewise; similar(ly).

E'BERHARD von FREI'SINGEN. Benedictine Monk, 11th century.
> "Wrote on the scale of organ pipes and on bell-founding."

E'BERL, Anton. Vienna, 1766-1807. Pianist and composer; friend of Gluck and Mozart. Capellmeister, St. Petersburg, 1796-1800.
> Works: 5 operas, *Die Zigeuner* (1782), *La Marchande de Modes* (1783); symphonies, pf. concertos, pf. sonatas, songs, &c.

E'BERLIN (EBERLE), Johann E. *B.* Swabia, 1702; *d.* 1762. Capellmeister to the Archbishop of Salzburg.
> Works: toccatas and fugues for organ, motets, sonatas, 13 oratorios (in MS.), a miserere, &c.

E'BERS, Carl F. *B.* Cassel, 1770; *d.* 1836. Capellmeister at the Schwerin and Pesth Theatres.
> Works: 4 operas, symphonies, overtures, and several popular transcriptions for pf.

E'BERWEIN, Karl. Weimar, 1786-1868. Court musician; friend of Goethe.
> Works: 2 operas, cantatas, a flute concerto, songs, &c.

E'BERWEIN, Traugott Maximilian. *B.* Weimar, 1775; *d.* 1831. Capellmeister to the Prince of Rudolstadt, 1817.
> Works: 11 operas, symphonies, songs, a Mass in A? (his best work), &c.

Ebollimen'to *(I.)* ⎫ Ebullition. A sudden and
Ebollizio'ne *(I.)* ⎭ energetic expression of emotion.

Ecart *(F.).* A wide stretch on the piano.

EC'CARD, Johannes. *B.* Thuringia, 1553; *d.* 1611. Pupil of Lassus. Capellmeister to the Elector, Berlin, 1608. "An eminent composer of sacred music."
> Works: 20 sacred odes a motet, numerous Lieder and Festlieder, choruses, songs, &c.

Ecceden'te *(I.).* Augmented (of intervals).

Ecche'ia. Vases used by the Greeks and Romans in their theatres to augment the sound of the voices of the actors.
> They were tuned in proportions of 4ths, 5ths, and 8ths, and placed in niches between the seats of the spectators.

EC'CLES, John. 1668-1735. Son of S. (below). Master of the Queen's band, 1704.
> Wrote several masques and stage pieces (*The Way of the World, Don Quixote, The Mad Lover,* &c.); collections of songs, &c. He was "one of the most popular composers of his day."

EC'CLES, Solomon. Violinist; London, 1618-83. Turned Quaker and destroyed his insts.

Ecclesiastical Modes. The old church or Gregorian modes. (See **Mode.**)

Ec'co *(I.).* An echo.

Echappée *(F.).* A "hanging" or "anticipatory" note.
> "If from a *broderie* the return-note, the repetition of the original note, is taken away, what remains is the *échappée.*"—*Lavignac.*

Broderies. *Echappées.*

[music]

Echappement *(F.).* An escapement. The "hopper" of a pf.

Echeggia're *(I.).* To echo; to resound.

Echelette *(F.).* A xylophone *(q.v.).*

Echelle *(F.).* A scale.
> *Echelle chromatique.* Chromatic scale.
> *Echelle diatonique.* Diatonic scale.

Echelon *(F.).* A degree of the scale.

Echo. (1) A reflected sound. (2) A *piano,* or *pianissimo* repetition of a short fragment of music. (3) An echo stop on the organ. (4) A kind of mute placed within the bell of a Cornet-à-pistons to produce echo effects. (5) A contrivance on some old harpsichords to subdue the sounds. (6) An old term for *piano, i.e., soft.*
> Of natural echoes there is one at Milan which repeats the report of a pistol 56 times; another at Wood-

stock, Oxfordshire, which repeats 50 times. "On firing a cannon at the head of Echo Lake, New Hampshire, the report is so bandied about from mountain to mountain as to produce an effect like thunder . . . expiring in the distance . . . not louder than a whisper."—*Moore*. It is also said that there are some remarkable echoes which repeat sounds at a different pitch !

Echo Organ. (1) A set of pipes enclosed in a box ; the precursor of the Swell Organ. (2) A separate organ placed at a distance from the main organ.

Echo Cornet. (See *Cornet*.)

Echt, Ech′ten *(G.).* Genuine.
Nach ein′er ech′ten Zigeu′ner-Melodie′. From a genuine Gipsy melody.

ECK, Franz. Brother and pupil of J. F. (below). *B.* Mannheim, 1774 ; *d.* insane, 1804. Fine violinist ; taught Spohr (1802-3). Played chiefly at Munich and St. Petersburg.

ECK, Johann F. *B.* Mannheim, 1766; *d.* abt. 1809. Remarkable violinist ; court musician at Munich, 1780. Afterwards " dramatic director " at the National and Court Theatres (to 1801).
Works : 6 violin concertos and a symphonie-concertante for 2 violins.

ECK′ER, Karl. Freiburg, Baden, 1813-1879. Wrote popular male quartets and songs.

ECK′ERT, Karl A. F. *B.* Potsdam, 1820 ; *d.* 1879. Considered a musical prodigy at 6 ; wrote an opera at 10, and an oratorio at 13 ! Afterwards studied under Mendelssohn at Leipzig. Capellmeister, Court Opera, Vienna, 1853 ; Court Capellmeister, Berlin, 1869.
Works : 4 operas, 2 oratorios, several psalms, &c. of little value ; and several highly-esteemed songs.

Eclat *(F.).* Brilliancy ; dash.

Eclatant(e) *(F.).* Piercing ; loud.

Eclisses *(F.).* Sides, or ribs, of a violin, guitar, lute, &c.

Eclogue *(F.).* A pastoral, or shepherd's song ; or a piece in imitation of one.

E′co *(I.).* Echo. (Also *Ec′co*.).

Ecole *(F.).* A school ; especially a particular style or " school " of composition.

Ecossaise *(F.).* (1) Scotch. (2) A lively dance in $\frac{2}{4}$ time.
A l'écossaise (F.). In the Scotch style.

Ed *(I.).* And ; used before a vowel.

EDDY, Clarence H. Distinguished American organist ; *b.* Greenfield, Mass., 1851.
Gave a series of 100 organ recitals (Chicago, 1879), without repeating a single program-number ! Has pub. several org. pieces, &c.

E′del *(G.).* Noble ; refined, lofty.

EDGCUMBE. (See **Mount-Edgcumbe**.)

EDMESTON, Jas. Architect ; 1791-1867. Wrote some 2,000 hymns, including " Saviour, breathe an evening blessing."

EDSON, Lewis. *B.* Bridgewater, Mass., 1748 ; *d.* 1820.
Composed the hymn - tunes " Bridgewater " and " Lenox," at one time very popular.

EDWARDS, Frederick Geo. *B.* London, 1853.
Author of " United Praise," " Musical Haunts in London," &c. Editor *Musical Times*.

EDWARDS, Henry J. *B.* Barnstaple, 1854. Mus.Doc. Oxon, 1885. Conductor Exeter Oratorio Society.
Works : oratorio *(The Ascension)*, anthems, &c.

EDWARDS, Henry Sutherland. *B.* Hendon, 1829 ; *d.* 1906.
Works : "History of the Opera " (2 vols., 1862), " Life of Sims Reeves," and several other works.

EDWARDS, Julian. *B.* Manchester, 1855. Produced 2 operas in America, *Madeleine* (Boston, 1894), *Brian Boru* (New York, 1896).

EDWARDS (EDWARDES), Rd. English poet and madrigalist ; 1523-66.
Wrote words, and probably music, of " In going to my lonely bed."

EE′DEN, J. B. van den. *B.* Ghent, 1842. Studied at Ghent and Brussels. Appointed Director Mons Cons., 1878.
Works : opera, *Numance* (Antwerp, 1897) ; several oratorios *(Brutus, Judith,* &c.) ; cantatas, orch. music, part-songs, songs, &c.

Effekt′ *(G.).* *(F., Effet ; I., Effet′to.)* Effect, impression.
" The most general mistake of composers, in their pursuit of this great object, is the being more solicitous to load their scores with numerous parts and powerful combinations, than to produce originality, purity, and sweetness of melody."—*Moore*.

Effleurez très légèrement *(F.).* Touch ("graze") very lightly.

E flat. The flat of E.

E flat major. (1) The key or scale requiring 3 flats. (2) The chord

E flat minor. (1) The relative minor of G♭ major (signature 6 flats). (2) The chord

Egalité *(F.).* Equality, evenness, smoothness.

EG′GELING, Eduard. *B.* Brunswick, 1813 ; *d.* 1885.
Published some valuable pf. studies and instruction books.

EGG′HARD, Julius. (Pseudonym of Count **Hardegen**). Vienna, 1834-67. Pupil of Czerny.
Wrote several popular *salon* pf. pieces.

E′GLI, Joh. H. 1742-1810. Swiss composer of popular vocal music—sacred and secular.

Eglise *(F.).* A church : *Musique d'église*, church music.

Eglogue *(F.).* (See **Eclogue**.)

Eguaglian′za *(I.)* ⎫ Equality, smoothness,
Egualez′za *(I.)* ⎭ evenness.

Egua′le *(I.).* Equal.
Vo′ci egua′li. Equal voices.

Egualmen′te *(I.).* With evenness, &c.

Egyptian Music.
The history of civilisation—as far as it has been traced—exhibits a series of " cycles of alternate elevation and depression." The glories of ancient Greece and Rome expired in barbarism ; the dawn of Christianity was obscured by the darkness of the Middle Ages, which in turn was gradually superseded by the light of the Renaissance and

the Protestant Reformation. So, in all probability, has been the history of music. For many generations it was customary to trace the growth of music from the ancient Greeks; among whom, as a matter of fact, music never reached a high level. Modern researches in Assyria, Babylonia, and Egypt have considerably modified the views of thoughtful musical antiquarians. The "seven sacred sounds" were prescribed in Egyptian music as long ago as 3892 B.C.; and there is no doubt that the Egyptians "had attained a high degree of refinement . . . at a time when the whole Western world was still involved in barbarism, . . . and when the history of Greece had not yet begun." Music was an integral part of the Egyptian temple ritual from the most remote times. The favourite instrument used by the priests was the harp, which was probably invented in Egypt. It reached a point of development and beauty which has rarely been equalled. The finest harps were taller than a man; they had many strings, and were most beautifully ornamented; answering "in the houses of Egyptian grandees to the splendid grand pianos which adorn our modern residences." As the players are represented in the ancient rock-tombs as using *both* hands, quite in the modern manner, it is incredible to suppose that these magnificent instruments were used for melody only. Chords of some sort must inevitably have been struck! Even more remarkable were instruments of the lute kind, "with long necks (fingerboards), round or arched bodies," and sometimes "sound-holes." "Instruments of this kind, from which sounds of different pitch were obtained by shortening the strings, were utterly unknown to the Greeks" (*Riemann*). The "Lady Maket" double flutes discovered by Prof. Flinders Petrie in a tomb at Kahun (date abt. 1100 B.C.) show that the Egyptians "certainly employed the intervals we now use" (*Musical Times*, Dec., 1890). More extraordinary still is the pipe with 11 holes found at Panopolis in 1888, "which gives a complete scale of semitones and two enharmonic intervals." The date of this flute is given by Egyptologists as 1500 B.C. It is absurd to suppose that all these highly-developed instruments were used to play melodies "restricted to the compass of a tetrachord!" When it is also remembered that the construction of the Great Pyramids presents mechanical problems which modern engineering science is unable to solve, it is only natural to infer that the ancient Egyptians possessed a far more elaborate system of music than has usually been supposed; possibly, in many respects quite equal to our own! The decadence of Egyptian music dates from abt. 527 B.C.

EH'LERT, Ludwig (or **Louis**). *B.* Königsberg, 1825; *d.* 1884. Studied under Schumann and Mendelssohn. Lived in Berlin as teacher and critic, 1850-63. Conductor Cherubini Society, Florence, to 1869. Settled finally at Wiesbaden.
Works: valuable treatises, "Briefe über Musik" (1859), "Römische Tage" (1867), "Aus den Tonwelt" (1877): a *Spring Symphony* and a *Requiem für ein Kind* are his best compositions.

EHNN-SAND, Bertha. Operatic soprano; *b.* Pesth, abt. 1845-48. From 1868 *prima donna*, Court Opera, Vienna.

EHR'LICH, Alf. Heinrich. "First-rate critic and writer about music." *B.* Vienna, 1822; *d.* 1899. For some years court pianist at Hanover. Pf. teacher Stern Cons., Berlin, 1864-72 and 1886-98.
He wrote several pf. works, and his critical essays for the *Berliner Tageblatt*, &c., are widely esteemed.

EI'BENSCHÜTZ, Albert. Pianist; *b.* Berlin, 1857. Prof. Stern Cons., Berlin, 1896.

EI'BENSCHÜTZ, Ilona. Cousin of A.; *b.* Pesth, May 8th, 1872. Highly distinguished pianist; played at a concert with Liszt in her 5th year. Studied under Madame Schumann (1885-9). First appearance in London, 1891.
Her playing exhibits "a charming individuality of style, and the highest artistic ideals."

EICH'BERG, Julius. *B.* Düsseldorf, 1824; *d.* Boston, Mass., 1893. Violinist and composer. Settled in Boston, 1859. Director of the Museum Concerts and of the Boston Cons. Also Superintendent of Music in the Public Schools.
Works: 4 operettas; studies, &c., for violin; string quartets, songs, &c.

EICH'BERG, Oscar. Pianist; *b.* Berlin, 1845.

EICH'BORN, Hermann L. *B.* Breslau, 1847. Invented the Soprano Waldhorn in F used in many Silesian bands. Has composed many songs, &c., and is a well-known writer on musical subjects (for the Leipzig *Zeitschrift fur Instrumenten-bau*, &c.).

EICH'HORN, Johann G. E. (Coburg, 1822-44), and **Joh. K. E.** (1823-97). Two brothers who gave violin performances together in 1829 (one being 7, the other 6). They toured till 1835, and were afterwards members of the Court Orchestra.

Ei'ferig, Ei'frig *(G.).* Passionate, ardent, full of zeal, eager.

Ei'gentlich *(G.).* Real, actual, proper.

Ei'genton *(G.).* The natural, or fundamental tone of an instrument, or hollow space.

Eight-foot octave. Notes from ♩ to the lowest of these being produced by an organ pipe 8 ft. long. (See **Acoustics.**)

Eight-foot pitch. Unison pitch; *i.e.*, producing the notes "as written."

Eight-foot tone. Tone of unison pitch produced by stopped pipes. (See **Acoustics.**)

Eighth. An octave. The interval of an octave.
Eighth-note. A quaver, ♪
Eighth-rest. A quaver rest, ╕

Ei'len *(G.).* To accelerate.
Ei'lend. Same as *accelerando* or *stringendo*.
Ei'lig. In a hurried or swift manner.

EI'LERS, Albert. *B.* 1830; *d.* Darmstadt, 1896. Basso cantante; studied Milan Cons.
Chosen by Wagner to take the part of the giant *Fasolt*, Bayreuth, 1876. Wrote a successful comic opera, &c.

Ein, Ein'e, Eins *(G.).* One.
Ein'chörig. (1) One string to each note. (2) For an undivided choir.
Ein'e Sai'te. (On) one string.
Ein'fach. Simple; not compound or florid.
Ein'falt. Simplicity.
Ein'gang. Introduction, preface, preamble.
Ein'gangs-schlüs'sel. Introductory key (or clef).
Ein'gestrichen. "Once stroked," as g', a', &c.
Ein'gewebe. Episode.
Ein'greifen. To touch or sound strings; to cross hands.
Ein'halt. A pause.
Ein'heit, Ein'igkeit. Unity, harmony.

Ein'igem Pomp, Mit. "With something of pomp;" *i.e.* in a rather pompous manner.

Ein'klang. Unison, concord, agreement.

Ein'lage. A short piece between two longer ones.

Ein'laut. Monotonous.

Ein'leitungssatz. An opening piece; overture, introduction, prelude, &c.

Ein'mal. Once.

Ein'müthigkeit. Unanimity.

Ein'saiter. A monochord.

Ein'sang. A solo.

Ein'satz. The entry or attack of a voice or inst.

Ein'satzstück. A crook (as of a horn).

Ein'schlafen. To diminish in speed or loudness.

Ein'schlagend. Striking inwards (a beating reed as opposed to a *free* reed).

Ein'schmeichelnd. Insinuating.

Ein'schnitt. (1) A pause at the end of a phrase. (2) An incomplete *motiv* or theme.

Ein'setzen. To enter (after a rest); to attack.

Ein'stimmen. To tune with others; to chime in.

Ein'stimmig. For one voice (or part); in unison.

Ein'tracht. Accord.

Ein'tritt. The beginning; the entrance.

Ein we'nig. A little.

Ein we'nig leben'dig. Rather lively.

Ein we'nig mäs'siger als zuvor'. A little slower than before.

Ein'zeln } Single, alone. (1) Solo. (2) With one
Ein'zelne } voice (or instrument) to each part.

Ein'zelstim'me. A single voice; a solo.

Ein'zug. Entry, entrance.

Ein' Fes'te Burg. The "Reformation hymn." Luther's version of Ps. 46; abt. 1538.

The fine tune—also popularly ascribed to Luther—has been repeatedly employed by composers; notably, Bach (*Church Cantata*), Mendelssohn (*Reformation Symphony*), Meyerbeer (*Les Huguenots*), Wagner (*Kaisermarsch*), and overtures by Nicolai and Raff. As modernized it commences thus :—

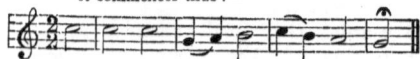

Ein'ige *(G.).* Some.

Ein'ige Contrabässe stim'men die E Sai'te nach D um. Some of the double-basses tune the E string down to D.

E'is *(G.).* E♯ (E sharp).

E'iseis, or **E'isis** *(G.).* E× (E double-sharp).

Ei'senvioline *(G.).* An iron fiddle; nail-fiddle. (See **Nagelgeige.**)

EIS'FELD, Theodor. *B.* Wolfenbüttel, 1816; *d.* 1882. Capellmeister Wiesbaden Court Theatre, 1839-43. Lived in New York (1848-66), conducting the Harmonic Society and the Philharmonic.

EISS'LER, Marianne. Violinist; *b.* Brünn, 1865.

Eistedd'fod. A Welsh gathering for the election of the chief Bard, &c., characterised by poetical and musical competitions.

Hence, a musical competition of the nature of a musical festival.

EIT'NER, Robert. *B.* Breslau, 1832. Settled in Berlin, 1853, and established a pf. school, 1863. *D.* Templin, 1905.

Eitner devoted himself chiefly to musical literature. His "Quellen Lexicon" is a standard work, being especially valuable for its complete lists of old composers' works and their whereabouts. (See *Dictionaries, Musical.*)

Eklo'g(u)e *(G.).* (See **Eclogue.**)

E la. (See **Alt.**)

Elargi *(F.).* Broadened, slackened.

EL'DERING, Bram. Violinist; *b.* Groningen, 1865.

Electric Organ. An organ in which the keys, stops, &c., are connected with the pallets and slides by means of electricity.

Elégant *(F.).* } Elegant, graceful.
Elegan'te *(I.).* }

Elégamment (F.) }
Elegantemen'te (I.) } In an elegant, graceful style.
Elegan'za, Con (I.) }

Elegi'a *(I.).* } (1) A dirge. (2) A composition
Elégie *(F.).* } of a commemorative and
El'egy. } mournful character.

Elegi'ac } In the style of an elegy;
Elegi'aco *(I.).* } mournful.

Elemens *(F.); Elements.* Rudiments.

E'LERS (ELERUS), Franz. *B.* Uelzen, abt. 1500; *d.* 1590. Cathedral mus. director, Hamburg.

Published a comprehensive "Gesangbuch" (1588).

Eleva'tio *(L.).* } (1) An up-beat. (2) A com-
Elevazio'ne *(I.).* } position to accompany the "Elevation of the Host" in the Roman Catholic ritual.

Elevation. } (1) Same as **Elevatio.** (2) The
Elévation *(F.).* } name of 2 obsolete graces.

Eleva'to *(I.).* Elevated, sublime.

Elève *(F.).* A pupil.

Eleventh. The interval of a compound 4th (or an octave and a 4th).

The *Chord of the Eleventh* is classed by Macfarren among the Fundamental Discords (*q.v.*). It is usually taken on the Dominant, and the complete chord is rarely found—the major 3rd being generally omitted :—

With root and 3rd omitted, and 7th placed in the bass, it becomes the chord of the "added 6th"—

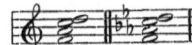

(See *Added Sixth.*)

The 11th, like all other Fundamental Discords, admits of several different resolutions. (See *Harmony.*)

EL FARABI. (See **Alfarabi.**)

Elf'te *(G.).* Eleventh.

ELGAR, Sir Ed. Wm. *B.* Broadheath, near Worcester, June 2nd, 1857. Mus.D.Cantab. (*honoris causâ*), 1900; knighted, 1904.

Chief works: *The Light of Life* (Worcester Festival, 1896); *Caractacus* (Leeds, 1899); *The Dream of Gerontius* (Birmingham, 1900); *Cockaigne* overture (1901); *Pomp and Circumstance* marches (1901); trilogy, *The Apostles* (Parts 1 and 2, Birmingham, 1903; Part 3, *The Kingdom*, 1906); Symphony in A♭ (1908); also songs, part-songs, pf. pieces, &c.

ELIAS SALOMONIS. Monk of Périgord.

Wrote "Scientia artis Musicæ" (1274); "of peculiar value as the oldest work giving rules for improvised counterpoint."—*Baker.*

E'licon *(I.).* Helicon (*q.v.*).

ELIJAH. Mendelssohn's chief oratorio; 1st performance, Birmingham Festival, Aug. 26th, 1846.

ELLA, John. *B.* Thirsk, Yorks, 1802; *d.* London, 1888. Violinist, King's Theatre,

1822 ; afterwards at the Concerts of Antient Music and the Philharmonic.
Instituted a series of "Musical Winter Evenings" (1845-59). Lecturer on Music, London Institution, 1855. Founded and directed the Musical Union, aristocratic chamber concerts.
Works : "Musical Sketches abroad and at home" (3 editions) ; "Lectures on Dramatic Music," &c., and a series of analytical programmes for his "Musical Winter Evenings." These were the first analytical programmes used in London, and were an improvement on those of J. Thompson, Edinburgh, 1837. The earliest known were by Reichardt, Berlin, 1783.

ELLER, Louis. *B.* Graz, 1819 ; *d.* 1862. Violinist ; toured through Austria, Switzerland, and Southern Europe.
Wrote descriptive pieces for violin ("Valse diabolique," "Menuet sentimental," &c.).

ELLERTON, Rev. John, M.A. ; 1826-93. Wrote several hymns—"The day Thou gavest," "Now the labourer's task is o'er," &c.

ELLERTON, John L. *B.* Chester, 1801 ; *d.* 1873. Studied at Rome.
Works : 11 operas, an oratorio *(Paradise Lost)*, 5 symphonies, 44 string quartets, 13 sonatas, 144 duets and glees, &c.

ELLICOTT, Rosalind F. Daughter of Bishop Ellicott ; *b.* Cambridge, 1857. Composer and pianist ; has written cantatas, orch. pieces, songs, &c.

ELLIOTT, Charlotte ; 1789-1871. Wrote "Just as I am," "Thy will be done," and many other favourite hymns.

ELLIOTT, Jas. Wm. *B.* Warwick, 1833. Pupil of G. A. Macfarren.
Has written 2 operettas, nursery rhymes, pieces for harm., services, anthems, part-songs, &c.

ELLIOTT, Lionel. Pen name of **J. Williams** *(q.v.).*

ELLIS, Alexander John, F.R.S. London, 1814-1890. Noted writer on musical science.
Works : "The Basis of Music" (1877) ; "Pronunciation for Singers" (1877) ; a translation of Helmholtz's great work on Acoustics (1875) ; "The Musical Scales of Various Nations" (1885) ; and numerous other treatises, essays, &c.

ELLIS, William Ashton. Critic and writer ; *b.* 18—. Author of "A Life of Wagner," &c.

ELM'BLAD, Johannes. Operatic bass ; *b.* Stockholm, 1853.

ELMAN, Mischa. Distinguished precocious violinist ; son of a poor Jewish schoolmaster. *B.* Talnoje, Sth. Russia, 1891.

Eloge *(F.).* Praise, eulogy.

ELOUIS, J. Celebrated French harpist ; end of 18th century.

EL'SENHEIMER, Nicholas J. *B.* Wiesbaden, 1866. Prof. Cincinnati College of Music, 1891.
Has written cantatas, orchestral works, &c.

ELS'NER, Jos. X. *B.* Silesia, 1769 ; *d.* 1854. Was Chopin's teacher at Warsaw. Established there a school for organists, which afterwards became the Cons. of which he was director to 1830.
Works : 19 operas ; ballets, symphonies, cantatas, &c. ; and 2 essays on the "Polish Language in Vocal Music."

ELSON, Louis Chas. *B.* Boston, Mass., 1848. Writer and lecturer on mus. history, &c.
Works : "Curiosities of Music," "History of German Song," "The Realm of Music," "A Music Dictionary," "Great Composers and their Work" (1899). &c. Has also translated and arranged over 2,000 songs, operas, &c.

EL'TERLEIN, Ernst von (real name **Ernst Gottschald).** *B.* Elterlein, Saxony, 1826.
Published "An Æsthetic Analysis of Beethoven's Pianoforte Sonatas" (1857).

ELVEY, Sir George J. *B.* Canterbury, 1816 ; *d.* 1893. Chorister Canterbury Cathedral. Studied R.A.M. under Dr. Crotch. Org. and Master of the Boys, St. George's, Windsor, 1835-82. Mus.D. Oxon, 1840 ; knighted, 1871.
Works : anthems, services, chants, glees, &c.

ELVEY, Stephen. Brother of G. J. *B.* Canterbury, 1805 ; *d.* 1860. Org. New Coll., Oxford, 1840 ; Mus.D., 1838 ; Choragus, 1848-60.
Works : anthems, services, hymns, songs, and a popular "Psalter."

ELWART, Antoine A. E. Paris, 1808-77. Apprenticed to a mechanic at 13 ; but ran away, and joined the orchestra of a small theatre as violinist. Studied Paris Cons. 1825-34, taking *Grand Prix de Rome*. Afterwards Prof. in the Cons. (to 1871).
Taught Gouvy, Grisar, and Weckerlin.
Works : an opera, oratorios, cantatas, chamber music, &c., and several treatises : "Theory of Chords, Thorough - Bass, Counterpoint, and Fugue," "Transposition," "Vocal Studies," "A Short Manual of Instrumentation," &c.

ELWES, Gervase. (See **Cary-Elwes.**)

Embellimen'ti *(I.).* Embellishments.

Embellir *(F.).* To embellish ; to add ornaments and graces.

Embouchure *(F.).* (1) The mouthpiece of a wind instrument. (2) The method of adjusting the mouth, lips, teeth, &c., in producing tone on a wind instrument ; also called "lipping."

EMERSON, Luther O. *B.* Parsonsfield, Mass., 1820. Composer and compiler of collections of simple popular songs and hymntunes—"The Golden Wreath," "The Golden Harp," "Sabbath Harmony," &c.

EMERY, Stephen A. *B.* Paris, Maine, 1841 ; *d.* Boston, 1891. Studied at Leipzig and Dresden. Prof. of Harmony and Counterpoint, Boston University ; assistant editor, Boston *Musical Herald*.
Published "Foundation Studies in Pianoforte Playing," and "Elements of Harmony."

EM'MERICH, Robert. *B.* Hanau, 1836 ; *d.* 1891. Capellmeister Magdeburg Theatre, 1878-9 ; Conductor Stuttgart Male Choral Union, 1879-89.
Works : 3 operas, 2 symphonies, a cantata, &c.

Emozio'ne *(I.).* Emotion. *Con emozio'ne*, with emotion.

Empâter les sons *(F.).* To produce the sounds (especially in singing) in a *portamento* or very *legato* style.
Execution empâtée. A performance lacking in distinctness ; too much slurred.

Emperor's Hymn. The Austrian national hymn; music by Haydn, 1797.

Empfin'dung *(G.).* Feeling, emotion, passion, sensation, sensitiveness.
Empfin'dungsvoll. Full of emotion, &c.
Ton'empfindungen. "The sensations of tone." Term used by Helmholtz in his great treatise on Acoustics.

Empfind'sam *(G.).* Sensitive, emotional.

Emphasis. *(G., Empha'se; F., Emphase.)* Stress laid on certain notes. (See **Accent.**)

Emphatique *(F.);* **Emphat'isch** *(G.).* Emphatic.

Empi'to *(I.).* Impetuosity.

Emporté (e) *(F.).* Carried away by emotion or excitement; fiery, passionate.

Empressé (e) *(F.).* Urgent, eager, hurried.

Emu *(F.).* Moved, affected.

En *(F.).* In; in the style of.
En badinant. Playfully, jestingly; *scherzando.*
En bousculade. Precipitately.
En cédant. Slackening (the speed).
En chantant. In singing style.
En chœur. In chorus.
En diminuant la force. Diminuendo.
En élargissant beaucoup. With much more breadth.
En mesure. A tempo; in time.
En passant. In passing; by the way.
En rondeau. In the style of a rondo.

Enarmo'nico *(I.).* Enharmonic.

EN'CKE, Heinrich. *B.* Neustadt, Bavaria, 1811; *d.* 1859. Pianist; pupil of Hummel.
Published pf. études and pieces, and fine four-hand arrangements of classical works.

ENCK'HAUSEN, Heinrich F. *B.* Celle, 1799; *d.* Hanover, 1885. Director of the Berlin Singakademie and Court Pianist.
Works: opera, *Der Savoyard* (1832); a standard book of chorals, &c.

Encore *(F.).* "Again! Repeat!" Still.
Used chiefly in England. The Germans use the term *Da capo*; and the French, *Bis.*
Encore plus vite. Still faster.

End'e *(G.).* End.

Energi'a *(I.),* **Energie** *(F.).* Energy.
Energicamen'te (I.). } With energy and emphasis.
Con energi'a (I.).

Ener'gico *(I.).* } Energetic; with vigour and
Ener'gisch *(G.).* } distinctness.

ENESCO, Georges. Composer; *b.* Roumania, 1881.

Enfant de Chœur *(F.).* A choir-boy.

Enfa'si *(I.).* Emphasis.
Con enfa'si } With emphasis.
Enfaticamen'te }
Enfa'tico. Emphatic, earnest.

Enfla'tamente *(I.).* Proudly.

Enfler *(F.).* To swell; *crescendo.*

Eng, Eng'e *(G.).* Narrow, close.
Eng'e Harmonie'. Close harmony.
Eng geschrei'bene Partitur'. A condensed (short) score.

ENG'EL, David H. *B.* Neuruppin, 1816; *d.* 1877. Org. Merseburg Cathedral, 1848.
Works: comic opera (*Prinz Carneval*), oratorio (*Winfried*),a choralbuch, psalms, org.pieces,&c.

ENG'EL, Gustav Ed. *B.* Königsberg, 1823; *d.* 1895. Settled in Berlin as singing teacher and critic. Prof. in the Hochschule, 1874.
Works: Vocal Exercises, treatises on the Voice and Vocal Culture, an "Æsthetik der Tonkunst " (1884), &c.

ENG'EL, Karl. Musical historiographer; *b.* near Hanover, 1818; settled in London, 1850; *d.* (by his own hand), 1882.
Works: "Music of the most Ancient Nations" (1864), "Introduction to the Study of National Music " (1866), "Musical Instruments of all Countries " (1869), "Musical Myths and Facts " (1876), "Researches into the early history of the Violin Family " (1853), &c.

ENG'ELSBERG, E. S. (pseudonym of **Dr. Ed. Schön.**) Silesia, 1825-79.
Wrote popular humorous male-voice quartets.

Eng'elstimme *(G.).* The *Vox Angelica (q.v.).*

Eng'führung *(G.).* The *stretto* of a fugue.

ENGLE, Marie. Vocalist; *b.* 18—. *Début*, 1887.

Eng'lisch (es) Horn *(G.).* } The *cor anglais.*
English Horn } *(q.v.)*

English Music. England was well to the front in vocal music during the 15th century, and in instrumental music during the 16th century.
It has long been celebrated for its church services, anthems, and glees; it has also achieved considerable success in the domains of song, opera, cantata, oratorio, and organ music. In pf. music, chamber music, and orchestral music (symphonies, &c.), it can hardly be said to occupy a distinctive place.
Chief Composers.—Dunstable (1380-1453), Gilbert Banister (abt. 1450-90), Fairfax (abt. 1470-1529[30]) John Taverner (16th cent.), Dr. Tye (1497-1572), Marbeck(s) (1523-85), Tallis (abt. 1510-85), Farrant (abt. 1530-80), Parsons (abt. 1535-69), Byrde (1543-1623), Sheppard (16th cent.), Wm. Munday (abt. 1540-91), Dowland (1562-1626), Morley (1557-1604), Wilbye, Kirbye (abt. 1565-1634), Bennet, Weelkes (1578-1623), Gibbons (1583-1625), H. Lawes (1600-62), Child (1606-97), Lock (1620-77), Wise (1638-87), Humphrey (1647-74), Aldrich (1647-1710), Blow (1648-1708), Purcell (1658-95), Weldon (1676-1736), Croft (1677-1727), Greene (1696-1765), Boyce (1710-79), Arne (1710-78), Webbe (1730-1816), Jackson of Exeter (1730-1803), Cooke (1739-93), Arnold (1740-1802), Dibdin (1745-1814), Shield (1754-1829), Stevens (1756-1837), Danby (1757-1798), Dr. S. Wesley (1766-1837), Callcott (1766-1821), Attwood (1767-1838), Spofforth (1768-1827), Horsley (1774-1858), Crotch (1775-1847), John Field (1782-1837), Bishop (1786-1855), Goss (1800-80), John Barnett (1802-90), Balfe (1808-70), S. S. Wesley (1810-76), G. A. Macfarren (1813-87), Wallace (1814-65), Hatton (1815-87), Sterndale Bennett (1816-75), Ouseley (1825-89), Barnby (1838-96), J. F. Barnett (1838-), Stainer (1840-1901), Sullivan (1844-1900), Bridge (1844-), Mackenzie (1847-), Parry (1848-), Cowen (1852-), Stanford (1852-), Elgar (1857-), Ed. German (1862-), Coleridge-Taylor (1875-).

Enguichure *(F.).* Mouthpiece of a trumpet.

Enharmon'ic. *(G., Enharmon'isch; F., Enharmonique; I., Enarmo'nico.)* (1) One of the three ancient Greek *genera*: enharmonic, diatonic, chromatic.
(2) An instrument or scale having intervals smaller than a semitone.
(3) A change of notation without a change of sound.
In acoustical theory, or just temperament, there is a difference of pitch between C♯ and D♭, D♯ and E♭, F♯ and G♭, &c. (See *Temperament.*) An attempt to apply temperament to all the scales in modern use leads to such complications that, as far back as the time of J. S. Bach, it began to be abandoned in favour of a division of the octave into 12 equal semitones, and Bach wrote his 48 Preludes and Fugues for the "well-tempered" Clavier. This *Equal Temperament* is now universal on keyboard instruments (pianos, harmoniums, organs), and the same key stands for

C♯ and D♭, for D♯ and E♭, &c., these pairs of notes being regarded as *Enharmonic Equivalents*.

Table showing all the Enharmonic names which keys (notes) may have without going beyond the double sharp and double flat :—

B×	F♭♭	E×	C♭♭		
D♭	E♭	G♭	A♭	B♭	
C♯	D♯	F♯	G♯	A♯	

C	D	E	F	G	A	B
B♯	C×	D×	E♯	F×	G×	A×
D♭♭	E♭♭	F♭	G♭♭	A♭♭	B♭♭	C♭

Enharmonic varieties of notation are common in full scores; they do not imply, as some old theorists imagined, "some mysterious and subtle interval," but, as Berlioz says, "on such occasions the orchestra becomes a large temperamented instrument." The composer has simply selected the notation most easy to read for each individual part :— (See *Expedient Notation*.)

VOICES. *Les Huguenots.* MEYERBEER.

INSTS.

BASSI. *Freyschutz.* WEBER.

TROMBONES.

VOICES. *Golden Legend.* SULLIVAN.

BELLS. &c.

Enharmonic Change. A change caused by altering the notation of a note or chord :—

Enharmonic Chords. Chords alike in sound but written differently. (See *Diminished 7th Chord*.)

Enharmonic Di'esis. (See *Diesis*.)

Enharmonic Equivalents. (1) Notes having the same sound on the pf. but written differently, as B♭, A♯. (2) Keys or scales sounding the same, but having different key-signatures, as F♯ and G♭ :—

(3) Enharmonic chords.

Enharmonic Interval. (1) The real acoustical interval between two enharmonic forms of a note, as C♯, D♭; or (2) any other interval formed by enharmonic change of notation.

Enharmonic Modulation. A modulation made by means of enharmonic notation. (See *Modulation*.)

Enharmonic Organ. An organ constructed with more than 12 keys to the octave, providing separate keys for C♯ and D♭, &c.

Enigmatical Canon. (See *Canon*.)

Enlevez la sourdine *(F.).* "Take off the mute."

EN'NA, August. *B.* Nekskov, Denmark, 1860. Son of a poor shoemaker. After several early struggles—including "the playing of the big drum before a circus tent"—his compositions attracted Gade's attention, and Enna was awarded the "Ancker Scholarship," with two years' instruction in Germany (1888-9).

His opera, *The Witch* (Copenhagen, 1892), was a brilliant success.

Other works: operas (*Cleopatra, Aucassin and Nicolette*, &c.), violin concerto in D, &c.

ENOCH & Co. Founded 1869.

Enoncer *(F.).* To enunciate.

En scène *(F.).* On the stage.

Enseignement *(F.).* Instruction.

Enseigner *(F.).* To instruct.

En s'éloignant *(F.).* Growing fainter.

Ensemble *(F.).* "Together." (1) The general unity, proportion, and balance of a composition; or (2) its general effect. (3) The harmonious working together of all the performers in the rendering of a composition, or work.

Morceaux d'ensemble. Concerted pieces.

En serrant*(F.).* *Stringendo;* hurrying the pace.

Entfernt *(G.).* Distant, remote, far off; "echo-like."

Enthal'len *(G.).* To sound forth.

Entr'acte *(F.).* A piece to be played between the acts of an opera, drama, &c.

Entran'te *(I.)* ⎱ (1) An overture, prelude, in-
Entra'ta *(I.)* ⎰ troduction, &c. (2) The en-
Entrée *(F.)* try of an actor, or part.
(3) An old dance in 4-4 time.

Entrechats *(F.).* "The peculiar bounds with which a dancer leaps across the stage on entering."—*Stainer and Barrett*.

Entreme'se *(S.).* A short burlesque musical interlude or *entr'acte*.

Entremet*(F.).* A short entertainment between two longer ones.

Entry. The point of commencement, or "coming-in" of any voice or instrument (especially after a rest).

The "order of entry" is an important consideration in the construction of a fugue.

Entschie'den *(G.).* Decided, resolute.

Entschla'fen *(G.).* To die away.

Entschlos'sen *(G.).* Determined, resolute.

Mit Entschlos'senheit. With firmness and decision.

Entusia'smo *(I.)* ⎱ With enthusiasm.
Entusia'stico *(I.)* ⎰

Entwurf *(G.).* A sketch, design, plan, &c.

Entzück'end *(G.).* Charming, delightful.

Enunciation. (See **Voice-production**.)

Enuncia'to *(I.).* Enunciated.

Envoys. "One of the names given to old English ballads."—*Stainer and Barrett*.

Eolian Harp. (See **Æolian Harp**.)

Eolian Mode. (See **Æolian Mode**.)

Epic *(I., Epi'co).* In heroic, narrative style.

In poetry, *Epic* is opposed to *Lyric* and *Dramatic*.

Epice'dion *(Gk.).* A funeral dirge, or elegy.

Epigo'neion *(Gk.).* An ancient Greek lyre said to have had 40 strings.

Ep'ilogue. " An after-word ; " a peroration ; a concluding speech (or song).
Sullivan's *Golden Legend* ends with a " Choral Epilogue."

EPINE, Francesca M. de l' (Mrs. J. C. Pepusch). Soprano ; *b.* Italy, ab. 1672 ; *d.* London, 1746.

Epinette *(F.).* A spinet, or small variety of harpsichord.

Epini'cion *(Gk.).* (1) A song of victory. (2) The *Sanctus* in the Gk. Church ritual.

Epio'dion *(Gk.).* A funeral lament.

Ep'isode. *(G., Zwisch'ensatz ; F., Episode ; I., Divertimen'to.)* A digression ; an incidental passage. (1) A short passage introduced between the main divisions of a fugue, generally based on some portion of the subject or countersubject. (See **Fugue.**) (2) The subject or passage between any two repetitions of the principal theme of a rondo. (See **Rondo.**) (3) Any incidental or connective passage.
Movement of Episode. Name given to a movement developed from a short "motive" (or motives) without extended themes (as many of Bach's *Preludes*, &c.).

Epis'trophe *(Gk.).* A refrain.

Epit'asis *(Gk.).* (1) The progress of the plot in a play or poem. (2) The raising of the voice.

Epithala'mion *(Gk.).* ⎫ A nuptial poem or
Epithala'mium *(L.).* ⎭ song.

Ep'ode *(Gk.).* An "after-song." (1) A refrain. (2) The third portion (stanza) of a Greek ode ; *stro'phe, antis'trophe, ep'ode.*

E poi *(I.).* And then.
E poi la co'da. And then (go on to) the Coda.

EPSTEIN, Julius. Distinguished pianist ; *b.* Agram, 1832. Prof. of Pf. Vienna Cons. since 1867 ; taught I. Brüll and M. Sembrich.

Eptacorde *(F.).* ⎫ (1) A heptachord, or scale of
Eptacor'do *(I.).* ⎭ 7 notes. (2) The interval of a 7th.

Equa'bile *(I.).* Even, uniform, equable.

Equabilmen'te *(I.).* Evenly, equably, &c.

Equal temperament. The division of the octave into 12 equal parts (semitones). (See **Temperament**, and **Enharmonic.**)

Equal voices. Voices of the same class. (1) Children's voices. (2) Female voices. (3) Men's voices.
Strictly speaking, equal voices are those of the same pitch and compass; but the term is generally used as above.

E'quisonance *(F., Equisonnance ; I., Equiso'no).* In unison (or octaves).

Equivocal, or Doubtful chords. (1) Chords common to two or more keys. (2) Chords susceptible of various resolutions.

ÉRARD, Sébastian. Renowned maker of harps and pianos ; *b.* Strasburg, 1752 ; *d.* near Paris, 1831. At 16, on the death of his father, he was engaged in a Paris harpsichord factory, but was dismissed "for wanting to know everything." In 1777, under the patronage of the Duchess

of Villeroy, he completed " the first pf. made in France," and perfected the " double-action harp "—for which he is specially famous—in 1811.
He also made many other improvements in pf. mechanism, &c.

ERATOS'THENES. *B.* Cyrene, 276 B.C. ; *d.* Alexandria, 195 B.C.
Custodian of the Alexandrian Library ; wrote on Greek music and musical instruments. His division of the tetrachord is quoted by Ptolemy.

ERB, M. Jos. *B.* Strasburg, 1860. Studied in Paris.
Has published a Suite for Orchestra, a Mass, violin pieces, and several *salon* pieces for pf.

ERBA, Dionigi. Milanese priest, abt. 1700.
Believed to be the composer of a *Magnificat* utilized by Handel in *Israel in Egypt.*

ER'BACH, Christian. *B.* about 1560; *d.* 1628. Organist Augsburg Cathedral from 1600. Published a valuable collection of motets (*Cantica Sacra*), 1600-11.

ERD'MANNSDÖRFFER, Max. *B.* Nuremberg, 1848. Studied Leipzig Cons. Court Capellmeister, Sondershausen, 1871-80. Director Imperial Musical Society, Moscow, 1882. Capellmeister Court Theatre, Munich, 1896.
Works : several "legends" for soli, chorus, and orchestra ; overtures, pf. and violin pieces, male choruses, songs, &c.
His wife, **Pauline Fichtner,** is a distinguished pianist.

Erfreu'lich *(G.).* Joyous.

Ergriff'en *(G.).* Stirred, agitated, moved.
Mit Ergrif'fenheit. With agitation, emotion, &c.

Erha'ben *(G.).* Sublime, exalted, lofty.
Mit Erha'benheit. With sublimity, exaltation, &c.

Erhöh'ung *(G.).* "Elevating." In music, raising the pitch ; sharpening.
Erhöh'ungszeichen. A chromatic sign for raising the pitch, as ♮, ♯, x.

Erin'nerung *(G.).* Reminiscence.

ERK, Friedrich A. Brother of L. (below). *B.* Wetzlar, 1809 ; *d.* 1879. Teacher in the Realschule, Düsseldorf.
Published collections of lieder, school songs (in his brother's books), and (with Silcher) a "Lahrer Commersbuch."

ERK, Ludwig Ch. *B.* Wetzlar, 1807; *d.* Berlin, 1883. Conductor of liturgical singing, Domchor, Berlin, 1836-40. Teacher, Berlin R. Seminary, 1837. Founded the Erk Männergesangverein, 1843 ; and the Erk Gesangverein (mixed voices), 1852.
Published numerous popular song books for schools, and several highly valuable collections of German folk-songs and chorals.

ER'KEL, Alexander (or Alexius). Son of F. (below). *B.* Pesth, 1846 ; *d.* 1900. Musikdirektor, Pesth Royal Opera, 1896.
Wrote an opera, *Tempetöi*, 1883.

ER'KEL, Franz (or Ferencz). "The creator of Hungarian national opera." *B.* Gyula, Hungary, 1810 ; *d.* Pesth, 1893. Conductor, Pesth National Theatre, 1837. "He brought the opera orchestra to a high state of efficiency," and founded the Philharmonic concerts.
Works : 9 operas, *Hunyády László* (1844), *Bank Bán* (1861), *King Stefan* (1874(, &c.; and numerous popular national songs.

Erkling'en *(G.)*. To sound, resound.

ERLANGER, Camille. Composer ; *b.* Paris, 1863. Naturalized Englishman.

Works : *Saint-Julien* (3-act dramatic legend), *Kermaria* (3-act lyric drama), &c.

ERLANGER, Baron Frédéric d'. Operatic composer ; *b.* Paris, 1868.

Erleich'terung *(G.)*. Simplified arrangement.

ER'LER, Hermann. *B.* near Dresden, 1844. Founded a music publishing house (now Ries & Erler), Berlin, 1873. Edited the *Neue Berliner Musik-Zeitung.*

Erlösch'end *(G.)*. Extinguished ; *calando ;* gradually dying away.

Ermat'tet *(G.)*. Wearied, exhausted, jaded.

Ernie'drigung *(G.)*. "Lowering, depressing." In music, flattening.

Ernie'drigungszeichen. A chromatic sign for lowering the pitch, as ♮, ♭, ♭♭.

Ernst *(G.)*. Earnest, grave, serious, solemn.

ERNST II. 1818-93. Duke of Saxe-Coburg-Gotha.

Composed *Diana von Solange* and 4 other operas, 2 operettas, several cantatas, songs, hymns, &c,

ERNST, Alfred. French writer and critic ; about 1855-98. "A passionate admirer and defender of Wagner."

Chief works : "Rd. Wagner et le drame contemporain" (1887), "L'art de Rich. Wagner" (1893), and "L'œuvre dramatique de H. Berlioz" (1884).

ERNST, Franz A. Bohemian violinist ; 1745-1805.

Wrote a fine violin concerto in E♭.

ERNST, Heinrich Wilhelm. Famous violinist ; *b.* Brünn, 1814 ; *d.* Nice, 1865. Studied under De Bériot. From 1834-50 he toured as a concert violinist, and afterwards settled in London.

Of his numerous brilliant works for violin, the "Elegie," the "Concerto in F♯ min.," and the "Carnaval de Venise" are among the best.

Ernst'haft *(G.)*. Serious, earnest, solemn, &c.

Ernst'haftigkeit. Seriousness, gravity, severity, &c.

Ernst'lich. Seriously, earnestly, ardent(ly).

Ern'telied *(G.)*. Harvest song.

Eröff'nung *(G.)*. Introduction ; opening.

Ero'ica, Ero'ico *(I.)*. Heroic ; illustrious.

Ero'ica Symphony *(Sinfo'nia Ero'ica).* Beethoven's third symphony (in E♭), finished 1804. Original title, "Bonaparte. Louis van Beethoven."

Erot'ic. *(F., Erotique ; I., Ero'tico.)* From Gk. *eros,* love. (1) Amatory. (2) A love song.

ERRANI, Achille. *B.* Italy, about 1823 (?) ; *d.* New York, 1897. Tenor singer ; teacher of Minnie Hauck and other American singers.

Erregt' *(G.)*. Excited, agitated.

Er'satz *(G.)*. A substitute, equivalent.

Erst, Er'ste, Er'ster, Er'stes *(G.)*. First.

Er'ste Ausgabe. 1st edition, arrangement, &c.

Er'ste Stim'me. The highest part.

Ers'tes Zeit'mass. Tempo primo *(q.v.).*

Er'sterben(d) *(G.)*. Dying away ; *morendo.*

Erweck'ung *(G.)*. Animation, awakening.

Erwei'tern *(G.)*. To expand, to augment.

Erwei'tert *(G.)*. Expanded, augmented, amplified.

Erzäh'ler *(G.)*. The *Narrator* (Evangelist) in a Passion, or Passion-play.

Erz'laute *(G.)*. An archlute.

Es *(G.)*. It.

Es folgt. It follows ; *segue.*

Es *(G.)*. E♭.

*Esacor'do *(I.)*. (1) A hexachord. (2) Interval of a 6th.

Esaltazio'ne *(I.)*. Exaltation, sublimity.

Esat'ta, Esat'to *(I.)*. Exact, true.

Essat'ta intonazio'ne. Just intonation.

ESCH'MANN, Joh. K. Swiss pianist ; 1826-82. Published a Pf. Method, pieces for violin and pf., songs, pf. music, &c.

Esclama'to *(I.)*. Well declaimed ; *marcato.*

ESCUDIER, Marie (1819-80), and **Léon** (1821-81). Two brothers, natives of Castelnaudary, Aude. Started *La France Musicale,* Paris, 1838, and opened a music shop.

Published "Biographical Studies," a "Dict. of Music," a "Life of Rossini," &c.

Es dur *(G.)*. E♭ major.

Esecuto're *(I.)*. A performer.

Esecuzio'ne *(I.)*. Execution, technique ; rendering, performance.

Esegui're *(I.)* To execute or perform a piece.

Esem'pio, Esem'mpio *(I.)*. An example.

Eserci'zio *(I.)*. An exercise ; practice.

Es'es *(G.)*. E♭♭.

ESLA'VA, Don Miguel H. *B.* in Navarre, 1807 ; *d.* Madrid, 1878. Chorister and violinist, Pampeluna Cathedral, 1824. Maestro, Ossuna Cathedral, 1828 ; Sevilla, 1832, Court maestro, 1844.

Works : 3 operas, organ pieces, a fine collection of Spanish church music, "Lira Sacro Hispana" (1869) ; a "Metodo de Solfeo," a "School of Harmony and Composition," &c.

Es moll *(G.)*. E♭ minor.

Espace *(F.)*. A space of the staff.

Espagnol *(F.)*. Spanish.

Espagnuo'lo (I.). } In Spanish style.

A l'espagnol (F.). }

Espansio'ne *(I.)*. Expansion, breadth.

Con espansio'ne. With breadth of style.

Espiran'do *(I.)*. Expiring, dying away.

ESPOSI'TO, Michele. Pianist and composer ; *b.* nr. Naples, 1855.

Espressio'ne *(I.)*. Expression.

Con espressio'ne } With expression.

Espressi'vo }

Essai *(F.)*. An essay ; a trial piece.

Esse'mpio *(I.)*. Same as **Esempio** *(q.v.).*

Essential harmony. The plain chords divested of grace notes, passing-notes, appoggiaturas, &c., all of which are classed as *non-essential* notes.

Essential discord. Term used by Macfarren to signify a prepared 7th or 9th added to any diatonic triad, the whole chord being resolved on another chord with its root a 5th lower (or 4th higher) than that containing the discord.

Essential discords thus differ from passing-notes, appoggiaturas, and fundamental discords.

Essential 6th and 7th. The notes **f** and **se** in the minor scale.

⁜ Note that *s* takes the place of *x* in Italian words.

ES'SER, Heinrich. *B.* Mannheim, 1818; *d.* 1872. Capellmeister, Court Opera,Vienna, from 1857, and conductor of the Philharmonic.
Works: 3 operas, orchestral music, chamber music, popular male quartets, songs, &c.

ESSI'POFF (or ESSIPOVA), Annette. *B.* St. Petersburg, 1851. Distinguished pianist. *Début,* St. Petersburg, 1874, followed by successful concert tours. Married her teacher, Leschetizky, 1880. Prof. of pf., St. Petersburg Cons., 1893.

ESSIPOFF, Stepán, Pen-name of **Burnand** (*q.v.*).

ESTE, EST, EAST, or EASTE, Thomas. Celebrated music printer, London (about 1550-1609).
Among the most interesting of his publications were Byrd's "Psalmes, Sonets, and Songs of Sadness and Pietie" (1588), and "The Whole Booke of Psalmes; with their wonted Tunes . . . composed in foure Parts" (1592), commonly known as "Este's Psalter." (See *Hymn.*)

Estensio'ne *(I.).* The "extension" or compass of a voice (or instrument).

ES'TERHAZY, Prince Nicholas. 1765-1849. Friend and patron of Haydn (*q.v.*).

ESTHER. Handel's first Eng. oratorio, 1720.

Estinguen'do *(I.).* Dying away; being extinguished.

Estin'to *(I.).* (Almost) "extinct;" as soft as possible.

Estravagan'za *(I.).* An **Extravaganza** (*q.v.*).

Estremamen'te *(I.)* Extremely.

E'stro poe'tico *(I.).* Poetic frenzy or fervent passion.

Esultazio'ne *(I.).* Exultation.

Et *(L.* and *F.).* And.

Eteignez le son *(F.)* Let the sound die away.

Etendu (e) *(F.).* (1) Extended. (2) Compass.

Et Incarna'tus est *(L.).* Part of the *Credo* in a Mass.

Etouffé (e) *(F.).* Stifled, damped, muted.

Etouffoirs *(F.).* Dampers.

Et resurrex'it *(L.).* Part of the *Credo.*

ETT, Caspar. *B.* Bavaria, 1788; *d.* 1847. Court organist, St. Michael's, Munich, from 1816.
Was especially noted for "reviving the church music of the 16th to 18th centuries."

Etude *(F.).* A study, exercise, or lesson, intended to afford practice in some special difficulty.
Etude de concert. A study, or characteristic piece, intended for concert performance.

Et vi'tam ventu'ri *(L.).* Conclusion of the *Credo;* usually set to a fugue.

Et'was *(G.).* Somewhat, rather.
Et'was bele'bend. Slightly accelerating.
Et'was betont', doch sehr in'nig. Somewhat accented, but very feelingly.
Et'was bewegt'. Rather animated.
Et'was breit in Zeit'mass. Somewhat broad (moderate) in tempo.
Et'was dräng'end. Hurrying a little.
Et'was deut'licher und allmäh'lich aus'drucksvoller. A little more distinct, and gradually more full of expression.
Et'was flüs'siger als zu An'fang. Rather more flowing (smooth) than at the beginning.
Et'was gedehnt'. Rather drawn out (*i.e.,* a little *rallentando*).
Et'was geschwind'. Rather quick.
Et'was lang'sam. Rather slow.

Et'was lang'samer als das The'ma. A little slower than the theme.
Et'was lang'samer und ruh'ig. Rather slower, and quietly.
Et'was leb'haft, und mit in'nigster Empfin'dung. Rather quick, and with the deepest feeling (emotion).
Et'was leich'ter und beweg'ter. Rather lighter and quicker.
Et'was rallent. Becoming gradually a little slower.
Et'was rasch'er. Rather quicker.
Et'was sanf'ter. Rather softer.
Et'was schnell. Rather quick.
Et'was zö'gernd und sehr ruh'ig. Somewhat retarding and very tranquil(ly).

EUCLID. Renowned Greek geometrician, Alexandria (abt. 300 B.C.)
Wrote *Sectio Canonis* (on the "Division of the Monochord").

Eufo'nia *(I.)* ⎫ (1) Pleasant sound. (2) A
Euphonie *(F.).* ⎬ consonant and agreeable
Eu'phony ⎭ combination of sounds.

Eufo'nio *(I.).* Euphonium.

EUGEN ONÉGIN. Opera by Tschaikowsky; composed 1877-8.

Euharmon'ic. Producing perfect harmony; *i.e.,* with pure, just intervals, instead of tempered ones. Same as **Enharmonic** [2].
Euharmonic organs have been constructed, but they are too complex for practical use.

EUING, Wm. *B.* nr. Glasgow, 1788; *d.* 1874. Founded a musical scholarship, Anderson's College, Glasgow, and bequeathed his valuable musical library to the same institution.

EU'LENBURG, Philip, Graf zu. *B.* Königsberg, 1847.
Works: several sets of songs (both words and music).

EU'LENSTEIN, Chas. Noted performer on the Jew's Harp (*q.v.*). *B.* Heilbronn, 1822; *d.* 1890.

EU'LER, Leonhardt. Celebrated mathematician; *b.* Basel, 1707; *d.* 1783.
Said to have been the first to use logarithms to express differences of pitch.

EUOUAE. (See **Evovae.**)

Euphone. A 16 ft. free-reed organ stop.

Eupho'nious. Sweetly sounding.

Eupho'nium. The smaller bass instrument of the Saxhorn family.
It is usually in C or B♭, and is furnished with 3 or (more often) 4 valves. It has a larger bore and much fuller tone than the baritone, and possesses a very extensive compass. In the brass band it is indispensable, and it is also much used in modern orchestras.

EUTER'PE. One of the 9 muses.
She presided over Joy and Pleasure, and was the patroness of flute players.

Evacua'tio *(L.).* "An emptying." In medieval music, reducing the time value of a note by writing it in outline; ♦ ♢

EVANS, David Emlyn. Self-taught composer and writer; *b.* Cardiganshire, 1843.

EVANS, Harry. Orgt. and condr.; *b.* Dowlais, Glam., 1873.

Eveillé *(F.).* Sprightly, lively, quick.

EVERARD, Camille François. Fine dramatic bass singer; *b.* Dinant, 1825. *Début,* Naples, 1847. Sang at Vienna (1852-67),

Madrid (1868-70). Prof. of Singing, St. Petersburg Cons., 1870-90; Kiev Cons., 1890.

EVERS, Karl. *B.* Hamburg, 1819; *d.* Vienna, 1875. Pianist; studied under Mendelssohn (1839).
Concert giver, music dealer, and composer of pf. pieces (12 "chansons d'amour," &c.).

Ever'sio, Evolu'tio *(L.).* Inverting the parts in double counterpoint.

EVESHAM, Monk of. (See **Odington.**)

Evira'to *(I.).* A *castra'to* or *mu'sico.*

EVOVAE, or EUOUAE. An abbreviation consisting of the vowels of " Seculorum Amen"—the last two words of the "Gloria Patri"—much used in medieval music.

EWER & CO. Founded 1820.
United with Novello & Co. (1867) as Novello, Ewer & Co.

E'WEYCK, Arthur van. Baritone; *b.* Milwaukee (U.S.), 1866.

EWING, Alexander. *B.* Aberdeen, 1830; *d.* 1895. Composed the tune "Ewing," usually sung to "Jerusalem the Golden."

Exactement *(F.).* Exactly; with precision.

Exalté *(F.).* Exalted; inspired, over-elevated.

Exécutant(e) *(F.).* Performer.

Execution. The technique and style of a musical performance.
The due execution of a vocal solo demands "*just intonation, taste, grace, feeling,* and *expression.*"—*Moore.*

Exercise. *(G., Übung, Übungsstück; F., Exercise; I., Eserci'zio.)* A short composition, *étude,* or technical study to train the fingers, voice, &c.

Exercise. A composition forming one of the requirements for a musical degree.
Perhaps the shortest exercise ever written was that submitted by Haydn, 1791, when he was created Doctor of Music at Oxford :—

Canon Cancrizans, a tre.

Thy voice. O har-mo - ny, is div - ine.

Expedient Notation. A term used by the Day-Macfarren school for enharmonic varieties of notes, not theoretically correct, but used to save accidentals or to render a passage (or chord) easier to read. Called also *False Notation.* (For examples see **Enharmonic.**)

EXPERT, Henri. Historical and critical writer on music; *b.* Bordeaux, 1863.

Explosive Tone (Note). A tone delivered with special emphasis; a sudden diminuendo on a single note or chord—

Exposition. *(G., Er'ste Durch'führung.)* (1) The first portion of a fugue. (See **Fugue.**)
(2) The first part (up to the double bar) of the 1st movement of a sonata, &c. *(Sir H. Parry).* (See **Sonata.**)
Exposition *(G., Exposition')* is also sometimes used for *development* generally.

Expressif et largement chanté *(F.).* Expressive(ly), and in a broad singing style.

Expression. "The spirit of music, as opposed to the mere mechanical production of sound "—*Stainer & Barrett.*
By analogy, melody constitutes the *outline* or *form* of music; harmony its *substance, framework,* or *body;* time and rhythm give *life* and *animation;* expression is the *soul.*
The **means of expression** are variations of speed (*rallentando, accelerando, tempo rubato, pause,* &c.), variations of accent (see **Accent**), variations of force (see **Dynamics**), and combinations of all these. Articulation (proper delivery of *legato, staccato, portamento,* &c.), technique, clear enunciation (of words), beauty of tone, neat rendering of graces and embellishments—though more properly included under *style*—are all aids to effective expression. The signs used to indicate expression (*p, f, cres., accel.,* &c.) are included under the general name of *expression marks;* and the term *nuances* is applied both to these and to those delicate shades of expression which can hardly be written down, but which differentiate the *artist* from the mere *performer.*
Rules to cover all the shades of expression are impossible; the following — in addition to those given under **Accent**— are the most usual. They apply, of course, chiefly to solo performances :—

(1) CRESCENDO AND ACCELERANDO.
These frequently, but not invariably, go together. They imply *increased excitement*—some difficulty to be overcome, or a working-up to a climax of intensity or development, and are most appropriate in *ascending* passages :—

Speed to your own courts my light, &c.

And the de-sire

For now is Christ risen, for now is Christ risen.

(2) DIMINUENDO AND RALLENTANDO.
These naturally imply *relaxation of effort,* and are most appropriate in *descending* passages :—

Messiah. HANDEL.

cres. . . *dim. e rall.*

the earth. upon the earth.

Rallentando is always combined with *diminuendo* in such terms as *calando, morendo,* &c. It is, however, often used with *crescendo* in connective passages leading up to a fresh theme (or to the re-entry of some theme previously employed); and also at the end of a movement which leads directly into another movement. In such cases it implies, as it were, "a gathering-up of one's energies," "pulling one's self together for a more vigorous effort."

As Riemann observes: "The natural dynamic shading of a musical phrase is *crescendo* up to the point of climax, and *diminuendo* from there to the end," and "a composer indicates, for the most part, any deviation from these general rules."

(3) THE SWELL.

This is used, especially in vocal music, for all long sustained tones, and occasionally for shorter ones. (See *Dynamics.*)

(4) REPEATED NOTES.

Oft-repeated notes like the following should be given *crescendo* and rather *staccato*:—

Messiah. HANDEL.

Blessing and honour, glory and pow'r be unto Him.

When of a quieter and more sustained character, *organ tones* are more appropriate:—

HANDEL.

(5) REPEATED PASSAGES.

A repetition of a passage is generally given with some variation of force, speed, or style.

(6) PAUSE. All notes requiring very marked emphasis (see *Accent*), and all notes of the nature of a climax—especially long high notes—are naturally prolonged; and this is particularly the case in vocal solos. (See also *Tempo Rubato.*) In songs of the *bravura* style there is generally some note near the end which is specially prolonged. It is often marked with a hold, ⌒, and sometimes followed by a *cadenza* (*q.v.*).

For a more detailed analysis of musical expression, see Curwen's "Musical Theory," Book IV, and Lussy's "Musical Expression" (Novello & Co.). A careful study of the expression marks in Beethoven's pf. sonatas will also well repay the student.

Expression Stop. A stop on the harmonium which brings the pressure of wind on the vibrating reeds directly under the player's control.

Expression, Verbal. (See **Verbal Expression.**)

Expressive Organ. (*G., Expressiv' Orgel; F., Orgue expressif.*) The harmonium.

Extem'pore. Without previous preparation; "on the spur of the moment."

Extemporise. (*G., Extempori(e)'ren.*) To play *extem'pore.*

Among the greatest of extempore players were Bach, Mozart, Clementi, Beethoven, Mendelssohn, Hummel, Moscheles, Liszt, and Wesley (organ).

Extemporising Machine. A machine to record extempore playing. (See *Melograph.*)

Extended Compass. (1) A wide compass. (2) A range beyond ordinary limits.

Extended Harmony. Dispersed or "wide" harmony.

Extended Phrase, Theme, Subject. (See **Thematic Development.**)

Extension. Specially, the stretch of the little finger to play the ♯ on the E string of the violin; also the wide pf. arpeggios introduced by Chopin (1st and 11th Études).

Extension Pedal. Another name for the "loud" pf. pedal.

Extent of Transition. Mr. Curwen distinguishes between "Cadence Transition," "Passing Transition," and "Extended Transition." (See **Transition.**)

Extraneous Modulation. A modulation to an extreme or unrelated key.

Extravagan'za. An extravagant farcical, or fantastic composition; a burlesque.

Extreme. (1) Of intervals, augmented. (2) Of keys, remote, unrelated. (3) In part-music, the outer parts; *i.e.*, the highest and lowest.

Extreme Flat. Old term used for diminished intervals; extreme flat 3rd, extreme flat 4th, extreme flat 7th, and extreme flat 8th.

Extrêmement lent (*F.*). Extremely slow.

Extreme Sixth, Chord of the. Another name for the chord of the Augmented Sixth.

The Chord of the Augmented or Extreme Sixth is used chiefly on the Minor 6th and Minor 2nd of the scale. It has 3 forms:—

(1) *Italian* 6th (with 3rd only). (2) *French* 6th (with 3rd and 4th). (3) *German* 6th (with 3rd and perf. 5th).

fe¹	t	fe¹	t	fe¹	t
d¹	f	r¹	s	ma¹	la
la	ra	d¹	f	d¹	f
		la	ra	la	ra

By enharmonic change a German 6th becomes a Dominant 7th (or *vice versa*):—

Hence the chord is of great value in modulation. (See *Modulation.*)

EY'BLER, Joseph (afterwards **Edler von Eybler**). *B.* nr. Vienna, 1765; *d.* 1846. Studied under Albrechtsberger; intimate friend of Haydn and Mozart. Court Capellmeister, Vienna, 1824.

Of his numerous works only his church compositions (2 oratorios, 32 masses, 7 Te Deums, &c.) are now known.

EY'KEN (or **EYCKEN**), **Simon van**; also known as **Du CHESNE.** (See **Quercu.**)

EY'KEN (or **EIJKEN**), **Jan A. van.** *B.* Amersfoort, Holland, 1822; *d.* 1868. Celebrated organist. Org. at Elberfeld from 1854.

Works: *Lucifer* (a tragedy), quartets, songs, &c., and several well-known organ pieces.

EYMIEU, Henri. French composer and writer; *b.* 1860.

Writes critical essays, &c., for the leading Parisian musical papers, and has published numerous pf. pieces, &c.

EYRE, Alf. Jas. *B.* Lambeth, 1853. Orgt. Crystal Palace, 1880-94.

F

F. (*Ger. F; Fr.* and *I., Fa.*) (1) The 4th note of the scale of C.

(2) The *final* (or lowest note) of the Lydian Mode. (See **Mode.**)

F clef. The Bass clef.

F dur (*G.*). F major.

F holes. The *f*-shaped holes in a violin, &c.

F-Löcher (*G.*). F holes.

F major. (1) The key or scale requiring one flat; signature

(2) The chord—

F minor. (1) The relative minor of A♭ major; signature—

(2) The chord—

F moll (*G.*). F minor.

F quadra'ta (*L.*). Old name for F♯.

F-Schlüssel (*G.*). The F clef. (See **Clef.**)

f. Forte.

ff or *fff*. Fortissimo.

ff **principalmen'te il bas'so** (*I.*). Very loud, especially the bass.

Fa. (1) The 4th of Guido's syllables; *ut, re, mi, fa, sol, la.* (2) The name of F in "fixed-*do*" systems.

Fa-be-mi. }
Fa-ut. } (See **Alt.**)
Fa be'mol (*F.*). F♭.
Fa dièse (*F.*). F♯.
Fa feint (*F.*). }
Fa fic'tum (*L.*). } Old name for any flattened note.
Fa mi. A semitone (descending) in solmisation.

FA'BER, Fredk. Wm., D.D. 1814-1863. Established the London Oratorians. Wrote "Was there ever kindest Shepherd?" and other favourite hymns.

FA'BER, Heinrich. *D.* Saxony, 1552. Pub. "Compendiolum musicæ pro incipientibus" (1548), and "Ad musicam practicam introductio" (1550).

FA'BER, Nickolaus (or **Nicol**). Priest; built (Halberstadt, 1539-61) what is thought to be the first German organ, "with 20 bellows, keys 3 inches broad and ½ in. apart."

FA'BIO. (See **Ursillo.**)

FA'BRI, Stefano (the Elder). Maestro at the Vatican, Rome, 1599-1601. Pub. 2 books of "Tricinia" (church compositions for 3 voices).

FA'BRI, Stefano (the Younger). Rome, 1606-58. Pupil of Nanini. Published Motets and "Salmi Concertati" (for 5 voices).

FABRI'CIUS, Werner. *B.* Itzehoe, 1633; *d.* Leipzig, 1679. Orgt. of the *Nicolai-kirche* (Leipzig), and mus.-director of the *Paulinerkirche*. Works: a "Collection of Pavanes, Allemandes, &c., for viols and other instruments" (1656);

collections of lieder, arias, dialogues, &c.; also motets and other church music.

His son, **Johann Albert,** was an eminent Hebrew and Greek scholar.

Fa'burden. (*F., Faux bourdon; I., Fal'so bordo'ne.*) (1) One of the medieval systems of harmonizing a *canto fermo*; (chiefly) by the addition of 3rds and 6ths above:

TONE II (Hypo-Dorian).

Glo-ri-a Pat-ri, et Fi-li - o, et Spi-ri-tu-i Sancto.
C.F.

(From Rockstro's "History of Music.")

(2) A drone bass, or *burden*.

"In the 16th century, any slow Psalm Tune was called a *Faux-bourdon*, provided it was written entirely—or even chiefly—in the First Order of Counterpoint."—*Rockstro.*

Façade d'orgue (*F.*). Front of an organ case.

FAC'CIO, Franco. *B.* Verona, 1841; *d.* 1891. Studied Milan Cons.; intimate friend of, and co-worker with Boito. Toured in Scandinavia as concert conductor, 1866-8. Prof. of harmony, Milan Cons., 1868. Conductor, *La Scala,* Milan, 1872. Works: operas, *I profughi fiamminghi* (1863), *Amleto* (1865); Symphony in F; act-tunes, a string-quartet, vocal pieces, &c.

Face (*F.*). Appearance; presentation.

Faces d'un accord (*F.*). Positions of a chord; viz., its root position and inversions. In Sol-fa, the *a, b, c, d* positions, &c.

Fach (*G.*). Suffix, "fold;" as *Drei'fach,* 3-fold.
Drei'fach. Of an organ "mixture," 3 ranks.
Zwei'fach. Of an organ "mixture," 2 ranks.

Fäch'erförmiges Pedal' (*G.*). "Fan-shaped pedal." A radiating pedal-board.

Facile (*F.*), **Fa'cile** (*I.*). Easy, fluent.
Facilement (*F.*). } Easily, fluently.
Facilmen'te (*I.*). }
Facilità (*I.*). Facility, fluency of execution.
Facilita'to (*I.*). Simplified.
Facilité (e) (*F.*). (1) Same as *Facilità.* (2) A piece made easy by some re-arrangement. (3) An easy *alternative* of a difficult passage.

Fack'eltanz (*G.*). A *Marche aux flambeaux,* or "torch-dance."
A kind of *polonaise* in march-time played in connection with a torch-light procession on German festal occasions.

Facteur (*F.*). Maker. **Facteur d'orgue,** organ builder.

Factitious notes. Notes producible on brass insts. by modified "lipping."
They "form no part of the natural scale."

Facture (*F.*). (*G., Faktur'; I., Fattu'ra*). Structure. (1) The plan, design, form, workmanship of a piece of music. (2) The "scale" of an organ pipe.

Fa'ding. (1) The burden or refrain of a song (Old English). (2) An old Irish dance.
"I will have him dance *fading; fading* is a fine jig."—*Beaumont and Fletcher.*

FAEL'TEN, Carl. *B.* Thuringia, 1846. From 1882 actively engaged in America as pianist and teacher. Founded the Faelten Pf. School (for teachers), Boston, 1898.

Has published "The Conservatory Course for Pianists" (a series of some 16 text-books).

FAGE. (See **Lafage.**)

FAGGE, Arthur. Conductor; *b.* Margate, 1864.

Faggio'lo (*I.*). A flageolet.

FA'GO, Nicolo. *B.* Tarento, 1674 (hence known as **Il Tarentino**); *d.* abt. 1730. Prolific composer; pupil of A. Scarlatti; teacher of Leonardo Leo.

Best known works: oratorio (*Faraone sommerso*); operas (*Eustachio, Astarte*, &c.); masses, cantatas, psalms, motets, &c.

Fagott' (*G.*). \
Fagot'to (*I.*). / The Bassoon.

"The name is said to be derived from its resemblance to a *faggot*, or bundle of sticks."

Fagotti'no (*I.*). A small bassoon.
Fagott'ist (*E.* and *G.*) \
Fagottis'ta (*I.*). / A bassoon player.
Fagotto'ne (*I.*). A double bassoon.
Fagott'zug (or *Fagott'*) (*G.*). An organ reed-stop.
Quint'fagott (*G.*) \
Tenor'fagott (*G.*) / (See *Basson quinte*.)

Fah. The Tonic Sol-fa spelling of *fa*, the name of the fourth note of the major scale (standing a diatonic semitone, or "little step," above **me**).

FAHR'BACH, Jos. Vienna, 1804-83. Distinguished flute and guitar player; pub. several works for flute.

FAHR'BACH, Philipp (Senr.). Vienna, 1815-85. Conductor and composer.

Wrote 2 operas and a large number of popular dance pieces.

FAHR'BACH, Philipp (Junr.). Son of preceding; Vienna, 1843-94.

Wrote over 300 popular dances, marches, &c.

Fah're sogleich' fort (*G.*). Go on with the next movement at once.

Faible (*F.*). Weak, feeble.

Temps faible. A weak or unaccented beat.

FAIGNIENT, Noë. 16th cent. Flemish Contrapuntist.

Works: motets, arias, madrigals, chansons, &c.

Faire (*F.*). To make, do, execute.

Faire des fredons. A trill.
Faire ressortir le chant. Bring out the melody.
Faites bien sentir la mélodie. Make the melody very distinct.

FAIRFAX (FAYRFAX), Robert. Mus.Doc. Cantab. abt. 1501; *d.* 1529.

Wrote a volume of songs, several masses, motets, &c.

FAIRLAMB, James R. American musician; *b.* Philadelphia, 1837. Orgt. St. Ignatius, New York, from 1884.

Works: an opera (*Valéne*); over 100 songs, choral works, pf. pieces, &c.

FAISST ("ai" like "i" in *spiced*), **Dr. Immanuel G. F.** Orgt. and composer; chiefly self-taught. *B.* Würtemberg, 1823; *d.* 1894.

Founded a Society for classical church music, Stuttgart, 1847. Promoted the establishment of the Stuttgart Cons., 1857; was the first prof. of org. playing and composition, and (1859) Director.

Edited (with Lebert) the "Cotta" edition of classical pf. works; wrote cantatas, motets, choruses for male voices, songs, organ pieces, pf. pieces, &c., and treatises on musical theory.

Faktur' (*G.*). (See **Facture.**)

Fa la, or **Fal la.** A short song, or a madrigal, with a *fa la* refrain at the end of each line or stanza. Morley's ballets are good specimens.

J. Savile, 1667.

Here's a health unto His Majesty, With a fa la la la la
Con - fu-sion to his enemies, With a fa la la la la

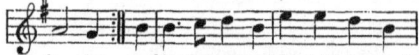

la   la; And he that will not drink this health, I

wish him neither wit nor wealth, Nor yet a rope to

hang himself, With a fa la la, la la la la la la

la, With a fa la la' la la la   la!

FALCKE, Henri. Distinguished pianist; *b.* Paris, 1866; *d.* 1901. Studied at the Cons. He had an immense repertory.

Published a valuable "School of Arpeggios" (English edition, 1895).

FALCON, Marie C. Celebrated operatic soprano; Paris, 1812-97. *Début*, Paris Grand Opéra, as "Alice" in Meyerbeer's *Robert*, 1832.

Sang at the Opéra with brilliant success until 1837, when she unfortunately lost her voice. Dramatic soprano parts are still called "Falcon *rôles*" in France.

FALK, Mad. (See **Anna Mehlig.**)

Fall. (1) The hinged cover of a pf. keyboard. (2) A lowering of the voice. (3) A cadence.

"That strain again: it had a dying *fall*."—*Shakespeare, Twelfth Night.*

FALLERSLEBEN. (See **H. A. Hoffmann.**)

Fal'sa (*L.* and *I.*) (*G., Falsch*). False, defective.

Mu'sica fal'sa (*L.*) \
Mu'sica fic'ta (*L.*) / (See *Musica ficta*.)
Quin'ta fals'a (*L.*). (See *False fifth*.)

False. (*G., Falsch*; *F., Faux, fausse*; *I., Fal'so,-a.*) Defective, imperfect; out of tune.

False cadence. An interrupted cadence.
False chord. (See *False triad*.)
False fifth. (*G. Fal'sche Quin'te*.) A diminished fifth.
False harmony. False relation; the inclusion of wrong notes.
False intonation. *False notes.* Playing or singing (1) out of tune, or (2) with a faulty tone.
False notation. (See *Expedient notation*.)
False string. A badly-constructed (violin) string which gives faulty notes.
False triad. The leading-note triad.

False relation, Cross relation, or **Inharmonic relation.** A note of the same letter-name, chromatically altered (as C♯, C♮ ; B♮, B♭ ; &c.), used in successive chords, *but not in the same part.*

HANDEL. *Judas.* (a)   BACH. (b) Prelude, F min.

MENDELSSOHN. (c)   BRAHMS. Requiem. (d)

Of these examples, (a) and (b) are decidedly *rough*; but (c) and (d) are quite harmonious. The rule forbidding false relations admits of so many exceptions, that experience, judgment, and a wide knowledge of musical construction can alone determine whether any given instance is objectionable or not.

False relation of the Tritone. *Mi contra Fa.* A forbidden succession of two major 3rds in two-part counterpoint when the lower part rises or falls a whole tone :

The older contrapuntists regarded the tritone in harmony or melody as *Diabolus in Musica.*

Falset'to (*I.*). (*G., Falsett' ; F., Voix de fausset.*) The high artificial notes in men's voices—employed by male altos.

Falsett'stimme (*G.*). A falsetto voice.

Fals'o bordo'ne (*I.*). (See **Faburden.**)

FALTIN, Rd. Fr. *B.* Danzig, 1835. Condr. of the Finnish Opera, Helsingfors.

Works : Finnish folk-songs, a Finnish song-book.

Fa majeur (*F.*). F major.
Fa mineur (*F.*). F minor.

FAMIN'TZIN, Alex. S. Russian composer and writer ; *b.* Kaluga, 1841 ; *d.* 1896. Prof. of Mus. Hist. St. Petersburg Cons. 1865 ; Sec. Russian Mus. Soc. 1870.

Works : operas, *Sardanapal* (1875), *Uriel Acosta* (1883), a symphonic poem, orchestral and chamber music, songs, pf. pieces, critical contributions to music periodicals, &c.

Fancy. Old English name for a short piece on an original theme ; a fantasy.

Fandan'go (*S.*). A lively Spanish dance in 3-4 time accompanied by castanets or a tambourine. It was derived from the Moors.

  "The Fandango is generally danced by a male and female ; the dance alternates with vocal couplets, both dance and song having a guitar accompaniment."—*Baker.*

Fanfa'ra (*I.*) ⎱ (1) A brass band. (2) A
Fanfare (*F.*) ⎰ fanfare (*Old E.* "tucket").

Fan'fare. (1) A flourish of trumpets. (2) A trumpet call.

FANING, Jos. Eaton. *B.* Helston, 1850. Studied R.A.M. 1870-6. Mendelssohn Scholar, 1873. Music Director, Harrow School,1885-1901. Mus.D.Cantab.1900.

Works : operettas, cantatas, part-songs (*Song of the Vikings,* &c.), songs, &c.

Fantasi'a (*I.*) ⎫   "According to fancy."
Fantaisie (*F.*) ⎬ (1) An impromptu or
Fantasie' (*G.*) ⎭ improvisation. (2) An
Phantasie' (*G.*) old composition in "free imitation." (3) A *potpourri,* extravaganza, or other piece not in strict "form."

Con fantasi'a (*I.*). With fancy, spirit, freedom.
Fantasie'ren (*G.*). (See *Phantasieren.*)
Fantasie'stück (*G.*). (See *Phantasiestück.*)
Fantasticamen'te (*I.*) ⎫ Fantastic(ally) ; "giving
Fanta'stico (*I.*) ⎬ free rein to fancy,"
Fantastique (*F.*) ⎭ In a grotesque manner.
Fantas'tisch (*G.*)
Fan'tasy. (See *Fantasia.*)
Free fantasia. That portion of a "first movement" in "Sonata Form" which follows the first double bar. It comes between the *Exposition* and the *Reprise,* and is more frequently called the Development Portion. (See *Sonata.*)

FARABI. (See **Alfarabi.**)

FARADAY, Philip M. Composer ; *b.* London, 1875.

Farando'la (*I.*) ⎱ An exciting
Farandoule (Farandole) (*F.*) ⎰ circle dance in rapid 6-8 time, common in Southern France and Northern Italy.

Far'be (*G.*). Colour, tint.
Klang-farbe. Tone-colour.

Farce. (*I., Far'sa in Mu'sica.*) A musical burlesque.

FARINEL'LI (Real name, **Carlo Bro'schi**). Famous male soprano ; *b.*Naples, 1705 ; *d.* Bologna, 1782. Pupil of Porpora (and afterwards of his own celebrated rival, Bernacchi). *Début,* Rome, 1722.

Sang in London (against Handel's party), 1734-6. Visited Madrid, 1736 ; by his wonderful singing cured King Philip V of his melancholy, and was thenceforth retained by that grateful monarch at a salary of 50,000 francs as the "King's friend and confidential adviser." Farinelli, at his best, was "in every way the first European singer of his time." He excelled in *bravura* and *coloratura.*

FARINEL'LI, Giuseppe. *B.* Este, 1769 ; *d.* 1836. Studied Cons. Turchini, Naples. Maestro Cath. S. Giusto, Trieste, 1819.

Works : about 70 operas (chiefly comic), including *Il Dottorato di Pulchinella* ; oratorios, cantatas, masses, &c.

FARJEON, Harry. Composer ; *b.* Hohokus (U.S.), 1878.

FAR'KAS, Edmund. Hungarian composer ; *b.* 1852.

Works : operas, *Bayader, Feenquelle, Die Büsser, Bulassa Bálint ;* ballads, lieder, orch. works, string quartets, choruses, &c.

FARMER, Henry. Nottingham, 1819-91. Violinist and organist.

Works : a Mass in B♭, violin pieces, glees, songs, &c. ; and instruction books for violin.

FARMER, John. Nephew of H. *B.* Nottingham, 1836; *d.* 1901. Studied Liepzig and Coburg. Music master at Harrow, 1862-85 ; afterwards orgt. Balliol Col., Oxford.
Works : oratorio (*Christ and His Soldiers*), cantatas, nursery rhymes, chamber music, school song books, &c.

FARNABY, Giles. *B.* Truro, 16th century.
Works : canzonets, madrigals, pieces in the Fitzwilliam Virginal Book, &c.

Farneticamen'te (*I.*). Deliriously.

FARRANT, Richard. *B.* abt. 1530 ; *d.* 1580. Orgt. St. George's Chapel, Windsor.
Works : services, anthems, &c., including "Lord, for Thy tender mercies' sake."

FARRAR, Geraldine. Soprano ; *b.* Melrose (U.S.), 1882.

FARRENC, Jacques H. A. *B.* Marseilles, 1794 ; *d.* Paris, 1865. Flute player, composer, and historiographer. Edited a great collection of pf. music.
The biographical materials collected by him "were generously turned over to Fétis for the second edition of his great work."

FARRENC, Jeanne Louise (*née* **Dumont**). Remarkable pianist and composer ; wife of preceding. Paris, 1804-75. Prof. of pf. Paris Cons. 1842-73.
Works : symphonies, overtures, much chamber music, sonatas for pf. and violin, pf. pieces, &c.

FARWELL, Arthur. American writer and composer ; *b.* 1872.

FASCH, Carl F. Ch. *B.* Zerbst, 1736 ; *d.* Berlin, 1800. Asst. Cembalist to Frederick the Great, 1756 (under C. P. E. Bach). Capellmeister, Berlin Opera, 1774-6. Cond., "Singakademie" from its foundation, 1792.
His church music was pub. in 6 vols., 1839.

Fa'scia (*I.*). A tie or bind.

Fa'scie (*I.*). The ribs of a violin, &c.

Fast dassel'be Tem'po (*G.*). Almost the same speed.

Fastosamen'te (*I.*). ⎱ Proud(ly) ; in a stately
Fasto'so (*I.*). ⎰ or pompous style.

Fatigue call. A military signal, calling to fatigue-duty.

Fattu'ra (*I.*). (See **Facture.**)

FAULKES, Wm. Orgt. and composer ; *b.* Liverpool, 1863.

FAURÉ, Gabriel U. *B.* Pamiers, 1845. Orgt. Madeleine (Paris), 1896, and Prof. of Composition, &c., at the Cons.
Works: an opera (*l'Organiste*) ; a requiem, a violin concerto, a symphony, and other orchestral music, ballads, songs, pf. quartets, &c. ; and much chamber music, including a popular violin sonata.

FAURE, Jean B. *B.* Moulins, 1830. Baritone singer ; studied Paris Cons. Sang at the Opéra Comique, 1852-76.
Has pub. a useful instruction book, "L'Art du Chant."

Fausse (*F.*, *Masc.* **Faux**). False, defective.
Fausse corde. A false string.
Fausse quinte. A diminished 5th.

Fausset (*F.*). Falsetto.

FAUST. Opera by Gounod, 1859.
Of other operas with the same title, those of Spohr (1818) and Lindpaintner (1832) are noteworthy. Schumann and Lassen wrote music to the play. Berlioz's *Faust* is a kind of oratorio.

FAUST, Karl. 1825-92. Bandmaster successively at Luxemburg, Frankfort, Breslau, Waldenberg, &c.
Wrote popular marches and dance music.

FAUSTI'NA. (See **Hasse, Faustina.**)

Faux (*F.*). False ; out of tune.
Faux accord. A discord.
Faux bourdon. (See *Faburden.*)

FAVARGER, René. *B.* Paris, 1815 ; *d.* 1868.
Wrote popular pf. pieces.

FAVRE, Jules. Pen-name of **W. M. Watson** (*q.v.*).

FAWCETT, John, D.D. 1740-1817. Baptist minister.
Wrote the hymn "Lord, dismiss us with Thy blessing."

FAWCETT, John. *B.* Kendal, 1789 ; *d.* 1867. Shoemaker ; afterwards music teacher in Bolton.
Works : oratorio (*Paradise*) ; collections of anthems, hymn-tunes, &c., all of an easy and popular character. His music was at one time greatly in vogue.

His son **John** (1824-57) studied at the R.A.M., and graduated Mus.B. Oxon (1852).

FAY, Amy. *B.* Missouri, 1844. Studied the pf. under Tausig, Kullak, and Liszt.
Pub. "Music Study in Germany" (Chicago, 1881), an exposition of the Deppe system of pf. playing.

FAY, Guillaume de. (See **Dufay.**)

FAYOLLE, François J. M. Paris, 1774-1852. Writer on music.
Pub. (with Choron) "Dictionnaire des Musiciens" (1810-11); "Corelli, Tartini, Viotti," &c. ; and other works.

FAYRFAX. (See **Fairfax.**)

F-clef. (*G.*, *F-schlüssel ; F.*, *Clef de fa ; I.*, *Chia've di bas'so.*) (See **Clef.**)

fe (pron. *fee*). The sharp of **fah** in Tonic Sol-fa.

Feathering. Light, detached vn. bowing.

FECH'NER, G. T. Prof. of Physics ; *b.* 1801 ; *d.* Leipzig, 1887.
His *Vorschule der Aesthetik* is a valuable work.

FEDE'LE. (See **Treu.**)

Fe'derclavier, Fe'derklavier (*G.*). A spinet.

FEDERI'CI, Vincenzo. *B.* Pesara, 1764 ; *d.* Milan, 1826 (or 7). Left an orphan at 16, he came to London, was appointed Cembalist at the Italian opera, and produced his first opera, *l'Olimpiade* (1790). Returned to Italy, 1803 ; Prof. Milan Cons. 1809 ; Director, 1825.
Works : 14 serious operas (including *l'Olimpiade*), and a comic opera (*La locandiera Scaltra*, 1812).

Féerie (*F.*). A fairy opera or play.

Fei'er (*G.*). Festival, holiday, celebration.
Fei'ergesang. Solemn hymn.
Fei'erl.ch. "Festival-like ;" solemn.

Feigned Treble. Falsetto.

Fel'len (*G.*). "To file." To polish, touch up, refine.

Fein (*G.*). Fine, refined, delicate.

Feld (*G.*). A field. "The disposition of pipes in an organ."—*Stainer and Barratt.*

Feld'flöte. A fife ; a rustic pipe or flute.

Feld'musik. Military music.

Feld'pfeife. The *flauto traverso* ; a fife, or rustic flute.

Feld'stück. A military signal or call.

Feld'ton. The key of Eᵇ; so called because German military bugles, &c., are often in this key.

Feld'trompete. A military trumpet.

FELIX, Dr. Hugo. Composer ; *b.* Vienna, 1866.

Feminine cadence. A cadence falling on a weak accent. (See **Cadence.**)

Feminine rhythm. A rhythm (phrase, figure, &c.), ending on a weak or unaccented note.

FENARO'LI, Fedele. Celebrated Italian teacher of composition ; 1730-1818. Taught Cimarosa, Zingarelli, Mercadente, and other eminent musicians. Prof. Cons. della Pietà, Naples, 1775-1818.

Works : motets, cantatas, masses, &c., and theoretical treatises.

FENTON, Lavinia. The original "Polly Peachum" in the *Beggars' Opera,* 1728. *D.* 1760, Duchess of Bolton.

FE'O, Francesco. Singing teacher and composer ; *b.* Naples, abt. 1685 ; *d.* abt. 1740.

Works : an oratorio, masses, &c. ; and several operas (*L'Amor tirannico,* 1713).

Ferial. Ordinary, as opposed to *festal* (Anglican Service).

Fermamen'te (*I.*). } Firmly, with decision.
Ferma'to (*I.*) }

Ferma're il tuo'no (*I.*). (See **Messa di voce.**)

Ferma'ta (*I.*). } A hold, or pause, ⌒.
Ferma'te (*G.*). }

Fermez'za (*I.*). Firmness.

Con fermez'za. With decision and firmness.

Fer'mo (*I.*). Firm, fixed.

Can'to fer'mo. The fixed song.

Fer'ne (*G.*). Distance.

Wie aus der Fer'ne. As if from a distance ; soft, subdued.

Fern'flöte. A kind of "echo" flute, 8-ft. pitch and soft tone.

Fern'werk. (1) "Echo" work generally. (2) The echo-organ.

Fero'ce (*I.*). Wild, fierce, cruel.

Ferocemen'te. Fiercely, vehemently.

Ferocità'. Wildness, fierceness.

Con ferocità'. With wildness, &c.

FERRABOS'CO (or **FERABOSCO**), **Alfonso.** 16th century Italian composer.

Works : madrigals in from 4 to 8 parts.

FERRABOS'CO, Alfonso. Probably son of preceding ; *b.* Greenwich, 1580 ; *d.* 1652. Tutor to Prince Henry (abt. 1605).

Works : a vol. of "Ayres" (1609), "Lessons for 1, 2, and 3 viols," "Fancies for Viols," &c.

FERRABOS'CO, Domenico M. 16th cent. Roman composer. Member Papal Choir, 1550-5.

Wrote motets and madrigals.

FERRAN'TI. (See **Zani.**)

FERRA'RI, Benedetto (known as **Della Tiorba**). *B.* Reggio, 1597 ; *d.* 1681. Fine *theorbo* player. Maestro succ. at Modena, Vienna, and Ratisbon.

Works : opera *libretti,* operas and ballets (*Dafne,* &c.), and "Musiche varie a voce sola."

FERRA'RI, Carlo. *B.* Piacenza, abt. 1730 ; *d.* 1789. Fine 'cellist.

Said to be "the first 'cellist to use his thumb as a *Capotasto*" (or temporary nut).

FERRA'RI, Carlotta. Dramatic composer ; *b.* Lodi, 1837.

She has written the words and music of 3 successful operas (*Ugo, Sofia, Eleonora d'Arborea*); also masses, songs, &c.

FERRA'RI, Domenico. Fine violinist ; brother of Carlo. *B.* Piacenza ; *d.* Paris, 1780. Pupil of Tartini ; composed violin sonatas, &c.

FERRA'RI, Francisca. Harpist ; *b.* Christiania, abt. 1800 ; *d.* Silesia, 1828.

Played "with brilliant success," Leipzig (1826), Magdeburg (1827).

FERRA'RI, Giacomo G. *B.* Tyrol, 1759 ; *d.* London, 1842. Accompanist to Queen Marie Antoinette ; afterwards settled in London.

Works : operas and ballets ; pieces for pf., harp, flute, &c. ; songs, and instruction books on singing.

FERRA'RI, Serafino Amadeo de'. Genoa, 1824-85 ; Director of the Genoa Cons.

Works : operas, *Don Carlo* (1853), *Pipele* (1856), *Il matrimonio per concorso* (1858), &c.; a ballet, masses, songs, &c.

FER'RI, Baldassare. Male soprano ; Perugia, 1610-80. Entered the service of Cardinal Crescenzio, Orvieto, at 11, and remained there until 1655 ; afterwards sang in Vienna (under Ferdinand III).

He had a voice of incomparable beauty, and was regarded as "one of the most extraordinary singers who ever lived."

FER'RI, Nicola. *B.* Italy, 1831 ; *d.* London, 1886. Lived chiefly in Paris and London (where he was a Prof. at the G.S.M.).

Works : operas (including *Luigi Rolla,* composed at the age of 16), and several interesting songs.

FERRIER, Paul R. M. M. *B.* Montpellier, 1843.

"Author of a vast number of light comedies and many libretti for operas and operettas of temporary vogue in Paris."—*Baker.*

FERRO'NI, Chevalier Vincenzo E. C. *B.* S. Italy, 1858. Studied Paris Cons. (1876-83). Since 1888, Prof. Milan Cons.

Works : operas, *Rudello* (1892), *Ettore Fieramosco* (1896); orchestral music, songs, pf. pieces, organ music, chamber music, &c.

Fer'tig (*G.*). Lively, dexterous ; ready, finished ; accomplished.

Fer'tigkeit. Readiness, finish, dexterity.

Ferven'te (*I.*). Fervent, ardent.

Ferventemen'te } Fervently, ardently.
Fervidamen'te }

Fervo're. Fervour.

Con fervo're. With fervour, &c.

Fes (*G.*). The note F♭.
Fes'es. F♭♭.

FES'CA, Alex. Ernst. Son of F. E. (below). *B.* Carlsruhe, 1820; *d.* 1859. Pianist, pupil of Schneider and Taubert, Berlin. Toured, 1839-40; chamber pianist to Prince Fürstenburg, 1841.
Works : 4 operas, chamber music, and very many popular songs.

FES'CA, Friedrich Ernst. *B.* Magdeburg, 1789; *d.* 1826. Violinist; played at Magdeburg, Leipzig, Cassel, Vienna, &c.; afterwards leader of Carlsruhe orch.
Works : 2 operas, 3 symphonies, and other orchestral pieces, and some fine chamber music (20 quartets, 5 quintets, &c.).

Fest (*G.*). (1) A festival.
Fest'lich. Festive; pompous, solemn.
Fest'lied. A festal song.
Fest'gesang. A festival cantata.
Musik'fest. A musical festival.

Fest (*G.*). (2) Firm, strong, sure.
Fest'er Gesang'. Canto fermo (*q.v.*).
"Ein fest'e Burg" (*q.v.*). "A safe (sure) stronghold."
Fest'halten. To hold fast, maintain.

FES'TA, Costanzo. Noted composer of madrigals, &c.; *b.* Rome, abt. 1490; *d.* 1545. Singer, Pontifical Chapel from abt. 1517. He is regarded as a forerunner of Palestrina.
Works : motets, madrigals, litanies, a Te Deum (still sung in the Papal chapel), &c.
"His madrigal 'Down in a flow'ry vale' enjoys the distinction of being the most popular piece of this description in England."—*Grove.*

FES'TA, Giuseppe M. *B.* Trani, 1771; *d.* 1839. Distinguished violinist and conductor. Settled in Naples, 1805.

Feste'vole (*I.*). Joyful, merry.

FEST'ING, Michael C. London, 1680 (?)- 1752. Violinist; pupil of Geminiani. Conductor, Ranelagh Gardens, 1742.
Promoted (with Dr. Greene and others) the establishment of the " Society of Musicians " (1738) for the maintenance of decayed musicians and their families.
Works : solos, concertos, sonatas, &c., for violin; odes, cantatas, songs, &c.

Festivamen'te (*I.*). In festival style; *i.e.* (1) solemn, or (2) festive.

Festività (*I.*). Mirth, festivity.
Con festività. With mirth; gaily.
Festi'vo } Same as *Festlich* (*q.v.*).
Festo'so }

FÉTIS, François Joseph. Celebrated musical historian and theorist; *b.* Mons, 1784; *d.* Brussels, 1871. Organist at 9. Studied Paris Cons., 1800-3, and afterwards at Vienna. Visited Paris, 1818, and brought out some successful operas. Prof. of composition, Paris Cons., 1821; Librarian, 1827. Director Brussels Cons., 1833—a position he held with distinguished ability for 38 years !
Works : "Biographie universelle des musiciens" (8 vols., 1837-44) ; "Treatise on Counterpoint and Fugue;" "Elementary Method of Harmony and Accompaniment;" Treatises on "Solfeggio," "Playing from Score," "The Principles of Music," &c.; "Manual for Young Composers;" Methods for pf., singing, and plain chant; a "Complete Treatise on the Theory and Practice of Harmony," a " General History of Music" (5 vols. to 15th century completed); &c.
He also composed 6 operas, orchestral and chamber music, pf. music, masses, motets, a requiem, &c. In 1827 he founded *La Revue Musicale,* and edited it alone for 5 years ! "His industry was untiring; he worked from 16 to 18 hours a day."

His sons, **Edouard L. F.** (*B.* 1812) and **Adolphe L. E.** (1820-73) were also musicians and writers.

Feu'er (*G.*). Fire, passion, eagerness.
Feu'(e)rig. With fire, ardour, &c.
Feu'rig schwung'voll. Passionately impetuous.
Sehr feu'rig. Very impetuously ; *con fuo'co.*

Feuillet (*F.*). A leaf.
Feuillet d'album. Album-leaf.

FÈVRE, Le. (See **Lefèvre.**)

Fiac'ca, Fiac'co (*I.*). Faint, languishing.

FIA'LA, Joseph. Eminent Bohemian oboist ; 1749-1816. Friend of Mozart.

Fias'co (*I.*). "A flask, a bottle ; " used in the sense of a "broken bottle." A failure ; a ridiculous breakdown.
The Italians cry *"Ola, ola, fiasco"* when a singer makes a false note, or fails to please.

Fia'to (*I.*). Wind ; breath.
Stromen'to da fia'to. A wind instrument.
In u'no fia'to. In one breath.

FI'BICH, Zdenko. "One of the foremost of the young Czech composers ; " *b.* Bohemia, 1850 ; *d.* 1900. Asst. Capellmeister, Prague National Theatre, 1876 ; "dramaturgist," 1899.
Works : operas, *Sarka* (1898) and several others; symphonic poems and other orchestral pieces; choral ballads, chamber music, choruses, songs.

FI'BY, Heinrich. *B.* Vienna, 1834. City musical director, Znaim, 1857.
His male-voice part-songs are widely known in Austria.

FICHT'NER, Pauline. (See **Erdmannsdörffer.**)

Fic'ta,-um (*L.*). False ; feigned.
Fic'ta Mu'sica. (See *Musica ficta.*)

Fiddle. (*G., Fi'del, Fie'del ; A.S., Fidhele ; Dan., Fiddel ; Dutch, Vedel ; Low Lat., Vidula.*) A violin (*q.v.*).
Old spellings : *fidel, fedele, fithel, fithele, fithul, fydel, fydyll, fythel,* &c.
Fiddle-bag. Formerly an important part of a Fiddler's equipment.
Fiddle-bow, Fiddle-stick. A bow.
Fiddle-de-dee } Nonsense ; trifling.
Fiddle-faddle }
Fiddle-string. The catgut string of a violin.

Fiddle G. The note

The swell on some old organs does not go below " fiddle G."

Fiddler, Fitheler, Fydelare, Fydeler. A violinist.

FIDE'LIO. Beethoven's only opera ; produced Vienna, 1805 (as *Leonore*).

Fi'dicen (*Mas.*) (*L.*). } A player on a stringed
Fi'dicina (*Fem.*) (*L.*). } instrument (lute, harp, &c.).

Fidu'cia (*L.* and *I.*). Trust, faith, confidence.

Fie'del (*G.*). Fiddle.
Fie'delbogen. Violin bow.
Stroh'fiedel. A xylophone (*q.v.*).

FIED'LER, August Max. Pianist and composer ; *b.* Zittau, 1859.

FIELD, John. Celebrated pianist and writer of nocturnes ; *b.* Dublin, 1782 ; *d.* Moscow, 1837. Studied under Clementi, by whom he was employed in his salerooms "to show off pianos to customers." Visited Paris with Clementi (1802), and St. Petersburg (1804), where he remained as a teacher and concert player. Played in Moscow, 1823, and in London, 1832 ; afterwards in Paris, Belgium, Italy, Vienna, &c. As a composer for the pf. his nocturnes are specially noteworthy ; they initiated the style so successfully adopted by Chopin.
He also wrote concertos, sonatas, rondos, romances, fantasias, &c., for pf., still used as teaching-pieces on the Continent.

FIELD, John T. Orgt. and composer ; *b.* nr. Manchester, 1850.

FIE'LITZ, Alex. von. Noted contemporary composer of songs and pf. pieces ; *b.* Leipzig, 1860.

Fier, Fière (*F.*). Proud, fierce, haughty.

Fie'ro, Fie'ra (*I.*). Haughty, bold, fierce, vigorous.
Fieramen'te ⎱ Boldly, with fierceness, &c.
Con fierez'za ⎰

FIERRABRAS. Opera by Schubert, 1823.

Fife. (*G.*, *Pfei'fe*, *Quer'pfeife* ; *F.*, *Fifre* ; *I.*, *Pif'fero*, *Fif'faro*.) (1) A small flute, with or without keys.
The *Pic'colo* or *Flau'to pic'colo*, also meaning "a small flute," is a special variety of the fife.
(2) Formerly any kind of musical pipe.
(3) An organ stop of 2 ft. pitch.

Fif'faro (*I.*). ⎱ A fife.
Fifre (*F.*). ⎰

Fifteenth. (1) (*G.*, *Quint'dezime* ; *F.*, *Quinzième* ; *I.*, *Quindice'sima*.) The interval of a double-octave, or bis-diapason.
(2) A 2 ft. organ stop.

Fifth. (*G.*, *Quin'te* ; *F.*, *Quinte* ; *I.*, *Quin'ta*.) An interval comprising 5 scale-degrees (or letter-names). (See **Interval**.)

Perfect 5th. Diminished 5th. Augmented 5th.
Defective fifth. A diminished fifth.
Extreme sharp fifth. Augmented.
False fifth ⎱
Flat fifth ⎰ Diminished.
Imperfect fifth ⎰
Major fifth. Perfect.
Minor fifth. Diminished.
Pluperfect fifth ⎱
Redundant fifth ⎰ Augmented.
Superfluous fifth ⎰
Sharp fifth. Augmented ; sometimes used for perfect, as opposed to *flat*.

Fifths, Circle of. If a series of Perfect 5ths and 4ths (the inversions of 5ths) be written down, commencing with C, they

form (in equal temperament) a complete octave of semitones :—

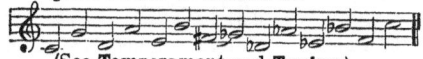

(See **Temperament** and **Tuning**.)
Arranged in a Circle, these notes become a "Circle of Fifths : "—

The Chinese are said to have had a Circle of 5ths "thousands of years ago ! "
(See also **Keys, Circle of**.)

Fifths, Consecutive, or Parallel. A succession of perfect 5ths between any two parts which rise or fall together :

Acoustically, there is no reason why consecutive 5ths should not be as pleasing as consecutive 3rds or 6ths ; in fact, they ought to be *more pleasing !* In the early days of harmony consecutive 5ths and 8ves were employed as follows :—

And Gounod uses similar progressions in the *Angels' Chorus* of *Faust* to produce an archaic effect :—

With the growth of counterpoint, consecutive 5ths came to be entirely forbidden, although numerous instances of their intentional or accidental employment may be found in the works of the greatest masters. It was formerly supposed that consecutive 5ths were bad because they suggested two different keys at the same time. Sir John Stainer proved conclusively, however, that this was not necessarily the case (*Theory of Harmony*, p. 130), and it has been abundantly shown that the uneducated ear does not find them at all objectionable !
The rule prohibiting their use is therefore evidently based upon artistic and æsthetic considerations. Consecutive 5ths have been well described as the "*bête noire*" of the young composer !

Fifths, Ill-approached. (See **Hidden Fifths**.)

FI'GARO. (See **Nozze di Figaro**.)

Figur' (*G.*). A group of notes. (See **Figure**.)

Figu'ra (*L.*). "A figure ;" specially in old music, a note.

Figu'ra mu'ta. A rest.
Figu'ra liga'ta) Notes connected by) Terms used
Figu'ra obli'qua) a "ligature.") in medieval
Figu'ra simplex. A note standing by) notation.
itself. (See *Musical Notation*.)

Fig'ural.) Florid ; embellished. Used,
Fig'urate.) at first especially, to dis-
Figura'to (*I*.).) criminate between the
Figuré (*F*.).) "figured" added counter-
Figured.) points and the plain,
Figuriert' (*G*.).) simple notes of the
Canto Fermo.

Figural'-gesang (G.))
Cantus figura'lis (L.)) Mensurable music (*q.v.*).
Figural'-musik (G.).) Florid counterpoint.

Figuration. (1) The development of florid
counterpoint by the introduction of
figures, runs, passing-notes, &c.
(2) Embellishing a theme by adding varied
figures of accompaniment, &c., or by
ornamenting the melody with grace-
notes, runs, florid passages, cadenzas, &c.
(3) The working-out of a figured bass.

Figure. (*G*., *Figur'*; *F*., *Figure*; *I*., *Figu'ra*).
(1) Any distinct and significant group of
notes. (2) A motive (or germ) for development. (3) A "form" of accompaniment.

(*a*) Melodic figures : BEETHOVEN.

MOZART.

(*b*) Rhythmic figures :

BEETHOVEN.

(*c*) Figures of Accompaniment :

(See also **Accompaniment, Leit-motiv,
Motive,** and **Rhythm.**)

Figure. (*G*., *Ziffer*; *F*., *Chiffre*; *I*., *Ci'fra*).
A numeral (or cypher) as in figured bass.

Figured Bass. (*G*., *Bezif'ferbass, General'-
bass*; *F*., *Basse chiffrée*; *I*., *Basso
conti'nuo, Basso cifra'to*.) A bass provided with figures to indicate the
chords.

EXAMPLE :
(*a*) Figured Bass.

6   6   6
5   7

(*b*) Solution.

Absence of figures implies the triad of the bass
note; *a* position. The figure 6 implies a 1st
version ; *b* position. The figures ⁶₄ imply a 2nd
inversion ; *c* position. The figure 7 implies a
triad with 7th added; ⁷S, ⁷R, &c. The figures ⁶₅
imply a 1st inversion of a 7th chord ; ⁷S*b*,
⁷R*b*, &c.
Chromatic alterations of notes are shown by
" chromatics " placed beneath or before
figures ; &c.
The upper notes may be arranged in any order as
long as the rules of harmony are observed.

Figures of Diminution. Figures indicating
triplets, quadruplets, quintuplets, &c.

Figure Solmization. (See **Chevé**.)

Fil (*F*.).) A thread.
Fi'lo (*I*.).)

Filar' (or *Affilar'*) *il tuo'no (I.).*) To "draw out" the
Filar' la vo'ce (I.).) voice. To produce
Filer un son (F.).) a steady sustained
Filer la voix (F.).) tone (in the Italian
method of singing). Also used to imply a *swell*
on a long note.
Fi'lo di vo'ce (I.). "A thread of a voice." The voice
as soft as possible.

FILIP'PI, Filippo. *B.* Vicenza, 1830 ; *d.*
1887. Editor *Gazzetta Musicale*, Milan,
1859. Warm partizan of Wagner.
Wrote chamber music, pf. pieces, and songs.

FI'LITZ, Dr. Friedrich. Critic and historian;
b. Arnstadt, 1804 ; *d.* Munich, 1876.

Filling-up Parts.
Parts without special melodic interest, added to
complete or enrich the harmony; or, in the
orchestra, to supply " orchestral colour."

FILLMORE, John C. American musician
and writer ; 1843-98. Founded the
Milwaukee School of Music, 1884.
Works : "Pianoforte music," &c. ; "Lessons in
Musical History ; " "A study of Omaha Indian
Music ; " English translations of Riemann's
Klavierschule and *Natur der Harmonik* ; &c.

FILL'UNGER, Marie. Soprano ; *b.* Vienna,
1850.

Fil'pen (*G*.). Same as **Fistulieren** (q.v.).

Fi'lum (*L*., "A thread.")**.** The stem of a note.

Fin (*F*.). (1) The end. (2) Fine, delicate.

Fin (*I*.). Abbn. of *Fino*, "Up to," "until."
Fin al seg'no. Up to the :S:
Fin qui. Up to here.

Final. The last note of a melody in any of
the church modes, answering to our
Tonic or key-note. (See **Mode**.)
Final Close. The concluding cadence.

Fina'le (*I.*). (1) Same as **Final.** (2) The concluding movement of a sonata, symphony, &c.; the last number of an act in an opera; the last piece on a program.

Operatic Fina'le. An *ensemble piece* at the end of an act (or opera), including soloists and chorus, and generally working up to a climax.

Grand Fina'le. A specially imposing, exciting, or dramatic close.

F in Alt. ; F in Altissimo (*I.*). (See **Alt.**)

FINCK, Heinrich. German contrapuntist; 15th and 16th centuries.

Works : songs, hymns, motets, &c.

FINCK, Henry T. Mus. Ed. New York *Evening Post ; b.* Bethel, Missouri, 1854.

Works : "Wagner and His Works" (2 vols. 1893), "Paderewski and His Art," &c.

FINCK, Hermann. Grand-nephew of Heinrich. *B.* Saxony, 1527 ; *d.* 1558.

Wrote a valuable work, "Practica Musica" (1556).

FIND'EISEN, N. F. *B.* St. Petersburg, 1868. Founder *Russische Musikzeitung,* 1893.

Fi'ne (*I.*). The end. It is sometimes indicated thus—

Da ca'po al fi'ne ; or D.C. al fi'ne. Repeat from the beginning of the piece to the *Fi'ne.*

Dal se'gno al fi'ne ; or D.S. al fi'ne. Repeat from the *Sign* (𝄋) to the *Fi'ne.*

Fi'ne del at'to. End of the act (of an opera), &c.

Fing'er (*G.*). A finger.

Fing'erbildner. A "finger-developer." Dumb-piano, Virgil Clavier, &c.

Fing'erbrett. A fingerboard (*q.v.*).

Fing'erfertigkeit. "Finger dexterity."

Fing'erleiter. A Chiroplast (*q.v.*).

Fing'er lie'gen las'sen. The finger to remain (on the string).

Fing'ersatz
Fing'erzetzung } Fingering (*q.v.*).

Eng'er Fing'erzetzung. Close fingering ; *i.e.*, with the fingers close together.

Gedeh'nter Fing'erzetzung. Wide fingering ; *i.e.*, including wide stretches, &c.

Fing'erwechsel. Change of fingers on the same note (key).

Fingerboard. (*G., Fing'erbrett, Griff'brett ; F., Touche, Manche ; I., Tastie'ra.*) (1) The piece of wood attached to the neck of a vn., guitar, mandoline, &c., over which the fingers are held so that they may press down and shorten the strings to produce the notes required.

When *frets* are used they are attached to the fingerboard.

(2) Also used for *Keyboard* (pf., org., &c.).

Finger cymbals. Small cymbals attached to the thumb and forefinger.

Fingering. (*G., Fing'ersatz, Fing'erzetzung, Applikatur'; F., Doigter ; I., Diteggiatu'ra.*) (1) The method of using the fingers in playing musical insts. (2) Marks to guide the player in using the fingers.

Cross fingering. Special devices of fingering to produce chromatic tones on wood-wind instruments not provided with keys for that purpose.

English fingering (pf.). Thumb marked + or × ; fingers 1, 2, 3, 4.

German or *Continental fingering (pf.).* Thumb marked 1 ; fingers 2, 3, 4, 5.

Fini're il tuo'no (*I.*). (See **Messa di voce.**)

Finite Canon. (See **Canon.**)

Fini'to (*I.*). Finished.

FINK, Gottfried W. *B.* Thuringia, 1783 ; *d.* 1846. Editor, *Allgemeine Mus. Zeitung,* 1827-41. Music-director, Leipzig Univ., 1842.

Works: pf. pieces, violin pieces, male-voice music, ballads, a collection of 1,000 German songs, &c. ; several works on musical theory ; and important contributions to musical Lexicons and journals. His old-fashioned views provoked Schumann to found an opposition paper.

FINK'ENSTEIN, Jettka. Contralto ; *b.* Seni, Russia, 1865.

Fi'no (*I.*). Up to, as far as, till, until.

Fin qui (*I.*). To this place.

Fin'ta (*Fem.*) (*I.*) } Feigned ; counter-
Fin'to (*Mas.*) (*I.*) } feited, hidden.

Caden'za fin'ta. A deceptive or interrupted cadence.

Fio'co, Fio'ca (*I.*). Hoarse, veiled, feeble.

Fiochet'to. A little hoarse, &c.

Fiochez'za. Hoarseness, &c.

Vo'ce fio'ca. A faint voice.

FIORAVAN'TI, Valentino. *B.* Rome, 1764 ; *d.* 1837. After engagements at Rome, Naples, Paris, and Lisbon, became Maestro at St. Peter's, Rome, 1816.

Works : a *Stabat Mater,* a *Miserere,* and other church music ; and about 50 operas—*Iviaggiatori ridicoli* (1785) being the first, and *Le cantatrici villane* (1799) the most successful.

FIORAVAN'TI, Vincenzo. Son of preceding. *B.* Rome, 1799 ; *d.* 1877.

Wrote about 40 operas, including *Pulcinella molinaro* (1819).

Fio're (*I.*). "Flower, bloom, blossom."

Fioreggia're. To embellish ; to figurate (with runs, &c.).

Fioret'to. An embellishment.

Fioriscen'te } Florid ; embellished, ornamented.
Fiori'to }

Fioritu're (Plur. of *Fioritu'ra*). Ornaments, embellishments, flourishes, cadenzas, runs, &c., added to a melody.

Fioret'ti (*I.*). Little vocal ornaments or graces.

FIORIL'LO, Federigo. Violinist. Son of Ignazio (below). *B.* Brunswick, 1753 ; *d.* 1812. Visited London abt. 1788, and played the viola in Salomon's quartet.

Works : chamber music, violin duets, &c., and a celebrated set of 36 caprices—"Etudes de Violon."

FIORIL'LO, Ignazio. *B.* Naples, 1715 ; *d.* 1787. Capellmeister, Brunswick, 1754 ; Cassel, 1762-80.

Works: oratorio (*Isacco*) ; masses, &c., and several operas (*Artimene,* 1738), &c.

Fipple Flute. Any flute of the *flûte-à-bec* or flageolet type.

FI'QUÉ, Karl. Pianist ; *b.* Bremen, 1861.

Firing. In bell-ringing, clashing all the bells at once.

First Flat Key. The key with a signature of one flat more (or one sharp less).

First-movement Form. (See **Sonata.**)

First Remove. A change of key to the "next" column to the right or left on the Tonic Sol-fa modulator.

First Sharp Key. The key with a signature of one sharp more (or one flat less).

Fis (*G.*). F♯.

Fis'fis, or Fis'is. Fx.

FISCH'ER, Adolf. *B.* Pomerania, 1827; *d.* 1893. Director Frankfort Singakademie, 1853; founded Silesian Cons., Breslau, 1880.
Wrote symphonies, motets, organ music, songs.

FISCH'ER, Christian W. Operatic *basso buffo;* 1789-1859. Sang chiefly in Dresden, Leipzig, and Magdeburg.

FISCH'ER, Gottfried E. Berlin, 1791-1841.
Works : motets, school songs, songs, theoretical treatises, &c.

FISCH'ER, Joh. Ch. Celebrated oboe player; *b.* Baden, 1733; *d.* London, 1800.
Wrote 10 oboe concertos, flute duets, flute solos, &c.

FISCH'ER, Josef. Stuttgart; 1828-85.
Composed the song "Hoch Deutschland, herrliche Siegesbraut."

FISCHER, Karl A. *B.* Saxony, 1828; *d.* 1892. Distinguished organist; toured successfully (1852-5); afterwards settled in Dresden.
Works : 3 organ concertos, a mass, symphonies for organ and orchestra, orchestral suites, &c.

FISCH'ER, Karl L. Bavarian violinist; 1816-77. Mus.-director of theatres at Cologne, Aix-la-Chapelle, Nuremburg, &c.; Court Capellmeister, Hanover, 1859.
Specially noted for his popular male-voice choruses.

FISCH'ER, Ludwig. Celebrated bass singer; *b.* Mayence, 1745; *d.* Berlin, 1825. Sang with great success in Germany, France, and Italy. Mozart wrote the part of "Osmin"(*Entführung*) especially for him.

" He was singing, one evening, an aria, in which he introduced the following passage : While waiting for the usual thunder of applause, a sailor in the upper gallery took up the tune, and closed the aria for him thus :— to the astonishment and mirth of the audience."—*Moore.*

FISCH'ER, Michael G. *B.* nr. Erfurt, 1773; *d.* 1829. Famous organist and condr.
Works : about 50 organ compositions; symphonies, concertos, chamber music, motets, pf. pieces, &c.

Fis dur (*G.*). The key of F♯ major.

FISHER, Henry. *B.* Blackpool, 1845. Mus.Doc. Cantab., 1878.
Author of " The Musical Profession," " The Candidate in Music," "The Harmony Player," "The Pianist's Mentor," " Psychology for Music Teachers," &c.

Fis moll (*G.*). The key of F♯ minor.

FISSOT, Alexis. H. French organist and pianist; 1843-96. Prof. of pf. Paris Cons. from 1887.
Published numerous pf. pieces (Ballades, Arabesques, Morceaux, Pièces de genre, &c.).

Fis'tel, Fis'telstimme (*G.*). Falsetto.

Fisto'la (*I.*), **Fis'tula** (*L.*). A pipe, or reed.
Fis'tula dul'cis (L.). A flûte-à-bec (q.v.).
Fis'tula, cui semper decrescit arundinis ordo (L.). Pan pipes.
Fis'tula pastori'cia (L.). A shepherd's pipe.

Fistuli(e)'ren (*G.*). (1) To sing falsetto. (2) To overblow an organ-pipe so as to produce one of its upper partials instead of the fundamental. (See **Acoustics.**)

FITELBERG, Geo. Composer; *b.* Dünaburg, 1879.

Fith'ele. (See **Fiddle.**)

FITZWILLIAM Collection. A collection of books, paintings, MSS.,&c., bequeathed by Viscount Fitzwilliam (*d.* 1816) to the Cambridge University; now contained in the Fitzwilliam Museum, Cambridge.
Among the musical MSS. are sketches by Handel, the great Virginall-Booke (recently edited by Squire and Fuller-Maitland), anthems in Purcell's hand-writing, &c.

Fixed Do.
In *fixed-do* systems C is always called *do* (or *ut*), D always called *re* (RAY), E always *mi* (ME), &c. whatever the key or mode may be; but in *movable-do* systems the name *do* is always given to the Tonic of any major key, and the other names in order of scale position. N.B.—In some systems the Tonic of minor keys is also called *do;* but in the Tonic Sol-fa system the minor Tonic is LAH. (See also *Movable-do.*)

Fixed-do solmisation; from *Hullah's Manual* (1849).

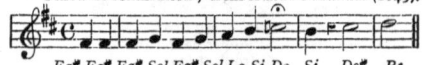

Fa♯ Fa♯ Fa♯ Sol Fa♯ Sol La Si Do Si Do♯ Re

The same in *Movable-do* solmisation.

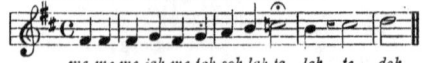

me me me lah me lah soh lah ta lah te doh

Flach-flö'te (*G.*). "Shallow flute." A flageolet; an organ stop.

Flag. Abbreviation for *Flageolet-tones*, or harmonics, in stringed inst. playing.

Flageolet. (*G., Flageolett; F., Flageolet; I., Flagiolet'ta.*) (1) A small *flûte-à-bec.* (See **Flute.**) (2) An org. stop, 2 ft. pitch.
The flageolet is essentially the same in construction as a tin whistle or an organ flue-pipe. The ordinary flageolet in D has the same pitch as the piccolo (*flauto piccolo*) in D, producing all sounds *an octave higher than the written notes.* Many flageolets are provided with alternative piccolo heads. The tone of the flageolet is softer than that of the piccolo, and very high notes are not easy to produce.
Double flageolet. A flageolet with one mouthpiece and two tubes.
Flageolet tones } The natural harmonics of stringed
Flageolet'töne (G.) } instruments.

FLAGLER, Isaac V. V. Orgt. and composer; *b.* Albany (U.S.), 1844.

Flaschinet' (*G.*). Old name for the flageolet.

Flat. (*G., Be; F., Bémol; I., Bemol'le.*) The sign ♭, which lowers a note a semitone from its pitch in the scale of C.
Double flat. The sign ♭♭, which lowers a tone two semitones.
Flat Keys. } Name sometimes given to all keys or
Flat Scales. } scales requiring *flats* in the signature.
Flat Key. In Sol-fa, a key to the *left* of any other on the Modulator.

Flat. Low.
Flat pitch. Any low pitch ; as *French Pitch* compared with *English Concert Pitch.*
Flat singing. Singing out of tune by not quite reaching the true pitch.
Flat tuning. Tuning at any pitch lower than the ordinary.

Flat. Old name for minor.
Flat third. A minor 3rd.
Flat seventh. A minor 7th.
Flat fifth. A minor fifth ; now usually called a diminished 5th.
Extreme flat. Diminished ; as *Extreme flat 7th,* a diminished 7th.

Flatter la corde (*F.*). "To caress the string ;" to play in an expressive and tender manner.

Flaut-à-becq. Same as *Flûte-à-bec* (*q.v.*).

Flautan'do, Flauta'to (*I.*). "Flute-like."
(1) To bow near the finger-board (of a vn., &c.) so as to produce somewhat dull, flute-like tones ; or (2) To use the harmonics, or flageolet-tones.

Flauti'na (or **Flauti'no**). A kind of accordion.

Fla'uto (*I.*). (*Sp., Flauta.*) A flute (*q.v.*).
Fla'uto a bec'co. Flûte-à-bec. (See *Flute.*)
Fla'uto ama'bile. A sweet-toned organ stop, generally 4 ft. pitch.
Fla'uto dol'ce. A sweet-toned organ stop, generally 8-ft. pitch on the pedal.
Fla'uto pic'colo. A little flute. (See *Piccolo.*)
Fla'uto ta'cere (or *ta'cet*). The flute to be silent (*i.e.,* not to be played).
Fla'uto traver'so. The ordinary concert-flute, held *transversely,* and blown across a hole near the top. It was formerly called a German flute, to distinguish it from a *flûte-à-bec.*
Flauti'no. A small flute, flageolet, or piccolo.
Flauti'sta. A flute player.
Flauto'ne. A large or bass flute.

Fle'bile (*I.*) } In a doleful, plaintive
Flebilmen'te (*I.*) } style.

FLÉGIER, Ange. French composer ; *b.* Marseilles, 1846.
Works : opera (*Fatima*) ; cantatas, orchestral pieces, pf. pieces, and several songs.

FLEI'SCHER, Oskar R. *B.* Saxony, 1856. Custodian of the Royal Collection of Mus. Insts., Berlin. Founder of the "International Music Society."
Works : a cantata (*Holda*) ; important studies in mus. history, organ pieces, motets, and songs.

Fleh'end (*G.*). Supplicating, imploring.

FLEM'MING, Friedrich F. *B.* Saxony, 1778 ; *d.* 1813.
Composed popular male-voice choruses ("Integer vitæ," &c.).

Flessi'bile (*I.*). Flexible.
Flessibilità. Flexibility.

FLETCHER, Chas. O. L. Violinist ; *b.* Somersetshire, 1846.

Flexibility. (From *L. flexibilis,* "easily bent.") Ability to render rapid passages easily and fluently.

Flick'oper (*G.*). A *Pasticcio* (*q.v.*).

Flicor'no (*I.*). Flügelhorn (*q.v.*).

FLIE'GENDE HOLL'ÄNDER, DER. "The Flying Dutchman." Opera, Wagner, 1843.

Flies'send (*G.*). Flowing ; smoothly, softly.
Flies'send, a'ber im'mer gemäs'sigt. Flowingly, but always in moderate time.

FLIGHT, Benjamin. Renowned English org. builder ; 1767-1847.

Fling. A spirited Highland dance in 4-4 time similar to the *Reel.*

FLINTOFT, Rev. Luke. *B.* Worcester, abt. 1670(?); *d.* 1727 ; B.A.,Cambridge,1700.
He is said to have invented or adapted the first double chant.

FLOOD, W. H. Grattan. *B.* Lismore, Ireland, 1859.
Orgt., successively at various Irish cathedrals (Enniscorthy Cath. 1895); Mus.D., R.U.I., 1907; &c.
Author of " The Story of the Harp," " A Hist. of Irish Music " (1905), &c.

FLORENCE, Evangeline (Mrs. Crerar). Soprano ; *b.* Cambridge (U.S.), 1873.

Florid. Embellished with runs, passages, &c.
Florid Counterpoint. (See *Counterpoint.*)

FLORI'DIA, Pietro. Pianist and composer ; *b.* Sicily, 1860.
Works : opera, *Maruzza* (Venice, 1894) ; several pf. pieces, &c.

FLO'RIMO, Francesco. *B.* Calabria, 1800 ; *d.* Naples, 1888. Librarian Naples College of Music, 1826-51.
Great friend of Bellini ; founded the "Bellini Prize" for young Italian composers.
Works : a musical history of Naples and its Conservatories, treatises on Bellini and Wagner, a "Metodo di Canto" (adopted by the Conservatoire), cantatas, church music, and several books of songs.

FLO'RIO, Caryl. (Real name **William Jas. Robjohn**.) *B.* Tavistock, 1843.
Has won distinction in America as organist, choirmaster, actor, critic, and composer.
Works : operas, operettas, symphonies, vocal music, pf. music, and chamber music (including a quintet for pf. and saxophones).

FLORIZEL. (See **Reuter.**)

Flö'te (*G.*). A flute.
Flö'tenartig. Flute-like.
Flö'tenbass. A bass flute.
Flö'ten-beglei'tung. Flute accompaniment.
Flö'tenspieler. A flute player.
Flö'tenstimme. An organ flute stop.
Flö'tenwerk. An organ with flue-pipes only (without reeds, &c.).
Flö'tenzug. Flute-stop (on an org., &c.).

FLO'TOW, Friedrich von. Operatic composer ; *b.* nr. Mecklenburg, 1812 ; *d.* Darmstadt, 1883. Studied Paris, under Reicha. First great success, *Le naufrage de la Méduse* (Paris, 1839). Intendant of Court music, Schwerin, 1856-63. Retired, 1868.
Works : about 30 operas, ballets, &c., of which *Stradella* (1849) and *Martha* (his best work, Vienna, 1847) are the most important.

Flourish. (1) A call ; a trumpet fanfare or prelude. (2) An ornamental passage.

FLOWERS, Geo. French. *B.* Boston, Lincolnshire, 1811 ; *d.* 1872. Mus.D. Oxon, 1865. Successful singing teacher.

Flüch'tig (*G.*). Light, rapid. Also *adv.,* lightly, nimbly ; superficially.

Flue-pipe. (*G., Labial'pfeife ; F., Tuyau à bouche ; I., Can'na d'a'nima.*) An org.

pipe sounded on the same principle as a tin-whistle. (See **Organ.**)

Flue-stop. A stop consisting of flue-pipes.

Flue-work. (1) An organ containing flue-pipes only; *i.e.*, without reeds. (2) The flue-pipes of an organ; *i.e.*, all "non-reed" stops.

Flug′blatt (*G.*). A fugitive piece; a trifle.

FLÜ′GEL, Ernest P. Son of G. (below). B. Stettin, 1844. Founded the "Flügel-Verein" (a singing society), Breslau.

> Works: "The 121st Psalm," a pf. trio, pf. pieces, organ pieces, songs, &c.

FLÜ′GEL, Gustav. *B.* Nienburg-on-Saale, 1812; *d.* 1900. Cantor and orgt., Schloss-Kirche, Stettin, from 1859.

> Works: 112 *Choralvorspiele* and many other organ pieces, orchestral and chamber music, part-songs, and choruses, pf. pieces, songs, &c.

Flü′gel (*G.*). "A wing." Any wing-shaped inst., especially a harpsichord or grand pf. The wing-shaped "treble-piece" of a bassoon.

Flü′gelharfe. "A small triangular harp (or psaltery), to be set on a table."—*Baker.*

Flü′gelhorn. (1) A keyed bugle (*Klap′penhorn*). (2) An instrument of the saxhorn type, made in several sizes (soprano, alto, tenor, bass). The soprano (in B♭) is the only one commonly used.

Flüs′sig (*G.*). Fluid; flowing evenly.

Flute, Floyt, Floyte, Flowte. (*G., Flöte; F., Flûte; I., Fla′uto; Low L., Flau′ta,* from *flatus,* "a blowing;" *L., Cal′amus* ("a reed"), or *Ti′bia* ("a leg-bone"); *Dutch, Fluit; Gk., Au′los.*) One of the most ancient and universal of musical instruments.

> The ancient terms translated "flute" include all pipes, whether played with reeds of the oboe or clarinet type or blown so as "to whistle." The term is now restricted to the latter sense. Flute tone is produced by (1) blowing across the end of the pipe, as in the familiar *Pan-pipes* of the Punch and Judy show; (2) by using a mouth-piece of the flageolet or tin whistle type, as in all organ flue-pipes. Flutes of this kind were formerly called *Flûtes-à-bec,* or "beak" flutes; (3) by blowing across a hole near the top of the pipe, as in the ordinary orchestral (transverse) flute—*Fla′uto traver′so.* The development of the primitive whistling pipe into the complex modern organ—essentially "a box of whistles"—forms one of the most interesting chapters of musical history!

> The orchestral flute has a range of 3 octaves, with all the semi-tones:— It is a "non-transposing" instrument, playing all notes "as written."

> Its tone is almost "simple," the fundamental being accompanied by very few upper partials. (See *Acoustics.*)

> Flute stops on the organ consist of a special variety of flue-pipes, voiced so as to imitate the tone of the orchestral (or other) flute.

Alto flute. An obsolete flute similar to the *Flûte d′amour.*

Bass flute. (1) An obsolete flute used to play bass to a family of flutes. (2) An organ stop.

Beak flute. A *flûte-à-bec.* (See *Flute.*)

Cross flute. *Flauto traverso.* (See *Flute.*)

Direct flute. A *flûte-à-bec.*

Flûte-à-bec (*F.*). (See *Flute.*)

Flûte à cheminée (*F.*). An organ flute stop provided with "chimneys" (or tubes) at the ends of the pipes.

Flûte allemande (*F.*). A German flute; *Flauto traverso,*

Flûte-à-pavillon (*F.*). An organ stop, 8-ft.

Flûte d′amour (*F.*). (*a*) An old flute in A or B♭. (*b*) A sweet-toned organ stop.

Flûte d′Angleterre (*F.*). English flute. The flageolet or *Flûte-à-bec.*

Flûte dessus (*F.*). Treble flute (organ stop).

Flûte douce (*F.*). See *Flauto dolce.*

Flûte du Poitou (*F.*). The bagpipe, or cornamusa.

Flûte harmonique (*F.*). See *Harmonic flute* (below).

Flûte minor. A small flute stop; 4-ft. or 2-ft. pitch.

Flûte octaviante (*F.*). See *Harmonic flute.*

Flûte ouverte (*F.*). A flute stop with open pipes.

Flûte traversière (*F.*). *Flauto traverso.* (See *Flute.*)

Gedackt-flöte (*G.*). A flute stop with stopped pipes.

German flute. The *flauto traverso,* or ordinary flute.

Harmonic flute. A family of organ stops with pipes pierced in the middle so as to produce the octave instead of the fundamental tone.

Hohl′flöte (*G.*). "Hollow-toned flute." An organ stop which gives a fuller tone than the stopped diapason, and often takes its place on large organs.

Octave flute (or *Octave*). The piccolo.

Orchestral flute. (1) The ordinary concert flute. (2) A specially-voiced solo stop on the organ.

Quint flute } An organ stop sounding a 5th higher
Quint′flöte (*G.*) } than the written notes.

Wald′flöte (*G.*). (*Waldflute*). "A forest flute." An organ stop of broad scale, generally 4-ft. (or 2-ft.) pitch.

Flûté(e) (*F.*). Sweet, soft, flutelike.

Fly. The hinged cover, or flap, of a pf. or org. keyboard.

F. O. Full Organ.

Fo′co (*I.*). Fire, spirit, energy.

Foco′so } With spirit; ardently.
Focosamen′te }

FODOR, Joseph. Celebrated violinist; *b.* Venloo, 1752; *d.* 1828.

FODOR-MAINVIELLE, Josephine. Renowned singer; daughter of Jos. *B.* Paris, 1793; retired 1833.

FOERSTER, Adolf M. American musician; *b.* Pittsburg, 1854.

> Works: orchestral pieces, chamber music, violin pieces, pf. pieces, songs, &c.

FOGLIA′NI, Ludovici. *B.* Modena, 2nd half 15th century; *d.* 1540.

> Wrote a famous book, "Musica Theorica" (1529).

Fogliet′to (*I.*). A first vn. part showing the "points of entry" of the chief orch. insts. and marked with *cues,* &c., so as to serve as a "conductor's copy" in the absence of a full score.

FOIGNET, Chas. G. *B.* Lyons, abt. 1750; *d.* 1823.

> Wrote about 25 comic operas for the smaller Parisian theatres.

FOIGNET, François. Son of C. G.; about 1780-1845.

> Wrote comic operas, pantomimes, and melodramas.

Foire des enfants (*F.*). Toy symphony (*q.v.*).

Fois (*F.*). Time.

Dernière fois. Last time.

Première fois. First time.

Seconde fois. Second time.

FÖL′DESY. Noted contemporary 'cellist. Son of a military bandsman at Budapest. Successful London appearance, 1902.

FOLEY, Allan Jas. Bass singer; known as **Signor Foli.** *B.* Cahir, Ireland, 1835; *d.* 1899.

> His voice was powerful and of extensive compass; he was a favourite both as an operatic and concert singer.

Fol'ge (*G.*). Sequence, consecution.
Folgt lang'e Pau'se. A long pause follows.

Foli'a (*S.*). A Spanish dance in slow 3-4 time, similar to the *Fandango*.

Fo'liated. Ornamented ; florid.

Folk Song. (*G., Volks'lied.*) "A song of the people ; " a national song.

FOLVILLE, E. E. Juliette. Concert-pianist, violinist, conductor, and composer ; *b.* Liége, 1870. She was appointed Pf. Prof. Liége Cons., 1898.
Works : a successful opera, *Atala* (1892) ; orchestral suites, a violin concerto, songs, pf. music, organ music, &c.

Fondamental,-e (*F.*). ⎫
Fondamenta'le (*I.*). ⎬ Fundamental.
Basse fondamentale (*F.*) ⎫ The root or generator of a
Son fondamental (*F.*) ⎬ chord.

Fondamen'to (*I.*). (1) The fundamental bass. (2) The root or generator of a chord.

Fonds d'orgue (*F.*). The foundation stops. (See **Organ.**)

FONSECA. (See **Portogallo.**)

FONTAINE, Chas. Pen-name of **C. W. Smith** (*q.v.*).

FONTAINE, Mortier de. (See **Mortier.**)

FONTAINE, Hendrik. Bass singer ; *b.* Antwerp, 1857.
Specially good as *Lucifer* in Benoit's oratorio.

FONTA'NA, G. B. A very early composer for the violin ; *d.* Brescia, 1630.

Foot. (*G., Fuss ; F., Pied ; I., Pie'de.*) A group of syllables in poetry corresponding to a measure in music.
The poetical foot may begin on any kind of accent ; the musical measure, however, always begins on the strong accent. (See *Metre.*)

Foot. (*G., Stie'fel.*) The lower part of an organ-pipe.

Foot. Old term for a drone bass, or *burden.*
For the meaning of 8-ft., 4-ft., 16-ft., &c., in describing pitch, see *Acoustics.*

Foot-key. Name sometimes given to an organ pedal.

FOOTE, Arthur Wm. Prominent American organist and composer ; *b.* Salem, Mass., 1853.
Works : overtures, &c., for orchestra ; cantatas (*Wreck of the Hesperus, The Skeleton in Armour*) ; chamber music, pf. pieces, songs, &c.

FOOTE, Frank Barrington. Baritone vocalist ; *b.* Plymouth, 1855.

FORCH'HAMMER, Theodor. Orgt., composer, and writer ; *b.* Schiers, 1847.

FORD, Ernest A. C. Composer and conductor ; *b.* London, 1858.
Works : operas and operettas (*Daniel O'Rourke, Joan, Mr. Jericho,* &c.) ; ballet music, songs.

FORD, Henry Ed. *B.* Warlingham, 1822. Mus.D. Cantuar. Orgt. Carlisle Cath. since 1842.

FORD, Thomas. *B.* abt. 1580 ; *d.* 1648. Musician to Prince Henry and to Chas. I.
Famous for his madrigal, "Since first I saw your face."

Foreign. Not in the key ; as *Foreign chord, Foreign note.*

Forestroke. "An incidental note striking on an accented pulse or on the first part of a pulse."—*Curwen.*
Forestrokes are (1) horizontal, (2) oblique, (3) waving, or (4) unprepared.

FORKEL, Johann N. Famous mus. historian ; *b.* nr. Coburg, 1749 ; *d.* 1818. University orgst. and Mus. Director, Göttingen (1778).
Chief works : *Musikalisch-Kritische Bibliothek* (3 vols. 1778-9), *Allgemeine Geschichte der Musik* (2 vols.), *Allgemeine Litteratur der Musik* (1792, the first work of its kind), and a celebrated *Life of J. S. Bach* (1803).

Forla'na (*I.*). ⎫ A lively Italian dance in 6-8
Forlane (*F.*). ⎬ (or 6-4) time.

Form. The design, plan, or structure of a musical composition. "The shape and order in which musical ideas are presented."—*Stainer and Barrett.*
The chief factors of musical form are—
I. EXPOSITION : the orderly setting out of melody (See *Melody*) in portions of definite lengths (See *Metrical Form*), with a proper balance of keys and cadences, and with appropriate harmonies and accompaniments.
II. DEVELOPMENT. (See *Thematic Development.*)
III. RECAPITULATION : the repetition of the *Exposition*, either exactly as before, or with some variation of key, mode, *tempo*, or development.
Unity of design includes (1) *Mechanical Symmetry*, and (2) *Æsthetic Symmetry.*

The principal musical forms are (1) **Aria,** (2) **Canon** and **Fugue,** (3) **Minuet,** (4) **Overture,** (5) **Rondo,** (6) **Sonata** (including *Concerto, Symphony, Quartet, Quintet, Sextet, Septet,* and *Octet*), (7) **Song,** and (8) **Suite.** (See each under its own heading.)
(See also Allemande, Anthem, Arioso, Ballad, Bergamasca, Bolero, Bourrée, Cachucha, Capriccio, Cavatina, Chaconne, Chanson, Concert-stück, Country Dance, Courante, Etude, Fandango, Fantasia, Gavotte, Gigue, Glee, Ground Bass, Hornpipe, Hymn, Idyll, Impromptu, Intermezzo, Lied, Madrigal, March, Mazurka, Motet, Musette, Nocturne, Passacaglio, Pastoral, Polka, Polonaise, Potpourri, Prelude, Recitative, Reel, Rigadoon, Saltarello, Sarabande, Scherzo, Schottisch, Serenade, Siciliano, Sketch, Tarantella, Toccata, Trio, Variations, and Waltz.)

The higher forms have reached such a point of elaboration that much study is necessary to analyse and appreciate their structure and development. For the simpler forms of composition, however, the only indispensable requisite is *a proper balance of keys,* together with some amount of *metrical proportion.*
Musical form, as we now understand it, is of quite recent date. The old Latin melodies—except that they were written to hymns of formal construction and based on definite church modes—had very little of what can be called "form." Most of them appear to modern ears as "aimless wanderings among sounds ! " With the growth of counterpoint, the *motet* and *madrigal* assumed symmetry and proportion, and were at their best towards the end of the 16th cent. (See *Counterpoint, Golden Age of.*) In the meantime the secular music of the people began to foreshadow certain essentials of form, especially in regard to definite *tonality*, balance of *melodic outline*, and *metrical uniformity.*

The growth of modern forms dates from the invention of the new style of composition, about the year 1600. (See *Bardi, Caccini, Cavaliere,* and *Peri*). The *Aria da Capo,* invented by B. Ferrari (1597-1681), and used by Cavalli, was perfected by A. Scarlatti (1650-1725). The *Fugue* — gradually developed — reached its highest point with J. S. Bach. Bach (and Handel) also brought the *Suite* to its full development. The *Sonata*—the "classical form" *par excellence*—was moulded by Haydn and perfected by Mozart and Beethoven. The beauty and symmetry of this form were at once universally recognized, and its effect has ever since been felt in the shaping of all kinds of compositions, both instrumental and vocal.
Since the time of Beethoven the chief addition to musical forms has been the application of the *Leit-motiv*—especially by Wagner—to dramatic composition. (See *Leit-motiv.*)

Forma're il tuo'no (*I.*).   (See **Messa di voce.**)

FOR'MES, Karl J. Bass singer ; *b.* Mühlheim-on-Rhine, 1816 ; *d.* 1889.
Début as "Sarastro" in Mozart's *Magic Flute* (1841) ; sang in London, 1852-7.

FOR'MES, Theodor. Tenor singer ; brother of K. J. ; 1826-74.
After a brilliant career, died insane.

FORNA'RI, Vincenzo. Operatic composer ; *b.* Naples, 1848 ; *d.* 1900.
Works : several operas (most successful, *Un dramma in Vendemmia,* Florence, 1896).

FÖR'NER, Christian. Wettin, 1610-78. Organ builder ; invented the "windgauge," abt. 1675.

FOR'STER, Wm. (Senr.). Vn. maker ; *b.* Brampton, Cumberland, 1739 ; *d.* London, 1808 (where he established himself as a publisher and vn. maker, 1781).
His 'cellos and double basses—copies of Stainer and Amati—are rare and valuable.

FOR'STER, Wm. (Junr.). Son of preceding ; 1764-1824. Made some very fine vns.

FÖR'STER, A. M. (See **Foerster.**)

FÖR'STER, Alban. *B.* Saxony, 1849. Violinist and composer.
Works : operas (*Die Mädchen von Schilda,* &c.); orchestral pieces, chamber music, violin pieces, pf. pieces, and songs.

FÖR'STER, Christoph. Thuringian organist ; 1693-1745. Capellmeister, Rudolstadt, 1745.
Works : cantatas, overtures, symphonies, organ pieces, pf. pieces, &c. ; over 300 in all.

FÖR'STER, Emanuel A. Silesian composer and theorist ; *b.* 1748 ; *d.* Vienna, 1823.
Works : a notturno for strings and wind, 48 string quintets and quartets, a pf. sextet, pf. quartets, pf. sonatas, &c.

Fort *G.*). Off ; as *Flöte fort,* "flute off" (org. music).

Fort (*F.*). (1) Loud ; (2) strong ; (3) skilful, eminent.
Temps fort. The strong beat.

For'te (*I.*). Loud ; abbr. *f* or *for.*
For'te l'appoggiatu'ra. Strongly accent the appoggiatura.
Fortemen'te. Loudly, vigorously.
For'te-pia'no. Suddenly loud, then soft ; abbr. *fp* (*ffp, sfp*).
For'te possi'bile. As loud as possible.
Fortis'simo. Very loud ; *ff.*

Fortissis'simo. As loud as possible ; *fff,* or *ffff.*
Più forte. Louder.
Po'co for'te. "A little loud ;" rather loud.

For'te (*I.*). (1) Any loud passage or piece. (2) A device on the harmonium to produce a *forte* effect.

For'tepia'no (*I.*). Older Italian form (still used in Russia) of the word *Pianoforte.*

Fort'fahrend (*G.*). Resuming, going on.

FÖRTSCH, Johann P. Franconian physician, singer, and composer ; 1652-1732.
Wrote 12 operas, several concertos for clavichord, &c.

Fort'schreiten (*G.*). To progress.
Fort'schreitung. Progression.
Fort'schreitung einer Dissonanz'. The resolution of a dissonance (discord).

Fort'setzung (*G.*). Development, continuation, or expansion of a theme.

"Forty-eight, The." Bach's 48 Preludes and Fugues for the "well-tempered clavier."

Forty Parts.
With the development of counterpoint it was naturally considered a great achievement to be able to write in a multitude of parts—40 parts in particular being regarded as a veritable triumph of genius ! (See *Tallis.*) It is now very properly thought to be much better to write *four interesting parts* than any number of mechanical and uninteresting ones !

For'za (*I.*). Force, emphasis, energy.
Con for'za. With force and energy.

Forzan'do, Forza'to (*I.*). "Forcing, straining." Strongly accented ; *fz, ffz.* Also *Sforzando* and *Rinforzando ; sf, sfz, sff, rf.* Signs >, ∨, ∧.

Forzar' la vo'ce (*I.*). To force the voice.

Fougeux,-euse (*F.*). Ardent, impetuous.

FOSTER, Muriel (**Mad. L. Goetz**). Contralto singer ; *b.* Sunderland, 1877.

FOSTER, Myles Birket. *B.* London, 1851. Orgt. Foundling Hospital, 1880-92.
Works : services and anthems, several children's cantatas, songs, &c.

FOSTER, Stephen Collins. "Unique among American composers as a writer of songs." *B.* Lawrenceville (Pittsburg), 1826 ; *d.* 1864. Chiefly self-taught.
His numerous songs (over 160 published) include "My old Kentucky Home," "Old Dog Tray," "Willie, we have missed you," "Come where my love lies dreaming," "The Swanee River," and "Beautiful Dreamer" (his last, 1864).

FOULDS, J. H. 'Cellist and composer ; *b.* Manchester, 1880.

Foundation Chords. The triads of the tonic, dominant, and sub-dominant in any major or minor key.

Foundation Stops. (See **Organ.**)

FOUQUÉ, Pierre Octave. Distinguished French critic and writer ; 1844-83.
Wrote on "English Music before Handel," and a biography of Glinka ; musical critic to the chief Parisian papers.

Fourchette tonique (*F.*). A tuning-fork.

Fourlane (*F.*). Same as **Forlana** (*q.v.*).

FOURNEAU, Léon ("**Xanrof**"). Composer ; *b.* Paris, 1867.

FOURNIER, Pierre S. Maker of music type ; Paris, 1712-68.
Introduced round-headed notes in place of lozenge-shaped ones.

Fourniture (*F.*). A mixture-stop on the org.

Four Removes. A key with its tonic a major 3rd higher or lower than that of the original key ; as C to E ; C to A♭.

Fourth. (*G.*, *Quar'te* ; *F.*, *Quarte* ; *I.*, *Quar'ta.*) An interval comprising four letter-names or degrees. (See **Interval.**)

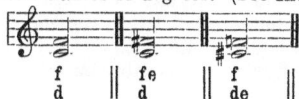

| f | | fe | | f | |
| d | | d | | de | |

Perfect 4th. Augmented 4th. Diminished 4th.

Defective fourth. Diminished.
Extreme (Extreme sharp) fourth. Augmented.
False fourth. ⎫
Flat fourth. ⎬ Diminished.
Major fourth. A perfect fourth.
Minor fourth. A diminished fourth.
Normal fourth. Perfect.
Pluperfect fourth ⎫
Redundant fourth ⎬ Augmented.
Sharp fourth ⎪
Superfluous fourth ⎭

FOWLES, Ernest. Pianist and composer ; *b.* Portsmouth, 1864.

FOX, George. English composer and singer ; *b.* abt. 1854 ; *d.* 1902.
Wrote *Robert Macaire*, *The Corsican Brothers*, and other operettas.

fp, fpp. Forte-piano ; forte-pianissimo. Loud, then immediately soft (over single notes or chords). (See **Explosive Tone.**)

FRANC, Guillaume. Contributor of tunes to Marot's Psalter, 1545. (See **Hymn.**)
He possibly composed the "Old 100th."

Française (*F.*). "French." A dance in triple time similar to the *Country-dance*.

Francamen'te (*I.*). With freedom ; boldly.

FRANCHET'TI, Baron Alberto. *B.* Turin, 1860. Operatic composer.
Most successful operas : *Asraële* (1888), *Colombo* (1892).

Franchez'za (*I.*) ⎫ Freedom, confidence,
Franchise (*F.*) ⎭ boldness.

FRANCHI'NUS. (See **Gafori.**)

FRANCHI-VERNEY, Giuseppe J., Count of Valetta. Composer and writer ; *b.* Turin, 1848. Established the "Accademia di Canto corale," 1876. Wrote a sketch of Donizetti (1897), and contributes to several musical papers.
His most successful composition is a ballet, *Il Mulatto* (Naples, 1896).

FRANCHOMME, Auguste. Celebrated 'cellist ; friend of Chopin. *B.* Lille, 1808 ; *d*, Paris, 1884. Studied Paris Cons., where he became 'cello teacher, 1846.
Wrote a concerto, variations, nocturnes, studies, &c., for 'cello.

FRANCK, César Auguste. One of the most distinguished of modern French composers. *B.* Liége, 1822 ; *d.* Paris, 1890.

At Paris Cons. took 1st prize for pf. playing (1838), and 2nd prize for composition (1839). Succeeded Benoist as Prof. of organ, 1872.
Works : symphonic poem, *Les Béatitudes* (his finest work) ; opera, *Hulda* (1894) ; oratorios, (*Ruth et Boaz* and *La Redemption*), symphonies, sonatas, chamber music, pf. pieces, songs, &c.

FRANCK, Eduard. *B.* Breslau, 1817 ; *d*, 1893. Pf. teacher and composer.
Works : a symphony ; a pf. concerto, a 'cello sonata, pf. sonatas, pf. duos, &c.

FRANCK, Joseph. Brother of C. A. B. Liége, abt. 1820. Parisian organist and teacher.
Works : cantatas, masses, motets, &c.; also two Manuals on Plain-song, a "Treatise of Harmony," and a "New Pianoforte Method."

FRANCK, Melchior. *B.* Zittau, abt. 1580 ; *d.* Coburg, 1639 (as Court Capellmeister.)
A voluminous and prolific composer of sacred and secular music, including psalms, magnificats, chorals, lieder (songs), melodies, duos, recreations, threnodies, convivial songs, &c., all of great antiquarian interest. "He did much to improve the instrumental accompaniment to songs."—*Grove.*

⎰ **FRANCO of Paris.** About 1100 (?).
⎱ **FRANCO of Cologne.** Prior of Cologne Benedictine Abbey, abt. 1260.
Both were progressive musicians who introduced improvements in notation. Franco of Cologne was the author of a famous work on Mensurable Music. (See *Mensurable Music.*)

FRANCŒUR, François. Paris, 1698-1787. Chamber musician to the King, one of the "24 violons du roi ;" Director of the Opéra (1751). Works : 10 operas (with Rebel), and 2 vols. of violin sonatas.

FRANCŒUR, Louis J. Violinist ; nephew of F. Paris, 1738-1804. Member of the Opéra orch. ; later, conductor and director.
Works : opera, *Ismène et Lindor*, &c.

FRANK, Ernst. *B.* Munich, 1847 ; *d.* insane, 1889. Capellmeister, operaconductor, &c., at Würzburg, Vienna, Mainheim, Frankfort, and Hanover.
Works : 3 operas (*Adam de la Halle*, *Hero*, and *Der Sturm*), and several beautiful songs.

FRANKENBERGER, Heinrich. Violinist ; *b.* Wümbach, 1824 ; *d.* 1885.
Works : 3 operas ; treatises on Instrumentation, Harmony, the Organ, &c.

FRANKLIN, Benjamin. *B.* Boston, Mass., 1706 ; *d.* 1790.
Invented the Harmonica (or "musical glasses"), and wrote on various musical subjects.

FRANSEL'LA, Albert L. Flautist and condr.; *b.* Amsterdam, 1865.

FRANZ, Robert. Celebrated song composer ; Halle, 1815-92. Pub. his first set of songs — "warmly praised by Schumann, Liszt, and Mendelssohn"— in 1843. Conductor of the Singakademie, and music-director, Halle University, to 1868.
Works : 257 songs, 117th Psalm (for double chorus *a cappella*), 12 part-songs, &c. ; and revisions with additional accompaniments of works by Bach and Handel.

FRANZL, Ferdinand. Violinist ; *b*. Palatinate, *1770* ; *d*. *1833*. Court Capellmeister, Munich, 1806-27.
Works : several concertos for violin, orchestral music, chamber music, songs, &c., and 6 operas.

Franz'ton (*G.*). French pitch. (See **Pitch.**)

Frappé (*F.*). "Struck, beaten." The down beat. *Levé*, up-beat.

Fra sè (*I.*). To one's self ; aside.

Fra'se (*I.*). A phrase. (See **Phrasing.**)
Fra'se lar'ga. In a broad style of phrasing.
Fraseggia're. To phrase.
Fra'si. Phrases.

Frau'enchor (*G.*). A female chorus.
Frau'enstimmen. Female voices.

FRAU'SCHER, Moritz. Operatic vocalist ; *b*. Austria, 1861.

Fred'do,-a (*I.*). Cold.
Freddamen'te } With coldness, indifference.
Con freddez'za }

FREDERICK II ("the Great"), of Prussia ; 1712-1786. Patron of music, composer, and skilful flautist. (See **K. P. E. Bach, Quantz,** and **Graun.**)

Fredon (*F.*). Old term for *vibrato* (*q.v.*). Also used for any extemporized vocal ornamentation.
Fredonnement. Trilling, warbling, humming.
Fredonner. To trill, hum, &c.

Free. (1) Not fettered by strict rule. (2) Abounding in violations of rules.
Free fugue. (See **Fugue.**)
Free parts. Parts added to a Canon or Fugue to complete the harmony.
Free reed. (See **Reed.**)
Free style. The modern "Harmonic" style, with all its freedom of progressions, &c., as opposed to the ancient "contrapuntal" style.

Fregiatu'ra (*I.*). An embellishment, grace.

Frei (*G.*). Free.
Frei'heit. A license, or freedom.
Frei'e Schreib'art. Free writing ; music in "Free Style."

Frei'em (*G.*). Freedom, boldness.
Mit Frei'em. With freedom ; boldly.

FREI'SCHÜTZ, DER. Romantic opera by Weber ; 1821.

Fremen'te (*I.*). Furiously.

Fremissement (*F.*). Humming ; singing in a low voice.

French flat tuning. (See **Pitch** and **Tuning.**)

French horn. (See **Horn.**)

French Music. Grace, piquancy, freshness, *sparkle*, are in general the characteristics of French music.
The following are the chief French composers (including Lully, Gluck, Meyerbeer, and Cherubini), who composed their best music in France) : De Meurs (1300?-1370?), Dufay (1400?-74), Okeghem (1430?-1496), Goudimel (abt. 1505-1572), Cambert (1628?-77), Lulli (Lully) (1633-87), Campra (1660-1738), Rameau (1683-1764), Rousseau(1712-78), Gluck(1714-87), Grétry (1741-1813), Cherubini (1760-1842), Méhul (1763-1817), Destouches (1772-1844), Nicolo (1775-1818), Boieldieu (1775-1834), Auber (1782-1871), Fétis (1784-1871), Hérold (1791-1833), Meyerbeer (1791-1864), Halévy (1799-1862), A. Adam (1803-56), Berlioz (1803-69), Felicien David (1810-76), Ambroise Thomas (1811-96), L. Wely (1817-70), Maillart (1817-71), Gounod (1818-93), Offenbach (1819-80), Massé (1822-84), César Franck (1822-90), Reyer (1823-), Gevaert (1828-), Lalo (1830-92), Lecocq (1832-), Saint-Saens (1835-), Delibes (1836-91), Dubois (1837-), Guilmant (1837-), Bizet (1838-75), Chabrier (1841-94), V. A Duvernoy (1842-), Massenet (1842-), Audran (1842-1901), Paladilhe (1844-), Widor (1845-), Salvayre (1847-), Planquette (1850-), Thomé (1850-), Pugno (1852-), Messager (1853-), G. Charpentier (1860-), Mlle. Chaminade (1861-) Leroux (1863-), Erlanger (1863-), Debussy (1862-).

French Sixth. (See **Extreme Sixth.**)

French Violin Clef. The G clef on the 1st line. (See **Clef.**)

FRÈNE, Eugène H. *B*. Strasburg, 1860 ; *d*. Paris, 1896.
Wrote a successful opera, *Quand on aime.*

Frene'tico (*I.*). Frantic(ally).

FRÈRE, Marguerite J. ("Hatto"). Soprano ; *b*. Lyons, 1879.

FRES'CHI, Giovanni Domenico. Vicenza, 1640-90.
Works : oratorio, (*Guiditta*), 11 operas, masses, &c.

Fres'co (*I.*). Fresh, cool.
Frescamen'te. Freshly, briskly.
Al fres'co. In the open air.

FRESCOBAL'DI, Girolamo. *B*. Ferrara, 1583 ; *d*. 1644. Pub. his first work, a colln. of madrigals, Antwerp, 1608. Orgt. St. Peter's, Rome, from 1608 to his death ; "his fame was already such, that 30,000 people are said to have attended his first performance." —*Baker*. He was the greatest Italian organist of his time, and an excellent composer.
Works : madrigals, canzoni, lamentations, magnificats, arias, &c. ; and a large number of organ pieces (toccatas, fugues, capriccios, &c.). He has been called the "Father of the organ voluntary."

Fret. (*G., Bund ; F., Touche ; I., Tas'to.*) One of the small ridges across the fingerboard of a mandoline, &c., to shorten the strings as required.

Fretel, Fretèle (*E.*). A sylvan, or Pan's pipe, with seven reeds.

Fret'ta (*I.*). Speed, haste, hurry.
Con fret'ta. With speed, &c.
Frette'vole }
Frettolo'so } Hurried, accelerated, quick.
Fretto'so }
Frettolosamen'te. Hurriedly, &c.

Freu'de (*G.*). Joy, rejoicing.
Freu'den-gesang'. A song of joy.
Freu'dig. Joyfully.

FREU'DENBERG, Wilhelm. *B*. Prussia, 1838. Opera conductor and composer. Founded a Cons., Wiesbaden, 1870.
Works : several operas, a symphonic poem, incidental music, songs, &c.

FREWIN, T. Harrison. Violinist and composer. "Balfe Scholar," R.A.M., 1885.
Works : orchl. pieces, vn. and pf. pieces, &c.

Fricassée (*F.*). A Parisian dance with pantomimic action (18th cent.).

FRICK'E, August G. L. *B*. Brunswick 1829 ; *d*. 1894. Bass singer ; *début* as

"Sarastro" (Mozart's *Magic Flute*), 1851. From 1856-86 principal bass, Berlin Court Opera.

FRICK'ENHAUS, Fanny (*née* Evans). Distinguished pianist; *b.* Cheltenham, 1849.

FRICKER, Anne. Song-writer; *b.* abt. 1820. Married Mr. Mogford.
Wrote a number of simple songs, once very popular (*Fading Away, Footprints in the Snow*, &c.).

FRICKER, Herbert A. *B.* Canterbury, 1868.
Mus.B. Durham, 1893. Orgt. Leeds Town Hall, since 1898; chorusmaster, Leeds Festival, 1904; condr. Leeds Municipal Orch., &c.

FRIED'HEIM, Arthur. Pianist; *b.* St. Petersburg, 1859.
Pupil of Liszt, whose pf. works he interprets with special distinction.

FRIED'LÄNDER, Arthur M. Composer; *b.* Clapham, 1868.

FRIED'LÄNDER, Max. Bass singer; *b.* Silesia, 1852. Pupil of Manuel Garcia, London. *Début,* Monday Popular Concerts, 1880.
Has written a biography of Schubert.

FRIED'RICH, Mad. (See **Amalie Materna.**)

Fries (*G.*). The purfling (of a vn., &c.).

FRIES, Wulf C. J. 'Cellist; *b.* Holstein, 1825. Went to Boston, 1847. Played in the Mendelssohn Quintet Club for 23 years (from 1849), and "took part in frequent concerts all over the New England States." He was also an excellent teacher. *D.* 1902.

Frisch (*G.*). Fresh, lively, vigorous.

FRITZ, Barthold. Brunswick, 1697-1766.
Celebrated self-taught maker of organs and clavichords.

FRIT'ZE, Wilhelm. Pianist and composer; *b.* Bremen, 1842; *d.* 1881.
Works: 2 oratorios, vn. concerto, pf. concerto, pf. pieces, songs, &c.

FRITZSCH, Ernst Wilhelm. *B.* Lützen, 1840; *d.* 1902. Took over the music publishing firm of Bomnitz, Leipzig (1866), under his own name.
By his influence and writings he did much to advance the music of Wagner, Rheinberger, Grieg, Cornelius, and others, and to promote modern musical development.

Fri'volo (*I.*). Trivial, frivolous.

FRO'BERGER, Johann Jakob. The most famous German organist of the 17th cent.; *b.* abt. 1605; *d.* 1667. Court orgt., Vienna, 1637; studied under the renowned Frescobaldi, Rome, 1637-41; returned to his post at Vienna, 1641-5 (and again 1653-7). He also made long concert tours.
Organ works: toccatas, fantasias, canzoni, fugues, &c.

Froh'bewegt (*G.*). Gaily animated.

Froh'gesang (*G.*). A joyous song.

Fröh'lich (*G.*). Frolicsome; gay, joyous.

FRÖ(H)LICH, Joseph. Würzburg, 1780-1862. Founded the students' "Akademische Bande," out of which eventually grew the Royal School of Music.
Published a biography of Vogler, a Vocal Method, separate methods for all instruments, &c.

Froidement (*F.*). Coldly.

FRONTI'NI, F. P. *B.* Catania, 1860.
Works: operas (*Malia*, 1893); oratorio (*Samsone*); a collection of "Canti popolari Siciliani," &c.

Front'pfeifen (*G.*). The front or display pipes of an organ.

Frosch (*G.*). The nut (of a bow).
Am Frosch. "On the nut." "Bow as near the nut as possible."

FROSCH'AUER, Johann. Augsburg; end of 15th cent.
Believed to have been the first printer to print music with movable types.

FROST, Chas. Jos. Organist and composer; *b.* Westbury-on-Trym, 1848. Mus.D. Cantab. 1882. Org. prof. G.S.M. since 1880.
Works: sacred music, songs, organ pieces, &c.

FROST, Henry F. Musical critic and writer; *b.* London, 1848; *d.* 1901.
Musical critic, *Weekly Despatch, Athenæum, Standard,* &c.; wrote a biography of Schubert ("Great Musicians" series).

Frot'tola (*I.*). A comic ditty; a ballad.

FROTZ'LER, Carl. Precocious composer; *b.* Stockerau, Lower Austria, 1873. Pupil, Vienna Con-., 1888. Capellmeister, City Th., Linz-on-Danube, 1897.
Works: operas (*Arnelda, Mathias Corvinus,* &c.); a symphony, masses, orch. music, &c.

Früh'er (*G.*). Before, earlier.
Früh'eres Zeit'mass. The previous *tempo.*
Wie früh'er. As before.

Früh'lingslied (*G.*). A spring song.

FRY, Wm. Henry. *B.* Philadelphia, 1813; *d.* 1864. For several years mus. critic *New York Tribune.*
Works: 2 operas, symphonies, cantatas, songs.

ften. (See **Tenuto.**)

F-Schlüs'sel (*G.*). The F clef (See **Clef.**)

FUCHS, Albert. Composer; *b.* Basle, 1858.

FUCHS, Anton. Operatic baritone; *b.* Munich, 1849.

FUCHS, Ferdinand K. Vienna, 1811-48.
Wrote 3 operas and several popular songs.

FUCHS, Joh. Nepomuk. *B.* Styria, 1842; *d.* 1899. Director, Vienna Cons., 1893.
Wrote an opera (*Zingara*), arranged for performance Handel's *Almira*, Schubert's *Alfonso and Estrella,* and Gluck's *Der betrogene Cadi.*

FUCHS, Karl D. J. Pianist, teacher, writer, and critic; *b.* Potsdam, 1838.
Works: valuable treatises on pf. technique, &c.

FUCHS, Robert. Brother of J. N. *B.* Styria, 1847. Prof. of theory, Vienna Cons., since 1875.
Works: 3 interesting serenades for strings, a symphony, chamber music, pf. music, 2 operas, &c.

FUEN'TES, Don Pasquale. Distinguished church composer; *b.* Albayda, Valencia, early part of 18th cent.; *d.* 1768.

FUER'TES, M. Soriano. (See **Soriano.**)

Fu′ga (*L.* and *I.*). A fugue.

Fu′ga ad octa′vam (*L.*). (See *Octave fugue.*)

Fu′ga ad quin′tam (*L.*). Fugue at the 5th ; *i.e.,* the ordinary interval of reply. (See *Fugue.*)

Fu′ga aequa′lis mo′tus (*L.*). A real fugue. (See *Fugue.*)

Fug′a al contra′rio (*L.*). ⎫ A fugue by inversion.
Fu′ga al rever′so (*I.*). ⎬ (See *Inversion.*)
Fu′ga al rove′scio (*I.*). ⎭

Fu′ga authen′tica (*L.*). With an authentic subject. (See *Authentic* and *Mode.*)

Fu′ga cano′nica (*L.*). A fugue in canon.

Fu′ga compo′sita (*L.*). Subject moves by conjunct degrees.

Fu′ga contra′ria (*L.*). A fugue by inversion.

Fu′ga del tuo′no (*I.*). A tonal fugue. (See *Fugue.*)

Fu′ga dop′pia (*I.*). A double fugue.

Fu′ga homopho′na (*L.*). With answer at the unison. A canon at the unison.

Fu′ga impro′pria (*L.*). A free fugue.

Fu′ga inaequa′lis (*L.*). A fugue by inversion.

Fu′ga incompo′sita (*L.*). Subject moves by skips (disjunct degrees).

Fu′ga in consequen′za (*I.*). A canon.

Fu′ga in contra′rio tem′pore (*L.*). With the subject and answer differently accented.

Fu′ga in no′mine (*L.*). A free fugue ; one "in name" only.

Fu′ga irregula′ris (*L.*). An irregular or free fugue.

Fu′ga li′bera (*L.* and *I.*). A free fugue.

Fu′ga liga′ta (*L.* and *I.*). "Tied ; bound." Entirely developed from subject and countersubject— without episodes.

Fu′ga mix′ta (*L.*). Employing various devices. (See *Fugue*: "Bach's B♭ minor.")

Fu′ga obbliga′ta (*I.*). (See *Fuga ligata.*)

Fu′ga ostina′ta (*I.*). A fugue maintaining a definite figure.

Fu′ga partia′lis (*L.*). A fugue proper as opposed to a canon.

Fu′ga per ar′sin et the′sin (*L.*). By inversion of accent or interval.

Fu′ga per augmentatio′nem (*L.*). Theme augmented. (See *Augmentation.*)

Fu′ga per diminutio′nem (*L.*). Theme diminished (See *Diminution.*)

Fu′ga per imitatio′nem interrup′tam (*L.*). The answer interrupted by breaks (or rests).

Fu′ga per mo′tum contra′rium (*L.*). By inversion.

Fu′ga perio′dica (*L.*). (See *Fuga partialis.*)

Fu′ga perpet′ua (*L.*). A canon (infinite).

Fu′ga plaga′lis (*L.*). With a plagal subject. (See *Authentic* and *Mode.*)

Fu′ga pro′pria (*L.*). A fugue in regular form.

Fu′ga rea′le (*I.*). ⎱ A real fugue. (See *Fugue.*)
Fu′ga rec′ta (*L.* ⎰

Fu′ga reddi′ta (*redita*) (*I.*). A fugue including a strict canon.

Fu′ga regula′ris (*L.*). A fugue in regular form.

Fu′ga retrogra′da (*L.*). Fugue by contrary motion.

Fu′ga ricerca′ta (*I.*). A strict scientific or "school" fugue, without episodes.

Fu′ga sciol′ta (*I.*). ⎱ A free fugue.
Fu′ga solu′ta (*L.*). ⎰

Fu′ga tota′lis (*L.*). A canon.

Fu′ga a tre vo′ci, con alcu′ne licen′ze (*I.*). Three-part fugue, with some licenses (*Beethoven*).

Fugal Imitation. (See **Imitation,** and **Fugue.**)

Fuga′ra. An organ stop ; a kind of *gamba* of 8 ft. or 4 ft. tone.

Fuga′to (*I.*). (1) In fugal style. (2) A short piece comprising free fugal imitations.

Fu′ge (*G.*). A fugue.

Fuggi′re la caden′za (*I.*). "To avoid the cadence." An interrupted cadence.

Fughet′ta (*I.*). ⎱
Fughet′to (*I.*). ⎬ A short fugue.
Fughet′te (*G.*). ⎰

Fugue. (*G., Fu′ge ; F., Fugue ; I.,* and *L., Fu′ga,* "a flight.") A composition developed from one or more short themes

according to the rules of counterpoint, and with the underlying principle of all the parts being equally important.

> " All that a good composer ought to know may find its place in a fugue ; it is the type of every piece of music ;....it should include all the resources of counterpoint,....and many other artifices peculiar to itself."—*Cherubini.*

The essential elements of a fugue are (1) the SUBJECT, (2) the ANSWER, and (3) the COUNTERSUBJECT.*

> The *Subject* is usually a short definite theme of from 4 to 8 bars.
>
> The *Answer* is the transposition of the Subject *into the Key of the Dominant.*
>
> If the answer is an exact repeat of the subject it is said to be a *Real* answer, and the fugue is a *Real* fugue.
>
> If slight modifications are made to allow of the original *tonic* being answered by its *dominant,* and *vice versa,* the answer is *Tonal,* and the fugue a *Tonal* fugue.

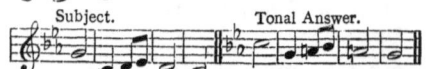

The *Countersubject* is the part which accompanies the *Answer* at its first entry. It is usually a continuation of the Subject, and is generally written in Double Counterpoint, so that it may be used regularly above or below the Subject and Answer at each successive entry :—

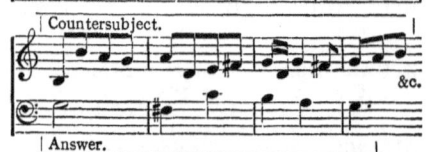

If the fugue is written in more than two parts other accompanying counterpoints are added as the various parts enter.

Other prominent—but not absolutely necessary—features of fugue are (1) EPISODE, (2) STRETTO, and (3) PEDAL (or ORGAN-POINT).

> *Episodes* are connective passages generally based on some fragment of the subject or countersubject, but they may be entirely new.
>
> *Stretto* is the bringing closer together of the entries of Subject and Answer :—

Cherubini enumerates the following "artifices" which may be employed in fugue :—

(1) Imitations of every kind. (See *Canon,* and *Imitation.*)

(2) Double Counterpoint. (See *Counterpoint.*)

(3) Inversion of the subject by contrary motion.

* Of Bach's " 48," 18 have no *regular* countersubject.

(4) Introduction of a new subject, which may be combined with the first subject and counter-subject.

(5) Combining the stretto in various ways.

(6) Using the subject and its inversion together in contrary motion.

(7) Combining subject, countersubject, and stretto on a pedal.

(8) Augmentation or Diminution of the subject.

"We must, however, make a choice, and not introduce them all ; . . . . the fugue would be too long. . . . and tiresome."—*Cherubini.*

To these well-known "artifices" every great composer adds others of his own invention. It follows, therefore, that hardly any two fugues are cast in precisely the same mould. The majority of "strict" fugues, however, conform more or less closely to the following general scheme.

(1) THE EXPOSITION, or first enunciation of the theme by all the parts in turn ; sometimes with an additional or "redundant" entry.

This may be followed by an *Episode,* and (in a very long fugue) by a *Counter-Exposition* in which the entries are in the same keys but in a varied order of parts.

(2) THE MIDDLE GROUP (of ENTRIES).

In a *major* fugue most of the entries in this part are in related minor keys ; in a *minor* fugue, in related major keys. The whole is freer in style ; foreshadowings of the stretto may appear ; a fresh countersubject is often employed ; the episodes are generally more fully developed ; inversions of the subject and other devices are introduced at pleasure.

(3) THE FINAL GROUP.

This includes various forms of stretto (if the subject admits of any), the closest imitations and overlappings being left until last.

If a "*Pedal-point*" is introduced, it generally occurs near the end of the stretti, the most involved imitations being taken "on the pedal." A short *Coda* often completes this part.

It will be seen from the above that "the interest of a fugue should grow from start to finish."

The following skeleton sketch-plan of Bach's Fugue for 4 voices (*i.e.* parts) in Bb minor (No. 22, Bk. II of the 48 Preludes and Fugues) differs considerably from the above. It is an example of a free yet perfectly consistent "fugue-form."

N.B.—The accompanying parts abound in the most scholarly imitations, &c., but only the entries of Subject and Answer are shown here.

(*a*) EXPOSITION.

(1) Subject in Alto, key Bb minor, bars 1–4.

(2) Answer in Treble, key F minor, bars 4–8.

(3) Subject in Bass, key Bb minor, bars 11–14.

(4) Answer in Tenor, keys F minor, bars 17–20.

(5) Episode, bars 21–26.

(*b*) THE SUBJECT IN IMITATION.

(1) Subject, Bb minor, in Tenor ; imitated one minim later, at the 7th above, in the Alto, bars 27–30.

(2) Subject, Db major, in Treble ; imitated one minim later, at the 9th (16th) below, in the Bass ; bars 33–36.

(3) Episode, bars 37–41.

(*c*) EXPOSITION OF THE INVERTED SUBJECT.

(1) Inverted Subject in Tenor ; key Bb minor, bars 42–45.

(2) Inverted Subject (or Answer) in Alto ; key Eb minor ; bars 46–49.

(3) Inverted Subject in Treble ; Bb minor to Gb major ; bars 52–55.

(4) Inverted Subject in Bass ; Ab minor ; bars 58–61.

(5) Episode, bars 62–66.

(*d*) THE INVERTED SUBJECT IN IMITATION.

(1) Inverted Subject in Tenor, key Bb minor, imitated one minim later at the 9th above in Treble, bars 67–70.

(2) Inverted Answer in Alto, F min., imitated one minim later at the 7th (14th) below, in Bass ; bars 73–76.

(3) Episode, bars 77–79.

(*e*) SUBJECT AND INVERTED SUBJECT COMBINED.

(1) Inverted Subject in Treble ; Subject one minim later in Tenor ; bars 80–83.

(2) Subject in Bass ; Inverted Subject one minim later in Alto ; bars 89–92.

(3) Subject in 6ths (and 3rds) Treble and Alto ; Inverted Subject in 3rds, Tenor and Bass ; Bars 96–99.

Accompanied Fugue. A choral fugue with free instrumental accompaniments ; *e.g.,* "Behold, now total darkness " (Mendelssohn's *St. Paul*).

Antecedent. Another name for *Subject.*

Choral Fugue. A fugue for voices.

Close fugue. One in which the Answer follows the Subject — overlaps in *Stretto* style — from the beginning :—

Codet'ta (I.). A short connective passage tacked on to the end of the Subject (or Answer) to lead more effectively to the next *Entry.*

Co'mes (L.). ⎱ "Companion." Other names for
Consequent. ⎰ *Answer.*

Double Fugue. A Fugue with two Subjects ; *e.g.,* "We worship God" (Handel's *Judas*).

Dux (L.). "Guide" or "Leader." Another name for *Subject.*

Free Fugue. One in which all the rules are not rigidly observed.

Fugue renversee (F.). An inverted fugue.

Octave Fugue. One in which the Answer follows the Subject at the Octave, instead of at the 4th or 5th ; *e.g.,* "Where warlike Judas" (Handel's *Judas*).

Quadruple Fugue. A fugue on 4 subjects.

Real Fugue. (See *Fugue,* above.)

Strict Fugue. One in which all the rules are rigidly observed.

Tonal Fugue. (See *Fugue,* above.)

Triple Fugue. One on three subjects ; *e.g.,* "Quam olim Abrahae" (Cherubini's *Requiem in C minor*).

Fugal Chorus. One in which fugal imitations and other devices are employed at the composer's discretion. It is often a fugal "exposition" only with much free episodical matter. Handel's "Hallelujah Chorus," for example, comprises two fugal expositions, the second theme being also used in stretto. (See also *Fuga.*)

The following easily accessible fugues should be studied, in addition to those given above :

INSTRUMENTAL FUGUES. Bach's 48 Preludes and Fugues, Bach's Organ Fugues, Mendelssohn's Organ Fugues, Mozart's Overture to *Zauberflöte* (a fugue combined with Sonata Form), Schumann's Fugues on *Bach*.

CHORAL FUGUES AND FUGAL CHORUSES. *Pignus Futuræ* (Mozart's *Litany in B♭*) ; the Fugues in Mozart's *Requiem* ; "Awake the Harp," and "Achieved is the glorious work" (Haydn's *Creation*) ; Fugues and Fugal Choruses in Bach's *Mass in B minor,* and those in Handel's *Messiah, Samson, Jephtha, Israel in Egypt,* &c. ; also the Fugal Choruses in Mendelssohn's *Elijah, St. Paul,* and *Hymn of Praise,* and in Beethoven's *Mass in D.*

Füh'rer (*G.*). " Leader, director." The subject of a fugue.

Füh'rung. Leading, conducting, guiding.

Die füh'rende Stim'me. The leading voice (or part).

FÜH'RER, Robt. *B.* Prague, 1807 ; *d.* 1861. Capellmeister, Prague Cath., 1839-45. Works : 20 masses, many organ pieces, treatises on the organ, &c.

Fulgen'te (*I.*). Effulgent, bright ; brilliant.

Full. Complete ; for all the performers (or parts).

Full anthem. (See *Anthem.*)

Full band. A complete band ; the whole band.

Full cadence. ⎱ A perfect cadence. (See *Cadence.*)
Full close. ⎰

Full choir. (1) The whole choir. (2) Of an organ, "draw all the stops of the Choir Organ."

Full chord. A complete chord. A chord for the full orchestra and choir.

Full great. On the organ, "draw all the *Great* stops."

Full orchestra. A complete orchestra. (See *Orchestra.*)

Full organ. With all stops and couplers drawn.

Full score. A score with each vocal and instrumental part on a separate staff. (See *Score.*)

Full service. (1) A church service including the canticles sung in chorus. (2) A church service with all available accompanying music.

Full swell. "Draw all the stops of the *Swell* organ."

Full to fifteenth. "All stops except reeds and mixtures."

Füll (*G.*). Added, extra ; accessory.

Füll'flöte. An org. flute stop of full tone.

Füll'pfeife. A "dummy" organ pipe.

Füll'quinte. A loud, piercing, "quint" stop, only drawn when many foundation stops are used.

Füll'stelle. A part added to "fill up." (See *Filling up.*)

Füll'stimme. An accessory part.

Füll'stimmen. Accessory parts.

FUMAGAL'LI. Four brothers ; *b.* Inzago, Italy.

(1) **Disma ;** 1826-93. Prof. Milan Cons. ; wrote over 250 pf. pieces.

(2) **Adolfo ;** 1828-56. Pianist ; known as the "Paganini of the Pianoforte." Wrote " elegant " popular pf. pieces.

(3) **Polibio ;** 1830-1900. Wrote some fine organ sonatas.

(4) **Luca ;** *b.* 1837. Pianist ; has written an opera, drawing-room pf. music, &c.

FUMAGAL'LO, Mario L. Noted baritone ; *b.* Milan, 1864.

FU'MI, Vinceslao. Renowned Italian operaconductor ; 1823-80.

Works : opera (*Atala*), orchestral pieces, songs.

Fundamental. (1) The root of a chord. (2) The generator of a series of partials. (See **Acoustics.**)

Fundamental bass. (*G., Fundamental'bass.*) The "root" bass as distinguished from the "continued" bass (or ordinary figured bass part.) (See **Rameau.**)

Example from Rameau's *Principles of Composition* :—

N.B.—Rameau regarded the sub-dominant as the root of the "added 6th."

Fundamental chord. ⎱ A chord in its root (or "*a*")
Fundamental position. ⎰ position.

Fundamental'ton (G). (1) The root of a chord. (2) The tonic of a key. (Also *Grund'ton.*)

Fundamental tones. (1) Roots. (2) Generators. (3) Tonics.

Fundamental Discords. Term used in the Day-Macfarren system for a series of discords supposed to be derived from the "Chord of Nature" (see **Acoustics**), used on the Dominant, Supertonic, and Tonic of any major or minor key.

Fundamental discords need no preparation, as "Nature itself is presumed to have already prepared them." Reading upwards from the root, every fundamental discord implies a major 3rd, a perfect 5th, and a minor 7th, being in these respects identical with the dominant 7th chord. To these notes a major or minor 9th, an 11th, and a major or minor 13th, may be added. The complete series includes :—

(1) Dominant 7ths, 9ths, 11ths, and 13ths.

(2) Supertonic 7ths, 9ths, 11ths, and 13ths.

(3) Tonic 7ths, 9ths, 11ths, and 13ths.

(4) Augmented 6ths on the minor 2nd and minor 6th of the key (these being derived from *double-roots*). (See *Extreme Sixth.*)

All the Supertonic and Tonic discords belong to the list of "Borrowed Chords" (*q.v.*).

As complete 9ths, 11ths, and 13ths include more notes than can be used in 4 parts, one, two, or three of the notes are omitted, the number of various presentations and inversions of the chords being almost endless !

Simple rules for finding the root, which apply in most ordinary cases, are given by Prof. Prout :—

(1) If the combination includes diatonic notes only the root is the dominant.

(2) If it includes the sharpened 4th of the key—*fe* (or *re* in minor keys)—the root is the supertonic.

(3) If it includes the flattened 7th—*ta* (or *s* in minor)—the root is the tonic. (See also Macfarren's *Rudiments of Harmony.*)

Funèbre (*F.*).

Fune'bre (*I.*). } Funereal, dirge-like.

Funera'le (*I.*).

Marche funèbre (*F.*). A funeral march.

Fünf' (*G.*). Five.

Fünf'fach. Five-fold. An org. *mixture* of 5 ranks.

Fünf'stimmig. In five parts.

Fünf'stufige Ton'leiter. A pentatonic scale. (See *Pentatonic.*)

Funf'te (*G.*). A fifth.

Funzio'ni (*I.*). Functions, duties. Applied to the services, &c., of the Roman Church.

Fuo'co (*I.*). Fire, energy, spirit.

Con fuo'co } With fire, &c.
Fuoco'so }

Fuo'ri di sè (*I.*). As if dreaming ; absently.

Für (*G.*). For.

Für Harmonie'musik. For wind instruments.

Für die lin'ke Hand allein'. For the left hand alone.

Für die rech'te Hand allein'. For the right hand alone.

Fureur (*F.*).), **Fu'ria** (*I.*). Fury, rage, vehemence.

Con fu'ria (*I.*). }
Furibon'do (*I.*). }
Furiosamen'te (*I.*). } With fury, passion, rage, &c.
Furio'so (*I.*). }
Furiosis'simo (*I.*). With the utmost fury, &c.

Furiant, Furie. A spirited Bohemian dance with changing rhythm and accent.

Furla'na,-o. (See **Forlana.**)

FURLANET'TO, B. (Known as **Musin.**) Composer and singing teacher ; Venice, 1738-1817.

Wrote several oratorios and cantatas.

Furniture. A mixture-stop on the organ.

FUR'NO, Giovanni. *B.* Capua, 1748 ; *d.* 1837. Prof. of Compn. at various Italian schools of music.

Among his pupils were Bellini, Mercadente, Costa, Petrella, and Rossi.

Furo're (*I.*). (1) Fury, passion, &c. (2) Enthusiasm, passionate fondness.

Con furo're. With passionate enthusiasm, &c.

FURSCH-MA'DI, Emmy. *B.* Bayonne, 1847 ; *d.* 1894. Fine dramatic soprano ; a favourite in London and New York.

She created the *rôle* of "Aida" at Verdi's request, in his opera of that name.

Für'sich (*G.*). Aside.

FÜRST'ENAU, Anton B. Son of K. (below); *b.* Münster, 1792 ; *d.* 1852. "Solo concert-flautist from the age of 7."

Pub. some 150 valuable compositions for flute.

FÜRST'ENAU, Kaspar. *B.* Münster, 1772 ; *d.* 1819. Famous flautist ; pub. abt. 60 flute pieces.

FÜRST'ENAU, Moritz. Son of A. B. ; Dresden, 1824-89. Flautist and musical historian ; fl. teacher Dresden Cons., from 1858.

Works : historical treatises on church music, operatic music, the construction of musical instruments, &c.

Fu'sa (*L.*). A quaver, or 8th note, ♪

Fusée (*F.*). A roulade, shake, rapid ascending or descending passage, slide, &c.

Fusel'la (*L.*). A semiquaver, ♫.

Fusel'lala. A dimisemiquaver, 𝅘𝅥𝅲

Fuss (*G.*). Foot.

Acht'füssig } 8-ft. ; unison pitch. (See *Acoustics.*)
8'-füssig }

Fuss'klavier. "Foot-klavier." (Organ) pedals.

Fuss'ton. "Foot-pitch ;" as 16-*Fuss'ton*, 16-ft. pitch.

FUSSELLE, Kate. Soprano vocalist ; pupil of Sainton-Dolby ; *b.* Harrow, 1860.

Füt'terung (*G.*). The "linings" of a vn., &c.

Future, Music of the. A term applied formerly to Wagner's music, and also to that of Liszt, Berlioz, &c.

FUX, Johann Joseph. Learned theorist ; *b.* Upper Styria, 1660 ; *d.* Vienna, 1741. First Capellmeister to the Vienna Court, 1715. This office—the highest position attainable by a musician—he held under 3 successive emperors.

Of his 405 works (including 18 operas, 10 oratorios, 50 masses, 57 vespers and psalms, 38 sacred sonatas, &c.), the most famous is his treatise on counterpoint, "Gradus ad Parnassum," which was studied by Mozart and Haydn, and recognised by Cherubini, Albrechtsberger, Martini, and Vogler. Though based on the old Church Modes, it may be regarded as the fountain-head of all contrapuntal systems.

Fz. Abbreviation of *Forzando* (*q.v.*).

G

G (*I.* and *F. Sol*). (1) The 5th note of the scale of C. (2) The 4th (lowest) string of the violin. (3) The *final* of the Mixo-Lydian Mode. (See **Mode.**)

Fiddle G. (See under *F.*)

G Clef. The treble clef

G dur (*G.*). The key of G major.

G major. The key or scale requiring one sharp; signature. The chord

G minor. The relative minor of B♭ major; signature. The chord

G moll (*G.*). The key of G minor.

G. (Abbn. of *gauche*). Left; *m.g.*, Left hand.

G. Great (organ).

G.O. (*Grand-orgue*.) Full organ.

G.-Schlüssel (*G.*). G clef.

Ga'bel (*G.*). A fork.

Ga'belklavier. A keyboard inst. with tuning-forks instead of strings.

Ga'belton. "Tuning-fork" tone; generally the A of a tuning-fork.

Ga'belgriffe. Cross-fingering.

Stimm'gabel. A tuning-fork.

GA'BRIEL, Mary A. Virginia. (**Mrs. G. E. March.**) *B.* Banstead, 1825; *d.* 1877. Wrote several songs, some of which are still sung ("Cleansing Fires," &c.).

GABRIE'LI, Andrea. Venice, 1510(?)-1586. Pupil of Willaert. Most eminent orgt. of his time; taught Leo Hassler.

Works: masses, psalms, madrigals, &c., and a large number of org. pieces.

GABRIE'LI, Domenico. Bologna, abt. 1640-90. Fine 'cellist; President Bologna Philharmonic Academy, 1683.

Works: 9 operas, motets, cantatas, and instrumental music.

GABRIE'LI, Giovanni. Venice, 1557-1612 (13)? Nephew of A. Organist of St. Mark's; chief composer of the Venetian School; teacher of H. Schütz.

Works: madrigals, "*Symphoniæ Sacræ*" (in from 6 to 19 real parts for voices and insts.), "Canzoni e sonate a 3-22 voci," choruses for 2 and 3 choirs, org. pieces, &c.

GABRIEL'LI, Catterina. Rome, 1730-96. Brilliant operatic singer, noted for her skill in *coloratura* (*q.v.*).

GABRIEL'LI, Francesca. *B.* Ferrara, 1755; *d.* 1795. Celebrated lady *buffa.* Sang in London, 1786.

GABRIEL'LI, Count Nicolo. Naples, 1814-91. Prolific writer of operas and ballets of no great merit.

GABRIEL'SKI, Johann W. 1791-1846.⎱
GABRIEL'SKI, Julius. 1806-78. ⎰
Brothers; distinguished flautists; members of the Berlin Royal Orch.

GABRILO'VITCH, Ossip S. Pianist; *b.* St. Petersburg, 1878.

GABUS'SI, Vincenzo. *B.* Bologna, 1800; *d.* London, 1846. Wrote several songs, which were once thought to rival Schubert's!

GA'DE, Niels Wilhelm. Copenhagen, 1817-90. Distinguished composer; "founder of the Scandinavian School of Music." Son of a joiner and inst. maker. Set to learn his father's trade at 15, but after 6 months gave it up for music. Joined the Court Orch., and at 16 appeared as concert violinist. Attracted general attention by his "Ossian" overture, 1840. Went to Leipzig, 1843, and became an intimate friend of Mendelssohn and Schumann. Conductor of the Gewandhaus Concerts at Mendelssohn's death, 1847. Returned to Copenhagen, 1848. Visited Birmingham, 1876, to conduct his works (*Zion* and *The Crusaders*). Voted a life pension by the Danish Government, 1876.

Works: orchestral overtures (*Ossian, Im Hochlande*, &c.); 8 symphonies; cantatas (*Zion, The Crusaders, Psyche*, &c.); string quartets, quintets, sonatas, &c.; a vn. concerto; klavierstücke; songs, part-songs, male choruses; pf. sonatas, arabesques, novelletten, &c.

GADSBY, Henry Robert. *B.* Hackney, 1842; *d.* 1907. Works: cantatas (*The Lord of the Isles, Columbus, The Cyclops*, &c.), overtures, church music, part-songs, &c.

GAD'SKI, Johanna E. A. (**Frau Tauscher.**) Fine soprano; *b.* Pomerania, 1871.

GAFU'RIUS, Franchinus. Also known as **Gaforio, Gafori, Gafuri,** and **Gaffurio.** Celebrated theorist; *b.* Lodi, 1451; *d.* Milan, 1522. Founded a music school, Milan, 1485. Chief work: "Practica Musicæ" (in 4 vols. with "mensural notation in Block print"), 1496.

Gagliar'da (*I.*). ⎱ A galliard (*q.v.*).
Gagliar'de (*G.*). ⎰

Gagliardamen'te (*I.*). ⎱ Briskly, merrily.
Gagliar'do (*I.*). ⎰

GAH'RICH, Wenzel. Bohemian composer; 1794-1864. Ballet master, Berlin Court Opera, 1845-60. Works: ballets, symphonies, dances, songs, &c.

Gai (*F.*). Gay, brisk, lively, joyous.

Gaiement. Gaily, briskly, merrily.

GAÏL, Edmée Sophie (*née* **Garre**). Paris, 1775-1819. Composer and singer. Wrote successful operas, songs, &c.

GAILHARD, Pierre. Noted operatic baritone; *b.* Toulouse, 1848.

Gaillarde (*F.*). A galliard (*q.v.*).

Gai'ta (*S.*). (1) A bagpipe. (2) A flageolet.

Gajamen'te (*I.*). Gaily, merrily.

Ga'jo,-a. Gay, merry, joyful.

Di ga'la. Merrily, gaily.

Galamment (*F.*). ⎱ Gallantly, gracefully,
Galantemen'te (*I.*). ⎰ in good taste.
Con galante'ria (*I.*).

GALANDIA. (See **Garlandia.**)

Galant,-e (*F.*), **Galan'te** (*I.*). Gallant, graceful, pretty.

Galant' (*G.*). Free.
Galan'te Fu'ge. A free fugue.
Galan'ter Stil. Free style (of composition).
Gebun'dener Stil. Old strict style (of composition).

GALEAZ'ZI, Francesco. Italian violinist, 1758-1819.
Wrote one of the first vn. methods (Rome, 1791).

GALILE'I, Vincenzo. Florence, abt. 1533-1600. Lutenist and violinist ; father of **Galileo Galilei**, the famous astronomer. One of the chief of Bardi's artistic circle who initiated the modern style. (See **Bardi, Caccini,** and **Peri.**)
Galilei's compositions for voice and lute are regarded as the starting point of the new style. He also wrote several interesting treatises on music.

GALIN, Pierre. French mathematician, 1786-1821. Originated the method of teaching afterwards carried out by Paris and Chevé. (See **Chevé.**)

GALI'TZIN, Nicholas B. Russian Prince. Patron of Beethoven, who dedicated some of his later compositions to him.

GALI'TZIN, Georg. Son of preceding. St. Petersburg, 1823 - 1872. Imperial Chamberlain.
Formed a choir of 70 boys, and an orchestra, with which he travelled in Europe and America giving concerts of Russian music. Wrote masses, orchestral pieces, &c.

GALLAY, Jacques F. *B.* Perpignan, 1795 ; *d.* 1864. Famous horn player ; Prof. Paris Cons., 1842.
Wrote concertos, quartets, études, nocturnes, &c., for horn ; and a "Complete Method" for the inst.

GALLAY, Jules. 1822-97. Wealthy French amateur.
Collected and published a number of valuable works on Lutes and Lute-playing.

GAL'LENBERG, Wenzel R. von. *B.* Vienna, 1783 ; *d.* 1839. Married Countess Guicciardi (to whom Beethoven dedicated his Sonata, Op. 27, No. 2).
Works : abt. 50 successful ballets and some pf. music.

GAL'LI, Amintore. *B.* Talamello (Rimini), 1848. Composer and writer.
Works : A useful treatise on "Harmony, Counterpoint, and Fugue," &c.

GAL'LI, Filippo. *B.* Rome, 1783 ; *d.* 1853. Fine *buffo* singer.
Rossini wrote several parts especially for him.

Gal'liard. (*G.*, *Gagliar'de ; F.. Gaillarde ; I.*, *Gagliar'da.*) An old French dance.
It was for 2 dancers, in 3-4 time, and of spirited though not rapid *tempo.* It was also called a *Romane'sca*, and is regarded as the precursor of the minuet. In Elizabethan music-books it always follows a Pavan.

GAL'LIARD, Johann E. *B.* Hanover, 1687 ; *d.* London, 1749. Oboe player ; orgt. at Somerset House.
Wrote cantatas, church music, and music to several masques and pantomimes.

GAL'LICO, Paolo. Pianist ; *b.* Trieste, 1868.

GALLI-MARIÉ, Célestine (*née* **Marié d'Isle**). Renowned mezzo ; *b.* Paris, 1840. Created the rôles of "Mignon" (1866) and "Carmen" (1875).

GAL'LO, Ignazio. Fine teacher ; pupil of A. Scarlatti. *B.* Naples, 1689 ; *d.* (?).

GAL'LUS, Jacobus. (Real name, **Jacob Händl.**) *B.* Carniola, abt. 1550 ; *d.* 1591.
"Eminent contemporary of Palestrina and Lassus." Wrote fine masses, motets, &c.

Gal'op. (*G.*, *Galopp'; F.*, *Galop, Galopade ; I.*, *Galop'po.*) A very lively round dance in 2-4 time.
It is supposed to be of German origin, and has been popular in France from the beginning of the 19th cent.

Galoubé, Galoubet (*F.*). A Provençal fife, with 3 finger-holes and a very shrill tone.

GALUP'PI, Baldassare. *B.* Burano, nr. Venice, 1706 ; *d.* 1785. (Known as **Il Buranel'lo**) Composer of comic operas and harpsichord music. Visited England, 1741.
Of his 54 operas the most successful was *Dorinda* (Venice, 1729).

Gam'ba. (1) A *Viola da Gamba* (*q.v.*). (2) An organ stop with a "stringy" pungent tone.
The pipes are of small scale, and "cut up high" at the mouth. Varieties are the *Bell-gamba* and *Cone-gamba.* Some modern organs have pedal stops of gamba tone (*Violone, Contrabass, Contraviolone*).

Gam'be (*G.*). (1) A leg. (2) A *Viola da Gamba* (*q.v.*).
Gam'benstimme. A gamba stop.
Gambet'te. An octave gamba stop (4 ft.).
Gambvio'le. Viola da gamba.

GAMBI'NI, Carlo A. Genoese composer ; 1819-65.
Works : an oratorio (*La Passione*) ; 4 operas, a symphonic ode, masses, pf. music, &c.

Gam'bist. A *Viola da Gamba* player.

GAMBLE, John. English violinist and composer ; 17th cent.
Published "Ayres and Dialogues," 1656 and 1659.

Gam'ma. (1) The Greek letter G. (2) The entire musical scale, or *Gamut.*
In mediæval music the name *Gamma* was given to the lowest note then used. This note being also the lowest *Ut* of Guido's system, became known as *Gamma-ut* or *Gamut.* (See *Alt, Guido,* and *Gamut.*)

Gamme (*F.*). (1) The whole musical scale, or *Gamut.* (2) A scale (used in the ordinary sense).
Gamme chromatique. Chromatic scale.
Gamme diatonique. Diatonic scale.
Gamme descendante. Descending scale.
Gamme montante. Ascending scale.

GAMUC'CI, Baldassare. Florence, 1822-92. Founded the "Società Corale del Carmine," 1849, which afterwards became an important branch of the Florence Musical Institute.
Works : masses, psalms, pf. pieces ; a treatise on the "Life and Works of Cherubini," &c.

Gam'ut. From *Gamma-ut*. (See **Gamma.**)
(1) The note G ♭⊜♯ (2) The entire musical scale. (3) The Staff.
(4) Old name for key G.
Also used by analogy for any complete range or compass, as "The whole gamut of human emotion."

Ganascio'ne (*I*.). A lute.

GANAS'SI, Silvestro. *B*. nr. Venice abt. 1500.
Wrote two works of great antiquarian interest—"A Method for Flute" (explaining the graces), and "A Method for Viola and Bass-viol."

GANDILLOT, Léon. *B*. Paris, 1862.
Writer of vaudevilles (*La Tortue, Madame Jalouette*, &c.).

GANDI'NI, Alessandro. Modena, 1807-71. Maestro to the Duke of Modena.
Works : 8 operas (*Demetrio*, 1828) ; "History of the Theatres of Modena from 1539 to 1871."

Gang (plur. *Gäng'e*) (*G*.). (1) A passage.
(2) Rate of movement.

GANNE, Louis G. *B*. 1862. Studied Paris Cons. Composer of light popular music.
Works : Comic opera (*Rabelais*) ; vaudevilles, ballets, operettas, pf. pieces, &c.

GÄNS'BACHER, Johann. *B*. Tyrol, 1778 ; *d*. Venice, 1844. Friend and fellow-pupil of Weber and Meyerbeer. Capellmeister of St. Stephen's, Vienna, 1823.
His 216 works include 15 masses, 4 requiems, a symphony, pf. pieces, songs, &c., few of which are of much value.

GANTIER, Felix. Pen-name of **S. R. Glover** (*q.v.*).

Ganz (*G*.). (1) Whole, complete. (2) Very.
Ganz' Note
Ganz'ze Takt'note. } A whole note, or semibreve.
Ganz'er Ton
Ganz'ton } A whole tone.
Ganz'ze stär'ke. Very loud.
Ganz lang'sam. Very slow.
Ganz lei'se. Quite soft.
Gänz'lich verkling'end. Completely dying away.
Ganz'es Werk. Full organ.
Ganz'schluss. Final cadence.

GANZ, Adolf. *B*. Mayence, 1796 ; *d*. London, 1870. Violinist and condr.

GANZ, Leopold. Brother of A. *B*. Mayence, 1810 ; *d*. 1869. Violinist. Concertmeister Berlin Court Orch., 1840.

GANZ, Moritz. Brother of the preceding. *B*. Mayence, 1806 ; *d*. 1868. Fine 'cellist ; member Berlin Court Orch.
Wrote some good 'cello music.

GANZ, Chevalier Wilhelm. Son of A. *B*. Mayence, 1833. Pianist and conductor. Prof. G.S.M.
Has written *Salon* pieces for pf.

GARAT, Pierre Jean. *B*. Basses-Pyrénées, 1764 ; *d*. Paris, 1823. A wonderful "tenor-baritone" singer ; for 20 years the foremost male singer on the French concert stage. Prof. of Singing Paris Cons. Teacher of Nourrit, Levasseur, and Ponchard.
Garat was destined for the law, but his musical inclinations developed early, and he was aided in his efforts by Count d'Artois and Queen Marie Antoinette.

GARAUDÉ, Alexis de. *B*. Nancy, 1779 ; *d*. 1852. Prof. of Singing, Paris Cons., 1816-41.
Works : a mass, chamber music, songs, solfeggi, a "Méthode de Chant," works on the piano and harmony, &c.

Gar'bo (*I*.). Elegance, gracefulness.
Garbatamen'te
Garba'to } In graceful, elegant style.
Con garbo }

GAR'CIA, Albert. Baritone ; son of G. *B*. London, 1877.

GAR'CIA, Don Francisco S. Known as "Padre Garcia." *B*. Nalda, Spain, 1731 ; *d*. 1809. Maestro Saragossa Cathedral, 1756.
Works : masses, motets, &c., mostly in 8 parts.

GAR'CIA, Gustave. Baritone ; son of M. P. R. *B*. Milan, 1837.

GAR'CIA, Manuel del Popolo Vicente. Celebrated tenor and teacher of singing. *B*. Seville, 1775 ; *d*. Paris, 1832. Chorister Seville Cath. at 6 ; singer, composer, and conductor at 17. After singing with great success in Paris and London, he toured with other distinguished artists in America and Mexico ; afterwards settling in Paris as a teacher. His two daughters, Madame **Malibran** and Madame **Pauline Viardot-Garcia**, were among the most celebrated singers of all time.
He wrote a large number of operas, ballets, &c., all now forgotten.

GAR'CIA, Manuel P. R. Son of preceding. *B*. Madrid, 1805 ; *d*. London, 1906. Started as a singing-teacher, Paris, 1829. Invented the *Laryngoscope*. Prof. Paris Cons., 1847. Settled in London, 1850. His most distinguished pupil was Jenny Lind.
His wife Eugénie (*née* **Mayer**), 1818-80, was an operatic soprano.

GAR'CIA, Marie Félicité. (See **Malibran.**)

GAR'CIA, Pauline. (See **Viardot-Garcia.**)

GARCIN, Jules A. S. French violinist and conductor ; 1830-96. Vn. prof. Paris Cons. from 1890.
Wrote a *Suite Symphonique* for orch. and several compositions for vn.

GARDA'NO (or **GARDA'NE**), **Antonio.** Venice, abt. 1500-1571 (?).
"One of the earliest and most celebrated Italian music printers."

GARDEN, Mary. *B*. Aberdeen, 1877. Soprano singer. *Début*, Paris, 1900.
Has sung in America, Paris, and London.

Garde Republicaine. Famous French military band.
Originated 1848 ; officially organised under Nap. III with 55 members ; now comprises 84 picked musicians, mostly prizemen from the Paris Cons. First performed in London, 1871.

Garder (*F*.). To keep, hold.
Gardez la sourdine. Keep (on) the mute.

GARDINER, Chas. Pianist ; *b*. Greenwich, 1836.

GARDINER, H. Balfour. Composer; *b.* London, 1877.

GARDINER, Wm. Leicester, 1770-1853. Clever amateur; published "The Music of Nature," 1832, and arrangements of Haydn, Mozart, and Beethoven.

GARDO'NI, Italo. *B.* Parma, 1821; *d.* 1882. "One of the most fascinating tenors that ever lived."—*Lavignac.*

Gariglio'ne (*I.*). A chime.

GARLANDIA, Johannes de. English author of works on plain-song and mensural music. Settled in France abt. 1210.

GARNIER, F. J. Vaucluse, 1759-1825 (?). 1st oboe player at the Paris Grand Opéra, 1786. Wrote a good "Méthode pour le hautbois."

GARRETT, George Mursell. *B.* Winchester, 1834; *d.* Cambridge, 1897. Orgt. St. John's Coll., Cambridge, 1857. Mus.Doc., 1867. Orgt. to the University. 1873. Works: oratorio (*The Shunammite*), services and other church music, org. pieces, &c.

Garri're (*I.*). To chirp, chatter, warble. *Garren'do.* Chattering, rustling, &c.

GASPA'RI, Gaetano. Bologna, 1807-81. Composer and musical historian. Librarian Bologna *Liceo Musicale*, 1855. Works: masses and other church music, and several historical treatises on musical subjects.

GASPARI'NI (or GUASPARINI), Francesco. *B.* nr. Lucca, 1668; *d.* Rome, 1737. Pupil of Corelli. Maestro Lateran, Rome, 1735. Teacher of B. Marcello. Works: a celebrated "Method of Thorough-Bass Playing," 40 successful operas, an oratorio (*Moses*), masses, motets, &c.

GASPARI'NI, Michelangelo. *B.* Lucca, 1685; *d.* 1732. Male contralto, and excellent singing teacher. Founded a singing school at Venice; teacher of Faustina Bordoni. He also wrote 5 operas (performed in Venice).

GASPA'RO da SALÒ (Family name, **BERTOLOT'TI**). *B.* Salò (Brescia), abt. 1542; *d.* 1609. Renowned maker of viols, viole da gamba, and contrabass viols. He is said to have introduced several of the improvements which gave the vn. its modern shape. "Dragonetti's favourite double-bass was an altered *viola contrabassa* of Gasparo's." —*Baker.*

Gas'senhauer (*G.*). Formerly a popular street song or dance; now applied to any trite vulgar melody.

GASSIER, Ed. Noted baritone; *début*, 1845; *d.* 1871.

GASS'MANN, Florian Leopold. *B.* Bohemia, 1723; *d.* 1774. Taught by Padre Martini. Court Capellmeister, Vienna, 1771. Founded what is now the "Haydn Society" for the relief of the widows and orphans of musicians. Taught Salieri. Works: 23 operas, much church music, orch. and chamber music, &c.

GASS'NER, Ferdinand S. *B.* Vienna, 1798; *d.* 1851. Violinist. Music director, Geissen Univ., 1818. Joined the Court Orch., Darmstadt, 1826. Pub. and edited musical journals, wrote a "Treatise on Scoring," "A Musical Lexicon," &c., and composed 2 operas and several ballets.

GASTAL'DON, Stanislas. *B.* Turin, 1861. Works: an opera, pf. pieces, and songs (some of which have proved very popular).

GASTINEL, Léon G. C. *B.* Villers, nr. Auxonne, 1823. Pupil of Halévy, Paris Cons. Works: oratorios, masses, orchestral pieces, &c., and successful comic operas and ballets (*Titus et Bérénice, Le rêve,* &c.).

GASTOL'DI, Giovanni G. Italian poet and composer; abt. 1556-1605. Works: masses, madrigals, psalms, canzoni, &c.

GATAYES, Guillaume P. A. Guitar player; Paris, 1774-1846. Wrote 3 Guitar Methods, a Harp Method, and much music for guitar and harp, both *soli* and in combination with other insts.

GATAYES, Joseph Léon. Son of G. Paris, 1805-77. Fine harpist. Wrote solos, duets, and *études* for harp.

GATAYES, Félix. Brother of preceding; *b.* Paris, 1809. Pianist. Toured for 20 years in Europe, America, &c. Works: overtures, symphonies, military music.

GATES, Bernard. 1685-1773. Master of the Choristers, Chapel Royal. Handel's *Esther* was performed at his house.

Gathering-note. Name sometimes given to the first note of a hymn tune, or the *reciting-note* of a chant.

GA'THY, August. *B.* Liége, 1800; *d.* 1858. Pub. a valuable "Musikalisches Conversationslexikon."

GATTY, Alfred Scott. *B.* Ecclesfield, 1847. Works: popular songs ("True till Death," &c.), pf. pieces, &c.

GATTY, Nicholas C. Composer; *b.* Bradfield, 1874. Works: Operas, songs, &c.

Gauche (*F.*). Left. *La main gauche.* *Main gauche.* }The left hand. *M.G.*

GAUCQUIER, Alard. (Also known as **Dunoyer** (his real name), **Nuceus,** and **Insulanus.**) Famous 16th cent. contrapuntist; *b.* Lille. Served under Ferdinand I, Maximilian II, and the Archduke Matthias. Works: magnificats, masses, &c., up to 8 parts.

Gauden'te (*I.*). } Jubilant, joyous, blithe. **Gaudio'so** (*I.*). }

Gauge. A small instrument for measuring the thickness of strings.

GAUL, Alfred Robert. *B.* Norwich, 1837. Mus.Bac. Cantab., 1863. Conductor Walsall Philharmonic, 1887. Works: oratorio (*Hezekiah*); several popular cantatas (*The Holy City, Ruth,* &c.), part-songs, songs, church music, &c.

GAULTIER (or GAUTIER). Name of a family of eminent French lute-players.

(1) **Jacques.** *B.* Lyons, abt. 1600 ; *d.* Paris, abt. 1670. Royal lutenist, London, 1617-47. Called "Gotire" by Herrick.

(2) **Denis.** Cousin of J. *B.* Marseilles, abt. 1600-10 ; *d.* Paris (date unknown). Established with Jacques a school for lute-playing, Paris, 1647.
Two of his pub. collns. of lute music are still known.

(3) **Ennémond.** Son of J. *B.* 1635. Royal Chamber lutenist, Paris, 1669.
Pub. 2 collns. of music in lute-tablature. (See *Tablature.*)

GAULTIER, Abbé A. E. C. *B.* Italy, abt. 1755 ; *d.* Paris, 1818.
Pub. a new method of teaching music to children, 1789.

Gau'menton (*G.*). A throaty, guttural tone.

GAUNTLETT, Henry John. *B.* Wellington, 1805 ; *d.* Kensington, 1876. Mus.D. Lambeth, 1843.
A fine organist, and well-known composer and arranger of hymn-tunes and congregational music. With Wm. Hill, the org. builder, he was mainly instrumental in promoting the general adoption of "C" organs in England (in place of the old F or G organs).

GAUTHIER, Gabriel. Blind organist and teacher ; *b.* Saône-et-Loire, 1808.
Works : "Répertoire des maîtres de chapelle" (5 vols.), &c.

GAUTIER, Felix. Pen-name of **W. M. Watson** (*q.v.*).

GAUTIER, Jean F. E. *B.* nr. Paris, 1822 ; *d.* 1878. Pupil, and afterwards prof., Paris Cons.
Works : an oratorio (*La Mort de Jésu*) ; 14 comic operas, &c.

GAUTIER, Théophile. Distinguished French writer on dramatic art, 1811-72.
Pub. "Histoire de l'art dramatique en France depuis 25 ans." Unfortunately hated music.

GAVEAUX, Pierre. French operatic tenor ; 1761-1825.
Composed 33 operas.

GAVINIÉS, Pierre. *B.* Bordeaux, 1726 ; *d.* Paris, 1800. Brilliant violinist ; chiefly self-taught. Viotti called him "The French Tartini," and he is considered the founder of the French school of vn. playing. Prof. Paris Cons., 1795.
Works : comic opera (*Le Prétendu*), 6 vn. concertos, 9 vn. sonatas, 24 "Matinées," and much other vn. music (including the celebrated " Romance de Gaviniés ").

Gavot'. (*F., Gavote* or *Gavotte ; I., Gavot'ta.*) An old French dance.
The Gavotte is usually in 2-2 (or 4-4) time, and should commence at the half bar (thus differing from the *Bourrée*). It is in regular sections of 2 or 4 bars. The "trio" portion is often a *Musette* (on a drone bass). The gavotte was much used by Bach and Handel in their Suites, and Handel also used the form in vocal music.

GAVRON'SKI, Woitech. Composer ; *b.* nr. Vilna, 1868.

GAWLER, Wm. Lambeth, 1750(?)-1809.
Published "Hymns and Psalms," &c.

GAYARRE, Julian. 1844-90. Successful tenor ; son of a poor blacksmith.
Educated at Madrid Cons. Sang Covent Garden, 1877-70.

Ga'zel. (See **Ghazel.**)

GAZTAMBI'DE, Josquin. Spanish composer ; 1822-70.
Works : 40 very successful operettas (or "zarzuelas").

Gazouillant (*F.*). Chattering, warbling ; babbling, rustling.

GAZZANI'GA, Giuseppe. *B.* Verona, 1743 ; *d.* 1819. Pupil of Porpora. Maestro Crema Cath., 1791.
Works : 33 operas (including *Don Giovanni Tenorio*, which has the same story as Mozart's *Don Giovanni*), masses, and other church music.

G-clef. (*G., G'-Schlüssel ; F., Clef de sol ; I., Chia've di sopra'no.*) The treble clef. (See **Clef.**)

GEAR, George F. *B.* London, 1857.
Mus.-director, German Reed Co., 1876-92.

GEAUSSENT, Geo. F. Pianist ; *b.* London, 1852.

GEB'AUER, Franz X. *B.* Eckersdorf, 1784 ; *d.* Vienna, 1822. Friend of Beethoven.
Founded Vienna " Concerts Spirituels," 1819.

GEBAUER, Michel Joseph. *B.* La Fère, 1763 ; *d.* 1812 (during the retreat from Moscow). Oboist and violinist ; Prof. Paris Cons., 1794-1802. Bandmaster Garde des Consuls, and afterwards of the Imperial Guard.
Works : over 200 popular marches, several duets for various insts., &c.

His three brothers were also talented musicians.

(1) **François R.** 1773-1845. Bassoonist.
Wrote a "Method for Bassoon," and several compositions for wind insts.

(2) **Etienne F.** 1777-1823. Flautist.
Wrote over 100 flute solos, &c.

(3) **Pierre Paul.** *B.* 1775 ; died young.
Wrote 20 horn duets.

GE'BEL, Franz X. *B.* nr. Breslau, 1787 ; *d.* 1843. Capellmeister at various theatres ; pf. teacher, Moscow, 1817.
Works : operas, 4 symphonies, chamber music, pf. pieces.

GE'BEL, Georg (Senr.). Breslau, 1685-1750.
Invented a clavichord with quarter tones. Wrote several compns., including canons *up to 30 parts*.

GE'BEL, Georg (Junr.). Son of preceding. *B.* Silesia, 1709 ; *d.* 1753. Held several appointments as organist and capellmeister. Prolific composer.
Works : 12 operas, numerous sets of cantatas, over 100 orch. pieces, &c.

Geberd'enspiel (*G.*). Pantomime, dumb show.
Geberd'ensprache. The language of gesture.

GEBHAR'DI, Ludwig Ernst. *B.* Thuringia, 1787 ; *d.* 1862. Orgt. Erfurt Seminary.
Works : collections of org. pieces, school songs, an org. Method, a Method of Thorough-bass. &c.

Geblet'erisch (*G.*). Commanding, peremptory, domineering.

Gebla'se (*G.*). Blowing, trumpeting.

Geblä'se (*G.*). Bellows, blast of wind.

Geblümt' (*G.*). Flowered ; embellished.
Gebroch'en (*G.*). Broken.
Gebroch'ene Akkord'e. Broken chords ; arpeggios.
Gebun'den (*G.*). Tied, bound, sustained, syncopated, slurred.
Gebun'dene Dissonanz'. A prepared (tied) dissonance.
Gebun'dene No'te. A tied note.
Gebun'denes Spiel. Legato playing.
Gebun'dener Stil. The "strict" style (of composition).
Geburts'lied (*G.*). Birthday song.
Gedacht', Gedackt' (*Gedact, Gedakt*) (*G.*). Covered, stopped. Lit. "decked ;" used of organ pipes.
Lieb'lich Gedacht'. Beautiful (toned) stopped (diapason).
Gedacht' Flöte. A stopped flute (org. stop).
GÉDALGE, André. Parisian composer ; *b.* 1856.
Works : Orchestral music, dramatic music, pf. pieces, &c.
Gedämpft' (*G.*). Damped, muffled, muted.
Gedeckt' (*G.*). Same as **Gedacht.**
Gedehnt' (*G.*). Prolonged, sustained ; slow.
Gedicht' (*G.*). A poem.
Gefähr'te (*G.*). A fugal *Answer.* (See **Fugue.**)
Gefal'len (*G.*). To suit, to please.
Gefäl'lig. Pleasing, attractive, agreeable.
Nach Gefal'len. At pleasure ; *ad lib.*
Gefeil'ter Strich (*G.*). "Detached stroke," in vn. playing.
Gefie'del (*G.*). Fiddling, scraping.
Gefühl' (*G.*). Feeling, emotion, expression.
Gefühl'voll. \
Mit Gefühl'. / With feeling, &c.
Gegei'ge (*G.*). Fiddling.
Ge'gen (*G.*). Against ; same as **Contra** (*q.v.*).
Ge'genbewe'gung. Contrary motion.
Ge'genfuge. A fugue by inversion. (See *Fugue.*)
Ge'gengesang. Antiphonal singing.
Ge'genharmonie. \ A counter-subject ; a contrasted
Ge'gensatz. } part ; a contrapuntal accom-
Ge'genstimme. / panying melody.
Ge'genpunkt. Counterpoint.
Gehal'ten (*G.*). Sustained, held ; steady.
Gehaucht' (*G.*). Very soft and light ; whispered.
Wie gehaucht'. Like a whisper.
Geheim'nisvoll (*G.*). Mysterious.
Geh'end (*G.*). *Andante ;* Lit. "going."
Et'was geh'end. "Somewhat going ;" *andantino.*
Gehör'ig (*G.*). Suitable, convenient.
GEH'RING, Franz. 1838-84. Mathematical lecturer Vienna Univ.
Wrote a Biog. of Mozart ("Great Musicians" Series), and articles for Grove's Dictionary.
GEIBEL, Adam. Composer ; *b.* Neuenheim, 1855.
Geig'e (*G.*). A violin.
Gei'genblatt. Fingerboard.
Gei'genbogen. Bow.
Gei'genharz. Resin (Rosin).
Gei'gensaite. Violin string.
Gei'gen principal. Violin diapason (org. stop).
Gei'gensattel. Violin bridge.
Gei'genschule. A vn. method.
Gei'genspieler. Violinist.
Gei'genstück. A composition for vn.
Gei'genwirbel. The vn. peg.
Gei'genzettel. The "label" or "inscription."
GEI'JER, E. G. 1783-1847. Prof. of History Upsala Univ.
Published and edited important collections of Swedish folk-songs.

GEIS'LER, Paul. *B.* Pomerania, 1856.
Works : operas (*Die Ritter von Marienburg*, &c.) ; several symphonic poems, "cycles" for voices and orch., songs, &c.
Geist (*G.*). Soul, spirit ; genius, intellect.
Geis'terharfe. Eolian harp.
Geist'lich. Sacred, spiritual, religious.
Geist'gesänge. Psalms, hymns.
GEIS'TINGER, Marie C. C. *B.* Graz, Styria, 1836 ; *d.* 1903. Brilliant soprano singer. Sang in New York, 1897.
Gekling'el (*G.*). Tinkling.
Gekneipt' (*G.*). Pizzicato (*q.v.*).
Gelas'sen (*G.*). Calm, tranquil.
Gelas'senheit. Tranquillity ; deliberateness.
Geläu'fig (*G.*). Fluent ; easy, rapid.
Geläu'figkeit. Fluency, velocity.
Geläut'(e) (*G.*). A peal of bells.
Gelin'de (*G.*). Soft, gentle, tender.
Gelin'digkeit. Sweetness, gentleness.
GE'LINEK, Hermann A. Bohemian priest ; 1709-79. Tired of monastic life, he fled to Naples ; became noted as a violinist under the assumed name of **Cervetti.**
GE'LINEK, Abbé Joseph. *B.* Bohemia, 1758 ; *d.* 1825. "Claviermeister," on Mozart's recommendation, to Count Kinsky.
Wrote much showy music "of slight artistic value."
Gel'len (*G.*). To sound loudly, to yell.
Gel'lenflöte. A clarinet.
GELLERT, Christian F. 1715-69. Prof. Leipzig Univ.
Wrote the hymn " Jesus lives."
GEL'LER-WOL'TER, Luise. Contralto ; *b.* Cassel, 1863.
Gel'tung (*G.*). (Time) value of a note or rest.
Gemäch'lich (*G.*). (1) Gentle, convenient, easy ; slow. (2) Gradually, by degrees.
Gemäh'lig (*G.*). Gradually.
Gemäs'sigt (*G.*). *Moderato* (*q.v.*).
Gemebon'do (*I.*) \ Moaning ; plaintive, dole-
Gemen'do (*I.*) / ful.
Gemes'sen (*G.*). Measured ; *moderato.*
GEMINIA'NI, Francesco. *B.* Lucca, abt. 1680 ; *d.* Dublin, 1762. Violinist ; pupil of Scarlatti and Corelli. Settled in London, 1714.
Pub. 18 concertos, 24 solos, and 12 sonatas for vn.; 6 solos for 'cello ; 12 trios for 2 vns. and 'cello ; the earliest known Vn. Method, 1740 ; and several other theoretical works.
Gemisch'te Stim'men (*G.*). (1) Mixed voices. (2) Organ mixture stops.
Gems'horn (*G.*). (1) A chamois horn. (2) An org. stop with tapering metal pipes, and light clear tone quality.
GEMÜN'DER, August. Renowned violin maker ; *b.* Württemberg, 1814 ; *d.* New York, 1895.
Gemüt'(h) (*G.*). Heart, soul, mind, temperament ; feeling.
Mit Gemüth \
Gemüt'(h)lich / With feeling ; expressive(ly).

GENAST', Eduard F. Operatic baritone;
B. Weimar, 1797; *d.* 1866. Sang from
1829 at the Weimar Court Theatre.
Finest rôle, *Don Giovanni.*
Wrote 2 operas and some songs.

GENÉE, Franz F. R. *B.* Danzig, 1823; *d.*
1895. Capellmeister successively at
several theatres.
Wrote some 15 operettas (*Der Geiger aus Tirol,
Der Seedakett, Die Dreizehn,* &c.).

Ge'nera. Plural of *Genus* (*q.v.*).

General'bass (*G.*). Thorough-bass. (See
Figured Bass.)
General'bassschrift. Thorough bass notation.
General'pause. A pause, or hold, for the whole orch.
General'probe. A final rehearsal.

GENERA'LI, Pietro. (Real name **Mercan-
det'ti.**) *B.* Piedmont, 1783; *d.* 1832.
Works : an oratorio (*Il voto di Jette*) ; over 50
operas, the best being *I Baccanali di Roma*
(1815); masses, psalms, &c.

Generator. (*F., Générateur*). (1) The root of
a chord. (2) The fundamental or
ground tone of a series of partials.
(See **Acoustics.**)

Ge'nere (*I.*). (1) A key or mode. (See
Genus.) (2) Style.

Genero'so,-a (*I.*). Generous, noble, free,
ample.

GENET. (See **Carpentras.**)

Genial' (*G.*). Showing genius; talented,
spirited.

Génie (*F.*). **Genie'** (*G.*). **Ge'nio** (*I.*). Genius,
talent, spirit; capacity.

Genius.
" Seek not, young artist, what meaning is expressed by genius. If you are inspired with it,
you must feel it in yourself. Are you destitute
of it, you will never be acquainted with it.
The genius of a musician submits the whole
universe to his art."—*Rousseau.*

GENOVE'VA. Opera by Schumann; Leipzig, 1850.

Genre (*F.*). (1) Style. (2) Key or mode;
diatonique, chromatique, enharmonique.
(See **Genus.**)
Genre expressif. The Expressive Style.

GENSS, Hermann. *B.* Tilsit, 1856.
Works : orch. and chamber music, songs, &c.

Gentil,-le (*F.*). **Genti'le** (*I.*). Graceful,
dignified, delicate, refined.
Gentilment (*F.*).
Gentilmen'te (*I.*).   With grace, dignity, elegance.
Con gentilez'za (*I.*).

Ge'nus (*L.*) (plur. *Ge'nera*). Sort, class;
mode.
The Greeks recognized 3 genera; diatonic, chromatic, and enharmonic.

GEORGES, Alexandre. *B.* Arras, 1850.
Prof. of harmony, Niedermeyer School,
Paris.
Works : operas (*Le Printemps, Poèmes d'amour,
Charlotte Corday*), songs, &c.

Gera'de (*G.*). Straight, regular, even.
Gera'de Bewe'gung. Similar motion.
Gera'de Takt'art   Duple or Quadruple Time.
Gera'der Takt

GÉRARD, Henri P. *B.* Liége, 1763; *d.*
1848. For over 30 years Prof. of Singing, Paris Cons.
Chief work : a "Méthode de Chant," 1819.

GÉRARDY, Jean. Belgian violoncellist;
b. Spa, 1877(8?).

Geraub'tes Zeit'mass (*G.*). *Tempo rubato*
(*q,v.*).

GER'BER, Heinrich N. *B.* nr. Sondershausen, 1702; *d.* 1775. Org. pupil of
J. S. Bach. Wrote org. music.

GER'BER, Ernst Ludwig. Son of H. N.;
Sondershausen, 1746-1819. 'Cellist and
organist.
Compiled a "Biographical Dict. of Musicians" (2
vols., 1790-2), and a supplementary edition (4
vols., 1812-14), both containing much material
still valuable.

GER'BERT (von HORNAU), Martin. Benedictine monk ; *b.* Horb-on-Neckar,
1720 ; *d. 1793.* Prince-Abbot of the
monastery of St. Blaise, 1764.
His "Scriptores Ecclesiastici de Musica Sacra
potissimum" (3 vols., 1784), is one of the most
important sources of musical history It is a
colln. of treatises by all the chief authors of the
middle ages, given *verbatim*, with all the original
mistakes ! Reprinted, 1905.

GER'HARDT, Paul. 1607-76. German
hymn-writer ; ranking next to Luther.
Wrote "O sacred Head," "Commit thou all thy
griefs," &c.

GE'RICKE, Wilhelm. *B.* Graz, Styria, 1845.
Talented conductor ; "Gesellschaft-
Concerte," Vienna (succeeding Brahms),
1880-4, and again 1889-95; Boston
(Mass.) Symphony Orch., 1884-9, and
again 1898.

GER'LACH, Dietrich. 16th century music-
printer, Nuremburg.

GER'LACH, Theodor. *B.* Dresden, 1861.
Conductor and composer.
Works : opera (*Matteo Falcone*, 1898); cantatas
symphonies, chamber music, songs, &c.

GER'LE, Hans. Celebrated maker of lutes
and violins ; *d.* Nuremburg, 1570.
Pub. several works in lute-tablature which are
historically valuable.

GERMAN, J. Edward. *B.* Whitchurch,
Shropshire, 1862. Studied R.A.M.
Works : incidental music to several of Shake-
speare's plays; orch. music; pf. music, songs.

German Flute. (See **Flute.**)

German Music. In classical music Germany
(with Austria) stands pre-eminent,
claiming most of the "Great Composers" in addition to many others of
considerable fame. (It attained pre-
eminence in the 18th cent.)
Chief musicians : Hasler (1564-1612), Fux (1660-
1741), J. S. Bach (1685-1750), W. F. Bach
(1710-84), C. P. E. Bach (1714-88), J. C. Bach
(1735-82), Handel (1685-1759), Hasse (1699-
1783), Graun (1701-59), Gluck (1714-87),
Marpurg (1718-95), Kirnberger (1721-83), J.
Haydn (1732-1809), Albrechtsberger (1736-
1809), M. Haydn (1737-1806), Vogler (1749-
1814), Mozart (1756-91), Steibelt (1765-1823),
Beethoven (1770-1827), Romberg (1770-1841),

J. B. Cramer (1771-1858), Hummel (1778-1837), Ferd. Ries (1784-1838), Spohr (1784-1859), Weber (1786-1826), Czerny (1791-1857), Meyerbeer (1791-1864), Moscheles (1794-1870), Schubert (1797-1828), Herz (1806-88), Mendelssohn (1809-47), Nicolai (1809-49), Schumann (1810-56), Hiller (1811-85), Liszt (1811-88), Thalberg (1812-71), Flotow (1812-83), Wagner (1813-83), Heller (1815-88), Suppé (1820-95), Raff (1822-82), Schulhoff (1825-98), Bülow (1830-94), Joachim (1831-), Brahms (1833-97), Max Bruch (1838-), Rd. Strauss (1864-).

German Scale. The scale of the natural notes is A, H, C, D, E, F, G; B being our B♭. (See **H.**)

German Sixth. One of the forms of the Augmented or Extreme Sixth Chord. (See **Extreme Sixth.**)

GER′MER, Heinrich. *B.* Saxony, 1837; pf. teacher at Dresden.

Works : a pf. method, and treatises on pf. technique, &c.

GERNS′HEIM, Friedrich. *B.* Worms, 1839. Director, Rotterdam Cons., 1874 ; Prof. Stern Cons., Berlin, 1890.

Works : symphonies, overtures, a pf. concerto, a violin concerto, chamber music, cantatas, songs, &c.

GERS′BACH, Jos. *B.* Säckingen, Baden, 1787 ; *d.* 1830.

Pub. several collns. of school songs.

GERS′BACH, Anton. *B.* 1801 ; *d.* 1848. Brother of J., whom he succeeded as music teacher at the Karlsruhe Teachers' Seminary.

Pub. school songs, a pf. method, pf. pieces, &c.

GER′STER, Etelka (Madame **Gardi′ni-Gerster**). *B.* Kaschau, Hungary, 1857. Distinguished operatic soprano; opened a singing school, Berlin, 1896.

GERVASO′NI, Carlo. Milan, 1762-1819.

Wrote treatises on musical theory.

GERVI′NUS, George G. *B.* Darmstadt, 1805 ; *d.* 1871. Prof. Heidelberg Univ. One of the founders of the Leipzig "Händel-Verein."

Wrote "Händel und Shakespeare : zur Ästhetik der Tonkunst."

Ges (*G.*). The note G♭.

Gesang′ (pl. *Gesäng′e*) (*G.*). Singing ; a song, melody, hymn, air, &c.

Gesang′artig. In a singing style.
Gesang′buch. Song book ; hymn book.
Gesangs′kunst. The art of singing.
Gesang′(s)mässig. Melodious ; *cantabile.*
Gesang′reich. Very smooth and *cantabile.*
Gesang stimme. Voice part, vocal part.
Gesang′verein. A singing society.
Gesang′voll, mit in′nigster Empfin′dung. Very singingly, and with sincere (heartfelt) emotion.
Gesang′weise. Tune, melody. In song style.

Gesäu′sel (*G.*). Murmuring, rustling.

Geschlecht′ (*G.*). Genus ; mode, species.

Geschleift′ (*G.*). Slurred ; *legato.*

Geschlos′sene Löch′er (*G.*). Closed holes (of a flute, clarinet, &c.).

Geschmack′ (*G.*). Taste.

Geschmack′voll. With taste ; tastefully.

Geschnell′ter Dop′pelschlag (*G.*). The turn of 5 notes played very quickly. (See **Turn.**)

Geschwind′ (*G.*). Quick, rapid, prompt.

Geschwind′marsch. A quick march.
Geschwind′, doch nicht zu sehr, und mit Entschlos′senheit. Quick, but not too much so, and with decision.
Nicht zu geschwind′. Not too quick.

Ges dur (*G.*). G♭ major.

Gesell′schaft für Mu′sikforschung. "Society for the Investigation of Music." Founded, Berlin, 1868. Reprinted many important older works.

Bach-Gesell′schaft. A Bach Society.

GESEL′SCHAP, Marie. Pianist ; *b.* Batavia, 1874(?).

Ges′es (*G.*). G♭♭.

Gesicht′ (*G.*). Front ; face.

Gesichts′pfeifen. Front pipes of an organ.

Gesing′e (*G.*). Bad singing.

GE′SIUS (or **Göss**), **Bartholomäus.** Abt. 1555-1613. Cantor, Frankfort-on-Oder.

Pub. (1588-1624) collns. of psalms, chorals, motets, masses, &c.

Gespon′nen (*G.*). Spun.

Gespon′nene Sai′te. A covered string.
Gespon′nener Ton. (*F.*, *Son filé*). A tone "spun out," *i.e.*, drawn out to a mere thread.

Gesproch′en (*G.*). Spoken.

Gestei′gert (*G.*). Crescendo ; *sforzando.*

Gestopft′ (*G.*). Stopped (as horns).

Gestos′sen (*G.*). Staccato, detached.

Gestrich′en (*G.*). (1) Stroked (through). (2) Cut, cut out.

Eingestrich′ene Okta′ve. The "once accented" octave ; c¹, d¹, &c.

GESUAL′DO, Don Carlo. Prince of Venosa ; *d.* before 1626. "One of the most enlightened musicians " of the *New Style.* (See **Bardi, Caccini, Peri.**)

Pub. 6 vols. of madrigals *a* 5 (1594, &c. ; in score, 1613.)

Getern, Getron. Old English names for the Guitar.

Get(h)eilt′ (*G.*). Divided ; *divisi.*

Geteil′te Violinen. Violins divided. (See *Divisi.*)
Geteil′te Stim′men. Divided, or partial, org. stops.

Getra′gen (*G.*). Sustained ; *sostenuto.*

Getrost′ (*G.*). Confident, trustful.

GEVAERT, François Auguste. *B.* nr. Oudenarde, 1828 ; *d.* Dec. 1908. Studied Ghent Cons., won *Grand Prix de Rome* for composition. Brought out 9 operas in Ghent from 1852 to 1861. *Chef de Chant,* Paris Grand Opéra, 1867. From 1871, Director Brussels Cons.

Works : about a dozen operas (*Quentin Durward,* &c.); cantatas (*De nationale verjaerdag*) ; ballads, songs, &c. ; also several theoretical treatises, including the finest work on "Instrumentation and Orchestration" that has yet been written.

GEWAND′HAUS Concerts. Celebrated concerts held in the Hall of the Gewandhaus (Ancient Armoury), Leipzig. They date from 1781, and among the conductors have been Mendelssohn (who introduced beating time, 1835), Hiller and Gade.

Gewandt′ (*G.*). Active, nimble, dexterous.

Gewicht′ig (*G.*). Heavily ; *pesante.*

Gewid′met (*G.*). Dedicated (to).

Gewir'bel (*G.*). Roll of drums.

Gewiss' (*G.*). Firm, sure, resolute.

Geworf'ener Strich (*G.*). A light dancing stroke, or *saltato* (*q.v.*) in vn. playing.

Gezo'gen (*G.*). Drawn out, sustained.

G Flat. (1) The flat of G. (2) The Major key with signature of 6 flats.

G Gamut. (See **Gamut.**)

Ghaz'al, Ghaz'el. An Arabic melody with a short oft-recurring theme or refrain.

GHEYN, Matthias van den. *B.* Brabant, 1721; *d.* 1785. Celebrated organist and *Carilloneur* at Louvain.

Ghiribiz'zo (*I.*). Caprice, whim.

Ghiron'da (*I.*). Hurdy-gurdy.

GHISELING (GHISELIN, GHISELINUS), Jean. Noted Netherland contrapuntist, 16th to 17th cents.

GHISLANZO'NI, Antonio. *B.* Lecco, 1824; *d.* 1893.
For several years Editor Milan *Gazzetta Musicale;* wrote the *libretti* of over 80 operas (including Verdi's *Aïda*).

GHIZZO'LO, Giovanni. Italian monk; *b.* abt. 1560.
Pub. masses, motets, *falsi bordoni,* &c.

GHY'MERS, Jules E. Pianist and critic; *b.* Liége, 1835.

GHYS, Joseph. Violinist; *b.* Ghent, 1801; *d.* 1848.
Wrote a concerto, and several other works for vn.

GIACOMEL'LI, G. *B.* Parma, 1686; *d.* 1743. Opera composer.
Chief operas : *Ipermnestra, Cesare in Egitto.*

GIALDI'NI, Gialdino. *B.* Pescia, 1843. Distinguished conductor.
Has pub. a collection of the "Folk-songs of Lombardy."

GIANEL'LI, Pietro. Italian writer, abt. 1770-1822(?).
Pub. the oldest Italian Dict. of Music and Biography (3 vols.), Venice, 1801; 2nd edn. (8 vols.), 1820.

GIANETTI'NI (Zanettini), Antonio. *B.* Venice, 1649; *d.* 1721. Capellmeister, Modena, 1686.
Works : 6 operas, 6 oratorios, cantatas, psalms, &c.

GIARDI'NI, Felice de'. *B.* Turin, 1716; *d.* 1796. Violinist; leader, Italian Opera, London, 1752; Manager, 1756. Returned to concert giving, 1765.
Works : oratorio (*Ruth*) ; 5 operas, songs, and much good vn. music (including 12 concertos).

GIBBONS, Rev. Edward. Abt. 1570-1650(?) Mus.B.Oxon, 1592. Orgt. Bristol Cath., 1592-1611 ; Exeter Cath., 1611-44.

GIBBONS, Orlando. "The English Palestrina." Brother of E. *B.* Cambridge, 1583; *d.* Canterbury, 1625. Chorister, King's Coll., Cambridge, 1596; Orgt. Chapel Royal, 1604; Mus.B. Cantab., 1606; Mus.D. Oxon, 1622. Orgt. Westminster Abbey, 1623.
Works : "Fantasies for Viols" (the earliest engraved English music), church services and anthems, harpsichord pieces, madrigals, &c.
On his monument (Canterbury Cath.) is the following quaint inscription : *To Orlando Gibbons of Cambridge, Born among the Muses and Musick; Organist of the Royal Chapel, emulating, by the Touch of his Fingers, the Harmony of the Spheres ; A man of integrity, whose manner of Life, and sweetness of Temper, vy'd with that of his Art ; being sent for to Dover to attend the Nuptials of King Charles and Mary, he died of the Small-Pox and was conveyed to the heavenly Choir on* Whit-Sunday, Anno 1625.

GIBBONS, Christopher. Son of Orlando ; London, 1615-76. Orgt. Chapel Royal, 1660-76; orgt. Westminster Abbey, 1660-5. Mus.D. Oxon, 1664.

GI'BEL (GIBE'LIUS), Otto. 1612-82. School rector at Minden.
Pub. "Sacred Harmonies for 1-5 voices with and without instruments."

GIBERT, Paul César. *B.* Versailles, 1717 ; *d.* 1787.
Wrote several operas for the Comédie Italienne, a colln. of solfeggi, &c.

GIBSON, George Alf. *B.* Nottingham, 1849. Fine violinist and viola player.

GIBSONE, Guillaume I. *B.* London, abt. 1826. Pianist ; pupil of Moscheles.
Works : pf. pieces, songs, &c.

Gichero'so,-a (*I.*). Merry.

GIDE, Casimir. Paris, 1804-68.
Works : 6 successful operas (*Les trois Marie, Belphégor,* &c.), and 7 ballets.

GIFFE, Wm. Thos. Composer ; *b.* Portland (U.S.), 1848.

Gi'ga (*I.*). (See **Gigue.**)

Gigeli'ra (*I.*). A Xylophone (*q.v.*).

GIGLIUC'CI, Countess. (See **Clara Novello.**)

GIGOUT (pron. *Zhē-goo*), **Eugène.** Distinguished orgt. and mus. critic. *B.* Nancy, 1844. Pupil and afterwards Prof. Niedermeyer School, Paris ; orgt. St. Augustin Church, 1863. Founded an org. school, Paris, 1885.
Works : an "Album Grégorien," over 300 Plainsong compns., and numerous org. pieces.

Gigue (*F.*). (*I., Gi'ga.*) (1) Old name for *Viol.* (2) A jig.
The Gigue was a lively dance form often employed as the last movement of a suite. It was usually in 6-8, or 12-8 time, but 3-8, 3-4, 4-4, 6-4, 9-16, and 12-16 were also employed.
Numerous examples occur in the Suites of Bach and Handel. They are generally written in a bright, playful, imitative style—are constructed in two repeated portions—and vary in length from 12 to 143 bars.

GIL, Francisco A. *B.* Cadiz, 1829. Prof. of Harmony, Madrid Cons.
Works : several operas, a Spanish trans. of Fétis' "Harmony," &c.

GILBERT, William Schwenck. *B.* London, 1836.
Wrote the libretti of most of Sullivan's operas.

GILCHRIST, William Wallace. Distinguished American orgt. and conductor ; *b.* Jersey City, N.J., 1846.
Works : cantatas, odes, church music, songs, &c.

GILES, Nathaniel. *B.* nr. Worcester, abt. 1550 ; *d.* 1633. Mus.B. Oxon, 1585. Orgt. St. George's, Windsor, 1595.

Master of the Children, Chapel Royal, 1597. Mus.D. Oxon, 1622.
Works: anthems, services, &c. Hawkins gives a quaint "Lesson of Descant of thirtie-eighte Proportions of sundrie kindes, made by Master Giles."

GILL, Allen C. H. Condr.; *b.* Devonport, 1864.

GILL, Thos. H. *B.* Birmingham, 1819. Wrote "We come unto our fathers' God," and other hymns.

GILLES (G. Brebos); known as **Maitre Gilles.** Famous 16th cent. org. builder at Louvain and Antwerp. *D.* 1584.

GILLET, Ernest. 'Cellist and composer; *b.* Paris, 1856.

GILMORE, Patrick Sarsfield. *B.* Co. Galway, 1829; *d.* St. Louis, 1892. Organised "Gilmore's Band," Boston (U.S.), 1859. Conducted 2 "monster Peace Festivals," Boston, 1869 and 1872; the latter with an orchestra of 2,000 and chorus of 20,000. "The orchestra was reinforced by a powerful organ, cannon fired by electricity, anvils, and chimes of bells." —*Baker.* Made successful tours with his band, visiting Europe, 1878.
Wrote much band music, and some popular songs.

GILSON, Paul. Belgian operatic composer; *b.* Brussels, 1865.

G in Alt, G in Altis'simo. (See **Alt.**)

Gio'co (*I.*). A joke, jest, banter.
Con gio'co ⎱ Playfully, merrily, jestingly.
Gioche'vole ⎰
Giocon'do,-a ⎱ Jocose, playful, &c.
Gioco'so,-a ⎰
Giocondamen'te ⎱ Playfully, merrily, &c.
Giocosamen'te ⎰
Gioconda'to. Playful, happy.
Giocondez'za. Mirth, &c.

Gio'ia, Gio'ja (*I.*). Joy, delight.
Con gio'ja, Giojan'te, Giojo'so,-a, Giojosamen'te. Joyfully, mirthfully.

GIORDA'NI, Tommaso. (Real name **Carmine.**) *B.* Naples, 1740; *d.* Dublin, abt. 1806. Sang in opera buffa at the Haymarket, London, 1762.
Works: oratorio (*Isaac*), an opera, flute duets, pf. pieces, songs.

GIORDA'NI, Giuseppe (known as **Giordanel'lo**). Brother of T. *B.* Naples, 1744; *d.* 1798. Fellow-student of Cimarosa and Zingarelli, Loreto Cons. Popular teacher in London, 1772-82.
Works: abt. 30 operas (*Il Bacio*, 1794, &c.); much chamber music, 6 vn. concertos, 5 books of canzonets, pf. pieces, &c.

GIORDA'NO, Umberto. Operatic composer; *b.* Foggia, 1867.
Most successful work, a 4-act serious opera *Andrea Chenier.*

GIORGI. (See **Banti-Giorgi.**)

GIORNOVI'CHI. (See **Jarnovic**).

GIOR'ZA, Paolo. *B.* Milan, 1838.
Works: dances, marches, and over 40 ballets (many of them very successful).

GIO'SA. (See **De Giosa.**)

GIOVANEL'LI, Ruggiero. *B.* Velletri, abt. 1560; *d.* Rome, abt. 1620. One of the most distinguished composers of the Roman School. Succeeded Palestrina as Maestro at St. Peter's, 1594.
Works: madrigals, motets, *Sdruccioli*, *Villanelle*, &c. Prepared a new edition of the Graduals for Pope Paul V.

Giovia'le (*I.*). Jovial, pleasant, cheerful.
Con giovialità'. With cheerfulness, &c.

Giraffe. An old form of upright spinet.

GIRALDO'NI, Leone. *B.* Paris, 1824; *d.* 1897. Baritone vocalist; taught for several years at Moscow Cons.
Wrote "A Theoretical and Practical Guide for Singers," &c.

Gi'ro (*I.*). A turn (*q.v.*).

Gis (*G.*). G♯.
Gis moll. G♯ minor.
Gis'is. G×.

Gita'na (*I.*). ⎱ A Spanish gipsy dance.
Gitta'na (*I.*). ⎰

Gittern, Gitteron, Gittron. A kind of guitar; like the Cittern, but gut-strung.

Giubili'o, Giu'bilo, Giubilazio'ne (*I.*). Joy, jubilation.
Con Giu'bilo ⎱
Giubilan'te ⎬ Joyously; with jubilation.
Giubilo'so,-a ⎰

Giulli'vo (*I.*). Joyful, mirthful.
Giulivamen'te. Pleasantly, gaily.

Giuocan'te (*I.*). ⎱ Jokingly, playfully;
Giuoche'vole (*I.*). ⎰ banteringly.

Giu'sto,-a (*I.*). Just, strict, accurate, suitable. (In Handel, 4-4 time.)
Alle'gro giu'sto. Moderately quick.
A tem'po giu'sto. In moderate, strict time.
Con giustez'za ⎱ With precision and accuracy.
Giustamen'te ⎰

Giving out.
"A term used by organists to signify the preluding performance by which the Psalm Tune about to be sung is announced, or *given out*, to the congregation."—*Moore.*

Gix'er (*G.*). The "goose" note (clarinet, &c.).

GIZZIEL'LO (G. Conti). *B.* nr. Naples, 1714; *d.* 1761. Male soprano; "one of the greatest singers of the 18th century." Sang in London, 1736.

GLADSTONE, Francis Edward. *B.* Summertown, 1845. Organist; pupil of Dr. S. S. Wesley. Mus.D. Cantab., 1879. Prof. of harmony and counterpoint R.C.M.
Works: "The Organ Student's Guide," church music, org. pieces, &c.

Glais (*F.*). The passing bell.

Glänz'end (*G.*). Brilliant, resplendent.

Glapissant (*F.*). Shrill.

GLAREA'NUS, Henricus. (Henrich Lo'ris. Also known as **Loritus.**) *B.* Glarus, 1488; *d.* 1563. Poet-laureate, Cologne, 1512.
His "Dodecachordon" (1547) is a valuable historical work; it deals with "church modes, mensural music, notation, and early music printing." Reprinted in German, 1888.

GLA'SENAPP, Carl F. *B.* Riga, 1847. Has written "Wagner's Life and Work," and a "Wagner-Lexikon."

GLÄ'SER, Franz. *B.* Bohemia, 1798; *d.*
1861. From 1832, Royal conductor,
Copenhagen.
Works: 13 operas (*Des Adlers Horst*, 1833, the
best), and other dramatic music.
Glas'harmonika (*G.*). (See **Harmonica.**)
Glasses, Musical.
"Glasses tuned by partially filling with water, and
played by rubbing their edges evenly with a wet
finger."—*Hughes.*
Glatt (*G.*) Smooth, even.
GLAZOU'NOW (GLAZUNOV) (pron. *Gla-tsoo'-nov*), **Alexander.** Distinguished
Russian composer; *b.* St. Petersburg,
1865. First symphony produced, 1881;
fourth given under his *báton* by the
London Philharmonic, 1889. Prolific
composer of instrumental music. Hon.
Mus.D. Cantab., 1907.
Chief works : 7 symphonies; several symphonic
poems, suites, and other orch.works; overtures;
chamber music of all kinds; pf. pieces (preludes,
nocturnes, waltzes, études, &c.).
GLEASON, Fredk. G. American composer;
b. Middletown, Conn., 1848. Pupil of
Dudley Buck; studied also at Leipzig,
Berlin, and London. *D.* Chicago, 1903.
Works: operas, overtures, cantatas, church music,
org. pieces, songs, chamber music, pf. pieces,&c.
Glee. A composition for 3 or more solo voices
(properly without accompaniment).
The Glee is peculiarly an English form of composition; its best period was from 1760 to
1830; it has now been practically superseded
by the part-song.
TYPICAL GLEES : "Which is the properest day to
sing?" Dr. Arne, 1750; "Where the bee sucks,"
W. Jackson, 1760; "Dame Durden," Harring-
ton, 1760; "In summer's cool shade," Dr. S.
Arnold, 1760; "Glorious Apollo," Webbe,
1770; "When winds breathe soft," Webbe;
"Thy voice, O harmony," Webbe; "Let me
careless," T. Lindley, 1770; "O happy fair,"
Shield, 1775; "Here in cool grot," Ld. Morn-
ington, 1775; "Breathe soft, ye winds," S.
Paxton, 1775; "Ye shepherds, tell me," J.
Mazzinghi, 1775; "Five times by the taper's
light," Storace, 1775; "The Red Cross Knight,"
J. W. Callcott, 1780; "Hark, the lark," Dr.
Cooke, 1780; "Awake, Æolian lyre," Danby,
1780; "From Oberon," Stevens, 1780; "Hail,
smiling morn," Spofforth, 1805; "Mynheer
Van Dunck," Bishop, 1805; "The bells of St.
Michael's Tower," Knyvett, 1830; "Ossian's
Hymn," Goss, 1830.
Gleemen. Old name for minstrels.
GLEESON-WHITE, Cicely Rose. Soprano;
b. Christchurch, Hants., 18—.
Gleich (*G.*). Equal; like, similar.
Glei'cher Klang. Consonance; unison.
Glei'cher Kon'trapunkt. Equal counterpoint, *i.e.*, 1st
species.
Gleich'schwebende Temperatur'. Equal temperament.
Glei'che Stim'men. Equal voices.
Gleich'tönend. In unison.
GLEICH, Ferdinand. *B.* Erfurt, 1816; *d.*
1898. Critic *Dresdner Anzeiger.*
Works : symphonies, songs, pf. pieces, "A Hand-
book of Modern Instrumentation," &c.
Gleich'mässig (*G.*). Equal, uniform, similar;
even.
Immer gleich'mässig p. Uniformly *p* throughout.
Gleich'sam (*G.*). As it were; almost.
GLEISS'NER, Franz. *B.* Neustadt, 1760;
d. Munich (after 1815).
The first lithographic music printer.

Glei'ten (*G.*). Same as **Glissando** (*q.v.*).
GLEITS, Karl. Composer; *b.* nr. Cassel,1862.
GLEN. Family of Scotch bagpipe makers,
and publishers of music for that inst.
(1) **Alexander.** *B.* Fife, 1801; *d.* 1873.
(2) **Thos. Macbean.** Bro. of A. 1804-73.
Established a musical inst. business,
Edinburgh, 1827; made bagpipes, &c.,
and invented the serpentcleide, (a
wooden ophicleide).
(3) **John.** Son of T. M. *B.* Edinburgh,
1833. Succeeded to the business 1866,
with Robert (4). *D.* 1904.
(4) **Robert.** *B.* Edinburgh, 1835.
The firm of J. and R. Glen has issued much
valuable music for the bagpipes.
Gli (*I.*). The; as *gli stromen'ti*, the instruments.
Gli accompagnmen'ti p stacca'ti e sem'pre arpeggia'ti.
The accts. (to be) soft, staccato, and always
arpeggiated.
Glide. A slur from one note to another, as in
the *portamento* (*q.v.*) or *glissando* (*q.v.*).
GLIÈRE, Reinhold. Russian Composer;
b. Kieff, 1874. Studied Moscow Cons.
Works: a symphony in E♭ (London, 1906), &c.
GLIN'KA, Michail Ivanovitch. *B.* nr. Smo-
lensk, June 1, 1804; *d.* Berlin, Feb. 15,
1857. A nobleman by birth; "the
pioneer Russian national composer."
Studied the pf. under Field, Moscow,
1822. Travelled in Italy, 1830-4.
Studied under Dehn, Berlin, 1834.
Gave orch. concerts, Paris, 1844,
"which aroused Berlioz's enthusiasm."
Works: 2 operas, *A life for the Czar*, or *Ivan
Sussanina* (the first Russian national opera,
St. Petersburg, 1836), and *Russlan and Ludmilla* (1842). Also numerous orch. pieces, a
septet and other chamber music, pf. pieces,
romances, and songs.
Glissade (*F.*). } (1) A rapid slur, or *porta-*
Glissan'do (*I.*). *mento*, in vn. playing.
Glissa'to (*I.*). (2) A rapid,gliding scale-
Glissican'do (*I.*) passage on the pf. pro-
duced by running the
Glissica'to (*I.*). tip of the thumb or
finger (frequently the "finger-nail"),
along the white keys, instead of striking
each note separately. (3) Any smooth,
flowing rendering of a passage.
Glissé (*F.*). Glissando.
Glisser. To slide, to glide.
Glock'e (*G.*). A bell.
Glöck'chen. A little bell.
Glockenist'. A bell ringer.
Glock'enspiel. (1) A carillon (*q.v.*). (2) A set of tuned
bells or metal rods, used in military bands and
orchestras. (3) A set of small bells operated on by
the keyboard of an org. (4) An old org. *mixture.*
Glo'ria in Excel'sis De'o (*L.*). "Glory to God
in the highest." Part of the Roman
mass.
Generally referred to as " the Gloria." (See also
Doxology.)
Glotte (*F.*). } The opening between the
Glot'tis. } vocal cords (*q.v.*).
Coup de Glotte (*F.*). "The shock of the glottis."
(See *Voice Production.*)

GLOVER, Mrs. F. (See **E. Harraden.**)

GLOVER, Sarah Ann. *B.* Norwich, 1785; *d.* Malvern, 1867. Invented the Tonic Sol-fa Notation afterwards developed by the Rev. John Curwen. (See **Tonic Sol-fa.**)

Pub. "A Manual of the Norwich Sol-fa System," 1845, and a "Development of the Tetrachordal System," 1850.

GLOVER, Stephen R. London, 1812-1870.

Wrote popular songs, duets, &c., and some drawing-room pf. pieces.

GLOVER, Wm. Howard. *B.* London, 1819; *d.* 1875. Violinist; for some years critic for the *Morning Post;* settled in New York, 1868.

Works: an opera (*Ruy Blas*), operettas, pf. pieces, songs, &c.

GLUCK, Christoph Wilibald (Ritter von). *B.* Weidenwang, nr. Neumarkt, Upper Palatinate, July 2, 1714; *d.* Vienna, Nov. 25, 1787. Renowned dramatic composer.

" The opera, when he took it up, was the laughing-stock of Europe. It left his hands a serious form of art, carefully thought out in all its details, with a new method and unity of purpose. . . All the serious dramatists—Beethoven, Wagner, Weber, Berlioz—had their way made easier by the labour of Gluck."— *Ernest Newman.*

Son of a game-keeper. Sent to the Komotau Jesuit College (1726-32), where he learnt the vn., harpsichord, and organ. In 1736 entered the service of Prince Melzi (Vienna), who sent him to Milan to complete his mus. education under Sammartini. Visited London, 1745, and wrote 2 operas for the Haymarket. Director Court Opera, Vienna, 1754-64. Handel's contemptuous criticism led Gluck to adopt his "new style," and his first really great opera, *Orfeo*, was given at Vienna, 1762. In 1774 he went to Paris. Piccinni came also to Paris to contest Gluck's supremacy, but was finally completely overwhelmed by the latter's superiority. The war of the *Gluckists* and *Piccinnists* is historically famous. In 1780 Gluck retired to Vienna.

Chief operas: *Artaserse*, Milan, 1741; *Demetrio*, 1742; *Artamene*, 1743; *Alessandro nell' Indie*, 1745; *La Caduta dei Giganti*, London, 1746; *La Semiramide Riconsciuta*, 1748; *Telemaco*, 1750; *Il re pastore*, 1756; *Orfeo (Orpheus)*, 1762; *Alceste*, 1766; *Iphigénie en Aulide*, Paris, 1774; *Armide*, 1777; *Iphigénie en Tauride* (his masterpiece), Paris, 1779. Of these, the last 5 are the works on which Gluck's fame rests.

Glüh'end (*G.*). Glowing, ardent.

Gnac'care, Gnac'chere (*I.*). Castanets (*q.v.*).

GNEC'CO, Francesco. *B.* Genoa, 1769; *d.* 1810. Opera composer.

Chief work : *La prova d'un' opera seria.*

GOB'BAERTS, J. L. *B.* Antwerp, 1835; *d.* 1886. Pianist; studied Brussels Cons. Wrote abt. 1,200 light, popular pf. pieces.

GOB'BI, Aloys. Violinist; *b.* Pesth, 1844.

GOB'BI, Henri. Brother of A.; *b.* Pesth, 1842. Pupil of Liszt.

Works : male choruses, pf. pieces, &c.

GÖBEL, Karl H. E. *B.* Berlin, 1815; *d.* 1879. Capellmeister Dantzig Theatre.

Works : 2 operas, chamber music, songs, &c.

GOCK'EL, August. Westphalia, 1831-61. Pianist; pupil of Mendelssohn.

Wrote a pf. concerto.

GODARD, Benjamin L. P. *B.* Paris, 1849; *d.* 1895. Played the vn. in public at 9. Studied Paris Cons. under Vieuxtemps, with whom he twice toured in Germany. Won the *Prix Chartier* from the Institut de France "for merit in the department of chamber music."

Works : 8 operas (*La Vivandiere*, 1895, very successful); 6 symphonies, orch. suites, "Ouverture dramatique," "Concerto romantique" for vn., a pf. concerto, pf. pieces, &c., and over 100 songs.

GOD'DARD, Arabella. *B.* nr. S. Malo, 1836. Fine pianist; played in public at the age of 4; at 8 played before Queen Victoria, 1860. Married to J. W. Davison, 1860. Retired 1880.

Made numerous concert tours, including a "tour of the world," 1873-6.

GODDARD, Jos. Critic and writer; *b.* 1833.

GODEBRYE. (See **Jacotin.**)

GODEFROID, Jules J. *B.* Namur, 1811; *d.* 1840.

GODEFROID, D. J. G. Félix. 1818-1897. Brothers; celebrated harpists and composers of harp music. Also wrote operas.

GODFREY, Daniel. *B.* London, 1831; *d.* 1903. Bandmaster, Grenadier Guards, 1856.

Works : dance music, and arrangements for military bands.

GODFREY, Adolphus Fred. 1837-82.

GODFREY, Charles. *B.* 1839. Brothers of D. Conductors.

GODFREY, Daniel E. Son of D. Condr.; *b.* London, 1868.

GODFREY, Percy. Vocal and instl. composer; *b.* Walton-on-Trent, 1859.

GODOW'SKI (pron. *God-off-'skee*), **Leopold.** *B.* Vilna, Poland, 1870. Fine pianist; began composing at 7. Head of pf. dept. Chicago Cons., 1895.

Has published pf. pieces and songs.

GOD SAVE THE KING. The English "National Anthem."

"No definite solution of the problem of the authorship of either words or music has been made. . . Henry Carey divides about equally with Dr. John Bull the credit of its composition."—*Grove's Dict.*, 1906. It became popular in 1745, when it was said to have been originally written and composed for Jas. II, 1688.

GOEP'FART, Christian H. Organist and conductor; *b.* Weimar, 1835; *d.* Baltimore, 1890.

GOEP'FART, Karl E. Son of C. H. *B.* Weimar, 1859.
Works: an opera (*Sarastro*), choral works, &c.

GOEP'FART, Otto E. Composer; *b.* Weimar, 1864.

GOE'THE, Wolfgang von. Great German poet; 1749-1832.

GOE'THE, Walther W. von. Grandson of the poet; *b.* Weimar, 1818; *d.* 1885. Studied under Mendelssohn at Leipzig.
Works: 3 operettas, 10 books of songs, &c.

GOETSCHIUS, Percy. American musician; *b.* Paterson, N. J., 1853. Studied Stuttgart Cons. Since 1896, private teacher, Boston, U.S.
Works: pf. pieces, org. pieces, a "Critical Revision of Mendelssohn's Complete pf. Works," and several theoretical treatises (including an excellent book on "The Homophonic Forms of Musical Composition").

GOETZ, Mad. L. Muriel Foster (*q.v.*).

GOETZ, Hermann. Talented composer; *b.* Königsberg, Prussia, 1840; *d.* 1876. Studied under Louis Köhler.
Works: *The Taming of the Shrew*, 1874 (one of the finest of modern operas), a symphony in F, a vn. concerto, a pf. concerto, choral works, chamber music, pf. music, songs, &c.

GOET'ZE. (See **Götze**.)

Go'la (*I.*). "The throat." A throaty, guttural voice.

GOLD'BECK, Robert. Pianist; *b.* Potsdam, 1839. Prod. an operetta, *The Soldier's Return*, London, 1856. Went to New York, 1857. Founded Conservatories in Boston, 1867, and Chicago, 1868.
Works: 2 operas, a cantata, orch. pieces, 2 pf. concertos, abt. 140 pf. pieces, songs, &c.

GOLD'BERG, Johann Gottlieb (Theophilus). Renowned organist and clavichord-player; *b.* Königsberg, abt. 1730; *d.* abt. 1760. Pupil of J. S. Bach; "an extraordinary improviser and sight-reader."

GOLD'BERG, Jos. P. Vienna, 1825-90. Violinist, bass vocalist, and singing teacher.
Wrote a Triumphal March for Victor Emmanuel's entry into Rome.

GOLD'MARK, Karl. Hungarian violinist, pianist, and composer; *b.* 1832. Studied Vienna Cons. His first opera, *Die Königin von Saba*, 1875, made him famous.
Works: other operas (*The Cricket on the Hearth*, 1896, specially successful); symphonies, overtures, chamber music, pf. solos and duets, vn. concerto, male choruses, songs, &c.

GOLD'SCHMIDT, Adalbert von. *B.* Vienna, 1851; *d.* 1906. "Amateur, and ardent Wagnerite."
Best-known work, cantata *Die Sieben Todsünden*, Berlin, 1875.

GOLD'SCHMIDT, Hugo Dr. *B.* Breslau, 1859. Co-director, Scharwenka-Klindworth Cons., Berlin, 1893.
Has written treatises on singing methods, &c.

GOLD'SCHMIDT, Otto. *B.* Hamburg, 1829. Pianist; pupil of Mendelssohn and

Chopin. Married Jenny Lind, 1852. Member London Philharmonic Soc., 1861; Vice-principal, R.A.M., 1863; founded the Bach Choir, 1875. *D.* 1907.
Published pf. pieces, songs, &c.

GOLDWIN (or GOLDING), John. *B.* 1670; *d.* Windsor, 1719. Orgt. St. George's, Windsor, 1697.
Wrote anthems, &c.

GOLINEL'LI, Stefano. *B.* Bologna, 1818. After tours as a concert pianist, he became pf. professor, Bologna Liceo Musicale. Retired 1870; *d.* 1891.
Works: abt. 300 pf. pieces of all kinds (greatly esteemed in Italy).

GOLL'MICK, Adolf. Pianist. Son of K. (below). *B.* Frankfort-on-Main, 1825; *d.* 1883. Settled in London, 1844.
Works: 3 comic operas, a symphony, cantatas, pf. pieces, songs.

GOLL'MICK, Karl. *B.* Dessau, 1796; *d.* 1866.
Works: pf. solos and duets, a "Singing Method," "Kritische Terminologie für Musiker und Musikfreunde," a "Handlexikon der Tonkunst," &c.

GOL'TERMANN, Georg Ed. *B.* Hanover, 1824; *d.* 1898. Distinguished 'cellist; Capellmeister City Th., Frankfort-on-Main, 1874.
Works: a symphony, overtures, songs, and several 'cello pieces (including 6 concertos).

GOL'TERMANN, Johann A. J. *B.* Hamburg, 1825; *d.* 1876. 'cellist; Prof. Prague Cons., 1850-62; 1st 'cello, Stuttgart, 1862.

GOMBERT, Nicolas. Celebrated Flemish contrapuntist; pupil of Josquin Despres. *B.* Bruges, abt. 1495; *d.* after 1570. Master of the boys, Imperial Chapel, Madrid, 1530. Fétis regards him as "a forerunner of Palestrina."
Works: motets, masses, chansons, &c.

GO'MES, Antonio C. Brazilian opera composer, 1839-96. Studied Milan Cons. Apptd. Director, Pará Cons., 1895; died shortly after.
Chief operatic works: *A noite do Castello*; a "Rivista" (including the very popular "Song of the Needle-gun"); *Salvator Rosa, Marie Tudor*, and *Lo Schiavo* (his greatest success).

GO'MEZ, Alice (Mrs. T. H. Webb). Mezzo-soprano vocalist; *b.* Calcutta.
First appearance in England, 1885.

GOM'PERTZ, Rd. Violinist; *b.* Cologne, 1859.

Gon'dellied (*G.*). } Gondolier's song. Same
Gondolie'ra (*I.*). } as **Barcarolle** (*q.v.*).

Gon'dolin. A variety of the zither.

Gong. (*F. & G., Tam-tam.*) An inst. of percussion. A plate of metal struck by a drumstick.
The best metal is 80 parts of copper to 20 of tin.

GOODBAN, Thos. Canterbury, 1784-1863.
Works: glees, songs, pf. music, instruction books, &c.

GOODRICH, Alfred J. American theorist; *b.* Ohio, 1847.
Works: "The Art of Song," "Analytical Harmony," &c.

GOODSON, Katherine. (See **Mrs. A. Hinton.**)

GOODWIN, Amina Beatrice (Amy). Pianist; *b.* Manchester, 1863(7?).
Played in public at the age of 6. First appearance in London, Covent Garden, 1883.

GOODWORTH, W. G. Waller. *B.* London, 1858.
Edited "Musicians of all Times," 1907.

Goose. (*F., Couac.*) The harsh squeak produced on a reed inst. by bad blowing.

GOOSENS, Eugène. Condr.; *b.* Bordeaux, 1867.

GOOVAERTS, Alphonse J. M. A. *B.* Antwerp, 1847. Musical historian. Royal archivist, Brussels, 1887.
Works: church music, songs, treatises on musical history, &c.

GÖP'FERT, Karl A. *B.* nr. Würzburg, 1768; *d.* 1818. Clarinet player.
Wrote an opera, 4 clar. concertos, chamber music, songs, &c.

GÖP'FERT, Karl G. *B.* nr. Dresden, 1733; *d.* 1798. Violinist.
Wrote 6 polonaises for vn.

GORDIGIA'NI, Luigi. *B.* Modena, 1806; *d.* 1860.
Works: 7 operas, an oratorio, 3 cantatas, &c., and a large number of Tuscan popular songs (*Canti popolari Toscani*) set to old folk-songs.

GORDON, Wm. *B.* end of 18th cent.; *d.* abt. 1839.
Flute player; made improvements in flute mechanism similar to those of Boehm.

Gorgheg'gio (I.). A florid passage.
Gorgheggia're. To perform florid vocal music.
Gorgheggiamen'to. The art of singing florid music.

GO'RIA, Alexandre E. Parisian pianist; 1823-60.
Works: several popular pf. pieces.

GOR'LITZ, Mrs. H. (See **Amy Sherwin.**)

GÖ'ROLDT, Joh. H. *B.* nr. Stolberg, 1773; *d.* abt. 1835(?).
Wrote a horn method, works on composition, &c., and some church music.

GORRIA, Tobio. *Nom de plume* of **A. Boito.**

GOR'TER, Albert. *B.* Nuremburg, 1862. Capellmeister, Leipzig Opera, 1899.
Works: operas (*Harold*, &c.), symphonic poems, choral works, pf. pieces, songs.

Gosier (*F.*). The throat.

GOSS, (Sir) John. *B.* Fareham, Hants, 1800; *d.* Brixton, 1880. Chorister, Chapel Royal, 1811. Orgt. St. Paul's Cath., 1838-72. Knighted, 1872. Mus.Doc. Cantab., 1876.
Works: services, anthems, hymn-tunes, chants, &c., glees, madrigals; a work on "Harmony," a "Church Psalter and Hymn-book," &c. Several of his anthems are still extremely popular.

GOSSEC (or GOSSÉ), François Joseph. *B.* Vergnies, Belgium, Jan. 17th, 1734; *d.* Passy, Feb. 16, 1829. Chorister, Antwerp Cath., 1741-9. Through Rameau's interest became conductor of La Popelinière's private orch., Paris, 1751. Conductor Prince Conti's orch., 1762. Founded the Concerts, des Amateurs,

---

1770. Established the Ecole Royale de Chant ("the germ of the Conservatoire") 1784. Retired 1815.
Works: 27 symphonies, 3 oratorios, masses, motets, Te Deums, choruses, string quartets, several operas (*Les Pêcheurs*, 1766), a fine *Messe des Morts*, &c. His first symphonies, 1754, were published 5 years before Haydn's.

GOST'LING, Rev. John. *D.* 1733. Bass singer, celebrated for his extensive compass. Purcell wrote a song for him ranging from—

Goto. A Japanese dulcimer.

GÖT'TERDÄM'MERUNG. "The Dusk of the Gods." Fourth and last division of Wagner's *Ring des Nibelungen*, Bayreuth, 1876.

GOTT'SCHALG, Alex. W. *B.* nr. Weimar, 1827. Orgt. and critic.
Pub. (with Liszt) a fine "Colln. of Modern Organ Music."

GOTT'SCHALK, Louis M. Pianist; *b.* New-Orleans, 1829; *d.* 1869. Studied in Paris; pianistic *début*, 1845. Toured in France, Switzerland, Spain, and through the United States.
Works: 2 operas, 2 symphonies, abt. 90 pf. pieces, songs, &c.

GÖTZ. (See **GOETZ.**)

GÖT'ZE, Emil. Fine operatic tenor; *b.* Leipzig, 1856; *d.* 1901.

GÖT'ZE, Franz. 1814-88. Leading tenor Weimar, 1836-52. Singing teacher, Leipzig Cons., 1853-67.
Auguste, his daughter (*b.* 1840), is a distinguished teacher of singing.

GÖT'ZE, Joh. N. K. Violinist; Wiemar, 1791-1861.
Works: 4 operas, chamber music, vaudevilles, &c.

GÖT'ZE, Karl. *B.* Weimar, 1836; *d.* 1887. Pupil of Töpfer and Liszt.
Works: 4 successful operas (*Judith*, 1887), a symphonic poem, pf. pieces, songs.

GOUDIMEL, Claude. *B.* Vaison, nr. Avignon, abt. 1505; killed in the St. Bartholomew massacre, Lyons, 1572.
Works: masses, motets, chansons, &c., and settings of the Psalms of David (some of which are still sung).

GOULD, Baring. (See **Baring-Gould.**)

GOULD, Nathaniel D. American musician; 1781-1864.
Edited several collections of hymn-tunes.

GOUNOD, Charles François. *B.* Paris, June 17, 1818; *d.* there Oct. 17, 1893. One of the most distinguished of French composers. Entered Paris Cons. 1836; won *Grand Prix de Rome*, 1839. Conductor, Paris "Orphéon," 1852-60. Achieved world-wide renown with the opera *Faust*, 1859. Founded "Gounod's Choir" (now the "Royal Choral Society"), London, 1870. Returned to Paris, 1875.
Chief works: oratorios, *The Redemption* (Birmingham, 1882), *Mors et Vita* (Birmingham 1885); a requiem, a *Messe Solennelle*, and

other masses; operas, *Sapho* (1851), *Le Médecin malgré lui* (1858), *Faust* (1859, his finest work), *Philémon et Baucis* (1860), *Mireille* (1864), *Roméo et Juliette* (1867), *Cinq Mars* (1877); several cantatas (*Gallia*, 1871); many songs (*Nazareth, There is a green hill, O Divine Redeemer*, &c.); orch. pieces (*The Funeral of a Marionette*), &c.

GOURRON, Albert R. Contemporary tenor vocalist; *b.* Bordeaux.

Goût (*F.*). Taste, judgment.

GOUVY, Louis T. *B.* nr. Saarbrücken, 1819; *d.* 1898. Pianist and composer.
Works: church music, dramatic cantatas (*Œdipus, Iphegénie, Elektra*), 7 symphonies, overtures, chamber music, pf. pieces, and songs. Gouvy's music is popular in France and Germany.

Governing Tone. The Tonic or Key-note. —*Curwen.*

GOW, George Coleman. American musician; *b.* Massachusetts, 1860.
Works: part-songs, songs, a text-book on "The Structure of Music," &c.

GOW, Niel. Scottish violinist; 1727-1807.
Pub. six collns. of "Strathspey Reels."

GOW, Nathaniel. 1763-1831. Violinist; son of preceding.
Composed the song "Caller Herrin'."

GOW, Niel (Jnr.). 1795-1823. Violinist; son of Nathaniel.
Composed "Flora Macdonald's Lament" and other songs.

G. P. Abbn. of *Generalpause* (*q.v.*).

GRA′BEN-HOFF′MANN, Gustav. *B.* nr. Posen, 1820; *d.* 1900.
Composed many popular songs, and some pf. music.

Grab′gesang (*G.*). } A funeral song, a dirge.
Grab′lied (*G.*). }
Grab′es-stim′me. Sepulchral voice.

Grace. (*G., Verzie′rung; F., Ornement, Agrément; I., Abbellimen′to, Fioret′to.*) An ornamental note (or notes) to embellish the melody. (See **Ornaments.**)
Grace notes are usually printed or written smaller than the principal notes which they precede (or occasionally follow).

Gracieux, Gracieuse (*F.*). Gracious; graceful.

Gra′cile (*I.*). Graceful, delicate, slender.
Vo′ce gra′cile. A thin slender voice.

Grad (*G.*). A grade; a degree (of the staff).
Grad′leiter. A scale.

GRÄ′DENER, Hermann T. O. Son of Karl (below); *b.* Kiel, 1844. *Lector* in harmony and counterpoint, Vienna Cons., 1899. Conductor, Vienna *Singakademie.*
Works: orch. and chamber music, pf. pieces, songs, &c.

GRÄ′DENER, Karl G. P. *B.* Rostock, 1812; *d.* 1883. For 10 years Mus.-director Kiel Univ. Prof. of singing and theory, Vienna Cons., 1862, and Hamburg Cons., 1865.
Works: oratorio (*Johannes der Täufer*), 2 symphonies, a pf. concerto, much chamber music, pf. pieces, a text-book of Harmony, &c.

Grade′vole (*I.*). Agreeable, pleasing.
Gradevolmen′te. Pleasingly, gracefully.

13

Graditamen′te (*I.*). Sweetly, graciously.

Gra′do (*I.*). A step, a degree.
Gradatamen′te. By steps, gradually.
Gra′do ascenden′te. An ascending step (of the scale).
Gra′do descenden′te. A descending step.
Di gra′do. Stepwise. Opposed to *di salto*, by skip.

Gradual (Grail). } (1) An antiphon sung after
Gradual′e (*L.*). } reading the Epistle. (2) A book containing the graduals, introits, and other antiphons of the Mass.

Graduellement (*F.*). Gradually.

Gra′dus ad Parnas′sum (*L.*). "The road to Parnassus." Name often given to textbooks; Fux's (1715) and Clementi's (1817) are famous.

GRAEW. (See Bacfart.)

GRAFFI′GNA, Achille. 1816-1896. Conductor of various Italian theatres.
Wrote operas and songs.

GRÄ′FINGER. (See Grefinger.)

GRAHAM, Geo. F. Edinburgh, 1789-1867. Composer and critic.
Wrote the art. "Music" in the 7th and 8th edns. of the *Ency. Brit.* (See also *Scottish Music.*)

Graillement (*F.*). A hoarse sound.

GRAIN, Corney. Musical entertainer; *b.* Teversham, 1844; *d.* 1895.

GRAINGER, Percy. Pianist; *b.* Melbourne, 1883.

GRAM′MANN, Karl. *B.* Lubeck, 1844; *d.* 1897.
Works: several operas (*Melusine, Ingrid*), 2 symphonies, chamber music, &c.

Grammatical Accent. Metrical accent. (See **Accent.**)

Gra′mophone. (See also **Phonograph.**)
A sound-recording and sound-reproducing machine introduced by Dr. Berliner in 1887; perfected in its present form, 1897. The "records" are made on metal discs, and it is regarded as the best type of "talking-machine."

Gran (*I.*). Large, grand.
Gran canto′re. A fine, or great singer.
Gran Cas′sa } Big drum.
Gran Tambu′ro }
Gran d′organo. Great organ.
Gran gu′sto. Applied to a piece or performance showing specially fine taste. Also used ironically for anything affected or exaggerated.
Gran pro′va. Final rehearsal.

Grand (*F.*). Large, great.
Grand bourdon. Double bourdon (*q.v.*).
Grand chantre. Precentor.
Grand chœur. Full organ, full choir.
Grandement. Grandly; with dignity and force.
Grand Jeu. (1) Full organ. (2) A harmonium stop which brings on the full power of the inst.
Grande mesure à deux temps. Duple time.
A grand orchestre. For full orchestra.
Grand orgue. (1) Full organ. (2) Great organ. (3) A pipe organ.

Grand. A grand pianoforte.
Concert Grand. A large-size grand piano for concert use.
Grand action. The mechanism (action) of a grand pf.

Grandeur (*F.*). Size (applied to the size of intervals).

Grandez'za (*I.*). Grandeur, dignity.

GRAN'DI, Allesandro de'. *D.* Bergamo, 1630. Pupil of G. Gabrieli.

Works: madrigals, Psalms, Te Deums, motets, masses, &c.

Grandio'so (*I.*). Majestic, grand, pompous.

Grandisonan'te (*I.*). "Grand-sounding." Loud, resonant, sonorous, re-echoing.

Grand Opera. A serious opera without spoken dialogue.

Grand stave. The great stave or staff of 11 lines. (See **Stave.**)

GRANDVAL, Marie F. C. de Reiset, Vicomtesse de. *B.* Sarthe, 1830. Pupil of Flotow and Saint-Saëns.

Works: operas (*Piccolino, Mazeppa*); oratorio (*La Fille de Jaïre*), a mass, a Stabat Mater, symphonic works, songs, &c.

GRANJON, Robt. Celebrated French music printer, 16th cent.

Printed notes with "round" heads (instead of lozenge-shaped ones), and introduced other improvements.

GRANT, Sir Robt. 1785-1838.

Wrote the hymns "O worship the King" and "Saviour, when in dust to Thee."

Granula'to (*I.*). Disconnected; slightly staccato.

Graph'ophone. (See **Phonograph.**)

Grap'pa (*I.*). A brace or bracket.

GRAS. (See **Dorus-Gras.**)

GRASSE, Edwin. Blind violinist; *b.* New York, abt. 1874. *Début*, Berlin, 1902.

Grasseyer (*F.*). To pronounce *r* and *l* thickly in singing.

GRASSINEAU, James. *B.* London, abt. 1715; *d.* 1769.

Pub. "A Musical Dictionary," London, 1740, mainly a translation of Brossard's Dict.

GRASSI'NI, Josephina. Noted singer; *b.* Varese, Lombardy, 1773; *d.* 1850. Sang in London, 1804, from March to July, for £3,000, then a prodigious salary.

GRATIANI. (See **B. Graziani.**)

Gra'tias a'gimus (*L.*). "We give thanks (to Thee)." Part of the *Gloria.*

Gratio'so (*I.*). Same as *grazioso* (*q.v.*).

GRAU'MANN. (See **Marchesi.**)

GRAUN, Joh. G. 1698(?)-1771. Violinist; brother of Karl (below). Leader, Royal Orch., Berlin, from 1740.

Works: 40 symphonies, 20 vn. concertos, 24 string quartets, &c.

GRAUN, Karl Heinrich. Noted composer; *b.* Wahrenbrück, Saxony, 1701; *d.* Berlin, 1759. Operatic tenor, Brunswick, 1725; afterwards vice-Capell-

meister. Capellmeister, Berlin (under Frederick the Great), from 1740.

Works: 34 operas (*Pollidoro, Rodelinda, Semiramide*, &c.); passion oratorio (*Der Tod Jesu* 1755, extremely popular in Nth. Germany), a fine *Te Deum* (1756), several church cantatas, motets, church melodies, &c.

GRAUP'NER, Christoph. *B.* Kirchberg, Saxony, 1683; *d.* 1760. Capellmeister, Darmstadt, 1711.

Works: 6 operas, several compns. for harpsichord, a choralbuch, &c.

Grave Mixture. An org. stop of 2 ranks, 12th and 15th.

Gra've (*I.*). (1) In *pitch;* low, deep. (2) In *tempo;* slow, heavy. (3) In *expression;* serious, grave, solemn, ponderous.

Alle'gro modera'to e gra've (*I.*). Moderately quick, and weighty in style (impressively).
Gravement (*F.*).
Gravemen'te (*I.*). } Slowly, seriously; with majesty.
Con gravità' (*I.*). }
Gravicem'balo (*I.*). A harpsichord.
Grav'is (*L.*). Heavy, ponderous.
Gravisonan'te (*I.*). Loud, or heavy-sounding.

GRAY, Alan. *B.* York, 1855; Mus. Doc. Cantab., 1889.

Conductor Cambridge Univ. Mus. Soc., 1892.

GRAY, Hamilton. Pen-name of **W. H. P. Jones** (*q.v.*).

Gra'zia (*I.*). Grace, elegance.

Con gra'zia
Grazio'so,-a } Gracefully, &c.
Graziosamen'te

GRAZIA'NI (or **GRATIA'NI**), **Bonafacio.** *B.* Marino, abt. 1606; *d.* 1664. Maestro at Rome.

Works: motets, psalms, masses, &c.

GRAZIA'NI, Francesco. *B.* Fermo, 1829. Baritone singer.

GRAZIA'NI, Ludovico. Fermo, 1823-85. Brother of F. Fine tenor singer.

Verdi wrote for him the part of Alfredo (in *Traviata*).

GRAZIA'NI, Padre Tommaso. Italian maestro, 16th to 17th cents. At Milan, 1617.

Wrote masses, madrigals, vespers, &c.

Graziös' (*G.*). Graceful, gracefully.

GRAZZI'NI, Reginaldo. *B.* Florence, 1848. Artistic director, Liceo Benedetto Marcello, Venice.

Works: symphonies, church music, pf. music, &c.

Great. That part of an organ comprising the heavier manual stops. (See **Organ.**)

Great Manual. The keyboard operating on the Great organ (generally the middle row of keys when there are 3 manuals).

Great Octave. The 8-ft. octave:—

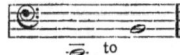

Great Sixth. Another name for the **Added Sixth** (*q.v.*).

Greater. Old name for major.

Greater Third, Major 3rd. *Lesser Third*, Minor 3rd.

Greatest Composers. Sir Hubert Parry (*Studies of Great Composers*) gives the following :—

Palestrina (1526-1594), Handel (1685-1759), J. S. Bach (1685-1750), Haydn (1732-1809), Mozart (1756-1791), Beethoven (1770-1827), C. M. Weber (1786-1826), Schubert (1797-1828), Mendelssohn (1809-1847), Schumann (1810-1856), Wagner (1813-1883). Gounod considered Mozart and Mendelssohn the two greatest.

GREAT'OREX, Thos. *B.* North Wingfield, Derby, 1758 ; *d.* 1831. Orgt. Westminster Abbey from 1819.

Works : glees, psalms, chants, " Parochial Psalmody," &c.

Grec (*F.*). Greek.

À la grec. In Greek style.

GRECHAN'INOV, Alex. T. Prolific composer of pf. music ; *b.* Moscow, 1864.

GRE'CO (or **GREC'CO**), **Gaetano.** *B.* Naples, abt. 1680. Pupil of A. Scarlatti ; teacher of Pergolesi and Durante.

Works : litanies, harpsichord music, org. music (toccatas, fugues, &c.).

GREEF, Ernest de. Distinguished contemporary. Belgian violinist.

Greek Music.

Though much has been written, very little is known, concerning the music of the ancient Greeks. They valued and encouraged the study of music, produced skilful flute players, were acquainted with the divisions of a stretched string and the ratios of intervals, and possessed philosophical systems of scales. But the nature of their melodies, and whether they used chords or any kind of "harmony," as we understand the term, remain matters of speculation. It is the opinion of modern musical scholars that "Greece, the cradle of art and beauty, pre-eminent in sculpture, architecture, and dramatic poetry, attained only a very moderate level in the art of music."

The following summary is based on G. A. Macfarren's *Musical History*.

(1) SYSTEM OF THE SEVEN-STRINGED LYRE (and the Music of the Spheres) taught by Pythagoras (585 B.C.).

NETE ; lowest (shortest) string, highest note ; likened to the *Moon*.

PARANETE ; next to lowest (string) ; likened to *Venus*.

PARAMESE ; next to Mese ; likened to *Mercury*.

MESE ; middle string ; principal or key-note ; likened to the *Sun*.

LICHANOS ; forefinger string ; likened to *Mars*.

PARHYPATE ; next to Hypate ; likened to *Jupiter*.

HYPATE ; highest (longest) string ; lowest note ; likened to *Saturn*. (See also *Music of the Spheres*.)

(2) GREEK GREATER SYSTEM.

The lowest A was called *Proslambanom'enos*.

(3) GREEK SCALES, OR MODES.

N.B.—The 4 Authentic Scales are tranpositions of one another, each consisting of the intervals

l t d r m f s l ;

and similarly with the Plagal Scales.

(1) DORIAN.
(2) PHRYGIAN.
(3) LYDIAN.
(4) MIXO-LYDIAN.
(5) HYPO-DORIAN.
(6) HYPO-PHRYGIAN.
(7) HYPO-LYDIAN.
(8) HYPO-MIXO-LYDIAN.

These should be compared with the Church Modes (see *Mode*), which have similar names but quite different intervals.

GREEN, Rd. Baritone ; *b.* London, 1866.

GREEN, Samuel. *B.* London, 1730 ; *d.* 1796. Celebrated org. builder ; adapted the " Venetian " swell to the organ.

GREEN, Wm. Tenor ; *b.* Bolton, 1867.

GREENE, Harry Plunket. Favourite bass singer ; *b.* County Wicklow, 1865.

GREENE, Dr. Maurice. London, 1695(6)-1755. Orgt. St. Paul's Cath., 1718 ; Chapel Royal, 1727 ; Cambridge Prof. of Music, 1730 ; Master of the King's Band, 1735.

Works : 2 oratorios, an opera, masques, 40 anthems, odes, catches, songs, church services, &c.

GREENWOOD, James. Orgt. and singing teacher ; *b.* Lancashire, 1837 ; *d.* 1894.

Author of " Lancashire Sol-fa " (Novello's Primers) &c.

GREETING, Thos. Teacher of the flageolet, London, 17th cent. ; taught Pepys.

GRE'FINGER, (or GRÄFINGER) Joh. W. Viennese composer, 16th cent.

Edited the *Psalterium Pataviense* (1512), a rare work.

GREGH, Louis. *B.* 1843. Parisian composer of ballets, vaudevilles, &c.

GRÉGOIR, Jacques M. J. *B.* Antwerp, 1817 ; *d.* 1876. Pianist ; pupil of Herz.

Works : an opera, a pf. concerto, many pf. pieces (études, fantasias, &c.).

GRÉGOIR, Edouard G. J. Brother of J. ; 1822-90. Composer and writer.
Works : 8 operas, orch. pieces, over 100 male choruses, vn. pieces, songs, and numerous historical and biographical treatises.

Grego'rian. (*G.*, *Gregorian'isch* ; *F. Gre'gorien* ; *I.*, *Gregoria'no.*) Introduced or regulated by Pope Gregory the Great. (See **Plain Chant, Mode,** and **Gregory.**)

GREGO'ROVITCH, Charles. Violinist ; *b.* St. Petersburg, 1867.

GREGORY I, "the Great." *B.* Rome, 540. Pope, 590-604. He reformed and set in order the musical service of the Roman Church, and is reputed to have established the Ecclesiastical Modes.
Under his supervision antiphons, offertories, responses, &c., were prescribed for the whole year's ritual, the music being still known as *Gregorian Chant*, or Plain-Song. He is said to have added 4 *plagal* modes to the 4 *authentic* modes of St. Ambrose, thus providing 8 Gregorian modes (or "tones"). (See *Mode*.)

Grei'fen (*G.*). To finger. To stretch. To grasp. To stop. (See **Griff.**)

Grell' (*G.*). Shrill, harsh, hard.
Grel'heit. Shrillness, sharpness.

GRELL, Dr. Eduard August. *B.* Berlin, 1800 ; *d.* 1886. Royal music-director, Berlin, 1838 ; Court Cath. Orgt., 1839. teacher of compn. at the Akademie, 1851 ; professor, 1858. "He considered vocal music the only music worthy of the name."
Works : a mass for 16 voices, an oratorio, psalms, cantatas, hymns, songs, an arrangement of the Lutheran *Gesangbuch* for 4-part male chorus, &c.

Grelots (*F.*). Sleigh bells.

GRENIÉ, Gabriel J. *B.* Bordeaux, 1757 ; *d.* Paris, 1837.
Invented the *Orgue expressif* (harmonium) afterwards improved by Érard.

GRENVILLE, Arthur. Pen-name of **J. Williams** (*q.v.*).

GRESNICH, Antoine F. *B.* Liége, 1755 ; *d.* Paris, 1799. Visited London ; apptd. mus.-director by the Prince of Wales, 1786-91. *Chef d'orchestre*, Grand Theatre, Lyons, 1793.
Wrote over 20 operas (*l'Amour à Cythère*), &c.

GRETCHANI'NOV, Alex. A. Composer ; *b.* Moscow, 1864.

GRÉTRY, André Ernest M. "The Molière of Music ; " founded the school of French comedy-opera. *B.* Liége, 1741 ; *d.* Montmorency, 1813. The success of a Mass, Liége (1759), induced Canon du Harlez to send him to Rome for study. First dramatic work, *Le Vendemmiatrice* (Rome, 1765), praised by Piccinni. *Le Huron* (Paris Opéra-Comique, 1768), "commenced a series of successes seldom equalled." Made privy councillor by the Bishop of Liége, 1784 ; had a street named after him in Paris, 1785 ;

Inspector of the Cons., 1795 ; Chevalier of the Legion of Honour, 1802, with a pension of 4,000 francs from Napoleon.
Works : 50 operas (*Richard Cœur de Lion*, 1784, is still performed), church music, 6 symphonies, chamber music, and pf. sonatas. The Belgian Government is issuing a complete edition.

GREU'LICH, Adolf. *B.* Silesia, 1836 ; *d.* 1890. Capellmeister, Breslau, 1884. Wrote much sacred music.

GRICE, Robt. Bar. vocalist ; *b.* Leeds, 1859.

GRIEG, Edvard Hagerup. Eminent Norwegian composer ; Bergen, 1843-1907. Studied Leipzig Cons., 1858, and under Gade, Copenhagen, 1863. Formed a Musical Union, Christiania, 1867, and conducted it till 1880. Later, lived chiefly in Bergen. First visited London in 1888, playing his pf. concerto at a Philharmonic concert. Received the honorary degree of Mus.Doc. from Cambridge Univ., 1894. Grieg's music evinces strong Scandinavian characteristics and much originality. His pf. pieces and songs are "among the most charming compositions of their kind."
Chief works : "Peer Gynt" Suite, No. 1 ; "Peer Gynt" Suite, No. 2 ; symphonic dances, "Lyrische Stücke," popular Norwegian melodies, "Albumblätter," romances, &c., for pf. ; and a large number of beautiful "Lieder" (songs) for voice and pf.

GRIE'PENKERL, F. K. *B.* nr. Brunswick, 1782 ; *d.* 1849.
Edited with Roitzsch the Peters' "Critical Edition" of J. S. Bach's instrumental works.

GRIES'BACH, John H. *B.* Windsor, 1798 ; *d.* 1875. 'Cellist ; member of the Queen's Band, 1810-18.
Works : oratorio (*Daniel*) ; operatic music, cantatas, anthems, songs ; "An Analysis of Musical Sounds," &c.

GRIE'SINGER, Georg A. *D.* Leipzig, 1828. Wrote the first biography of Haydn (1810).

Griff (*G.*). Fingering ; touch, grip, stretch. (Compare **Griefen**).
Griff'brett. Fingerboard.
Griff'loch. A finger hole (of a flute, &c.).

GRIFFIN, Thos. English org. builder ; 18th cent.

GRIFFITH, Frederick W. Fine flautist ; *b.* Swansea, 1867.

GRIFFITHS, Robt. *B.* Carmarthen, 1824 ; *d.* London, 1903.
Able secretary, Tonic Sol-fa College, 1875-1900.

GRILL, Leo. *B.* Pesth, 1846. Teacher of choral singing and harmony, Leipzig Cons., 1871.

GRILLET, Laurent. French composer ; *b.* 1851.
Works : opera (*Graciosa*, 1892) ; ballets, &c.

Gril'lig (*G.*). Capricious, whimsical.

GRIMAL'DI. (See **Nicolini**.)

GRIMM, F. M., Baron von. *B.* Ratisbon, 1723 ; *d.* 1807. Writer ; lived in Paris, 1747-93 ; friend of Diderot and Rousseau. Supported *Opera Buffa* as against *Opera Seria*.

GRIMM, Julius Otto. Livonian composer; *b.* 1827; *d.* 1903. Royal Music-director, Münster Academy, 1878.
Works: a symphony in D minor, 2 fine suites for string orch., pf. pieces, songs, &c.

GRIMM, Karl. Fine 'cellist; *b.* Hildburghausen, 1819; *d.* 1888.
Published several good 'cello pieces.

GRIMM, Karl K. L. Berlin, 1820-82. First harpist, Court Orch.

GRIM'MER, Ch. F. Mulda, Saxony, 1800-50.
Song composer.

GRIMSHAW, Arthur E. Composer; *b.* Leeds, 1864.

Gringotter (*F.*). To hum.

GRISAR, Albert. B. Antwerp, 1808; *d.* 1869. Prolific dramatic composer.
Works: abt. 33 operas (*Le Mariage impossible*, 1833; *Le Carilloneur de Bruges*, 1852; *Douze innocentes*, 1865); over 50 *romances*.

GRISART, Charles J. B. 1838-1904. Parisian composer of light operas, pf. pieces, &c.

GRI'SI, Giudetta. Dramatic mezzo-soprano; *b.* Milan, 1805; *d.* 1840.

GRI'SI, Giulia. Sister of Giudetta. Celebrated dramatic soprano; *b.* Milan, 1811; *d.* 1869. Sang in Italy, Paris, and London (1832-49). Wife of Mario.

Grisoller (*F.*). To warble.

Grob (*G.*). Coarse, wide; as *Grob'gedacht*, a wide-scale stopped org. pipe.

GROD'SKI, Boleslas. Composer; *b.* St. Petersburg, 1865.

Grooves. (*G., Kansel'le.*) Channels in the wind chest of an org. to convey the wind to the required pipes.

Groppet'to (*I.*). Same as **Gruppetto** (*q.v.*).

Grop'po (*I.*). Same as **Gruppo** (*q.v.*).

GROS'HEIM, Georg C. Cassel, 1764-1847. Composer and writer.
Works: 2 operas (*Titania*), org. pieces, school songs, a Choralbuch, &c.

GROSJEAN, Ernest. Nephew of J. R. (below). Organist; *b.* Vagney, 1844.
Works: org. pieces, a Treatise on the Acct. of Plain Chant, &c.

GROSJEAN, Jean R. Organist; *b.* Vosges, 1815; *d.* 1888.
Works: "Album d'un organiste catholique," the "Noëls" of Lorraine, &c.

GROSS, Peter. Composer; *b.* 1824; *d.* Strasbury, 1867.

Gross (*G.*). (*F., Gros, Grosse; I., Gros'so.*) Great, large, grand, heavy; major.
In org. stops, same as *Grob* (*q.v.*).
Grosse-caisse (*F.*). Big drum.
Gros-Fa. The large square notation used in old church music.
Gros'se Okta've (*G.*). Great octave.
Gros'se Sona'te (*G.*). Grand sonata.
Gros-tambour (*F.*). Bass drum.
Gros'se Terz (*G.*). Major third.
Gros'se Trom'mel (*G.*). Big drum.

GROS'SI. (See **Siface** and **Viadana**.)

GROS'SI, Carlotta. (**Charlotte Grossmuck**). Stage singer; *b.* Vienna, 1849; *d.* 1900.

GROSSMITH, George. Humorous vocalist; *b.* 1847.

Gröss'ter (*G.*). Greatest.
Mit gröss'ter Energie'. With the greatest energy.

Grottes'co (*I.*). Grotesque, humorous.

Ground Bass. (*I., Bas'so ostina'to.*) A short theme repeated over and over again in the bass with varied melodic and harmonic accompaniments.
Fine examples of a ground bass are Purcell's "When I am laid in earth," *Dido*; Handel's "Envy, eldest born," *Saul*; "The many rend the skies," *Alexander's Feast*; Bach's "Crucifixus," *Mass in B minor*; and his great *Passacaglia* in C minor for the organ.

Group. (*F., Groupe; I., Grup'po.*) Any short series of rapid notes; a division, run, series of grace notes, &c.
Specially, a number of quavers, semiquavers, &c. with joined stems—

The grouping of notes is regulated (1) by the metrical accent, and (2) by the rhythm. (See *Accent* and *Rhythm*.)

GROVE, Sir George. B. Clapham, 1820; *d.* 1900. Civil engineer. Sec. Society of Arts, 1850; Sec. Crystal Palace Co., 1852; wrote excellent analytical programmes for the Crystal Palace concerts. Editor *Macmillan's Magazine* for 15 years. D.C.L., Durham, 1875.
Director of the Royal College of Music (opened 1883); knighted, 1883. LL.D., Glasgow, 1885. Editor-in-chief of "Grove's Dictionary" (1876-89), for which he wrote many fine articles; published "Beethoven and his Nine Symphonies" (1896), &c.

GROVER, Geo. F. Orgt. and writer; *b.* London, 1860.

GRU'A, C. L. P. 1700-1755. Court conductor, Mannheim.

GRU'A, Paul. Son of C. L. P. B. Mannheim, 1754; *d.* 1833. Capellmeister, Munich, 1779.
Wrote an opera, 31 orch. masses, and much other church music, concertos, &c.

GRUEN'BERG, Eugene. Violinist; *b.* Lemberg, 1854. Pupil, Vienna Cons. For 10 years member of the Gewandhaus Orch., Leipzig. Settled in America, 1891.
Works: a symphony, vn. pieces, songs, "The Violinist's Manual," &c.

GRÜN, Friederike. Operatic soprano; *b.* Mannheim, 1836.

GRÜN'BERG, Paul E. M. Violinist and teacher; *b.* Berlin, 1852.

GRÜN'BERGER, Ludwig. Prague, 1839-96. Pianist.
Works: opera (*Die Heimkehr*, 1894); pf. and chamber music, and many songs.

Grund (*G.*). Ground, foundation, fundamental note, generator.
Grund'akkord. A chord in its root, or *a* position.
Grund'bass. (1) Fundamental bass (*q.v.*). (2) A ground bass.
Grund'lage. Root position (of a chord)

Grund'stimme. (1) Same as *Grund'bass.* (2) A bass part. (3) A foundation stop on the organ (*q.v.*).
Grund'ton. (1) Root, or generator. (2) Tonic.
Grund'tonart. The principal key in a piece.

GRUND, Friederich W. Hamburg, 1791-1874. Founded the Hamburg *Sing-akademie*, 1819.
Works: cantatas, symphonies, church music, pf. pieces, songs, &c.

GRÜN'FELD, Alfred. *B.* Prague, 1852. Concert pianist.
Works: several pf. pieces.

GRÜN'FELD, Heinrich. Brother of A.; *b.* Prague, 1855. Fine 'cellist.

Gruppet'to (*I.*). (1) A group (*q.v.*). (2) A turn (*q.v.*).
Gruppet'to all' ingià. Ordinary turn.
Gruppet'to all' insù. Inverted turn.
Gruppet'to ascenden'te. Back, or inverted, turn.
Gruppet'to discenden'te. Ordinary turn.

Grup'po (*I.*). (See **Group.**)

GRÜTZ'MACHER, Friedrich W. L. *B.* Dessau, 1832. 1st 'cello, Gewandhaus Orch., 1849; 'cello teacher, Leipzig Cons. Settled in Dresden, 1860; *d.* 1903.
Works: a concerto and other 'cello pieces, pf. pieces, songs, &c.

GRÜTZ'MACHER, Leopold. Brother of preceding; *b.* Dessau, 1835; *d.* 1900.
'Cello player and composer of 'cello pieces.

GRÜTZ'MACHER, Fredrich. Son of Leopold. 'Cello teacher, Cologne Cons., 1894.

G Sai'te (*G.*). G string.

G'-Schlüs'sel (**G.**). The G clef—

Gt. Abbreviation of **Great** (*q.v.*).

Guara'cha (*S.*). A quick Spanish dance partly in triple and partly in duple time.

GUARNE'RI (*I.*, **GUARNIE'RI**; *L.*, **GUARNE'RIUS**). Celebrated family of violin makers, Cremona.
(1) **Pietro Andrea.** *B.* abt. 1630. Pupil of Nicolo Amati.
His violins date from 1650-1695.
(2) **Giuseppe.** Son of P. A. *B.* 1660. Worked 1690-1730.
(3) **Pietro.** 2nd son of P. A. *B.* abt. 1670.
(4) **Pietro.** Son of G. (2).
(5) **Giuseppe Antonio.** Nephew of P. A. *B.* 1683; *d.* abt. 1745. "The most celebrated of the family."

GU'DEHUS, Heinrich. Operatic tenor; *b.* nr. Hanover, 1845.
Created the *rôle* of *Parsifal*, Bayreuth, 1882.

Gue. A kind of vn. with two horsehair strings, formerly in use in the Shetlands.

GUER'CIA, Alfonso. *B.* Naples, 1831; *d.* 1890.
Wrote several popular songs.

GUÉRIN, Emmanuel. 'Cellist; *b.* Versailles, 1799; *d.* (?).
Wrote numerous 'cello solos and duets.

GUERRE'RO, Francisco. Seville, 1528-99. Pupil of Morales.
Works: psalms, masses, motets, &c.

Guerrie'ro (*I.*). Warlike, martial.

GUEST, Ralph. *B.* Shropshire, 1742; *d.* 1830.
Works: "The Psalms of David," glees, songs, &c.

Guet (*F.*). A flourish of trumpets.

GUEYMARD, Louis. Distinguished French tenor; 1822-80.
Sang Grand Opéra, Paris, 1848-68).

GUEYMARD, Pauline (*née* **Lauters**). Wife of L.; *b.* Brussels, 1834.
Operatic mezzo-soprano; Paris Grand Opéra, &c.

GUGLIEL'MI, Pietro. *B.* Massa di Carrara, 1720 (or 1727); *d.* Rome, 1804. Prolific composer; studied under Durante. Maestro at the Vatican, 1793.
Works: nearly 200 operas, 5 oratorios (*Debora e Sisara* (1794), his finest work), a mass, &c.

GUGLIEL'MI, Pietro Carlo. Son of the preceding; *b.* Naples, abt. 1763; *d.* 1827. Known as **Guglielmi'ni.** Vocal teacher in London for some years.
Wrote 25 operas.

GUI (or **GUI'DO**) **de CHÂLIS.** Abbot of Châlis, Burgundy, 12th cent.
Wrote treatises on Plain-chant and Discant.

Gui'da (*I.*). (*F.*, *Guide.*) (1) Subject of a fugue; antecedent of a Canon. (2) A Direct (*q.v.*). (3) A sign marking the points of entry in a canon or round (✳, ✛, &c.).

Gui'da ban'da (*I.*). A conductor's condensed score.

Guide (*E.*). Same as **Guida** (2) and (3).
In Sol-fa theory, the "link" connecting the Bridge (*q.v.*) with the 2nd Principal subject.

GUIDET'TI, Giovanni. *B.* Bologna, 1532; *d.* Rome, 1592. Pupil of Palestrina and member of the Papal choir.
Published several works on church music.

GUI'DO d'Arezzo (or **GUI'DO Areti'nus**). *B.* abt. 995; *d.* 1050(?). Monk in the Benedictine Monastery, Pomposa. Called to Rome by Pope John XIX to explain his new method of teaching singing. (Believed by many to have come from Paris.)
Gui'do developed the staff from the two lines of earlier date, viz., a *red* line for F, and a *yellow* line for C. (See *Notation.*) He is therefore generally said to have "invented" the staff! He also introduced a system of *Solmization;* the syllables *ut, re, mi, fa, sol, la,* being taken from the hymn to St. John.
Ut queant laxis
Resonare fibris
Mira gestorum
Famuli tuorum
Solve polluti
Labii reatum,
Sancte Johannes.
(See *Hexachord* and *Tonic Sol-fa Syllables.*)

GUI'DO de CHÂLIS. (See **Gui.**)

Guidon (*F.*). A Direct (*q.v.*).

Guido'nian Hand. A diagram of the hand, with Guido's syllables marked in order on the successive finger-joints. (See **Guido** and **Hexachord.**)

Guildhall School of Music. (See **Diplomas.**)

GUILLAUME TELL. Rossini's finest opera (1829).

GUILMANT, Alexandre Félix. Celebrated organist; *b.* Boulogne, 1837. Organ prof., Paris Cons., 1896. As a child, he practised on the organ for 8 to 10 hours at a time, and at the age of 12 he was a competent church organist.

His numerous compositions and arrangements for the organ are widely known and appreciated. They include several fine organ sonatas.

Guimbard. (*F.*, *Guimbarde*.) A Jew's-harp.

GUINDA'NI, Eduardo. 1854-97. Italian composer. Wrote the opera *Agnese.*

GUIRAUD, Ernest. *B.* New Orleans, 1837; *d.* Paris, 1892. Precocious composer; produced the opera *Le roi David* at the age of 15. Studied in Paris and Rome. Prof. of Harmony, Paris Cons., 1876.

Works : some 10 operas (*Gretna Green, Frédégonde*, &c.), an overture, a solemn mass, &c.

Guitar'. (*S.*, *Guitar'ra* ; *G.*, *Guitar've* ; *F.*, *Guitare* ; *I.*, *Chitar'ra*.) An inst. of the lute family, used as a solo inst. and in accompanying songs.

The Spanish guitar has 6 strings tuned as below, each string sounding an octave lower than the written note :—

E A D G B E

By means of the *Capotasto* (*q.v.*) the pitch of all the strings can be raised a semitone.
Music for the guitar is written with the G clef; the finger-board is provided with frets (like the mandoline); and the sounds are produced by plucking the strings with the finger-tips, striking them with the backs of the fingers, or sweeping the thumb across them in *arpeggio.*

Guitare d'Amour (*F.*). ⎱ An *Arpeggio'ne*
Guitar violoncello. ⎰ (*q.v.*)

GUL'BRANSON, Ellen. Distinguished soprano in Wagnerian *rôles ; b.* Stockholm, 1863. *Début* in opera, 1889.

GULLI, Luigi. Eminent Italian pianist ; *b.* 1859.

GUM'BERT, Ferdinand. Berlin, 1818-96. Singer, teacher, and critic.

Wrote abt. 500 songs, "some eminently popular."

GUM'PELTZHAIMER, Adam. *B.* Bavaria, 1559 ; *d.* 1625. Cantor at Augsburg, 1581. Church composer and theorist.

Revised Faber's "Compendium Musicæ."

GUM'PERT, F. A. Horn player ; *b.* Thuriniga, 1841.

Works : a "Praktische Hornschule," a "Solobuch" for horn, &c.

GUM'PRECHT, Dr. Otto. Critic ; *b.* Erfurt, 1823 ; *d.* 1900.

Anti-Wagnerian ; in 1866 called *Lohengrin* " a frosty sense-and-soul-congealing tone-whining."

GUNGL (or GUNG'L), Joseph. *B.* Zsámbék, Hungary, 1810 ; *d.* 1889. Bandmaster.

Wrote over 300 marches, dances, &c.

GUNGL, Johann. Nephew of Joseph. 1828-83.

Composed favourite dance music.

GUNN, Barnabas. *D.* 1743. Organist, Gloucester Cath, 1730.

Noted for his fine extempore playing.

GUNN, John. *B.* 1765(?) ; *d.* Edinburgh, abt. 1824. 'Cello teacher.

Works : a pf. Method, "Forty favourite Scotch Airs," "School for the German Flute," treatises on the 'cello, &c.

Gunst (*G.*). Grace, tenderness.

GÜN'THER, H. (See **Herther.**)

GÜNTHER, Dr. Otto. Leipzig, 1822-97.

For several years President of the Cons. and the Gewandhaus.

GUNTRAM. Opera by Rd. Strauss ; 1894.

GUNZ, Gustav. *B.* Lower Austria, 1831 ; *d.* 1894. Fine tenor singer ; pupil of Jenny Lind.

Sang in Hanover, London, &c.

GU'RA, Eugen. Operatic baritone. *B.* nr. Saatz, Bohemia, 1842. *D.* 1906.

Specially good in Wagnerian rôles ("Hans Sachs" in *Die Meistersinger,* &c.).

GURICKX, Camille. Pianist ; *b.* Brussels, 1849.

GUR'LITT, Cornelius. *B.* Altona, 1820. Prof. Hamburg Cons. and Royal Mus. Director, 1874 ; *d.* 1901.

Wrote several instructive pf. pieces.

GURNEY, Edmund. *D.* Brighton, 1888.

Wrote "The Power of sound," 1880.

GUSIKOW, M. J. *B.* Poland, 1806 ; *d.* 1837.

Celebrated for his performances on the *Strohfiedel* (*q.v.*).

Gu'sto (*I.*). Taste.

Di buon gu'sto. In good taste.
Gusto'so. Tastefully.
Gran Gu'sto. (See *Gran.*)

G-ut. (See **Gamma.**)

Gut (*G.*). Good, well ; very.

Gut betont'. Well accented.
Gu'ter Takt'eil. The strong beat.
Gut gehal'ten. Well sustained.
Gut gestos'sen. Very staccato.
Gut hervor'tretend. Well brought-out.
Gut stim'men. To play in tune.
Mit gut'em Humor. With much humour.

Gut. Catgut.

Gut strings are usually made from the entrails of sheep or lambs, the latter yielding the finest strings. Genuine " Roman" strings are the best.

GUT'MANN, Adolf. 1819-82. Pupil and friend of Chopin. Wrote much pf. music.

Gut'tural. Throaty ; produced in the throat.

The "gutturals" are *g, k, c* (as in cat), *ch* (as in chasm), *ng* (nasal guttural), and *h* (aspirate).

GUY d'Arezzo. (See **Guido.**)

GUY, Henry. Tenor ; *b.* Oxford, 1847.

GWYN, Eira. Young Welsh contralto. First London appearance, 1907.

GYE, Mrs. E. (See **Albani.**)

GY'ROWETZ (pron. *Ghee'-ro-vets*), **Adalbert.** *B.* Bohemia, 1763 ; *d.* Vienna, 1850. Became known through the friendship of Mozart. Capellmeister, Vienna Court Opera, 1804-31.

Works : 30 operas (*Der Augenarzt,* the best), 40 ballets, 60 symphonies, &c., now mostly forgotten.

H

H. The German name for B♮. (See **B**, and **German Scale**.)

H. An abbn. for horn, heel, or hand.

HAAS, Madame Alma (*née* **Hollaender**). Pianist; *b.* Ratibor, Silesia, 1847. Settled in England, 1870.

Habane'ra. A Cuban contra-dance in 3-4 or 6-8 time.

HA'BENECK, François A. Distinguished conductor; *b.* Ardennes, 1781; *d.* Paris, 1849. Permanent concert director Paris Cons., 1828; conductor, Grand Opéra for 20 years (from 1826). Introduced Beethoven's Symphonies to the French public.
Pub. some vn. and orchestral music.

HA'BERBIER, Ernst. *B.* Königsberg, 1813; *d.* 1869. Concert pianist.
Pub. pf. pieces, études, &c.

HA'BERL, Franz X. *B.* Lower Bavaria, 1840. Became a priest, and was made Canon of Ratisbon. Theorist and writer; great authority on Catholic music.
Editor of *Musica Sacra* and (formerly) of the *Kirchenmusikalisches Jahrbuch*. Founded a Palestrina Society, 1879. Directs a school of church music.
His works include an edition of the "Works of Palestrina," "Magister Choralis," a "Psalterium Vespertinum," &c.

HA'BERMANN, Franz J. *B.* Bohemia, 1706; *d.* 1783. Capellmeister and composer.
Works: an opera, 12 masses, 6 litanies, &c.

Ha'ber-rohr (*G.*). A shepherd's flute or pipe.

Hack'(e)brett (*G.*). A dulcimer.

Hack'e (*G.*). The heel.

HACKH, Otto C. *B.* Stuttgart, 1852. Went to New York, 1880.
Works: abt. 200 pf. pieces.

HADDEN, Jas. Cuthbert. Musician and writer; *b.* nr. Aberdeen, 1861.

HADDOCK, Edgar A. Violinist; *b.* Leeds, 1859.

HADDOCK, Geo. Percy. Violinist; brother of E. A.; Leeds, 1860-1907.

HADOW, Wm. Hy. *B.* Ebrington, 1859. Mus.B.Oxon, 1890.
Works: "Studies in Modern Music," hymns, cantatas, chamber music, "National Songs," &c. Editor of the "Oxford Hist. of Music." Chairman "Church Music Society."

HAES'CHE, Wm. E. Condr. and composer; *b.* New Haven (U.S.), 1867.

HAESSLER, J. W. (See **Hässler**.)

HÄFF'NER, Johann C. F. *B.* nr. Suhl, 1759, *d.* Upsala, 1833. Cath. orgt., Upsala, 1808; Music-director of the Univ., 1820.
Works: 3 operas, collections of Swedish Folk Songs, a "Svensk Choralbok," &c.

Ha'gebüchen (*G.*). Coarse, clumsy.

HA'GEMANN, Maurice L. Pianist and violinist; *b.* Zutphen, 1829. Founded a Cons. of Music, Leeuwarden, 1875.
Works: an oratorio, cantatas, pf. pieces, songs.

HA'GEN, Adolf. *B.* Bremen, 1851. "Artistic manager," Dresden Cons., 1884.
Works: a 2-act comic opera, &c.

HA'GEN, Friedrich H. von der. *B.* Ukraine, 1780; *d.* 1856. Prof. of German Literature, Berlin Univ.
Pub. a valuable work in 5 vols. on the "Minnesingers and their Music."

HA'GER, Johannes (Johannes von Hasslinger-Hassingen). Vienna, 1822-98. Pupil of Mendelssohn.
Wrote an oratorio, 2 operas, chamber music, &c.

HAGUE, Chas. *B.* Tadcaster, 1769; *d.* 1821. Mus.Doc. Cantab., 1801. Prof. of Music, Cambridge University, 1799.

HAHN, Reynaldo. *B.* Caracas, Venezuela, 1874. Pupil, Paris Cons.
Works: stage music, pf. pieces, and several songs.

Hahn'büchen (*G.*). Coarse, clumsy.

HÄH'NEL. Jacobus Gallus (*q.v.*).

Hail, Columbia. American patriotic song; composed 1798.

HAINL, Georges F. Distinguished French 'cellist; 1807-73. Chef de orchestre, Grand Opéra, Paris, 1863.
Conducted the Court concerts and the concerts of the Paris Cons. for some years.

HAI'ZINGER (or **HAITZINGER**), **Anton.** Operatic tenor; *b.* Wilfersdorf, 1796; *d.* 1869. Sang principally at Carlsruhe; also in London, Paris, and Vienna.

Halb, Hal'be (*G.*). Half.
Hal'be Applikatur'. A half shift (on the vn., &c.).
Halb'bass. A small double bass.
Halb'cadenz. (See *Halbkadenz*.)
Halb'cello. A small 'cello.
Halb'gedeckte Stim'me. An org. stop, with the pipes "half-stopped."
Halb'kadenz. A half-close (Dominant Cadence).
Hal'be No'te. A minim ($\mathbf{\cdot}$).
Hal'be Or'gel. An organ without 16 ft. pipes.
Hal'be Pau'se. A minim rest.
Halb'schluss. A half-close.
Halb'schreitig. Proceeding by semitones; chromatic.
Halb'stark. Half loud; *mf*.
Hal'be Stim'me. An incomplete organ stop.
Hal'be Takt'note. A minim ($\mathbf{\cdot}$).
Halb'tenor. A baritone.
Halb'ton } A semitone.
Hal'ber Ton }
Halb'violine. A small violin for children.
Halb'violon. Same as *Halb'bass*.
Halb'werk. Same as *Hal'be Or'gel*.

HALE (or **HALLE**). (See **Adam de la Hale**.)

HALE, Philip. American musician and writer; *b.* Norwich, Vermont, 1854.
Critic, *Boston Home Journal, Boston Post, New York Musical Courier*, &c. Editor, *Boston Musical Record* (1897).
"One of the most forceful and brilliant writers for the American musical press."—*Baker*.

HALÉVY, Jacques François F. E. Distinguished dramatic composer; *b.* Paris, May 27, 1799; *d.* Nice, March 17, 1862. Son of a Jew. Entered Paris Cons. at 10. Studied counterpoint under Cherubini. Won the *Prix de Rome*, 1819, and studied for 3 years in Italy. Prof. of

Harmony, Paris Cons., 1827; and of counterpoint and fugue, 1833.

Chef de Chant, Paris Opéra, 1830. Succeeded Reicha as a member of the Académie, 1836; appointed secretary for life, 1854.
Chief operas: *Pygmalion, l'Artisan* (1827), *Clari* (1829), *Manon Lescaut* (1830), *La langue Musicale* (1831), *Les Souvenirs de Lafleur* (1832), *La Juive* (1835), *l'Eclair* (1835), *La Reine de Chypre* (1841), *Charles VI* (1843), *Le Val d'Andorre* (1848), *La Fée aux roses* (1849), *Le Juif errant* (1852), *Valentine d'Aubigny* (1856), *La Magicienne* (1857).
Of these, *La Juive* was his masterpiece. He also wrote pf. pieces, part-songs, cantatas, and a popular Text Book on Singing.
His music exhibits great artistic refinement and true dramatic power.

Half Beat. Old name for a short appoggiatura (or acciaccatura).

Half Cadence. ⎫ (See **Cadence.**)
Half Close. ⎭

Half-note. (1) A minim (𝅗𝅥). (2) Old name for a semitone.

HALFORD, Geo. Jn. Orgt., pianist, and condr.; *b.* Warwickshire, 1858.

Half-rest. A minim rest

Half-shift. (See **Shift.**)

Hälf'te (*G.*). A half.

Half-tone. A semitone.

HALIR', Karl. Distinguished Bohemian violinist; *b.* 1859. Leader, Weimar Court Orchestra.

HALIR', Theresa (*née* **Zerbst**). Soprano; wife of preceding; *b.* Berlin, 1859.

Hall, Hal'le (*G.*). Sound, clang, resonance.
Hal'len. To sound, to clang, to resound.

HALL, Chas. King. London, 1845-95. Orgt. and composer.
Works: "Harmonium Primer" (Novello), several popular operettas for the *German Reed* Entertainments, church music, songs, &c.

HALL, Elsie M. S. Pianist; *b.* Australia, 1877.

HALL, Marie. Distinguished violinist; *b.* Newcastle-on-Tyne, 1884.

HALL, W. H. *B.* Nottingham, 1842. "Father of the I.S.M."

HALLE. (See **Adam de la Hale.**)

HALLÉ, Sir Charles. *B.* Hagen, Westphalia, 1819; *d.* Manchester, 1895. Infant prodigy; studied under Rink. Went to Paris, 1836; established a reputation as a pianist, and was friendly with Cherubini, Chopin, and Liszt. Came to London, 1848; and founded "Charles Hallé's Orchestra," Manchester, 1857. Knighted, 1888; married **Madame Norman-Neruda**, 1888.
He was a sound "classical" pianist, and a fine interpreter of Beethoven. He edited and pub. many pf. works.

Hallelujah. (See **Alleluia.**)

HALLÉN', Anders. Swedish dramatic composer; *b.* Gotenburg, 1846. Conductor, Stockholm Royal Opera, 1892.
Works: operas (including *Hexfallen*, 1896), orchestral pieces, ballad-cycles for voices and orch., songs, &c,

HAL'LER, Michael. *B.* Upper Palatinate, 1840. Teacher at the school of Church Music, Ratisbon.
Works: masses, motets, &c., and several treatises on church music.

HALLEWELL, Fredk. Jn. Bass singer; *b.* Leeds, 1846. Went to Australia, 1880.

Hal'ling. A Norwegian country dance, generally in 4-4 time.

HALL'STRÖM, Ivar K. Swedish dramatic composer; *b.* Stockholm, 1826; *d.* 1901.
Chief operas: *Mountain King* (1874), *Bride of the Gnome* (1875), *Vikings' Voyage* (1877), *Nyaga* (1885), *Granada's Daughter* (1892).

HALM, Anton. *B.* Styria, 1789; *d.* 1872. Intimate friend of Beethoven.
Works: chamber music, pf. pieces, études, &c.

Halm'pfeife (*G.*). A shepherd's pipe.

Hals (*G.*). The neck of an inst.

Halt (*G.*). A hold, or pause, ⌢.
Halt'en. To hold, sustain.

HAM'BOURG, Mark. Pianist; *b.* South Russia, 1879. Pupil of Leschetizky.

HAMBOYS. (See **HANBOYS.**)

HA'MEL, Eduard. *B.* Hamburg, 1811. Violinist, Grand Opéra, Paris, for several years.
Works: an opera (*Malvina*), pf. pieces, songs, &c.

HAMEL, M. P. *B.* Auneuil, 1786; *d.* 1875(?) Expert on organ building.
Wrote a valuable work on "Organ construction from the time of Dom Bedos," with an historical account of the org. and biographies of the chief org. builders.

HA'MEL, Margarethe. (See **Schick.**)

HA'MERIK, Asger. *B.* Copenhagen, 1843. Pupil of Gade and Bülow. Director Cons. of Peabody Institute, Baltimore, 1871.
Works: operas (*La Vendetta*, &c.); cantatas, symphonies, chamber music, &c.

HAMILTON, David. Organ builder; Edinburgh, 1803-63.
Invented the *Pneumatic Lever* for organs.

HAMILTON, James Alexander. London, 1785-1845. Son of a dealer in second-hand books. Wrote and translated numerous works, some of which are still in vogue. He was unfortunately of intemperate habits, and died in want and misery.
Works: Modern Instruction for the Pf.; Catechisms of Singing, Harmony, Counterpoint, Double Counterpoint, Writing for an Orchestra, &c.; a Dictionary of Musical Terms; translations of Cherubini's Counterpoint, Baillot's Violin Method, &c.

HAMILTON, John. *B.* 1761; *d.* Edinburgh, 1814.
Wrote several Scots songs, and pub. collections of Scottish music.

HAM'MA, Benjamin. Composer; *b.* Friedingen, 1831.

Hammer. (*G.*, *Ham'mer*; *F.*, *Marteau*; *I.*, *Martel'lo.*) (See **Pianoforte.**)
Ham'merclavier (G.) ⎫ Early name for the pf.
Ham'merklavier (G.) ⎭

HAM'MERSCHMIDT, Andreas. Bohemian organist ; 1611-75.
His numerous compositions are of considerable antiquarian and historical value.

Hanac'ca (*I.*). (*F., Hanaise ; G., Hana'-kisch.*) A Moravian dance in 3-4 time, somewhat like a *Polonaise*, but quicker.

Al'la hanac'ca (*I.*). In *hanac'ca* style.

HANBOYS (or **HAMBOYS**), John. Doctor of Music ; abt. 1470.
Wrote a Latin treatise describing the musical notation then in use.

Hand, Harmonic. (See **Guidonian Hand.**)

HAND, Ferdinand G. *B.* Saxony, 1786 ; *d.* 1851.
Pub. a suggestive work on "Musical Æsthetics."

Hand'bassl (*G.*). An obsolete bass inst. between a viola and a 'cello.

Hand'bildner. }
Hand'leiter. } " Hand-guide." (See *Chiroplast.*)

Hand'glocke. A hand-bell.

Hand'lage. Position of the hand in playing.

Hand'stücke. Short pf. exercises for "forming" the hand.

Hand'tasten. Fingerboard.

Hand'trommel. A tambourine.

Hän'de (*G.*). Hands.

Zu 2 Hän'den }
Zwei'händig } For 2 hands.

HANDEL, George Frederick. (*G.,* **Hän'del, Georg Friedrich.**) One of the great masters of music ; *b.* Halle, Feb. 23, 1685 ; *d.* London, April 14, 1759. His father, surgeon and valet to the Prince of Saxe-Magdeburg, intended Handel to be a lawyer. The boy, however, secretly learnt to play the harpsichord ; and at the age of 7 so astonished the Duke of Saxe-Weissenfels by his organ playing that the Duke persuaded the unwilling father to let his gifted son have a sound musical education—still with the understanding on the father's part that he should eventually become a lawyer and not a musician. Placed under Zachau, orgt. of Halle Cath., he studied counterpoint, &c., and practised diligently on the organ, harpsichord, and oboe. Was apptd. asst. organist, and "for three years wrote a motet for every Sunday." In 1696 the Elector Frederick offered to send Handel to Italy, but his father declined. The father died in 1697 ; but in pursuance of his wishes Handel took up and continued his legal studies until 1703. Went to Hamburg, 1703, as violinist, and afterwards clavecinist, under Keiser, director of the German opera. Here he produced two operas, 1704-5. Went to Italy (1706) and brought out his first Italian opera, *Rodrigo*, Florence, 1707. Returned to Germany, 1709, as Capellmeister to the Elector of Hanover. Visited England, 1710, and produced *Rinaldo* at the Haymarket. Again visited London, 1712, and having written an ode for the Queen's birthday and a *Te Deum* and *Jubilate* for the Peace of Utrecht was awarded an annuity of £200, which caused him to "conveniently forget" to return to Hanover. By the death of Queen Anne, 1714, the Elector succeeded to the throne of England as Geo. I. Handel had naturally incurred the King's displeasure, but the intervention of powerful friends and the success of his "Water-Musick" re-instated him in the monarch's favour. The annuity also was confirmed ! Appointed Chapel-master to the Duke of Chandos, 1718 ; wrote his first great English oratorio, *Esther*. Was also music-master to the daughters of the Prince of Wales ; and was apptd. Director of the new Royal Academy of Music. *Radamisto* (1720) was the first of a series of operas Handel wrote for the Royal Academy ; this period of his career is noted for the war between his supporters and those of Bononcini and Ariosti (his rivals). Bononcini, however, left London in 1731. (See **Bononcini.**) In 1733, Handel undertook the management of opera on his own account ; but renewed opposition, his own unyielding temper, a failure of health (1737), and other causes, led to financial ruin ; and in 1741 he abandoned opera for oratorio. The *Messiah* (Dublin, April 13, 1742) restored him to popular favour. In 1752 he wrote his last oratorio, *Jephtha*. He was much troubled during the composition of this work by failing eyesight, and three operations for cataract resulted in total blindness. He still, however, continued playing the organ at his oratorio performances, playing for the last time at a performance of the *Messiah* on April 6, 1759—eight days before his death. He was buried in Westminster Abbey, having been naturalized as an Englishman in 1726.

The German Händel Society's complete edition of Handel's works (Dr. Chrysander) comprises 100 large folio vols. The following are his most important compositions :—

Operas : *Almira* (1704), *Rodrigo* (his first *Italian* opera, 1707), *Agrippina* (Venice, 1708), *Rinaldo* (Haymarket, 1710), *Radamisto* (1720), *Scipione* (1726), *Alcina* (1735), *Serse* (1738), *Deidamia* (1741), and some 30 others.

Serenatas : *Aci, Galatea, e Polifemo* (1708), *Parnasso in Festa* (1734), *Acis and Galatea* (1721), *Semele* (1743), *The Choice of Hercules* (1750).

Oratorios : *Passion according to John* (1704), *Il Trionfo del Tempo e del Disinganno* (Rome) 1707), *La Resurrezione* (1708), *Passion Oratorio* (1717), *Esther* (his first Eng. oratorio, 1720), *Deborah* (1733), *Athaliah* (1733), *Saul* (1738), *Israel in Egypt* (1738), *Messiah* (1741 ; 1st performance Dublin, 1742), *Samson* (1741), *Joseph* (1743), *Hercules* (1744), *Belshazzar* (1744), *Occasional* (1746), *Judas Maccabæus* (1746), *Alexander Balus* (1747), *Joshua* (1747), *Solomon* (1748), *Susanna* (1748), *Theodora* (1749), *Jephtha* (1752, his last).

Odes: *Alexander's Feast* (1736), *St. Cecilia's Day* (1739), *L'Allegro, Il Penseroso, ed Il Moderato* (1740).

Te Deums, Anthems, &c.: 12 Chandos anthems (1718-20), 4 Coronation anthems (1727), *Utrecht Te Deum* (1713), *Dettingen Te Deum* (1743), &c.

Miscellaneous Vocal Music: 25 Chamber duets, 12 Hanover cantatas (1711), 79 Italian cantatas (1706-12), various songs, and detached pieces, &c.

Instrumental Music: 12 harpsichord sonatas (1732), 6 hautboy concertos (1734), 6 organ concertos (1734), 7 sonatas for 2 vns. and 'cello (1735), 12 grand concertos (1739), 6 organ concertos (1741), a third set of org. concertos 3 other organ concertos, "Water Musick" (1715), "Forest Musick" (1741-2), "Firework Musick" (1749), 16 harpsichord suites (1720-1733), 6 fugues, 3 sets of "Lessons," &c.

Handel Commemoration. A festival performance of Handel's works in Westminster Abbey, 1784. (Also 1785, 1786, 1787, and 1791.)

Handel Festival. The 1st "Great Handel Festival" was held at the Crystal Palace (1857) under Costa. Since 1862 it has been held triennially.

Hand-guide. (See **Chiroplast.**)

Hand-harmon'ica. An Accordion.

Hand-horn. (See **Horn.**)

HÄNDL. (See **Gallus.**)

HAND'LO, Robt. de. English musician, 14th cent.
Wrote a Commentary on Franco's System of "Mensurable Music."

Hand'lung (*G.*). Action, plot; a drama.

Hand-note. A "stopped" note on the horn.

Hand Organ. A barrel-organ; especially a *small* portable barrel-organ.

Hand Piano (Handle-piano). A mechanical pf. on the "barrel-organ" principle.
It is capable of great facility of execution, but little expression.

HAND'ROCK, Julius. B. Naumburg, 1830; d. 1894. Wrote instructive pf. pieces.

Hand-signs.
These signs, used in teaching Tonic Sol-fa, are suggestive of the "Mental Effects" of the tones of the scale; thus, the *firm* Doh is represented by the closed fist; the *steady, calm* Me by the level hand, &c. Analogous signs, "finger signs," are used for time; the thumb is kept out of sight, and each of the 4 fingers represents a *quarter-pulse.*

HÄ'NEL von CRO'NENTHAL, Julia. B. Graz, 1839. Studied in Paris.
Works: symphonies, pf. sonatas, &c.

HANF'STÄNGEL, Marie (*née* **Schröder**). B. Breslau, 1848, retired 1897. Fine soprano; *début* as "Agathe," Weber's *Der Freischütz*, Paris, 1867.

Hanging-tone. An "after-stroke" auxiliary note one degree above (or below) the harmony note which it follows.
It may be consonant or dissonant, and is often of the nature of an *anticipation* :—

✳ HANDEL.

HAN'KE, Karl. B. Rosswalde, 1754; d. 1835. City music-director, Hamburg.
Works: operas, ballets, and other stage music; symphonies, chamber music (including some 300 horn duets), songs, &c.

HANKEY, Katherine.
Author of "Tell me the old, old story," pub. 1866.

HÄN'SEL und GRE'TEL. Fairy opera by Humperdinck (Weimar, 1893).

HANS'LICK, Dr. Eduard. Distinguished critic and writer; b. Prague, 1825; d. 1904. Musical editor (of conservative opinion) Vienna *Neue Freie Presse,* 1864.
His most influential work is a treatise on "Musical Æsthetics," which claims that "the beauty of a musical composition lies wholly in the music itself without reference to extraneous non-musical ideas." It has been translated into several languages.

HANS'SENS, Chas. Louis Joseph. B. Ghent, 1777; d. 1852. For some time director of the Royal Orch. and Inspector of the Cons., Brussels.
Works: operas, masses, &c.

HANS'SENS, Chas. Louis. 'Cellist; b. Ghent, 1802; d. 1871. Conductor, Theatre de la Monnaie, Brussels, 1848-69.
Works: 8 operas, symphonies, concertos, masses, cantatas, &c.

HARCADELT. (See **Arcadelt.**)

Hard. (1) Of tones: coarse, harsh, strident. (2) Of touch: heavy, wanting in delicacy and variety. (3) Of execution: unsympathetic, without expression.

HAR'DEGEN. (See **Egghard.**)

d'HARDELOT, Guy (Mrs. Rhodes). Contemporary song composer; b. Chateau d'Hardelot, nr. Boulogne-sur-Mer.

Hardiment (*F.*). ⎫ Boldly; with vigour,
Avec hardiesse (*F.*). ⎭ hardihood.

HARDING, Henry Alfred. B. Salisbury, 1855. Mus.D. Oxon, 1882. Sec. R.C.O. 1908.
Author of an "Analysis of Beethoven's pf. sonatas," &c.

HARDY, Jos. N. B. nr. Leeds, 1860. Orgt. Wakefield Cath. since 1886.

Har'fe (*G.*). The harp.
Har'fenbass. Same as *Alberti Bass* (*q.v.*).
Harfenett'. (See *Spitzharfe.*)
Har'fen Instrumen'te. Instruments whose sounds are produced by plucking the strings.
Har'fenmässig. Harp-like; *arpeggiando.*
Har'fenspieler. Harp player.

HARGITT, Chas. J. Orgt., condr., and composer; b. Edinburgh, 1833.

HARINGTON (or **HARRINGTON**), **Henry.**
B. Kelston, Somersetshire, 1727 ; *d.*
1816.
Wrote hymn-tunes, glees, catches, rounds, &c.

Harm. Abbn. of *Harmonic.*

Harmoni'a (*Gk.* and *L.*). Harmony.

Harmon'ic, Harmon'ick (*adjective*). (*L., Harmon'icus ; Gk., Harmon'ikos ; G., Harmo'nisch ; F., Harmonique ; I., Armo'nico.*) Pertaining to harmony or chords ; as opposed to *Melodic*, pertaining to melody.

Harmonic figuration. Broken chords, *arpeggios.*
Harmonic flute. (See *Harmonic Stops.*)
Harmonic hand. (See *Guidonian Hand.*)
Harmonic interval. A consonant interval.   o
Harmonic mark. In vn. music, &c., a
    small *o* placed above a note to show
    that a harmonic note is required :—
Harmonic note. } Also *Flageolet* tone. (See the Nuon
Harmonic tone. } *Harmonic,* below.)
Harmonic reed. (See *Harmonic Stops.*)
Harmonic scale. The natural series of "Partials."
    (See *Acoustics.*)
Harmonic stops. Org. stops whose pipes have a small
    hole pierced midway, so as to give sounds an
    octave higher.
Harmonic triad. A common chord.

Harmonic (*noun*). (*a*) *Natural* harmonic.
(1) (*G., O'berton ; F., Son harmonique ; I., Suo'no armo'nico*). An "upper partial."
(See **Acoustics.**)
(2) (*G., Flageolet'ton, Harmo'nikaton ; F., Son harmonique ; I., Suo'no armon'ico.*)
An upper partial produced by lightly touching an open string while bowing.
Thus : By lightly touching a string at the middle
    the octave is produced ; by touching it at one
    third of its length, the 12th is produced, &c.
    These "harmonics" are sweet and delicate, with
    a "fluty" tone (especially on the 'cello and
    double bass) ; hence the term *flageolet* tones
    (or *flautato*). They were brought into practical
    use by Paganini.
(*b*) *Artificial Harmonic.* A note produced by stopping a
    string, and also touching it lightly at some aliquot
    part of the vibrating portion.

Harmonic Chromatic Scale. }
Harmonic Minor Scale. } (See **Scale.**)

Harmon'ica. An inst. developed from the "Musical Glasses" (*q.v.*) by Dr. Benjamin Franklin.
Mouth Harmonica. (See *Mouth.*)

Harmonicel'lo. An inst. of the 'cello kind with 5 gut and 10 wire strings.

Harmon'ichord. }
Harmonicorde (*F.*). } A Piano-violin (*q.v.*).

Harmon'icon. Name applied to the mouth-harmonica, the orchestrion, and various other instruments.

Harmoni-cor (*F.*). A wind inst. blown through a mouthpiece, and fitted with a set of clarinet-shaped reed pipes to supply the different sounds.

Harmonics. (1) The science of music. (2) Plur. of Harmonic (*q.v.*).

Harmo'nicum. A development of the *Bandonion* (*q.v.*).

Harmonie' (*G.* & *F.*). (1) Harmony ; chord. (2) The wind insts. of an orchestra. (3) Music for wind insts.

Harmonie'eigen. Chordal, harmonic ; proper to a
    chord.
Harmonie'gesetze. The rules of harmony.
Harmonie'fremd. Foreign to a chord.
Harmonie'lehre. A harmony text book ; a theory of
    harmony.
Harmonie'musik. Music for wind insts.
Harmonie'regeln. The rules of harmony.
Harmonie'trompete. An instrument between the horn
    and a trumpet.

Harmonieux,-ieuse (*F.*). Harmonious.

Harmo'nika (*G.*). A concertina or accordion.
Holz'harmonika. A Xylophone (*q.v.*).
Mund'harmonika. A Mouth harmonica (*q.v.*).
Zieh'harmonika. An accordion.

Harmon'iphon. (*G., Klavier'oboe.*) A wind inst. with a keyboard, and oboe-shaped reed pipes.

Harmonique (*F.*). Harmonious.
Sons harmoniques. Harmonics (2).

Harmoni'(e)ren (*G.*). To harmonize.

Harmo'nisch (*G.*). Harmonic ; harmonious.
Harmo'nische Töne. Harmonics (2).

Harmo'nium. A keyboard inst., patented by A. Debain, Paris, 1843, provided with bellows worked by the feet to force the air outwards through a series of free reeds. (See **Reed Organ.**)
In harmonium music figures enclosed in circles are
    used to indicate the stops :—

On the Bass side :	On the Treble side
(1) Cor Anglais.	(1) Flute.
(2) Bourdon.	(2) Clarinet.
(3) Clarion.	(3) Piccolo.
(4) Bassoon.	(4) Oboe.

Stops (1) and (4) on each side are of 8ft. (or
    unison) pitch ; stop 2 of 16ft. pitch ; stop 3 of
    4ft. pitch.

Harmonize. (1) To agree ; to form part of a chord. (2) To arrange or compose harmony ; especially to add other parts to a given melody or bass.

Harmony. (1). (*L.* and *Gk., Harmoni'a ; G., Harmonie'; F., Harmonie ; I., Armoni'a.*) "Notes in combination."— *Macfarren.* "The system of forming chords, with their proper movement or progression according to key-relationship."—*Stainer.*

(A) HISTORY.—The history of harmony may be
    divided into three stages.
(1) The contrapuntal, polyphonic, ancient, or
    strict style :
Harmony a combination of intervals result-
    ing from the superposition of melodies ;
    music regarded *horizontally ;* tonality vague,
    based largely on the old modes (see *Modes*) ;
    little idea of definite chord-progression or key-
    relationship.
(2) The harmonic, homophonic, modern, or free
    style :
Harmony built up on "roots" of chords (Ra-
    meau's *Traité d'Harmonie,* 1722) ; harmonic
    structure regarded *vertically ;* definite tonality,
    the modern major and minor keys fixed ;
    chord-progressions systematized ; clearly de-
    termined key-relationship.

(3) The ultra-modern tendency or "harmony of the future" (Wagner to Rd. Strauss):

Re-action against definite tonality and key-relationship ; harmonies built up on the "semi-tonic" scale ; any concord or discord can be used *in any key* ; any chord can be followed by *any other chord* ; two (or more) keys can be even employed simultaneously (as in Strauss).

(B) MATERIALS.

The materials of harmony are concords and discords. Excluding enharmonic varieties of notation there are 12 *major* common chords—one on each semitone of the chromatic scale—and 12 *minor* common chords. Add to these 24 "first inversions" (or "*b*" positions) and 24 "second inversions" ("*c*" positions), also 12 first inversions of diminished triads, and we have a total of 84 possible concords, of which only 24 are direct chords.

The number of possible discords is, however, *infinite ;* a Wagner, Debussy, or Rd. Strauss is always inventing some new combination, and text-books of harmony have to be continually revised in the endeavour to explain and systematize the fresh developments. Concords are the foundation of harmony, the "substantial food" of music, so to speak ; discords set off the concords ; they are the "seasoning." Discords vary considerably in their dissonant effect ; some are noble and sonorous (as Dominant 7ths) ; others harsh, and essentially displeasing to the ear. A succession of concords becomes monotonous ; a succession of discords soon tends to disagreeable unrest ; the best effects of harmony are produced by a due admixture of both, and that musical taste is undoubtedly a depraved one which is constantly endeavouring "to startle the ear by the introduction of far-fetched and incoherent cacophony."

(C) SYSTEMS.

Systems of harmony may be arranged in two classes.

I. ROOT THEORIES (best exemplified in the Day-Macfarren System).

(1) Concords: (*a*) The common chords of the key and their inversions, and the 1st inversion of diminished triads. (*b*) Chromatic concords "borrowed" from other keys, but not implying a change of key.

(2) Prepared Discords : (*a*) Suspensions (resolved in the same chord). (*b*) Essential 7ths and 9ths (resolved on another chord).

(3) Discords which do not need preparation : (*a*) Fundamental discords derived from the "Chord of Nature" (see *Acoustics*), and available on the dominant, supertonic, and tonic of the key ; they include 7ths, 9ths, 11ths, and 13ths (see *Fundamental Discords*). (*b*) Passing-notes, appoggiaturas, and auxiliary notes generally.

II. ALTERED CHORD THEORIES.

(1) Diatonic triads of the key and their inversions.
(2) Chords by chromatic alterations of triads ; *e.g.* :—

&c.
(See *Altered Chords*.)

(3) Suspensions, or chords by substitution.
(4) Chords by addition (or superposition) ; *e.g.* :—

(5) Various combinations of 2, 3, 4 :—

(*a*) (*b*)

(*a*) Alteration and addition.
(*b*) Substitution and chromatic addition.

(6) Combinations formed by passing notes, &c.

N.B.—The advanced student of harmony should study not only English treatises, but German, French, and Italian works (as, for example, those of Jadassohn, A. Lavignac, and A. Galli).

Artificial Harmony. A mixture of concords and discords (as opposed to *natural* harmony).

Broken Harmony. In arpeggios.

Chromatic Harmony. (1) Containing chromatic notes. (2) The modern style.

Close Harmony. With the parts in close position (near together in pitch).

Compound Harmony. With two or more constituent notes.

Diatonic Harmony. (1) Consisting of diatonic notes. (2) The ancient style.

Dispersed Harmony. }
Extended Harmony. } Same as *open* harmony.

Essential Harmony. The chords divested of passing notes, auxiliary notes, &c.

Figured Harmony. Ornamented with passing-notes, grace-notes, &c.

Free Harmony. (1) Not bound by strict rules. (2) The modern style.

Natural Harmony. Consisting of common chords.

Open Harmony. The parts at wide intervals from one another.

Perfect Harmony. Same as *Pure Harmony.*

Plain Harmony. The opposite of figured harmony.

Pure Harmony. Harmony in pure, or just intonation.

Spread Harmony. Same as *open* harmony.

Strict Harmony. With the rules strictly observed (the opposite of *Free* harmony).

Tempered Harmony. As performed on equally tempered insts. (pf., org., &c.).

Harmony. (2). Agreement, concord ; a chord. (3) Music in general.

Harmony Analysis. The analysis of chords and harmonic progressions by means of figures or other symbols.

Three methods of Harmony Analysis are in common use :—

(1) FIGURED BASS (*q.v.*).

(2) GOTTFRIED WEBER'S METHOD :

(*a*) The triads of a key are indicated by Roman numerals ; major triads by large capitals ; minor triads by small capitals :—

I II III IV V VI

I IV V VI

(*b*) A small *o* shows a diminished triad, as VII° ; a 7th, 4th, 9th, &c., is shown by a corresponding figure, as V₇ (Dominant 7th).

(*c*) The prevailing key is indicated by *Italics*, capitals for major keys, small letters for minor.

(3) CURWEN'S METHOD :

This is essentially the same as Weber's, but is more definite and complete.

(*a*) The sol-fa name of the chord is shown by a capital letter, *e.g.*, D, chord of *Doh ;* S, chord of *Soh*, &c.

(*b*) The position (or inversion) of the chord is indicated by a small letter *a, b, c, d,* &c., *after* the capital ; and 7ths, 9ths, &c., are shown by corresponding figures *before* the capital.

The following shows the 3 methods :—

(1)   6   6   6   7 ♮7   6   5   7
        4   ♯   4   3
        2

(2) C: I V I V₇ I II₇ V₇ vi IV I   V V₇ I
(3)   D Sb D ⁷Sd Db⁷fᶜR ⁷S L F Dc   S ⁷S D

Methods (2) and (3) are equally available for indicating chords to accompany a melody :—

From BUSSLER-CORNELL's *Musical Form.*

e: II°7 (V)   C: III   II   I V I

By combining Weber's and Curwen's methods—and adding several features of his own—Prof. Prout has developed an exceedingly elaborate "Harmony Analysis," of which the following is a specimen :—

Harmony: 16th Edition, p. 245.

e: V7b   vii° 7   ♯iv° 7d) a: vii° 7
           (V9b)   a: ♯iii° 7c }   (V9b)

V 13g   1b   ♯iv° 7b) Bb: ♯iv°b7b
           Bb : vii°b7d }   (IIb9c)

Harmony, False. (1) False relation (*q.v.*). (2) Wrong or discordant notes, caused by mistakes, or ignorance of rules.

Harmony of the Spheres.
    A "grand world music," held by ancient nations (Chinese, Greeks, &c.) to be produced by the harmonious motions of the heavenly bodies. (See *Greek Music.*)
"There's not the smallest orb which thou behold'st
But in his motion like an angel sings,
Still quiring to the young-eyed cherubins."
                                    Shakespeare.

HARM'STON, John W. *B.* London, 1823 ; *d.* Lübeck, 1881. Pupil of Sterndale Bennett. Wrote pf. pieces and songs.

Harp, Harpe. (*O. Eng., Hearp* ; *L., Har'pa* ; *G., Har'fe* ; *F., Harpe* ; *I., Ar'pa.*) A stringed inst. of triangular form, furnished with a number of gut strings which are plucked by the thumb and first three fingers of each hand.
    The harp is one of the most ancient and universal of insts. (see *Egyptian Music*), and several varieties of it are still in use.
    The orchestral, or "double action" harp (see *Erard*) has 46 or 47 strings—a range of 6½ octaves—and is furnished with 7 pedals. When all the pedals are raised to their highest position the instrument stands in the key of C♭, and

gives the major scale without any chromatic notes. Compass—

Each pedal acts simultaneously on all the strings of the same letter name ; *i.e.*, one acts on all the C's, another on all the D's, &c. By depressing a pedal to its first "notch" it raises all the strings connected with it by a semitone. Thus when all seven pedals are lowered to the 1st notch, the harp stands in the key of C major. By depressing a pedal to its 2nd notch the corresponding strings are raised another semitone. Thus by suitable combinations of pedals any desired key or chromatic note can be obtained.
Single-Action Harp. Stands in E♭ ; compass 5 octaves. Each pedal can raise the pitch of its corresponding strings by *one* semitone only.
Double Harp. A harp with two rows of strings tuned dissimilarly.
Triple Harp. A harp with 3 rows of strings tuned dissimilarly.
Æolian Harp. (See *Æolian.*)
Chromatic Harp. Recently invented by M. Gustave Lyon. It gives a complete chromatic scale, having 12 strings to each octave and no pedals. The strings for the "sharps" cross the others diagonally.
Couched Harp. A spinet (*q.v.*).
Dital Harp. A kind of lute provided with *Ditals,* or Finger keys, to raise the pitch a semitone.
Jews' Harp. See under "J."
Welsh Harp. A triple harp. Two of the rows of strings are tuned diatonically ; the third provides the "accidentals."

Harp Pedal. Name given to the "soft" (or left) pedal of the pf.

Harpe (*F.*). A harp.
Harpe d'Eole } Æolian harp (*q.v.*).
Harpe éolienne }

Harpeg'gio. Same as **Arpeggio.**

HARPER, Thomas. Celebrated trumpet-player ; *b.* Worcester, 1787 ; *d.* 1853.

HARPER, Thos. J. Trumpet-player ; *b.* London, 1816 ; *d.* 1898.

Harpicor'do. Same as **Arpicordo.**

Harp-lute. See **Dital-harp** (above).

Harpo-lyre (*F.*). A kind of large guitar with 21 strings and 3 necks.

Harp'sichon, Harp'sicon. Old name for the harpsichord or spinet.

Harpsichord, Arpsichord, Harpsechord. (*G., Kiel'flügel ; F., Clavecin ; I., Arpi-cor'do, Clavicem'balo.*) The precursor of the Grand pf. The strings were plucked by means of quills attached to "jacks." (See **Pianoforte.**)
Harpsichord Graces. Old graces specially used in harpsichord music.
Vis-à-vis Harpsichord. With two keyboards at opposite sides or ends.

Harp-way tuning. Special tunings of the *Viola da Gamba* to facilitate arpeggio playing.

HARRADEN, Ethel. (Mrs. Frank Glover.) Contemporary composer ; has written cantatas, songs, pf. pieces, &c.

HAR'RADEN, Samuel. *B.* Cambridge, abt. 1821 ; *d.* 1897. Orgt. Old Mission Church, Calcutta, 1846. Founded the first Calcutta "Glee Club."

HARRIERS - WIPPERN, Luise (*née* Wippern). *B.* Hildesheim, 1837 ; *d.* 1878. Charming soprano ; *début* as "Agathe" (Weber's *Der Freischütz*), Royal Opera, Berlin, 1857 (where she was afterwards permanently engaged).

HARRINGTON. (See **Harington.**)

HARRIS. Family of organ-builders.
The most noted was *Renatus* (or *René*), who returned to England abt. 1660, and was a formidable rival to Father Smith (*q.v.*).

HARRIS, Sir Augustus. *B.* Paris, 1852 ; *d.* 1896.
" One of the most celebrated theatrical managers of the 19th century." Drury Lane, 1879 ; Her Majesty's Theatre, 1887 ; &c.

HARRIS, Clement Antrobus. Musical litterateur ; *b.* York, 1862.
Author of " Curios of Mus. History," " Chart of Mus. History," "Snippet Thoughts of a Country Orgt.," &c.

HARRIS, Clement Hugh Gilbert. *B.* 1871 ; killed at Pentepizendia, 1897. Pianist ; pupil of Mad. Schumann.
Works : 4 concert-studies for pf., a Symphonic Poem, &c. –showing great promise.

HARRIS, Cuthbert. *B.* London, 1870. Mus.Doc. Durham, 1899. Orgt., comp., and writer.

HARRIS, Wm. Victor. American orgt. and song composer ; *b.* New York, 1869.

HARRISON, Annie Fortescue (Lady Arthur Wm. Hill). Song composer.
"In the gloaming" (1877) was very popular.

HARRISON, Beatrice. 'Cellist ; *b.* Roorkee, India, 1892.

HARRISON, Julius A. *B.* Stourport, 1885.
Prize cantata *Cleopatra*, Norwich, 1908.

HARRISON, May. Contemp. violinist. Won the " Open Scholarship," R.C.M., 1904. Prof. *début*, 1907.

HARRISON, Samuel. Tenor singer ; *b.* Belper, Derbyshire, 1760 ; *d.* 1812.

HARRISON, Walter. *B.* London, 25 April, 1859. B.A. Cantab, 1893 ; Mus.B. Oxon, 1895 ; M.A. Cantab, 1897. Appointed Secretary Tonic Sol-fa College, 1900, in succession to Mr. Robt. Griffiths.

HARRISON, Wm. Fine tenor singer and actor ; *b.* Marylebone, 1813 ; *d.* 1868.

HARRISS, Dr. Chas. A. E. Organist ; *b.* London, 1862. Settled in Montreal, 1883.
Works : Coronation Mass, an opera, anthems, pf. music, songs, &c.

HARROP, Sarah (Mrs. Joah Bates). Soprano singer ; *d.* London, 1811.

Hart (*G.*). Hard, harsh, abrupt, unprepared ; major.
Har'te To'nart. Major key (mode).
Hart'klingend. Harsh.
Hart vermin'derter Drei'klang. A diminished triad with a major 3rd :—

HART, Andro. Published Hart's Scottish Psalter, Edinburgh, 1611.

HART, George. London, 1839-91. Son of J. T. (below).
Wrote "The Violin: Its Famous Makers and their Imitators," and "The Violin and its Music."

HART, James. Bass singer. Sang at York Minster, the Chapel Royal, and Westminster Abbey. *D.* 1718.
Works : Songs in "Choice Ayres, Songs, and Dialogues" (1676-84), &c.

HART, John Thos. English vn. maker, and famous vn. expert ; 1805-74.

HART, Philip. Organist ; probably son of James.
Works : anthems, odes, org. fugues, &c.

HÄR'TEL, Benno. *B.* Silesia, 1846. Prof. Berlin Royal Hochschule.
Works : pf. pieces, songs, &c.

HÄR'TEL, Gustav A. Violinist ; *b.* Leipzig, 1836 ; *d.* 1876. Capellmeister, Homburg, 1873.
Works : opera (*Die Carabiner*), operettas, vn. pieces, &c.

HÄR'TEL, Luise (*née* HAUFFE). Pianist ; 1837-82. Wife of Dr. H. Härtel of the firm of Breitkopf & Härtel.

HART'MANN, Emil. Son of J. P. E. (below). Copenhagen, 1836-98.
Works : operas (*Runenzauber*, &c.), orchestral and chamber music, &c.

HART'MANN, Johan P. E. Danish composer ; *b.* Copenhagen, 1805 ; *d.* 1900.
Director Copenhagen Cons., 1840 ; Royal Capellmeister, 1849. Gade was his son-in-law.
Works : operas (*The Corsairs*, 1835, &c.), orchestral and chamber music, pf. pieces, songs, &c.

Hart'näckige Bass (*G.*). A ground bass (*q.v.*).

HAR'TOG, Edouard de. *B.* Amsterdam, 1826. Settled in Paris, 1852.
Works : operas (*l'Amour et son Hôte*, 1873, &c.), orchestral and chamber music, songs, pf. pieces, &c.

HAR'TOG, Jacques. *B.* Zalt-Bommel, Holland, 1837. Prof. of mus. hist., Amsterdam School of Music.
Works : Dutch translations of Lebert and Stark's *Klavierschule*, Langhans' " Hist. of Music," &c.

HART'VIGSON, Fritz. Pianist ; *b.* Jutland, 1841. Settled in London, 1864. Pianist to the Princess of Wales, 1873 ; Prof. Norwood Coll. for the Blind, 1875 ; Pf. prof. Crystal Palace, 1887.

HARTY, H. Hamilton. Composer ; *b.* Hillsborough, Ireland, 1881.

HARTY, Mrs. H. H. (See **Agnes Nicholls.**)

HARWOOD, Basil. *B.* Olveston, Gloucestershire, 1859. Orgt. Christ Church Cathedral, Oxford, 1892 ; Mus.Doc., 1896.

HARWOOD, Edward. *B.* nr. Blackburn, 1707 ; *d.* 1787.
Wrote the popular music to " Vital spark of heavenly flame."

Harz (*G.*). Resin ; rosin.

HÄ'SER, August F. *B.* Leipzig, 1779 ; *d.* 1844. Capellmeister, Weimar Court Theatre.
Works : oratorio (*Der Triumph des Glaubens*), masses, Te Deums, &c. ; orchestral music, 3 operas, pf. music, songs, &c.

HÄ'SER, Charlotte H. Celebrated singer ; sister of A. F. ; *b.* Leipzig, 1784 ; *d.* 1871.

HAS'LER (or **HASS'LER**), **Hans Leo von.**
Distinguished early German composer ;
one of the founders of German music.
B. Nuremburg, 1564 ; *d.* Frankfort,
1612. Studied in Italy. Court musician
at Prague, 1601-8.
Works : canzonette, Cantiones Sacræ, madrigals,
masses, psalms, and sacred songs, litanies,
motets, &c. His music exhibits fine scholarship, many pieces being in 12-part counterpoint.

HAS'LER, Jakob. Brother of H. L. ; *b.*
Nuremburg, 1566 ; *d.* 1601. Famous
organist ; composed church music.

HAS'LER, Kaspar. Brother of the above ;
Nuremburg, 1570-1618.
Edited a collection of church music.

HAS'LINGER, Tobias. Music publisher,
Vienna ; *b.* Zell, 1787 ; *d.* 1842. Inti-
mate friend of Beethoven.
His son **Karl**, 1816-68, wrote an opera
(*Wanda*), and about 100 other works.

HAS'SE, Faustina (*née* Bordo'ni). *B.* Venice,
1693 (or 1700) ; *d.* 1783. Famous
mezzo-soprano ; sang for Handel,
London, 1726-8. Married J. A. Hasse
(below), 1730.
"In her zenith, she was unrivalled in the brilliance
and finish of her vocalization."—*Baker.*

HAS'SE, Gustav. Song composer ; *B.*
Brandenburg, 1834 ; *d.* 1889.

HAS'SE, Johann Adolph. *B.* Bergedorf, nr.
Hamburg, 1699 ; *d.* Venice, 1783. Son
of a schoolmaster. Sang under Keiser,
Hamburg Theatre, 1717-21. Prod. his
1st opera, *Antigonus*, Brunswick theatre,
1723. Studied in Italy (1724) with
Porpora and A. Scarlatti. Prof. Scuola
degl'Incurabili, Venice, 1727. Married
Bordoni (see above), Venice, 1730.
Capellmeister and opera director, Dresden, 1731. Invited to London by
Handel's enemies, but recognised his
own inferiority and returned to Dresden,
1739. Remained there with his wife—
popular favourites — till 1763, afterwards retiring to Vienna. Spent the
last 10 years of his life at Venice.
Works : over 100 operas, including *Il Sesostrate*
(Naples, 1726), *Attalo, re di Bitinia* (Naples,
1728), *Dalisa, Artaserse, Ruggiero* (1744, his
last), &c. ; 10 oratorios, 5 Te Deums, cantatas,
masses, misereres, psalms, concertos, &c. His
melodies were delightful ; two of them were
sung every evening for 10 years by Farinelli
(*q.v.*), to soothe the melancholy of his royal
master, Philip of Spain.

HAS'SELBECK, Rosa. (See **Sucher.**)

HAS'SELT-BARTH, Anna M. W. (*née* **Van
Hasselt**). Celebrated soprano. *B.*
Amsterdam, 1813 ; *d.* 1881. *Début*,
Trieste, 1831.

HASS'LER. (See **Hasler.**)

HÄSS'LER, Johann W. *B.* Erfurt, 1747 ;
d. 1822. Son of a cap maker. Studied
the org. and became orgt. at Erfurt at
the age of 14. Founded Winter Concerts, Erfurt, 1780. Imperial Capell-

meister, St. Petersburg, 1792 ; settled
in Moscow as a pf. teacher, 1794.
His pf. works form a link between those of Bach
and Beethoven. The best known is a *Gigue in
D minor ;* he also wrote sonatas, concertos,
fantasias, &c.

HASS'LINGER-HASS'INGEN. (See **Hager.**)

HAST, Thos. Gregory. Tenor ; *b.* London,
1862.

Hast'ig (*G.*). Quick, hasty, impetuous.

HASTINGS, Thos. Self-taught American
musician, 1787-1872.
Wrote "The History of Forty Choirs," a "Dissertation on Musical Taste," &c.

HAST'REITER, Helene. Contralto singer ;
b. Louisville, Kentucky, 1858. Has
sung with great success in Italy.

HATCHARD, Caroline. Contemp. vocalist.
Pupil of Agnes Larkcom ; 3rd appearance at Covent Garden, 1908.

Hâte (*F.*). Speed, haste.

HATHAWAY, Jos. W. G. Orgt. and composer ; *b.* 1870. Mus.D. Oxon, 1906.

HATHERLY, Rev. Stephen G. *B.* Bristol,
1827 ; *d.* 1905. Mus.Doc., St. Andrew's,
1893.
His treatise on "Byzantine Music" is a scholarly
work.

HATTO. (See **M. J. Frère.**)

HATTON, John Liptrot. *B.* Liverpool, 1809 ;
d. 1886. Self-taught musician. Conductor, Drury Lane, 1842. Music-
director, Princess' Theatre, 1853-8.
Works : Sacred drama (*Hezekiah*), operettas, and
other stage music, many successful part-songs,
very popular songs, &c.

HATT'STAEDT, John J. *B.* Monroe, Michigan, 1851. Director, American Cons.,
Chicago, 1886.

Hau'chen (*G.*). To breathe, exhale, aspirate.

HAUCK, Minnie. Soprano ; *b.* New York,
1852. *Début* as "Norma," 1869. Has
sung with great success in London,
Vienna, Berlin, &c.

HAUFF, Johann C. Frankfort, 1811-91.
One of the founders, Frankfort School
of Music.
Wrote a "Theorie der Tonsetzkunst" (3 vols.).

HAUF'FE, Luise. (See **Härtel.**)

Haupt (*G.*). Head, chief, principal.
Haupt'accent. The primary or *strong* accent of a
  measure.
Haupt'akkord. (1) Tonic triad. (4) A fundamental
  chord. (See *Acoustics.*)
Haupt'gesang. } The leading melody.
Haupt'melodie }
Haupt'kadenz. A full close.
Haupt'kirche. Cathedral.
Haupt'manual. The "great" organ manual. (*Man.* 1
  in German editions.)
Haupt'note. (1) The principal note (of a chord,
  melody, or measure). (2) The essential note in a
  turn, shake, &c.
Haupt'prinzipal. An 8-ft. diapason on an org.
  manual ; a 16-ft. diapason on the pedal.
Haupt'probe. "Chief proof ;" a full or final rehearsal.
Haupt'sängerin. Prima donna.
Haupt'satz. Chief theme ; *motive.*
Haupt'schluss. A full close.
Haupt'septime. The dominant 7th.
Haupt'stimme. The principal part (vocal or instru-
  mental).

Haupt'thema. The 1st or principal theme (or subject).
Haupt'ton. (1) Root of a chord. (2) Key-note. (3) Generator.
Haupt'tonart. The chief key of a composition.
Haupt'werk. The great organ. (H.W. in German editions.)
Haupt'zeitmass. The prevalent *tempo* of a piece.

HAUPT, Karl A. *B.* Silesia, 1810; *d.* 1891. Fine organist; played at various Berlin churches; had many distinguished pupils.

    Pub. a "Choralbuch" (1869), part-songs, songs, &c.

HAUPT'MANN, Dr. Moritz. *B.* Dresden, 1792; *d.* Leipzig, 1868. Studied the vn. and compn. under Spohr, 1811.

    Musik-direktor, Thomasschule, Leipzig, 1842, and prof. of counterpt. and compn. at the Cons. Among his distinguished pupils were Ferd. David, Burgmüller, Joachim, Sullivan, Bülow, and Cowen.
    Works: an opera, chamber music, church music, songs, a valuable treatise on "Die Natur der Harmonik und Metrik," &c.

HAUPT'NER, T. Berlin, 1825-89.
    Pub. a "Deutsche Gesangschule," &c.

HAU'SE, Wenzel. *B.* Bohemia, abt. 1796. Prof. of the double-bass, Prague Cons.
    Wrote a valuable "Contrabass-schule."

HAU'SEGGER, Siegmund von. Talented German composer; *b.* 1872.
    Has written fine symphonic poems.

HAU'SER, Franz. Dramatic baritone; *b.* nr. Prague, 1794; *d.* 1870.
    Sang in London, 1832. Director and singing teacher, Munich Cons., 1846-64. Formed a fine collection of Bach's works, autographs, &c.

HÄU'SER, Johann E. *B.* nr. Quedlinburg, 1803; *d.* (?) . Teacher, Quedlinburg Gymnasium.
    Works: a "A Musical Lexicon" (2 vols.), a "Neue Pianoforteschule," &c.

HAU'SER, Miska. Hungarian violinist; 1822-87. Toured (1840-61) through Europe, America, Australia, &c.
    Works: an operetta, and numerous vn. pieces.

HAUS'MANN, Robt. 'Cellist; *b.* Rottlebe-rode, Harz Mts., 1852; *d.* 1909. From 1879, 'cellist in the Joachim Quartet.

HAUS'MANN, Valentin. The name of five musicians " in direct lineal descent."

(1.) *B.* Nuremburg, 1484. Friend of Luther and Walther; wrote chorals.

(2.) Son of (1). Organist at Gerbstädt wrote motets, canzonets, and dance music.

(3.) Son of (2). Organist at Löbejün; expert on organ building.

(4.) Son of (3). Organist at Alsleben; wrote a treatise on solmization.

(5.) Son of (4). *B.* Löbejün, 1678; orgt. at Merseburg, Halle, and Lauchstädt.

Hausse (*F.*). Nut (of a violin bow, &c.).
Hausser. To raise the pitch.

Haut,-e (*F.*). High.
Haut-contre. (1) Counter tenor, or Alto. (2) An alto viola.
Haut-dessus. High soprano; 1st soprano.
Haute-taille. High tenor; 1st tenor.

Hautbois (*F.*). An oboe (*q.v.*).
Hautbois baryton. A modern baritone oboe an octave lower than the ordinary one.
Hautbois d'amour. A small obsolete form of oboe.

Haut'boy (pron. *Hō-boy*). Old English spelling of oboe (*q.v.*).

Hautement (*F.*). Haughtily.

HAUTIN (or **HAULTIN**), **Pierre.** *B.* La Rochelle, abt. 1500; *d.* Paris, 1580.
    The earliest founder of musical types in France (1525).

Havanaise (*F.*). A Habanera (*q.v.*).

HAVERGAL, Frances Ridley. 1836-79. (Daughter of Rev. W. H.).
    Wrote several hymns: " I could not do without Thee," " Master, speak," &c.

HAVERGAL, Rev. Wm. H. *B.* High Wycombe, 1793; *d.* 1870.
    Wrote services, hymns, chants, &c. Edited a reprint of Ravenscroft's Psalter.

HAWEIS, Rev. Hugh R. *B.* London, 1838; *d.* 1901. Amateur violinist.
    His "Music and Morals" and "My Musical Life" are interesting works, though quite untrustworthy.

HAWES, Wm. London, 1785-1846. Chorister, Chapel Royal, 1793-1801; violinist, Covent Garden, 1802; Gentleman, Chapel Royal, 1805; Master of the Choristers, St. Paul's, 1814; Master of the Children, Chapel Royal, 1817; Layvicar, Westminster Abbey, 1817-20; Director of English opera, Lyceum, 1824-36.
    Works: comic operas, glees, madrigals, &c.

HAWKINS, Sir John. *B.* London, 1719; *d.* 1789. Attorney and ardent musical amateur. Knighted, 1772.
    Wrote a "General History of the Science and Practice of Music," in 5 vols. (1776; repub. by Novello & Co., 1875).

HAWKS, Annie S. New York, 1835-72.
    Wrote the hymn " I need Thee every hour."

HAWLEY, Chas. Beach. Song composer; *b.* Brookfield, Mass., 1858.

HAWLEY, H. Stanley. Pianist and composer; *b.* Ilkeston, 1867.

HAY'DN, Franz Josef. "The father of modern instrumental music." *B.* Rohrau, Lower Austria, Mar. 31, 1732; *d.* Vienna, May, 31 1809. Second son of a wheelwright, who was also the organist and sexton of the village church. Commenced to learn music under his cousin, Johann Mathias Frankh, at the age of 5. At 8, sent to Vienna, as chorister at St. Stephen's Church, under George Reutter, who, however, taught him very little. Wrote a mass at 13. In 1748 his voice began to break, and he was dismissed. Some poor, but generous friends, gave him shelter, and he managed to gain a bare pittance (and to continue his musical studies) by giving lessons. He was soon able to rent an attic for himself, which was fortunately in the house where the poet Metastasio lived. The poet taught the youth Italian, and procured him an engagement as teacher in a Spanish family. Here he became acquainted with Porpora, who in return for various menial services, gave him instruction in composition, and procured him a stipend of 50 francs a month from the Venetian ambassador. In 1752 he was engaged by Countess Thun as harpsichordist and singing master ; and in 1758 Count Ferdinand Maximilian Morzin appointed him Musik-direktor, at Lukavec (nr. Pilsen). In 1760, he entered the service of Prince Paul A. Esterházy, Eisenstadt, as 2nd, and afterwards 1st Capellmeister. The "great" Nicholas Esterházy succeeded his brother in 1762, and henceforward Haydn's musical career and fame were established. The Prince maintained an adequate orchestra, and Haydn's duties at the new Esterház palace included "two weekly operatic performances and two formal concerts" in addition to the "daily music." Prince Nicholas died in 1790, but Haydn was retained at a salary of 1,400 florins. His duties were nominal, and he settled in Vienna. In 1791-2 and again in 1794 he visited England, where he wrote 12 of his finest symphonies, and received the honorary degree of Mus.D. Oxon. In 1797 he composed the " Emperor's Hymn," now the National Hymn of Austria ; in 1798, his *Creation* was produced, and in 1801 *The Seasons*. His last appearance in public was at a performance of the *Creation*, 1808.

Works : (*a*) Instrumental : 125 symphonies (some with titles : *e.g.*, *Farewell*, *Oxford*, *Toy*, *Surprise*, *Military*), *The Seven Last Words*, 9 vn. concertos, 6 'cello concertos, 16 other concertos for various insts., 77 string quartets, 32 trios, 4 vn. sonatas, 20 pf. concertos, 38 pf. trios, 53 pf. sonatas and divertimenti, 4 sonatas for vn. and pf., 175 pieces for barytone (a kind of *Viola da Gamba*), &c.
(*b*) Vocal : 3 oratorios (*Creation*, *Seasons*, *Il ritorno di Tobia*), 14 masses, several cantatas, 2 Te Deums, 13 offertoires, motets, &c. ; about 25 operas and operettas (of little permanent value), 22 arias, 12 canzonets, 36 German songs, duets, trios, collections of Scotch and Welsh songs, &c.

Haydn-form.
The form of the *First Movement* of a sonata, symphony, &c., of which the general plan was definitely established by Haydn. (See *Form* and *Sonata*.)

HAY'DN, Johann Michael. Brother of F. J. ; *b.* Rohrau, 1737 ; *d.* Salzburg, 1806. Chorister, St. Stephen's, Vienna, 1745-55. Concertmeister, Salzburg, 1762 ; orgt. of Salzburg Cath. and St. Peter's Church, 1777. His wife, **Maria Magdalena** (*née* Lipp), was a fine soprano.
Works : about 360 church compositions (oratorios, masses, &c.), operas, operettas, songs, &c.; 30 symphonies, chamber music, org. pieces.

HAYES, Catherine. Distinguished soprano ; *b.* Limerick, 1825 ; *d.* 1861.

HAYES, William. *B.* Hanbury, Worcestershire, 1706; *d.* 1777. Orgt. Worcester Cath., 1731-4 ; Magdalen Coll., Oxford, 1734 ; Univ. Prof. of Music, 1742 ; Mus.Doc., 1749.
Works : a masque (*Circe*), psalms, cantatas, glees, anthems, &c.

HAYES, Philip. Son of preceding ; *b.* Oxford, 1738 ; *d.* 1797. Gentleman, Chapel Royal, 1767 ; Orgt. New Coll., Oxford, 1776 ; orgt. Magdalen Coll. and Univ. Prof. of Music, 1777 ; Mus.Doc., 1777 ; orgt. St. John's Coll., 1790.
Works : an oratorio (*Prophecy*), anthems, services, odes, glees, 6 concertos for org. or harpsichord, &c.

HAYM (or **HENNIUS**), **Gilles.** Belgian composer.
Published masses, motets, &c. (1620-51).

HAYM (or **AIMO**), **N. F.** *B.* Rome, abt. 1679 ; *d.* London, 1729.
Wrote opera libretti for Handel, Bononcini, Ariosti, and others.

HAYNES, Walter Battison. *B.* Kempsey, 1859 ; *d.* 1900. Prof. of counterpoint and harmony, R.A.M., 1890.
Works : cantatas for female voices, church music, songs, org. music, &c.

HAYS, Wm. Shakespeare. Song composer ; *b.* Louisville, Kentucky, 1837.
His numerous simple popular songs include " Driven from home," " Write me a letter from home," " Mollie darling," &c.

Head. (1) The point of a bow. (2) The part of a vn., &c., which includes the pegs and scroll. (3) The membrane of a drum. (4) The part of a note which indicates its pitch.
Head-voice } Opposed to chest voice, &c. (See *Voice*
Head-tones } *Production*.)

HEAP, Chas. Swinnerton. *B.* Birmingham, 1847 ; *d.* 1900. Studied Leipzig Cons.; Mus.Doc. Cambridge, 1872.
Works : oratorio (*The Captivity*), cantatas, overtures, anthems, pf. pieces, songs, &c.

HEATHER. (See **Heyther**.)

HE'BENSTREIT, Pantaleon. *B.* Eisleben, abt. 1669 ; *d.* 1750.
Celebrated performer on the "Pantalon," an improved dulcimer of his own invention.

HEBER, Reginald, D.D. 1783-1826. Vicar, Hodnet, 1807. Bishop, Calcutta, 1823.
Wrote many fine hymns : " Holy, holy, holy," " Brightest and best," " From Greenland's icy mountains," &c.

HEBRIDES. Concert overture by Mendelssohn, 1830. Called also " Fingal's Cave."

HECHT, Eduard. *B.* Dürkheim, 1832 ; settled in England, 1854 ; *d.* 1887.
Works : cantatas, chamber music, pf. pieces, &c.

HECK'EL, Wolf. Pub. a colln. of old songs and dances for lute (Strasburg, 1562).

Heck'elphon (*G.*), An inst. similar to the Hautbois Baryton (*q.v.*).
Used by Strauss in *Elektra*, 1909.

HECK'MANN, Georg J. R. Violinist; *b.* Mannheim, 1848; *d.* 1891.

HEDGCOCK, Walter Wm. *B.* Brighton, 1864. Orgt. Crystal Palace, 1894.
Works: songs and pianoforte pieces.

HED'MONDT, E. C. Tenor; *b.* Maine (U.S.), 1857.

HEDOUIN, Pierre. Lawyer. *B.* Boulogne, 1789; *d.* 1868.
Wrote several works on musicians and musical subjects. Also wrote libretti for several operas, and composed songs.

HEER'MANN, Hugo. Violinist; *b.* Heilbronn, 1844. Chief vn. teacher, Hoch Cons., Frankfort-on-Main, 1878.

Heer'pauke (*G.*). Army drum; large kettle-drum, &c.

Hef'tig (*G.*). Impetuous, passionate, boisterous, vehement, fervent.
Hef'tig bele'bend } Becoming intensely ani-
Hef'tig beschleun'igend } mated.
Hef'tigkeit. Vehemence, passion, impetuosity.

HE'GAR, Emil. 'Cellist and singing teacher; *b.* Basle, 1843.

HE'GAR, Friedrich. Brother of E. *B.* Basle, 1841. Studied Leipzig Cons. Settled in Zurich as conductor and teacher, 1863; founded a Cons. there, 1875.
Works: dramatic poems, hymns, &c., for voices and orchestra; male choruses, songs, a vn. concerto, pf. pieces, &c.

HEGEDÜS, Ferencz. Violinist; *b.* Hungary, 1872(?). London *début*, 1901.

HEG'NER, Anton. 'Cellist; *b.* Copenhagen, 1861.
Works: 2 'cello concertos, chamber music, songs.

HEG'NER, Otto. *B.* Basle, 1876. Precocious pianist; first appearance in England, 1888. *D.* 1907.

Hehr'messe (*G.*). High Mass.

Heim'lich (*G.*). Mysterious, stealthy; homely.

HEI'NE, Heinrich. 1801-55. Poet.
Wrote many of the finest German songs ("Lorelei," &c.).

HEI'NEFETTER, Sabine. *B.* Mayence, abt. 1805; *d.* insane, 1872.
As a young girl she was a strolling harpist; her beautiful voice was noticed by a Frankfort musician, and after some training she became a brilliant operatic soprano.

HEI'NEMANN, Alex. Vocalist and composer; *b.* Berlin, 1873.

HEI'NEMEYER, Ernst Wm. Distinguished flautist; *b.* Hanover, 1827; *d.* 1869.
Wrote concertos and other flute music.

HEI'NICHEN, Johann David. *B.* nr. Weissenfels, 1683; *d.* 1729. Court Capellmeister, Dresden, 1718.
Works: church music, operas, cantatas, concertos, a "Treatise on Thorough Bass," &c.

HEIN'RICH, Johann G. Silesia, 1807-82.
Works: cantatas, psalms, org. pieces, an "Organ Instructor," &c.

HEIN'RICH, Max. Baritone singer; *b.* Chemnitz, 1853.
Works: several songs.

HEIN'RICHS, Anton P. *B.* Bohemia, 1781; *d.* New York, 1861.
Works: songs, pf. pieces, &c.

HEIN'ROTH, Johann A. G. *B.* Nordhausen, 1780; *d.* 1846. Music-director, Göttingen Univ., 1818.
Reorganised the Jewish Liturgy, and composed several melodies still sung in Jewish synagogues. Also wrote part-songs, male choruses, and theoretical works.

HEINTZ, Albert. *B.* Eberswalde, 1822. Orgt. Petrikirche, Berlin.
Writer on Wagner's works, &c.

HEIN'ZE, Gustav A. *B.* Leipzig, 1820; *d,* 1904. Capellmeister, German opera. Amsterdam, 1850; director, Euterpe Liedertafel, 1853; conductor, Excelsior Singing Society, 1868.
Works: oratorios, masses, cantatas, male choruses, &c.

HEI'SE, Peder Arnold. Copenhagen, 1830-79.
Chief works: 2 operas (*The Pasha's Daughter*, *King and Marshal*), and many songs.

HEI'SER, Wilhelm. Berlin, 1816-97.
Wrote over 500 songs—some very popular.

Heiss (*G.*). Hot, ardent, burning.

Hei'ter (*G.*). Cheerful, serene, bright.

HEL'DENLEBEN, Ein. Tone poem by Rd. Strauss; Frankfort, 1899.

Held (*G.*). A hero.
Hel'dendichter. Epic poet.
Hel'denlied. A hero song.
Heldenmässig. Heroic; in heroic style.
Hel'dentenor. A dramatic *tenore robusto.*

Hel'icon. (*G., Helikon.*) A circular monster bombardon carried over the shoulder.

Hell (*G.*). Bright, clear, sonorous.

HELL'ER, Stephen. Esteemed pianist and composer; *b.* Pesth, 1815; *d.* Paris, 1888. Played in public at 9; made a concert tour with his father, 1829-32.
Went to Paris, 1838, and became acquainted with Liszt, Chopin, and Berlioz. Visited London, 1849, and again in 1862, spending the rest of his life in Paris.
Wrote several hundred pf. pieces, including *Promenades d'un Solitaire*, ballades, études, mazurkas, waltzes, Songs without words, variations, caprices, &c. Only the *études* and a few detached pieces are now popular.

(1) **HELL'MESBERGER, Georg** (Senr.). Celebrated vn. teacher; *b.* Vienna, 1800; *d.* 1873.
His pupils include Ernst, Hauser, Joachim, and his own sons (see below).

(2) **HELL'MESBERGER, Georg** (Junr.), Son of (1). Fine violinist; *b.* Vienna. 1830; *d.* 1852.
Produced 2 operas at Hanover.

(3) **HELL'MESBERGER, Joseph** (Senr.). Son of (1). Distinguished violinist; Vienna, 1829-93. 1st vn. of the "Hellmesberger Quartett," 1849-87. Director Vienna Cons. till 1893. Hofkapellmeister, 1877. President of the Jury for Mus. Insts., Paris Exhibition, 1855.

(4) **HELL'MESBERGER, Joseph** (Junr.), Son of (3). Vienna, 1855-1907. Court Opera Capellmeister, 1886; leader of the "Hellmesberger Quartett," 1887.
Works: several operettas, ballets, &c.

(5) **HELL'MESBERGER, Rosa.** Daughter of (2). Operatic singer; *début*, Vienna Court Opera, 1883.

HELL'WIG, Karl F. L. *B.* Kunersdorf, 1773; *d.* 1838. Orgt. Berlin Cath,, 1813.
Works: operas (*Don Sylvio,* 1822), masses, motets, songs, male choruses, &c.

HELM, Theodor. Highly esteemed musical critic; *b.* Vienna, 1843.
Chief work: a "Technical Analysis of Beethoven's Quartets."

HELM'HOLTZ, Hermann L. F. Famous scientist; *b.* Potsdam, 1821; *d.* 1894.
His "Sensations of Tone as a Physiological Basis for the Theory of Music (1863; Eng. translation by Ellis, 1875) is the standard work on Acoustics.

HELMORE, Rev. Thos. *B.* Kidderminster, 1811; *d.* 1890.
Published several works on Plain-Song (" The Hymnal Noted,") &c.

Helpers. Pipes sometimes used in organs to sound with other pipes, to increase the volume or brilliancy of tone, or to promote quick " speech."

Hemi (*Gk.*). Half.
Hemidemisemiquaver. A note equal to 1-8th of a quaver—
Hemidiapen'te (*Gk.*). A diminished 5th.
Hemidi'tone (*Gk.*). A minor 3rd.
Hem'iphrase. A half phrase.
Hem'itone. A semitone.

HEMPSON (or **HAMPSON**), **Denis.** One of the last of the Irish bards; *b.* nr. Garvagh, Londonderry, 1695; *d.* 1807, at the great age of 112. He played on his harp the day before his death.

HEMY, Henri F. Composer and writer; *b.* Newcastle, 1818.

HENDERSON, J. Dalgety. Tenor singer; *b.* Montrose, 1856.

HENDERSON, Wm. Jas. American musician and writer; *b.* Newark, New Jersey, 1855. Lecturer on Musical Hist., New York Coll. of Music; writes for most of the leading musical magazines.

HEN'KEL, Michael. Fulda, 1780-1851.
Wrote church music, org. pieces, &c.

HEN'KEL, Dr. Georg A. Son of preceding; Fulda, 1805-71.
Wrote masses, motets, male choruses, org. pieces, pf. pieces, &c.

HEN'KEL, Heinrich. Pianist; son of M.; *b.* Fulda, 1822; *d.* 1899. Royal Musik-director, Frankfort, 1883.
Works: a pf. method, songs, pf. pieces, vn. pieces, &c.

HENLEY, John. Wesleyan minister. 1800-42.
Wrote the hymn "Children of Jerusalem."

HEN'NES, Aloys. *B.* Aix-la-Chapelle, 1827; *d.* 1889.
Wrote some useful educational pf. pieces.

HEN'NIG, Karl. Berlin, 1819-73. Royal Music-director, 1863.
Wrote psalms, cantatas, songs, male choruses, &c.

HEN'NIG, Karl Rafael. Son of preceding; *b.* Berlin, 1845. Founded the "Hennig" Vocal Society, Posen, 1873.
Author of a profound analysis of Beethoven's 9th symphony, &c.

HEN'NIUS. (See **Haym.**)

HENRY VIII. 1491-1547. King of England.
Composed motets, and other pieces.

HEN'SCHEL, Isidor Georg. Fine baritone singer; *b.* Breslau, 1850. Studied at Leipzig and Berlin. Resided in London 1877-80; conductor, Boston Symphony Orchestra, 1881-4; settled in London, 1885; founded the London Symphony Concerts; Prof., R.C.M., 1886-8.
Works: an opera, a comic operetta, an oratorio, orchestral pieces, psalms, and several songs.

HEN'SCHEL, Lillian (*née* **Bailey**). Soprano singer; wife of preceding; *b.* State of Ohio, 1860; *d.* 1901.

HEN'SEL, Fanny Cecilia. *B.* Hamburg, 1805; *d.* Berlin, 1847. Brilliant pianist and clever composer; eldest sister of Mendelssohn. Married the Prussian artist, Hensel, 1829.
Her sudden death so affected Mendelssohn that his health broke down, and he died 6 months later.

HEN'SELT, Adolf von. Distinguished pianist; *b.* Bavaria, 1814; *d.* 1889. Studied under Hummel. Toured in Germany, 1837; went to St. Petersburg, 1838; was appointed chamber pianist to the Empress, and held other positions at the Imperial Court.
His compositions for the pf. include a concerto in F minor, and some very fine études.

HENT'SCHEL, Theodor. *B.* Upper Lusatia, 1830; *d.* Hamburg, 1892. Theatre Capellmeister successively at Leipzig, Bremen, and Hamburg.
Works: 5 successful operas (*Lancelot,* 1878), orchestral pieces, pf. music, songs, &c.

Hep'tachord. (1) A scale of 7 notes. (2) The interval of a 7th. (3) An instrument with 7 strings.

HEPTINSTALL, John. The first English music type-printer to unite quavers and semiquavers into groups by joining their stems. London, abt. 1690.

Herab'strich (*G.*). The down-bow ("downstroke.").
Herab'stimmung. Lowering the pitch.

Herauf'gehen (*G.*). To ascend.

Herauf'strich (*G.*). The up-bow.

HER'BECK, Johann F. von. Celebrated conductor; Vienna, 1831-77. Son of a poor tailor; chiefly self-taught. Chorus master Vienna *Männergesang-verein,* 1856; Prof. at the Cons., and conductor of the *Singverein,* 1858; conductor, *Gesellschaft der Musikfreunde* 1859; chief Court Capellmeister, 1866.
Works: numerous part-songs, church music, orchestral music, &c.

HERBERT, John Bunyan. Composer; *b.* U.S., 1852.

HERBERT, Victor. *B.* Dublin, 1859. Solo 'cellist, Metropolitan Orchestra, New York, 1886; bandmaster, 22nd Regiment (succeeding Gilmore), 1894; conductor, Pittsburg Orchestra, 1898.
Works: an oratorio (*The Captive*), comic operas, a 'cello concerto, songs, &c.

HE'RING, Karl Friedrich A. Violinist; *b.* Berlin, 1819; *d.* 1889. Founded the Berlin *Sonatenverein*, 1848.
Works: symphonies, masses, chamber music, songs, a vn. method, &c.

HE'RING, Karl Gottlieb. *B.* Schandau, Saxony, 1765; *d.* 1853. Principal of Zittau Seminary, and chief teacher of harmony, from 1811.
Works: theoretical treatises, text books, pf. pieces, &c.

HE'RING, Karl Eduard. Son of preceding; *b.* Oschatz, Saxony, 1809; *d.* 1879.
Works: pf. pieces, part-songs, songs, school chorals, &c.

HERITES, Marie. Violinist; *b.* Wodnian, Bavaria, 1884(?).

HER'MAN, Robert. *B.* Berne, Switzerland, 1869.
Works: a symphony in C (Berlin, 1895), and other orchestral pieces, a pf. quintet, pf. pieces, songs, &c.

HER'MANN, Friedrich. Violinist; *b.* Frankfort, 1828. Studied under Mendelssohn, Leipzig Cons.; member of the Gewandhaus Orchestra, 1846-75; Prof. at the Cons., 1848.
Works: a symphony, chamber music, &c.

HER'MANN, Johann D. Pianist; *b.* Germany, abt. 1760; *d.* Paris, 1846. Teacher of Marie Antoinette.
Wrote pf. concertos, sonatas, &c.

HER'MANN, Johann G. J. Philologist and Greek scholar; Leipzig, 1772-1848. Wrote valuable works on Metre.

HER'MANN, Matthias. Netherland contrapuntist; 16th cent.
Wrote motets, &c., and a "Musical Battle Sketch" (an early attempt at "program music").

HER'MANN, Reinhold L. Violinist; *b.* nr. Brandenburg, 1849. Resided in New York, 1871-8; Director, Stern Cons., Berlin, 1878-81; returned to New York; conductor of "Handel and Haydn Society," Boston, 1898.
Works: operas, cantatas, overtures, chamber music, songs, &c.

HER'MESDORFF, Michael. Trier (Trèves), 1833-85. Noted authority on Gregorian music.
Edited the "Gradual ad usum Romanum cantus S. Gregorii," &c.

HERM'STEDT, Johann S. Clarinettist; *b.* nr. Dresden, 1778; *d.* 1846. Made improvements in the clarinet, and wrote concertos, &c., for it. Spohr wrote for him a clarinet concerto.

HERNAN'DEZ, Pablo. *B.* Saragossa, 1834. Studied Madrid Cons.
Works: Spanish operettas (or *Zarzuelas*), church music, org. pieces, an organ method, &c.

HERNAN'DO, Rafael J. M. *B.* Madrid, 1822. Sec. Madrid Cons., 1852, and afterwards Professor of Harmony.
Works: successful *Zarzuelas*, cantatas, hymns, &c.

Heroic. (*G., Hero'isch; F., Héroïque; I., Ero'ico,-a.*) Imposing, noble, bold, brave.

HÉROLD, Louis Joseph Ferdinand. Distinguished operatic composer; *b.* Paris, 1791; *d.* 1833. Entered Paris Cons., 1806; took 1st prize for pf. playing, 1810; won *Grand Prix de Rome*, 1812; produced his 1st opera, *La gioventù di Enrico*, Naples, 1815. *Chef du Chant*, Paris Grand Opéra, 1827.
Chief operas: *Les Rosières* (1817), *La Clochette* (1817), *Marie* (1826), *l'Illusion* (1829), *Zampa* (1831), *Le Pré aux Clercs* (1832). He also wrote several graceful ballets and pf. pieces.

HERON-ALLEN. (See **Allen.**)

HERR'MANN, Gottfried. Violinist and pianist; *b.* Sondershausen, 1808; *d.* 1878. Studied the vn. under Spohr. Orgt. and mus. director, Marienkirche, Lübeck, 1831; city Capellmeister, 1852.
Works: operas, songs, orchestral music, &c.

HERR'MANN, Hans. Popular song composer; *b.* Leipzig, 1870.
Has published over 100 songs of all kinds.

HERR'MANN, J. Z. (See **J. Zeugheer.**)

HER'SEE, Rose. Soprano; *b.* London, 1845.

Her'strich (*G.*). "Hither stroke." The down bow on 'cello and bass.

HER'TEL, Joh. C. Distinguished performer on the *Viola da Gamba*. *B.* Oettingen, 1699; *d.* 1754.

HER'TEL, Joh. Wilhelm. Son of preceding; *b.* Eisenach, 1727; *d.* 1789.
Concertmeister (1757) to the Duke of Mecklenburg-Schwerin.
Works: 8 oratorios, 12 symphonies, 6 pf. sonatas, songs, &c.

HER'TEL, Peter L. Berlin, 1817-99. Ballet-director, Berlin Court Opera, 1860-93.
Works: several successful ballets.

HER'THER, F. Operatic composer; *b.* Leipzig, 1834; *d.* 1871.

HERTZ'BERG, Rudolph von. Berlin, 1818-1893. Conductor, cáth. choir, 1851-89.
Edited "Musica Sacra" (a valuable collection of sacred music).

Herun'terstrich (*G.*). The down-bow on the violin or viola.

HERVÉ (pen name of **Florimond RONGER**). "The creator of French operetta." *B.* nr. Arras, 1825; *d.* Paris, 1892.
Conducted the Covent Garden Promenade Concerts, 1870-1; music-director, Empire Theatre, 1871-4.
Wrote some 50 operettas (*Vade au Cabaret, Fifi et Nini, Le petit Faust, Le roi Chilpéric, Les Bagatelles*, &c.).

HER'VEY, Arthur. *B.* Paris, 1855. Musical critic, *Morning Post*, 1892.
Works: songs, pf. pieces, &c. Author of "Masters of French Music."

Hervor'geho'ben (*G.*). With emphasis. *Den Rhyth'mus scharf hervor'gehoben.* The rhythm sharply emphasized.
Hervor'tretend. Brought out, made prominent.

HERZ, Henri ("Heinrich"). Pianist; *b.* Vienna, 1806; *d.* Paris, 1888. Pf. professor, Paris Cons., 1842-74.
His numerous pf. pieces—at one time very fashionable—are of little intrinsic value. Except some useful études, they are already practically forgotten.

Herz'haft (*G.*). Brave, bold, courageous.

Herz'lich (*G.*). Heartily.

Her'zig (*G.*). Heartily and ingenuously ; tenderly ; charming, dear, sweet.

HER'ZOG, Emilie. Brilliant stage singer ; *b.* Thurgau, abt. 1860. *Début* in *Les Huguenots*, at Munich.

HER'ZOG, Johann G. Bavarian organist ; *b.* 1822.
Works : collections of preludes, chorals, &c., for the organ ; an "Orgelschule," &c.

HER'ZOGENBERG, Heinrich von. *B.* Graz, Styria, 1843 ; *d.* 1900. One of the founders of the *Bach-Verein*, Leipzig, 1874. Prof. of composition, Berlin Hochschule für Musik, 1885-92.
Works : an oratorio, symphonies, psalms, and other choral works, chamber music, &c.

Hes (*G.*). H♭ ; *i.e.*, same as English B♭.
Hes'es. H♭♭ ; *i.e.*, B♭♭.

HESS, Joachim. For 44 years (1766-1810) organist and carillonneur at Gouda, Holland.
Wrote several works on organ construction, &c.

HESS, Willy. Fine violinist ; *b.* Mannheim, 1859. Led Sir Chas. Hallé's Orchestra for 7 years (from 1888). Leader of the Symphony Orch., Boston (U.S.), 1904.

HES'SE, Adolf F. Celebrated organist ; Breslau, 1809-63. Visited Paris, 1844 ; England, 1852. For several years Director, Breslau Symphony Concerts.
Works : cantatas, symphonies, chamber music, an "Orgelschule," organ pieces, &c.

HES'SE-WAR'TEGG, Baroness. Minnie Hauck (*q.v.*).

HETSCH, K. F. Ludwig. *B.* Stuttgart, 1806 ; *d.* 1872.
Wrote an opera, oratorios, symphonies, songs, &c.

HEU'BERGER, Richard F. J. *B.* Graz, Styria, 1850. Conductor, Vienna Singakademie, 1878.
Works : operas, *Mirjam* (1894), *Die Lautenschlägerin* (1896)), cantatas, orchestral pieces, songs, &c.

HEUB'NER, Konrad. *B.* Dresden, 1860. Director, Coblenz Cons., 1890. *D.* 1905.
Works : a symphony in A, overtures, chamber music, songs, &c.

HEU'GEL, Jacques L. *B.* La Rochelle, 1815 ; *d.* Paris, 1883. Editor of the musical journal *Le Ménestrel* from 1834.
Founded the publishing house of Heugel et Cie., which issues all the "Méthodes" of the Paris Cons.

Heu'len (*G.*). (1) To howl, scream. (2) Ciphering (in an organ).

HEU'MANN, Hans. *B.* Leipzig, 1870.
Works : over 100 songs, &c.

Hex'achord. (1) A scale of 6 notes. (See **Guido**, and **Tonic Sol-fa Syllables**.) (2) The interval of a 6th.

Hexam'eter. A line of poetry containing *six* "feet ; " one of the chief forms used in classical poetry.

HEY, Julius. Renowned singing teacher ; *b.* Lower Franconia, 1832. Ardent disciple of Wagner, who considered him "the chief of all singing teachers." His pupils are to be found in all the important German theatres.
Chief work : a "Singing Method" (4 parts, 1886).

HEY'DRICH, Bruno. Dramatic tenor ; distinguished exponent of Wagner's *rôles*. *b.* Leuben, Saxony, 1865.
Works : an "opera-drama" (*Amen*), songs, &c.

HEY'MANN, Karl. Pianist ; *b.* nr. Posen, 1854.
Works : several brilliant pf. pieces.

HEYTHER (or **Heather**), **Wm.** *B.* Middlesex, abt. 1584 ; *d.* 1627. Mus. Doc. Oxford, 1622 ; founded the "Music Lecture" there (1626-7), and endowed it with £17 6s. 8d. per annum.

Hia'tus. A gap.

HICKFORD'S ROOM. "One of the first regular public concert rooms in London," 1713 to 1775 (after which it gradually fell into disuse). "Master Mozart" (8 years of age) and "Miss Mozart" (13 years of age), "Prodigies of Nature," gave a concert here, May 13, 1765.

Hidden. Term sometimes applied to 5ths and 8ths approached by similar motion.

Macfarren called them exposed 5ths and 8ths ; Curwen, "badly-approached" 5ths and 8ths. Old books on harmony were much cumbered with rules prohibiting these hidden consecutives even between inner parts. The first two examples are only objectionable between *extreme* parts ; and only then when the 2nd chord has no very definite relationship to the preceding. The 3rd example is bad between any two vocal parts.

HIED'LER, Ida. Soprano ; *b.* Vienna, 1867.

Hier (*G.*). Here. **Hier'ab.** From here.
Von hier im Zeit'mass. From here in strict time.
Von hier'ab in Tempo und Aus'druck stei'gern bis zu völ'ligen Ü bermut. From here in strict time, and with increasing excitement up to complete abandonment.

HIERON'YMUS de Moravia. Dominican Friar, Paris, abt. 1260. One of the earliest writers on Mensurable music.

Hift-horn (*G.*). A wooden hunting horn.

Highland Fling. A characteristic Scottish dance.
It is generally danced to a *Strathspey* (*q.v.*).

HIGGS, James. Organist and writer ; London, 1829-1902.

HIGNARD, J. L. Aristide. Dramatic composer ; *b.* Nantes, 1822 ; *d.* 1898. Pupil of Halévy, Paris Cons.
Works : operas (*Hamlet*, 1888, the best), pf. pieces, songs, &c.

HILARY, St. Bishop of Poitiers ; *d.* 367.
Said to have written the first Latin hymns, 355.

HIL'DACH, Eugen. Fine baritone ; *b.* Wittenberge-on-Elbe, 1849. His wife **Anna** (*née* **Schubert**), *b.* Königsberg, 1852, is a mezzo-soprano.

HIL'DEBRAND, Zacharias. Celebrated org. builder; *b.* Saxony, 1680; *d.* 1743. His son, **Johann Gottfried**, built the fine org. at St. Michael's Church, Hamburg.

HILES, Henry. *B.* Shrewsbury, 1826; *d.* 1904. Orgt. St. Paul's, Manchester, 1864-7; Mus.Doc. Oxon, 1867. Prof. of harmony, &c., Owen's Coll., Manchester, 1876; and in 1879 at Victoria University.
Works: "Grammar of Music," "Harmony of Sounds," "Part-writing, or Modern Counterpoint;" 2 oratorios, cantatas, anthems, hymns, part-songs, &c.

HILES, John. Brother of preceding; *b.* Shrewsbury, 1810; *d.* 1882. Organist.
Works: catechisms of harmony, part-singing, pf., organ, thorough bass, &c.; a Dictionary of Musical Terms; pf. pieces, and songs.

HILF, Arno. Violinist; *b.* Bad Elster, Saxony, 1858. Studied Leipzig. Leader Gewandhaus Orchestra, Leipzig, 1888.

Hilfs (*G.*). Helping, auxiliary.
Hilfs'linie. A leger line.
Hilfs'note. An auxiliary note.
Hilfs'stimme. A mutation stop (mixture, quint, tierce).

HILL, Lady Arthur. (See **A. F. Harrison.**)

HILL, John. Norwich, 1797-1846. Founded the Norwich Choral Society.

HILL, Junius W. American musician; *b.* Massachusetts, 1840. Studied Leipzig Cons. Prof. of music, Wellesley Coll., Boston, 1886-97.
Works: female choruses, pf. pieces, &c.

HILL, Karl. Fine baritone; *b.* Idstein, 1840; *d.* 1893. Wagner selected him for the *rôles* of "Alberich" in *Der Ring*, Bayreuth, 1876, and "Klingsor," in *Parsifal*, 1882.

HILL, Thos. Hy. Weist. Violinist; London, 1828-91. First Principal, Guildhall School of Music, 1880-91.

HILL, Urell C. New York, 1802(?)-75. Violinist; pupil of Spohr. First President, New York Philharmonic Society, 1842.

HILL, Wm. Organ builder; London, 1800-70.
With Dr. Gauntlett introduced the CC organ keyboard (in the place of the old G or F keyboards), the system now generally adopted.

HILL, Wm. Ebsworth. Renowned violin maker; London, 1817-95.

HIL'LE, Gustav. Violinist; *b.* nr. Berlin, 1851. Studied under Joachim. Now resides in America.
Works: concertos and other vn. pieces, pf. pieces, songs, &c.

HIL'LEMACHER, Paul J. G. (*b.* Paris, 1852), and **Lucien J. E.** (*b.* Paris, 1860), Brothers; well-known operatic composers who write all their works in collaboration. Pupils of the Paris Cons.; the elder took the *Grand Prix de Rome* in 1876, and the younger in 1880.
Works: Symphonic Legend *Loreley* (1882); operas *St. Mégrin* (1886), *Le Drac*, &c., songs, orchestral music, &c.

HIL'LER, Ferdinand von. *B.* Frankfort, 1811; *d.* Cologne, 1885. Of Jewish descent; played a Mozart pf. concerto in public at 10. Pupil of Hummel, 1825. "As a boy of 15 saw Beethoven on his death bed." Lived in Paris, 1828-35, where he was renowned as an interpreter of Beethoven's pf. works. Conducted his oratorio *Die Zerstörung Jerusalems*, at Mendelssohn's invitation, Leipzig Gewandhaus, 1840. Capellmeister, Cologne, 1850; organized the Cologne Cons.; conducted the Lower Rhine musical festivals, Gürzenich Concerts, &c. Retired 1884.
Works: 6 operas, 2 oratorios, 6 cantatas, church music, choral music, over 100 songs, pf. music (including the concerto in F# minor), some fine chamber music, 3 overtures, 3 symphonies, &c. He also wrote several musical papers, essays, &c., and was an able lecturer.

HIL'LER, Friedrich A. Son of J. A. below; *b.* Leipzig, 1768; *d.* 1812. Music-director, Schwerin Theatre, 1790; Altona, 1796; Königsberg, 1803. Wrote 4 operettas, 6 string quartets, pf. music.

HIL'LER (HÜLLER), Johann A. *B.* nr. Görlitz, 1728; *d.* Leipzig, 1804. After early struggles, settled in Leipzig (1758) and revived the "Subscription Concerts" (1763), which developed into the famous "Gewandhaus Concerts." Hiller was the first conductor. He was also Music-director at the Thomasschule, 1789-1801. He originated the German "Singspiel" or "song play;" many of his songs are still very popular.
Works: several *Singspiele* (*Lottchen am Hofe* (1760), &c.), a Passion cantata, symphonies, a "choralbuch," many arrangements of classical compositions, &c. He also wrote and edited numerous theoretical works.

HIL'PERT, W. K. F. 'Cellist; *b.* Nuremberg, 1841; *d.* 1896.
One of the founders of the "Florentine Quartet." Prof. Royal Music School, Munich, 1884.

HIL'TON, John. English musician; *d.* 1657. Mus.B. Cantab, 1626. Organist, St. Margaret's, Westminster, 1628.
Works: madrigals, "Ayres, or Fa-las for 3 Voyces" (1627), catches, services, anthems.

HILTON, Robt. Bass vocalist; *b.* Preston, 1840. Vicar-choral, Westminster Abbey, since 1870.

HIM'MEL, Friedrich H. Pianist; *b.* nr. Brandenburg, 1765; *d.* 1814. Court Capellmeister, Berlin, 1795; visited St. Petersburg (1798) and Riga (1799). Visited London 1801.
Works: several operas, *Il primo navigatore* (Venice, 1794), *Alessandro* (St. Petersburg, 1798), *Fanchon, das Leiermädchen* (his best, Berlin, 1804), &c., an oratorio, church music, chamber music, and many songs.

Himm'lisch (*G.*). Heavenly, celestial, ethereal.

Hinauf'strich (*G.*). Up-bow (violin, &c.).
Hinauf'stimmen. To raise the pitch
Hinauf'ziehen. An upward *portamento.*

HINCKLEY, Allen C. Baritone; *b.* Boston (U.S.), 1877.

HINE, Wm. *B.* Brightwell, Oxfordshire, 1687; *d.* 1730. Orgt. Gloucester Cath., 1712. Pub. "Select Anthems in Score."

HINGSTON, John. Composer of "Fancies for the Viol." Orgt. to Oliver Cromwell, and taught his daughter; *d.* 1683.

HIN'KE, Gustav A. Oboist; *b.* Dresden, 1844; *d.* 1893.
Said to have introduced the Bass-tuba into the Dresden orchestra.

Hinster'bend (*G.*). Dying away.

Hin'strich (*G.*). Up-bow ('cello and bass).

Hin'ter der Sce'ne (or **Sze'ne**) (*G.*). Behind the scenes.

HINTON, Arthur. Composer; *b.* Beckenham, 1869.

HINTON, Mrs. A. (See **K. Goodson.**)

HINTON, John Wm. *B.* Edmonton, 1849. Mus.D., Dublin, 1874. An expert on organ construction.

Hinun'terziehen (*G.*). A downward *portamento*.

HIP'KINS, Alfred James. *B.* Westminster, 1826; *d.* 1903. An expert on the construction of pianofortes and other instruments. For many years with the firm of Broadwood & Sons.
Works: "Musical Instruments, Historic, Rare, and Unique" (1888), "A Description and Hist. of the Pf. and the older Keyboard stringed Instruments" (1896). Articles in the Encyclopædia Britannica, Grove's Dictionary, &c.

HIRSCH, Carl. *B.* Wemding, Bavaria, 1858. Noted conductor and teacher. Specially known for his male-voice music, which is popular throughout Germany.
Works: several cantatas, and some hundreds of choruses for male voices; numerous songs, &c.

HIRSCH, Dr. Rudolf. Musical critic; *b.* Moravia, 1816; *d.* Vienna, 1872.
His chief work, *Galerie der lebenden Tondichter* (1836), is noted for its original criticisms.

HIRSCH'BACH, Hermann. *B.* Berlin, 1812; *d.* 1888. Founded and edited the "Musikalisch-Kritisches Repertorium," Leipzig, 1843-5. Schumann expected much from him.
Wrote 14 symphonies, 2 operas, and much characteristic chamber music.

HIRSCH'FELD, Dr. Robert. *B.* Moravia, 1858. Teacher of Musical Æsthetics, Vienna Cons., 1884.
Chief work: a pamphlet in defence of old *a-cappella* music.

Hirt'enflöte (*G.*). A shepherd's flute.

Hirt'engesang, Hirt'enlied (*G.*). A Pastoral Song.

Hirt'lich (*G.*). Rural, pastoral.

His (*G.*). H♯; *i.e.*, B♯.
His'is. Hx; *i.e.*, Bx.

Histories of Music, Chief.
The most important are marked *.
Tinctor, *De Origine Musicæ*, 15th cent.
Sethus Calvisius, *De initio et progressu Musices*, 1600.
Praetorius, *Syntagma Musicum*, 1615.
Kircher, *Masurgia*, 1650.
Meibomius, *Antiquæ Musicæ*, 1652.
Printz, *History of Music, &c.*, 1690.
Bonnet, *Histoire de la Musique*, 1715-16.

Bourdelot, *Histoire de la Musique*, 1743.
Marpurg, *Critical History of Music, &c.*, 1754-78.
*Padre Martini, *Storia della Musica* (3 vols.), 1757-81.
*Burney, *General History of Music* (4 vols.), 1776-89.
*Hawkins, *History of Music* (5 vols., 1776).
*Gerbert, *Scriptores*, 1784.
Forkel, *Allgemeine Geschichte der Musik*, 1788-1801.
Vogler, *History of Music*, 1814.
Schilling, *History of Music*, 1841.
*Coussemaker, various works, 1852-1874.
Marx, *Music of the 19th century*, 1855.
Hullah, *History of Modern Music*, 1862.
*Reissmann, *General History of Music*, 1863-4.
C. Engel, *Music of the Most Ancient Nations*, 1864.
*Ambros, *Geschichte der Musik* (4 vols.), 1864-78.
Hullah, *Transition Period of Musical History*, 1865.
Fétis, *General History of Music*, 1869-76.
Chappell, *History of Ancient Music*, 1874.
*Ritter, *Students' History of Music*, 1875-80.
Gevaert, *History of the Music of Antiquity*, 1875-81.
Hunt, *Concise History of Music*, 1879.
Naumann, *History of Music*, 1880-5.
Clement, *Histoire de la Musique*, 1885.
Rowbotham, *History of Music*, 1885-7.
*Davey, *History of English Music*, 1895.
Matthew, *Handbook of Musical History and Bibliography*, 1898.
*Hadow (editor), *Oxford History of Music*, 1905.
Walker, *History of English Music*, 1907.

HLAWATSCH, Woizech I. Composer; *b.* Leditsch, 1849.

HOARE, Margaret. Soprano; *b.* London, 1852.

HOBBS, Jn. Wm. Tenor; *b.* Henley, 1799; *d.* 1877. Gentleman, Chapel Royal, 1827; Lay Vicar, Westmr. Abbey, 1836.
Wrote over 100 songs ("Brave old Temeraire," "Phyllis is my only joy," &c.).

HOBDAY, Mrs. A. (See **Ethel Sharpe.**)

Hobo'e (*G.*) } The oboe (*q.v.*).
Ho'boy (*Old E.*) }

HOBRECHT, Jakob. (Also **Obrecht, Obreht, Obertus, Hobertus.**) Famous Netherland contrapuntist; *b.* Utrecht, abt. 1430; *d.* Antwerp, abt. 1506. Capellmeister, Utrecht, 1465; *Notre Dame*, Antwerp, 1492.
Works: masses, motets, hymns, &c.

HOBY. (See **Hothby.**) ..

Hoch (*G.*). High, sharp; lofty, sublime.
Hoch'amt. High mass.
Hoch fei'erlich. Very solemn.
Hoch'gesang } An ode, or hymn.
Hoch'lied }
Höchst lang'sam. Very slow.
Höchst leb'haft. Very lively.
Hoch und mit'tel. High and medium (pitch).
Hoch und tief. High and low (pitch).
Hoch'zeitsmarsch. A wedding march.

HOCH'BERG, Bolko Graf, von. (Composed under the name of **J. H. Franz.**) *B.* Silesia, 1843. Founded the Silesian Music Festivals, 1876. General-intendant, Prussian Court Theatres, 1886.
Works: operas, symphonies, songs, &c.

HODGES, Edward. *B.* Bristol, 1796; *d.* 1867. Mus.Doc. Cantab, 1825. Orgt. Toronto (Canada), 1839; New York, 1839-63.
Wrote "An Essay on the Cultivation of Church Music."

Hof (*G.*). A court.
Hof'dichter. Poet laureate.
Hof'kapelle. Court band and singers.
Hof'kapellmeister. Director of a Court orchestra.
Hof'organist. Court organist.

HOFF'MANN, Ernst Theodor A. W. *B.*
Königsberg, 1776; *d.* Berlin, 1822. A man
of wonderful versatility; in turn music
teacher, journalist, poet, composer,
caricaturist, conductor, and lawyer.
He had a passionate love of Mozart, and was
himself admired by Beethoven, Weber, Schumann, and Carlyle.
Works: 9 operas (*Undine*, Berlin, 1816, his best),
a ballet, a mass, a symphony, pf. sonatas, &c.

HOFF'MANN, Heinrich A. Poet and philologist; *b.* Fallersleben, Hanover, 1798;
d. 1874.
Pub. collections of German church songs, folksongs, children's songs, &c.

HOFF'MANN, Karl. Violinist; *b.* Prague,
1872.

HOFF'MANN, Richard. Pianist; *b.* Manchester, 1831. Went to New York, 1847,
and became the "head of the Pianistic
fraternity." Accompanied Jenny Lind
on her American tours.
Works: anthems, part-songs, songs, pf. music.

HOFF'MEISTER, Franz A. *B.* 1754; *d.*
Vienna, 1812. Estab. a "Bureau de
Musique," Leipzig, 1800, now Peters's.
Works: 9 operas; orchestral pieces; 30 concertos, 18 quintets, 156 quartets, 44 trios, and
96 duos for flute; pf. music, chamber music
(42 string quartets), much church music, songs.

**HOF'HAIMER (Hofheimer, Hofhaymer),
Paulus von.** Salzburg, 1459-1537.
Court organist, Vienna. "An unrivalled organist and lutenist, and the
best composer of his age."—*Baker.*
Works: odes for 4 voices, German *Lieder* for 4
voices, chorals, lute music, org. music, &c.

Höf'lich (*G.*). Graceful, courteous.

HOF'MANN, Heinrich K. J. Pianist and
composer; *b.* Berlin, 1842; *d.* 1902.
Works: operas: *Cartouche*, 1869; *Der Matador*,
1872; *Armin*, 1872; *Donna Diana*, 1886;
Lully, 1889, &c.; oratorio (*Prometheus*), 1896;
several cantatas (*Song of the Norns*, &c.),
Music-drama (*Editha*), part-songs, vocal scenas.
songs, &c.; "Frithjof" symphony (1874),
"Hungarian" Suite (1873), and other orchestral
music; pf. duets and solo pieces, much
chamber music, &c.

HOF'MANN, Joseph. Pianist; *b.* Cracow,
1877. Infant prodigy; played in
public at 6; toured through Europe at
9. After a period of further study in
Berlin, resumed concert playing, 1894.
Works: pf. pieces.

HOF'MANN, Richard. *B.* Prussian Saxony,
1844. Music teacher at Leipzig.
Chief work: a valuable "Praktische Instrumentationsschule" (1893).

HOGARTH, George. Writer and critic;
father-in-law of Chas. Dickens. *B.* nr.
Oxton, Berwickshire, 1783; *d.* London,
1870. Musical critic, *Morning Chronicle*
1834; *Daily News*, 1846-66. Secretary,
Philharmonic Society, 1850.
Works: "Musical History, Biography, and
Criticism," "Memoirs of the Opera," &c.

HOGG, James. The "Ettrick Shepherd."
Scotch poet and musician; 1770-1835.
Pub. collns. of "Scottish Songs and Melodies," &c.

Höh'e (*G.*). Acuteness, high register.
Obo'enhöhe. The highest notes of the oboe.

Hohl'flöte (*G.*). "Hollow flute." An organ
stop consisting of open flue pipes of
broad scale, and a somewhat hollow
tone; generally of 8 ft. pitch.
In large organs it often takes the place of the
stopped Diapason on the Great.

Höh'nend (*G.*). Sneering, scoffing.

HOL, Richard. *B.* Amsterdam, 1825; *d.* 1904.
City music director, Utrecht, 1862;
cathedral orgt. 1869; Director of the
School of Music, 1875.
Chief works: oratorio (*David*), opera (*Floris V*),
2 symphonies, masses, chamber music, ballads
for voices and orchestra (*De vliegende Hollander*,
&c.), choral music, songs, &c.

HOLBROOKE, Joseph C. Composer; *b.*
Croydon, 1878.
Works: symphonic poems (*Skeleton in Armour*,
&c.), an "Illuminated" symphony, choral
works (*The Bells*), songs, &c.

Hold. (*G., Ferma'te; F., Point d'arret;
I., Ferma'ta, Coro'na.*) A pause;
marked ⌢ or ⌣.
When placed over a double bar it indicates (1) a
slight pause before attacking the next section,
or (2) that the place so marked is the end (*Fine*),
after *D.C.* or *D.S.*

HOLDER, Rev. Wm., D.D. 1614-97.
Pub. "A Treatise on the Natural Grounds of
Harmony," &c.

Holding-note. A note continued in one
part while the others proceed in shorter
notes:—

HOLLAND, Edwin. Singing teacher; *b.*
London, 1845.

HOL'LÄNDER, Alexis. Pianist; *b.* Ratibor,
Silesia, 1840. Conductor, "Cäcilienverein," Berlin, 1870.
Works: pf. pieces, part-songs, songs, &c.

HOL'LÄNDER, Alma. (See **Mad. Haas.**)

HOL'LANDER, Benno. Violinist and composer; *b.* Amsterdam, 1853.

HOL'LANDER, Christian J. Netherland
composer, abt. 1520-70.
Wrote motets, "Cantiones Variæ," &c.

HOL'LÄNDER, Gustav. Violinist; *b.* Leobschütz, Upper Silesia, 1855. Pupil of
David and Joachim. Director, Stern
Cons., Berlin, 1894. Concertmeister,
Hamburg, 1896.
Has published several works for vn. and pf.

HOL'LÄNDER, Victor. *B.* Leobschütz,
1866.
His compositions include the comic opera *Carmosinella*, and an operetta *The Bey of Morocco*
(London, 1894).

HOLLINS, Alfred. Blind pianist and orgst. ; *b.* Hull, 1865. Studied Royal Normal Coll. for the Blind, Upper Norwood. At 16, played to Queen Victoria at Windsor.
Has written several excellent org. compositions.

HOLL'MANN, Jos. 'Cellist and composer ; *b.* Maestricht, 1852.

HOL'LY, Franz A. *B.* Luba, Bohemia, 1747 ; *d.* 1783.
Wrote popular *Singspiele* for Prague, Berlin, and Breslau theatres.

HOLMES, Alfred. Violinist ; *b.* London, 1837 ; *d.* 1876. Settled in Paris, 1864.
Works : an opera (*Inez de Castro*, Paris, 1875), symphonies, overtures, &c.

HOLMES, Edward. Teacher and writer ; *b.* nr. London, 1797 ; *d.* (U.S.) 1859.
Works: "A Ramble among the Musicians of Germany," "The Life of Mozart," "Life of Purcell," &c.

HOLMES, Henry. Violinist ; brother of Alfred ; *b.* London, 1839 ; *d.* 1906.
Works : 4 symphonies, a vn. concerto, cantatas, songs, &c.

HOLMES, Oliver Wendell. M.D., LL.D. 1809-1904. Noted American writer.
Wrote some fine hymns.

HOLMES, Wm. Henry. Pianist ; *b.* Sudbury, Derbyshire, 1812 ; *d.* 1885. For many years pf. prof. at the R.A.M. Among his pupils were Sterndale Bennett and the two Macfarrens.
Wrote pf. pieces, songs, &c.

HOLMÈS (or **HOLMES**), **Augusta Mary.** *B.* (of Irish parents) Paris, 1847 ; *d.* 1903. Studied under César Franck.
Works : symphonies and symphonic poems (*Héro et Léandre*, 1874), *Lutece, Les Argonautes, Les 7 Ivresses, Irlande* (1885), *Lutin, Roland,* &c., an allegorical cantata, and over 100 songs.

HOLST, Edvard. *B.* Copenhagen, 1843 ; settled in New York abt. 1874 ; *d.* 1899.
Wrote over 2,000 pieces "of a light description," including a comic opera (*Our Flats*), pf. pieces, and songs.

HOLZ'BAUER, Ignaz. *B.* Vienna, 1711 ; *d.* 1783. Capellmeister successively at Vienna, Stuttgart, and Mannheim. His works were highly praised by Mozart.
Works : 12 operas, 5 oratorios, 26 orchestral masses, 37 motets, 196 symphonies, 18 quartets, 13 concertos, &c.

Holz'bläser (*G.*). Abbn. *Hlzbl.*, or *Hzbl.* Players on wood-wind instruments.
Holz'blasinstrumente. Wood-wind instruments. (The "wood-wind" of the orchestra.)

Holz'schlägel (*G.*). A wooden beater (for drums, cymbals, &c.).

Höl'zernes Geläch'ter (*G.*)   } A Xylophone
Holz'harmonica (*G.*)   }   (*q.v.*).
Holz'flöte (*G.*). Wood-flute ; an organ stop.

Home, sweet Home. Favourite Eng. song ; words by an American, John Howard Payne, music by Sir Henry Bishop (from a Sicilian air), about 1823.

HOMER, Sidney. Composer ; *b.* Boston (U.S.), 1864.

HOMER, Mme. Louise. Wife of S. Contralto ; *b.* Pittsburg, Pa., abt. 1874 (?).
Sang Covent Garden, 1900.

HO'MEYER, Paul J. M. *B.* Osterode, Harz, 1853; *d.* 1908. Orgt. at the Gewandhaus, and org. teacher at the Cons., Leipzig.

HOMI'LIUS, Gottfried A. *B.* Rosenthal, Saxony, 1714 ; *d.* 1785. Pupil of J. S. Bach. Orgt. Frauenkirche, Dresden, 1742 ; cantor, Kreuzschule, and musicdirector of the 3 chief churches, 1755.
Works : a Passion cantata, a Christmas oratorio, motets, chorals, &c.

Homophone (*F.*). The enharmonic equivalent of a note ; as $Cx = D$.
On the harp, two strings tuned to the same (enharmonic) pitch (as D$\sharp$, E$\flat$).

Homophon'ic. Like or similar in sound.
The contrapuntal style of music (1400-1600) is *polyphonic* ("many sounding"), as it is essentially a combination of a number of equally important melodies. (See *Counterpoint.*) The modern style initiated by Peri, Caccini, &c., about 1600, consists rather of *one principal melody* with an *accompaniment* of chords. Hence this style is said to be *homophonic.* Bach and Handel successfully fused the two styles.

Ho'mophony. Homophonic music.

Ho'nigstimme (*G.*). Sweet, "honied" voice.

HOOD, Helen. Composer ; *b.* Chelsea, Massachusetts, 1863. Resides in Boston.
Works : part-songs, pf. pieces, chamber music, songs, &c.

Hook. (*G., Fah'ne, Fähn'chen ; F., Crochet.*) The "crook" on the stem of a quaver (♪).
A semiquaver has 2 hooks, a demisemiquaver 3 (♪, ♪).

HOOK, James. *B.* Norwich, 1746 ; *d.* 1827. Music-director, Marylebone Gardens, 1769-73 ; Vauxhall Gardens, 1774-1820.
Wrote over 2,000 songs, catches, cantatas, &c. "Within a mile of Edinboro' town" and "Sweet Lass of Richmond Hill" still survive.

HOPE'KIRK, Helen. Pianist ; *b.* Edinburgh, 1856. *Début,* Leipzig Gewandhaus, 1878.
Works : orchestral pieces, pf. pieces, songs, &c.

HOP'FFER, Ludwig B. *B.* Berlin, 1840 ; *d.* 1877.
Wrote 3 operas, a festival play, choral works, symphonies, chamber music, songs, &c.

HOPKINS, Edward Jerome. American musician ; *b.* Burlington, Vermont, 1836 ; *d.* 1898. Orgt. at 10. Founded the "American Music Association," the "Orpheon Free Schools" (New York), the popular "Lecture Concerts," the *New York Philharmonic Journal,* &c.
Wrote over 700 works, mostly in MS.

HOPKINS, Edward John. *B.* Westminster, 1818 ; *d.* 1901. Chorister, Chapel Royal, 1826-33. Orgt. Mitcham Church, 1834 ; St. Peter's, Islington, 1838 ; St. Luke's, Berwick Street, 1841 ; Temple Church, 1843-98. Mus.Doc. Canterbury, 1882.
Works : anthems, hymn tunes, chants, org. pieces and arrangements ; and (with Dr. Rimbault) "The Organ : its History and Construction" (a standard work).

HOPKINS, Harry P. Composer ; *b.* Baltimore, 1873.

HOPKINS, John. Orgt.; brother of Edw. John; *b.* Westminster, 1822; *d.* 1900.
Works : church services, hymn tunes, &c.

HOPKINS, John Larkin. *B.* Westminster, 1819; *d.* 1873. Mus.Doc. Cantab, 1867.
His "Te Deum in G" is very popular.

HOPLIT. (See **Pohl, Rd.**)

Hop'ser, or **Hops'tang** (*G.*). A country dance.

Ho'ræ cano'nicæ (*L.*). The canonical hours of the Roman Church.

Horizontal Preparation. A dissonant note sounded as a consonant note in the previous chord and in the same part. (See **Suspension.**)

Horn. In general, any instrument consisting of a tube sounded by means of a cupped mouthpiece ; as *Bass-horn, Bugle-horn, Hunting-horn, Sax-horn, Tenor-horn, Russian-horn,* &c. (See each under its own heading.)
Horn Diapason. A variety of org. diapason of "horny" or "stringy" quality.

Horn, Orchestral. (*I., Cor'no ; F., Cor ; G., Horn.*) One of the chief brass wind instruments in an orchestra.
The tone of the horn is mellow, sonorous, and "romantic," and it blends well with every "voice" in the orchestra. The older masters used two horns in their scores ; in modern orchestral music 4 are generally employed.
(1) The *Natural,* or *French* horn (*F., Cor de Chasse ; G., Wald'horn*), gives the notes of the "Chords of Nature" (see *Acoustics*), from the 2nd partial to about the 16th.

N.B.—The notes marked * are a little out of tune and the last 5 are difficult to produce.
Most of the notes missing from the above series can be supplied (and the " out of tune " notes remedied) by placing the hand in the "bell" of the instrument ; these "stopped" notes are of a dull sombre quality.
The horn is furnished with a number of crooks by which its pitch can be changed from B♭ *Alto* to *A basso.* The horn in F is the one most used.
(2) The *Valve,* or *Chromatic* horn is the same as above, but it is provided with valves or pistons so that all the missing tones and semitones can be produced as "open" notes.
All orchestral horns are transposing instruments, *e.g.* :—

Written notes.

Actual sounds on Corno in B♭ alto.

Actual sounds on Corno in F.

Actual sounds on Corno in D.

Actual sounds on Corno in B♭ Basso.

Horn-band, Russian. A band of hunting horns, each horn limited to one note.
The method of performance is analogous to hand-bell ringing, or change ringing on a peal of bells.

HORN, August. *B.* Freiberg, Saxony, 1825 ; *d.* 1893. Pupil of Mendelssohn.
His pf. arrangements of classical compositions are favourably known.

HORN, Chas. Ed. Son of Karl F. (below). *B.* London, 1786 ; *d.* Boston (U.S.), 1849. Singer and composer ; produced several operas at New York.
Works : 3 oratorios, 26 operettas, glees, songs ("Cherry Ripe," "Allan Water," &c.).

HORN, Karl F. *B.* Nordhausen, Saxony, 1762 ; *d.* Windsor, 1830. Came to London, 1792. Orgt. St. George's, Windsor, 1823.
Edited (with Wesley) Bach's "Wohltemperirtes Clavier ; " wrote pf. sonatas, &c., and a treatise on "Thorough Bass."

HORNER, Egbert F. Orgt. and composer ; Mus.Doc. Durham, 1900.

HORNER, Ralph J. *B.* Newport, Monmouth, 1848. Mus.Doc. Durham, 1898.
Works : cantatas, pf. pieces, songs, &c.

Hör'ner (*G.*). Horns. (Abbn. *Hr.*)

Horn'musik (*G.*). Same as **Harmonie'musik.**

Hornpipe. (1) An old Eng. wind instrument of the *chalumeau* character. (2) An Eng. dance in lively 3-2 or 4-4 time.
The 4-4 hornpipe is popular as a sailors' dance.

Horn'sordin (*G.*). A mute for a horn.

HORN'STEIN, Robt. von. *B.* Stuttgart, 1833 ; *d.* 1890. Teacher, Munich Royal School of Music.
Wrote operas (*Adam and Eva,* &c.), pf. pieces, and songs.

HORROCKS, Amy E. Pianist and composer ; *b.* (of British parents), Brazil, 1867.

HORSLEY, Chas. Ed. Son of Wm. (below). *B.* London, 1822 ; *d.* New York, 1876.
Works : 3 oratorios (*Gideon, David, Joseph*), odes, songs, and a "Text Book of Harmony."

HORSLEY, William. Famous glee composer ; London, 1774-1858. Mus.B. Oxon, 1800.
Works : 5 collections of glees, 40 canons, psalm-tunes, pf. pieces, songs, an "Introduction to Harmony and Modulation," &c.

HORTON, Priscilla. (See **Mrs. G. Reed.**)

HORVÁTH, Géza. Hungarian composer ; *b.* 1868.

HOR'WITZ, Benno. Violinist and composer ; *b.* Berlin, 1855.

Hosan'na. Part of the *Sanctus* in a mass.

HOSTIN'SKY, Dr. Ottokar. *B.* Bohemia, 1847. Prof. of Musical Æsthetics, Prague University, 1884.

HOTH'BY (HOTHOBUS, OTTEBY, OTTOBI), Johannes (Real name **Hoby**). Englishman ; "famous for his skill in the science of music." *D.* London, 1487. Carmelite friar, Lucca, 1467-86.
Two of his treatises, "De proportionibus et cantu figurato" and "Calliopea leghale" (printed by Coussemaker), are of historical value.

HOTTETERRE, Louis. Finest flute player of his period ; chamber musician to Louis XIV and XV.
Pub. (abt. 1700 to 1738) important works on the *flauto traverso, flûte-à-bec, hautbois,* and *musette.*

HO'VEN, J. (See **Vesque von Püttlingen.**)

HOW, William W. D.D. 1823-97. Bishop of Bedford, 1879 ; of Wakefield, 1888.
Wrote several hymns : "On wings of living light," "For all the saints," &c.

HOWARD, George H. *B.* Norton, Massachusetts, 1843. Founded the Boston School for Teachers of Music, 1891.

HOWARD, Samuel. London, 1710-82. Mus.Doc. Cantab, 1769.
Works : anthems, songs, &c.

HOWELL, Mrs. A. (See **Rose Hersee.**)

HOWELL, Edw. 'Cellist and writer ; *b.* London, 1846.

HOYTE, William Stevenson. Organist ; *b.* Sidmouth, 1844. Mus.D., Cantuar, 1905.

HRIMA'LY, Adalbert. *B.* Pilsen, 1842. Conductor, Gothenburg Orchestra, 1861 ; Prague Nat. Theatre, 1868 ; Prague German Theatre, 1873 ; &c.
Chief works : opera (*Der verzauberte Prinz*), "Tonale und rhythmische Studien für die Violine."

HU'BAY (HUBER), Karl. *B.* Varjas, Hungary, 1828 ; *d.* 1885. Conductor, Nat. Theatre, Pesth.
Works : operas (*Szekler Mädchen*, &c.).

HU'BAY, Jenö. (German name, **Eugen Huber.**) Son of Karl. *B.* Budapest, 1858. Violin prof., Brussels Cons., 1882 ; Pesth Cons., 1886.
Works : operas (*Der Geigenmacher von Cremona,* 1893 ; *Der Dorflump,* 1896, &c.), a symphony, vn. music, songs, &c.

HU'BER, Felix. Swiss poet and song composer ; *d.* Berne, 1810.

HU'BER, Ferdinand. Swiss song composer ; 1791-1863.
"His songs were highly praised by Mendelssohn."

HU'BER, Dr. Hans. Swiss dramatic composer ; *b.* nr. Olten, 1852. Director, Basle Music School, 1896.
Works : operas : *Weltfrühling,* 1894 ; *Gudrun,* 1896 ; symphonies, concertos, cantatas, chamber music, pf. music, &c.

HU'BER, Karl. (See **Hubay.**)

HU'BERMANN, Bronislaw. Violinist ; *b.* nr. Warsaw, 1882.

HUBER'TI, Leon G. *B.* Brussels, 1843. Won the *Prix de Rome,* Brussels Cons., 1865. Prof. at the Cons., 1899.
Works : oratorios, dramatic and symphonic poems (*Fiat Lux,* &c.), orchestral suites, a concerto, and other pf. pieces, chamber music, and numerous songs.

Hübsch (*G.*). Charming, dainty.
Hübsch vor'tragen. In a dainty manner.

HUCBALD (HUGBALD'US, UBALDUS, UCHUBALDUS). *B.* abt. 840 ; *d.* St. Amand, nr. Tournay, 930 or 932.
His work "Harmonica Institutio" (or "Liber de Musica") contains the earliest known attempts to indicate pitch by means of parallel lines. (See *Notation.*)

Huchet (*F.*). A postman's horn.

HÜE, Georges A. Dramatic composer ; *b.* Versailles, 1858. *Grand Prix de Rome,* Paris Cons., 1879.
His *La Belle aux bois dormant* (1894) is specially noteworthy.

HUEF'FER, Dr. Francis. *B.* Münster, 1843 ; *d.* London, 1889. Settled in London, 1869 ; *Times* musical critic, 1878-89. Did much to advance English opera and an appreciation of Wagner's music.
Works : libretti of Mackenzie's *Colomba* and *Troubadour,* and Cowen's *Sleeping Beauty ;* "Richard Wagner and the Music of the Future," "Musical Studies," a translation of the "Correspondence of Wagner and Liszt," &c.

Hue'huetl. A large drum anciently used in Mexico and Central America.

Hüft'horn (*G.*). A bugle horn.

HUGUENOTS, Les. Opera by Meyerbeer, 1836.

HUHN, Bruno S. Pianist ; *b.* London, 1871.

Huitième de Soupir (*F.*). A demisemiquaver rest.

Huit-pieds (*F.*). "Eight feet." Same as **Halbe Orgel** (*q.v.*).

Hul'digungsmarsch (*G.*). "Homage March." Name of a composition written by Wagner on his becoming a Bavarian subject.

Hülfs- (*G.*). Same as **Hilfs-** (*q.v.*).

HULL, Arthur Eaglefield. Orgt., condr., and composer. Mus.D. Oxon, 1903.
Editor, Breitkopf & Härtel's "Concert Guides."

HULLAH, John Pyke. *B.* Worcester, 1812 ; *d.* London, 1884. Became known as a composer of English operas, 1836. Opened his "Singing School for Schoolmasters," Exeter Hall, 1841. Introduced Wilhem's "Fixed Do" system of sight-singing from the staff. Prof. of Singing, King's Coll., 1844-74. Orgt. Charter House, 1858. Inspector of Music in Training Colleges, 1872. LL.D., Edinburgh, 1876. Although a persistent and rather bitter opponent of Tonic Sol-fa, Hullah did much good work in popularising sight-singing.
Works : operas (*The Village Coquettes, The Barbers of Bassora, The Outpost*), collections of vocal music, "Wilhem's Method of Teaching Singing," "A Grammar of Vocal Music," "The History of Modern Music" (1862), "The Transition Period of Musical History," &c. He also wrote many songs ("The Three Fishers," "The Storm," &c.).

HÜL'LER, J. A. (See **Hiller.**)

HÜLL'MANDEL, Nicholas J. Celebrated performer on the harmonica ; *b.* Strasburg, 1751 ; *d.* London, 1823. Also noted as a pianist.

HÜLL'WECK, Karl. 'Cellist ; *b.* Dresden, 1852.
Works : pieces for 'cello and pf., &c.

Humane Music.
Ancient term for vocal music, "to distinguish it from instrumental music and the music of the spheres."

HUME, J. Ord. Bandmaster and arranger of band music ; *b.* Edinburgh, 1864.

HUMFREY (HUMPHREY, HUMPHRYS), Pelham. *B.* London, 1647 ; *d.* Windsor, 1674. Chorister, Chapel Royal, 1660. Sent to Paris by Chas. II (1664) to study under Lully. Master of the Children, Chapel Royal, 1672.
Works : services, odes, anthems, songs. His early death cut short a very promising career.

Hum'mel, Hüm'melchen (*G.*). (1) A small bagpipe. (2) A drone ; or an imitation of one.

HUM'MEL, Ferdinand. *B.* Berlin, 1855. Harp virtuoso at the age of 7. Toured Europe with his father, 1864-7.
Works : operas (*Mara*, 1893 ; *Assarpai*, 1898, &c.) ; works for chorus and orches. ; overtures ; chamber music, pf. pieces, harp pieces, songs.

HUM'MEL, Johann Nepomuk. "One of the most famous pf. virtuosi and extemporists of his period. . . At one time considered the equal of Beethoven." *B.* Pressburg, 1778 ; *d.* Weimar, 1837. Instructed by Mozart for 2 years ; *début* (1787) at a concert given by Mozart in Dresden. Deputy Capellmeister for Haydn (*q.v.*). 1804-11. Court Capellmeister, Stuttgart, 1816 ; Weimar, 1819. Made several professional tours ; visited London, 1830 and 1833, and conducted a season of German opera at the King's Theatre.
Of his 124 compositions the chief are : 3 masses, 7 pf. concertos, some pf. sonatas, a septet in D minor, and an "Instruction Book for the Pf."

Humor' (*G.*). Humour.

Humoresque. (*G.*, *Humores'ke*.) A humorou or whimsical composition ; a *Caprice.*

HUM'PERDINCK, Engelbert. *B.* Siegburg, nr. Bonn, 1854. Won the Mendelssohn Prize, Berlin, 1878, and the Meyerbeer Prize, 1880. Made pf. arrangements of Wagner's works (1881-2), and assisted him in the preparation of *Parsifal* for the stage. Prof. Barcelona Cons., 1885-6 ; Hoch Cons., Frankfort, 1900.
His best-known work is the 2-act fairy opera *Hänsel und Gretel.* He has also written other operas, orchestral music, &c.

Hum'sen (*G.*). To hum, buzz, drone.

HUN'EKER, James G. *B.* Philadelphia, 1860. 10 years pf. teacher, National Cons., New York; musical critic of the *Musical Courier, New York Sun, New York Recorder* (1891-5), *Morning Advertiser* (1895-7), etc.

Hungarian (or Gipsy) Scale. A characteristic scale common in Hungarian music :—

l₁　t₁　d　re　m　f　se　l

HUNT, Rev. H. G. Bonavia. *B.* Malta, 1847. Mus.Doc. Dublin, 1887.
Author of a "Concise History of Music," &c.

HUNT, Wm. Hy. Composer and teacher ; *b.* London, 1852 ; *d.* 1894. Mus.D. Lond., 1886.

HÜN'TEN, Franz. Coblenz, 1793-1878. Pianist ; studied Paris Cons.
Wrote a "Methode nouvelle pour le piano," and several pleasing pf. pieces.

HUNTLEY, George Frederic. Organist and composer ; *b.* Datchet, 1859. Mus.Doc. Cantab, 1894.

Hüp'fend (*G.*). Springing, skipping.
Hüp'fender Bo'gen. With springing bow.

Hunts-up (Hunt's up). Old Eng. morning hunting song.

Hurdy-gurdy. (*G.*, *Dreh'leier, Bau'ernleier ; F., Vielle ; I., Li'ra tede'sca.*) A kind of lute or guitar whose strings are made to sound by turning a rosined wheel.

HURLSTONE, William Yeates. Pianist and composer ; *b.* London, 1876 ; *d.* 1906.
Works : pf. concerto in D, a fairy suite (*The Magic Mirror*), a suite for cl. and pf., songs, &c.

Hur'tig (*G.*). Quick, nimble ; *presto.*
Hur'tigkeit. Agility, promptness, dash.

HUSK, Wm. Henry. London, 1814-87. Librarian Sacred Harmonic Soc., and writer.

HUSS, Henry H. American pianist and composer ; *b.* Newark, New Jersey, 1862.
Works : a pf. concerto, pf. pieces, songs, &c.

HUTCHINSON, Mrs. R. H. P. (*née* **Alwina Valleria Lohmann**). Soprano ; *b.* Baltimore (U.S.), 1848.

HUTCHINSON, Thos. *B.* Sunderland, 1854. Mus.Doc. Oxon, 1894 ; Orgt. and composer.

HUTCHISON, Wm. M. Composer ; *b.* Glasgow, 1854.

HUTS'CHENRUIJTER, Willem. Celebrated horn and trumpet player ; Rotterdam, 1796-1878.
Wrote an opera, 4 symphonies, numerous works for wind-band, masses, songs, &c.

HÜT'TENBRENNER, Anselm. Pianist ; *b.* Graz, Styria, 1794 ; *d.* 1868. Friend of Beethoven (who died in his arms), and of Schubert.
Wrote 4 operas, 9 masses, 5 symphonies, 300 male choruses, 200 songs, &c.

Hydrau'lic Organ. (See **Organ.**)

HYL'LESTED, August. Concert pianist ; *b.* Stockholm, 1858. Court pianist to Princess Louise of Denmark.
Works : symphonic poem (*Elizabeth*)) pf. pieces, songs.

Hymn. (*Gk.*, *Hum'nos ; L., Hym'nus ; G., Kirch'enlied, Kirch'engesang ; F., Hymne ; I., In'no.*) Originally, "an ode of joy." In general, a song to some Superior Being whom it is desired to honour or propitiate.
From the most ancient times, hymns have been sung either to the Creator, or to some ancestor, god, hero, king, or saint, whom the piety, fear,

or superstition of man has led him to address in praise or supplication.

N.B.—In the Anglican Church only the metrical psalms were sung for long after the Reformation. Watts introduced hymns, but they were not established till about 1860. (Dr. Pearce played from *Tate and Brady* at St. Martin's, Salisbury, as late as 1870!)

COLLECTIONS OF HYMNS, PSALTERS, &c., OF HISTORIC VALUE.

The Persian *Gathas;* Zoroaster, who wrote the first of these, is said to have lived in the 14th cent. B.C.—*Ency. Brit.*

The Jewish *Psalms;* David was king of Israel abt. 1055 B.C.

The Hindu (or Sanskrit) *Rig-Veda;* between 1000 and 500 B.C.

Chinese *Book of Odes*, arranged by Confucius, abt. 550-478 B.C.

The *Buddhist Hymns*, from the 5th cent. B.C.

The Grecian *Homeric Hymns;* probably not all written by Homer, but already old in the time of Thucydides (*b*. abt. 471 B.C.).

Odes of Pindar ; abt. 522-443 B.C.

Hymns of Callimachus of Cyrene, 3rd cent. B.C.

The *"Orphic" Hymns* of the Alexandrian School. Scholars are not agreed whether they are earlier or later than the Christian era.

Hymns of Catullus, abt. 87-53 B.C.

The *Carmen Sæculare* of Horace, 65-8 B.C.

Fragments of hymns in the *New Testament ;* Eph. v. 14 ; 1 Tim. iii. 16 ; 1 Tim. vi. 15, 16 ; 2 Tim. ii. 11-13.

The *Latin Hymns*, or *Hymns of the Western Church*, dating from the 4th to the 12th cents. Chief hymn writers, St. Hilary, St. Ephraim of Edessa, St. Chrysostom, St. Ambrose, St. Augustine, St. Gregory the Great, Prudentius, and V. Fortunatus. The melodies were based on the Church modes (see *Mode*) ; among the most celebrated are *Veni Redemptor Gentium* (4th cent.), *Veni Creator Spiritus* (8th cent.), *Jesu Dulcis Memoria* (12th cent.), *Sanctorum Meritis* (Salisbury Hymnal), and *Vexilla Regis* (fine settings by Palestrina and Gounod, "March to Calvary"). (See the *Vesperale Romanum*, Mechlin edit., 1848.)

Lutheran Chorals ; from 16th century. Words arranged by Luther, Walther, and others ; many of the tunes based on the old Latin melodies, others original. Typical chorals : *Ein Feste Burg* (Luther, 1535), *Nun danket alle Gott* (J. Crüger, 1649), *Passion Choral* (Hassler, 1601?), *Sleepers, wake* (Nicolai, abt. 1599) (See Bach's *Choralgesänge*, 2 vols., Peters.) The Lutheran Chorals are the National Hymns of Germany, and represent in many respects the noblest type of hymn-tune ; originally "rhythmic" (following the natural accents of the words), they gradually altered to the present form of "balanced musical phrases" during the 17th century.

Marot and Beza's Psalter, with tunes adapted by Guillaume Franc, Geneva, 1542. Contains the oldest version of the "Old 100th" (*q.v.*).

Goudimel's arrangement of the same, 1565.

Claudin le Jeune's arrangement, Leyden, 1633.

Sternhold's 51 *Psalms*, 1549.

Daye's (or *Day's*) *Psalter*, containing the *Whole Booke of Psalmes* by Sternhold and Hopkins (and others) —now called the *Old Version*, 1562. This Psalter contains melodies to the Psalms, taken from French and German sources.

Daye's Harmonized Psalter, 1563 ; "the first book of hymn tunes ever pub. in Eng. for 4 voices."

Este's (*Est's*) *Psalter*, 1592. Includes 57 different tunes arranged for 4 voices by 10 of the best Elizabethan composers (J. Dowland, G. Farnaby, G. Kirbye, &c.).

Ravenscroft's Psalter, 1621 (2nd edit. 1633). Contains 98 different tunes arranged for 4 voices.

Hart's Scotch Psalter, with melodies only, 1615.

Hart's Scotch Psalter, harmonized edit., 1635.

Playford's Psalter, 1677, arranged for 3 voices. In this Psalter the principal melody is given to the *Treble*, instead of the Tenor as in previous Psalters.

Tate and Brady's Version of the *Psalms*, "The New Version,' 1696.

Of the numerous Hymn books and Collections of hymn tunes of modern times the following may be mentioned :—

Hymns (1707-9) ; *Psalms* (1719), Dr. Watts.

The Foundery Tunes (1742) and *Sacred Melody* (1761), published by J. Wesley.

The Olney Hymns, Cowper and Newton, 1779.

A Collection of Hymns for the People called Methodists, John Wesley, 1779.

The Hymnal Noted, Helmore, 1853.

The Union Tune Book, 1854.

Goss and Mercer's Psalter and Hymn Book, 1857.

Hymns Ancient and Modern, 1861.

The Bristol Tune Book, 1863.

Church Hymns with Tunes, Sullivan, 1874.

(For an exhaustive account of Christian Hymns and Hymn Writers, see Julian's *Hymnology*).

Hymnaire (*F.*)   A hymn-book.

Hymn of Praise.   (See **Lobgesang.**)

Hypa'te (*Gk.*).   (See **Greek Music.**)

Hy'per (*Gk.*).   Above.

Hyperdiapa'son.   The octave above.

Hyperdiapen'te.   The 5th above.

Hy'po (*Gk.*).   Below.

Hypodiapa'son.   The octave below.

Hypodiapen'te.   The 5th below.

In the old church modes the term *hypo* was prefixed to the names of all the plagal varieties, which were a 4th below the authentic. (See *Mode*.)

I

I (*I.* pl.). The; as *I Puritani*, the Puritans.

Iam'bus. A metrical foot of two syllables; short, long (∪ —).
Iambic verse is the commonest form of English poetry. In hymnody, it includes Short Metre, Common Metre, Long Metre, and 6-8's.

Ias'tian. Same as **Ionian** (*q.v.*).

I'BACH, J. Adolf. 1766-1844. Founded a pf. and org. manufactory, Barmen, 1794.

IBOS, Guillaume. Vocalist; *b.* 1862; *début,* 1885.

Ic'tus. Accent, stress, emphasis.

Idea. A theme, subject, figure, phrase, or motive.

Idée fixe (*F.*). Berlioz's name for a constantly recurring theme or figure.
"A fundamental and recurrent theme" (*Lavignac*). It is a kind of *Leit-motiv* (*q.v.*).

IDOMENE'O. Opera by Mozart, 1780.

I'dyl, I'dyll. (*G., Idyl'le ; F., Idylle ; I., Idil'lio.*) A pastoral or romantic composition.

IGGULDEN, Athelstan G. *B.* Herne Bay, 1870. Mus.D. Durham, 1901.

Il (*I.*). The ; *Il Trovatore*, the Troubadour.
Il Bas'so sem'pre pia'no e leggieris'simo. The bass to be always soft and as light (delicate) as possible.
Il can'to. The melody, the song.
Il dop'pio movimen'to. Twice as fast.
Il fi'ne. The end.
Il più. The most.
Il più for'te possi'bile. As loud as possible.
Il più pia'no possi'bile. As soft as possible.

Ilarità (*I.*). Hilarity.

Il faut (*F.*). It is necessary.
Il faut 3 timbaliers. It is necessary to have 3 kettle-drummers.

I'LIFFE, Frederick. *B.* Smeeton-Westerby, Leicester, 1847. Mus.Doc.Oxon. 1879.
Works : oratorio (*The Vision of St. John*), orchestral music, "Critical Analysis of Bach's well-tempered Clavichord," &c.

ILIN'SKI, Count J. S. *B.* Poland, 1795; *d.* (?). Studied under Beethoven.
Works : 3 masses, and other church music ; a symphony, overtures, 2 pf. concertos, 8 string quartets, songs, &c.

Ill-approached Intervals. (See **Hidden.**)

Il ponticel'lo (*I.*). "The little bridge."
Old name for the "break" between the natural voice and the *falsetto.*

ILYN'SKY, Alex. A. Composer ; *b.* Tsarskoe Selo, Russia, 1859.

Im (*G.*). In ; in the. *Im tem'po,* in strict time.
Im An'fang nicht zu rasch. Not too fast at the commencement.
Im gemes'senen Schritt. In precise *tempo.*
Im gemüt'(h)lichen Menuet'tempo. In easy-going Minuet time.

IMBART de la TOUR, Georges J. B. Operatic tenor ; *b.* Paris, 1865. *Début,* 1891.

IMBERT, Hughes. French mus. critic and littérateur ; 1842-1905.
His writings on Brahms, Wagner, Berlioz, &c. are valuable.

Imboccatu'ra (*I.*). (1) Mouthpiece of a wind instrument. (2) Lipping ; *embouchure.*

Imbro'glio (*I.*, "confusion "). Conflicting, contrasted, or *cross* rhythms :—

Imitan'do (*I.*). Imitating.
Imitan'do la vo'ce. Imitating the voice.

Imitation (*L., Imita'tio ; F., Imitation ; G., Nach'ahmung ; I., Imitazio'ne*). The repetition of a passage (theme, &c.), in another part, or at a different pitch in the same part.
The various forms of repetition and imitation are an important feature of musical development.

A. REPETITION.
(1) Exact, same pitch. "Blue Bells of Scotland."

Repetition.

(2) Exact, different octave. BEETHOVEN. Op. 27.

(3) In the Relative Major or Minor. "St. Bride."
A minor.   C maj. (Relative).

(4) In the Tonic Major or Minor.
A minor.   A major.

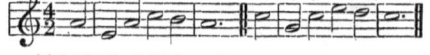

            BEETHOVEN. Op. 31, No. 1.
G major.   G minor.   G major.

(5) In another part. (See *Imitation* (below) and *Canon.*
(6) In another key. SCHUMANN. "Reaper's Song."

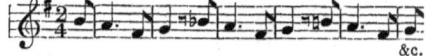

Key G.

Key C.

Then, after 8 bars of different melody :

Key F.

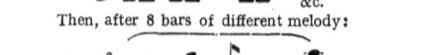

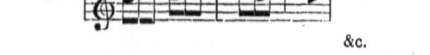

&c.

(7) *Varied.* Repetition may be varied infinitely; an altered ending or continuation is extremely common.

SCHUMANN.

Many extended melodies consist almost entirely of varied repetitions of the first 4 measures.

Dal Tuo Stellato. ROSSINI.

(*a*) 1st Section, G minor.

(*b*) Repetition, with

varied ending in B♭ major.

(*c*) Repetition in B♭ major.

Cadence, B♭.   Repeat, G min.

(*d*) Repetition of (*a*) in G major.

(*e*) Repetition of (*c*)

in G major.

(*f*) Added passage.

(*g*) Repetition, with varied ending.

B. IMITATION.
(1) *Sequential.* (See *Sequence.*)
(2) *Fugal.* (See *Fugue.*)
(3) *Strict.* (See *Canon.*)
(4) *Free.* Imitation in *Canonic style*, but not strict as to interval (and sometimes also with variations of time, accent, &c.), is more frequent and more valuable in modern music than Strict Canon. All the devices of Canon and Fugue may be employed (as *Inverse, Retrograde,* Imitation by *Augmentation* or *Diminution,* &c.), while the composer is free to vary the notes at pleasure.

BEETHOVEN.   Op. 2.

WAGNER.   Symphony in C.

Free inverse imitation.

(See also *Melody, Motive,* and *Thematic Development.*)

Imitation by Augmentation
Imitation by Diminution
Imitation by Inversion } (See *Canon.*)
Imitation, Retrograde,
Imitation, Strict.
Imitation, Free. (See above.)
Imitation, Tonal. When the key is not changed.
Imitation, Rhythmic. Repetition of a "Rhythm" with different melody :—

Imitation, Transitional. Imitation in another key.

Imitative Music. The imitation of natural sounds, as thunder, the singing of birds, the rushing of the wind, &c.

Elaborate treatises have been written attempting to prove that all music is derived by imitation from various natural sounds. As nearly all these sounds may, however, be classed either as *noises* or *inflections;* as music is based on scales of definite tonality and relative pitch ; and, further, as these definite musical scales are nowhere found in nature, it is evident that the art of music is only remotely connected with such sounds. It is true, that *by judicious selection,* the notes of the major and minor scales can be picked out of the "Chord of Nature" (see *Acoustics*), but this discovery(?) was not made until the scales had been in use for generations!

How far realistic imitations are allowable in music has long been a matter of controversy. "The Imitation of a Farmyard" on the violin, "The Battle of Prague" on the piano—thought by many uneducated lovers of music to be wonders of art and skill—are regarded by critics as mere vulgar clap-trap. Yet Beethoven's "Pastoral Symphony," which under the name of " Descriptive " or " Program " music is essentially the same in principle, attracts large audiences of distinguished musicians to our chief concert halls. The undoubted popularity of descriptive music may perhaps be accounted for by (1) the comparatively small number of listeners with sufficient musical education and taste to enable them to thoroughly appreciate and enjoy the beauties of pure absolute music ; and (2) the natural "law of association" which delights in connecting the sounds heard with some special object, place, event, action, idea, feeling, or "program."

The following are celebrated examples of realistic imitation :—

"La Bataille à Quatre;" Jannequin, 1545.
The cackling of a hen; part-song by A. Scandelli, 1570.

"The Cat's Fugue;" A. Krieger, 1667.

Mi - - - - au, mi - - - au!

The leaping of frogs, the buzzing of flies, &c. ; Handel's *Israel in Egypt.*
The howling of Cerberus ; Gluck's *Orfeo.*

Voices.

Strings.

The crowing of the cock ; Haydn's *Seasons.*

The roaring of the lion, &c. ; Haydn's *Creation.*

The cuckoo, nightingale, and quail ; Beethoven's *Pastoral Symphony.*

Nightingale.

Flute.

Oboe.

Cl. in Bb.

Quail &c.

Cuckoo. &c.

"The Battle of Prague ;" Kotzwara.
The braying of the ass ; Mendelssohn's Overture, *Midsummer Night's Dream.*
The Bells of Strasburg Cathedral ; Sullivan's *Golden Legend.*
(See also *Leit Motiv, Program Music,* and *Word Painting.*)

Imita'to (*I.*).   Imitated.

Im klagen'den Ton (*G.*).   In a sorrowful tone (or style).

Im lang'samer Marsch'takt. In rather slow march time.
Im leb'haftesten Zeit'masse. As quick as possible.
Im legen'den Ton. In the style of a romance or legend.
Im Marsch'zeitmass. In march time.
Im mäs'sigen Tem'po. In moderate time.

Im'mer (*G.*).   Always, continually.

Im'mer beweg'ter bis zum En'de. With increasing emotion to the end.
Im'mer gleich'mässig leicht. Always light throughout.
Im'mer gleich'mässig p. Uniformly *p* throughout.
Im'mer lang'sam. Slow throughout.

Im'mer lang'samer. Continually slower ; *rallentando.*
Im'mer le'bendiger. Stringendo (*q.v.*).
Im'mer p. a'ber deut'lich. Always *p,* but distinct.
Im'mer stärk'er wer'dend. Continually louder; *crescendo.*
Im'mer schwäch'er. Becoming softer and softer.
Im'mer sehr weich gebun'den. Always very softly sustained.

Immuta'bilis (*L.*).   (See **Accent.**)

IM'MYNS, John.   Attorney and lutenist ; *b.* 1700(?) ; *d.* London, 1764.
Founded the Madrigal Society, 1741. Taught himself the lute at 40, and became lutenist to the Chapel Royal, 1752.
He was a connoisseur and collector of ancient music, and acted as amanuensis to Dr. Pepusch.

Imparfait (*F.*).   Imperfect.

Impazien'te (*I.*).   Impatient, restless.
Impazientemen'te. Impatiently, hurriedly.

Imperfect.   Defective, incomplete, inconclusive.
Imperfect Cadence. (See *Cadence.*)
Imperfect Chord. A chord with one (or more) of its constituents omitted.
Imperfect Consonances (Concords). Major and minor 3rds and 6ths ; so called to distinguish them from the Perfect Consonances (4ths, 5ths, 8ves).
Imperfect Fifth. Diminished 5th.
Imperfect Fourth. Diminished 4th.
Imperfect Measure ⎱ Duple. Triple time was origin-
Imperfect Time ⎰ ally called "Perfect Time" in allusion to the "Trinity."
Imperfect Stop. An incomplete organ stop.
Imperfect Triad. Diminished Triad (*b₇ r f*).

Imperfect Method of Writing Transitions.
In Sol-fa, the use of "accidentals" at a change of key instead of the "perfect" method of using bridge-notes.

Imperfet'to (*I.*).   Imperfect.

Imperio'so,-a (*I.*).   Imperious, haughty, dignified.
Imperiosamen'te. In a haughty, dignified style.

Imperturba'bile (*I.*).   Quiet, imperturbable.

Im'peto (*I.*).   Impetuosity.
Con im'peto, Con impetuosità, Impetuosamen'te, Impet-uo'so,-a. With impetuosity.

Implied discord.   A concord which becomes a discord by the addition of another note (or notes).
Thus the major 3rd becomes an augmented triad by the addition of another major 3rd :

Implied intervals.   Intervals "understood" in Thorough-bass but not marked in the figuring.

The figure 6 implies also the 3rd ; the figure 2 implies also the 6th and 4th ; &c.

Imponen'te (*I.*).   Imposingly ; emphatically.

Imponi(e)'rend (*G.*).   Imposing, majestic.

Impresa'rio (*I.*).   Manager (conductor, agent) of a concert or opera company.

Impressing musicians.
In 1454 musicians were "impressed" for the Chapel Royal and cathedrals in England ; and this practice continued till after the reign of Queen Elizabeth.

Impromp'tu.   (1) Off-hand, *extempore.* (2) An improvisation. (3) A piece in the style of an improvisation or *fantasia.*

Impropé'ria (*L.*).   "The Reproaches" sung in Roman Catholic churches on Good Friday morning instead of the daily mass.

15

Im'provise. To extemporise; to play without previous preparation.

All' improvvis'ta (I.). Extempore.

Improvisateur (F.)
Improvvisato're (I.) } "One who has the gift of improvising."
Improvvisatri'ce (I.) }

Improvvisa're (I.) } To improvise.
Improviser (F.) }

Improvvisamen'te (I.). Unprepared, extempore.

Improvvisa'ta (I.). An improvisation.

Improvisier'maschi ne (G.). A melograph (*q.v.*).

Im ruh'igen Tem'po (*G.*): In tranquil time.

Im Studen'tenton (*G.*). In the *pupil's* style (as opposed to the style of a *master*).

Im Tact, Im Takt (*G.*). In time.

Im Volks'ton (*G.*). In folk-song style.

Im Zeit'mass (*G.*). In time.

Inacuti're (*I.*). To sharpen.

In ab'wechselnden Chör'en (*G.*). For alternate choirs; antiphonally.

In alt (*I.*), **In altis'simo** (*I.*). (See **Alt.**)

In battu'ta (*I.*). In strict time.

In'brunst (*G.*). Fervour, ardour.

Inbrün'stig. Ardent, fervent.

Incalcan'do, Incalzan'do (*I.*). Increasing in speed (and force); *stringendo*.

Incantazio'ne (*I.*). Songs of incantation.

Inchoa'tio (*L.*). The introductory notes of a Plain-song Chant; called also the **Intonation.**

Inch of Wind. (See **Weight.**)

Incidentals. Term used by Mr. Curwen for passing-notes, appoggiaturas, auxiliary notes, &c.; *i.e.*, for all notes except *essential* notes (*q.v.*).

Inci'so,-a (*I.*). Incisive; well emphasised.

INCLEDON, Chas. B. Tenor vocalist; renowned as a ballad singer; *b.* St. Keverne, Cornwall, 1763; *d.* 1826.

Incomincia'ndo (*I.*). Commencing.

Incomplete stop. An organ stop which does not extend through the complete compass of the manual.

Inconsola'to (*I.*). Mournful, disconsolate.

Incon'sonant. Discordant.

Incorda're (*I.*). To string (an instrument).

Incrociamen'to (*I.*). "Encroaching;" crossing.

Indeci'so (*I.*). Undecided, capricious.

Indegna'to (*I.*) } Wrathfully, indig-
Indegnatamen'te (*I.*) } nantly.

Indifferen'te (*I.*) } With assumption
Indifferentemen'te (*I.*) } of indifference;
Indifferen'za, Con (*I.*) } carelessly.

In distan'za (*I.*). At a distance.

Index. A direct (*q.v.*).

d'INDY, P. M. T. Vincent. *B.* Paris, 1851. Studied Paris Cons.; chorus-master (under Colonne), 1875. Music inspector of Paris schools; Chevalier of the Legion of Honour, &c.

Works: opera, *Fervaal* (Brussels, 1897); symphonic poems and *Legends* for orches.; overtures, suites, romances, songs, &c.

Infe'rior (*L.*). Lower (as of parts).

Inferna'le (*I.*). Infernal, hellish.

Infervora'to (*I.*). Fervent, impassioned.

Inflammatamen'te (*I.*). Ardently.

Infinite canon. (See **Canon.**)

Inflati'lia (*L.*). "Inflatile," *i.e.*, *wind* insts.

Inflection. (1) Gradual rising and falling in pitch without determinate sounds or intervals, as in speech. (2) The change from monotone in chanting.

Inflexion. Same as **Inflection** (*q.v.*).

In'fra (*L.*). Beneath, below.

Infrabass' (*G.*). "Sub-bass." A 16ft. org. stop.

In fret'ta (*I.*). In haste; hurriedly.

Infurian'te (*I.*), **Infuria'to** (*I.*) Furious.

Ingan'no (*I.*). "A deception."

Ingan'no Cadence } A deceptive cadence. (See
Caden'za d'ingan'no (I.) } Cadence.)

INGEGNE'RI, Marco Antonio. Celebrated early North Italian composer; abt. 1540-91. Monteverde was his pupil.

Wrote masses, motets, madrigals, "Sacræ Cantiones," Responses, &c.

Ingeg'no (*I.*). Art, skill, discretion.

In geh'ender Bewe'gung (*G.*). "In going (walking) movement." *Andante.*

In geh'ender Bewe'gung, doch mit Aus'druck. Same as *Andante espressivo* (*q.v.*).

INGEMANN, Bernhardt S. 1789-1862. Danish professor.

Wrote the hymn "Through the night of doubt and sorrow" (Eng. trans. by S. Baring-Gould.)

Ingenuamen'te (*I.*). Naturally, ingenuously.

In gleich'er Stär'ke, oh'ne An'schwellen (*G.*). With even force, without (any) *crescendo*.

INGLOTT, Wm. Renowned organist; 1554-1621. Orgt. Norwich Cath., 1608.

INGRAM-ADAMS, Mrs. W. (See **Amy Goodwin.**)

In'halt (*G.*). Contents; subject-matter.

In'harmonic relation. False relation (*q.v.*).

In höch'ster Angst (*G.*). In deepest anguish.

In lontanan'za (*I.*). Same as **In distanza.**

In mo'do popola're (*I.*). In popular style.

In Musik' set'zen (*G.*), To set to music.

Inner parts. All parts except the highest and lowest.

Many progressions are allowed between inner parts which are not good between the "outer" or "extreme" parts.

Inner pedal. A pedal-point in one of the inner parts. (See **Pedal.**)

In'nig (*G.*). Inmost; heartfelt; sincere.

In'nigkeit. Deep, heartfelt emotion.

In'niglich. Same as *innig.*

Mit in'nigem Aus'druck. With fervent, heartfelt expression.

In'no (*I.*). Hymn, canticle, ode.

Innocen'te (*I.*). Innocent, natural, unaffected.

Innocentemen'te } In an artless, childlike style.
Innocen'za, Con }

In no'mine (*L.*). "In the name." A kind of free fugue popular in the 16th cent.

In pal'co (*I.*). On a stage.

In parti'to (*I.*). In score.

Inquie'to (*I.*). Restless, agitated.

INSAN'GUINE, Giacomo. (Called "Monopoli.") *B.* Monopoli, 1744; *d.* 1795.

Works: Psalm 71 (his best work), abt 20 operas, hymns, masses, &c.

Insects, Music of. The musical notes of insects are produced (1) by striking rapidly a series of hard plates attached to the abdomen, after the manner of Spanish castanets ; (2) by rubbing the wings against small bridge-like edges or ridges attached to the abdomen, after the manner of a violin. Some insects of this kind have "veritable bows" covered with fine ridges attached to the wings ; and in almost all "there is a parchment-like part of the body which acts as a kind of sounding-board."

Many insects sing by day, others only at night. The performers are always male, "female insects contenting themselves with staying at home looking after the children, instead of standing at the front door singing like their lords and masters."—*Scientific American.*

Insensi'bile (*I.*) } Imperceptibly ; very
Insensibilmen'te (*I.*) } gradually.

Insie'me (*I.*). Ensemble (*q.v.*).

Insisten'do (*I.*). Urgently, insistently.

In'ständig (*G.*) } Instant ; urgent, pressing.
Instan'te (*I.*) }
  Instantemen'te (*I.*). Urgently, vehemently.

Instrument. (*G., Instrument' ; F., Instrument ; I., Instrumen'to, Istrumen'to, Stromen'to, Strumen'to.*)

Instrumen'tal } For an instrument (or
Instrumenta'le (*I.*) } instruments).

This term was formerly specially used for the instrumental bass as opposed to the vocal bass.

Instrumental forms.

The chief forms of instrumental music are:— Ballade, Concerto, Dance Music (*q.v.*), Fantasia, Intermezzo, March, Minuet, Nocturne, Octet, Offertoire, Overture, Partita, Prelude, Quartet, Quintet, Rondo, Scherzo, Septet, Serenade, Sextet, Sonata, Suite, Symphony, Tone-poem, Trio, Toccata, Variation, Voluntary. (See each under its proper heading.)

Instrumentation. (*G., Instrumentie'rung ; F., Instrumentation ; I., Istrumentazio'ne.*) (1) The knowledge of the pitch, compass, capabilities, and effects of instruments. (2) Orchestration.

Instrumentation and orchestration are generally regarded as the same ; but Gevaert distinguishes between them. (See *Orchestration.*)

Intavola're (*I.*). To set out or copy notes ; to score.

The following classified list of musical instruments is adapted and amplified from Gevaert's *Nouveau Traité d'Instrumentation.*

I.—STRINGED INSTRUMENTS.

A.	Rubbed	(a) By a bow	Violin, Viola, Violoncello, Double-bass, Viola d'Amour, Viols generally.
		(b) By a wheel	Hurdy-gurdy, Piano-violin.
B.	Plucked	(a) By the fingers, with or without a plectrum.	Harp, Guitar, Mandolin, Zither, Banjo, Lute, Auto-harp.
		(b) By keyboard mechanism.	Harpsichord.
C.	Struck	(a) By a hammer	Dulcimer, Zimbalon, Xylophone, Gondolin.
		(b) By keyboard mechanism acting on hammers.	Pianoforte.

II.—WIND INSTRUMENTS.

A.	With mouth-hole.	(a) Lateral		Flutes, Piccolos, Fifes.
		(b) With beak		Flûtes-à-bec, Flageolet, Whistle.
B.	With reed	(a) Cylindrical tube, and single beating reed.		Chalumeau, Clarinet, Alt-clarinet (or Basset-horn), Bass Clarinet.
		(b) Conical tube and single beating reed.		Saxophones (Sopranino, Soprano, Alto, Tenor, Barytone and Bass),
		(c) Conical tube and double reed.		Oboe, Hautbois d'amour, Alt-oboe (or Cor Anglais), Musette, Sarrusophones, Bassoon, Tenoroon, Double-bassoon.
C.	With "cup" mouthpiece.	(a) Natural		Post-horn, Military Bugle, Natural Horn, Natural Trumpet.
		(b) Chromatic	(1) With slide.	Trombone, Slide-trumpet.
			(2) With keyed holes.	Key-bugle (or Trumpet), Serpent, Ophicleide.
			(3) With valves or pistons.	Valve-horn, Valve-trumpet, Valve-trombones (Alto, Tenor, Bass), Cornets, Saxhorns (Alto, Tenor, Baritone, Bass), Euphonium, Bombardon, Helicon, Tuba, &c., Flugel-horns.
D.	Polyphonic	(1) With tubes (pipes).		Organ.
		(2) Without tubes.		Harmonium, Vocalion, American Organ, Mustel Organ, Accordeon, Melodeon, English Concertina, German Concertina, Flutina.

III.—PERCUSSION INSTRUMENTS.

A.	With a membrane.	(a) Determinate pitch.	Kettledrums.
		(b) Indeterminate pitch	Bass-drum, Side-drum, Tambourine, &c.
B.	Autophonic	(a) Determinate pitch.	Bells, Carillons, Glockenspiel, Keyed Harmonica, Hand Bells, &c.
		(b) Indeterminate pitch.	Triangle, Gong, Cymbals, Tam-tam, Castanets, Jingle Bells, &c.

IV.—TOY INSTRUMENTS.

Mouth-harmonica, Panpipes, Picco-pipe, Bird Organ, Cuckoo, Fairy Bells, Nightingale, Rattle, Quail, &c.

V.—MECHANICAL AND AUTOMATIC INSTRUMENTS.

Orchestrion, Barrel-organ, Barrel-piano, Organette, Autophon, Piano-player, Gramophone, Musical-box, &c. Many other varieties of instruments are mentioned under their proper headings.

Instrument à l'archet (*F.*) } A bowed instrument.
Instrumen'to d'ar'co (*I.*) }
Instrumen'to a corda (*I.*) } A stringed instrument.
Instrument à cordes (*F.*) }
Instrument à vent (*F.*) } A wind instrument.
Instrumen'to da fia'to I.) }
Instrument à percussion (*F.*) } A percussion instrument.
Instrumen'to da percotimen'to (*I.*) }
Instrumen'to da pen'na (*I.*). A spinet.
Instrumen'to da tas'to (*I.*). A keyed instrument.

Intavolatu'ra (*I.*). (1) Notation. (2) Figured Bass. (3) Tablature (*q.v.*).

In tem'po (*I.*), **A tempo.** In strict time.
  In tem'po, ma po'co più len'to. In strict time, but a little slower.

Intendant (*F.*) } Manager, director, conductor.
Intenden'te (*I.*) }

Intenziona'to (*I.*). With emphasis.

Interchange of notes. Transferring the notes of a chord from one part to another.

Interligne (*F.*). A space between staff lines.

In'terlude ⎫ "Played between." A
Interlu'dium (*L.*) ⎭ piece between the acts of a drama, the verses of a hymn, &c.

Intermède (*F.*). (1) An interlude. (2) A one-act operetta.

Interme'dio (*I.*). An interlude.
   Intermediet'to.   A short interlude.

Intermez'zo (*I.*). (1) An interlude ; an *entr'acte.* (2) A short operetta.

Interrot'to (*I.*). Interrupted.

Interrupted cadence. (See **Cadence.**)

Interruzio'ne (*I.*). Interruption; pause.
   Sen'za interruzio'ne.   Go straight on without pause or interruption.

Interval ⎫
Intervall' (*G.*) ⎪ The difference in pitch
Intervalle (*F.*) ⎬ between two sounds.
Interval'lo (*I.*) ⎭

(1) TABLE OF INTERVALS USED IN PRACTICAL MUSIC :

NAME OF INTERVAL	No. OF SEMI-TONES	EXAMPLE
(Perfect) Unison, or Prime	0	
Augmented Prime, or Chromatic Semitone	1	
Minor 2nd (Diatonic Semitone)	1	
Major 2nd	2	
Augmented 2nd	3	
Diminished 3rd	2	
Minor 3rd	3	
Major 3rd	4	

NAME OF INTERVAL	No. OF SEMI-TONES	EXAMPLE
Augmented 3rd	5	
Diminished 4th	4	
Perfect 4th	5	
Augmented 4th	6	
Diminished 5th	6	
Perfect 5th	7	
Augmented 5th	8	
Diminished 6th	7	
Minor 6th	8	
Major 6th	9	
Augmented 6th	10	
Diminished 7th	9	
Minor 7th	10	
Major 7th	11	
Diminished 8ve	11	
Perfect 8ve	12	
Augmented 8ve	13	

The following *Compound Intervals* (see below) are used in Systems of Harmony :

Minor 9th (or Compound Minor 2nd)	
Major 9th (Compound Major 2nd)	
(Perfect) 11th (Compound Perfect 4th)	
Minor 13th (Compound Minor 6th)	
Major 13th (Compound Major 6th)	

(2) TABLE OF INTERVALS referred to in Acoustics and other theoretical investigations, with the vibration-ratio of each Interval, and its comparative value in terms of an equally-tempered semitone (*i.e.*, the semitone of the pianoforte). (Adapted from Dr. A. J. Ellis.)

NAME	RATIOS	VALUE COMPARED TO A SEMITONE
Skhisma	32805 : 32768	$\frac{1}{53}$ or (·2)
Comma of Didymus.	81 : 80	$\frac{11}{50}$ (·22)
Comma of Pythagoras	531441 : 524288	$\frac{6}{25}$ (·24)
Septimal Comma....	64 : 63	$\frac{27}{100}$ (·27)
aQuartertone	246 : 239	$\frac{1}{2}$ (·5)
bSmall Semitone	25 : 24	$\frac{7}{10}$ (·7)
Pythagorean Limma	256 : 243	$\frac{9}{10}$ (·9)
Small Limma	135 : 128	$\frac{46}{50}$ (·92)
aEqual Semitone	89 : 84	1
bDiatonic Semitone ..	16 : 15	$1\frac{3}{25}$ (1·12)
Apotome	2187 : 2048	$1\frac{7}{50}$ (1·14)
Trumpet three-quarter tone ..	12 : 11	$1\frac{51}{100}$ (1·51)
bMinor Tone	10 : 9	$1\frac{41}{50}$ (1·82)
aEqual Tone	449 : 400	2
bMajor Tone	9 : 8	$2\frac{1}{25}$ (2·04)
Sub-minor Third	7 : 6	$2\frac{67}{100}$ (2·67)
aEqual Minor 3rd	44 : 37	3
bJust Minor 3rd......	6 : 5	$3\frac{4}{25}$ (3·16)
Zalzal's Neutral 3rd .	49 : 22	$3\frac{11}{20}$ (3·55)
bJust Major 3rd.....	5 : 4	$3\frac{43}{50}$ (3·86)
aEqual Major 3rd ..	63 : 50	4
Pythagorean Major 3rd	81 : 64	$4\frac{2}{25}$ (4·08)
Grave 4th	320 : 243	$4\frac{19}{25}$ (4·76)
bJust 4th	4 : 3	$4\frac{49}{50}$ (4·98)
aEqual 4th	303 : 227	5
Septimal 5th	7 : 5	$5\frac{83}{100}$ (5·83)
bJust Tritone	45 : 32	$5\frac{9}{10}$ (5·9)
aEqual Tritone	140 : 99	6
Grave 5th	40 : 27	$6\frac{4}{5}$ (6·8)
aEqual 5th	433 : 289	7
bJust 5th	3 : 2	$7\frac{1}{50}$ (7·02)
Acute 5th	248 : 160	$7\frac{1}{25}$ (7·04)
aEqual Minor 6th....	100 : 63	8
bJust Minor 6th......	8 : 5	$8\frac{7}{50}$ (8·14)
Zalzal's Neutral 6th	18 : 11	$8\frac{53}{100}$ (8·53)
bJust Major 6th	5 : 3	$8\frac{21}{25}$ (8·84)
aEqual Major 6th ...	37 : 22	9
Pythagorean Major 6th	27 : 16	$9\frac{3}{50}$ (9·06)
Sub-minor, or Harmonic Minor 7th	7 : 4	$9\frac{69}{100}$ (9·69)
bJust Minor 7th......	16 : 9	$9\frac{24}{25}$ (9·96)

NAME	RATIOS	VALUE COMPARED TO A SEMITONE
aEqual Minor 7th ...	98 : 55	10
bJust Major 7th	15 : 8	$10\frac{22}{25}$ (10·88)
aEqual Major 7th ...	168 : 89	11
Pythagorean Major 7th	243 : 128	$11\frac{1}{10}$ (11·1)
Octave	2 : 1	12

Intervals marked (*a*) are the equally-tempered intervals of the piano ; those marked (*b*) are the true Acoustical Intervals. (See *Acoustics*.)

Disguised Intervals. Many *Doubly-augmented* (or even *Doubly-diminished*) intervals may be found in modern printed music caused by two parts moving semitonically in contrary motion or by the "Expedient Notation" (*q.v.*) of a chord.

* Doubly-augmented 4th. † Doubly-diminished 8ve.

Such intervals do not need classification, as they are ordinary intervals "disguised" by the notation. Thus the Doubly-augmented 4th at (*a*) in the following is really a "perfect 5th," E♮ being written instead of F♭ :—

BEETHOVEN · *Pf. Sonata, Op.* 57.

Note the "disguised" consecutive 5ths at (*a*) (*b*).

Peculiar intervals are also often caused by the use of appoggiaturas, or other incidental (or non-essential) notes :—

SCHUMANN : *Pilgrimage of the Rose.*

(*a*) Doubly-augmented unison (prime); B♮ an appoggiatura.

(*b*) Doubly-augmented 5th; G♯ a chromatic waving-tone.

(*c*) Doubly-diminished 8ve ; two chromatic "waves."

Interval, augmented. Greater than perfect, or greater than major.

Interval, chromatic. (See *Chromatic*.)

Interval, compound. An interval greater than an octave.

Interval, consonant. (See *Consonance*.)

Interval, diatonic. (See *Diatonic*.)

Interval, diminished. Less than perfect, or less than minor.

Interval, dissonant. Requiring resolution.
Interval, enharmonic. (See *Enharmonic.*)
Interval, extreme. Augmented (or diminished). (See *Extreme.*)
Interval, flat. (See *Flat.*)
Interval, harmonic. When both notes are sounded together.
Interval, imperfect. (See *Imperfect.*)
Interval, inverted. (See *Inversion.*)
Interval, melodic. When the 2 notes are sounded in succession.
Interval, pluperfect. An augmented interval.
Interval, simple. An interval not greater than an octave.

Intervals of the Scale. (See **Acoustics.**)

Intime (*F.*) ⎫
In'timo (*I.*) ⎬ Same as **In'nig** (*q.v.*).

Intimis'simo (*I.*). With very much feeling and expression.

Intona're (*I.*). To tune; to sing; to intone; to sound the key-note.

Intona'tion. (1) The method of tone production of a voice or instrument. (2) Pitch. (3) Tone quality or *timbre*. (4) The opening notes of a Gregorian chant.

Intonation is *correct, just, pure, true,* &c., when the pitch is exact and the tone quality good; otherwise it is incorrect, impure, false, &c.
Fixed intonation. Absolute pitch. (See *Pitch.*)

Intona'to (*I.*). Set to music; tuned.

In'tonator. A monochord (*q.v.*) with a movable bridge.

By placing the bridge in a suitable position any note of a scale can be accurately obtained.

Intonatu'ra (*I.*) ⎫
Intonazio'ne (*I.*) ⎬ Intonation; pitch.

Intonie'ren (*G.*). To intone; to voice (organ pipes).

Inton'ing. A method of chanting (mostly in monotone) employed in church ritual.

Intra'da (*I.*) ⎫ (*F., Entrée*). A prelude or
Intra'ta (*I.*) ⎬ overture; an opening
Intra'de (*G.*) ⎭ movement.

Intre'ccio (*I.*). "An intrigue." A short stage piece.

Intrepidamen'te (*I.*) ⎫
Intrepidez'za, Con (*I.*) ⎬ With boldness, daring, courage.
Intrepi'do (*I.*) ⎭

Introduction ⎫ A phrase, theme, or
Introducimen'to (*I.*) ⎬ movement, to announce the commencement of a work (or any important division of a work).
Introduzio'ne (*I.*) ⎭

The introduction may vary in length from two or three chords (to summon attention) to a lengthy overture. In operas the name "Introduction" is often given to the whole of the 1st scene.

Introit' ⎫ (1) A short anthem, anti-
Intro'ito (*I.*) ⎬ phon, psalm, &c., sung
Intro'itus (*L.*) ⎭ while the officiating priest proceeds to the altar to celebrate the Holy Communion. In the R.C. Church, a selection from the Bible sung before the Kyrie. (2) An introduction.

Intuona're (*I.*). To intone.

Inven'tio (*L.*) ⎫ (1) A suite (*q.v.*). (2) A
Invention ((*E.* ⎬ composition of a fanciful
Invenzio'ne (*I.*) ⎭ or impromptu character.

Bach's Inventions are the most famous pieces of this kind; those for 3 parts he called "symphonies."

Inver'sio (*L.*), **Inverzio'ne** (*I.*). Inversion.

Inversion. (1) Of a theme, or subject. An imitation in contrary motion.

Of strict inversions there are two common varieties:—

(*a*) Tonic and Dominant interchangeable:—

Each of these examples is an inversion of the other.

(*b*) Tonic and Mediant interchangeable:—

It will be seen that (*b*) is "absolutely strict" as to interval. (See also *Canon* and *Fugue.*)
Free inversions of themes are also frequently employed. (See *Imitation.*)

(2) Of parts. A rearrangement, so that an *upper* part becomes a *lower* or *middle* one, &c. (See **Counterpoint, Double.**)

(3) Of a chord. All "positions" except the "Root" or "*a*" position.

Thus a triad has 3 positions, viz., the Root pos'tion and the 1st and 2nd Inversions; a chord of 4 notes has 4 positions, including a 3rd inversion; &c.

Root	1st	2nd		1st	2nd	3rd
pos.	Inv.	inv.		Inv.	inv.	inv.
s	d^l	m^l		f	s	t	r^l
m	s	d^l		r	f	s	t
d	m	s		t$_l$	r	f	s
				s$_l$	t$_l$	r	f
D(*a*)	D*b*	D*c*		7S(*a*)	7S*b*	7S*c*	7S*d*

(4) Of an Interval. The difference between the interval and a perfect octave.

A *simple* interval is inverted by writing its lower note an octave higher, or its higher note an octave lower. A *compound* interval must first be reduced to a *simple* interval.

When inverted,
Minor intervals become Major.
Major intervals become Minor.
Diminished intervals become Augmented.
Augmented intervals become Diminished.
Perfect intervals remain Perfect.

Inverted Cadence. (See **Cadence.**)

Inverted pedal. (See **Pedal.**)

Inverted turn. (See **Turn.**)

Invitato′rium (*L.*) ⎫ An introductory anti-
Invi′tatory   ⎭ phon, psalm, &c.
    (1) Roman Catholic Church, The *Venite*. (2)
    Greek Church, "O come, let us worship."
    (3) Anglican Church, "Praise ye the Lord,"
    "The Lord's name be praised."

Invoca′to (*I.*)   ⎫ A prayer, an invocation.
Invocazio′ne (*I.*) ⎭

In zwei Ab′teilungen (*G.*). In two parts.

Io′nian Mode. One of the later Church
modes. (See **Mode.**)
    It commences on the note C, and is identical with
    our modern scale of C major.

IONS, Thos. Organist and composer; *b.*
Newcastle, 1817; *d.* 1857. Mus.Doc.
Oxford, 1854.

IPHIGÉNIE EN AULIDE. Opera by Gluck;
Paris, 1774.

IPHIGÉNIE EN TAURIDE. Opera by Gluck;
Paris, 1779.

I′po (*I.*) Same as Gk. *hypo;* as *Ipofri′gio*,
Hypo-phrygian.

IPPOLITOV-IVANOV, Michail M. Russian
composer; *b.* Gatshin, 1859. Prof. of
harmony and composition Moscow
Cons., 1893.
    Works: operas, orch. pieces, chamber-music,
    choruses, songs, &c.

I′ra (*I.*). Anger, wrath.
Con i′ra   ⎫
Iracondamen′te ⎬ Angrily, with wrath.
Iratamen′te   ⎪
Ira′to,-a   ⎭

IR′GANG, Friedrich Wm. *B.* Hirschberg,
Schleswig, 1836. Founded a school for
pf. playing and theory, Görlitz, 1863.
    Works: an "Allgemeine Musiklehre," a "Har-
    monielehre," pf. pieces, &c.

Irish Music.
    The following are among the most noted Col-
    lections of Ancient Irish Music.
    (1) Bunting's "Music of Ireland," 3 vols.
    (1796-1840).
    (2) Moore's "Irish Melodies" with accts. by
    Stevenson and others (1808-34).
    (3) G. Thomson's Collection; Beethoven's accts.
    (1814).
    (4) G. Petrie's Collection (1855; completed edn.,
    1903).
    Irish Bagpipe. The Irish bagpipe differs from the
    Scotch as follows :—(1) It is blown with bellows
    instead of the mouth; (2) The
    reeds are more delicate and
    the tone softer. (3) The scale
    extends from
    with all the semitones. (4) It
    is furnished with a kind of harmony :—

    N.B.—The ancient Irish bagpipe " was inflated
    by the mouth, and was in every respect the
    same as the Highland bagpipe of to-day."
    (For a full account of Irish pipes and the
    distinction between "War" pipes and
    "Uilleann" pipes, see Dr. Grattan Flood's
    Hist. of Irish Music.)
    Irish Harp. The ancient Irish harp was triangular in
    shape, possessed from 30 to 50 strings, and was
    usually set in the key of G. It stands as the em-
    blem of Ireland on the Royal Standard.

Irlandais,-e (*F.*) ⎫ Irish. An air or dance
Ir′ländisch (*G.*) ⎭ tune in Irish style.
A l′irlandaise (*F.*). In the Irish style.

Iron fiddle ⎫
Iron harp ⎬ (See **Nail fiddle.**)

Iro′nia (*I.*). Irony, dissimulation.
Con iro′nia   ⎫
Ironicamen′te ⎬ Ironically.
Iro′nico,-a   ⎭

IRONS, Wm. Josiah, D.D. 1812-83. Prebendary, St. Paul's Cath.
    Trans. the *Dies Iræ* of Thomas of Celano; "Day
    of wrath."

Irregular Accents. Syncopated notes, &c.
(See **Accent.**)

Irregular Cadence. (See **Cadence.**)

Irrelative. Term applied to two chords
which have no note in common.

Irresolu′to (*I.*). Undecided, hesitating.

ISAACS, Edw. Pianist and composer; *b.*
Manchester, 1881.

**I′SAAK (ISAAC, IZAK, YZAK, YSACK),
Heinrich.** Eminent contrapuntist; abt.
1450-1517. Known in Italy as **Arrigo
Tedesco**; *Latin name*, **Arrighus.** Maestro to "Lorenzo the Magnificent," 1477-
1490; afterwards lived at Rome and
Innsbruck.
    Works: 23 masses; motets, psalms, introits,
    graduals, chorals, &c. Also a large number of
    very fine part-songs (*Liedlin*), including the
    choral " Innsbruck."

ISAYE. (See **Ysaye.**)

Isde′gno (*I.*). Indignation.

Islan′cio (*I.*). Same as **Slancio** (*q.v.*).

Ismani′a (*I.*). Madness, wildness.

ISME′NIAS. Celebrated Theban flute player
who is said to have given three talents
(£581 5s.) for a flute.

Isoch′ronal ⎫ Uniform in time; together;
Isoch′ronous ⎭ simultaneous.

I′son (*Gk.*). The key-note of a chant. (See
also **Chant en ison.**)
    At the Westminster Cath. Sept. 12, 1908,
    " Eastern custom was followed with regard to
    the employment of the accompaniment called
    Ison. The melody is allotted to the choir,
    while boys' voices sustain one note—generally
    the dominant—of the scale."

Isoton′ic. (From Gk. " Equal toned.")
Applied to the equally-tempered scale
of 12 semitones.

ISOUARD, Niccolò. *B.* Malta, 1775; *d.*
Paris, 1818. Studied at Palermo and
Naples. Private secretary to Gen.
Vaubois, Paris, 1799.
    Works: 33 French operas (including *Cendrillon*,
    1810; *Joconde*, 1814; and *Jeannot et Collin*,
    1814); masses, psalms, &c. His music was
    melodious, and he had a "fine dramatic taste."
    He was a keen rival of Boieldieu.

ISRAEL, Karl. Critic and writer on musical
bibliography; *b.* Electoral Hesse, 1841;
d. 1881.

ISRAEL IN EGYPT. Oratorio by Handel;
1st performance, April 4, 1739.

Istes'so (*I*.). The same.

L'istes'so tem'po } (1) The same time as before.
Lo stes'so tem'po } (2) The duration of the *beat* to be the same as before; thus, ♩ = ♪, crotchet equal preceding minim; ♩. = ♩, dotted crotchet equal preceding crotchet, &c.

L'istes'so tem'po poi a poi di nuo'vo viven'te. The same time, with gradually increasing animation.

L'istes'so tem'po di ario'so. The same time as the *Arioso.*

L'istes'so tem'po del'la Fu'ga. The same time as the *Fugue.*

Istrepi'to (*I*.). Noise, bluster.

Istromen'to (*I*.) }
Istrumen'to (*I*.) } An instrument.

Istrumenta'le (*I*.). Instrumental.

Istrumentazio'ne (*I*.). Instrumentation.

Italian mordent. A short trill or shake with the note *above.* (See **Mordent.**)

Italian Music.

Italy, "the Land of Song," was for several centuries (above all in the 17th cent.) the leading musical country of Europe. From about the time of J. S. Bach, however, Germany gradually acquired that pre-eminence which she has ever since maintained. Italian music has always been justly celebrated for its charming and spontaneous melody.

CHIEF COMPOSERS: C. Festa (1490-1545), Palestrina (abt. 1526-94), Zarlino (1519-90), Galilei (abt. 1533-1600), Merulo (1533-1604), Gabrieli (1540-1612), Cavalieri -e (1550-1600?) Marenzio (1550?-99), Peri (1560?-1630), Croce (1560-1609), Monteverde (1567(8)-1643), Allegri (1580?-1662), Frescobaldi (1583-1644), Carissimi (1604-74), Lulli (1633-87; see *French Music*), Colonna (1640-95), Stradella (1645-81?), A. Scarlatti (1650-1725), Corelli (1653-1714), Bononcini (1660-1750?), Perti (1661-1756), Geminiani (1680-1761), D. Scarlatti (1683-1757), Durante (1684-1755), Marcello (1686-1739), Porpora (1686-1767), Tartini (1692-1770), Leo (1694-1746), Martini (1706-84), Pergolesi (1710-36), Jomelli (1714-74), Piccinni (1728-1800), Sacchini (1734-86), Boccherini (1740-1805), Paisiello (1741-1816), Cimarosa (1749-1801), Salieri (1750-1825), Clementi (1752-1832), Zingarelli (1752-1837), Viotti (1753-1824), Cherubini (1760-1842; see *French*

Music), Spontini (1784-1851), Carafa (1787-1872), Rossini (1792-1868), Mercadente (1797-1870), Donizetti (1798-1848), Bellini (1801-35), Verdi (1813-1901), Boito (1842-), Leoncavallo (1858-), Mascagni (1863-), Busoni (1866-), Perosi (1872-).

Italian sixth. A variety of the chord of the Augmented (or Extreme) sixth. (See **Extreme sixth.**)

Italian strings. Catgut strings of superior quality, mostly made in Rome.

Italia'no (*I*.) }
Italie'nisch (*G*.) } In the Italian style.
Italienne, A l' (*F*.) }

I'te, mis'sa est (*L*.). "Go, (the congregation) is dismissed." The final words of the Mass.

The name " mass " is said to be derived from the word "missa" in this passage.

IVANOV (or **IWANOW**), **Michail M.** Russian composer and writer; *b.* Moscow, 1849. Pupil of Tschaikowsky.

Works: operas, symphonies, overtures, pf. pieces, songs, &c.

IVANOVI'CI. Popular waltz composer. *D.* Roumania, 1902.

IVES, Joshua. Organist and composer; *b.* Hyde, Cheshire, 1854. Prof. of Music, University of Adelaide, 1884.

IVES, Simon. Noted composer of catches, rounds, &c. He was a vicar choral of St. Paul's Cath., and died in 1662.

IVIMEY, John Wm. Conductor and composer; *b.* West Ham, 1868.

IVRY, Marquis **Richard d'.** Operatic composer; *b.* Beaune, 1829; settled in Paris, 1854; *d.* 1903.

Works: operas, *Fatma* (1854), *La Maison du docteur* (1855), *Les Amants de Vérone* (1867), &c.; also orchestral music, songs, &c.

IZAC. (See **ISAAK.**)

J

J. Sometimes used for "I" at the end of Italian and German words; as *Esercizj*, Exercises.

Jach, Jäh (G.). Precipitate, hasty.

JACHET. (See **Berchem.**)

JACH'MANN-WAGNER. (See **J. Wagner.**)

Jack. The "hopper" at the end of a harpsichord key, carrying the quill which plucked the string.
Shakespeare confuses the jacks with the keys.

JACKSON, Arthur Herbert. Composer and pianist; *b.* Brighton, 1852; *d.* 1881.
Works: *Lord Ullin's Daughter* (Choral Ballad), orchestral pieces, &c.

JACKSON, B. *B.* Birstwith, Yorks, 1869. Exhibitioner, R. C. M., 1887-1890; F.R.C.O., 1889. Solo-orgt. People's Palace, London, since 1889.
Works: org. pieces, anthems, songs, &c.

JACKSON, Edwin W. Pubd. a "Complete Manual of Finger Gymnastics," 1866.

JACKSON, J. P. *D.* 1902. Author of "Album of the Passion-play at Oberammergau," 1873; Wagner's *Ring of the Nibelung*, 1882; Eng. trans. of *Parsifal*, &c.

JACKSON, Leonora. Violinist; *b.* Boston (U.S.A.), 1879.

JACKSON, Samuel P. *B.* Manchester, 1818; *d.* Brooklyn, 1885.
"A well-known teacher of pf., org., and harmony; for many years music-proof reader to G. Schirmer, New York."—*Baker.*
Published organ voluntaries, &c.

JACKSON, Seymour. Tenor vocalist; stage *début*, 1886.

JACKSON, Thos. Composer; *b.* abt. 1715; *d.* 1781.
Wrote the hymn-tune "Jackson's," chants, &c.

JACKSON, Wm. "Jackson of Exeter." Exeter, 1730-1803. Orgt. Exeter Cath. from 1777.
Works: *The Lord of the Manor*, and other operas; odes, pretty songs, madrigals, &c., and much church music (including the well-known service, "Jackson in F"); also essays.

JACKSON, Wm. "Jackson of Masham." *B.* Masham, Yorkshire, 1815; *d.* 1866. Self-taught musician. Conductor Bradford Choral Union; Choirmaster Bradford Festivals.
Works: 2 oratorios, 2 cantatas, church music, songs, glees, &c.

JACKSON, Wm. *B.* 1828; *d.* Girvan, 1876.
Composed the once-popular song "The dear little Shamrock."

JACOB, Benjamin. London, 1778-1829. Famous organist and recitalist. Orgt. Surrey Chapel, 1794-1825. Conductor Lenten Oratorios, Covent Garden, 1818.
Works: "National Psalmody" (1819), glees, songs, &c.

JACOB, F. A. L. (See **Jakob.**)

JACO'BI, Georges. *B.* Berlin, 1840. Settled in London as violinist and conductor, 1870. *D.* 1906.
Works: numerous ballets, &c., produced at the Alhambra.

JACOBS, Edouard. *B.* Hal, Belgium, 1851. Fine 'cellist; 'cello-professor, Brussels Cons., 1885.

JAC'OBSTHAL, Gustav. *B.* Pomerania, 1845. Lecturer on Music, Strasburg Univ., 1872.
Chief work: "Mensural Music in the 12th and 13th centuries."

JACOTIN. (Real name **Jaques Godebyre.**) Celebrated Flemish contrapuntist; *b.* abt. 1445; *d.* 1529. Singer at *Notre-Dame*, Antwerp.
Works: masses, motets, chansons, &c.

JACQUARD, Léon J. Eminent 'cellist; Paris, 1826-86. Prof. Paris Cons., 1877.

JACQUES, Edgar F. Musical critic and lecturer; *b.* 1850; *d.* 1906.

JACQUES-DALCROZE, Emile. Noted song writer; *b.* Vienna, 1868. Prof. Mus. Theory, Geneva Cons., 1892.
Works: 2 operas, many pf. pieces, and numerous songs.

JA'DASSOHN, Salomon. Renowned teacher and writer; *b.* Breslau, 1831; *d.* 1902. Prof. of Harmony, Counterpoint, Composition, and Instrumentation, Leipzig Cons. from 1871.
Works: Text-books on "Harmony" (1883), "Counterpoint" (1884), "Canon and Fugue" (1884), "Form" (1889), and "Instrumentation" (1889). All these have been translated into English. His compositions—over 130—include 4 symphonies, 4 serenades, 2 overtures, a pf. concerto, much chamber music, "The 100th Psalm" (for double chorus and orch.), motets, songs, pf. pieces, &c.

JADIN, Hyacinthe. *B.* Versailles, 1769; *d.* 1802. Pianist; Prof. Paris Cons., from its foundation, 1795.
Wrote pf. concertos, pf. sonatas, string quartets.

JADIN, Louis E. Brother of H. *B.* Versailles, 1768; *d.* 1853. Prof. Paris Cons., 1802.
Wrote about 40 operas and operettas, orchestral and chamber music, songs, &c., and many pieces for the band of the *Garde Nationale*, of which he was for some time a member.

JAELL, Alfred. Pianist and composer; *b.* Trieste, 1832; *d.* Paris, 1882. *Début*, Venice, 1843. Toured successfully through Europe and America. Married **Marie Trautmann**, 1866.
Works for pf.; valses, notturnos, &c., and clever transcriptions from Wagner, Schumann, &c.

JAELL-TRAUTMANN, Marie. Fine pianist; wife of preceding. *B.* Alsace, 1846.
Works: a pf. concerto, waltzes, characteristic pf. pieces, &c.

JAF'FE, Moritz. Violinist and composer; *b.* Posen, 1835.
Works: successful operas, chamber music, songs, &c.

JAFFÉ, Sophia. Violinist; *b.* Odessa, 1872.

Jagd (G.). The chase; hunting.

Jä'ger (G.). Huntsman, sportsman.
Jagd'horn. Hunting horn.
Jagd'ruf. Sound of the horn.
Jagd'sinfonie. Hunting symphony.
Jagd'stück. Hunting piece.
Jä'gerchor. Hunting chorus.
Jä'gerhorn. Hunting horn.

JAHN, Otto. Learned critic and writer on music ; *b.* Kiel, 1813 ; *d.* 1869. Prof. of Archæology at various universities.

His *magnum opus* is the "Biography of Mozart" (4 vols.)—a standard work. A critical edition of *Fidelio* (Beethoven) is also valuable.

JÄHNS, Friedrich W. Distinguished singing-teacher ; *b.* Berlin, 1809 ; *d.* 1888. Teacher of rhetoric, Scharwenka's Cons., Berlin, 1881.

He was a "Weber" enthusiast; wrote "C. M. von Weber in seinen Werken" (1871), and made a colln. of all obtainable works by Weber or referring to him—a valuable colln. now in the Royal Library, Berlin. He composed pf. pieces and numerous vocal works.

JA'KOB, F. A. L. Writer and composer ; *b.* nr. Liegnitz, 1803 ; *d.* 1884.

His works include a valuable "Reformirtes Choralbuch," (Calvinist Hymn Book).

Jale'o (*S.*). A Spanish national dance in triple time.

Jalousie'schweller (*G.*). A "Venetian-blind" swell in an organ.

JAMES, Frederic. *B.* Rotherham, 1858. Mus.B. Cantab, 1885 ; music master, Woodhouse Grove School, 1884.

Works : cantatas, anthems, hymn-tunes, &c.

JAMES, W. N. Flautist.

Pub. "A word or two on the Flute" (1826).

Jäm'merlich (*G.*). Lamentable, deplorable.

Jam'mernd (*G.*). Wailing, lamenting.

JAN, Dr. Karl von. Author of several works on Ancient Greek Music. *B.* Schweinfurt, 1836 ; *d.* 1899.

JANIEWICZ (or **Yaniewicz**), **Felix.** Polish violinist, 1762-1848.

Wrote concertos, &c., for violin.

Janitscha'renmusik (*G.*) ⎫ Turkish music.
Jan'izary music ⎭ Used for big drum, cymbals, triangle and other insts. of percussion.

The Janizaries were a privileged class of Turkish soldiers suppressed in 1826.

JANKÓ, Paul von. *B.* Totis, Hungary, 1856.

Invented the "Janko Keyboard," 1882.

Jankó Keyboard.

Six rows of keys "in step-like succession." The 1st, 3rd, and 5th rows are exactly alike ; as are also the 2nd, 4th, and 6th. Successive keys on the same row are a whole tone apart.
　　2nd (4th and 6th)—C♯ D♯ F G A B
　　1st (3rd and 5th)—C D E F♯ G♯ A♯ C
The fingering of all diatonic scales is the same; chromatic scales are played by taking notes alternately on any two adjoining rows. A 10th is the same stretch as an 8ve on the ordinary piano, so that large hands can easily stretch a 13th.

JANNACO'NI, Giuseppe. One of the last Italian composers in the style of Palestrina. *B.* Rome, 1741 ; *d.* 1816.

Was a distinguished composer of church music, and scored many of Palestrina's works for modern use.

JANNEQUIN (**Janequin, Jennekin**), **Clement.** Contrapuntist ; 16th cent.

Noted for having written some of the earliest attempts at "Program music : " "La Bataille," "La Guerre," "La Chasse de lièvre," "Le chant des oiseaux," &c.

JANO'THA, Nathalie. Pianist ; *b.* Warsaw, 1856. Pupil of Madame Schumann. *Début,* Leipzig Gewandhaus, 1874.

JANOW'KA, T. B. Bohemian organist.

Pub. "Clavis ad Thesaurum Magnæ Artis Musicæ" (1701), the earliest musical lexicon except Tinctor's.

JAN'SA, Leopold. Celebrated violinist ; *b.* Wildenschwert, Bohemia, 1795 ; *d.* Vienna, 1875. Director of Music, Vienna Univ., 1834. Banished for taking part in a concert on behalf of the Hungarian revolutionists in London, 1849. Resided in London, 1849-68. Returned to Vienna, 1868.

Works : 2 vn. concertos, 36 vn. duets, many other vn. pieces, 8 string quartets, &c.

JAN'SEN, F. Gustav. Orgt. and writer ; *b.* nr. Hanover, 1831.

Noted for his writings on Schumann.

JANS'SEN, Julius. Condr. and song composer ; *b.* Venloo, Holland, 1852.

JANS'SENS, J. F. Joseph. Antwerp, 1801-35. Legal student and notary ; composed "in his leisure hours." The value of his music was not recognized till after his death.

Works : 4 operas (*Le père rival, La jolie fiancée,* &c.), 2 cantatas, 2 symphonies, 5 masses, motets, songs, &c.

JANUSCHOW'SKY, Frau Georgine von. Dramatic soprano ; famous in Wagnerian *rôles;* *b.* Austria, abt. 1859. Prima donna, Imperial Theatre, Vienna, 1893-5.

Japanese Music.

A full and complete Japanese orchestra "consists of 1 flute, 1 large drum, 2 bell-rattle insts., 2 wooden clappers, 2 small drums."—*Naumann.*
The following is the melody of their National Anthem.

Slow.

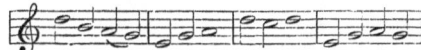

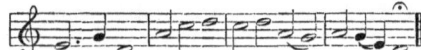

JA'PHA, Georg J. Violinist and teacher ; *b.* Königsberg, 1835 ; *d.* 1892. Toured in Germany, Russia, London, &c.

JA'PHA, Louise. *B.* Hamburg, 1826. Distinguished pianist and composer ; studied under Robt. and Clara Schumann. Married W. Langhans, 1858. After brilliant concert tours, settled in Wiesbaden, 1874.

Works : an opera, string quartets, songs, pf. pieces.

JAQUES-DALCROZE. (See **Dalcroze**.)

JAREC'KI, Henri. Condr. and composer ; *b.* Warsaw, 1846.

JARMAN, Thomas. *B.* Clipston, abt. 1788 ; *d.* 1862.

Wrote a number of hymns and anthems once very popular.

JÄR'NEFELT, Armas. Composer; *b.* Viborg, 1869.

JARNOVIC (Giornovicchi), Giovanni M. *B.* Palermo, 1745; *d.* 1804. Violinist; pupil of Lolli. Won fame at the *Concerts Spirituels*, Paris, 1770. Undertook long concert tours; visited London, 1792.
Wrote 16 vn. concertos and much other vn. music.

JARVIS, Chas. H. Noted American pianist; Philadelphia, 1837-95. Played in public at 7; founded the Philadelphia Quintet Club, 1862.

JARVIS, Stephen. Composer; *b.* 1834; *d.* Lewisham, 1880.
Works: string quintets, pf. pieces, songs.

Jauch'zend (*G.*). Shouting, joyful.

Jaw's-harp. (See **Jew's-harp.**)

JAY, John. Pianist and composer; *b.* Essex, 1770; *d.* 1849. Mus.Doc.Cantab., 1811.
Wrote pianoforte and vocal music.

JEAN de MURIS. (See **Muris.**)

JEDLIC'ZKA, Ernest. Pianist; *b.* Poltawa, 1855.

Jedoch' (*G.*). Yet; however; nevertheless.

JEFFRIES, Geo. Orgt. to Chas. I, 1643.
Wrote a large number of anthems and motets.

JEFFRIES, Jn. Ed. *B.* Walsall, 1863. Orgt. Newcastle cath. since 1895.

JÉHIN (Jéhin-Prume), Frantz H. Celebrated violinist; *b.* Spa, Belgium, 1839; *d.* Montreal, 1899. Studied under his uncle, Liége Cons., at 5; gave a public concert at 6. Studied also under De Bériot, Léonard, Vieuxtemps, and others. Made his *début* as a virtuoso at 16; toured successfully through Europe and America. Settled in Montreal, 1887. Isaye was one of his pupils.
Works: 2 vn. concertos, about 30 vn. solos. songs, &c.

JÉHIN, Léon. Condr. and violinist; *b.* Spa, Belgium, 1853.

JE'KYLL, Chas S. Orgt. and composer; *b.* Westminster, 1842.

JE'LINEK, Franz X. Noted Bohemian oboist; 1818-80. From 1841, librarian at the "Mozarteum," Salzburg.
Wrote church music, oboe solos, male choruses.

JENKINS, David. Composer; *b.* Trecastell, Brecon, 1849. Mus.Bac. Cantab., 1878.

JENKINS, John. *B.* Maidstone,, 1592; *d.* 1678. Lutenist and player on the "lyra-viol" to Chas. I and Chas. II.
Works: many "Fancies" for viols or organs, "Rants" (quick dances), "12 Sonatas for 2 vns. and a Base, with a Thorough Base for the Organ or Theorbo" (the 1st Eng. composer of this kind of music).

JENNEKIN. (See **Jannequin.**)

JEN'SEN, Adolf. Distinguished song composer; *b.* Königsberg, 1837; *d.* 1879. Passionate admirer of Schumann, and afterwards of Wagner; Capellmeister,

Posen, 1857; spent 2 years with Gade, 1858-60; Prof. of Advanced Compn., Tausig's School, Berlin, 1866-8.
Works: a concert overture, much interesting music for pf. (4 hands and pf. solo), about 160 songs for solo voice and pf., a *Nonnengesang* (for soprano solo, female chorus, 2 horns, harp, and pf.), *Jephthas Tochter* (for soli, chorus, and orch.), 2 sets of 8 four-part songs, part-songs for female voices, &c. His music is characterized by deep "emotional originality."

JEN'SEN, Gustav. Violinist; *b.* Königsberg, 1843; *d.* 1895. Pupil of Joachim. Prof. of Counterpoint, Cologne Cons., 1872-5.
Works: Symphony in B♭, and other orch. music; chamber music, characteristic vn. pieces, pf. pieces, songs, &c.

JEPHTHAH. Handel's last oratorio, 1751-2.

JESSON'DA. Opera by Spohr, 1823.

Jeu (*F.*). Style of playing.

Jeu (*F.*). A stop (harmonium, organ, &c.).
Jeu à bouche. A flue stop.
Jeu céleste. Céleste stop.
Jeu d'anche. Reed stop.
Jeu d'ange. Vox angelica (*q.v.*).
Jeu de flûtes. Flute stop.
Jeu de mutation. Mutation stop (*q.v.*).
Jeu d'orgues. An organ stop.
Jeu de timbres. Glockenspiel (*q.v.*).
Jeu de violes. A consort of viols (*q.v.*).
Jeu de voix humaine. Vox humana.
Jeux de fonds. The foundation stops (of an org.).
Jeux doux. Sweet, soft stops.
Jeux forts. Loud stops.
Grand Jeu } Full organ; full power of the inst.
Plein Jeu }
Demi Jeu. Half power.

JEUNE. (See **Lejeune.**)

Jewish Music.

" It was with the Israelites that music became the connecting link between man and his Maker." —*Naumann.*

"It has been clearly proved that the chants of the early Christians were derived from the Temple melodies."—*De Sola.*

Hence the special interest of Jewish music. Of the ancient Jewish melodies we have very few authentic examples. The following, which has been transmitted with religious care and veneration from one generation to another, is said to be identical with that sung daily in the temple by the priestly choirs to bless the people (Numbers VI. 22-26). We find that, with slight alterations, it is still used for the same purpose throughout the Jewish world.

BIRKAT COHANIM.

"The Lord bless thee, and keep thee; The Lord make His Face to shine upon thee, and be gracious unto thee; The Lord lift up His countenance upon thee, and give thee peace."

Jew's-harp. } (G., _Maul'trommel, Ju'den-_
Jew's trump. } _harfe ; F., Trompe, Guimbarde ; I., Trom'ba._) Possibly a corruption of Jaw's harp or _Jeu trompe._
　"A soldier of Frederick the Great of Prussia so
　charmed the King by his performance on two
　Jew's-harps that he gave him his discharge,
　. . . and he subsequently amassed a fortune
　by playing at concerts."
　"In 1827-8 Chas. Eulenstein appeared in London
　and by using 16 Jew's-harps produced extra-
　ordinary effects."—_Grove's Dict._

JEWSON, Frederick B. Pianist and composer ; _b._ Edinburgh, 1823 ; _d._ 1891.

Jig. (_F._ and _G., Gigue ; I., Gi'ga._) A
lively dance. (See **Gigue.**)
　The word _Jig_ is supposed to be derived from
　Geige, a fiddle.

JIM'MERTHAL, Hermann. Organist and
expert on organ building ; Lübeck,
1809-86. Pupil of Mendelssohn.
　His writings on organ matters include a mono-
　graph on Buxtehude.

Jingles. The metal discs attached to the
hoop of a tambourine.

Jingling Johnny. A _Turkish Crescent (q.v.)._

JIRÁNEK, Josef. Bohemian pianist; _b._
1855. Pupil of Smetana.
　Works : pf. pieces, "Studies in Touch," &c.

JO'ACHIM, Joseph. Eminent classical
violinist ; _b._ Kittsee, nr. Pressburg,
1831. Began the study of the violin at
5 ; appeared in public at 7 ; entered
Vienna Cons. at 10 ; played in Leipzig
at a concert given by Viardot Garcia at
12, and shortly after (with pronounced
success) at the Gewandhaus. Made
Leipzig his home until 1849, enjoying
the friendship of Schumann, Mendels-
ssohn, and David. During this period
he paid his first visit to London, 1844.
Concertmeister, Weimar orch., 1849 ;
solo violinist to the King of Hanover,
1854 ; married **Amalie Weiss**, 1863 ;
temporary head of the "Hochschule für
ausübende Tonkunst," Berlin, 1868 ;
made permanent director, 1895, and
became "the life and soul of the institution." Honorary Mus.Doc. Cantab.,
1877. _D._ 1907.
　Works : "Hungarian" Concerto (perhaps his best
　work), other concertos, many solos for vn. with
　orch. or pf. acct., overtures, pieces for viola
　and pf., &c.

JO'ACHIM, Amalie (_née_ **Weiss**). Fine contralto singer ; _b._ Marburg, Styria, 1839;
_d._ 1899.
　"Her interpretation of Schumann's songs was
　unrivalled."

JOÃO IV. King of Portugal ; 1604-56.
　Theorist and composer ; gave a fine musical
　library very rich in Eng. music (destroyed by
　the earthquake, 1755). Catalogue published,
　1649; reprinted, 1874.

JOBLIN, Fredk. Wm. _B._ Bonchurch, I. of W.,
1860. Orgt. at Sunderland since 1881.

JÖCH'ER, C. G. Leipzig, 1694-1758.
　Wrote "Allgemeines Gelehrten-Lexicon" (4 vols.),
　1750,

Joco'sus (_L._). Merry, jocose.

Jo'deln (_G._) } To yodel. A peculiar method
Jö'dl (_G._) } of singing practised by the
Jo'dle (_G._) } Swiss and Tyrolese herdsmen, consisting of rapid alternations of
the natural and falsetto voice.

CHANSON D'APPENZELL.

Jo'dler (_G._) } A song or refrain sung in the
Yo'del (_G._) } above style.

**JOHAN'NES DAMASCE'NUS (Saint John of
Damascus).** _D._ abt. 780. "The
greatest poet of the Greek church."
　Arranged the Greek Church liturgical music, and
　reformed its notation. Wrote some fine hymns
　still in use.

JOHAN'NES de GARLAN'DIA. (See **Garlandia.**)

JOHAN'NES de MU'RIS. (See **Muris.**)

JOHNS, Clayton. American composer ; _b._
New Castle, Delaware, 1857.
　Works : Over 100 songs ; pf. pieces, pieces for
　vn. and pf., &c.

JOHNSON, Edward. Mus.Bac. Cantab.,
1594. Composer of madrigals, &c.
One of the contributors to Este's
Psalter, 1592.

JOHNSON, Jas. Engraver and publisher ;
_b._ Ettrick district of Scotland, 1753(?) ;
_d._ 1811. (See **Scottish Music,** No. 2.)

JOHNSON, Robert. 16th cent. composer of
motets, part-songs, madrigals, &c.

JOHNSON, Robt. 16th and 17th cents.
　Composer of original music for Shakespeare's
　plays, "As I walked forth one summer's day,"
　&c.

JOHNSON, W. Noel. 'Cellist and composer;
_b._ Repton, 1863.

Joie (_F._). Joy, gladness.

JOLLEY, Chas. Edward. Orgt. and condr. ;
_b._ Higham Ferrers, N. Hants., 1860 ;
Mus. Doc. Oxon, 1899. Organist, St.
George's, Hanover Square, 1892.

JOMMEL'LI (Jomel'li), Nicola. Opera composer ; called the "Italian Gluck."
_B._ Aversa, nr. Naples, 1714; _d._ 1774.
Produced his first opera at 23 (_L'Errore
amoroso_, Naples, 1737). Visited Rome,
1740 ; Bologna, where he received

valuable advice from Martini, 1741 ; Venice, 1743 ; Vienna, 1745 ; at each of these places bringing out fresh operas with triumphant success. Maestro St. Peter's, Rome, 1749-54. Capellmeister to the Duke of Wurtemburg, 1754.

Works : operas, *Odoardo* (1738), *Esio*, (1741), *Eumene* (1742), *Merope* (1743), *Artaserse* (1749), and about 45 others ; 4 oratorios, several cantatas, a Miserere for 2 soprani and orch. (considered his best work), Magnificats, hymns.

JONÁS, Alberto. Pianist ; *b.* Madrid, 1868. Settled in Michigan (U.S.), 1894, as pf. professor, &c.

JONAS, Emile. Composer ; *b.* Paris, 1827. Studied Paris Cons. ; prof. of solfeggio, &c., 1847-70. Music-director, Portuguese Synagogue. *D.* 1905.

Works : over 20 successful light comic operettas (*Le Duel de Benjamin*, 1855 ; *La Parade*, 1856 ; *Javotie*, 1871, afterwards given in London as *Cinderella*), &c.

JONCIÈRES, Félix L. V. de (F. L. Rossignol). Paris, 1839-1903. Composer ; Wagner enthusiast ; distinguished musical critic.

Works : operas, *Sardanapale*, *Dimitri*, *Lancelot du lac*, &c. ; orch. music, a violin concerto, &c.

Jonction (*F.*). Blending of (vocal) registers ; *l'union des registres.*

JONES, Arthur Barclay, Composer ; *b.* London, 1869.

JONES, Edward ("Bardy Brenin"). Musician and writer ; *b.* Llanderfel, Merionethshire, 1752 ; *d.* 1824. Welsh Bard to the Prince of Wales, 1783.

Works : " Musical and Poetical Relicks of the Welsh Bards " (4 vols., containing 225 Celtic melodies) ; " Lyric Airs " (specimens of national melodies of all countries), &c.

JONES, German Ed. Ed. German (*q.v.*).

JONES, Griffith Rhys ("Caradog"). Noted Welsh conductor ; *b.* Trecynon, 1834.

Conducted the victorious Welsh choir, Crystal Palace, 1872-3.

JONES, Hirwen. Tenor singer ; *b.* nr. Cardigan, 1857.

JONES, John. English organist ; 1728-96. Orgt. St. Paul's, 1755 .

Pub. Chants, Lessons for Harpsichord, songs.

JONES, Robert. Lutenist ; Mus.Bac.Oxon. 1597.

Works : Books of " Ayres," " Madrigals for Viols and Voices, or for Voices alone, or as you please " (1607), and several other Collns. with acct. for Lute and Viols.

JONES, Sidney. Contemporary composer of light opera. *B.* London, 1861.

Chief works : *The Gaiety Girl* (1893), *The Geisha* (1896).

JONES, William ("Jones of Nayland"). *B.* Lowick, 1726 ; *d.* 1800. Curate of Nayland, Suffolk, from 1779.

Works : " A Treatise on the Art of Musick," org. pieces, anthems, &c.

JONES, William P. H. ("Hamilton Gray"). Song composer ; *b.* Flint, 1871.

JONES, Sir Wm. Indian judge ; *b.* London, 1746 ; *d.* 1794.

Wrote a valuable treatise on "The Musical Modes of the Hindus," 1784.

Jongleurs (*F.*) ⎫ Wandering minstrels (11th,
Jonglours (*F.*) ⎭ 12th, and 13th cents.).

Later they degenerated into jugglers or mountebanks.

JORDAN, Charles Warwick. Organist and composer ; *b.* Clifton, 1840. Mus.Doc. Cantuar, 1886.

JORDAN, Jules ("Julian Jordan"). Tenor singer ; *b.* Connecticut, 1850.

Works : opera (*Rip van Winkle*), cantatas, songs, &c.

Jorram. A Highland boat-song, generally in flowing 12-8 time.

JOSEF'FY, Rafael. Pianist ; *b.* Miskoles, Hungary, 1853. Fine interpreter of Chopin ; settled in New York abt. 1879.

Works : salon pieces for pf.

JOSEPH (Saint) of the Studium. *B.* Sicily ; a slave in Crete ; founded a monastery, Constantinople. *D.* 883. Prolific hymn writer.

Wrote the hymn "Safe home, safe home in port " (Eng. trans. by Dr. Neale).

JOSHUA. Oratorio by Handel ; 1747.

JOSQUIN. (See **Deprés.**)

Jo'ta (*S.*). A Spanish dance somewhat resembling a waltz.

Jouer (*F.*). To play (an instrument).

Jouer ces petites notes à defaut du contre-basson. Play these small notes when there is no double-bassoon.

Joueur d'instrumens (*F.*). A player on instruments.

JOULE, Benjamin St. John Baptist. Orgt. ; *b.* Salford, 1817 ; *d.* 1895.

Pub. a valuable colln. of chants, church music, &c.

JOURET, Léon. *B.* Ath, Belgium, 1828. Prof. Brussels Cons.

Works : operas (*Quentin Metsys*, *Le Tricorne enchanté*), cantatas, songs, &c.

JOURNET, H. J. Marcel. Noted bassocantante ; *b.* Alpes Maritimes, 1869. *Début*, Montpellier, 1893.

JOUSSE, J. *B.* Orléans, 1760 ; *d.* London, 1837.

Works : "Lectures on Thorough Bass," &c.

Jovia'lisch (*G.*). Jovial, merry.

Joyeusement (*F.*). Joyously.

JOZÉ, Thomas R. G. Composer and orgt. ; *B.* Dublin, 1853. Mus.Doc. Dublin, 1877.

Ju'ba. A negro dance.

JU'BAL. "The father of such as handle the harp and organ" (Gen. iv-21).

This is the earliest mention of musical insts. in the Bible.

Ju'bal (*G.*). An organ stop ; 4 ft. or 2 ft. pitch.

Ju'balflöte. A variety of Doppelflöte (*q.v.*).

Ju'bel-gesang' (*G.*) ⎫
Ju'bel-lied (*G.*) ⎭ A song of jubilee.

Ju'belhorn (*G*.). A key-bugle, or *Klappen-horn* (*q.v.*).

Ju'belnd (*G*.). Rejoicing, jubilation.

Jubila'te De'o. The 100th Psalm, sung after the 2nd Lesson of the Morning Service (Anglican Church).

Jubila'tio (*L*.). The ending of the "Alleluia" in the Roman Catholic Ritual.

JUBILEE OVERTURE. Weber; 1818.

Jubilo'so (*I*.). Same as **Giubiloso** (*q.v*).

Ju'bilus (*L*.). (1) Same as *Jubilatio*. (2) An ornamental phrase in old antiphons.

JUCH, Emma. Vocalist; *b.* 1863; *début,* 1881.

JUDAS MACCABÆUS. Oratorio by Handel, 1746.

JUDE, William Herbert. Composer; *b.* Westleton, Suffolk, 1851.

Ju'denbass (*G*.). A very deep bass voice.

Ju'denharfe (*G*.). Jew's harp.

Ju'gend (*G*.). Youth.

JUIVE, La. Opera by Halévy, 1835.

JULIEN (or **Jullien**), **Louis Antoine.** *B.* Sisteron, Basses-Alpes, 1812; *d.* 1860. Entered Paris Cons., but preferred writing dance tunes to serious study. Left the Cons. and established "dance-concerts," which became very popular. Came to London to escape his creditors, 1838; got together a fine orchestra and established a great reputation as a conductor (largely on account of his extravagant manners and pretensions). Wrote an opera, which, by the expenses of its production, ruined him. He returned to Paris and died insane.

Jullien is now chiefly regarded as a musical *mountebank;* but, with all his bombast, he undoubtedly did useful work in introducing many excellent compositions of the great masters.

JULLIEN, J. L. Adolphe. Distinguished musical critic and writer; *b.* Paris, 1845.

His works include "Richard Wagner, sa vie et ses œuvres" (1886), "Hector Berlioz" (1888) and numerous essays on the rise and progress of opera in the 16th, 17th, 18th, and 19th cents.

JUMILHAC, Dom Pierre Benoit de. *B.* nr. Limoges, 1611; *d.* 1682.

Wrote a learned work on the "Science and Practice of Plain Chant" (1673).

Jump. (1) A leap or skip in melody. (2) Same as **Dump** or **Dumpe** (*q.v.*)

JUNCK, Benedetto. Italian composer; *b.* Turin, 1852; *d.* 1905.

Jung'fernregal (*G*.) ⎫ The *Vox Angelica*
Jung'fernstimme (*G*.) ⎭ (*q.v.*).

JUNG'MANN, Albert. *B.* Langensalza, Prussia, 1824; *d.* 1892. Founded the firm of Jungmann & Lerch.

Published pianoforte pieces and songs.

JÜNGST, Hugo. Condr. and composer; *b.* Dresden, 1853.

Works : choruses for male voices.

Junk. An Arabian harp.

JUNKER, Karl L. *B.* Öhringen, abt. 1740; *d.* 1797.

Works : cantatas, 3 pf. concertos, &c., and several treatises on musical subjects.

JUON, Paul. Composer and writer; *b.* Moscow, 1872.

JUPITER SYMPHONY. Mozart's last symphony, in C major.

The last movement, based on the theme—

is noted for its wonderful "Quintuple counterpoint."

JUPIN, Chas. F. *B.* Chambéry, 1805; *d.* 1839. Precocious violinist; 1st prize, Paris Cons., 1823.

Works : a comic opera (*La Vengeance Italienne*), a vn. concerto, pf. and vn. pieces, &c.

JÜR'GENSON, Peter I. *B.* Reval, 1836. Founded a music pub. house (Moscow, 1861), which specially produces works by Russian composers. *D.* 1904.

Jusqu'à (*F*.). Until, up to.

Jusqu'à la fin. Up to (until) the end.

Just ⎫ Accurate, true, in tune; perfect
Juste (*F*.) ⎭ (of intervals).

Just Intonation. Exact pitch, &c. (See **Intonation.**)

Justesse (*F*.). Correctness, purity, equality.

Justesse de la voix. Accuracy and purity of intonation.
Justesse de l'oreille. Correctness of ear.

Ju'sto, Con (*I*.). With precision, exactness.

K

K. Many German words are spelt either with "C" or "K." (In general, *both* spellings will be found in this work.)

KA'AN, Heinrich von ("Albést-Kahn"). Pianist; *b.* Galicia, 1852. Prof. Prague Cons., 1890.
Works: ballet (*Bojaja*); pf. concertos, chamber music, &c.

Kaba'ro. An Egyptian and Abyssinian drum.

KA'DE, Dr. Otto. Composer and writer, *b.* Dresden, 1819; *d.* 1900. Grand-Ducal mus.-dir., Schwerin, 1860.
Works: many valuable historical writings; a *Choralbuch*, and other collns. of melodies; an important collection of the early settings of the *Passion*, &c.

Kadenz' (*G.*). (1) Cadence. (2) Cadenza.
Ab'gebrochene Kadenz'. An interrupted cadence. (See *Cadence*.)
Auf'gehaltene Kadenz. The hold ⌒ before a cadenza.
Plagal'kadenz. Plagal cadence.
Trug'kadenz. Deceptive cadence.
Un'vollkommene Kadenz'. Imperfect cadence. } (See *Cadence*.)
Voll'kommene Kadenz. Perfect cadence.

KAEMP'FER, Jos. Celebrated Hungarian double-bass player; lived in London for some years from 1783.

KAF'KA, J. N. Bohemian composer of *salon* pf. music; 1819-86.

KAH'LERT, Karl A. T. Breslau, 1807-64.
Wrote treatises on music ("Tonleben," 1838), and songs.

KAHN, Robert. Pianist; *b.* Mannheim, 1865. Founded a Ladies' Choral Union, Leipzig, 1891; pf. teacher Berlin Hochschule, 1893.
Works: orchestral, chamber, and pf. pieces; *Mahomet's Gesang* for chorus and orch.); choruses for female voices, songs.

KAH'RER. (See **Rappoldi-Kahrer**.)

KAI'SER, Fr. Emil. *B.* Coburg, 1850. Regimental bandmaster, Prague.
Works: successful operas (*Der Trompeter. von Säkkingen*, 1882, &c.).

Kai'sermarsch (*G.*). An imperial march.

KAJA'NUS, Robt. Condr. and composer; *b.* Finland, 1856.

Kalama'ika. A Hungarian dance in lively 2-4 time.

KAL'BECK, Max. Musical critic and writer; *b.* Breslau, 1850.
Works: Studies on Wagner's *Nibelungen* and *Parsifal*; German translations of many standard operas, &c.

KALINNIKOV, Basil S. Composer; *b.* Voina, Russia, 1866; *d.* 1901.

KA'LISCH, Paul. Tenor; *b.* Berlin, 1855.

KA'LISCH, Frau. Lilli Lehmann (*q.v.*).

KA'LISCHER, Dr. Alfred. Writer and teacher; *b.* Thorn, 1842.
Works: treatises on Beethoven, Luther, *Musik und Moral*, &c.

Kalkant' (*G.*). Bellows-treader.
Kalkan'tenglocke. Bell signal to blower.

KALK'BRENNER, Christian. *B.* Minden, Hanover, 1755; *d.* 1806. *Chef de chant*, Paris Opéra, 1799.

KALK'BRENNER, Friedrich W. M. Son of preceding; *b.* 1788; *d.* nr. Paris, 1849. Took 1st prize for pf. playing, Paris Cons., 1801. Toured as concert pianist. Resided in London, 1814-23; adopted and simplified Logier's *Chiroplast*, 1818. Settled in Paris, 1824.
The *Chiroplast* method of teaching has long been discarded, but Kalkbrenner did much good work in developing left-hand technique. Of his numerous pf. pieces, his *études* are still valuable.

Kalliope. (See **Calliope**.)

KALLIWO'DA, Johann Wenzel. Distinguished pianist; *b.* Prague, 1801; *d.* 1866. Capellmeister to Prince Fürstenberg, Donaueschingen, 1823-53.
Works: 2 operas, 6 symphonies, 14 overtures, 13 fantasias for orch., a vn. concerto, a concerto for 2 vns., vn. solos, chamber music, choruses, songs, &c.

KALLIWO'DA, Wilhelm. Son of preceding; 1827-93.
Works: light pf. pieces, songs, fine male choruses.

KALL'WITZ (KAL'WITZ). (See **Calvisius**.)

KAMIEN'SKI, Mathias. "The first composer of Polish opera;" *b.* Ödenburg, Hungary, 1734; *d.* Warsaw, 1821.
Chief works: 6 Polish operas, *Nedza uszczesliwiona* ("Comfort in misfortune") being his first (1828).

Kam'mer (*G.*). Same as *I.* **Camera**; a chamber, small hall, &c.
Kam'merconcert'. (See *Kammerkonzert*, below.).
Kam'merkanta'te. Chamber cantata.
Kam'merkomponist'. Court composer.
Kam'merkonzert'. A chamber concert, or concerto.
Kam'mersik } Chamber music (*q.v.*).
Kam'merspiel }
Kam'mermu'sikus. Member of a Court private band.
Kam'mersäng'er. Court singer.
Kam'mersängerin. Female court singer.
Kam'merstil. The style of chamber music (as opp. to the theatrical style, &c.).
Kam'merton. Concert pitch.

KAM'MERLANDER, Karl. Swabian composer; 1828-92.
Works: songs, church music, male choruses.

Kandele, or **Kantele.** (1) Ancient Finnish harp. (2) A kind of dulcimer.

KAN'DLER, Franz S. *B.* Lower Austria, 1792; *d.* 1831.
Wrote several critical works on the History of Italian music.

Ka'non (*G.*). Canon (*q.v.*).
Kano'nik. Canonic.

Kanoon', or **Kanun'.** A Turkish dulcimer. (See **Canun**.)

Kanta'te (*G.*). Cantata.

Kan'tor (*G.*). Cantor; conductor, trainer, or director of a choir.

Kanzel'le (*G.*). A channel or groove in the wind chest of an organ.

Kan'zel-lied (*G.*). Hymn before the sermon.

Kanzo'ne (*G.*). Canzona (*q.v.*).

Kapel'le (*G.*). "Chapel." Originally a private band or company of musicians connected with a court or church. Now applied to any band or orchestra.
Kapell'knabe. Choir boy.
Kapell'meister. (See *Capell'meister*.)

Kapell'meistermusik. " Band-master's music ; " un-inspired "routine" compositions and arrangements.
Kapell'musik. (See *Capell'musik.*)
Kapell'stil. Same as *A cappella* (*q.v.*).

Kapodas'ter (*G.*). Capotasto (*q.v.*).

KAPS, Ernst. 1826-87.
Established a piano factory, Dresden, 1859.

KAPS'BERGER, Johann H. von. *D.* Rome, abt. 1633. Noted performer on the theorbo, chittarone, and lute.
Wrote sacred music ; also pub. many collns. of airs, villanellas, &c., for the above insts.

KARASOW'SKI, Moritz. 'Cellist and writer; *b.* Warsaw, 1823 ; *d.* 1892.
Works : "History of the Polish Opera," "Life of Mozart," " F. Chopin, sein Leben, seine Werke und Briefe," &c.

Karfrei'tag (*G.*). Good Friday.

KARGA'NOFF, Genari. Russian pianist; 1858-90. Wrote several pf. works.

KARL, Tom. Tenor singer ; *b.* Dublin, 1846. Settled in New York. Director, Operatic School, Carnegie Hall, 1899.

KARN, Fred. Jas. Orgt. and composer ; *b.* Leatherhead, 1862.

KASATCHEN'KO, Nicolai I. Russian composer; *b.* 1858. Chorus-master Imperial Opera, St. Petersburg.

KASAU'LI, Nicolai I. Condr. and composer ; *b* Tiraspol, Russia, 1869.

KASHKIN, Nicholas D. Pianist and writer; *b.* Voronezh, 1839.
Works : " Reminiscences of Tschaikovsky " &c.

KAS'KEL, F. Karl von. *B.* Dresden, 1866.
His operas *Hochzeitsmorgen* (1893), and *Sjula* (1895) were very successful.

Kassation' (*G.*). (See **Cassation.**)

KÄSS'MEYER, Moritz. Violinist and composer ; Vienna, 1831-85.
Wrote a comic opera, symphonies, church music, &c., and a number of "humorous pieces" for pf. (4 hands), with string quartet, &c.

Kastagnet'ten (*G.*). Castanets (*q.v.*).

Kas'ten (*G.*). Case (for an instrument).

KAST'NER, Emmerich. *B.* Vienna, 1847.
Pub. a "Richard Wagner-Katalog."

KAST'NER, Johann Georg. Bandmaster, composer, and theorist ; *b.* Strasburg 1810 ; *d.* Paris, 1867. Went to Paris 1835, and settled there as teacher. Specially interested in military music ; originated competitions of bands of all nations (Paris Exposition, 1867).
Works : "Traité général d'instrumentation," "Grammaire musicale," Methods of harmony singing, piano, violin, flute, clarinet, horn, 'cello, ophicleide, oboe, saxophone, &c.; 8 or 9 operas, 2 collns. of male choruses, symphonies, overtures, songs, &c.; and several "Livres-partitions" (vocal and instrumental symphony cantatas preceded by explanatory essays), including *Les Danses des morts, La Harpe d'Éole, Les voix de Paris,* &c.

Katalek'tisch (*G.*). Catalectic ; wanting a syllable at the end.

KA'TÉ, André ten. 'Cellist ; *b.* Amsterdam, 1796 ; *d.* 1858.
Works : operas, *Seid e Palmira* (1831), *Constantia* (1835), &c. ; part-songs.

Kathedra'le (*G.*). } Cathedral.
Kathedral'-kir'che(*G.*) } Cathedral.

Kat'zenmusik (*G.*). "Cat's music." (See **Callithumpian.**)

KATZ'MAYR, Marie. Soprano ; *b.* Vienna, 1869.

KAU'ER, Ferdinand. *B.* Moravia, 1751 ; *d.* Vienna, 1831.
Wrote about 200 operas and operettas (*Singspiele*), 20 masses, cantatas, symphonies, songs.

KAUFF'MANN, Dr. Emil. Son of E. F. (below) ; *b.* Ludwigsburg, 1836. Music-director, Tübungen Univ., 1877.
Works : Lieder, male choruses, pf. pieces, essays on musical subjects.

KAUFF'MANN, Ernst F. *B.* Ludwigsburg, 1803 ; *d.* 1856.
Composed 6 sets of beautiful songs while in prison (1838-42) on account of his connection with the Revolutionists.

KAUFF'MANN, Fritz. *B.* Berlin, 1855 ; won the Mendelssohn prize for composition, 1881. Conductor Magdeburg "Gesell-schaftsconcerte," 1889.
Works : a comic opera, a symphony, vn. concerto, pf. concerto, chamber music, organ music, pf. pieces, songs, &c.

KAUF'MANN, Friedrich. Inventor ; Dresden, 1785-1866.
From one of his inventions, the "Symphonion," his son (F. THEODOR) developed the "Orchestrion."

KAUF'MANN, J. G. Maker of musical clocks ; Saxony, 1751-1818.

Kaum (*G.*). Hardly, scarcely.
Kaum hör'bar. Scarcely audible ; very soft.
Kaum merk'lich beweg'ter. A very little faster.

KAUN, Hugo. Composer ; *b.* Berlin, 1863.

Kavati'ne (*G.*). Cavatina (*q.v.*).

KAY'SER, Fried. Emil. (See **Kaiser.**)

KAY'SER, Heinrich E. Pianist ; friend of Goethe ; *b.* Frankfort, 1755 ; *d.* 1823.

KEARNS, Wm. Hy. Irish musician ; *b.* 1794 ; *d.* London, 1846.
Wrote operettas, songs, &c.

KEARTON, Jos. Harper. Tenor singer ; *b.* Knaresborough, 1848.

KEBLE, John M. A. 1792-1866. Vicar of Hursley, 1836. Wrote *The Christian Year,* 1827.
His hymn, "Sun of my soul," is of world-wide popularity.

Keck (*G.*). Bold, confident, audacious, pert.
Keck'heit. Boldness, vigour, audacity.
Mit Keck'heit vor'getragen. With bold and vigorous execution.

KEEBLE, John. Organist ; *B.* Chichester, 1711 ; *d.* 1750.
Pub. a "Theory of Harmonics," 5 books of org. pieces, &c.

KEELEY, Mrs. **(Mary Anne Goward).** Operatic soprano, and distinguished actress ; *b.* Ipswich, 1805 ; *d.* 1899.

Keeners. Irish mourners "hired to howl at funerals" (*Stainer* and *Barrett*).

KEETON, Haydn. *B.* Mosborough, nr. Chesterfield, 1847 ; orgt. Peterboro' Cath., 1870 ; Mus.Doc. Oxon, 1877.

Keh'le (*G.*).   The throat.
Kehl'fertigkeit.   Vocal skill.
Kehl'kopf.   The larynx.
Kehl laut.   Guttural (throaty) sound.
Kehl'schlag.   The "shock of the glottis." (See *Glottis.*)

Keif'end (*G.*).   Nagging, scolding, bickering.

KEIGHLEY, Thomas. Orgt., condr., and composer; *b.* Stalybridge, Cheshire, 1869. Hargreave Exhibitioner, Owens Coll., Manchester, 1896-8; Mus.D. 1901.

Kein'eswegs schnell (*G.*).   By no means fast.

KEIN'SPECK (KEIN'SBECK, KÜNSPECK), Michael.
Author of one of the earliest printed works on Gregorian chant (Basle, 1496).

KEI'SER, Reinhard. Renowned composer; *b.* nr. Weissenfels, 1674; *d.* 1739. Lived in Hamburg the whole of his life from 1694, except an interval of 6 years (1722-8) which he spent at Copenhagen as conductor to the King. "He was the first German to employ popular subjects in opera;" and "in melody, orchestration, and dramatic expression he was easily the foremost German opera composer of the day."
Wrote some 120 operas; *Ismene* (1692), the first; *Circe* (1734), the last; also oratorios, cantatas, motets, psalms, *Divertimenti* for insts., songs.

KEITH, Charlton. Pianist and accompanist; *b.* Dundee, 1882. Studied Hampstead Cons. under Michael Hambourg. London *début*, 1903.

KÉLER-BÉLA (Albert von Kéler). Composer of dance music and conductor; *b.* Hungary, 1820; *d.* 1882.

KEL'LER, Gottfried (Godfrey). *B.* Germany; settled in London as harpsichord teacher.
Pub. "Rules for a Thorow-bass," 1707.

KEL'LER, Karl. Flautist; *b.* Dessau, 1784; *d.* 1855.
Works: 3 concertos and much other flute music; part-songs, several popular songs, &c.

KEL'LER, Max. Bavarian organist; 1770-1855.
Works: 6 Latin masses, 6 German masses, and other church music; also organ pieces.

KEL'LERMANN, Berthold. Pianist; *b.* Nürnberg, 1853. Wagner's Secretary, 1878-81.

KEL'LERMANN, Christian. Noted 'cellist; *b.* Randers, Jutland, 1815; *d.* 1866. Soloist, Royal Orch., Copenhagen, 1847.

KELLEY, Edgar S. American composer and writer; *b.* Sparta, Wisconsin, 1857. Lecturer on Music, New York Univ. Extension, 1896.
His comic opera *Puritania* has been very successful.

KELLIE, Lawrence. Baritone singer and song composer; *b.* London, 1862.

KELL'NER, Ernst August. Precocious

16

pianist; probably a grandson of J. C. (below); *b.* Windsor, 1792; *d.* 1839.
Began the study of the pf. at 2! Played a Handel concerto before the Court at 5. Studied in Italy. In 1820 returned to England as baritone vocalist and pianist; toured with Catalani; afterwards visited Venice (1824), St. Petersburg (1828), and Paris (1833); his success both as singer and player was "phenomenal." Orgt. Bavarian Chapel, London, 1834.

KELL'NER, Joh. Christoph. Son of **Johann Peter** (1705-88); *b.* Gräfenroda, Thuringia, 1735; *d.* 1803. Court organist, Cassel.
Works: opera, *Die Schadenfreude;* concertos, sonatas, &c., for harpsichord; org. pieces, &c.

KELLOGG, Clara Louise. Distinguished dramatic soprano; *b.* Sumterville, S. Carolina, 1842. *Début*, New York, 1861; London *début*, Her Majesty's Th., 1867, as "Margherita" in *Faust.*

KELLY, Michael. Tenor singer and composer; *b.* Dublin, 1762; *d.* Margate, 1826. Studied singing in Italy. Sang Vienna Court Opera for 4 years; was there friendly with Mozart, and sang the part of "Basilio" at the 1st performance of *Figaro*, 1786. Sang leading tenor *rôles*, Drury Lane, from 1787 to 1811. His first stage piece was prod. 1789. The failure of a music business (1802-11) led him to become a wine merchant. Sheridan proposed that he should style himself, "Michael Kelly, composer of wines and importer of music."
He wrote 62 stage pieces, and many songs (including "The Woodpecker" and "Rest, warrior, rest ").

KELLY, Thos. 1769-1854.
Wrote the hymn "Through the day Thy love hath spared us."

KEL'WAY, Jos. *B.* abt. 1702; *d.* 1782. Harpsichord teacher to Queen Charlotte.
Wrote harpsichord sonatas and lessons.

KEL'WAY, Thos. Brother of J.; orgt. Chichester Cath., 1720; *d.* 1749.
Wrote services and anthems.

Kemangeh'. A Turkish stringed inst.

KEMP, Joseph. *B.* Exeter, 1778; *d.* London, 1824. Orgt. Bristol Cath., 1802; Mus.Doc. Cantab., 1809. "One of the earliest promoters of music instruction by classes."
Wrote anthems, chants, songs, &c.

KEMP, Robert. Shoe dealer; known as "Father Kemp;" *b.* Wellfleet, Massachusetts, 1820; *d.* Boston, 1897.
Founded the "Old Folks' Concerts," Boston, 1854.

KEMP, Stephen. Pianist and composer; *b.* Yarmouth, 1849.

KEMP'TER, Lothar. Bavarian conductor and composer; *b.* 1844. Chief Capellmeister, Zurich City Theatre, 1874.
Works: Fairy opera, *Das Fest der Jugend* (1895); orchestral pieces, vn. and pf. pieces, songs, male choruses, &c.

KEN, Thos. D.D. 1637-1711. Bishop of Bath and Wells ; imprisoned in the Tower, 1688.

Wrote the morning and evening hymns "Awake, my soul" and "Glory to Thee, my God, this night."

Ken'et. An Abyssinian trumpet.

KENNEDY, Arnold. Pianist and teacher ; *b.* London, 1852.

KENNEDY, David. Tenor singer ; *b.* Perth, 1825 ; *d.* Ontario, 1886.

Ken'ner (*G.*). "One who knows." An expert, a connoisseur.

KENNERLEY-RUMFORD. (See **Rumford.**)

Kent bugle. (*G.*, *Kent'horn.*) A keyed bugle invented about 1814(5). (See **Bugle.**)

KENT, James. Winchester, 1700-76. Orgt. Trinity Coll., Cambridge, 1731; Winchester Cath., 1731-74.

Works : Services in C and D, anthems, &c.

KEP'LER, Johannes. Great astronomer ; 1571-1630.

Wrote "Harmonices Mundi."

Kera'na } A Persian horn sounded at sun-
Kerre'na } set and midnight.

Kera'nim. The Hebrew sacred trumpets.

Keras (*Gk.*). A horn. (Specially an inst. made from the horn of an animal.)

Kerau'lophon. An 8 ft. org. stop invented by Gray and Davison.

"A species of soft full-toned Gamba."—*Hinton.*

Keren. A Hebrew trumpet (originally a ram's horn, afterwards made of metal).

KERFOOT, Jos. Blind organist ; for over 53 years orgt. Parish Church, Leigh, Lancs. *D.* 1884.

KERLE, Jacques de. Netherland composer, 16th cent. *Maitre de chapelle* to the Emperor Rudolph II.

Pub. masses, motets, madrigals, hymns, &c. (1562-83).

KERLL (or **KERL, KHERL, CHERL**), **Johann Caspar.** Noted organist; *b.* nr. Ingolstadt, 1627 ; *d.* Munich, 1693. Court Capellmeister, Munich, 1658-73.

Works : masses, kyries, organ music, pieces for harpsichord, &c.

Kern (*G.*). The *languid* (or *language*) of an organ pipe.

Kern'stimmen. The fundamental ("foundation") stops of an organ.

Ker'nig (*G.*). With decision, firmness ; *deciso.*

Ker'ophone. A free-reed org. stop of horn-like quality.

KES, Willem. Violinist ; *b.* Dordrecht, 1856. Studied under David, Wieniawski, and Joachim. Conductor, Glasgow Orch., 1895 ; Director, Moscow Cons., 1898.

Kes'sel (*G.*). "A kettle." The mouthpiece, or cup, of a brass wind inst.

Kes'selpauke (*G.*). A kettle-drum.

KESS'LER, Friedrich. Westphalian preacher.

"Active propagandist of Natorp's figure notation." Pub. several works in this notation, 1829-38.

KESS'LER (*Kötz'ler*), **Jos. Christoph.** Pianist ; *b.* Augsburg, 1800 ; *d.* 1872. Taught in Lemberg, 1835-55 ; then settled in Vienna.

Wrote valuable études for pf., which were utilized by Moscheles and commended by Liszt ; also preludes, nocturnes, &c.

Ketch. Old name for **Catch** (*q.v.*).

KETHE, Wm. Protestant exile at Frankfort, 1555. Rector, Childe Okeford, 1561. *D.* abt. 1608.

Wrote the hymn "All people that on earth do dwell" (Psalm 100).

KETTEN, Henri. *B.* Hungary, 1848 ; *d.* Paris, 1883. Wrote graceful pf. pieces.

Ket'tentriller (*G.*). A chain of shakes or trills.

Ket'tengesang. A catch (*q.v.*).

KETTENUS, Aloys. Belgian violinist ; 1823-96. From 1855 member of Sir C. Hallé's orchestra.

Wrote an opera, a vn. concerto, &c.

KETTERER, Eugène. *B.* Rouen, 1831 ; *d.* Paris, 1870.

Wrote nearly 300 *salon* pf. pieces, many of which became popular.

KETTLE, Chas. Ed. Orgt. and composer ; *b.* Bury St. Edmunds, 1833 ; *d.* 1895.

Wrote hymn tunes, chants, &c.

Kettle-drums. (*G.*, *Pau'ken ;* *F.*, *Timbales ;* *I.*, *Tim'pani.*) The ordinary drums of the orchestra.

Every complete orchestra has 2 kettledrums; the larger can be tuned from

the smaller from—

Formerly they were always tuned to the Tonic and Dominant of the prevailing key—

Timp. in D and A. Handel—*Dettingen Te Deum.*

Modern composers sometimes tune them differently :—

Timp. in F and F. Beethoven—*Scherzo, 9th Sym.*

Timp. in C and F♯. Wagner—*Siegfried.*

&c.

In large modern orchestras there are generally 3 (or more) kettledrums :—

Wagner—*Die Walküre*, Act II.

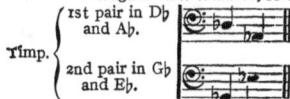

Timp. {
1st pair in D♭ and A♭.
2nd pair in G♭ and E♭.

In the "Tuba Mirum" of his *Requiem,* Berlioz employs 16 kettledrums and 10 drummers, so as to obtain chords from drums alone.

N.B.—"Chromatic" kettledrums are now made provided with pedals by means of which the tuning can be instantly changed.

KEUR'VELS, Ed. H. J. *B.* Antwerp, 1853. Pupil of Benoît: Condr. Nat. Flemish Th., Antwerp, 1882.

Works: operas (*Parisina, Hamlet, Rolla*); operettas, songs, &c.

Key. (1) A tuning key. (2) A clef (*Cla'vis*).

Key (3). (*G., Tast'e ; F., Touche ; I., Ta'sto.*) (*a*) A digital or "finger-key" of a pf., org., &c. (*b*) A pedal or "foot key."

"Those little pieces in the fore-part of an organ, spinnet, or harpsichord, by means whereof the jacks play, so as to strike the strings of the instrument; and wind is given to the pipes by raising and sinking the sucker of the sound board."—*Grassineau.*

Key (4). (*G., Klap'pe ; F., Clé, Clef ; I., Chia've.*) "A mechancal appliance for closing or opening ventages" (holes) in wind insts.

Key (5). (*G., Ton'art ; F., Mode, Ton ; I., Mo'do, To'no.*) The scale, chords, and tonal relationships grouped round a given Tonic or key-note.

All keys are either major or minor, according to their scale; and, in addition to its own proper chords, any key may "borrow" a number of others without causing a "change of key." (See *Borrowed Chords* and *Chromatic Chords.*) The various scales on which keys are based are given under *Scale* (*q.v.*).

CHART OF KEYS. (Relative minors are given in Italic Capitals.)

No. of flats in signature.								No. of sharps in signature.						
7	6	5	4	3	2	1		1	2	3	4	5	6	7
C♭	G♭	D♭	A♭	E♭	B♭	F	C	G	D	A	E	B	F♯	C♯
A♭	E♭	B♭	F	C	G	D	A	E	B	F♯	C♯	G♯	D♯	A♯

Attendant Keys. The 5 nearest keys. It will be seen from the above chart that the 5 attendant keys of F major (for example) are C and B♭ major, and G, A, and D minor; those of E minor are B and A minor and G, D, and C major, &c. (See also *Attendant Keys,* under *A*).

Extreme Key. One remote from the principal key; as F♯ compared with C, &c.

Fundamental Key. The principal key of a composition.

Major Key. A key with major 3rd and major 6th.

Minor Key. A key with minor 3rd and minor 6th.

Natural Key. The key of C major.

Parallel Keys. The major and minor keys of the same keynote; as C major, C minor.

Related Key. (1) A relative major or minor. (2) An attendant key.

Relative Keys. The major and minor keys with the same signature; as C major and A minor.

Remote Key. An extreme key (*q.v.*).

Removes of Key } The relationship of keys can be
Relationship of Keys } seen from the above *Chart of Keys,* or from the following *Circle of Keys* (minor keys in small italics) :—

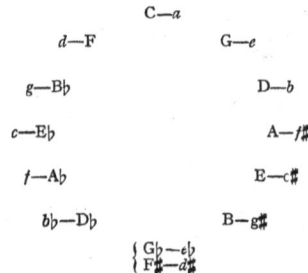

C—a

d—F   G—*e*

g—B♭   D—*b*

c—E♭   A—*f♯*

f—A♭   E—*c♯*

b♭—D♭   B—*g♯*

{ G♭—*e♭*
{ F♯—*d♯*

The number of "sharp" removes is found by reading the chart "from left to right" (or round the circle in the direction of the hands of a watch); the number of "flat" removes is found by reading from "right to left" (or round the circle backwards).

Examples :
B♭ major to F major; 1 sharp remove.
B♭ major to D major; 4 sharp removes.
A major to F♯ major; 3 sharp removes.
F major to E minor; 2 sharp removes "with modulation to the minor."
G minor to D major; 4 sharp removes "with modulation to the major."
D major to F major; 3 flat removes.
A major to E♭ major; 6 flat removes (enharmonically the same as 6 "sharp" removes).

Flat Key.—(1) A key with "flats" in its signature. (2) A minor key. (3) In Tonic Sol-fa, any key to the "left" of any other on the Modulator.

Sharp Key.—(1) A key with "sharps" in its signature. (2) A major key. (3) In Tonic Sol-fa, any key to the "right" of any other on the Modulator.

N.B.—"Key sharp," "Key flat" (for Major or Minor) was often added at the end (or beginning) of old psalm-tunes, &c.

Key-action. The entire mechanism of a keyed inst.

Keyboard. (*G., Klaviatur' ; F., Clavier ; I., Tastatu'ra, Tastier'a.*) (1) A row of keys (pf., &c.). (2) An organ "manual." (3) The whole set of manuals of an organ.

"The modern standard keyboard is the product of an evolution extending over 1000 years."— *Baker.*

Key-bugle. (See **Bugle.**)

Key-chord. The tonic triad; *d m s* or *l₁ d m.*

Key Colour. The characteristics of keys.

Volumes have been written concerning the mental effects—real or imaginary—of various keys. F. Grœnings (*Mus. Times,* Nov., 1886) affirms that "Key or scale colour in the *abstract* does not and cannot exist;" but he admits that differences of key-colour are caused by peculiarities in the construction of instruments, and the methods of employing the fingers and thumbs in playing. Most players *feel,* for example, that the key of D♭ on the pf. or harmonium is distinctly different in its mental suggestions from that of D. On the flute, the keys of E♭ and A♭ are "extremely favourable to the velvet sounds of this instrument" (*Berlioz*); and on the violin, keys which admit of many open notes must obviously differ in effect from those which require much "stopping." And, even apart from these "accidental" peculiarities, every composer has an intuitive perception that keys have different complexions; the key of F♯ major, for example, differs from that of F major; they conjure up *different mental atmospheres,* suggest different planes of thought—different melodies, harmonies, and modulations; even the mere printed notes seem pregnant with contrasted pictures. Beethoven felt this strongly; *e.g.,* "B minor is a black key;" "I have set the tune in *a suitable key ;* " &c. Lavignac ("Music and Musicians"), while admitting that it cannot be explained, affirms that there is a "mysterious law which assigns to each key a peculiar aspect, a special 'colour,'" but that "each person will regard this aspect according to his own personal temperament."

The "preponderating shades" of the various keys as given by different writers are shown in the following table. The second column is from Gardiner's "Music of Nature;" the key-colours given by Berlioz refer especially to the violin.

MAJOR KEYS.

	LAVIGNAC.	GARDINER.	BERLIOZ (for Violin).
C	Simple, naive, frank; or flat and commonplace.	Bold, vigorous, commanding.	Grave, but dull and vague.
C♯ D♭	Charming, suave, placid.	Awfully dark.	Less vague, and more elegant. Majestic.
D	Gay, brilliant, alert.	Grand and noble.	Gay, noisy, and rather commonplace.
D♯ E♭	Sonorous, vigorous, chivalrous.	Full, soft, beautiful.	Dull. Majestic, tolerably sonorous, soft, grave.
E	Radiant, warm, joyous.	Bright, pellucid, brilliant.	Brilliant, pompous, noble.
F	Pastoral, rustic.	Rich, mild, contemplative.	Energetic, vigorous.
F♯ G♭	Rugged. Gentle and calm.		Brilliant, incisive. Less brilliant; more tender.
G	Rural, merry.	Gay, sprightly.	Rather gay, and slightly commonplace.
G♯ A♭	Gentle, caressing; or pompous.	Unassuming, delicate, tender.	Dull, but noble. Soft, veiled; very noble.
A	Frank, sonorous.	Golden, warm, sunny.	Brilliant, elegant, joyous.
B♭	Noble and elegant; graceful.	Deficient in fire.	Noble; but without distinction.
B	Energetic.		Noble, sonorous, radiant.
C♭			Noble, but not very sonorous.

MINOR KEYS.

	LAVIGNAC.	GARDINER.	BERLIOZ (for Violin).
C	Gloomy, dramatic, violent.	Complaining.	Gloomy; not very sonorous.
C♯ D♭	Brutal, sinister; or very sombre.		Tragic, sonorous, elegant. Serious; not very sonorous.
D	Serious, concentrated.	Solemn, grand.	Lugubrious; sonorous; somewhat commonplace.
D♯ E♭	Profoundly sad.		Dull. Very vague, and very mournful.
E	Sad, agitated.	Persuasive, soft, tender.	Screamy, and slightly commonplace.
F	Morose, surly; or energetic.	Penitential, gloomy.	Not very sonorous; gloomy, violent.
F♯ G♯	Rough; or light, aërial. Melancholy, shy.	Mournfully grand. Replete with melancholy.	Tragic, sonorous, incisive. Melancholy, tolerably sonorous, soft.
G♯	Very sombre.		Not very sonorous; mournful, elegant.
A♭	Doleful, anxious.		Very dull and mournful, but noble.
A	Simple, naive, sad, rustic.	Plaintive, but not feeble.	Tolerably sonorous, soft; mournful, rather noble.
B♭	Funereal or mysterious.		Gloomy, dull, hoarse; but noble.
B	Savage or sombre, but vigorous.	Bewailing.	Very sonorous; wild, rough, ominous, violent.

Though the above descriptions are occasionally contradictory, there is, on the whole, a very striking unanimity of feeling. There seems to be abundant evidence that composers and performers recognize and appreciate key-colour; how far it is *discerned by listeners* is another question !

Key-harp. (*F., Clavi-harpe.*) A kind of pf. with tuning-forks instead of strings.

Key-note. The tonic.

Key-plan. The arrangement and distribution of keys and modulations in a composition.

> Key-plan is a very important element of musical form. It has, indeed, been said that "it is the *only essential* of form;" certainly "there is no greater proof of ignorance of the principles of composition than an aimless wandering from key to key." The older masters (Bach, Handel, &c.) rarely modulated beyond the five "attendant" keys (except for dramatic purposes); later composers often employ much more remote ones.
> The key-plan of a *Fugue* or *Sonata* is based upon regular rules; that of a *Fantasia* or *Impromptu* is not restricted.
> The most generally observed rule as to key-plan is that " a piece of music should begin and end in the same key." (If it begins in a minor key, it may end in the *Tonic Major*, and *vice versa*.)

Keyship. Tonality (*q.v.*).

Key-signature. (See **Signature** and **Scale**.)

Key-stop violin. A vn. with 33 stop-keys acting on the strings.

Key-tone. Same as key-note.

Key-trumpet. A trumpet with keys, pistons, or valves.

Khal'il. A Hebrew flute or oboe.

Kicks (*G.*). "Fault, blunder," The *couac*, or goose-note, of a clarinet or oboe.

KIDDLE, Fredk. B. Pianist; *b.* Frome,1874.

KIDNER, Walter J. Condr. and teacher; *b.* Bristol, 1851.

KIDSON, Frank. Authority on British National Music; one of the Founders of the Folk-song Society; *b.* Leeds, 1855. Author of " Old Eng. Country Dances, &c.,' (1890); " Traditional Tunes of Yorkshire, &c." (1891); " British Music Publishers " (1900); numerous Articles in Grove's Dict., &c.; also (with A. Moffat) " The Minstrelsy of England" (1902), "Songs of the Georgian Period," " British Nursery Rhymes," " Songs of Long Ago," &c.

KIEL, Friedrich. *B.* nr. Siegen, 1821 ; *d.* Berlin, 1885. Self-taught pianist and composer ; son of a village schoolmaster. Settled in Berlin as pf. teacher, 1844 ; teacher of composition, Berlin Hochschule für Musik, 1870.
Works : 2 requiems, an oratorio (*Christus*), motets, a pf. concerto, chamber music, vn. sonatas, pf. works, songs, &c.

Kiel′flügel (*G.*). A wing-shaped harpsichord.

KIE′NE. (See **Bigot.**)

KIEN′LE, Ambrosius. Authority on Gregorian music ; *b.* Siegmaringen, 1852.

KIENZL, Dr. Wilhelm. *B.* Waizenkirchen, Upper Austria, 1857. Opera Capellmeister successively at Amsterdam, Crefeld, and Hamburg ; Hofkapellmeister, Munich, 1892-3 ; afterwards settling in Graz.
Works : successful operas, *Heilmar, der Narr* (1892), *Der Evangelimann* (1895), &c. ; much light pf. music, about 100 songs, &c.

KIE′SEWETTER, Raphael G. Distinguished writer on music ; *b.* Holleschau, Moravia, 1773 ; *d.* 1850. **Ambros,** the historian, was his nephew.
Works : standard treatises on " Netherland Music," " Greek Music," " Guido d'Arezzo," "History of the Music of Modern Europe, with Examples," &c.

KILBURN, Nicholas. Condr. and writer ; *b.* Bishop Auckland, 1843.
Author of "¦Wagner, a Sketch of his Life and Works," &c.

KIMBALL, Josiah. Composer of psalm tunes ; Topsfield, Massachusetts, 1761-1826.

Kin, or **Kin chi.** A Chinese inst. shaped like a dulcimer, with from 5 to 25 silk strings plucked by the fingers.

KIND, Johann F. *B.* Leipzig, 1768 ; *d.* 1843.
Wrote the words of Weber's *Der Freischutz.*

KINDER, Ralph. Orgt. and composer ; *b.* Stalybridge, 1876.

KIN′DERMANN, August. Baritone singer ; *b.* Potsdam, 1817 ; · *d.* 1891.
"A prime favourite at the Munich Court Opera."

KIN′DERMANN, Hedwig. (See **Frau Reicher.**)

KIN′DERMANN, Joh. Erasmus. Nuremberg orgt. and song composer ; 1616-1655(?).

Kind′erscenen (*G.*). "Childhood scenes."
Kind′erstück. A "child's piece ; " an easy piece.
Kind′erübungen. Exercises for children.
Kind′lich. Childlike ; simple.

King, or **King chi.** A Chinese inst. of percussion consisting of a number of tuned stones struck by a hammer.

KING, Alfred. *B.* Shelley, Essex, 1837 ; Mus.Doc. Oxon, 1890. Orgt. Brighton Corporation, 1878.
Composer of sacred and secular choral works.

KING, Chas. *B.* Bury St. Edmunds, 1687 ; *d.* 1748. Master of the Choristers, St. Paul's Cath., 1707 ; Vicar-choral, 1730.
Published services and anthems.

KING, Frederick. Baritone singer ; *b.* Lichfield, 1853 ; Prof. of singing, R.A.M., 1890.

KING, Julie. (See **Rivé-King.**)

KING, Matthew P. London, 1773-1823.
Wrote about a dozen English operas, an oratorio (*The Intercession*), pf. sonatas, a " General Treatise on Music," &c.

KING, Oliver A. Pianist and composer ; *b.* London, 1855.
Works : cantatas ; "The 137th Psalm" (Chester Festival, 1888), orchestral music, church music, pf. music, &c.

KING, Robert. Member of the private band of William and Mary, and of Queen Anne. Mus.Bac. Cantab., 1696.
Pub. "Songs for 1, 2, and 3 Voices, Composed to a Thorough Basse for ye Organ or Harpsichord ; " &c.

KINGDOM, The. Oratorio by Elgar ; Birmingham Festival, 1906.

King's Band of Music, The.
An ancient institution. Ed. IV had 13 minstrels, "whereof some be trumpets, some with shalmes and smalle pypes." The band of Chas. II (in imitation of Louis XIV) consisted of 24 performers on vns., tenors and basses, known as "the four-and-twenty fiddlers." At present the King's band consists of 30 members.— *Grove.*

KINGSBURY, Fredk. Pianist and condr. ; *b.* Taunton, abt. 1815; *d.* London, 1892.
Professor of Pianoforte, G.S.M., 1882.

KINGSTON, Wm. Beatty. *B.* London, 1837 ; *d.* 1900. Member Austrian Consular Service, 1856.
Wrote " Music and Manners" (2 vols.).

Kinn′halter (*G.*). A chin-rest (for a vn.).

Kin′nor. The first stringed inst. mentioned in the Bible.

KINROSS, John. Pianist and composer ; *b.* Edinburgh, 1848 ; *d.* London, 1890.

Kin′tal. Small Indian cymbals.

KIP′PER, Hermann. Composer of male-voice comic operettas. *B.* Coblenz, 1826.

KIRBY, John. Orgt. York Minster, late 16th and early 17th cent., succeeding Wyrnal (*q.v.*).
"An excellent chanter and incomparable orgt. The boast, glory, and honour of his church."

KIRBYE, George. 16th cent. composer ; one of the 10 contributors to "Este's Psalter," 1592. Wrote madrigals, &c.

Kir′che (*G.*). A church.
Kir′chenarie. A church aria ; sacred aria.
Kir′chendienst. A church service.
Kir′chenfest. A church festival.
Kir′chengesänge. Sacred songs, hymns, chorals.
Kir′chenkantate. A church cantata.
Kir′chenkomponist. Composer of church music.
Kir′chenlied. A sacred song, hymn, canticle.
Kir′chenmusik. Church music, sacred music.
Kir′chensänger. A chorister.
Kir′chenschluss. A plagal cadence.
Kir′chenstil. (1) The style of church music. (2) The style of the old modes.
Kir′chenstück. A church composition.
Kir′chenton. A church mode.
Kir′chenweise. A church melody.

KIR′CHER, Athanasius. Jesuit ; *b*. nr. Fulda, 1602 ; *d*. Rome, 1680. Wrote a celebrated "Musurgia Universalis" **ἰ** (1650), containing many quaint remarks on the "Miraculous Effects of Music," &c.

KIRCHL, Adolf. *B*. Vienna, 1858. Works : songs for male voices.

KIRCH′NER, Hermann. Tenor singer ; *b*. Thuringia, 1861.

KIRCH′NER, Theodor. Noted composer ; *b*. nr. Chemnitz, 1824. Friend of Mendelssohn and Schumann. Director, Würzburg Cons., 1873-5 ; settled in Hamburg, 1890. *D*. 1903. Works : numerous pf. works (nocturnes, legends, preludes, album-leaves, *Lieder ohne Worte*. Studies, &c.) ; string quartets and trios ; songs.

KIRK′MAN (KIRCHMANN), Jacob. Founded the firm of Kirkman & Sons, harpsichord makers, London, abt. the middle of the 18th cent.

KIRN′BERGER, Johann Philipp. Theorist ; *b*. Saalfeld, Thuringia, 1721 ; *d*. 1783. Pupil of Bach. Capellmeister to Princess Amalie, Berlin, 1754. Wrote valuable works on Thorough-bass and Composition, Harmony, Fugue, &c.

Kis′sar. The 5-stringed Nubian lyre.

KIST, F. C. *B*. Arnheim, 1796 ; *d*. 1863. Physician, flautist, and horn player. Founded *Cicilia*, the leading Dutch music periodical, 1844.

KIST′LER, Cyrill. *B*. nr. Augsburg, 1848. Teacher, Sondershausen Cons., 1883-5 ; editor *Musikalische Tagesfragen*, 1884-1894. *D*. 1907. Works : operas and music dramas, orch. works, choruses, songs, &c.

KIST′NER. Leipzig music pub. firm ; estab. abt. 1823.

Kit. (*G., Ta′schengeige ; F., Pochette ; I., Sordi′no.*) The small "pocket-fiddle" formely used by dancing masters.

Kitar′ } An Arabian guitar.
Kitra′ }

KITCHINER, Wm. Physician and amateur musician ; London, 1775-1827. Works : an operetta, a music drama, glees, songs, "Observations on Vocal Music," "Sea Songs of Chas. Dibdin," &c.

Ki′thara (*Gk.*). An inst. of the harp or lyre kind used by the ancient Greeks.

KITSON, Chas. H. "De Grey" Exhibitioner, Oxford Univ., 1893-7. Mus.D. Oxon, 1902. Author of, "Counterpoint....as a Decorative Principle," &c.

KIT′TEL, Johann Christian. Organist ; Erfurt, 1732-1809. J. S. Bach's last pupil. Teacher of Rinck. Works : organ sonatas, preludes, and fugues ; a "Practical Organ School," &c.

KIT′TL, Emmy. (See **Emmy Destinn**.)

KIT′TL, Joh. F. Bohemian composer ; 1806-68. Director, Prague Cons., 1843-65. Works : operas, *Bianca und Giuseppe* (1848; text by Rd. Wagner), *Die Bilderstürmen* (1854), &c. ; also masses, symphonies, chamber music.

KITZ′LER, Otto. 'Cellist and composer ; *b*. Dresden, 1834. Teacher of **A. Bruckner.** Works : orch. music, pf. pieces, songs.

KIVER, Ernest. Pianist ; *b*. London, 1864.

KJE′RULF (pron. *k'yay′roolf*), **Halfdan.** Distinguished Norwegian composer ; *b*. 1818 ; *d*. Christiania, 1868. He is chiefly famous for his songs, which were popularized by Jenny Lind, Nilsson, and Sontag. He also wrote much pf. music.

KLAF′SKY, Katharina. (**Lohse-Klafsky.**) Hungarian dramatic soprano ; *b*. 1855 ; *d*. Hamburg, 1896. Sang in Wagnerian *rôles* ; visited London, 1892-4.

Kla′ge (*G.*). Lamentation.
Kla′gend } Plaintive, mournful, wailing.
Klä′glich }
Kla′ge-gedicht } An elegy, lamentation, dirge.
Kla′ge-lied }
Kla′gestimme. A plaintive voice.
Kla′ge-ton } A plaintive melody.
Klag′ton }

Klam′mer (*G.*). A brace, or bracket.

Klang (*G.*). (1) A sound. (2) A composite musical tone consisting of a fundamental with its partials. (See **Acoustics** and **Clang**.)
Klang′boden. A sound board.
Klang′farbe. "Clang-tint," tone colour ; *timbre*.
Klang′folge. The tonality of a chord progression.
Klang′figuren. The modal figures shown by sand on a vibrating plate.
Klang′gebend. Sonorous.
Klang′geschlecht. A mode, or genus (major, minor, &c.).
Klang′lehre. Acoustics.
Klang′leiter. A scale.
Klang′los. Soundless, mute.
Klang′saal. A concert room.
Klang′stufe. A degree ; an interval.
Klang′verwandschaft. Chord relationship.
Klang′voll. Sonorous, full-sounding.

Klang′los (*G.*). Soundless.

Klap′pe (*G.*). A key or valve of a wind inst.
Klap′penflügelhorn. Keyed bugle.
Klap′penhorn. Keyed horn.
Klapp′trompete. Keyed trumpet.

Klar (*G.*). Clear, bright, limpid.
Klar′heit. Clearness, distinctness, brightness.
Klär′lich. Clearly.
Klar′stimme. A clear voice.

Klarinet′te (*G.*). A clarinet.

Klas′sisch (*G.*). Classical.

Klau′sel (*G.*). A cadence.
Bass′klausel (*G.*). The progression from Dominant to Tonic in a final cadence.

KLAU′SER, Karl. Teacher and editor ; *b*. St. Petersburg, 1823 ; settled in America 1850.

KLAU′SER, Julius. Teacher and writer ; *b*. New York, 1854. Author of a manual of harmony.

KLAU′WELL, Dr. Otto. Composer and writer ; *b*. Thuringia, 1851. Prof. of pf., theory, and history, Cologne Cons., 1875 ; director of the teachers' pf. classes, 1885. Works : a romantic opera, overtures, pf. pieces, songs, &c. ; "Der Vortrag in der Musik," "Der Fingersatz des Klavierspiels" "Form in Instrumental Music," &c.

Klaviatur' (*G*.). A keyboard.
Klaviatur'harfe. (See *Klavierharfe*, below.)
Klaviatur'zither. A zither with keyboard attached.

Klavier' (*G*.). (1) A keyboard. (2) A keyboard inst.; especially clavichord, harpsichord, or pianoforte.
Klavier'abend. An evening pf. recital.
Klavier'auszug. An "arrangement" for pf.; a pf. score.
Klavier'auszug mit Text. A vocal score with pf. acct.
Klavier'harfe. A harp with keyboard attachment.
Klavier'harmonium. A combination of the pf. and harmonium.
Klavier'hoboe. The harmoniphon (*q.v.*).
Klavier'mässig. In pf. style; suitable for pf.
Klavier'satz. Pf. music; pf. style.
Klavier'schlüssel. A tuning-key.
Klavier'schule. A method (instruction book) for pf.
Klavier'sonate. Pf. sonata.
Klavier'spieler. A pf. player.
Klavier'stuck. A pf. piece.
Klavier' vier'händig } A pf. duet.
Klavier' zu 4 Händ'en }
Klavier'violoncello. A 'cello with keyboard attachment.
Klavier'viola. A viola with keyboard.

KLEE, Ludwig. *B*. Schwerin, 1846.
Author of a work on the "Pf. graces from Bach to Beethoven."

KLEE'BERG, Clotilde. (**Mad. C. Samuell.**)
Concert pianist; *b*. Paris, 1866; *d*. 1909.
Brilliant *début* at the age of 12 with Beethoven's Concerto in C minor.

KLEE'MANN, Karl. Condr. and composer; *b*. Rudolstadt, 1842.

KLEF'FEL, Arno. *B*. Thuringia, 1840.
Teacher of theory, Stern's Cons., Berlin, 1892.
Works: an opera, overtures, pf. pieces, songs, &c.

Klein, Klei'ne (*G*.). Small; minor.
Klein'bass }
Kleinbass'geige } Violoncello.
Klei'ne Flöte. The Piccolo.
Klei'ne Terz. Minor 3rd.
Klein'gedackt. A small stopped diapason; a stopped flute stop.
Klein'er Halb'ton. A minor semitone.
Klei'ne Lie'der. Little songs.
Klei'ne Trom'mel. Small drum.
Klein'laut. Small in volume; low or timid in sound (speech, voice).
Klein'er No'nenakkord. Chord of the minor 9th.

KLEIN, Bernhard. *B*. Cologne, 1793; *d*. 1832. Studied under Cherubini, Paris Cons. Settled in Berlin, 1818; apptd. director and singing teacher at the Univ., 1820.
Works: 3 oratorios, *Jephtha, David,* and *Job;* 2 operas; motets for male voices; an 8-part paternoster, psalms, hymns, pf. pieces, &c.

KLEIN, Bruno Oscar. Pianist and composer; *B*. Osnabrück, 1858. Went to America, 1878; settled in New York, 1883; Prof. of Counterpoint, &c., National Cons., 1887-92. Has made successful tours.
Works: opera, *Kenilworth;* pf. pieces, songs, &c.

KLEIN, Hermann. Critic and singing teacher; *b*. Norwich, 1856; Prof. of Singing, G.S.M., 1887.

Klei'ne Flö'te (*G*.). (1) A piccolo. (2) A small flute stop (org.).

KLEIN'MICHEL, Rd. *B*. Posen, 1846; *d*. 1901. Mus.-director, Leipzig City Th., 1882; then Magdeburg.
Works: operas, *Manon* (1883), *Der Pfeiffer von Dusenbach* (1891); symphonies, characteristic pieces and études for pf., songs, &c.

KLENG'EL, August A. Dresden, 1784-1852. Pianist and orgt; visited England, 1815.
Works: canons, fugues, concertos, &c., for pf.

KLENG'EL, Julius. Gifted 'cellist; *b*. Leipzig, 1859; 1st 'cello, Gewandhaus Orch., and Prof. at the Cons.
Has pub. 3 'cello concertos, and much other music for 'cello and orch., and 'cello and pf.

KLENG'EL, Dr. Paul K. Pianist, violinist, and conductor; elder brother of J. *B*. Leipzig, 1854.

KLENOV'SKI, Nicolai S. *B*. Odessa, 1857. Cond. Imperial Th., Moscow, 1883-93; asst. cond. Court Choir, St. Petersburg, 1902.
Works: ballets, incidental stage music, cantatas, orch. music, songs, &c.

KLIND'WORTH (pron. *klint'vort*), **Karl.** *B*. Hanover, 1830. Self-taught pianist and violinist; at 17, to earn his living, became a condr. of a travelling opera troupe. Afterwards studied under Liszt, and secured the firm friendship of Wagner. Visited London, 1854; remained there until 1868 as pf. teacher and concert pianist. Pf. prof., Imperial Cons., Moscow, 1868-82. Settled in Berlin, 1882; conducted for 10 years the concerts of the *Wagnerverein* and the Philharmonic Society, and established a "Klavierschule." Retired to Potsdam, 1893.
His numerous "monumental" arrangements for the pf. (including Wagner's Music Dramas, a complete revised edition of Chopin's compositions, a revised edition of Beethoven's Sonatas, &c.), are "world renowned."

KLING, Henri. *B*. Paris, 1842.
Author of a popular work on Instrumentation.

Kling'bar (*G*.). Resonant, sonorous.
Kling'el. A small bell.
Kling'eln. To jingle, to tinkle.
Kling'en ei'ne Okta've hö'her als notiert'. To sound an octave higher than written.
Kling'end. Sonorous, resonant.
Kling'ende Stim'men. Speaking pipes (as opposed to *dummy* pipes).
Kling'klang. Tinkling; jangle; ding-dong.
Kling'spiel. The noise (or sound) of insts.

KLING'EMANN, Carl. *B*. Limmer, Hanover, 1798; *d*. London, 1862 as Secretary to the Hanoverian Legation.
Great friend of Mendelssohn's; accompanied him on his Scotch tour and wrote the words of several of his songs.

KLO'SE, Friedrich. Composer; *b*. Carlsruhe, 1862.

KLOSÉ, Hyacinthe E. Clarinettist; *b*. Corfu, 1808; *d*. Paris, 1880.
Improved the mechanism of the clarinet, and wrote for it a "Grande Méthode" and several solos and études.

KLOTZ (**KLOZ**, or **CLOTZ**). A family of Bavarian violin makers.
MATTHIAS (a pupil of Stainer), whose vns. date from about 1660-96, and SEBASTIAN, his son, are the most renowned members of the family.

KLUG'HARDT, August F. M. *B.* Köthen, 1847. Studied at Dresden. Court Capellmeister, Neustrelitz, 1873 ; afterwards at Dessau. *D.* 1902.
Works : operas, *Miriam* (1871), *Iwein* (1879), *Gudrun* (1882), *Die Hochzeit des Mönchs* (1886) ; symphonic poem, *Leonore ;* symphonies, overtures, an orch. suite, a vn. concerto, chamber music, pf. pieces, songs, &c.

KNA'BE, Wm. *B.* nr. Oppeln, 1803 ; *d.* Baltimore, 1864.
Founded a pf. manufactory at Baltimore, 1839.

Kna'benstim'me (*G.*). A boy's voice ; a counter-tenor or male alto.

KNAPP, Wm. *B.* Wareham, 1698 ; *d.* 1768.
Composed hymn tunes (including "Wareham").

KNAPTON, Philip. *B.* York, 1788 ; *d.* 1833.
Composed the song "There be none of beauty's daughters," &c.

Knar're (*G.*). A rattle.

KNATCHBULL, Mrs. (*née* **Dora E. Bright**). Pianist ; *b.* Sheffield, 1863.

KNECHT, Justin Heinrich. Organist ; rival of **Abbé Vogler.** *B.* Biberach, 1752 ; *d.* 1817.
Works : treatises on Harmony and Composition, an "Organ School," psalms, motets, cantatas. He "taught chord building by thirds up to chords of the 11th on all degrees of the scale."—*Baker.* Some of his psalm-tunes are found in English collections. One of his pieces "anticipated Beethoven's *Pastoral Symphony.*"

Knee-stop ⎱ A knee lever on a harmonium
Knee-swell ⎰ or American organ, to act on the "swell," or to bring on all the stops.

Knel'fend (*G.*). Plucking ; *pizzicato.*

KNEI'SEL, Franz. Precocious violinist ; *b.* Roumania, 1865. Leader and soloist, Boston Symphony Orch., 1885. Organized the "Kneisel Quartet," 1886.
"He has done and is doing important service to the cause of chamber music in America."— *Baker.*

Knell. The tolling of a funeral bell.

KNELLER HALL.
A "Military School of Music," near Hounslow, opened for the training of bandmasters and bandsmen, 1857.

Knicky-nackers. The "bones."

Knie (*G.*). Knee.
Knie'geige. A Viola da gamba (*q.v.*).
Knie'guitarre. A large guitar held between the knees.
Knie'zug. A knee stop.

KNIE'SE, Julius. *B.* Roda, nr. Jena, 1848. Chorusmaster, Wagner "Festival-plays," Bayreuth, from 1882. *D.* 1905.
Published songs, &c.

KNIGHT, Rev. Jos. Philip. *B.* Bradford-on-Avon, 1812 ; *d.* 1887.
Wrote 200 songs, including "Rocked in the cradle of the deep," and "She wore a wreath of roses."

Knoll. Old form of **Knell** (*q.v.*).

Knopf'regal (*G.*). An old organ reed stop.

KNORR, Iwan. Composer ; *b.* Mewe, Prussia, 1853.

KNORR, Julius. Leipzig, 1805-61. Celebrated pf. teacher ; intimate friend of Schumann.
His numerous works include "A new Pianoforte School," and "A Methodical Guide to the Study of the Pf." His preparatory technical exercises for the pf. are highly esteemed.

KNOWLES, Chas. R. Baritone ; *b.* Leeds, 18—.

KNYV'ETT, Chas. Tenor singer ; *b.* 1752 ; *d.* London, 1822. Orgt. Chapel Royal; 1796.
Est. (with S. Harrison) the "Vocal Concerts," 1791-4.

KNYV'ETT, Chas. Organist and teacher ; son of preceding ; 1773-1852.
With his brother William, and others, revived the "Vocal Concerts," 1801.

KNYV'ETT, William. Alto singer ; brother of preceding ; 1779-1856. Gentleman, Chapel Royal, 1797 ; afterwards lay-vicar, Westminster Abbey.
Conducted the Concerts of Antient Music, 1832-40, and the Birmingham Festivals, 1834-43.

KOB'BÉ, Gustav. American musican and writer ; *b.* New York, 1857.
Author of "Wagner's Life and Works" (2 vols, 1890) ; &c.

Kob'sa. A primitive Russian lute.

KOCH, Eduard E. Pastor ; *b.* nr. Stuttgart. 1809 ; *d.* 1871.
Author of a valuable work on the "Sacred Songs of the German Lutheran Church."

KOCH, Franz. 'Cellist and composer ; *b.* Berlin, 1862.

KOCH, Heinrich Christoph. Violinist and theorist ; Rudolstadt, 1749-1816.
Works : a "Musical Lexicon" (1802), a "Guide to Composition" (3 parts, 1782-93), a "Handbook of Harmony" (1811), &c.

KOCHAN'SKI, Paul. Violinist ; *b.* Orol, Russia, 1887.

KÖCH'EL, Ludwig, Ritter von. Gifted amateur ; *b.* Lower Austria, 1800 ; *d.* Vienna, 1877.
Author of a "Systematic, chronological, and complete Catalogue of Mozart's Works," 1862.

KOCHETOV, Nicholas R. Composer and critic ; *b.* Oranienbaum, 1864.

KO'CIAN, Jaroslav. Bohemian violinist ; *b.* 1884. *Début,* 1901.

KOCZAL'SKI, Raoul A. G. Precocious pianist ; *b.* Warsaw, 1885. Played in public at 4 ; and was at once regarded as an "infant phenomenon." After playing in most of the great European cities, he became Court Pianist to the Shah of Persia.
Works : an opera, and several pf. pieces.

KOEM'MENICH, Louis. *B.* Elberfeld, 1866.
Since 1890 has done good work as conductor and teacher in New York.

KOE'NEN, Friedrich. *B.* nr. Bonn, 1829; *d.* 1887. Capellmeister, Cologne, 1863 ; founded the *Cäcilienverein*, 1869.
Works : 2 masses for male voices, 5 for mixed choir ; motets, psalms, organ pieces, songs, &c.

KOESS'LER, Hans. Condr. and composer ; *b.* Waldeck, Bavaria, 1853.

KO'FLER, Leo. Writer, critic, and singing teacher ; *b.* Austrian Tyrol, 1837 ; *d.* 1908. From 1877, orgt. in New York.
Author of "The Art of Breathing as the Basis of Tone Production," &c.

KÖH'LER, Ernst. Orgt. and composer ; *b.* Silesia, 1799 ; *d.* 1847.
Wrote org. and pf. pieces, orch. music, church music, &c.

KÖH'LER, C. Louis H. (Ludwig). Pianist, composer, and critic ; *b.* Brunswick, 1820 ; *d.* 1886. Settled in Königsberg, 1847, and founded a School for Pf. Playing and Theory. Teacher of **Hermann Goetz.** As a pf. teacher he has been called "the heir of Czerny."
Works : pf. pieces and valuable studies ; 3 operas, orchestral music, songs, &c., and several theoretical treatises.

KOHOUT' (pron. *ko-hoot'*), **Franz.** Dramatic composer ; *b.* Bohemia, 1858. Condr. Deutsches Theater, Prague.
Stella (Prague, 1896) is his most successful opera.

Kokett' (*G.*). Coquettish(ly).

KOL'BE, Oskar. Composer and writer ; Berlin, 1836-78.
Works : an oratorio, works on Thorough Bass and Harmony, pf. music, songs, &c.

KOLFF, J. van Santen. *B.* Rotterdam, 1848 ; *d.* 1896.
Author of a ",History of the *Leit-motiv* before Wagner," numerous writings on "Wagner and his Works," &c.

Kollectiv'zug (*G.*). A composition pedal on the organ.

KOL'LING, Karl W. P. *B.* Hamburg, 1831.
Wrote a successful operetta, *Schmetterlinge* (1891).

KOLL'MANN, August F. K. *B.* Hanover, 1756 ; *d.* London, 1829. Orgt. German Chapel, St. James's.
Works : The *Shipwreck* (a program-symphony) ; 100 Psalms harmonized in 100 ways ; guides to Thorough-bass, Harmony, Composition, &c.

Kol'lo. A Japanese inst. of the harp kind.

Kol'lern (*G.*). To sing in a thin reedy voice.

Kom'isch (*G.*). Comical, Comic.
Kom'ische Op'er. Comic opera.

Kom'ma (*Gk.* and *G.*). (See **Comma.**)

Komödiant' (*G.*). A comedian.

KÖM'PEL, August. Violinist ; called "Spohr's best pupil ; " *b.* Brückenau, 1831 ; *d.* 1891.

Komponi(e)'ren (*G.*). To compose.
Komponirt'. Composed.
Komponist'. A composer.

Komposi'tion (*G.*). A composition.
Komposi'tionlehre. The art of composition; a treatise on composition.

KO'NING, David. Pianist, teacher, and composer ; *b.* Rotterdam, 1820 ; *d.* 1876. President, Amsterdam Cecilia Society.
Works : vocal music, pf. études, &c.

KONIUS, George E. Composer ; *b.* Moscow, 1862.

KÖN'NEMANN, Arthur. *B.* Baden-Baden, 1861. Theatre condr. in various German towns.
Works : operas (*Der tolle Eberstein*, 1898), orches. pieces, pf. pieces, choruses, songs, &c.

KON'RADIN, Karl F. *B.* nr. Baden, Lower Austria, 1833 ; *d.* 1884.
Produced 11 operettas at Vienna.

Konservato'rium (*G.*). (See **Conservatory.**)

Kon'tra (*G.*). (See **Contra.**)
Kontrabass,`Kontrafagott, Kontraoktave, Kontrapunkt, Kontrasubjekt, Kontratöne* (see under *Contra*).

Kon'tretanz (*G.*). (See **Contre-danse.**)

KONT'SKI, Antoine de. Fine pianist ; *b.* Cracow, 1817 ; *d.* 1899 ; Pupil of Markendorf and Field. Taught advanced pf. playing in London ; toured round the world at 80.
His pf. works are showy but superficial.

KONT'SKI, Apollinaire de. Brother of Antoine ; precocious violinist ; Paganini's favourite pupil ; Warsaw, 1825-79. Founded Warsaw Cons., 1861.
Two other brothers were musicians ; CHARLES, violinist, 1815-67 ; and STANISLAS, violinist, *b.* 1820.

Konzert' (*G.*). A concert ; a concerto.
Konzert'meister. (See **Concertmeister.**)
Konzert'oper. A "concert" opera without stage accessories.
Konzert'stück. (See **Concertstück.**)
Konzert'ton. Concert pitch.

KOPECK'Ý (pron. *ko-pet'-shee*), **Ottokar.** Bohemian violinist ; *b.* 1850. Now conductor to the King of Greece.

Kopf'stimme (*G.*; *I.*, *Vo'ce di te'sta*). The head voice ; falsetto.

Kop'pel (*G.*). An organ coupler.
Kop'pel ab. "Coupler off."
Kop'pel an. " Draw coupler."

KOPYLOFF, Alex. Composer ; *b.* St. Petersburg, 1854.

KOR'BAY, Francis A. Tenor singer and pianist ; *b.* Pesth, 1846. Settled in New York, 1871 ; in London, 1894.

KORES(H)TSHEN'KO, Arseni N. Russian composer ; *b.* Moscow, 1870.
Works : operas, orch. pieces, pf. pieces, songs, &c.

KÖR'NER, Christian G. Song composer ; *b.* Leipzig, 1756 ; *d.* 1831.
Father of the poet Theodor Körner.

Kornett' (*G.*). A *Cornet-à-pistons.*
Kornett'bläser. Cornet player.

Koryphæ'us (*Gk.*). (See **Coryphæus.**)

Kos. A Hungarian dance.

Kosa'ke. (*G.*, *Kosa'kisch.*) A national Cossack dance in 2-4 time.

KO'SCHAT, Thos. Bass singer and composer ; *b.* nr. Klagenfurt, 1843. Member of the Cathedral choir, Vienna, 1874, and the Hofkapelle, 1878. Organized the "Kärnthner Quintet," 1875.
He has written words and music of over 100 immensely popular "Carinthian" quartets for men's voices. Also operas, &c.

KÖSELITZ, Heinrich. Opera composer ; *b.* Saxony, 1854.

KOS'LECK, Julius. Trumpet and cornet player ; *b.* Neugard, Pomerania, 1835. Founder of the famous " Kaiser-Cornett-Quartett," 1871.

KOSSMALY, Carl. Writer ; *b.* 1812 ; *d.* Stettin, 1893. Capellmeister at Wiesbaden, Mayence, Amsterdam, Bremen, Detmold, and Stettin.
Works : orch. music, songs, &c. ; a "Musical Lexicon," treatises on the works of Mozart, Wagner, &c. He was an anti-Wagnerian.

KÖST'LIN, Frau. (See **Josephine Lang.**)

KOST'LIN, Heinrich Adolf. Preacher and writer ; *b.* Tübingen, 1846. Organized the Württemberg Lutheran "Kirchengesangverein," 1877
Author of works on "Musical Æsthetics," &c.

KO'THE, Aloys. *B.* Gröbnig, Silesia, 1828 ; *d.* 1868.
Pub. a mass for men's voices ; songs, pf. pieces.

KO'THE, Bernhard. Brother of A ; *b.* Gröbnig, 1821 ; *d.* 1897. Founded the Cäcilien-Verein for Catholic church-music, Breslau.
Works : organ music, sacred songs for men's voices, pamphlets on Catholic church music, &c.

KO'THE, Wilhelm. Brother of preceding ; *b.* Gröbnig, 1831.
Works : Methods for violin and voice ; songs, and pf. music.

Ko'to. A Japanese "Zither harp" with 13 silk strings.

KOTSHETOV. Same as **Kochetov** (*q.v.*).

KOTT'HOFF, Lawrence. Critic and teacher; *b.* Eversburg, Germany, 1862. Settled in St. Louis, Missouri, 1886.
He is known as a "Bach Specialist."

KÖTT'LITZ, Adolf. Precocious violinist ; *b.* Trier, 1820 ; killed while hunting in Siberia, 1860. Played vn. concertos in his 7th year ; gave public concerts at 10. Leader, Königsberg Th., 1848-56.

KOT'ZELUCH (KOZ'ELUCH), Leopold A. Pianist and composer ; *b.* Wellwarn, 1752 ; *d.* Vienna, 1814. Court composer, succeeding Mozart, Vienna, 1792.
Works : numerous operas and ballets (including *Le Mazet* (1780), &c.), an oratorio, cantatas, 30 symphonies, over 40 pf. concertos, chamber music, &c.

KOT'ZOLT, Heinrich. Teacher and conductor ; *b.* Upper Silesia, 1814 ; *d.* Berlin, 1881. Founded the "Kotzolt Gesangverein," Berlin, 1849, and conducted it till his death.
Pub. a "Method for *a cappella* singing."

KOTZSCH'MAR, Hermann. *B.* Finsterwalde, 1829. Went to America, 1848 ; settled in Portland, Maine, 1849 ; Orgt. First Parish Church, and conductor "Haydn Association."

KOTZWA'RA, Franz. *B.* Prague, abt. 1750 ; *d.* Dublin, 1791.
Wrote a once celebrated pf. piece, "The Battle of Prague."

KO'VAROVIC, Karl. Noted opera composer ; *b.* Prague, 1862. Cond. Nat. Bohemian Th., Prague, 1899.

KOVEN, Henry L. R. de. Composer ; *b.* Middletown (U.S.), 1859.

KOWAL'SKI, Henri. Pianist, and composer of light pf. pieces ; *b.* Paris, 1841.

KOZ'ELUCH. (See **Kotzeluch.**)

Kräch'zen (*G.*). To croak ; to sing in a croaking voice.

Kraft (*G.*). Energy, force, vigour, strength.
Kräf'tig ⎫
Kräf'tiglich ⎬ Powerful, energetic, vigorous.
Kräf'tig, doch nicht zu schnell. Energetic, but not too fast.
Kräf'tig gestos'sen. Forcibly detached.
Kräf'tig und bestimmt'. Vigorous and decided.
Kräf'tig und feu'rig. Vigorous and spirited.
Mit al'ler Kraft. As loud as possible ; with full force.

KRAFT, Anton. 'Cellist ; *b.* nr. Pilsen, 1752 ; *d.* 1820. Studied composition under Haydn. Member of Prince Esterházy's Orch. 1778-90.
Works : a concerto, and other pieces for 'cello, &c.

KRAFT, Nicolaus. 'Cellist ; son and pupil of A. ; *b.* Esterház, Hungary, 1778 ; *d.* 1853. Played in Dresden with Mozart, 1789 ; member of the "Schuppanzigh Quartet" (famous for the production of Beethoven's works) ; successful concert tourist, &c.
Works : 5 concertos, and much other interesting 'cello music.

Krako'viak ⎫
Krakovienne (*F.*) ⎬ (See **Cracoviak.**)
Krako'wiak ⎭

KRANTZ, Eugen. Pianist ; fine interpreter of Bach ; Dresden, 1844-98. Director Dresden Cons., 1890.
Published a pf. method, songs, &c.

KRAUS, K. F. H. Ernst. Operatic tenor ; *b.* Erlangen, Bavaria, 1863. Stage *début*, Mannheim, 1893.

KRAU'SE, Anton. Pianist ; *b.* Geithain, Saxony, 1834. Conductor Liedertafel, Leipzig, 1856 ; Director, Singverein and Concertgesellschaft, 1859-97. *D.* 1907.
Works : *Prinzessin Ilse* (for soli, female chorus, and pf.), choral music, songs, numerous instructive pf. pieces, &c.

KRAU'SE, Emil. Pianist ; *b.* Hamburg, 1840. Teacher of pf., Hamburg Cons., 1885.
Works : cantatas, chamber music, songs, pf. pieces; treatises on pf. playing, harmony, &c.

KRAU'SE, Martin. Pianist and teacher; *b.* Lobstedt, nr. Leipzig, 1853. Made Liszt's acquaintance in 1882, and for three years studied his methods closely. Chief promoter of the establishment of the Lisztverein, Leipzig, 1885.
As teacher and writer he is held in high esteem.

KRAU'SE, Theodor. Rector; *b.* Halle, 1833. Organized the choirs of the Nikolaikirche and the Marienkirche, Berlin. R. Music-director, 1887.

Kräu'sel (*G.*). A mordent (*q.v.*).

KRAUSS, Dr. Felix. Operatic bass; *b.* Vienna, 1870.

KRAUSS, Gabrielle. Distinguished dramatic soprano; *b.* Vienna, 1842; *d.* 1906. After brilliant sucesses at Vienna, Baden, Milan, &c., sang at the Paris Grand Opéra, 1875-86.
Her charming voice had a compass of over two full octaves from B₁.

KREBS, Carl August. (Real name **Miedcke.**) Pianist; *b.* Nuremburg, 1804; *d.* 1880. Hof - Kapellmeister, Dresden Opera, 1850-72.
Works: 2 operas, pf. pieces, very popular songs.

KREBS, Johann L. Organist; thought by J. S. Bach to be his best pupil; *b.* Thuringia, 1713; *d.* 1780.
Wrote org. music, clavier music, flute trios, &c.

KREBS, Dr. Karl. Musical critic; *b.* Hanseberg, 1857.

KREBS, Marie. Fine pianist; daughter of Carl A.; *b.* Dresden, 1851; *d.* 1900. *Début* at 12. After long tours, settled in Dresden as teacher.

Krebs'gängig (*G.*). Backward, retrograde, crab-like. (See **Canon.**)
Beethoven uses the device in the fugue of his Op. 106, writing the theme backwards.

KREĆMAN. (See **Kretschmann.**)

KREH'BIEL, Hy. Ed. American writer; *b.* Michigan, 1854. Musical critic, New York *Tribune*.
Pub. "Technics of violin playing" (1880).

KREHL, Stephen. Pianist; *b.* Leipzig, 1864. Teacher of pf. and theory, Carlsruhe Cons., 1889.
Works: characteristic pieces, Lieder, Kinder-stücke, &c., for pf.

KREI'PL, Jos. Tenor singer; *b.* 1805; *d.* Vienna, 1866.
Wrote some beautiful songs, including "Das Mailüfterl."

Kreis (*G.*). A circle, a ring.
Kreis'fuge. A canon.
Kreis'lieder. A series, or cycle of songs.
Kreis'tanz. A circle dance.

Kreis'chend (*G.*). Shrieking, harsh, strident.

KREIS'LER, Fritz. Violinist; *b.* Vienna, 1875.

KREISS'LE von Hellborn, Heinrich. Schubert's biographer; *b.* Vienna, date uncertain; *d.* there, 1869.
He was a secretary in the Ministry of Finance.

KREJČI (pron. *kray'-tchee*), **Josef.** Distinguished organist; *b.* Bohemia, 1822; *d.* Prague, 1881.

KREM'PELSETZER, Georg. Composer of successful operettas; Vilsbiburg, Bavaria, 1827-71. Capellmeister at Munich, Görlitz, and Königsberg.

KREM'SER, Eduard. *B.* Vienna, 1838. Chorusmaster of the "Männergesang-verein" since 1869.
Works: operettas; a cantata, celebrated *Altneider-ländische Volkslieder* and other part-songs, pf. music, &c.

KRENN, Franz. Renowned organist and conductor; *b.* Dross, Lower Austria, 1816; *d.* 1897.
Wrote 2 oratorios, cantatas, 15 masses, 3 requiems a symphony, part-songs, pf. and org. pieces, an org. method, &c.

Kreol. A Danish reel.

KRETSCH'MANN, Theobald. 'Cellist; *b.* nr. Prague, 1850.

KRETSCH'MER, Edmund. *B.* Ostritz, Saxony, 1830. Court orgt., Dresden, 1863-90. Founded the "Cäcilia" Singing Society. *D.* 1908.
Works: operas, *Die Folkunger* (1874), *Heinrich der Löwe* (1877), &c.; pieces for soli, chorus, and orch.; masses, orchestral music, &c.

KRETZSCH'MAR, Dr. A. F. Hermann. *B.* Olbernhau, Saxony, 1848. Org. teacher, Leipzig Cons., 1871; Mus.-director, Leipzig Univ., 1887. Organized the "Akademische Orchesterconcerte," 1890.
Works: org. pieces, part-songs; critical essays.

KREUBE, Charles F. *B.* Lunéville, 1777; *d.* 1846.
Produced 16 comic operas, Paris Opéra-Comique.

KREUT'ZER, Auguste. Violinist; *b.* Versailles, 1781; *d.* 1832.
Succeeded his brother Rodolphe (below) as vn. teacher, Paris Cons., 1826.

KREUT'ZER (or **KREUZER**), **Conradin.** *B.* Mösskirch, Baden, 1780; *d.* Riga, 1849. Studied counterpoint 2 years under Albrechtsberger. Capellmeister at various theatres, 1812-40.
Wrote 30 operas, including *Das Nachtlager von Granada* (1834, his best), *Verschwinder* (1836), and *Jery und Bätely*; an oratorio, fine male choruses, &c.

KREUT'ZER, Léon C. F. Composer and critic; son of A.; *b.* Paris, 1817; *d.* 1868.

KREUT'ZER, Rodolphe. Celebrated violinist, to whom Beethoven dedicated the Kreutzer Sonata; *b.* Versailles, 1766; *d.* 1831. Solo violin, Théâtre Italien, 1790; Opéra, 1801. Condr. Opéra, 1817. Also chamber musician to Napoleon and Louis XVIII.
Works: 43 operas, including *Lodoïska*; 40 "Etudes ou Caprices," and much other vn. music; joint author with Rode and Baillot of the standard Vn. Method of the Paris Cons.

KREUTZER SONATA. Beethoven's Sonata for vn. and pf. in A, Op. 47.

Kreuz. (*G.*). (Pron. *kroitz*). The sharp (♯).

Dop'pelkreuz
Kreuz-dop'peltes } The double-sharp (x or 𝄪).

Kreuz'tonart. Sharp key.

KREUZ, Emil. Viola player and composer; *b.* Elberfeld, 1867.

KREU'ZER. (See **Kreutzer.**)

KRIE'GER, Adam. Court orgt. Dresden; *b.* Driesen, Neumark, 1634; *d.* 1666.

KRIE'GER, Ferdinand. *B.* Franconia, 1843. Pub. "The Elements of Music," "A Harmony Course," &c.

KRIE'GER, Johann. Famous contrapuntist; brother and pupil of J. P. (below); *b.* Nuremberg, 1652; *d.* 1736. Orgt. and mus.-director, Zittau, 1681.

KRIE'GER, Johann Philipp. *B.* Nuremberg, 1649; *d.* 1725. Capellmeister and orgt. at various Courts. Wrote several operas, 24 sonatas for 2 vns and bass, &c.

Krie'gerisch (*G.*). Martial, warlike.

Kriegs'gesang }
Kriegs'lied } A soldier's song.

Kriegs'spieler. A military musician.

KRI'GAR, J. Hermann. Pianist; Berlin, 1819-80. Pupil of Schumann and Mendelssohn. Conducted singing societies at Berlin. Wrote motets, psalms, pf. pieces, songs, &c.

KRIZKOW'SKY, Paul. Augustine monk; *b.* 1820; *d.* Brünn, 1885. Composer of national *Czech* music.

KROE'GER, Ernest R. Composer; *b.* St. Louis (U.S.), 1862.

KROLL, Franz. Pianist; pupil of Liszt; *b.* Bromberg, 1820; *d.* 1877. Edited "Bach's well-tempered Clavichord," and other pf. works for the Bach-Gesellschaft (Breitkopf & Härtel); also for the Peters' edition.

KRO'LOP, Franz. Dramatic bass singer; *b.* Troja, Bohemia, 1839; *d.* 1897. Sang Berlin Court Opera from 1872.

Kro'me (*G.*). A quaver (♪).

KROM'MER, Franz. Organist, violinist, conductor, and bandmaster; *b.* Kamenitz, Moravia, 1760; *d.* 1831. Imperial Capellmeister, Vienna, 1814. Works: 5 symphonies, 5 vn. concertos; 69 string quartets, and much other chamber music, &c.

Kro'ne (*G.*). A corona or pause; ⌒.

KRON'KE, Emil. Pianist; *b.* Danzig, 1865. A zealous student of Liszt's works. Works: pf. pieces.

Krotalon. (See **Crotalum.**)

KRÜCKL (KRÜKL), Franz. Noted baritone singer; *b.* Moravia, 1841; *d.* 1899. Director, Municipal Th., Strasburg, 1892.

KRUG, Arnold. Son of D. (below); *b.* Hamburg, 1849; Won the Mozart Scholarship, Leipzig Cons., 1869. Teacher, Hamburg Cons., 1885. *D.* 1904. Works: orchestral music, choral works (*Sigurd*, &c.), a vn. concerto, pf. music, songs, &c.

KRUG, Dietrich. Pianist and teacher; Hamburg, 1821-80. Pub. "Melodious Studies for Pf.," &c.

KRUG, Friedrich. Baritone singer; *b.* Cassel, 1812; *d.* 1892. Court music director, Carlsruhe. Wrote some fairly successful operas.

KRUG, Wenzel Joseph (known as **Krug-Waldsee**). *B.* Waldsee, Swabia, 1858. Capellmeister, Brünn Th., 1892-3; Nuremberg, 1894; Augsburg, 1896; Magdeburg, 1901. Works: important concert-cantatas (*Dornröschen Seebilder*, &c.), operas and ballets; orch. music, songs, &c.

KRÜGER, Gottlieb. Fine harpist; Stuttgart, 1824-95.

KRÜ'GER, Wilhelm. Pianist; brother of G.; Stuttgart, 1820-83. Lived in Paris, 1845-70; then Court pianist, Stuttgart, and teacher at the Cons. Pub. 168 works for pf., and an edition in 2 vols. of Handel's Harpsichord works.

KRUIS, M. H. van. Orgt., teacher, and writer; *b.* Oudewater, Holland, 1861. Founded a mus. monthly, *Het Orgel*, 1886. His works include the opera *De bloem van Island*.

Krumm (*G.*). Curved, bent, crooked.

Krumm'bogen (*G.*). A crook of a horn or trumpet.

Krumm'horn (*G.*). "Crooked horn." A mediæval inst. The word "Cremona" (org. stop) is a corruption of *Krummhorn*.

KRUMP'HOLTZ, Johann Baptist. Celebrated harpist; *b.* nr. Prague, abt. 1749; *d.* Paris, 1790. Had composition lessons from Haydn, and was a member of Prince Esterhàzy's Orch., 1773-6. Afterwards, with his wife, gave brilliant concerts in Paris, &c. He invented a harp with soft and loud pedals, and stimulated Erard to the invention of the present double-action harp. He also wrote 6 concertos and many other harp pieces.

KRUMP'HOLTZ, Wenzel. Violinist; brother of J. B.; *b.* abt. 1750; *d.* 1817. He was a friend of Beethoven, who dedicated to him his "Gesang der Mönche."

KRU'SE, Joh. S. Violinist; *b.* Melbourne, 1859. Pupil of Joachim. Leader, Bremen Orch., 1892.

Krus'tische Instrumente (*G.*). Percussion insts.

KU'BELIK (pron. *koo'-bĕ-lĭk*), **Johann.** Distinguished Bohemian violinist; *b.* Michle, nr. Prague, 1880. Son of a gardener. *Début*, Vienna, 1898; London, 1900. Was awarded the "Beethoven Medal" by the London Phil. Soc., 1902.

KUCHARŽ, Joh. Baptist. *B.* Chotecz, Bohemia, 1751 ; *d.* 1829. Condr., Prague Opera, 1791-1800.

KÜCK'EN, Friedrich Wm. Song composer ; son of a peasant ; *b.* Bleckede, Hanover, 1810 ; *d.* 1882. Capellmeister, Stuttgart, 1851-61.
Works : operas (*Der Flucht nach der Schweiz*, 1839), vn. sonatas, male-voice quartets, and numerous very popular songs.

Kuckuck (*G.*). Same as **Kuk-kuk** (*q.v.*).

KUCZYN'SKI, Paul. Polish composer ; *b.* 1846.

KUDEL'SKI, Karl M. Violinist ; *b.* Berlin, 1805 ; *d.* 1877. Dirctor, Imperial Th., Moscow, 1841-51.
Wrote vn. concertos, pf. trios, a Harmony text book, &c.

KUF'FERATH, Hubert F. Pianist and orgt.; *b.* Mühlheim-on-Ruhr, 1818 ; *d.* 1896. Studied Leipzig under Mendelssohn ; Condr. Cologne Männergesangverein, 1841-4 ; Prof. Brussels Cons., 1872.
Wrote symphonies, pf. concertos, pf. pieces and études, &c.

KUF'FERATH, Joh. Hermann. Brother of H. F. ; violinist ; pupil of Spohr. *B.* Mühlheim, 1797 ; *d.* 1864.
Wrote a "Jubelcantate," a "Manuel de Chant," &c.

KUF'FERATH, Louis. Pianist ; brother of the two preceding ; *b.* Mühlheim, 1811 ; *d.* 1882. Director, Leeuwarden Cons., 1836-50.
Works : cantata (*Artevelde*), 250 canons, pf. pieces, songs, &c.

KUF'FERATH, Maurice ("Maurice Reymont"). 'Cellist and writer ; son of H. F. ; *b.* Brussels, 1852. Editor, *Guide Musicale*, Brussels, 1873.
Works : essays on Wagner, Berlioz, Schumann, Brahms, &c. He is a critic of "thoroughly modern spirit."

KÜFF'NER, Jos. Prolific composer ; Würzburg, 1776-1856.
Works : 2 operas, 7 symphonies, 10 overtures, &c.

KUH'E, Wilhelm. Pianist ; *b.* Prague, 1823. Prof. R.A.M., 1886.
Works : graceful drawing-room pf. pieces.

Kuh'horn (*G.*). "Cow horn ; " Alpine horn.

KUH'LAU, Friedrich. Flautist ; *b.* Uelzen, Hanover, 1786 ; *d.* Copenhagen, 1832. Court composer, Copenhagen, 1818.
Works : half-a-dozen operas ; 3 quartets, and numerous other pieces for flute ; 8 vn. sonatas ; several instructive sonatas and sonatinas for pf., male quartets, songs, &c.

KÜHM'STEDT, Friedrich. Theorist ; *b.* Oldisleben, 1809 ; *d.* 1858.
Wrote valuable org. music.

Kuhn (*G.*). Dashing, audacious, bold.

KUH'NAU, Johann. Noted organist ; *b.* Geysing, Saxony, abt. 1667 ; *d.* Leipzig, 1722. Orgt. Thomaskirche, Leipzig, 1694; Cantor (Bach's predecessor), 1700.
Pub. the first "Harpsichord Sonata," 1695; also some early examples of "program music" in the

form of "Biblical Sonatas" (*The Fight between David and Goliath*, *Jacob's Wedding*, *David's Cure of Saul*, &c.), 1700.

Kuh'reigen (*G.*) ⎫
Kuh'reihen (*G.*) ⎬ **Ranz des Vaches** (*q.v.*).

Kuja'wiak. A Polish dance similar to the Mazurka (*q.v.*).

Kuk-kuk (*G.*). The cuckoo.

KU'LENKAMPF, Gustav. Pianist and composer ; *b.* Bremen, 1849. Organized the Kulenkampfscher Frauenchor, Berlin.
Works : operas, *Der Page* (1890), *Die Braut von Cypern* (1897), &c. ; female choruses, songs, &c.

KUL'LAK, Dr. Adolf. Brother of T. (below) ; *b.* Meseritz, 1823 ; *d.* 1862.
Wrote a valuable "Æsthetik des Klavierspiels."

KUL'LAK, Franz. Pianist ; son of T. (below) ; *b.* Berlin, 1842. Director of his father's Academy, 1882-90 (when it was dissolved.)
Works : an opera (*Ines de Castro*), pf. pieces, songs.

KUL'LAK, Theodor. Pianist ; *b.* nr. Posen, 1818 ; *d.* 1882. After touring in Austria, settled in Berlin. Court pianist, 1846 ; founded (with J. Stern and B. Marx) the Berlin (later Stern) Cons., 1850 ; founded his "Neue Akademie der Tonkunst," 1855. Among his numerous pupils were the two Scharwenkas, and M. Moszkowski.
Wrote about 130 pf. works, including several valuable Studies (notably the "School of Octave Playing" and "Seven Studies in Octave Playing").

KUM'MEK, Fr. August. Eminent 'cellist ; *b.* Meiningen, 1797 ; *d.* 1879. For many years 'cello teacher, Dresden Cons.
Wrote numerous fine pieces for 'cello, a 'cello Method, &c.

KÜM'MERLE, Salomon. *B.* nr. Stuttgart, 1838 ; *d.* 1896.
Pub. an "Encyclopedia of Lutheran Church Music," &c.

KÜN'DINGER, Alex. Violinist ; *b.* Kitzingen, 1827.

KÜN'DINGER, Kanut. Bro. of preceding ; 'cellist ; *b.* Kitzingen, 1830.

KÜN'DINGER, Rudolf. Bro. of preceding ; pianist ; *b.* Nordlingen, 1832. Prof. St. Petersburg Cons., 1879.

KUN'KEL, Franz Jos. Teacher and writer ; *b.* Drieburg, Hesse, 1804 ; *d.* 1880.

Kunst (*G.*). Art, skill ; knowledge.
Künst'fuge. An artistic, scholarly fugue.
Künst'kenner. A connoisseur.
Künst'ler. An artist.
Künst'lied. An art song (as opposed to *Volkslied*, a folk-song.)
Künst'pfeifer. A town musician.
Kunst'werk der Zu'kunft. "The art work of the future."—*Wagner.*

Kunst der Fu'ge, Die. (See **Art of Fugue, The.**)

KUNT'ZE, Carl. Orgt. ; *b.* Trier, 1817 ; *d.* 1883. Wrote humorous male choruses.

KUNZ, K. M. *B.* Schwandorf, 1812; *d.* 1875. Conductor, Munich *Liedertafel.*

Works: "200 canons for pf." (recommended by von Bülow), popular male quartets, &c.

KUN'ZEN, Adolf C. Precocious pianist; *b.* Wittenberg, 1720; *d.* 1781. Toured in Holland and England at 8. Finally orgt., Marienkirche, Lübeck.

Works: pf. sonatas, &c.

KUN'ZEN, F. Ludwig A. Son of the preceding; operatic composer; *b.* Lübeck, 1761; *d.* 1817. Court conductor, Copenhagen, 1795.

Works: several operas (including *Holger Danske*, 1789); oratorios, overtures, pf. sonatas, &c.

KUP'FER-BER'GER, Ludmilla. Operatic soprano; *b.* Vienna, 1850. *Début* as "Marguerite" (*Faust*), 1868.

Kup'pel (*G.*). Same as **Koppel** (*q.v.*).

KURPIN'SKI, Karl. *B.* nr. Posen, 1785; *d.* 1857. Conductor Warsaw Nat. Th., 1825-41.

Wrote 24 Polish operas, and several ballets.

KURSCH'MANN. (See **Curschmann.**)

KURTH, M. A. Otto. *B.* Triebel, Brandenburg, 1846. Prof. Teachers' Seminary, Lüneburg, 1871.

Works: operas, oratorio (*Isaaks Opferung*), symphonies, chamber music, sonatas for pf. and vn., &c.

Kurz (*G.*). Short, detached; *staccato.*

Kur'zeflöte. "Short flute." A piccolo (org. stop).
Kür'zen. To abbreviate.
Kur'zer Mor'dent. A short mordent.

Kur'ze No'te. An *Acciaccatura.*
Kur'ze Okta've. A short octave.
Kur'zer Vor'schlag. Short appoggiatura.
Kurz und bestimmt'. Short and decided.
Kur'zung. An abbreviation.
Kur'zungzeichen. A sign of abbreviation.

KUS'SER (or **COUSSER**), **Johann S.** *B.* Pressburg, abt. 1657; *d.* Dublin, 1727. Conductor, Hamburg Opera, 1693-5; Stuttgart Opera, 1698-1704; Viceroy's Orch., Dublin, 1704.

Works: 5 operas (produced at Hamburg), 6 operatic overtures, &c.

Kussir'. A Turkish musical inst.

KÜS'TER, Hermann. *B.* Templin, Brandenburg, 1817; *d.* 1878. Settled Berlin, 1852; founded the "Berliner Tonkünstler-Verein;" Court Cathedral, orgt., 1857.

Works: 7 oratorios, orch. music, church music, songs; treatises on "Handel's *Israel in Egypt*," "Form in Music," &c.

Kus'tos (*G.*). (1) A cue. (2) A direct (*q.v.*).

KWAST, Jas. Pianist; *b.* Nijkerk, Holland, 1852. Pf. teacher, Hoch Cons., Frankfort, 1883.

Works: a concerto and other pf. music.

Ky'rie elei'son(*Gk.*). "Lord have mercy upon us." (1) The 1st movement of a Mass. (2) The response sung at the end of each of the Commandments. (Generally called " Kyrie " only.)

"Lord, have mercy upon us; and incline our hearts to keep this law."

Kyrielle (*F.*). A Litany.

L

L. Abbrevn. of *Left*. *L. H.*, left hand.

L' or l'. Abbrevn. of *Le*, *La*, or *Lo*, "the."
L'accompagnamen'to sem'pre leggieris'simo (I.) The accompaniment always very light.

La. (1) The 6th of Guido's syllables. (See **Guido.**) (2) (*F. & I.*) The note A. (3) Spelt "Lah;" the Tonic Sol-fa name of the 6th note of the major scale, and the Tonic of the minor scale.

La bémol (F.) ⎫
La bemol'le (I.) ⎬ The note A♭.

La bémol majeur (F.) ⎫
La bemol'le maggio're (I.) ⎬ Key of A♭ major.

La bémol mineur (F.) ⎫
La bemol'le mino're (I.) ⎬ Key of A♭ minor.

La dièse (F.) ⎫
La die'sis (I.) ⎬ The note A♯.

La (*adj., I. & F.*). The.
La chasse (F.). "The chase;" a piece in hunting style.
La de'stra (I.). The right hand.
La vo'ce (I.). The voice.

LABARRE, F. Théodore. Renowned harpist; Paris, 1805-70. Lived alternately in Paris and London, 1824-51. Conductor, Louis Napoleon's orch., 1851. Works: a "Méthode complète" and numerous compositions for harp.

LABATT', Leonard. Operatic tenor; Stockholm, 1838-97. Member, Vienna Court Opera, 1869-83.

Labeceda'tion ⎫
Labecedisa'tion ⎬ (See **Bebisation.**)

La'bial. Lipped; with lips.
Labial'pfeife (G.). ⎫
Labial'stimme (G.). ⎬ A lipped pipe; a *flue* pipe.
Labial'werk (G.). Flue-work.

La'bien (*G.*). Pipes.

Labisa'tion. (Same as **Bebisation**, *q.v.*)

LABITZ'KY, Joseph. B. nr. Eger, 1802; *d.* 1881. Wrote popular dance music.

La'bium (*L.*). "A lip." Specially, the lip of an organ pipe.

LABLACHE, Luigi. Celebrated bass singer; *b.* Naples, 1794; *d.* 1858. Commenced his public career at 18; sang in Milan, Venice, Vienna, Paris, St. Petersburg, London, &c. Retired 1852.
He had a voice of wonderful power and flexibility, with a compass from E♭¡ to E♭¹, and was considered the finest dramatic basso of his day.

LA'BOR, Josef. Blind pianist and organist; *b.* Horowitz, Bohemia, 1842.
Works: pianoforte music, songs, &c.

LABORDE, Jean B. de. Composer and writer; Paris, 1734-94. Pupil of Rameau; chamberlain to Louis XV.
Works: 11 comic operas, chansons, an "Essay on Ancient and Modern Music" (4 vols., 1780), &c.

LACH'MUND, Carl V. Composer; *b.* Booneville (U.S.), 1854.

LACH'NER, Franz. B. Rain,'Bavaria, 1803; *d.* Munich, 1890. Orgt. Protestant Ch., Vienna, 1822; intimate friend of Schubert's, and an acquaintance and profound admirer of Beethoven. Capellmeister, Kärnthnerthor Theatre

(1826), Mannheim (1834); Court-Capellmeister, Munich, 1836-68.
Works: 8 fine orchestral suites; 4 operas, 2 oratorios, a requiem, masses, symphonies, overtures, chamber music, songs, &c.

LACH'NER, Ignaz. Brother of preceding; *b.* Rain, 1807; *d.* 1895. Capellmeister, Hamburg City Theatre, 1853; Court Conductor, Stockholm, 1858; Capellmeister, Frankfort, 1861-75.
Works: 3 operas; several *Singspiele* (including '*s letzte Fensterle*); ballets, symphonies, masses, pf. pieces, &c.

LACH'NER, Vincenz. Brother of preceding; *b.* Rain, 1811; *d.* 1893. Court Capellmeister, Mannheim, 1836-73. Cond. German Opera, London, 1842.
Several 4-part male choruses; symphonies, chamber music, songs, &c.

LACK, Théodore. B. Quimper, Finisterre, 1846. Studied Paris Cons. Officier de l'Instruction publique, 1887.
Works: numerous graceful *salon* pieces for pf.

LACOMBE, Louis. (**Brouillon-Lacombe.**) B. Bourges, France, 1818; *d.* 1884. Pianist; pupil of Zimmermann, Paris Cons. After long tours, settled in Paris.
Works: operas, dramatic symphonies, choruses, numerous pf. pieces ("Grand étude en octaves"), &c.

LACOMBE, Paul. Pianist; *b.* Carcassonne, Aude, France, 1837.
Works: fine chamber and pf. music; symphonies·

LACOME, Paul. (**P. J. J. Lacome de l'Estaleux.**) B. Houga, France, 1838.
Works: about 20 light operas (*Jeanne, Jeannette et Jeanneton*, 1876, &c.); orchestral and chamber music; pf. pieces; over 200 songs, &c.

Lacrimo'sa (*L.*). "Weeping." Part of the *Dies Iræ* in a *Requiem*.

Lacrimo'so (*I.*) ⎫
Lacriman'do (*I.*) ⎬ Mournfully, tearfully.

LACY Fredk. St. John. Composer and writer; *b.* nr. Cork, 1862.

La'de (*G.*). A wind chest (of an organ).

LA'DEGAST, Friedrich. Noted organ builder; *b.* nr. Leipzig, 1818.
Built the fine org. Nikolaikirche, Leipzig (1859-62) with 4 manuals and 85 stops.

LADUR'NER, Ignaz A. F. X. Pianist and renowned teacher; *b.* Aldein, Tyrol, 1766; *d.* 1839. Lived in Paris, 1788-1836. Auber was his pupil.
Works: sonatas for pf., pf. and vn., &c.; also 2 operas.

LAFAGE, Juste A. L. de. Distinguished writer; *b.* Paris, 1801; *d.* 1862.
Works: important treatises on Plain Chant; "Manuel complet de musique vocale et instrumentale" (6 vols.), "A General History of Music and the Dance" (2 vols.), sketches of the Lives of Great Composers, &c.

LAFONT, Chas. Philippe. Concert violinist; *b.* Paris, 1781; *d.* 1839.
Works: several vn. pieces (including 7 concertos), about 200 songs, &c.

La'ge (*G.*). Position. (1) Of a chord. (2) Of the hand in "shifting" on the violin.
Eng'e La'ge. Close harmony; close position.
Wei'te La'ge. Open harmony; extended position.

La'genwechsel (*G.*). Shifting (in vn. playing).

Lagne'vole (*I.*) } Plaintive, doleful.
Lagno'so,-a (*I.*) }

Lagnosamen'te. Dolefully, mournfully.

La GRANGE, Anna C. de. Operatic soprano ; *b.* Paris, 1825.

Lagriman'do (*I.*) } Tearfully, mournfully,
Lagrimo'so,-a (*I.*) } sadly.

LAH. Tonic Sol-fa spelling of **La** (3) (*q.v.*).

LAHEE, Henry. *B.* Chelsea, 1826. Orgt. Holy Trinity, Brompton, 1847-74.
Works : cantatas (*The Building of the Ship, The Sleeping Beauty*, &c.), anthems, part-songs, &c.

Lai (*F.*). A lay, song, ditty ; *Lied*.

LAIDLAW, Anna Robena (Mrs. Thomson). Pianist ; *b.* Bretton, Yorkshire, 1819. Schumann inscribed to her his *Phantasiestücke*, Op. 12. *D.* 190-(?).

Laisser (*F.*). To allow ; to let.
Laisser vibrer. Allow (the note, drum, &c.) to vibrate.

LAJEUNESSE. (See **Albani.**)

LALANDE, Michel Richard de. Eminent church composer ; Paris, 1657-1726.
Orgt. of 4 churches in Paris ; music master to the Princesses ; *chef de musique* to Louis XIV, 1683.

LALANDE (Méric-Lalande), Henrietta C. Brilliant soprano ; *b.* Dunkirk, 1798 ; *d.* 1867.
Was renowned in Italy, Vienna, and Paris.

LALO, Edouard V. A. Distinguished composer ; *b.* Lille, 1823 ; *d.* 1892. Lived in Paris as violinist and teacher.
Works : operas (*Le Roi d'Ys*, &c.) ; a ballet ; "Rhapsodie norvégienne," for orch. ; a pf. concerto, 2 noted vn. concertos, chamber music, pf. and vn. music, &c.

La majeur (*F.*). The key of A major.

La MARA. (See **Lipsius, Marie.**)

LAM'BERT, Alexander. Concert pianist ; *b.* Warsaw, 1862. Director, New York Coll. of Music, 1888.
Works : pf. pieces, &c.

LAMBERT, George J. Beverley, 1794-1880. Orgt. Beverley Minster, 1818-75.
Wrote chamber music, pf. pieces, &c.

LAMBERT, Lucien. *B.* Paris, 1861. Took the *Prix Rossini*, Paris Cons., 1883.
Works : operas (*Brocéliande*, 1893, *Le Spahi*, 1897, &c.) ; orch. pieces, pf. pieces, &c.

LAMBERT, Michel. Celebrated singing teacher ; father-in-law of Lully. *B.* Poitou, 1610 ; *d.* Paris, 1696.

LAMBER'TI, Giuseppe. *B.* Cuneo, Italy, 1820 ; *d.* 1894.
Wrote 2 successful operas, sacred music, &c.

LAMBILLOTTE, Pere Louis. *B.* Charleroi, 1797 ; *d.* 1855.
Works : 4 grand masses, and other sacred music ; several works on Gregorian music (including an "Antiphonaire de saint Grégoire, facsimile du manuscrit de Saint-Gall").

L'ame (*F.*). Sound post (of a violin, &c.).

La melodi'a ben marca'ta (*I.*). The melody (to be) well emphasized.

Lament. A Scotch song or melody of a melancholy or mournful character.

Lamentazio'ne (*I.*) } A lamentation, dirge
Lamen'to (*I.*) } elegy, complaint.

Lamenta'bile
Lamentabilmen'te
Lamentabon'do
Lamentan'do } Mournfully, plaintively, com-
Lamente'vole } plainingly, sadly.
Lamentevolmen'te
Lamento'so

LA'MIA. Most celebrated female flute player of ancient Greece ; *b.* 4th cent. B.C.

La mineur (*F.*). The key of A minor.

LAMOND', Frederic A. Concert pianist ; *b.* Glasgow, 1868. *Début*, Berlin, 1885.
Works : a symphony, an overture, pf. pieces, &c.

LAMOTHE, Georges. French composer of dance music ; 1837-94.

LAMOUREUX, Chas. Celebrated cond. ; *b.* Bordeaux, 1834 ; *d.* Paris, 1899. Est. the famous "Concerts Lamoureux," Paris, 1881.

LAMPADA'RIUS, Johannes. Constantinople, 14th cent.
Wrote a work on the Music of the Greek Church.

LAMPA'DIUS, Wilhelm A. Lutheran pastor; 1812-92.
Author of a work on Mendelssohn.

LAMPE, John Frederic. *B.* Saxony, 1703 ; came to England abt. 1725 ; *d.* 1751.
Wrote stage pieces, &c. ; was associated with the Wesleys in the production of their books of hymn-tunes.

Lam'penfieber (*G.*). Stage fright.

LAM'PERT, Ernst. Pianist and violinist Gotha, 1818-79. Pupil of Hummel and Spohr. Concertmeister (1844), Capellmeister (1855), to the Court, Gotha.
Works : operas, chamber music, pf. pieces, &c.

LAMPER'TI, Francesco. Renowned teacher of singing ; *b.* Savona, 1813 ; *d.* 1892. Among his pupils were Albani, Mme. Artôt, the two Cruvellis, and Campanini.
Published several works on the Art of Singing.

Lam'po (*I.*). A flash of lightning.

Lampon (*F.*). A drinking song.

LAMPUGNA'NI, Giovanni Battista. *B.* Milan, 1706 ; *d.* abt. 1780. Conductor, Italian Opera, London, 1743 ; Maestro, "La Scala," Milan, 1779.
Wrote about 15 serious operas.

Lancashire Sol-fa.
A system of solmization by means of tetrachords (using only the names *mi, fa, sol, la*), formerly popular in Lancashire. The place of the leading-note was always indicated by the syllable *mi*. The scale of C, read upwards, was *fa, sol, la, fa, sol, la, mi, fa*.

LANCIA, Florence. Soprano vocalist; *b.* London, 1840. *Début*, Turin, 1858. Sang in the 1st series of Monday Popular Concerts, 1859. Retired 1874. *D.* 1907.

Lancers. (*F., Lanciers.*) A set of quadrilles.

Lan'cio (*I.*). Spring, enthusiasm, glow.

LAND, Dr. Jan P. N. Philologist ; *b.* Delft, 1834 ; *d.* 1897.
Wrote valuable works on "Arabic Music," &c.

Län'derer (G.). ⎫ A popular Styrian pea-
Länd'ler (G.). ⎭ sants' dance; a kind of
slow waltz in 3-8 or 3-4 time.
Lan'derisch. In the style of a rustic dance.
Länd'lich. Rural, pastoral.
Länd'lied. A rustic song.

LAN'DI, Camilla. Soprano; b. Geneva,1866.

LAN'DI, Stefano. Noted church composer;
pupil of Nanini ; b. Rome, abt. 1590 ;
d. abt. 1655. Singer in the Papal
Chapel, Rome, from 1629.
Works : a pastorale (*La Morte di Orfeo*), madrigals, masses, arias, &c.

Lan'du. A Portuguese dance in duple time.

Lan'dums. Portuguese music of a sentimental character.

Lang (G.). Long. (See **Lange Fermata**, and
Langsam.)

LANG, Benjamin Johnson. Distinguished
American musician ; b. Salem, Massachusetts,1837; d. 1909. Condr. "Handel
and Haydn Society," Boston, 1895. "As
a pianist, teacher, conductor, and
organizer, he has been in the first rank
of Boston's musicians for over a third
of a century."—*Baker.*
Works : oratorio (*David*), orch. music, pf. pieces,
songs, &c.

LANG, Josephine. (**Lang-Köstlin.**) Song
composer ; pupil of Mendelssohn ; b.
Munich, 1815 ; d. 1880.

LANG, Karl. Tenor ; b. Waiblingen, 1860.

LANG, Margaret R. Song composer ;
daughter of Benj. J. ; b. Boston, 1867.

LANG'DON, Richd. B. Exeter, abt. 1729 ;
d. 1803. Orgt. Exeter Cath., 1753-77 ;
Bristol Cath., 1777-81 ; Armagh Cath.,
1782-94. Mus.Bac. Oxon, 1761.
Works : "Divine Harmony" (a colln. of psalms
and anthems), 2 cantatas, 12 songs, 12 glees, &c.

LANG'E, Daniel de. 'Cellist, pianist, conductor, and critic ; b. Rotterdam, 1841.
Director, Amsterdam Cons., 1895.
Works : an opera, church music, cantatas, orch.
and chamber music, songs, &c.

LANG'E, Gustav F. B. nr. Erfurt, 1830 ; d.
1889.
Wrote over 400 graceful pf. pieces.

LANG'E, Mad. (*née* **Aloysia M. A. Weber**).
Soprano ; sister-in-law of Mozart ; b.
Mannheim, 1750 ; d. 1839.

LANG'E, Samuel de. Noted organist ;
brother of Daniel ; b. Rotterdam, 1840.
Teacher, Cologne Cons., 1876 ; Vice-
director, Stuttgart Cons., 1893.
Works : oratorio (*Moses*), a symphony, a pf.
concerto, some fine organ sonatas, &c.

Lang'e Ferma'ta (G.) ⎫
Lang'e Halt'en (G.) ⎬ A long hold or pause.
Lang'e Pau'se (G.) ⎭

LANG'ER, Ferdinand. 'Cellist ; b. nr.
Heidelberg, 1839.
Works : successful operas for the Mannheim Court
Theatre.

LANG'ER, Dr. Hermann. Organist and conductor ; b. nr. Tharandt, Saxony, 1819 ;

d. 1889. Mus.-director, Leipzig Univ.,
1857. Conductor for some years of the
"Euterpe" Concerts.
Published works on Choral Singing, &c.

LANG'ER, Victor. B. Pesth, 1842 ; d. 1902.
Works : numerous Hungarian songs, dances,
choruses, &c., which are very popular.

LANG'ERT, J. August (Adolf). B. Coburg,
1836. Capellmeister at various theatres;
afterwards Court Conductor, Gotha.
Works : several operas (*Die Fabier*, &c.).

Lang'es Schwei'gen (G.). A long silence.

LANG'HANS, Dr. F. Wilhelm. Violinist,
conductor, and writer ; b. Hamburg,
1832 ; d. 1892. Settled in Berlin, 1871.
Prof. of Hist., Kullak's Academy, 1874;
Scharwenka's Academy, 1881.
Wrote "A History of Music in the 17th, 18th, and
19th centuries" (a continuation of Ambros'
Hist.), "12 Lectures on Musical Hist.," &c.

LANGHANS, Frau F. W. (See **Luise Japha.**)

LANGLÉ, Honoré F. M. B. Monaco, 1741 ;
d. 1807. Librarian, Paris Cons.
Wrote a "Traité d'harmonie et de modulation,"
works on Fugue, Singing, Figured Bass, &c.

LANGLEY, Beatrice C. A. Violinist ; b.
Devonshire, 1872.

Lang'sam (G.) Slow ; *largo*.
Lang'samer. Slower.
Lang'samer wer'dend. Becoming slower.
Lang'sam und getra'gen. Slow and sustained.
Lang'sam und mit Aus'druck spiel'en. To be played
slowly and with expression.
Lang'sam und sehn'suchtsvoll. Slow and with intense
yearning.
Et'was lang'sam. Rather slow.
Sehr lang'sam. Very slow.

Language ⎫ Probably a corruption of *Lingua*
Languid ⎭ "a tongue." The partition
between the foot and body of an organ
flue pipe.

Languemen'te (I.) ⎫ In a languishing, plain-
Languen'do (I.) ⎬ tive style ; love-sick.
Languen'te (I.) ⎭

Languette (F.). "A little tongue." (1) The
tongue of a reed (org. or harm.). (2) A
key or valve of a wind instrument.

Languid. (See **Language.**)

Langui'do (I.). Faint, weak ; languishing.
Langui'do e ruba'to. Languidly and in *rubato* tempo.

Languo're (I.). Languor.
Con languo're
Languidamen'te ⎬ Languidly.
Langui'do ⎭

LANIÈRE (Lanier or Lanieri), Nicholas.
One of a French family of musicians
from Rouen ; Master of the King's
Musick under Chas. I and Chas. II.
B. London(?), 1588 ; d. 1666.
Said to have introduced *Recitative* into England
(in his *Masques*).

LAN'NER, Joseph F. K. Famous dance composer ; "created the modern Viennese
Waltz." B. nr. Vienna, 1801 ; d. 1843.
He was the leader of a quartet in which Johann
Strauss played the viola. The quartet developed into an orchestra, and Lanner (and afterwards Strauss) wrote for it the dance music
which soon became of world-wide popularity.

17

Lan'tum. A kind of large hurdy-gurdy.

LAPORTE, Jo;eph de. Jesuit writer ; *b.* Béfort, 1713 ; *d.* Paris, 1779.
Works : "Anecdotes dramatiques," "Dictionnaire dramatique," " Historic Calendar of French Operas," &c.

LARA, Adelina de (*nee* **Preston**). Concert pianist ; *b.* Carlisle, 1872.

LARA, Isidore de. (Real name **Cohen.**) *B.* London, 1860.
Works : 6 operas (*Amy Robsart, Sanga*), &c.

La pri'ma intenzio'ne (*I.*). The form of a composition as originally designed by the composer.

La pri'ma par'te sen'za repetizio'ne (*I.*)
La pri'ma par'te sen'za re'plica (*I.*)
The first part not to be repeated.

Largamen'te (*I.*)   Slowly, broadly.   (See
Largamen'to (*I.*)   **Largo**.)

Largan'do (*I.*). (Getting) slower and more impressive. (See **Largo**.)

Large. A note in mediæval notation equal in duration to two Longs. (See **Long**.)

Large (*F.*). Same as **Largo** (*q.v.*).

Largement (*F.*). Same as **Largamente** (*q.v.*).
Largement chanté. Sung with breadth.

Largeur (*F.*). Breadth.

Larghet'to (*I.*). Rather slow. Dim. of **Largo** (*q.v.*).

Larghez'za (*I.*). Breadth, fulness, stateliness. (See **Largo**.)
Con larghez'za. Slow, and with breadth, &c.

Larghis'simo (*I.*). Very slow. Superlative of **Largo**.

Lar'go (*I.*). Large, broad, stately, slow.
Lar'go andan'te. Slow and measured.
Lar'go assa'i. With due breadth and slowness ; deliberate(ly).
Lar'go di mol'to. Very slow.
Lar'go e me'sto. Slowly and sadly.
Lar'go ma non trop'po. Slow, but not too slow.
Po'co lar'go. Rather broad (but not necessarily slow).

Larigot (*F.*). (1) Old name for the flageolet. (2) An organ stop of 1⅓ ft. pitch.

Larin'ge (*I.*). The larynx (*q.v.*).

LARKCOM, C. Agnes. Contemporary soprano vocalist ; *b.* nr. Reading.

Larmoyant (*F.*). Weeping ; tearfully.

LAROCHE, Hermann A. Esteemed critic ; *b.* St. Petersburg, 1845.
Writer on Glinka, &c.

La RUE, Pierre de. (Known also as **Pierchon, Pierson, Pierzon, Perizone,** or **Pierazon de la Ruellien ;** Latin name, **Petrus Platensis.**) Distinguished Netherland Contrapuntist ; pupil of Okeghem. Chapel singer, Burgundy, 1492-1510.
Works : several fine masses ; motets, madrigals.

Laryng'oscope. An instrument with a reflecting mirror for examining the larynx ; invented by Garcia, 1854.

Larynx. The upper part of the trachea, or windpipe, containing the vocal cords.

La SALETTE, Joubert de. Brigadier-general ; Grenoble, 1762-1832.
Works : " A Consideration of the different systems of music, Ancient and Modern," " The Greek System of Notation," &c.

La secon'da par'te u'na vol'ta (*I.*). The 2nd part once only.

Lascia'te s(u)ona're (*I.*). Let (the note, drum, cymbals, &c.), vibrate (resound). and not be damped,

LAS'NER, Ignaz. Bohemian 'cellist ; *b.* 1815 ; *d.* Vienna, 1883.
Wrote some good 'cello music.

LAS'NER, Karl. Son of I. ; 'cellist ; *b.* Vienna, 1865.

LASSALLE, Jean. Baritone ; *b.* Lyons, 1847.

LAS'SEN, Eduard. *B.* Copenhagen, 1830. Studied Brussels Cons. ; 1st prize for pf., 1844 ; *Prix de Rome*, 1851. Court Capellmeister, Weimar (succeeding Liszt), 1861-95. *D.* 1904.
Works : operas (*Le Captif*, 1865, &c.) ; music to *Oedipus, Faust*, and other plays ; characteristic pieces, symphonies, and overtures for orches. ; cantatas (*Die Künstler*, &c.) ; many fine songs.

LAS'SO, Orlando di. (Latin, **Orlandus Lassus;** originally **Roland de Lattre.**) The greatest composer of the Netherland school ; after Palestrina, the greatest composer of the 16th cent. *B.* Mons, Hainault, 1532 ; *d.* Munich, 1594. It is said that while a choir boy at St. Nicholas Church, Mons, "he was thrice kidnapped on account of his beautiful voice." Accompanied Ferdinand de Gonzaga to Milan and Sicily; lived in Naples, Rome, &c.; Antwerp, 1554-7 ; entered the service of Duke Albert V, Munich, 1557, and was Court Capellmeister from 1562 until his death. His works are characterised by beautiful harmonies and great fluency of "melodic invention." His contemporaries styled him the "Belgian Orpheus."
His 2,500 compositions include 336 Latin motets (many in 12 parts), masses, passions, magnificats, madrigals, &c., and "The Penitential Psalms of David" (his most celebrated work).

His eldest son, **Ferdinand,** was Court Capellmeister at Munich, where he died, 1609. His second son, **Rudolf,** was an orgt. and composer ; *d.* 1625.

LA'SUS. Said to be the 1st Greek writer on the theory of music ; abt. 548 B.C.

LATIL'LA, Gaetano. Operatic composer ; *b.* Bari, 1713 ; *d.* Naples, 1789. Second Maestro, St. Mark's, Venice, 1762-72.
Wrote about 30 operas, including *Demofoonte* (1738) and *Orazio* (1738).

La TOMBELLE. (See **Tombelle**.)

LATROBE, Rev. C. I. *B.* Fulneck, 1758 ; *d.* 1836. Wrote anthems, hymns, &c.

LAUB, Ferdinand. Famous violinist ; *b.* Prague, 1832 ; *d.* 1875. Played in public at 11. Visited London, 1851 ; Concertmeister, Weimar, 1853 ; Leader Royal Orchestra, Berlin, 1856 ; Violin prof., Moscow Cons., 1866.
Works : an opera, solo pieces for vn., 2 collections of Czech melodies, &c.

Lau'd (*Spanish*). A lute (*q.v.*).

Lauda'mus Te. "We praise Thee." Part of the *Gloria* in a mass.

LAU'DA SI'ON. A Sequence sung at High Mass (Feast of Corpus Christi); set by Mendelssohn, 1846.

LAU'DI SPIRITUA'LI (*L.*). Specially, the canticles, hymns, &c., sung by the priests in the Oratory. (See **Oratorio.**)

Laudis'ti (*L.*). Psalm singers.

Lauds. (*L.*, *Lau'des.*) Hymns of praise.

Lauf (*G.*). The peg box of a guitar or vn. (2) A run, division, trill, or *roulade* in singing.

Läu'fer (*G.*). Plural of **Lauf** (2).

Lauf'tanz (*G.*). "A running dance." A courante (*q.v.*).

Lau'nenstück (*G.*). A voluntary.

Lau'nig (*G.*). Lightly, gaily ; *facile*, humorous.

LAURENCIN, Graf. Ferd. P. *B.* Moravia, 1819 ; *d.* 1890. Son of Archduke Rodolph.
Author of "A Hist. of Italian and German Church Music," "Schumann's *Paradise and the Peri*," "The Harmony of Modern Times," &c.

LAURENS, Edmond. Noted French composer ; *b.* Bergerac, 1851.
Works : opera (*La harpe et la glaive*), pf. pieces songs, &c.

LAURENT de RILLE, F. A. *B.* Orleans, 1828. Inspector of vocal music, Paris schools.
Works : operettas and male-voice choruses.

LAUREN'TI, B. G. Bologna, 1644-1726.
Early composer of chamber sonatas for vn. and 'cello, &c.

LAU'SKA, Franz S. I. Pianist and teacher ; *b.* Brünn, Moravia, 1764 ; *d.* 1825. Pupil of Albrechtsberger. Settled Berlin, 1798 ; teacher of Meyerbeer.
Works : a pf. method; pf. sonatas, 4-hand pieces, rondos, &c.

Laut (*G.*). (1) Loud, *forte*. (2) A sound.
Laut'heit. Sonorousness, loudness.
Laut'los. Soundless, mute.

Lau'te (*G.*). A lute (*q.v.*).
Laut'en-gei'ge. A viol (*q.v.*).
Laut'en-instrumente. Instruments whose strings are plucked.
Lautenist' } A lute player.
Laut'enspieler }
Laut'en-ma'cher. (See *Luthier*.)

Läu'ten (*G.*). To ring, to toll, to sound.

LAU'TERBACH, Joh. Christoph. Bavarian violinist ; *b.* 1832. Pupil of Fétis and de Bériot. Prof. Dresden Cons., 1860-77; Concertmeister, Dresden, 1860-89.
Works : concert pieces, &c., for vn.

LAVALLÈE, Calixa. Concert pianist ; *b.* Verchères, Canada, 1842 ; *d.* 1891. *Début* at 10.
Wrote 2 operas, an oratorio, orch. pieces, pf. études, &c.

LAVENU, Louis Hy. 'Cellist ; *b.* London, 1818 ; *d.* Sydney, 1859.
Works : an opera, songs, pf. pieces.

LAVI'GNA, Vincenzo. *B.* Naples, 1777 ; *d.* abt. 1837. Singing teacher, Milan Cons., 1823. Verdi was his pupil.
Works : 9 operas (*La Muta per amore*, 1802).

LAVIGNAC, A. J. Albert. *B.* Paris, 1846. Prof. of Harmony, Paris Cons.
Pub. a "Cours complet de dictée Musicale" (1882), which led to the adoption of "Musical Dictation" in all the great modern schools of music ; also a thoughtful work on "Music and Musicians " (1895), &c.

LAVIGNE, Jacques E. Operatic tenor ; Pau, 1782 ; 1855. Sang Paris Grand Opéra, 1809-25.
He was known as "l'Hercule du chant" on account of his powerful voice.

LAVOIX, Henri M. F. Paris, 1846-97. From 1865, librarian, National Library. Wrote a "Histoire de l'instrumentation," "Music in Nature," &c.

Lavol'ta (*I.*). An old Italian dance in triple time, characterized by "quick turns and high leaps."

Lavora're (*I.*). To work, to labour.

LAW, Andrew. The "pioneer singing teacher in New England."—*Baker.* *B.* Cheshire, Connecticut, 1748 ; *d.* 1821.
Works : Collections of hymn tunes, "Rudiments of Musick," &c.

LAWES, Henry. *B.* Dinton, nr. Salisbury, 1595 ; *d.* 1662. "Epistler" of the Chapel Royal, 1626; afterwards "gentleman" and "clerk of the cheque." Great friend of Milton, who addressed a sonnet to him.
Works : music to Milton's *Comus*, psalm tunes, songs, "Ayres and Dialogues," &c.

LAWES, Wm. Elder brother of H. ; *b.* Salisbury, 1582 ; killed, siege of Chester. 1645. Gentleman Chapel Royal, 1602.
Works : masques, "Ayres and Dialogues," "Consorts for viols," &c.

LAWROWSKA'JA (Lavrovska'ja), Eliz. A. (Princess **Zeretelev**). Distinguished Russian operatic soprano ; *b.* Kaschin, Tver, 1845. *Début*, 1867.

LAWSON, Malcolm L. Condr. and composer ; *b.* Wellington, Shropshire, 1849.

Lay. A song, a ditty, a ballad ; a tune.

Lay Clerk.
"A vocal officiate in a cathedral, who takes part in the services and anthems, but is not of the priesthood."

LAYOLLE (Layole, dell'Aiole, Ajolla), François. 16th cent. Florentine composer of masses, motets, madrigals, &c.

LAZARE, Martin. Pianist; Brussels, 1829-97.
Works : an opera, chamber music, pf. music (études, &c.).

LAZARUS, Henry. Fine clarinettist ; London, 1815-95. From 1840 to 1891 the leading English clarinet player.

LAZZA'RI, Sylvio. Composer ; *b.* Botzen, 1858.

Le (*F.* and *I.*). The.
Le pius léger possible (*F.*). As lightly as possible.
Le vo'ci (*I.*). The voices.

LEACH, Jas. *B.* nr. Rochdale, 1762; *d.* 1798. Hand-loom weaver; afterwards member of the King's band and tenor vocalist.
Wrote anthems and hymn tunes.

Lead. (1) The announcement of a theme, or subject, in any vocal or instrumental part (as in a fugue, &c.). (2) A cue.

Leader. (1) Conductor. (2) The principal 1st vn. of an orchestra. (3) The 1st cornet of a brass band. (4) The chief clarinettist of a military band. (5) The leading 1st soprano in a chorus.

Leading-note. (*G., Leit'ton ; F., Note sensible ; I., No'ta sensi'bile.*) The note a diatonic semitone below the tonic of any major or minor scale (**te** in the major scale ; **se** in the minor).
Pope John XXII issued a futile "ed.ct against the licentious use of the leading-note," 1322.

Leading theme. (See **Leitmotiv.**)

Leaning-note. An **appoggiatura** (*q.v.*).

Leaning-tones. In Tonic Sol-fa theory **t**, **r**, **f**, and **l** are the leaning tones of the scale ; **d**, **m**, and **s**, the *strong* tones; **te** and **fah** have the "most marked leaning tendency."

Leap. (1) A skip in melody. (2) Lifting the hand clear of the keyboard between two notes (or chords) in pf. playing.

Leathering. Fixing a strip of leather to the upper lip of an org. pipe to improve or modify its tone.

Le BÉ, Guillaume. Early French founder of music types.
His types of 1540 printed the notes and lines together ; those of 1555 printed them separately.

Le BEAU, Louise Adolpha. Pianist and composer ; *b.* Rastatt, Baden, 1850. Pf. pupil of Kalliwoda and Madame Schumann. Her concerts at Berlin, Leipzig, &c., have been very successful.
Works : chamber music, a choral work (*Hadumoth*), and several pf. pieces (including a very popular gavotte).

Le'ben (*G.*). (1) Life. (2) To live, to be alive.
Le'bend. Living; active, lively.
Le'bendig. Lively, animated; *Allegro.*

LE'BERT (properly **LEVY**), **Siegmund.** Pianist and teacher ; *b.* nr. Stuttgart, 1822 ; *d.* 1884. One of the founders of the Stuttgart Cons. (1856-7).
Works : a "Grosse Klavierschule" (Lebert and Stark), an "Instructive Edition" of classic pf. works, &c.

Le'bewohl (*G.*). Farewell !
BEETHOVEN, Op. 81 (a).
Adagio.

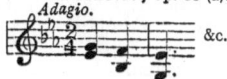
&c.
Le - be - wohl!

Leb'haft (*G.*). Lively, quick ; *vivace.*
Leb'haft, aber nicht zu sehr. Quick, but not too much so.
Leb'haft bewegt'. With lively animation.
Leb'haft doch gewich'tig. Quick, but with weight.
Leb'haft, doch nicht zu schnell. Lively, but not too fast.
Leb'hafter. More lively, quicker.
Leb'haftesten. Very quick.

Leb'haftigkeit. Liveliness, vivacity.
Leb'haft mit Stei'gerung. Lively and with exaltation.
Leb'haft rasch. Very quickly.
Mit Leb'haftigkeit und durchaus' mit Empfin'dung und Aus'druck. With animation, and throughout with feeling and expression.

LEBLANC, Georgette. *B.* Rouen, abt. 1873(?). *Début*, Paris, 1893.
Noted for her "song-recitals in costume."

LEBORNE (or **Le BORNE**). **Fernand.** *B.* Paris, 1862. Studied Paris Cons.
Works : pastoral drama (*Daphnis et Chloé*), symphonies, suites, chamber music, motets, &c.

LEBRUN, Louis S. Tenor singer ; Paris, 1764-1829.
Wrote the 1-act opera *Le Rossignol*, and 13 others.

LEBRUN, Ludwig A. Oboist; *b.* Mannheim, 1746 ; *d.* 1790. Visited London, 1781. He is said to have been "the greatest oboist of the 18th century."
Wrote 7 oboe concertos, 12 trios for oboe, vn., and 'cello, &c.

LEBRUN (*née* **Danzi**), **Franciska.** Wife of preceding ; *b.* Mannheim, 1756 ; *d.* 1791. Distinguished soprano singer.

Le CARPENTIER, Adolphe C. Pianist ; Paris, 1809-69.
Wrote a "Pf. method for Children," 2 collections of études, and some 300 fantasias, arrangements, &c.

LECLAIR, Jean M. Noted violinist ; *b.* Lyons, 1697 ; assassinated, Paris, 1764. Wrote an opera ; an opera ballet ; concertigrossi for 3 vns., viola, 'cello, and org.; numerous vn. trios, duos, &c. ; and 48 fine sonatas for vn. and basso-continuo.

LECOCQ, Alex. Charles. Renowned opera composer ; *b.* Paris, 1832. Studied Paris Cons., where he won several prizes. Chevalier of the Legion of Honour, 1894.
Works : about 40 comic operas, operettas, &c. The most popular are *Fleur-de-Thé* (1868), *La Fille de Madame Angot* (1872), and *Giroflé-Girofla* (1874).

Leçon (*F.*). A lesson, exercise, study.

Le COUPPEY, Felix. Paris, 1814-87. Teacher, pf. and harmony, Paris Cons.
Pub. several educational works and studies for pf.

LE'DERER, Georg. Tenor ; *b.* Marienburg, 1843.

LE'DERER, Victor. Contemporary songcomposer.

Ledger (or **Leger**) **lines.** Short lines drawn above or below the staff to increase its compass.
Ledger (or *Leger*) *space.* A space between ledger lines, or between the staff and a ledger-line.

LEDUC, Alphonse. Pianist and bassoonist ; *b.* Nantes, 1804 ; *d.* 1868. Founded a music business, Paris, 1841.
Works : 632 dances, 328 pf. pieces, 13 pieces for bassoon, 52 for guitar, 38 for flute, 94 vocal pieces, an "Elementary Pf. Method," &c.

LEE, Ernest Markham. *B.* Cambridge, 1874; Mus.Doc. Cantab., 1899.
Works : cantatas, part-songs, songs, &c.

LEE, George Alexander. London, 1802-51. Lessee and conductor of various London theatres.
Works : English operas and operettas, and numerous songs.

LEE, Louis. Fine 'cellist; *b*. Hamburg, 1819; *d*. 1896. 'Cello teacher at the Cons. and 1st 'cello Philharmonic Society.
Works : orch. music, chamber music, 'cello solos, pf. pieces, &c.

LEE, Maurice. Brother of L. ; *b*. Hamburg, 1821 ; *d*. London, 1895.
Composer of *salon* music for pf.

LEE, Sebastian. Brother of preceding ; Hamburg, 1805-87. Solo 'cellist, Grand Opéra, Paris, 1837-68.
Works : an excellent "Method for 'cello," 'cello music, &c.

Leeds Musical Festival. First given 1858; established 1874.

Leer (*G*.). Empty, hollow ; open.
Lee're Sai'ten. Open strings.

LEFÉBURE, Louis F. H. Paris, 1754-1840. Government official.
Works : 2 oratorios, cantatas, &c. ; and a "Nouveau Solfège."

LEFÉBURE-WÉLY, Louis J. A. Distinguished organist ; Paris, 1817-69. Played in public at 8. Took first prizes for pf. and org., Paris Cons., 1835. Orgt. La Madeleine Church, 1847-58 ; St. Sulpice, 1863.
In addition to much org. music, he wrote an opera, masses, symphonies, vocal music, pf. études, and numerous *salon* pf. pieces.

LEFEBVRE, Chas. E. *B*. Paris, 1843. *Grand Prix de Rome*, Paris Cons., 1870.
Works : operas, orchestral and chamber music.

LEFEBVRE (or **Le Febvre**), **Jacques.** (Jacobus Faber ; Stapulensis.) *B*. Etaples ; *d*. Nérac, 1537 (or 47).
Wrote "Elementa Musicalia," 1496.

LEFÈVRE, Jean X. Distinguished clarinettist ; *b*. Lausanne, 1763 ; *d*. 1829. Prof. Paris Cons., 1795-1825.
Added a 6th key to the clarinet ; wrote the clarinet method adopted at the Cons. (1802).

Leg. Abbn. of *Legato*.

Lega'bile ⎱ Tied, smooth, connected ; *Legato*.
Legan'do ⎰

Lega're (*I*.). To bind, to tie.

Lega'to (*I*.). Bound, smooth, connected, gliding ; opposed to *staccato* and indicated by a *slur* :—

Lega'to assa'i ⎱ Very legato ; exceedingly smooth and
Legatis'simo ⎰ connected.

Lega'to-bo'gen (*G*.). A legato mark, or slur.

Lega'to touch. Prolonging each note on the pf. its full and exact length so as to connect it with the next.

Legatu'ra (*I*.). A ligature (*q.v.*), tie, brace, or slur ; a syncopation.
Legatu'ra di vo'ce. Binding the voice ; singing several notes in one breath.

Légend, Légende (*F*.) ⎱ A piece in narra-
Légen'de (*G*.) ⎰ tive or romantic style.
Legen'denton, In romantic style. (See *Romantic Music*.)

Léger (*F*.) ⎱ Light, nimble, agile.
Légère (*F*.) ⎰
Légèrement (*F*.). (1) Lightly, nimbly, gracefully. (2) Slightly.
Très légèrement retenu (*F*.). Very slightly slackened (in speed).
Léger et animé (*F*.). Light and animated.
Légèreté (*F*.) ⎱ Agility, lightness, rapidity.
Leggerez'za (*I*.) ⎰
Leggeramen'te (*I*.). Lightly.
Leggeran'za (*I*.) ⎱ Lightness.
Leggerez'za (*I*.) ⎰

Leger lines. (See **Ledger Lines.**)

LEGGE, Robin H. Writer on Music ; *b*. nr. Liverpool, 1862.
Author of articles on Musicians in the Dict. of Nat. Biography, &c.

Leggen'da (*I*.). A legend.

Legge'ro (*I*.). Same as **Leggiero** (*q.v.*).

Leggia'dro (*I*.). Handsome, beautiful, graceful ; nice, agreeable.
Leggiadramen'te. Gracefully, charmingly.
Leggiadret'to. Graceful, agreeable.

Leggie'ro (*I*.). Light, swift, delicate, easy.
Leggieramen'ie. ⎱
Leggiermen'te. ⎬ Lightly, swiftly, easily, delicately.
Leggie're. ⎭
Leggieres'za,Con
Leggieris'simo. Very lightly, &c.
Leggie'ro con moto. Lightly and swiftly.
Leggieruco'lo. Rather light and swift.

Leg'gio (*I*.). A music stand, desk, &c.

LEGIN'SKA, Ethel (Ethel Liggins ; Mrs. Whithorne). Pianist ; *b*. Hull, 1886.

Le'gno (*I*.). Wood.
Col le'gno. "With the wood." A direction in vn. playing to strike the strings with the back of the bow.
Le'gni. Plur. of *Le'gno.* The wood-wind insts.

LEGREN'ZI, Giovanni. Noteworthy composer ; *b*. nr. Bergamo, abt. 1625 ; *d*. Venice, 1690. Maestro, St. Mark's, Venice, 1685.
Works : 18 operas ; motets, concerti (for voices and insts.), cantatas, sonatas, &c.

LEHAR, Franz. *B*. Komorn, Hungary,1870.
Works : several operas (*Merry Widow*, &c.).

LEH'MANN, George. Violinist, teacher, and critic ; *b*. New York, 1865. Studied Leipzig and Berlin.
Works : "True Principles of the Art of Violin Playing," &c.

LEH'MANN, Lilli. Operatic soprano ; *b*. Würzburg, 1848. Took principal parts at the first Wagner Festival, Bayreuth, 1876. First sang in London, 1880.

LEH'MANN, Liza (Mrs. Herbert Bedford). *B*. London, 1862.
Composer of songs and song-cycles ; " In a Persian Garden " is perhaps her best work.

LEH'MANN, Mrs. R. (" A. L.") (*née* Amelia Chambers). Composer ; mother of preceding.

Leh're (*G*.). System of instruction ; text book ; model.

Leh'rer (*G*.). (*Fem.*, *Leh'rerin*.) A teacher, master.

Leich (*G*.). (1) A lay. (2) A funeral.
Lei'chengesang. A dirge, elegy.
Lei'chenmusik. Funeral music.
Lei'chenton, A mournful, lugubrious sound.

Leicht (*G.*). Light, easy, brisk; slight.
Leicht beschwingt'. Slightly quickened.
Leicht bewe'glich }
Leicht bewegt' } Somewhat animated.
Leicht'fertig. Light, careless, playful.
Leicht gestos'sen. Lightly detached.
Leicht'heit }
Leicht'igkeit } Lightness, facility.
Leicht lich. Lightly, easily.
Leicht schwe'bend. Lightly gliding.
Leicht und luf'tig. Light and airy.
Leicht und zart. Light and delicate.

Lei'denschaft (*G.*). Fervency, passion, intense feeling, rage.
Lei'denschaftlich. Passionately, &c.
Lei'denschaftlich bewegt'. Passionately animated.
Mit lei'denschaftlichen Vor'trag. With fervent, passionate expression.

Lei'er (*G.*). A Lyre, hurdy-gurdy, hackneyed tune, old song.
Lei'erkasten }
Lei'erorgel } A hand organ.
Lei'erspieler. Lyre player.

LEIGHTON, Sir Wm. "Gentleman pensioner."
    Pub. "The Teares or Lamentacions of a Sorrowfull Soule; composed with Musicall Ayres and Songs both for Voyces and Divers Instruments" (1614).

Lei'ne (*G.*). A line of the staff.

Lei'se (*G.*). Low, soft, light, gentle.
Lei'se bewegt'. Gently animated.
Lei'se und sehr egal' zu spiel'en. To be played lightly and very evenly.
Leise, wie für Sich. Sotto voce; softly, as if to oneself.

LEI'SINGER, Elizabeth. Operatic soprano; *b.* Stuttgart, 1864. Member Berlin Court Opera since 1884.

Leis'tung (*G.*). Performance, rendering.

Leit'akkord (*G.*). A leading or guiding chord; especially the chord of the Dominant 7th.

Lei'ten (*G.*). To lead, guide.

Lei'ter (*G.*). A leader, guide, &c.; a ladder; a scale.
Lei'tereigene Akkor'de. The diatonic chords proper to any scale or key.
Lei'terfremd. Foreign to the scale.
Ton'leiter. A scale.

LEI'TERT, Johann Georg. Pianist; *b.* Dresden, 1852. *Début,* 1865; successful tour in England, 1867. Afterwards studied under Liszt. *D.* 1901.
    Works: numerous characteristic pieces for pf.

Leit'motif' (*G.*) } (pron. *Light'-moteef'*). A
Leit'motiv' (*G.*) } "leading theme." A typical theme, figure, or motive, recurring repeatedly throughout a work, and representative of some person, action, mood, or sentiment.
    A *Leitmotiv* may consist of 2 or 3 notes, or it may be an extended theme. It may be repeated without variation; or it may be developed, transformed—*metamorphosed*—in every possible way that ingenuity can devise! (See *Thematic Development.*)
    Although "Leading themes" were used before the time of Wagner (as in Weber's *Der Freischütz,* or the *Idée fixe* of Berlioz's *Symphonie Fantastique*), he used them so characteristically and consistently that it is with his name that they are chiefly associated. "In fact, any suggestions Wagner may have received from other composers were so slight that the leading-motive in the modern sense may unhesitatingly be said to be his invention."
    A *Leitmotiv* must not be regarded either as a mere label to be crudely displayed whenever the person, action, &c., which it typifies is referred to; nor as a piece of vulgar word-painting. (Hence the failure of so many would-be imitators of Wagner!)
    It should be a "suggestion" of quality, character, mood, &c., and rarely a realistic imitation. (See *Imitative Music.*)
    With Wagner "a leading-motive is a musical searchlight or X-ray which illuminates and enables us to look deep into every character, thought, mood, purpose, idea, and impulse in the drama."—*G. Kobbé.*
    Compare the yearning, fascinating "Love-potion" theme with which *Tristan und Isolde* opens (and which forms the key of the whole work)—

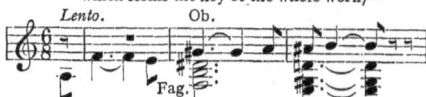

pp 'Cello.
with the "Death-motive,"

or with the dignified melody typifying *Siegfried* as "mature hero" in the *Ring*:—

(The first appearance of this "Hero-Siegfried" theme occurs in *Die Walküre.*)

and the "matured" theme, above, is an easily intelligible example of the "metamorphosis" of a *Leitmotiv.*)
    Since the time of Wagner almost every prominent composer has availed himself of the *Leitmotiv* as a valuable means of *Musical Characterization.*

Leit'ton (*G.*). Leading-note (*q.v.*).

Le JEUNE, Claudin. French contrapuntist; *b.* Valenciennes, abt. 1530; *d.* abt. 1600.
    Works: "40 Psalms of David," 1601; &c.

LEKEU, Guillaume. Composer of great promise; *b.* nr. Verviers, 1870; *d.* 1894.
    Works: Lyric poem (*Andromeda*); symphonic studies, and other orchestral works, &c.

LELY, Durward. (See Lyall.)

LEMAIRE (or **Le MAIRE**). French musician; 16th-17th cents.
    Said to have suggested the name "*si*" or "*za*" for the 7th note of the scale,

LEMAIRE, Théophile. French singing teacher ; *b.* 1820.
Author of "Le principes et l'histoire du chant."

Le MAISTRE (or Le MAÎTRE), Mattheus. Netherland contrapuntist ; *d.* 1577.
Works : masses, motets, magnificats, &c.

LEMARE, Edwin H. Distinguished orgt. ; *b.* Ventnor, 1865.
Works : several fine organ pieces.

LEMARE, William. *B.* Godalming, 1839. Mus.Doc. Cantuar, 1888.
Works : operettas, anthems, songs, &c.

LEM'MENS, Jacques Nicolas. Celebrated organist ; *b.* Zoerle-Parwys, Belgium, 1823 ; *d.* 1881. Prof. of Org., Brussels Cons., 1849 ; married Miss Sherrington, 1857.
Works : an "Ecole d'orgue" (adopted Paris Cons.), about 60 org. compositions, pf. pieces, songs.

LEM'MENS-SHER'RINGTON. (See **Sherrington.**)

LEMMONÉ, John. Flautist and composer ; *b.* Ballarat, Australia, 1862.

LEMOINE, Antoine M. Guitar player ; Paris, 1763-1817.
Founded the music pub. business known by his name.

LEMOINE, Henri. Son of preceding ; Paris, 1786-1854. Pianist ; pupil Paris Cons., Succeeded to his father's business, 1817.
Works : Methods for pf., harmony, and solfeggio ; pf. pieces, &c.

LEMOINE, Mad. (See **L. Puget.**)

LEMOYNE (or MOYNE), Jean B. *B.* Périgord, 1751 ; *d.* 1796.
Wrote several successful operas (*Nepthé*, Grand Opéra, Paris, 1789 ; &c.).

LENAERTS, Constant. *B.* Antwerp, 1852. Pupil of Benoît.
Director, Flemish Nat. Th. at 18. Afterwards teacher, Antwerp Cons.

LENEPVEU, Chas. F. *B.* Rouen, 1840. Won *Grand Prix de Rome*, Paris Cons., 1865 ; Harmony prof., 1891.
Works : operas, *Le Florentine* (Opéra-Comique, 1874), *Velleda* (Covent Garden, London, 1882) ; lyric drama (*Jeanne d'Arc*) ; a requiem, odes.

Lenez'za. (See **Leno.**)

LENGYEL von BAGOTA, Ernst. Highly-gifted pianist ; *b.* Vienna, 1893.
Début at 5 ; 1st London appearance 1907.

Le'no (*I.*). Weak, feeble, dull, faint.
Con lenez'za. In a quiet, gentle style.

Lent, Lente (*F.*) }
Len'to (*I.*) } Slow.
Lentamen'te (*I.*). Slowly, gently.
Lentan'do (*I*). Slower by degrees ; *rallentando.*
Len'te (*I.*). Slow.
Lentement (*F.*) } Slowly.
Lentemen'te (*I.*) }
Avec lenteur (*F.*) } "With slowness ;" slowly, de-
Con lentez'za (*I.*) } liberately.
Len'to assa'i (*I.*) }
Len'to di mol'to (*I.*) }
Lentis'simo (*I.*) } Very slow.
Len'to len'to }
Tres lentement (*F.*) }

LENZ, Wilhelm von. *B.* Russia, 1804 ; *d.* 1883. Pianist ; pupil of Liszt and Chopin. Russian Councillor, St. Petersburg.
Works : "Beethoven and his three styles" (2 vols.) ; "Beethoven : an art study" (5 vols.) ; "The great pianoforte virtuosi of our Epoch" (sketches of Liszt, Chopin, &c.). These are all standard works.

LE'O, Leonardo. Eminent composer ; *b.* nr. Brindisi, 1694 ; *d.* Naples, 1746. Pupil of A. Scarlatti. Prof. Cons. La Pieta di Turchini, Naples, 1716 ; Orgt. Royal Chapel, 1716. Capellmeister Santa Maria della Solitaria, and Prof. San Onofrio Cons., 1717. Among his pupils were Pergolesi, Jommelli, Piccinni, and Sacchini.
Works : 4 oratorios, nearly 60 operas (*Sofonisbe*, Naples, 1718 the first), much church music (including a celebrated 8-part *Miserere* for double choir), organ fugues, 'cello concertos, clavichord toccatas, &c.

LÉONARD, Hubert. Distinguished violinist; *b.* nr. Liége, 1819 ; *d.* Paris, 1890. Chief vn. prof. Brussels Cons., 1848-67.
Works : a vn. method ; 5 vn. concertos, a serenade for 3 vns., pieces for vn. and pf., numerous technical vn. studies, &c.

LEONCAVAL'LO, Ruggiero. Pianist and renowned dramatic composer ; *b.* Naples, 1858.
His operas include *I Pagliacci* (1892, his one success), and *Tommaso Chatterton* (revised 1896). He has also written orchestral music and several songs.

LE'ONHARD, Julius E. *B.* Laubau, 1810 ; *d.* 1883. Pf. professor, Munich Cons., 1852 ; Dresden Cons., 1859.
Works : an oratorio, cantatas, a symphony, chamber music, &c.

LEO'NI, Carlo. Contemporary Italian composer of operas : *Urbano* (1896), &c.

LEO'NI, Franco. Composer ; *b.* Milan, 1864.
Works : *Rip van Winkle* (1897), *L'Oracolo* (1906).

LEO'NI, Leone. Maestro Vicenza Cath.
Pub. madrigals, motets, psalms, &c., 1588-1623.

LÉONORE (Leono'ra). The original name of Beethoven's opera *Fidelio.*

LEONO'WA (Leono'va), Dapya Mikailovna. Dramatic contralto ; *b.* Tver, 1825 ; *d.* 1896. Studied 5 years with Glinka. *Début* at 18 in *A life for the Czar.*

LEROUX, Xavier H. N. *B.* Papal States, 1863. *Grand Prix de Rome*, Paris Cons., 1885.
His dramatic works include the 5-act opera *Cléopâtre* (1890), *Le Chemineau* (1908), &c.

Les (*F.*). "The" (plural).
Les pp. doivent être pris brusquement. The *pp.* should be taken suddenly.

LESCHETITZ'KY, Theodor. Famous pf. teacher ; *b.* Langert, Austrian Poland, 1830. Began teaching in his 15th year. Teacher St. Petersburg Cons., 1852-78. Married Annette Essipoff, 1880, and settled in Vienna as teacher ; afterwards removing to Wiesbaden. His most famous pupil is **Paderewski.**
Works : an opera, and some pf. pieces.

LESLIE, Fred. (Real name **Hobson**.) Baritone singer and burlesque actor ; *b.* Woolwich, 1855 ; *d.* 1897(?).

LESLIE, Henry David. *B.* London, 1822 ; *d.* 1896. Organized "Leslie's Choir" (1855) which won the 1st prize, Paris International Exhibition, 1878.
Works : effective part-songs (*The Lullaby of Life,* &c.) ; also cantatas, 2 oratorios, &c.

Lesser. Old term for Minor.
Lesser Third. Minor 3rd.
Lesser Sixth. Minor 6th.
Lesser appog'giatu'ra. Short appoggiatura.

LESS'MANN, W. J. Otto. Musical critic ; *b.* Rüdersdorf, nr. Berlin, 1844. Since 1882, proprietor and editor of the *Allgem. Musik-Zeitung.*
Works : several songs, &c.

Lesson (*F., Leçon*). (1) An exercise or study. (2) Any movement in old music for the harpsichord, lute, &c.
In Bunyan's *Pilgrim's Progress,* Christiana played "a lesson" on the viol.

Less Mode. Minor mode.

Le'sto (*I.*). Light, gay, cheerful, quick.
Lestamen'te. Quickly.
Lestis'simo.
Le'sto le'sto } Very quick.

Le SUEUR (or LESUEUR), Jean Francois. *B.* nr. Abbéville, 1764(0?); *d.* Paris, 1837; Maitre de musique at various cathedrals. Maitre de Chapelle, Notre Dame, Paris, 1786. Inspector at the Cons., 1795 ; dismissed 1802 ; spent 2 years in poverty ; Maitre de Chapelle to Napoleon, 1804 ; superintendent and composer, Chapelle du Roi, 1814-30. As a composer he is regarded as the "precursor of Berlioz."
Works : operas, *La Caverne, Paul et Virginie, Télémaque,* and 5 others ; several oratorios, much church music, &c. ; also numerous theoretical works.

L'été (*F.*). A movement in a quadrille.

Letter-name. The alphabetical name of a note (A, B, &c.), as opposed to its Sol-fa name (*lah, te,* &c.).

Letter-note Notation. (See **Notation.**)

Leu'to (*I.*). A lute.

LE'VA, Enrico de. Pianist and composer ; *b.* Naples, 1867.

Leva're (*I.*). To raise, lift, remove.
Leva'te i ma'ni. Lift the hands.
Leva'te i sordi'ni. Take off the mutes.

LEVASSEUR, Jean H. 'Cellist; *b.* Paris, 1765 ; *d.* 1823. Prof. of 'cello, Paris Cons. ; "co-editor" of the 'cello method used there. Wrote sonatas, études, &c., for 'cello.

LEVASSEUR, Nicholas Prosper. Fine operatic bass ; *b.* Picardy, 1781. Studied Paris Cons. ; *début,* Grand Opéra, 1813; sang in London, 1816. Sang, Paris Opéra, in leading *rôles,* 1828-45.

Levé (*F.*). " Raised." The up beat.

LEVERIDGE, Rd. Bass singer ; *b.* 1670 ; *d.* London, 1758.
Wrote stage pieces, and several songs ("All in the Downs," "The Roast Beef of old England," &c.).

LEVEY, Wm. Chas. *B.* Dublin, 1837 ; *d.* London, 1894. Conductor, Haymarket, Covent Garden, &c.
Works : several operas and operettas (*Fanchet.e,* 1864), pantomimes, pf. pieces, songs.

Levez (*F.*). Raise, take off.
Levez les mains. Lift the hands.
Levez les sourdines. Take off the mutes.

Levez'za (*I.*). Lightness.

LEVI, Hermann. Conductor ; *b.* Giessen, 1839; *d.* 1900. Cond. German Opera, Rotterdam, 1861-4. Court Capellmeister, Carlsruhe, 1864-72 ; Munich, 1872-96.

LEVI, LEVY, or LEWY. (See **Lebert.**)

LEWANDOW'SKI, Louis. *B.* Wreschen, Posen, 1823 ; *d.* 1894. Mus.-director, Berlin Synagogue from 1840.
Co-founder and active supporter of the "Institute for Aged and Indigent Musicians."

LEWIS, Chas. Hutchins. Composer ; *b.* London, 1853.

LEWIS, Jas. H. Composer and writer ; *b.* Gt. Malvern, 1856.

LEWY, Chas. Pianist ; *b.* Lausanne, 1823 ; *d.* 1883. Wrote *salon* pf. pieces.

LEWY, Richard. Brother of C. ; Vienna, 1827-83. Singing teacher.
Madame Sembrich was one of his pupils.

LEWYS, Dyved. (**David Lewis.**) Tenor singer ; *b.* Llanerwys, Carmarthen, 1865.

LEY'BACH, Ignace X. J. Pianist ; *b.* Alsace, 1817 ; *d.* 1891. Pupil of Kalkbrenner and Chopin. Orgt. Toulouse Cath., 1840.
Works : an organ method, songs, &c. ; and numerous "easy, pretentious, and pleasing" pf. pieces.

Ley'er (*G.*). Old spelling of **Leier** (*q.v.*).

Leziosamen'te (*I.*). Affectedly.

Lezzio'ni (*I.*). Lessons.

L'HOMME ARMÉ. An old French Chanson often used as the theme of scientific masses by 15th and 16th cent. composers.

LI'ADOFF (or LIADOW), Anatole. *B.* St. Petersburg, 1855. Prof. of Harmony, St. Petersburg Cons., 1878.
Works : original and elegant pf. pieces.

Liaison (*F.*). (1) A bind or tie. (2) A syncopation. (3) A slur.
Liaison de chant. The *sostenuto* style of singing.

LIA'PUNOV (or NOW), Serge M. *B.* Jaroslavl, 1859. Studied Moscow Cons. Sub-director, Imperial Choir, St. Petersburg.
Works : pf. pieces, a "Collection of Russian Folk-songs," &c.

LIBE'LIUS. (See **Sibelius.**)

Liberamen'te (*I.*). **Librement** (*F.*) Freely.
Librement déclamé (*F.*). Freely declaimed; not in strict time.

Libertà (*I.*). Liberty, freedom.
Con libertà. Freely.

Lib'itum (*L.*). Pleasure.
Ad libitum (*ad lib.*). At pleasure.

Libret'to (*G., Text'buch; F., Livret.*) The book of words of an opera, oratorio, &c.
Libret'tist. The writer or compiler of the words.

Licence (*G., Frei'heit; F., Licence.*) }
Licen'za (*I.*) } A disregard of some rule of harmony, &c.
"As the greatest part of the rules of harmony are founded on arbitrary principles, what is a licence at one time is not so at another."—*Rousseau.*
Con alcu'na licen'za. With some freedom.

Lice'o (*I.*). Academy, lyceum.

Lich'anos (*Gk.*). One of the strings of the Greek Lyre. (See **Greek Music.**)

LICH'TENBERG, Leopold. Concert violinist; *b.* San Francisco, 1861. Played in public at 8 ; pupil of Wieniawski at 12, and later studied under him at Brussels. After successful tours, was appointed head of the vn. department, New York National Cons.

LICH'TENSTEIN, Karl A., Freiherr **von.** *B.* Franconia, 1767 ; *d.* 1845. Intendant of Court Theatres at Dessau (1798). Vienna (1800), Bamberg (1811), and Berlin (1823).
Works : 11 operas and numerous vaudevilles.

LICH'TENTHAL, Peter. *B.* Pressburg, 1780; *d.* 1853. Settled in Milan, 1810.
Works : operas and ballets, pf. pieces ; a "Dictionary and Bibliography of Music" (4 vols.), treatises on "The Healing Power of Music," &c.

LIDDELL, Mrs. A. L. Emily Shinner (*q.v.*).

LIDDLE, Robt. W. *B.* Durham, 1864. Orgt. Southwell Cath. since 1888.

LIDDLE, Samuel. Pianist and song composer ; *b.* Leeds, abt. 1868. Studied R.C.M.
Most popular song, "Abide with me" (written for Madame Clara Butt).

Lié (*F.*). Tied, syncopated ; *Legato.*
Lié coulant. Flowing, slurred.

LIE (pron. *Lee*). **Erica.** (Madame **Nissen.**) Pianist and teacher ; *b.* nr. Christiania, 1845; *d.* 1903.

LIE'BAU, Julius. Tenor-buffo ; *b.* Lundenburg, 1857.

LIE'BAU-GLO'BIG, Helene. Soprano ; *b.* Berlin, 1866.

Lie'be (*G.*). Dear, beloved, valued, good.
Lie'besflöte. (See *Flöte d'amour.*)
Lie'beslied. A love song.
Lie'bevoll. Very lovingly, "full of love."

LIE'BICH, Ernst J. G. Noted violin maker ; Breslau, 1830-84.

LIE'BIG, Karl. Oboist ; *b.* Schweldt, 1808 ; *d.* 1872.
Founded a famous orchestra, the Berlin "Symphoniekapelle," 1843.

Lieb'lich (*G.*). Lovely, sweet, charming.
Lieb'lich Gedackt. Sweet-toned stopped diapason.
Lieb'lich Geschallt'. A very small-scaled Echo Lieblich Gedackt.

LIEB'LING, Emil. Concert pianist ; *b.* Silesia, 1851. Settled in America, 1867.
Works : pf. pieces, songs, &c.

LIEB'LING, Georg L. *B.* Berlin, 1865. Court pianist to the Duke of Coburg 1890
Works : pf. pieces, the "Lieblingswalzer" (often sung by Nikita), &c.

Lied (*G.*) (plur. *Lie'der*). A song ; a song-like composition ; a lyric, a ballad.
Durch'komponier'tes Lied. "Through-composed song." A song with different music for each verse (stanza).
Geist'liches Lied. Psalm, hymn.
Lied'chen. A little song, or melody.
Lie'derabend. "A song evening;" a song recital by one singer.
Lie'derartig. In ballad style.
Lie'derbuch. A book of songs; a hymn-book.
Lie'derbund. A society of song singers.
Lie'dercyclus } A cycle (or circle) of songs.
Lie'derkreis }
Lie'derkranz. (1) A glee club. (2) A choral society. (3) A set of songs.
Lie'der ohl'ne Wor'te. Songs without words.
Lie'dersammlung. A collection of songs.
Lie'dersänger. Song singer, ballad singer.
Lie'derspiel. A "song play." An operetta including popular songs, a ballad opera.
Lie'dertafel. A (male) singing society.
Lie'dertanz. A dance combined with songs.
Lied'form. Song-form (*q.v.*) ; ballad-form.
Kunst'lied. An "art" song (as opposed to the *Volks'lied*).
Stro'phenlied. A ballad (a song with the same melody for each stanza).
Volks'lied. A folk-song, a people's song.
Volks't(h)ümliches Lied. (See under *V.*)

Lie'gend (*G.*). Lying, horizontal.
Lie'gender Bo'gen. Legato bowing, with the bow "lying well on the strings."

Lier (*Dutch*). A lyre.

Lie'to (*I.*). Blithe, joyous, merry.

Lie've (*I.*). Light, easy.
Con lievez'za } Lightly, delicately, softly.
Lievemen'te }

Liga'to (*I.*). Same as **Legato** (*q.v.*).

Lig'ature. (*G., Ligatur'; F., Ligature ; I., Ligatu'ra.*) (1) A tie, or bind.
(2) See **Notation.**

Ligne (*F.*). A staff line.
Ligne additionelle
Ligne ajoutée } A leger line.
Ligne postiche
Ligne supplémentaire

LI'LIENCRON, Rochus, Freiherr **von.** Noted writer on music ; *b.* Plön, Holstein, 1820. *D.*{190-(?).
Chief works : "German Folk-songs of the Middle Ages" (4 vols.), "Select Folk-songs of the 16th cent. with Melodies," works on church and concert music, &c.

Lilliburle'ro. A jingle of rhymes with tune from Purcell which "contributed not a little towards the Great Revolution of 1688."

LIL'LO, Giuseppe. *B.* Galatina, Italy, 1814; *d.* 1863. Studied under Zingarelli, Naples Cons. ; Prof., 1859.
Works : symphonies, pf. music, &c. ; and 16 operas (*L'osteria d'Andujar*, 1840, being the best).

Lilt. A lively tune, a lay, a song ; to sing or play merrily. The "spring," "go," "pulsation," "rhythmic swing," of a poem or tune.

LIM'BERT, Frank L. Condr. and composer; *b.* New York, 1866; lived in Germany since 1874.

Lim′ma (*Gk.*). A to B♭ in old Greek systems. (See **Interval**, Table II.)

LIMPUS, Rd. D. *B.* 1824 ; *d.* 1875. One of the founders of the Coll. of Organists ; was first secretary, 1864-75.

LIN′CKE, Joseph. *B.* Trachenberg, Silesia, 1783 ; *d.* Vienna, 1837. 'Cellist in the famous quartet of Prince Rasoumowsky which played Beethoven's works under "the great composer's own supervision." Beethoven was very fond of Lincke and wrote a comic canon embodying his name.

LINCOLN, Henry J. Lecturer and writer ; *b.* London, 1814 ; Mus. critic, *Daily News*, 1866-86. *D.* 1901.

LIND, Jenny. "The Swedish Nightingale." *B.* Stockholm, Oct. 6, 1820 ; *d.* Wynds Point, Malvern Wells, Nov. 2, 1887. Marvellous soprano ; gave indications of a wonderful voice at the age of 2. *Début*, Stockholm Court Theatre as "Agathe" in Weber's *Der Freischütz*, 1838. Studied under Manuel Garcia, Paris, 1841. Sang in Berlin "with great applause," 1844 ; and made a "triumphant progress" through Hamburg, Cologne, Coblenz, Copenhagen, Leipzig, and Vienna. London *début* as "Alice" in Meyerbeer's *Robert*, Her Majesty's Theatre, 1847. Her success was probably unprecedented ; she at once became, and remained until her retirement, "a public idol." Left the operatic for the concert stage, 1849. Toured the United States, 1850-2. Married Otto Goldschmidt, Boston, 1852. Returned to London,1856. Last public performance, Düsseldorf, 1870. Led the Bach Choir in London.

Her voice, from

soprano of bright, thrilling, and remarkably sympathetic quality ; her private life was as admirable as her public repute."

LIND′BLAD, Adolf F. *B.* nr. Stockholm, 1801 ; *d.* 1878. Works : an opera, a symphony, &c.; and numerous fine songs with national Swedish colour, which were popularised by Jenny Lind (his pupil). He is called "The Schubert of the North."

LIN′DEN, Karl van der. Noted bandmaster and conductor ; *b.* Dordrecht, 1839. Works : cantatas and numerous songs.

LIND′LEY, Robert. 'Cellist ; *b.* Rotherham, 1776 ; *d.* London, 1855. Principal 'cellist at the Opera and at all the chief musical festivals, 1794-1851. Published 'cello music, songs, &c.

LIND′NER, Ernst O. T. Editor and writer ; *b.* Breslau, 1820 ; *d.* 1867. Wrote treatises on Meyerbeer, German Lieder, &c.

LIND′PAINTNER, Peter Joseph von. *B.* Coblenz, 1791 ; *d.* 1856. Capellmeister, Stuttgart, from 1819. Works : 21 operas (*Der Vampyr, Lichtenstein,* &c.) ; ballets, melodramas, 2 oratorios, masses, orches. music, songs, &c,

LINDSAY, Miss M. (Mrs. J. Worthington Bliss.) Writer of trivial once-popular songs. "The Bridge" and "Excelsior" are still sung.

Li′nea (*I.*)   }
Li′nie (*G.*)   } A line.
Li′niensystem (*G.*)   The staff of five lines.

Linez′za. Same as **Lenezza** (See **Leno**).

Lin′gua (*L.* and *I.*). "Tongue." The tongue of an organ reed-pipe. *Linguet′ta* (*I.*). A small reed (tongue).

Lingual′pfeife (*G.*) A reed-pipe.

Lin′gula (*L.*). The Glottis (*q.v.*).

Link, Links (*G.*). Left. *Lin′ke Hand.* Left hand. Abbreviation—L.H.

LINLEY, Eliza Ann. Daughter of Thomas (sen.). Soprano ; the famous "Maid of Bath." *B.* Bath, 1754 ; *d.* 1792. Married Sheridan, 1773.

LINLEY, George. Poet and composer ; *b.* Leeds, 1798 ; *d.* 1865. Works : operas and operettas (*La Poupée de Nuremberg,* Covent Garden, 1861, &c.), part-songs, hymns, songs.

LINLEY, Thomas (Senr.). *B.* Bath, 1725 (32?); *d.* 1795. Works : songs and ballads, madrigals, &c. ; and several English operas produced at Drury Lane.

LINLEY, Thos. (Junr.). Son of preceding ; *b.* Bath, 1756 ; *d.* 1778. Wrote an oratorio (*The Song of Moses*), music to *The Tempest*, &c.

Li′nos (*Gk.*). (1) A rustic air. (2) A dirge.

LIN′TERMANS. Renowned singing teacher; *b.* Brussels, 1808 ; *d.* 1895.

LIPIN′SKI, Karl Joseph. Distinguished violinist ; *b.* Radzyn, Poland, 1790 ; *d.* 1861. Concertmeister, Dresden, 1839-59. Works : 4 vn. concertos, vn. solos, a collection of Galician folk-songs, &c.

Lip′pe (*G.*). Lip. *Lip′penpfeife.* A flue pipe.

LIP′SIUS, Marie. (Pen-name, **"La Mara."**) Writer ; *b.* Leipzig, 1837. Works : "Musikalische Studienköpfe" (5 vols.), a German transl. of Liszt's "Chopin," writings on Wagner, the Bayreuth Festival (1877), &c.

Lip, To } (*G., An′satz ; F., Embouchure ;*
Lipping } *I., Imboccatu′ra.*). The art of adjusting the lips in playing a wind instrument.

Lips. The flat places above and below the mouth of an organ flue pipe.

Li′ra (*I.*). A lyre. N.B.—The ancient lyre was a harp-like inst. [See *Lyre.*] The mediæval *lira* was a kind of viol played with a bow. *Li′ra Barberi′ni.* A small lyre named after Cardinal Barberini. *Li′ra da brac′cio.* A kind of tenor violin (or viola) with 7 strings. *Li′ra dop′pia.* A double lyre. *Li′ra da gamba.* A kind of 'cello with from 12 to 16 strings. *Li′ra tede′sca.* A hurdy-gurdy.

Lire (*F.*). A lyre or harp.

Lires′sa (*I.*). A lyre or harp of inferior quality.

Li'rico,-a (*I.*). Lyrical, lyric.

Liro'ne (*I.*). A large bass lyre. (See **Accor'do**.)

LISCHIN, Grigory A. Russian composer; *b.* 1853; *d.* St. Petersburg, 1888.
Chief opera, *Don César de Bazan*, 1888.

Lis'cio (*I.*). Smooth.

Lis'pelnd (*G.*). Lisping, whispering.

L'ISLE. (See **Rouget de l'Isle**.)

LISSEN'KO, N. V. Russian composer; *b.* Grinjki, 1842.
Works : popular operas, numerous songs, &c.

LISS'MANN, Heinrich F. Baritone; *b.* Berlin, 1847.
His wife **Annie M.** is an esteemed soprano.

LIS'TEMANN, Bernhard. Violinist; *b.* Schlotheim, Thuringia, 1841. Concertmeister, Rudolstadt, 1859-67. Went to America (1867) ; founded the "Listemann Quartet," Boston.
"One of the most prominent violinists and teachers in America."—*Baker.*

LIS'TEMANN, Franz. 'Cellist ; son of B. ; *b.* New York, 1873.

LIS'TEMANN, Fritz. Violinist ; brother of B. ; *b.* Schlotheim, 1839. Went to New York, 1867. Has played mostly in New York and Boston, with occasional concert tours.
Works : violin pieces and songs.

LIS'TEMANN, Paul. Violinist ; son of B. ; *b.* Boston, 1871.

L'istes'so (*I.*). The same. (See **Istesso**.)
L'istess'o tem'po di Ario'so. The same tempo as the *Arioso.*

LISZT, Franz. Famous pianist ; *b.* Raiding, nr. Ödenburg, Hungary, Oct. 22, 1811 ; *d.* Bayreuth, July 31, 1886. Began to learn the pf. at 6 ; played in public at 9 ; studied pf. under Czerny, and theory under Salieri, Vienna, 1821-2 ; by his pf. playing attracted the attention and admiration of Beethoven. Gave his first public concerts in Vienna, 1823 ; their success determined his father to take him to the Paris Cons., but Cherubini, who was opposed to "infant phenomena," refused him admission. Franz, left to develop his genius in his own way, brought out an operetta *Don Sancho* (1825) ; spent 2 years in concert tours ; and, on the death of his father (1827), settled in Paris. After a period of *St. Simonism*, when he neglected music, he was received "into the highest circles of letters and art." The influence of Paganini and Berlioz was soon felt in his "unheard-of feats in piano technique" and his poetic feeling and expression. Toured Europe (1839-49), famed as the "greatest pianist who has ever lived." Court Capellmeister, Weimar, 1849-59. This part of his career is famous for the production of the works of Wagner and

Berlioz ; it is not too much to say that "the merits of these great composers were *revealed* to the world by Liszt." From 1859 to 1870 he lived mostly at Rome, where Pius IX conferred on him the title of Abbé. Appointed President of the Hungarian Academy of Music, Pesth, 1875. Liszt was the founder of "transcendental" or "orchestral" pf. playing ; and as a composer he invented the *Symphonic Poem.*
Works : symphonic poems (*Dante, Faust, Tasso, Orpheus, Hamlet,* &c.) ; marches, waltzes, &c. for orches. ; concertos, rhapsodies, fantasias, études, &c., and many brilliant paraphrases and transcriptions for pf. ; masses ; 3 oratorios (*St. Elizabeth, Stanislaus,* and *Christus*) ; psalms, cantatas, about 60 fine songs, &c. ; a "Life of Chopin," and numerous writings on Wagner, Franz, Field, &c.

Litanei' (*G.*)
Lita'nia (*L.*) } A litany, a solemn supplication.
Litanie (*F.*)

LITOLFF, Henry Chas. Pianist ; *b.* London, 1818 ; *d.* Paris, 1891. Played in public at 12 ; went to Paris at 17 ; made successful concert tours, 1840-1. Condr., Warsaw, 1841-4. Visited London, 1846. Married the widow of Meyer, the mus. pubr., Brunswick, 1851, and changed the name of the firm to "H. Litolff." He was "one of the pioneers of cheap music." Returned to Paris, 1860.
Works : operas and operettas (*Héloise et Abélard,* &c.) ; an oratorio, orch. music, and much excellent pf. music.

LIT'TA, Duca Giulio, Visconte Arese. Operatic composer ; *b.* Milan, 1822 ; *d.* 1891.

LITTLE, Henry Walmsley. Organist ; *b.* London, 1853. Mus.Doc. Oxon, 1885.
Works : cantatas, part-songs, pf. pieces, &c.

Little Step. The Tonic Sol-fa name for a diatonic semitone.
The "little steps," major scale, are *m-f,* and *t-d'.*

Lit'urgy. (*I., Liturgi'a ; F. and G., Liturgie'.*) The prescribed ritual for public worship in various churches.
Liturgique (*F.*) } Liturgical.
Litur'gisch (*G.*)

Lit'uus (*L.*). A Roman crooked trumpet.

LIT'VINNE, Mad. (*née* Felia Schütz). Soprano ; *b.* St. Petersburg, 18—.

Liu'to (*I.*). A lute (*q.v.*).
Liuta'io. Same as *Luthier* (*q.v.*).
Liuti'sta. A lute player.

LIVERA'TI, Giovanni. Tenor singer ; *b.* Bologna, 1772 ; *d.* 1817. Conductor at Potsdam, Prague, &c.
Works : 14 operas, 2 oratorios, 'cello music, &c.

Livre (*F.*). A book.
A livre ouvert. At first sight.

Livret (*F.*). A libretto (*q.v.*).

LJA'DOFF. (See **Liadoff.**)

LJA'PUNOV. (See **Liapunov.**)

LLOYD, Chas. Harford. *B.* Thornbury, Gloucestershire, 1849. Mus.Doc.Oxon, 1891. Orgt. Gloucester Cath., 1876; Christ Church, Oxford, 1882; Precentor and mus. instructor, Eton, 1892.
Works: cantatas (*Hero and Leander*, &c.); church music, part-songs, &c.

LLOYD, Edward. Distinguished tenor singer; *b.* London, 1845. Choir-boy, Westminster Abbey. Came prominently into notice at the Gloucester Festival, 1871.

LLOYD, John A. *B.* Mold, 1815; *d.* 1874.
His cantata, *The Prayer of Habakkuk*, was the first work of its kind produced in Wales.

Lo (*I.*). The. Also an abbn. of *Loco*.

LO'BE, Johann Christian. Flautist, viola player, composer, and writer; *b.* Weimar, 1797; *d.* 1881. Edited the Leipzig *Allgem. Mus. Zeitung*, 1846-8.
Works: 5 operas, orchestral music, fl. pieces, &c. His writings include a "Text Book on Musical Composition" (4 vols.), a "Catechism of Music," a "Catechism of Composition," &c.

Lob'gesang (*G.*) ⎱ A hymn or song of praise.
Lob'lied (*G.*) ⎰ Mendelssohn's "Lobgesang" was first performed in 1840.

LOB'KOWITZ, Prince J. F. Maximilian. *B.* 1772; *d.* 1816. Intimate friend and patron of Beethoven, who dedicated several works to him.

LO'BO (or **Lopez, Lupus**), **Duarte.** 17th cent. Portuguese composer.
Published magnificats, masses, &c.

Lob'singen (*G.*). To sing praises.

LOCATEL'LI, Pietro. Violinist; *b.* Bergamo, 1693; *d.* 1764. Pupil of Corelli. He was a wonderful player for his time, and Paganini is said to have "profited by his innovations."
Wrote 12 concerti-grossi, and numerous other works for violin.

Loch. (*G.*, *plur.* *Löch'er*). An opening. (1) Ventage of a wind-inst. (2) Sound-hole (of a violin, &c.).

Lo'chrian ⎫
Lo'crian ⎬ (See **Mode.**)
Lo'krisch (*G.*) ⎭

LOCK, Matthew. *B.* Exeter, abt. 1632; *d.* 1677. Chorister, Exeter Cath.; composer to Chas. II, 1661.
Works: music to *Macbeth* and *The Tempest;* masques; "Consorts for viols;" anthems; the first English work on Thorough-bass (1673), &c.

Lo'co (*I.*). In its proper place; play or sing the notes as written.
Used after 8va, &c.

LO'DER, Edward Jas. *B.* Bath, 1813; *d.* 1865. Condr. Princess' Theatre, &c.
Works: operas for Drury Lane and Covent Garden (*Puck, Raymond and Agnes*, &c.), a masque, string quartets, and songs ("The Brave Old Oak," "The Diver," &c.).

LO'DER, Kate Fanny. (See **Lady H. Thompson**).

LOEB, Jules. Noted French 'cellist; *b.* Strasburg, 1857.
Solo 'cellist, Paris Opéra, Cons. concerts, &c.

LOEFFLER-TORNOV, Chas. M. Violinist and composer; *b.* Mühlhausen, 1861.

LOEILLET, Jean B. Flautist and harpsichord player; *b.* Ghent; *d.* London, 1728. Gave weekly amateur concerts at his house in London from 1710.
Works: sonatas for fl., ob., and vn.; 12 suites of lessons for harpsichord, &c.

LOESCH'HORN. (See **Löschhorn.**)

LOEWE. (See **Löwe.**)

Lo'geum (*L.*). The stage of a Greek theatre.

LO'GIER, Johann Bernhard. *B.* Cassel, 1777; *d.* Dublin, 1846. Ran away from home at the age of 10; was taken to England; joined a regimental band as flautist (1805), and after various wanderings invented a hand guide for piano practice—"The Chiroplast"—patented 1814. Notwithstanding much opposition, this invention was extensively patronised in Britain, Ireland, Germany, and Paris, and brought its "author" fame and fortune.
Logier wrote several works to accompany and explain his invention and his method of teaching; also a work on Thorough-bass.
The "Chiroplast" has long been discredited; Liszt, in particular, called it an "Ass's Guide."

LOGROSCI'NO, Nicola. Dramatic composer; Naples, abt. 1700-63. Pupil of Durante. Introduced the *ensemble* conclusion of the act of an opera.
Works: over 20 operas (*Inganno per inganno* (1738), *Il Governatore* (1747), &c.

LO'HENGRIN. Romantic drama by Wagner; composed 1847; prod. Weimar, 1850.

LOH'MANN, Peter. German poet; *b.* Westphalia, 1833.
Several of his dramas have been set to music.

LÖHR, George A. *B.* Norwich, 1821; *d.* 1897. Asst. orgt. Norwich Cath. for 10 years.

LÖHR, Hermann. Song composer; *b.* Plymouth, 1872.

LÖHR, Richd. Harvey. *B.* Leicester, 1856. Studied at the R.A.M.
Works: pf. pieces, songs, &c.

LOH'SE, Otto. *B.* Dresden, 1859. Capellmeister, Strasburg Theatre.
Wrote the successful opera *Der Prinz wider Willen* (1898).

Lointain (*F.*). In the distance; an echo effect.

LOL'LI, Antonio. Violinist; *b.* Bergamo, abt. 1730 (or 40); *d.* Palermo, 1802. Made several concert tours; was a special favourite of Catherine II, St. Petersburg.
Wrote vn. concertos, sonatas, &c.

LOL'LI, Mad. (See **Scalchi.**)

LOMAGNE, B. de. Pen-name of **Soubies** (*q.v.*).

LOMAKIN, Gabriel G. Noted Russian teacher of singing classes; 1812-85.

LOMBARD, Louis. Born of poor parents in France; made a princely fortune in America; maintains a large private orchestra at the Castle of Trevano, nr. Lugano, Switzerland.

LOMBAR'DI, I. Opera by Verdi, 1843.

Long. (*L., Lon'ga.*) In mediæval music a note equal to 2 (or 3) Breves.
Double Long. A *Large*; equal to 2 *Longs*.

Long appoggiatura. The ordinary appoggiatura (*q.v.*).

Long drum. (See **Drum.**)

Long metre. A stanza of 4 lines in Iambic measure (see **Iambic**), each line consisting of 8 syllables.

Long mordent. A mordent of 4 notes. (See **Mordent.**)

LONGHURST, Wm. Hy. *B.* Lambeth, 1819; *d.* 1904. Choirboy, afterwards orgt. Canterbury Cath., 1828-98; Mus.Doc. Cantuar, 1875.
Wrote church music, &c.

Longue pause (*F.*). A long pause; *lunga pausa*.

Lonta'no (*I.*). (As if) in the distance; *Piano.*
Da lonta'na } *Piano;* as if from a distance.
In lontanan'za }
Lontanis'simo. (As if) very far away; *pp.*
Trom'ba da lonta'no. A trumpet played in the distance.

LOOMIS, Harvey W. Composer; *b.* Brooklyn (U.S.), 1865.

LOPEZ. (See **Lobo.**)

LO'RENZ, Carl A. Conductor and composer; *b.* Pomerania, 1837. Condr. Stettin *Musikverein,* 1864; municipal mus.-director, Stettin, 1866.
Works: 2 successful operas, a Stabat Mater, concert-cantatas, &c.

LO'RENZ, Julius. Condr. and composer; *b.* Hanover, 1862.

LO'RIS; LORI'TUS. (See **Glareanus.**)

LORT'ZING, G. Albert. Actor, singer, conductor, and opera composer; Berlin, 1803-51. Almost wholly self-taught.
Chief operas: *Die Beiden Schützen* (1837), *Czar und Zimmermann* (1839), *Der Wildschütz* (1842), *Regina, oder die Marodure* (prod. Berlin, 1899 —nearly 50 years after his death). His operas are extremely popular in Germany.

Los (*G.*). (1) Free, unfettered. (2) " Play up." " Begin."

LÖSCH'HORN, K. Albert Pianist; *B.* Berlin, 1819; *d.* 1905. Pf. teacher, Royal Inst. for Church Music, Berlin, 1851.
Works: numerous excellent pf. studies; effective *salon* pf. pieces, suites, sonatas, &c.

Lo stes'so tem'po (*I.*). At the same speed. (See **Istesso.**)

LOTT, Edwin Matthew. *B.* St. Helier, Jersey, 1836; *d.* 1902. Orgt. St. Saviour's, Holborn, 1883.
Works: anthems, services, songs, numerous pf. pieces, a "Dict. of Mus. Terms," &c.

LOTT, John B. *B.* Faversham, 1849. Orgt. Lichfield Cath. since 1881.

LOT'TI, Antonio. Distinguished organist and composer; *b.* Hanover (?), abt. 1667; *d.* Venice, 1740. Produced an opera at Venice at the age of 16. From 1704-36 organist, St. Mark's, Venice. As a composer, he stands midway between the old "strict" style and the modern "free" style.
Works: 4 oratorios, many masses, motets, &c.; 20 operas. His most famous work is a *Miserere* (with a *Crucifixus* in 12 parts).

LOT'TO, Isidor. Violinist; *b.* Warsaw, 1840.

Loud pedal. The right pedal of a pf., which raises all the dampers from the strings.

LOULIÉ, Etienne. Music master to Mlle. de Guise abt. 1700.
Invented the "Chronomètre," the precursor of the metronome.

Lourde (*F.*). Heavy.
Lourdement. Heavily.

Loure (or **Louvre**) (*F.*). (1) An ancient French bagpipe. (2) An old dance named from this instrument.

Louré (*F.*). Slurred, *legato*; in organ-tones (*q.v.*).

LOVER, Samuel. Novelist; *b.* Dublin, 1797; *d.* 1868.
Wrote music to several Irish plays, songs, &c.

LÖW, Joseph. Pianist; Prague, 1834-86.
Works: about 450 *salon* pf. pieces.

Low (1). (*G., Lei'se; F., Douce; I., Pia'no.*) Soft.

Low (2). (*G., Tief; F., Bas, Basse; I., Bas'so,-a.*) Deep; grave in pitch.

LOWE, Edward. *B.* Salisbury, abt. 1610; *d.* 1682. Choragus and Prof. of Music, Oxford, 1662.
Works: anthems, "A short Direction for the Performance of the Cathedral Service," &c.

LOWE, C. Egerton. Composer and writer; *b.* London, 1860.

LÖWE, Dr. J. Carl G. Celebrated song composer; *b.* nr. Halle, 1796; *d.* 1869. Town music-director, Stettin, 1821-66.
Works: operas, oratorios, several fine songs (his most characteristic compositions), string quartets, pf. sonatas, &c.; and a number of theoretical treatises.

LOWTHIAN, Caroline. (Mrs. C. A. Prescott.) Contemporary song composer. ("The Gates of the West," "Sunshine," &c.)

LUARD-SELBY. (See **Selby.**)

LÜ'BECK, Ernst. *B.* The Hague, 1829; *d.* 1876. Settled in Paris as a favourite concert pianist.

LÜ'BENAU, L. Pen-name of **S. Jadassohn.**

LUCANTO'NI, Giovanni. Singing teacher ; *b.* Rieti, Italy, 1825. From 1857 resided chiefly in Paris and London.
Works : a ballet, a mass, songs, pf. pieces, &c.

LUCAS, Chas. 'Cellist ; *b.* Salisbury, 1808 ; *d.* 1869. Member of Queen Adelaide's band, 1830. Condr. R.A.M., 1832 ; Principal, 1859-66.
Works : opera (*The Regicide*), anthems, songs, &c.

LUCAS, Clarence. *B.* Canada, 1866.
Works : operas, pf. pieces, songs.

LUCAS, Stanley. Son of Charles ; *b.* 1834. Sec. R. Soc. of Musicians, 1861 ; Phil. Soc., 1866-80. *D.* 1903.

LUC'CA, Pauline. Celebrated dramatic soprano ; *b.* Vienna, 1841. Commenced her public career in *Der Freischütz*, 1859. Very distinguished in the *rôle* of "Selika" in Meyerbeer's *l'Africaine*. First sang in London, 1863. *D.* 1908.

LU'CIA, Fernando de. Tenor ; *b.* Naples, 1860(?).

LÜCK, Stephan. *B.* Linz-on-Rhine, 1806 ; *d.* Trier, 1883.
Noted for his "reforms in Catholic church music."

Lu'dus (*L.*). Play.
Lu'di moderato. Organist.
Lu'di spiritua'li. Sacred plays (mysteries ; miracle plays).

LUD'WIG, August. Composer and writer ; *b.* Waldheim, 1865.

LUDWIG, Jos. Violinist and composer ; *b.* Bonn, 1844.

LUD'WIG, Paul. 'Cellist ; son of J. ; *b.* Bonn, 1872.

LUÈRES, Mad. F. (See **Camilla Urso.**)

Luf'tig (*G.*). Light, airy, vaporous.

Lugu'bre (*I.* and *F.*). Doleful, lugubrious, mournful, dreary.

LUIGI'NI, Alex. C. L. J. Noted condr. ; *b.* Lyons, 1850.

LUI'NI, Carl. Pen-name of **H. Brinley Richards** (*q.v.*).

LUKE, Mrs. Jemima (*née* Thompson). 1813-1906. Married Rev. Samuel Luke, 1843.
Wrote the hymn, "I think when I read," 1841.

Lullaby. A cradle song ; a *Berceuse.*

Lul'len (*G.*). To lull, sing to sleep.
Lull'gesang. A lullaby.

LULLY (or **LULLI**), **Jean Baptiste de.** "The founder of French grand opera ; " *b.* Florence, 1633 ; *d.* Paris, Mar. 22, 1687. At 13 entered the service of Mlle. de Montpensier as page. Here, after performing many menial duties, he attracted the notice of influential personages who secured his admission to "la grande bande" (the King's private orchestra). Was made the head of this "corps of 24 violins," 1652 ; he organized a second band of 16—'les petits violons"—which became under his direction the finest orchestra in France. Apptd. Court Composer, 1653 ; wrote masques, &c., in which Louis XIV took part. The King preferred Lully's music to all other, and in 1672 granted him letters patent for an "Académie royale de musique"—now the Grand Opéra. "From this time dates Lully's real fame as the creator of French opera." He moulded the overture, wrote his music to suit the *genius* of the French language, improved the orchestra and the scenic arrangements, and introduced dramatic effects previously unknown.
Of his numerous operas, which kept the stage for nearly a century, *Armide et Renaud* (1686) is perhaps the best. He also wrote ballets, symphonies, church music, &c.

Lu-lu. Chinese official collection of musical treatises and laws.

LUM'BYE, Hans Christian. Copenhagen, 1810-74.
Called the "Northern Strauss" on accouut of the popularity of his dance music.

Lun'du. A Portugese dance in duple time.

LUNN, Chas. Singing teacher ; *b.* Birmingham, 1838 ; *d.* 1906.
Wrote "The Philosophy of the Voice," 1874.

LUNN, Rev. Jn. Robt. Composer and writer ; *b.* Cleeve Prior, Worcester, 1831.

LUNN, Henry Chas. Pianist and critic ; *b.* London, 1817 ; *d.* 1894.
Wrote "Musings of a Musician," &c.

LUNN, Mad. Kirkby. (See **Mrs. W. J. K. Pearson.**)

Lun'go,-a (*I.*). Long.
Lun'ga pau'sa. A long pause.
Lun'ghe (plur.). Drawn out.

Luo'go (*I.*). Same as **Loco** (*q.v.*).

LUPORI'NI, Gaetano. Italian composer ; *b.* Lucca.
Works : operas, *I dispetti amorosi* (1894), *La Collana di Pasqua* (1896).

LUPOT, Nicolas. Violin maker ; the "French Stradivarius." *B.* Stuttgart, 1758 ; *d.* Paris, 1824.

Lur. An ancient Scandinavian trumpet or horn.

Lusing. An abbreviation of **Lusingando.**

Lusingan'do (*I.*). ⎫ Coaxingly, caressingly,
Lusingan'te (*I.*). ⎭ flatteringly.
Lusinghe'vole ⎫
Lusinghevolmen'te ⎰ Coaxingly, &c.
Lusinghie're ⎱
Lusinghie'ro ⎭

LUSSAN, Zélie de. Dramatic soprano ; *b.* New York, 1863. Concert *début* at 16 ; stage *début*, 1885 ; sang in London, 1889.

LUSSY, Matthis. Pf. teacher and writer ; *b.* Stans, Switzerland, 1828. Settled Paris, 1847.
Author of an excellent "Traité de l'expression musicale" (1873), a "Histoire de la notation musicale" (1882), &c.

Lus'tig (*G.*). Merry, gay, jocund, playful.
Lus'tig und im'mer schnel'ler und schmet'ternder. Gaily, and always faster and more resounding (resonant).

Lust'lied (*G.*). A gay, merry song.

LÜST'NER, Ignas Peter. Violinist ; *b.* nr. Jauer, 1792 ; *d.* 1873. Founded a School of Vn. Playing, Breslau, 1844.

His five sons, **Karl, Otto, Louis, Georg,** and **Richard,** all became prominent musicians.

L'ut de poitrine (*F.*). The high C "from the chest" (*i.e.,* not in *falsetto*).

Lute. (*G., Lau'te ; F., Luth ; I., Liu'to.*) A very ancient pear-shaped inst. of the guitar and mandoline family, with a neck and fretted fingerboard.
> The largest form was the *Theorbo, Arch-lute,* or *Chittaro'ne,* which sometimes had as many as 13 pairs of strings, played as in the guitar.
> Lute music was written in *Tablature (q.v.).*
> "The *Lutes* of *Boulogne* are esteemed the best, on account of the wood, which is said to have an uncommon disposition for producing a sweet sound."—*Grassineau.*
> *Lutanist* ⎰ A lute player. (Also *Lutist, Luter, Lu-*
> *Lutenist* ⎱ *tinist.*)
> *Luti'na.* A small lute.

Luth (*F.*). A lute.

LUTHER, Martin. The great Church Reformer ; *b.* Eisleben, 1483 ; *d.* 1546.
> Wrote or arranged the words of many of the finest of the German Chorals, and perhaps composed the music of about 13 of them. He was ably seconded by Johann Walther.

Luthier (*F.*). A lute maker ; a violin maker.
> For a list of the greatest makers of *Lutherie,* see *Violin.*

LÜTSCHG, Waldemar. Pianist ; *b.* St. Petersburg, 1877.

LUTTMAN, Willie. Org. scholar, Cambridge Univ., 1894-7 ; Mus.B. Cantab., 1903. Orgt. St. Albans Cath., 1907.

Lut'to (*I.*). Grief, sorrow, mourning.
> *Lutt(u)osamen'te* ⎰ Sadly, mournfully, plaintively.
> *Lutt(u)o'so* ⎱

LUTZ, Wm. Meyer. *B.* Männerstadt, Kissingen, 1829. Settled in England, 1848. Conductor Surrey Theatre (1851-55), Gaiety Theatre (1869). *D.* 1903.
> Works : operas and operettas, stage music, &c.

LÜT'ZEL, Johann H. *B.* nr. Speyer, 1823 ; *d.* 1899. Organized the "Evangelischer Kirchenchor," Zweibrücken, 1854. (In 1880 it "had spread over the whole Palatinate.")
> Pub. a "Choralbuch" (1858), "Der Praktische Organist," school song-books, &c.

LUX, Friedrich. Organist ; *b.* Thuringia, 1820 ; *d.* 1895. Capellmeister, City Theatre, Mayence, 1851-77 ; condr. Oratorio Society, 1867-91.
> Works : 4 operas, orchestral and chamber music, organ pieces, pf. music, songs, &c.

LUZZA'SCHI (LU ZZA'SCO). Pupil of Rore ; orgt. at Ferrara, 1580. Taught Frescobaldi.

LUZ'ZI, Luigi. Italian composer ; 1828-76.
> Wrote 3 operas, orch. music, pf. pieces, and several fine songs.

LVOFF (or **LWOFF**), **Alexis von.** Composer of the Russian National Anthem ; *b.*

Reval, 1799 ; *d.* 1870. Major-General and Adjutant to the Emperor Nicholas. Conductor, Court Choir, 1836-55.
> Works : operas, vn. music, Russian part-songs, essay on "Old Russian Church Song," &c.

LYALL, Jas. Durward (**Durward Lely**). Tenor vocalist ; *b.* Arbroath, 1857.

Lydian Mode. The Church mode beginning on F. (See **Mode.**)

LYNES, Frank. American organist and conductor ; *b.* Cambridge, Massachusetts, 1858. Studied Leipzig Cons. (1883-5). Afterwards settled in Boston.
> Works : vn. and pf. pieces, pf. music, part-songs, about 50 songs, &c.

LYON, James. *B.* Manchester, 1872. Mus.D. Oxon, 1904.
> Works : anthems, songs, pf. pieces, 4 orchestral suites (" The Pearl of Sicily," " The Warden of of the Cinque Ports," " The Legend Beautiful"), an organ sonata and other organ pieces, an overture in G min. (Sheffield, 1908), &c.

Ly'ra (*Gk., L.,* and *G.*). A lyre (*q.v.*).
> *Ly'ra dop'pia* (*I.*). (See *Lira doppia.*)
> *Ly'ra mendicor'um* (*L.*). A hurdy-gurdy.
> *Ly'ra-vi'ol.* An English viol with frets added. (See also *Lira.*)

Ly'ra. A lyre-shaped variety of Stahlspiel (*q.v.*) used in military bands.

LY'RA, Justus W. Pastor ; composer of German "Student Songs ; " *b.* Osnabrück, 1822 ; *d.* 1882.
> 5 vols. of his extremely popular songs were published, 1896.

Lyre. (*G.* and *L., Ly'ra ; F., Lyre, Lire ; G., Lei'er ; I., Li'ra.*) One of the most ancient of stringed instruments.
> It is fabled to have been invented by Mercury, about 2,000 B.C., from a dried up tortoise. Much confusion has been caused by the careless use of the words *lyre* and *lute.* The *lyre* is of the nature of a *harp,* from which it chiefly differs in having fewer strings. It differs essentially from the *lute* in having no fingerboard. In the middle ages, however, the term *lira* (or *lyra*) was applied to several bowed insts. which were really *viols* or "bowed" *lutes.* *Luthier* means either a lute maker or a violin maker. (See *Lira* and *Lyra.*)

Lyr'iker (*G.*), **Lyrique** (*F.*), **Lyr'isch** (*G.*) Lyric, lyrical.
> Poetry that expresses feeling, passion, emotion, and sentiment, "fitted to be sung to the lyre ; " as opposed to "epic" poetry which is of the nature of *narrative.*
> *Lyric drama.* Opera.
> *Lyric opera.* An opera in which the lyric elements predominate.

LYS'BERG (or **BOVY**), **Chas. Samuel.** Pianist ; *b.* Lysberg, nr. Geneva, 1821 ; *d.* 1873. Pupil of Chopin.
> Works : numerous favourite pf. pieces, and a comic opera.

LYTE, Henry Francis. 1793-1847. Curate Lower Brixham, Devon.
> Wrote "Abide with me," and other popular hymns.

LYTH, John. D.D. 1821-86. Wesleyan minister.
> Wrote the hymn " There is a better world," 1845.

LYTTLETON, Claude. Pen-name of **W. H. P. Jones** (*q.v.*).

M

M. Abbn. of *mezzo, mano* (or *main*), *manual*.
M. or **M.M.** Maelzel's Metronome. (See **Metronome.**)
m. The note *me* in Tonic Sol-fa.
Ma (*I.*). But.
  Alle'gro ma non trop'po. Quick, but not too much so. *Ma po'co.* But (only a) little.
MAAS, Joseph. Tenor singer ; *b.* Dartford, Kent, 1847 ; *d.* 1886. *Début,* St. James's Hall, 1871.
  His early death cut short a very promising career.
MAAS, Louis P. O. Pianist ; *b.* Wiesbaden, 1852 ; *d.* 1889. Settled in Boston (U.S.), 1880.
  Wrote pf. pieces, vn. sonatas, songs, &c.
MABELLI'NI, Teodulo. Operatic composer ; *b.* Pistoia, 1817 ; *d.* Florence, 1897. Condr. Filarmonica, Florence ; Court composer, &c.
  Works : 9 successful operas (*Rolla,* 1840, &c.) ; an oratorio, cantatas, chamber music, pf. pieces, &c.
MACBETH, Allan. Organist and composer ; *b.* Greenock, 1856. Studied Leipzig Cons. Principal, School of Music, Glasgow Athenæum, 1890.
MacCARTHY, Maud. Violinist ; *b.* Clonmell, 1884.
McCLELLAND, Herbert W. Mus.D. Dublin, 1905. Orgt., St. Canice Cath., Kilkenny, 1906.
McCORMACK, John F. Tenor ; *b.* Athlone, 1884. Won 1st prize, Feis Ceoil, Dublin, 1903. *Début* in opera, Dublin, 1905 ; London *début,* 1907.
MacCUNN, Hamish. *B.* Greenock, 1868. Studied R.A.M., 1883-6 ; Prof. of Harmony, 1888-94. Condr. Carl Rosa Opera Co., 1898.
  Works : operas (*Jeanie Deans,* 1894) ; cantatas (*Lord Ullin's Daughter, The Lay of the Last Minstrel,* &c.) ; orch. music, part-songs, songs.
MacDOWELL, Edward Alexander. Distinguished American pianist and composer ; *b.* New York, 1861. Studied Paris Cons. and Frankfort. Head teacher of pf. Darmstadt Cons., 1881-2. Prof. of music Columbia Univ., New York, 1896. *D.* 1908.
  Works : orchestral pieces (symphonic poems, suites, &c.) ; choruses ; pf. pieces (concertos, suites, sonatas, études, &c.) ; several fine songs.
MACE, Thos. 1619-1709. Clerk of Trinity Coll., Cambridge.
  Author of " Musick's Monument," (1676), an instruction book for the lute.
McEWEN, John B. Composer ; *b.* Hawick, 1868.
MACFARLANE, Thomas. Organist ; *b.* Horsham, 1808 ; retired 1882.
  Pub. numerous collections of Psalm tunes, &c.
MACFARLANE, Wm. C. Organist ; *b.* London, 1870. Taken to New York, 1874, and educated there.

MACFARREN, Sir Geo. Alexander. London, 1813-87. Studied R.A.M., where he became Prof., 1834 ; Principal, 1876 ; Prof. of Music, Cambridge Univ., 1875 ; Mus. Doc., 1876 ; Knighted, 1883.
  Works : English operas, *The Devil's Opera, Robin Hood, Jessy Lea, Helvellyn,* &c. ; oratorios, *St. John the Baptist* (1873), *Joseph* (1877), *King David* (1883), &c. ; 6 cantatas ; services, anthems, overtures, chamber music, part-songs, songs, &c. His writings include "Rudiments of Harmony" (1860), "Six Lectures on Harmony" (1867), "A History of Music," and "A Treatise on Counterpoint."
MACFARREN, Natalia (Lady). Wife of preceding ; *b.* Lübeck.
  Works : English translations of German songs, cantatas, &c.
MACFARREN, Mrs. John (*née* **Emma Marie Bennett**). Pianist and lecturer ; London, 1824-95. Married John Macfarren (brother of Sir G. A.), 1846.
  Pub. pf. pieces under the name of *Jules Brissac.*
MACFARREN, Walter Cecil. Pianist and teacher (brother of G. A.). *B.* London, 1826 ; *d.* 1905. Chorister, Westmr. Abbey, 1836-41 ; pupil, R.A.M., 1842-6 ; pf. Prof., R.A.M., from 1846.
  Works : a symphony, 7 overtures, a concertstück for pf. and orch., pf. and vn. pieces, numerous pf. pieces, services, anthems, part-songs, and songs.
M'GUCKIN, Barton. Tenor vocalist ; *b.* Dublin, 1853(2?).
Machê'te. A small Portuguese guitar.
Machine-head. (*G., Mecha'nik*). A mechanical arrangement for tuning the strings of the double-bass, guitar, and mandoline (instead of tuning-pegs).
Ma'chol. An ancient Hebrew inst.
Mach'werk (*G.*). "Manufactured stuff." Contemptuous expression for laboured, as opposed to spontaneous composition.
MACINTYRE, Margaret. Soprano vocalist; *b.* of Scottish descent in India ; *Début* Covent Garden, 1888.
MACIRO'NE, Clara Angela. Pianist and teacher ; *b.* London, 1821. Student, afterwards pf. prof., R.A.M.
  Works : church music, pf. pieces, songs, and several successful part-songs.
MACKAY, Angus. 1813-59. Piper to Queen Victoria. Pub. a colln. of "Highland Pipe Music."
McKAY, Ivor. Tenor singer ; *b.* Dublin. First important engagement, Leeds Festival, 1886.
MACKENZIE, Sir Alex. Campbell. *B.* Edinburgh, 1847. Won the King's Scholarship, R.A.M., 1862. Mus.Doc., St. Andrew's, 1886 ; Cambridge, 1888 ; Edinburgh, 1896. Principal R. A. M. (succeeding Macfarren), 1888 ; knighted 1894.
  Works : oratorios, *The Rose of Sharon* (1884), *Bethlehem* (1894) ; 2 operas (*Colomba,* 1883 ; &c.) ; several cantatas (*Jason, The Dream of Jubal,* &c.) ; orch. music, chamber music, anthems, part-songs, songs, &c.

MACKENZIE, Marian (Mrs. R. S. Williams). Contralto singer; *b.* Plymouth, 1858. Sang Norwich Festival, 1890; Leeds, 1892; Birmingham, 1894, &c.

MACKINTOSH, John. Celebrated bassoonist; *b.* Scotland, 1767; *d.* London, 1844.

MACKINLAY. (See Sterling.)

McLACHLAN, Jessie N. (Mrs. R. Buchanan). Soprano; *b.* Oban, 1866.

MACLAGAN, Wm. Dalrymple. D.D. *B.* 1826. Archbishop of York, 1891–1908.
Author of the hymn, "The saints of God."

MACLEAN, Alick. Son of C. D. (*below*); *b.* Eton, 1872.
Works: operas, *Quentin Durward* (1895), *Petruccio* (1895); songs, &c. *Petruccio* won the Moody-Manners £100 prize.

MACLEAN, Chas. D. *B.* Cambridge, 1843; Mus.Doc. Oxon, 1865. Orgt. and Mus.-director Eton Coll., 1871-5. Eng. Edtr. International Mus. Society since 1899.
Works: numerous orchl. pieces, &c.

MACLEOD, Peter. Composer of Scottish songs; *b.* Midlothian, 1797; *d.* 1859.

McMURDIE, Joseph. *B.* London, 1792; *d.* 1878. Mus.B. Oxon, 1814.
Works: glees, part-songs, hymn tunes, &c.

McNAUGHT, Wm. Gray. *B.* London, 1849. Mus.Doc. Cantuar, 1896. Editor *School Music Review*, 1892.
Has translated a large number of standard works into Sol-fa (*Novello's Sol-fa Series*), and is well-known as an adjudicator at choir competitions.

MACPHERSON, Chas. Orgt. and composer; *b.* Edinburgh, 1870.

MACPHERSON, Chas. Stewart. *B.* Liverpool, 1865. Studied R.A.M.; Prof. 1889. Condr. Westminster Orchestral Society, 1885.
Works: orch. pieces, pf. pieces, songs, a "Practical Harmony," &c.

MA'DER, Raoul M. Operatic composer; *b.* Pressburg, Hungary, 1856. Studied Vienna Cons., 1879-82: won the Liszt prize for pf. playing, 1880. Condr. Royal Opera, Pesth, 1895.
Works: opera (*Die Flüchtlinge*), ballets, operettas, choruses, songs, &c.

Ma'dre, Al'la (*I.*). "To the mother." Hymns, &c., to the Virgin Mary.

Madria'le (*I.*). (1) A madrigal. (2) A kind of **Intermezzo** (*q.v.*).
Madrialet'to. A short madrigal.

Mad'rigal. (*G.* and *F., Madrigal'; I., Madriga'le, Madria'le, Mandria'le*). A vocal (unaccompanied) composition, generally in imitative counterpoint in from 3 to 8 parts, especially characteristic of the 16th and early 17th centuries.
The madrigal is closely allied to the motet; it differs from the *Glee* in that it is best sung by a *Chorus*, while the *Glee* is intended for a solo voice to each part.
The following are among the finest specimens: " Il bianco e dolce cigno," Arcadelt; " O'er Desert Plains," Waelrent; "Down in a flowery vale," Festa; "Vezzosi augelli," Marenzio; "All creatures now are merry," Benet; "The silver swan," Gibbons; " In going to my lonely bed," Edwardes; " Flora gave me fairest flowers," Wilbye; "Welcome, sweet pleasure," Weelkes.

Madrigales'co (*I.*). In the style of a madrigal.

Madrigal'etto (*I.*) ⎱
Madrialet'to (*I.*) ⎰ A short madrigal.

MAEL'ZEL. (See Mälzel.)

Maestà (*I.*). Majesty, dignity.

Con maestà
Con maesta'de ⎱
Maeste'vole ⎰ With dignity, &c.
Maestevolmen'te

Maesto'so (*I.*). Majestic, dignified; with grandeur.
Maestosamen'te. Majestically.

Maestra'le (*I.*). Masterly.
Stret'to maestra'le. A fugal stretto in canon form.

Maestri'a (*I.*). Mastery, skill, address.

Mae'stro (*I.*). A master.
Mae'stri secola'ri. Teachers of secular music.
Mae'stro al cem'balo ⎱ The cembalist (or pianist) in an
Mae'stro al pia'no ⎰ opera orchestra, who formerly also conducted.
Mae'stro dei put'ti. Master of the boys.
Mae'stro del co'ro ⎱
Mae'stro di cappel'la ⎰ (See *Capellmeister.*)
Mae'stro di can'to. Singing master.

Mag'adis. An ancient Greek lyre with 20 strings, on which music could be played in 8ves.
Magadization. Playing in 8ves. Hence, by extension, the early attempts at harmony in 8ves, 5ths, and 4ths. (See *Organum.*)

Magazin'balg (*G.*). The reservoir-bellows of an organ.

MAGGI'NI (MAGI'NI, MAGI'NO), Giovanni Paolo. Famous Italian vn. maker; *b.* Bottocino-Marino, 1580; *d.* Brescia, abt. 1631(28?).

Maggiola'ta (*I.*). A May song.

Maggio're (*I.*). Major (*q.v.*).

Mag'got. Old name for impromptu fancies, ayres, &c.

Magisco'ro (*I.*). The chief of a choir.

Magistra'le (*I.*). Same as **Maestra'le** (*q.v.*).

MAGNARD, Lucien D. G. A. Composer; *b.* Paris, 1865.

Magni'ficat (*L.*). The hymn or song of the Virgin Mary (Luke i. 46-55).
Sung at Vespers in the Roman, and Evensong in the Anglican churches. Elaborately set by many composers.

Ma'gno (*I.*). Grand, great.

MAGNUS, Désiré. (Magnus Deutz.) Concert pianist; *b.* Brussels, 1828; *d.* 1884.
Works: a "Méthode élémentaire de piano," pf. pieces, &c.

Magre'pha. "An organ mentioned in the Talmud as having been in existence in the 2nd cent."—*Stainer and Barrett.*

MAHAFFY, Rev. John P. D.D.; Mus.Doc., 1891. *B.* 1839. Prof. of Ancient Hist., Trinity College, Dublin.

MAHILLON, Chas. Victor. *B.* Brussels, 1841. Custodian, Museum of Mus. Insts., Brussels Cons., 1877.
Works: a "Synoptical Table of Voices and Instruments," "Éléments d'acoustique," &c.

18

MAH'LER, Carl. Pen-name of **W. Small-wood** (*q.v.*).

MAH'LER, Gustav. *B.* Bohemia, 1860. Capellmeister at various theatres; Director, Court Opera, Vienna, 1897-1903.
Works : 2 operas, 6 symphonies, songs, &c.

Maid MARIAN. The "Queen of the May" in the old Morris dances, &c.

MAI'ER, Julius Joseph. *B.* Freiburg, Baden, 1821 ; *d.* 1889. Musical Custodian, Munich Library, 1857-87.
Pub. historical treatises on music.

MAIL'HAC, Pauline. Soprano ; *b.* Vienna, 1858.

MAILLART, Louis (Aimé). Operatic composer ; *b.* Montpelier, 1817 ; *d.* 1871. *Grand Prix de Rome*, Paris Cons., 1841.
Works : 6 operas (*Gastibelza*, 1847, &c.).

MAILLY, Alphonse J. E. Fine organist ; *b.* Brussels, 1833. Org. Prof. Brussels Cons., 1868.
Works : org. pieces, pf. pieces, &c.

Main (*F.*). The hand.
A quatre mains. For 4 hands (pf. duet, &c.).
Main droite, or *M.D.* The right hand.
Main gauche, or *M.G.* The left hand.
Main harmonique. Guido's "harmonic" hand.

MAIN'ZER, Abbé Joseph. *B.* Trier, 1807 ; *d.* Manchester, 1851. Established successful singing classes, Manchester ; also *Mainzer's Musical Times,* now the *Musical Times* (Novello & Co.).
Wrote several educational works on sight-singing, including "Singing for the Million" (1842).

Mais (*F.*). But.
Andante mais sans lenteur. Rather slow, but without dragging.
Piano (or *p*) *mais bien marqué.* Piano, but well marked.

MAIT'LAND, John Alexander Fuller. Critic and writer ; *b.* London, 1856. Succeeded Hueffer as *Times* music critic, 1890.
Edited the Appendix of Grove's Dict., 1st edn ; and is editor of the 2nd edn. Author of "Schumann" ("Great Musicians" series), "Masters of German Music ;" trans. (with Clara Bell) Spitta's "Life of Bach," &c.

Maître (*F.*). A master, a director.
Maître de chappelle. Same as *Capellmeister* (*q.v.*).
Maître de musique. Musical director, or teacher.

Maîtrise (*F.*). A cathedral music school.

Majestà (*I.*)
Majestät' (*G.*) } Majesty, grandeur.
Majesté (*F.*)
Majestueux (*F.*) } Majestic, noble, stately.
Majestä'tisch (*G.*) }

Majeur (*F.*). Major (*q.v.*).

MA'JO, Francesco di. *B.* Naples, 1745(?) ; *d.* 1770.
Works : 13 operas (*Astrea placata*), 5 masses, &c.

Major. (*G., Dur ; F., Majeur ; I., Maggio're.*) "Greater," as opposed to Minor, "less."
Major Bass. An organ pedal stop (16 ft. open diapason, wood).
Major cadence. One closing on a major chord.
Major chord } One with a major 3rd and perfect 5th.
Major triad }

Major key } (See *Key* and *Scale*.)
Major scale }
Major tone. The greater tone, ratio 9 : 8. (See *Acoustics.*)

Major fourth. A perfect fourth.
Also used for augmented 4th.

MA'JOR, Julius J. Composer ; *b.* Kaschau, Hungary, 1859.

Major Mode. The major key or scale.

MAJORA'NO. (See **Caffarelli.**)

Mal (*G.*). Time.
Zum ers'ten Mal. For the first time.

Malagueña (*S.*). A fandango (*q.v.*).

Malanconi'a (*I.*). Melancholy. (See **Malinconia.**)

MALASCHKIN, Leonid D. Popular Russian song composer ; 1842-1902 .

MALCOLM, Alexander. *B.* Edinburgh, 1687. Wrote "A Treatise on Music," 1721.

MAL'DER, Pierre van. Early composer of chamber music and symphonies; Brussels, 1724-68.
Works : 18 symphonies, 6 string quartets, 6 sonatas for 2 vns. and bass, &c.

MALHERBE, Charles T. Composer and writer ; *b.* Paris, 1863. Asst. archivist, Grand Opéra, 1896; editor *Le Ménestrel.*
Works : pf. pieces, vn. pieces, songs, transcriptions, &c.; writings on Wagner, the Opera-Comique, the works of Donizetti, &c.

MALIBRAN, Alexandre. Violinist ; Paris, 1823-67. Pupil of Spohr.
Wrote a "Life of Spohr," 1860.

MALIBRAN, Maria Felicità (*née* **Garcia**). Famous dramatic contralto ; *b.* Paris. 1808 ; *d.* Matlock, 1836. Daughter of Manuel del Popolo V. Garcia ; played a part in Paer's *Agnese* at 5. *Début,* H.M.'s Theatre, London, 1825. During the next two years she was a popular favourite in New York (where she married M. Malibran, a French merchant). From 1829 she sang every season in London, varied by engagements at Rome, Naples, Milan, &c. In London, 1835, she received £2,775 for 24 nights.
Her voice was of extraordinary compass, and she was also a marvellous actress.

Malinco'lico (*I.*) }
Malinconi'a (*I.*). } Melancholy.
Con malinconi'a
Malinconicamen'te
Malinco'nico } In a melancholy, dejected
Malinconio'so } manner.
Malincono'so
Also *Melanconi'a, Melenco'nico,* &c.

MAL'LING, Otto V. *B.* Copenhagen, 1848. Pupil of Gade and Hartmann.
Works : a symphony, and other orch. music, pf. pieces, songs, &c.

MAL'LINGER, Mathilde (*née* **Lichtenegger**). Operatic soprano ; *b.* Agram, 1847. Singing teacher, Prague Cons., 1890.
Sang in the part of "Eva" in Wagner's *Meister-singer*, 1868.

MALLINSON, Albert. Notable contemporary song composer.
Several vols. of his songs are pub. by The F. Harris Co.

MAL'TEN, Therese. Soprano ; *b.* Prussia, 1855. *Début*, Dresden, 1873.
Sang in the *rôle* of "Kundry" (*Parsifal*), Bayreuth, 1882.

MÄL'ZEL, Johann Nepomuk. *B.* Ratisbon, 1772 ; *d.* 1838.
Perfected the "Metronome," 1816 ; invented a "Pan-Harmonium," an automatic chess player, &c. ; also made ear trumpets.

Man (*I.*). Same as **Mano** (*q.v.*).

Man and Music.
"Our bodies are constructed on musical principles ;....the destruction of health, as regards both body and mind, may be well described as being out of tune.....There is every probability that a general improvement in our taste for music would really improve our morals."—*Moore.*

Mancan'do (*I.*). ⎫ Decreasing in loudness,
Mancan'te (*I.*). ⎭ dying away.

Manche (*F.*). Neck (of a violin, &c.).

MANCINEL'LI, Luigi. Famous conductor ; *b.* Orvieto, Papal States, 1848. From the age of 15 "earned his living for 8 years by 'cello playing, teaching, and song writing." 2nd condr., Opera, Rome, 1874 ; 1st condr. 1875. Director Bologna Cons., 1881. Condr. Drury Lane, 1886-8 ; Royal Th., Madrid, 1888-95 ; Covent Garden, from 1888.
Works : stage music, operas (*Ero e Leandro*), two oratorios, songs, &c.

MANCI'NI, Francesco. Naples, 1674-1739.
Wrote about 20 operas.

MANCI'NI, Giambatista. Singing teacher; *b.* Ascoli, 1716; *d.* Vienna, 1800.
Wrote a work on "Il Canto Figurato."

Mand°. Abbn. of *Mancando.*

Mando'la (*I.*). A large kind of mandolin.

Mandolconcel'lo, Mandolo'ne. Large varieties of the mandolin.

Man'dolin, Man'doline (*I., Mandoli'no*). An inst. of the lute family, with a fretted fingerboard, and a number of pairs of wire strings played by means of a plectrum.
The Neapolitan Mandolin has 4 pairs of strings tuned like those of the vn. ; the Milanese Mandolin has 5 or 6 pairs.

Mandolina'ta (*I.*). (1) An imitation of the mandolin in pf. playing. (2) A quiet piece for mandolin.

Mando'ra, Mando're. Same as **Mando'la.**

MANDYCZEW'SKI, Dr. E. Editor and writer; *b.* Czernowitz, 1857.

MAÑEN. Spanish violinist; *b.* 1884. Studied Paris Cons.
Works : 2 operas (*Akté*), trios and quartets for strings, &c.

MANGEOT, Edouard J. *B.* Nantes, 1834 ; *d.* 1898.
Invented a pf. with a double keyboard (Paris Exposition, 1878).

MAN'GOLD, J. Wilhelm. Darmstadt, 1796-1875. Court Capellmeister, 1825-58.
Works : an opera (*Merope*), chamber music, overtures, &c.

MAN'GOLD, Karl L. A. Brother of J. W. ; *b.* Darmstadt, 1813 ; *d.* 1889. Studied Paris Cons. Court Music Director, Darmstadt, 1848-69 ; and condr. of the chief singing societies.
Works : 4 operas (*Tannhäuser*, &c.), 3 oratorios, 4 concert dramas, 2 symphonies, chamber music, popular male quartets, songs, &c.

Ma'ni (*I.*). Plur. of *Ma'no,* the hand.
A du'e ma'ni. For two hands.
A quat'tro ma'ni. For four hands.

Ma'nica (*I.*). Fingering; a shift (on vn., &c.).

Man'ichord. (*L., Manichor'dium.*) Name applied to various obselete precursors of the harpsichord and pf.

Ma'nico (*I.*). (*F., Manche.*) Neck (of a violin, &c.).

Manier' (*G.*). (1) An **Agrément** (*q.v.*). (2) Style, manner.
Manie'ren. Ornaments, graces.

Manie'ra (*I.*). (*F., Manière.*) Manner, style, method (of performance).
Con dol'ce manie'ra. In a sweet, delicate style.
Manie'ra affetta'ta. An affected style.
Manie'ra langui'da. A languid style.

Manière (*F.*) "Mannered," affected.

Manifold Fugue. One with 2 or 3 subjects.

MANN, Arthur Henry. *B.* Norwich, 1850. Orgt. King's Coll., Cambridge, 1876. Mus.Doc. Oxon, 1882.
Works : church music, org. pieces, part-songs, &c.

Män'nerchor (*G.*). A male chorus.
Männergesang'verein. A male choral society.
Män'nerstimmen. Male voices.
The Vienna *Männergesangverein,* founded 1843, is one of the most celebrated of male-voice societies. Schumann, Mendelssohn, Meyerbeer, Liszt, and Wagner dedicated works to it.

MANNERS, Charles. (Southcote Mansergh). Bass vocalist; *b.* London, 1857. Joined the Carl Rosa Opera Co., 1887. Married **Miss Fanny Moody** (*q.v.*), 1890 ; and estd. the Moody-Manners Opera Co.

Männ'liche Stim'me (*G.*). A male voice.

MANNS, Sir August Friedrich. *B.* Stolzenberg, nr. Stettin, 1825. Son of a poor glass-blower ; taught the vn., clar., and fl., by the village musician of a neighbouring hamlet. 1st vn. Gungl's orch., Berlin, 1848 ; condr. Kroll's Garden, 1849-51 ; sub-condr. Crystal Palace Band, London, 1854. Director of the Crystal Palace music, 1855. Knighted, 1904; *d.* 1907.
He conducted over 12,000 concerts at the Crystal Palace, and introduced very many new works to English audiences, specially assisting English composers.

Manns'stimme (*G.*). Male voice.

MANN'STÄDT, Franz. Condr.; *b.* Hagen, 1852.

Ma'no (*I.*). The hand.
Ma'no de'stra, Man de'stra ⎫ The right hand.
Ma'no dirit'ta, Man di'ritta ⎪
Ma'no drit'ta, Man drit'ta ⎭ Abbn. M.D.
Ma'no sini'stra, Man sinis'tra. The left hand.
Abbn. M.S.

Manrit'ta (*I.*). The right hand.

MANS'FELDT, Edgar. (See **Pierson.**)

MANSFIELD, Orlando A. Composer and writer ; *b.* Horningsham, 1863.

MAN'TIUS, Eduard. Noted tenor singer ; *b.* Schwerin, 1806 ; *d.* 1874.

MANTOVA'NO. (See **Ripa.**)

Man'ual. (1) (*G., Manual' ; F., Clavier ; I.* and *L., Manua'le*). An organ keyboard. (2) A digital, or finger key.
Man'ual key. A finger key.
Manual'iter (*G.*). On the manuals alone ; without pedals.
Manual'koppel (*G.*). A manual coupler (org.).
Manualmen'te (*I.*). With the hands.
Manual'taste (*G.*). A finger key.
Manual'untersatz (*G.*). A 32-ft. stop (organ).
Manua'li accoppia'ti (*I.*). The manuals coupled.

Manual Signs. (See **Hand-Signs.**)

MANZUO'LI, Giovanni. Distinguished male soprano ; *b.* Florence, abt. 1725. Sang in London, 1764-65.

MAPLESON, Mrs. H. (See **Marie Roze.**)

MAR, Mad. J. R. de la. (See **Nordica.**)

MA'RA, Gertrud Elizabeth (*née* **Schmeling**). Phenomenal soprano ; *b.* Cassel, 1749 ; *d.* Reval, 1833. Crippled by a fall in infancy, she took to the violin, and appeared as a prodigy at 9. Taught singing in London by Paradisi. Sang Leipzig, 1766-71 ; Berlin Court Opera, 1771-1780. Married Mara, a 'cellist, 1773. Sang in London, 1784-1802 ; afterwards made a long European tour, and lost all her property at the burning of Moscow, 1812. Died poor at the age of 84. Her wonderful voice had the marvellous compass of—

MA'RA, La. (See **Marie Lipsius.**)

MARAIS, Marin. "The greatest *viola-da-gamba* player of his time ; " Paris, 1656-1728. Soloist, Royal Orch., 1685-1725.
Works : 5 books of pieces for Gamba, numerous pieces for Gamba with other insts., 4 operas, &c.

MARBECK (or **MERBECKE**), **John.** Orgt., St. George's, Windsor ; *b.* 1523 ; *d.* abt. 1585. Chorister, St. George's, 1531 ; "narrowly escaped burning as a heretic," 1544 ; Mus.B. Oxon, 1550.
Chief work : " The Booke of Common Praier Noted."

Marcan'do (*I.*) ⎱ Marked, accented, empha-
Marca'to (*I.*)   ⎰ sized. (Abbn., *Marc.*)
Ben marca'to. Well emphasized.
Marcatis'simo ⎱ Very strongly accented.
Marca'to assa'i ⎰
Marca'to e lega'to il bas'so. The bass emphasized, but smooth.
Marca'to il can'to ma pia'no l'accompagnamen'to. The melody marked, but the acct. soft.

MARCEL'LI, Marthe. Violinist ; *b.* Roubaix, 1895(4?).
First London appearance, 1908.

MARCEL'LO, Benedetto. Composer and poet ; *b.* Venice, 1686 ; *d.* 1739. Studied music under Gasparini and Lotti. Held various Government positions.
Works : "Music to the first 50 Psalms" (his most famous work), " Concerti grossi," canzoni, cantatas, &c. ; also polemical writings.

March. (*G., Marsch ; F., Marche ; I., Mar'cia.*) A composition suitable to accompany marching. "The metre and cadence of the drums, which is properly the march."—*Rousseau.*
The rhythm of a march should be clearly defined, and arranged in sections of 4 or 8 bars. The modern march is usually preceded by an *Introduction* or a *Fanfare ;* it has a *Trio* of subdued character alternating with the first part ; and there is generally a *Coda.* In form the March is analagous to the Minuet and Trio. (See *Minuet.*)
Slow March (Parade March). (*G., Para'demarsch ; F., Pas ordinaire*). About 75 steps to the minute.
Quick March (Quickstep). (*G., Geschwind'marsch ; F., Pas redoublé.*) About 108 steps.
Double or *Charge.* (*G., Sturm'marsch ; F., Pas de charge.*) About 120 steps.
Funeral or *Dead* Marches are slower, and more solemn in character.

MARCH, Mrs. G. E. (See **Virginia Gabriel.**)

MARCHANT, Arthur Wm. *B.* London, 1850. Mus.Doc. Oxon, 1898.
Works : church music, pf. pieces, org. pieces, "500 Fugue Subjects," &c.

Marche (*F.*). (1) A march. (2) A progression or sequence.
Marche des accords. A sequence or progression of chords.
Marche harmonique. A harmonic progression.
Marche redoublée. A quick step.
Marche triomphale. A triumphal march.

Mär'chen (*G.*). Tale, legend, fable.

MARCHE'SI, Luigi (known as **Marchesi'ni**). Celebrated male soprano ; *b.* Milan 1755 ; *d.* 1829. In 1780, was considered the greatest singer in Italy. Sang for several years in London, from 1788.

MARCHE'SI de Castrone, Mathilde (*née* **Graumann**). Renowned singer and teacher ; *b.* Frankfort-on-Main, 1826. Married Salvatore Marchesi (below), 1852.
Works : a Vocal Method, 24 books of Vocalizes, "Marchesi and Music," &c.

MARCHE'SI de Castrone, Salvatore. (Cavaliere Salvatore de Castrone, Marchese della Rajata). Baritone singer and teacher ; *b.* Palermo, 1822. *D.* 1908. Married Mathilde Graumann (see above), 1852. After singing together at Berlin, Brussels, London, &c., they taught singing at Vienna, Cologne, &c., settling in Paris, 1881.
Works : songs, vocalizes, a Vocal Method, &c.

Madame **Blanche Marchesi** is the 10th and only surviving child of the above.

MARCHESI'NI. (See **Luigi Marchesi.**)

MARCHET'TI, Filippo. Operatic composer ; *b.* Bolognola, Italy, 1835 ; *d.* 1902. Director Royal Accademia di S. Cecilia, Rome, 1881.
Chief operas : *Gentile da Varano* (1856), *Giulietta e Romeo* (1865), *Ruy Blas* (1869).

MARCHET'TUS of Padua. Abt. 1250-1300(?). Wrote 2 early essays on music, dated 1283.

MAR'CHI, Emilio de. Noted tenor ; *b.* Piedmont, 1866.

Mar'cia (*I.*). A march.
Marcia D.S. al fi'ne. Repeat the March from the ⸙ to the *fi'ne.*
Mar'cia fune'bre. A funeral march.
Marcia'le ⎫
Marzia'le ⎬ In march style.
Al'la mar'cia ⎭
Marcia'ta. A march.

MARÉCHAL, Henri Chas. *B.* Paris, 1842 ; *Grand Prix de Rome*, Paris Cons., 1870.
Works : operas (*La Taverne des Trabans, l'Etoile, Calendal*), stage music, pf. pieces, songs, &c.

MAREN'CO, Romauldo. *B.* Novi Ligure, 1841. Ballet Director, La Scala, Milan, 1873.
Works : over 20 ballets and half-a-dozen operas.

MAREN'ZIO, Luca. Famous composer of madrigals ; *b.* nr. Brescia, abt. 1550 ; *d.* 1599. Maestro to Cardinals d'Este and Aldobrandini, Rome, 1591 ; cantor, Papal Chapel, 1595. His madrigals are among the finest ever written.
Works : 17 books of madrigals, 3 books of motets, 6 books of "Villanelle ed Arie," &c.

MAREŠ, Joh. A. *B.* Bohemia, 1719 ; *d.* St. Petersburg, 1794.
Invented the Russian *Hunting-horn Music*, " in which each player blows a single tone."

MARIA'NI, Angelo. " The Prince of Italian conductors;" *b.* Ravenna, 1822 ; *d.* 1873. Pupil of Rossini.
Conductor at Messina, Milan, Vicenza, Copenhagen, Venice, Geneva, &c.

MARIMON, Marie. Soprano ; *b.* Paris, abt. 1835.

MARIN, Marie M. M. de. Distinguished harpist ; *b.* Bayonne, 1769 ; *d.* (?).
Wrote several sonatas, variations, &c., for harp.

Marine band. The band of a warship.

Marine trumpet. (See **Tromba marina.**)

MA'RIO, Giuseppe, Conte di Candia. Renowned operatic tenor ; *b.* Cagliari, Sardinia, 1810 ; *d.* 1883. *Début*, Paris Opéra, 1838. A great favourite in London and St. Petersburg. Married **Giulia Grisi** (*q.v.*).
His voice was fresh and powerful, and his vocal style finished and charming.

MARITA'NA. Opera by Wallace, 1845.

Mark, Division. The figure over any irregular group of notes ; *e.g.—*

Mark, Harmonic. The sign o indicating a "harmonic" on a vn., &c.

Mark, Metronome. (See **Metronome.**)

Marki(e)'ren (*G.*). To mark, emphasize, accent, make prominent.
Markiert' ⎫ Well marked, emphasized, &c.
Markirt' ⎭
Markie'rt und kräf'tig. Emphasized and vigorous.

Mar'kig (*G.*). "Marrowy." Sturdy, vigorous ; with much emphasis.
Im'mer mar'kig gestrich'en. Always with vigorous bow-strokes.

Marks of Expression. (See **Dynamics.**)

MARKULL', Friedrich W. *B.* nr. Elbing, 1816 ; *d.* 1887. Orgt. Marienkirche, Dantzig, 1836 ; Royal Mus.-director, 1847.
Works : 3 operas, 2 oratorios, symphonies, pf. pieces, org. pieces, songs, a "choralbuch," &c.

MARMONTEL, Antoine François. Pianist and teacher ; *b.* Puy-de-Dôme, 1816 ; *d.* 1898. Studied Paris Cons. ; succeeded Zimmermann as pf. teacher, 1848. Among his most celebrated pupils were Bizet, J. Wieniawsky, Dubois, Guiraud, Paladilhe, T. Lack, F. Thomé, &c.
Works : much educational pf. music ; "L'art classique et moderne du piano," "Eléments d'esthétique musicale," &c.

MAR'PURG, Friedrich Wm. Eminent theorist ; *b.* Seehausen, 1718 ; *d.* 1795. Director Prussian Lottery, Berlin, 1763.
His numerous theoretical works include "Die Kunst, das Clavier zu spielen," " Anleitung zum Clavierspielen," a treatise on Fugue (his greatest work), a " Handbook of Generalbass and Composition," &c.

MAR'PURG, Friedrich. Great grandson of preceding ; *b.* Paderborn, 1825 ; *d.* 1884. Violinist and pianist ; studied under Mendelssohn at Leipzig. Capellmeister at various theatres. Wrote 3 operas, &c.

Marqué (*F.*). Marked, accented, emphasized.
Marquez un peu la mélodie. Emphasize the melody a little.

MARRIOTT, Annie Augusta (Mrs. P. Palmer.) Soprano vocalist; *b.* Nottingham, 1859.

MARRIOTT, John. 1780-1825. Rector, Church Lawford.
Wrote the hymn "Thou whose almighty word."

Marsch (*G.*). (Plur. *Mär'sche.*) A march.
Märsch'artig ⎫ In the style of a march.
Märsch'mässig ⎭
Marsch'takt ⎫ March time.
Marsch'zeitmass ⎭

MARSCH'NER, Heinrich A. Distinguished dramatic composer ; *b.* Zittau, 1795 ; *d.* Hanover, 1861. Entered Leipzig Univ. as a law student, 1813, but soon gave up law for music. Choirmaster under Weber and Morlacchi, German and Italian operas, Dresden, 1823. Capellmeister, Leipzig Th., 1826. Court Capellmeister, Hanover, 1831-59.
Works : about 20 operas (including *Der Vampyr*, 1828 ; *Der Templer und die Jüdin*, 1829 ; and *Hans Heiling*) ; 10 sets of four-part male choruses, 20 sets of songs, &c.

MARSDEN, George. Organist ; *b.* Staly-bridge, 1843 ; Mus.Doc. Cantab., 1882.
Works : church music, pf. pieces, part-songs.

Marseillaise, La. The French National Song, written and composed by Rouget de Lisle, 1792.

MARSH, Alphonso. 1627-81. Gentleman, Chapel Royal. Wrote songs, &c.

MARSHALL, Julian. *B.* Headingly, Leeds, 1836 ; *d.* 1903.
Wrote articles for Grove's Dict., &c.

MARSHALL, Mrs. J. (See **F. A. Thomas.**)

MARSHALL, Wm. Violinist ; *b.* Focha-bers, 1748 ; *d.* 1833.
Works : several collections of Scotch Reels, Strathspeys, &c.

MARSICK, Martin P. J. Fine violinist ; *b.* nr. Liége, 1848. Orgt. Liége Cath. at 12 ; afterwards studied Paris Cons., taking 1st prize for vn. playing. Violin Prof. Paris Cons., 1892.
Works : several vn. pieces, including 3 concertos.

MARSTON, George W. American orgt. and composer ; *b.* Sandwich, Mass., 1840 ; *d.* 1901.

MARTEAU, Henri. Violinist ; *b.* Rheims, 1874. 1st prize for vn. playing Paris Cons., 1892. Has toured in Europe and America.

Marteau (*F.*). (1) The hammer of a pf. key. (2) A tuning hammer.

Martelé (*F.*) ⎫ " Hammered ; " accented
Martella'to (*I.*) ⎭ with special force.

Martellan'do (*I.*). Hammering.
Martella're (*I.*). To hammer. Also applied to staccato vn. bowing.
Martellement (*F.*). (1) The "crush-note" or *acciacca-tura* in harp playing. (2) A *mordent* in old music.

MARTHA. Opera by Flotow, 1847.
"The last Rose of Summer" made it successful.

MARTIN, Sir George Clement. *B.* Lambourne, Berks, 1844. Mus.Doc.Cantuar, 1883. Orgt. St. Paul's Cath., 1888.
Works : church music, org. pieces, part-songs, &c.

MARTIN, Jean Blaise. Famous baritone ; *b.* nr. Lyons, 1768 ; *d.* 1837.

MARTIN, Pierre Alex. Organ builder ; *d.* Paris, 1879.
Invented the harmonium " percussion action."

MARTIN Y SOLAR, Vicente. Opera composer ; *b.* Valencia, 1754 ; *d.* 1806.
Works : 10 operas (including *La Cosa rara*).

MARTI'NI, Giambattista. (Padre Martini.) Distinguished theorist ; Bologna, 1706-1784. Maestro, San Francesco Ch., 1725 ; took Holy Orders, 1729. Among those who received instruction from him were Gluck, Mozart, and Grétry.
His compositions are now forgotten ; of his numerous valuable writings the "Storia della Musica" (3 vols. completed), and "Examples of Counterpoint," are the most important.

MARTI'NI, Jean P. E. (Schwar'zendorf.) *B.* Freistadt, Palatinate, 1741 ; *d.*

Paris, 1816. Military officer ; Inspector Paris Cons., 1794-1802. Royal Intendant, 1814.
Works : 12 operas (*l'Amoureux de quinze ans*), church music, military music, &c.

Martra'za (*I.*). A Spanish dance.

MARTUC'CI, Giuseppe. *B.* Capua, 1856. Pupil, afterwards Prof., Naples Cons. ; Director Bologna Cons., 1886.
Works : orchestral music, chamber music, songs, interesting pf. pieces, &c.

MARTY, Georges E. *B.* Paris, 1860 ; *d.* 1908. *Grand Prix de Rome*, Paris Cons., 1882 ; Prof. of chorus singing, 1894.
Works : stage pieces, orchestral suites, pf. pieces, songs, &c.

MARX, Adolf Bernhard. Celebrated theorist; *b.* Halle, 1799 ; *d.* Berlin, 1866. Co-founder and editor of the *Berliner allgemeine musikalische Zeitung*, 1824-30. Music director, Berlin Univ., 1832. Co-founder of the Berlin Cons., 1850.
Works : "Musical Composition" (4 vols.), "All-gemeine Musiklehre," "The Music of the 19th Cent.," treatises on Beethoven and Gluck, &c.

MARXSEN, Eduard. *B.* nr. Altona, 1806; *d.* 1887. Teacher of Brahms.

Marzia'le (*I.*). Martial ; in march style.

MARZIALS, Theodor. Song composer ; *b.* Brussels, 1850. Superintendent Music Dept., British Museum, 1870.

MAR'ZO, Eduardo. *B.* Naples, abt. 1855. Went to New York as a "boy pianist," 1867, and has made a reputation there as conductor, accompanist, teacher, and composer.

MASANIE'LLO. Opera by Auber, 1829.
Called in France, *La Muette de Portici* ; in Germany, *Die Stumme von Portici*. It occasioned the Belgian revolution.

MASCA'GNI, Pietro. Renowned opera composer ; *b.* Leghorn, 1863. After many early struggles, his *Cavalleria Rusticana* (Rome, 1890), gained him world-wide fame.
His other operas include *L'Amico Fritz* (1891), *I Rantzau* (1892), *Guglielmo Ratcliff* (1895), and *Iris* (1898).

Masche'ra (*I.*). A mask.
Maschera'ta. A masquerade.

MASCHERO'NI, Angelo. Song composer ; *b.* Bergamo, 1856 ; *d.* 1905.

MASCHERO'NI, Edoardo. Conductor and composer ; *b.* Milan, 1857.

Maschi'nen (*G.*). Pistons (of a cornet, &c.).
Maschi'nen-pau'ken. Kettle drums with machine adjustment.

Ma'schio (*I.*). Manly, noble.

MASET'TI, Umberto. *B.* Bologna, 1869. Prof. of Singing, Bologna Cons., 1895.
Works : opera (*Vindice*), church music, songs, &c.

MASI'NI, Angelo. Tenor ; *b.* Forli, 1845.

Mask. (See **Masque.**)

MASON, Lowell. Teacher of class-singing, and composer of simple popular music ; *b.* Boston, Mass., 1792 ; *d.* 1872. Self-taught musician. Founded the Boston Acad. of Music, 1832.

Works : numerous collections of hymns, school songs, &c.

MASON, Luther W. *B.* Turner, Maine, 1828; *d.* 1896. Invented "The National Music Course." Settled in Boston, 1865, and "reformed musical instruction in the Primary Schools." Visited Japan, 1879, and worked there for 3 years as Inspector of School Music.

In Japan, school music is still called "Mason song."

MASON, William. Pianist and teacher ; son of Lowell Mason ; *b.* Boston, Mass., 1829; *d.* 1908. Studied Leipzig, 1849, and afterwards under Liszt at Weimar. After concert tours, settled in New York, 1855.

Works : pf. pieces, "Touch and Technic, a Method for Artistic Piano Playing," &c.

Masque (*F.*). (*G.*, *Mas'kenspiel.*) Originally a stage performance with masks. Afterwards a kind of cantata based on some mythological or allegorical subject.

The Elizabethan masques were specially elaborate.

Mass (*G.*). Time, measure. (See *Zeitmass.*)

Mass. (*L.*, *Mis'sa* ; *G.*, *Mes'se* ; *F.*, *Messe* ; *I.*, *Mes'sa.*) (1) The celebration of the Lord's Supper or Eucharist.

Generally, but not necessarily, applied to the Roman service.

(2) A musical setting of portions of the liturgy of the Mass.

The chief musical divisions of the mass are (1) *Kyrie,* (2) *Gloria,* (3) *Credo,* (4) *Sanctus,* (5) *Agnus Dei.* Each of these is generally divided into two or more parts.

(3) A church festival or feast-day ; as Candlemas, Christmas, Michaelmas, &c.

High Mass. One with music and incense.
Low Mass. One without music.
Requiem Mass. (See *Requiem.*)

Mass book. The Missal of the Roman Church.

MAS'SA, Nicolò, Italian opera composer ; 1854-94.

MASSART, Lambert Jos. Distinguished violinist ; *b.* Liége, 1811 ; *d.* 1892. Vn. Prof. Paris Cons., 1843-90.

Among his pupils were H. Wieniawski and Sarasate.

MASSÉ, Félix M. (known as **Victor Massé**). Renowned opera composer ; *b.* Lorient, France, 1822 ; *d.* Paris, 1884. *Grand Prix de Rome,* Paris Cons., 1845. Chorusmaster, Opéra, 1860 ; Prof. of Counterpoint, Paris Cons., 1866.

Chief operas : *La Chambre gothique* (1849), *Les Noces de Jeannette* (1853).

MASSENET, Jules E. F. Distinguished composer ; *b.* nr. St. Etienne, 1842. Won

Grand Prix de Rome, Paris Cons., 1863 ; Prof. of Compn., 1878-96.

Works : several operas (*Don César de Bazan,* 1872 ; *Le Cid,* 1885 ; *La Navarraise,* 1894 ; *Sapho,* 1897 ; &c.) ; sacred drama (*Marie-Magdeleine*) ; *Eve,* a mystery ; oratorio (*La Vierge*) ; orchestral suites, overtures, &c.

MASSIE, Rd. 1800-87. Trans. Spitta's *Psalter und Harfe,* 1860 (including " O, how blest the hour, Lord Jesus").

Mäs'sig (*G.*). (1) Moderate. (2) "Appropriate to," suitable.

Hel'denmässig. Hero-like, heroic.
Klavier'mässig. Suitable for the Clavier (pf., &c.).
Marsch'mässig. In march style.
Mäs'sig bewegt' } Moderately quick.
Mäs'sig geschwind' }
Mäs'sig lang'sam. Moderately slow.
Mäs'sig leb'haft. Moderately lively.
Mäs'sig und ru'hig. Moderately and tranquilly.

Mäs'sigen (*G.*). To diminish in speed and loudness.

Mäs'siger (*G.*). More moderate, slower.

Mas'sima (*I.*). A semibreve, or whole note.

Masterchord. The chord of the dominant (or the dominant 7th).

Master-fugue. A learned *fuga ricercata.* (See **Fuga.**)

Master note. Old name for **Leading-note.**

Master of Music. A musical degree between that of Bachelor and Doctor.

Mastersinger. (See **Meistersinger.**)

Masu're (*G.*)
Masu'reck (*Polish*) } A mazurka (*q.v.*).
Masu'rek (*G.*) }
Masur'ka (*G.*)

MASZYN'SKI, Peter. Pianist and composer ; *b.* Warsaw, 1855.

Mat'alan. A small Indian flute.

Matelotte (*F.*). A sailor's dance ; a hornpipe (*q.v.*).

MATER'NA, Amalie. Celebrated operatic soprano ; *b.* Styria, 1847. *Prima donna* Vienna Court Opera, 1869-96.

Her Wagnerian *rôles* were specially fine ; she created the part of "Brünnhilde," Bayreuth, 1876, and "Kundry," 1882.

MATHER, William. 1756-1808. Orgt. at Sheffield. Wrote several psalm tunes.

MATHEWS, Wm. S. B. American critic and writer ; *b.* New London, N.H., 1837.

Works : "Outlines of Mus. Form," "How to Understand Music," &c.

MATHIAS, Georges A. S. C. *B.* Paris, 1826. Prof. of pf. at the Cons., 1862.

Works : a symphony, overtures, pf. concertos, numerous pf. studies, &c.

MATHIEU, Emile L. V. *B.* Lille, 1844. Studied Brussels Cons. Director Louvain Music School, 1881-98. Director Royal Cons., Ghent, 1898.

Works : operas, ballets, cantatas, symphonic poems, male choruses, songs, &c.

Matina're (*I.*). To sing matins.

Matina'ta (*I.*). A morning song; an *Aubade*.

Matinée (*F.*). An entertainment during the daytime.

Matinée musicale. A musical *matinée.*

Matines (*F.*). Matins (*q.v.*).

Mat'ins, Mat'tins. The 1st of the "Canonical hours." The hymns and prayers at early morning service.

MATTAUSCH. Magdeburg composer. His opera, *Bridal Night*, was successfully produced, 1906.

MATTE'I, Abbate Stanislao. Bologna, 1750-1825. Pupil of Padre Martini; Prof. of Counterpoint, Liceo Filarmonico, from 1804. Taught Rossini and Donizetti.

Works : sacred music, a treatise on "Figured Bass," &c.

MATTE'I, Tito. Pianist; *b.* nr. Naples, 1841. Settled in London abt. 1865.

Works : 2 operas, a ballet, pf. pieces, songs.

MATTE'IS, Nicola. Italian violinist; settled in London, 1672. His son, **Nicola** (*d.* 1749), was the teacher of Dr. Burney.

MATTHAY, Tobias Augustus. Pianist; *b.* Clapham, 1858. Prof. R.A.M., 1880.

Works : orch. pieces, pf. pieces, "Touch in Pf. Playing," &c.

Matt'herzig (*G.*). Faint-hearted, spiritless.

MAT'THESON, Johann. Composer and writer; Hamburg, 1681-1764. Operatic tenor, 1697-1705; befriended Handel, 1703, "but afterwards broke with him." Music-director, Hamburg Cath., 1715-1728.

Works : 8 operas, 24 oratorios and cantatas, clavichord suites,12 sonatas for fl. and vn., &c. ; treatises on the orchestra, the organ, thoroughbass, "Georg Friedrich Händel's Lebensbeschreibung," &c.

MATTHIAS Le Maître. (See **Le Maistre.**)

MAT'THISON, Arthur. *B.* Birmingham, 1826; *d.* 1883.

"A versatile vocalist, actor, composer, and writer."

MAT'THISON-HAN'SEN, Hans. Danish organist; *b.* Flensburg, 1807; *d.* 1890. Orgt. Roeskilde Cath., 1832.

Works : an oratorio, church music, org. pieces.

MAT'THISON-HAN'SEN, Gotfred. Orgt.; son of preceding; *b.* Roeskilde, 1832. Org. teacher, Copenhagen Cons., 1867.

Works : org. pieces, pf. pieces, &c.

Maul'trommel (*G.*). A Jew's harp.

MAUNDER, John Henry. Organist and composer; *b.* Chelsea, 1858.

Works : church cantatas, anthems, services, &c.

MAUREL, Victor. Distinguished baritone singer; *b.* Marseilles, 1848. Studied Paris Cons. *Début*, Paris Opéra, 1867.

MAU'RER, Ludwig Wm. Violinist; *b.* Potsdam, 1789; *d.* 1878. Toured in Russia, Berlin, Paris, &c.

Works : symphonie concertante for 4 vns. and orch. ; vn. concertos, chamber music, &c.

Max'ima (*L.*). The Large (*q.v.*). The longest note in mediæval notation; equal to 8 semibreves.

MAY, Edward Collett. Organist and singing teacher; *b.* Greenwich, 1806; *d.* 1887. Orgt. Greenwich Hospital, 1837-69. He was " a disciple of Hullah," and did much " to popularize singing among the masses."

MAY, Florence. Daughter of E. C. Contemp. pianist, composer, writer, &c.

MAYBRICK, Michael. Baritone singer, and composer of exceptionally popular songs (under the name of **Stephen Adams**). *B.* Liverpool, 1844.

MAY'ER, Chas. Pianist; pupil of Field; *b.* Königsberg, 1799; settled in Russia; *d.* 1862.

Works : about 350 pf. works, including studies, concert pieces, fantasias, &c.

MAY'ER, Emilie. *B.* Friedland, Mecklenburg, 1821.

Works : symphonies, overtures, chamber music, pf. pieces, over 150 songs, &c.

MAY'ER, Karl. Baritone; *b.* Sondershausen, 1852.

MAY'ER, Wilhelm. (Pen name **W. A. Remy.**) *B.* Prague, 1831; *d.* 1898. Renowned teacher of pf. and composition; taught Busoni, Weingartner, Kienzl, &c.

Works : orch. music, part-songs, pf. music, songs, &c.

MAY'ERHOFF, Franz. Composer and condr.; *b.* Chemnitz, 1864.

MAYNARD, Walter. Pen name of **T. W. Beale** (*q.v.*).

MAYR, J. Simon. Distinguished teacher; *b.* Mendorf, Bavaria, 1763; *d.* 1845. Settled in Venice, where he brought out abt. 70 operas, then in Bergamo. His most renowned pupil was Donizetti.

Chief opera, *Saffo* (1794); he also a wrote "Brief Historical Notice of the Life and Works of Haydn," &c.

MAYR'BERGER, Karl. *B.* Vienna, 1828; *d.* 1881. Capellmeister, Pressburg Cath., 1864.

Works : operas, male choruses, songs, &c.

MAY'SEDER, Joseph. Distinguished violinist; Vienna, 1789-1863. *Début* at 11; solo violinist, Vienna Court Opera, 1820. Imperial Chamber virtuoso, 1835.

Works : vn. concertos, chamber music, pf. music, vn. solos and studies, &c.

MAZAS, Jacques F. Violinist; *b.* Béziers, France, 1782; *d.* 1849. Pupil of Baillot, Paris Cons. Director, Music-school, Cambrai, 1837-41.

Works : a vn. method, vn. studies, concertos, fantasias, &c. ; a Viola Method; 3 operas.

Mazourk' (*G.*)
Mazour'ka (*G.*)
Mazur' (*G.*)
Mazur'ca (*G.*)
Mazur'ka (*G.*)
Mazur'ke (*G.*) A lively Polish national dance in triple time, with much varied rhythm. It is quicker than the *Polonaise* or *Polacca*, and considerably slower than the waltz. Among the most characteristic rhythms are—

MAZZIN'GHI, Joseph. *B.* London, 1765 ; *d.* 1844. Pupil of J. C. Bach ; music teacher to the Princess of Wales.
> Wrote English operas, melodramas, &c. ; also pf. music, glees, songs, &c.

MAZZOC'CHI, Domenico. *B.* Civita Castellana, Rome, abt. 1590 ; *d.* abt. 1650.
> Pub. a book of madrigals (1640), in which the following signs are used for the first time:— *f, p, tr,* < >

MAZZOLA'NI, Antonio. Composer of successful operas, songs, &c. Ferrara, 1819-1900.

MAZZUCA'TO, Alberto. *B.* Udine, 1813, *d.* 1877. Violinist ; leader, La Scala; Milan, 1859-69. Director, Milan Cons., 1872.
> Works : operas (*La Findanzata di Lammermoor*, &c.), an "Atlas of Ancient Music," several translations of theoretical works, &c.

M.D. "Main Droite ; " right hand.

M.D.C. Abbn. for *Menuetto da Capo* (*q.v.*).

Me. The Tonic Sol-fa spelling of *Mi*, the 3rd note of the Major scale.

MEAD, Olive. Talented concert violinist ; *b.* Cambridge, Massachusetts, 1874.

Mean. Inner ; midway. (1) Middle voices ; as *Tenor* or *Alto*. (2) The middle strings of insts.
Mean Clef. The "C" clef. (See *Clef.*)
Mean parts. Middle parts.
Mean-tone system. (See *Temperament.*)

Means of Expression. (See **Expression** and **Dynamics.**)

Measurable. (See **Mensurable.**)

Measure. (1) (*G., Takt ; F., Mesure ; I., Misu'ra*). A metrical unit.
> The Measure is commonly called a "Bar." It consists of a division of time "from one strong accent to the next," and occupies the space between two successive "Bar-lines." (For the different kinds of Bars, or Measures, in Staff Notation, see *Time.*)
> In Tonic Sol-fa, 6 kinds of Measure are employed
> (1) Duple, or two-pulse Measure :—
> | : ‖
> (2) Triple, or Three-pulse Measure.—
> | : : ‖
> (3) Quadruple, or Four-pulse Measure—
> | : | : ‖
> (4) Compound Duple, or 6-pulse Measure—
> | : : | : : ‖
> (5) Compound Triple, or 9-pulse Measure—
> | : : | : : | : : ‖
> (6) Compound Quadruple, or 12-pulse Measure—
> | : : | : : | : : | : : ‖
> N.B.—A measure of music is somewhat analogous to a "foot" in poetry ; but the measure always

commences with a *strong* accent, while the poetical "foot" may commence on *any kind* of accent. Also, a measure of music may correspond to two or more feet of poetry.

(2) Speed ; rate or style of movement ; *e.g.,* " *a slow and stately measure.*"

(3) Name for an old dance of the nature of a *Minuet*.

(4) The metre of poetry.
> The terms *Common Measure, Long Measure,* &c., are sometimes used instead of the preferable *Common Metre, Long Metre,* &c. (See *Metre*.)
Measure-accents. The accents proper to each kind of measure. (See *Accent, Metrical.*)
Measure-note. The "beat-note" of any bar. In 3-4 time, for example, the measure-note is a crotchet ; in quick 6-8, a dotted-crotchet ; in slow 6-8, a quaver ; &c.

Mécanisme (*F.*)
Meccani'smo (*I.*) Mechanical dexterity : technique.

Mecha'nik (*G.*)
Mechanism (1) The "action" of a pf. or org. ; the "machine-head" of a double bass ; &c.

(2) Technique ; the method of using the fingers, &c., in playing.

Meck'ern (*G.*). To bleat, to tremolo.

Mede'simo (*I.*)
Mede'smo (*I.*) The same.

Mede'simo movimen'to.
Mede'simo tem'po. The same speed as before.

Me'dial. (1) Intermediate ; half way. (2) Pertaining to the mediant.

Mediant
Médiante (*F.*)
Median'te (*G.* and *I.*) The 3rd note of any major or minor scale ; the middle note between tonic and dominant.

Medium Accent. (See **Accent.**)

Medium Voice. A voice of moderate pitch—neither very high nor very low.

Mediation. The part of a chant between the reciting note and the next cadence.

Me'dius (*L.*). (1) The "mean" or tenor part. (2) One of the Ecclesiastical Accents. (See **Accent.**)

Medley. "A conglomeration of unrelated but usually familiar tunes ; " a *pot-pourri*.

MEE, Rev. John Hy. Composer and writer ; *b.* Derbyshire, 1852. Mus.Doc. Oxon, 1888. Precentor Chichester Cath., 1889. Coryphæus, Oxford Univ., 1890.

MEEN, J. Fountain. Organist ; *b.* London, 1846. Prof., G.S.M., 1886.

MEERENS, Chas. *B.* Bruges, 1831.
> Works : several treatises on Acoustics, &c.

Meer'trompe'te (*G.*)
Meer'horn (*G.*) A sea trumpet ; speaking trumpet.

MEERTS, Lambert J. Violinist ; Brussels, 1800-63. Prof. Brussels Cons., 1835.
> Wrote several excellent educational vn. studies.

MEES, Arthur. *B.* Columbus, Ohio, 1850. Conductor Cincinnati, New York, Albany, Chicago, &c.
> Works : "Piano Studies," analytical programs.

MEFISTOFE'LE. Opera by Boito, 1868.

MEGO'NE, Norfolk. Condr. ; *b.* London, 1850.

MEH'LIG, Anna (Mad. Falk). Pianist ; pupil of Liszt ; *b.* Stuttgart, 1843.

Mehr *(G.).* More (than one) ; several.
Mehr'chörig. For several choirs.
Mehr'fach. Manifold.
Mehr'faches Intervall'. A compound interval.
Mehr'facher Ka'non. A canon with more than 2 subjects.
Mehr'facher Kon'trapunkt. Counterpoint with several invertible parts.
Mehr'fache Stim'me. A compound organ stop.
Mehr'ho'he, hel'le, schar'fe Stim'men. More clear and bright stops.
Mehr lang'sam, oft zurück'haltend. Slower, with frequent retardations.
Mehr'stimmig. For several voices ; polyphonic.
Mehr'stimmige Musik'. Part-music.
Mehr'stimmiger Gesang'. A glee or part-song.
Mehr'stimmigkeit durch Bre'chung. Polyphony in broken chords.
Mehr tie'fe, vol'le Stim'men. More deep and full-toned stops.

MEHR'KENS, Friedrich A. *B.* Neuenkirchen, 1840 ; *d.* 1899. Condr. *Bach-Gesellschaft,* Hamburg, from 1871.
Works : a symphony, a Te Deum, &c.

MÉHUL, Étienne Nicolas. Distinguished operatic composer ; *b.* Givet, Ardennes, 1763 ; *d.* Paris, 1817. Organist at 10. Took up dramatic composition on the advice of Gluck. Apptd. one of the Inspectors, Paris Cons., 1795, and also elected a member of the Académie. His operas show " a robust dramatic style and fine orchestral effects," but his later works met with comparatively slight success.
Chief operas : *Euphrosyne et Coradin* (1790), *Stratonice* (1792), *Le Jugement de Pâris* (1793), *Phrosine et Mélidore* (1794), *Le jeune Henri* (1797), *Joseph* (his greatest work, 1807).

MEI'BOM (MEIBO'MIUS), Marcus. Learned philologist ; *b.* Schleswig, 1626 ; *d.* 1711.
Edited "Antiquæ Musicæ Scriptores," containing the writings on music of seven Greek and Latin authors (Euclid, Aristoxenus, &c.).

MEI'FRED, Joseph J. P. E. Horn-player ; *b.* Basses-Alpes, 1791 ; *d.* 1867.
Wrote Methods for Horn ; solos, duets, &c.

MEINAR'DUS, Ludwig S. *B.* Oldenburg, 1827 ; *d.* 1896. Studied Leipzig Cons. ; afterwards under Liszt. Condr. Glogau Singakademie, 1853-65 ; then teacher, &c., at Dresden and Hamburg.
Works : 5 oratorios (*Simon Petrus, Gideon,* &c.) ; choral ballades, 2 symphonies, chamber music, pf. pieces, songs ; theoretical treatises.

MEI'NERS, Giovanni. *B.* Milan, 1826 ; *d.* 1897. For some years Prof. at the G.S.M., London.
Works : 6 operas (*Riccardo III,* 1857).

MEISS'LER, Josef. Pen-name of **W. H. Hutchinson** *(q.v.).*

MEI'STER, Karl S. *B.* Königstein, 1818 ; *d.* 1881. Town music-director, Montabaur, 1851.
Wrote male-voice hymns, org. pieces, &c., and a work on German "Church Songs."

Mei'ster *(G.).* Master, teacher.
Mei'sterfuge. A "fuga ricerca'ta." (See *Fuga.*)
Mei'stergesang. A master's song ; a minstrel's song.
Mei'sterhaft } Masterly, skilful.
Mei'sterlich }
Mei'stersinger. } The chief musician of a German
Mei'stersänger. } town or district in the middle ages. The *Meistersingers* were the successors of the *Min'nesingers* (*q.v.*). They formed important "guilds" in most of the great German towns, especially in the 15th and 16th cents. Hans Sachs (*q.v.*) was a notable *Meistersinger.* The last Guild, at Ulm, dissolved 1839.
Mei'sterspieler. A virtuoso.
Mei'sterstück. A masterpiece.

MEI'STERSINGER von NURN'BERG, DIE. Opera by Wagner, 1867.

ME'LA, Vicenzo. *B.* nr. Verona, 1821 ; *d.* 1897.
Works : 6 operas (*Il Casino di Campagna,* 1865).

Melancoli'a *(I.)* } Melancholy. (See **Malin-**
Mélancolie *(F.)* } **coni'a.**)

Mélange *(G.).* A medley, or *potpourri.*

MELA'NI, Amelia. Soprano ; *b.* Pistoia, 1876.

MEL'BA, Madame Nellie. Operatic soprano; *b.* nr. Melbourne, 1859. (Real name **Mrs. Armstrong** (*nee* **Mitchell**), " Melba " (being an imitation of Melbourne). Studied under Mme. Marchesi in Paris ; *début,* Brussels, 1887. First London appearance, Covent Garden, May, 1888.

MEL'CER, Heinrich von. Pianist ; *b.* Warsaw, 1869.
Chief work : *Concertstück* in E minor for pf. and orch.

MELCHIOR, Edwd. Teacher and writer ; *b.* Rotterdam, 1860.

MELCHIO'RI, Antonio. Italian composer of *Balli Teatrali, Ballabili,* &c. ; 1827-97.

MELGOU'NOW, Julius von. Pianist and writer on rhythm, &c. ; *b.* Russia, 1846.

Melis'ma *(Gk.).* (1) A melodic ornament or embellishment. (2) A *Cadenza* (*q.v.*).
Melismat'ic. (1) Embellished. (2) With two or more notes to a syllable ; opposed to *syllabic.*

Melismatik *(G.).* The art of florid vocalisation or *fioratura.*

MELL, Davis. Violinist and clockmaker ; London, 17th cent.

Mellif'luous. Very sweet and melodious.

MELLON, Alfred. Violinist and condr. ; London, 1821-67.

Melo'de *(I.)* } Melody ; the air or tune.
Melodi'a *(I.)* }

Melo'deon. (1) Old name for American organ. (2) A variety of accordeon.

Melo'dia. An org. stop resembling the Clarabella, Waldflöte, or Hohlflöte.

Melo'dica. A small pipe organ invented by Stein, Augsburg, 1770.

Melo'dico *(I.)* } In a singing style ; *can-*
Melodico'so *(I.)* } *tando* (*q.v.*).

Melod'icon. A key-board inst. with tuning forks instead of strings.

Melod′ics. The theory of melody.

Melodic Stop } A device on some harmoniums,
Melody Attachment } positive organs, &c., by which only the highest (melody) note of a chord speaks in connection with the particular "melodic" stop drawn. Thus, other stops not being affected, it is possible to play a melody and its accompaniment (on other stops) on the same manual.

Mélodie (*F.*). Melody ; the air or tune.

Mélodie bien sentie. The melody (to be) well accented.
Mélodieuse. Melodious.
Mélodieusement. Melodiously.

Melo′dik (*G.*). Melodics (*q.v.*).

Melo′diograph. (See **Melograph.**)

Melo′dion. Name given to various insts. of the harmonium or concertina family.

Melodio′so (*I.*) }
Melo′disch (*G.*) } Melodious, sweet.

Melodi′sta (*I.*) } A melodist; one who in-
Mélodiste (*F.*) } vents good melodies.

Melo′dium. (See **Melo′dion.**)

Mel′odrama. (*G., Me′lodram ; F., Mélo-drame ; I., Melodram′ma.*) (1) Originally, the opera. (2) Spoken drama with musical accompt. (3) A sensational play.

Melody. (*G., Melodie′; F., Mélodie ; I., Melodi′a.*)

(1) "Notes in succession."—*Macfarren.*
(2) A tune ; an air ; a song.
(3) The leading part ; the air ; the theme.
(4) Any one of the parts of a composition.

Though, in its broadest sense, any *successive musical sounds* may be said to constitute melody, yet it must be understood that "artistic melody" implies arrangement, order, design. "The invention of a beautiful, singing, and expressive melody is one of the surest signs of genius ; but even the greatest genius will be anxious to purify, strengthen, and vary the melody by means of art and science."—*Pauer.*
Melody may be—
1. (*a*) Diatonic ; or (*b*) Chromatic.
2. (*a*) Conjunct, *i.e.*, proceeding (mainly) by steps of a second ; or (*b*) Disjunct, *i.e.*, proceeding (mainly) by leaps or skips.
The *Factors of Melody* are (*a*) Ascending Passages, (*b*) Descending Passages, (*c*) Repeated Notes, (*d*) Prolonged Single Notes. (For the distinctive character of each of these see *Expression.*)
Many melodies are based on a harmonic substructure ; *i.e.*, they consist largely of forms of *arpeggio.*

SCHUMANN.

Tonic Chord.   Subdominant.   Tonic.

Domt. 7th   Tonic.

Embellishments of all kinds may be used in melody. Formerly it was the custom to indicate most of them by small notes or signs. Modern composers are more sparing in the use of ornaments, and generally write them in full, *exactly as they should be performed.*

Extended melodies are often developed from little "germs" or "motives" (see *Thematic Development*), or by various forms of "Imitation" (see *Imitation*).
Wide skips and augmented intervals are generally reckoned "unmelodious," but they may be used for special effects.
For the formal arrangement of melodies in "groups of measures" see *Metrical Form.*

Melody in Speech. (1) The characteristic "sing-song" of the speech of different races or localities. (2) Street cries, &c.

It was long ago discovered by itinerant vendors of wares that the singing or chanting voice carries further than the speaking voice, and with much less effort.
The following "cries" are interesting and typical :—

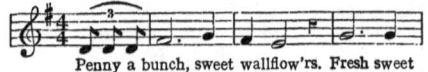

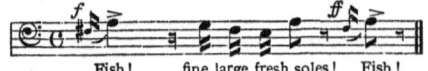

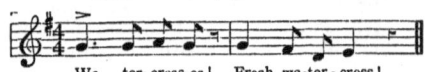

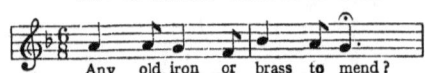

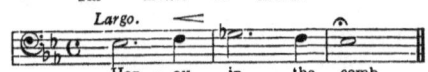

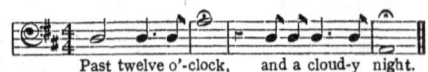

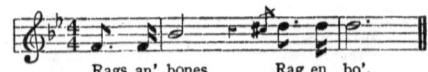

Wa - ter - cress-es.

Penny a bunch, sweet wallflow'rs. Fresh sweet

wallflow'rs, Penny a bunch, sweet wallflow'rs.

Fish!   fine large fresh soles !   Fish !

Wa - ter-cress-es!   Fresh wa-ter-cress!

Any old iron or brass to mend ?

Tin   kittles   to   mend ?

Largo.
Hon - ey   in   the   comb.

New   boil'd   shrimp.

Past twelve o'-clock,   and a cloud-y night.

Chel-sea bun, Chelsea bun, O Chelsea bun. A

pen-ny,   Chel - sea   bun !

Rags an' bones,   Rag en bo'.

Catch 'em a - loive, catch 'em a - loive!

Catch 'em all a-loive, Catch 'em all a - loive!

The following, described by the *Musical Times* as "unfruitful and fanciful speculation," is, perhaps, not without some interest. " Mr. F. Weber, organist of the Danish service, Marlborough House Chapel, has just published a book on how to learn to think and speak in music, which is to be used in the schools at Sandringham by command of the Queen. Mr. Weber's book is an attempt to teach children—and, indeed, adults—how to speak melodiously in from ten to twelve tones instead of the usual half a dozen or so. We print the following question and answer as a good example of Mr. Weber's system :—

Shall we have a game?

No; I think we'd better have a walk.
—*Daily News, Feb.* 1906.

Melody, Leading. (1) The chief melody in a composition for several "parts." (2) A *Leit-motiv* (q.v.).

Melody Organ } An American organ or
Melody Harmonium } harmonium so constructed as to bring out the upper notes of chords with special prominence.

Mel'ograph. An inst. to record improvised playing.
Many attempts have been made in this direction, the most successful being the *Phonautograph* (q.v.).

Mel'ologue. (*I., Melo'logo.*) Recitation or recitative with accompanying music.

Melope'a (*I.*) } Vocal declamation ;
Mélopée (*F.*) } melody. The art of
Melopœ'a (*Gk.*) } composing melody.

Mel'ophone. (1) A variety of concertina. (2) A string-tone org. stop of delicate tone-quality (a combination of string and flute tones).

Melopia'no. A pf. in which the tone of the strings is sustained by rapidly repeated blows of small hammers.

Melopom'enos (*Gk.*). Vocal melody.

Me'los (*Gk.*). Song ; declamation.
Wagner applies the term to the vocal phrases in his later operas, "which have not the form or symmetry of regular tunes."

Mel'otrope. (See **Melograph.**)

MELPOM'ENE. (See **Muses.**)

MELUZ'ZI, Salvatore. Church composer ; Rome, 1813-97. Director for 45 years of the Capella Giulia.
Works : masses, motets, psalms, a fine *Miserere*.

MEMBRÉE, Edmond. Operatic composer ; *b.* Valenciennes, 1820 ; *d.* 1882.

Même (*F.*). The same.
À la même. Tempo primo.
Même mouvement. The same *tempo.*
Même mouvement que précédement. The same *tempo* as the preceding.

Men (*I.*). Abbn. of **Me'no** ; less.
Men alle'gro. Less quick.

MEN'DEL, Hermann. Editor and writer ; *b.* Halle, 1834 ; *d.* 1876. Pupil of Mendelssohn and Moscheles.
Chief work : "Musikalisches Conversations-Lexikon," 1870-83.

MEN'DELSSOHN, Arnold. Grand nephew of F. (below). *B.* Ratibor, 1855.
Works : 2 operas, cantatas, &c.

MEN'DELSSOHN, Felix. (Full name **Jacob Ludwig Felix Mendelssohn-Barthol'dy.**) *B.* Hamburg, Feb. 3, 1809 ; *d.* Leipzig, Nov. 4, 1847. Son of Abraham Mendelssohn, a banker ; grandson of Moses Mendelssohn, the philosopher. Received his first pf. lessons from his mother ; afterwards taught pf. by Berger, theory by Zelter, and violin by Heunings. Pianistic *début*, Berlin, 1818. Joined the Berlin Singakademie as an alto, 1819 ; his setting of the 19th Psalm was given at the Akademie the same year. He also regularly composed pieces for a small orchestra which met on Sundays at his father's house.
Wrote the overture to *A Midsummer Night's Dream*, his first really great work, 1826. Secured a performance of Bach's *Passion*, 1829 (the first performance for many years, giving "the initial impulse to the successful Bach propaganda in which Mendelssohn was long the leading figure"). First visit to England, 1829 ; toured through Germany, Austria, Italy, and France, 1830-2. Condr., Lower Rhine Festival, Düsseldorf, 1833 ; Cologne, 1835. Conductor Gewandhaus Orch., Leipzig, 1835 ("an epoch-making point"). Produced *St. Paul*, Düsseldorf, 1836 (given under his baton, Birmingham, 1837). Chief organizer of the Leipzig Cons., opened 1843. Here he himself taught "when his other manifold duties permitted." Conducted the Philharmonic Concerts, London, 1844. Conducted the first performance of *Elijah*, Birmingham, August, 1846. His death the following year, largely the result of overwork, was accelerated by the sudden death of his favourite sister **Fanny** (1805-47).
Mendelssohn, in spite of numerous detractors, is long likely to be included among the "Great Composers ; " he was also an eminent conductor, a pianist of the highest rank, and a finished organist.
Works : ORATORIOS AND CANTATAS—*St. Paul, Elijah, Christus* (unfinished), *Hymn of Praise, The First Walpurgis Night, Athalie.* Music to

A Midsummer Night's Dream, Antigone, Œdipus in Colonos. OTHER CHORAL WORKS—*To the Sons of Art, Festgesänge, The Wedding of Camacho,* fragments of an opera (*Lorelei*), *Lauda Sion, Hear my Prayer,* several Psalms and Motets, 28 quartets for male voices, 28 quartets for mixed voices, 13 duets, 83 songs. ORCHESTRAL—4 symphonies (including the *Scotch, Italian,* and *Reformation*), 6 concert overtures (*Fingal's Cave, The Fair Melusina, Ruy Blas, &c.*) ; 2 concertos, 2 capriccios, and a Rondo Brillant for pf. and orchestra ; a vn. concerto in E minor (one of the finest works of its kind). CHAMBER MUSIC—An octet, 2 quintets, a pf. sextet, 7 string quartets, 3 pf. quartets, 2 pf. trios ; 2 trios for clarinet, basset horn, and pf. ; 2 sonatas for 'cello and pf., &c. PIANOFORTE MUSIC—3 sonatas, Rondo Capriccioso, 8 books of "Songs without Words" (*Lieder ohne Worte*), fantasias, caprices, preludes and fugues, variations, &c. ; 4-hand variations in B♭, 4-hand Allegro Brillant, and a *Duo concertant* for 2 pfs. ORGAN MUSIC— 3 preludes and fugues, 6 sonatas, preludes in C minor.

Ménestrel (*F.*). A minstrel (*q.v.*).

Ménétrier,-triere (*F.*). (1) A wandering fiddler. (2) A village musician.

MENGAL, Martin J. Horn player ; Ghent, 1784-1851. Director Ghent Cons. from 1835.

Wrote 5 operas, horn concertos, &c.

MENG'ELBERG, Wm. Jos. Condr. and composer ; *b.* Utrecht, 1870.

MEN'GEWEIN, Karl. Composer ; *b.* Thuringia, 1852.

MENGOZ'ZI, Bernardo. Singer and composer ; *b.* Florence, 1758 ; *d.* 1800. Prof. of singing, Paris Cons., 1795.

Works : 13 operas, a "Méthode de Chant," &c.

Me'no (*I.*). Less. When used *alone* it means "slower."

Me'no forte. Less loud.
Me'no mos'so. Less moved ; slower.
Me'no pia'no. Less soft.
Me'no sono'ro. Less sonorous ; softer.
Me'no to'sto. Less quick.
Me'no vi'vo. Not so fast.

Men'schenstim'me (*G.*). (1) The human voice. (2) A *vox humana* org. stop.

Mensur' (*G.*). Measure ; measurement, gauge, distance.

Applied to the relative duration of notes, the gauging of strings, the scale of org. pipes, the spacing of holes on wind insts., &c.

Mensu'ra (*L.*). Measure, time.

Men'surable Music ⎫
Mensural'gesang (*G.*) ⎬ Rhythmic or measured chant.
Mensural'musik (*G.*) ⎭

Before the middle of the 12th cent. musical notes merely indicated pitch. Franco of Cologne, in his *Cantus Mensurabilis* (abt. 1200), introduced the following "Time Table" :—

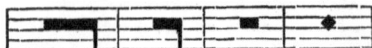

| Maxima, Double-Long, or Large. | Longa, or Long. | Brevis, or Breve. | Semi-Brevis, or Semibreve. |

Each of these notes might be *Perfect* or *Imperfect.* A perfect note was equal in duration to 3 of the

following denomination, an imperfect note to 2. Thus, a perfect Long was equal to 3 Breves, an Imperfect Long to 2 Breves, &c.

N.B.—"Until the close of the 16th cent. bars were only used to indicate convenient places for taking breath." For the development of modern notes, see *Notation* and *Time.*

Mensural'notenschrift (*G.*). The notation of Mensurable ·(or measured) music ; applied specially to mediæval notation.

Mental Effect. The "special effect on the mind" of any particular note, chord, progression, &c.

An appreciation of mental effects is of the utmost value in "ear-training," and is not to be lightly disregarded by the would-be composer.
What is called "Tonality" is merely a systematic grouping of the mental effects of notes and chords round some "governing-note" (called the key-note or Tonic).
(1) STRONG AND LEANING TONES. "When the ear is once filled with the key," the 1st, 3rd, and 5th notes of the scale are easily recognized as STRONG ; the others "are felt to be dependent or *Leaning.*"
(2) THE ALPHABET OF TUNE.—Mr. Curwen gives the following "*proximate* effects" of the tones of the Major Scale when sung slowly :—*Doh,* Strong or Firm ; *Ray,* Rousing or Hopeful ; *Me,* Steady or Calm ; *Fah,* Desolate or Awe-inspiring ; *Soh,* Grand or Bright ; *Lah,* Sad or Weeping ; *Te,* Piercing or Sensitive.
These effects are modified by mode, pitch, harmony, quality of tone, accent, and speed.
(3) MENTAL EFFECTS OF CONSONANCES.—Thirds and Sixths are "sweet," Perfect 5ths are "firm," Perfect 4ths are "negative."
(4) MENTAL EFFECTS OF DISSONANCES.—These have never been completely tabulated ; but it is generally conceded that dissonances from the "Chord of Nature" (*q.v.*) are less harsh than most others, and the effect of a discord is much modified by "preparation."
(5) MENTAL EFFECTS OF CHORDS.—Major chords are "bright ;" Minor chords more "dull and sombre." In general, the mental effect of a triad is analogous to that of its root.
(6) MENTAL EFFECTS OF CHANGE OF KEY.— Change to a sharper key, or from Minor to Major, generally "enlivens the music ;" change to a flatter key, or from Major to Minor generally subdues or "depresses" the effect.

Men'te (*I.*). Mind, memory.

Al'la men'te. Improvised.

MEN'TER, Joseph. 'Cellist ; *b.* Bavaria, 1808 ; *d.* 1856.

MEN'TER (Menter-Popper), Sophie. Fine pianist ; daughter of J. B. Munich, 1848. *Début,* 1863. Married the 'cellist Popper, 1872 (divorced 1886). Pf. prof. St. Petersburg Cons., 1878-87(?).

Menuet (*F.*) ⎫
Menuett' (*G.*) ⎬ A minuet (*q.v.*).
Menuet'to (*I.*) ⎭

Menuet'to da Ca'po (*I.*). Repeat the *Menuet'to* (*i.e.,* after playing the *Trio* part).
Menuet'to da Ca'po, sen'za re'plica (*I.*). Play the Minuet again without repeating each separate portion of it.

MER'BECKE, John. (See **Marbeck.**)

MERCADAN'TE, Francesco S. R. Operatic composer ; *b.* Altamura, 1795 ; *d.* Naples, 1870. Favourite pupil of Zingarelli. First opera, *L'apoteosi d'Ercole* (Naples, 1819). Lived in turn at Rome, Bologna, Turin, Milan, Venice, Madrid, Lisbon, Paris, and Vienna, composing operas in each city. Director, Naples Cons., 1840.

Works : about 60 operas (including *Elisa e Claudio*, 1821 ; *I Briganti*, 1836 ; *Il Giuramento*, 1837, considered his best ; and *Il Bravo*) ; 20 masses, and much other church music ; orchestral fantasias, songs, &c.

MÉREAUX, Jean A. L. de. Pianist ; *b.* Paris, 1803 ; *d.* 1874.

Pub. "Les clavecinistes de 1637 à 1790" (an interesting collection of pieces).

MEREDITH, Edward. Noted bass singer ; *b.* nr. Wrexham, 1741 ; *d.* 1809.

MÉRIEL, Paul. *B.* Mondoubleau, 1818 ; *d.* 1897. Director Toulouse Cons.

Works : an oratorio (*Cain*), comic operas, &c.

MERK, Joseph. 'Cellist ; *b.* Vienna, 1795 ; *d.* 1852. Teacher, Vienna Cons., 1834.

Wrote some excellent études for 'cello, &c.

MER'KEL, Gustav A. *B.* Oberoderwitz, Saxony, 1827 ; *d.* 1885. Pupil of Schneider ; befriended by Schumann. Orgt. Kreuzkirche, Dresden, 1860 ; Catholic Court .Ch., 1864. Prof. in the Cons., 1861.

Works : 9 org. sonatas, 3 fantasias, 30 pedal studies, an org. method, &c. ; pf. pieces, songs.

MERKLIN', Jos. Noted organ builder ; *b.* Oberhausen, Baden, 1819.

MÉRÖ, Iolanda. Pianist ; *b.* Budapest, 1887(?). London *début*, 1908.

MERSENNE (MERSEN'NUS), Marie. Learned French monk ; *b.* 1588 ; *d.* Paris, 1648.

Chief work : "Harmonie universelle" (2 large folio vols. with illustrations of all the insts. of the 17th cent., &c.).

MERT'KE, Eduard. Pianist ; *b.* Riga, 1833 ; *d.* 1895. Played in public at 10 ; after successful tours, &c., teacher of pf., Cologne Cons., 1869.

Works : an opera, 2 cantatas, pf. pieces and arrangements, a colln. of "Melodies of the Ukraine," &c.

ME'RULA, Tarquinio. Native of Bergamo.

Pub. 4 books of vn. sonatas (1623-51), and other early compositions for the violin.

Mer'ula. "A blackbird." (See **Vogelgesang.**)

ME'RULO (or **MERLOT'TI**), **Claudio.** Known as "**Da Correggio.**" *B.* Corregio, 1533 ; *d.* 1604. Chief organist, St. Mark's, Venice, 1566-86. He was recognized as the "head of the Venetian School," and was "one of the greatest organists of the time."

Works : Toccatas, Fugues, &c., for organ ; an opera, madrigals, motets, canzoni, &c.

Mescolan'za (*I.*). Cacophony ; a medley.

Me'se (*Gk.*). The middle string (and keynote) of the Greek lyre. (See **Greek Music.**)

Me'sochorus. Same as **Coryphæus** (1).

Mes'sa (*I.*). (*G., Mes'se ; F., Messe.*) A Mass.

Mes'sa bas'sa. Low Mass (or a "silent Mass whispered by the Priest").

Mes'sa da re'quiem. A Requiem Mass.

Mes'sa di vo'ce (*I.*). The "swell" on a long note in singing :

$pp \overbrace{} ff \overbrace{} pp$

The attack and *crescendo* are called *forma're il tuo'no ;* the sustaining of the *ff, ferma're il tuono ;* the *diminuendo* and finish, *fini're il tuono.*

MESSAGER, André C. P. Distinguished operatic composer ; *b.* Montluçon, Allier, 1855. Orchestral conductor, Paris Opéra-Comique, 1898.

Of his numerous operas and operettas the following have been most successful : *Les Michu* (1897), *Véronique* (1898), and *La Basoche* (1890).

MESSAGER, Mad. A. C. P. Hope Temple (*q.v.*).

MES'SERSCHMIDT - GRÜN'NER, Frau. Vienna, 1847-95.

Organized the 1st Viennese Ladies' orch., 1870.

MESSIAH. Handel's chief oratorio ; 1742.

"The old work still holds on like the 'some tall rock' of the poet, its head lifted into eternal sunshine, while angry waves dash impotently against its base."—*Daily Telegraph*, Oct. 5, 1906.

Mes'singinstrumente (*G.*). Brass insts.

Mesti'zia (*I.*). Sadness, melancholy.

Me'sto (*I.*) }
Mesto'so (*I.*) } Sad, pensive, melancholy.

Con mesti'zia }
Mestamen'te } Sadly, plaintively.

Mesure (*F.*). Measure ; a bar (or measure).

A la mesure. In time ; same as a *tem'po*, or *a battu'ta.*
Mesure à deux temps. Duple time.
Mesure à trois temps. Triple time.
Mesuré. Measured ; (1) *moderato ;* (2) precise.
Allegro mesuré. Allegro moderato.

Met. Abbn. of *Metronome* (*q.v.*).

METASTA'SIO, Pietro A. D. B. Celebrated poet and dramatist ; *b.* Rome, 1698 ; *d.* 1782. Court poet, Vienna, 1730-82.

Wrote the *libretti* of 34 operas, including Mozart's *La Clemenza di Tito.*

Metal'lo. (*I., Metal.*) A metallic ringing tone.

Bel metal'lo di vo'ce. A brilliant, clear ringing voice.

Metal'lophone. (1) A kind of pf. with tuned steel bars instead of strings. (2) A species of Xylophone with metal bars.

Metamor'phose. A melody (subject, theme) evolved from another melody by changing the accent or rhythm (or both), while retaining the same melodic outline. (See **Leit-motiv.**)

METH'FESSEL, Albert G. *B.* Thuringia, 1785 ; *d.* 1869. Court composer, Brunswick, 1832-42.

Works : an opera, an oratorio, pf. pieces, partsongs, songs.

Méthode (*F.*) }
Me'todo (*I.*) } (1) A method (or instruction book). (2) A school or style of music ; *e.g.*, the *Italian* method, the *French* method, &c.

MÉTRA, J. L. Olivier. *B.* Rheims, 1830; *d.* 1889. Violinist, 'cellist, and condr. in Parisian music halls and minor theatres.

Wrote operettas, ballets, &c., and numerous popular pf. dances.

Metre. Measured time. (1) In music, the arrangement of measures and groups of measures in regular and symmetrical succession. (See **Accent (metrical)** and **Metrical Form**). (2) In poetry, the arrangement of "feet" in regular order and grouping, so as to form "stanzas" (commonly called "verses").

THE CHIEF METRES of poetry are—

(1) (*a*) *Iam'bic*; short, long; or weak, strong (∪ —); *e.g.*, "Awake my soul and sing."
   (*b*) *Trocha'ic*; strong, weak (— ∪); *e.g.*, "Come, my soul, thy suit prepare."
   The Tro'chee is the converse of the Iam'bus.
(2) (*a*) *Dactyl'lic*; strong, weak, weak (— ∪ ∪); "Over the mountains and over the waves."
   (*b*) *Amphibrach'ic*; weak, strong, weak (∪ — ∪); "We sing of the realms of the blest."
   (*c*) *Anapœ'stic*; weak, weak, strong (∪ ∪ —); "He is gone o'er the mountain."
   The Am'phibrach and An'apæst may be regarded as varieties of the Dac'tyl.

THE CHIEF IAMBIC METRES, with the number of syllables in each line, are as follows :—

(1) Short Metre : 6,6,8,6.
(2) Common Metre : 8,6,8,6.
(3) Long Metre : 8,8,8,8.
(4) Six-Lines-Eights: 8,8,8 ; 8,8,8 ; or 8,8 ; 8,8 ; 8,8.

Special names are not now usually given to the numerous other metres of hymns ; figures showing the syllabic arrangement are generally employed, and may be found in any modern hymn book.

Metrical Accent. (See **Accent.**)

Metrical Form. The arrangement of measures in "groups."

Melody has a strong tendency to arrange itself in successive portions each *four measures* (or *bars*) *in length*. The "4-bar section" may therefore be called the "typical factor of metrical form." The section may begin at *any part of a bar*, and the end of it is generally marked by some sort of cadence.

N.B.—In slow music (or in Compound Times) a "2-bar section" may take the place of the ordinary "4-bar section ;" and occasionally a measure of, say, 12-8 time forms a complete section of itself.

The nomenclature of metrical form is, unfortunately, vague, and often contradictory. The following scheme is, however, coherent and easy of application :—

(1) A Section may be divided into *Sub-sections*.
(2) A Sub-section may consist of "*Germs*," "*Motives*," or "*Figures*."
(3) Two or more (generally 4) Sections form a *Sentence*.
(4) Two or more Sentences form a *Period*.
(5) Two or more Periods form a *Strain*.
6) Two or more Strains form a *Movement*.

Many short tunes (hymn-tunes, national songs, and the like), consist of *One Sentence of Four Sections*. In National songs, the 2nd section is often a repetition (or varied repetition) of the 1st ; the 3rd Section is generally *contrasted* in melodic outline ; while the 4th may be a repetition of the 1st (or 2nd), or it may be of the nature of a *Refrain*.

1st Section.
Sub-section.   Sub-section.

2nd Section.
Sub-section.   Sub-section.

3rd Section.

Sub-section.   Sub-section.
Figure.   Figure.   Figure.

4th Section.

In marches, and in all kinds of dance music, the 4-bar section reigns supreme. And in most other forms of composition sections of 4 (or 2) bars are more often employed than any others. Variety is secured in long works—and the "monotonous squareness" of 4-bar sections avoided—by the use of Introductory passages, Links, Codettas, Irregular sections of 3, 5, 6, 7, 8, or 9 bars, Overlapping sections, Extended sections, Canonic and Fugal imitations, &c.

Me'trik (*G.*). The science and art of metre.
Metrisch. Metrical.

Me'tro (*I.*). Metre, verse.

Metrome'ter (*G.*)
Métromètre (*F.*)   } A metronome.
Metrome'tro (*I.*)

Met'ronome. (*G., Metronom'; F., Métronome ; I., Metrono'mo*). A little mechanical inst. for beating time.

Maelzel's Metronome (see *Mälzel*) consists of a pendulum, which by means of a clockwork mechanism and a sliding weight, can be adjusted to beat from 40 to 208 times per minute. A *Bell Metronome* has an attachment by means of which a bell may be made to ring at every 2nd, 3rd, 4th, or 6th tick of the pendulum.

Metronome Mark. An indication of the rate of movement of a piece. Formerly the letters M.M. (standing for "Maelzel's Metronome") were used, or the letter M. (for Metronome). This was followed by the "beat-note," and the number of beats per minute ; thus M.M. ♩ = 60 means "60 beats per minute." It is now usual to omit the M.M. or M. Thus, ♩. = 72 means "72 dotted crotchets per minute ;" ♩ = 80 means "80 minims per minute ;" &c.

Metronome Values. The following approximate indications are given on the "scale" of the metronome :—*Adagio*, 40 to 72 ; *Largo*, 72 to 100 ; *Larghetto*, 100 to 126 ; *Andante*, 126 to 154 ; *Allegro*, 154 to 164 ; *Presto*, 164 to 208.

Metronom'isches Zei'chen (*G.*). Metronome mark.

Met'rum (*L.*). Metre.

Met'te (*G.*). Matins.

METTENLEITER, Johann G. Erudite church composer ; *b.* nr. Ulm, 1812 ; *d.* 1858. Orgt. Ratisbon Cathedral.

Met'tere in mu'sica (*I.*). To set (words) to music.

Met'ter la vo'ce (*I.*). Same as **Mes'sa di vo'ce** (*q.v.*).

Met'tete (*I.*). Put, place, set.
Met'tete i sordi'ni. Put on the mutes (vn.).
Met'tete le peda'li. Put down the pedals (pf.).

Mettez (*F.*). "Draw" (a stop).

Mettre d'accord (*F.*). To tune (an inst.).

Mettre en musique (*F.*). To set to music.

METZ'DORFF, Rd. *B.* Danzig, 1844. Capellmeister successively at Düsseldorf, Berlin, Nuremburg, Brunswick, and Hanover.
Works: operas (*Hagbart und Signe*), orch. music, chamber music, pf. pieces, songs.

Met'zilloth, Met'zillthaim. Ancient Jewish cymbals.

METZ'LER and Co. Founded by **Valentine Metzler** abt. 1790.

MEU'SEL, Joh. G. *B.* Eynchshof, 1743; *d.* 1820.
Works: a "Deutsches Künstler-Lexikon" (2 vols.), "Das gelehrte Deutschland," &c.

MEY'ER, Gustav. *B.* Königsberg, 1859. Capellmeister, Leipzig City Th., 1895.
Works: operetta (*Der Hochstapler*, 1897), stage music, songs, &c.

MEY'ER, Jenny. Berlin, 1834-94. Singing teacher, Stern Cons., 1865; owner and directress, 1888.

MEY'ER, Julius E. Vocal teacher; *b.* Altenburg, 1822; *d.* Brooklyn, 1899. Pupil of Schumann, David, &c., at Leipzig. Settled in Brooklyn, 1852.

MEY'ER, Leopold von (also known as **de Meyer**). Pianist; pupil of Czerny; *b.* nr. Vienna, 1816; *d.* 1883.

MEY'ER, Waldemar. Violinist; pupil of Joachim; *b.* Berlin, 1853.

MEY'ERBEER, Giacomo. (Real name, **Jakob Liebmann Beer.**) Famous opera composer, of Jewish descent. *B.* Berlin, Sept. 5, 1791; *d.* Paris, May 2, 1864. Played the pf. in public at 7. Studied theory under Zelter, Anselm Weber, and Abbé Vogler (1810-12). C. M. Weber was one of his fellow pupils. While studying with Vogler, he wrote an oratorio and two operas. Visited Venice, 1815, to study the Italian style (being much influenced by the success of Rossini). He now wrote a series of Italian operas, of which *Il crociato in Egitto* (Venice, 1824), was "an immense success." A visit to Weber induced him to abandon the light Italian style, and to "unite the flowing melody of the Italians with the solid harmony of the Germans and the pathetic declamation and varied, piquant rhythm of the French." *Robert le Diable* (Grand Opéra, Paris, 1831), the first work in his "third style," "fairly electrified the Parisians." It inaugurated the series of great operas which

made Meyerbeer's name famous. In 1842 he was appointed "General Music Director" to King Friedrich Wm. IV, Berlin. Visited London, 1847.
Chief works: operas, *Robert* (1831), *Les Huguenots* (1836), *Le Prophète* (1842-3), *Das Feldlager in Schlesien* (1843), *L'Etoile du Nord* (1854), *Dinorah* (1859), *l'Africaine* (prod. 1865, a year after his death).
He also wrote cantatas, odes, incidental music, psalms, choruses *a cappella*, orch. marches, &c. By his will he left £1,500 for the foundation of a Meyerbeer Scholarship.

MEY'ER-HEL'MUND, Erik. *B.* St. Petersburg, 1861.
Works: operas and ballets (*Rübezahl*, 1893), and over 60 songs.

MEY'ER-LUTZ. (See **Lutz.**)

MEY'ER-OL'BERSLEBEN, Max. *B.* nr. Weimar, 1850. Teacher of Counterpoint and Composition, Royal Cons., Würzburg, 1877; Condr. "Würzburger Liedertafel," 1879.
Works: operas, orch. music, chamber music, choruses (including 22 for male voices), pf. pieces, songs.

Mez. An abbreviation of **Mez'zo.**

MÉZERAY, Louis C. L. C. de. *B.* Brunswick, 1810; *d.* 1887. 1st *Maitre de chappelle* Grand Théâtre, Bordeaux, 1843. Founder Société Sainte-Cécile, 1843.

Mez'za (*I.*) } Half. When used alone it is
Mez'zo (*I.*) } equivalent to *mf* or *mp*.
A mez'za a'ria. Same as *Aria parlante* (*q.v.*).
Mez'za bravu'ra } With a moderate degree of ex-
Mez'zo carat'tere } pression and execution.
Mez'zo for'te (*mf*). "Half loud;" moderately loud.
Mez'zo lega'to. "Rather *legato*;" smooth and connected, but not so much so as in *legato*.
Mez'zo ma'nica. The half shift in vn. playing.
Mez'za orche'stra. With half the (string) orchestra.
Mez'zo pia'no (*mp*). "Half soft;" not quite so loud as *mf*.
Mez'zo respi'ro. A rapid half breath in singing.
Mez'zo sopra'no. The female voice between the contralto and soprano; compass about—

A   F or G

Mez'zo stacca'to. (See *Staccato.*)
Mez'zo teno're. A baritone voice (*q.v.*).
Mez'zo tuo'no. A semitone.
Mez'za vo'ce. With half the power of the voice; also used for half the power of an inst.

Mez'zo (*I.*). The middle.
Nel mez'zo del ar'co. In (or with) the middle of the bow.

mf (or **M.F.**). Abbn. of **Mez'zo for'te**; moderately loud.

M.G. Main gauche; the Left Hand.

Mi. (1) The 3rd of the Aretinian Syllables. (See **Guido.**) (2) The Italian and French name of the note E. (3) See **Me.**
Mi bémol (*F.*). } The note E♭.
Mi bemol'le (*I.*). }
Mi dièse (*F.*). } The note E♯.
Mi die'sis (*I.*). }
Mi contra fa (*L.*). The tritone (*q.v.*).
Mi contra fa est diabolus in musica (*L.*). "Mi against fa is the devil in music;" a mediæval "objurgation" against the use of the tritone (especially in melody).

MICE'LI, Giorgio. Opera composer ; b. Reggio di Calabria, 1836 ; d. 1895.
Of 8 operas the most successful were *Zoe* (1852), *Il Conte di Rossiglione* (1854), and *La Sonnambule* (1869).

MICHAE'LIS, Theodor. B. Ballenstedt, 1831 ; d. 1887.
Wrote popular open-air pieces.

MICHEL. (See **Yost.**)

MICHE'LI, Romano. Roman contrapuntist; abt. 1575-1660. Noted writer of canons.
Works : 50 motets and artistic canons, madrigals in canon form, masses, psalms, &c.

MICK'WITZ, Harald von. Pianist ; b. Helsingfors, 1859. Teacher of advanced pf. playing, Carlsruhe Cons., 1886 ; Wiesbaden Cons., 1893.

Mi'crophone. An acoustical inst. for intensifying feeble sounds.

Middle C. The note midway between the bass and treble staves.
This is the "pitch" of the C clef, wherever it is placed. (See *Clef.*)

Middle parts } Tenor, alto, mezzo-so-
Middle voices } prano, &c.

MIDGLEY, Samuel. Pianist and writer ; b. Brierley, Yorks, 1849.

MIDSUMMER NIGHT'S DREAM Music. Written by Mendelssohn. Overture composed, 1826 (when he was 17).

MIEKSCH. (See **Miksch.**)

Mignon (*F.*). (1) Favourite, charming. (2) Delicate, dainty.

MIHA'LOVICH, Edmund von. B. Slavonia, 1842.
Works : operas, *Hagbarth und Signe* (1882), *Toldi* (1893), &c. ; orch. ballads, pf. pieces, &c.

MIKSCH, Johann A. Singing teacher ; b. Georgenthal, Bohemia, 1765 ; d. 1845. Teacher of **Schröder-Devrient.**

MI'KULI, Karl. Pianist ; b. Czernowitz, 1821 ; d. 1897. Pupil of Chopin. Artistic drector, Lemberg Cons., 1858. Founded a music school, 1888.
Pub. a standard edition of Chopin's pf. works (with marginal notes showing the emendations made by Chopin on Mikuli's copies).

MILANOL'LO. Two sisters ; violinists.
(1) **Teresa**, b. nr. Turin, 1827 ; d. 1904.
(2) **Maria**, b. 1832 ; d. 1848.

MILCH'MEYER, Philipp J. B. Frankfort-on-Main, 1750 ; d. 1813.
Invented a 3-manual pianoforte.

MIL'DE, Hans F. von. Baritone singer ; b. Petronek, nr. Vienna, 1821 ; d. 1899.
Created the part of "Telramund" (Wagner's *Lohengrin*), Weimar, 1850.
His wife **Rosa** (*née* Agthe), b. Weimar, 1827, created the part of "Elsa" in the same opera.

MIL'DE, Rudolf. Operatic baritone ; son of preceding ; b. Weimar, 1859.

MIL'DER-HAUPT'MANN, Pauline Anna. Operatic soprano ; b. Constantinople,

1785 ; d. Berlin, 1838. *Début*, Vienna, 1803.
"Her voice was so powerful that Haydn once said to her, 'Liebes Kind, Sie Haben eine Stimme wie ein Haus' (Dear child, you have a voice like a house)."—*Baker.*
Beethoven wrote for her the part of "Fidelio."

Milieu (*F.*). Middle.
Milieu de l'archet. The middle of the bow.

MILILOT'TI, Leopoldo. Singing teacher ; b. Ravenna, 1835.
Works : 2 operettas, and numerous songs.

Militaire (*F.*). Military.
Militairement (*F.*) }
Militarmen'te (*I.*) } In military (martial) style.
Alla milita're (*I.*) }

Militär'musik (*G.*). (1) Military music. (2) A military band.

Military band. A "wind band."
English military bands comprise the insts. of a brass band, *plus* reed insts., flutes, &c. ; and when not used for marching purposes a double bass is often added to give "bite" to the tone of the bombardons, and to enrich the tone-quality. The Grenadier Guards Band—65 players—comprises 3 flutes and piccolos, 3 Eb clarinets, 2 oboes, 11 1st Bb clarinets (some playing saxophones, when required), 5 2nd Bb clarinets, 4 3rd Bb clarinets, 4 bassoons, 4 1st cornets, 3 2nd cornets, 3 trumpets, 6 French horns, 4 tenor trombones, 1 bass trombone, 3 euphonuims, 6 bombardons, 2 side drums, bass drum, and cymbals. The band of the New York 22nd Regt. comprises 66 insts. as follows : 2 piccolos, 2 flutes, 2 oboes, 1 Ab piccolo clarinet, 3 Eb clarinets, 16 Bb clarinets, 1 alto clarinet, 1 bass clarinet, 4 saxophones, 2 bassoons, 1 contra-bassoon, 1 Eb cornet, 4 Bb cornets, 2 trumpets, 2 flügel-horns, 4 French horns, 2 Eb alto horns, 2 Bb tenor horns, 2 euphoniums, 3 trombones, 5 bombardons, 3 drums, 1 pair cymbals.

MILLAR, Webster. Tenor ; b. Manchester. *Début*, Hallé concerts, 1901.

MIL'LARD, Harrison. Tenor singer , Boston, Mass., 1830 ; d. 1895.
Works : an opera, church music, nearly 400 songs

MILLER, Edward. B. Norwich, 1735 ; d. 1807. Studied under Dr. Burney. Orgt. Doncaster, 1756-1807. Mus.Doc. Cantab., 1786.
Works : harpsichord sonatas, flute solos, church music, songs, &c. Also works on Theory.

MILLER, Geo. John. Bandmaster and composer ; b. London, 1853. Mus.B. Cantab., 1892.

MILLEVIL'LE, Francesco. Organist ; b. Ferrara, abt. 1565.
Works : madrigals, masses, psalms, &c.

MIL'LÖCKER, Karl. B. Vienna, 1842 ; d. 1899. Theatre Capellmeister, Vienna.
Works : numerous operettas (*Der Bettelstudent*, 1881), musical farces, pf. pieces, &c.

MILLS, R. Watkin. Basso-cantante ; b. Painswick, Gloucestershire, 1856. *Début* Crystal Palace, 1884.

MILLS, Sebastian Bach. Pianist ; b. Cirencester, 1838 ; d. 1898. Pupil of Sterndale Bennett ; played before Queen Victoria at 7. Settled (1859) in New York, where he "did yeoman service in the cause of good music."
Works : pf. pieces.

19

MILMAN, Henry Hart, D.D. 1791-1868. Dean of St. Paul's, 1849.
Wrote "Ride on ! ride on in majesty," and other hymns.

Milo´te (*S.*). An Indian dance.

MIL´TON, John. Father of the poet ; *b.* nr. Oxford, abt. 1563 ; *d.* March, 1647.
Wrote a fine 6-part madrigal, motets, psalm-tunes (in Ravenscroft's Psalter), &c.

MILTON, John. Famous English poet ; 1608-74. Skilled amateur musician.
Wrote many odes, hymns, &c., which have been set to music.

Mi majeur (*F.*). The key of E major.

Mi mineur (*F.*). The key of E minor.

Mimes. Mimic actors.

Mi´modrama }
Mimodrame (*F.*) } A pantomime.

Minaccian´do (*I.*).

Minacc(i)e´vole (*I.*)
Minaccio´so (*I.*)
Minacc(i)evolmen´te (*I.*)
Minacciosamen´te (*I.*)
} Menacingly, threateningly.

Mind´er (*G.*). Minor, less.
Mind´er schnell. Less fast.

Mineur (*F.*). Minor.

MINGOT´TI, Regina (*née* **Valentini**). Celebrated soprano ; *b.* Naples, 1728 ; *d.* 1807. Pupil of Porpora. Sang in Dresden, Madrid, London, &c.

Miniatur´ Aus´gabe (*G.*). Miniature edition (of a full score, &c.).

Minim. (*G., Hal´be Not´e ; L.* and *I. Mi´nima ; I., Bian´ca ; F., Minime ; Blanche.*) The note 𝅗𝅥 (or 𝅗𝅥), equal to two crotchets (or quarter-notes).
The minim is also called a "half-note."

Minne´lied (*G.*). A love song.

Min´nedichter (*G.*)
Min´nesänger (*G.*)
Min´nesinger (*G.*)
} A German troubadour (12th to 14th cents.).
The Minnesingers were often of noble birth ; they composed both words and music of their "pure love" songs, and accompanied them on a small kind of harp or viol. They were succeeded by the Meistersingers (*q.v.*).

MINO´JA, Ambrosio. Singing teacher ; *b.* nr. Lodi, 1752 ; *d.* 1825. Maestro, La Scala, Milan, 1789-1809.
Works : a fine collection of Solfeggi, &c.

Minor } (*G., Klein, Moll ; F., Mineur.*)
Mino´re (*I.*) } Smaller ; less.
Minor interval. An interval a semitone less than a major interval. (See *Interval.*)
Minor key }
Minor mode } A key or mode whose *third* is minor.
Minor scale. A scale with a minor third between its first and third notes.
Minor semitone. A "chromatic semitone" (*q.v.*).
Minor tone. The smaller tone, ratio 10 : 9. (See *Acoustics.*)
Minor triad. A triad with a minor 3rd and perfect 5th.

MINSHALL, Ebenezer. *B.* Oswestry, 1845. Orgt. City Temple, 1876-93.
Editor, (*Nonconformist*) *Musical Journal.*

Minstrels. The wandering poets, musicians, bards, &c., 10th to 14th centuries. (See **Minnesinger, Meistersinger, Troubadour,** &c.).

Minuet´. (*G., Menuett´; F., Menuet ; I., Menuet´to, Minuet´to.*) A graceful rather slow dance in triple (generally 3-4) time, invented about the middle of the 17th century.
The original Minuet consisted of two portions of 8 bars, each repeated. Later, a 2nd Minuet in some related key (and generally of a quieter character) was alternated with the 1st ; this was called the Trio (see *Trio*). The Minuet and Trio formed a part of many of the old *Suites*, and became with Haydn a regular movement in the Sonata, Symphony, &c. Beethoven developed the Minuet into the *Scherzo* (*q.v.*). The MINUET AND TRIO FORM, as exemplified in Haydn and Mozart, is as follows :—
I. MINUET : (*a*) First portion, 8 to 24 bars ; repeated ; (*b*) Second portion, generally longer than the first ; repeated.
II. TRIO : Exactly similar in construction to the Minuet. Sometimes in the same key ; sometimes in a nearly-related key.
III. DA CAPO of the Minuet ; generally without repeating the two separate portions.
A CODA is sometimes added, to be played after III. The Minuet and Trio Form (with modifications of time, rhythm, &c.) is much used for Marches, all kinds of Dance Music, Drawing-room pf. pieces, and sometimes Songs.

Minu´ge (*I.*). Strings of insts. ; catgut.

MIOLAN - CARVALHO. (See **Carvalho-Miolan.**)

Miracle Play. (See **Mystery.**)

Miraculous Effects of Music. (See under **Music.**)

MIRANDA, Countess. (See **Christine Nilsson.**)

MIRANDE, Hippolyte. *B.* Lyons, 1862. Studied Paris Cons. Prof. of Mus. Hist. Lyons Cons., 1890.
Chief work : ballet, *Une fête Directoire* (1895).

MI´RUS. Baritone singer and composer ; *b.* Klagenfurt, 1856.

MI´RY, Karel. Ghent, 1823-1889.
Wrote 18 Flemish operas and operettas.

Miscel´la. A mixture stop (org.).

Mise de voix (*F.*). Same as **Messa di voce** (*q.v.*).

Mise en scène (*F.*). The stage setting (mounting) of a play, opera, &c.

Misere´re. A musical setting of the 51st Psalm, "Miserere mei, Domine."
Sung at the end of the office of Tenebræ. (See *Allegri.*)

Misericor´dia (*L.*). A Miserere.

Mis´sa (*L.*). A Mass.
Mis´sa bre´vis. A short Mass.
Mis´sa pro defunc´tis. A Requiem Mass.
Mis´sa solem´nis }
Mis´sa solem´nis } A solemn Mass ; High Mass.

MIS´SA, Edmond J. L. *B.* Rheims, 1861. Studied Paris Cons.
Works : orch. pieces, pf. music, songs, and several operas.

MIS´SA PA´PÆ MARCEL´LI. Celebrated Mass by Palestrina, 1565.

Mis´sal. (*G., Mis´sel ; L., Missa´le.*) A mass-book.

Miss'hällig (*G.*) } Discordant ; dissonant.
Miss'hellig (*G.*)

Mis'halligheit } Dissonance, discord.
Miss'klang
Miss'laut. Discordant sound.
Miss'stimmen. To tune badly, put out of tune, be discordant.
Miss'stimmung } Discord, dissonance.
Miss'ton

Miste'rio, Miste'ro (*I.*). Mystery.

Con miste'ro
Misteriosamen'te } Mysteriously.
Misterio'so

Mis'to (*I.*). Mixed.

Misu'ra (*I.*). (1) Measure. (2) A measure, a bar.

Misura'to. Measured ; in strict time.
Sen'za misu'ra. Ad lib. ; not in strict time.

Mit (*G.*). With.

Mit al'ler Kraft. Tutta forza (*q.v.*).
Mit äu'sserst stark'er Empfin'dung. With extremely strong emotion.
Mit Beglei'tung. With accompaniment.
Mit Bewe'gung. With animation.
Mit dem Bo'gen geschla'gen. Struck with the (back of the) bow.
Mit dem Griff. With the grip, finger, touch. *Pizzicato* in violin playing.
Mit der ganz'en Kraft. With the whole force; *tutta forza.*
Mit Empfin'dung. With feeling, emotion.
Mit er'sticker Stim'me. In a weak voice.
Mit Frei'em. With freedom, boldness.
Mit gros'sem Aus'druck. With great expression.
Mit gröss'ter Energie'. With the greatest energy (force).
Mit hal'ber Stim'me. With half the voice; *mezza voce.*
Mit heil'iger Rüh'rung. With holy (devout) feeling.
Mit Holz'schlägel. With a wooden beater (drum cymbals, &c.).
Mit in'nigster Empfin'dung. With innermost (deepest) emotion.
Mit'klang. Resonance.
Mit Kraft. With strength ; powerfully.
Mit'laut. Concord ; consonance.
Mit Leb'haftigkeit und durchaus' mit Empfin'dung und Aus'druck. With animation, and with feeling and expression throughout.
Mit leid'enschaftlichem Vor'trag. With passionate execution.
Mit sanf'ten Stim'men. With soft stops.
Mit stark'en Stim'men. With loud stops.
Mit zar'tem Vor'trag. With delicate execution.
   N.B.—*Mit* is used with many other German words given under their proper letters.

Mit'leidig (*G.*) } Compassionate.
Mit'leidsvoll (*G.*)

Mit'tel (*G.*). Middle ; half.

Mit'telcadenz'. A half close. (See *Cadence.*)
Mit'tellaut. Mediant.
Mit'telstark. Moderately loud.
Mit'telstim'me. (1) A middle (or inner) part. (2) A medium voice.
Mit'telstück. An interlude.
Mit'telton. The Mediant (*q.v.*).

MIT'TERWURZER, Anton. Baritone singer ; *b.* Tyrol, 1818 ; *d.* 1872.
   Sang Dresden Court Opera, 1839-70.

Mixed Cadence. (See **Cadence.**)
Mixed chorus } A choir with both female
Mixed voices } and male voices.

Mixolyd'ian. (See **Mode.**)

Mixture. (*G., Mixtur'; F., Fourniture ; I., Ripie'no, Accor'do.*) An org. stop with two or more pipes to each note.
   Each pipe gives one of the upper "partials" (see *Acoustics*) of the tone represented by the organ key.

MLYNAR'SKI, Emil. Condr. and composer ; *b.* Poland, 1870.

Mocking Bird.
   The American mocking-bird is the prince of song birds, and can imitate all sorts of sounds from the exquisite warbling of the blue-bird to the mewing of a cat or the crowing of a cock. He also repeats any tune taught him with perfect accuracy.

M.M. Abbn. for Maelzel's Metronome (*q.v.*).

Mo'bile (*I.*). Facile ; emotional, impulsive.

MOCQUEREAU, Dom André. Benedictine monk. *B.* nr. Cholet (Maine et Loire), 1849. Founded and edited a "Paléographie musicale" (1875) for the reproduction of ancient MSS.

Mod. Abbn. of *Moderato.*

Mode. (*L., Mo'dus.*) (1) Key. (2) Scale. (3) Specially, the order and arrangement of the steps forming a scale.

   A. GREEK MODES. (See *Greek Music.*)
   B. MODERN MODES: (1) *Major Mode:* the ordinary Major Scale. (2) *Minor Mode:* the ordinary Minor Scale.
   C. CHURCH MODES (also called GREGORIAN TONES or ECCLESIASTICAL MODES). Eight different scales were in use in early church music ; 4, called *Authentic,* said to have been introduced by St. Ambrose ; and 4, called *Plagal,* said to have been added by Gregory the Great.

AUTHENTIC MODES.
I. Dorian : Final, D ; Dominant, A.

*r   m   f   s   l   t   d¹   r¹

PLAGAL MODES.
II. Hypodorian : Final, D ; Dominant, F.

l₁   t₁   d   r   m   f   s   l

III. Phrygian : Final, E ; Dominant, C.

m   f   s   l   t   d¹   r¹   m¹

IV. Hypophrygian : Final, E ; Dominant, A.

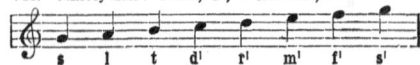
t₁   d   r   m   f   s   l   t

V. Lydian : Final, F ; Dominant, C.

f   s   l   t   d¹   r¹   m¹   f¹

VI. Hypolydian : Final, F ; Dominant, A.

d   r   m   f   s   l   t   d¹

VII. Mixolydian : Final, G ; Dominant, D.

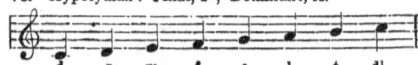
s   l   t   d¹   r¹   m¹   f¹   s¹

VIII. Hypomixolydian : Final, G ; Dominant, C.

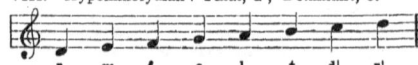
r   m   f   s   l   t   d¹   r¹

   * The Sol-fa initials are added to make clear the exact order of intervals in each mode.

The *Final,* answering to our Tonic (or key-note), was the same for any Plagal mode as for its relative Authentic mode. The *Dominant* (or *Reciting Note*) was a 5th above the Final in Authentic modes, unless it fell on B, and then C was taken instead; the Dominant of a Plagal mode was a 3rd lower than the Dominant of the Relative Authentic mode (unless this 3rd fell on B, when C was taken). In Mediæval music, B♭ was occasionally allowed in the Dorian and Hypodorian modes, showing an approach to modern tonality. From about the 16th cent. other modes were added—Æolian (Final, A), Locrian (Final, B), Ionian (Final, C), also Hypoæolian, Hypolocrian, and Hypoionian—but these had little recognized status in Gregorian music.

Doh Mode. The Major Scale.
Lah Mode. The Minor Scale.
Ray (or *Rah*) *Mode.* The Dorian Mode (see above).
Me Mode. The Phrygian Mode (see above).

Modera'to (*I.*). Moderate; at moderate speed.

Alle'gro modera'to. Moderately quick.
Con moderazio'ne ⎰ Moderately (fast) ; with moderate
Moderatamen'te ⎱ expression.
Moderatiss'imo. Very moderate; rather slow.
Modera'to assa'i con mol'to sentimen'to. In very moderate time, with much feeling.
Tem'po modera'to ⎰
A tem'po modera'to ⎱ In moderate *tempo.*

Modéré (*F.*). Moderate.

Modérément animé. Moderately quick (animated).
Modérément lent. Moderately slow.

Modern Music.

" The chief forces which have influenced modern music are (1) The Romanticists ; (2) the advent of programme music ; (3) Berlioz, from whom are to be dated several points of departure that are still being exploited ; (4) Liszt, with his new form, the Symphonic Poem and his Rhapsodies, full of fresh turns and surprising advances in the technique of the art ; and (5) the commanding figure of Wagner, whose operas, in their sequence, are themselves an example of individual development equalled only by that of the great Beethoven himself.', —*Sir A. C. Mackenzie, Jan.,* 1907.

Moder'no,-a (*I.*). Modern.

Al'la moder'na. In the modern style.

MODER'NUS, Jacobus. Music printer, Lyons, 1732-58.

Pub. works by French contrapuntists.

Mode'sto ⎰ Modestly; quietly ;
Modestamen'te (*I.*) ⎱ moderately.

Modifïcazio'ne (*I.*). Light and shade (in expression).

Mo'do (*I.*). Mode ; manner, style.

Mo'do maggio're. Major mode.
Mo'do mino're. Minor mode.

Modola're (*I.*) ⎰ To modulate (the voice) ;
Modula're (*I.*) ⎱ to change the key.

Modulation. (1) The rise and fall of the voice in speaking, reading, or reciting. (2) (*G., Modulation'; F., Modulation, Transition ; I., Modulazio'ne.*) Any change of key or mode.

(Mr. Curwen defines Modulation as "a change of Mode, from Major to Minor, or from Minor to Major ;" he calls a change of key (from Major to Major, or from Minor to Minor) "Transition ;" while a change of both key and mode is a "Transitional Modulation." In common usage the term "modulation" covers all these various meanings.)

A fine modulation is one of the most striking effects in music. The older composers (including Bach and Handel) rarely modulated beyond the five "Attendant Keys." (See *Keyplan.*) Modern composers modulate much more freely ; but it must be borne in mind that "excessive modulation causes music to become incoherent and vague," and that "the finest modulations lose their effect if introduced too often."

"To abandon a key which has scarcely been propounded ; to skip to and fro, merely to leave a place in which you are incapable of maintaining a footing ; in short, to modulate for the sake of modulation, betrays an ignorance of the art and a poverty of invention."—*Moore.*

Modulation may be (1) *gradual,* or (2) *sudden.* A sudden modulation to a remote key is sometimes called a "Transition." (N.B.—Not in Mr. Curwen's meaning of the term.)

The three chief methods of modulation are (1) *diatonic* (or *natural*), (2) *chromatic,* (3) *enharmonic.*

I.—DIATONIC MODULATION.
Example : C major to E minor.

Here the chord marked * is approached as the chord of the Sub-mediant in C major and quitted as the chord of the Sub-dominant in E minor. The modulation is said to be "established" by the *Perfect Cadence* in the new key.

II.—CHROMATIC MODULATION.
Transient modulation to B♭, C, D minor, and E♭.

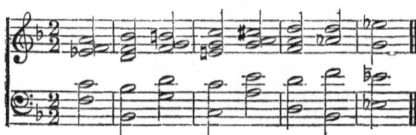

From C major to A♭ major.

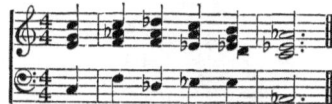

From D♭ major to C minor.

III.—ENHARMONIC MODULATION.
F major to E major.

The B♭ at * is quitted as if it were A♯ ; the whole chord being treated as an Augmented 6th (C, E, G, A♯) on the "flat 6th" of E major.

A very useful modulating formula — perhaps rather overdone in modern music—is a progression of semitones until the required key is reached.

From *Lavignac*..

&c.

From *Lavignac*.

&c.

Fine examples of every kind of Modulation may be found in Bach's *fantasias* and Beethoven's pf. sonatas. Spohr's *Last Judgment* may also be studied for striking illustrations of chromatic and enharmonic treatment. (See also *Transition*.)

Abrupt Modulation. Abrupt change to an extreme key.
Extended Modulation. Extending over several bars.
Extraneous Modulation } A modulation to an "ex-
Extreme modulation } treme" or unrelated key.
Final Modulation. An extended modulation.
Natural Modulation. See *Diatonic Modulation* (above).
Passing Modulation
Transient Modulation } For a few bars or chords only.
Transitory Modulation

Modulator. A chart for teaching tune.
The Sol-fa Modulator, perfected by the Rev. John Curwen, is a highly-ingenious and useful contrivance. In its extended form it shows at a glance the construction of each scale (major and minor) and the relationship of all the scales one to another. It also pictorially represents the scientific (acoustical) measurement of all intervals (major and minor tones, diatonic and chromatic semitones, kommatic differences of pitch, &c.). (See *Appendix*.)
STAFF MODULATOR. The simplest form consists of a staff with a black square (or squares) showing the position of *Doh*:—

 &c.

The Modulator adopted by the Staff Sight-singing College is as follows (with extensions on either side for the other keys):—

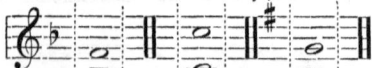

The sharps of notes are "pointed" to the right of the dotted line ; flats of notes to the left.

Modulazio'ne (*I.*). A modulation.
Moduli(e)'ren (*G.*). To modulate.
Mo'dus (*L.*). Mode (*q.v.*), or Mood (Time).
MOF'FAT, Alfred Ed. *B.* Edinburgh, 1866.
Works : cantatas, songs, trios, duets, pieces for vn. and pf., collections of folk-songs, &c.
Mög'lich (*G.*). Possible.
Mog'lichst gebund'en. As smooth(ly) as possible.
So rasch wie mög'lich. As quickly as possible.
MOHR, Hermann. *B.* Nienstedt, 1830 ; *d.* Philadelphia, 1896.
Wrote male choruses, pf. pieces, &c.
Moh'rentanz (*G.*). A Morris dance (*q.v.*).
Mohr'entrommel. Tambourine.
MÖH'RING, Ferdinand. *B.* Alt-Ruppin, 1816 ; *d.* 1887.
Wrote many popular male choruses,

Moins (*F.*). Less.
Moins vite. Less quick.
MOIR, Frank L. Song composer ; *b.* Market Harborough, 1852 ; *d.* 1904.
Moitié (*F.*). Half.
La moitié des premiers violons. Half the 1st vns.
MOLIQUE, Wm. Bernard. Violinist ; *b.* Nuremberg, 1802 ; *d.* Kannstadt, 1869. Trained by Rovelli, Munich. Member Vienna Court Orch., 1818 ; leader Munich Orch., 1820 ; leader Stuttgart, under Lindpaintner, 1826. After extended tours, lived in London, 1849-66.
Works : oratorio (*Abraham*, Norwich, 1860) ; 2 masses, a symphony, chamber music, and many fine compositions for vn. (including 6 concertos.)
Moll (*G.*). Minor.
Moll'akkord } A minor triad, minor chord.
Moll'dreiklang }
Molle (*F.*). (1) Soft, sweet, mellow, delicate.
Mol'le (*L.*). "Soft." (1) A mode, or a hexa-chord, with B♭ instead of B♮. (2) Minor.
Mollemen'te (*I.*). Softly, sweetly, &c.
MOL'LENHAUER, Eduard. *B.* Erfurt, 1827. Violinist ; pupil of Ernst and Spohr. Est. a vn. school for advanced students, New York, 1853.
Works : operas (*The Corsican Bride*, 1861) ; vn. pieces, songs, &c.
MOL'LENHAUER, Emil. Violinist and conductor ; *b.* Brooklyn, N.Y., 1855.
Mol'lis (*L.*). Soft. (See **Mol'le.**)
MOLLOY, James Lynam. Song composer *b.* King's Co., Ireland, 1837 ; *d.* 1909.
Moll'tonart (*G.*). A minor key.
Moll'tonleiter. A Minor Scale.
Molos'sus (*Gk.*). A metrical foot of three long syllables.
Mol'to,-a (*I.*). Much ; very, extremely.
Di mol'to. Exceedingly ; extremely.
Mol'to accenta'to il can'to. Accent the melody very much.
Mo'lto ada'gio. Very slow.
Mol'to canta'bile. Very singingly.
Mol'to me'no mos'so. Much less animated.
Mol'to più mos'so qua'si dop'pio tem'po. Much quicker ; almost twice as fast.
Mol'to sostenu'to. Well sustained.
Mol'to sot'to vo'ce. Very softly.
Mol'to viva'ce. Very quick and lively.
Moltisonan'te. Very sonorous ; resounding.
MOMIGNY, Jérome J. de. *B.* Philippeville, 1762 ; est. a mus. business, Paris, 1800 ; *d.* (?).
Wrote a "Cours Complet d'harmonie," 1822.
Monacor'do (*I.*). (See **Monochord.**)
MONASTE'RIO, Gesú. Violinist ; *b.* Potes, Spain, 1836 ; *d.* 1903. *Début*, 1845 ; "infant prodigy." After brilliant tours, founded the Madrid Quartet Society, 1861. Director, Madrid Cons., 1894.
Works : popular vn. pieces (*Adieux à l'Alhambra*).
Monau'los (*Gk.*). An ancient **flûte-à-bec,**

MONBEL'LI, Marie. Operatic soprano ; *b.* Cadiz, 1843. *Prima donna,* Covent Garden, 1869.

MONDONVILLE, Jean J. Cassanea de. Violinist ; *b.* Narbonne, 1711 ; *d.* 1772. Intendant, Musique de la Chapelle, Versailles, 1744 ; Condr. Concerts Spirituels, 1755-72.

Monferi'na (*I.*). An Italian peasant dance.

MONIUSZ'KO, Stanislaw. Organist and composer ; *b.* Lithuania, 1813(20?) ; *d.* 1872. Director Warsaw Opera, 1858.

Works : 15 national Polish operas (*The New Don Quixote, The Gipsies, The Paria, The Haunted Castle,* &c.) ; cantatas, church music, several songs, &c.

MONK, Edwin George. *B.* Frome, 1819 ; *d.* 1900. Mus.Doc. Oxon, 1856. Orgt. York Minster, 1858-83.

Works : church music, "Anglican Chant Book," "Anglican Hymn Book," "The Psalter and Canticles" (with Ouseley), &c.

MONK, Mark Jas. Orgt., composer, and condr. ; *b.* Hunmanby, Yorks, 1858. Mus.D. Oxon, 1888. Orgt. Truro Cathredral since 1889.

MONK, Wm. Henry. Organist ; London, 1823-89. Prof. of Vocal Music, King's College, London, 1874. Prof. Nat. Training College, 1876. Mus. Doc. Durham, 1882.

Works : church music, hymns, &c. ; musical editor of "Hymns, Ancient and Modern."

Mon'ochord. (*F., Monocorde ; I., Monocor'do, Monacor'do*). (1) An ancient inst. for measuring intervals, consisting of a single string stretched over a sound-box, with a movable bridge. (2) A tromba marina (*q.v.*).

A monocorde (*F.*).
A monocor'do (*I.*). } On one string (vn., &c.).

Monodi'a (*I.*). A plaintive song for a single voice. (See also **Monody.**)

Monodie (*F.*). (See **Monody.**)

Mon'odrama. (*G., Monodram' ; F., Monodrame.*) A dramatic piece for a single performer.

Mon'ody. (*G., Monodie'; F., Monodie ; I., Monodi'a.*) Same as **Homophony.**

Monody is the name given to the new style of *Recitative* invented in Italy abt. 1600. (See *Cavaliere, Bardi, Caccini.*)

Monoph'onous. Able to produce only one tone at a time (as an oboe, &c.) ; opp. to **Polyphonous** (as a pf., &c.).

Mon'otone. (1) The repetition of a single sound. (2) Recitation, intoning, or chanting, on one tone.

MONSIGNY, Pierre A. One of the creators of French comic opera ; *b.* nr. St. Omer, 1729 ; *d.* 1817. Orphaned at an early age, he supported his mother and the rest of the family by working as a clerk. In 1759, after studying a few months under Gianotti, a 1-act comic opera met with remarkable success.

This was followed by several others (principally for the Comédie Italienne, Paris), culminating

in *Félix, ou l'enfant trouvé,* 1777, his last and best work. After the Revolution he was pensioned by the Opéra-Comique and made an Inspector of the Cons.

Montant (*F.*). "Ascending." (See **Monter.**)

MONTE, Filippo de (Philippe de Mons). *B.* Mons (or Malines), 1521 ; *d.* Vienna, 1603. Celebrated contrapuntist ; Capellmeister to Maximilian II and Rudolf II.

Works : masses, motets, madrigals, canzonets, French chansons, "Sonnets de Pierre de Ronsard," &c.

MONTÉCLAIR, M. P. de. *B.* Chaumont, 1666 ; *d.* 1737. "One of the earliest players on the modern double-bass."

Wrote 3 operas, cantatas, 6 trios for 2 vns. and bass, an early Vn. Method (1720), &c.

Monter (*F.*). (1) To mount up ; to ascend. (2) To raise the pitch. (3) To set up an inst. (put strings on, &c.).

Montant. Ascending ; going up by steps (or skips).

Monter in ut, re, mi, &c. (*F.*). To sing " up the scale."

MONTEVER'DE (Monte'ver'di), Claudio G. A. *B.* Cremona, 1567 ; *d.* Venice, 1643. One of the most distinguished composers of the new style invented by Bardi, Peri, Caccini, and others, about 1600. He was one of the first to introduce unprepared discords ; he greatly improved the style of *Recitative ;* he employed the first *tremolo* of strings ; he enlarged the orchestra, and combined and contrasted the insts. with such skill that he is called " the Father of the Art of Instrumentation." Maestro to the Duke of Mantua, 1603 ; Maestro, St. Mark's, Venice, 1613.

Chief works : operas, *Orfeo* (1608) ("received with unbounded enthusiasm," and still regarded as an "epoch-making" work), and about 8 others ; madrigals, masses, vespers, motets, hymns, &c. The first opera house was opened at Venice, 1637, largely as a result of Monteverde's successes.

Montez (*F.*). Raise.

Montez la fa grave au la. Raise the low F to A (drum, &c.).

MONTGOMERY, James. 1771-1854. Editor, *Sheffield Iris.*

Wrote "Hail to the Lord's anointed," and many other hymns.

MONTIGNY, Mad. (See **F. M. C. Rémaury.**)

Montre (*F.*). " Set up, displayed." The open diapason of an org., generally " set up " or " displayed " on the organ case.

Mood (*E.*). Used by early writers instead of Mode in speaking of the *Time-Table,* when the Large, Long, and Breve might be divided into 2 or 3.

MOODY, Chas. H. *B.* Stourbridge, 1874. Orgt. Ripon Cath. since 1902.

MOODY, Fanny. Soprano vocalist ; *b.* Redruth, Cornwall, 1866. *Début* in opera, Liverpool, 1887. Married **Charles Manners** (*q.v.*) 1890,

Moonlight Sonata. " Fancy " name given —not by the composer—to Beethoven's Pf. Sonata in C♯ minor (Op. 27, No. 2).

MOORE, Graham Ponsonby. Pianist and composer ; *b.* Ballarat, 1859.

MOORE, Thomas. Poet ; *b.* Dublin, 1779 ; *d.* 1852.
> Wrote 125 songs, many of which were set to National Irish melodies and pub. as the well-known "Moore's Irish Melodies."

Mor. Abbn. of *Morendo*.

MORA′LES, Christofano (or Christofero). Eminent Spanish contrapuntist ; member Papal Chapel, Rome, abt. 1540. Some of his works are still sung there.
> Wrote masses, motets, Magnificats, &c.

Moralities. (See **Mysteries.**)

MO′RALT. A celebrated quartet of four brothers at Munich.
(1) **Joseph.** 1st violin ; 1775-1828.
(2) **J. Baptist.** 2nd violin ; 1777-1825.
(3) **Philipp.** 'Cello ; 1780-1847.
(4) **Georg.** Viola ; 1781-1818.

MO′RAN-OL′DEN, Fanny. (Frau Bertram.) Operatic soprano ; *b.* Oldenburg, 1855. *Début* Gewandhaus, Leipzig, 1877.

Morbidez′za, Con (*I.*) ⎫ Morbidly ; softly,
Mor′bido (*I.*) ⎭ tenderly.

Morceau (*F.*). "A morsel." A short composition ; a dainty passage.
> *Morceau d'ensemble*. A piece for several voices (or parts).
> *Morceau de genre*. A characteristic piece.
> *Morceau élégant*. A drawing-room piece.

Mordant (*F.*). An old French " grace." (See **Ornaments.**)

Mordent. (*G., Mor′dent, Bei′sser ; F., Pincé ; I., Morden′te.*) From *F. Mordre*, " to bite." A short trill.

(1) SHORT MORDENT. (*a*) German "Stroked" Mordent :—
Written.

Played.

(*b*) *Inverted* or Italian Mordent (without the " *stroke* ") (Called also a *Praller* or *Pralltriller*.) :—
Written. ♭   Played.

In very quick time this mordent is played as a triplet :—
Presto.   Played.

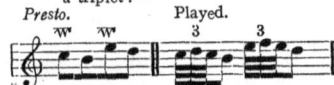

(2) LONG, or DOUBLE MORDENT.
Written.   Played.

MORE, Félicité. (See **Pradher.**)

MOREL, Auguste F. Self-taught composer ; *b.* Marseilles, 1809 ; *d.* 1881. Director Marseilles Cons., 1852.
> Works : a grand opera, chamber music, symphonies, cantatas, songs, &c,

MORELOT, Stephen. Writer ; *b.* Dijon, 1820 ; *d.* 1899.
> Works : "The Music of the 15th Century," a treatise on the "Accompaniment of Plain Chant," &c.

Moren′do (*I.*) ⎫ Dying away ; gradually
Morien′te (*I.*) ⎭ softer (and slower).

Mores′ca (*I.*) ⎫ Moorish ; a Morris dance
Moresque (*F.*) ⎭ (*q.v.*).

MORET′TI, Giovanni. *B.* Naples, 1807 ; *d.* 1884.
> Wrote 22 operas, 12 masses, a Requiem, &c.

MORGAN, George W. *B.* Gloucester, 1822 ; *d.* (U.S.), 1892. Settled in New York, 1853, as an organist.
> Wrote church music, org. music, and songs.

MORGAN, John Paul. Organist ; *b.* Oberlin, Ohio, 1841 ; *d.* 1879.
> Works : an English translation of Richter's "Harmony," church music, &c.

MORGAN, Robt. Orlando. Pianist ; *b.* Manchester, 1865.

Mor′gengesang (*G.*) ⎫ A morning song.
Mor′genlied (*G.*) ⎭

Mor′gen-ständ′chen (*G.*). A morning serenade ; an *Aubade*.

MORHANGE. (See **Alkan.**)

Moris′co (*I.*). Moorish (same as **Mores′ca**).

MORLAC′CHI, Francesco. *B.* Perugia, 1784 ; *d.* 1841. Capellmeister, Dresden Italian Opera, 1810.
> Works : 10 grand masses, 2 oratorios (*Isacco*, and *La Morte di Abele*), church music, org. pieces, songs, and over 20 operas.

MORLEY, Chas. Pen-name of **F. Behr** (*q.v.*).

MORLEY, Thomas. One of the best English musicians of his time ; *b.* 1557(8?) ; *d.* abt. 1604. Pupil of Byrd ; Mus.Bac. Oxford, 1588. Orgt. St. Paul's Cathedral ; Gentleman Chapel Royal, 1592.
> Works : "A Plaine and Easie Introduction to Practicall Musicke" (1597), "Aires or Songes," canzonets, madrigals, ballets, "Consort Lessons," &c.

Mormoramen′to (*I.*). A murmur.
> *Mormoran′do* ⎫
> *Mormore′vole* ⎬ In a gentle murmuring style.
> *Mormoro′so* ⎭

MORNINGTON, G. C. Wellesley, Earl of. Father of the Duke of Wellington ; *b.* Dangan, Ireland, 1735 ; *d.* 1781. Prof. of Music, Dublin Univ., 1764-74.
> Works : glees ("Here in cool grot"), hymns, chants, &c.

MORRIS, Herbert C. *B.* Coventry, 1873. Orgt. St. David's Cath. since 1896.

Morris-dance. (**Morrice-dance, Moriske-dance.**) An old English rustic dance in 4-4 time, supposed to be of Moorish origin.
> The performers formerly wore bells at their ankles. With other Old Eng. dances, the Morris-dance is being revived at pageants, &c.

MORROW, Walter. Fine trumpet player ; *b.* Liverpool, 1850.

MORSE, Chas. Hy. Organist ; *b.* Bradford, Mass., 1853 ; Director North-western Cons., Minneapolis, 1875-84 ; organist Brooklyn, 1891.
Works : sacred music, collections of org. music.

MORTELMANS, Lodewijk. Composer ; *b.* Antwerp, 1868.

MORTIER de FONTAINE, H. L. S. Pianist ; fine interpreter of Beethoven. *B.* Russia, 1816 ; *d.* London, 1883. *Début* Dantzig, 1832.

MORTIMER, Peter. *B.* Putenham, Surrey, 1750 ; *d.* 1828.
Wrote a treatise on the old Church modes.

MORTIMER, Philip. Pen-name of **J. P. Knight** (*q.v.*).

MOSCA, Giuseppe. *B.* Naples, 1772 ; *d.* 1839. Mus. Director, Messina Th., 1823.
Works : about 50 operas and ballets.

MOSCA, Luigi. Brother of G. Naples, 1775-1824.
Works : an oratorio, a mass, 16 operas, &c.

MO'SCHELES, Ignaz. *B.* Prague, 1794 ; *d.* Leipzig, 1870. Son of a Jewish merchant. Played a pf. concerto of his own composition in public at 14. Shortly after, went to Vienna as pianist and teacher. While there "prepared the pf. score of Beethoven's *Fidelio* under the composer's supervision." After Continental tours, lived mostly in London (1821-46) as teacher and composer. Gave Mendelssohn pf. lessons, Berlin, 1824. Pf. professor, Leipzig Cons., 1846. He was a brilliant and sympathetic player, and an excellent teacher.
Works : 8 pf. concertos ; a grand septuor, a grand sextuor, and other chamber music ; works for 2 pfs. (8 hands), pf. duets, numerous characteristic pieces for pf. solo, 24 excellent études still in general use, &c.; in all, 142 works.

MO'SENTHAL, Joseph. Violinist ; pupil of Spohr ; *b.* Cassel, 1834 ; *d.* 1896. Went to America, 1853 ; orgt. Calvary Ch., New York, 1860-87. Condr. New York "Mendelssohn Glee Club," 1867-96.
Wrote church music, part-songs, songs.

MO'SER, Karl. Violinist ; Berlin, 1774-1851.

MOSE'WIUS, Johann T. *B.* Königsberg, 1788 ; *d.* 1858. Est. the Breslau Sing-akademie, 1825 ; Univ. Mus.-dir., 1829.
Wrote treatises on Bach's church music.

MOSON'YI. (Michael Brandt.) Hungarian composer ; *b.* 1814 ; *d.* Pesth, 1870.
Works : opera (*Szep Ilonka*, 1861), a symphonic poem, a funeral symphony, pf. pieces, &c.

MOS'SEL, Jan. 'Cellist ; *b.* Rotterdam, 1870.

Mos'so (*I.*). " Moved." With animation.
Me'no mos'so. Less moved ; slower.
Più mos'so. More moved ; quicker.
Po'co mos'so. A little moved ; rather quick.
Allegret'to po'co mos'so. A little quicker than *allegretto*.
Mol'to mos'so. Very quick.

Mo'stra (*I.*). A direct (*q.v.*).

MOSZKOW'SKI (pron. *Môsh-koff'-shki*), **Alexander.** Critic and editor ; *b.* Pilica, Poland, 1851. Resides in Berlin.

MOSZKOW'SKI, Moritz. Pianist ; brother of A. ; *b.* Breslau, 1854. *Début*, Berlin, 1873 ; after successful tours settled in Paris, 1897.
Works : an opera (*Boabdil*, 1892), numerous elegant pf. pieces (*Spanish Dances, studies, waltzes,* &c.) ; also orchestral suites, symphonic poems, &c.

MOSZ'KWA, Jos. Napoleon Ney, Prince de la. Son of Marshall Ney ; *b.* 1803 ; *d.* 1857.
Est. and conducted the " Soc. de musique vocale, religieuse et classique," 1843. Wrote 2 successful operas.

Motet'. (*G.*, *Motet'te ; F.*, *Motet ; I.*, *Motet'to.*) A composition in contra-puntal style, sung in Catholic and Lutheran services.
The older motets were generally unaccompanied (*a cappella*). In England the place of the motet was taken by the *Anthem* (*q.v.*).
Motet'stil (*G.*). Motet-style ; used by German writers for pieces in which the accts. simply double the voice-parts.

Motif (*F.*). A motive (*q.v.*).

Motion. (1) The progression of a single part.
(*a*) *Conjunct* motion ; by steps—

(*b*) *Disjunct* motion ; by skips—

(2) The progression of one part in relation to another (or others).
(*a*) *Similar* or *Direct* motion ; 2 (or more) parts rising or falling together :—

(*b*) *Contrary* motion ; parts moving in opposite directions : —

(*c*) *Oblique* motion ; one part stationary while another moves :—

(*d*) *Parallel* motion ; specially used for consecutive 8ves or 5ths in similar motion ; *i.e.*, when both parts ascend or descend by the same interval :—

(3) Harmonic motion. The simultaneous motion of several parts.
Also the correct progression and resolution of chords and discords, &c.

Mo′tive. (Also pron. *Moteev′*.) (*G., Motiv′*; *F., Motif; I., Moti′vo*.) A short theme, passage, figure, &c., from which a longer theme is developed. (See **Leitmotiv,** and **Thematic Development**.)

Mo′to (*I.*). (1) Motion.
Mo′to contra′rio. Contrary motion.
Mo′to obbli′quo. Oblique motion.
Mo′to perpe′tuo. Perpetual motion.
Mo′to ret′to. Similar motion.

Mo′to (*I.*) (2) Movement, speed, *tempo*.
Con mo′to. With animation.
Lo stes′so mo′to. The same speed (as before).
Mo′to preceden′te. The previous *tempo* (speed).

Motor. A small bellows forming part of the pneumatic action in an organ.

Mottegian′do (*I.*). Jocularly, banteringly.

MOTTL, Felix. Distinguished conductor; *b.* nr. Vienna, 1856. Court Capellmeister, Carlsruhe, 1880. General Music-director, 1893. Conductor-inchief, Bayreuth, 1886. First conducted in London, 1893.

Mo′tus (*L.*). Motion.
Mo′tus contra′rius. Contrary motion.
Mo′tus obli′quus. Oblique motion.
Mo′tus rec′tus. Similar motion.

MOUNSEY, Ann S. (See **Mrs. Bartholomew.**)

MOUNT-EDGCUMBE, Richard, Earl of. B. 1764; *d.* 1839.
Wrote "Musical Reminiscences of an Amateur" (1823).

Mounted Cornet. A mixture stop in old organs "mounted" on a separate soundboard.

MOUNT OF OLIVES. English name of Beethoven's *Christus*.

MOUSSORGSKY. (See **Mussorgski.**)

Mouth. The opening in the front of an organ pipe.
Mouth Organ. (1) Pan's pipes (*q.v.*). (2) A small toy inst. with free reeds.

Mouthpiece. (*G., Mund′stück; F., Embouchure; I., Imboccatu′ra*.) The part of a wind inst. applied to the lips. (The "cup"of a brass inst., &c.).

MOUTON (Jean de Hollingue). Contrapuntist; *b.* nr. Metz abt. 1475; *d.* St. Quentin, 1522. Pupil of Josquin; teacher of Willaert.
Works: masses, motets, psalms, hymns, &c. According to Macfarren he was the "first composer to introduce the unprepared Dominant Seventh."

Mouvement (*F.*). (*I., Movimen′to*.) (1) Motion (*q.v.*). (2) Movement; speed.
Mouvement de l'archet. Bowing; the movement of the bow.
Bien mouvementé. In well-regulated elegant rhythm.

Movable Do (or **Doh**). Any system of sight-reading which calls the tonic of any (major) key "Doh," instead of restricting that name to "C" as in fixed-do systems. (See **Fixed-do.**)

Movement. (*G., Bewe′gung; F., Mouvement; I., Movimen′to, Tem′po, Mo′to*.) (1) Rate of speed; *tempo*. (2) Special style of rhythmical flow; *e.g., Waltz*

movement, Minuet movement. (3) (*G., Satz; F., Phrase; I., Tem′po*.). An important division of a composition (practically complete in itself); *e.g.*, the *First movement* of a symphony, the *Slow movement* of a sonata, &c.

Movimen′to contra′rio (*I.*). Contrary motion. (See **Motion.**)

MOZART, J. G. Leopold. (German pron. *Mō′tsart*; Eng. pron. *Mozart′*). Father of the great composer; *b.* Augsburg, 1719; *d.* 1787. Son of a poor bookbinder; choir-boy at Augsburg and at Salzburg. Violinist in the Prince-Bishop's Orch., Salzburg, 1743; court composer, 1762. Married Anna M. Pertlin, 1747; of their 7 children "only two, Nannerl and Wolfgang, passed the age of one year." (See **W. A. Mozart.**)
Works: 12 oratorios, symphonies, concertos, chamber music, org. music, a celebrated "Vn. Method," &c.

MOZART, Maria Anna. (Pet name **Nannerl**). Daughter of preceding; *b.* Salzburg, 1751; *d.* 1829. Precocious pianist; toured with her brother. (See **W. A. Mozart.**) Married Baron von Berchtold zu Sonnenberg, 1784. After his death resumed teaching until her eyesight failed in 1820.

MOZART, Wolfgang Amadeus. (Baptized as **Johannes Chrysostomus Wolfgangus Theophilus.**) "One of the brightest stars in the musical firmament." B. Salzburg, Jan. 27, 1756; *d.* Vienna, Dec. 5, 1791. Taught the clavichord by his father from his fourth year (at which age he also began "to compose little pieces.") In 1762, Wolfgang being 6 and "Nannerl" 10½, their father took them on a concert tour to Munich and Vienna. (While in Vienna, Wolfgang learned to play both the violin and organ without instruction.) In 1763 the gifted children were taken to Paris, "giving concerts on the way." In Paris Wolfgang's first published compositions (2 harpsichord sonatas, with vn. *ad lib.*) appeared. The travellers visited England in 1764, and remained here abt. 15 months, their phenomenal performances being greatly admired. "Our high and mighty Wolfgang," writes his father, "knows everything in this his 8th year, that one can require of a man of forty." Returned to Salzburg, 1766. Mozart composed his first oratorio, 1767. Revisited Vienna, 1768; wrote his first opera, *La finta semplice* (performed, Salzburg, 1769). Concertmeister to the Archbishop of Salzburg, 1768. Started (with his father) on an Italian tour, 1769. "This journey was a veritable triumphal progress." Received from the Pope the "Order of the Golden

Spur ; " was elected a member of the Bologna Philharmonic Academy. While in Rome, wrote out from memory the score of Allegri's famous *Miserere,* after hearing it twice. Returned to Salzburg, 1771. The archbishop died, 1772, and his successor "cared little for Mozart's genius." Insufficient income led Mozart to resign, 1777. The death of his mother, 1778, and the failure of expectations elsewhere, led him to resume the post ; he resigned finally, 1781, and settled in Vienna. Married Constance Weber, 1782 ; they were both rather improvident and experienced much real poverty. The unexampled success of *Don Giovanni,* Prague, 1787, led the Emperor to appoint Mozart Chamber Composer, with a yearly salary of 800 florins. King Friedrich William II offered him the post of Royal Capellmeister, 1789 (with a salary of 3,000 Thaler), but misplaced confidence in the Emperor led him to refuse this benevolent offer. His last work, a *Requiem Mass,* was written when the hand of death was upon him. He was buried in a pauper's grave.

" I consider Mozart the greatest purely musical genius that has ever showered blessings on the world. . . . . He was music personified."—*Felix Mottl,* 1906.

Breitkopf & Härtel's complete edition of Mozart's works includes :—

(1) CHURCH MUSIC—15 masses, 4 litanies, and about 40 other works.

(2) STAGE MUSIC—operas : *Idomeneo, Il Seraglio, Le nozze di Figaro, Don Giovanni, Cosi fan tutte, La clemenza di Tito, Die Zauberflöte,* and 14 others.

(3) VOCAL CONCERT MUSIC—44 arias, 2 duets, 6 terzets, 1 quartet, 35 songs, 20 canons, &c.

(4) ORCHESTRAL—41 symphonies (including the "Jupiter," G minor, and Eb) ; 31 divertimenti, &c. ; and about 45 other pieces.

(5) CONCERTOS WITH ORCHESTRA—6 vn. concertos 2 fl. concèrtos, 4 horn concertos, a clar. concerto, 25 pf. concertos, and about 15 others for other insts.

(6) CHAMBER MUSIC—11 quintets, 30 quartets, 42 vn. sonatas, and some 15 other works.

(7) PIANOFORTE MUSIC — 5 sonatas and an *Andante* for 4 hands, a fugue and a sonata for 2 pfs., 17 solo sonatas, 15 sets of variations, 4 fantasias, numerous miscellaneous pieces.

(8) 17 organ sonatas.

The best biography of Mozart is Otto Jahn's (Eng. translation, 3 vols., 1882).

MOZART, Wolfgang Amadeus. Son of the great composer ; *b.* Vienna, 1791 ; *d.* 1844. Talented pianist ; founded the "Cecilia Society," Lemberg.

Mozarteum. A Musical Institute at Salzburg, consisting of an orchestral society, a music school, and a museum of Mozart relics.

Mozart Scholarship. Founded Frankfort, 1838, to aid "gifted young composers of limited means."

mp. Abbn. of *Mezzo-piano,* moderately soft.

m.s. Abbn. of *Mano sinistra,* left hand.

MUCK, Dr. Karl. *B.* Darmstadt, 1859. Court Capellmeister, Berlin Royal Opera, 1892.

Muck'sen (*G.*). To mutter, to utter a faint sound.

MUDIE, Thomas M. London, 1809-76· Prof. of pf. R.A.M., 1832-44.
Wrote 4 symphonies, pf. music, songs, &c.

MUECKE, Mrs. F. F. (See **Ada Crossley.**)

Mue de voix (*F.*). The mutation, " break," of the voice. (See **Mutation.**)

MUF'FAT, August G. Son of G. (below). *B.* Passau, 1690 ; *d.* 1770. Imperial Court orgt., Vienna, 1717-64.
Wrote org. pieces and harpsichord pieces.

MUF'FAT, Georg. *D.* Passau, 1704. Orgt. and Capellmeister.
Wrote Instrumental Sonatas, dance pieces for 4 and 8 violins, org. pieces, 12 concertos for strings, &c.

Müh'(e)los (*G.*). Easily ; without effort.

MÜHL'BERGER-LEI'SINGER. See **Leisinger.**

MÜHL'DÖRFER, Wilhelm K. *B.* Graz, Styria, 1837. Capellmeister, Cologne, Th., 1881.
Works : operas (*Iolanthe,* 1890), overtures, incidental stage music, songs, &c.

MÜHL'FELD, Richard. Fine clarinet player ; *b.* Salzungen, 1856 ; *d.* 1907.

MÜH'LEN, Raimond. (See **Zur Mühlen.**)

MÜH'LING, August. 1786-1847. Royal Mus.-director, Magdeburg.
Works : 2 oratorios, orch. pieces, songs, &c.

MÜL'LER, Adolf (Junr.). *B.* Vienna, 1839 ; *d.* 1901. Condr. German Opera, Rotterdam, 1875.
Works : operas and operettas (*Der Blondin von Namur,* 1898).

MÜL'LER, August. Fine double-bass player ; *b.* 1810 ; *d.* Darmstadt, 1867.

MÜL'LER, August E. *B.* nr. Hanover, 1767 ; *d.* 1817. Capellmeister, Weimar, 1810.
Works : church cantatas, numerous pf. pieces, a pf. method, &c.

MÜL'LER, Carl Christian. *B.* Saxe-Meiningen, 1831. Went to New York, 1854. Prof. of Harmony, New York Coll. of Music, 1879.
Works : a trans. of Sechter's "Fundamental Harmony ; " pf. pieces, chamber music, org. pieces, choruses, songs.

MÜL'LER, Christian. Built the renowned org. at Haarlem (60 stops), 1738.

MÜL'LER, Franz K. F. Weimar, 1806-76. Govt. councillor ; "one of the first to recognize Wagner's real importance."
Works : numerous treatises on Wagner's music dramas (*Tannhäuser, Der Ring, Tristan, Lohengrin,* &c.).

MÜL'LER, Friedrich. Clarinettist ; *b.* Orlamünde, 1786 ; *d.* 1871. Capellmeister, Rudolstadt, 1831-54.
Works : orchestral music, 2 concertos and other compositions for clar., male choruses, &c.

MÜL'LER, Dr. Hans. *B.* Cologne, 1854 ; *d.* 1897.

> Wrote historical works on "Hucbald," "Mensural Music," &c.

MÜL'LER, Ivan (or Iwan). *B.* Reval, 1786 ; *d.* 1854. Greatly improved the clarinet (increasing the number of keys to 13), and invented the "alt-clarinet."

> Works : methods for clarinet and alt-clarinet, pieces for clar. and other insts., flute concertos.

MÜL'LER, Peter. *B.* nr. Hanau, 1791 ; *d.* 1877. Pastor at Staden, 1839.

> Works : an opera, 7 string quintets, male choruses, org. pieces, and a number of celebrated "Jugendlieder."

MÜL'LER Quartets. (1) Four brothers ; *b.* Brunswick. **Karl,** 1797-1873 ; **Gustav,** 1799-1855 ; **Theodor,** 1802-75 ; **Georg,** 1808-55. Toured in Germany, Austria, France, Russia, &c.

(2) The four sons of **Karl. Karl,** *b.* 1829 ; **Hugo,** 1832-86 ; **Bernhard,** 1825-95 ; **Wilhelm,** 1834-96. Toured, &c., 1855-1873. **Karl** is also known as a composer under the name of **Müller-Berghaus.**

MÜL'LER, Wenzel. *B.* Moravia, 1767 ; *d.* 1835. Capellmeister, Leopoldstadt Th., Vienna, from 1813.

> Wrote 200 popular operas and *Singspiele.*

MÜL'LER, William. Tenor singer ; *b.* Hanover, 1845. "The son of a shoemaker, and by trade a thatcher." Permanently engaged, Berlin Court Opera, 1876.

MÜL'LER - BERG'HAUS. (See **Müller Quartets.**)

> Works : an operetta, a cantata, a symphony, vn. pieces, songs, &c.

MÜL'LER-HAR'TUNG, Karl W. *B.* Sulza, 1834. Founded an Orchestra and Music School, Weimar, 1872.

> Works : org. sonatas, church music, male choruses.

MÜL'LER-REU'TER, Theodor. Pianist ; *B.* Dresden, 1858. Teacher, Dresden Cons., 1892.

> Works : operas, church music, female choruses, male choruses, pf. pieces, songs.

MUNCK. (See **De Munck.**)

Mund (*G.*). Mouth.

> *Mund' harmonica.* Mouth harmonica.
> *Mund'loch.* The mouth of an organ pipe.
> *Mund'stück.* Mouthpiece.

Mundane Music. Music of the Spheres (*q.v.*).

MUNDELLA, Emma. Pianist and composer ; *b.* Nottingham, 1858 ; *d.* 1896.

MUNDY, John. Organist, St. George's, Windsor, 1585 ; Mus.Doc. Oxon, 1624 ; *d.* 1630.

> Works : "Songs and Psalms," anthems, program music, &c.

Mun'ter (*G.*). Lively, gay, animated.

> *Mun'ter und straff.* Lively and precise.
> *Sehr mun'ter.* Very lively, &c.

MUNZ'INGER, Edgar. Pianist and composer ; *b.* Olten, Switzerland, 1847.

MURDOCH, Wm. Mc. Violinist ; *b.* Glasgow, 1870.

MU'RIS, Johannes (Jean) de. Author of "Speculum Musicæ," abt. 1325.

> This famous work treats of intervals, musical ratios, consonance and dissonance, ancient music, church modes, solmisation, measured music, and discant.

Murky. A harpsichord piece with a *murky-bass.*

> *Murky-bass.* A bass in broken octaves (*q.v.*).

Mur'meln (*G.*). To murmur, whisper.

Murmuran'do (*I.*). (See **Mormorando.**)

MUR'SKA, Ilma di. Dramatic soprano ; *b.* Croatia, 1836 ; *d.* 1889. *Début,* Florence, 1862. London *début,* 1865, at Her Majesty's Th. Sang frequently in London up to 1873.

Mu'sa (*L.*). A song.

MUSARD, Philippe. Famous dance composer ; the "King of Quadrilles ; " Paris, 1793-1859. Conducted Drury Lane Promenade Concerts, 1840-41.

Mu'sars. Ballad singers of the time of the Troubadours.

Mus.Bac., or **Mus.B.** Bachelor of Music.

Mus.Doc., or **Mus.D.** Doctor of Music.

Muse. The nozzle or tube of the bagpipe.

Muses. In Greek mythology, the 9 sisters who presided over the fine arts.

> Apollo presided over the Muses : Clio, the Muse of History ; Euterpe, of Lyric Poetry ; Thalia, of Comedy and Idyllic Poetry ; Melpomene, Tragedy ; Terpsichore, of Music and Dancing ; Erato, of Erotic Poetry ; Calliope, of Epic Poetry ; Urania, of Astronomy ; Polyhymnia, of Singing and Harmony.

Muset'ta (*I.*.) } (1) A primitive pastoral oboe.
Musette (*F.*.) } (2) A kind of bagpipe. (3) A piece with a drone bass, often used as the 2nd part of a gavotte. (4) An organ reed stop.

Music. (From *Gk. Mousikos,* pertaining to the muses ; *L.* and *I., Mu'sica ; G., Musik'; F., Musique ;* old spellings, *musick, musicke, musyk, musike,* &c.) (1) The art and science of producing, arranging, and combining sounds. (2) A taste for music. (See **Musical Perception.**) (3) Printed or written musical notation, compositions, &c.

> An all-embracing definition of music is impossible. The following quotations exemplify its many-sided character :—
> "The poetry of sound."—*Ency. Brit.*
> "The art of the beautiful and pleasing."—*Quintilian.*
> "The artistic union of inarticulate sounds and rhythm."—*Nat. Ency.*
> "The universal language which, when all other languages were confounded, the confusion of Babel left unconfounded."—*Prof. Wilson,*

"Miraculous rhetoric! excelling eloquence!—
Izaac Walton.
"A kind of inarticulate, unfathomable speech,
which leads us on to the edge of the infinite."
—*Carlyle.*
"The mysterious language of a remote spiritual
realm."—*Hoffmann.*
"All deep thought is music."—*Carlyle.*
"The harbinger of eternal melody."—*Mozart.*
"Next to theology."—*Luther.*
"The highest of all science."—*Bach.*
"The fine art which more than any other ministers
to human welfare."—*Herbert Spencer.*
"The worth of art appears most eminent in
music."—*Goethe.*
"What passion cannot music raise and quell?"—
Dryden.
"Exalts each joy, allays each grief."—*Armstrong.*
"Thou Queen of Heaven, care-charming spell!"
—*Herrick.*
"The medicine of the breaking heart."—*Hunt.*
"The sweet companion of labour."—*Sir J.
Lubbock.*
"A genuine and natural source of delight."—
—*Sir J. Hawkins.*
"The chief recreation of tired humanity."—*Kay.*
"Of all delights the most exquisite."—*Dr.
Tulloch.*
"Has the power of making heaven descend to
earth."—*Japanese Proverb.*
"The voice of Liberty."—*W. S. Walker.*
"The sacred emblem of Truth, Peace, and Order."
—*E. Smith* (1707).
"There is no truer truth obtainable
By man than comes of music."—*Browning.*
"The seed of many virtues is in such hearts as are
devoted to music."—*Luther.*
"One of the most forcible instruments for training,
for arousing, and for governing the mind and
the spirit of man."—*W. E. Gladstone.*
"The voice of prayer."—*Sherer.*
"The handmaid of Religion."
"Rouses the soul to fearless deeds of daring and
valour."—*Acton.*
"The man that hath no music in himself,
Nor is not moved with concord of sweet sounds,
Is fit for treasons, stratagems, and spoils."
—*Shakespeare.*
Yet, "Nothing that has ever been written of
Music has adequately expressed what it has
meant to mankind."—*Ency. Brit.*

Mu'sica (*L.* and *I.*). Music.

Mu'sica anti'qua (*L.*). Ancient music (Greeks, &c.).
Mu'sica arithmet'ica (*L.*). Musical ratios, intervals,
&c., considered mathematically.
Mu'sica artificia'le (*I.*). (1) Complex. (2) Instru-
mental music.
Mu'sica atti'va (*I.*). Practical music.
Mu'sica chora'ica (*L.*). Music proper for dancing.
Mu'sica chora'le (*I.*). Plain-song.
Mu'sica chroma'tica (*L.*). Chromatic music.
Mu'sica colora'ta (*I.*). Ornamented music.
Mu'sica combinato'ria (*L.*). The art of rhythmical
variety.
Mu'sica contemplati'va (*L.*). Theortical music.
Mu'sica da cam'era (*I.*). Chamber music.
Mu'sica da chie'sa (*I.*). Church music.
Mu'sica da tea'tro (*I.*). Operatic music.
Mu'sica diaton'ica (*I.*). Diatonic music.
Mu'sica didac'tica (*L.*). The quantities, proportions,
and qualities of sounds.
Mu'sica di gat'ti (*I.*). Cats' music.
Mu'sica drama'tica (*L.*). Theatrical music.
Mu'sica ecclesias'tica (*L.*). Church music.
Mu'sica enharmon'ica (*L.*). Enharmonic (*q.v.*).
Mu'sica ennunciati'va (*L.*). Musical signs and
characters.
Mu'sica figura'lis (*L.*) ⎫ Ornamented music.
Mu'sica figura'ta (*I.*) ⎭
Mu'sica harmon'ica (*L.*). Harmony.
Mu'sica histo'rica (*L.*). Musical history.
Mu'sica instrumenta'lis (*L.*). Instrumental music.
Mu'sica maniero'sa (*I.*). In some special style.
Mu'sica melisma'tica (*L.*) ⎫ A melody; a single part.
Mu'sica melo'dica (*I.*) ⎭

Mu'sica melopoe'tica (*L.*). The art of making melody.
Musica mensurab'ilis (*L.*). ⎫ Measured; in time.
Mu'sica mensura'ta (*L.*). ⎭
Mu'sica met'rica (*L.*). Poetic metre; a song com-
posed to poetry.
Mu'sica moder'na (*I.*). The music of modern Europe.
Mu'sica modulato'ria (*L.*). The art of modulating the
voice.
Mu'sica monda'na (*I.*). The "harmony of the
spheres."
Mu'sica natura'le (*I.*). (1) Simple. (2) Vocal music.
Mu'sica organ'ica (*L.*). Music for insts.
Mu'sica pie'na (*I.*) ⎫ Plain chant.
Mu'sica pla'na (*L.*) ⎭
Mu'sica poe'tica. The art of composition.
Mu'sica pra'tica (*I.*). Practical music.
Mu'sica recitati'va (*I.*). Recitative.
Mu'sica rhyth'mica (*L.*). The metre of prose; a song
to prose words.
Mu'sica sce'nica (*I.*). Theatrical music.
Mu'sica signato'ria (*L.*). Musical signs and characters.
Mu'sica speculati'va (*L.*). Theoretical music.
Mu'sica theatra'le (*I.*). Theatrical music.
Mu'sica theor'ica (*L.*). Theoretical music.
Mu'sica tra'gica (*L.*). Sad, sorrowful music.
Mu'sica voca'le (*I.*). Vocal music.

Musical box. A clockwork mechanism
enclosed in a box, with a metal cylinder
fitted with pins which operate upon a
series of accurately-tuned steel tongues
as the cylinder revolves.

Musical Dictation. A system of ear-training
in tune, time, and musical memory.

Musical Form. (See **Form.**)

Musical Glasses. (See **Glasses.**)

Musical Notation. (See **Notation.**)

Musical Perception. (See **Ear for Music.**)
"Men without taste or ears for music ever comfort themselves with imagining that their
contempt for what they neither feel nor understand is a mark of superior wisdom."—*Dr.
Burney.*
It is stated, however, by medical men and
physiologists that "a lack of musical sensibility is the result of defective brain development."—*Dr. Walshe* on "Dramatic Singing."

Musical Periodicals.

BRITISH:
British Bandsman. Weekly, 1d. 210 Strand, W.C.
Y Cerrdor. Monthly, 2d. Wrexham.
Cornet. Monthly, 1d. Sibsey, Boston, Lincs.
Cremona. Monthly, 2d. 11 Cursitor Street, E.C.
Monthly Musical Record. Monthly, 2d. 6 New
Burlington Street, W.
Music. Monthly, 2d. 4 Gough Square, E.C.
Music Trades Review. Monthly, 4d. 13 Bream's
Buildings, E.C.
Musical Budget. Monthly, 1d. 20 Paternoster
Row, E.C.
Musical Herald. Monthly, 2d. 24 Berners Street, W.
Musical Home Journal. Weekly, 1d. La Belle
Sauvage, E.C.
Musical Journal. Monthly, 2d. 22 Paternoster
Row, E.C.
Musical News. Weekly, 1d. 4 Bell's Buildings,
Salisbury Square, E.C.
Musical Opinion. Monthly, 2d. 35 Shoe Lane, E.C.
Musical Standard. Weekly, 2d. 83 Charing Cross
Road, W.C.
Musical Star. Monthly, 1d. 101 Leith Street,
Edinburgh.
Musical Times. Monthly, 4d. 160 Wardour Street, W.
Organist and Choirmaster. Monthly, 3d. 60 Berners
Street, W.
Piano and Music Trades Journal. Monthly, 6d. 164
Aldersgate Street, E.C.
School Music Review. Monthly, 1½d. 169 Wardour
Street, W.

Strad. Monthly, 2d. 186 Fleet Street, E.C.
Wright and Round's Brass Band News. Monthly, 3d. Liverpool.
In addition, several musical colleges, academies, and societies issue journals to their members.

FOREIGN. The following are among the most important :—

FRENCH : *Le Ménestrel* (Paris) ·· *Le Monde Musical* (Paris) ; *Revue Internationale de Musique* (Paris) ; *Le Courrier Musical* (Paris) ; *Revue Musicale d'histoire et de critique* (Paris) ; *Le Guide Musical* (Brussels).

GERMAN : *Signale für die Musikalische Welt* (Leipzig); *Deutsche Musikzeitung* (Vienna) ; *Musikalisches Wochenblatt* (Leipzig) ; *Bayreuther Blätter* (Bayreuth) ; *Internationale Musik-Gesellschaft* (Eng. Edn., Breitkopf & Härtel, London) ; *Die Musik* (Berlin).

ITALIAN : *Rivista Musicale* (Turin).

AMERICAN : *Church Music* (Philadelphia); *The Etude* (Philadelphia) ; *The Musician* (Boston) ; *The New Music Review* (New York) ; *The Musical Courier* (New York) ; *Musical America* (New York) ; *Music Trade Review* (New York) ; *Musical Age* (New York) ; *The Presto* (Chicago) ; *Musical Canada* (Toronto).

Musicalement (*F.*). Musically, harmoniously.

Musica're (*I.*). To perform music ; to sing or play.

Musica're u'na canzo'ne. To set a song to music.

Music, Miraculous Effects of.

Nearly all primitive nations invested music with supernatural attributes, originating largely, no doubt, in its unquestioned and unparalleled effects on the emotions. The ancient Hindoo "Ragas" were supposed to be capable of producing miraculous effects ; some forced men, animals, and even inanimate nature to move at the will of the singer ; others called down rain or "terror-striking" darkness ; others could not be sung by mortals without the risk of being consumed by flames. "The singer Naik-Gobaul tried to sing a forbidden Raga by standing up to his neck in the river Jumna, but was nevertheless consumed by fire." Astounding stories are also told by the Greeks and Romans.

" Orpheus with his lute made trees
And the mountain tops that freeze
  Bow themselves when he did sing ;
To his music plants and flowers
[Ever sprung, as sun and showers
  There had made a lasting spring.
Everything that heard him play,
Even the billows of the sea,
Hung their heads and then lay by."
         —*Shakespeare.*

Many of the marvels related by Kircher and others —of " a certain Peter, a Dutchman, who broke a glass by the sound of his voice," of " a large stone which trembled at the sound of a certain organ pipe," of " a kind of waggon which the playing of an organ shook as if it had been an earthquake," of " a pillar in the church at Rheims which sensibly shakes at the sound of a certain bell "—are now easily explained by the phenomenon of *Resonance* (or *Sympathetic Vibration*). (See *Acoustics.*)

Mu'sico (*I.*). (1) A musician. (2) A Castrato.

Music of Nature. (See **Nature's Music.**)

Music of the Spheres. (See **Harmony of the Spheres.**)

Music-recorder. (See **Melograph.**)

Musik' (*G.*). Music.

Musik'alien. Music, notes ; musical compositions.
Musika'lisch. Musical.
Ein musika'lisches Gehör'. A musical ear.
Mu'sikant. Musician.

Mu'siker. A musician, composer.
Musik'fest. Musical festival.
Mu'sikino. A little musician.
Musik'lehrer. A music teacher.
Musik'kenner ⎱ An amateur ; a lover of music.
Musik'liebhaber ⎰
Musik'meister. A conductor, or teacher.
Musik'stimme. A part.
Musik'stück. A piece of music.
Musik'unterricht. Instruction in music.
Mu'sikus. Member of an orchestra.
Musik'verein. A musical society.
Muzik'zeichen. A musical character (note, sign, &c.).
Musik'zeitung. A musical journal.

Musika'lisches Op'fer (*G.*). "Musical Offering." A work by Bach containing fugues, &c., on a subject given him by Frederick the Great, 1747.

MUSIN, B. (See **Furlanetto.**)

MUSIN, Ovide. Violinist ; *b.* nr. Liége, 1854. Won the 1st prize for vn., Liége Cons., at 11. After numerous successes as concert violinist, apptd. Violin Prof. Liége Cons., 1898.

MU'SIOL, Robert P. J. *B.* Breslau, 1846 ; *d.* 1903.
Author of a "Catechism of Music," a "Music Lexicon," &c. ; editor of Tonger's " Conversations-Lexikon" and the 10th edition of Schubert's " Musikalisches Conversations-Lexikon."

Musique d'eglise (*F.*). Church music.

MUSSORG'SKI, Modest Petrovitch. *B.* Pskov, Russia, 1839 ; *d.* 1881.
Wrote 2 operas (*Boris Godunoff*, 1874), pf. pieces, and songs.

MUSTEL, Victor. Harmonium maker and inventor; *b.* Havre, 1815; *d.* Paris, 1890.

Mustel Organ. An improved variety of harmonium capable of producing numerous orchestral effects.

Mu'ta, Muta'no (*I.*). " Change."
A direction to a player on a trumpet, horn, or kettle-drums, to change the "crook" or alter the pitch of his instrument (or instruments). Thus : *Muta in D ;* "change the crook to D ;" *Timp. in F, C, muta in E♭, B♭ ;* "alter the tuning of the kettledrums from F and C to E♭ and B♭.

Muta'tion. (1) (*G., Mutie'rung ; F., Mue; I., Mutazio'ne.*) Change ; the change of the voice at puberty.
(2) (*G., Mutation'; F., Mutation ; I., Mutazio'ne.*) Shifting in vn. playing.

Mutation Stop. An org. stop not in unison (or 8ves) with the foundation stops ; as a *quint, tierce,* &c.

Mutazio'ne (*I.*). (See **Mutation**).

Mute. (*G., Däm'pfer ; F., Sourdine ; I., Sordi'no.*) A mechanical contrivance for softening the tone of an inst.
The mute of a vn., when attached to the bridge, decreases the amount of vibration of the whole inst. When it has to be used the direction *Con sordi'no* is given. *Sen'za sordi'no* means "without the mute." (See *Sordino*).
N.B.—In modern scores, the mute is sometimes used to *modify* rather than soften the tone. Thus, trumpets " con sordini," and *ff* (Elgar's Symphony in A♭, Op. 55).

Mutes. In speech, those letters which have no sound of their own apart from the vowels ; *e.g.*, k, d, t, b, p.

The letters f, r, th, s, z, j, &c., are called *Semi-mutes*, or *Spirants (q.v.).*

Muth (*G.*). Courage, spirit, boldness.

Mu'thig. With spirit ; bold, daring.
Muth'los. Dejected, spiritless.

Muth'willig (*G.*). Lively, mischievous.

MU'ZIO, Emanuele. Singing teacher ; *b.* nr. Parma, 1825 ; *d.* 1890. Adelina Patti and Clara Louise Kellog were his pupils.

Wrote 3 operas, and several songs and pf. pieces.

MYSLI'WECZEK, Joseph. *B.* nr. Prague, 1737 ; *d.* 1781.

Wrote about 30 popular operas, 2 oratorios, 6 symphonies, 12 string quartets, 6 trios, pf. music, &c.
Mozart "greatly admired his pf. sonatas."

Mysteries
Moralities } Mediæval dramas.
Miracle plays

The *Mysteries* dealt with the Last Judgment, &c. ; the *Moralities* with allegorical impersonations of virtues, vices, &c.; the *Miracle-Plays* with Christ's miracles. (See also *Passion-Play.*) The Mysteries, Moralities, and Miracle-Plays may be regarded as rudimentary forms of the oratorio (*q.v.*).

N

NAAFF, Anton E. A.   Poet and writer on music ; *b.* German Bohemia, 1850.

Nab′la ⎰ A 10-stringed inst. of the ancient
Nab′lium ⎱ Jews.

Nacaire (*F.*).   A kind of kettledrum.

Nac′care (*I.*) ⎱
Gnac′care (*I.*) ⎰ Castanets (*q.v.*).

Naccheˊra (*I.*)   A small military drum ; a kettledrum.
Naccheroˊne. A large military drum.

Nach (*G.*).   After ; following ; agreeably to ; in imitation of ; to.
E nach F. Change the tuning (of the drum, &c.) from E to F.
Nach′ahmung. Imitation. (*q.v.*).
Nach Belie′ben. "As you like :" *ad libitum.*
Nach bestimmt′en Zeit′mass. In exact time.
Nach′druck. Accent ; emphasis, vigour.
Nach′drücklich. With emphasis, energetic.
Nach ein′er ech′ten Zigeu′ner-Melodie′. From (in imitation of) a genuine gipsy-melody.
Nach Gefal′len. Ad libitum.
Nach′gebend. Rallentando.
Nach′gehend. Following, with.
Nach′gesang. Aftersong ; epode.
Nach′hall. Reverberation, echo.
Nach′klang. Resonance.
Nach′lassend. Slackening the speed ; *rallentando.*
Nach′lässig. Carelessly, negligently.
Nach′ruf. A farewell, a refrain.
Nach′satz. An "after theme ;" a responsive theme or section.
Nach′spiel. A postlude, a concluding voluntary.
Nach′stimmen. To tune one instrument with another.
Nachst′verwand′te Tö′ne. Attendant keys (*q.v.*).
Nach′tönen. To resound.
Nach und nach. Gradually ; step by step.
Nach und nach beleb′ter ⎱ Gradually quicker.
Nach und nach im′mer beweg′ter ⎰
Nach und nach im′mer lang′samer wer′dend. Gradually slower.
Nach und nach mehr′ere Sai′ten. Gradually more strings ; *i.e.,* gradually release the left pedal.

NACH′BAUR, Franz.   Dramatic tenor ; *b.* nr. Friedrichschafen, 1835 ; *d.* 1902. Sang Munich, 1866-90 ; then pensioned. Created the part of "Walther," Wagner's *Die Meistersinger,* 1868.

NA′CHEZ, Tivadar.   (Theodor Na′schitz.) Distinguished violinist ; *b.* Pesth, 1859. Pupil of Joachim and Léonard.
Works : concertos for vn. and orch. ; Hungarian Rhapsodies, &c., for vn. ; a Requiem ; songs.

Nach′schlag (*G.*).   An after-note.

(1)

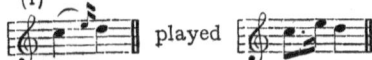

played

(2) The auxiliary note at the end of a trill or shake.

Nacht (*G.*).   Night.
Nacht′horn ⎱ "Night horn ;" an organ stop re-
Nacht′schall ⎰ sembling the tone of the *Hohl′flöte,* or the *Quintatön.*
Nacht′igall. The nightingale.
Nacht′musik. "Night music ;" a serenade.
Nacht′stück. A nocturne (*q.v.*).

NADAUD, Gustave.   Celebrated composer of *Chansons ; b.* Roubaix, 1820 ; *d.* Paris, 1893.
Works : 3 operettas and over 300 *chansons.*

NA′DERMANN, François J.   Paris, 1773-1835. Court harpist, 1816 ; Prof. at the Cons., 1825.
Published much harp music.

Nae′nia (*Gk.*).   A dirge.

Nagâ′rah.   A Moorish drum.

Nagaret′, Nagareet′.   An Abyssinian drum.

NA′GEL, Dr. Willibald.   *B.* Mühlheim-on-Ruhr, 1863.
Works : "Johannes Brahms" "History of Eng. Music" (to the death of Purcell), &c.

Na′gelgeige (*G.*) ⎱
Na′gelharmonika (*G.*) ⎰ A nail-fiddle (*q.v.*).

NÄ′GELI, Johann Hans Georg.   *B.* Wetzikon, nr. Zurich, 1773 ; *d.* 1836. Renowned teacher of singing on the "Pestalozzian System."
Works : treatises on the Pestalozzian System, a "Gesangbuch" songs, &c.
A monument was erected to his memory at Zurich, 1848.

Na′he (*G.*).   Near.
Na′he dem Chor. Near the choir (chorus).

Naïf (*F.*) ⎱
Naïve (*F.*) ⎰ Artless, natural, unaffected.
Naïv′ (*G.*) ⎰
Naïvement (*F.*).   Naturally, artlessly, &c.
Naïveté (*F.*).   Simplicity, artlessness, &c.

Nail Fiddle.   (*G., Na′gelgeige.*) An inst. with 16 to 20 metal pins sounded by a bow. The tone resembles the "musical glasses."

Naked.   Bare ; unaccompanied.
Naked fifth. The interval of a fifth (without a 3rd or other note).
Naked fourth. The interval of a fourth (without any other note).

Na′ker.   Old name for kettledrum.

Nan′ga.   A negro harp.

Nä′nien (*G.*).   Dirges.   (See **Naenia.**)

NANI′NI, Giovanni B.   Brother of G. M. (below).   *B.* Vallerano, abt. 1560 ; *d.* Rome, abt. 1618.
Works : psalms, madrigals, motets, showing a "falling away from strict polyphony."

NANI′NI, Giovanni Maria.   Eminent Italian contrapuntist ; *b.* Vallerano, abt. 1540 ; *d.* Rome, 1607.   Member of the Papal Choir, 1577 ; *Maestro di cappella,* 1604.
Works : motets, madrigals, Lamentations, psalms, canzonets, &c. His 6-part motet "Hodie nobis" is still sung in the Sistine Chapel every Christmas morning.

NAPOLEON, Arthur.   Pianist ; *b.* Oporto, 1843.   After concert tours throughout Europe and America, settled in Rio Janiero (abt. 1870).

NÁPRA′VNIK, Eduard F.   Pianist ; *b.* nr. Königgrätz, 1839.   Capellmeister to Prince Yussupoff, St. Petersburg, 1861 ; 1st condr. Russian Opera, 1869.   Condr. Musical Society's Symphony Concerts, 1870-82.
Works : operas (*Dubroffsky,* &c.) orchestral music, chamber music, Bohemian and Russian songs, pf. music.

NARDI'NI, Pietro. Violinist ; *b.* Tuscany, 1722 ; *d.* 1793. Pupil of Tartini. Court Maestro, Florence, 1770.
Works : concertos, sonatas, solos, and duets for vn. ; string quartets flute solos &c.

NARES, James. *B.* Stanwell, Middlesex, 1715 ; *d.* 1783. Orgt. York Minster, 1734 ; Orgt. and composer, Chapel Royal, 1757 ; Master of the Children, 1757-80 ; Mus.Doc. Cantab.,1757.
Works : Lessons for Harpsichord ; "A Regular Introduction to Playing on the Harpsichord or Organ ;" 2 treatises on singing ; several anthems, services, &c., and a collection of catches, canons, and glees.

NARET-KONING, Johann J. D. Violinist ; *b.* Amsterdam, 1838. Pupil of David ; Leader City Theatre, Frankfort.

Narquois (*F.*). Crafty, cunning.

Narran'te (*I.*). In narrative style ; well declaimed.

Narra'tor. The singer of the "narrative" texts in a Passion-play (or oratorio).

Nar'rentanz (*G.*). A fool's dance.

Nasal Tone. The result of a loose or "flabby" soft palate.
"That tone which is produced when the voice issues in too great a degree from the cavities of the nose. In singing, this tone, or *twang*, must be avoided."—*Moore.*
Nasal tone can generally be cured by suitable vocal exercises for hardening the soft palate and keeping it "well up."

Nasard (*F.*). (Also **Nassat, Nasarde, Nazard,** &c.) An org. stop of 2⅔ ft. pitch, sounding a 12th above the written notes.

Naset'to (*I.*). The point of a bow. (See **Punta d'arco.**)

NASOLI'NI, Sebastiano. *B.* Piacenza, abt. 1768 ; *d.* (?).
Produced about 30 operas, 1788-1816.

Na'son } A 4 ft. flute stop on some old
Na'son flute } organs.

Nassat, Nasat. (See **Nasard.**)

NATHAN, Isaac. *B.* Canterbury, 1792 ; *d.* Sydney, 1864.
Works : *Sweethearts and Wives*, and other stage music ; "Hebrew Melodies," songs, &c.

National Anthem. (See **"God save the King."**)

National'-lied (*G.*). A national song.

National Music. (1) The popular traditional melodies, folk-songs, &c., of a country. (2) The style of music peculiar to a country ; as Chinese music, Turkish music, Hungarian music, Italian music. (3) So-called "National Anthems."
Of National anthems the following are among the most celebrated :—
GREAT BRITAIN : "God save the King," "Rule Britannia."
AMERICA : "The Star-spangled Banner," "Hail, Columbia," "Yankee-Doodle."
RUSSIA : "God, the All-terrible."

DENMARK : "King Christian."

AUSTRIA : Haydn's "Emperor's Hymn." (See *Austrian Hymn.*)
FRANCE : "La Marseillaise" (*q.v.*) ; "Partante pour La Syrie."
GERMANY : "The Watch on the Rhine."

National Hymn—"Nun Danket."

PRUSSIA : "Heil dir im Siegeskranz," sung to our "God save the King."
BELGIUM : "La Brabançonne." (See *Brabançonne.*)
NORWAY :

SWEDEN :

SPAIN : "Royal March."

HOLLAND : National Hymn.

JAPAN : (See *Japanese Music*).

National Training School for Music. Opened 1876 ; succeeded by the Royal College of Music, 1882.

NA'TORP, Bernhard C. W. Pastor ; *b.* Werden-on-Ruhr, 1774 ; *d.* 1846.
Pub. works on church singing, choral books, collections of sacred songs, &c. He did much to "improve singing in churches and schools."

Natur' (*G.*). Nature.
Natur'horn. Natural horn.
Natür'lich. Natural ; *loco.* (See *Naturale.*)
Natur'liche. Natural.
Natur'liche Ton'leiter. The natural scale (of C).
Natur'töne. See *Natural Tones* (below).

Natural. (*G., Auf'lösungszeichen ; F., Bé-carre ; I., Bequa'dro.*) The sign ♮, which restores any note previously flattened or sharpened to its "natural" pitch in the scale of C major. (See **Notation.**)
All the white keys of the pianoforte are called "naturals."
Natural harmonics. The "upper partials" of any fundamental tone. (See *Acoustics.*)
Natural hexachord. One beginning on C. (See *Hexachord.*)
Natural horn. A hand horn ; the French horn without pistons. (See *Horn.*)
Natural interval. Any interval found in a major scale.
Natural key. The key of C major.
Natural modulation. (1) Diatonic modulation. (See *Modulation.*) (2) Modulation to a nearly-related key.
Natural pitch. The fundamental pitch (of an organ pipe, &c.).
Natural scale. The scale of C major.
Natural tones. The natural harmonics of a horn, trumpet, &c.
Natural voice. Opposed to *Falsetto.*

Natura′le (*I.*). Natural; unaffected.

Also used in scores to indicate the "natural" or "usual" method of producing tones. Thus, with strings, to contradict the use of mutes or any unusual method of bowing; with horns to contradict "stopped" notes; with percussion insts., to contradict any unusual method of striking, &c.

Do natura′le. C natural.

Naturalmen′te. Unaffectedly.

Naturalist′ (*G.*). A self-taught musician; not trained in any particular "school" or "method."

Naturalis′tisch. Amateurish; untrained.

Naturel, Naturelle (*F.*) ⎰ Natural; unaffected.
Natür′lich (*G.*) ⎱ Also used for *loco.*

Son naturel (*F.*). An open note on a brass inst.

Ut naturel (*F.*). C♮.

Nature's Music.

The following, selected from various sources, are among the most interesting records of the "Voices of Nature." The musical notes are, of course, only approximate indications, as nearly all natural sounds are *inflected, i.e.,* graded by infinitely small intervals.

Partridge. *accel. e cres. f presto.*
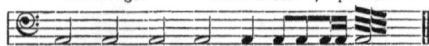
Boom, boom, boom, boom, boo boo burr . . .

Screech Owl. *Simile.*

Ah - - - - - oo, Ah - oo, Ah - oo.

Whip-poor-Will. *Vivace.*

Whip-poor-will, Whip-poor-will.

Night-hawk. *f* Crow.

Boo-oo-m! Caw, Caw, Caw,

Wood Thrush.
8ve higher.

Linnet.

Skylark.
8va.

&c.

Goldfinch.
8ve higher.

8va..........
Sparrow.

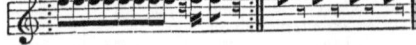

Yellowhammer.
8va.

Lit-tle bit of bread and no cheese!

Gnat.
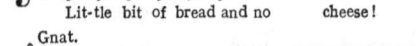

Horse cantering.

Man sneezing.

Dog barking for joy.
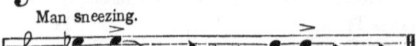

Cow lowing.

Horse neighing.

Grasshopper.

Fly buzzing.

Water dripping.
8ve higher.

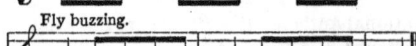
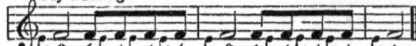
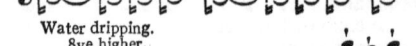

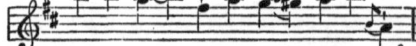
&c.

(See also *Bird Music, Cuckoo's Song, Imitative Music, Program Music,* and *Word Painting.*)

NAU, Maria Dolores B. J. Soprano singer; *b.* New York, 1818. *Début,* Paris Opéra, 1836. Retired, 1856.

NAU'BERT, Friedrich A. Noted song composer ; *b.* Saxony, 1839 ; *d.* 1897.

NA'UDIN, Emilio. Dramatic tenor ; *b.* Parma, 1823. Created the *rôle* of "Vasco," Meyerbeer's *l'Africaine*, 1865.

NAU'E, Johann F. Halle, 1787-1868. Wrote historical works, a Choralbuch, &c.

NAU'ENBURG, Gustav. Baritone singer ; *b.* Halle, 1803. Wrote some valuable singing studies.

Naufra'gio (*I.*). "A shipwreck ; " a *fiasco* (*q.v.*).

NAU'MANN, Dr. Emil. Grandson of J. G. (below). *B.* Berlin, 1827 ; *d.* 1888. Mus. director, Court Church, Berlin, 1856 ; Lecturer on Mus. Hist., Dresden Cons., 1873. Works : oratorio (*Christus der Friedensbote*), motets, psalms, &c., and numerous historical works (including a "History of Music," pub. in English by Cassell & Co.).

NAU'MANN, Johann Gottlieb. *B.* Blasewitz, nr. Dresden, 1741 ; *d.* 1801. Court composer, Dresden, 1763 ; Capellmeister, 1776 ; Capellmeister-in-chief, 1786. Works : 23 operas, 10 oratorios, 18 symphonies, church music, chamber music, songs, &c.

NAU'MANN, Dr. Karl Ernst. Grandson of J. G. *B.* Freiberg, Saxony, 1832. "Professor," Jena Univ., 1877. Works : valuable revisions of classical works for the "Bach-Gesellschaft," &c. ; choral works, chamber music.

NAVA, Franz. Pen-name of **E. F. Rimbault** (*q.v.*).

NA'VA, Gaetano. Singing teacher ; Milan, 1802-75. Prof. of Solfeggio, Milan Cons., 1837. Works : a "Practical Method of Vocalization," church music, songs, pf. pieces, numerous excellent *solfeggi*, &c.

NAVÁL, Franz. Tenor singer ; *b.* Laibach, Carniola, 1865. *Début*, Frankfort-on-Main, 1888.

NA'VRÁTIL, Karl. *B.* Prague, 1867. Works : operas, symphonies, poems, concertos, male choruses, songs, &c.

Nay. An Egyptian flute.

NAYLOR, Edmund Woodall. *B.* Scarborough, 1867 ; Mus.Doc. Cantab, 1899. His opera *The Angelus* won Ricordi's £500 prize, 1908.

NAYLOR, John. *B.* Stanningley, nr. Leeds, 1838 ; *d.* 1897. Mus.Doc. Oxon, 1872 ; Orgt. York Minster, 1883. Works : 4 cantatas, church services, anthems, part-songs, organ pieces, chants, &c.

NAYLOR, Sidney. Organist and pianist ; London, 1841-93.

NAYLOR, Mrs. S. (*née* **Blanche Cole**). Soprano ; *b.* Portsmouth, 1851 ; *d.* 1888.

Nazard. (See **Nasard.**)

NEALE, John Mason, D.D. 1818-66. Warden, Sackville Coll., East Grinstead. Eminent translator of Latin hymns. "The strain upraise," "O come, O come, Immanuel," "Brief life is here our portion," &c.

Neapolitan School. The chief representatives are the following :— A. Scarlatti, Durante, Leo, Feo, Porpora, Pergolesi, Logroscino, Jomelli, Piccinni, Sacchini, Traetta, Paesiello.

Neapolitan Sixth. A chord consisting of the subdominant with its minor 3rd and minor 6th. The Neapolitan 6th is more frequent in minor keys, but it is also used in major keys. It admits of several resolutions.

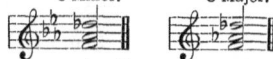

Macfarren regards the Neapolitan 6th as the "first inversion of a major common chord on the minor 2nd of the key," but the root position is rarely employed. Beethoven uses the chord on a tonic pedal, with fine effect, at the end of his Funeral March :—

NEATE, Chas. Pianist ; *b.* London, 1784 ; *d.* 1877. Pupil of Field. *Début*, Covent Garden, 1800. Works : pf. pieces, chamber music, songs, &c.

Nebel. A Hebrew stringed inst.

Ne'ben (*G.*). Near ; adjoining ; accessory ; secondary.
Ne'bendominant. The "dominant of the dominant ; " as D in key C.
Ne'bendreiklang. A secondary triad.
Ne'bengedanken. Accessory or subordinate themes or ideas.
Ne'benklang. An accessory or subordinate accompanying sound.
Ne'benlinie. Leger line.
Ne'bennote. An auxiliary note.
Ne'bensatz. A subsidiary phrase.
Ne'benseptimen. Secondary chords of the 7th.
Ne'benstimmen. (1) Subordinate or accessory parts. (2) Accessory organ stops.
Ne'benthema. A subsidiary theme.
Ne'bentonart. A relative key (or mode).
Ne'benwerk. The Choir Organ. (See *Organ.*)

Necessa'rio (*I.*). Necessary ; *obbligato.*

Nech'iloth. Hebrew for "wind insts."

Neck. (*G., Hals; F., Manche; I., Ma'nico.*) The part of a stringed inst. to which the fingerboard is attached.

NEEB, Heinrich. *B.* Lich, Upper Hesse, 1807 ; *d.* 1878. Works : 4 operas, a cantata, and several popular ballads.

NEEDHAM, Mrs. Alicia (*née* **Montgomery**). Contemp. song composer ; *b.* Co. Meath, Ireland.

NEE'FE, Christian Gottlob. *B.* Chemnitz, 1748 ; *d.* 1798. Electoral Music-director, Bonn, 1782 ; taught Beethoven. Condr. Dessau Opera, 1796. Works : 8 vaudevilles and operas ; a concerto for pf., vn., and orch. ; pf. pieces, songs, &c.

Ne′fer. An Egyptian guitar.

Neg′inoth. Ancient Hebrew stringed insts.

Ne′gli (*I. plural*). In the, at the.

Negligen′te (*I.*). Negligent; careless.
Negligentemen′te. Negligently.
Negligen′za. Negligence, carelessness.

Negro Music. "Nearest approach to *folk-music* in the United States."—*Grove.*
The best known collection is "The Music of the Jubilee Singers of the Fisk University."

Neh′iloth. Same as Nechiloth (*q.v.*).

Neh′men (*G.*). Take; take up; resume.
Neh′men wie′der gros′se Flö′te. Take up again the large flute.

NEHR′LICH, Christian G. Singing teacher; *b.* Upper Lusatia, 1802; *d.* 1868.
Wrote a work on the "Art of Singing."

Ne′i (*I.*). Same as Negli.

NEID′LINGER, Wm. Harold. American composer; pupil of Dudley Buck. *B.* Brooklyn, 1863.
Works: church music, choruses, numerous songs.

NEIT′HARDT, August H. *B.* Schleiz, 1793; *d.* 1861. Bandmaster, Kaiser Franz Grenadiers, 1822-40; Condr. Berlin Cath. Choir, 1845.
Works: an opera, military music, male choruses, songs, &c.; and a collection of sacred music ("Musica Sacra.")

NEIT′ZEL, Otto. Conductor and composer; *b.* Falkenburg, Pomerania, 1852.
His operas have had fair success.

Nel, Nel′la, Nel′le, Nel′lo, Nell' (*I.*). In the, at the.
Nel bat′tere. On the down-beat.
Nel′lo stes′so tem′po. In the same time.
Nel mede′simo. In the same time.
Nel sti′lo anti′co. In the ancient style.
Nel tem′po. In time; same as *a tem′po.*

NEL′LI, Romilda. Soprano; *b.* Italy, 1882(?).

NELSON, Sidney. *B.* 1800; *d.* London, 1862.
Works: operettas; treatises on singing; several songs ("Mary of Argyle," &c.).

Ne′nia (*L.*). (See Naenia.)

NEN′NA, Pomponio. *B.* Bari, Naples.
Published several madrigals, 1585-1631.

Neo-German School. The romantic school, or "programmists," followers of Liszt.

NE′RI, Filippo. Priest; *b.* Florence, 1515; *d.* Rome, 1595. Established the "Oratory" lectures at San Girolamo for which Animuccia (*q.v.*) composed his "Laudi Spirituali."
These lectures with musical illustrations gradually grew into the oratorio, the word "oratorio" being the Italian for "oratory."

Ne′ro (*I.*). A black note, or crotchet (♩).
Bian′ca, a white note, or minim (♩).

NERU′DA, Franz. Brother of Wilma (below); fine 'cellist; *b.* Brünn, 1843.

NERU′DA, Wilma Maria F. (Madame Normann-Neruda; Lady Hallé). Distinguished violinist; *b.* Brünn, 1839. Played in public at Vienna, 1846. First appearance in London, 1849. Married Ludwig Normann, 1864. Since 1869 has played regularly in London, where she is a popular favourite. Married the pianist, Sir Chas. Hallé (*q.v.*), 1888.

NESS′LER, Victor E. *B.* Alsace, 1841; *d.* 1890.
Works: several popular but commonplace operas and operettas (*Der Rattenfänger von Hameln,* 1879; *Der Trompeter von Säkkingen,* 1884; &c.); choruses for male voices, songs, &c.

NESVAD′BA, Joseph. *B.* Bohemia, 1824; *d.* 1876.
His Bohemian songs and choruses are popular.

NESVE′RA, Joseph. *B.* Bohemia, 1842.
Works: opera (*Perdita*), church music, choruses, songs, pf. pieces, &c.

Net, Nette (*F.*) ⎱ Neat, clean.
Nett (*G.*) Net′to (*I.*) ⎰
Nettamen′te (I.). Neatly, distinctly.
Nett′heit (G.). Neatness.

Ne′te. (See Greek Music.)

Netherland School.
Chief composers: Busnois, Binchois, Dufay, Okeghem, Hobrecht, Josquin, Gombert, Clemens non Papa, Willaert, Arcadelt, Goudimel, Lasso, Verdonck.

NET′ZER, Joseph. *B.* Tyrol, 1808; *d.* 1864.
Works: operas, symphonies, overtures, &c., and over 100 songs.

Neu (*G.*). New.
Neu′deutsche Schu′le. The Neo-German School (*q.v.*).

NEU′BAUER, Franz C. *B.* Horzin, Bohemia, 1760; *d.* 1795. Violinist; taught by the village schoolmaster. Succeeded C. F. Bach as Court Capellmeister at Bückeburg.
Works: 12 symphonies, 10 string quartets, concertos, songs, &c.

NEU′ENDORFF, Adolf. *B.* Hamburg, 1843; *d.* New York, 1897. Went to America, 1855; became noted as a pianist, violinist, and conductor. Under his direction, *Lohengrin, Die Walküre,* and other works were given for the first time in America.
Works: 4 operas, 2 symphonies, male quartets, songs, &c.

NEU′KOMM, Sigismund (Ritter von). *B.* Salzburg, 1778; *d.* 1858. Studied under M. Haydn and J. Haydn. Condr. German Opera, St. Petersburg, 1807; visited Paris, 1809, and became pianist to Talleyrand. Court Music Director, Rio Janiero, 1816-21. Resumed service under Talleyrand, and remained with him till 1826; afterwards went on extensive tours.
Works: 7 oratorios, 15 masses, 5 cantatas, 10 operas, several orch. pieces, concertos, chamber music, pf. pieces, 57 org. pieces, 200 songs, &c., "now mostly consigned to oblivion."

NEU'MANN, Angelo. Tenor singer and operatic manager; *b.* Vienna, 1838. Manager, Prague German Opera, 1885. Enthusiastic Wagnerian propagandist. "To his stupendous energy were due the first representations of the *Ring* in London," 1882.
Author of "Personal Recollections of Wagner" (Eng. Edn., 1909).

NEU'MARK, Georg. Poet and composer; *b.* Langensalza, 1621; *d.* 1681.
Works: several collections of poems with melodies, 1649-62.

Neumes. (Sing. *Neu'ma, Neume,* or *Neum.*) The dots, dashes, &c., of the 8th to 12th centuries which were gradually developed into notes. (See **Notation.**)

Neun (*G.,* pron. *"noyn"*). Nine.
Neun'ach'telkakt. Nine-eight time.
Neun'stimmig. For nine voices.
Neun'te. A ninth.

NEU'PERT, Edmund. Pianist; *b.* Christiania, 1842; *d.* New York, 1888.
Wrote instructive studies for pf.

NEU'SIEDLER, Hans. Lute maker; *d.* Nuremberg, 1563.
Pub. a valuable work in Lute-Tablature, with explanations.

NEU'SIEDLER, Melchior. Lutenist; *d.* Nuremberg, 1590.
Pub. works in Lute-Tablature, 1566-87.

Neutral Ground. A small margin allowed by the ear in tuning intervals.
"On CC of the Open Diapason (when tuned with its octave) there are nearly two commas of neutral ground, *representing about an inch of length in the pipe.*"—*Dr. Hinton.*

Neutralizing Sign. The natural (♮).

Neuvième (*F.*). The interval of a 9th.

NEUVILLE, Valentin. *B.* Rexpoede, Belgium, 1863.
Works: an oratorio, several operas, symphonies, pf. pieces, songs, &c.

NEVA'DA, Emma. (Emma Wixon.) Operatic soprano; *b.* Nevada, U.S., abt. 1860; *début,* London, 1880.

NEV'IN, Ethelbert W. American composer of songs and pf. pieces; *b.* Edgeworth, Penn., 1862; *d.* 1901.

NEWBOULT, Henry. Orgt. and writer; *b.* Bradford, 1858.

NEWELL, Jos. E. Orgt. and composer; *b.* Hunslet, 1843.

NEWMAN, Ernest. Critic and writer; *b.* Liverpool, Nov. 30, 1869.
Mus. critic, *Manchester Guardian,* 1905-6; *Birmingham Daily Post,* since 1906. Author of "Gluck and the Opera," 1895; "A Study of Wagner," 1899; "Wagner," 1904; "Musical Studies," 1905; "Elgar," 1906; "Hugo Wolf," 1907; "Rd. Strauss," 1908, &c.

NEWMAN, John Henry. D.D. 1801-90. Cardinal of the Roman Church, 1879.
Author of "Lead, kindly Light," 1833; "The Dream of Gerontius" (set by Elgar, 1900), &c.

NEWMARCH, Rosa. Contemporary writer.
Author of "Jean Sibelius," "Tschaikovsky," "Art-songs of Russia," &c.

NEWSIDLER } (See **Neusiedler.**)
NEYSIDLER }

NEWTH, Robert B. Tenor vocalist; *b.* Worcester,abt. 1860(?). Sang Gloucester Festival, 1883, &c.

NEWTON, John. 1725-1807. Curate of Olney, 1764; pubd. "Olney Hymns," 1779.
Wrote "Safely through another week," &c.

NEY, Jos. (See **Moskwa.**)

NICCOLI'NI, Giuseppe. (See **Nicolini.**)

NICCOLÒ DE MALTA. (See **Isouard.**)

NICETA, St., of Remésiana. Dacian Bishop, 392-414.
Most probable author of the "Te Deum Laudamus," long ascribed to St. Ambrose and St. Augustine. (See *Te Deum Laudamus.*)

NICH'ELMANN, Christoph. *B.* nr. Brandenburg, 1717; *d.* 1762. Pupil of Bach; 2nd cembalist to Frederick the Great, 1744-56. Wrote a work on "Melody."

NICHOL, Henry Ernest. *B.* Hull, 1862. Mus.B. Oxon, 1888. Organist Hull Harmonic Society.
Works: cantatas, anthems, part-songs, songs, &c.

NICH'OLL, Horace Wadham. *B.* Tipton, 1848. Went to America, 1871; Orgt. at Pittsburg. Settled in New York, 1878. Successful teacher and writer.
Works: a cycle of 4 oratorios, a mass, orch. tone-poems, symphonies, concertos, pf. pieces, org. pieces, songs, &c.

NICHOLL, J. Weston. *B.* Halifax, 1875. Instl. composer, orgt., and condr.; Dover Festival Prize (1904), orchl. tone-picture "In summer seas" (1908), &c.

NICHOLL, Wm. Tenor vocalist; *b.* Glasgow, 1851. *Début,* Glasgow, 1884.

NICHOLLS, Agnes H. (Mrs. H. H. Harty). Soprano vocalist; *b.* Cheltenham, 1877.

NICHOLS, Marie. Violinist; *b.* Chicago, 1879. *Début,* Boston, 1899.

NICHOLSON, Charles. Flautist; *b.* Liverpool, 1795; *d.* 1837. Played at Drury Lane, Covent Garden, Philharmonic, &c.
Pub. numerous works and collections for flute, including a "School for the Flute" (1836).

NICHOLSON, Sydney H. Orgt. and composer; *b.* London, 1875. Mus.B.Oxon, 1902; Orgt. Manchester Cath. 1908.

NICHO'MACHUS. Greek writer on music, 2nd cent. A.D.

Nicht (*G.*). Not.
Nicht anschwel'len las'sen. Without swelling (on the note).
Nicht ei'len. Without hurrying.
Nicht schlep'pen. Without dragging.
Nicht schnell. Not quick.
Nicht zu geschwind'. Not too quick.
Nicht zu geschwind' und sehr sing'bar vor'getragen. Not too quick, and very *cantabile* in performance.
Nicht zu lang'sam. Not too slow.
Nicht zu rasch. Not too quick.
Nicht zu stark. Not too loud.

NICODÉ, Jean Louis. Noted pianist; *b.* Jerczik, nr. Posen, 1853. Pf. teacher, Dresden Cons., 1878-85.
Works: orchestral pieces, pf. pieces, songs, &c.

NI'COLAI, Otto. Operatic composer ; *b.* Königsberg, 1810 ; *d.* 1849. Studied under Zelter and Klein, Berlin. Capellmeister, Vienna, 1837-8.

Works : several operas (including the popular *Merry Wives of Windsor*, 1849, and *Der Templer*), a mass, orchestral pieces, pf. pieces, part-songs, songs, &c.

NI'COLAI, Willem F. G. *B.* Leyden, 1829 ; *d.* 1896. Director, Hague Royal Music School, 1865. Edited the *Cicilia* for 25 years.

Works : an oratorio, cantatas, overtures, songs.

NICOLI'NI (or **NICCOLI'NI), Giuseppe.** Piacenza, 1762-1842. Maestro, Piacenza Cath., 1819.

Works : about 70 operas, 7 oratorios, 40 masses, 100 psalms, pf. sonatas, string quartets, canzonets, &c.

NICOLI'NI. Stage name of **Ernest Nicholas.** Operatic tenor ; *b.* St. Malo, 1834 ; *d.* 1898. Married **Adelina Patti,** 1886. Sang for several years (from 1871) at Drury Lane and Covent Garden.

NICOLÓ. (See **Isouard.**)

Ni'colo (*I.*). A precursor of the bassoon.

NIECKS, Frederick. *B.* Düsseldorf, 1845. Orgt. at Dumfries, 1868. "Reid Professor" of Music, Edinburgh Univ., 1891.

Works : "Dict. of Mus. Terms," "Frederic Chopin," lectures, essays, &c.

NIE'DEN, ZUR. (See under **Z.**)

Nie'der (*G.*). Down ; low.
Nie'derschlag. The down beat.
Nie'derstrich. The down bow.
Nie'dertakt. The down beat.

NIE'DERMEYER, Louis. *B.* Nyon, Switzerland, 1802 ; *d.* 1861. Pupil of Moscheles, Fioravanti, and Zingarelli ; intimate with Rossini. Settled in Paris, 1823 ; organized the "Ecole Niedermeyer" (an institute for church music now subsidized by Government).

Works : 4 unsuccessful operas ; masses, motets, hymns, &c. ; several popular romances ; pf. pieces, org. pieces ; a "Méthode d'accompagnement du Plain Chant," &c.

Nie'drig (*G.*) Low or deep in voice.

NIELD, Jonathan. Tenor singer ; *b.* 1769 ; *d.* London, 1843. Gentleman Chapel Royal, 1795. For many years chief tenor at the "Ancient Concerts," &c.

NIEL'SEN, Carl. Danish composer ; *b.* 1865.

Works : an opera, orch. pieces, pf. pieces, songs, &c.

NIE'MANN, Albert. Operatic tenor ; *b.* nr. Magdeburg, 1831. Engaged by Wagner to create the parts of "Tannhäuser" (Paris, 1861), and "Siegmund" (Bayreuth, 1876). Retired, 1889.

NIE'MANN, Rudolf F. Pianist ; *b.* Wesselburen, 1838 ; *d.* 1898. Toured (with Wilhelmj) in Germany, Russia, and England. Wrote pf. pieces and songs.

Nien'te (*I.*). Nothing.
Qua'si nien'te. "As if nothing ; " extremely soft ; barely audible.

NIE'TZSCHE. Noted philosopher ; *b.* nr. Lützen, 1844 ; *d.* 1900. At first an ardent Wagnerite ; afterwards changed his opinions and wrote "Der Fall Wagner" (bitterly hostile to his "former demigod.")

NIG'GLI, Arnold. *B.* Aarburg, Switzerland, 1843. Sec. to the Aarburg Town Council, 1875.

Works : several valuable contributions to musical history (including works on Chopin, Schubert, Mara, Meyerbeer, Jensen, &c.).

NIGHTINGALE, John Chas. *B.* abt. 1785 ; *d.* abt. 1837. Orgt. Foundling Hospital.

Works : Handel's overtures and choruses arranged for org. and pf. ; hymn-tunes, songs, &c.

NIK'ISCH, Arthur. Violinist and esteemed conductor ; *b.* Szent Miklos, Hungary, 1855. Studied Vienna Cons. ; 1st Capellmeister, Leipzig Th., 1882-9 ; Conductor, Boston Symphony Orch., 1889-93 ; Director, Pesth Royal Opera, 1893-5 ; Condr. Gewandhaus Concerts, Leipzig, 1895.

NIKI'TA. Stage name of **Louisa M. Nicholson.** Operatic soprano ; *b.* Philadelphia 1872. "Prima donna soprano," Paris Opéra, 1894.

NIKO'MACHUS. (See **Nichomachus.**)

NIL'SSON, Christine. Celebrated soprano ; *b.* nr. Wexiö, Sweden, 1843. *Début* in *La Traviata*, Paris Th.-Lyrique, 1864. In London, she created the part of "Edith" in Balfe's *Talismano* (1874), and was successful as "Elsa" in Wagner's *Lohengrin* (1875). Married Count Miranda.

Her voice is " sweet, brilliant, and even," with a compass of 2½ octaves ; she excels as " Marguerite" in Gounod's *Faust*.

Nimmt (*G.*). Takes ; takes up.
Piccolo nimmt 3te Flö'te. The piccolo player takes the third flute.

Nine-eight Time. (See **Time.**)

Nineteenth. An interval of 2 octaves and a 5th. A **Larigot** (*q.v.*).

NI'NI, Alessandro. *B.* Fano, Romagna, 1805 ; *d.* 1880. Director, School of Singing, St. Petersburg, 1830-7 ; Maestro, Bergamo Cath., 1843.

Works : 7 operas ; masses, requiems, a fine *Miserere*, &c.

Nin'na-Nan'na (*I.*). Cradle song ; a lullaby.

Ninth. (*G., No'ne ; F., Neuvième ; I., No'na.*) The interval of an octave and a second.

Major Ninth. An octave and a major second ; a compound major second :—

Minor Ninth. An octave and a minor second; a compound minor second:—

Chord of the Ninth. (1) DIATONIC : any triad of the key with the 7th and 9th added.

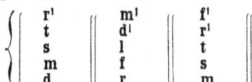

r¹	m¹	f¹
t	d¹	r¹
s	l	t
m	f	s
d	r	m

N.B.—Also called "Chords of the 7th and 9th."

(2) FUNDAMENTAL : a chord on the dominant, supertonic, or tonic of any key, including a major 3rd, a perfect 5th, a minor 7th, and either a major or minor 9th. (See *Fundamental Discords.*)

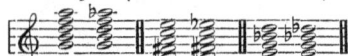

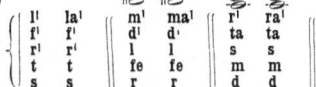

l¹	la¹	m¹	ma¹	r¹	ra¹
f¹	f¹	d¹	d¹	ta	ta
r¹	r¹	l	l	s	s
t	t	fe	fe	m	m
s	s	r	r	d	d

Suspended Ninth. A prepared 9th resolved on the 8th of the chord. It is not accompanied by a 7th unless the latter is specially marked in the figuring. (See *Suspension.*)

NISARD, Théodore. *Nom-de-plume* of Abbé **Théodule E. X. Normand.** *B.* nr. Mons, 1812.

   Author of several valuable works on the history, notation, and accompaniment of Plain Chant. Discovered the "Antiphonary of Montpellier" (in Neumes and Letter Notation).

NIS'SEN, Erica. (See **Lie.**)

NIS'SEN, Georg N. von. Danish Councillor ; 1761-1826. Married Mozart's widow, 1809.

NIS'SEN (NIS'SEN-SA'LOMAN), Henriette. Distinguished stage singer ; at one time "rivalled Jenny Lind in popularity ; " *b.* Gothenburg, Sweden, 1819 ; *d.* 1879. Pupil of Chopin and Manuel Garcia. *Début,* 1843. Toured successfully throughout Europe. Teacher of Singing, St. Petersburg Cons., 1859.

   Author of a "Vocal Method."

NIVERS, Guillaume G. *B.* nr. Melun, 1617 ; *d.* (?). Orgt. St. Sulpice, 1640 ; Singer, Royal Chapel, 1642 ; Orgt. to the King, 1667.

   Pub. several works on Singing and Plain Chant, 3 books of org. pieces, &c.

NIXON, Henry George. *B.* Winchester, 1796; *d.* 1849. Orgt. in various London churches.

   Works : 5 masses, and other church music ; pf. arrangements, songs, &c.

NIXON, Henry Cotter. Son of preceding ; *b.* London, 1842 ; *d.* 1907(?). Mus.Bac. Cantab, 1876. Conductor Hastings and St. Leonard's Orch. Society.

   Works : part-songs, pf. pieces, songs.

NÖB, Victorine. (See **Stoltz.**)

Nobilità (*I.*). Nobility, dignity, grandeur.

No'bile (*I.*). Noble, impressive, lofty, &c.
Nobilmen'te (*I.*). | Nobly, grandly, &c.
Noblement (*F.*). |

NOBLE, Thos. Tertius. *B.* Bath, 1867. Orgt. Ely Cath., 1892 ; York Minster, 1898.

   Works : church music, organ pieces, &c.

Noch (*G.*). Still, yet ; in addition.

Noch beweg'ter, sehr lei'denschaftlich. Still more animated, and with much passion.
Noch dräg'ender. Still more hurried.
Noch ein'mal, da Capo. Da capo once more.
Noch lang'samer. Still slower.
Noch lei'ser. Still softer.
Noch mehr nach'lassend. Still more *rallentando.*
Noch schnel'ler. Still quicker.
Noch stark'er. Still louder.

Nocturn. Part of the Catholic office of Matins.

Nocturne (*F.*). (*G., Noktur'ne, Nacht'stück ; I., Nottur'no.*) "A night piece." A piece of a quiet, gentle character.

Node. (*L., No'dus ; G., Kno'tenpunkt ; F., Nœud ; I., No'do.*) A "point of rest" in a vibrating string, column of air, &c. (See **Acoustics.**)

No'dus (*L.,* "a knot."). An enigmatical canon (*q.v.*).

Noël (*F.*) | "Good news." (1) A refrain
Nowell (*E.*) | to a Christmas carol. (2) A Christmas carol.

   "The airs should have a rural and pastoral character, suitable to the simplicity of the words, and to that of the shepherds, who, we suppose, sung them at going to pay homage to the infant Jesus in the manger."—*Rousseau.*

Nœud (*F.*). (1) A node. (2) A turn (*q.v.*).

NOHL, Dr. K. F. Ludwig. Lawyer and musician ; *b.* Iserlohn, 1831 ; *d.* 1885. Prof. Heidelberg Univ., 1880.

   Works : "Life of Beethoven" (3 vols.), "Life of Mozart," "Letters of Beethoven," "Letters of Mozart," "Beethoven, Liszt, Wagner," &c.

Noire (*F.*). "Black." The black note, or crotchet (♩).

Blanche. The white note, or minim (♩).

Noise. An old English name for music.

Noise and Music.

   A musical tone is produced by regular and continuous vibration ; noise by irregular vibration. Musical sounds, if exceedingly loud or shrill, are also regarded as noises ; thus, loud or screamy music is often called "noisy music."

Nom de plume (*F.*). A "pen-name" adopted by a composer or writer.

Nom de théâtre (*F.*). A "stage-name" adopted by a singer or actor.

No'menclature of Music. Names of notes, rests, and other musical signs ; and musical terms in general.

Non (*I.*). Not.

Non assa'i. Not very (much).
Non mol'to. Not much.
Non tan'to. Not too much.
Non trop'po. Not too much.
Non trop'po pres'to. Not too fast.

No'na (*I.*) ⎫
No'ne (*G.*) ⎬ A ninth.

No'nenakkord (*G.*). A chord of the ninth.
Nonett' (*G.*) ⎫
Nonet'to (*I.*) ⎬ A piece for nine insts. or voices.

Non'nengeige (*G.*). A nun's fiddle. (See **Tromba marina.**)

Non'ny   ⎫ "A common burden to old
Hey non'ny ⎬ English ballads."—*Stainer.*

Nono'le (*G.*) ⎫ A group of nine notes to be
Non'uplet ⎬ performed in the time of
8 (or 6) of the same kind.

NORBLIN, Louis P. M. Noted 'cellist ; *b.* Warsaw, 1781 ; *d.* 1854.

NORDICA, Madame. Stage name of **Lillian Norton ;** distinguished American soprano ; *b.* Farmington, Me., 1859. *Début,* Boston, 1876. Sang at Covent Garden, 1887. She is a favourite in opera, oratorio, and concert singing.

NORD'QUIST, Johan C. Condr. and composer ; *b.* Venersburg, Sweden, 1840.

NORD'RAAK, Rd. 1842-66 ; called the "Father of Norwegian Modern Music." Composed the Norwegian National Hymn.

NOR'MA. Opera by Bellini, 1832.

Normal Position of a Chord. A chord in its closest position ; as—

Normal (*F.*) ⎫
Normal' (*G.*) ⎬ Normal, standard, regular.

Normal Major Scale. The scale of C major.
Normal Minor Scale. The scale of A minor.
Normal'ton (*G*). The note A, to which the insts. of an orch. are tuned.
Normal'tonarten (*G*). The standard keys of C major and A minor.
Normal'tonleitern (*G*). The scales of C major and A minor. The "Diapason Normal" adopted in France (1879) and at Vienna (1887) regulates the pitch of A at 435 vibrations per second. (See *Acoustics.*)

NORMAND. (See **Nisard.**)

NOR'MAN(N), Ludwig. *B.* Stockholm, 1831 ; *d.* 1884. Condr. Stockholm New Phil. Soc., 1859 ; condr. of the Opera, 1861. Married Wilma Neruda (see **Neruda**), 1864.
Works : chamber music, pf. pieces, pf. arrangements of Swedish melodies, &c.

NORRIS, Homer A. American composer ; *b.* Wayne, Maine, 1860.

NORRIS, Thos. Tenor singer ; *b.* nr. Salisbury, abt. 1741 ; *d.* 1790. Orgt. Christ Ch., Oxford, 1765 ; Mus.Bac. Oxon, 1765 ; Orgt. St. John's Coll.,

1765. Sang at the Handel Commemoration, 1784.
Works : 6 symphonies for 2 vns., 2 hautboys, 2 horns, a tenor, and a bass ; glees, anthems, songs, &c.

NORTH, Roger. 1650-1733.
Left in MS. "Memoirs of Music," printed by Dr. Rimbault, 1846.

NORTON, Hon. Mrs. (Lady W. Stirling-Maxwell). *B.* 1809 ; *d.* 1877. Composed songs, and wrote the words of a number of others.

NORTON, Lillian B. (See **Nordica.**)

NOSZKOW'SKI, Sigismund. *B.* Warsaw, 1848. Director, Mus. Society, Warsaw, 1881 ; Prof. at the Cons., 1888.
Works : opera (*Livia*), orch. pieces, pf. pieces, a "Musical Notation for the Blind," &c.

NOSZ'LER, Karl E. *B.* Reichenbach, Saxony, 1863. Orgt. and Mus.-director, Bremen Cath., 1893 ; Condr. Bremen Neue Singakademie, 1896.
Works : orch. pieces, choruses, songs, pf. pieces

No'ta (*L.* and *I.*). A note.
No'ta bian'ca (*I.*). A white note, or minim (♩).
No'ta buo'na (*I.*). An accented note.
No'ta cambia'ta (*I.*). A changing note (*q.v.*).
No'ta caratteris'tica (*I.*). The leading-note (or other characteristic note).
No'ta catti'va (*I.*). An unaccented note.
No'ta corona'ta (*I.*). A note marked with a corona, ⌒.
No'ta d'abellimen'to (*I.*). A grace note.
No'ta di passa're (*I.*). A passing note.
No'ta di piace're (*I.*). An optional grace note.
No'ta fal'sa (*L.*). A changing note (*q.v.*).
No'ta lega'ta (*I.*). A tied or slurred note.
No'ta martella'ta (*I.*). A hammered note.
No'ta principa'le (*I.*). A principal or essential note.
No'ta sensi'bile (*I.*). ⎫ The leading-note.
No'ta sensi'bilis (*L.*). ⎬
No'ta sostenu'ta (*I.*). A sustained note.

Notation.

The development of symbols to represent musical pitch may be divided into three stages.

I.—Letters of the alphabet, in direct or inverted positions.

(1) Greek notation. (Hawkins gives 540 letter-signs used by the ancient Greeks, who probably derived their system from some eastern nation.)

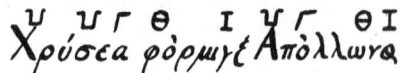

Χρύσεα φόρμιγΣ Ἀπόλλωνα

(2) The Romans substituted their own letters, and perhaps reduced the number to the first seven of the alphabet (Virgil's "Septem discrimina vocum"), doubled in the higher octave.

(3) Letters continued in use to the 8th century (or later), though in the meantime other systems had been introduced.

II.—Dots, dashes, &c., called *Neums*, or *Neumes* (*Neuma, Pneumata*). " The Neume System," says Naumann, "dates from the end of the 4th century," and the neumes were probably at first mere accent marks (grave and acute).

Ambrosian Missal, 9th Cent.

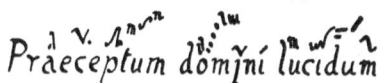

III.—THE STAFF.

(1) About the year 900 A.D. a *red line* was introduced for F; higher or lower sounds were represented by Neumes above or below the line.

Antique Missal abt. 900 (Martini).

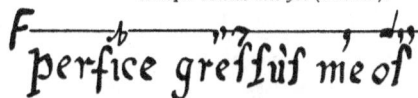

(2) A *yellow line* was next placed above the red one and called C. (N.B.—Each line marked the place of a *semitone.*)

(3) Two *black lines* were subsequently added for A and E; the variously-coloured lines soon gave way to the uniform black or red staff of 4 lines, which is still in use for Gregorian or Plainsong music. The Neumes placed on the lines and spaces gradually developed into modern notes. (See *Note.*)

(5) After the invention of printing (in the 15th cent.), the number of lines—except for Gregorian music—gradually became fixed at five, as at present. But in the meantime, and indeed later, staves of 3, 6, 7, 8, 10, or even 12 lines had been used.

(6) Attempts had also been made to indicate pitch by placing the syllables in the spaces of a staff, or by points on the lines only (without using the spaces); but these attempts led to nothing permanent.

From Hucbald, 10th cent.

A		a			
G		da	te		num
F	Lau			mi	de
E			do		e
D					cœlis

From Martini ("Storia della Musica").

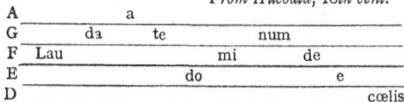

For the origin of the clefs, see *Clef.*

THE CHROMATIC SIGNS were all derived from B, the only inflected note in early music. (1) B *molle* answered to our B flat, and was represented by a "round" or Roman ♭ (*L., B rotundum; F., Bé rond; I., B rotondo.*) B *molle* became the ♭ of modern music.

(2) B *durum* (*L., B quadratum; F., Bé carre; I., Be quadro*) was represented by a "square" Gothic ♭, or ♭, which became the modern ♮.

(3) B *cancellatum*, perhaps a square B cancelled, ♭, became the modern ♯.

N.B.—All sharp and flat notes were formerly called "fictitious" notes.

Braille Notation. A system of raised characters for the use of the blind, invented by M. Braille, a Frenchman, 1834.

Chevé Notation. (See *Chevé.*)

Letter-note Notation. A system of notation with the Sol-fa initial printed within the head of each staff note.

Mensurable Notation } (See *Mensural Music.*)
Mensural Notation

Tonic Sol-fa Notation. (See *Tonic Sol-fa.*)

SPECIMENS OF OTHER MUSICAL NOTATIONS, with European equivalents.

CHINESE :

ARMENIAN :

GREEK CHURCH :

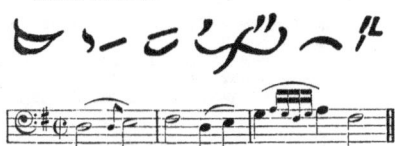

Notazio'ne Musica'le (*I.*).   Musical notation.

Note.   (*L., No'ta; F., Note; I., No'ta.*)
(1) A musical sound. (2) The written or printed character representing a musical sound. (3) Formerly (and still occasionally) used for the interval of a whole tone; *e.g.*, "Take the piece a note higher."

N.B.—Mr. Curwen and some other writers distinguish between a musical sound and its symbol, calling the former a musical "tone" and the other a "note."

DEVELOPMENT OF NOTES FROM NEUMES.   (See *Notation.*)

(1) Neumes :

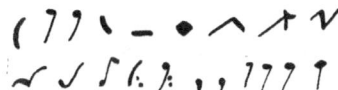

(2) On 2-lined staff :

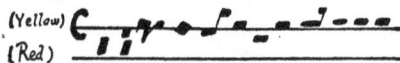

(3) On 4-lined staff :

(4) Ligatures and Obliquities; 11th cent. and onwards.

(5) Gothic. "Horse-shoe and Nail;" 12th to 16th cents.

(6) Open and black notes combined :

(See also *Mensural Music.*)

TABLE OF NAMES OF NOTES.

ENGLISH	ITALIAN	FRENCH	GERMAN
C	Do	Ut	C
D	Re	Re	D
E	Mi	Mi	E
F	Fa	Fa	F
G	Sol	Sol	G
A	La	La	A
B flat	Si bemolle	Si bémol	B
B	Si	Si	H

For " flat," the Italian is *bemol'le ;* French, *bémol;* German, *es.*
For " double flat," the Italian is *bemol'le dop'pia ;* French, *double bémol ;* German, *eses.*
For " sharp," the Italian is *die'sis ;* French, *dièse;* German, *is.*
For " double sharp," the Italian is *die'sis dop'pio ;* French, *double dièse ;* German, *isis.*

Thus :

	ITALIAN	FRENCH	GERMAN
C♭♭	Do bemol'le dop'pia	Ut double bémol	Ceses
C♭	Do bemol'le	Ut bémol	Ces
C♯	Do die'sis	Ut dièse	Cis
C✕	Do die'sis dop'pio	Ut double dièse	Cisis

For the Duration Names of Notes, see *Time.*

Clef note. The note corresponding to the pitch of the Clef.
Half note. A minim.
Note accidentée (F.). An accidental.
Note bonne (F.). An accented note.
Note changée (F.). A changing-note (*q.v.*).
Note couronnée (F.). A note with a corona (⌒).
Note dièsée (F.). A sharpened note.
Note d'agrément (F.) } A grace note ; an embellish-
Note de goût (F.) } ment.
Note de passage (F.). A passing note.
Note liée (F.). A tied or syncopated note.
Note piquée (F.). A staccato note.
Note sensiblé (F.). The leading-note.
Note syncopée (F.). A syncopated note.
Open note. (1) A semibreve or minim. (2) A note produced on an open string.
Quarter note. A crotchet.
Whole note. A semibreve.

No'te (*G.*). A note.

Erhöh'te No'te. Raised note, sharpened note.
Ganz'e No'te. A semibreve (whole note).
Geschwänz'te No'te. A quaver.
Halb'e No'te. A minim.
In No'ten set'zen. To note down an air ; to set to music.
Nach No'ten spiel'en. To play at sight.
Nach No'ten sing'en. To sing at sight.
No'ten. (1) Notes. (2) Pieces of music.
No'tenblatt. A sheet of Music.
No'tenplan. A scale.

No'tenschlüssel. A clef.
No'tenschrift. Musical manuscript.
No'tensing'en. To sing at sight.
No'tenspielen. To play at sight.
No'tensystem. The staff.
Schwar ze No'te. A crotchet.
Von No'ten spiel'en. To play at s'ght.
Von No'ten singen. To sing at sight.

Noter (*F.*). To write music.

NOT'KER. Monk of St. Gallen ; known as Balbulus ; *b.* 840 ; *d.* 912.

Composed "Sequences ;" wrote treatises on "The Division of the Monochord," &c.

No'tograph. Same as Melograph (*q.v.*).

NOT'TEBOHM, Martin G. *B.* Westphalia, 1817 ; *d.* 1882. Pupil of Schumann and Mendelssohn. Settled in Vienna as teacher and writer, and became renowned as a "Beethoven Specialist."

Works : "Beethoven's Sketch Books," a "Thematic Catalogue of Beethoven's Works," "Beethoveniana," "Beethoven's Studies," "Thematic Catalogue of Schubert's Works," &c., all very valuable.

Nottur'no (*I.*). A Nocturne (*q.v.*).

Notturni'no. A little nocturne.

Nourri (*F.*). Nourished. (The "inner parts" rich and full.)

Un son nourri. A full, well-sustained tone.

NOURRIT, Adolphe. Celebrated tenor ; *b.* Paris, 1802 ; *d.* 1839. Trained by Garcia. *Début,* Paris Grand Opéra, 1821. Singing teacher, Paris Cons., for 10 years. The tenor *rôles* of several French operas were specially written for him.

Nour'surgh. A Hindu straight horn.

No'va (*I.*). A small flute.

NO'VÁČEK, Ottokar E. Violinist ; *b.* Hungary, 1866 ; *d.* 1900. Won the Mendelssohn Prize, Leipzig Cons., 1885. Went to America, 1891.

Works : 3 fine string quartets, a pf. concerto, pieces for vn. and pf., &c.

NOVÁK, Vitězslav. Composer; *b.* Kamenitz, Bohemia, 1870.

NOVAKOV'SKI (or NOWAKOW'SKI), Josef. Pianist ; *b.* Mniszck, Poland, 1805 ; *d.* 1865. After successful concert tours, pf. professor Alexandra Inst., Warsaw.

Works : chamber music, a pf. method, and numerous pf. pieces (including 12 grandes études).

Novelet'te } Name given by Schumann to the
Novellet'te } compositions of his Op. 21.

They are free in form and romantic in character.

NOVEL'LO, Clara Anastasia. Daughter of V. (below).; distinguished soprano ; *b.* London, 1818 ; married Count Gigliucci, 1843 ; retired 1860; *d.* 1908.

Sang at all the principal English musical festivals and concerts from the age of 14.

NOVEL'LO, Joseph Alfred. Son of F. V. (below) ; *b.* London, 1810 ; *d.* 1896. Entered his father's business at 19 ; "did much to popularize classic music in England by publishing cheap oratorio scores."

NOVEL'LO, F. Vincent. *B.* London, 1781 ; *d.* 1861. Founder of the firm of **Novello & Co.,** 1811 ; Pianist to the Italian Opera, 1812 ; co-founder of the Philharmonic Society ; Orgt. Moorfields R. C. Chapel, 1840-3. Retired 1849.

Works : masses, motets, anthems, hymns, &c. ; also edited and published numerous collections of sacred and secular music.

Novemo'le (*G.*). A nonuplet (*q.v.*).

NOVERRE, Jean G. Introduced the "ballet-pantomime ; " *b.* Paris, 1727 ; *d.* 1810. Ballet - master, Paris Opéra-comique, 1749 ; London, 1755 ; Grand Opéra, Paris, 1776-80 ; &c.

Pub. "Lettres sur la danse et les ballets."

Nowell. (See **Noel.**)

NOWOWIE'JSKI, Felix. *B.* Wartenburg, 1875.

Works : an oratorio (*Quo vadis*), 2 symphonies.

NOZ'ZE DI FI'GARO, Le. Opera by Mozart, 1786.

Nuances (*F.*). Lights and shades of musical expression. Especially " those indefinite and delicate shades of tone-colour and æsthetic significance at the command of the cultured executant."

La nuance bien indiquée. The shading of expression well marked.

Nunc dimit'tis (*L.*). The first 2 words in the " Canticle of Simeon" (Luke ii. 29-32).

Nun's-fiddle. (See **Tromba marina.**)

Nuo'vo (*I.*). New.

Di nuo'vo. Afresh, anew ; again.

Nur (*G.*). Only.

Nur halb'er Frau'enchor. Only half the female chorus.

Nut. (*G., Sat'tel ; F., Sillet ; I., Capota'sto.*) The ridge at the end of the fingerboard of a vn., &c.

Nutri'to,-a (*I.*). Fed, nourished.

Nutren'do. Nourishing, sustaining (the sounds).

NUX, Paul V. de la. Parisian opera composer ; *b.* 1853.

Works : opera (*Zaire*), stage music, pf. pieces, &c.

O

O. (1) The old sign for "perfect" or triple time (see **Circolo**). (2) A small circle is used to signify (*a*) an open string (vn., &c.), or (*b*) a "harmonic" note (see **Harmonic**); also (*c*) in Harmony Analysis (*q.v.*), a diminished triad.

O (or Od) (*I.*). Or.
Fla'uto o violi'no. Flute or violin.

OAKELEY, Sir Herbert S. *B.* Ealing, 1830; *d.* 1903. Studied Dresden and Leipzig. Reid Prof. of Music, Edinburgh Univ., 1865-91. Mus.Doc. Cantuar and Cantab., 1871; knighted, 1876; Mus.Doc. Oxon, 1879; &c.
Works: anthems, part-songs, orchestral pieces, hymn-tunes, songs, &c.

OAKEY, George. *B.* London, 1841; Mus.Bac. Cantab., 1877. Prof. of Harmony and Composition, City of London College.
Works: anthems, part-songs, hymns, &c.; text-books of Harmony, Counterpoint, Musical Elements, Figured Bass, Harmony Analysis.

Oaten-pipe. The primitive form of reed instrument. (See **Reed**.)

Ob. Abbn. of *Oboe* (or *Oboi*).

Obb. Abbn. of *Obbligato*.

Obbliga'to (*I.*). Necessary, indispensable. A part "that cannot be dispensed with."
Violin obbliga'to. An essential part for a violin.
N.B.—Note that this word is often spelt incorrectly with one "b." The German and French have one "b" (see *Obligat'*), the Italian two. "Latterly the term *obbligato* has almost come to mean *optional*."—*Hughes.*

Obbli'quo (*I.*) } Oblique.
Obli'quo (*I.*) }
Mo'to obbli'quo. Oblique motion.

O'ber (*G.*). Over, above; higher, upon.
O'berdominan'te } The over-dominant and under-
Un'terdominan'te } dominant; *i.e.*, the dominant and sub-dominant.
O'berlabium. The upper lip of an org. pipe.
O'bermanual. Upper manual.
O'berstimme } The upper (highest) part.
O'bertheil }
O'bertaste. An upper "black" key of a pf. or org. keyboard. Compare *Tas'te* and *Ta'sto.*
O'bertöne. Overtones, upper partials, harmonics.
O'berwerk (abbn. *Obw.*, or *O.W.*). "Upper work." In Germany, it refers on a 2-manual organ to the "Choir;" on a 3-manual org., to the "Swell;" on a 4-manual org., to the "Solo."—*Baker.*

OBERON. Opera by Weber, 1826.

Obertas. A popular national Bohemian dance (in the style of a waltz).

O'BERTHÜR, Karl (Charles). Distinguished harpist; *b.* Munich, 1819; *d.* 1895.
Works: 2 operas, cantatas, orch. music; a concertino for harp and orch.; trios, duets, and numerous solos for harp; pf. pieces, songs.

OBIN, Louis H. Operatic baritone; *b.* nr. Lille, 1820; *d.* 1895. *Début*, Paris Opéra, 1844; Prof. Paris Cons., 1871-91.

Objective Music.
Music of "universal" character which "appeals directly to the senses;" *e.g.*, Handel's Choruses. It is the opposite of *Subjective Music* (*q.v.*).

Obligat' (*G.*), **Obligé** (*F.*). Obbligato (*q.v.*).

Oblique motion. (See **Motion**.)

Oblique pianoforte. An upright pf. with the strings arranged diagonally to secure greater fulness of tone.

Obli'quus (*L.*). Oblique.

O'boe (pron. *Ō'-bŏ*). (*Old Eng., Hautboy; F., Hautbois; G., Hobo'e; Obo'e; I., Oboè*.) (1) An orchestral wood-wind inst. with a conical bore and a double reed.
The oboe is the natural treble of the bassoon. It has from 9 to 14 keys, and gives the complete chromatic scale from

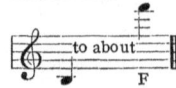

or even higher with solo players. The upper notes are, however, "difficult and hazardous," and it is rarely written for above

The tone is rich in partials (both odd and even), and is of very "characteristic" quality. (See *Acoustics*.)
(2) An organ reed stop of 8 ft. pitch.
Alt-oboe } An alto oboe, or *Cor'no Ingle'se*
Oboè da cac'cia (*I.*) } (*q.v.*); it is a 5th lower than the ordinary oboe, and was formerly used in hunting.
Oboè bas'sa (*I.*) } A large "bass" oboe, now
Grand hautbois (*F.*) } obsolete.
Hautbois d'amour (*F.*) } "Oboe of love;" an oboe of
Oboè d'amor'e (*I.*) } tender tone-quality, a
Oboè lun'go (*I.*) } minor third (in pitch) below the ordinary oboe; used by Bach, and recently revived.
Orchestral Oboe. A delicate "solo" stop on the organ, voiced to imitate the oboe.

Obo'er (*G.*) } Oboe player.
Obois'ta (*I.*) }

O'BRECHT. (See **Hobrecht**.)

Obw. Abbn. of *Oberwerk*. (See **Ober**.)

Ocari'na (*I.*). A small wind inst. of fluty tone (generally made of terra-cotta), pierced with small holes for the fingers.
It is practically a toy instrument, and has no great musical value.

O'CAROLAN, Turlogh. One of the last wandering Irish bards; *b.* Newtown, Meath, 1670; *d.* 1738. Blind from 16. Called the "Irish Handel." "Composer of the tune known as *The Arethusa*."—*Flood.*

OCCASIONAL ORATORIO. Handel, 1746.

OCHS, Siegfried. *B.* Frankfort-on-Main, 1858. Condr. "Philharmonischer Chor," Berlin.
Works: opera (*Im Namen des Gesetzes*), operettas, male choruses, and numerous songs.

OCK'ENHEIM. (See **Okeghem**.)

Oct'achord. (1) An inst. with 8 strings. (2) A diatonic scale of 8 sounds.

Oc'tain. "A section of 8 measures."—*Curwen.*

Octa'va (*L.*). An octave.

Octave. (*G., Okta've; F., Octave; I., Otta'va.*) (1) The interval of an eighth; the Greek *diapason.*
The octave may be either perfect, augmented, or diminished. (See *Interval.*) A perfect octave

above any sound is produced by "twice as many vibrations per second ; " an octave below by "half as many vibrations per second." (See *Acoustics*.)

The "octave" of a sound has been called its "repetition," "miniature," or "replicate," on account of the perfect blending of the two sounds. In most systems octaves have the same letter (or other) name, as C¹ C ; G₁ G ; Doh₁ Doh ; &c.

(2) A scale of eight notes in diatonic succession.

(3) An org. stop of 4 ft. pitch on the manuals, or 8 ft. pitch on the pedals.

(4) Old name of the piccolo, or "octave flute."

Octave. The "eight days" following a great Church Festival.

At the octave. Same as *All'otta'va.* (See *Otta'va.*)
Blind octaves. (See under B.)
Broken octaves. (See *Broken.*)
Consecutive (or parallel) octaves. Two (or more) parts rising or falling together in perfect octaves.
Double octave. The interval of two octaves.
Exposed octaves ⎫
Hidden octaves ⎬ Octaves approached by similar
Ill-approached octaves ⎭ motion.

Octave coupler. An organ coupler which causes pipes to speak which are an octave higher or lower than the notes represented by the keys touched.
Octave flute. The piccolo.
Octave marks. Figures 1, 2, &c., used after the Sol-fa initials to indicate higher or lower octaves ; as d₁ s¹ t₂, &c.
Octave scale. A complete scale of an octave.
Rule of the octave. (See *Rule.*)
Short octave. In old organs, the lowest octave, which was often incomplete.
Sub-octave. The octave below.
Super-octave. The octave above.

Octavia'na. A piccolo.

Octavin'. (1) A piccolo. (2) An inst. somewhat like a clarinet, invented by O. Adler, 1893.

Octavi'na. A small spinet, an octave higher than the ordinary one.

Octa'vo attachment ⎫ A mechanical con-
Octave pedal ⎭ trivance on some pfs. by means of which the octave of any note sounds simultaneously with the note struck.

Octet'. (*G., Octett', Oktett'; F., Octette, Octuor ; I., Ottet'to.*) A piece of music for 8 voices or insts.

Octo-bass ⎫ A large kind of double-
Octo-basse (*F.*) ⎭ bass (a third lower in pitch than the ordinary double-bass), invented by Vuillaume, 1851.

Oct'ochord. (See **Octachord.**)

Octo'le. (See **Octuplet.**)

Oc'tuor. (See **Octet.**)

Octuple Time. (See **Beating Time.**)

Oc'tuplet. A group of 8 notes to be performed in the time allotted to 6 of the same kind :—

Od (*I.*). Or ; as *Vno· od ob.*, violin or oboe.

Ode. (1) A short poem or song ; a lyric poem in strophes (stanzas). (2) An elaborated musical setting of such a poem—"almost a cantata."
O'dische Mu'sik (*G.*). Music set to an ode.

O'dem (*G.*). Breath.

O'DENWALD, Robert T. Noted trainer of choral societies, and teacher of singing ; *b.* nr. Gera, 1838 ; *d.* 1899.
Works : psalms, part-songs, &c.

Ode'on. (*G., Odei'on ; L., Ode'um.*) In ancient Greece a building where poets and musicians contended for prizes ; a concert hall ; a theatre.

O'der (*G.*). Or ; or else ; otherwise.
Für ein o'der zwei Clavie're. For one, or for two manuals.

Ode-symphonie (*F.*). A symphony with vocal chorus.

O'DINGTON, Walter. Monk of Evesham ; lived at Oxford, 1316-30.
Wrote a learned treatise on mensural music and discant, "De Speculatione Musicæ."

ODO of Clugny (Cluny), Saint. Abbot of Clugny, 927 ; *d.* 942.
Wrote "Dialogus de Musica" (including a Letter-notation based on the first seven letters of the alphabet.)

OEGLIN, Erhard. "The first German printer to print figured music with types ; " (1) wooden types, Augsburg, 1507 ; (2) metal types, 1512.

OEL'SCHLÄGEL, Alfred. *B.* Anscha, Bohemia, 1847.
Works : operettas (*Der Landstreicher*, 1893, &c.).

OELS'NER, F. Bruno. *B.* Neudorf, Saxony, 1861. Vn. teacher, Darmstadt Cons., 1882.
Works : operas (*Der Brautgang*), songs, &c.

OES'TEN, Theodor. Berlin, 1813-70.
Wrote light *salon* pf. pieces.

OE'STERLE, Otto. Flautist ; *b.* St. Louis, 1861 ; *d.* 1894.
Played mostly at New York and Brooklyn. Fl. Prof. National Cons., New York.

OE'STERLEIN, Nikolaus. *B.* 1840 ; *d.* Vienna, 1898. "Indefatigable collector of everything relating to Wagner."
The catalogue of his "Wagner Museum," Eisenach, fills 4 vols.

OET'TINGEN, Arthur J. von. Noted writer on acoustics, &c. ; *b.* Dorpat, 1836.

Œuvre (*F.*). A work, or "opus" (*q.v.*).
Première œuvre. A first work ; Opus 1 (or Op. 1).
Chef-d'œuvre. A masterpiece.

Of'fen (*G.*). Open.
Of'fenflöte. An "open" flute stop (on the organ).

OF'FENBACH, Jacques. "The creator of French burlesque opera." *B.* Cologne, 1819 ; *d.* Paris, 1880. Son of a Jew ; studied Paris Cons. Condr. Théâtre Francais, 1849 ; ran a theatre of his own, 1855-66 ; manager, Théâtre de la Gaîté, 1872-6.
His music, immensely popular at the time, is sprightly and humorous, but often

trivial and vulgar. The phrase "from Bach to Offenbach" is used to express the opposite poles of musical intellectuality.

Of his 102 stage works the best are *Orphée aux enfers* (1858), *La belle Hélène* (1864), *Barbe-Bleue* (1866), *La vie Parisienne* (1866), *La grande Duchesse* (1867), and *Madame Favart* (1879).

Of'fenbar (*G.*). Open, evident, manifest.
Of'fenbare Okta'ven. Consecutive (parallel) octaves.
Of'fenbare Quin'ten. Consecutive (parallel) fifths.

Offertoire (*F.*) ⎱ (1) An "offering," or "col-
Offerto'rio (*I.*) ⎰ lection " of alms, &c.,
Offerto'rium (*L.*) ⎱ taken during Holy
Offertory ⎰ Communion or some other church service. (2) A piece of music played during the offertory. (3) A movement in a *Requiem Mass*.

Offic'ium (*L.*). A mass ; a service.
Offic'ium defuncto'rum. A funeral service ; a *requiem*.
Offic'ium diur'num. The ordinary daily service hours.

Officle'ida (*I.*) ⎱ An ophicleide (*q.v.*). Also
Oficle'ida (*I.*) ⎰ spelt *Officleide* or *Oficleide*.

OGIN'SKI, Michael Casimir. Warsaw, 1731-1803. Said to have "invented the pedals of the harp."

OGIN'SKI, Prince Michael Cleophas. Nephew of preceding ; noted writer of Polonaises ; *b.* nr. Warsaw, 1765 ; *d.* 1833.

O'gni (*I.*). All, each, every.
Per o'gni tem'pi. (Suitable) for any occasion.

Oh'ne (*G.*). Without.
Oh'ne Beglei'tung. Without accompaniment.
Oh'ne Ei'le. Without haste.
Oh'ne Pedal das ganz'e Stück. Without pedal throughout the piece.
Oh'ne Peda'le. Without pedals.
Oh'ne Sordi'ne. Without the mute.
Oh'ne Wort'e. Without words : *e.g.*, *Lied oh'ne Wor'te,* " a song without words."
O 'ne zu schlep'pen. Without dragging (the time).

O'KEGHEM (OKEKEM, OKENGHEN, OCKENHEIM, &c.), **Jean de** (or **Joannes**). Celebrated Netherland contrapuntist ; *b.* abt. 1430 ; *d.* Tours, 1495(?). Chorister, Antwerp Cath., 1443-4; pupil of Dufay abt. 1450; royal *Maître de chapelle*, Paris, 1465 ; probably retired about 1490. Teacher of Josquin.

Extant works : 17 masses, 7 motets, a nine-fold canon in 36 parts, 19 chansons, &c.

Old Hundredth. The tune set to the " Old Version " of the 100th Psalm (Sternhold and Hopkins, 1562).

CELEBRATED VERSIONS OF THE MELODY.
(1) The oldest known form : Marot and Beza's Genevan Psalter, 1542-3.

(2) Sternhold and Hopkins' Psalms, 1562.

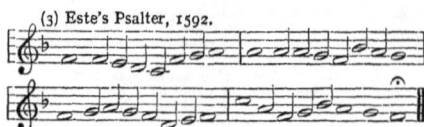

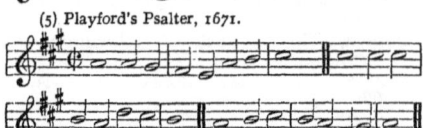

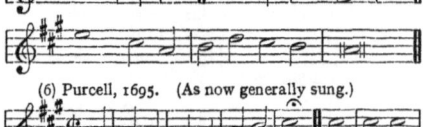

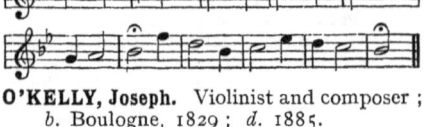

(3) Este's Psalter, 1592.

(4) Ravenscroft's Psalter, 1621.

(5) Playford's Psalter, 1671.

(6) Purcell, 1695. (As now generally sung.)

(7) Bach, 1730.

O'KELLY, Joseph. Violinist and composer ; *b.* Boulogne, 1829 ; *d.* 1885.

Okta've (*G.*). Octave (*q.v.*).
Oktav'enfolgen. Consecutive octaves.
Oktav'engänge. A succession of octaves.
Oktav'flöte. Piccolo.
Oktav'koppel. Octave coupler.
Oktav'parallel'en. Consecutive (parallel) octaves.

Oktavin'. (See **Octavin.**)

OLD, John. Composer and conductor ; *b.* Totnes, 1827 ; *d.* 1892. Founded the Layston Coll. of Music, Reading.
Works : opera (*Herne the Hunter*), songs, pf. pieces, &c.

O'LEARY, Arthur. Pianist ; *b.* Tralee, 1834. Professor, R.A.M., 1856.
Works : numerous pf. pieces, orchestral pieces, songs, &c.

O'LEARY, Mrs. A. (See **Rosetta Vinning.**)

OLE BULL. (See **Bull.**)

O'lio. A miscellaneous collection.

OL'IPHANT, Thos. *B.* Condie, Perthshire, 1799 ; *d.* London, 1873. For 40 years secretary, afterwards president, of the London Madrigal Society.
Edited a colln. of the words of 400 madrigals ; collns. of madrigals, glees, catches, &c.

Ol'iphant (or **Olifant**). A horn made of an elephant's tusk.

OLIT'ZKA, Rosa. Operatic contralto ; *b.* Berlin, 1873.

OLIVER, Henry K. *B.* Beverly, Mass., 1800; *d.* Boston, 1885.
Works : a colln. of church music, original hymn-tunes, &c.

OLIVERS, Thos. 1725-99. One of Wesley's preachers.
Wrote the fine hymn, "The God of Abraham praise."

Ol'la-podri'da (*S.*). A medley ; an *olio* (*q.v.*).

d'OLLONE, Max. Composer ; *b.* Besançon, 1875. *Grand Prix de Rome*, Paris Cons., 1897.

OL'SEN, Ole. Norwegian composer ; *b.* Hammerfest, 1851.
Works : orch. music, pf. pieces, &c.

O'MARA, Joseph. Tenor vocalist ; *b.* Limerick, 1866.
Created the part of "Mike Murphy" in Stanford's *Shamus O'Brien*, 1896.

Om'bi. West African negro harp.

Om'bra (*I.*). Shade (in expression).

Om'nes (*L.*)　⎫
Om'nia (*L.*)　⎬ " All ; " chorus or *Tutti*.

Om'nitonic　⎫ Capable of producing all the tones
Omnitonique (*F.*)　⎬ (and semitones).
Cor omnitonique (*F.*). (1) A "chromatic" or valve horn.
(2) A horn that can be set to any key.

Once-marked Octave, &c. (See **Pitch.**)

Ondeggiamen'to (*I.*)　⎫ Waving, undulating,
Ondeggian'te (*I.*)　⎬ trembling ; *tremolo*.

ON'DRICZEK, Franz. Violinist ; *b.* Prague, 1859. Won 1st prize for vn. playing, Paris Cons.

Ondulation (*F.*). Undulation, waving, &c.

Ondulé (*F.*). Undulating ; same as **Ondeggiamento** (*q.v.*).

Onduli(e)'ren (*G.*). To tremolo, to undulate.

O'NEILL, Arthur. Irish harpist ; 1726-1816. Collected a large number of traditional Irish melodies.

O'NEILL, Norman H. Composer and singer ; *b.* Kensington, 1875.

Ongare'se (*I.*)　⎫ Hungarian.
Onghere'se (*I.*)　⎬

ONSLOW, George. Grandson of the 1st Lord Onslow ; *b.* Clermont-Ferrand, 1784 ; *d.* 1852. Member of the French Académie, 1842.
Works : 3 comic operas, 34 string quintets (and much other chamber music), 4 symphonies, pf. pieces, &c.

Onzième (*F.*). An interval of an eleventh.

Ood, or **Oud.** An Egyptian guitar.

Op. Abbn. of *Opus* (*q.v.*).

Open. Free, untouched, not closed, &c.
Open diapason. The chief foundation stop of an organ. (See **Organ.**)
Open harmony. With the notes of the various chords as equidistant as possible. (See **Harmony.**)
Open key. Name sometimes given to the key of C major.

Open note. One produced on an "open" string (see below) ; or on a horn, trumpet, &c., without the use of valves or stopping with the hand.
Open order. Same as open harmony (see above).
Open pedal. The "Loud" pedal of a pf.
Open pipe. An organ pipe not closed (or "stopped") at the top.
Open score. With each part on a separate staff. (See *Score.*)
Open string. Not "stopped" or pressed by the finger.
Open tone. (1) Same as open note (above). (2) In singing, a "forward" tone with the mouth well open.

Op'era. (*G., O'per, Musik'drama ; F., Opéra ; I., O'pera, Dram'ma per mu'sica.*) A drama set to music for voices and instruments, with action (and generally scenery).
An opera, like a play, is divided into Acts and Scenes. It generally commences with an *Overture* or *Prelude ;* it contains *Recitatives, Solos, Duets, Trios,* &c.; also *Ensemble Pieces* and *Choruses ;* and there is generally a *Finale* to each Act.
The opera had its origin in "Bardi's attempt to restore the style of declamation peculiar to ancient Greek Tragedy. (See *Bardi, Caccini, Cavaliere, Galilei,* and *Peri.*)
The first opera publicly performed was Peri's *Euridice,* Florence, 1600. (N.B.—The 1st oratorio was performed the same year at Rome.) Peri's chief co-worker was Caccini. Their operas consisted mostly of a kind of recitative (called "*Musica parlante*") with a slight instrumental accompaniment. Monteverde added several improvements in harmony, expression, and orchestration ; and with the development of the "New Style" of music, the composition of opera gradually spread throughout Italy, France, Germany, &c.
NOTEWORTHY OPERAS, with date of first performance. (See also under each composer's name.)
PERI : *Euridice,* Florence, 1600 (the 1st Italian opera ; *Dafne,* 1597, was an experiment).
MONTEVERDE : *Arianna,* Mantua, 1607 ; *Orfeo,* 1608 ; *Tancredi e Clorinda,* Venice, 1624.
GIACOBBI : *Andromeda,* Bologna, 1610.
MANELLI : *Andromeda,* Venice, 1637.
CAVALLI : *Le Nozze di Peleo,* 1640.
ABBÉ MAILLY : *Akebar,* Carpentras, 1646 (the 1st French opera).
CESTI : *L'Orontea,* Venice, 1649.
CAMBERT : *Pomone,* Paris, 1669.
LULLY : *Atys,* Paris, 1676 ; *Armide,* 1686.
STRADELLA : *La Forza dell'Amor paterno,* Genoa, 1678.
J. THEILE : *Adam und Eva,* Hamburg, 1678 (1st German "Singspiel").
FRESCHI : *Berenice,* Padua, 1680.
A. SCARLATTI : *L'Onestà nell'Amore,* Rome, 1680 ; *La Principessa fedele,* Venice, 1705(?).
PURCELL : *Dido and Æneas,* 1688(90?) ; *King Arthur* (1691).
B. KEISER : *Basilius,* Wolfenbüttel, 1693.
HANDEL : *Rinaldo,* London, 1711 ; *Radamisto,* 1720.
DR. PEPUSCH : *Beggar's Opera,* London, 1727.
PERGOLESI : *Sallustia,* Naples, 1732 ; *La serva padrona,* 1734.
ARNE : *Artaxerxes,* 1762.
GLUCK : *Orfeo,* Vienna, 1762 (revised, Paris, 1774) ; *Armide,* 1777 ; *Iphigénie en Tauride,* 1778.
CIMAROSA : *Il Matrimonio segreto,* Vienna, 1792.
MOZART : *Le Nozze di Figaro,* Vienna, 1786 ; *Don Giovanni* (*Don Juan*), Prague, 1787 ; *Die Zauberflöte* (*Il Flauto Magico*), Vienna, 1791.
CHERUBINI : *Les deux Journées,* , Paris, 1800.
BEETHOVEN : *Fidelio* (*Leonora*), Vienna, 1805 (revised, 1814).
SPONTINI : *La Vestale,* 1807.
MÉHUL : *Joseph,* 1807.
ROSSINI : *Il Barbiere,* Rome, 1816 ; *Semiramide,* 1823 ; *William Tell,* Paris, 1829.

WEBER : *Der Freischütz*, Berlin, 1821.
SPOHR : *Jessonda*, Cassel, 1823.
PACINI : *Niobe*, 1826.
MERCADENTE : *Nitocri*, 1826.
MARSCHNER : *Der Vampyr*, 1828.
AUBER : *Fra Diavolo*, 1830 ; *Crown Diamonds*, 1841 ; *Masaniello*, 1828.
HEROLD : *Zampa*, Paris, 1831.
BELLINI : *La Sonnambula*, Milan, 1831 ; *Norma*, Milan, 1832.
MEYERBEER : *Robert de Diable*, Paris, 1831 ; *Les Huguenots*, 1836 ; *Le Prophète*, 1849.
HALÉVY : *La Juive*, 1835.
DONIZETTI : *Lucia di Lammermoor*, Naples, 1835 ; *The Daughter of the Regiment*, Paris, 1840.
GLINKA : *A Life for the Czar*, 1st Russian National Opera, 1836.
BALFE : *Bohemian Girl*, 1843.
WAGNER : *Der Fliegende Hollander*, Dresden, 1843 ; *Tannhäuser*, Dresden, 1845 ; *Lohengrin*, Weimar, 1850 ; *Tristan*, Munich, 1865 ; *Die Meistersinger*, Munich, 1868 ; *Der Ring des Nibelungen* (entire work produced Bayreuth, 1876) ; *Parsifal*, 1882.
ERKEL : *Hunyády László*. First Hungarian National Opera, 1844.
WALLACE : *Maritana*, 1845.
FLOTOW : *Martha*, Vienna, 1847.
SCHUMANN : *Genoveva*, Leipzig, 1850.
VERDI : *Il Trovatore*, Rome, 1853 ; *Otello*, Milan, 1887 ; *Falstaff*, 1893.
CORNELIUS : *Der Barbier von Bagdad*, 1858.
GOUNOD : *Faust*, Paris, 1859 ; *Roméo et Juliette*, 1867.
MACFARREN : *Robin Hood*, 1860.
BENEDICT : *Lily of Killarney*, 1862.
AMBROISE THOMAS : *Mignon*, Paris, 1866.
BOITO : *Mefistofele*, Milan, 1868.
SEROV : *The Power of the Enemy*, St. Petersburg, 1871.
BIZET : *Carmen*, Paris, 1875.
SULLIVAN : *Pinafore*, 1878 ; *Mikado*, 1885 ; *Ivanhoe*, 1891.
DÉLIBES : *Lakmé*, Paris, 1883.
MACKENZIE : *Colomba*, 1883.
GORING THOMAS : *Nadeshda*, 1885.
MASSENET : *Le Cid*, Paris, 1885.
MASCAGNI : *Cavalleria Rusticana*, Rome, 1890.
LEONCAVALLO : *I Pagliacci*, Milan, 1892.
HUMPERDINCK : *Hänsel und Gretel*, Weimar, 1893.
GIORDANO : *Andrea Chenier*, 1896.
STANFORD : *Shamus O'Brien*, 1896.
PUCCINI : *La Bohème*, Turin, 1896.
CHARPENTIER : *Louise*, Paris, 1900.
DEBUSSY : *Pelléas et Mélisande*, 1902.
VINCENT D'INDY : *L'Etranger*, 1903.
RD. STRAUSS : *Salome*, Dresden, 1905.
ETHEL SMYTH : *The Wreckers*, Leipzig, 1906.
Burlesque Opera. Same as *Opéra bouffe*.
English Opera. Formerly, a spoken drama interspersed with ballads.
Grand Opera } Serious, grand, tragic ; without
Heroic Opera } spoken dialogue.
Lyric Opera. One chiefly " lyrical," and without much dramatic action.
Opéra bouffe (F.) } Comedy opera ; farcical opera.
O'pera buf'fa (I.) }
Opéra comique (F.). An opera with spoken dialogue.
O'pera dramma'tica (I.). Romantic opera (*q.v.*).
O'pera Se'ria (I.). A grand opera (*q.v.*).
Romantic Opera. One in which the incidents are supernatural, mythical, &c., as *Der Freischütz*.
Singspiel (G.). A German "ballad" opera.
Tragic Opera. A grand opera with a tragic issue, as *Les Huguenots.*

Operet'ta (I.) } A little opera, generally of
Opérette (F.) } a light and playful
Operet'te (G.) } character.

O'pern-haus (G.). Opera house.

O'pern-kom'ponist (G.). Opera composer.

O'pern-säng'er (*Fem., Säng'erin*) (G.). Opera singer.

Oph'icleide. (1) The bass of the key-bugle. The ophicleide is now little used, its place in the orchestra being taken by the Bass-tuba. Mendelssohn wrote for the ophicleide in *Elijah*, and in the overture to the *Midsummer Night's Dream* (where it comically imitates the braying of the donkey).

(2) A powerful org-stop on the Pedals ; the bass of the Tuba.

Opp., Oppu're (I.). Same as **Ossia** (*q.v.*).

Op'us (L.). A work ; abbn. *Op.*
Composers number their publications Op. 1, Op. 2, &c. ; an *opus* may be a large and important work or a mere trifle. Viadana numbered his works in the modern way ; but Beethoven was the first great composer to use *opus* numbers regularly.
Mag'num op'us. "Great work;" a masterpiece.

Opus'culum (L.). A short work.

Orage (F.). A storm, tempest.

O'ra pro no'bis (L.). "Pray for us." A response in the Roman Catholic service.

Orato'rio. (L. and G., *Orato'rium ; F., Oratoire ; I., Orato'rio*.) A sacred work analogous to an opera, but without action, scenery, or costume.
The words of an oratorio (which, in England especially, represents the highest type of musical composition) are taken from the Bible, the life of a saint, or some other religious source. It takes its name from the *oratory* in which San Filippo Neri (*q.v.*) gave his religious lectures (16th cent.). To accompany these lectures "Laudi Spirituali" were composed by Animuccia (*q.v.*), who has been called the "Father of the Oratorio."
The first "oratorio," in the modern sense of the term, was written by Emilio del Cavaliere (*q.v.*), Rome, 1600. The music was in the "New Style," as in the 1st opera, Florence, 1600. (See *Opera*.)
Concert oratorios were the invention of Handel. Lutheran settings of the *Passion* are usually reckoned oratorios.
NOTEWORTHY ORATORIOS. (See also under each composer's name.)
CAVALIERE : *Rappresentazione dell'anima e del corpo*, Rome, 1600.
H. SCHUTZ : *Die Auferstehung Christi*, Dresden, 1623 (1st true German oratorio).
MAZZOCCHI : *Querimonia di S. Maria Maddelena*, abt. 1630.
CARISSIMI : *Jephtha*, abt. 1660.
STRADELLA : *San Giovanni Battista*, abt. 1676.
A. SCARLATTI : *I Dolori di Maria sempre Vergine*, 1693.
R. KEISER : *Passions Dichtung*, Hamburg, 1704.
CALDARA : *Sisera*, abt. 1720.
BACH : *Passion* (St. John), 1724 ; *Passion* (St. Matthew), 1729.
LEO : *Santa Elena al Calvario*, abt. 1725(?).
HANDEL : *Israel*, 1739 ; *Messiah*, 1741 ; *Samson*, 1743 ; *Judas*, 1747 ; *Jephthah*, 1752.
GRAUN : *Der Tod Jesu*, Berlin, 1755.
ARNE : *Judith*, 1764.
SACCHINI : *Esther*, abt. 1770.
PAISIELLO : *Passione*, abt. 1780(?).
CIMAROSA : *Judith*.
HAYDN : *Creation*, 1798.
BEETHOVEN : *Mount of Olives*, abt. 1800.
CROTCH : *Palestine*, 1812.
F. SCHNEIDER : *Das Weltgericht*, 1819.
SPOHR : *Last Judgment*, 1826 ; *Calvary*, 1835.
MENDELSSOHN : *St. Paul*, 1836 ; *Elijah*, 1846.
BERLIOZ : *Childhood of Christ*, 1854.
COSTA : *Eli*, 1855.
OUSELEY : *St. Polycarp*, 1855.
F. HILLER : *Saul*, 1858.

MOLIQUE : *Abraham*, 1860.
LISZT : *St. Elizabeth*, 1865.
STERNDALE BENNETT : *Woman of Samaria*, 1867.
SULLIVAN : *Prodigal Son*, 1869 ; *Light of the World*, 1873 ; *Golden Legend*, 1886.
BENEDICT : *St. Peter*, 1870.
MACFARREN : *St. John the Baptist*, 1873.
GOUNOD : *Redemption*, 1882 ; *Mors et Vita*, 1885.
DVORAK : *St. Ludmila*, 1886.
COWEN : *Ruth*, 1887.
PARRY (SIR H.) : *Judith*, 1888.
BRIDGE : *Repentance of Nineveh*, 1890.
STANFORD : *Eden*, 1891.
MACKENZIE : *Bethlehem*, 1894.
ELGAR : *Dream of Gerontius*, 1900 ; *The Apostles*, 1903 ; *The Kingdom*, 1906.

Orchésographie (*F.*). The science and theory of dancing.

Orchestique (F.). Relating to dancing.
Orchestik' (G.). Art of rhythmical motion.

Orches'ter (*G.*)
Or'chestra (*E.*)
Orche'stra (*I.*)
Orchestre (*F.*)
"Dancing place." (1) In the ancient Greek theatre the place in front of the stage allotted to the "chorus." In modern theatres and concert rooms the place allotted to the "band." Hence (2) the band itself, and the instruments in general.

The "Classical" full orchestra, as established by Beethoven, consists of 3 main divisions :—
(1) The "wood-wind ; " 2 flutes (*flauti*, abbn. *fl.*), 2 oboes (*oboi, ob.*), 2 clarinets (*clarinetti, clar., cl.*), and 2 bassoons (*fagotti, fag.*).
(2) The " brass " (and percussion insts.) ; 2 (or 4) horns (*corni, cor.*), 2 (or 3) trumpets (*trombe, tr.*), 3 trombones (*tromboni, tbi.*), 2 (or 3) kettledrums (*timpani, timp.*).
(3) The "strings ; " 1st violins, 2nd violins, violas, violoncellos, and double-basses (varying in number according to the "size" of the orch.).
In the *Finale* of his 9th Symphony, Beethoven also employs a piccolo, a contrafagotto, a triangle, cymbals, and a big drum.
More recent composers occasionally add considerably to Beethoven's orchestral resources.
Wagner's "grand orchestra" in the *Ring des Nibelungen* consists of 1 piccolo, 3 flutes 3 oboes, 1 cor anglais, 3 clarinets, 1 bass clarinet, 3 bassoons, 8 horns, 3 chromatic trumpets, 1 bass chromatic trumpet, 3 trombones, 1 contrabass trombone, 5 tubas, 4 kettledrums, triangle, cymbals, bass drum, 6 harps, 16 first vns., 16 second vns., 12 violas, 12 'cellos, 8 double-basses.
Berlioz "sighed for an ideal Festival orchestra" to consist of 120 violins, 40 violas, 45 'cellos, 18 three-stringed basses, 15 four-stringed basses, 4 octo-basses, 6 large flutes, 4 third flutes, 2 piccolos, 2 piccolos in Db, 6 oboes, 6 corni Inglesi, 5 saxophones, 4 tenoroons, 12 bassoons, 4 clarinets in Eb, 8 ordinary clarinets, 3 bass clarinets, 16 horns, 8 trumpets, 6 cornets-à-pistons, 12 trombones, 3 ophicleides, 2 bass tubas, 30 harps, 30 pianofortes, 1 organ, 8 pairs of kettledrums, 6 drums, 3 long drums, 4 pairs of cymbals, 6 triangles, 6 sets of bells, 12 pairs of antique cymbals, 2 very low great bells, 2 gongs, and 4 Turkish Crescents.

Orches'ter-Beglei'tung (*G.*). Orchestral accompaniment.
Orches'ter-Partitur' (*G.*). A full orchestral score.
Orches'tersatz. An orchestral piece ; a concerted piece.
Orches'ter-stim'men (*G.*). Orchestral parts.
Orches'ter-verein (*G.*). An orchestral society.
Small orchestra. A "classical" orchestra (as above), with trombones (and perhaps clarinets and drums) omitted, and only 2 horns and 2 trumpets.
String orchestra. An orchestra of strings only.

Orches'tral colour. (See **Colour.**)

Orches'tral oboe
Orches'tral flute } Organ stops specially voiced to imitate the orchestral instruments.

Orchestral Score. (See **Score.**)

Orchestras, Finest.
The finest orchestras in the world are (1) The orchestra of the Casino, Monte Carlo ; (2) Lamoureux orchestra, Paris ; (3) Philharmonic orchestra, Berlin ; (4) Châtelet Theatre, Paris (under M. Colonne) ; (5) Boston Symphony Orchestra ; (6) New York Philharmonic Orchestra.—*London Evening News*, Aug., 1906.
Mr. Henry Wood's Queen's Hall Orchestra and the Orchestra of the Paris Cons. should also be mentioned.

Orchestration. The art of writing for the orchestra.
Often called *Instrumentation.* (For Gevaert's distinction see *Instrumentation.*)
Or'chestrate (E.)
Orchestri(e)'ren (G.)
Orchestrer (F.)
Orchestra're (I.)
} To write, or arrange music for an orchestra.

Orchestre (*F.*). Orchestra.
À grand orchestre. For full orchestra.

Orchestri'na
Orches'trion
} A large automatic barrel organ imitating a full orchestra.

Orchestri'no (*I.*). A piano-violin, invented 1808.

OR'DENSTEIN, Heinrich. *B.* Worms, 1856. Studied Leipzig Cons. and Paris, Founded the Carlsruhe Cons., 1884.

Ordinaire (*F.*). Ordinary.
Cors ordinaires. Natural horns.
Sons ordinaires. The " open " or natural sounds of instruments.

Ordina'rio (*I.*). Ordinary.
A tem'po ordina'rio. At a moderate speed ; 4-4 time.

Ordre (*F.*). A suite.

Orec'chia,-o (*I.*)
Oreille (*F.*)
} The ear.
Orec'chia musica'le (I.)
Oreille musicale (F.)
} An ear for music.
Orecchian'te (I.). One who performs or judges music "by ear ; " *i.e.*, without musical training.

Or'gan. (*L., Or'ganum ; G., Or'gel ; F., Orgue ; I., Or'gano.*)
The development of the "King of Instruments " —essentially " a box of whistles "—from the primitive "whistling reed" represents one of the highest achievements of human ingenuity. The first organs of which we have any *authentic* records date from about the 4th century, A.D. (A so-called "hydraulic" organ was invented by Ctesibius an Egyptian (3rd cent. B.C.), but our knowledge of the details of its construction is vague and uncertain.) The early organs were naturally very crude instruments in comparison with our present magnificent church and concert organs. They had from 8 to 30 pipes, and the keys were so clumsy and broad (4 to 6 inches) that they had to be struck by the fists or elbows. Hence the performers on these organs were known as "organ beaters." Pedals were invented about 1325, and reed pipes probably in the 15th century.
The CONSTRUCTION of an organ falls conveniently under 4 heads :—
(1) *The Pipes.* These are of 2 kinds. (*a*) Flue pipes, constructed on the same principle as the ordinary tin whistle, and either *open* or *stopped.* (See *Acoustics* and *Pipe.*) (*b*) Reed pipes, constructed on the principle of the clarinet. A group of pipes of the same tone-quality forms a *Register* or *Stop*, and a number of different

Registers is allotted to each "Manual." (See *Console*, below.) Pipes are constructed either of wood or of metal.

(2) The *Wind-supply*; including bellows, wind-trunks, and wind-chest.

(3) The *Console*. This is the part of the organ under the immediate control of the player. It includes the rows of keys, called "Manuals" (of which there may be any number from 1 to 5), the "Pedals" for the feet, the "Draw Knobs" or "Stops" connected with the various registers, the "Couplers," and other "Accessory Movements," and the "Swell Pedal." In an "Electric" or "Pneumatic" organ, the Console is sometimes placed at a distance from the main body of the inst.

(4) *The Action*. This includes all the mechanism connecting the keys with the pipes (and by means of which any required pipe or pipes can be made to sound.)

Three kinds of "Action" are in common use: (a) Tracker-action; by means of slender rods called "trackers," "stickers," and "pull-downs." (2) Pneumatic action; by means of compressed air. (3) Electric action.

Organ Manuals are named (in order of importance) *Great, Swell, Choir, Solo*, and *Echo*.

Each manual controls a separate section of the instrument, which has the same name; *Great Organ, Swell Organ*, &c.

ENGLISH	GERMAN	FRENCH	ITALIAN
Great(Gt.)	Haupt'werk (Man. 1)	Grand orgue	Principa'le
Swell (Sw.)	Schwell'werk (Man. 3)	Clavier de récit.	Or'gano d'espressio'ne
Choir (Ch.)	Un'terwerk (Man. 2)	Positif	Or'gano di co'ro
Solo	So'loklavier' (Man. 4)	Clav. des bombardes	Or'gano d'asso'lo
Echo	E'choklavier' (Man. 5)	Clav. d'écho	Or'gano d'e'co
Pedal (Ped.)	Pedal'klaviatur	Clav. des pédales	Pedalle'ra

The largest organ in the world was built for the St. Louis Exposition, 1904, by the Los Angeles Organ Co., California. It was "voiced" by Mr. J. W. Whiteley, an Englishman, and cost 100,000 dollars (£20,000). The organ is 70 ft. wide, 50 ft. high, and 30 ft. deep; weight of largest wood pipe, 1735 ℔; largest metal pipe, 840 ℔; smallest, half-an-ounce. It has five manuals, 140 speaking stops, 99 accessory stops, and 10,059 pipes. There are 30 stops on the Pedal organ alone (including one of 64 ft. pitch, and 4 of 32 ft. pitch). In addition to the ordinary Console, there is a special Console for an "Automatic Self-playing Attachment," and the builders claim that it is "the most complete and perfect organ ever fabricated by the hand of man."

Barrel-organ. (See under "B.")
Buffet-organ. A very small organ.
Cabinet-organ. (See *Reed Organ*.)
Enharmonic organ } (See *Enharmonic and Eu-
Euharmonic organ } *harmonic*.)
Full-organ. The full power of the organ.
Organet'to (I.). A small organ.
Organier (F.). An organ builder.
Organique (F.). Relating to the organ.
Organi'sta (I.). (1) An organist. (2) Formerly, a composer.
Organ-loft. The part (of a church, &c.) where the organ is placed.
Organ metal. A mixture of tin and lead used for organ pipes; "the more tin the better it is."
Organ point. (See *Pedal point*.)
Organ tone. A tone sustained with even (or uniform) power; shown thus—

Pair of organs. Used in the sense of "a pair of steps;" an organ with a complete set of pipes.

Organ Builders in England.

Pre-Restoration Organ *Makers*—
JN. ROOSE, York, 1457.
GEO. GAUNTE, York, 1470.
RD. SOWERBY, York, 1473.
JN. BORTON, of Stowmarket, 1482.
JN. HOWE,* London, 1485.
WM. WOTTON, Magdalene Coll. organ, Oxford, abt. 1486-7.
JOHN CHAMBERLYN (CHAMBERLAINE) and THOS. SMYTH, St. Margaret's, Westminster, 1514.
ANTHONY DADDYNGTON, of London; built org. at All Hallows, Barking, 1519.
JOHN DE JOHN, mentioned in 1526 and 1531.
ROBARTT, of Crewkerne, Somerset, about 1535.
WM. BETON (BETUN), mentioned 1537-44.
WYGHT (WHITE), *circa* 1531-45.
BROUGHE, St. Margaret's, Westminster, 1590.
JOHN CHAPINGTON, Westminster Abbey, 1596.
GIBBS, Dulwich Coll. Chapel, 1618.
JN. BURWARD, of London, built an org. for Chirk Castle, 1631; repaired the org. at Westminster Abbey under the direction of Orlando Gibbons.
PRESTON, York, 17th cent.
THAMAR, Peterboro', 17th cent.
JOHN LOOSEMOORE (1613-81), Exeter Cath., 1665.
ROBT. DALLAM, 1602-65.
FATHER SMITH, 1630-1708.
RENATUS HARRIS (*q.v.*), built from abt. 1660.
JOHN HARRIS (son of Renatus).
JOHN BYFIELD (*q.v.*), 18th century.
CHRIS. SCHRIDER, succeeded Father Smith, 1708.
THOS. SCHWARBROOK, *d.* abt. 1750.
JORDAN (father and son), built organs 1700-33.
RD. BRIDGE, built organs from 1729; then joined with Byfield, senr., and the Jordans.
JN. BYFIELD, junr., *d.* 1774.
GLYN & PARKER, 1730-49.
JN. SNETZLER, built organs from 1749.
CRANG & HANCOCK, best work abt. 1770.
SAMUEL GREEN (*q.v.*), 1730-96.
JOHN AVERY (*q.v.*), 18th century.
ENGLANDS, father and son, built organs from 1760-1812.

Of more recent London and Provincial builders the following may be mentioned :—

BEVINGTON & SONS, established 1794.
J. C. BISHOP, invented composition pedals, 1809.
C. S. BARKER (*q.v.*), 1806-79, invented the pneumatic lever.
ELLIOTT & HILL, York Minster, 1829.
HENRY WILLIS (*q.v.*), 1821-1901.
LEWIS & CO.
J. W. WALKER & SONS.
HILL & SONS, Westminster Abbey, 1908-9.
GRAY & DAVISON.
FOSTER & ANDREWS.
BRYCESON & CO.
NORMAN & BEARD.
HOPE-JONES & CO.
KIRTLAND & JARDINE, Manchester.
HELE & CO., Plymouth.
HARRISON & HARRISON, Durham.
ABBOTT & SMITH, Leeds.
J. BINNS, Leeds.
BRINDLEY & FOSTER, Sheffield.
NICHOLSON & CO., Worcester.
WADSWORTH BROS., Manchester.
ALBERT KEATES, Sheffield.
P. CONACHER & CO., Huddersfield.
H. S. VINCENT & CO., Sunderland.
MORGAN & SMITH, Brighton.
NICHOLSON & LOW, Walsall.

Organe (F.). An organ.

Organ'ic music. Old term for instrumental music.

* "Undoubtedly the Henry Willis of his day."—*Dr. C. W. Pearce*.

Orga'nicen (*L.*). Organ player.

Organist'rum (*L.*). An old form of hurdy-gurdy (abt. 1100 A.D.).

Organists, Royal College of. Founded 1864.

Or'gano (*I.*). Organ.

Or'gano di campa'na (*I.*). An organ with bells.
Or'gano di le'gno (*I.*). (1) A Xylophone (*q.v.*). (2) The flue-work of an organ.
Organo espressi'vo (*I.*). The swell organ.
Or'gano pie'no (*I.*) ⎱ Full organ (see above).
Or'gano ple'no (*I.*) ⎰
Or'gano porta'bile (*I.*). A small portable organ. (See Portative.)
Organi voca'li (*I.*). The vocal organs.
In or'gano (*L.*). An old term for "more than two parts" (from Organum, 2).

Organochor'dium. A combination of pf. and pipe org. invented by Abbé Vogler.

Or'ganum (*L.*). (1) (*Gk.*, *Or'ganon*.) At first, any instrument; later, the organ.

Or'ganum hydrau'licum. Hydraulic (water) organ.
Or'ganum pneumat'icum. Ordinary (wind) organ.

Or'ganum. (2) Early attempts at improvised counterpoint; called also *Diaphony*.

It consisted of 8ves and 5ths (or 4ths) added to the "Plain-song."

Example from Hucbald, abt. 900 A.D.

Tu Pa-tris sem-pi-tern-us es Fi-li-us.

Or'gel (*G.*). Organ.

Or'gel-bälge. Organ-bellows.
Or'gelgehäuse. Organ-case.
Or'gelklang. The tone of an organ.
Or'geln. To play on the organ.
Or'gelpfeife. An organ pipe.
Or'gelpunkt. Organ point. (See Pedal point.)
Or'gelregister. Organ stop.
Or'gelschu'le. An organ "Method."
Or'gelspieler. Organ player.
Or'gelstim'me. A row of organ pipes; a stop.
Or'gelwolf. "Ciphering" on the organ.
Or'gelzug. Organ draw-stop.

ORGE'NI (ORGENYI), Aglaia. Operatic soprano; *b.* Galicia, 1843. *Début*, Berlin Opera, 1865; first appearance in London, Covent Garden, 1866; vocal teacher Dresden Cons., 1886.

Orgue (*F.*). Organ.

Orgue de Barbarie. (1) A hurdy-gurdy. (2) A barrel-organ.
Orgue de salon ⎱ Harmonium.
Orgue expressif ⎰
Orgue à percussion. Harmonium with percussion attachment (Alexandre, Paris).
Orgue plein. Full organ.
Orgue pòrtatif. A portable organ.
Orgue positif. (1) The Choir Organ. (2) A small fixed organ.

Orguette (*F.*). An ancient portable organ.

Orguinette (*F.*). A kind of reed organ played with a crank, with perforated sheets of paper or metal to admit air to the reeds as required.

ORIAN'A, The Triumphs of. "A collection of 25 madrigals in praise of Queen Eliza-

beth," composed by 23 of the most famous musicians of the period.

Orical'chi (*I.*). Brass instruments; the "brass" of an orchestra.

Original' Aus'gabe (*G.*). Original edition, arrangement, setting.

Origin of Music.

Ancient nations ascribed the invention of music to the gods! It is probable that the existence of some form of music is coeval with that of man himself, and that the art was a gradual development determined largely by accident and environment. The following speculations from Moore's *Encyclopædia* are not without interest.

"With respect to the origin of music, one need seek no other cause than the natural constitution of man. He is so formed as to receive a mechanical delight from the perception of sweet and melodious sounds; the laws of concord and discord, and of rhythm, are founded in his nature. He seeks as naturally for the gratification of music as for food to allay his hunger, or for drink to quench his thirst.

Vocal music, or some kind of singing, is practised everywhere, even among the most rude and barbarous nations, but if a model were wanting to suggest the art, it is provided by nature in the sweetness and variety of the singing of birds; which might have prompted men to try the melody of their voices. Man—predisposed to take delight in musical sounds—would also embrace the first hint that might suggest any method of producing them artificially, as the whistling of wind through a hollow reed. The trumpet was an imitation of the horns of animals, which, when blown into, produce a powerful sound. Thus flutes and trumpets, with drums, were the only instruments known in primitive ages. Stringed instruments seem to have been a much later invention."

OR'LOW, Count Gregor V. *B.* 1777; *d.* St. Petersburg, 1826.

Wrote a "History of Music in Italy," (2 vols., 1822).

Ornament. (*G.*, *Verzie'rung*; *F.*, *Ornement*; *I.*, *Ornamen'to*, *Abbellimen'to*, *Abbellitu'ra*.) A grace, an embellishment; an accessory note.

The principal ornaments—*Acciaccatura*, *Anschlag*, *Appoggiatura*, *Arpeggio*, *Mordent*, *Nachschlag*, *Shake*, *Trill*, and *Turn*—are given under their respective names.
The following are also occasionally met with in old music:—

Accents.

Played.

Aspiration.   Beat.

Played.

Cadence, or Cadent.   Cadence liée.

Played.

Backfall. Double Backfall. Balancement.

Played.

Downward Arpeggio. Martellement. Pincé.

Played.

Pincé lié. Port de voix.

Relish. Slide.

In pf. music "groups" of ornamental notes are frequently written. Their performance is in a great measure *ad libitum*; as, however, they are difficult for beginners, various revised editions have been prepared by eminent authorities.

EXAMPLES: (1) Chopin, Valse, Op. 34, No. 1.

Klindworth's Edn.

(2) Chopin, Nocturne, Op. 32, No. 1.

Klindworth's Edn.

&c.

&c.

Von Bulow's edition of Beethoven's pf. works is similarly suggestive.

N.B.—All ornaments and graces are subject to a "wide diversity of intrepretation," and it is becoming more and more the custom of composers to write out all embellishments " in full," *i.e.*, exactly as they should be played. " It is an extremely false taste to overload every performance with a profusion of ornament. The violation of this rule, if it procure, by chance, a momentary applause from a mixed audience, will never insure a lasting reputation."
—*Moore.*

Ornamen'te (*I.*)
Orna'to,-a (*I.*) } Ornamented, embellished; ornate.
Orné (*F.*)

Ornements (*F.*). Ornaments, graces, &c.

ORNITHOPAR'CUS. (Real name **Andreas Vogelsang.**) Native of Memmingen. Wrote "Musicæ activæ micrologus" (1516); translated into English by Dowland, 1609.

Orphar'ion. A variety of the zither (*q.v.*).

Orphéon (*F.*). (1) A male-voice singing society. (2) A piano violin.

Orpheo'reon. Same as **Orpharion** (above).

OR'PHEUS. Fabled son of Apollo; "said to have accompanied the Argonauts on their expedition," 1350 B.C. The classic story of "Orpheus and Eurydice" has often been set to music.

Orpheus with his lute made trees,
And the mountain tops that freeze,
Bow themselves when he did sing;
To his music, plants and flowers
Ever sprung; as sun and showers
There had made a lasting spring.
Every thing that heard him play,
Even the billows of the sea,
Hung their heads and then lay by.
Shakespeare.

ORTH, John. *B.* Bavaria. Pianist and teacher, Boston, Mass., since 1875.
Works: graceful *salon* pf. pieces.

ORTIGUE, Joseph L. d'. Noted writer on Church music; *b.* Vaucluse, 1802; *d.* Paris, 1866.
Founded (with Niedermeyer) a periodical for church music (1857), and edited it 1858-60.

Osan'na (*I.*). Hosanna.

OSBORNE, George Alexander. Pianist; *b.* Limerick, 1806; *d.* 1893. Settled in London, 1848.
Works: a sextet, several fine duets for pf. and vn., and other chamber music; numerous *salon* pieces for pf., &c.

OSCH'WALD (*née* **Wedekind**), **Frau Erica.** (See **Erica Wedekind.**)

Oscillation. (*G.*, *Oszillation'.*) Vibration ; beating.

Oscu'ro (*I.*). Obscure ; dull.

OSGOOD, George L. *B.* Chelsea, Massachusetts, 1844. Settled in Boston as singing teacher, 1872.
Works : " Guide in the Art of Singing," anthems, part-songs, songs, &c.

Osi'a (*I.*). Same as **Ossia** (*q.v.*).

Osservan'za (*I.*). Care, observation, attention.
Con osservan'za } With care and exactness.
Osserva'to }
Sti'le osserva'to. The strict style.

Ossi'a (*I.*). Or ; or else ; otherwise.
Ossi'a più fa'cile. Or else (this) more easy (note or passage).
Ossia indicates an easier or alternative note or passage (which is generally given in smaller type).

ÖS'TEN. (See **Oesten.**)

Os'terlied (*G.*). Easter Hymn.

Ostina'to (*I.*). "Obstinate ; " frequently repeated, continuous.
Bas'so ostina'to. A Ground Bass (*q.v.*).

OSTLERE, May. Contemporary composer of *salon* pf. pieces.

O'SULLIVAN, Dennis. Baritone vocalist ; *b.* San Francisco, 1868 ; *d.* 1908.

OSWALD (Hatch), Arthur L. Baritone vocalist ; *b.* Brighton, 1858 ; Prof. R.A.M., 1886 ; G.S.M., 1896.

OSWALD, James. *B.* Scotland, 1710(11?) ; *d.* 1769. Chamber-composer to Geo. III.
Pub. several collections of Scots tunes.

Ôtez (*F.*). " Off," (as an org. stop).
Ôtez les anches. " Shut off the reeds."
Ôtez la tirasse. "Shut off the pedal coupler."
Ôtez les sourdines. "Take off the mutes."

OTH'MAYER, Caspar. *B.* Amberg, 1515 ; *d.* Nuremberg, 1553.
Wrote several esteemed vocal pieces (motets, songs, &c.).

OTHO. (See **Odo.**)

OTTA'NI, Bernardini. *B.* Bologna, 1735 ; *d.* 1827. Pupil of Padre Martini. Maestro at Bologna and Turin.
Works : 12 operas, 2 oratorios, 46 masses, &c.

Otta'va (*I.*). An octave. Abbn. 8*va* or 8.
All'otta'va. "At the octave ; " an octave higher than written.
Coll' otta'va. "With the octave ; " in octaves.
Otta'va al'ta (8va). (1) The higher octave. (2) An octave higher.
Otta'va bas'sa (8va bas'sa). (1) The lower octave. (2) An octave lower.
Otta'va ri'ma. An Italian 8-lined poetical stanza, each line consisting of 11 syllables.
Otta'va so'pra. The octave above.
Otta'va sot'ta. The octave below.

Ottavi'na. (See **Octavina.**)

Ottavi'no (*I.*) }
Ottavi'no fla'uto (*I.*) } The piccolo.

Ottemo'le (*G.*). An **Octuplet** (*q.v.*).

Ottet'to (*I.*). (See **Octet.**)

ÖT'TINGEN. (See **Oettingen.**)

OT'TO, E. Julius. *B.* Königstein, Saxony, 1804 ; *d.* 1877. Cantor, Kreuzkirche, Dresden, 1830-75 ; condr., Dresden " Liedertafel."
Works : 2 operas, 3 oratorios, masses, &c. ; numerous admirable male choruses and " cycles ; " songs, pf. pieces, &c.

OT'TO, Franz. *B.* Kö igstein, 1809 ; *d.* 1841. Wrote male-voice choruses.

OT'TO, Rudolf K. J. Tenor singer ; *b.* Berlin, 1829. Member Berlin *Domchor.* Teacher Stern Cons., 1852 ; Royal *Hochschule*, 1873.

OT'TO-ALVS'LEBEN (*née* **Alvsleben**), **Melitta.** Operatic soprano ; Dresden, 1842-93. *Prima donna*, Hamburg City Theatre, 1875-6 ; Dresden Court Th., 1877-83.

Otto'ne (*I.*). Brass.
Strumen'ti d'otto'ne. Brass instruments.

Ou (*F.*). Or. (See **Ossia**).

OUDIN, Eugène E. Baritone vocalist ; *b.* New York, 1858 ; *d.* London, 1894. Sang frequently in London (from 1886).

OUDRID Y SEGURA, Cristobal. Composer and condr. ; *b.* Badajoz, 1829 ; *d.* 1877.
Works : over 30 "zarzuelas" (operettas) prod. at Madrid.

Ouïe (*F.*). Soundhole (of a vn., &c.).

OULD, Chas. Noted 'cellist ; *b.* Romford, Essex, 1835.

OULIBICHEF. (See **Ulibisheff.**)

OURY, Madame (*née* **Anna C. de Belleville**). Noted pianist ; *b.* Bavaria, 1808 ; *d.* 1880.

OUSE'LEY, Sir Frederick Arthur Gore. *B.* London, 1825 ; *d.* 1889. Mus.D. Oxon, 1854 ; Prof. of Music, Oxford Univ., 1855 ; Mus.Doc. Cantab., 1862 ; &c.
Works : 2 oratorios (*St. Polycarp, Hagar*), church services, anthems ; "The Psalter," "Anglican Psalter Chants," "Cathedral Services," "Colln. of Anthems ; " organ pieces, chamber music, part-songs, songs ; treatises on Harmony, Counterpoint, Musical Form ; articles in Grove's Dict. ; &c.

Outer parts } The highest and lowest parts
Outer voices } (or voices).

Ouvert (*F.*). Open.
Accord à l'ouvert. A chord on the open strings (of a vn., &c.).
À livre ouvert. At (first) sight.

Ouverture (*F.*) }
Overtu'ra (*I.*) } The instrumental "opening
O'verture (*E.*) } number" of an opera,
Overtür'e (*G.*). } oratorio, or play.

(1) "LULLY," or FRENCH OVERTURE. 1st movement, *Grave* ; 2nd movement, *a Fugue* ; sometimes followed by a *Minuet*. Examples : Handel's *Messiah, Judas,* and *Samson.*
(2) "SCARLATTI," or ITALIAN OVERTURE. 1st movement, *Allegro* ; 2nd movement, *Slow* ; 3rd movement, *Allegro* or *Presto.* Example : Handel's *Athaliah.*
(3) CLASSICAL, or SYMPHONIC OVERTURE. In the form of the 1st movement of a sonata (*q.v.*) or symphony, but without repetition of the 1st part, and generally less developed in the *Free*

Fantasia. Examples : Mozart's *Don Giovanni, Figaro,* &c.; Beethoven's 4 overtures to *Fidelio.* The overture to Mozart's *Zauberflöte* is a fine example of a classical overture combined with a Fugue.

(4) CONCERT OVERTURE. An overture in classical form, not connected with any particular work, but written for concert performance. It is generally of a descriptive, romantic, or program character. Examples : Gade's *Ossian,* Mendelssohn's *Hebrides,* &c.

(5) POTPOURRI OVERTURE. A loosely connected string of melodies from the work ; as most overtures to light and comic operas.

(6) "WAGNERIAN" PRELUDE. A *symphonic poem* treating and blending themes occurring in the musical drama, " to prepare the hearers for the coming action." Examples : All Wagner's later operas.

Overtu'ra di bal'lo (I.). An overture in dance music style.

Overblow. On wind insts., org. pipes, &c., to accidentally produce an "upper partial" (see **Acoustics**) instead of the fundamental note.

Overlapping. (1) Of parts.

A lower part ascending to a higher note than that assigned to a higher part in the previous chord; or *vice versa* in descending.

(2) Of sections.

" It is common in instrumental music to make the end of one section the beginning of the next." This is called " overlapping."

Overspun. " Covered ; " *e.g., Covered strings.*

Overstrung. Applied to pianofortes where additional depth of tone is secured by crossing the longer strings diagonally over or under the others.

Overtone. An "upper partial." See **Acoustics.**)

Ov'vero (I.). Or ; same as **Ossia** (*q.v.*).

O.W. (*G.*). Abbn. for *Oberwerk* (*q.v.*).

OWEN, John (**Owain Alaw**). *B.* of Welsh parents, Chester, 1821 ; *d.* 1883.

Works : oratorio (*Jeremiah*), cantatas (including the 1st Welsh secular cantata, *Prince of Wales,* 1862) ; anthems, glees, collns. of Welsh melodies, &c.

P

P. *P.* or *Ped..* Abbn. of *Pedal.*
In French organ music, P stands for *Positif, i.e.,* Choir organ.

P. or *p.* Abbn. of *Piano ;* soft.

pp. *Pianissimo ;* very soft.
ppp, pppp, or even *ppppp* may be found in modern music to indicate " extremely soft," " scarcely audible."

Paar (*G.*). A pair (of drums, &c.).

PABST, August. *B.* Elberfeld, 1811 ; *d.* 1885. Director Riga Cons.
Three of his operas were performed.

PABST, Paul. Pianist ; son of A. *B.* Königsberg, 1854 ; *d.* 1897. Pf. prof., Moscow Cons., 1878 ; later, Director.

Pacatamen'te (*I.*). Peacefully, placidly, calmly, quietly.

Paca'to (*I.*). Quiet, tranquil, placid,

PACCHIAROT'TI, Gasparo. Celebrated male soprano ; *b.* nr. Ancona, 1744 ; *d.* Padua, 1821. Was a great favourite in London (1778-85 and 1790-1800).

PACH'ELBEL, Johann. Nuremberg, 1653-1706. Orgt. successively at Vienna, Eisenach, Erfurt, Stuttgart, and Nuremberg.
Works : chaconnes, toccatas, chorals, &c., for organ ; pieces for 2 vns. and bass ; &c. His org. chorales are much in the style of Bach.

PACH'ELBEL, Wilhelm H. Son of J. ; *b.* Erfurt, 1685 ; *d.* 1764.
Wrote pieces for organ or clavichord.

PACH'MANN, Vladimir de. Distinguished pianist ; fine interpreter of Chopin ; *b.* Odessa, 1848. Has toured with great success in Russia, Germany, France, England, America, &c.

PACHUL'SKI, Heinrich. Pianist ; *b.* Lasa, Russia, 1859. Pf. prof. Moscow Cons., 1886.
Works : suite for orch. ; numerous pf. pieces ; arrangements of Tschaikowski's works for pf. ; songs, &c.

PACI'NI, Emilio. Brother of G. (below) ; *b.* 1810 ; *d.* nr. Paris, 1898. Librettist ; wrote the libretto of Verdi's *Il Trovatore.*

PACI'NI, Giovanni. Noted opera composer ; *b.* Catania, 1796 ; *d.* Pescia, 1867. Studied at Bologna and Venice. Est. a school of music nr. Lucca, 1835.
Works : over 80 operas (including *Annetta e Lucinda,* his first (1813) and *Saffo,* his best (1840). (The latter, written in 28 days, is still performed.) Also numerous oratorios, cantatas, masses, &c. ; much chamber music, and several arias and duets.

PA'CIUS, Friedrich. Fine violinist ; pupil of Spohr ; *b.* Hamburg, 1809 ; *d.* 1891. Mus.-director, Helsingfors Univ. from 1834. Composed the 1st Finnish opera, 1852.
Works ; 2 operas (including *Loreley,* 1857).

PADEREW'SKI (pron. *Paderess'kĭ*),* **Ignace Jan.** Celebrated pianist ; *b.* Podolia, Poland, 1860. Pupil at Warsaw and Berlin, and afterwards of Leschetitzki at Vienna (1878-83). As a concert pianist he is especially popular in England and the United States.
Works : several pf. pieces, some songs, a fantasia for pf. and orch., a symphony, &c.

Paderewski Fund. Est. by Paderewski after his American tour (1895-6) ; the interest to be devoted to the award of prizes " to composers of American birth."

Padiglio'ne (*I.*). The bell of an inst.
Padiglio'ne Chine'se. The Turkish Crescent.

Padoua'na (*I.*) ⎫
Padova'na (*I.*) ⎬ A *Pavan* (*q.v.*).
Padua'na (*I.*) ⎭

Pæ'an (*Gk.*). A song of invocation or triumph addressed to Apollo before or after a battle.

Pæ'on (*Gk.*). A metrical foot of one long and three short syllables :
| — ∪ ∪ ∪ | or | ∪ — ∪ ∪ | &c.

PAËR, Ferdinando. Operatic composer ; *b.* Parma, 1771 ; *d.* Paris, 1839. Court Capellmeister, Dresden, 1802 ; *Maître de Chapelle* to Napoleon, Paris, 1807.
Wrote 43 operas (*Camilla, ossia il sotteraneo,* 1799, his best), 2 oratorios, a Passion, 10 cantatas, orchl. and military music, pf. variations, &c.

PAESIEL'LO. (See **Paisiello.**)

PAGANI'NI, Niccolò. Famous violinist ; *b.* Genoa, 1782 ; *d.* Nice, 1840. Son of a poor shopkeeper ; appeared in public as a violinist at 11. Ran away from home, 1798, and started concert touring on his own account. Returned home, 1804 ; resumed touring, 1805, "arousing unbounded enthusiasm." Remained in Italy until 1828 ; then visited Vienna, Berlin, Paris, and London (1831). "Within a year he amassed a fortune in Britain." Retired 1834. As a soloist " he was the most wonderful and original of violin players." His technique was marvellous ; and together with his personal eccentricities, his "tricks of virtuosity," and his "dazzling genius," made him the "wonder of his age." His remarkable performances "on a single string" have probably never been equalled.
His compositions for the vn. were not numerous, and they were of an ephemeral character.

PAGE, Arthur J. Orgt. and composer ; *b.* Ipswich, 1846.

PAGE, John. *B.* abt. 1750 ; *d.* London, 1812. Lay clerk, St. George's, Windsor, 1790 ; Gentleman, Chapel Royal ; Vicar-choral, St. Paul's, 1801.
Works : "Harmonia Sacra" (74 anthems in score by Eng. composers, 3 vols.) ; collns. of glees, madrigals, hymns, psalms, &c.

* This is the *correct* pronunciation as given by Paderewski,

PAGE, Nathan C. *B.* San Francisco, 1866.

Pa'gina d'al'bum (*I.*). An album leaf (*q.v.*).

PAINE, John Knowles. Distinguished American orgt. and composer; *b.* Portland, Maine, 1839; *d.* 1906. Studied Berlin, 1858-61. Teacher of music, Harvard Univ., 1862; Professor, 1876 (the first musical professorship in any American Univ.).
Works : an oratorio (*St. Peter*), cantatas, a mass, 2 symphonies, 2 symphonic poems, overtures, chamber music, organ pieces, pf. pieces, songs.

Pair of organs. Old name for an organ "having a complete set of pipes."— *Stainer and Barrett.*

PAISIBLE. Eminent flautist.
Composed overtures, &c., in London from 1690 to 1703.

PAISIBLE, N. Violinist; *b.* Paris, 1745; *d.* (by suicide), 1781.

PAISIEL'LO, Giovanni. Famous opera composer; *b.* Taranto, 1741; *d.* Naples, 1816. Studied Cons. di S. Onofrio, Naples, 1754-59. First comic opera, *La pupilla*, Bologna, 1764. Visited St. Petersburg, 1776, and lived there 8 years "on a princely salary." Maestro to Ferdinand IV, Naples, 1784-99. Napoleon's *Maître de Chapelle*, Paris, 1802-3; again Maestro at Naples, 1803-1815. He was one of the most popular composers of his time.
Works : about 100 operas, of which *La Serva Padrona* (Naples, 1769) is still performed; much church music, 12 symphonies, 6 pf. concertos, chamber music, pf. sonatas, &c.

PALADILHE, Émile. Distinguished French composer; *b.* Montpellier, 1844. Studied Paris Cons.; won *Grand Prix de Rome*, 1860.
Works : operas (*Suzanne*, 1878; *Patrie*, 1885; &c.) ; masses, orch. music, numerous songs, &c.

Palala'ïka. Same as **Balalaïka** (*q.v.*).

Pal'co (*I.*). A stage (of a theatre, &c.).

PALESTRI'NA, Giovanni Pierluigi da. The greatest composer of the Roman Catholic Church and of the "Golden Age of Counterpoint;" *b.* Palestrina, nı. Rome, abt. 1525; *d.* Rome, 1594. Orgt. at Palestrina Cath., 1544; married 1547. At Rome, 1551; maestro at the Lateran, 1555; Santa Maria Maggiore, 1561; St. Peter's (Rome), 1571-94. Married a rich widow, 1581.
Among his most famous works are the *Improperia* or "Reproaches," 1560 (still sung every Good Friday at the Sistine Chapel, Rome), and the *Missa papæ Marcelli* (written, 1565, for the College of Cardinals, to prove that music could be composed which was in every way appropriate for church performance). The success of this famous "Mass" earned for Palestrina the name of the "saviour of music." A complete edition of his works is published by Breitkopf & Härtel in 33 vols. They include over 250 motets, 45 hymns, 68 offertoires, 92 masses, 17 litanies, 35 magnificats, 90 secular and 56 church madrigals, and numerous miscellaneous pieces,

Palestri'nastil (*G.*). In the style of Palestrina ; *a cappella* (*q.v.*).

Palettes (*F.*). White keys (of a pf., &c.) ; *feintes,* black keys.

PALLAVICI'NI (or **-CI'NO**), **Carlo.** *B.* Brescia, 1630; *d.* 1688. Capellmeister, Dresden Italian Opera.
Works : over 20 operas (*La Gerusalemme liberata,* 1688, &c.).

Pallet. A spring valve in the wind chest of an organ, which when pulled down admits wind to a pipe (or pipes).

PALLISER, Esther (real name **Walters**). Contemporary soprano vocalist; *b.* Philadelphia, 1871.

PALLISER, Sybil. Contemporary song composer; *b.* London.

PALLO'NI, Gaetano. Singing teacher; *b.* Camerino, Italy, 1831.
Works : numerous songs and duets.

PAL'ME, Rudolf. Organist; *b.* Barby-on-Elbe, 1834.
Works : org. music, male choruses, songs, &c.

PALMER, Eliz. A. (" **Bessie** "). Contralto ; *b.* London, 1831.

PALMER, Horatio Rd. American teacher, composer, and conductor; *b.* Sherburne, N.Y., 1834.
Works : Methods of Class Teaching, &c. ; collns. of songs and choruses.

PALMER, Mrs. P. (See **Marriott.**)

PALMER, Mrs. R. (See **Emma Wixom.**)

PALO'SCHI, Giovanni. 1824-92 ; of the publishing house of Ricordi, Milan.
Compiled a valuable "General Musical Calendar" (1876).

PALOT'TA, Matteo. Noted contrapuntist ; *b.* Palermo, abt. 1688; *d.* Vienna, 1758.

PAL'SA, Johann. Celebrated horn player ; *b.* Bohemia, 1754; *d.* 1792.

Pam'be. A small Indian drum.

PAN. The god of Nature and "Nature's music."
The nymph Syrinx "whom he was pursuing prayed the Naiades, the nymphs of the water, to change her into a bundle of reeds, just as Pan was laying hold of her, who therefore caught the reeds in his hand, instead of her. The wind moving these reeds backward and forward, occasioned mournful but musical sounds, which Pan perceiving, he cut them down, and made of them reeden pipes." Hence the name Syrinx (*q.v.*).

Pandean pipes. Pan pipes (*q.v.*).

Pando'ra ⎫
Pando're ⎬ (See **Bando'la** and **Bando'ra.**)
Pandou'ra ⎭

Pan'flöte (*G.*) ⎫ A set of graduated reeds
Pans'flöte (*G.*) ⎪ blown by the mouth ;
Pan-pipes ⎬ the earliest compound
Pan's-pipes ⎭ wind inst. known. Also called a *Syrinx.* It was supposed to have been invented by the god *Pan.*
It is still the chief inst. used at "Punch and Judy" shows.

Panharmon'icon. An automatic orchestrion.

Panmelo′dion. A keyboard inst. invented in 1810. "The tone was produced by the friction of wheels on metal bars."

PAN′NY, Jos. Violinist ; *b.* Lower Austria, 1794 ; *d.* 1838.
Works : vn. pieces (including a "scena" written for Paganini), male choruses, &c.

PANOF′KA, Heinrich. Violinist ; *b.* Breslau 1807 ; *d.* 1887. Played in public at 10 ; resided in Paris 1834-44. Singing teacher in London, 1844-52. Afterwards lived in Paris and Florence.
Works : "The Practical Singing Tutor," several vocalises, &c., and numerous vn. pieces.

Panorgue (*F.*). A small harmonium to be attached to a pf.
Panorgue-piano. A combination of pf. and harmonium.

PANSERON, Auguste M. Renowned singing teacher ; Paris, 1796-1859. Won *Grand Prix de Rome*, Paris Cons., 1813 ; Prof. of Solfeggio, 1826 ; of vocalization, 1831 ; of singing, 1836.
Works : Méthode complète de vocalization, several books of *Solfège*, about 200 *Romances* (songs), &c.

Pantal′eon, or **Pantalon.** A kind of dulcimer, invented by Hebenstreit, 1690. It is regarded as one of the precursors of the pianoforte.

Pantalon (*F.*). A movement of a quadrille.

Pan′tomime. (*I.*, *Pan′tomima.*) An entertainment in "dumb-show," *i.e.*, expressed by mimicry and gesticulation without speech or song. It is generally accompanied by instrumental music.

PANZ′NER, Karl. Condr. ; *b.* Teplitz, Bohemia, 1866.

PA′PE, Johann H. Piano maker ; *b.* nr. Hanover, 1789 ; *d.* Paris, 1875.
Introduced improvements in piano making (including "padded hammers").

PAPE, Willy B. Composer of light pf. pieces ; *b.* Mobile (U.S.), 1850.

PAPIER, Rosa. Fine mezzo-soprano ; *b.* nr. Vienna, 1858. Married **H. Paumgartner**, 1881.

Papillons (*F.*). "Butterflies ;" light, graceful piano pieces.

PAPI′NI, Guido. Distinguished violinist ; *b.* nr. Florence, 1847. *Début*, Florence, at 13 ; first London appearance, 1874.
Works : vn. concertos, transcriptions, romances, nocturnes, &c.

PAP′PENHEIM, Eugénie. Soprano singer ; *b.* Austria. *Début*, 1872. Sang with great success in London, 1878-9.

PAP′PERITZ, Benj. Robt. *B.* Saxony, 1826; *d.* 1903. Studied Leipzig Cons. ; teacher of harmony and counterpoint, 1851. Orgt. Nikolaikirche, 1868-99.
Works : organ pieces, choral works, songs.

PAQUE, Guillaume. 'Cellist ; *b.* Brussels, 1825 ; *d.* London, 1876.

PARABOS′CO, Girolamo. Noted organist ; *d.* Venice, 1587.

PARADI′ES (or **PARADI′SI**), **Pietro D.** Harpsichord player ; *b.* Naples, 1710 ; *d.* 1792. Pupil of Porpora. Resided in London as harpsichord teacher for several years (from 1747).
Works : operas, harpsichord sonatas, &c.

PARADIS′, Maria T. von. Pianist, organist, and composer ; blind from her 5th year ; *b.* Vienna, 1759 ; *d.* 1824. Made successful tours to Paris, London, &c.
Works : an opera, a melodrama, an operetta, pf. pieces, songs, &c., all of considerable merit.

PARADI′SI. (See **Paradies**.)

Par′allel. Used of two parts moving upwards or downwards " by the same fixed interval." Latterly the term has been much used instead of "consecutive."

Parallel (or consecutive) Perfect 5ths.

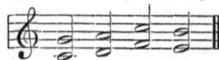

Parallel 8ves.

Parallel Major 3rds.

&c.

Parallel′bewe′gung (*G.*). (1) Similar motion. (2) Parallel motion.
Parallel′tonarten (*G.*). Related keys.

Par′aphrase. An arrangement or transcription of a composition ; generally of a showy and florid character.

PARE′PA-RO′SA (*née* **Parepa de Boyescu′**), **Euphrosyne.** Celebrated soprano ; *b.* Edinburgh, 1836 ; *d.* 1874. *Début* at 16, at Malta. A great favourite in London from her first appearance there, 1857. Married **Carl Rosa**, 1867. She had a sweet and powerful voice with a compass of 2½ octaves.

PARENT, Charlotte F. H. Pianist, teacher, and writer ; *b.* London, 1837. Studied Paris Cons.

Parfait (*F.*). Perfect, complete, true ; strong.
Cadence parfaite. A perfect cadence.
Temps parfait. (1) The strong beat. (2) Triple time.

Pa′ri (*I.*). Equal.
Tem′pi pa′ri. Equal, *i.e.*, "duple" times.
Vo′ci pa′ri. Equal voices.

PARISH-ALVARS, Elias. Noted harpist ; *b.* Teignmouth, 1810 ; *d.* 1849. After successful tours settled in Vienna as chamber harpist to the Emperor, 1847.
Wrote several fine pieces for harp and orch., and for harp solo.

PARISI′NI, Federigo. Bologna, 1825-91.
Works : treatises on harmony, choral singing, &c.

PARKE, John. Fine hautboy player ; *b.* 1745 ; *d.* London, 1829.

PARKE, Wm. Thos. Brother of J.; celebrated hautboy player; *b.* 1762; *d.* 1847.
Wrote "Musical Memories," songs, glees, &c. He extended the compass of the hautboy to G in alt (see *Alt*), E♮ having been the previous highest note.

PARKER, Henry. *B.* London, 1845.
Works: pf. pieces, songs (*Jerusalem*); "The Voice," &c.

PARKER, Horatio Wm. Distinguished American musician; *b.* Auburndale, Mass., 1863. Prof. of music, Yale Univ. 1894. Honorary Mus.D. Cantab., 1902.
Works: oratorios (*Hora novissima*), &c., several cantatas; male choruses, female choruses, orch. music, anthems, pf. pieces, songs, &c.

PARKER, James C. D. *B.* Boston, Mass., 1828. Studied at Leipzig. Settled in Boston, 1854; orgt. for several years to the Handel and Haydn Society.
Works: an oratorio, cantatas, church music; trans. of Richter's "Harmony," &c.

PARKER, Louis N. Composer and dramatist; *b.* Calvados, France, 1852.

PARKER, Wm. Frye. Violinist; *b.* Dunmow, Essex, 1855.

PARKI'NA. (Elizabeth Parkinson.) American soprano; *b.* Southern Missouri, 1881. *Début,* Paris Opéra-Comique, 1902; sang Covent Garden, 1904.

Parlan'do (*I.*) ⎫ "Speaking;" in a decla-
Parlan'te (*I.*) ⎭ matory or "recitative" style (sometimes marked ⏜ or ⌣).
Con u'na cer'ta espressio'ne parlan'te. With a certain "speaking" expression.
Parla'to. Spoken.

PARLOW, Kathleen. Precocious violinist; *b.* Calgary, Canada, 1890.
Début at 7; London *début,* 1907.

Parodi'a (*I.*). A parody; a burlesque.

PAROISSE-POUGIN. (See **Pougin.**)

Paroles (*F.*). Words.
Sans paroles. Without words.

Parolier (*F.*). A writer of words to be set to music.

PARRATT, Henry L. Huddersfield, 1834-1904.
Orgt. Huddersfie'd Parish Church for 42 years.

PARRATT, Sir Walter. Brother of H. L.; *b.* Huddersfield, 1841. Knew Bach's *Well-tempered Clavichord* by heart at 10; orgt. at 11. Orgt. St. George's, Windsor, 1892; knighted, 1892; "Master of the Queen's Musick," 1893. Prof. of Music, Oxford Univ., 1908.
Works: anthems, pf. pieces, org. music, songs, &c.

PARRY, Sir Chas. Hubert Hastings. *B.* Bournemouth, 1848. Mus.Bac.Oxon at 18; M.A., 1874; Choragus to the Univ., 1883; Mus.Doc. Cambridge, 1883 (Oxon, 1884; Dublin, 1891); Director R.C.M., 1894; knighted, 1898. Prof. of Music, Oxford Univ., 1901-8. Made a baronet, 1903.
Works: symphonies, overtures, chamber music, pf. pieces, anthems, songs, &c.; oratorios

(*Judith,* 1888; *Job,* 1892; *King Saul,* 1894; &c.); several cantatas and odes, a *De profundis* for 3 choirs, music to Greek plays; also "Studies of the Great Composers," "The Art of Music," "Summary of Mus. Hist.," &c., and numerous excellent articles in Grove's Dict.

PARRY, John. Welsh bard; *b.* Ruabon; *d.* 1782.
Pub. collections of "Antient Welsh Airs," &c.

PARRY, John ("Bardd Alaw"). *B.* Denbigh, 1776; *d.* 1851. Treasurer, Royal Soc. of Musicians, 1831-49.
Works: "The Welsh Harper," "Cambrian Harmony," and other collections of Welsh music; harp sonatas, glees, songs, &c.

PARRY, John Orlando. Son of preceding; *b.* London, 1810; *d.* 1879. Harpist, pianist, and singer (German Reed Entertainments, 1860-9, &c.).
Wrote comic and sentimental songs.

PARRY, Joseph. *B.* Merthyr Tydvil, 1841; *d.* 1903. Son of a labourer; worked at a puddling furnace at 10. Through the influence of **Brinley Richards** (*q.v.*) entered the R.A.M., 1868. Mus.Bac. Cantab., 1871; Mus.Doc., 1878. Mus. Lecturer, Univ. Coll. of South Wales, Cardiff, 1888.
Works: oratorios (*Emmanuel, Saul of Tarsus*), 4 operas, cantatas, orch. pieces, pf. music, anthems, hymns, songs, &c.

PAR'SIFAL. A "stage-consecrating festival play." Wagner, 1879; 1st performance, 1882.

PARSONS, Albert R. Organist; *b.* Sandusky, Ohio, 1847. Studied Leipzig and Berlin. Settled in New York, 1871.
Works: vocal quartets, songs, translations of musical treatises, &c.

PARSONS, Robert. *B.* Exeter, abt. 1530; *d.* 1570.
Wrote church music, madrigals, &c.
N.B.—There were other musicians of this name.

PARSONS, Sir Wm. *B.* 1746; *d.* London, 1817. Master of the King's Musick, 1786; Mus. Doc. Oxon, 1790(?); knighted 1795.
It was wittily said that "he was knighted more on the score of his merits than because of the merits of his scores."

Part. (1) (*G., Part, Stim'me; F., Partie, Voix; I., Par'te, Vo'ce*). The music allotted to one voice or instrument; as *Soprano part, Flute part, Organ part,* &c. (2) A division of a work.
Part-book. (1) (*G., Stimm'buch.*) A book containing the music of any one vocal or instrumental part. (2) (*G., Chor'buch.*) A book in which all the parts were written (not in score, but separately), on the same opening, so that 4 singers sitting at 4 sides of a table could sing from the same book.

Par'te (*I.*) ⎫
Partie (*F.*) ⎭ (See **Part.**)
Par'te cantan'te (*I.*). Vocal part; the chief melody.
Col'la par'te (*I.*). "With the (principal) part;" the accompanist to follow the solo part.
Par'ti d'accompagnamen'to (*I.*). Accompanying parts (or voices).
Par'ti di ripie'no (*I.*). Supplementary parts.
Parties de remplissage (*F.*). Filling-up parts.

Partial stop. An incomplete org. stop ; one that does not "run through" the complete scale of the organ.

Partial tones, or **Partials.** (See **Acoustics.**)

Partial Dissonance. A dissonance caused by any two partials of a compound tone.

Participating tone. An accessory or auxiliary tone.

Partimen'ti (*I.*). Figured basses (for playing or accompanying from).

Parti'ta (*I.*). (*G., Partie'.*) (1) A Suite (*q.v.*). (2) A set of variations.

Partiti'no (*I.*). A small supplementary score containing parts omitted from the full score.

Partition (*F.*)
Partitur' (*G.*)
Partitu'ra (*I.*) } A full score. (See **Score.**)
Partizio'ne (*I.*)

Partition d'orchestre (*F.*). Full orchestral score.
Partition piano et chant (*F.*). A vocal score with pf. accompaniment.
Partitu'ra d'orchestra (*I.*). Full orchl. score.

Part-music. Music (especially vocal music) in 2 or more parts.

Part-song. A piece for 3 or more voices, in which the melody is the principal part and the other parts of the nature of chordal accompaniment.

Like the *Madrigal,* the part-song may have any number of voices to each part ; but the style is essentially *harmonic* rather than *contrapuntal.* The *Glee* differs from the part-song in having only a *solo* voice to each part.

Part-writing. Writing in parts.

Part-writing, as we now understand it, is the fusion of the best features of counterpoint with the resources of modern harmony. Bach and Handel were the first great composers to initiate modern part-writing. The *spirit* of counterpoint is retained by making each part interesting and melodious ; but all sorts of chords and progressions are freely introduced. It is sometimes called "Free Counterpoint" as opposed to "Strict Counterpoint."

Pas (*F.*). (1) A step ; a dance. (2) Not.

Pas de charge. A double quick march.
Pas de deux. A dance for two performers.
Pas ordinaire. Ordinary march time.
Pas redoublé. A quick step ; quick march.
Pas seul. A dance for one performer.
Pas trop lent. Not too slow.
Pas trop vite. Not too quick.

PASCAL, Florian. Pen-name of **J. Williams** (*q.v.*).

PASCH, Oskar. Orgt. and singing teacher ; *b.* Frankfort-on-Oder, 1844.

Works : a symphony, oratorios, motets, vaude-villes, &c.

PASCUC'CI, Giovanni C. Composer of light operas ; *b.* Rome, 1841.

PASDELOUP, Jules E. Fine conductor ; *b.* Paris, 1819 ; *d.* 1887. Student, afterwards Prof., Paris Cons. Organized the symphony concerts of the "Société des jeunes élèves du Cons." (1851), which afterwards became the "Popular Classical Concerts" at the "Cirque d'hiver."

These were " a pioneer series of good, cheap, popular concerts," and the best classic music

was performed. They were afterwards superseded by the concerts of Colonne and Lamoureux.

PASH'ALOFF, Victor N. Composer of popular Russian songs ; 1841-85.

PASMORE, Henry B. *B.* Jackson, Wisconsin, 1857. Studied in Leipzig and London. Settled in San Francisco as organist, singing teacher, &c.

Paspy. Same as **Passepied** (*q.v.*).

PASQUA'LI, Nicolo. *B.* Italy, abt. 1718 ; *d.* Edinburgh, 1757.

Works : " Thorough-bass ; " 12 overtures for horns ; vn. sonatas ; trios for 2 vns., viola, and basso-continuo ; &c.

PASQUÉ, Ernst. Baritone singer ; *b.* Cologne, 1821 ; *d.* 1892. Début Mayence, 1844. Stage manager, Weimar, 1856-72.

Works : a "Geschichte des Theaters zu Darmstadt, 1559-1710," &c.

PASQUI'NI, Bernardo. Famous organist ; *b.* Tuscany, 1637 ; *d.* 1710. Organist, S. Maria Maggiore, Rome ; chamber musician to Prince G. Borghese. Durante was his pupil.

Works : an oratorio, 2 operas, toccatas and suites for Clavecin, &c.

Passaca'glia (*I.*)
Passaca'glio (*I.*)
Passacal'le (*S.*)
Passagal'lo (*I.*) } (*G., Gas'senhauer.*) A stately dance in triple time, generally constructed on a Ground Bass. Bach's *Passacaglia* in C minor for the organ is a notable work ; fine examples may also be found in Handel's Harpsichord Suites.
Passecaille (*F.*)
Passe-rue (*F.*)

Passage. (*G., Gang ; I., Passag'gio ; F., Passage.*) (1) A (short) melodic or harmonic portion of a piece. (2) A figure or embellishment. (3) A run. (4) A change of key.

Scale passage. A run ; a series of notes in scalewise progression.
Notes de passage (*F.*). Grace notes, embellishments.

Passage-boards. Boards in an organ on which the tuner can walk so as to reach the pipes or mechanism.

Passamez'zo (*I.*) } A lively dance in triple
Passepied (*F.*) } time, the precursor of the *Minuet* (*q.v.*). It is said to have been invented in Bretagne.

Pas'send (*G.*). Suitable, convenient ; fit.

Passing. Transient, non-essential.

Passing discord. (1) A dissonant passing-note (see below). (2) A transient dissonant chord.
Passing modulation. A transient modulation.
Passing shake. A short trill (*q.v.*).

Passing notes. Notes " passing," generally by step, from one essential note to another.

Passing notes may be (1) accented or unaccented ; (*b*) diatonic or chromatic ; (*c*) consonant or dissonant. Accented passing notes are also called " notes of transition." Macfarren includes among passing notes (1) Appoggiaturas and acciaccaturas (which, if unprepared, he calls "passing notes by skip ")" ; (2) Changing notes ; (3) Hanging notes. Curwen includes the name "waving" notes (see the following examples) :—

(a) Unaccented, dissonant ; (b) Accented, consonant ; (c) and (d) Dissonant ; (e) Hanging ; (f) Waving (downward) ; (g) Waving (upward) ; (h) Changing note ; (j) Chromatic ; (k) Diatonic and chromatic ; (l) by skip in tenor ; (m) Chromatic waving.

N.B.—In French text books, *waving notes* are called *broderies*. Anticipations are also classed by many theorists among passing notes.

Passion. (*I., Passio'ne.*)
The story of Christ's sufferings and death, as told in the four Gospels, is recited in Roman Catholic services during Holy week. It was originally chanted by three priests ; harmonized passages were introduced in the 16th cent. (the oldest setting being by Richd. Davy). In the Lutheran services Chorales and reflective passages were added, till the *Passions* became complete oratorios.
The finest is Bach's *St. Matthew Passion*. Works in similar style are now sung in Anglican churches.

Passio'ne (*I.*).   Passion ; fervour ; deep feeling.
Con passio'ne.
Passionatamen'te
Passiona'te
Passiona'to,-a
} In a fervent, impassioned style.
Passionné (*F.*).   Impassioned, fervent.

Passion-play.   A dramatic form of the Passion with stage setting and action.
The most renowned Passion play is the one given at Oberammergau, but this is not by any means the only one.
" In the village of Selzach, in the Canton of Soleure, a passion play is enacted every Sunday during the entire season. The actors to the number of 400 are all inhabitants of Selzach and the neighbouring villages. There are no grand scenic effects nor talented acting, as at Oberammergau, but the sacred scenes are produced simply and faithfully with great effect. The singing and music are much above the average, and the performers are all chosen for their fine physique."—*Daily News.*

Pas'so (*I.*).   A step.
Pas'so a cin'que.   A dance for 5 performers.
Pas'so ordina'rio.   Common time.
Passo raddoppia'to,   A quick step.

Passu'na.   Same as **Posaune** (*q.v.*).
Passy-measure (*Old E.*).   A corruption of *Passamez'zo* (*q.v.*).
PA'STA (*née* **Negri**), **Giuditta.**   Celebrated operatic soprano ; b. Como, 1798 ; d. 1865. Her *début* (1815) was not a success, but after further study she reappeared (Paris, 1822) as a " vocal phenomenon."
Her voice from 1822-29 was unrivalled, and the parts of *La Sonnambula, Norma,* and *Anna Bolena* were specially composed for her.

Paste'te (*G.*)
Pastic'cio (*I.*)
Pastiche (*F.*)
} A "patch-work" ("pie") composition (opera, cantata, &c.), made up of the works of different composers, or detached fragments from the same composer. (Also *G., Flick'oper.*)

Pas'toral
Pastorale (*F.*)
Pastora'le (*I.*)
} (1) A melody in rustic style, generally in 6-8 (or 12-8) time. (2) A cantata, or operetta, based on rural incidents. (3) An instrumental piece imitating or suggesting pastoral or rural scenes ; as Beethoven's *Pastoral Symphony* (1808).
Pastorel'la (*I.*)
Pastorelle (*F.*)
} A short pastoral.
Pastoral organ-point.   The tonic and dominant sustained together to form a kind of *Drone-bass.*

Pastori'ta (*I.*).   (1) A shepherd's pipe. (2) The *Nachthorn* (*q.v.*).
Pasto'so,-a (*I.*).   Mellow, soft.
Pastourelle (*F.*).   (1) A shepherdess. (2) A movement of a quadrille. (3) A pastoral.

Pate'tica,-o (*I.*)
Pathétique (*F.*)
Pat(h)e'tisch (*G.*)
} Pathetic ;   *e. g.,* Beethoven's *Sonate pathétique,* Tschaikowsky's *Pathetic Symphony.*
Pateticamen'te (*I.*)
Pathétiquement (*F.*)
} Pathetically.

PATEY (*née* **Whytock**), **Janet M.**   "The foremost English contralto from 1870 to 1894 ;" b. London, 1842 ; d. 1894.
Sang Worcester Festival, 1866 ; married John Patey (bass vocalist), 1866 ; thenceforward sang at all the chief festivals and concerts.

Patimen'to (*I.*).   Grief, suffering, pain.
Con espressio'ne di patimen'to.   With plaintive, mournful expression.

Patter-song.   A humorous song characterised by rapidly enunciated words on repeated notes.

PATTERSON, Annie W.   B. Lurgan, Ireland, 1868. Mus. Doc. Royal Univ. of Ireland, 1889.

PATTERSON, Alexander.   Baritone vocalist ; b. Glasgow, 1847.

PATON, Mary Ann (Mrs. Wood).   Soprano singer ; b. Edinburgh, 1802 ; d. 1864.
Sang in public at 8 ; *début,* Covent Garden, 1822. Created the part of "Rezia," Weber's *Oberon,* Drury Lane, 1826.

Patouille (*F.*).   A Xylophone (*q.v.*).

PAT'TI, Adelina. **(Adela Juana Maria.)**
Great soprano singer ; *b.* Madrid, 1843.
Début, New York at 16 ; London, Covent Garden,
at 18 ; Paris at 19. Married the Marquis de
Caux, 1868. Her second husband, the tenor
Nicolini, died in 1898 ; she married Baron
Cederström, a Swedish nobleman, 1899.
" Her voice is of wide compass and matchless
sweetness, wonderfully flexible, and perfectly
even throughout."

PAT'TI, Carlotta. Charming concert soprano :
sister of Adelina ; *b.* Florence, 1840 ;
d. Paris, 1899. *Début*, New York, 1861.
Married the 'cellist De Munck, 1871.

PAT'TISON, John N. American concert
pianist ; *b.* Niagara Falls, 1845.
Works : orch. pieces, and numerous pf. pieces.

PATTISON, Thos. Mee. *B.* Warrington, 1845.
Works : cantatas, anthems, &c.

PAU'ER, Ernst. *B.* Vienna, 1826 ; *d.* 1905.
Director, Mayence Musical Societies,
1847-51 ; settled in London, 1851 ;
Prof. of pf. R.A.M., 1859 ; Prof.
National Training School, 1867 ; R.C.M.
1883-96.
Works : Primers on "Musical Forms," " Pf.
Playing," "The Beautiful in Music ; " numerous
editions of classical pf. pieces, and arrangements
for pf. of classical symphonies and overtures ;
also original pianoforte studies and solos,
chamber music, &c.

PAU'ER, Max. Pianist and teacher ; son of
E. ; *b.* London, 1866. Pf. Prof. Cologne
Cons., 1887 ; chamber virtuoso to the
Grand Duke of Hesse, 1893 ; Pf. Prof.
Stuttgart Cons., 1897.
Works : pf. pieces and arrangements.

Pau'ken (*G.*). (1) Kettledrums. (2) To
thump on the piano. (3) To speechify.
Pau'kenklang) Sound of a kettledrum
Pau'kenschall)
Pau'kenschlägel. Kettle-drum stick.
Pau'kenschlä'ger) Kettle drummer.
Pau'ker)
Pau'kenwirbel. Roll on a kettledrum.

PAUL, Dr. Oscar. *B.* Freiwaldau, 1836 ; *d.*
1898. Lecturer, Leipzig Univ., 1866 ;
teacher in the Cons., 1869.
Works : trans. of Boetius' "De Musica," "Lehrbuch der Harmonik," "Geschichte des Claviers,"
"Handlexikon der Tonkunst" (1873), &c.

PAUL, St.) Oratorio by Mendelssohn ;
PAULUS) produced 1836.

PAU'MANN, Conrad. Born blind, Nuremberg, abt. 1410 ; *d.* 1473.
"Author of the oldest extant organ book"
(exercises, preludes, &c).

PAUM'GARTNER, Dr. Hans. *B.* 1844 ; *d.*
Vienna, 1896. Chorusmaster, Vienna
Court Opera ; esteemed pianist and
mus. critic.
Works : chamber music, songs, pf. pieces.

PAUR, Emil. Conductor ; *b.* Czernowitz,
1855. Studied Vienna Cons. Capellmeister, Leipzig City Th., 1891. Conductor Boston Symphony Orch., 1893-8 ;
New York Philharmonic Concerts, 1898.
Director National Cons., New York,
1899 (succeeding Dvorak).
Works : vn. pieces, pf. pieces, songs.

PAUR, Marie (*née* **Bürger**). Pianist ; wife
of preceding ; *b.* Gengenbach, Black
Forest, 1862 ; *d.* 1899.

Pau'ra (*I.*). Dismay, fear.
Pauro'so. Fearful, timid.

Pau'sa (*L.*). A rest.

Pa'usa (*I.*). (1) A rest. (2) A hold ($\curvearrowright$).
Lun'ga pa'usa. A long rest or pause.
Pa'usa genera'le. A pause or rest for all the per-
formers.

Pause (*F.* and *G.*). (1) A rest or pause.
(2) A semibreve rest. (3) A bar's rest.
Demi-pause (*F.*). A minim rest.
Gan'ze Pau'se (*G.*). A semibreve rest.
G. P., or *General' Pau'se* (*G.*). A rest for all the
performers.
Hal'be Pau'se (*G.*). Minim rest.

PAU'WEIS, Jean E. Violinist ; Brussels,
1768-1804. Conductor Brussels Opera,
1794.
Works : 3 operas, a vn. concerto, 6 vn. duets, &c.

Pavan') A stately dance in 2-2 or 3-4
Pava'na (*I.*)) time, said to have been
Pavane (*F.*)) invented at Padua.

Paventa'to (*I.*)) Fearful, timorous ; with
Pavento'so (*I.*)) anxiety.

PAVE'SI, Stefano. *B.* Casaletto Vaprio,
1779 ; *d.* 1850. Maestro, Crema Cath.,
1818.
Works : over 60 operas (*Ser Marcantonio*, 1810),
symphonies, church music, &c.

Pavillon (*F.*). The "bell" of a wind inst.
Flûte à pavillon. An organ stop, the pipes of which
have a bell-shaped top.
Pavillon chinois. A number of crescent-shaped plates
hung with little jingling bells, and attached to a
staff. Also called a Turkish Crescent.
Pavillon en l'air. A direction to horn players to "turn
the bell upwards."

PAXTON, Stephen. Glee composer ; *b.*
1735 ; *d.* London, 1787.

PA'YER, Hieronymus. *B.* nr. Vienna, 1787 ;
d. 1845. Teacher of pf. and singing,
Paris, 1825 ; Conductor Paris German
Opera, 1831-2 ; Capellmeister, Joseph-
stadt Th., Vienna, 1832-8.
Works : operas, operettas, masses, chamber
music, org. pieces, pf. pieces, &c.

PAYNE, Arthur W. Violinist and Condr. ;
b. London, 1866.

PAZ. (See **Valle de Paz.**)

PEACE, Albert Lister. Distinguished orgt. ;
b. Huddersfield, 1844. Orgt. Holmfirth
Parish Church at 9 ; Mus.Doc. Oxon,
1875. Orgt. Glasgow Cath., 1873 ; St.
George's Hall, Liverpool (succeeding
Best), 1897.
Works : church music, cantatas, org. pieces, &c.

Peal. (1) A " ring " of bells. A set of bells
tuned to successive notes of the major
scale and hung for the special requirements of change ringing. (2) A series
of " changes " rung on such a set of
bells.

Pean. A Pæan (*q.v.*).

PEARCE, Chas. Wm. *B.* Salisbury, 1856. Mus.Doc. Cantab., 1884. Dean, Trinity Coll., London, 1891 ; Hon. Treasurer Union of Musical Graduates, 1894 ; Prof. of Harmony, G.S.M., 1898. Director of Examinations, T.C.L., 1908.
Works : church cantatas, services, anthems, org. pieces ; "Students' Counterpoint," "Composers' Counterpoint," "Organ Acct. to the Psalms," and several other text-books.

PEARCE, Stephen A. *B.* London, 1836 ; *d.* 1900. Mus.Doc. Oxon, 1864. Settled in America, 1872. Orgt. New York (1879-95), and contributor to several musical journals.
Works : an opera, an oratorio, orch. pieces, cantatas, songs, a "Dict. of Mus. Terms," &c.

PEARSALL, Robert Lucas de. *B.* Clifton, 1795 ; *d.* 1856.
Works : madrigals, glees, part-songs, choral songs, a Catholic Hymn-book, &c.

PEARSON, H. Hugo. (See **Pierson.**)

PEARSON (PEERSON, or PIERSON), Martin. Composer ; *b.* nr. Cambridge, abt. 1590 ; *d.* abt. 1650.

PEARSON, Mrs. W. J. K. (Mad. Kirkby Lunn). Mezzo-soprano ; *b.* Manchester, 1873.

PEARSON, Wm. Webster. *B.* Bishop Auckland, 1839.
Works : org. music, pf. music, songs, numerous part-songs, &c.

PEASE, Alf. H. Noted American pianist ; *b.* Cleveland, Ohio, 1838 ; *d.* 1882. Studied Berlin.
Works : orch. pieces, numerous pf. pieces, songs.

PECHATSCHEK, François. Violinist and composer ; *b.* Vienna, 1793 ; *d.* 1840.

Ped. Abbn. of *Pedal.*

Ped'al. (*G., Pedal'; F., Pédale ; I., Peda'le.*) In general, any mechanism controlled by the foot (or feet).
Balance swell-pedal. An org. swell pedal which remains at rest wherever the foot leaves it.
Combination pedal) An org. pedal which acts upon a
Composition pedal) number of stops together, or, occasionally, on one special stop.
Crescendo pedal. An org. pedal which gradually brings on the full power of the organ.
Damper pedal) The "right" pedal of the pf. ; also
Forte pedal) called the "open," "loud," or "extension" pedal.
Harp pedal. Name sometimes given to the "soft" pedal of the pf.
Inverted pedal. (See *Pedal-point*, below).
Loud pedal) (See *Damper pedal*, above).
Open pedal)
Organ pedal. (1) A foot-key on the organ. (2) The whole pedal keyboard.
Pedal-action. The mechanism connected with a set of pedals.
Pedal-board. Same as *Pedal-keyboard* (*q.v.*).
Pedal coupler. A coupler connecting one of the manuals of an organ with the pedals.
Pedal-keyboard. A complete set of pedals, including from 30 to 32 foot-keys.
Pedal-organ. All the pipes and stops connected with the pedals.
Pedal-piano. A pf. with a pedal keyboard attached.
Pedal-point (or simply *Pedal*). (*F., Pédale.*) A sustained note (generally in the bass part) which is continued through varying harmonies either consonant or dissonant with it. The "Pedal" is

generally the Tonic or Dominant (or both) ; but modern composers occasionally employ other notes as pedals. A pedal in an upper part is called an "Inverted Pedal."
Piano pedal.) The " left " pedal of the pf.
Soft pedal.)
Swell pedal. A pedal which controls the "shutters " of the swell-box of an organ, producing effects of *crescendo, diminuendo, p, f,* &c.

Pedal' (*G.*). Pedal. Plur., *Peda'le.*
Pedal'bezeich'nungen. Marks to indicate pedalling.
Pedal' Cla'ves)
Pedal'claviatur' }The pedal keyboard of an organ.
Pedal'klaviatur')
Peda'le dop'pelt. Double pedals ; with both feet at once (org. or pf.).
Pedal'flügel. A grand pf. with pedal-board attachment.
Pedal'harfe. A pedal harp. (See *Harp.*)
Pedal'pfeife A pedal pipe.
Pedal'ton (*I.*). (1) A pedal note. (2) A fundamental tone on a brass inst.
Pedal'tritt) A pedal stop.
Pedal'zug)

Pédale (*F.*). Pedal. Plur., *Pédales.*
Clavier des pédales. Pedal keyboard.
Pédale a chaque mesure. Press down the "loud" pf. pedal at the beginning, and release it at the end of each measure (bar).
Pédales de combinaison. Composition pedals. (See *Ped'al.*)
Petite pédale. The " soft " pedal (pf.).

Peda'le (*I.*). Pedal. Plur., *Peda'li.*
Col peda'le e u'na cor'da. With both pf. pedals down.
Peda'le dop'pio. Double pedals ; with both feet at once (org. or pf.).
Peda'le d'or'gano. Organ pedals.
Ped. a tut'ta le battu'te) Press the right pf. pedal at
Peda'le a o'gni battu'ta } (the beginning of) each measure (or fresh chord).
Peda'li) A pedal keyboard.
Pedalier'a)

Pedalier') A set of pedals attached to a
Pédalier (*F.*) } pf., and acting on the bass
Pedal'ion) strings.

Pedal-sign. When the right pf. pedal is to be pressed down the abbn. *Ped.* is used ; when released, the sign ✳.

Pedant'isch (*G.*). Pedantic.

PEDRELL', Felipe. Noted Spanish musician and writer ; *b.* Tortosa, 1841. Prof. of Musical Hist. and Æsthetics, Madrid Royal Cons., 1894.
Works : numerous treatises, including a "Diccionario Tecnico de la Musica ;" 5 operas, a dramatic trilogy, orch. music, church music, songs, &c. Also valuable historical writings and editions.

PEDROT'TI, Carlo. Operatic composer ; Verona, 1817-93. Director Turin Cons., and Condr. Royal Th., 1868 ; Director Liceo Rossini, Pesaro, 1882.
Works : nearly 20 operas (*Lina,* 1840 ; *Tutti in maschera,* or *Les Masques,* 1856 ; &c.) ; church music, romances, &c.

Peg. (*G., Wir'bel ; F., Cheville ; I., Bi'schero.*) Tuning peg (of a vn., &c.).

Pe'gli (*I.*). Abbn. of *Per gli,* "for the."

Pek'tis. A Greek lute or dulcimer.

Pel (*I.*). Contraction of *per il,* " for the."
Pel mandoli'no. For the mandolin.

PÉLISSIER, Harry G. Song composer ; *b.* Finchley (London), 1874.

PELLEGRI'NI, Felice. Basso buffo ; *b.* Turin, 1774 ; *d.* 1832. Prof. of singing, Paris Cons., 1829.

PELLEGRI'NI, Giulio. Bass vocalist ; *b.* Milan, 1806 ; *d.* 1858. *Début*, Turin, at 16.

Pellito'ne (*I.*). A kind of bombardon.

Pel'lo (*I.*). *Per lo,* " for the."

PEM'BAUR, Joseph. *B.* Innsbruck, 1848. Director Innsbruck Music School, 1875.
Works : masses (for male chor. and orch., and for mixed voices), a successful opera (*Ziguener-leben*), orch, pieces, songs, &c.

PEÑA y GONI, Antonio. *B.* San Sebastian, 1846 ; *d.* 1896. Mus. critic of the Madrid *Imparcial* for over 30 years. Champion of Wagner ; friend of Wagner and Gounod.
Wrote a "Hist. of Opera in Spain ; " composed the "Basque National Anthem," pf. pieces, &c.

PENDLETON, Mrs. W. F. (See **Blauvelt, Lillian.**)

PENFIELD, Smith Newell. Prominent American musician ; *b.* Oberlin, Ohio, 1837. Settled in New York, 1882. President Music Teachers' National Association, 1885.
Works : Church music, pf. pieces, songs, &c.

Penillion singing. Originally, improvised Welsh singing.
In modern practice its improvised character is practically obsolete.

Pen'na (*I.*). " A feather ; " a quill, a plectrum.

PEN'NA, Frederic. Baritone vocalist ; *b.* London, 1831.

PEN'NA, Lorenzo. *B.* Bologna, 1613; *d.* 1693.
Wrote masses, psalms, &c., and treatises on music.

Pen'nant. The "hook " of a quaver (♫).

Penorçon (*F.*). An obsolete form of guitar.

Pensiero'so (*I.*) ⎫
Pensif,-ive (*F.*) ⎬ Pensive, thoughtful.
Penso'so (*I.*) ⎭

Pen'tachord. (1) An inst. with 5 strings. (2) A diatonic scale of 5 notes.

Pentam'eter ⎫
Pentame'tro (*I.*) ⎬ In poetry, a line of 5 feet.

Pen'tatone. An interval of 5 whole tones ; an augmented 6th.

Pentaton'ic scale. A scale of 5 notes.
The pentatonic scale is common to many ancient nations, and is still used by the Chinese. It is a characteristic of many old *Scotch* tunes. It is essentially the same as the modern major scale with the 4th and 7th (*fa* and *te*) omitted :

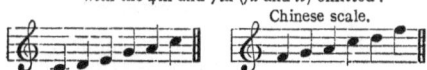

The " black " keys of the pf., starting on F♯, give the pentatonic scale.

Pen'te (*Gk.* " five "). A quint (*q.v.*).

PEPO'LI, Countess. (See **Alboni.**)

PEPPERCORN, Gertrude. Pianist ; *b.* West Horsley, Surrey, 1878.

PE'PUSCH, John Christopher. *B.* Berlin, 1667 ; *d.* 1752. Settled in London, 1700 ; in turn violinist, cembalist, and composer at Drury Lane. One of the founders of the "Academy of Antient Music," 1710. Orgt. and composer to the Duke of Chandos, 1712 (preceding Handel) ; Mus.Doc. Oxon, 1713 ; for several years Director Lincoln's Inn Th. ; Orgt. Charterhouse, 1737-52. He was "a learned but conservative musician."
Works : " A Treatise on Harmony," masques, ballad-operas, odes, &c. His most celebrated work is *The Beggars' Opera,* a setting of Gay's words to popular ballads, &c.

PE'PUSCH, Mrs. J. C. (See **Epine.**)

Per (*L.*). By.
Per ar'sin et the'sin. By reversal of accents. (See *Canon.*)
Per augmentatio'nem. By augmentation (*q.v.*).
Per diminutio'nem. By diminution (*q.v.*).
Per inversio'nem. By inversion (*q.v.*).
Per rec'te et re'tro. (See *Canon.*)

Per (*I.*). By, for, through.
Per fini're. For finishing; to finish (with).
Per il fla'uto solo. For solo flute.
Per il violi'no. For the violin.
Per interval'li giu'sti. By exact intervals (as in canonic imitation).
Per l'or'gano. For organ.
Per la misu'ra si con'ta nel Lar'go sem'pre quat'tro semicro'me, ciò è ; ♩♩♩♩ Count the time in the *Largo* in groups of 4 semiquavers. (Beethoven, Sonata, Op. 106.)
Per o'gni tem'pi. (Suitable) for any occasion.

PER'ABO, J. Ernst. Pianist and teacher ; *b.* Wiesbaden, 1845. Studied Leipzig Cons. Settled in Boston (U.S.), 1866.
Works : pf. pieces, transcriptions and arrangements for pf., &c.

Percussion. (*I., Percussio'ne.*) " Striking together." (See **Suspension.**)
Percussion instruments. Drums, gongs, triangle, &c. The pianoforte may be regarded as the highest type of percussion inst.
Percussion stop. An ingenious mechanism in some harmoniums whereby a small hammer strikes the reed at the moment of pressing the key, thus securing prompt " speech."

PERCY, John. Composed the song "Wapping Old Stairs ; " *b.* abt. 1749; *d.* 1797.

Perden'do (*I.*) ⎫ " Losing itself ; "
Perden'dosi (*I.*) ⎬ softer and slower;
Perden'do le for'ze (*I.*) ⎭ dying away.
Perden'dosi po'co a po'co. Dying away by degrees.

Per'egrine Tone. A "foreign" tone added to the eight regular Plain-song tones. (See **Mode.**)

PERE'IRA, Domingos N. *B.* Lisbon ; *d.* 1729. Maestro Lisbon Cath.
Works : requiems, responses, villancicos, &c.

PEREPELIT'ZIN, Polycarp de. Russian colonel ; *b.* Odessa, 1818.
Works : a "Dict. of Music," an "Illustrated Hist. of Mus. in Russia," &c.

PE'REZ, Davide. *B.* (of Spanish parents), Naples, 1711 ; *d.* 1778. Maestro Palermo Cath., 1739 ; Palermo Court Orch., 1740-8 ; Court Th., Lisbon,1752.
Works : 30 operas (*Siroe*, 1741 ; *Demofoonte*, &c.); church music, &c.

PERFALL', Karl von. Munich, 1824-1907. Conductor Munich Liedertafel, 1850 ; founded the "Oratorio Soc.," 1854. Intendant Munich Court Th. (1867-93).
Works : 4 operas, cantatas and melodramas, fine songs, &c.

Perfect. (*G., Rein ; F., Parfait : I., Perfet'to.*) Complete.
Perfect cadence. A full close. (See *Cadence.*)
Perfect concords } Unison, perfect 4th, perfect 5th,
Perfect consonances } and octave.
Perfect fifth. A fifth comprising 3 whole tones and 1 semitone (or 7 semitones).
Perfect fourth. A fourth comprising 2 whole tones and 1 semitone (or 5 semitones).
Perfect octave. A complete octave (12 semitones).
Perfect time. An old name for triple time. In medieval music, the division of the Breve into 3 semibreves.
Perfect triad. Name sometimes given to a major common chord (as *d m s*).

Perfect Method. In Tonic Sol-fa, the proper notation of a change of key by means of bridge-notes. (See **Imperfect Method.**)

Perfet'to (*I.*). Perfect, complete.
Tem'po perfet'to. Triple time.

PER'GER, Rd. von. *B.* Vienna, 1854. Pupil of Brahms. Director Rotterdam Cons., 1890-5 ; Condr. Vienna Gesellschafts-Concerte, 1895.
Works : opera, *Der Richter von Granada*, Cologne, 1889 ; a vn. concerto, chamber music, a vaudeville, &c.

PERGOLE'SI (or PERGOLE'SE), Giovanni Battista. Celebrated composer ; *b.* Jesi, Papal States, Jan. 4, 1710 ; *d.* Pozzuoli, Mar. 16, 1736. Studied under Durante and Feo, Cons. dei Poveri di Jesu Cristo, Naples. Became famous through his *Solemn Mass* performed after the great Naples earthquake (1731), and the opera buffa *La Serva Padrona* (Naples, 1733).
Works : several operas (none very successful during his life except *La Serva Padrona*) ; a fine *Stabat Mater* (finished 5 days before his death) ; masses, kyries, and much other church music (including an oratorio, *La Nativita*) ; 30 trios for vns. and bass, cantatas, a vn. concerto, &c.

PE'RI, Jacopo. Composer of the "first opera." *B.* of noble family, Florence, abt. 1560 ; *d.* there abt. 1633. Maestro at the courts of Ferdinando I and Cosimo II de' Medici, and (from 1601) at the Court of Ferrara. He was one of the "distinguished circle" who met at the houses of the Counts Bardi and Corsi to discuss the revival of ancient Greek declamation. Their efforts resulted in the "New style" of composition. (See **Bardi, Caccini, Cavaliere,** and **Galilei.**) The music to *Dafne*, 1594(97?), was written by Peri, Caccini, and Corsi. This was the first "drama with music" in the new ("monodic") style, and

was the precursor of Peri's *Euridice* (Florence, 1600) which is regarded as the "first opera." (See **Opera.**)
Peri also wrote madrigals, &c.

PE'RI, Achille. Reggio, Southern Italy, 1812-80.
Works : about 10 operas (*Circe, Rienzi*, &c.), and a Biblical drama, *Giuditta.*

Périgourdine. An old Flemish dance, of cheerful character, in triple time.

Pe'riod (*E.*)
Periode (*F.*) } A period. (See **Metrical**
Perio'do (*I.*) } **Form.**)
Pe'riod'enbau (*G.*). The construction and arrangement of melodic periods.

Periodicals, Musical. (See **Musical Periodicals.**)

PERKINS, Chas. W. *B.* Birmingham, 1855. Orgt. Birmingham Town Hall, 1888.

PERKINS, Henry S. American conductor and critic ; *b.* Stockbridge, Vermont, 1833. Founded the Chicago National Coll. of Music, 1890.
Works : collections of songs, hymns, &c. ; vocal quartets and songs.

PERKINS, Julius Edson. Brother of H. S. ; *b.* Stockbridge, 1845 ; *d.* Manchester, England, 1875. Bass singer ; *début* 1868 ; *Primo basso*, Italian opera, London, 1873 ; married Marie Roze, 1874.

PERKINS, William O. Brother of preceding ; *b.* Stockbridge, 1831 ; settled in Boston (U.S.) as conductor, &c. D. 1902.
Works : about 40 collns. of songs, anthems, &c.

Perlé (*F.*) } Brilliant ; like a "string of
Per'lend (*G.*) } pearls."
Cadence perlée (*F.*). (See *Cadence.*)
Pearly touch. A light, delicate, bright pf. touch.
Per'lendes Spiel (*G.*). Tasteful, masterly playing.

PERNE, François L. Paris, 1772-1832. Prof. of Harm., Paris Cons. ; Inspector General, 1816 ; Librarian, 1819.
Works : a *Grand Festival Mass*, a "Cours d'harmonie et d'accompagnement," 2 pf. methods, pf. pieces, &c.

PERO'SI, Don Lorenzo. Priest and noted Italian composer ; *b.* Tortona, 1872. Maestro, St. Mark's, Venice, 1897 ; honorary Maestro Papal Choir, 1898.
Works : a trilogy, *La Passione di Cristo* (Milan, 1897) ; oratorios (*La Trasfigurazione*, 1898 ; *La Risurrezione di Lazaro*, 1898 ; *Il Natale del Redentore*, 1899 ; &c.) ; also 15 masses.

PEROT'TI, Giovanni A. *B.* Vercelli, 1760(9?) ; *d.* 1855. Maestro St. Mark's, Venice, 1817.
Works : an opera (*La Contadina nobile*, 1795), much church music, a treatise on "Music in Italy," &c.

Perpetual Canon. (See **Canon, Infinite.**)

Perpe'tuo (*I.*). Perpetual, infinite. (See **Canon.**)
Mo'to perpe'tuo. "Perpetual motion." A spirited piece without break in its impetuous movement.

PER'RIN, Harry Crane. *B.* Wellingborough, 1865. Orgt. Canterbury Cath., 1898-1908. Mus.Doc. Dublin, 1901.

PERRIN, Pierre. *B.* Lyons, abt. 1620; *d.* Paris, 1675.
Wrote the libretti for Cambert's operas (known as the "first French operas ").

PERRONET, Edwd. 1726-92. Methodist preacher; friend of J. Wesley.
Wrote the hymn "All hail the power of Jesu's name."

PERRY, ₤Ed. Baxter. Blind American pianist; *b.* Haverhill, Mass., 1855. Studied under Madame Schumann and Liszt. Gave 1,200 concerts—"lecture-recitals"— in America in 10 years.

PERRY, Geo. F. *B.* Norwich, 1793; *d.* 1862. Mus. director, Haymarket Th., 1822; Condr. Sacred Harmonic Soc., 1848.
Works : 4 oratorios, 2 operas, a cantata, anthems, pf. pieces, songs, &c.

PERSIA'NI (*née* **Tacchinardi**), **Fanny.** Celebrated operatic soprano; *b.* Rome, 1812; *d.* Passy, 1867. *Début*, Leghorn, 1832; great favourite in London and Paris, 1837-48.

Persisting tone. A short tonic or dominant pedal.
"When the persistence of tonic or dominant does not extend beyond a single measure, we call it a *persisting tone*."—*Curwen*.

Personag'gio (*I.*). A "character" in a play or drama.

PER'TI, Jacopo A. Distinguished composer; Bologna, 1661-1756. Maestro San Pietro, 1690; San Petronio, 1696.
Works : 21 operas, 4 oratorios, cantatas, masses.

Pes (*L.*). A foot. A kind of "burden" (*q.v.*) in Old English music.

Pesamment (*F.*) ⎫ Weightily, impres-
Pesan'te (*I.*) ⎬ sively; firm and
Pesantemen'te (*I.*) ⎭ vigorous.

PESCET'TI, G. B. *B.* Venice, 1704; *d.* 1766. Pupil of Lotti. Lived for some years in London.
Wrote several operas for Venice and London.

PESCH'KA-LEUT'NER, Minna. Fine operatic soprano; *b.* Vienna, 1839; *d.* 1890. *Début*, Breslau, 1856. Sang in London, 1872.

PESSARD, Emile L. F. *B.* Montmartre, 1843. *Grand Prix de Rome*, Paris Cons., 1866; Prof. of Harmony, 1881.
Works : several comic operas; masses, orch. pieces, pf. pieces, songs, &c.

PES'TER - PROS'KY, Bertha. Dramatic soprano; *b.* Frankfort-on-Main, 1866.

Petac'cha (*I.*). A plectrum.

PETERS. Leipzig music pub. firm; founded by Carl F. Peters, 1814. Dr. Max Abraham became sole proprietor, 1863.
The firm established its reputation by publishing a "Complete critical edition of Bach's works." The issue of the well-known "Edition Peters" dates from 1868.

PE'TERSEN, Margarete. Contralto; *b.* nr. Copenhagen, 1869.

PETERSI'LEA, Carlyle. Pianist and teacher. *b* Boston, Mass., 1844; *d.* 1903.

Studied Leipzig; estab. an Academy of Music, Boston, 1871-86. Spent the last 11 years of his life in California.
Wrote pf. studies, &c.

PETERSON, Franklin S. *B.* Edinburgh, 1861. Mus.B. Oxon, 1892. Prof. of Music, Melbourne Univ., 1901.
Works : "Elements of Music," anthems, songs.

Petit, Petite (*F.*). Small.
Petit chœur. A small choir (originally in 3 parts only).
Petit détaché. Light *staccato* bowing with the point of the bow.
Petite flûte. The piccolo flute.
Petite flûte-a-bec. A flageolet.
Petite mesure à deux temps. 2-4 time.
Petite note. The small note representing an appoggiatura, acciaccatura, &c.
Petites notes. Grace notes.
Petite pédale. Soft pedal (of the pf.).
Petits riens. Light, trifling pieces.

PETREL'LA, Enrico. Operatic composer; *b.* Palermo, 1813; *d.* 1877. Studied Naples Cons., 1825-30. Although for many years "he vied with Verdi in Italian favour," he died "in extreme poverty."
Works : over 20 operas, including *Il Diavolo color di Rosa* (1829), *Le Miniere di Freiburg* (1839, his finest "buffo" opera), and *Elnava* (his best "serious" opera).

PE'TRI, Henri W. Violinist; pupil of David; *b.* Zeyst, nr. Utrecht, 1856. Leader Dresden Court Orch., 1889.
Works : studies and pieces for violin.

PETRIE, Geo. Noted collector of Irish folk-music; Dublin, 1789-1866.

PETRIE, Robert. Violinist; *b.* Perth, Scotland, 1767; *d.* 1830.
Pub. 4 collections of reels, strathspeys, &c.

PETRI'NI, Franz. Harpist; *b.* Berlin, 1744; *d.* Paris, 1819.
Works : 4 concertos, 8 sonatas, and other pieces for harp; a harp method and a manual of harmony.

PETRUC'CI, Ottaviano de. Inventor of movable types for music printing; *b.* Fossombrone, 1466; *d.* 1539. The Council of the Republic of Venice granted him (1498) the privilege of printing music by his new process for 20 years.
He worked in Venice (1501-11), and afterwards at Fossombrone (1513-23). His editions were "printed with great neatness," and are now rare and valuable.

PE'TRUS PLATEN'SIS. (See **La Rue**.)

PETSCH'KE, Dr. Hermann T. *B.* Bautzen, 1806; *d.* 1888.
Wrote fine male-voice choruses.

PETSCH'NIKOFF, Alex. Precocious Russian violinist; *b.* Jeletz, Russia, 1873. Successful German tour, 1895-6

Pet'to (*I.*). The chest.
Di pet'to ⎫ The chest voice.
Vo'ce di pet'to ⎭

PETZ'MAYER, Johann. Famous zither player; son of an innkeeper; *b.* Vienna, 1803; *d.* (?).

PET'ZOLD, Eugen K. *B.* nr. Altenburg, 1813 ; *d.* 1889.
"Active promoter of music" at Zofingen, Switzerland ; composer, orgt., and director.

PET'ZOLD (or PET'ZHOLD), Wilhelm L. Early Parisian pf. maker ; *b.* Saxony, 1784 ; *d.* (?).

Peu (*F.*). Little ; a little.
Peu à peu. Little by little ; gradually. Same as *poco a poco.*
Un peu. A little.

PEVERNAGE, André. *B.* Courtray, Belgium, 1543 ; *d.* 1591. Choirmaster Notre-Dame, Antwerp.
Works : chansons, Laudes, motets, masses, &c.

PE'ZEL (or PEZE'LIUS), Johann. Town musician at Bautzen (1686), and later at Leipzig.
Wrote numerous instrumental compositions of historic interest.

Pezza, Pez'zo (*I.*) ⎱ A piece.
Pez'zi (*I.*) ⎰ Pieces.
Pezzet'to. A short piece.
Pez'zi concertan'ti. Concerted pieces (with occasional solos for each inst.).
Pez'zi di bravu'ra. "Show pieces." (See *Bravura.*)
Pez'zi stacca'ti. Detached pieces.
Pez'zo d'insie'me. An ensemble piece.

P.F. or *pf.* Abbn. of *Pianoforte ;* also occasionally used for *più forte,* or *poco forte.*
pf or *pff* over a single note or chord means "first soft, then immediately loud." (See *Pressure note.*)

Pfei'fe (*G.*). A fife, pipe, or small flute.
Pfei'fen, To pipe, to whistle.
Pfei'fenboden. Sound-board of an organ.
Pfei'fenwerk. The pipe work of an organ.
Pfei'fer. Fifer, piper ; whistler.

PFEIFFER, Jean Georges. Pianist ; *b.* Versailles, 1835. *Début,* 1862. *Prix Chartier* for chamber music, Paris Cons.
Works : an oratorio (*Hagar*), operas, orch. pieces, pf. concertos, chamber music, &c.

PFEIF'FER, Karl. *B.* 1833(?) ; *d.* 1897. Chorus-director Vienna Imperial Opera for 30 years.
Works : a mass, part-songs, songs, &c.

PFEIL, Heinrich. Mus. editor ; Leipzig, 1835-99.
Works : numerous male-voice choruses.

Pfif'fig (*G.*). Artful, sly, cunning.

PFITZNER, Hans E. Pianist, teacher, and conductor ; *b.* Moscow, 1869.
Works : a successful "music-drama," *Der Arme Heinrich,* 1895 ; orch. pieces, pf. pieces, songs.

PFLUG'HAUPT, Robt. Pianist ; *b.* Berlin, 1833 ; *d.* 1871. Left his fortune to found a "Beethoven Scholarship."
Works : pf. pieces (valses, mazurkas, polkas, &c.).

PFLUG'HAUPT, Sophie (*née* Stschepin). Fine pianist ; pupil of Henselt and Liszt ; *b.* Dünaburg, Russia, 1837 ; *d.* 1867.

PFOHL, Ferdinand. *B.* Elbogen, Bohemia, 1863. Mus. editor *Hamburger Nachrichten,* 1891.
His writings include useful "guides" to Wagner's *Tannhäuser* and *Die Meistersinger.*

PFUNDT, Ernst G. B. *B.* nr. Torgau, 1806 ; *d.* 1871. Kettle-drummer, Leipzig Gewandhaus Orch., from 1835.
Wrote a method for kettledrum, and invented its "machine-head."

Phantasie' (*G.*). A fantasy or fantasia.
Phantasie'bilder ⎱ Fanciful pieces with no strict form.
Phantasie'stücke ⎰
Phantasi(e)'ren. To improvise.

PHASEY, Alf. Jas. *D.* Chester, 1888.
Euphonium player ; so much improved that inst. that he was "practically its inventor."

PHELPS, Ellsworth C. Noted American orgt. and teacher ; *b.* Middletown, Conn., 1827. Settled in Brooklyn, 1857.
Works : some 200 compositions of various kinds.

Phil'harmon'ic. Music-loving.

PHILIDOR (properly DANICAN). Famous family of French musicians.
Over 20 members of the family were noted musicians ; the following were the most celebrated.

(1) **Jean Danican Philidor.** Piper, King's military band ; *d.* Paris, 1679.

(2) **André Danican Philidor.** *B.* abt. 1647 ; *d.* 1730. Member of Louis XIV's *three* bands, playing "bassoon, cromorne, oboe, marine-trumpet, or drums, as required."
Composed masques, ballets, military music, &c., and "made a fine collection of old instrumental pieces" for the Royal Mus. Library, Versailles.

(3) **Anne Danican Philidor.** Eldest son of André ; Paris, 1681-1728. Flute player ; composed 3 operas, and music for fl., vn., and oboe ; founded the "Concerts spirituels."

(4) **Pierre Danican Philidor.** Flute player ; 1681-1731. Pub. duets and trios for flute.

(5) **François André Danican Philidor.** Youngest son of André (2) ; "greatest of the family." *B.* Dreux, 1726 ; *d.* London, 1795. Started his career as a chess player ; achieved great renown, and was pensioned by the London Chess Club (abt. 1750). Returning to Paris 1754, he commenced to compose with great ardour, and produced a long series of successful operas which entitle him to rank as "one of the greatest operatic composers of his period."
Of some 25 operas (immensely popular at the time) the best are *Le Marechal* (1761), *Le Sorcier* (1764), *Tom Jones* (1764), and *Ernelinde* (1767, his finest work).

PHILIPP, Isidor E. Fine pianist ; *b.* Pesth, 1863. Took 1st prize for pf. playing, Paris Cons., 1883.
Works : orch. pieces ; pf. pieces, studies, and exercises.

PHILIPPE de Mons. (See **Monte.**)

PHILIPPE de Vitry. (See **Vitry.**)

PHILIPPS, Peter. (**Petrus Philippus ; Pietro Filippo.**) Noted English contrapuntist ; *b.* abt. 1560 ; *d.* abt. 1633. Catholic priest. Orgt. vice-royal Chapel, Antwerp ; afterwards Canon at Soignies.
Works : madrigals, motets, &c., and "the earliest regular fugue known."

22

PHILLIPPS, Adelaide. Dramatic contralto ; *b.* Stratford-on-Avon, 1833 ; *d.* 1882. *Début*, Milan, 1854. Lived chiefly in America from 1840.

PHILLIPS, Chas. Baritone ; *b.* Ayr, 1866.

PHILLIPS, Mrs. C. (See **Ethel Barns.**)

PHILLIPS, Henry. Baritone singer and song composer ; *b.* Bristol, 1801 ; *d.* 1876.

PHILLIPS, Montague F. Composer ; *b.* Tottenham, 1885.

PHILLIPS, Wm. Lovell. 'Cellist ; *b.* Bristol, 1816 ; *d.* 1860. Musical director at various London theatres.
Works : dramatic music, a symphony, songs, &c.

PHILLIPS, W. R. Teacher and writer ; *b.* London, 1851.
Author of "Vocal Interval Practice," "Pupil Teachers' Notes," "Staff Notation Theory," &c.

Philome'la (*L.*). (1) The nightingale. (2) An ancient inst. of the vn. species with wire strings. (3) A large-scaled solo stop on some modern organs akin to the Doppel- flöte or Stenterphon (*q.v.*).

Philosophical pitch. A standard of pitch often employed in acoustical investi- gations.
It fixes for the vibration-number of each "C" some power of 2 ; thus, 16 ft. C, 32 vibrations ; 8 ft. C, 64 ; 4 ft. C, 128 ; 2 ft. C (or "Middle C"), 256 ; &c.

PHILP, Elizabeth. *B.* Falmouth, 1827 ; *d.* 1885. Wrote part-songs, songs, &c.

Phonas'cus (*L.* from *Gk.*). A singing master.

Phonaut'ograph. A " self-music-recorder."
In the form invented by Fenby for keyboard insts., a stud is attached to each key, which, " by electric connection, marks on prepared paper lines corresponding to the duration of the notes."

Pho'ne (*Gk.*). (1) Sound, tone, voice. (2) The "clang" (klang) or compound (*com- posite*) tone of a note and its upper partials. (See **Acoustics.**)
Phonet'ics, Pho'nics. The science of sounds.
Phoneu'ma. An organ stop of 8 ft. or 16 ft. tone, in- vented by Hope-Jones. It is analogous to the *Quintatön* (*q.v.*), but more "stringy" in character.
Pho'nikon. A metal wind inst. with a globular bell, invented 1848.
Phonom'eter. (*F., Phonomètre*). An inst. for counting vibrations.

Phonograph. A " sound-writer."
Edison's phonograph (1877) may well be regarded as one of the most remarkable inventions of the 19th century.
" The records are made by a steel point working upon tubes of wax." In its modern forms, under the names of *Talking machine*, *Graphophone*, &c., the phonograph not only " records " but " reproduces " sounds of all kinds, although at present (1909) some of the reproductions can only be fairly described as "caricatures." From the improvements con- tinually being made it seems probable, however, that the phonograph will eventually become a " real musical inst." (See also *Gramophone.*)

Phor'minx. An ancient Greek lyre.

Phrase. A term variously used by different writers to mean a *Motive*, a *Sub-section*,

a *Section*, or even a complete *Musical Sentence*. (See *Metrical Form*.)
A phrase is perhaps best defined as " a definite musical thought or idea," or as a "passage of melody complete in itself and unbroken in con- tinuity." It may vary in length from two or three notes to a whole section (or extended section), as in the following :—

Each of the portions (*a, b, c, d*) is complete in itself, and hardly susceptible of further sub- division. The passage, therefore, consists of 4 phrases.
N.B.—It is difficult to see how a whole musical sentence can fairly be called a "phrase" in the modern sense ; but the whole terminology of *Musical Form* is almost hopelessly vague and indefinite, and hardly any two authorities agree *completely* as to the meanings of the terms used.

Phrasing. (*G., Phrasi(e)'rung ; F., Frasé.*)
(1) Musical punctuation.
This includes (*a*) the more or less emphatic delivery of phrases (whether *motives, sub- sections, figures, subjects,* or *sections*) with regard to their relative importance ; (*b*) the "attack" of each phrase (see *Accent, Rhyth- mical*), and its "release" (by slightly cutting short the final note) ; (*c*) the marks, if any, used by composers to indicate phrases.

(2) Musical articulation.
This includes the proper delivery of the individual notes (especially in instrumental music).
The following, for example, are a few different "phrasings" of the same passage :—

Phrase marks.
Composers generally add the marks for " articu- lation," but rarely those for " punctuation." Occasionally, however, a tick (✓) shows the beginning of a phrase ; or a curved line (like a *slur* or *legato-mark*) is drawn above the whole phrase, and articulation marks also given :—

Schumann's pf. works are models of phrasing.

Phry'gian. (See **Mode**.)

Phrygian Cadence. A cadence on the major triad of the mediant (in a major key), seM.

Physharmo'nica. (1) One of the precursors of the harmonium. (2) A free-reed organ stop.

Piace're (*I.*). Pleasure.

A piace're. At pleasure (as regards time) ; *ad lib.*

Piace'vole (*I.*) ⎫
Con piacevolez'za (*I.*) ⎬ Pleasantly ; in a light, graceful, smooth style ;
Piacevolmen'te (*I.*) ⎭
suavely.

Piacimen'to (*I.*). Same as **a piacere** (*q.v.*).

Piagen'do (*I.*). Same as **piangendo** (*q.v.*).

Piagne'vole (*I.*). Same as **piangevole** (*q.v.*).

Pianamen'te (*I.*) ⎫
Pianen'te (*I.*) ⎬ Gently, softly.

Pianette (*F.*). A small pf.

Piangen'do (*I.*). Plaintive, weeping, tearful.

Piangen'te
Piange'vole ⎬ Sadly, mournfully, dolefully.
Piangevolmen'te

Piani'no (*I.*). Same as **pianette** (*q.v.*).

Pian'ist (*E.*)
Pianiste (*F.*) ⎬ A player on the piano.

Pia'no (*I.*). Soft. Abbn. *P.* or *p.* "Soft and sweet, by way of an echo."— *Grassineau.*

Pia'no assa'i
Pianis'simo, pp ⎬ Very soft.

Pianis'simo quan'to possi'bile. As soft as possible.

Pianis'simo sem'pre sen'za sordi'ni. Very soft, and always without the dampers (*i.e., con pedale*).

Piano ed egualmen'te. Soft, and evenly.

Pianissis'simo, ppp, pppp, ppppp. As soft as possible ; extremely soft.

Piano pedal. The soft pedal of the pf.

Piano piano. Softer ; very soft.

Pia'no, sem'pre stacca'to e marca'to il bas'so. Soft, but with the bass always *staccato* and well marked.

Piano, Pianoforte. (Abbn. *Pf. ; G., Clavier', Klavier', Pianofor'te ; F., Piano, Piano-forté, Forté-piano ; I., Pia'no, Pia'nofor'te.*) The highest development of the dulcimer.

The piano—"the orchestra of the home"—is too well-known to need a detailed description. Though it owes much in shape and mechanism to the *Harpsichord* and *Spinet* (both of which it superseded), it is essentially "a large dulcimer

with a keyboard," and is a direct descendant of the *Clavichord* (*q.v.*). Cristofori (*q.v.*) of Padua invented (1710-11) a *Clavicembalo con piano e forte, i.e.,* a Clavicembalo which could play "soft or loud." The name was soon shortened into *Piano e forte,* and this again into *Pianoforte,* or simply *Piano.* Cristofori's invention was adopted by Silbermann in Germany, by Stein (who invented the *soft pedal*), by Erard, Schudi, and Broadwood (who invented the "damper" or "loud" pedal) ; but the piano did not make much headway until Clementi and Beethoven "threw their powerful influence on its side." Cristofori's idea, "with many improvements in detail but little fundamental change, persists in the magnificent instruments of to-day." The piano has a complete chromatic scale of 7 octaves or more ; every kind of music can be played on it ; "except the organ, it is the only self-supporting instrument ; it is capable of a rapidity and celerity of utterance of which the organ is incapable ; and no other inst. but the organ approaches its resources in chords, range, and brilliance."—*Hughes.*

The pf. is said to have been first heard in England at Covent Garden, 1767.

Boudoir piano. A small grand pf.
Cabinet piano. An old style of upright pf.
Concert grand. The largest size grand pf. for concert purposes.
Cottage piano. A small upright piano.
Dumb piano. A pf. keyboard without strings, for practice of scales, &c.
Flü'gel (*G.*). "A wing ; " a grand pf.
Grand piano. A large, horizontal, harp-shaped pf.
Oblique piano. With the strings running obliquely to obtain greater length.
Overstrung piano. With some strings running obliquely over others for greater length and fulness of tone.
Pedal piano. See *Pedal.*
Piano à archet (*F.*). A piano-violin (*q.v.*).
Pia'no a co'da (*I.*) ⎱ "Tailed" piano ; *i.e.,* a grand
Piano à queue (*F.*) ⎰ piano.
Piano carré (*F.*). A square pf.
Piano droit (*F.*). An upright pf.
Piano mecanique (*F.*). A mechanical or automatic pf.
Piano muet (*F.*). A dumb piano. (See above.)
Pianoforte score. An arrangement of the accompaniments of a work in "short score" for pf. (See *Score.*)
Pian'ograph. A melograph (*q.v.*).
Piano-organ. The ordinary "street" piano.
Trichord piano. A pf. with three wires to each note (except in the lower octaves).
Semi-grand piano. Same as *Boudoir pf.* (see above).
Virgil Clavier. An improved dumb piano. (See *Virgil.*)

Pia'nofortebeglei'tung (*G.*). Pf. accompt.

Piano Music.

Paderewski ranks Beethoven, Mozart, Liszt, Schumann, Chopin, and Grieg as the greatest composers for the piano.—*Daily Telegraph,* 1907.

Piano-player. An automatic device for playing the piano.

Under the names of *Pianola, Æolian, Cæcilian, Auto-player,* &c., many mechanical piano-players are now before the public. The *Pianola* is in shape like a small harmonium ; it is provided with 65 mechanical "fingers," and 4 stops (*Piano, Forte, Tempo,* and *Accent*) ; the motive power is supplied by two treadles worked by the feet, and the "music" consists of perforated rolls of paper. The most elaborate pieces of music can be performed.

Piano study.

"There are two main points to be attended to in the education of a pianoforte player—the finger and the taste."—*Mus. Magazine,* 1855.

"Skilled masters of the inst. no longer burden their pupils with futile finger exercises ; and the precious morning hours . . . are now utilized for the memorizing of a *répertoire* and the study of especial difficulties in a composition. Most of the vast and useless *étude* literature has been sent to Limbo ; for *in music itself*—after the independence of the fingers, the scales in single and double notes, arpeggios and octaves have been thoroughly mastered—may be studied the precise technical difficulty to be overcome."—*J. Huneker*, 1903.

Piano-violin. A development of the hurdy-gurdy applied to the piano.

Pian'to (*I.*). Weeping, lamentation.

Piat'ti (*I.*). Cymbals.

Sen'za piat'ti. The bass drum alone, without the cymbals. (Used when the same player performs on bass drum and cymbals.)

PIAT'TI, Carlo Alfredo. 'Cellist ; *b.* Bergamo, 1822 ; *d.* 1901. First London appearance, 1844. Played regularly in the Monday and Saturday Popular Concerts from 1859 to 1897.

Works : concertos, fantasias, capriccios, &c., for 'cello.

Pib'corn (*Welsh*). A hornpipe (*q.v.*).

Pi'broch. A set of variations played on the Scotch bagpipe.

Piccanteri'a, Con (*I.*). With piquancy.

Picchiettan'do (*I.*) }
Picchetta'to (*I.*) } Detached. In violin
Picchietta'to (*I.*) } playing, *semi staccato.*

PICCIN'NI (PICCI'NI, PICIN'NI), Nicola. Celebrated opera composer ; *b.* Bari, Jan., 1728 ; *d.* Passy, May, 1800. Favourite pupil of Leo and Durante, Cons. de San Onofrio, Naples, for 12 years (from the age of 14). First opera, *Le donne dispettose*, Naples, 1754. After great successes at Naples and Rome he settled in Paris, 1776. The opponents of **Gluck** rallied round Piccinni (who was himself of an amiable and generous disposition, and took no part in the quarrel), and the famous controversy between the "Gluckists" and "Piccinnists" ended in Gluck's complete triumph with *Iphigénie en Tauride*, 1779. (See **Gluck.**) Piccinni continued to compose for some years after this, but never recovered his former prestige.

Of his 133 operas, the best were *Il curioso* (1755), *La buona figliuola* (1760), *Il Re pastore* (1760), *L'Olimpiade* (1761), *Didone abbandonata* (1767), *Antigone* (1771), *I Viaggiatori* (1774), *Le fat méprisé* (1779), *Atys* (1780), and *Didon* (1783).

PICCIN'NI, Luigi. Son of Nicola ; *b.* Naples, 1766 ; *d.* 1827. Wrote about 15 operas.

PICCIN'NI, Louis A. Grandson of Nicola ; Paris, 1779-1850. *Chef de Chant*, Paris Opéra, 1816-26.

Wrote about 200 operas, operettas, ballets, &c.

Piccio'lo (*I.*). Small.

Violin'o piccio'lo. A small violin.

Pic'co pipe. A small whistle with 3 holes.

Pic'colo (*I.*). Small, light, delicate.

Pic'cola no'ta. Same as *Petite note* (*q.v.*).
Pic'colo piano. A small pf.
Violi'no pic'colo. A small violin.

Pic'colo. A 2 ft. organ stop of bright tone.

Pic'colo } (*G.*, *Oktav'flöte*, *Pick'elflöte ;*
Pic'colo flute } *F.*, *Petite flûte ; I.*, *Ottavi'no*, *Fla'uto pic'colo.*) A small flute an octave higher in pitch than the ordinary orchestral flute.

PICCOLO'MINI, M. Pen-name of **Pontet-Piccolomini** (*q.v.*).

PICCOLO'MINI, Maria. Soprano singer ; *b.* Sienna, 1836 ; *d.* 1899. *Début*, Florence, 1852 ; retired, 1863.

Pic'corn. A hornpipe (*q.v.*).

PICH'EL (or PICHL), Wenzel. Violinist ; *b.* Bechin, Bohemia, 1741 ; *d.* 1805. Chamber composer to Archduke Ferdinand, Milan, 1775-96 ; violinist, Court Th., Vienna, 1796.

His 700 compositions include 88 symphonies, 13 serenades, concertos for various insts., much chamber music, 4 masses, 20 operas, &c.

PICIN'NI. (See **Piccinni.**)

Pick. (1) A plectrum. (2) To pluck (strings).

Pick'elflöte (*G.*). The piccolo flute.

Pièce (*F.*). A piece ; a play.

Pièce de théatre. A play.
Suite de pièces. A set of pieces.

Pied (*F.*). A foot.

Avec les pieds. "With the feet ; " *con peda'le.*

PIEL, Peter. *B.* nr. Bonn, 1835.

Works : several masses and motets, 8 magnificats, &c. ; org. pieces, a "Harmonielehre," &c.

Pie'na,-o (*I.*). Full, complete.

A pie'na orche'stra. For full orchestra.
A vo'ce pie'na. With full voice.
Pie'no co'ro. Full chorus.
Pie'no or'gano. Full organ.
Pie'no spi'rito. Full (of) spirit.

Pierced Organ Pipes.

Pipes with a " slot " cut in the side of the pipe near the top, to modify the tone or to facilitate tuning. Gambas, viols, and dulcianas are generally " slotted."

PIERCY, Henry R. Tenor vocalist ; *b.* Birmingham. Sang Bristol Festival, 1885 ; Birmingham, 1888 ; Leeds, 1889 ; &c.

PIERNÉ, H. C. Gabriel. *B.* Metz, 1863. Won *Grand Prix de Rome*, Paris Cons., 1882. Succeeded César Franck as orgt. Ste.-Clothilde, 1890.

Works : several stage pieces (*Vendée*, 1897), orch. pieces, a pf. concerto, &c.

PIERPONT, Bantock. Baritone vocalist ; *b.* Runcorn, 1856.

PIERRE, Constant. Bassoon player ; *b.* Passy,1855. Editor, *Le Monde Musical*, Paris.

Works : essays on "Popular Noëls," a "History of the Opéra Orchestra," &c.

PIERSON. (See **La Rue.**)

PIERSON (PEARSON), Henry Hugo. *B.* Oxford, 1815 ; *d.* Leipzig, 1873. Wrote under the name of "**Edgar Mansfeldt.**" Lived mostly in Germany.

Works : 4 operas, 2 oratorios (*Jerusalem*, Norwich 1852) ; a symphony, 4 overtures, church music, part-songs, songs, &c.

PIERSON-BRE'THOL, Bertha. Soprano ; *b.* Vienna, 1861.

Pietà (*I.*). Pity, compassion.

Pietosamen'te } With pity ; tenderly, sympathetically.
Pieto'so

Pif'faro, Pif'fera, Pif'fero (*I.*). (1) A primitive form of oboe, still used by the peasants of Italy and the Tyrol. (2) A fife.

Piffara'ri } Players on the *Piffaro.*
Piffera'ri
Piffera'ta. (1) An air for the *Piffero.* (2) An imitation of one (on the pf., &c.).
Pifferi'no. A small *Piffero.*

Piki(e)'ren (*G.*). (See **Piqué.**)

Pilea'ta (*L.*). "Capped" (as an organ pipe.)

PILGER, Karl. (See **Spazier.**)

Pil'gerchor (*G.*). " Pilgrims' Chorus." A kind of *Vox humana* on old German organs.

PILKINGTON, Francis. Madrigalist ; *b.* abt. 1570 ; *d.* Chester, 1638. Mus.B. Oxon, 1595 ; lutenist and member of the choir, Chester Cath.

PILOT'TI, Giuseppe. Bologna, 1784-1838 ; Prof. of Counterpoint at the Liceo Filarmonico, 1829.

Works : 2 operas, much church music, &c.

H.M.S. PINAFORE. Comic opera by Gilbert and Sullivan, 1878.

Pincé (*F.*). "Pinched." (1) Plucked (as a harp, &c.). (2) Pizzicato (*q.v.*). (3) An old harpsichord ornament like a short trill or mordent. (See **Ornaments.**)

Pincé bemolisé. A *pincé* with a flattened auxiliary note.
Pincé dièse. A *pincé* with a sharpened auxiliary note.
Pincé etouffé. An acciaccatura.
Pincement. Same as *Pincé.*
Pincé renversé. An inverted mordent (*q.v.*).
Pincés. General name for insts. played by plucking the strings.

Pincer (*F.*). To pluck.

Pincer la harpe. To play the harp.

PINDAR, The greatest lyric poet of ancient Greece ; *b.* Thebes abt. 520 B.C.

PINEL'LI, Ettore. Violinist ; *b.* Rome, 1843. Pupil of Joachim. Founded the "Società Orchestrale Romana" (Rome, 1874), which he still conducts ; also conductor of the Court Concerts (with Sgambati).

Works : orchestral pieces, chamber music, &c.

PIN'NER, Max. Noted pianist ; *b.* New York, 1851 ; *d.* 1887. Studied in Leipzig and Berlin ; settled in New York, 1877.

PINSU'TI, Ciro. *B.* Sinalunga, Florence, 1829 ; *d.* 1888. Studied in Rome, London, and Bologna ; private pupil of Rossini. Divided his time between England and Italy. Prof. of Singing, R.A.M., 1856.

Works : 3 operas, numerous popular part-songs, and over 200 songs (many of them standard favourites).

PIN'TO, George F. Grandson of T. (below) ; London, 1786-1806. Precocious violinist and pianist.

PIN'TO, Thomas. Violinist ; son of a Neapolitan ; *b.* England, 1714 ; *d.* 1779. Played in public at 11 ; leader at the principal festivals, &c.

Pipe. (1) A bagpipe. (2) Any primitive wind inst. ; as a *flageolet, oboe, shawm, shepherd's pipe,* &c.

Organ pipe. (G., *Or'gelpfeife ;* F., *Tuyau d'orgue ;* I., *Can'na d'or'gano*). Organ pipes are of two kinds : (*a*) FLUE PIPES, constructed on the principle of the tin-whistle, and (*b*) REED PIPES, constructed on the principle of the clarinet, with a "beating" reed. A few large organs have also "stops" (see *Organ*) with "free" reeds, like those of the harmonium. (For the distinction between "open" and "stopped" pipes see *Acoustics.*)

PI'PEGROP, Heinrich (known as **Baryphonus**). Esteemed contrapuntist ; *b.* Wernigerode, 1581 ; *d.* Quedlinburg, 1655.

Pipes of Pan. (See **Pan-pipes.**)

Pique (*F.*). (1) The peg or "standard" of a 'cello. (2) The dash or dot indicating *staccato.*

Piqué (*F.*). The *mezzo-staccato* in vn. playing. (See **Picchietta'to.**)

Piquer (*F.*) }
Piqui'ren (*G.*) } To play *piqué.*
Pikie'ren (*G.*) }

PIRA'NI, Eugenio. Pianist ; *b.* Bologna, 1852. Pf. teacher, Kullak's Academy, Berlin, 1870-80. Returned to Berlin, 1895.

Works : orch. pieces ; pf. trios, studies, and solos ; songs, &c.

PIRRO, André. *B.* St. Dizier, Haute Marne, 1869. Director " Schola Cantorum," Paris, 1896.

Chief work : " The Organ of J. S. Bach " (1894, Eng. trans. 1902).

PI'SA, Agostino. "Author of the earliest-known treatise on the details of conducting" (2nd edition, Rome, 1611).

PISA'RI, Pasquale. Rome, 1725-78. Bass singer in the Papal Chapel.

Works : a series of motets for the whole year, a "Dixit" in 16 real parts (for 4 choirs), &c. Martini called him " the Palestrina of the 18th century."

PISARO'NI, Benedetta R. Fine singer ; Piacenza, 1793-1872. *Début* as a high soprano, Bergamo, 1811 ; after a severe illness reappeared as a " magnificent contralto."

PI'SCHEK, Johann B. Fine baritone ; *b.* Melnick, Bohemia, 1814 ; *d.* 1873. First appearance in England, 1845.

PI'SENDEL, Joh. G. Violinist ; pupil of Vivaldi ; *b.* Carlsburg, 1687 ; *d.* 1755. Leader Electoral Orch., Dresden, 1728. Wrote a symphony, vn. concertos, &c.

PISTOC'CHI, Francesco A. Famous singing teacher ; *b.* Palermo, 1659 ; *d.* 1726. Capellmeister, Ansbach, 1697-9. Founded at Bologna, abt. 1700, " the first school of music in which systematic vocal instruction was given in classes."

Works : 3 oratorios, 4 operas ; a "Collection of French, Italian, and German Airs," &c.

Piston. (1) (See **Valve.**) (2) A *cornet à pistons.*

Pistonbläser (G.). A cornet player.
Piston-solo (G.). A solo for *Cornet à pistons.*
Piston (*Pistons*) in French scores signifies a brass inst.

Pisto'ne (I.). Generally used as equivalent to the soprano cornet (in E♭ or F).
Pistoni'no. A small cornet.

Pitch. (*G., Ton'höhe ; F., Hauteur du ton ; Diapason.*) (1) The acuteness or gravity —highness or lowness—of a musical sound. (2) The tuning of an inst.

Absolute pitch depends upon the number of air-vibrations per second (the more rapid the vibrations, the higher the pitch). (See *Acoustics* and *Temperament*).

Relative pitch is the interval between one sound and another. (See *Interval.*)

There are many ways of naming the different octaves in absolute pitch ; the best and simplest is the "foot pitch" of the notes given by open organ pipes (and named after the "C" in each case). The following table gives most of the usual names : —

C Double C.	Gamut G.	C Tenor C.	Fiddle G.	C Middle C.	C Treble C.
C D E F G A B		c d e f g a b		c' d' e' f' g' a' b'	c'' d'' e'' f'' g'' a'' b''
Great octave.		Small octave.		{ Once-marked octave. { Once-accented octave.	{ Twice-marked octave. { Twice-accented octave.

Tonic Sol-fa } Letter names. }	C₂ D₂ E₂ F₂ G₂ A₂ B₂	C, D, E, F, G, A, B,	C D E F G A B	C' D' E' F' G' A' B'
	8ft. octave.	4ft. octave.	2ft. octave.	1ft. octave.

The octave below the 8 ft. octave is the 16 ft. octave (CCC, DDD, &c.) ; the octave below the 16 ft. is the 32 ft. octave (CCCC, DDDD, &c.). The octave above the 1 ft. octave is the 6 inch or "thrice accented" octave, &c. (See also *Alt.*)

French pitch. The French *diapason normal* fixes A in

the 2nd treble space at 435 vibrations per second. This pitch (adopted by America as "International Pitch") is being rapidly accepted as the "Standard of Pitch" by all countries.

N.B.—Other standards of pitch are given under the letter "A."

Pitch-fork. A tuning-fork.

Pitch-pipe. A small wooden or metal pipe giving various tones of fixed pitch.

The pitch-pipe was formerly much used by Precentors in starting Psalm tunes, &c., and

also by violinists to get the correct tuning for their strings.

PITO'NI, Giuseppe O. *B.* Rieti, Italy, 1657 ; *d.* Rome, 1743. Maestro, Collegio di S. Marco, Rome, 1677. Among his pupils were Durante, Leo, and Feo.

Works : a Dixit for 4 choirs (in 16 parts) still sung annually during Holy Week at St. Peter's, Rome ; over 40 masses and psalms in 12 parts (for 3 choirs), and over 20 in 16 parts (for 4 choirs) ; psalms and motets up to 36 parts ; and an unfinished mass in 48 parts. Also vespers, hymns, requiems, &c.

PITT, Percy. *B.* London, 1870.

Works : symphonic poems, pf. pieces, songs, &c·

PITTMAN, Josiah. 1816-86. Organist ; pupil of S. S. Wesley.

Works : anthems, hymns, services, &c.

PIT'TRICH, George W. *B.* Dresden, 1870. Chorusmaster, Dresden Court Opera, 1890 ; Capellmeister, Cologne Opera, 1899.

Works : an opera, incidental music to several plays, orch. pieces, songs, &c.

Più (I.). More. When used alone it means *più mos'so,* quicker.

Più alle'gro. Quicker.
Più for'te. Louder.
Più len'to. Slower.
Più len'to e sotto vo'ce. Slower, and in an undertone.
Più marca'to del princi'pio. More *marcato* than the 1st time.
Più mos'so. "More moved ; " quicker.
Più mos'so su'bito. Suddenly quicker.
Più pia'no. Softer.
Più sensi'bile. The melody more prominent.
Più stret'to. Accelerating.
Più to'sto alle'gro. Rather quicker.
Più vi'vo. More lively, more animated.

PIU'TTI, Karl. *B.* Thuringia, 1846 ; *d.* 1902. Teacher Leipzig Cons., 1875 ; Orgt. Thomaskirche, Leipzig, 1880.

Works : numerous org. pieces, and a work on "Musical Theory."

Pi'va (I.). (1) A bagpipe. (2) A hautboy.

Pivot-note. A note about which a passage of melody "turns ; " as G in the following :—

This kind of melody is common in variations, &c.

PIX'IS, Johann Peter. Pianist ; *b.* Mannheim, 1788 ; *d.* 1874.

Works : much pf. music (sonatas, *salon* pieces, a concerto, &c.) ; also 3 operas.

PIZ'ZI, Emilio. *B.* Verona, 1862. Director Bergamo Music School, 1897. Has won several valuable prizes for operas and other compositions.

Works: operas (*Guglielmo Ratcliff,* 1889; *Gabrielli,* written for Adelina Patti, 1893; *Rosalba,* 1896; &c.); chamber music.

Pizzican'do (*I.*) ⎱ Abbn. *Pizz.* Pinched,
Pizzica'to (*I.*) ⎰ plucked. A direction to violinists to pluck the string with the finger instead of bowing it.

When bowing has to be resumed, the direction *Arco* (or *Coll'arco*) is given.

Placa'bile (*I.*). ⎱ Calmly, peacefully.
Placabilmen'te (*I.*). ⎰

Placenteramen'te (*I.*). Pleasingly; joyfully.

Placidez'za (*I.*). Placidity, quietness, &c.

Con placidez'za ⎫
Placidamen'te ⎬ Placidly, peacefully, calmly.
Pla'cido ⎭

Pla'cito (*I.*). Pleasure.

A be'ne pla'cito. *Ad lib.* as to *tempo,* embellishments, &c.

Pla'gal. Sidewise; collateral; relative. (See **Mode.**)

Plagal cadence. (See *Cadence.*)
Plagal melody. A melody ranging (chiefly) from the under-dominant to the over-dominant. (See *Authentic.*)

Plaga'lisch (*G.*). Plagal.

Plagiau'los (*Gk.*). A *Flauto traverso.* (See **Flute.**)

PLAI'DY, Louis. Pianist and teacher; *b.* Hubertsburg, Saxony, 1810; *d.* 1874. Pf. instructor Leipzig Cons. (on Mendelssohn's invitation), 1843-65.

Works: a "Pianoforte Teacher's Guide," and a book of "Technical Studies" (the well-known "Plaidy's Exercises").

Plain. Simple, unadorned.

Plain-beat. (See *Ornaments.*)
Plain-chant. (1) A canto fermo. (2) Plain song.
Plain counterpoint. Simple counterpoint.
Plain Chant; Plain Song. (*L., Can'tus pla'nus, Can'tus choral'is; I., Mu'sica pla'na.*) The old "Gregorian" ecclesiastical music, based on the 8 modes of Ambrose and Gregory. (See *Mode.*) The music is written on a four-line staff, and two clefs are used; Ut, Do, or C clef, 𝄢; Fa, or F clef,
Plain trill. A trill ending without a turn. (See *Trill.*)

Plainte (*F.*). A lament; an elegy.
Plaintif. Plaintive.

Plainti'vo (*I.*). Plaintive(ly), expressive(ly).

Plaisant (*F.*). Pleasing, merry, sportive.

Plaisanterie (*F.*) ⎱ A "cheerful melody" for
Pleas'antrie (*E.*) ⎰ a solo instrument (especially a harpsichord).

Plan. "Form" in musical composition. (See **Form, Key-plan, Metrical Form, Sonata.**)

Planchette (*F.*). A mechanical pf.

PLANÇON, Pol H. Fine bass singer; *b.* Ardennes, 1854. After singing for 10 years in the Paris Grand Opéra, he went to New York, 1893. He has several times sung at Covent Garden, London.

PLANQUETTE, J. Robt. Opera composer; Paris, 1850-1903. Studied Paris Cons.

His numerous successful operas include *Les Cloches de Corneville* (1877; given 400 times running), *Le Talisman* (1892), *Panurge* (1895); also two written for London, *The Old Guard* (1887), *Paul Jones* (1889).

PLANT, Arthur B. Organist; *b.* Lichfield, 1853. Mus.Doc. Oxon, 1896.

PLANTADE, Chas. Henri. *B.* Pontoise, 1764; *d.* 1839. *Maitre de chant,* Paris Opéra, 1812-15; Prof. of Singing, Paris Cons., 1816-28. Mme. Cinti-Damoreau was his most famous pupil.

Works: operas, masses, motets, romances, vocal duets, &c.

PLANTÉ, François. Distinguished pianist; *b.* Orthez, 1839; *d.* 1898. Studied Paris Cons.

Works: excellent transcriptions of classical pieces.

Planx'ty. Name given by the old Irish and Welsh bards to a kind of "lament."

Plaqué (*F.*; from *plaquer,* "to strike at once.") Notes of chords to be struck simultaneously, without *arpeggio* or other embellishment.

Plär'ren (*G.*). To bleat, bawl, sing badly.

PLATA'NIA, Pietro. *B.* Catania, 1828. Director Palermo Cons., 1863; Dir. Royal Coll. of Music, Naples, 1888.

Works: operas, orch. pieces, a requiem, a treatise on "Canon and Fugue," &c.

PLATEL, Nicolas J. 'Cellist; *b.* Versailles, 1777; *d.* 1835. 1st 'cello, Antwerp Opera, 1813; Brussels (abt. 1819); 'cello professor, Brussels Royal School of Music (now the Brussels Cons.).

Works: concertos, sonatas, romances, &c., for 'cello; chamber music.

PLA'TO. Greek philosopher; 429-347 B.C.

In his system of harmony "he likened the movements of music to those of the soul;" the soul might therefore be developed by musical training.

Plaud'ernd (*G.*). Babbling, prattling.

PLAYFORD, John. 1623-86(?). London music publisher.

Chief pubs.: "Breefe Introduction to the Skill of Musick for Song or Viall" (1654; about 25 editions to 1730); and "Playford's Psalter." The tunes in this Psalter are arranged in simple 3-part harmony, and the melody is placed in the treble (instead of in the tenor as in all previous psalters) (See *Hymns.*)

PLAYFORD, Henry. John's son and successor; *b.* 1657; *d.* abt. 1710.

Pub. "The Theatre of Musick," "The Banquet of Musick," several of Purcell's works, &c.

Playhouse tunes. Pieces performed "between the acts" in old London theatres.

Plectrum. A piece of ivory, quill, wood, or metal, for plucking the strings of a mandolin, &c.

Plein (*F.*). Full.

Plein jeu. (1) With the full power. (2) Full organ. (3) A harmonium stop bringing on the full power of the inst. (4) A full mixture.

Ple'no orga'no (*L.*). Full organ.

Plet'tro (*I.*). A plectrum.

PLEY'EL, Camille. Son of Ignaz (below) ; pianist ; *b.* Strasburg, 1788 ; *d.* 1855. Skilfully managed the pf. business established by his father.

PLEY'EL, Ignaz Joseph. Prolific composer ; *b.* nr. Vienna, 1757 ; *d.* 1831. Studied under Haydn's care for 5 years (from his 15th year). Private Capellmeister to Count Erdödy, his patron, until 1781. 2nd Capellmeister, Strasburg Minster, 1781 ; 1st Capellmeister, 1789. Visited London, 1791-2. Founded the pf. factory now known as "Pleyel, Wolff & Co.," Paris, 1797. (Up to 1889 the firm had sold 100,000 pianos.)
Works : 29 symphonies, much chamber music (including 5 books of string quintets and 45 string quartets), 2 vn. concertos, 7 "symphonies concertantes," 2 pf. concertos, sonatas for pf. and vn., much pf. music of all kinds, &c.

PLEY'EL, Marie F. D. (*née* **Moke**). Wife of Camille ; celebrated pianist ; *b.* Paris, 1811 ; *d.* 1875. Pupil of Herz, Kalkbrenner, and Moscheles. Made a "sensational" tour in her 15th year. Prof. Brussels Cons., 1848-72.

Plinti'vo (*I.*). Same as **Plainti'vo** (*q.v.*).

Plock-flöte. Corruption of **Blockflöte** (*q.v.*).

Plötz'lich (*G.*). Suddenly ; at once.
Plötz'lich an'haltend. Suddenly restraining (the speed).
Plötz'lich et'was breit'er. Suddenly somewhat broader (in style or *tempo*).
Plötz'lich schnel'ler. Suddenly quicker.
Plötz'lich wie'der im Zeit'mass. Suddenly again in (strict) *tempo*.

PLÜD'DEMANN, Martin. *B.* Kolberg, 1854 ; . *d.* 1897.
Works : popular male choruses, and numerous fine songs.

Plu'res ex u'na (*L.*). "Many from one." Old name of a canon written on one line.

Plus (*F.*). More.
Plus animé. More animated ; quicker.
Plus de chaleur. With more warmth.
Plus de largeur. } With more breadth.
Plus large. }
Plus lentement. Slower.
Plus modéré. Rather slower.
Plus vite qu'au début. More animated than at the beginning.

Pneu'ma. (See **Neume**.)

Pneumatic action. Mechanism by means of compressed air to lighten the touch, &c., in organs.

Pneumatic organ. (1) The ordinary organ blown by wind. (2) An organ with pneumatic action.

Pochet'ta (*I.*) }
Poche (*F.*) } " A pocket." A small "pocket fiddle," or *kit*,
Pochette (*F.*) } formerly much used by dancing masters.

Pochetti'no (*I.*) } A very little. (See **Poco**.)
Pochet'to (*I.*) }
Ritard un pochetti'no. Make a very slight *rallentando*.

Pochis'simo (*I.*). As little as possible ; a very little.

Po'co (*I.*). A little ; rather, somewhat.
Po'co allegret'to e grazio'so. Graceful and rather quick.
Po'co anima'to. Rather animated.
Po'co a po'co. By degrees ; gradually.
Po'co a po'co du'e ed allo'ra tut'te le cor'de. (See *Poi e poi tutte le corde*.)
Po'co a po'co crescen'do. Gradually louder and louder.
Po'co a po'co crescen'do e stringen'do. Gradually louder and quicker.
Po'co a po'co più calan'do sin al fi'ne. Gradually dying away until the end.
Po'co a po'co, più di fuo'co. Gradually increasing in animation and fire (energy).
Po'co len'to. Rather slow.
Po'co pia'no. Rather soft.
Po'co ritenen'te (Po'co rit.). Retard a little.
Po'co ritenu'to. A little slower (at once).

Po'co me'no (*I.*). A little less. (When used *alone*, same as **Poco meno mosso**.)
Po'co me'no mos'so. Rather less quick ; a little slower.
Un po'co me'no Andante, ciò è : un po'co più Ada'gio co'me il te'ma. A little less "walking ;" that is, a little slower than the theme.
Un po'co me'no for'te. A little less loud.

Po'co più (*I.*). A little more. (When used *alone*, same as **Poco più mosso**.)
Po'co più alle'gro } A little quicker.
Po'co più mos'so }
Po'co più anima'to, ma po'co. A little quicker, but (only a) little.
Po'co più len'to del'la 1ma vol'ta. A little slower than the 1st time.
Po'co più for'te. A little louder.

PODBERT'SKY, Theodor. *B.* Munich, 1846. Favourite composer of male-voice choruses, &c.

Poème Symphonique (*F.*). A symphonic poem.

Poe'ta (*L.*). A "maker." A poet, writer, composer, &c.
Poe'ta nas'citur non fit. "The poet is born, not made" (Latin proverb). "No one has ever become a great man without some degree or measure of divine inspiration."—*Cicero*.

Poetic Basis of Music. (See **Program-music**.)

Poggia'to (*I.*). Leant upon ; dwelt upon ; impressive.

POHL, Karl Ferdinand. *B.* Darmstadt, 1819 ; *d.* 1887. Librarian, "Gesellschaft der Musikfreunde," Vienna, 1866.
Works : "Mozart and Haydn in London," the 1st Vol of a "Biography of Haydn," &c.

POHL, Dr. Richard. (*Nom - de - plume*, "**Hoplit**.") *B.* Leipzig, 1826 ; *d.* 1896. Distinguished critic and writer ; great friend of Liszt ; ardent upholder of the modern "romantic" German school.
Chief works : "Richard Wagner" (1883), "Franz Liszt" (1883), "Hector Berlioz" (1884), a German translation of Berlioz's "Collected Writings," &c. He composed a melodrama, male choruses, songs, &c.

POH'LENZ, Christian A. *B.* Saalgast, 1799 ; *d.* 1843. Orgt. Thomaskirche, Leipzig ; Dir. Gewandhaus Concerts, 1827-35.
Works : male choruses and popular songs.

Po'i (*I.*). Then.
Menuet'to D.C. e po'i la co'da. Repeat the Minuet and then (go on to) the Coda.
Pia'no po'i for'te. Soft, then loud.
Po'i a po'i. By degrees.
Po'i a po'i di nuo'vo viven'te sem'pre u'na cor'da. Gradually more lively, but always with the soft pedal.

Po'i a po'i tut'te le cor'de. Gradually lead up to "all the strings" (after *u'na cor'da* on the pf.), *i.e.*, Gradually release the soft pedal.
Po'i la co'da. (And) then the coda.
Po'i se'gue. Then follows ; here follows.

Point. (1) A dot. (2) A mezzo-staccato mark. (3) Old name for " note."

Point (*F.*). A dot, a point.
Point d'arrêt. The sign ⌒.
Point d'augmentation. A dot after a note.
Point d'orgue. (1) A pedal point (*q.v.*). (2) A pause.
Point de repos. A pause, a rest.
Pointé. Dotted.
Points detachés. Staccato dots.

Pointe (*F.*). A point. Abbn. *p.* The toe (in organ playing).
Pointe d'archet. The point of a bow.

Pointer (*F.*). (1) To dot. (2) To perform in a *staccato* manner.

Pointing. (1) An arrangement of the Psalms, Canticles, &c., for chanting, showing what portions should be taken on the reciting-notes and cadences. (2) The marks indicating such arrangement.

POISE, Jean A. F. *B.* Nîmes, 1828 ; *d.* 1892. Studied Paris Cons.
Works : 14 operas and operettas (*Bonsoir*, 1853 ; *Le Médecin malgré lui*, 1887 ; &c.).

POISOT, Chas. E. Pianist ; Dijon, 1822-1904. Studied Paris Cons. ; Co-founder "Soc. des Compositeurs ; " founder and director Dijon Cons.
Works : operas, chamber music, church music, &c.

Poitrine (*F.*). The chest.
Ut de poitrine. The high C in the chest voice.
Voix de poitrine. The chest voice.

Polac'ca (*I.*) Polish ; a *Polonaise*.
Al'la polac'ca. In the style of a polonaise.

Polac'co,-a (*I.*). Polish ; in Polish style.

POLE, Wm. *B.* Birmingham, 1814 ; *d.* 1900. Mus.D. Oxon, 1864 ; Examiner in Music, London Univ., 1876-90.
Works : "Philosophy of Music" (1879), "The Story of Mozart's Requiem," &c.

Polichinelle (*F.*). A clown dance.

POLIDO'RO, Federigo. Lecturer and writer; *b.* Naples, 1845 ; *d.* 1903.
Works : Sketches of Beethoven, Mozart, Mendelssohn, Wagner, &c. ; studies in Mus. Hist. and Musical Æsthetics, &c.

Polifo'nico,-a (*I.*). Polyphonic (*q.v.*).

Polka. (*I.*, *Pol'ca.*) A popular Bohemian dance in lively 2-4 time. Its characteristic rhythm is—

$$\begin{array}{c}{}^9_4\end{array}$$ &c.

Polka-mazurka. A slower dance in triple time, accented on the last beat of the bar.

POL'KO, Elise (*née* **Vogel**). *B.* nr. Dresden, 1826 ; *d.* 1899. Mezzo-soprano singer and writer of numerous " musical novels."
Her works include " Musikalische Märchen," "Faustina Hasse," "Erinnerungen an F. Mendelssohn-Bartholdy," "Die Classiker der Musik," &c.

POLLARO'LO, Carlo F. *B.* Brescia, 1653 ; *d.* 1722. Singer, orgt., and vice-maestro St. Mark's, Venice, from 1665.
Prod. 64 operas at Venice.

POLLE'DRO, Giovanni B. Violinist ; *b.* nr. Turin, 1781 ; *d.* 1853. Capellmeister Dresden, 1814-24 ; Maestro, Turin Court Orch., 1824-44.
Works : a "Sinfonia pastorale," a mass, a miserere, 5 vn. concertos, vn. studies, &c.

Pol'lice (*I.*). The thumb.

POLLI'NI, Bernhard. (Family name, **POHL.**) Tenor singer and impresario ; *b.* Cologne, 1838 ; *d.* 1897. Director Hamburg City Th. ; 1874 ; Manager Altona Th., 1876 ; "Thalia" Theatre, Hamburg, 1894.

POLLI'NI, Cesare, Cavaliere de'. *B.* Padua, 1858. Director chief Cons. at Padua, 1883-5. Afterwards devoted himself to writing, &c.
Works : a "General Theory of Music," a "Dict. of Musical Terms in Italian and German," &c.

POLLI'NI, Francesco G. Pianist ; pupil of Mozart ; *b.* Laibach, 1763 ; *d.* Milan, 1846. Prof. of pf. Milan Cons., 1809. He is said to have been the first composer to use 3 staves for pf. music.
Works : A Stabat Mater ; much good pf. music, including toccatas, sonatas, caprices, variations, &c. ; and a pf. method.

POL'LITZER, Adolf. Violinist ; *b.* Pesth, 1832 ; *d.* London, 1900. Orch. leader Her Majesty's Th., London, 1851 ; afterwards to the New Philharm. Soc.
Wrote vn. solos and arrangements, &c.

Pol'nisch (*G.*). Polish ; in Polish style.

Po'lo, or O'le. A Spanish dance with singing.

Polonaise (*F.*) } (*G.*, *Polonä'se ;* *I.*, *Po-*
Polonoise (*F.*) } *lac'ca.*) A Polish dance in 3-4 time and moderate *tempo*.
Chopin's Polonaises are the best classical examples of this dance. Schubert's are also noteworthy.

Polska. A Swedish dance in triple time.

Pol'ychord. An inst. "like a double-bass without a neck" with 10 strings ; invented by Hillmer, Leipzig, 1799.

Polymor'phous. Having many forms ; generally used in reference to Canons.

Polypho'nia (*Gk.*) } (1) A combination of
Pol'yphony. } several sounds. (2) Music in several parts.
The term "polyphonic" is applied to the ancient contrapuntal style in which all the parts are of equal interest, as opposed to the modern "homophonic" style in which the highest part (air, treble, melody), is paramount.

Polyphon'ic. (1) See **Polyphony.** (2) Any inst. capable of producing several tones simultaneously ; as the pf., organ, &c.

POMASAN'SKI, Ivan A. *B.* nr. Kiev, 1848.
Works : pf. pieces, several songs, &c.

Pom'mer (*G.*). A *Bombard* (*q.v.*).

Pom'pa (*I.*). (*F. Pompe*). Pomp ; dignity.
Con pom'pa } Pompously ; with dignity and
Pomposamen'te } breadth.
Pompo'so. }

Pom'pös (*G.*). Pompous, majestic.

PONCHARD, Louis A. E. Tenor singer; Paris, 1787-1866. Prof. of singing, Paris Cons., 1819.

PONCHIEL'LI, Amilcare. *B.* nr. Cremona, 1834; *d.* Milan, 1886. Studied Milan Cons., 1843-54. Maestro, Piacenza Cath., 1881. Next to Verdi, he is regarded in Italy as the greatest modern opera composer.
Chief operas : *I promessi Sposa* (1872), *Le due gemelle* (1873), *La Gioconda* (1876), *Marion Delorme* (1885).

Ponctuation (*F.*). Phrasing (*q.v.*).

Pondero'so (*I.*). Ponderous; with weight and impressiveness; well-marked.

PONIATOW'SKI, Jozef M. X. F. J., Prince of Monte Rotondo. Tenor singer; *b.* Rome, 1816; *d.* Chislehurst, 1873.
Works : a dozen operas (*Esmeralda; Gelmina,* London, 1872, &c.) ; also some popular songs.

PO'NITZ, Franz. Noted harpist; *b.* W. Prussia, 1850.

PONS, Jose. Spanish composer; *b.* Gerona, 1768; *d.* 1818.
Wrote notable "Vilhancicos," or short Christmas oratorios.

PON'TE, Lorenzo da. *B.* nr. Venice, 1749; *d.* (in destitution) New York, 1838. Court poet to Joseph II., Vienna; intimate with Mozart, for whom he wrote the libretti of *Figaro, Don Giovanni,* and *Così fan tutte.*

PONTÉCOULANT, Louis A. le Doulcet, Marquis de. *B.* Paris, 1794; *d.* 1882.
Wrote several essays on musical hist. and the construction of mus. insts.

PONTET-PICCOLO'MINI, Henri T. A. M. J. Song composer; *b.* Dublin, 1840(35?); *d.* 1902.

Ponticel'lo (*I.*). "A little bridge." (1) The bridge (of a vn.). (2) The "break" in the voice. (See **Break.**)
Sul ponticel'lo. "Bow near the bridge." (The notes thus produced are more cutting and metallic).

Poo'fye. A Hindoo "nose"-flute.

POOLE, Elizabeth. Mezzo soprano; fine ballad singer; *b.* London, 1820.

POOLE, Fanny Kemble (*nee* **Barnett**). Contralto vocalist; *b.* London, 1845.

Popola're (*I.*). Popular.

POP'PER, David. Distinguished 'cellist; *b.* Prague, 1845; 1st 'cello Vienna Court orch., 1868-73. He has played with great success in all the important capitals of Europe.
Works : a 'cello concerto, a suite for 'cello and pf., numerous 'cello solos, &c.

Popular Music.
Immediate popularity, though it sometimes awaits a new melody or work, is no infallible criterion of the merits of a composition. It is too often true that "a popular air is that which echoes in empty heads."—*H.S.Merriman.*

PORGES, Heinrich. Critic and writer; *b.* Prague, 1837.
Zealous partisan of Wagner.

POR'PORA, Niccola Antonio. *B.* Naples, 1686; *d.* 1766 (or 7). Studied Cons. di San Loreto. Maestro to the Portuguese Ambassador, Naples,1709; opened a vocal school in Naples, abt. 1712 ; singing teacher, Cons. di San Onofrio, 1719; singing teacher, Cons. degli Incurabili, Venice, 1725-8; singing master, Electoral Princess, Dresden, 1728 ; visited London, 1729, and produced several operas ; being unable to obtain a footing in opposition to Handel he left London, 1736, and became Director of the Cons. del' Ospedaletto, Venice. Resided in Vienna, 1745-8, Haydn being his pupil during part of that time ; Capellmeister, Dresden, 1748-51. Director Cons. de San Onofrio, Naples, 1760. His fame rests chiefly on his great ability as a singing teacher. (Among the pupils trained at his Vocal School were Farinelli, Caffarelli, Senesino, Uberti, and Tosi).
Works : about 50 operas (*Berenice,* 1710 ; *Faramondo,* 1719 ; *Ariadne,* 1733 ; *Agrippina,* 1735 ; &c.) ; 6 oratorios ; cantatas for vocal solo, with harpsichord acct. ; 12 vn. sonatas with bass ; 6 fugues for harpsichord, &c.

PORPORI'NO. (See **Uberti.**)

POR'TA, Padre Constanza. Renowned Contrapuntist ; pupil of Willaert ; *b.* Cremona, abt. 1530 ; *d.* Padua, 1601. Maestro successively at Padua, Osima, Ravenna, and Loreto.
Works : motets, masses, introits, madrigals, hymns, psalms, &c.

POR'TA, Francesco della. Milan, 1590(?)-1666.
Works : villanelle, psalms, motets, &c.

POR'TA, Giovanni. *B.* Venice, abt. 1690 ; *d.* 1755. Chorus-master Cons. della Pietà, Venice, abt. 1717-37 ; Court Capellmeister, Munich, 1737.
Wrote about 20 operas.

Portamen'to (*I.*). Gliding by imperceptible degrees from one note to another in solo singing, violin playing, &c.
The *Portamento* is sometimes marked by a slur over the two notes, but more often left to the discretion of the performer. In solo singing it is a beautiful and expressive ornament, very different from the *drawling* of untrained singers.
N.B.—*Portamento,* literally "carrying," is generally used much in the above sense. It is also used for a proper management of the hands, or feet, in playing.
Portamen'to del'la ma'no. Proper use of the hand. In pf. playing this often means "carrying the hand smoothly from note to note, or chord to chord,"
Portamen'to de' pie'di. Correct manner of pedalling.

Portan'do la vo'ce (*I.*). (1) Sustaining ("carrying") the voice. (2) *Portamento.*

Porta'ta (*I.*). The staff.

Porta'te la vo'ce (*I.*). "A direction to *more than one singer to sing portamento.*"—*Baker.*

Por'tative-organ. (*F., Portatif; G., Portativ'.*) A small portable organ.

Porta′to (*I.*). Sustained, held out ; lengthened.

Port de voix (*F.*). "Carrying the voice." (1) *Portamento* (*q.v.*). (2) An obsolete "grace" (a kind of *appoggiatura*).

Portée (*F.*). (1) The staff. (2) *Portamento* (*q.v.*).

PORTER, Samuel. *B.* Norwich, 1733 ; *d.* 1810. Orgt. Canterbury Cath., 1757-1803.
Works : "Cathedral Music" (anthems, chants, &c.)

Porter la voix (*F.*). Same as *Portando la voce* (*q.v.*).

PORT′MANN, Johann G. *B.* Oberlichtenau, Saxony, 1739 ; *d.* 1798.
Pub. treatises on Harmony and Composition, a " Gesangbuch," &c.

PORTOGAL′LO (or **PORTUGAL**), **Marcos Antonio da Fonseca.** The greatest Portuguese composer ; *b.* Lisbon, Mar. 24, 1762 ; *d.* Rio de Janeiro, Feb. 7, 1830. Pupil, Priest's Seminary, Lisbon ; cembalist Madrid Opera, 1782. Studied in Italy, 1787. Condr. San Carlos Th., Lisbon, 1799-1810. Followed the Portuguese Court to Rio de Janeiro, 1810 ; Director Vera Cruz Cons., 1813.
Works : about 40 operas (*L'Astuto*, Florence, 1790 ; *Il filosofo secudente*, Venice, 1798 ; *Le donne cambiate*, &c.) ; operettas, masses, Te Deums, psalms, &c.

Portunal-flute. An organ stop of open wood pipes larger at the top than at the mouth.

Portu′nen (*G.*). A *Bourdon* (*q.v.*).

Pos. Abbn. of *Posaune* (*q.v.*).

Posa′to (*I.*). Reposefully, sedately.

Posau′ne (*G.*). (1) A trombone. (2) A powerful reed stop on the organ ; generally 8 ft. on the manuals and 16 ft. on the pedals.
Posau′nen. To play the Trombone.
Posau′nenbass. An organ reed-stop.
Posau′nenbläser } A trombonist.
Posau′ner }

Poschet′te (*G.*). Same as *Pochette* (*q.v.*).

Posément (*F.*). Gravely, sedately, steadily.

Poser la voix (*F.*). "To poise the voice ; " to attack clearly and with precision in singing.

Positif (*F.*). (1) A chamber organ. (2) The " choir " organ.

Position. (1) Of a chord—
When the *root* of a chord is also the *bass*, it is said to be in its root, original, 1st, or *a* position ; when the 3rd of the chord is in the bass, it is in its 2nd, or *b* position (or 1st inversion) ; when the fifth of the chord is the bass, it is in its 3rd, or *c* position (or 2nd inversion) ; &c.
(2) In violin playing (*G.*, *La′ge* ; *F.*, *Position* ; *I.*, *Posizio′ne*)—
When the left hand is in its ordinary or normal place, it is said to be in the 1st position ; when "shifted" so that the 2nd finger falls on C it is in the 2nd position ; &c.
Close position. Same as *Close harmony* (*q.v.*).
Open position. Same as *Open harmony* (*q.v.*).

Position in singing.
The body should be erect, the head up (but not back), the shoulders back (but not up), the mouth freely open (teeth at least a finger's breadth apart), the tongue flat ; and the singer should " look pleasant."

Positiv′ (*G.*). Same as **Positif** (*q.v.*).

Positive organ. (1) Originally a "fixed" organ as opposed to a *Portative* organ. (2) Old name for the "choir" organ. (See **Organ.**)

Posizio′ne (*I.*). Position (*q.v.*).

Possi′bile (*I.*). Possible.
For′te possi′bile. As loud as possible.
Il più pres′to possi′bile. As fast as possible.
Pianis′simo possi′bile. As soft as possible.

Post-horn. A horn consisting of a single straight tube without valves or pistons.

Posthume (*F.*) } Published after the com-
Pos′thumous (*E.*) } poser's death.

Post′lude } (*G.*, *Nach′spiel* ; *F.*,
Postlu′dium (*L.*) } *Clôture.*) A concluding piece ; an organ voluntary at the end of a service.

POTHIER, Dom Joseph. Noted writer on Gregorian music, neume notation, &c. ; *b.* Bouzemont, nr. Saint-Dié, 1835. Prof. of Theology, Solesmes monastery, 1866.

Potpourri (*F.*). A medley ; a loosely connected succession of tunes or fragments of tunes.

POTTER, P. Cipriani H. Pianist ; London, 1792-1871. Visited Beethoven. Pf. teacher, R.A.M., 1822 ; Principal, 1832-59.
Works : orch. music, chamber music, and numerous pf. pieces.

POTT′GEISSER, Karl. *B.* Dortmund, 1861.
Works : operas, male choruses, songs, &c.

Pouce (*F.*). The thumb.

POUGIN, Arthur. Noted writer and critic ; *b.* Châteauroux, Indre, France, 1834. Studied Paris Cons. ; devoted himself to musical literature, &c., from 1863. Active contributor to the leading French musical journals.
His numerous writings include many "Biographical Sketches," an "Almanac of Music," "Music in Russia," the supplement to Fetis' "Biographie universelle," &c.

Poule, La (*F.*). One of the movements of a quadrille.

POUNDS, Chas. C. Tenor vocalist ; *b.* London, 1869.

Pour (*F.*). For ; to.
Pour finir. "To finish ; " a bar or chord to close the piece.
Pour la première fois. For the first time (only), when there is a repetition.

Poussé (*F.*). "Pushed ; " the up-stroke of the bow (vn., &c.).

POWELL, Maud. Violinist ; *b.* Peru (U.S.), 1868.

POWELL, Thos. Violinist; *b.* London, 1776; *d.* after 1860.
Works: 15 vn. concertos, pf. and vn. sonatas, overtures, &c.

Power of notes. An old term used to signify the various time-values of notes as determined by their shape.

pp, ppp, &c. Abbns. of *Pianissimo.*

Präch'tig (*G.*). In a majestic, dignified style.
Pracht'voll. In a very stately, dignified style.

Präcis' (*G.*). Exact, precise.
Sehr präcis' im Rhyth'mus. Very exact in rhythm.

PRADHER (or **PRADÈRE**), **Louis Barthélemy.** Pianist; *b.* Paris, 1781; *d.* 1843. Pf. prof. Paris Cons., 1802-27.
Works: 7 comic operas, much pf. music, and 22 sets of songs.

PRAE'GER (or **PRÄ'GER**), **Ferdinand C. W.** Pianist; *b.* Leipzig, 1815; *d.* London, 1891. Settled in London as a teacher; English contributor to Schumann's *Neue Zeitschrift für Musik;* early and ardent supporter of Wagner.
Works: orch. pieces, pf. pieces, "Wagner as I knew him," &c.

PRAETO'RIUS (or **PRÄTOR'IUS**), **Hieronymus.** Hamburg, 1560-1629. Organist; town cantor, Erfurt, 1580; asst. orgt. Jacobikirche, Hamburg, 1582; orgt. 1586.
Works: Cantiones Sacræ, magnificats, a "Choralbuch," &c.

PRAETO'RIUS (or **PRÄTOR'IUS**), **Michael.** Celebrated writer and composer; *b.* Kreuzberg, Thuringia, 1571(?); *d.* Wolfenbüttel, 1621. Capellmeister, Lüneberg; afterwards orgt. and capellmeister to the Duke of Brunswick.
Works: "Syntagma Musicum," in 3 vols. (vol. II contains 42 woodcuts of the principal insts. known at the period, and is invaluable as a work of reference); also numerous compositions and collections, including "Musæ Sionæ" (1,244 vocal pieces), madrigals, motets, psalms, hymns, &c.

Prall'triller (*G.*). An inverted *Mordent.* (See **Mordent.**)

Prälu'dien (*G.*). Preludes.
Präludi(e)'ren. To prelude; to play a prelude.

Prä'stant (*G.*). Same as **Prestant** (*q.v.*).

Pra'tico (*I.*) } Practical.
Prat'tico (*I.*) }

PRATT, Silas G. American composer; *b.* Addison, Vermont, 1846. Studied chiefly at Berlin. Pf. prof. New York Metropolitan Cons., 1890.
Works: 2 operas; symphonies and symphonic suites; pf. pieces, part-songs, songs, &c.

PRATTEN, Robt. S. Distinguished flute player; *b.* Bristol, 1824; *d.* 1868.

Präzis' (*G.*). Exact, precise.

Preamble } An introductory voluntary; a prelude.
Préambule (*F.*) }
Pream'bulum (*L.*) }

Precen'tor } Leader of a choir; director and manager of the choir of a church, &c.
Præcen'tor }
Préchantre (*F.*) }

PRECIO'SA. Opera by Weber, 1820.

Precipitazio'ne (*I.*). Precipitation, impetuosity.
Con precipitazio'ne (*I.*) }
Precipitan'do (*I.*) }
Precipitatamen'te (*I.*) } Hurriedly, impetuously, with precipitation.
Precipita'to (*I.*) }
Précipité (*F.*) }
Precipito'so (*I.*) }

Con precisio'ne (*I.*) } With precision and exactness.
Preci'so (*I.*). } exactness.

PREDIE'RI, Luca A. Bologna, 1688-1769.
Wrote 11 operas, an oratorio, &c.

Prefazio'ne (*I.*) Preface.

Prefect'us cho'ri (*L.*). Precentor.

Pregan'do (*I.*). "Praying;" in a devotional, prayerful style.

Preghie'ra (*I.*). A prayer; a piece in devotional style.

PREIND'L, Joseph. *B.* Marbach, Austria, 1756; *d.* 1823. Choirmaster, St. Peter's, Vienna, 1780; Capellmeister, St. Stephen's, 1809.
Works: masses, pf. concertos, a treatise cn "Strict Composition," &c.

PREITZ, Franz. Orgt. and composer; *b.* Zerbst, 1856.

PRELL, Johann N. Fine 'cellist and teacher; Hamburg, 1773-1849.

Prel'ude. (*I., Prelu'dio; L., Prelu'dium; G., Vor'spiel.*) (1) An introduction. (2) An overture (*q.v.*). (3) A movement in a Suite or Partita (*q.v.*). (4) A preliminary trial of an inst. (See **Assaying.**) (5) An introductory voluntary.

Premier, Première (*F.*). First. (Abbns, *1er, 1ère.*)
A première vue. At first sight.
Premier dessus. 1st treble.
Première fois. 1st time.

PRENDERGAST, Arthur H. D. Composer of madrigals, &c.; *b.* London, 1833.

PRENDERGAST, William. *B.* Burneston, Yorks, 1868. Orgt. Winchester Cath., 1902. Mus.D. Oxon, 1904.

PRENTICE, T. Ridley. Pianist; *b.* Ongar, Essex, 1842; *d.* 1895. Pupil of the Macfarrens, R.A.M.; orgt. Christ Ch., Lee, 1872; Pf. prof. R.A.M., 1880.
Works: "The Musician" (a pf. student's guide, with analyses, in 6 grades); pf. pieces, part-songs, &c.

Preparation. (*G., Vor'bereitung; F., Préparation; I., Preparazio'ne.*) Causing a dissonant note to be previously heard as a consonant note. (See **Suspension.**)

Prepared shake } A shake or trill with preparatory grace notes—
Prepared trill }

Préparez (*F.*). Prepare, get ready.
Préparez le ton de sol. Prepare the key of G (for a harp, horn, &c.).

PRES, Josquin des. (See **Deprès.**)

Pre'sa (*I.*). A sign showing the "points of entry" in a canon or round.

PRESCOTT, Oliveria L. Composer and writer ; *b.* London, 1842.
Works : cantatas, anthems, symphonies and overtures, a work on "Form and Design in Music," &c.

Près de (*F.*). Near.
Près de la touche. Near the fingerboard.
Près de la chevalet. Near the bridge.

Pressan'do (*I.*) } "Pressing on ; " *acceler-*
Pressan'te (*I.*) } *ando,* or *stringendo.*

PRES'SEL, Gustav A. *B.* Tübingen, 1827 ; *d.* Berlin, 1890.
Wrote 2 operas, several songs, &c. ; "his researches proved that Mozart wrote the whole of his celebrated Requiem."

PRESSER, Theodore. *B.* Pittsburg, 1848. Founded *The Etude,* a journal for pf. teachers and students, Philadelphia, 1883.

Pressez (*F.*). *Accelerando, stringendo.*
Pressez peu à peu. Quicken by degrees.
Pressez toujours. Quicken continually.
Pressez un peu. A little accelerated.

Pressi'ren (*G.*). To hurry the time ; *accelerando.*

Pressure-note. A sudden *crescendo ;* marked $\overset{\leq}{\rightleftharpoons}$ $\overset{\leq}{\rightharpoondown}$ or, $\overset{pf.}{\rightleftharpoons}$ $\overset{pff.}{\rightharpoondown}$.

Prestamen'te (*I.*) } Hurriedly, quickly.
Con prestez'za (*I.*) } (See also **Presto.**)

Prestant (*F.*). An open diapason (org. stop); same as the "Principal" on English organs.

Pres'to (*I.*). Fast ; quick, nimble.
Più pres'to qua'si prestis'simo. More quickly, as if *prestissimo.*
Prestis'simo } (Superlative of *Presto.*) Very fast.
Presto presto }
Prestissimamen'te. As fast as possible.
Pres'to al'la tedes'ca. Fast, and in the German (waltz) style (allowing of changes of *tempo*).
Pres'to assa'i. Very fast.
Pres'to parlan'te. Rapid utterance (in Recitative, &c.).

PRESTON, Jas. M. Orgt. and composer ; *b.* Gateshead, 1860.

PRÉVOST, Eugène P. Conductor ; *b.* Paris, 1809 ; *d.* New Orleans, 1872. *Grand Prix de Rome,* Paris Cons., 1831. Lived chiefly in Paris and America.
Works : oratorios, masses ; and several operas (for Paris and New Orleans).

PREVO'STI, Franzeschina. Soprano ; *b.* Leghorn, 1866.

PREY'ER, Gottfried von. *B.* Hausbrunn, Lower Austria, 1809 ; *d.* 1901. Director Vienna Cons., 1844-8 ; Court orgt., 1846; pensioned, 1876; ennobled, 1893.
Works : oratorio (*Noah*), 3 operas, a symphony, masses, hymns, pf. and org. pieces, songs, &c.

PRICE, Daniel. Baritone vocalist ; *b.* Dowlais, Glamorgan, 1862. Member Westminster Abbey Choir, 1888.

Prick-song } Term used in Elizabethan times
Prickt song } for "written" music as opposed to improvised descant. (See **Descant.**)

Prière (*F.*). A prayer.

PRILL, Karl. *B.* Berlin, 1864. Violinist ; pupil of Joachim ; Leader Gewandhaus Orch., Leipzig, 1891.

Pri'ma, (*I., Feminine.*) First, chief. (See also **Primo.**)
Pri'ma buf'fa. Chief comic actress or lady singer.
Pri'ma don'na. Chief lady singer in an opera.
Pri'ma op'era. A first work.
Pri'ma vi'sta. (At) first sight.
Pri'ma vol'ta (abbn. 1ma volta, or 1). The first time (of a passage which is repeated).

Pri'mary accent. The strong accent of a bar, directly following the bar-line.

Primary dissonance. The dissonance between two dissonating tones when placed in their closest position.

Primary triads. The triads of the Tonic, Dominant, and Sub-dominant of any key (major or minor).

Prime. (1) A tonic, root, or generator. (2) The lower note of an interval. (3) A unison.
Augmented prime. A chromatic semitone.

Primer (*F., Primaire ; I., Prima'rio*)· (1) A small prayer book ; an office of the Virgin Mary. (2) An elementary text-book.

Prim'geiger (*G.*). Leading 1st vn. ; leader·

Primice'rio (*S.*) } The cantor, precentor,
Primice'rius (*L.*) } or succentor of a cathedral.

Primitive chord. A chord with its root in the bass.

Pri'mo. (*I., Masculine.*) First ; chief. (See also **Prima.**)
Co'ro pri'mo. The first chorus.
Pri'mo buf'fo. Chief comic actor or male singer.
Pri'mo can'to. First treble.
Pri'mo mu'sico } Chief male singer in an opera.
Pri'mo uo'mo }
Tem'po pri'mo } The original (or first) rate of speed.
Prim. tempo }
Violi'no pri'mo. First violin (of an orch., &c.).

Prin'cipal. (1) Old Eng. name for the subject of a fugue. (2) Old name for a trumpet playing the lowest part.

Principal (*F.*) } An open diapason ; 8 ft.
Prinzipal' (*G.*) } on the manuals, 16 ft. on the pedals.
Prinzipal'stimme. Solo, or leading part.

Prin'cipal. On Eng. organs, a 4 ft. open diapason on the manuals, or 8 ft. on the pedals.
The "scale" of tuning is first set on the *Principal,* and all the other stops are then tuned in unison or octaves with it.

Prin'cipal }
Principa'le (*I.*) } Chief.
Principal violin } The leading violin.
Violi'no principa'le (*I.*) }

Principal subject, or theme. One of the chief themes of a movement in "sonata" form, as opposed to *subordinate, accessory,* or *subsidiary* themes. (See **Sonata.**)

Princi'pio (*I.*). The beginning ; the first time.
Più marca'to del princi'pio. More *marcato* than the 1st time.

PRINGLE, Godfrey. Composer ; *b.* 1867.

PRINGLE, Lemprière. Bass vocalist ; *b.* Hobart, Tasmania, 1869.

PRINGUER, Henry Thos. Composer and conductor ; Mus.D. Oxon, 1885.

PRINTZ, Wolfgang C. *B.* Waldthurn, 1641 ; *d.* 1717.

Wrote treatises, &c., interesting to musical antiquarians.

Prise (*F.*). Entry. *Reprise*, re-entry.

Prise du sujet. Entry of the subject.

Proas'ma. (1) A prelude, or introduction. (2) A short symphony.

Pro'be (*G.*). " A proof ; " a rehearsal.

General'probe. A full rehearsal.

Probi(e)'ren. To rehearse, try over.

Procel'la (*I.*). A storm, a tempest.

PROCH, Heinrich. *B.* Böhmisch-Leipa, 1809 ; *d.* Vienna, 1878. Capellmeister, Vienna Court Opera, 1840-70. Among his pupils was Tietjens (*q.v.*).

Works : 4 operas, and several once-popular songs.

PROCHÁZ'KA, Clementine. (See **Frau Schuch.**)

PROCHAS'KA, Ludwig. Prague, 1837-88. A "noted composer of Bohemian songs and duets."

PROCHÁZ'KA, Rudolf, Freiherr von. *B.* Prague, 1864.

Noted as a song composer ; also a "Mystery," operas, male choruses, orch. and chamber music ; writings on Mozart, Franz, &c.

PROCTER, Adelaide Ann. 1825-64. Wrote the words of "The Lost Chord," several hymns, &c.

PRODHOMME, Jacques G. Musical historian ; *b.* Paris, 1871. Lived in Munich, 1897-1900.

Chief works : " Studies of Berlioz," " Analysis of Wagner's *Götterdämmerung.*"

Profa'no,-a (*I.*). Secular.

Professeur de chant (*F.*). A singing master.

Pro'gram
Programm' (*G.*)
Program'ma (*I.*)
Programme (*F.*) } A list of the pieces to be performed at a concert, &c.

Pro'gram Music. (*G., Programm'musik.*) Instrumental music illustrating a "program" of events, scenes, or emotions.

Program music includes both " Imitative music" (*q.v.*) and "music with a poetic basis."
" The passion for realism in art, and especially in the art of music, seems universal ; . . . . pure music the mass of us cannot grasp ; we prefer that which humbly waits upon legend or poem, the character of a crazy knight-errant, or the proceedings of a day in a composer's household. . . . Between music pure and free (as the C minor symphony of Beethoven, for example), and that which is the slave of a programme, there is no comparison. . . . Abstract music, the fine flower of the art, we now seem to be in danger of losing, . . . a sign of non-attainment certain to be removed as culture progresses."— *Daily Telegraph, Dec.,* 1906.

Progres'sio Harmon'ica. An org. mixture stop " which, instead of *breaking,* increases in the number of ranks as the pitch rises."

Progression. (*G., Fort'schreitung ; F., Progrès, Marche ; I., Progressio'ne.*) The movement from one note or chord to another.

Melodic progression. The succession of notes forming a melody.

Harmonic progression. Progression from chord to chord.

Progressions'-schweller (*G.*). A kind of *crescendo* swell pedal invented by Abbé Vogler. (See **Organ,** and **Pedal.**)

Progressive notes. Old name for diatonic notes. (See **Diatonic.**)

Proibi'to (*I.*). Forbidden.

Interval'lo proibi'to. A forbidden interval ; in ancient counterpoint, the tritone, *the major 6th,* the 7th, 9th, &c.

PROKSCH, Josef. Pianist ; *b.* Bohemia, 1794 ; *d.* 1864. Became blind 1811 ; founded a "School of Pf. Playing," Prague, 1830.

Wrote several treatises on pf. playing, &c. ; a concerto for 3 pfs., sonatas, masses, cantatas, vocal pieces, &c.

Prola'tio (*L.*). In early mensural music " the subdivision of a semibreve into 2 or 3 minims."

Prologue. An introduction, a prelude.

Prolongement (*F.*). A *sostenuto* pf. pedal.

Prolongement Harmonique. A mechanical device— rarely employed—for sustaining a chord or note on an organ or harmonium.

PROME'THEUS. Beethoven's only ballet, 1800.

Promptement (*F.*)
Prontamen'te (*I.*)
Pron'to (*I.*) } Promptly, readily, quickly.

Pronunciation of Musicians' Names.

Without some knowledge of German, French, and Italian, it is often impossible to pronounce foreign names quite correctly. The following, from the most reliable sources, afford, however, an approximate guide ; and names not in this list can be fairly pronounced by means of the accent marks given with them (in their proper places).
The vowel marked ĕ or ŭ is the obscure sound of *e* in " shrapnel," " partner," &c., as ordinarily pronounced in speaking.
N.B.—Many of the best-known names are allowed by custom to be pronounced as if English.

ÆRTS : Erts.
ALLEGRI : Al-lay'-gree.
AMATI : Ah-mah'-tee.
ANIMUCCIA : Ahn-ee-moot'-chah (*ch* as in "church").
ARENSKY : Ah-ren-shkĭ (*ĭ* as in "pin').; or Ah-ren'-skee.
ARTOT : Ar-to (*o* as in "toe").
AUBER : O-bair (*ai* as in "pair").
AUER : Ow'-er (*ow* as in "cow").
BACH : Bahkh.
BACHE : Baych (*ch* as in "church").
BALAKIREV : Bah-lah-kee'-reff.
BARTHOLDY : Bar-tol-dee (*o* as in "wrong").
BATISTE : Ba-teest'.
BECHSTEIN : Bekh'-s(h)tine.
BEETHOVEN : Bayt'-ho-vn (*o* as in "so").
BELLINI : Bel-lee'-nee.
BENOÎT : Bŭh(ng)-wah'.
BERLIOZ : Bair-li-ose (*ai* as in "pair" ; *ose* as in "rose")."
BIANCHI : Bee-ahn'-kee.
BIZET : Bee-zay'.
BOËLLMANN : Bwell'-mahn.
BOIELDIEU : Bwall-dyu'.
BOÏTO : Bo-ee'-to (*o* as in "toe").

BONONCINI : Bo-non-chee'-nee (*ch* as in "church").
BORODIN : Bo'-ro-deen (*o* as in "toe").
BREMA : Bray'-mah.
BRUCH : Brookh (*oo* as in "boot").
BRUCKNER : Brook'-ner (*oo* as in "boot").
BRÜLL : Brill.
BUSONI : Boo-so'-nee.
CACCINI : Caht-chee'-nee (*ch* as in "church").
CALVÉ : Cal-vay.
CARISSIMI : Cah-ris'-see-mee.
CARRENO : Car-rain'-yo (*ai* as in "pain").
CAVAILLÉ-COLL : Ca-vy-yay-coll (*vy* rhymes with "my").
CHAMINADE : Sham'-i-nahd'.
CHERUBINI : Kay-roo-bee'-nee.
CHEVÉ : Shŭ-vay.'
CHLADNI : Klaht'-nee ; *or* Klahd'-nee.
CHOPIN : Sho-pa(ng).
CHORON : Sho-ro(ng) ; *or* Ko-ron.
COENEN : Koo'-nen ; *or*, Kö'nen.
COUPERIN : Coo-pŭ-ra(ng).
CRAMER : Crah'-mer.
CRANZ : Krahnts.
CUI : Kwee.
CZERNY : Chair'-nee.
DANNREUTHER : Dahn'-roy-ter.
DARGOMIJSKY : Dar-go-meesh'-shkee.
DEHN : Dane.
DELIBES : Dŭ-leeb'.
DE RESZKE : Dŭ Resh'-kay.
DIENEL : Dee'-nel.
DOHNANYI : Doh-nahn'-yee.
DONIZETTI : Doh-nee-tset'-tee.
DRAESEKE : Dray'-zě-kě.
DREYSCHOCK : Dry'-shock.
DUBOIS : Du-bwah'.
DUPUIS : Du-pwee'.
DUSSEK : Doo'-shek.
DVORAK : Dvor-shahk'.
EAMES : Aims.
EBERWEIN : A'-ber-vine (*a* as in "ale").
EGGHARD : Egg'-hart.
EIBENSCHUTZ : I'-ben-shüts (*I* as in "ice" ; modified German *ü*).
ERLANGER : Er-lah(ng)-zhay.
EULENBURG : Oi'-len-boorkh.
EULER : Oiler.
FAURÉ : Fo-ray (*o* as in "foe").
FAUST : Fowst (*ow* as in "cow").
FÉTIS : Fay-teece'.
FIBICH : Fee'-bĭkh (*i* as in "pin").
FLOTOW : Flow'-to (*ow* as in "flow" ; *o* as in "toe").
FRANZ : Frahnts.
FUX : Fooks (*oo* as in "fool").
GADE : Gah'-dě.
GALILEI : Gah-lĭ-lay'-ee.
GAUTIER }
GAULTIER } Goat-yay.
GAUTHIER }
GEDALGE : Zhay-dahlzh.
GENÉE : Zhŭ-nay'.
GEVAERT : Zhŭ-vart, *or* Gay'-vart.
GLUCK : Glook (*oo* as in "boot").
GOETZ : Gets.
GOSSEC : Goss'-sek.
GOUNOD : Goo-no.
GRAUN : Grown (rhyming with "crown").
GRIEG : Greeg.
GRISI : Gree'-zee.
GUIDO : Gwee'-doh.
GUILMANT : Geel-mah(ng) (*G* hard, as in "geese").
GUNGL : Goong'-l (*oo* as in "boot").
HALEVY : Ă-lay-vee.
HANDEL : *E.* Han'-dl.
HÄNDEL, *or* HAENDEL : *G.* Hayn'-dtl.
HASSE : Hahss'-sě.
HAUPTMANN : Howpt'-mahn (*ow* as in "cow").
HAUSMANN : House'-mahn.
HAYDN : *G.* High'-dn ; *E.* Hay'-dn.
HÉROLD : A-rol (*a* as in "fate" ; *o* as in "wrong").
HILLER : Hill'-ler (*i* as in "pin").
HUMMEL : Hoom'-mel (*oo* as in "boot").
HUTSCHENRUIJTER : Hoot'-shen-roy-ter.
IBACH : Ee'-bahkh.
ISOUARD : Ee-zoo-ar'.

JADASSOHN : Yah'-dahs-zone.
JAELL : Yale.
JAHN : Yahn.
JANKÓ : Yahng'-ko.
JANOTHA : Yah-no'-tah.
JÉHIN : Zhay-an(g).
JENSEN : Yen'-sen.
JOACHIM : Yo'-ah-kheem.
JOMMELLI : Yom-mel'-lee.
JOSEFFY : Yo-sef'-fi.
JUL(L)IEN : Zhül-yah(ng).
KES : Case.
KIND : Kĭndt (*i* as in "pin").
KIRCHNER : Keerkh'-ner.
KJERULF : K'yay'-roolf.
KLINDWORTH : Klint'-vort.
KÖHLER : Ku(r)'-ler.
KOPECKÝ : Ko-pet'-skee.
KREU(T)ZER : Kroy'-tser.
KUBELIK : Koo'-bě-lĭk.
KUHLAU : Koo'-low (*ow* as in "allow").
LABLACHE : Lah-blash'.
LAMOUREUX : Lam-oo-rü' (modified French *ü*).
LANGE : Lahng'-ě.
LAURENT DE RILLE : Lo-rah(ng) dŭ Ree'-yŭ.
LEFÉBURE WÉLY : Lŭ-fay'-bür-Vay'-lee.
LESCHETITSKY : Lesh-ě-tit'-shkĭ (*or* "skee").
LINDPAINTNER : Lĭndt'-pint-ner (*i* as in "pin" ; i as in "pint").
LISZT : List (better than "Least").
LOESCHHORN }
LÖSCHHORN } Lesh'-horn.
LULLI : Lool'-lee (*oo* as in "boot").
MAILLY : My-yee.
MALIBRAN : *F.*, Mal-ĭ-brah(ng) ; *E.*, Mal'-I-bran.
MARA : Mah'-rah.
MARCHESI : Mahr-kay'-zee.
MASCAGNI : Mahs-kahn'-yee.
MASSENET : Mass-nay.
MATTEI : Maht-tay'-ee.
MAUREL : Mo-rel.
MÉHUL : May-ül.
MENDELSSOHN : *G.*, Men'-d'l-zone ; *E.*, Men'-dl-sn.
MERKEL : Mair'-kěl (*ai* as in "pair").
MESSAGER : Mes-sa-zhay.
MEYERBEER : My'-er-bair (*ai* as in "pair").
MOLIQUE : Mol-eek'.
MONSIGNY : Mon-seen-yee.
MONTEVERDE : Mon-tay-vair'-dee.
MOSCHELES : Mosh'-ě-less.
MOSZKOWSKI : Mosh-koff'-shkĭ (*or* "skee").
MOZART : *G.*, Moat'-sahrt ; *E.*, Mo-zahrt'.
MYSLIWECZEK : Mee-slee'-vay-chek.
NÁCHEZ : Nat'-ches (*ch* as in "church").
NAUMANN : Now'-mahn.
NEUKOMM : Noy'-komm.
NICODÉ : Nee'-ko-day.
NICOLAI : Nee'-ko-li (*i* as in "light").
NIECKS : Neeks.
NIKISCH : Nik'-ish.
NOSZKOWSKI : Nosh-koff'-shkĭ (*or* "skee").
NOTTEBOHM : Not'-tě-boam (*oa* as in "boat").
OELSNER : Else'-ner.
ONDRICZEK : On'-drĭ-chek (*i* as in "pin" ; *ch* as in "church").
PACHMANN : Pahkh'-mahn.
PADEREWSKI : Pah-der-ess'-kĭ (*or* "kee").
PALADILHE : Pal-ah-deel.
PALESTRINA : Pah-less-tree'-nah.
PASDELOUP : Pah-dŭ-loop.
PAUER : Power.
PEPUSCH : Pay'-poosh.
PERGOLESI : Pair-go-lay'-see.
PERI : Pay'-ree.
PIZZI : Pid'-zee.
PLANQUETTE : Plahn(g)-ket.
PONCHIELLI : Pon-ki-el'-lee.
PONIATOWSKI : Po-nĭ-ah-toff'-shkĭ (*or* "skee").
PUGNO : Pün-yo.
QUANTZ : Kvahnts.
QUINAULT : Kee-no.
RAMEAU : Rah-mo.
REGER : Ray'-ger (*g* as in "get").
REICHA : Righ'-khah (*igh* as in "high").
REINECKE : Righ'-ně-kě (*igh* as in "high").

REISS : Rice.
REUBKE : Royp'-kĕ.
RHEINBERGER : Rhine'-berkh-er.
RICHTER : Rĭkh-ter (*i* as in "pin").
RIEMANN : Ree'-mahn.
ROECKEL } Rek'-el.
RÖCKEL }
ROSENTHAL : Ro'-zen-tahl.
ROSSINI : Ross-see'-nee.
ROUSSEAU : Roos-so.
RUBINSTEIN : Roo'-bin-stine (*or* "shtine").
SACCHINI : Sahk-kee'-nee.
SACHS : Zahkhs ; *E.*, Sahks.
SAINT-SAËNS : San(g)-Sah'(ng).
SALVAYRE : Sal-var'.
SARASATE : Sah-rah-sah'-tĕ.
SAUER : Zow'-er (*ow* as in "cow").
SAURET : So-ray.
SAX : Sacks.
SCHARWENKA : Shahr-ven'-kah.
SCHNEIDER : Shny'-der.
SCHUBERT } Shoo'-bĕrt (*oo* as in "boot").
SCHUBERTH }
SCHULTZ } Shoolts (*oo* as in "boot").
SCHULZ }
SCHUMANN : Shoo'-mahn.
SEIDL : Zight'-'l.
SICARD : See-car.
SINDING : Zĭnt'-ĭng ; *E.*, Sĭnd'-ing (*i* as in "pin").
SMETANA : Smay'-tah-nah.
STAVENHAGEN : S(h)tah'-fĕn-hah-gĕn (*g* as in "get").
STORACE : Sto-rah'-chee (*ch* as in "church").
STRAUSS : Strowss (*ow* as in "cow").
TAMAGNO : Tah-mahn'-yo.
TAUBERT : Tow'-bert (*ow* as in "cow").
TCHAIKOVSKY } Tshah-ee-koff'-shkĭ (*or* " skee)."
TSCHAIKOWSKI } *E.*, Chi-koff'-skee (*chi* as in "child").
THALBERG : Tahl'-berkh ; *E.*, Tal'-berg.
THOMÉ : Toe-may.
TIETJENS : Teet'-yĕns.
TINEL : Tee-nell'.
TOMBELLE : To(ng)-bell.
UBERTI : Oo-ber'-tee.
URSPRUCH : Oor'-sprookh.
VACCAI } Vahk-kah'-ee.
VACCAJ }
VERDI : Vair'-dee ; *E.*, Ver'-dee.
VIARDOT : Vĭ-ar'-doh.
VIEUXTEMPS : V'yŭ-tah(ng).
VOGEL : Foe'-gĕl ; *E.*, Vo'-gel.
VOGLER : Fōkh'-lĕr (*o* as in "folk") ; *E.*, Voh'-gler.
VOLKMANN : Folk'-mahn (*o* as in "wrong" ; *l* sounded).
VUILLAUME : Vwee-yome (*o* as in "home").
WAGNER : Vahkh'-nĕr ; *E.*, Vahg'-ner.
WALTHER : Vahl'-tĕr ; *E.*, Wall'-ter, *or* Wall'-ther.
WEBER : Vay'-bĕr.
WEINGARTNER : Vine'-gahrt-nĕr.
WIDOR : Vee-dor.
WIECK : Veek .
WIENIAWSKI : V'yay-nee-ahff'-shkĭ (*or* "skee").
WILHELMJ : Veel-hell'-mee.
WINTER : *G.*, Vin'-ter ; *E.*, Winter.
WOLLENHAUPT : Vol'-len-howpt (*o* as in "wrong" ; *ow* as in "cow").
WÜLLNER : Vill'-nĕr.
YSAYE : Ee-sigh'-yŭ.
ZAJIC : Zah'-yeach (*each* as in "peach").
ZELTER : Tsell'-tĕr.
ZICHY : Tsee'-shee.
ZÖLLNER : Tsell'-nĕr.
ZUMPE : Tsoom'-pĕ.

Pronunzia'to (*I.*). Marked, pronounced ; emphasized.

Ben pronunzia'to. Well enunciated ; well emphasized.

Proper-chant. Old name for a chant in C major.

PROPHÈTE, Le. Opera by Meyerbeer, 1849.

Proportion. Ratio ; balance, symmetry.

In medieval music, a highly-complex system of ratios for determining intervals, proportions of rhythms and cross rhythms, duple and triple

divisions of notes, &c. The science of Acoustics, and our modern Time-table and Time-signatures have fortunately superseded this " intricate pedantry of Mensural Music."

Propo'sta (*I.*). The subject of a fugue.

Pro'sa (*L.*). (*F., Prose.*) A hymn sung before the Gospel in the Roman Catholic service.

Pro'sae sequen'tiæ (*L.*). } A book of "proses."
Prosa'rium (*L.*). }

Prosce'nio (*I.*) } (1) The space *behind* the
Prosce'nium } stage. (2) The "stage front" from the curtain to the foot-lights. (The word is generally used in this sense.)

Prose. (See **Prosa**.)

PROS'KE, Karl. *B.* Gröbnig, 1794 ; *d.* Ratisbon, 1861. Canon and Capell-meister, Ratisbon Cath., 1830.

Pub. valuable reprints of sacred classics, includ-ing Palestrina's *Missa Papæ Marcelli*, and "Musica Divina" (master works of the 16th and 17th cents.) in 4 vols.

Proslambanom'enos (*Gk.*). "Additional." (See **Greek Music**.)

Pros'ody. (*L.* and *I., Prosodi'a :* *G., Prosodie'; F., Prosodie.*) The science of Metre (*q.v.*) ; especially the laws of versification.

Prospekt' (*G.*). Front of an organ.

PROUDMAN, Joseph. Condr. and teacher ; London, 1833-91.

PROUT, Ebenezer. *B.* Oundle, Northamp-tonshire, 1835. Chiefly self-taught. B.A., London, 1854 ; Orgt. Union Chapel, Islington, 1861-73 ; Pf. prof. Crystal Palace School of Art, 1861-85 ; Prof. of Harmony and Counterpoint National Training School, 1876 ; Prof. R.A.M., 1879 ; Condr. Hackney Choral Association, 1876-90 ; Editor, *Monthly Mus. Record*, 1871-4 ; Critic, *Academy* (1874-9), *Athenæum* (1879-89). Prof. of Music, Dublin Univ., 1894 ; Mus.Doc. (Dublin and Edinburgh), 1895.

Works : 4 symphonies, 2 overtures, &c. ; 2 org. concertos ; chamber music ; cantatas (*Alfred*, 1882 ; *Red Cross Knight*, 1887 ; &c.) ; church music, anthems, org. arrangements, &c. Also valued treatises on "Instrumentation," "Har-mony," "Counterpoint," "Fugue," "Musical Form," "The Orchestra," &c.

PROUT, Louis B. Son of preceding ; *b.* London, 1864.

Author of " Harmonic Analysis," " Sidelights on Harmony, &c.

Pro'va (*I.*). "A proof ; " a rehearsal.

Pro'va in costu'me. Dress rehearsal.
Pro'va genera'le. Full rehearsal.

Provençales. The early troubadours of Provence.

" In this country the rhymers and minstrels of mediæval times seem to have had their origin." —*Stainer and Barrett.*

PRUCK'NER, Caroline. Renowned soprano; *b.* Vienna, 1832. Suddenly lost her

voice, 1855 ; started a School of Opera, Vienna, 1870.
Wrote a valuable "Theory and Practice of the Art of Singing," 1872.

PRUCK'NER, Dionys. Distinguished pianist and teacher ; *b.* Munich, 1834 ; *d.* 1896. Pupil of Liszt, 1852-6. Teacher, Stuttgart Cons., 1859 ; Court pianist, 1864 ; "Royal Professor," 1868.

PRUDENT, Emile. Pianist ; *b.* Angoulême, 1817 ; *d.* 1863. 1st prize, Paris Cons., 1833, for pf. playing. After successful tours settled in Paris as teacher.
Wrote pf. pieces (études, *salon* music, &c.).

PRÜ'FER, Dr. Arthur. *B.* Leipzig, 1860. Lecturer and prof. Leipzig Cons.
Works : treatises on musical subjects, a collection of "Schein's Complete Works," &c.

PRUME, François H. Violinist ; *b.* nr. Liége, 1816 ; *d.* 1849.
Works : pieces for vn., with pf. or orch., &c.

PRUMIER, Antoine. Harpist ; Paris, 1794-1868. Harpist, Opéra-Comique, &c. ; Prof. at the Cons. (1835).
Works : about 100 harp pieces.

PRUMIER, Ange C. Son of Antoine ; Paris, 1821(?)-1884. Harpist, Opéra-Comique, &c. ; Prof. at the Cons. (1870).
Works : harp pieces and studies ; sacred songs.

Psalm. (*Gk., Psal'mos,* to play on a stringed inst ; *G., Psal'm ; F., Psaume.*) An ode, song, or hymn. (See **Hymn.**)
Psallettes. Mediæval schools for teaching descant.
Psal'mbuch (*G.*). A Psalter.
Psal'mgesang (*G.*). Psalmody.
Psalm'ist. A writer of psalms.
Psalm-melod'icon. An inst. imitating different orchl. wind insts., invented by Weinrich, 1828.
Psalm'ody. The singing of psalms and hymns.
Psal'msammlung (*G.*). A collection of psalms.
Psal'ter. A book of psalms (often with the music).
Psalte'rium (*L.*). (1) A psalter. (2) A psaltery.
Psaume des morts (*F.*). A funeral hymn or psalm.

Psalmody Island.
An island in the ancient diocese of Nismes which derived its name from a monastery founded there in the 14th cent. by a Syrian monk. A "perpetual psalmody" was enjoined called "*Laus perennis.*"

Psal'tery. An ancient Hebrew stringed inst. (the Kinnor).

Psal'triæ (*L.*). Female musicians at the old Roman banquets.

Psautier (*F.*). A Psalter.

PTOL'EMY, Claudius. Alexandrian astronomer, mathematician, &c. Wrote a treatise on music, 2nd cent. A.D.

PUCCI'NI, Giacomo. Prominent opera composer ; *b.* Lucca, 1858. Studied Milan Cons. under Ponchielli ; Prof. of Composition, Milan Cons., 1893.
Chief operas : *Edgar* (Milan, 1889), *Manon Lescaut* (Turin, 1893), *La Bohème* (Turin, 1896), *La Tosca* (1899), *Madama Butterfly* (Milan,1904).

PUCHAL'SKI, Vladimir V. Russian pianist ; *b.* Minsk, 1848.
Works : an opera, orch. music, pf. pieces, songs.

PU'CHAT, Max. Pianist ; *b.* Breslau, 1859. Won the Mendelssohn prize, Berlin, 1884.
Works : symphonic poems, a pf. concerto, songs.

PUCIT'TA, Vincenzo. *B.* Civitavecchia, 1778 ; *d.* 1861. Cembalist, Italian Opera, Paris. Wrote about 30 operas.

PU'DOR, Dr. Heinrich. "Voluminous and eccentric writer on musical subjects ; " *b.* Dresden, abt. 1860.

PUGET, Loïsa (Mad. Lemoine). Composer ; Paris, 1810(?)-1889.

PUGET, Paul C. M. *B.* Nantes, 1848. *Grand Prix de Rome,* Paris Cons., 1875.
Works : operas, incidental stage music, songs, &c.

PUGNA'NI, Gaetano. Noted violinist ; Turin, 1731-98. Leader, Court Orch., Turin, 1752 ; toured from 1754 ; leader, Italian Opera, London, for some years ; Maestro, Turin Court Theatre, 1770 . Also founded a school for violinists ; Viotti was his pupil.
Works : several operas ; 9 vn. concertos ; 14 vn. sonatas ; 12 octets for strings, 2 oboes, and 2 horns ; vn. trios, duets, solos, &c.

PUGNO, Raoul. Fine pianist ; *b.* Montrouge, 1852. Studied Paris Cons. ; took 1st pf. prize (1866), 1st harmony prize (1867), and 1st organ prize (1869) ; Prof. of pf., Paris Cons., 1896 ; officer of the *Académie.*
Works : an oratorio, stage pieces (operettas, vaudevilles, &c.), pf. pieces, songs.

PULI'TI, Leto. Florence, 1818-75.
One of his numerous essays gives valuable information concerning Cristofori (*q.v.*).

Pulpi'tum (*L.*). (1) The stage of an ancient Greek theatre. (2) A *Motet.*

Pul'satile. Instruments of percussion ; drum, cymbals, gong, &c.

Pulsa'tor organo'rum (*L.*). "Organ beater." (See **Organ.**)

Pulse. "The time between one accent, of whatever kind, and the next."—*Curwen.*
The pulse in simple times is generally the same as a "beat." In quick compound times the pulse is "one-third of a beat." In Tonic Sol-fa, measures are described by the number of pulses they contain ; thus—2-pulse measure, 3-pulse measure, &c. (See *Measure.*)

Pult (*G.*). A desk.
Pult'virtuos. A distinguished conductor.

Punc'tus (*L.*).
Punc'tum (*L.*) }A point, a dot ; a neume.
Punc'tus con'tra punc'tum. "Point against point ; " counterpoint.

Punkt (*G.*). A dot, a point.
Punkti(e)rt'. Dotted.
Punkti'rte No'ten. Dotted notes.

Pun'ta (*I.*). A point.
Col'la pun'ta dell' ar'co. With the point (tip) of the bow in vn. playing.
Pun'ta d' or'gano. An organ-point (*q.v.*).
Punta'to. Pointed, detached ; *staccato.*

Pun'to (*I.*). A dot, a point.
Pun'to corona'ta. A hold (⌒).

PUN'TO, Giovanni. (See **Stich.**)

23

Pupitre (*F.*). (1) A motet. (Same as **Pulpitum** (2)). (2) A music desk.

PUP'PO, Giuseppe. Eccentric violinist ; *b*. Lucca, 1749 ; *d*. in poverty, 1827.
For several years a "fashionable" teacher in London and Paris.

PURCELL, Daniel. Brother of Henry (below) ; London, 1660-1717.
Wrote anthems, odes, incidental stage music, &c.

PURCELL, Henry. "The most original and extraordinary musical genius that our country (England) has produced."— *Grove's Dict*. *B*. St. Ann's Lane, Old Pye Street, Westminster, 1658 ; *d*. Dean's Yard, Westminster, Nov. 21, 1695. Chorister, Chapel Royal, 1664 ; wrote his first dramatic music, 1676 ; Orgt. Westminster Abbey, 1680 ; Composer-in-Ordinary to the King, 1683 ; pub. his first chamber music (sonatas for 2 vns. and org. or harpsichord), 1683, and from this date composed with "extraordinary activity" till his death. He was buried in Westminster Abbey. His memorial tablet bears the following quaint inscription :—"Here lyes Henry Purcell, Esq., who left this life, and is gone to that blessed place where only his harmony can be exceeded."
Chief works : *Timon of Athens* (1678), *Dido and Æneas* (1688(90?), *The Tempest* (1690), "The Yorkshire Feast Song" (1690), *Dioclesian* (1690), *King Arthur* (1691), *Bonduca* (1695) ; 28 odes ; ayres, songs, &c. ; services, abt. 50 anthems, sacred songs, psalms, hymns ; sonatas for vn. and bass, Harpsichord Lessons, &c. Beside those given above, Purcell wrote the music to about 30 dramatic works.

Purcell Society. Founded 1876, "to publish and perform Henry Purcell's works."

PURDAY, Chas. H. *B*. Folkestone, 1799 ; *d*. London, 1885.
Works : songs, hymns, collections of Psalmtunes, &c.

Purfling. The ornamental border of vns.,&c.

Put'ti (*I.*), Small boys ; choir boys, &c.

PYCHOW'SKI, Jan N. Pianist ; *b*. Bohemia, 1818 ; *d*. 1900. Settled in America, 1850, as teacher, &c.

PYE, Kellow John. *B*. Exeter, 1812. Mus.Bac. Oxon, 1842. *D*. 1901.
Works : anthems, pf. pieces, songs, &c.

Pyk'non (*Gk.*). The "close note" in ancient Greek music. In mediæval music, a semitone.

PYNE, James Kendrick. Organist ; *b*. London, 1810 ; *d*. 1893. Orgt. Bath Abbey for half a century (from 1839).

PYNE, James Kendrick. Son of preceding ; *b*. Bath, 1852. Orgt. Manchester Cath., 1876-1908. Mus.D. Cantuar, 1900.

PYNE, Louisa Fanny (Mrs. F. Bodda). Soprano singer ; *b*. England, 1828 ; *d*. 1904. First public appearance at 9 ; operatic *début*, Boulogne, 1849, in *La Sonnambula*. Sang frequently in London theatres from 1849 to 1868.

Pyram'idon. A pedal stop invented by Ouseley.
The pipes are "stopped" and are of the shape of an inverted pyramid, the top being about 4 times as wide as the mouth. Very deep tones are produced, but they have little " weight." It is believed that the stop " never passed the experimental stage."

Py'rophone. An inst. invented by Kastner. The tones are produced by gas jets burning under resonant tubes.

Pyr'rhic. (1) An ancient Greek dance with lyre or flute accompt. (2) A metrical foot of two short syllables (U U).

PYTHA'GORAS. Greek philosopher ; abt. 582 to 500 B.C. Reputed originator of the idea of the "Music of the Spheres." (See **Greek Music**.)
The idea probably originated in China more than a thousand years earlier.

Pyth'ian Games. Ancient Greek games in honour of Apollo, including musical contests.
Strabo, the famous geographer (*d*. abt. 25 A.D.), mentions a hymn called the *Pythian Nome*, sung to celebrate Apollo's victory over the serpent *Python*. It was a kind of cantata—or piece of "program-music"—consisting of five parts : (1) *The Prelude*, or preparation for the fight ; (2) *The Onset*, or beginning of the combat ; (3) *The Heat of the Battle* ; (4) *The Song of Victory* ; (5) *The Hissing of the Dying Monster*.

Q

Q. Abbn. of *quick* in old music ; Q.T. "quick time."

ᖩ. (Q inverted.) A direction in 'cello music to lay the thumb across the strings as a temporary " nut."

Quad'rain. " A section of 4 measures."— *Curwen.*

Quadrat' (*G.*) ⎫
Quad'rate (*E.*) ⎬ "A square." A natural
Quadra'tum (*L.*) ⎭ (♮) (*B Quadratum*).

Quadra'tum (*L.*). In mensural music, a breve (▰).

QUA'DRI, Domenico. *B.* Vicenza, 1801 ; *d.* 1843. Teacher of harmony ; advocated chord-building by thirds.
Wrote two treatises on his theories.

Quad'rible. (See **Quatrible.**)

Quadricin'ium (*L.*). A piece for 4 parts (voices).

Quadrille. (*I., Quadri'glia.*) A dance in 5 movements or figures.
The figures are : (1) *Le Pantalon*, (2) *L'Eté*, (3) *La Poule*, (4) *La Pastourelle* (or *La Trenise*), and (5) *Le Finale.*

Quadripar'tite. (1) For 4 parts. (2) In 4 divisions or movements.

Quadriv'ium (*L.*). The 4 "highest branches of learning" in ancient times ; *viz. :* music, arithmetic, geometry, and astronomy.

Quad'ro (*I.*) ⎫ (1) A natural (♮). (2) A
Quad'rum (*L.*) ⎬ tableau or picture.

Quad'ruple. Four-fold.
Quad'ruple counterpoint. (See *Counterpoint.*)
Quad'ruple croche (*F.*) ⎫ A hemidemisemiquaver, or
Quad'ruple quaver (*E.*) ⎬ 64th note ; (♬)
Quad'ruple rhythm ⎫ Any time with " four beats to
Quad'ruple time ⎬ the measure ; " 4-4, 4-2, 12-8, 12-16, &c. (See *Time.*)

Quad'ruplet. A group of 4 equal notes to be performed in the time allotted to 3 (or 6) of the same kind.

Quad'ruplo (*I.*). Quadruple.

QUAGLIA'TI, Paolo. Cembalist ; *d.* Rome, abt. 1660.
Works : motets, canzonets, &c., and one of the earliest musical dramas (*Carro di fedeltà d'amore*).

Qual (*G.*). Agony, torment.
Qual'voll. Full of agony.

Quality of Tone. (*G., Ton'farbe ; F., Timbre; I., Tim'bro.*) (See **Timbre.**)

Quantity. Correct emphasis. In Greek and Latin verse, the long and short time-values of syllables.
There is no precise equivalent of quantity in modern poetry or music ; accented and un-accented syllables (or notes) now roughly represent the long and short syllables of classical " quantity."

Quan'to (*I.*). As much as ; as far as.
For'te quan'to possi'bile. As loud as possible.

QUANTZ, Johann Joachim. Famous flautist; teacher of Frederick the Great ; *b.* Oberscheden, 1697 ; *d.* Potsdam, 1773. Played the double-bass at 8 ; joined the Dresden Town Orch., 1716 ; oboist, Royal Polish Orch., Warsaw and Dresden, 1718 ; soon afterwards took up the flute. Visited London 1726. Flute player, Dresden Orch., 1728. Engaged by Frederick the Great to teach him the flute, 1728. Chamber musician and court composer, Berlin, 1741-73.
Works : abt. 500 flute pieces—mostly written for his royal master—including 300 concertos ; also church music, a flute method, &c. He added a key and a tuning slide to the flute.

QUARAN'TA, Francesco. Singing teacher ; *b.* Naples, 1848 ; *d.* 1897.
Works : an opera, a grand mass, and numerous songs.

QUAREN'GHI, Guglielmo. *B.* Casalmaggiore, 1826 ; *d.* 1882. Studied Milan Cons. 1st 'cello, La Scala, Milan, 1850; 'cello prof. Milan Cons., 1851 ; Maestro, Milan Cath., 1879.
Works : an opera, church music, 'cello pieces, a 'cello method, &c.

QUARLES, Chas. Orgt., Trinity College, Cambridge ; Mus.B., 1698. Orgt., York Minster, 1722 ; *d.* 1727.

Quarree (*F.*). Old name for a breve.

Quart(*G.*). Abbn. of *Quartett* (*q.v.*).
In German " arrangements " of orchl. music, *Quart* means "the strings."

Quart. The interval of a 4th.
Quart flute. A flute a 4th higher than the ordinary flute.

Quart (*F.*). A quarter.
A un quart de voix. Very softly ; in a whisper.
Quart de mesure. A crotchet rest.
Quart de soupir. A semiquaver rest.
Quart de son ⎫ A quarter-tone.
Quart de ton ⎬

Quar'ta (*L.* and *I.*). (1) The interval of a 4th. (2) Fourth.
Quar'ta abun'dans (*L.*). ⎫ An augmented 4th.
Quar'ta ecceden'te (*I.*) ⎬
Quar'ta defi'ciens (*L.*) ⎫ A diminished 4th.
Quar'ta diminui'ta (*I.*) ⎬
Quar'ta mo'di (*I.*) ⎫ The subdominant.
Quar'ta to'ni (*I.*) ⎬

Quarte (*F.*) ⎫ The interval of a 4th.
Quar'te (*G.*) ⎬
Quarte augmentée (*F.*). An augmented 4th.
Quarte de nazard (*F.*). An org. stop a 4th above the nazard (or 12th).
Quarte diminuée (*F.*). A diminished 4th.
Quarte du ton (*F.*). The subdominant.
Quar'tenfolgen (*G.*) ⎫ Consecutive or parallel 4ths.
Quar'tenparallelen (*G.*) ⎬
Quart'fagott (*G.*). A bassoon a 4th higher than the ordinary one.

Quart'flöte (*G.*). A flute a 4th higher than the ordinary one.

Quart'geige (*G.*). A small fiddle.

Quart'posaune (*G.*). A trombone (or organ stop) a 4th lower than usual.

Ü'bermässige Quar'te (*G.*). Augmented 4th.

Vermin'derte Quar'te (*G.*). D:minished 4th.

Quarter-note. (*G.*, *Vier'telnote*, *Vier'tel* ; *F.*, *Noire* ; *I.*, *Ne'ra*.) A crotchet (♩).

Quarter-rest. A crotchet rest (𝄽 or 𝄼).

Quarter-tone. An interval equal to half a semitone.

     There are no *exact* quarter tones used in music ; the term is loosely used for intervals less than a semitone, as, for example, the enharmonic intervals possible on vns. (between C♯ and D♭. &c.).

Quartet' (*E.*).

Quartett' (*G.*)

Quartette (*F.*)   }   A composition for four solo voices or insts.

Quatuor (*F.*)

Quartet'to (*I.*)

Double quartet. A piece for 8 solo voices or insts.

Pianoforte (or *pf.*) *quartet.* A composition for pf. and 3 other insts. (generally strings).

Quartetti'no (*I.*). A short quartet.

String quartet. A quartet for 1st and 2nd vns., viola, and 'cello.

Wind quartet. A piece for 4 wind insts.

     N.B.—In German full scores *Quartett'*, (or *Quart.*) means " all the strings of the orchestra." *i.e.*, the "string band."

     Vocal Quartets are not written in any special form. Nearly all classical instrumental quartets are in "Sonata Form." (See *Sonata.*)

Quarti'no (*I.*). A high clarinet in E♭.

Quar'to (*I.*). (1) A fourth. (2) A crotchet.

Quar'to d'aspet'to. A semiquaver rest (𝄾).

Quar'to di tuo'no. A quarter tone.

Quarto'le (*G.*). A quadruplet (*q.v.*).

Quartsext'akkord (*G.*). A six-four chord ; a second inversion.

Qua'si (*I.*). As if ; almost ; like ; in the style of.

Andan'te qua'si len'to. *Andante*, almost *lento* ; *i.e.*, a slow *Andante*.

Qua'si ad lib. As if *ad lib.* ; almost at pleasure.

Quasi allegret'to. Somewhat *allegretto* ; rather quick.

Qua'si caden'za. In the style of a cadenza ; *ad lib.*

Quasi chitar'ra. Imitating a guitar.

Qua'si fantasi'a. In the style of a *fantasia*. (1) Not in strict form. (2) Somewhat *ad lib.* in performance.

Quasi lonta'na. As if in the distance.

Qua'si nien'te. "As if nothing ; " as soft as possible.

Qua'si parla'to. As if spoken.

Qua'si recitati'vo. In the style of a recitative.

Qua'si sona'ta. Somewhat in sonata form, but not strictly so.

Qua'si trom'be. "Like trumpets ; " bright, clear, ringing.

Quatorzième (*F.*). The interval of a 14th.

Quat'rain. A poetical stanza of 4 lines rhyming alternately.

Quatre (*F.*). Four.

A quatre mains. For 4 hands (as a pf. piece).

QUATREMAYNE, Frank. Bass vocalist ; *b.* Devonport, 1848.

     Author of "Correct Voice Production," &c.

Quat'rible. In old descant, singing in 4ths with the Plain-song.

Quatrici'nium (*L.*). (See **Quadricinium.**)

Quattricro'ma (*I.*). A hemidemisemiquaver.

Quat'tro (*I.*). Four.

A quat'tro ma'ni. For 4 hands.

Quatuor (*F.*). (See **Quartet.**)

Qua'ver. (*G.*, *Acht'elnote* ; *F.*, *Croche* ; *I.*, *Cro'ma.*) An eighth-note (♪).

Quaver rest. The sign 𝄾.

     N.B.—In vocal music quavers "which have to be sung to separate syllables are written detached, while those which are sung to a single syllable are grouped." (See also *Slur.*)

Let us go to the woods with song,   and

Quavering. "The act of trilling or shaking, or running a division with the voice." —*Grassineau.*

QUEIS'SER, Carl T. Great trombone player ; *b.* nr. Leipzig, 1800 ; *d.* 1846. He is said to have " created " trombone playing.

     " There is a story to the effect that at the first rehearsal of Mendelssohn's *Lobgesang*, Queisser led off as follows, to the Composer's infinite amusement."—*Grove.*

Quel'lenlexikon (*G.*). (See **Eitner.**)

Quer (*G.*). Oblique, transverse, queer.

Quer'flöte. The (ordinary) transverse flute. (See *Flute.*)

Quer'pfeife. The ordinary transverse fife.

Quer'stand. False relation.

Quer'strich. (1) The oblique stroke joining the stems of quavers, &c.; or drawn across the stem of a minim, &c., to divide it into shorter notes :

 or 𝄿

     (2) A leger-line.

QUERCU, Simon de. *B.* Brabant.

     Pub., 1509, "Opusculum Musices" (a work on Gregorian music).

Ques'ta,-o. This, that ; yonder.

Da ques'ta par'te fi'no al Maggio're po'co a po'co più anima'to e più for'te. From this place up to the major (portion), gradually quicker and louder.

Ques'te no'te ben marca'te. These notes well accented.

Queue (*F.*). "A tail." (1) The stem of a note. (2) The tail piece of a vn., &c.

Piano à queue. A grand piano.

Quet'schung (*G.*). An acciaccatura (*q.v.*).

Quick step. A quick march. (See **March.**)

QUIDANT, Alfred (or **Joseph**). Pianist ; *b.* Lyons, 1815 ; *d.* Paris, 1893.

     Works : Popular light pf. music.

Quie'to (*I.*). Calm, quiet.

Quietamen'te. Calmly, quietly.

Quietis'simo. Very calmly, quietly, &c.

QUILTER, Roger C. Composer ; *b.* Brighton, 1877.

QUINAULT, Jean B. M. *D.* Gien, 1744. Singer and actor, Paris Théâtre Francais, 1712-33.

     Works : a grand 4-act ballet ; over 20 *intermèdes*, ballets, &c.

QUINAULT, Philippe. Paris, 1635-88.
Wrote the libretti of several of Lully's operas.

Quinde'cima (*I.*). Same as **Quinta decima** (below).
A la quinde'cima. At the double octave.

Quinde'zime (*G.*). (1) The interval of a 15th. (2) A 15th.

Quin'ible. In old descant, singing in 5ths above the Plain-song.

Quin'que so'li (*I.*). For 5 solo voices or insts.

Quint (*E.* and *G.*) ⎫ (1) The interval of a
Quin'ta (*L.* and *I.*) ⎪ 5th. (2) An organ
Quinte (*F.*) ⎬ stop sounding a 5th
Quin'te (*G.*) ⎭ higher than the unison
stops. (3) The E string of a violin.

Quint'absatz (*G.*) ⎫ A half-close or dominant
Quint'abschluss (*G.*) ⎭ cadence. (See *Cadence.*)
Quint'bass (*G.*). A pedal stop on the org. a 5th above 16 ft. pitch.
Quint'fagott (*G.*). (See *Basson quinte.*)
Quint'flöte (*G.*). An org. flute stop a 5th above unison pitch.
Quint'fuge (*G.*). A fugue in which the subject is answered (regularly) at the 5th.
Quint'gedackt (*G.*) ⎫ An org. stop a 5th above unison
Quint'stimme (*G.*) ⎭ pitch.
Quint'saite (*G.*). The E string of a vn.
Quint stride. A skip of a 5th in melody.
Quint vio'la. An org. stop of the "viol" or gamba kind, a 5th above unison pitch.
Al'la quin'ta (*I.*). At the 5th; as *Fu'ga al'la quin'ta, a* fugue answered at the 5th.
Quin'ta de'cima (*I.*). (1) A double octave or 15th. (2) An organ stop sounding two octaves above the unison stops.
Quintade'na. (See *Quintaton,* below.)
Quin'ta diminui'ta (*I.*). A diminished 5th.
Quin'ta ecceden'te (*I.*). Augmented 5th.
Quin'ta fal'sa (*I.*). A diminished 5th.
Quin'ta mo'di (*I.*) ⎫ The dominant.
Quin'ta to'ni (*I.*) ⎭
Quinte octaviante (*F.*). The interval of a 12th (5th and octave).
Quin'tenfolgen (*G.*)
Quin'tenfortschreitung (*G.*) ⎬ Consecutive (parallel) 5ths.
Quin'tenparallelen (*G.*)
Quin'ten-zir'kel (*G.*). Circle of fifths (*q.v.*).
Quinter (*F.*). To sing in 5ths (same as *quinible.*)
Quintes cachées. Hidden 5ths.
Quintes consécutives (*F.*). Consecutive 5ths.
Quinti(e)'ren (*G.*). To overblow a stopped pipe or clarinet and sound the 12th.
Quintoier (*F.*) ⎫ (1) To sing in descant at the 5th.
Quintoyer (*F.*) ⎭ (See *Quinible.*) (2) To overblow and sound the 12th.
Rei'ne Quin'te (*G.*). Perfect fifth.
Vermin'derte Quin'te (*G.*). Diminished fifth.

Quin'tain. "A section of 5 measures."— *Curwen.*

Quin'tatön (*G.*). An organ stop so voiced as to make the 12th specially prominent.

Quint Coupler. An org. coupler bringing on the "fifth" of any stop (or stops) instead of the unison or octave.
"Judiously employed, it is capable of producing many curious and by no means displeasing effects.'—*Wedgwood.*

Quinte (*F.*). (1) See above. (2) A viola.

Quinter'na, Quin'terne, or **Chiter'na.** A kind of lute or guitar with from 3 to 5 pairs of gut strings, and sometimes 2 wire-covered single strings in addition.
It was very popular in Italy in the 17th and 18th centuries.

Quintet' (*E.*) ⎫
Quintett' (*G.*) ⎪
Quintette (*F.*) ⎬ A composition for 5
Quintuor (*F.*) ⎪ solo voices or insts.
Quintet'to (*I.*) ⎭
Pf. quintet, string quintet, wind quintet, &c. See remarks on *Quartet.* The classical instrumental quintet, like the quartet, is in sonata form. The string quintet is usually for 2 violins, 2 violas, and violoncello; sometimes 2 violins, 1 viola, and 2 'cellos (*e.g.,* Schubert, Boccherini). Onslow's quintets are for the usual quartet and double-bass.

Quin'to (*I.*). A 5th.

Quin'tole (*E.*) ⎫
Quinto'le (*G.*) ⎬ Same as **Quintuplet** (*q.v.*).

Quinton (*F.*). A five stringed viol.

Quintuor (*F.*). (See **Quintet.**)

Quin'tuple rhythm, Quin'tuple time. A rather rare measure of "5 beats in the bar."
Quintuple time is generally accented on the 1st and 3rd (or 1st and 4th) beats; *i.e.,* as 2 + 3, or 3 + 2, in each bar. Perhaps the most famous instance of this time is the slow movement of Tschaikowsky's *Pathetic Symphony.* (See *Time.*)

Quin'tuplet. A group of 5 equal notes (to be performed in the time allotted to 4, 3, or 6 of the same kind)—

Quintvio'le (*G.*). (See **Quintviola** (above).

Quinzième (*F.*). The interval of a 5th.

Quire. Old English spelling of *Choir.*

Quirister. A chorister.

Qui tollis (*L.*). Part of the *Gloria* in a Mass.

Quitter (*F.*). To leave, to quit.
Sans quitter la corde. Without quitting the string (in vn. playing).

Quod'libet. A medley ; a *pot-pourri.*

Quo'niam tu so'lus. Part of the *Gloria* in a Mass.

q.v. Abbn. of *Quod vi'de* (*L.*). "Which see."
These letters in brackets, thus (*q.v.*), refer the reader to the word (or phrase) after which they are placed.

R

R. Abbreviation for *Right* (*G.*, *Rech'te*). *R.H*, or *r.h.* Right hand.

R. Ripieno (*q.v.*).

R. In French organ music, stands for *Clavier de récit.* "Swell."

RAAFF (or **RAFF**), **Anton.** Operatic tenor; *b.* nr. Bonn, 1714; *d.* 1797. In 1778 he went to Paris with Mozart, who wrote for him the part of " Idomeneo."

Raban'i } A small Hindu drum (or tam-
Raban'na } bourine).

Rab'bia (*I.*). Fury, rage, frenzy, madness. *Con rab'bia.* With fury, &c.

Raccol'ta (*I.*). A collection. *Raccol'ta di pez'zi.* Collection of pieces. *Raccol'ta di sona'te.* Collection of sonatas.

Raccontan'do (*I.*). As if reciting or nar-rating ; in a descriptive style.

Raccon'to (*I.*). A tale, a story.

Raccourcir (*F.*). To abridge.

RACHMANI'NOFF, Sergei Vassilievitch. Pianist ; *b.* Novgorod, Russia, 1873. Won the " great gold medal," Moscow Cons., 1891. Works : opera, *Aleko ;* a symphony; a pf. concerto, and numerous other pf. pieces (*Prelude in C# minor*, &c.).

Rackett' (*G.*) } (1) An obsolete form of
Rankett' (*G.*) } bassoon or bombard. (2) An obsolete organ reed-stop.

Racler (*F.*). To saw, to scrape. *Racleur.* A bad fiddler, a "scraper."

RADCLIFF, John. Flautist; *b.* Liverpool, 1842; *d.* (?).

Raddolcen'do (*I.*) } Growing gradually
Raddolcen'te (*I.*) } sweeter and softer. *Raddolcia'to* } More sweet and calm ; pacified. *Raddolci'to* }

Raddopplamen'to (*I.*). Doubling (the notes of chords, &c.). *Raddoppia'te no'te.* Repeated notes. *Raddoppia'to.* Doubled, increased ; compound (of intervals). *Pas'so raddoppia'to.* A quick march.

RA'DECKE, A. M. Robert. *B.* Dittmans-dorff, Silesia, 1829 ; *d.* 1893. Violinist and condr.; 1st vn.Gewandhaus, Leipzig, 1850; Court capellmeister, Berlin, 1871 ; director Royal Inst. for Church Music, Berlin, 1892. Works : a *Liederspiel*, orch. music, &c. ; fine part-songs and songs.

RA'DECKE, Dr. Ernst. Son of preceding ; *b.* Berlin, 1866. Town Mus. Director, Winterthur, Switzerland, 1893.

RA'DECKE, Luise. Operatic soprano ; *b.* Celle, Hanover, 1847. Prima donna, Munich, 1873-6.

Ra'del (*G.*). A solo with choral refrain. (See also **Rundgesang.**)

RADFORD, Robt. A. Bass vocalist; *b.* Nottingham, 1874.

Radiating pedals. A fan-shaped pedal keyboard.

Radical. A root. *Radical bass.* (1) The root, or generator, of a chord. (2) The fundamental bass (*q.v.*). *Radical cadence.* A cadence formed by any two chords with their roots in the bass. *Radical tones of the scale.* The tonic, dominant, and subdominant.

RADIGER, Anton. Composer of hymn-tunes ; *b.* Chatham, 1749 ; *d.* 1817.

Rad'leier (*G.*). A hurdy-gurdy.

RADOUX, Jean Théodore. *B.* Liége, 1835. Won the Prix de Rome, Liége Cons., 1859 ; director Liége Cons., 1872. Works : oratorio (*Cain*), operas, cantatas, symphonic-poems, church music, male choruses, songs, &c.

RAD'ZIWILL, Prince Anton H. *B.* Wilma, 1775 ; *d.* 1833. Patron of Beethoven and Chopin. Works : incidental music to Goethe's *Faust*, male quartets, " Complainte de Marie Stuart," &c.

RAFF, Anton. (See **Raaff.**)

RAFF, Joseph Joachim. Noted composer ; *b.* Lachen, Lake Zurich, May, 1822 ; *d.* Frankfort-on-Main, June, 1882. Starting as a school teacher, his early compositions became known through the friendly efforts of Mendelssohn, Liszt, and Von Bulow, and " he gave up school teaching for the career of a composer." Joined Liszt at Weimar, 1850, and became a champion of the " New German " school. Settled in Wiesbaden as pf. teacher, 1856. His first symphony, *An das Vaterland*, won the prize of the Vienna "Gesellschaft der Musikfreunde," 1863. Appointed director Hoch Cons., Frankfort, 1877. His works (over 230) include 11 symphonies, 4 suites, 9 overtures, and other orch. pieces ; a pf. concerto, vn. concerto, a 'cello concerto, &c. ; much chamber music, numerous pf. pieces, cantatas and other church music, many songs, 6 terzets for female voices, 30 male quartets, &c. His music is of " very unequal value ; " but it includes several " masterpieces," notably the 3rd and 5th symphonies, the overtures Op. 101 and Op. 194, the pf. concerto Op. 185, and the 'cello concerto Op. 193.

Raffrenan'do (*I.*). Checking ; slightly *rallentando.*

RAGGHIAN'TI, Ippolito. Violinist ; *b.* nr. Pisa, 1866 ; *d.* 1894. Wrote the lyric drama *Jean Marié.*

Raggio'ne (*I.*). Ratio, proportion.

Rago'ke. A small Russian horn.

Rag-time (corruption, **Rag-tune**). A broken, ragged, tattered, " snap " rhythm common in American coon songs, clog dances, &c.

Rah. The "grave" form of *Ray.* It is a " comma " (*q.v.*) lower than *Ray ;* and makes a perfect (acoustical) 5th with *Lah.*

RAIF, Oscar. Fine pianist ; *b.* The Hague, 1847 ; *d.* 1899. Pf. teacher Berlin Hochschule, from 1875. Wrote a pf. concerto, a sonata for pf. and vn., &c.

RAILLARD, Abbé F. *B.* Montormentier, France, 1804.
Author of several works on Gregorian notation, neumes, &c.

RAIMON'DI, Ignazio. Violinist; *b.* Naples, 1733; *d.* 1802.
Works: a symphony, an opera, 3 vn. concertos, 6 string quartets, &c.

RAIMON'DI, Pietro. Operatic writer and distinguished contrapuntist; Rome, 1786-1853. Studied at Naples, Rome, and Florence. Director Royal Theatres Naples, 1824-32; prof. of Counterpoint Royal Cons., 1825; Prof. of Counterpoint Palermo Cons., 1832-52; Maestro St. Peter's, Rome, 1852.
Works: about 60 operas and 21 ballets; a large number of astonishingly clever contrapuntal works, including a fugue in 64 parts (for 16 choirs), and a trilogy of 3 oratorios which were performed (Rome, 1852) "at first separately and then *simultaneously!*" Also 5 other oratorios, masses, requiems, the 150 psalms (15 volumes), a 16-part *Credo*, &c.

RAINFORTH, Catherine. Soprano singer; *b.* 1814; *d.* Bristol, 1877.
The original "Arline" in Balfe's *Bohemian Girl*, 1843.

Rake. (See **Rastrum**.)

Ralentir (*F.*). To slacken (the speed).

Rall. ⎱ Abbreviations of *Rallentan'do*.
Rallen. ⎰

Rallentan'do (*I.*) ⎱ Gradually slower.
Rall nta'to (*I.*) ⎰
Rallentamen'to. Slackening the time; retardation.
Rallentando al fi'ne. Gradually slower to the end.
Rallentan'do assa'i. Slacken very much.
Rallenta're. To become slower; to retard.
Rallenta'te. Retard the pace.
Sen'za rallenta're. Without slackening the speed.

RA'MANN, Bruno. Song composer; *b.* Erfurt, 1832.

RA'MANN, Lina. Cousin of B.; *b.* nr. Kitzingen, 1833. Founded (with Ida Volkmann) a music school, Nuremberg, 1865.
Works: "Bach and Handel," a "Biography of Liszt" (3 vols.), "Principles of Technique in Pf. playing," &c.

RAMEAU, Jean Philippe. "Creator of the modern science of harmony." *B.* Dijon, Sept., 1683; *d.* Paris, Sept., 1764. Could play on the harpsichord any music placed before him at 7. Wandered through France for several years as violinist and organist. Published his "Nouveau système de musique théorique," 1726. His opera *Hippolyte et Aricie* was given at the Paris Opéra, 1733, and his masterpiece, *Castor et Pollux*, in 1737. "For the next 30 years his operas dominated the French stage."
Works: about 30 operas; numerous pieces for the clavecin (with Tables of *Agrémens*, notes on fingering, &c.); several works on theory and harmony.
Rameau's system of harmony, instead of regarding chords as "combinations of intervals" (as in the old contrapuntal systems), reduced them to series of 3rds built up on "roots" (or "Fundamental Basses"), thereby reckoning a chord and all its inversions from the same root. His theory has—in some form or other

—been adopted by nearly all subsequent writers on harmony. (See *Root*.)

RANALOW, Fredk. B. Baritone; *b.* Kingstown, Ireland, 1873.

RANDALL, John. *R.* 1715; *d.* Cambridge, 1799. Prof. of music Cambridge Univ., 1755; Mus.Doc., 1756.
Wrote church music, songs, &c.

RAN'DEGGER, Alberto. Distinguished singing teacher; *b.* Trieste, 1832. Settled in London abt. 1854. Prof. of Singing R.A.M., 1868. Condr. Carl Rosa Opera Co., 1879-85.
Works: a grand opera, a comic opera (London, 1864), dramatic cantatas, songs, a Primer on Singing (Novello), &c.

RANDHART'INGER, Benedict. *B.* Lower Austria, 1802; *d.* 1894. Solo soprano Vienna Court Choir, at 10; tenor singer, 1832; vice-Hofkapellmeister, 1844; 1st Kapellmeister, 1862-6.
Works: an opera, 20 masses, 60 motets, 2 symphonies, chamber music, hundreds of songs and part-songs, pf. pieces, &c.; in all, over 600 works.

Rang (*F.*). A rank (of organ pipes, &c.).

Range. The compass or extent of a voice or inst.

Rank. A row, a set; a range.
Rank of pipes. A row of pipes belonging to an organ stop. Mixtures are of 2, 3, 4 (or more) ranks; *i.e.*, there are two or more pipes to each key.

RANSFORD, Edwin. Baritone vocalist and composer; *b.* Bourton-on-the-Water, 1805; *d.* 1876.

Rant. (1) An old country dance. (2) A Reel (*q.v.*). (3) Boisterous, empty, extravagant declamation.

Ranz des vaches (*F.*). (*G.*, *Kuh'reigen*, *Kuh'reihen*.) "Calling the cows." A simple melody played on the Alpine horn by the Swiss mountaineers.

The famous "Ranz de Vaches de l'Appenzel."

RAOUL de COUCY. (See **Coucy.**)

Rapidité (*F.*). Rapidity, swiftness.
Rapidement. Rapidly, quickly.

Rapi'do (*I.*). Rapid, quick.

Rapidamen'te
Con rapidità } Rapidly, quickly.

RAPPOL'DI, Edward. Violinist ; *b.* Vienna, 1839 ; *d.* 1903. Head vn. teacher Dresden Cons., 1893.

RAPPOL'DI - KAHRER, Laura. Distinguished pianist ; wife of preceding ; *b.* Vienna, 1853. Pupil of Liszt.

Rappel (*F.*). A military call.

Rapsodie (*F.*). A Rhapsody (*q.v.*).

Rare Chromatics.
In Sol-fa, *my*, sharp of *me; ty*, sharp of *te; du* (or *da*), flat of *doh; fu*, flat of *fah; sa*, flat of *soh; be*, sharp of *bah.*

Rasch (*G.*). Quick, rapid ; impetuous.
Ein we'nig rasch'er. A little quicker.
Noch rasch'er. Still faster.
Rasch bewegt'. In rapid *tempo.*
Rasch'er. Quicker.
Rasch, nicht zu has'tig. Quick, but not too hastily.
Rasch wie zuvor'. As quick as before.
So rasch wie mö'glich. As fast as possible.

Rasch'eln (*G.*). To rustle.

Ra'send *G.*). Raging, blustering ; mad.

Ra'segesang
Ra'selied } A wild song ; a dithyrambic.

Rasga'do (*S.*). An arpeggio on the guitar by sweeping the strings with the thumb.

Rastral' (*G.*). } " A rake." A 5-pointed
Ras'trum (*L.*). } device for ruling music staves.

RASUMOV'SKI (RASOUMOFF'SKY), Count A. K. *B.* 1752 ; *d.* 1836. Russian ambassador at Vienna, 1793-1809. Maintained the celebrated "Rasumovski Quartett" (afterwards the "Schuppanzigh Quartett"), 1808-16, himself playing 2nd violin.
Beethoven inscribed his 3 string quartets, Op. 59, to Rasumovski.

Rate of movement. (See **Tempo.**)

RATEZ, Emile P. *B.* Besançon, 1851. Studied Paris Cons. ; director of the Lille branch of the Cons., 1891.
Works : operas (*Lydéric*, 1895, &c.), orchestral works, chamber music, &c.

Räth'selcanon (*G.*) } A puzzle, or riddle
Rät'selkanon (*G.*) } canon. (See **Canon.**)

Ra'tio. Relative magnitude, value, or proportion.

Rattenen'do (*I.*) } Restraining or holding
Rattenu'to (*I.*) } back the *tempo; rallentando.*

Rattez'za (*I.*). Speed.

Rattle. (*G., Rat'sche, Schnar're.*)
The invention of the *Rattle* is ascribed to the Greek mathematician, Archytas (abt. 400 B.C.), " to prevent his children tumbling his things about the house."

RA'TZENBERGER, Theodor. Pianist ; pupil of Liszt ; *b.* Thuringia, 1840 ; *d.* 1879. Wrote pf. pieces and songs.

Raucedi'ne (*I.*). Harshness.

RAU'CHENECKER, Georg Wm. *B.* Munich, 1844. Mus. director, Elberfeld, 1889 ; *d.* 1906.
Works : operas (*Ingo*, 1893, &c.), popular string quartets, &c.

Ra'uco (*I.*)
Rauh (*G.*) } Hoarse, rough, harsh ; rude,
Rauque (*F.*) } raw, coarse.

Rausch'en (*G.*). To rush, rustle, ripple, roar.
Rausch'end und fest'lich. Dashing and festive.
Rausch'er. The rapid repetition of a note.

Rausch'flöte } A mixture stop of 2 ranks in old
Rausch'pfeife } organs, consisting either of a 12th
Rausch'quint } and 15th, or a 15th and octave
Rausch'werk } 12th.

RAUSCH'ER, Max. Conductor ; *b.* Wettstetten, 1860.

Räus'pern (*G.*). To clear the throat.

RAUZZI'NI, Venanzio M. Tenor singer ; *b.* Rome, 1747 ; *d.* Bath, 1810. Sang in London, 1774-8, and lived there as singing teacher until 1787 ; afterwards settled at Bath.
Works : 8 operas, chamber music, pf. pieces, &c.

Ravanas'tron. A Buddhist bowed string instrument.
" Possibly the progenitor of the violin." It is said to have been invented about 5000 B.C., in the time of Ravana, King of Ceylon.

RA'VENSCROFT, Thomas. London ; 1593-1635(?). Chorister St. Paul's Cathedral ; Mus.Bac. Cantab., 1607.
Pub. "Pammelia" (1609 ; the 1st colln. of rounds, catches, and canons printed in England) ; "The Whole Booke of Psalmes," 1621 ; &c.

RAVE'RA, Niccolo T. Opera composer ; *b.* Alessandria, Italy, 1851. Settled in Paris as Chef d'orchestre, Théâtre Lyrique de la Galérie-Vivienne.

RAVINA, Jean H. Pianist ; *b.* Bordeaux, 1818 ; Won 1st prize for pf. playing Paris Cons., 1834. Made long concert tours (to 1871) ; afterwards settled in Paris.
Works : a pf. concerto ; numerous pf. études, salon pieces, &c.

RAVO'GLI, Julia (Giulia). Contralto vocalist ; *b.* Rome, 1866.

RAVO'GLI, Sofia. Sister of J. ; Soprano vocalist ; *b.* Rome, 1865.

Ra(v)viva're (*I.*). To revive, to re-animate.
Ra(v)vivan'do
Rav(v)iva'to } Accelerando (*q.v.*).
Rav(v)ivan'do il tem'po.

RAWLINGS, Alfred. (See **Bonheur.**)

RAWSON, Geo. 1807-89. Solicitor, Leeds.
Wrote "God the Lord is King," and other hymns.

RAY. The Tonic Sol-fa spelling of **Re** (*q.v.*).

Ray, or Rah, Mode. The scale *r m f s l t d' r';* it is equivalent to the Dorian Mode. (See **Mode.**)

RAYMOND-RITTER, Fanny. (See **Ritter.**)

Re. (*F., Ré.*) (1) The note "D" in fixed doh systems. (2) The 2nd note of the scale in movable doh systems. In Sol-fa notation it is spelt *Ray* (written **r**).

Ré bémol (F.). } The note D♭.
Re bemol'le (I). }
Ré dièse (F.); } The note D♯.
Re die'sis (I.). }

Re (pron. *Ree*). The sharp of *Ray* in Tonic Sol-fa.

REA, Dr. Wm. Orgt. and condr.; *b.* London, 1827; *d.* 1903. Orgt. Harmonic Union, 1853; founded the Polyhymnian Choir, 1856; Corporation orgt., Newcastle, 1860; North Shields, 1864-78.

READ, Fredk. John. *B.* Faversham; Orgt. Chichester Cath., 1887. Mus.Doc. Oxon, 1891.

READ, Daniel. "Comb maker, composer, and music teacher;" *b.* Rehoboth, Mass., 1757; *d.* 1836.
<small>Pub. collns. of hymn-tunes, &c., and wrote several hymn-tunes still sung.</small>

READING, John. *B.* abt. 1645(?); *d.* Winchester, 1692. Orgt. Winchester Cath., 1675-81. Composed "Dulce Domum."

READING, John. Son of preceding; *b.* 1677; *d.* London, 1764. Chorister Chapel Royal; Orgt. Dulwich Coll., 1700-2; lay-vicar Lincoln Cath., 1702; afterwards orgt. of various London churches. Wrote anthems and songs.
<small>The tune "Adeste Fideles" has been ascribed to him.</small>

READING, John. Orgt. Chichester Cath., 1674-1720.

READING, Rev. John. Prebendary Canterbury Cath.
<small>Pub. a "Sermon on Church Musick," 1663.</small>

Real answer. } (See **Fugue**.)
Real fugue }

Rea'le (*I.*). Real; distinct.
A qua'tro vo'ce rea'le. In 4 real parts.
<small>N.B.—"Real" parts are separate and distinct melodies, as opposed to duplications at the unison or octave and "filling-up" parts; thus a composition for 30 or 40 different instruments may comprise only 1, 2, 3, 4, &c., "real" parts.</small>

Realism. In music, the attempt to represent natural sounds as they really are; the opposite of *Idealism*, or "absolute music" (*q.v.*).
<small>Realism in modern music is often carried to vulgar extremes; it has been called " imitative music run mad." (See *Imitative Music, Nature's Music, Word Painting, Programme Music*, &c.)</small>

REAY, Samuel. *B.* Hexham, 1822; *d.* 1905. Orgt. St. Andrew's, Newcastle, 1841; afterwards song-schoolmaster Newark Parish Church, and condr. Newark Philharmonic Soc. Mus.B. Oxon, 1851.
<small>Works : church music, part-songs, &c.</small>

Re'bab }
Re'bec } (*I., Ribe'ba, Ribe'ca ; S., Ra'be, Ra'bel*). A three-stringed bowed inst., probably of Arabian or Turkish origin. "It was the primitive pear-shaped violin of modern Europe." (See **Violin**.)
Rebec'ca }
Re'beck }
Re'bed }
Re'bet }

REBEL, François. Son of J. F. (below); Paris, 1701-55. Violinist Opéra Orch. at 13; leader, with Francœur, 1733-44; both were inspectors of the Opéra, 1744-53; directors, 1753-7. Rebel was also Intendant-in-chief of the King's music, and (1772-5) Administrator-general of the Opéra.
<small>Works : 10 operas (with Francœur) ; church music, cantatas, &c.</small>

REBEL, Jean F. Paris, 1669-1747. Chef d'orchestre of the Grand Opéra, and one of the " 24 violons du Roi."
<small>Wrote sonatas and trios for vns. and bass.</small>

REBEL'LO, João L. Distinguished early Portuguese composer ; teacher of King John IV. *B.* Caminha, 1609 ; *d.* 1661.
<small>Wrote psalms in 16 parts, masses, misereres, &c.</small>

Re bémol (*F.*). The note D♭.
Re bémol majeur. The key of D♭ major.

REBER, Napoléon H. *B.* Mühlhausen, Alsatia, 1807 ; *d.* Paris, 1880. Prof. of harmony Paris Cons., 1851 ; of composition, 1862. Elected member of the Académie, 1853.
<small>Works : a ballet, half-a-dozen operas ; 4 symphonies, and other fine orch. works ; chamber music, pf. music ; church music ; 33 songs, &c. Also an excellent "Treatise on Harmony."</small>

Re'bibe }
Re'bible } A small old Eng. Rebeck (*q.v.*).

RE'BIČEK, Josef. Violinist and Condr. *B.* Prague, 1844 ; *d.* 1904. Leader and opera-director, Imperial Theatre, Warsaw, 1882 ; Condr. National Theatre, Pesth, 1891 ; Condr. Wiesbaden, 1893 ; Capellmeister, Berlin Philharmonic Orch., 1897.
<small>Chief work : a symphony in D minor.</small>

RE'BIKOFF, Vladimir I. *B.* Krasnojarsk Siberia, 1866. His music is "weird, dissonant, and remarkable." It includes operas, songs, and numerous highly-original pf. pieces.

REB'LING, Friedrich. Tenor singer ; *b.* nr. Magdeburg, 1835 ; *d.* 1900. Teacher of singing Leipzig Cons., 1877.

REB'LING, Gustav. *B.* nr. Magdeburg. 1821 ; *d.* 1902. Orgt. Johanniskirche, Magdeburg, 1858-97.
<small>Works : psalms, motets, pieces for org. and pf., songs, &c.</small>

Recapitulation. The Reprise of a movement in Sonata Form. (See **Reprise** (3) and **Sonata**.)

Récension (*F.*). (1) An analytical criticism of a work. (2) A critically revised edition.

Reces'sional. A hymn sung as the clergyman, or choir, leaves the chancel after service.

Rechange (*F.*). "Exchange."
Corps de rechange } Crooks of the horn, trumpet, & c
Tons de rechange }

Rechanter (*F.*). To sing again.

Recheat' (Old *E.*). A huntsman's signal to recall the hounds.

Recherché (*F.*). " Sought out." (1) Rare ; elegant ; affected. (2) Same as **Ricercata** (*q.v.*).

Recht (*G.*). Right ; true, straight, proper.
Recht'e Hand. The right hand.
Recht lust'ig. Right cheerfully.

Récit (*F.*). (1) Recitative (*q.v.*). (2) A solo, or principal part. (3) A recital.
Clavier de récit. The swell manual of an organ.

Reci'tal. A concert by one performer (or from one composer's works).
The pf. recital is said to have been initiated by Liszt, 1840.

Recitan'do (*I.*) ⎱
Recita'to (*I.*) ⎬ In the style of a recitative;
Recitan'te (*I.*) ⎰ as if reciting.

Récitant,-e (*F.*). A solo singer (or player).

Récitatif (*F.*). Recitative (*q.v.*).

Recitative (pron. *Ress-it-a-teev'*). (*G., Recitativ', Rezitativ'* ; *F., Récitatif* ; *I., Recitati'vo.*) Musical declamation.

Recitative is the name commonly given to the *Musica Parlante* (*i.e.*, " spoken music ") invented by Peri, Caccini, Cavaliere, &c., about the year 1600. The earliest kind of recitative (*Recitati'vo sec'co*) consisted of a voice part with a very simple accompt. indicated by a figured bass :—

From Peri's *Euridice* (the first opera).

&c.

With the growth of opera and oratorio the accompt. gradually became richer, and "Accompanied Recitative" (*Recitati'vo accompagna'to*) was added to the composer's resources.

In most operas and oratorios both forms of recitative are still used.

Accompanied Recit. Handel's *Messiah.*

Com - - - - fort ye, my people.

Recitatives are often made up of a combination of *Recitati'vo sec'co* and *Recitati'vo accompagna'to* with little snatches of melody in regular time. (See *Arioso.*)

Unless the recit. is marked *a tempo* (or has a very important accompt.) it is performed *molto ad lib.*

N.B.—The recitatives of Bach and Handel were never performed *exactly as written.* A comparison, say, of Macfarren's "Performing Edition" of the *Messiah* with older editions, will enable the student to ascertain the most important rules of "traditional renderings."

Recitati'vo (*I.*). Recitative (*q.v.*).
Al'la recitati'vo (*I.*). In the style of a recitative.
Récitatif accompagné (*F.*) ⎱ Accompanied recitative.
Récitatif obligé (*F.*) ⎰
Recitati'vo accompagna'to (*I.*) ⎱
Recitati'vo con accompagnamen'to (*I.*) ⎬ Accompanied recitative.
Recitati'vo obbliga'to (*I.*) ⎰
Recitati'vo parlan'te (*I.*) ⎱
Recitati'vo sec'co (*I.*) ⎰ (See *Recitative.*)
Recita'tivo sen'za misu'ra. Recitative *very free* as to tempo.
Recitati'vo stromenta'to (*I.*). Accompanied recitative.
"Recitativos are what in our operas usually tire the audience, . . . but the songs make them some amends."—*Grassineau* (1740).

Réciter (*F.*). (1) To perform a *récit.* (*q.v.*). (2) To recite, to declaim.

Reciting-note. The 1st note of each section of a chant. (See **Chant.**)

Reclame (*F.*). The song of a bird.
Reclamer. To sing in imitation of a bird.

Recorder. (1) An obsolete form of flageolet (or *flûte-a-bec*). (2) An organ stop.
Record (Old *E.*). To play on the recorder.

Récréation (*F.*). A light pleasing pf. piece.

Rec'te et re'tro (*L.*). " Forward and backward." (See **Canon.**)

Rectus' (*L.*). Right, direct, straight.
Mo'tus rec'tus. Similar motion.

Recueil d'hymnes (*F.*). A hymn book.

Recurring bass. A ground bass (*q.v.*).

REDAN, Karl. (See **Converse.**)

Reddi'ta, Redi'ta (*I.*) ⎱
Redite (*F.*) ⎰ A repeat.

REDEMPTION, The. Sacred Trilogy by Gounod ; Birmingham Festival, 1882.

RE'DEKER, Louise D. A. Contralto ; *b.* nr. Hanover, 1853. *Début*, Bremen, 1873.

Re'dend (*G.*). (1) Speaking ; same as *Parlando* (*q.v.*). (2) Expressive.

REDFORD, John. *B.* abt. 1480. Orgt. St. Paul's Cath., 1530-40 ; *d.* abt. 1546.
Works : good organ pieces.

REDHEAD, Richard. Organist ; *b.* Harrow, 1820 ; *d.* 1901.
Works : church music (masses, hymn-tunes, &c.), organ pieces.

Redondil'la (*S.*). A roundelay (*q.v.*).

Redoubled interval. A compound interval.

Redoublement (*F.*). Doubling a note of a chord, a part, &c.

Red'owa ⎱ A lively Bohemian dance now
Redowak' ⎬ in 3-4 time ; originally in
Redowaz'ka ⎰ alternating 2-4 and 3-4 time.

Redublica'to (*I.*). Doubled (of chord notes, intervals, &c.).

Reduction. (*G., Reduk'tion ; F., Réduction ; I., Riduzio'ne.*) An arrangement of a composition in a condensed or simplified form.
Réduire (F.), Reduzi'(e)ren (G.). To reduce, condense, or re-arrange a work.

Redundant. Same as **Augmented** (*q.v.*).
Redundant 5th. An augmented 5th.

REE, Anton. Pianist ; *b.* Aarhus, Jutland, 1820 ; *d.* 1886. Settled in Copenhagen as teacher and writer, 1842.
Works : pf. pieces, études, &c.

REED, Andrew, D.D. 1787-1862. Congregational minister.
Wrote the hymn "Spirit Divine, attend our prayers."

REED, Thos. German. *B.* Bristol, 1817 ; *d.* 1888. Mus. director Haymarket Theatre, 1838-51. Started, with his wife (see below), the "German Reed Entertainments," 1855.

REED, Mrs. German (*née* **Priscilla Horton**)· Actress and contralto singer ; *b.* 1818 ; *d.* 1895.

Reed. (*G., Rohr'blatt, Zung'e ; F., Anche ; I., An'cia, Lin'gua.*) An elastic strip of cane, metal, &c., fixed at one end, and made to vibrate by a current of air.
In the human voice the vocal cords act as reeds ; in brass wind instruments the lips are the reeds.
Beating reed. One which in vibrating strikes against the edges of the slot over which it is placed ; as in the clarinet.
Double reed. Two reeds striking against each other ; as in the oboe and bassoon.
Free reed. A reed which does not strike the edges of the slot ; as in the concertina and harmonium.
Impinging reed } A beating reed.
Percussion reed }
Reed instrument. An instrument played by means of a single or double reed.
Reed orchestra. The oboes, clarinets, and bassoons of the ordinary orchestra.
Reed organ. A name specially applied to the harmonium, American organ, vocalion, &c.
Reed pipe } The reeds of the organ are generally
Reed stop } "beating," but occasionally "free" tongues are employed. (See *Organ.*)
Striking reed. A beating reed.

Reeds. (1) The reed insts. of an orchestra. (2) The reed stops of an organ.

Reel. A lively dance of rustic character in 4-4 (or 6-8) time.
It is especially popular in Scotland, though probably of Scandinavian origin.

REES, Robt. ("**Eos Morlais**"). Welsh tenor singer ; 1841-92.

REEVE, Wm. London, 1757-1815. Orgt. St. Martin's, Ludgate Hill, 1792 ; part-proprietor Sadler's Wells Th. from 1802.
Works : music to abt. 40 plays ; glees, songs, &c. "I am a friar of orders grey" is still popular.

REEVES, John Sims. Celebrated tenor singer ; *b.* Woolwich, 1818 ; *d.* 1900. Orgt. North Cray Church, at 14. *Début* as a *baritone*, Newcastle, 1839. *Début* as a tenor, La Scala, Milan, 1846. From 1848 to 1891 the leading English tenor.

Reflorimen'ti (*I.*). Arbitrary embellishments introduced during a performance.

Refrain. A chorus, or burden, often sung at the end of each verse of a ballad or other song.

Refret. A ritornello (*q.v.*).

Re'gal. (*G., Regal'; F., Régale.*) An obsolete small portable organ with beating reeds. (Also *Re'gall, Ri'gal, Ri'gole*).
It is regarded as a precursor of the harmonium.
Bi'belre'gal (*G.*). A small regal which could be folded up like a Bible.
Har'fenregal (*G.*). An obsolete reed-stop imitating the harp.
Gei'genregal (*G.*). An obsolete reed-stop imitating the violin.

RE'GAN', Anna. (See **Schimon-Regan**.)

Re'gel (*G.*). A rule, principle; order.
Re'gel der Okta've. The rule of the octave (*q.v.*). A harmonized (bass) scale.

Re'gens cho'ri (*L.*). A choirmaster.

RE'GER, Max. One of the most distinguished of modern composers ; *b.* Brand, Bavaria, 1873. Prof. of harmony, counterpoint, and organ, Royal Academy of Music, Munich ; condr. Porges' Singing Society.
Works : orchestral pieces ; numerous pf. pieces, over 200 songs, chamber music ; organ sonatas, fugues, preludes, &c. ; cantatas, male choruses, &c. His style is very complex, and his freedoms are even greater than those of Rd. Strauss.

Regi'na Cœ'li (*L.*). "Queen of heaven." A hymn to the Virgin Mary, sung at Compline.

Register. (*G., Regis'ter.*) (1) A set of organ pipes of the same tone quality (generally called a "stop"). (2) A distinct division of the tone quality of a voice, or inst. ; *e.g., chest* register, *head* register, *thick* register, *thin* register, *chalumeau* register (of the clarinet), &c. (3) Compass of a voice or inst. ; *e.g.,* extensive register, low register, &c.
Registration. The art of selecting and combining the stops in organ playing.
Regis'ter-knopf (*G.*). A stop-knob.
Regis'ter-stim'men (*G.*). Speaking stops (as opposed to couplers, &c.).
Regis'terzug. A draw-stop.

Registre (*F.*) } (1) A stop-knob. (2) Same
Regis'tro (*I.*) } as **Register** (2) and (3).
Regis'tri di ripie'no (*I.*). Mixture Stops.
Regis'tri dol'ci (*I.*). Soft, sweet stops.

Registri(e)'ren (*G.*). To select and combine org. stops.
Registri(e)'rung. Registration.

Règle (*F.*) }
Re'gola (*I.*) } Rule ; precept.
Règle de l'octave (*F.*). Rule of the octave (*q.v.*). To a mize a bass scale.

REGON'DI, Giulio. Noted concertina player ; *b.* Geneva, 1822 ; *d.* 1872.

REGNAL, Frédéric. Pen-name of **Baron d'Erlanger** (*q.v.*).

REGNART (or **REGNARD**), **Jacob.** Netherland contrapuntist ; *b.* 1540 ; *d.* abt. 1600. Imperial vice - capellmeister, Prague.
Wrote a large number of masses, motets, canzone, &c., and several books of German songs.

Regular fugue. A strict fugue. (See **Fugue.**)

Regular motion. Similar motion. (See **Motion.**)

REH'BAUM, Theobald. *B.* Berlin, 1835.
Works : 7 operas ; vn. pieces, part-songs, songs.

REH'BERG, Willy. Pianist ; *b.* Morges, Switzerland, 1863. Head pf. teacher Geneva Cons., 1890.
Works : pf. pieces and études, a sonata for pf. and vn., &c.

Rehearsal. (*G., Pro'be ; F., Répétition ; I., Pro'va.*) Practice of a work before performance.

REH'FELD, Fabian. Violinist and composer ; *b.* Tuchel, 1842.

REI'CHA, Anton J. Eminent theorist ; *b.* Prague, 1770 ; *d.* Paris, 1836. Flautist Bonn orchestra (in which Beethoven was a viola player), 1788 ; pf. teacher, Hamburg, 1794-9 ; lived in Vienna (1801-8) on friendly terms with Beethoven, Haydn, and Albrechtsberger. Afterwards settled in Paris as theorist and teacher ; Prof. of counterpoint and fugue Paris Cons., 1818; naturalized, 1829 ; member of the Académie, 1835.
Works : 2 symphonies, much chamber music (24 string quartets, 24 quintets, 24 trios for horns, 22 flute duets, &c.), pf. pieces (including 36 fugues) ; also several theoretical treatises, including a " Traité de haute composition musicale," which has been translated into several languages.

REI'CHARDT, Alexander. Operatic tenor ; *b.* Hungary, 1825 ; *d.* 1885. Sang yearly in London from 1851 to 1857.

REI'CHARDT, Gustav. *B.* nr. Demmin, 1797 ; *d.* Berlin, 1884. Music teacher to the late Emperor Frederick.
Wrote songs ("Was ist des Deutschen Vaterland," &c.).

REI'CHARDT, Johann F. *B.* Königsberg, 1752 ; *d.* 1814. Capellmeister to Frederick the Great, Berlin, 1775 ; founded the " Concerts Spirituels," (with analytical programs), 1783 ; dismissed by Fred. Wm. II, 1794. Afterwards Inspector of salt works (with other appointments) under Fred. Wm. III.
Works : numerous Italian and German operas ; a Passion ; cantatas, psalms, &c. ; and several fine songs. Also 7 symphonies, 14 pf. concertos, much chamber music, 17 pf. sonatas, and a number of theoretical works.

REI'CHARDT, Luise. Daughter of J. F. ; *b.* Berlin, 1788 ; *d.* 1826.
Wrote several charming songs.

REI'CHEL, Adolf H. J. *B.* Tursznitz, Prussia, 1816 ; *d.* 1896. Teacher of composition Dresden Cons., 1857-67 ; Municipal music-director, Berne, 1867.
Works : pf. pieces (concertos, sonatas, mazurkas, &c.) masses, songs.

REI'CHER, Frau E. (Hedwig Kindermann). Soprano ; *b.* Munich, 1853.

REI'CHERT, Matthieu A. Noted flautist and composer of flute music ; *b.* Maestricht, 1830.

REICH'MANN, Theodor. Operatic baritone; *b.* Rostock, 1849 ; *d.* 1903. Created the part of " Amfortas " in Wagner's *Parsifal,* Bayreuth, 1882.

REICH'WEIN, Leopold. Noted conductor ; *b.* Breslau, 1878. Conducted German Opera, Covent Garden, 1907.
Works : opera, *Vasantasena,* &c.

REID, Alan. Composer ; *b.* Arbroath, 1853.

REID, General John R. Musical amateur ; *b.* Perthshire, 1721(?) ; *d.* 1807. Left £52,000 to found a chair of music in Edinburgh Univ.
The present "Reid Professor" (1908) is Dr. Fr. Niecks.

Reif'tanz (*G.*). A circle dance ; a shepherds' dance ; a rustic dance.

Rei'gen .(*G.*) } A circular dance. A row or
Rei'hen (*G.*) } procession of dancers or singers. A refrain ; a roundelay.

REIJN'VAAN (or REYN'WAEN), J. V. Holland, 1743-1809. Projected the 1st Dutch Mus. Dict., completing A to M.

REI'MANN, Heinrich. Distinguished music critic ; son of Ignaz (below) ; *b.* Regensdorf, Silesia, 1850 ; *d.* 1906. Settled in Berlin, 1887 ; asst. librarian in the Royal Library, orgt. to the Philharmonic Society, &c.
Works : organ sonatas and studies, a "Biography of Schumann," a treatise on "Byzantine Music," &c.

REI'MANN, Ignaz. Prolific church composer ; *b.* Silesia, 1820 ; *d.* 1885.
Works : 18 masses, 4 requiems, 48 offertoires, 40 graduals, &c.

Rein (*G.*). Clear, pure, perfect,exact.
Rein'greifen. Accurate fingering, playing, &c.
Rein'e Stim'me. A clear voice.

REI'NAGLE, Alex. Robt. Son of J. (below) ; *b.* Brighton, 1799 ; *d.* 1877. Orgt. St. Peter's-in-the-East, Oxford, 1822-53.
Works : colln. of vn. pieces ; psalm-tunes (including the well-known " St. Peter "), &c.

REINAGLE, Joseph. 'Cellist and writer ; *b.* Portsmouth, 1762 ; *d.* 1836.
Works : a Violoncello Method, 6 string quartets.

REI'NECKE, Carl H. C. Distinguished pianist and teacher of composition ; *b.* Altona, 1824. Court pianist, Copenhagen, 1846-8 ; pf. teacher Cologne Cons., 1851 ; mus. director, Barmen, 1854 ; condr. Breslau Singakademie, 1859 ; condr. Gewandhaus concerts, Leipzig, 1860-95 ; prof. of pf. and composition Leipzig Cons., 1860.
Works : operas and operettas, an oratorio (*Belsazzar*), several cantatas ; song-cycles, concert arias, 20 canons for female voices, 2 masses ; symphonies and overtures for orch., chamber music, and much pf. music (4 concertos, sonatas for pf. and vn., serenades, solo sonatas, ballades, fantasias, &c.).

REI'NER, Jacob. Contrapuntist ; pupil of Lasso (or Lassus) ; *b.* Altdorf, Württemberg, abt. 1560 ; *d.* 1606.
Works : motets, psalms, masses, magnificats, songs, &c.

REIN'HARD, B. F. The first music printer to use the stereotype process ; Strasburg, 1800.

REIN'HOLD, Hugo. Composer ; *b.* Vienna, 1854.

REIN'HOLDT, Theodor C. Cantor, Kreuzkirche, Dresden ; *d.* 1755. Teacher of J. A. Hiller. Wrote motets, &c.

REIN'KEN (REIN'KE, or REIN'ICKE), Johann Adam. Celebrated organist ; *b.* Wilshausen, Alsace, 1623 ; *d.* 1722. Pupil of Scheidemann ; orgt. Katharinenkirche, Hamburg, 1663. J. S. Bach frequently walked from Lüneburg to hear him play.
Works : org. pieces ; quartets for 2 vns., viola, and bass, &c.

REINS'DORF, Otto. Musical editor and critic ; *b.* Köselitz, 1848 ; *d.* Berlin, 1890.

REIN'THALER, Karl M. *B.* Erfurt, 1832 ; *d.* 1896. Teacher of singing Cologne Cons., 1853 ; municipal music director and capellmeister at the cathedral, Bremen, 1857 ; member Berlin Akademie, 1882.
Works : 2 operas, an oratorio (*Jephtha*), the celebrated "Bismarck-Hymne," cantatas, a symphony, male choruses, songs, &c.

Reis'elied (*G.*). A travelling song ; a pilgrim's song.

REI'SENAUER, Alfred. Concert pianist ; *b.* Königsberg, 1863 ; *d.* 1907.

REI'SER, August F. *B.* Gammertingen, Württemberg, 1840. Editor Cologne *Neue Musikzeitung*, 1880-6.
Works : orchestral pieces, male choruses, &c.

REISET, Marie F. C. de. (See **Grandval**.)

REIS'SIGER, Friedrich A. *B.* nr. Wittenberg, 1809 ; *d.* 1883. Military bandmaster. Wrote many songs.

REIS'SIGER, Karl G. Brother of preceding ; *b.* nr. Wittenberg, 1798 ; *d.* 1859. Studied at Leipzig, Vienna, and Munich; organized a Cons. of Music at The Hague, 1826 ; mus. director German opera, Dresden, 1826 ; afterwards Court Capellmeister, Dresden.
Works : 9 operas (*Die Felsenmühle von Etalières*, &c.), an oratorio (*David*), 10 masses, a symphony, chamber music, pf. pieces, songs, &c.

REISS'MANN, Dr. August. Noted writer on music ; *b.* Frankenstein, Silesia, 1825 ; *d.* 1903. Lecturer on the Hist. of Mus. Stern Cons., Berlin, 1866-74 ; afterwards lived in Leipzig and Wiesbaden, and again in Berlin.
Works : 3 operas, an oratorio, choruses, songs, vn. pieces, pf. pieces, &c. His numerous treatises include "From Bach to Wagner" (1861), "A History of German Songs" (his best work), "A History of Music" (3 vols.), "Musical Composition" (3 vols.), "Musical Æsthetics" (1879), a "Handlexicon of Music," lives of Mendelssohn, Schubert, Haydn, Bach, Handel, Gluck, Weber, &c.

REI'TER, Ernst. Composer ; *b.* Wertheim, 1814 ; *d.* 1875.

REI'TER, Josef. Composer ; *b.* Braunau-on-Inn, 1862.
Works : operas, symphonies, cantatas, male choruses, pf. pieces, songs, &c.

Relation. (*G.*, *Verwand'schaft ; F.*, *Relation ; I.*, *Relazio'ne.*) Affinity.
Relation, False. (See *False Relation.*)

Rela'ted ⎱ Allied ; having a number of
Rel'ative ⎰ notes or chords in common.
Related keys. (See *Attendant keys.*)
Relative chord. A chord common to two (or more) keys.
Relative major ⎱ (*G.*, *Parallel'tonart ; F.*, *Mode*
Relative minor ⎰ *relatif ; I.*, *To'no relati'vo.*) A major and minor scale (or key) with the same key signature. Thus A minor is the relative minor of C major ; C major is the relative major of A minor, &c.

Rela'tio non harmon'ica (*L.*). False relation.
" False relation was formerly forbidden ; but modern composers, rejecting the rigorous trammels of early contrapuntists, have enlarged the bounds both of harmony and melody, and given them a freedom to which we owe many beauties unknown to the fathers of musical science."—*Moore.*

Relazio'ne (*I.*). Relation.

RELFE, John. *B.* Greenwich, 1763 ; *d.* abt. 1837. Teacher of pf. and harmony.
Works : harpsichord pieces, songs, " The Principles of Harmony," &c.

Religieux,-euse (*F.*) ⎱
Religio'so (*I.*). ⎬ Religious, devotional,
Religiös (*G.*) ⎰ solemn.
Religiosamen'te (*I.*). In devotional style.

Relish ⎱ Old harpsichord graces.
Double relish ⎰ (See **Ornament.**)

RELL'STAB, H. F. Ludwig. Son of J. K. F. (below) ; noted novelist ; Berlin, 1799-1860. Wrote musical criticisms, biographies of great composers, &c.
Violently opposed Chopin's music.

RELL'STAB, Johann K. F. Berlin, 1759-1813. Music printer and publisher ; lecturer on harmony, &c.
Wrote numerous musical criticisms, a work on "Pf. playing," &c.

Re majeur (*F.*). D major.

RÉMAURY, Fanny M. C. Pianist ; *b.* Pamiers, 1843.

REM'ENYI, Eduard. Distinguished violinist; *b.* Heves, Hungary, 1830 ; *d.* San Francisco, 1898. Banished for taking part in the Hungarian Revolution, 1848. Solo violinist to Queen Victoria, 1854. After the amnesty of 1860, became solo violinist to the Emperor of Austria. Toured with great success from 1865. " His technique was prodigious," and it was united with " vigour, passion, and pathos."
Works : a vn. concerto, vn. solos, &c.

Re mineur (*F.*). D minor.

REM'MERS, Johann. Chamber violinist at St. Petersburg ; *b.* Jever, 1805 ; *d.* 1847.

REM'MERT, Martha. Pianist ; pupil of Tausig and Liszt ; *b.* nr. Glogau, 1854.

Remote key. An unrelated key ; an extreme key (*q.v.*).

Removes of key. (See under **Key.**)

Remplissage (*F.*). " A filling up." (1) Middle parts (especially in orchestral scores). (2) Decorative flourishes, embellishments, &c. ; padding.
Parties de remplissage. Filling-up parts.

REMUSAT (or **REMUZAT**), **Jean.** Distinguished flautist ; *b.* Bordeaux, 1815 ; *d.* 1880. 1st flute at the Queen's Theatre, London, and (from 1853) at the Th.-Lyrique, Paris. He preferred the old style of flute to the Böhm system.
Wrote flute solos and duets, fl. and vn. pieces, a "Flute Method," &c.

REMY, W. A. (See **Mayer, Wm.**)

RÉNARD, Marie. Soprano ; *b.* Graz, 1864.

RENAUD, Albert. *B.* Paris, 1855. Musical critic of *La Patrie.*
Works : operas, ballets (*The Awakened Shepherd*, London, 1892), vaudevilles, &c.

RENAUD, Maurice A. Noted bass singer ; *b.* Bordeaux, 1862. Pupil Paris Cons. Has sung at the Paris Grand Opéra since 1891. His *repertoire* includes over 50 operas.

RENDA'NO, Alfonso. Pianist ; *b.* Calabria, 1853. Pupil of Thalberg.
Works : salon pieces for pianoforte.

Rendering ⎱ Interpretation ; method of
Rendition ⎰ performance ; *e.g.,* "artistic rendering," " new rendering," &c.

REN'NER, Josef. *B.* Bavaria, 1832 ; *d.* 1895. Organized the " Ratisbon Madrigal Quartet " to revive the old German madrigals.
Published collections of madrigals.

Rentrée (*F.*). A re-entry. (See **Reprise.**)

Renversement (*F.*). Inversion (*q.v.*).
Renversé. Inverted.
Renverser. To invert.

Renvoi (*F.*). A repeat ; a repeat-mark.

Re'ol. A Danish reel.

Repeat. (*G., Wiederho'lungszeichen ; F., Bâton de reprise ; I., Re'plica.*) A sign indicating repetition.

(a)   (b)   (c)   (d)

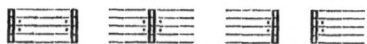

(a) Repeat the music between the two double bars.
(b) Repeat the parts before and after the double bar.
(c) Repeat the part before the double bar.
(d) Repeat the part after the double bar.
N.B.—Four dots are sometimes used instead of two, thus—

A repeat is also indicated by the word *Bis* (*q.v.*).
(See also *D.C.* and *D.S.*) A repetition of words is marked by the sign ://: (See **Signs.**)

Repeat 8va. Repeat an octave higher.

Repercussion. The repetition of the same sound ; or the regular re-entry of a theme.

Repertoire *F.*) ⎱ The pieces which a per-
Rep'ertory (*E.*) ⎰ former knows thoroughly. The stock pieces of an opera company.

Repetimen'to (*I.*) ⎱ Repetition.
Repetizio'ne (*I.*) ⎰
Sen'za repetizio'ne. Without repetition.

Répétiteur (*F.*) ⎱ Director of an opera
Repeti'tor (*G.*) ⎰ chorus.
Repetito're (*I.*) ⎰

Repetition. (See **Imitation.**)

Répétition (*F.*). A rehearsal.
Répétition générale. Dress rehearsal of an opera, &c.

Re'plica (*I.*). Reply, repetition.
Con re'plica. With repetition ; repeated.
Replica'to. (1) Repeated. (2) Doubled.
Replicazio'ne. Repetition.
Senza re'plica. Without repeating.

Rep'licate ⎱ " A repetition of a tone at a
Replique (*F.*) ⎰ different pitch." The octave, double octave, &c., of a note.
Replique (*F.*). (1) An answer. (2) A cue (*q.v.*).

Reply ⎱ The Answer of a Fugue.
Réponse (*F.*) ⎰ (See **Fugue.**)

Repos (*F.*). (1) A pause, or hold. (2) The end of a section, &c.

Reprendre (*F.*). To retake, to resume.

Reprise (*F.*). (1) A **Burden** (*q.v.*). (2) A repeat. (3) The re-entry (or recapitulation) of the principal subjects in the 2nd part of a movement in sonata form. (See **Sonata.**)
Reprise d'un opéra. The reproduction, or revival, of an opera.

Re'quiem (*L.*). (*L., Mis'sa pro defunc'tis ; G., Tod'tenmesse ; I., Mes'sa per i Defon'ti ; F., Messe de Morts.*) A mass for the dead.
Among the finest Requiems may be mentioned those of Vittoria, Colonna, Mozart, Gossec, Cherubini, Berlioz, and Verdi.

Requin'to (*S.*). The small E♭ clarinet.

Research. (1) An extemporized prelude on the organ or pf. introducing the leading themes of some composition to follow. (2) A **ricercata** (*q.v.*).

Resin. (See **Rosin.**)

Résolument (*F.*). Resolutely.

Resolu'tio (*L.*) ⎱ (*G., Auf'lösing ; F., Réso-
Resolu'tion ⎰ lution ; I., Risoluzio'ne.*) The progression of a dissonant note (or chord) to some other note (or chord) according to the laws and rules of harmony. (See also **Suspension.**)
N.B.—The resolution of a dissonant note may be *delayed,* or it may be *transferred* to another part.

Resoluzio'ne (*I.*). Energy, decision.

Res'onance. (*G., Resonanz' ; F., Resonnement.*) Sympathetic vibration. (See **Acoustics.**)
Resonance-body A sound-board (of a pf., &c.).
Resonance-box. The hollow part of a violin, &c.
Resonanz'boden (*G.*). Resonance-body (sound-board).
Resonanz'kasten (*G.*). Resonance-box.
Resonanz'saite (*G.*). A sympathetic string (in old harpsichords, &c.).

Res'onator. A hollow sphere of glass or metal with 2 orifices, one to insert in the ear, the other communicating with the air. It is tuned to a certain pitch, and powerfully reinforces any sound of that pitch ; so that partials or other accompanying sounds can be detected.

Resonner *F.*). To resound ; to echo.

Respiration. Breathing.

Respi'ro (*I.*). (1) A breath. (2) A semiquaver rest (⌐). (3) A breathing mark.

Responsay song. " An anthem in which the choristers and people sing by turns."— *Grassineau.*

Response. (*L.*, *Respon'sum ; I.*, *Responsio'ne, Respon'so.*) (1) The reply of choir or congregation to a passage read or chanted by the officiating minister. (2) The *Answer* in a fugue.

Responsi'vo (*I.*). Responsive(ly).

Resserrement (*F.*). A stretto ; in stretto style.

Ressort (*F.*). The bass bar (of a vn., &c.).

Ressortir, Faire (*F.*). To bring forward. *Faites ressortir le chant.* Bring out the melody.

Rest. (*G.*, *Pau'se ; F.*, *Silence ; I.*, *Pa'usa.*) A sign indicating silence.

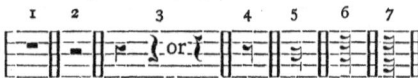

French form of crotchet rest : ⌐ ⌐ &c.

RESZKÉ. (See **De Reszké.**)

Retardation. (1) A gradual slackening of speed. (2) A kind of suspension (resolved *upwards*), caused by continuing one or more notes of a chord into the following chord.

Retentir (*F.*). To resound. *Retentissement.* Re-echoing ; pealing.

Retenu (*F.*). **Ritenuto** (*q.v.*). *En retenant.* Rallentando.

Retouche (*F.*). The addition of embellishments to a melody.

Retraite (*F.*). A retreat ; the military tattoo.

Re'tro (*L.*). Backwards. (See **Recte et retro.**)

Ret'rograde. (*L.*, *Retrogra'dus ; I.*, *Retrogra'do.*) Reversed, backward. *Mo'tus retrogra'dus* (*L.*). "Reading music backwards." *Imita'tio retrogra'da* (*I.*). Imitation *per recte et retro* (See *Canon* and *Imitation.*)

Ret'to (*I.*). Right, direct ; similar. *Mo'to ret'to.* Similar motion. (See *Motion.*)

REUB'KE, Adolf. Noted organ builder ; Halberstadt, 1805-75. Built the great organ (88 stops) in Magdeburg Cath.

English Name.	German.	French.	Italian.
(1) Semibreve, or Whole rest	Takt'pause	Pause	Pa'usa del'la Semibre've
(2) Minim, or Half rest	Hal'bepause, or Zwei'telpause	Demi-pause	„ „ Mi'nima
(3) Crotchet, or Quarter rest	Vier'telpause	Soupir	„ „ Semimi'nima (or Quar'to)
(4) Quaver, or Eighth rest	Acht'elpause	Demi-soupir	„ „ Cro'ma (or Mez'zoquar'to)
(5) Semiquaver, or 16th rest	Sech'zehntelpause	Quart de soupir	„ „ Semi-cro'ma (or Respi'ro)
(6) Demisemiquaver, or 32nd rest	Zwei'unddrei'ssigstelpause	Demi-quart de soupir	„ „ Biscro'ma
(7) Hemidemisemiquaver, or 64th rest	Vier'undsech'zigstelpause	Seizième de soupir	„ „ Semibiscroma

N.B.—Rests are sometimes "dotted" like notes. A semibreve rest is used in all kinds of time for a " bar's rest."

A rest of several bars' duration is generally shown in one of the following ways :—

Restez (*F.*). " Stay there ! " Keep to the same position, or on the same string, &c., in playing on a bowed inst. Also used in the sense of *Tenuto*, or *Sostenuto.*

Resul'tant tones ⎫ The accessory sounds pro-
Resul'tants ⎭ duced by two (or more) simultaneous sounds. (See **Acoustics.**)

Resurrex'it (*L.*). Part of the *Credo* in a Mass.

REUB'KE, Julius R. Fine pianist ; son of A. ; *b.* 1834 ; *d.* 1858. Wrote an org. sonata, a pf. sonata, songs, &c.

REU'LING, L. Wilhelm. *B.* Darmstadt, 1802 ; *d.* 1879. Capellmeister Josephstädter Th., Vienna, 1829 ; Kärnthnerthor Th., 1830-54. Works : 37 operas and operettas, 17 ballets, pantomimes, chamber music, &c.

REUSS-BEL'CE, Louise. Soprano ; *b.* Vienna. *Début* as "Elsa" (*Lohengrin*), Carlsruhe, 1884.

REU'TER, Florizel. Popular American " boy violinist ; " *b.* 1890(?).

REUT'TER, Georg. Vienna, 1656-1738. Theorbo player Court Orch., 1697-1703; Court orgt., 1710; capellmeister St. Stephen's, 1712; Cathedral capellmeister, 1715.

REUT'TER, J. A. C. Georg. Son of preceding; Vienna, 1708-72. Capellmeister St. Stephen's, 1738; Court capellmeister, 1746.

"It was he who engaged young Haydn for the choir, and treated him so badly."—*Baker.*

RÉV, Kálmán. Precocious violinist; *b.* Zemplener, North Hungary, Dec. 15, 1896. Pupil of Hubay. London *début,* 1909.

Reveil' (*Old E.*) ⎫ "Awakening." A mili-
Réveil (*F.*) ⎬ tary signal at day-
Reveil'le (*G.*) ⎭ break.

Revenez (*F.*). Return.
Revenez peu à peu au premier mouvement. Return by degrees to the first *tempo.*

R3verberi(e')ren (*G.*). To reverberate.

Rev'erie. A contemplative, quiet piece.

Reverse motion. Contrary motion (*q.v.*).

REY, Jean Baptiste. Noted conductor; *b.* Lauzerte, 1734; *d.* Paris, 1810. Asst. condr. Paris Grand Opéra, 1776; conductor, 1781-1806(?). Napoleon's Maître de chapelle, 1804.
Works : 2 operas ; masses, motets, ballets, &c.

REY, Jean Baptiste. *B.* Tarascon, abt. 1760. 'Cellist Paris Grand Opéra, 1795-1822.
Works : an "Elementary Treatise on Harmony," a " Pf. Primer," &c.

REYER (or **REY**), **Louis E. E.** One of the chief exponents of modern French romantic opera ; *b.* Marseilles, 1823 ; *d.* 1909. Embraced a musical career, 1848; member of the French Académie, 1876; chevalier and officer of the Legion of Honour.
Works : operas (*La Statue,* his best, 1861 ; *Salammbô,* 1890 ; &c) ; ballets, pantomimes, symphonic odes, cantatas, male choruses, &c.

REYNOLDS, Charles. Noted oboe player ; *b.* Stockport, 1850.
Prof. of Oboe, Royal Manchester Coll. of Music.

REYNOLDS, Charles T. *B.* Ross, Hereford, 1865; Mus.Doc. Oxon, 1895.

REYNOLDS, John. 18th cent. Composer; *d.* 1778(?). Gentleman, Chapel Royal, 1765-70. Composed "My God, look upon me."

REYNOLDS, Williamson J. *B.* London, 1861; Mus.Doc. London, 1889; Orgt. St. Michael's, Cornhill, 1891; Birmingham Parish Ch., 1900.

Rezitativ' (*G.*). Recitative (*q.v.*).

REZ'NICEK, Emil N. Freiherr von. Gifted opera composer ; *b.* Vienna, 1861. Studied Leipzig Cons.; 1st capellmeister Mannheim Court Th., 1896.
Works: operas (*Donna Diana,* 1894; &c.); a requiem, orchestral pieces, &c.

rf., rfz. Abbn. of *Rinforzando* (*q.v.*).

R.H. or *r.h.* Right hand.

Rhapsodie (*F.*) ⎫ A piece in the style of
Rhapsodie' (*G.*) ⎬ an improvization or
Rhap'sody (*E.*) ⎭ impromptu, with no regular form, and generally of brilliant character.
The ancient Greek *Rhapsodists* were reciters (especially of fragments of Homer's works). Their style was wild and disconnected ; and, like the later " Bards," they often worked themselves up into a frenzy.

RHAW (or **RHAU**), **Georg.** *B.* Eisfeld, Franconia, 1488 ; *d.* 1548. Cantor Thomasschule, Leipzig. Est. a music printing business, Wittenberg, 1524 ; pub. especially the works of Protestant composers.

RHEIN'BERGER, Joseph G. Distinguished organist ; *b.* Vaduz, Liechtenstein, 1839; *d.* 1901. Played the pf. at 5, and the organ at 7. Teacher of theory, Munich Royal School of Mus. (1859), and orgt. Court Ch. of St. Michael. Capellmeister Royal Chapel Choir, 1877.
Works : operas, an oratorio (*Christophorus*), masses, requiems, Stabat Maters, cantatas, orchestral works, chamber music, pf. sonatas and solos, and many fine organ pieces (including 2 concertos and 20 sonatas).

RHEIN'GOLD, Das. The Vorspiel, or Prelude, of Wagner's *Nibelungen Ring ;* 1st performance, Munich, 1869.

Rhet'oric. The science of oratory ; the art of speaking with propriety, elegance, and force.

RHIGI'NI, Mad. (See **Ella Russell.**)

RHODES, Benjamin. 1743-1815. One of Wesley's preachers.
Wrote the hymn " My heart and voice I raise."

RHODES, Mrs. W. T. (See **Guy d'Hardelot.**)

Rhyme. (1) Correspondence of sound in syllables ; *e.g.,* rain, *pain ;* go, *low ;* &c.
(2) An old spelling of rhythm.
False rhymes. Syllables spelt similarly but not agreeing in sound; as bread, *mead ;* bough, *cough.*
Feminine rhymes. Words rhyming the last two syllables, and accenting the last but one ; as remarker, *embar'ker.*
Masculine rhymes. Words rhyming in the last syllable only.

Rhythm. (L., *Rhyth'mus ;* G., *Rhyth'mus ;* F., *Rhythme ;* I., *Rit'mo.*) Movement in musical time. The word is specially used in two senses :—

(1) The varied contents of bars.
Various rhythmical arrangements of the scale (in 2-4 time).

(e)

(f)

(2) The division of melody into motives, figures, sub-sections, sections, &c.

Rythmical figures.

(a)   (b)   (c)

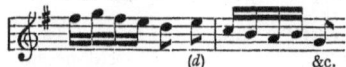

(d)   &c.

Examples of Three-bar rhythms.

(a)

(b)

A Five-bar rhythm (2 + 3).   Mendelssohn.

It will be seen that Rhythm cannot in modern music be dissociated from Metre and Metrical Formation, as "the Metre contains the Rhythm." (See also *Accent, Metre*, and *Metrical Formation.*)

Characteristic rhythms. The special forms of Rhythm used in various dances, national songs, &c.

(a) *Cracovienne—*

&c.

(b) *Polka—*

&c.

(c) *Mazurka—*

&c.

Rhyth'mical Accent. (See **Accent.**)

Rhyth'mic Imitation. The repetition of a rhythmical figure with different melody.

Rhyth'mics. The science of rhythm.

Rhythmique (*F.*) } Rhythmical.
Rhyth'misch (*G.*) }

Rhyth'misch bestimmt' (*G.*). Rhythmically accented. (See *Accent, Rhythmical.*)

24

Rhythmopœ'ia (*Gk.*). The regulation of quantity (accent) in metrical verse.

Rhyth'mus (*G.*). Rhythm.
Der Rhyth'mus scharf markie'rt. The rhythm strongly marked.

Ribat'tere (*I.*). To reverberate.
Ribattimen'to. Re-percussion ; reverberation.

Ribattitu'ra (*I.*) } " Restriking." The
Ribattu'ta (*I.*) } (rather) slow first notes of a shake. (See **Shake.**)
No'te ribattu'te. Repeated notes.

Ribe'ba (*I.*) } A Rebec (*q.v.*).
Ribe'ca (*I.*) }
Ribbechi'no. A small Rebec.

Ribs. (*G., Zar'gen; F., Eclisses; I., Fa'scie*).
(1) The curved sides of a vn., &c.
(2) The side supports of organ bellows.

RICCA'TI, Count Giordano. *B.* Castelfranco, Treviso, 1709 ; *d.* 1790.
Wrote on Counterpoint, Acoustics, Rameau's System of Harmony, &c.

RIC'CI, Federico. *B.* Naples, 1809 ; *d.* 1877. Pupil of Furno, Zingarelli, and Raimondi. Music director Imperial Theatres, St. Petersburg, 1853.
Of his numerous operas the following were the most successful : *La prigione d' Edinburgo* (1838), *Corrado d'Altamura* (1841), *Crispino e la comare* (1866), and *Una follia a Roma* (1869).

RIC'CI, Luigi. Eminent dramatic composer; brother of F.; *b.* Naples, 1805; *d.* 1859. Maestro Trieste Cath., and chorusmaster of the theatre, 1836.
His operas (about 30) include *Il Colombo* (1829), *Amina* (1829), *Chiara di Rosemberg* (1831), *Chi dura vince* (1834), *La festa di Piedigrotta* (1852), *Il diavolo a quattro* (1859). He also wrote masses, choruses, songs, &c.

RIC'CIUS, August F. *B.* Bernstadt, Saxony, 1819 ; *d.* 1886. Director "Euterpe" concerts, Leipzig, 1849. Capellmeister City Th., 1854-64; Hamburg Th., 1864.
Works : an overture, a cantata, incidental stage music, pf. pieces, songs, &c.

RIC'CIUS, Carl A. Nephew of preceding ; *b.* Bernstadt, 1830 ; *d.* 1893. Studied under Schubert, then at Leipzig Cons. Violinist Dresden Court Orch., 1847 ; chorus-master, 1863 ; librarian, Royal Music Library, 1889.
Works : operatic pieces, ballets, pf. pieces, songs.

Ricer'ca (*I.*) } " Seeking after ; " research,
Ricerca're (*I.*) } enquiry ; elaboration. A scholarly work.
Ricerca'ri. (1) Scholarly and elaborate embellishments. (2) Exercises.
Ricerca'ta. An elaborated toccata or fantasia.
Fu'ga ricerca'ta. A strict and learned fugue without episodes.

RICHARDS, H. Brinley. Pianist and teacher; *b.* Carmarthen, 1817 ; *d.* London, 1885. Won the "King's Scholarship," R.A.M., 1835 and 1837.
Works : a pf. concerto, orch. pieces, numerous graceful pf. pieces, part-songs, songs, &c. His best-known work is " God bless the Prince of Wales " (1862).

RICHARDS, Hy. W. Orgt., teacher, &c. ; *b.* London, 1865. Mus.D. Durham, 1903.

RICHARDSON, Alf. Madeley. *B.* Southend, 1868. Mus.D. Oxon, 1896. Orgt. Southwark Cath., 1897-1908.

RICHARDSON, Jas. Noted contemporary 'cellist ; *b.* Manchester, 18—.

RICHARDSON, Joseph. Flautist ; *b.* 1814 ; *d.* London, 1862.
Wrote studies, fantasias, &c., for flute.

RICHARDSON, Vaughan. *B.* London, abt. 1670 (?). Orgt. Winchester Cath., 1693 ; *d.* 1729.
Wrote anthems ("O how amiable," &c.), odes, cantatas, &c.

RICHAULT, Chas. S. *B.* Chartres, 1780 ; *d.* 1866. Founded the music publishing house known by his name, Paris, 1805.

RICHE, Antoine Le. (See **Divitis.**)

Richia'mo (*I.*). A bird call.
Richiama're. To imitate a bird call ; to warble.

RICH'TER (pron. *Rikh'-ter*), **Alfred.** Son of E. F. (below) ; *b.* Leipzig, 1846. Teacher Leipzig Cons., 1872-83 ; lived in London, 1883-97, afterwards returning to Leipzig.
Pub. supplements to his father's Manuals of Harmony and Counterpoint, &c.

RICH'TER, Ernst Friedrich E. Noted theorist ; *b.* Saxony, 1808 ; *d.* Leipzig, 1879. Son of a schoolmaster ; teacher of harmony and composition Leipzig Cons., 1843 ; condr. Singakademie, 1843-7 ; orgt. Petrikirche, 1851 ; Neukirche, 1862 ; music-director Nikolaikirche and Thomaskirche, 1868.
Works : Manuals of "Harmony," "Single and Double Counterpoint," and "Fugue"—all of which have been very popular. He also wrote an oratorio, masses, motets, string quartets, org. pieces, pf. pieces, &c.

RICH'TER, Ernst H. L. *B.* nr. Ohlau, 1805 ; *d.* 1876.
Wrote a comic opera, a mass, cantatas, male-voice part-songs, org. pieces, &c.

RICH'TER, Franz X. *B.* Moravia, 1709 ; *d.* 1789. Capellmeister Strasburg Cath., from 1774.
Works : 7 masses ; Te Deums, motets, &c. ; 26 symphonies, chamber music, a "Treatise on Harmony and Composition," &c.

RICH'TER, Dr.'Hans. Eminent conductor ; *b.* Raab, Hungary, 1843. Choir boy Court Chapel, Vienna, 1853. Studied with Wagner, 1866-7. Chorus-master Munich opera, 1867 ; Court conductor (under Bulow), 1868-9. Capellmeister Pesth Nat. Th., 1871-5 ; Imperial Op., Vienna, 1875. Chosen by Wagner to conduct the *Ring des Nibelungen*, Bayreuth (1876). Condr. Birmingham Festival since 1885. Mus.Doc. (*honoris causa*), Oxford, 1885. Director Manchester Orch. since 1897.

Richt'ig (*G.*). Right, accurate, exact.

RICIE'RI, Giovanni A. *B.* Venice, 1679 ; *d.* 1746. Teacher of Padre Martini ; composed several oratorios.

RICKARD, Richd. H. Pianist ; *b.* Birmingham, 1858 ; *d.* Brighton, 1907.
Composed pf. pieces.

Ricordan'za (*I.*). Recollection, remembrance.

RICOR'DI, Giovanni. Violinist ; Milan, 1785-1853. Founded the great music-pub. firm, Milan, 1808.

RICOR'DI, Giulio. Son of the above ; present head of the firm ; *b.* Milan, 1840. Editor-in-chief *Gazzetta Musicale.*
Works : salon pf. pieces, &c.

RIDDELL, John. Ayr, 1718-95. " Believed to have been blind from infancy."
Published collections of Scots Reels, &c.

RIDDELL, Capt. Robt. Friend of Burns ; *d.* nr. Dumfries, 1794.
Pub. collections of "Scotch, Galwegian, and Border Tunes," &c.

RIDDING, John A. Baritone vocalist ; *b.* Birmingham, 1862.

Riddo'ne (*I.*). A roundelay (*q.v.*).

Riden'do, Riden'te (*I.*). Laughing(ly).

RIDEOUT, Percy R. Pianist ; Mus.Doc., London, 1896. Orgt. West London Synagogue, 1904.

Ridevolmen'te (*I.*). Laughingly, pleasantly.

Ridicolosamen'te (*I.*). Ridiculously.

RIDLEY, Wm. *B.* Newark, 1820 ; *d.* 1886.
Published a collection of 301 chants, &c.

Ridot'to (*I.*). "Reduced." A reduction (*q.v.*); an arrangement ; an adaptation.

Riduzio'ne (*I.*). A reduction (*q.v.*) ; an arrangement.

RIE'CHERS, August. *B.* Hanover, 1836 ; *d.* 1893. Skilful maker and repairer of violins.
Pub. "The Violin and the Art of its Construction."

RIE'DEL, Dr. Carl. *B.* Kronenberg, nr. Elberfeld, 1827 ; *d.* 1888. Pupil, Leipzig Cons. ; organized the "Riedelverein " (choral society), 1854 ; president " Allgemeiner deutscher Musikverein," 1868 ; also president "Wagnerverein."
Works : Collections of German " Lieder," church melodies, &c.

RIE'DEL, F. E. A. *B.* Chemnitz, 1855. Town cantor and condr. of the Musikverein, Plauen, Saxony, 1890.
Works : cantatas, songs, part-songs, pf. pieces.

RIE'DEL, Hermann. Noted song composer; *b.* Burg, nr. Magdeburg, 1847. Court capellmeister, Brunswick.

RIEDT, Fr. Wm. Flautist ; Berlin, 1712-84. Chamber musician to Frederick the Great, 1741 ; director Berlin " Gesellschaft," 1750.
Works : symphonies, chamber music, flute music.

RIE'GO, Teresa del. Contemporary song composer ; *b.* London, 18—.

RIEHL, Wm. Heinrich von. *B.* Biebrich-on-Rhine, 1823 ; *d.* 1897.
Wrote on the "History of Civilization," "Musical History," &c. ; also pub. 2 vols. of songs.

RIEM, Friedrich Wm. *B.* Thuringia, 1779 ; *d.* 1857. Orgt. Thomaskirche, Leipzig. 1814 ; cath. orgt. Bremen, 1822.
Works : chamber music, pf. pieces, org. pieces, &c.

RIE'MANN, Dr. Hugo. Distinguished writer on music ; *b.* nr. Sondershausen, 1849. Lecturer on music Leipzig Univ., 1878-1880 ; teacher Hamburg Cons., 1881-90 ; Wiesbaden Cons. till 1895 ; resumed lecturing at Leipzig, 1895.
Works : pf. pieces, songs, chamber music, pf. studies, &c. ; historical treatises on music ; a method of "Harmony," a "Neue Schule der Melodik ;" works on Dynamics, Agogics, Phrasing, &c. ; a pf. method ; catechisms on musical instruments, musical forms, pf. playing, &c. ; works on Counterpoint and Modulation, a new edition of Marx's "Composition," &c. ; also a valuable "Musik-Lexikon" (chiefly biographical ; English edition, 1893).

RIEN'ZI. Early opera by Wagner; produced Dresden, 1842. He afterwards disowned it.

RIE'PEL, Joseph. *B.* Upper Austria, 1708 ; *d.* 1782. Chamber musician to the Prince of Thurn and Taxis.
Wrote numerous theoretical treatises.

RIES. Noted family of musicians—

(1) **Adolf.** Son of Hubert (5). *B.* Berlin, 1837. Pf. teacher in London.
Works : chamber music, songs, pf. pieces.

(2) **Ferdinand.** Eldest son of Franz (3). *B.* Bonn, 1784 ; *d.* 1838. Favourite pf. pupil of Beethoven. After pianistic tours, lived in London (1813-24) as performer and teacher. Afterwards settled at Frankfort. Conducted several of the Lower Rhine musical festivals.
Works : 3 operas, 2 oratorios, 6 symphonies, 9 pf. concertos, much chamber music, and many pf. pieces. His "Biography of Beethoven" is a valuable work.

(3) **Franz.** 1755-1846. Music director at Bonn ; friend of Beethoven.

(4) **Franz.** Son of Hubert (5). *B.* Berlin, 1846. Excellent violinist ; gave up playing and became a music publisher, 1875.
Works : orchestral and chamber music, pf. pieces, songs, &c.

(5) **Hubert.** Son of Franz (3). *B.* Bonn, 1802 ; *d.* 1886. Violinist ; pupil of Spohr. Leader Royal Orch., Berlin, 1836 ; teacher Royal "Theater-instrumentalschule," 1851-72.
Works : a vn. method, a large number of useful vn. studies, &c.

RIES, Louis. Violinist ; son of Hubert. *B.* Berlin, 1830. Settled in London, 1853.
2nd vn. Monday Pop. Concerts, 1859-97.

Rie'senharfe (*G.*). An Æolian harp.

RIETZ, Julius. *B.* Berlin, 1812 ; *d.* 1877. 2nd conductor (under Mendelssohn) Düsseldorf Opera, 1834 ; chief condr., 1835. Capellmeister Leipzig Th., 1847 ;

condr. Gewandhaus concerts, 1848. Court Capellmeister, Dresden, 1860 ; "General-musikdirector," 1874.
Works : 4 operas, 3 symphonies, several overtures, music to plays ; concertos for 'cello, vn., clarinet, and pf. ; chamber music, pf. sonatas, &c. ; much church music ; choruses, songs, &c. Of greater importance are his carefully-edited "Complete Works of Mendelssohn," "Mozart's Operas and Symphonies," "Beethoven's Symphonies," &c.

Rifacimen'to (*I.*). A restoration, rebuilding, or reconstruction of a work.

Rifiormen'to (*I.*). An ornament.
Rifiorimen'ti. Improvised or impromptu embellishments.

Ri'ga (*I.*). A line of the staff.

RI'GA, Frantz (or **François**). *B.* Liége, 1831 ; *d.* 1892.
Noted composer of male choruses.

Rigabel'lo (*I.*)
Rigabel'lum (*L.*) } A regal (*q.v.*).

Rigadoon' } An old Provençal dance
Rigaudon (*F.*) } of the nature of a jig, usually in lively 4-4 time.

Riga'ta (*I.*). The staff.

Ri'gal. A Regal (*q.v.*).

RIGBY, Geo. Vernon. Tenor vocalist ; *b.* Birmingham, 1840. *Début* Covent Garden, 1861.

RIGHI'NI, Vincenzo. Bologna, 1756-1812. Pupil of Bernacchi and Padre Martini. Singing master to the Archduchess Elizabeth, Vienna, 1780 ; Capellmeister Mayence, 1788-92 ; Capellmeister Berlin Court Opera, 1793.
Works : abt. 20 operas (*Tigrane*, 1799 ; *Gerusalemme liberata*, 1802 ; *La selva incantata*, 1802 ; &c.) ; a mass, a requiem, cantatas, arias, &c. and a fine collection of "Vocal Exercises" (1806).

Ri'go (*I.*). The staff.

Ri'gol. A Regal (*q.v.*).

Rigo're (*I.*). Strictness ; ·rigour.
Al rigo're di tem'po. In strict time.
Con rigo're. With exactness and precision.
Rigoro'so. Strict, exact.
Non rigoro'so in tempo. Not in strict time.

Rikk. A small Egyptian tambourine.

Rilascian'do (*I.*). } Relaxing the time ;
Rilassan'do (*I.*) } *rallentando.*
Rilascian'te. } Slower.
Rilassa'to }

Rilch }
Ril'ka } A Russian lute.

RILLÉ. (See **Laurent de Rillé.**)

Ri'ma (*I.*). Rhyme, verse, poem, song.

RIMBAULT, Ed. Francis. London, 1816-76. Orgt. Swiss Church, Soho, 1832 ; founded, with W. Chappell and others, the Musical Antiquarian Society, 1840 ; editor Motet Soc., 1841. LL.D. Harvard Univ., 1848. His numerous antiquarian and historical works, though by no means absolutely reliable, are of considerable value.

Chief works: "Bibliotheca Madrigaliana," "The Organ: its History and Construction," "The Pianoforte: its Origin, Progress, and Construction," Este's "Whole Book of Psalms," Merbecke's "Common Prayer" (in fac-simile), Purcell's *Bonduca*, "The Ancient Vocal Music of England," "The Rounds, Catches, and Canons of England," &c.

Rimembran'za (*I.*). Memory, remembrance; souvenir.

Rimetten'do (*I.*). } Abbreviation *Rimett.*
Rimetten'dosi (*I.*). } (1) Rallentando. (2) Returning, restoring.

Rimetten'dosi al Tempo I. Returning to the original speed.

RIM'SKY-KOR'SAKOV, Nikolas A. Distinguished composer; founded the Neo-Modern Russian school; *b.* Tikhvin, Novgorod, 1844; *d.* 1908. Prof. of composition and instrumentation St. Petersburg Cons., 1871; inspector of marine bands, 1873-84; Director Free School of Music, 1874-87; asst. condr. Imperial Orch., 1883; condr. Russian Symphony concerts, 1886.

Works: several successful operas; symphonies and other orch. works; a pf. concerto, church music, chamber music, choruses, songs, a collection of 100 popular Russian songs, &c.

RINAL'DI, Giovanni. Pianist; *b.* Reggiolo, 1840; *d.* 1895.

Wrote numerous "romantic" pf. pieces.

RINCK, Gustave. French pianist and composer.

Works: pf. concerto (1876), comic opera (*Bordeaux*, 1877), &c.

RINCK (or **RINK**), **Johann C. H.** Noted organist; *b.* Elgersburg, Thuringia, 1770; *d.* 1846. Town organist, Geissen 1790; Darmstadt, 1805; Court orgt., Darmstadt, 1813; chamber musician, 1817.

Of his numerous organ works his "Orgelschule" is still regarded as a standard guide to organ playing. He also wrote church music, chamber music, pf. sonatas, &c.

Rinforza're (*I.*). To reinforce; to emphasize (a note or passage).

Rinforzan'do
Rinforza'to
Rinfor'zo
Per rinfor'zo
} With special emphasis; same as *sforzando*, &c.; marked > ^ v. Abbns. *rinf.*, *rfz.*, *rf.*

N.B.—*Rinforzando* has been occasionally used in the sense of *crescendo*, as in Dussek's "La Consolation."

Ring (*G.*). A ring; a circle.

Ring'elgedicht. A roundelay.
Ring'elpauke. A Sistrum (*q.v.*).
Ring'elreim. A refrain, chorus.
Ring'elstück. A round, a rondo.
Ring'eltanz. A circle dance, round dance.

RINGEL, Federico. Pen-name of **Baron d'Erlanger** (*q.v.*).

Ring'en (*G.*). To ring, to sound.

Ringers. Bell ringers in churches, &c.

Formerly there were many "societies of ringers" in England. The "Ancient Society of College Youths," founded 1637, is at the present time the most mportant society in the kingdom.

RING'LER, Eduard. *B.* Nuremberg, 1838. Condr. Nuremberg Society for Classical Choral Works, 1890.

Chief work: 4-act grand opera (*Frithjof*).

RINK. (See **Rinck.**)

RINK'ART, Martin. 1586-1649. Lutheran pastor, Eilenberg.

Wrote "Nun danket alle Gott," the North German National Hymn of Thanksgiving.

RINUCCI'NI, Ottavio. Florence, 1562-1621.

Wrote the libretti of *Dafne* (1594), and Peri's *Euridice* (1600). (See *Peri.*)

RI'PA, Alberto de (also called **Alberto Mantovano**). Celebrated lute player; *b.* Padua; *d.* abt. 1580.

Pub. an important "Tablature de Luth," in 6 books (1533-8).

Ripercussio'ne (*I.*). Repercussion.

Ripete're (*I.*). To repeat; to rehearse.

Ripetitu'ra (*I.*) } (1) Repetition. (2) A
Ripetizio'ne (*I.*) } refrain.

Ripiane (*F.*). } Corruptions of **Ripieno.**
Ripiano (*E.*). }

Ripie'no (*I.*). (1) Additional, supplementary; filling up.

Ripie'nist. One who plays ripieno parts.
Violi'no ripie'no. An accessory violin; one played in full or tutti passages, choruses, &c., but not in accompanying soli, &c.
Ripieno Cornet. An accessory cornet in a brass band, with similar duties to *Violino ripieno.*

N.B.—*Ripieno* is sometimes used in scores as equivalent to *Tutti.*

Ripie'no (*I.*). (2) A mixture stop on Italian organs.

Ripie'no di du'e. A mixture of 2 ranks.
Ripie'no di tre. A mixture of 3 ranks.
Ripie'no di quat'tro, cin'que, &c. A mixture of 4, 5 ranks, &c.

Ripien'stimmen (*G.*). Ripieno parts.

Ripi'glio (*I.*). Repetition; reprise.

Ripo'so (*I.*). Repose.

Con ripo'so
Riposatamen'te
Riposa'to
} With repose.

RIPPON, John. Clergyman; 1751-1836.

Compiled books of hymn-tunes.

Ripren'dere (*I.*). To resume, to recommence.

Stringen'do per ripren'dere il pri'mo tem'po. Accelerating in order to resume the original *tempo.*

Ripre'sa (*I.*). (1) A burden. (2) A reprise (*q.v.*). (3) A repeat. (4) The sign 𝄋.

Riscaldan'do (*I.*). Becoming warmer; with more animation.

RISCH'BIETER, Wm. Albert. *B.* Brunswick, 1834. Teacher of harmony and counterpoint Dresden Cons., 1862.

Works: orch. pieces; treatises on Harmony, Counterpoint, Modulation, &c.

RISELEY, George. Orgt. and conductor; *b.* Bristol, 1845. Orgt. Colston Hall, Bristol, 1870. Condr. Bristol Orpheus Soc., 1878.

Risentitamen'te (*I.*) } With energetic ex-
Risenti'to (*I.*) } pression; brisk, lively. Resentful, spiteful.

RISLER, Edouard. Pianist; *b.* Baden-Baden, 1873.

Risolutez'za (*I.*) ⎫ Resolution, energy, de-
Risoluzio'ne (*I.*) ⎰ termination.
Con risoluzio'ne
Risolutamen'te ⎱ With resolution, energy, &c.
Risolu'to ⎰
Risolutis'simo. Very resolutely; strongly emphasized.

Risonan'za (*I.*). Resonance.

Risona're(*I.*). To resound.

Rispet'to (*I.*). A love ditty.

Rispo'sta (*I.*). A reply; the " answer " in a fugue. (See **Fugue.**)

Riss in der Stim'me (*G.*). A "crack," break, or gap in the voice in passing from one register to another.

RISTO'RI, Giovanni A. *B.* Bologna, 1692; *d.* 1753. Director Polish Orch., Dresden, 1717; chamber orgt. 1733; vice-capellmeister, 1750.
Works: 15 operas (including *Calandro*, 1726, and *Don Chisciotte*, 1727, two of the "earliest comic operas"), 3 oratorios, 16 cantatas, 11 masses.

Ristret'to (*I.*). A stretto (*q.v.*).

Risveglia're (*I.*). To rouse up, re-animate.
Risveglia'to. Animated, lively, excited.

Rit.
Ritard ⎱ Abbreviations of *Ritardando*, &c.

Ritarda're (*I.*). To retard or gradually slacken the pace.
Ritardan'do ⎫ Gradually slower and slower; *rallen-*
Ritarda'to ⎰ *tando.*
Ritardan'do al fi'ne. Gradually slower until the end.
Ritardazio'ne. Retardation; dragging.
Ritar'do. Retardation (*q.v.*).
Ritenen'do ⎫ Gradually slower and slower; *rallen-*
Ritenen'te ⎰ *tando.*

Ritenu'to (*I.*). Abbreviation *riten.* Immediately slower.
Note the special meaning of this term.
Ritenu'to mol'to. Much slackened (in speed).

Ritma'to (*I.*) ⎫ (1) Well balanced in
Ben ritma'to (*I.*) ⎰ rhythmical construction.
(2) With the rhythm well accentuated.

Rit'mo (*I.*). Rhythm, measure.
Rit'mico. Rhythmic.
Rit'mo di tre battu'te ⎫ (See under *Accent.*)
Rit'mo di quat'tro battu'te ⎰

Ritorna're (*I.*). To return, to repeat.
Ritordan'do al tem'po pri'mo. Returning to the original *tempo.*
Ritor'no al Tempo I. Return to the 1st *Tempo.*

Ritornel'
Ritornel'lo (*I.*) ⎫ Something returned to,
Ritournelle (*F.*) ⎰ or repeated. (1) A burden or refrain. (2) An introductory, connective, or concluding instrumental passage in an Aria or other song. (3) A *tutti* in a concerto. (4) A repeat.

RITSON, Joseph. Antiquary; *b.* Stockton, 1752; *d.* London, 1803.
His "Ancient British Songs" (1790) and "Scottish Songs" (1794) are valuable collections.

RIT'TER, Alexander. Russian violinist; *b.* Narva (or Reval), 1833; *d.* 1896. Leader at Meiningen, Weimar, Stettin,

and Würzburg (where he established a music business).
Works: 2 successful operas, orch. pieces, several fine songs, &c.

RIT'TER, August G. Noted organist; *b.* Erfurt, 1811; *d.* 1885. Orgt. successively at Erfurt, Merseburg, and Magdeburg.
Works: "The Art of Org. Playing" (2 vols.); organ sonatas, preludes, &c.; 4 choral books, orch. pieces, a pf. concerto, &c.

RIT'TER (or RAYMOND-RITTER), Fanny. *B.* England, 1840; *d.* 188-(?). Wife of Dr. F. L. Ritter (below).
Works: a trans. of Schumann's "Music and Musicians." "Some Famous Songs," &c.

RIT'TER, Dr. F. Louis. *B.* Strasburg, 1834; *d.* 1891. Went to Cincinnati, 1856; organized the Cecilia Vocal Soc., and the Philharmonic Orch.; settled in New York, 1861; condr. Sacred Harmonic Soc. and the "Arion." Prof. of music Vassar Coll., Poughkeepsie, 1874.
Works: a " Hist. of Music," "Music in America ;" orch. music, chamber music, psalms, numerous songs, &c.

RIT'TER, Georg W. *B.* Mannheim, 1748; *d.* 1808. Bassoonist Berlin Court Orch. from 1788.
Wrote 2 bassoon concertos, and 6 quartets for bassoon and strings.

RIT'TER, Hermann. Performer on the *Viola Alta ;* *b.* Wismar, 1849.

RIT'TER (real name Bennet), Théodore. Pianist; *b.* nr. Paris, 1841; *d.* 1886. Pupil of Liszt.
Wrote numerous pf. pieces.

RIT'TER-GÖT'ZE, Marie. Mezzo-soprano; *b.* Berlin, 1865.

Rit'terlich (*G.*). Knightly, chivalrous.

Rit'ual. The rites and ceremonies prescribed or observed in performing any particular form of church service.

RIVARDE, Serge A. Violinist; *b.* New York, 1865.

RIVÉ-KING, Julie. Pianist; *b.* Cincinnati, 1857. Has written popular pf. pieces.

River'so (*I.*) ⎫ Reversed ; retrograde.
River'scio (*I.*) ⎰

Rivolgimen'to (*I.*). The inversion of parts as in double counterpoint (*q.v.*).
Rivolta'to. Inverted as in double counterpoint.
Rivol'to. Same as *Rivolgimento.*

ROBERT le DIABLE. Opera by Meyerbeer, 1831.

ROBERTS, Arthur. Vocalist and comedian ; *b.* 1852.

ROBERTS, David A. *B.* Carnarvonshire, 1820; *d.* 1872.
Wrote a Welsh " Grammar of Music."

ROBERTS, Fred. Egbert. Bass vocalist ; *b.* Newtown, 1847. *Début* Crystal Palace, 1873.

ROBERTS, John Varley. *B.* Stanningly, nr. Leeds, 1841. Mus.Doc. Oxon, 1876; orgt. Magdalen Coll., Oxford, 1882.
Works: cantatas, church music, part-songs, &c.

ROBERTS, Richd. "The blind minstrel of Carnarvon;" 1796-1855.
Published a collection of Welsh airs.

ROBERTSON, John. *B.* Edinburgh, 1838. Mus.Doc. Cantab., 1884.

ROBINSON, Anastasia. (Countess of Peterborough). Celebrated contralto; *b.* abt. 1698; *d.* Southampton, 1750. Sang in Handel's operas, &c.

ROBINSON, Hamilton. *B.* Brighton, 1861. Mus.Doc. Dunelm, 1897. A.R.A.M. Prof. G.S.M.; Lecturer, King's Coll., London Univ.; Hon. Sec. I.S. Coll.
Works : orchl., pf., vocal, etc.

ROBINSON, John. 1682-1762. Organist Westminster Abbey, 1727. Composed chants, &c.

ROBINSON, Joseph. *B.* Dublin, 1816; *d.* 1898. Est. the "Antient Concerts," Dublin, 1834, and conducted them for nearly 30 years. Prof. of singing Royal Irish Academy of Music, 1856.
It was for Joseph Robinson that Mendelssohn scored for orchestra his *Hear my Prayer*, originally written with org. acct. only.

ROBINSON, Robert. 1735-90. Baptist minister, Cambridge.
Wrote the hymn, "Come, Thou fount of every blessing."

ROBJOHN. (See **Florio**.)

Robus'to (*I*.) Strong, powerful, robust.
Robustamen'te. Firmly, boldly.
Teno're robus'to. A tenor with a powerful voice; opposed to a light tenor, or *teno're leggie'ro*.

ROBYN, Alfred G. Composer; *b.* St. Louis, Missouri, 1860.
Works : 3 operas, 6 operettas, songs, &c.

Rocco'co (*I*.) ⎫ Eccentric; in extravagant
Roco'co (*I*.) ⎭ and debased taste; showy and superficial.

ROCH'LITZ, Johann F. Leipzig, 1769-1842. Founded the *Allgemeine Musikalische Zeitung*, 1798, and edited it till 1818.
Works : "Für Freunde der Tonkunst" (4 vols.; biographies, &c.); male choruses, libretti of operas, &c.

RÖCK'EL (or **ROECK'EL**), **Joseph L.** *B.* London, 1838. Teacher and pianist at Clifton.
Works : cantatas, songs, pf. pieces, &c.

ROECK'EL, Mrs. J. L. (*née* **Jane Jackson**). Pianist and composer; *b.* Clifton; *d.* 1907.

Rock harmonicon. A kind of dulcimer with tuned pieces of rock-crystal struck by a hammer.

ROCK'STRO (originally **RACK'STRAW**), **William S.** *B.* North Cheam, 1823; *d.* 1895. Studied Leipzig Cons.; Orgt. All Saints', Babbicombe, 1867; lived in London from 1891 as lecturer and teacher (R.A.M. and R.C.M.).
Works : "Practical Harmony," "Rules of Counterpoint," Lives of Handel and Mendelssohn, "General Hist. of Music" (1886), several articles in "Grove's Dict.," &c. He also wrote a cantata, songs, &c., and various settings of Gregorian melodies (on which he was a recognized authority).

Ro'co (*I*.). Harsh, hoarse, raucous.

RO'DA, Ferdinand von. *B.* Rudolstadt, 1815; *d.* 1876. Pupil of Hummel; founded the Bach-Verein, Hamburg, 1855. Mus.-dir. Rostock Univ., 1857.
Works : an oratorio, a Passion, and other church music; symphonies, pf. music, a cantata, &c.

RODDIE, William S. *B.* Glasgow, 1845.
Works : cantatas, operettas, school songs, &c.

RODE, J. Pierre J. Celebrated violinist; *b.* Bordeaux, 1774; *d.* 1830. Pupil of Viotti. *Début* Th. Feydeau, Paris, 1790. After tours in Holland, Germany, and London, appointed prof. of vn. Paris Cons., 1794. Solo violinist to Napoleon, 1800; resided in Russia, 1803-8; returned to Paris for 3 years, then toured in Germany. Beethoven wrote his *Romance* (Op. 50) for Rode.
Works : 13 vn. concertos; *Thèmes variés*, romances, études, &c., for vn.; a vn. method, and "24 caprices in the form of studies in the 24 major and minor keys" (a valuable work).

RO'DE, Johann G. Horn player and bandmaster; *b.* nr. Freiburg-on-Unstrut, 1797; *d.* 1857.
Wrote concertos for horn and for trumpet.

RO'DE, Theodor. Singing teacher; son of preceding; *b.* Potsdam, 1821; *d.* 1883.
Works : a "Singing Method," essays on Prussian Military Music, &c.

RO'DENBERG, Julius. *B.* Rodenburg, 1821. Founded the "Deutsche Rundschau;" wrote libretti, lyrics, &c.

RÖ'DER, Carl G. 1812-83. Founded the great Leipzig mus. printing establishment, 1846, "with one engraver's apprentice."

RÖ'DER, Georg V. *B.* Franconia, 1780; *d.* 1848. Capellmeister successively at Würzburg, Augsburg, and Munich.
Works : an oratorio, and much other church music; a symphony, an opera (*Die Schweden*).

RÖ'DER, Johann M. Org. builder, Berlin; *d.* abt. 1740.
Built the fine organ, St. Maria Magdalena, Breslau (58 stops).

RÖ'DER, Martin. *B.* Berlin, 1851; *d.* Boston, Mass., 1895. Chorus-master, Milan, 1873-80; teacher Scharwenka's Cons., Berlin, 1881-7; prof. Royal Academy of Music, Dublin, 1887; director vocal department, New England Cons., Boston, 1892.
Works : 30 operas, 2 mysteries; orch. music, chamber music, pf. pieces; also articles on theoretical subjects; &c.

RO'DIO, Rocco. Early Neapolitan contrapuntist; *b.* Calabria, abt. 1530.
Pub. a Treatise on Counterpoint, 9 masses, &c.

RODOLPHE (or **Rudolph**), **Jean J.** Violinist and horn player; *b.* Strasburg, 1730; *d.* 1812. Prof. of harmony "Ecole royale de chant" (afterwards the Paris Cons.), 1784.
Works : operas, ballets, horn concertos, vn. pieces, a treatise on "Accompaniment and Composition," &c.

ROD'WELL, George H. B. London, 1800-52. Mus.-director Covent Garden, 1836.
Works : several operettas, farces, songs, &c. ; the " Rudiments of Harmony," a " Guitar Method," &c.

ROECK'EL. (See **Röckel.**)

ROESS'LER, Ernestine. Contralto ; *b.* nr. Prague, 1861.

ROGEL, José. *B.* Orihuela, Spain, 1829.
Prod. 65 "Zarzuelas" (operettas), 1854-80.

ROGER, Frau. (See **Marie Soldat.**)

ROGER, Gustave Hippolyte. Famous dramatic tenor ; *b.* nr. Paris, 1815 ; *d.* 1879. Pupil Paris Cons. ; *début* Opéra-Comique, 1838. Prof. of singing at the Cons., 1868.
Created the part of the "Prophète" in Meyerbeer's opera, 1849.

ROGER, Victor. *B.* Montpellier, 1854 ; *d.* 1903. Musical critic of *La France.*
Works : numerous light operas and operettas (*La petite Tache*, 1898 ; *Poule blanche*, 1899 ; *Les Fêtards*, &c.).

ROGERS, Benjamin. *B.* Windsor, 1614 ; *d.* 1698. Orgt. Christ Church Cath., Dublin, 1639 ; gentleman St. George's, Windsor, 1641 ; Mus.Bac.Cantab., by command of Oliver Cromwell, 1658 ; orgt. Magdalen Coll., Oxford, 1664-85. Mus.Doc. Oxon, 1669.
Works : services, anthems, hymns, airs for violins, &c.

ROGERS, Clara K. (*née* **Barnett**). Soprano voct. ; *b.* Cheltenham, 1844 ; daughter of John Barnett. *Début*, Turin, 1863 ; After great success in Italy and London, went to New York, 1871 ; settled in Boston, 1873, as singer and teacher.
Works : songs, pf. pieces, &c.

ROGERS, Della. Soprano vocalist ; *b.* Denver, Colorado, abt. 1879.
Has sung in Italy, Russia, Turkey, &c.

ROGERS, Edmund. Organist ; *b.* Salisbury, 1851.
Works : sacred and secular cantatas ; operettas ; church music, part-songs, pf. pieces, &c.

ROGERS, James Hotchkiss. American orgt. and composer ; *b.* Fair Haven, Conn., 1857.

ROGERS, Roland. *B.* West Bromwich 1847. Orgt. Bangor Cath., 1871-92, and since 1906. Mus.Doc. Oxon, 1875.
Works : cantatas, church music, org. pieces, part-songs, songs, &c.

Roh (*G.*). Rough, coarse, rude.

ROH'DE, Eduard. *B.* Halle-on-Saale, 1828 ; *d.* 1883. Singing teacher.
Works : motets, part-songs, pf. music, &c.

Rohr (pl. *Röh're*). (*G.*). (1) A reed. (2) The tube of an inst.
Rohr'blatt. The reed of a clarinet, oboe, &c.
Rohr'flöte. " Reed flute ; " a sweet-toned half-stopped organ flute stop. A *Flûte à cheminée* (*q.v.*).
Rohr'ig. Reedy.
Rohr'pfeife. A reed pipe.
Rohr'quint. The same a 5th higher in pitch. (See *Quint.*)
Rohr'werk. The reed stops of an organ.

RO'LANDT - SCHAAF, Hedwig. Fine operatic soprano ; *b.* Graz, 1858.

Rola'ta (*I.*). A Roulade (*q.v.*).

Rôle (*F.*). A principal (solo) part in an opera or drama.
" The separated paper which contains the music that a concertant ought to execute is called a " part " in a concert, but a " roll " in an opera."—*Rousseau.*
Title rôle. The *rôle* (or part) which gives its name to an opera.

Roll ⎫ (*G.*, *Wir'bel* ; *F.*, *Roule-*
Rollan'do (*I.*) ⎬ *ment.*) The continuous
Rol'lo (*I.*) ⎭ sound produced by rapid strokes on the drum or tambourine. It is generally indicated in one of the following ways :—

ROL'LA, Alessandro, Violinist ; teacher of Paganini ; *b.* Pavia, 1757 ; *d.* 1841. Maestro La Scala, Milan, 1802 ; prof. of vn. and viola, Milan Cons., from its foundation, 1807.
Works : a ballet ; symphonies ; church music ; vn. concertos, viola concertos, 6 string quartets and other chamber music, &c.

Rol'le (*G.*). (1) A run ; a rapid succession of sequential figures or passages. (2) A *rôle* (*q.v.*).

ROL'LE, Johann H. *B.* Quedlinburg, 1718 ; *d.* 1785. Viola player Berlin Court Orch., 1741-6 ; town mus.-director, Magdeburg, 1752.
Works : 4 passions ; 20 oratorios and cantatas ; sets of church services for the whole year, &c.

Roller. (1) The " beard " of an org. pipe. (2) Part of a roller board.

Roller board. Part of the mechanism of a " tracker " organ. (See **Organ.**)

ROL'LIG, Carl L. Vienna, 1761-1804. Invented the " Orphika " and " Xanorphika "—" pianos with bows instead of hammers."
Wrote a comic opera, pieces for his new insts., &c.

Roma'ika. A modern Greek dance in which the dancers throw hankerchiefs at each other.

Roman' (*G.*) ⎫ (1) A composition of
Romance (*F.*) ⎪ romantic character ;
Roman'za (*I.*) ⎬ a popular tale in
Roman'ze (*G.*) ⎪ verse ; a " musical
Romaunt (*Old E.*) ⎭ story." (2) A love song.
Romance sans paroles (*F.*) ⎱ A story or song without
Roman'za sen'za paro'le (*I.*) ⎰ words.
Romanze'ro (*I.*). A suite of "romantic" pieces for pf.

Romanes'ca (*I.*) ⎱ An old Roman dance
Romanesque (*F.*) ⎰ resembling a Galliard.

ROMANIEL'LO, Luigi. Pianist ; *b.* Naples, 1860. Studied Naples Cons., 1876-80. Teacher at the Cons., musical critic, &c.
Works : operas, pf. pieces, a pf. method, pieces for vn. and pf., &c.

ROMANI'NI, Romano. Violinist ; *b.* Parma, 1864. Prof. of vn. Brescia Cons., 1890 ; director 1897.
Works: operas (*Al Campo*, 1895), orch. pieces, &c.

ROMA'NO, Giulio. (See **Caccini.**)

ROMANS.
The music of the ancient Romans was derived directly from that of the Greeks. They had the same scales and instruments (the flute and trumpet being the favourites). The Romans adopted the first 15 letters of the alphabet for the names of notes, that number being afterwards reduced to 7.

Roman School. The Roman composers from Festa and Palestrina to the 19th century. (See **Italian Music.**)

Roman strings. Gut strings for vns., &c., made in Italy.

Roman'tic
Romantique (*F.*)
Romantisch' (*G.*)
Romanzes'co (*I.*) } Legendary, mythical, supernatural ; fanciful, imaginative, mystic ; novel, strange, weird ; extravagant, fantastic, free from rule ; opposed to classical.
" In general, it means the striving after individuality, novelty, and personality of musical expression as opposed to the repetition of classic forms."—*Hughes.*
" The *Romanticists* of to-day are the *Classicists* of to-morrow."—*Baker.*
Thus the early Romantic composers, Weber, Chopin, and Schumann, are now regarded as *Classics ;* the *Neo-romanticists* (new-romanticists) being Berlioz, Liszt, and Wagner.

Romban'do (*I.*). Humming, droning, murmuring, buzzing.

ROM'BERG, Andreas J. *B.* Vechta, 1767 ; *d.* 1821. Violinist ; played in public at 7 ; toured 1784-90 ; member Electoral Orch., Bonn, 1790-3. Lived in Hamburg, 1801-15 ; court capellmeister, Gotha, 1815.
Works : 8 operas ; odes, cantatas, church music, much instrumental music (including 10 symphonies, 23 vn. concertos, and 33 string quartets), &c. The *Lay of the Bell* is his best known work.

ROM'BERG, Bernard. 'Cellist ; cousin of A. J. ; *b.* nr. Münster, 1767 ; *d.* 1841. 'Cello prof. Paris Cons., 1800-3 ; capellmeister Berlin Court Orch., 1815-19. Made numerous concert tours (many with A. J.).
Works : 9 'cello concertos, and several other 'cello pieces ; also operas, chamber music, &c.

Rome, Grand Prix de. An annual state prize for musical composition, providing for 4 years' residence and study in Italy and Germany, open to pupils of the Paris Cons.
A similar *Prix de Rome* is given by the Brussels Cons.

ROMER, Francis. *B.* London, 1810 ; *d.* 1889. Father of Lord Justice Romer.
Works : operas, cantatas, songs, a " School of Singing," &c.

Rome'ra. A Turkish dance.

Rö'misch (*G.*). Roman.
Rö'mischer Gesang'. Gregorian plain-song.

RONALD, Landon (**L. Russell**). Pianist and condr. ; son of Henry Russell (*q.v.*) ; *b.* London, 1873. Appeared in public at 14.
Works : songs, pf. pieces, &c.

RONCHET'TI-MONTEVI'TI, Stefano. *B.* Asti, 1841 ; *d.* 1882. Prof. of composition Milan Cons., 1850 ; director, 1877.
Works : excellent church music (including a motet in 16 parts), a national hymn " Per la patria il sangue han dato," &c.

RONCO'NI, Domenico. Operatic tenor and distinguished singing teacher ; *b.* Rovigo, 1772 ; *d.* 1839. After a successful career as a vocalist, he founded a singing school at Milan, 1829.
His vocal exercises are noteworthy.

RON'CONI, Giorgio. Son of D. ; baritone singer ; *b.* Milan, 1810 ; *d.* 1890. Singing teacher,Cordova, New York, &c.

Ron'da (*I.*). A round (*q.v.*).

Ronde (*F.*). A " round " note, or semibreve (○).
Ronde pointée, A dotted semibreve (○.).

Rondeau (*F.*)
Ron'do (*I.*) } (1) An old dance form with alternating solos and choruses. (2) A composition in which a principal theme occurs at least 3 times in the same key, with contrasting episodes between the repetitions.
The Rondo is often employed as the last movement of a sonata. The plan of Haydn's *Hungarian* (or "Gipsy") *Rondo*—an excellent type of early Rondo form—is as follows :—
(1) Principal Theme, G major.
(2) Responsive Theme, G major—a kind of continuation of (1).
(3) Episode, G minor.
(4) Principal Theme, G major.
(5) Episode, G minor and B♭ major.
(6) Principal Theme, G major.
(7) Short Coda.
Both Mozart and Beethoven considerably developed the resources of the simple Rondo, and the modern Rondo is often a combination of Rondo and Sonata form. (See *Sonata.*) The 1st episode is in the dominant key, afterwards recurring in the principal key as the 2nd episode, and there is generally much thematic development throughout.
This form of Rondo may be said to be in *Rondo-Sonata Form,* or *Sonata-Rondo Form,* and is generally very difficult for a beginner to analyse.
Rondos were the popular drawing-room music abt. 1800-30. They are now rarely composed.
Rondeau mignon (*F.*). A short easy Rondo.
Rondilet'ta (*I.*).
Rondinel'lo (*I.*).
Rondinet'ta (*I.*). } A short Rondo.
Rondi'no (*I.*).
Rondolet'to (*I.*).

Ronde'ña (*S.*). A Fandango (*q.v.*).

RONG, Wm. Ferdinand. Chamber musician; to Prince Heinrich of Prussia ; *d.* abt. 1821, aged 100 !
Wrote patriotic songs, a work on pf. playing, &c.

RONGER, Florimond. (See **Hervé.**)

RÖNT'GEN, Engelbert. Violinist ; *b.* Deventer, Holland, 1829 ; *d.* 1897. Pupil of David, Leipzig Cons .; member Gewandhaus Orch., 1850-69 ; afterwards concertmeister. Violin teacher, Leipzig Cons.

RÖNT'GEN, Julius. Pianist ; son of E. ; *b.* Leipzig, 1855. *Début*, Stuttgart, 1875. Teacher in the music school, Amsterdam, 1878. Condr. of various musical societies. One of the founders of the Amsterdam Cons., 1885.

Works : a pf. concerto, pf. sonatas, and other pf. pieces ; an operetta, chamber music, " Old Netherland Love Ditties," songs, &c.

Ronzamen'te (*I.*). Humming ; crooning.

ROOKE (or **ROURKE**), **Wm. Michael.** *B.* Dublin, 1794 ; *d.* 1847. Settled in England as chorus-master at Drury Lane, leader at Vauxhall Gardens, &c.

Works : English operas, songs, pf. music, &c.

Root. The fundamental bass or generator of a chord ; " the note on which a chord is built up."—*Stainer.*

The theory of " Roots " was first advanced by Rameau (*q.v.*). It has been very fully developed in the Day-Macfarren system, and a few modern theorists distinguish between the root and generator of some chords. It is, however, beginning to be widely felt that " the attempt to find a ' root ' for every combination of notes used in modern music is manifestly absurd." Many so-called " chords " are the result of appoggiaturas, passing-notes, &c., struck either with or instead of " essential notes " (*q.v.*).

ROOT, George Frederick. American composer of tuneful popular melodies ; *b.* Sheffield, Mass., 1820 ; *d.* 1895. Organist and teacher of singing.

Works : cantatas, numerous school songs, popular songs ("Tramp, tramp, tramp," " Just before the battle, mother "), &c.

ROOT, Fredk. W. Son of preceding ; *b.* Boston, Mass., 1846. Well-known as a singing teacher ; edited *The Song Messenger* for some years.

ROOTHAM, Cyril B. Son of D. W. (below). Orgt. and composer ; *b.* Bristol, 1875.

ROOTHAM, Daniel W. Baritone vocalist and condr. ; *b.* Cambridge, 1837. Condr. Bristol Madrigal Soc., 1865 ; Bristol Festival Choir, 1878.

ROOY. (See **Van Rooy**.)

ROPARTZ, J. Guy. Composer ; *b.* Guingamp, France, 1864. Director Nancy Cons., 1893.

ROQUET. (See **Thoinan**.)

RO'RE, Cipriano de. Distinguished contrapuntist ; *b.* Mechlin, 1516 ; *d.* Parma, 1565. Pupil of Willaert. *Chori praefectus* to the Duke of Parma.

Works : several books of madrigals (4 to 8 parts) ; motets, masses, cantiones sacræ, ricercari, passions, &c.

RO'SA (**ROSE**), **Carl.** '*B.* Hamburg, 1842 ; *d.* Paris, 1889. Started his career as a violinist ; played Crystal Palace,

London, 1866 ; married Miss E. Parepa, New York, 1867 ; started the " Parepa-Rosa English Opera Company." After his wife's death (1874) it became the well-known " Carl-Rosa Company."

RO'SA, Salvatore. *B.* nr. Naples, 1615 ; *d.* Rome, 1673. Celebrated painter ; also famous as a poet and musician.

Wrote some fine madrigals and songs.

Rosa'lia (*I.*). (*G., Rosa'lie, Schu'sterfleck,* or *Vet'ter Mi'chel.*) The frequent repetition of a passage " one degree higher."

The *Rosalia* is so easy of application that the term is often used to describe music " consisting of cheap and trite sequences and harmonies."

RÖSCH, Frederich. *B.* Memmingen, 1862. Works : humorous choral pieces, male-chorus madrigals, songs, &c.

ROSE, Algernon S. Writer on music ; *b.* London, 1859.

Works : " Talks with Bandsmen," essays, &c.

ROSÉ, Arnold J. Fine violinist ; *b.* Jassy, 1863. Leader Vienna Court Orch. since 1881 ; and Bayreuth Festivals since 1888.

ROSE, Henry R. Orgt. and composer ; *b.* Bedford, 1855.

ROSE, Mrs. H. R. (See **Clara Samuell**.)

ROSEINGRAVE, Thos. *B.* Dublin ; *d.* insane, 1750. Orgt. St. George's, Hanover Square, 1725-37.

Works : "Voluntarys and Fugues, made on purpose for the Organ or Harpsichord" (1730), flute pieces, harp music, &c.

RÖ'SEL, Rudolf A. Violinist ; *b.* nr. Gera, 1859. 1st vn. Hamburg City Th., 1879 ; leader, Rotterdam, 1884 ; Weimar Court Orch., 1888 ; prof. Weimar Music School.

Works : stage plays, orch. pieces, a vn. concerto, pieces for vn. and pf., songs, &c.

ROSELLEN, Henri. Pianist ; Paris, 1811-1876. Studied Paris Cons.

Works : a pf. method, a "Manuel des pianistes," and numerous pf. pieces (including 37 études and 76 fantasias on operatic airs),

RO'SENHAIN, Jacob (or **Jacques**). Pianist ; *b.* Mannheim, 1813 ; *d.* 1894. Made numerous tours.

Works : 4 operas ; 3 symphonies and other orch. works ; chamber music, pf. pieces, &c.

RO'SENTHAL, Moritz. Celebrated pianist ; *b.* Lemberg, 1862. Pupil of Liszt, 1876-1886. Has toured with great success in Europe and America.

ROSET'TI, F. A. *B.* Bohemia, 1750 ; *d.* 1792. Capellmeister, Schwerin, 1789.

Works : 2 oratorios, 19 symphonies, 9 string quartets ; concertos for flute, clar., horn, &c.

Ros'in. (*G., Kolophon'; F., Colophane, Resine ; I., Colofo'nio.*) The resin left after distilling off the volatile oil from turpentine ; used for string inst. bows.

RÖS'LER, Gustav. *B.* 1819 ; *d.* Dessau, 1882. His opera *Hermann und Dorothea* is popular.

ROSS, Wm. Baird. Mus.D. Oxon, 1904. Condr. Edinburgh Philharmonic Soc., 1906, &c.

ROSSA'RO, Carlo. Pianist ; *b.* Crescentino, 1828 ; *d.* Turin, 1878.
Works : an opera ; sonatas, character studies, fantasias, &c., for pf.

ROSSE, Jeanie (Mrs. H. A. Quinton). Contralto vocalist ; *b.* London, 1860.

ROS'SI, Carlo. Pianist ; *b.* Lemberg, 1839.

ROS'SI, Abbate Francesco. *B.* Bari, abt. 1645.
Works : 4 operas, an oratorio, a requiem, &c.

ROSSI, Countess. (See **Sontag.**)

ROS'SI, Gaetano. Dramatic poet ; Verona, 1780-1855.
Wrote over 100 opera *libretti* (for Donizetti, Mercadente, Meyerbeer, Rossini, &c.).

ROS'SI, Giovanni G. *B.* nr. Parma, 1828 ; *d.* 1886.
Works : 4 operas, an oratorio, a requiem, masses.

ROS'SI, Lauro. Operatic composer ; *b.* Macerata, 1812 ; *d.* Cremona, 1885. Maestro Teatro Valle, Rome, 1832. After touring in Mexico, New Orleans, Havana, &c., became director Milan Cons., 1850. Director Naples Cons., 1871-8.
Works : 29 operas (*I falsi monetari*, Milan, 1835 ; *La Contezza di Mons*, Turin, 1874 ; &c.) ; an oratorio (*Saul*), masses, cantatas, orch. works, vocalizes, songs, &c. ; and a "Guide to Harmony."

ROS'SI, Marcello. Violinist ; *b.* Vienna, 1862.

Rossignol (*F.*). The nightingale.
Rossignoler. To imitate the nightingale's song.

ROSSIGNOL, F. L. (See **Joncières.**)

ROSSI'NI, Gioachino Antonio. Celebrated opera composer ; called the "Swan of Pesaro." *B.* Pesaro, Feb. 29, 1792 ; *d.* nr. Paris, Nov. 13, 1868. A child of poor parents, his early instruction was very meagre. Entered Bologna Cons., 1807, and won a prize for a cantata the following year ; discontinued the study of counterpoint as soon as he knew enough for dramatic writing. First great success, *Tancredi*, Venice, 1813. *Il Barbiere*, "one of the finest specimens of Italian opera buffa," was hissed the first night (Rome, 1816), as Paisiello's setting was a favourite ; the second night's performance was, however, a "veritable triumph." From 1815 to 1823 he composed 20 operas, being "generally engaged in travelling from town to town in Italy" to bring out "his increasingly popular works." Came to London, 1823, and made £7,000 in 5 months. Afterwards settled in Paris as manager of the Théatre Italien, "Premier compositeur du Roi,"

and "Inspecteur-général du chant en France." His masterpiece, *William Tell*, was produced at the Opéra, 1829. In 1837 he retired from all active work.
Chief works : operas, *Tancredi* (Venice, 1813), *L'Italiana in Algeri* (1813), *Il Turco in Italia* (Milan, 1814), *Il Barbiere di Siviglia* (Rome, 1816), *Otello* (Naples, 1816), *La Cenerentola* (Rome, 1816), *La gazza ladra* (Milan, 1817), *Mosè in Egitto* (Naples, 1818), *La donna del lago* (Naples, 1819), *Semiramide* (Venice, 1823) *William Tell* (*Guillaume Tell*) ; 15 cantatas (*I Pastori*, &c.) ; the popular *Stabat Mater* ; canzonets, songs, solfeggi, hymns, &c.

RÖSS'LER' (See **Rosetti, F. A.**)

Ro'ta (*L.*) "A wheel." (1) A round
Rot'ta (*I.*)   (*q.v.*) or canon. (2) Any
Rote (*E.*)   composition with frequent
Rot'te (*G.*)   repeats, refrains, &c.
(3) Old Eng. name for hurdy gurdy.

ROTH (pron. *Rote*), **Bertrand.** Pianist ; *b.* St. Gallen, 1855. Pupil of Liszt. Teacher at Frankfort, Dresden, &c.

ROTH, Philipp. 'Cellist ; *b.* Silesia, 1853 ; *d.* 1898. Founded the Freie Mus. Vereinigung, Berlin, 1890.

ROTH-RONAY, Kalman. Violinist ; *b.* Veszprim, Hungary, 1869. Leader Covent Garden, 1893-4.

ROTHWELL, Alexander. Flute player.
Pub. "The Compleat Instructor for the Flute, . . with flourishes in every Key " (1698).

RO'TOLI, Augusto. Singing teacher ; *b.* Rome, 1847 ; *d.* 1904. Choir boy at St. Peter's. Vocal instructor New England Cons., Boston, 1885.
Works : a mass, numerous songs, &c.

Roton'do (*I.*). Round ; full.

ROT'TENBERG, Dr. Ludwig. Pianist and condr. ; *b.* Czernowicz, 1864.

ROT'TER, Ludwig. Vienna, 1810-95. Court orgt., Vienna, 1867.
Works : masses, requiems, offertories, &c. organ pieces, pf. pieces, a "Thorough Bass Method," &c.

Rot'to (*I.*). Broken, interrupted.

Ro'tulæ (*L.*). "Little rounds." Christmas carols.

Rotun'do (*I.*). Round.
B rotun'do. The "round" B ; B♭.
B quad'ro. B♮ ; "square" B.

ROUGET de l'Isle, Claude J. *B.* Lons-le-Saulnier, 1760 ; *d.* 1836. Composed the "Marseillaise," the national French song, 1792. He was at the time a military engineer at Strasburg.

Roulade (*F.*). A vocal flourish ; "a trilling or quavering ;" especially a series of rapid runs, divisions, &c.

Roulement (*F.*). A roll on the drum, &c.

Round. (1) A special kind of "perpetual canon at the unison " for two or more voices.

The voices enter one after the other singing the same music, forming in combination complete harmony. Perhaps the most widely known of all rounds is " Three blind mice."
A " Catch " is a round in which the words are so contrived that comic or ludicrous effects are produced by the voices "catching" at one another. (See also *Sumer is i-cumen in.*)

(2) A " round " dance (or circle dance).

Roundel ⎫ (1) A rustic song, or ballad,
Roundelay ⎬ with numerous repeats of
Roundley ⎭ the "burden" or refrain.
(2) A circular dance.

ROUSSEAU, Jean. Violinist ; pub. "Traité de la violé " (Paris, 1687), &c.

ROUSSEAU, Jean Jacques. Celebrated philosopher and self-taught musician ; *b.* Geneva, June, 1712 ; *d.* nr. Paris, July, 1778. His first great success in music was the opera *Le Devin du village*, 1752. He was a scathing critic of French as opposed to Italian music, and was " burnt in effigy " by the members of the Grand Opéra, 1753.
In addition to the opera mentioned he wrote *Pygmalion* (1773) in which he "created the melodrama," a " Dictionnaire de Musique " (1768), about 100 romances and duets (which he entitled " Les consolations des misères de ma vie "), &c.

ROUSSEAU, Samuel A. *B.* Aisne, 1853 ; *d.* 1904. Studied Paris Cons. ; chef d'orchestre Th. Lyrique, 1892.
Works : operas, *Mérowig, La cloche du Rhin*, &c. ; church music, songs, &c.

ROUSSEAU'S DREAM.
A favourite air adapted from J. J. Rousseau's *Le Devin du village*. It is not known whether he "dreamt" it or not.

&c.

ROUSSELIERE. Contemporary Paris Opéra Singer.
"Discovered" by M. Gailhard while singing at his anvil in an Algiers foundry, where he was engaged at 2s. 6d. per day.

ROUSSIER, Abbé Pierre J. *B.* Marseilles, 1716 ; *d.* 1790.
Wrote several treatises on "Chord Progressions," " Practical Harmony," " Antient Music," " Chinese Music," " Fundamental Bass," &c.

Rovesciamen'to (*I.*). (1) Retrograde motion. (See **Retrograde.**) (2) Inversion.

Rove'scio (*I.*). (1) Retrograde. (2) Inverted.
Al rove'scio. (1) Imitation by contrary motion. (2) Retrograde imitation. (See *Canon Cancrizans.*)

ROVET'TA, Giovanni. Pupil of Monteverde; Maestro St. Mark's, Venice, 1644 ; *d.* 1668.
Works : 2 operas ; psalms, madrigals, motets, &c.

ROWBOTHAM, John Fredk. Writer on music ; *b.* Edinburgh, 1854.
Works : " History of Music " (3 vols.), " The Troubadours, and the Courts of Love," articles in Chambers' Encyclopædia, &c.

ROWLAND, Alex. Campbell. Celebrated double-bass player ; *b.* Trinidad, 1826 ; *d.* Southampton, 1896.
Wrote a Double-Bass Method, &c.

ROWTON, Rev. Samuel Jas. *B.* London, 1844. Mus.D. Dublin, 1890 ; Orgt. Bradfield Coll., 1901-7.
Composer of chants, pf. pieces, &c.

Royal Academy of Music. Founded 1822 ; opened 1823. The first principal was Dr. Crotch, 1823-32.

Royal Society of Arts. (See **Diplomas.**)

Royal College of Music. Founded 1882 ; opened 1883. First director, Sir Geo. Grove, 1883-1894.

Royal College of Organists. (See **Diplomas.**)

ROZE, Marie (*née* **Ponsin**). Soprano ; *b.* Paris, 1846.

ROZKOŠ'NÝ, Josef R. Pianist ; *b.* Prague, 1833.
Works : several Bohemian operas (*St. Nicholas, Zavish of Falkenstein, Cinderella, Satanella*, &c.); overtures, masses, songs, pf. music, &c.

Rua'na. A Hindoo violin.

Ruban'do (*I.*). Robbing, stealing.

Ruba'to (*I.*). Robbed, stolen.
Tem'po ruba'to. Taking a portion of the time from one note of a melody and giving it to another, for the sake of expression. It is much employed in the playing of Chopin's music.
" It should not depart so far from strict *tempo* as to destroy the sense of rhythm."—*Hughes.*

Rubèbe (*F.*). A Rebec (*q.v.*).

RÜ'BEZAHL. Opera by Weber, 1804-6.

RUBINEL'LI, Giovanni B. Celebrated male contralto; *b.* Brescia, 1753 ; *d.* 1829. Sang in London, in Handel's operas, &c., with great success, 1786.

RUBI'NI, Giovanni B. Distinguished tenor ; *b.* nr. Bergamo, 1795 ; *d.* 1854. *Début*, Pavia, 1814. Teacher of Mario. Sang " with triumphant success " in Italy, Vienna, Paris, London, Berlin, &c.

RU'BINSTEIN, Anton Gregorovitch. Celebrated pianist and composer ; *b.* Wechwotynecz, Bessarabia, 1829 ; *d.* 1894. Began the study of the piano at 7 ; played at Paris before Chopin and Liszt, 1840 ; with his brother **Nicholas** (see below) studied Berlin, 1844 ; settled St. Petersburg, 1848 ; toured 1854-58 ; court pianist, St. Petersburg, 1858 ; director Russian Musical Soc., 1859 ; founded Imperial Cons., St. Petersburg, 1862. Toured in Europe, America, &c., 1867-87, " winning fame as a pianist hardly second to Liszt."
Works : 7 Russian operas (*The Demon*, 1875), 6 German operas (*The Maccabees*, 1875 ; *Nero*, 1879), 5 "sacred operas" or oratorios (*The Tower of Babel*, 1870 ; *Paradise Lost*, 1875 ; *Moses*, 1887) ; cantatas, scenas ; 6 symphonies ; concert overtures ; an orch. suite ; 5 pf. concertos, 2 'cello concertos, a vn. concerto ; an octet, a sextet, quintets, quartets, and other chamber music ; numerous pf. pieces, over 100 songs, &c.

RU'BINSTEIN, Nikolai (or **Nicholas**). Pianist ; brother of A. ; *b.* Moscow, 1835 ; *d.* 1881. Founded the Moscow Mus. Soc., 1859 ; this society founded the Moscow Cons. (1864), Rubinstein being director till his death.
Works : pf. pieces (mazurkas, valses, polonaises.

RU'BINSTEIN, Joseph. Russian pianist ; 1847-84. Friend of Wagner ; pianist at the preparatory rehearsals of the *Ring*, Bayreuth, 1874.
Made excellent pf. transcriptions of Wagner's *Ring*.

Rubinstein prizes.
Two prizes of 5,000 francs each, one for composition, the other for pf. playing, awarded quinquennially to young men of any nationality between 20 and 26 years of age.

RÜB'NER, Cornelius. Pianist and composer ; *b.* Copenhagen, 1853.

Rück (*G.*). Back.
Rück'bewegung. Retrograde movement.
Rück'erin'nerung. Reminiscence.
Rück'fall. A " Backfall " (*q.v.*).
Rück'gang. Going back to the repetition of a preceding theme.
Rück'positiv. A choir organ behind the player.
Rück'schlag. The Ribattuta (*q.v.*).
Rück'ung. Syncopation (*q.v.*).
Rück'ung, Enharmo'nische. Enharmonic change.
Rück'weiser. The sign $\mathcal{S}$.

RÜCK'AUF, Anton. Distinguished song composer ; *b.* Prague, 1855 ; *d.* 1903.
Works : an opera, about 80 fine songs, 5 duets, a pf. quintet, &c.

RÜCK'ERS. Antwerp family of clavecin-makers from abt. 1579-1667. Their harpsichords were the finest ever made.

Rudement (*F.*). Roughly.
Rudement accentué. Roughly accentuated.

RU'DERSDORFF, Hermine. Celebrated soprano ; *b.* Ivanowsky, 1822 ; *d.* 1882. After successes in Germany and London settled in Boston (Mass.), 1872, as a singing teacher.

RU'DORFF, Friedrich K. Pianist ; *b.* Berlin, 1840. Pf. teacher Cologne Cons., 1865 ; founded the Bach-Verein, 1867 ; head pf. teacher Berlin Hochschule, 1869. *D.* 190-(?).
Works : symphonies, overtures, and other orch. pieces ; part-songs, songs, &c.

RUE, Pierre de la (also known as **Pierchon, Pierson, Pierzon, Pierozon,** and **Petrus Platensis.**) Celebrated contrapuntist ; *b.* Picardy, abt. 1450(?) ; *d.* 1518.
36 of his masses still exist, besides motets, &c.

RUEG'GER, Elsa. 'Cellist ; *b.* Lucerne, 1881.

Ruf (*G.*). A call, cry, summons ; to voice ; to sound a trumpet call.
Ru'fer. A speaking-trumpet.

RÜ'FER, Philippe B. Pianist ; *b.* Liége, 1844. Teacher at Berlin from 1871.
Works : 2 operas, orch. music, chamber music, pf. pieces, songs, &c.

RUF'FO, Vincenzo. Maestro Verona Cath.
Pub. motets, madrigals, canzoni, &c. (1551-78).

RUGGE'RI (or **RUGGIE'RI**), **Giovanni M.** Venetian composer.
Works : 10 operas (1696-1712), sonatas for 2 vns. and basso continuo, 12 cantate, &c.

RUG'GI, Francesco. Naples, 1767-1845. Teacher of Bellini and Carafa.
Wrote 3 operas, an oratorio, church music, &c.

Ruh, Ruh'e (*G.*). Rest, repose ; calm.
Ruh'epunkt } " A point of repose ; " a pause ; a
Ruh'ezeichen } rest ; a cadence.
Ruh'ig. Quiet, calm, gentle ; reposeful.
Ruh'ig bewegt'. Quietly animated.
Ruh'ig geh'end. "Gently going ;" *Andan'te modera'to.*
Ruh'ig geh'end, nicht schlep'pend. Going gently, without dragging.
Ruh'ig und Sanft. Tranquil and soft.

RUHL'MANN, A. Julius. Dresden, 1817-77. Trombone, Royal Orch., 1841 ; prof. of pf. and mus. hist. at the Cons., 1856.
Wrote an illustrated " History of Bowed Instruments," valuable historical essays, &c.

Rüh'rung (*G.*). Emotion, feeling.

Rühr'trommel (*G.*). The tenor drum.

Rule. Old name for " Staff line."
" Five Rules are commonly used in the pricking or setting down of any Parte. . . . If any note happen to exceede this compas his Place is to bee notifyed by a short Rule drawn for the nonce, either aboov or below, as you shall have caus."—*Butler*, 1636.
" There is pleasure in writing notes on a neat ruling."—*Rousseau.*

Rule of the octave. The old rule for harmonizing a scale in figured bass playing.
Examples from Albrechtsberger.

Major Scale.

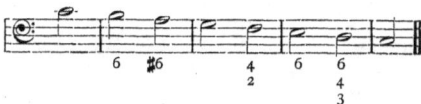

Minor Scale.

Rules of music.
Musical rules are based upon the formulas, progressions, &c., employed by great composers. These naturally vary from time to time, and the " forbidden progressions " of one age become the " accepted progressions " of the next. The beginner must, of course, follow the rules laid down in ordinary text-books ; but new resources necessitate new rules, and in spite of the objections of theorists who talk about " cacophony, horrid discords, earsplitting din," &c., it is no more binding on a Wagner or Strauss to observe the rules of a Tallis or Palestrina than it is incumbent on a modern Englishman to parade in the scanty costume of an ancient Briton.

Rule, Britannia. Music by Dr. Arne ; 1st performance, Aug. 1, 1740.

Rullan'do (*I.*) ⎫ Rolling.
Rullan'te (*I.*) ⎭
Tambu'ro rullan'te. A side drum.

RUM'FORD, R. Kennerley. Baritone singer; *b.* London, 1871 ; studied Frankfort, Berlin, and Paris. Married **Clara Butt,** 1900.

RUM'MEL, Frau. (See **Lillian Sanderson.**)

RUM'MEL, Franz. Noted pianist ; *b.* London, 1853 ; *d.* 1901. Won 1st prize Brussels Cons., 1872. Toured with great success in Holland and America.

Run. A rapid passage (especially a rapid scale passage).
In vocal music all the notes of a " run " are generally sung to the same syllable.

RUNCIMAN, John F. Contemporary music critic ; *b.* abt. 1866.

Rund (*G.*). (1) Round. (2) Smooth, flowing.
Rund'gedicht. ⎫ (1) A Rondo. (2) A solo song with a
Rund'gesang ⎬ " refrain " (or chorus).
Rund'tanz. ⎭ Round dance, circle dance.

Runes. The letters or characters of the ancient Teutonic and Scandinavian alphabets.
They are said to be the invention of the mystic Wodin or Odin.
Rune ⎫ Poetry expressed in runes; ancient
Runic rhyme ⎬ Gothic verse, &c.
Ru'ner. A Gothic bard.

RUNG, Henrik. Copenhagen, 1807-71. Founded the Cecilia Soc. for Old Church Music, 1852.
Works : 7 operas, several popular songs, &c.

RUNGENHA'GEN, Carl F. Berlin, 1778-1851. Vice-conductor Berlin Sing-akademie, 1815 ; chief condr., 1833.
Works : 4 operas, 3 oratorios, several cantatas, about 1,000 songs, &c.

Running. A dull humming of organ pipes caused by improper leakage of wind into the grooves.

Ruo'lo (*I.*). (1) A roll. (2) A kind of Italian waltz.

Russe (*F.*). Russian.
A la russe. In Russian style.

RUSSELL, Ella (Madame de Rhigini). Soprano vocalist ; *b.* Cleveland (U.S.), 1862. Educated Clevedon Cons. and Milan. First European tour, 1883; *début* Covent Garden, 1886.

RUSSELL, Henry. *B.* Sheerness, 1812(13?) ; *d.* 1900. Spent most of his active life touring as a singer in England, Canada, United States, &c.
Wrote about 800 songs, many of them " as familiar as household words," including " Cheer boys, cheer ! " " A life on the ocean wave," "Woodman, spare that tree," &c.

RUSSELL, Landon. (See **Landon Ronald.**)

RUSSELL, Louis A. American organist and condr. ; *b.* Newark, N.J., 1854.
Works : orch. pieces, anthems, songs, pf. pieces ; "Development of artistic pianoforte touch," &c.

RUSSELL, William. London, 1777-1813. Pianist, Sadler's Wells, 1800 ; Covent Garden, 1801 ; orgt. Foundling Hospital, 1801. Mus.Bac. Oxon, 1808.
Works : several operas, 3 oratorios, church music, org. pieces, glees, songs, &c.

Russian bassoon. A deep-toned inst. used in Russian military bands.

Russian horn band. A band of horns each of which can only produce a single note.

Russian music.
" Not so many years ago the music of Russia and its neighbourhood was reckoned to be on about a par with Japanese or Chinese. But now what a wonderful new kind of music has sprung up in this Slavonic school."—*H. W. Norton.*
The Russian school, though lacking a past, has already had a distinguished inauguration, and appears to have a great future before it. " Russian musicians are usually learned and scientific men, and men of rank and social prestige."—*Lavignac.*
Glinka was the " father of modern Russian music ; " the following is a list of its most noted composers :—
Glinka (1804-57), Dargomizsky (1813-67), Serov (1820-71), A. Rubinstein (1830-94), N. Rubinstein (1835-81), Borodine (1834-87), César Cui (1835-), Balakireff (1836-), Moussorgsky (1839-81), Tschaikowsky (1840-93), Rimsky-Korsakow (1844-), Arensky (1862-1906), Glazounow (1865-), Rachmaninoff (1873-). (See also *Lvoff, Jean* and *Ed. de Reszké, Essipoff, Sapelnikoff,* the brothers *Wieniawski, Petchnikoff,* and *Paderewski.*) (See *Appendix.*)

Russ'pfiefe (*G.*) ⎫ (See **Rauschquinte.**)
Rusz'pipe ⎭

RUST, Friedrich Wm. Violinist ; *b.* nr. Dessau, 1739 ; *d.* 1796. Court music director, Dessau, 1775.
Works : stage pieces, instrumental music, &c.

RUST, Wilhelm. *B.* Dessau, 1822 ; *d.* 1892. Condr. Bach-Verein, Berlin, 1862-74 ; teacher Stern Cons., 1870 ; orgt. Thomaskirche, Leipzig, 1878 ; cantor Thomasschule, 1880.
Works : church music, part-songs, songs, &c. ; and several carefully edited vols. of Bach's works.

Rustica'no (*I.*) ⎫ In a rustic pastoral style.
Ru'stico (*I.*) ⎭

RU'TA, Michele. Teacher and writer ; *b.* Caserta, 1827 ; *d.* 1896. Pupil Naples Cons. ; founder and editor of *La Musica* (Naples).
Works : several operas ; masses and other church music, patriotic songs, &c. ; treatises on " Harmony." " Composition," " Singing," &c.

RU'THARDT (pron. *Roo'tart*), **Adolf.** *B.* Stuttgart, 1849. Teacher of pf. Leipzig Cons., 1886.
Works : much pf. music (preludes, fugues, waltzes, sonatas, &c.).

Rut'scher (*G.*). (1) A Slider (*q.v.*). (2) A Galopade (*q.v.*).

Ru'vido (*I.*). Rough, coarse.
Ruvidamen'te. Roughly, coarsely.

RUZI'CKA, Wenzel. *B.* Moravia, 1758 ; *d.* Vienna, 1823.
Notable for having been for a short time the teacher of Schubert, of whom he remarked, " He knows everything already, God Almighty has taught him."

RYAN, Thos. *B.* Ireland, 1827 ; *d.* 1903. Went to America, 1844 ; clarinet and viola player " Mendelssohn Quintette Club, Boston, 1849. " This little band of excellent musicians has visited every town of any size in the United States." (*Baker*). Ryan was a member for over 50 years.

Wrote " Recollections of an Old Musician" (1899).

RYBA, Jakob J. *B.* Bohemia, 1765 ; *d.* 1815.

Works : much church music, 6 comic operas, 35 symphonies, 38 concertos, &c.

Rymour (*Old E.*) ⎫ A rural poet ; a bard, a
Rhymer   ⎭ minstrel.

Rythme (*F.*). Rhythm.

Rythme binaire. (1) Two-bar rhythm.   (2) Duple rhythm (or time)..

Rythme ternaire. (1) Three-bar rhythm. · (2) Triple rhythm (or time)

Rythmé (*F.*). Rhythmical.

Bien rythmé. (1) Well balanced in rhythmical con-·struction. (2) With due rhythmical accent. (See *Accent.*)

S

S. (1) An abbn. of *Segno*, as in *D.S.* (See **Segno.**) (2) An abbn. of *Senza* (*q.v.*). (3) An abbn. of *Sinistra* (*q.v.*), of *Solo*, or of *Sordino* (*q.v.*). (4) An abbn. of *Subito*, as in *V.S.*, *Volti Subito* ("turn over quickly").
N.B.—"S" is used as an "intensitive prefix" to many Italian words without materially altering their meaning, as *sforzato*, *slargando*, &c.

SAAR, Louis V. F. *B.* Rotterdam, 1868. Won the Mendelssohn Prize, 1891; settled in New York (1892) as teacher and critic.
Works: songs, pf. pieces, part-songs, &c.

SABBATI'NI, Galeazzo. Italian contrapuntist ; *b.* Pesaro.
Pub. madrigals, litanies, &c. (1627-39).

SABBATI'NI, Luigi A. *B.* nr. Rome, 1739 ; *d.* 1809. Pupil of Padre Martini ; maestro at Padua, 1780.
Pub. treatises on Musical Theory, Fugue, &c.

Sab'beka } A species of Hebrew harp.
Sab'eca }

Sabot (*F.*). An inferior violin.

Sacbut. (See **Sackbut.**)

Saccade (*F.*). A jerk, a sudden accent.
In bowed instruments a strong pressure of the bow, by means of which a note is forcibly accented, or 2 or more strings sounded together.
Saccadé. Forcibly accented.

SAC'CHI, Don Giovenale. Barnabite monk ; *B.* nr. Como, 1726 ; *d.* 1789.
Wrote treatises on "Musical Time," "Ancient Greek Music," "Consecutive 5ths in Cpt.," a "Life of B. Marcello," &c.

SACCHI'NI, Antonio M. G. Noted Neapolitan opera-composer; *b.* nr. Naples, 1734 ; *d.* Paris, 1786. Son of a poor fisherman, his singing attracted the attention of Durante, who secured his admission into the Cons. di S. Onofrio, Naples. First great success, *Semiramide*, Rome, 1762. *Alessandro nell'Indie* (1768) was so successful that he was appointed director Cons. dell'Ospedaletto, Venice. From 1772-82 he lived in London ; afterwards settled in Paris.
Works: over 50 operas (*Œdipe à Colone* (1786), his masterpiece) ; 6 oratorios, church music, chamber-music, 12 harpsichord sonatas, &c.

SACHS, Hans. "Chief of the Meistersingers ; " Nuremberg, 1494-1576. He is the central figure in Wagner's *Die Meistersinger von Nürnberg*.
Works: Over 4,000 poems, 1,700 tales, 200 dramatic poems, and numerous melodies.

SACHS, Melchior E. *B.* Lower Franconia, 1843. Condr. Munich Liederkranz, 1868-72 ; founder and condr. of the Tonkünstlerverein.
Works: an opera (*Palestrina*, 1886), orch. pieces, pf. pieces, songs, &c.

SACH'SE-HOF'MEISTER, Anna. Operatic soprano ; *b.* nr. Vienna, 1852. *Début* in *Les Huguenots*, Würzburg, 1870. Married the tenor **Sachse**, 1878. Prima donna Berlin Court Opera, 1883.

Sackbut. (1) A *Sabbeka* (*q.v.*). (2) The early form of the trombone.

Sack'geige (*G.*). A pocket fiddle (or *kit*).

Sack'pfeife (*G.*). Bagpipe (*q.v.*).

Sacque-boute (*F.*). A sackbut.

Sacred Harmonic Society. Founded London, 1832 ; dissolved 1882.

Sacred music. (*G.*, *Kir'chenmusik* ; *F.*, *Musique d'église* ; *I.*, *Mu'sica religio'sa.*) Church, or devotional music ; opposed to *secular* music.

Sa'cring bell } A small bell rung to
Saints' bell } indicate the various
Sanctus bell } stages of the Mass (in R. C. churches).

Sa'crist.
"A person retained in a cathedral . . . to copy out the music for the use of the choir, and take care of the books."—*Busby*.

Sadt. An old variety of **Gemshorn** (*q.v.*).

Saeng'erfest (*G.*). A musical and social festival.

SAF'FIEDDIN, Abdolmumin. An Arabian by birth ; founded the Persian School of Music (13th-14th centuries).
His "Sherefīie" is the greatest work on Persian musical theory.

SAFO'NOFF, Wasili de. Noted conductor ; *b.* Istchory, Caucasus, 1852. Director Moscow Cons. 1889.

Sa'ga. An ancient Scandinavian tale, legend, or poem.
Saga-man. A composer or reciter of *sagas*.

Sagbut, Sagbutt. Sackbut (*q.v.*).

Sag'gio (*I.*). A specimen, pattern, experiment ; a treatise.
Concer'to di sag'gio. A pupils' concert or trial performance.

SÁGH, Joseph. *B.* Pesth, 1852.
Pub. "An Hungarian Dict. of Musicians," 1877.

SAGITTA'RIUS. (See **Schütz.**)

SAH'LA, Rd. Violinist and composer ; *b.* Graz, 1855.

SAINT-AMANS, Louis J. *B.* Marseilles, 1749 ; *d.* 1820. Teacher Paris Cons., 1784-1802.
Works: 24 operas and ballets ; oratorios, chamber music, &c.

SAINT-AUBIN, Jeanne C. S. Noted actress and singer ; *b.* Paris, 1764 ; *d.* 1850.

SAINT-GEORGE, George. Violinist and viola d'amore player ; *b.* (of English parents), Leipzig, 1841. Settled in London.

SAINT-GEORGE, Henry. Violinist and Viola da Gamba player ; son of preceding ; *b.* London, 1866.

SAINT-GEORGES, Chevalier de. Violinist ; *b.* Guadeloupe, 1745 ; *d.* 1799.
Wrote sonatas, trios, concertos, &c., for violin.

SAINT-HUBERTY. (Antoinette C. Clavel.) *B.* Toul, abt. 1756 ; *d.* 1812. Celebrated soprano, Paris Grand Opéra, 1777-89.

SAINT-JOHN, Florence. (Maggie Grieg). Vocalist and actress ; *b.* Kirkcaldy. First London appearance, 1879.

SAINT-LUBIN, Leon de. Violinist ; *b.* Turin, 1805 ; *d.* 1850. Leader Königstädter Th., Berlin, 1830-47.
Works : 2 operas ; ballets and pantomines, 5 vn. concertos, 19 string quartets, &c.

ST. MAUR, Emlyn. Pen-name of **J. Williams** (*q.v.*).

SAINTON, Prosper P. C. Noted violinist ; *b.* Toulouse, 1813 ; *d.* London, 1890. 1st prize for vn. playing, Paris Cons., 1834 ; Prof. Toulouse Cons., 1840-4. Settled in England, 1844 ; Prof. R.A.M., 1845 ; leader, Philharmonic Orch., 1846-54 ; Covent Garden, 1847-1871 ; Her Majesty's, 1871-80. Married **C. H. Dolby** (below), 1860. Sir A. C. Mackenzie was one of his vn. pupils.
Works : 2 concertos, and other vn. pieces.

SAINTON-DOLBY, Charlotte Helen. Distinguished contralto singer ; London, 1821-85. Studied R.A.M., winning the King's Scholarship, 1837. *Début*, 1841 ; married **Sainton** (above), 1860.
Works : cantatas, songs, a "Singing Tutor," &c.

SAINT-SAËNS, Charles Camille. Eminent composer ; *b.* Paris, 1835. Began to learn the pf. at 2½ ; could play from a full operatic score at 5 ; entered Paris Cons. at 7 ; took 1st organ prize, 1851. Orgt. St. Méry, 1853 ; Madeleine, 1858. Produced his 1st symphony at 16. Commander, Legion of Honour, 1894.
Works : abt 8 operas (*Samson et Dalila, Etienne Marcel, Henri VIII*, &c.) ; ballets, incidental music to dramas, a *Christmas Oratorio*, a *Poème biblique* (*Le Déluge*), masses, odes, hymns, &c. ; 4 symphonic poems, 5 pf. concertos, 3 vn. concertos, much chamber music, pf. music, &c.

SAINTWIX, Thomas. One of the earliest Doctors of Music ; *d.* 1467. Master of King's Hall, Cambridge, 1463.

Sai'te (*G.*). A string ; *pl.*, **Sai'ten.**
Bespon'nene *Sai'ten.* Wire-covered strings.
Sai'tenfessel }
Sai'tenhalter } Tail-piece (of a vn., &c.).
Sai'ten *Instrument.* A stringed instrument.
Sai'tenklang }
Sai'tenton } The sound of a string.
Sai'tenspiel. Stringed inst. ; string music.
Sai'tenspieler. String inst. player.
Sai'tig. Stringed.
Sai'tenorgel. A "string organ" invented by Gümbel, Prussia, 1890.

SA'LA, Nicola. *B.* nr. Benevento, 1701 ; *d.* Naples, 1800.
Wrote several operas, and a celebrated "Rules of Practical Counterpoint" (3 vols.).

SAL'AMAN, Chas. K. Pianist and composer; London, 1814-1901.
Works : orch. and vocal music, pf. pieces, and numerous songs.

Sal'amanie. An Oriental flute.

Salamine. An echo salicional or echo dulciana organ stop.

Sal'cional } An organ flue-stop (of 8 ft.,
Sal'icet } 4 ft., or 2 ft. pitch) with a
Sali'cional { delicate and somewhat
Sol'cionell } "stringy" tone.

SALDO'NI, Don Baltasar. Eminent singing teacher ; *b.* Barcelona, 1807 ; *d.* 1890. Teacher of solfeggio Madrid Cons., 1830 ; 1st Prof. of Singing, 1840.
Works : church music, orch. pieces, operas, songs, pf. music, &c., and an excellent singing method ("Nuevo método de Solfeo y de canto").

SALE, François. Belgian contrapuntist. Tenor chapel-singer at Prague, 1594.
Wrote masses, motets, introits, &c.

SALE, John. Bass singer; London, 1758-1827. Sang at the Chapel Royal, St. Paul's, and Westminster Abbey. Secretary Catch Club, 1812.

SALE, John Bernard. Bass vocalist; brother of J. ; *b.* Windsor, 1779 ; *d.* 1856. Orgt. St. Margaret's, Westminster, 1809 ; Chapel Royal, 1838. Music teacher to Queen Victoria.

SALÉZA, Albert. Operatic tenor ; *b.* Bruges, Béarn, 1867(5?).
Studied Paris Cons., *Début*, Opéra Comique, 1883 ; engaged Grand Opéra, 1892.

Sal'icet. (See **Salcional.**)

SALIE'RI, Antonio. Distinguished opera composer ; *b.* Legnago, Verona, 1750 ; *d.* Vienna, 1825. Orphaned at 15 ; went to Venice, and was received into the San Marco Singing School ; was taken by Gassmann to Vienna, where he produced his 1st opera, *Le donne letterate*, 1770. Brought out 9 operas, 1770-4 ; produced *Tarare*, Paris, 1787 ; Court capellmeister, Vienna, 1788-1824. He was a fine teacher ; Schubert was one of his pupils.
Works : 40 operas ; oratorios, cantatas, masses, and other church music; a symphony, various concertos, &c.

SALIMBE'NI, Felice. Celebrated male soprano ; pupil of Porpora ; *b.* Milan, abt 1712 ; *d.* 1751. Sang in Italy, Berlin, Vienna, &c.

Salle de concert (*F.*). A concert room.

Salle de musique (*F.*). A music room.

Salm (*G.*), **Sal'mo** (*I.*). A psalm.

Salmi (*F.*). A Quodlibet (*q.v.*).

SALMON, Eliza (*née* **Munday**). Soprano singer ; *b.* Oxford, abt. 1787 ; *d.* 1858. *Début* Covent Garden, 1803.

SALMON, Thos. 1648-1708.
Wrote an essay advocating octaves instead of hexachords ; also a 6-lined stave, the lowest line to be always G ; instead of clefs the letters B, M, T (Bass, Mean, Treble). He was attacked by Lock (*q.v.*).

SALMOND, Norman. Bass vocalist ; *b.* Bradford, 1858. London *début*, 1890.

SALÒ, Gasparo de. (See **Gasparo.**)

SA'LOMAN, Siegfried. Violinist ; *b.* Tondern, Schleswig, 1816 ; *d.* 1899.
Works : operas (*The Diamond Cross*, 1847), vn. pieces, songs, &c.

SALOMÉ. Opera, Richard Strauss, 1905.
"This poem of hysterics is supported by a most extraordinary orchestra. It quivers, sings, yelps, howls, breaks out, thunders, calms down, works itself into a passion, coughs, sneezes. . . At one moment it sounds like

the slish-slash noise of silk being torn; at another like the smashing of a pane of glass. Or it is the wind howling, or wood creaking; then it resembles a peacefully flowing stream, which finally hastens its course, falling over a precipice with a noise like thunder. The greatest freedom reigns; while one group of instruments is wandering about in one key, another, without hesitation, moves about in a neighbouring key, while the voices go off in another direction. Often sweet, rapturous passages, which succeed cruelly lacerating sounds, enchant the ear. . . Anyhow, Dr. Richard Strauss has a wonderful talent."— *Saint-Saëns*, May, 1907.

SALOMÉ, Théodore C. Organist; *b.* Paris, 1834; *d.* 1896. Won 2nd *Grand Prix de Rome*, Paris Cons., 1861; 2nd orgt. La Trinité, Paris.
Works: a symphony and numerous org. pieces.

SALOMON, Hector. *B.* Strasburg, 1838. Studied Paris Cons.; 2nd chorus-master (1870), afterwards Chef de Chant, Paris Grand Opéra.
Works: operettas, pf. pieces, several songs, &c.

SA'LOMON, Joh. Peter. *B.* Bonn, 1745; *d.* London, 1815. Violinist, Electoral Orch., Bonn, 1758-65. Settled in London, 1781; gave a series of symphony concerts (Mozart, Haydn, &c.), 1786. Induced Haydn to visit London and write two sets of symphonies for his concerts (1791 and 1794). (The "Salomon" symphonies are Haydn's best orchestral works.) Co-founder, London Philharmonic Soc., 1813.

Salon-music. Music of a light and ephemeral character, composed for the *Salon* or *Drawing-room*.
Salon'flügel (*G.*). A parlour grand pf.
Salon'stück (*G.*). A piece of *salon* music.

Sal'pinx. An ancient Greek trumpet.

Salta're (*I.*). To leap, dance, skip.
Saltan'do ⎱ (1) With a dancing (or springing) bow
Salta'to ⎰ (in vn. playing). (2) Proceeding by skips.

Saltarel'la(*I.*) ⎫ (1) A light springing dance,
Saltarelle (*F.*) ⎬ usually in 6-8 time, with the
Saltarel'lo(*I.*) ⎭ "skipping" rhythm ♩♫ freely used. (2) An extended composition of similar nature. (3) A harpsichord jack.

Salteret'to (*I.*). The rhythmical figure ♩♫ (See **Saltarel'la**.)

Salte'rio, Salte'ro (*I.*). (1) A psalter. (2) A psaltery.
Salte'rio tede'sco. A dulcimer.

Sal'to (*I.*). A skip, leap, jump.
Di sal'to. A melody progressing by skips or leaps.
Sal'ti regola're. The skips allowed in early counterpoint; viz., minor 3rd, major 3rd, perf. 4th, perf. 5th, minor 6th, and octave.
Sal'ti irregola're. Skips allowed only "by licence" in later counterpoint; viz., tritone, major 6th, minor 7th, diminished 4th, diminished 5th (major 7th, rarely); and all intervals greater than an octave.

Salva're (*I.*). "To save." To resolve.
Salvar' una dissonan'za. To resolve a dissonance.

Salvation (*F.*). Resolution of a dissonance.

SALVAYRE, G. B. Gaston. Noted French composer; *b.* Toulouse, 1847. Won the *Grand Prix de Rome*, Paris Cons., 1872.
Works: operas (*Le Bravo*, 1877; *Richard III*, 1883; *La Dame de Montsoreau*, 1888; &c.); a Biblical symphony (*La Résurrection*); overtures, psalms, songs, &c.

Sal've Regi'na (*L.*). "Hail! Queen (of heaven.)" An antiphon sung to the Virgin Mary.

SAMA'RA, Spiro. Operatic composer; *b.* Corfu, 1861. Studied under Delibes, Paris Cons.
Works: operas (*Flora Mirabilis*, 1886, very successful); pf. pieces, numerous songs, &c.

Sambu'ca (*I.*) ⎱ A word of doubtful mean-
Sambu'ka (*I.*) ⎰ ing.
It was used in the middle ages for (1) a small psaltery, (2) a sackbut, (3) a bagpipe, or (4) a hurdy-gurdy.
Sambuci'stria. A player on the sambuca.

SAMMARTI'NI, Giovanni B. *B.* Milan, abt. 1705; *d.* abt. 1775. Prolific composer; "precursor of Haydn in symphonic and chamber music." Produced his 1st symphony, 1734; Gluck was his pupil.
Works: 24 symphonies, 12 trios for vns. and bass, &c.

SAMMARTI'NI, Giuseppe. Oboist; brother of preceding; *d.* London, 1740. Chamber musician to the Prince of Wales.
Works: 12 sonatas for 2 oboes and bass, 6 flute sonatas, 6 concerti grossi, 8 overtures, &c.

Samm'lung (*G.*). A collection, a set.
Samm'lung verschie'dener Musik'stücke. A miscellaneous collection of pieces of music.

Sämmt'lich (*G.*). Abbn. *Sämmtl.* All, all together; complete.

Sampo'gna (*I.*) ⎱ (1) A rustic flute or pipe.
Sampo'nia (*I.*) ⎰ (2) An Italian bagpipe.

SAMPSON, Brook. *B.* Leeds, 1848. Mus.B. Oxon, 1875.
Works: "Analyses of Bach's 48 Fugues," "Notes, Staves, and Clefs," a "Harmony Primer," &c.

SAMSON. Oratorio; Handel, 1743.
Handel esteemed it as much as the *Messiah*, and after his blindness wept when he heard the air "Total Eclipse."—*Grove.*

SAMUEL, Adolphe. *B.* Liége, 1824; *d.* 1898. Won the *Grand Prix de Rome*, Brussels, Cons. 1845; prof. of harmony, 1860. Founded the Brussels Popular Concerts, 1860; Director Ghent Cons., 1871.
Works: 5 operas, several cantatas, 7 symphonies, overtures, pf. pieces, string quartets, a "Course of Harmony and Figured Bass," &c.

SAMUEL, Mad. C. (See **Kleeberg.**)

SAMUELL, Clara. (**Mrs. H. R. Rose.**) Soprano vocalist; *b.* Manchester, 1857.

San'cho. A negro guitar.

SANC'TIS, Cesare de. Condr., composer, and writer; *b.* nr. Rome, 1830.

Sanc'tus (*L.*). "Holy." A movement of the Mass.

25

SAND'BERGER, Adolf. *B.* Würzburg, 1864. Prof. of Music Prague Univ., 1898.
Works : opera (*Ludwig der Springer*, 1895), orch. pieces, choruses, songs, a "Life of P. Cornelius," "Orlando di Lasso" (3 vols.), a complete edition of Lasso's works, &c.

SANDERS, James. *B.* 1816 ; *d.* Liverpool, 1891. Chorus-master Liverpool Festival, 1874.

SANDERSON, James. *B.* Workington, 1769 ; *d.* 1841. Violinist, theatre condr. (Newcastle and London), member Philharmonic Orch., &c.

SANDERSON, Lillian. Mezzo-soprano ; *b.* Milwaukee, 1867. *Début*, Berlin, 1890.

SANDERSON, Sibyl. Operatic soprano ; *b.* Sacramento, California, 1865 ; *d.* 1903. Paris *début*, Opéra-Comique, 1889.

SANDO'NI. (See **Cuzzoni.**)

SAN'DOW, Eugen. Violinist ; *b.* Berlin, 1856.

SANDT, Max van de. Pianist ; pupil of Liszt ; *b.* Rotterdam, 1863. Pf. teacher Stern Cons., Berlin, 1889.

Sanft (*G.*). Soft, smooth, delicate, gentle.
Mit sanft'en Stim'men. With soft stops.
Sanft belebt'. Gently animated.
Sanft bewegt'. With gentle motion (movement).
Sanft'flöte. A soft-toned flute.
Sanft'gedackt. A soft-toned stopped diapason (organ stop.)
Sanft hervor'tretend. Gently brought out.
Sanft'klagend. Plaintive, gently complaining.

Sanf'tig (*G.*). Soft, gentle, sweet.
Sanft müt(h)ig. Softly, gently.

Sang (*G.*). A song ; singing.
Mit Sang und Klang. With singing and music.
Sang'bar. Adapted for singing ; singable.
Sang'dichter. Lyric poet.
Säng'er. A singer, chorister, poet, bard.
Säng'erin. A female singer.
Säng'erbund } A singing society.
Säng'erverein }
Säng'er-fest. A choral festival.
Sang'spiel. Vocal music.
Sang'ständchen. A vocal serenade.
Sang'vogel. Song bird.
Sang'weise. Melody.

SÄNGER, Frau. (See **I. Sethe.**)

SANGIOVAN'NI, Antonio. *B.* Bergamo, 1831 ; *d.* 1892. Noted singing teacher ; prof. of singing, Milan Cons., from 1854.

Sanglot (*F.*). "A sob." An old form of portamento somewhat similar to the Irish "Ochone."

Och - one !

Sang Schools. "An old Scottish institution dating from the 13th cent."—*Grove.*
They became extinct abt. 1700.

SANGSTER, Walter Hay. Orgt. and composer ; *b.* London, 1835 ; *d.* Eastbourne, 1900. Mus.Doc. Oxon, 1877.

SANKEY, Ira D. Singing evangelist ; *b.* Edinburgh (U.S.), 1840 ; *d.* 1908.

Sans (*F.*). Without.
Sans hâte. Without haste.
Sans lenteur. Without slowness.
Sans pédales. Without the pedals.
Sans presser. Without hurrying.
Sans ralentir. Without slackening the speed.
Sans sourdine. Without the mute.

SANTI'NI, Abbate Fortunato. Rome, 1778-1862. Collected "one of the finest musical libraries ever formed," now at Münster,

SANT'LEY, Sir Chas. Distinguished baritone singer ; *b.* Liverpool, 1834. Studied Milan (1855-7) ; then with Garcia in London. *Début* as "Adam," Haydn's *Creation*, 1857. Stage *début*, Covent Garden, 1859 ; toured with the Carl Rosa Company for several years (from 1875). For many years he was the "foremost concert baritone" in England. Knighted, 1907.
Works : Some songs under the pseudonym of "Ralph Betterton," "Reminiscences," 1908.

San'toral (*S.*). A church choir-book.

SANTUC'CI, Marco. Noted contrapuntist ; *b.* Camajore, 1762 ; *d.* 1843. Maestro S. John Lateran, Rome (1797-1808), and afterwards at Lucca Cath.
Works : masses, motets (including a 16-part motet for 4 choirs), psalms, symphonies, organ sonatas, &c.

SAPELL'NIKOFF, Wassily. Noted concert pianist ; *b.* Odessa, 1868. *Début*, Hamburg, 1888.

SAPPHO (pron. *Saf'fo*). Famous Greek lyric poetess, abt. 600 B.C. ; called "The Tenth Muse."
She is credited with having invented "Sapphic Verse" and the Greek Mixolydian Mode.

Saquebut (*F.*). A sackbut (*q.v.*).

Sar'aband (*I.*) }
Saraban'da (*I.*) } A dance derived by the
Sarabande (*F.*) } Spaniards from the
Saraban'de (*G.*) } Moors. It is for a single performer, is in slow and stately 3-4 or 3-2 time, and is accompanied by castanets.
"A measure full of state and ancientry."— *Shakespeare.*
It has a strong accent on the 2nd beat of the bar, thus—

(See also *Suite.*)

SARAN, August F. *B.* Saxony, 1836.
Works : excellent arrangements of "Old German Songs ;" also pf. pieces, &c.

SARASA'TE, Pablo de. Celebrated violinist ; *b.* Pampeluna, Spain, 1844 ; *d.* 1908. Played before Queen Isabella at 10 ; took 1st prize, violin class, Paris Cons., 1857 ; and a *premier accessit*, 1859. He toured in all the principal countries of the world (1st visit to London, 1861), and was noted for "purity and beauty of tone, and perfection of technique."
Works : several vn. pieces and arrangements.

Sardo'nico (*I.*). Sardonic(ally), mocking(ly).

SARMIEN'TO, Salvatore. Operatic composer ; *b.* Palermo, 1817 ; *d.* 1869.

SARRETTE, Bernard. Founder of the Paris Cons. ; *b.* Bordeaux, 1765 ; *d.* 1858. Captain in the National Guard ; formed the famous band (1789) and started a school of music for the training of army bandsmen, from which the Conservatoire was developed, 1795.

SAR'RI, Domenico. *B.* nr. Naples, 1678; *d.* 1741 (?).

Wrote operas, oratorios, serenades, &c.

Sarrus'ophone. A kind of brass bassoon (with a double reed), invented by Sarrus, Paris, 1863.

It is made in various sizes, and is rarely used except in France.

Sartarel'la (*I.*) } A Neapolitan dance in
Sartarel'lo (*I.*) } quick 6-8 time, resembling the Tarantella (*q.v.*).

SAR'TI, Giuseppe. (Il Domenichi'no.) *B.* Faenza, 1729; *d.* Berlin, 1802. Pupil of Padre Martini; orgt. Faenza Cath. 1748-50. Director Italian Opera, Copenhagen, 1753; Court condr., 1755; condr. Court Opera, 1770-5. Maestro Milan Cath. 1779-84. Invited to St. Petersburg by Catherine II (meeting Mozart on his way at Vienna); lived there 18 years, raising the Italian opera "to an unexampled state of efficiency." Among his numerous pupils was Cherubini (who studied under him at Milan.)

His 40 operas (*Il re pastore*, Venice, 1753; *Armida*, 1786, &c.), were immensely popular at the time, but are now practically forgotten. He also wrote masses and other church music.

SARTO'RIO, Antonio. Operatic composer; Venice, abt. 1620-81.

SASS (or **SAX**), **Marie C.** Dramatic soprano; *b.* Ghent, 1838. *Début*, Paris Théâtre-Lyrique, 1859; sang at the Grand Opéra, 1860-71.

Sat'tel (*G.*). "A saddle." The "nut" (of a vn., &c.).

Sat'tel ma'chen. The use of the thumb as a temporary nut in 'cello playing.

Sat'tellage. The "half-shift," or 2nd position, in vn. playing.

SAT'TER, Gustav. Pianist; *b.* Vienna, 1832. Made several successful tours.

His compositions, "warmly praised by Berlioz," include an opera, symphonies, overtures, pf. sonatas, pf. quartets, &c.

Satz (*G.*). (1) A theme, subject, movement, or main division of a movement.

(2) A section answered by a responsive section; *Vor'dersatz* ("forephrase"), *Nach'satz* ("afterphrase").

(3) The science of harmony, art or style of composition, &c.

Satz'bildung. "Building-up" of sentences, &c.

SAU'ER, Emil. Distinguished pianist; *b.* Hamburg, 1862. Pupil of N. Rubinstein and Liszt. Has toured with great success since 1882.

SAU'ER, Wilhelm. Noted organ builder at Frankfort-on-Oder; *b.* Friedland, Mecklenburg, 1831.

SAUL. Oratorio; Handel, 1738.

Saun. A Burmese harp.

SAUNDERS, Chas. A. Tenor vocalist; *b.* Stratton, Cornwall, 1867.

SAUNDERS, Joseph Gordon. *B.* London, 1837. Mus.Doc. Oxon, 1878.

Works: "Examples in Strict Counterpoint" (Novello's Primer), "Fingering and Phrasing," org. pieces, part-songs, &c.

SAUREL, Emma. Brilliant opera singer; *b.* Palermo, 1850.

SAURET, Emile. Celebrated violinist; *b.* Dun-le-roi, Cher, France, 1852. Pupil of De Bériot; toured from the age of 8. London *début*, Covent Garden, 1866. Vn. professor R.A.M., 1890.

Works: a violinist's "Gradus ad Parnassum;" 2 concertos, and numerous vn. solos.

Säus'eln (*G.*). To rustle, murmur, sigh, hum.

Saut (*F.*). A leap; same as **Salto** (*q.v.*).

Sautereau. A "Jumper;" the jack of a harpsichord or spinet.

Sau'terie (*Old E.*). A dulcimer, or psaltery.

Sautillé (*F.*). With "springing bow" (in vn. playing); **Salta'to** (*q.v.*).

Sauver (*F.*). To resolve (save) a dissonance.

Suavement. Resolution (of a dissonance).

SAUVEUR, Joseph. *B.* La Flèche, 1653; *d.* Paris, 1716. A deaf mute; learned to speak in his 7th year. Became a great "acoustical investigator;" member of the Académie, 1696.

He pub. several treatises on acoustics, and was the first "to calculate absolute vibration-numbers and to explain scientifically the phenomena of overtones."—*Baker.*

SAUZAY, Chas. Eugene. Eminent violinist; *b.* Paris, 1809; *d.* 1901. 1st vn. to Louis Philippe, 1840; Prof. Paris Cons. 1860.

SAVARD, M. A. *B.* Paris, 1861; won *Grand Prix de Rome*, Paris Cons., 1886. Director Lyons Cons., 1902.

SAVARD, Marie G. A. Paris, 1814-81; Prof. of Harmony at the Cons.

Works: a "Complete Course of Harmony," "The Principles of Music," "First Notions of Music," "Studies in Practical Harmony" &c.

SAVART, Félix. *B.* Mézières, 1791; *d.* Paris, 1841. Prof. of Acoustics, Collège de France; member of the Académie, 1827.

Wrote several works on the Construction of Stringed and Bowed Insts.; the Communication of Vibrations in solids, liquids, and gases; the Human Voice; the Song of Birds; &c.

Save. To resolve a dissonance; to avoid breaking a musical rule.

Consecutive 5ths are said to be "saved" in cases like the following:—

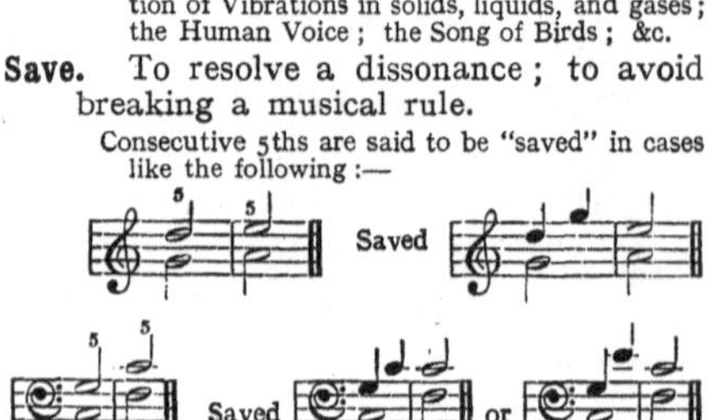

SAWYER, Frank Jos. Brighton, 1857-1908. Studied Leipzig Cons. Mus.Doc. Oxon, 1883. Prof. of Sight-singing, R.C.M. Hon. Sec, R.C.O., 1908.

Works : oratorio (*Star in the East*), cantatas, manuals of sight-singing, a "Graded School Song Book," anthems, part-songs, &c.

SAX, Chas. Jos. *B.* Dinant-sur-Meuse, Belgium, 1791 ; *d.* 1865. Established a factory (Brussels, 1815) for the manufacture of insts.—especially brass insts., which he greatly improved. Joined his son, Adolphe, Paris, 1853.

SAX, A. J. Adolphe. "The Christopher Columbus of Brass Insts. ; " son of the preceding ; *b.* Dinant, 1814 ; *d.* Paris, 1894. Studied Brussels Cons. Invented the **Saxophone** (*q.v.*), 1840. Settled in Paris, 1842, and with his father invented the **Saxhorn** and **Saxotromba** (see below). Teacher of Saxophone, Paris Cons., 1857.

SAX, Marie. (See **Sass.**)

Sax-horn. A horn with pistons, invented by Adolphe Sax. (See above.)

A "natural" horn gives only the series of notes known as the "Chord of Nature" (see *Acoustics*). The pistons invented by Sax enable the player "to supply the missing notes in this series" and thereby obtain a complete chromatic scale. As now used in English brass bands the Sax-horns include the following :—

(1) The Soprano Cornet in E♭ (*Sopranino Saxhorn ; petit Bugle à pistons*).
(2) The (ordinary) Cornet in B♭ (*Soprano Saxhorn ; Bugle tenor ;* &c.).
(3) The Tenor-horn in E♭ (*Alto Saxhorn ; Althorn in Es*).
(4) The Baritone in B♭ (*Tenorhorn in B ; Barytcn in Si♭*).
(5) The Euphonium in B♭ (*Bass Saxhorn ; Tuba-basse in Si♭*).
(6) The Bombardon in E♭ (*Low Bass Saxhorn ; Bombardon in Mi♭*).
(7) The Contrabass Bombardon in B♭ (*Contrabass Tuba ; Bombardon in Si♭ grave*).

Sax'ophone. (*G., Saxophon; I., Saxofo'nia.*) A brass inst. with conical tube and clarinet mouthpiece, invented by Sax, 1840.

It combines the tone qualities of the clarinet and 'cello, and is made in six sizes : (1) Sopranino, piccolo, or aigu ; (2) Soprano ; (3) Contralto; (4) Tenor ; (5) Barytone ; (6) Bass. It is, unfortunately, not much used in England.

Sax'otromba. An inst. invented by Sax, intermediate in tone between the Sax-horn and the trumpet.

It is made in seven sizes.

Saxtu'ba. (See **Tuba.**)
Say'nete (*S.*). Farces with music.
Sbal'zo (*I.*). A skip, leap, rebound.
Sbalza'to. Impetuous(ly).
Sbar'ra (*I.*). A bar-line.
Sbar'ra dop'pia. A double bar.
SBOL'CI, Jefte. 'Cellist ; Florence, 1833-95. Founded the Florentine "Società Orchestrale."
SBRI'GLIA, Giovanni. Noted tenor singer and teacher ; *b.* Naples, 1840.

Teacher of Jean de Reszké, Ed. de Reszké, Nordica, &c. Resides in Paris.

Scagnel'lo (*I.*). A bridge (vn., &c.).

Sca'la (*I.*). A scale or gamut. (See **Scale.**)
Sca'la croma'tica. Chromatic scale.
Scala diato'nica. Diatonic scale.
Scala, La. The celebrated opera house at Milan ; opened 1778.
Scald, Skald. A ancient Norse poet-musician, or bard.
SCAL'CHI, Sofia. Operatic mezzo-soprano ; *b.* Turin, 1850. *Début*, Mantua, 1866; London, 1868. Married Signor Lolli, 1875.
Scale. (1) (*G., Ton'leiter; F., Echelle, Gamme ; I. and L., Sca'la.*) A series of notes ascending or descending in regular order.

The scales in ordinary use are of 3 kinds : Major, Minor, and Chromatic.

I.—MAJOR SCALE :
In a major scale the interval between the 1st and 3rd notes is a major 3rd, and the "standard" major scale is represented by the notes :—

This is called the scale of "C major ; " the interval between the 3rd and 4th notes and between the 7th and 8th notes is a *semitone ;* the interval between any other pair of consecutive notes is a *whole tone* (2 semitones).

The "formula" of the Major *Tone-ladder* therefore reads : "TONE, TONE, Semitone ; TONE, TONE, TONE, Semitone."

The scale of C major includes all the "white" keys of the pf., harmonium, or organ.

Major scales of exactly similar structure are built up on the notes C♭, G♭, D♭, A♭, E♭, B♭, F ; G, D, A, E, B, F♯, and C♯, making 15 major scales in all. All these, except C major, require the use of one or more "black" keys to preserve the regular order of tones and semitones. (See *Signature.*)

The major scale, at whatever pitch, is represented in Tonic Sol-fa by the initials *d, r, m, f, s, l, t, d'.*

II.—MINOR SCALE :
In a Minor scale the interval from the 1st to the 3rd notes is a *Minor 3rd.* The standard scale is that of "A minor" (all white notes except the G♯) :—

1

Sol-fa: l₁ t₁ d r m f se l

The 6th and 7th notes of this scale are, however, *variable*, the 6th being sometimes sharpened and the 7th sometimes flattened.

2

l₁ t₁ d r m f s l

3

l₁ t₁ d r m ba se l l se ba m r d t₁ l₁

4

l₁ t₁ d r m ba se l l s f m r d t₁ l₁

No. 1 is called the "Modern" or "Harmonic" Minor scale ; No. 2 the "Ancient," or "Unaltered" minor scale. Nos. 3 and 4 are "Arbitrary," or "Melodic" forms (of which No. 4 is the usual "Melodic Minor," ascending by "sharpened" 6th and 7th and descending by "flattened" 7th and 6th).

N.B.—The Harmonic Minor Scale was long in "settling down" into its present form. Bach and Handel often (and even Mozart occasionally) used the the major triad of the sub-dominant; *i e.* with the major 6th of the minor scale as a harmony note.

For the signatures of the 15 minor scales, see *Signature.*

III.—CHROMATIC SCALE :

A chromatic scale is one that proceeds by semitones.

(*a*) The Melodic Chromatic scale is written with "sharps" in ascending and "flats" in descending, or *in any other way* at the composer's discretion.

N.B.—The "Day-Macfarren School" writes B♭ instead of A♯ in ascending, and F♯ instead of G♭ in descending.

(*b*) The Harmonic Chromatic Scale includes minor and major 2nd, minor and major 3rd, perfect and augmented 4th, minor and major 6th, minor and major 7th, all reckoned from the key-note (or Tonic).

d   ra   r   ma   m   f   fe   s   la   l   ta   t   d¹

d¹   t   ta   l   las   fe   f   m   mar   ra   d

ENHARMONIC SCALE. (Not used in practical music, but of theoretical importance).

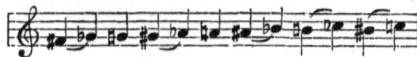

See also Greek Scales (under *Greek Music*) and Ecclesiastical Scales (under *Mode*).

Among other interesting scales may be mentioned: (1) The 84 Chinese scales (each "with a special philosophical signification"), including the following "pentatonic" scale, which is analogous to the old Scottish scale and that of many other ancient nations :—

(2) The Hindoo scales with intervals of "third-tones" and "quarter-tones."

(3) The Scottish Bagpipe scale. (See *Bagpipe.*)

(4) The chief Byzantine scale :—

(5) The Hungarian or Gypsy scale :—

(6) The 12 Arabic scales (with 9 or 10 notes to the octave).

(7) The Javanese scale of *six equal tones* :—

The music of any people is founded on its scales, and we naturally think that our scales are superior to all others ; that they are, in fact, "true, just, and natural." The Chinese, however, consider the music of Western Europe to be "barbaric and horrible."

"We cannot *prove* that the scales which we employ are better than those used by other races or at other epochs."—*Elson.*

"The final conclusion is that the Musical Scale is not one, not " natural," nor even founded necessarily on the laws....so beautifully worked out by Helmholtz, but very diverse, very artificial, and very capricious."—*Musical Scales of various Nations* ; Dr. A. J. Ellis F.R.S.

Aretinian Scale. (See *Guido's Scale,* below).

Chordal Structure of the Scale. A harmonic view of the scale which bases it on the triads of the Tonic, Dominant, and Sub-dominant.

Common Scale. The ordinary major scale.

Diatonic Scale. (See *Diatonic.*)

Dividing place of the scale. Between *f* and *s.*—*Curwen.*

German Scale. (See under *G.*)

Guido's Scale. The syllables *ut, re, mi, fa, sol, la* introduced by Guido (*q.v.*).

Harmonic Scale. (1) (See *Minor Scale*). (2) The series of " partials." (See *Acoustics.*)

Just Scale. The major scale derived from the "chord of nature." (See *Acoustics.*)

Laying a Scale. The tuner first "lays a scale" of one octave before proceeding with the tuning of the other notes.

Mixed Scale. A scale partly diatonic and partly chromatic.

Natural Scale. } The scale of C major.
Open Scale. }

Pentatonic Scale. (See *Pentatonic.*)

Relative Scales. Major and minor scales with the same signature.

Tempered Scale. Any scale based on the "12 equal semitones" of the pf., as opposed to a Just Scale. (See *Temperament.*)

Scale (2). The complete range or compass of a voice or inst.

Scale (3). (*G., Mensur'; F., Etalon.*) The dimensions and proportions of organ pipes, especially their width (or size of bore).

A *broad scale* gives a full, round, smooth tone ; a *narrow scale* is more bright and pungent.

Sca'len-schu'le (*G.*). A collection of " Scale exercises."

Scampana're (*I.*). To chime bells.

Scampa'nio. Chiming.

SCANDEL'LI, Antonio. *B.* Brescia, 1517 ; *d.* Dresden, 1580.

Pub. 2 books of Neapolitan Canzoni, and a large number of German sacred works (Passions, &c.).

Scannel'lo (*I.*) }
Scannet'to (*I.*) } Same as **Scagnel'lo** (*q.v.*).

Scan'sion. Discriminating (measuring) the "feet" of verse (poetry). (See **Foot.**)

SCA'RIA, Emil. Operatic bass singer ; *b.* Graz, 1840 ; *d.* 1886. *Début,* 1860, at Pesth. Excelled in Wagner *rôles ;* "created" the parts of "Wotan" (Bayreuth, 1876) and "Gurnemanz" (1882).

SCARLAT'TI, Alessandro. Eminent composer ; founder of the Neapolitan School ; *b.* Trapani, Sicily, 1659 ; *d.* Naples, 1725. Of his early life there is no authentic record. Maestro to Queen Christina of Sweden, Rome, 1684 ; Maestro to the Viceroy, Naples, 1694 ;

Asst. maestro (1703) and chief maestro (1707) S. Maria Maggiore, Rome. Afterwards maestro, Royal Chapel, Naples. Also taught at various Conservatories. His pupils include Durante, Leo, Feo, Hasse, and Porpora. He considerably improved the opera, perfected the *Aria da Capo* (*q.v.*), introduced Accompanied Recitative, and greatly enriched the orchestra.

Works : 115 operas (*Pompeo*, 1684 ; *La Rosaura*, 1690 ; *Teodora*, 1693 ; *Tigrane*, 1715 ; *Griselda*, 1721 ; &c.) ; 8 oratorios, 200 masses, and much other church music ; madrigals, serenatas, duets, and " a vast number of cantatas for solo voice with *basso continuo.*"

SCARLAT′TI, Domenico. Son of preceding ; called "the founder of modern pf. technique ; " *b.* Naples, 1683(5?) ; *d.* 1757. He made an early reputation as a harpsichord player, and when Handel visited Rome, 1709, Scarlatti was chosen to compete with him. On the organ Scarlatti was easily beaten, but on the harpsichord he fairly equalled his great opponent. Apptd. maestro, St. Peter's, Rome, 1715 ; cembalist, Italian Opera, London, 1719 ; court cembalist, Lisbon, 1721. Taught in Naples (1725-9) and Madrid (1729-54).

Works : 2 books of "Pieces for the Clavecin," and "Esercizi per Gravicembalo." Most of his pieces have been reprinted as "Harpsichord Lessons," "Sonatas," &c. They initiated the modern free style of pf. composition, and led to modern systems of fingering and pf. technique generally.

SCARLAT′TI, Giuseppe. Opera composer : grandson of A. ; *b.* Naples, 1712 ; *d.* Vienna, 1777.

Scel′ta (*I.*). Choice, selection.

A scel′ta del cantan′te. At the choice of the singer.

Seeman′do (*I.*). *Diminuendo* (*q.v.*).

Sce′na (*I.*) ⎱ (1) (*G.*, *Auf′tritt.*) A division
Scène (*F.*) ⎰ of a dramatic work "marked by the entrance or exit of one or more performers." (2) A dramatic vocal solo comprising *recitative* and *arioso*, and generally ending with a regular *aria*.

"The *Scena* is the largest and most brilliant solo form."—*Elson.* It may be an independent composition, or part of a work.
Scena d'entrata (*I.*) ⎱ The "entry song" of a soloist in
Scène d'entrée (*F.*) ⎰ an opera.
Sce′na ed a′ria (*I.*). (See *Scena*, 2.)

Scena′ril (*I.*). Side scenes.

Scena′rio (*I.*). (1) The plot or "skeleton libretto" of a work. (2) A play-bill.

Scena′rium. The full libretto, with directions for performance, &c.

Scene. (See **Scena.**)

Scenic music. Dramatic or stage music.

Schablo′ne (*G.*). A pattern, or stencil.

Schablo′nenmusik ⎱ Music without inspiration ;
Schablo′nenhafte Musik ⎰ "cut and dried" to pattern.

SCHACH′NER, Rudolf J. Pianist ; *b.* Munich, 1821 ; *d.* 1896. Settled in London as teacher, 1853.

Works : an oratorio ; 2 concertos and other pf. pieces.

SCHACK (or **CZIAK**), **Benedikt.** Operatic tenor ; *b.* Mirowitz, 1758 ; *d.* 1826.

Mozart wrote for him the part of "Tamino" in *The Magic Flute.*

SCHAD, Joseph. Pianist ; *b.* Steinach, Bavaria, 1812 ; *d.* 1879. Settled in Bordeaux as teacher, 1847.

Published numerous popular pf. pieces.

SCHA′DE (SCHADÄUS), Abraham. Pub. a Collection of 384 motets (1611-13).

SCHA′DE, Carl. Singing teacher ; Halberstadt.

Pub. several books on music for school classes (1828-31).

Schä′fer (*G.*). A shepherd, or swain.

Schä′fergedicht. "Shepherd Song"; an idyll, pastoral.
Schä′ferlied ⎱ A pastoral song ; a rural ditty.
Schä′ferspiel ⎰
Schä′fermässig. Pastoral.
Schä′ferpfeife. Shepherd's pipe.
Schä′ferstückchen. A little pastoral air (ditty).
Schä′fertanz. Shepherd's dance.

SCHÄF′FER, August. *B.* Rheinsberg, 1814 ; *d.* 1879. Pupil of Mendelssohn.

Works : operas, symphonies, chamber music, and popular humorous duets and quartets.

SCHÄF′FER, Dr. Julius. *B.* Crevese, 1823 ; *d.* 1902. Mus.-director to the Grand Duke of Schwerin, 1855 ; mus.-director Breslau Univ., and condr. of the Singakademie, 1860.

Works : songs, part-songs, choral books, writings on Robt. Franz., &c.

Schäff′lertanz (*G.*). An ancient festival dance of the Coopers' Guild, Munich.

SCHAF′HÄUTL, Karl F. E. von. Scientist and acoustician ; *b.* Ingolstadt, 1803 ; *d.* 1890.

Aided Böhm in the construction of his insts., and wrote several works on acoustics, &c.

Schaf′orgel (*G.*). A kind of bagpipe.

SCHALK, Josef. Condr.; *b.* Vienna. Condr. Covent Garden, 1898; New York, 1899 ; Berlin Court Opera, 1899, &c.

Schalk′haft (*G.*). Roguish(ly), sportive(ly), playful(ly), waggish(ly).

Schall (*G.*). Sound ; ring ; resonance.

Schall′becher. The "bell" of an inst.
Schall′becken. Cymbals ; generally called *Becken.*
Schall′boden. A sound-board.
Schall′brett. Wind chest of an organ.
Schall′glas. A musical glass.
Schall′horn. A trumpet or trombone.
Schall′lehre. Acoustics.
Schall′loch. Sound hole ; *f* hole.
Schall′rohr. (1) Speaking trumpet. (2) Wind inst.
Schall′stab. Triangle.
Schall′stück ⎱ Bell of an inst.
Schall′trichter ⎰
Schall′trichter auf. With the bell turned up (horns, &c.).

Schalmay′ (*G.*) ⎱
Schalmei′ (*G.*) ⎰ An oaten pipe. (See
Schalmey′ (*G.*) ⎰ **Chalumeau** and **Shawm.**)

Schanzu′ne (*G.*). A *Chanson* (*q.v.*).

Scharf (G.). Sharp, shrill, acute ; pointed ; exact, rigorous. A shrill mixture stop on the organ.

Scharf' betont'. Strongly accented.
Scharf'er Accent'. Acute accent.
Scharf gestos'sen. Sharply detached ; *staccatissimo.*
Scharf und spitz'ig. Sharp (sarcastic) and biting.

SCHAR'FE, Gustav. B. Saxony, 1835 ; d. 1892. Baritone singer, Dresden Court Opera ; teacher of singing at the Cons.

Wrote a work on "The Methodical Development of the Voice."

SCHAR'FENBERG, William. Pianist ; b. Cassel, 1819 ; d. 1895. Settled in New York, 1838 ; "for many years a leading teacher and player ; " musical editor to G. Schirmer & Co.

SCHÄR'NACK, Luise. Operatic mezzo-soprano ; b. Oldenburg, abt. 1860. *Début,* Weimar, in *Lohengrin :* sang in London, 1883.

SCHARWEN'KA, Franz Xaver. Noted pianist and composer; b. Samter, Posen, 1850. Studied Kullak's Academy, Berlin ; apptd. teacher there, 1868. Public *début,* 1869. Toured in Europe and America from 1874 ; founded with his brother L. P. (below) the "Scharwenka Cons.," Berlin, 1880, and the "Scharwenka Cons.," New York, 1891. Returned to Berlin, 1898, as director of the "Klindworth-Scharwenka Cons." (an amalgamation formed in 1893).

Works : opera, *Mataswintha,* 1896 ; a symphony in C minor ; 3 pf. concertos ; chamber music, many fine pf. pieces, church music, several songs, a "Critical Edition" of Schumann's pf. works, &c.

SCHARWEN'KA, Ludwig Philipp. Elder brother of preceding ; b. Samter, 1847. Studied Kullak's Academy, Berlin ; teacher of theory and composition, 1870. Joined his brother in founding the Cons. in Berlin, 1880, and New York, 1891. (See above.) Returned to Berlin, 1892.

Works : choral works ; symphonies, overtures, and other orch. pieces ; pieces for 'cello and pf., several pf. pieces, songs, &c.

Schat'tenhaft (G.). Shadowy.

Schau(e)'rig (G.). Weird, ghastly, horrible.

Schau'spiel (G.). A dramatic piece.

Schau'spieler. An actor.
Schau'spielerin. An actress.

SCHE'BEST, Agnes. Operatic mezzo-soprano ; b. Vienna, 1813 ; d. 1869. Sang at Dresden, Pesth, Vienna, &c.

SCHECH'NER-WAA'GEN, Nanette. Noted dramatic soprano ; Munich, 1806-60.

Celebrated in the *rôles* of Beethoven's *Fidelio* and Gluck's *Iphigenia.*

SCHEI'BE, Johann. D. Leipzig, 1748.

Built the organs in the Paulinerkirche and Johanniskirche, Leipzig ; J. S. Bach "considered the latter faultless."

SCHEI'BE, Joh. Adolf. Son of the preceding; b. Leipzig, 1708 ; d. 1776. Founded a musical paper *Der critische Musicus,* Hamburg, 1737.

Works : an opera, cantatas, sonatas, church music, songs, &c., and numerous musical essays.

SCHEI'BLER, Johann H. B. nr. Aix-la-Chapelle, 1777 ; d. 1838.

Invented an arrangement of 56 tuning-forks for tuning insts. in "Equal Temperament."

SCHEI'DEMANTEL, Karl. Operatic baritone ; b. Weimar, 1859. Member Dresden Court Opera since 1886.

SCHEIDT, Samuel. Halle-on-Saale, 1587-1654. Famous organist ; pupil of Sweelinck. Developed the choral on artistic lines, and "in true organ style."

Works : chorals, toccatas, fantasias ; cantiones sacræ, concerti sacræ ; psalms, songs ; 70 "Symphonien auf Concerten-Manier," &c.

SCHEIN, Joh. H. B. Saxony, 1586 ; d. Leipzig, 1630. Court capellmeister, Weimar, 1615 ; cantor Thomasschule, Leipzig, 1616.

Works : lieder, sacred songs, 20 suites ("interesting early German string music"), a Te Deum *a* 24, madrigals, Villanelle, a "Gesangbuch" (containing 313 sacred songs and psalms), &c.

Scheit'holt (G.). (See **Trumscheit.**)

SCHEL'BLE, Joh. Nepomuk. Singer and teacher ; b. Black Forest, 1789 ; d. 1837. Opera tenor, Vienna, 1813-16. Friend of Beethoven and Spohr. Founded the Frankfort Cäcilien-Verein.

Schel'len (G.). Bells, jingles ; sleigh-bells.

Schel'lenbaum. A Crescent (*q.v.*).
Schel'lentrommel. A tambourine.

SCHEL'LER, Jacob. Bohemian violinist ; b. 1759 ; d. (?).

Noted for his skill in double stopping and producing "harmonics."

SCHEL'LING, Ernest H. Pianist and composer ; b. Belvedere (U.S.), 1876.

Schelm'isch (G). Roguish, knavish.

SCHEL'PER, Otto. Fine operatic baritone ; b. Rostock, 1844.

Has sung principally at Bremen, Cologne, and Leipzig.

SCHENCK, Jean. Viola-da-Gamba player.

Pub. numerous works for Gamba, Amsterdam, 1688-93.

SCHENK, Johann. B. Wiener-Neustadt, 1761 (1753?) ; d. Vienna, 1836. " He was Beethoven's secret instructor while he (Beethoven) was taking lessons from Haydn."

Works : a mass (1778) and numerous popular operettas (*Der Dorfbarbier,* 1796).

Scherz (G.). Jest, joke, fun, raillery.

Scher'zend } Droll, playful, jocular, facetious,
Schers'haft } burlesque.
Schers'gedicht. A comic poem.
Schers'haftigkeit. Playfulness, sportiveness, &c.

SCHERZ'ER, Otto. B. Ansbach, 1821 ; d. 1886. Mus.-director Tübingen Univ., 1860-77.

Works : pf. pieces and several songs.

Scher'zo (*I.*) (pron. *sker'tzo*). A jest, a joke. (1) An instrumental piece of a piquant, playful, animated character. (2) A movement in a sonata or symphony characterized by the same qualities.

The *Scherzo* (of a symphony, &c.) was developed by Beethoven from the *Minuet and Trio* of Haydn and Mozart. The "form" is the same, but it is much extended ; and instead of being slow and stately it is extremely vivacious, full of contrasts of ryhthm and harmony, and abounding in light and delicate passages. The Scherzo is generally in quick 3-4 time (with occasional alternations of 2-4), and there is usually only "one beat in the bar."

Scherzi'no. A short scherzo.
Scherzan'do ⎫
Scherzan'te ⎬ Light, playful ; in the style of a
Scherze'vole ⎭ scherzo.
Scherzo'so
Scherzandis'simo ⎫ Very light, playful, &c.
Scherzevolmen'te ⎭
Scher'zo D.C. e poi la Co'da. Repeat the scherzo and then (go on to) the Coda.
Scher'zo da Ca'po sen'za repetizio'ne. Go back and play the scherzo without repeating its separate portions.

SCHET'KY, Christoph. 'Cellist ; *b.* Darmstadt, 1740 ; *d.* Edinburgh, 1773.
Works : 6 'cello sonatas, 6 string quartets, numerous pieces for 'cello with other insts., &c.

SCHICHT, Johann G. *B.* Reichenau, 1753 ; *d.* 1823. Pianist Gewandhaus Concerts, Leipzig, 1781 ; condr. 1785 ; cantor at the Thomaskirche, 1810 ; first editor of J. S. Bach's scores.
Works : 3 oratorios ; masses, choral-motets, Te Deums ; a collection of 1,285 chorals, several pf. pieces ; "The Ground-rules of Harmony," &c.

SCHICK (*née* Hamel), **M. Luise.** Noted soprano ; *b.* Mayence, 1773 ; *d.* 1809. Stage *début*, Mayence, 1791. Favourite *rôles* in Mozart's operas.

Schie'ber (*G.*). The slide of the bow (vn., &c.).

SCHIE'DERMAYER, Joseph B. Organist ; *d.* Linz-on-Danube, 1840.
Works : much sacred music ; symphonies, string trios, organ pieces, an edition of L. Mozart's violin method, &c.

SCHIED'MAYER & Söhne. Stuttgart firm of piano makers, founded 1781.

Schiettez'za (*I.*). Simplicity, plainness.
Con schiettez'za ⎫
Schiettamen'te ⎬ Simply, neatly, unembellished.
Schiet'to ⎭

SCHIE'VER, Ernst. Violinist ; *b.* Hanover, 1846.

SCHIKANE'DER, Emanuel J. Wrote the libretto of Mozart's *Zauberflöte* : *b.* Regensburg, 1751 ; *d.* 1812. Met Mozart at Salzburg, and afterwards induced him to compose the *Zauberflöte*, in which Schikaneder played the part of " Papageno." Died in great poverty.

SCHIL'LER, Madeline. Gifted pianist ; *b.* London. Brilliant *début*, Gewandhaus, Leipzig. Married Mr. Marcus Elmer Bennett of Boston, Mass. After numerous tours settled in New York.

SCHIL'LING, Bertha A. L. Lucienne Bréval (*q.v.*).

SCHIL'LING, Dr. Gustav. *B.* nr. Hanover, 1803 ; *d.* Nebraska, 1881. Settled in America, 1857(8?).
Works : a "Dictionary of Mus. Terms," an "Encyclopædic Dict. of Music" (7 vols.), a "Thorough-bass School," and numerous other works (Acoustics, Dynamics, Harmony, German Folk-music, &c.).

SCHIL'LINGS, Max. *B.* Düren, Rheinland, 1868. Chorus-trainer, Bayreuth, 1902.
Works : operas, orch. pieces, songs, &c.

SCHIM'MELPFEN'NIG von der OYE, Baroness. Mathilde Mallinger (*q.v.*).

SCHI'MON, Adolf. Noted singing teacher ; *b.* Vienna, 1820 ; *d.* 1887. Pupil Paris Cons. ; Maestro al cembalo, Her Majesty's, London, 1850-2 ; then at the Italian Opera, Paris. Married the soprano, **Anna Regan,** 1872. Afterwards taught at Leipzig and Munich.
Works : operas, songs, pf. pieces, &c.

SCHI'MON-RE'GAN. Celebrated soprano. (See above.) *D.* 1902.

SCHIN'DELMEISSER, Ludwig. *B.* Königsberg, 1811 ; *d.* 1864. Capellmeister at various German theatres.
Works : 6 operas, an oratorio, a concerto for 4 clarinets and orch., pf. pieces, songs, &c.

SCHIN'DLER, Anton. Violinist ; "Beethoven's faithful friend and biographer;" *b.* Moravia, 1796 ; *d.* 1864. Capellmeister, German Opera, Vienna ; afterwards at the cathedrals of Münster and Aix-la-Chapelle. During the last 10 years of Beethoven's life Schindler lived in the same house, and served Beethoven with untiring devotion.
Works : a "Biography of Beethoven" (1840), "Beethoven in Paris" (1842).

SCHI'RA, Francesco. Singing teacher ; *b.* Malta, 1809 ; *d.* 1883. Settled in London, 1840 ; condr. Princess Th., 1842 ; Drury Lane, 1847 ; Covent Garden, 1848.
Works : abt. 10 operas ; cantata (*The Lord of Burleigh*, Birmingham Festival, 1873), songs.

SCHIR'MACHER, Dora. Pianist ; *b.* Liverpool, 1857. *Début*, Leipzig Gewandhaus, 1877.

SCHIR'MER, G. Noted New York music publishing house, founded 1848.

SCHIR'MER, Gustav. Founder of the New York music pub. house ; *b.* Saxony, 1829 ; *d.* 1893.

Schis'ma, Skhis'ma (*Gk.*). The small interval (1-50th of a semitone) between a true perfect 5th and an "equally-tempered" perfect 5th.

Schlacht (*G.*). Battle, fight.
Schlacht'gesang. A war song.
Schlacht'hymne. Battle hymn.
Schlacht'lied. Battle song.
Schlacht'ruf. War-cry ; war signal.
Schlacht'stück. Battle piece.

Schlag (*G.*). A blow, stroke, pulse, beat. (See **Nachschlag, Vorschlag.**)
Schla'ger. A " hit," a successful piece.
Schlag'feder. A plectrum.
Schlag'instrument. An inst. of percussion.
Schlag'manie'ren. The various kinds of drum strokes.
Schlag'zither. The ordinary plectrum zither.

Schlä'gel (*G.*). Hammer, mallet, drumstick.
Schlä'ger. A drummer.

SCHLÄ'GER, Hans. *B.* Upper Austria, 1820; *d.* 1885. Capellmeister Salzburg Cath. and director of the "Mozarteum," 1861.
Works : operas, symphonies, masses, &c.

SCHLECHT, Raimund. Priest ; Eichstadt, 1811-91.
Pub. numerous works for the Roman Service.

Schlecht (*G.*). Bad ; weak.
Schlech'ter Takt'eil. A weak beat.

Schlei'fen (*G.*). To slide, to glide ; to slur.
Schleif'bogen. A " Slide-bow;" a slur.
Schleif'note. A tied or slurred note.
Schleif'strich. A dash indicating *staccato,* &c.
Schleif'zeichen } A slur (⌒).
Schleif'ungszeichen }

Schlei'fer (*G.*). (1) A slide (*q.v.*). (2) A Ländler, or slow German waltz. (3) A slurred note. (4) A turn at the beginning of a shake.

SCHLEI'NITZ, Heinrich C. *B.* nr. Döbeln, Saxony, 1807 ; *d.* 1881. Lawyer ; friend of Mendelssohn ; succeeded him as Director Leipzig Cons., 1847 (8?).

Schlep'pend (*G.*). Dragging (the time).
Nicht schlep'pend. In strict time, not dragging.

SCHLE'SINGER. (1) Mus. pub. firm, Berlin ; founded, 1810, by Adolf M. Schlesinger.
(2) Mus. pub. firm, Paris ; founded 1834, by a son, Adolf M.

SCHLE'SINGER, Sebastian B. *B.* Hamburg, 1837. German Consul, Boston (Mass.), for 17 years.
Works : pf. pieces and numerous songs.

SCHLET'TERER, Hans M. *B.* Ansbach, 1824 ; *d.* 1893. Mus.-director, Zweibrücken, 1847-53 ; Heidelberg Univ., 1854-8. Afterwards capellmeister Augsburg Protestant Church. Founded the Augsburg School of Music.
Works : operettas, cantatas, 17 books of choruses *a cappella,* a "Chorgesangschule" for male voices, a vn. method, several works on German sacred and secular songs ; essays on Pergolesi, Rousseau, Spohr, &c.

Schlicht (*G.*). Smooth, simple, even.

SCHLICK, Arnold. Court organist to the Elector Palatine.
Pub. rare and early examples of organ and lute tablature (1511-12).

SCHLIM'BACH, Georg C. F. *B.* Thuringia, 1760.
Pub. an interesting work on organ building (1801).

SCHLÖS'SER, C. W. Adolf. Pianist ; son of L. (below) ; *b.* Darmstadt, 1830 ; *début,* 1847. Settled in London, 1854 ; Prof. R.A.M.
Works : a pf. quartet ; a suite ; pf. studies and solos.

SCHLÖS'SER, Louis. Darmstadt, 1800-86. Court capellmeister, Darmstadt.
Works : several operas ; ballets, symphonies, overtures, string quartets, pf. pieces, songs, &c.

SCHLOTT'MANN, Louis. Fine pianist ; *b.* Berlin, 1826. After successful tours, settled in Berlin as teacher.
Works : orchl. and chamber music ; pf. pieces.

Schlum'merlied (*G.*). A slumber song.

Schluss (*G.*). End, conclusion ; *finale.*
Schluss'chor. A final chorus.
Schluss'fall. A cadence.
Schluss'kadenz. Closing (final) cadence.
Schluss'note. The final note.
Schluss'reim. A burden or refrain.
Schluss'satz. Concluding movement.
Schluss'stück. A *finale.*
Schluss'striche. A double-bar.
Schluss'zeichen. (1) A double bar. (2) A hold (⌒).

Schlüs'sel (*G.*). "A key." In music, a *Clef.* (See **Bass-schlüssel, C-Schlüssel,** &c.)
Schlüs'selfiedel. A nail fiddle.
Schlüs'sel-G. The note—

Schmach'tend (*G.*). Languishing(ly).

SCHME'DES, Erik. Pianist and dramatic singer ; *b.* Copenhagen, 1868.

Schmei'chelnd (*G.*). Caressing(ly), flattering(ly), coaxing(ly).

Schmei'zend (*G.*). (1) Melodious, mellow. (2) Melting away ; *calando.* (3) Languishing.

Schmerz (*G.*). Grief, pain, sorrow.
Schmerz'haft } Painful, plaintive, sorrowful.
Schmerz'lich }
Schmerz'voll. Full of grief ; dolefully.

Schmett'ernd (*G.*). Ringing, clanging, brassy, shrill.

SCHMIDT, Bernhardt ("Father Smith"). (See **Smith.**)

SCHMIDT, Gustav. *B.* Weimar, 1816 ; *d.* 1882. Condr. Frankfort Th. ; afterwards Court capellmeister, Darmstadt.
Works : operas (*Prinz Eugen,* 1845, &c.) ; male choruses, songs, &c.

SCHMIDT, Hermann. Berlin, 1810-45 ; Court composer, &c.
Works : operettas, ballets ; orchestral and chamber music.

SCHMIDT, Johann P. S. *B.* Königsberg, 1779 ; *d.* 1853. Government official.
Works : abt. 10 operas ; several cantatas ; oratorios, masses, symphonies, chamber music, critical articles on music, pf. arrangements of classical works, &c.

SCHMITT, Aloys. Pianist and teacher ; *b.* Erlenbach, Bavaria, 1788 ; *d.* 1866. Lived chiefly in Frankfort from 1816.
Works : 3 operas, 2 oratorios, masses, orchestral pieces, and much instructive pf. music (a Method, studies, rhapsodies, rondos, sonatinas).

SCHMITT, Georg Aloys. Pianist ; son of A. ; *b.* Hanover, 1827 ; *d.* 1902. After concert tours, condr. at various German theatres ; Court condr., Schwerin, 1857-1892 ; director "Mozartverein," Dresden, 1893.
Works : operas (*Trilby,* 1845), orchl. pieces, string quartets, pf. music, songs, &c.

SCHMITT, Hans. Pianist ; *b.* Koben, Bohemia, 1835. Won the silver medal for pf. playing, and appointed teacher Vienna Cons., 1862.

Works : "300 studies without octave stretches," and other instructive pf. works ; a vocal method, songs, &c.

SCHMITT, Jacob (Jacques). Brother of Aloys ; *b.* Obernburg, Bavaria, 1796 ; *d.* 1853. Noted pf. teacher.

Wrote 370 pf. works ; his "Method," studies, sonatinas, and short pieces are useful.

SCHMITT, Nikolaus. Bassoonist ; *b.* Germany ; Chef de musique, French Guards, 1779.

Pub. 3 bassoon concertos, 3 bassoon quartets ; quartets, quintets, octets, &c., for wind insts.

Schna'bel (*G.*). " A beak." Mouthpiece of a clarinet, flageolet, or saxophone.

Schna'bel-flöte. A *flûte-à-bec* (*q.v.*).

SCHNA'BEL, Jos. Ignaz. *B.* Silesia, 1767 ; *d.* 1831. Capellmeister, Breslau Cath.

Works : much church music ; male quartets, military marches, songs, &c.

Schnarr (*G.*). Rattle ; harsh jarring sound ; humming, droning.

Schnarr'bass. A drone bass.
Schnarr're. A rattle.
Schnarr'laut } Harsh, or rattling sound.
Schnarr'ton }
Schnarr'pfeifen } Reed pipes, reed work, of an organ.
Schnarr'werk }
Schnarr'trommel. A side drum.

Schnar'ren (*G.*). (1) To rattle, &c. (2) To sing falsetto.

SCHNECK'ER, Peter A. Organist and teacher ; *b.* Hesse-Darmstadt, 1850. Settled in America ; *d.* New York, 1903.

Works : collections of organ pieces ; pf. pieces, songs, &c.

SCHNEE'VOIGT, Georg. 'Cellist ; *b.* Viborg, 1872.

SCHNEI'DER, Georg A. Horn player ; *b.* Darmstadt, 1770 ; *d.* 1839. Capellmeister Berlin Court Opera, and Musikmeister of the Guards' regiments.

Works : operettas, ballets, 2 oratorios ; masses, cantatas, orchl. music, chamber music, &c.

SCHNEI'DER, Johann. Famous organist ; *b.* nr. Coburg, 1702 ; *d.* Leipzig, abt. 1775. Orgt. Nikolaikirche from 1730.

SCHNEI'DER, Joh. C. Friedrich. *B.* Saxony, 1786 ; *d.* 1853. Orgt. Paulinerkirche, Leipzig, 1807 ; Thomaskirche, 1812. Court capellmeister, Dessau, 1821 ; organized the Liedertafel ; founded a School of Music, 1829.

Works : several oratorios (*The Deluge*, &c.), 14 masses, 25 cantatas, 7 operas, 23 symphonies, 7 concertos, 400 male choruses, 200 songs, &c.

SCHNEI'DER, Joh. Gottlob. Brother of preceding ; *b.* nr. Zittau, 1789 ; *d.* 1864. Court organist, Dresden, 1825 ; Mendelssohn reckoned him "the finest German organist of the time." He played in London, 1833.

Works : fugues, fantasias, preludes, &c., for org. ; songs.

SCHNEI'DER, Joh. Julius. Pianist and orgt. ; Berlin, 1805-85.

Works : 2 operas, 2 oratorios ; 200 male choruses ; organ pieces, pf. pieces, chamber music.

SCHNEI'DER, Theodor. 'Cellist and cond. ; son of J. C. F. ; *b.* Dessau, 1827. Cantor and music-director, Jakobi-kirche, Chemnitz, 1860-96.

SCHNEI'DER, Wilhelm. *B.* Neudorf, Saxony, 1783 ; *d.* 1843. Organist and music-director, Merseburg.

Pub. numerous collections of org. pieces (chorals, preludes, &c.), a "Lehrbuch" for the org., a "Grammar of Music," a work on the "History and Construction of Mus. Insts.," &c.

Schnei'dig (*G.*). Piercing, cutting, energetic.

Schnell (*G.*). Quick, rapid ; *presto.*

Mäs'sig schnell. Moderately quick.
Schnell und bewe'glich. Quick and with feeling (emotion).
Schnell und dräng'end. Quick and hurried.
Schnell und spiel'end. Quick and playful ; *allegro giocoso.*
Schnell und stürm'isch. Quick and stormy.
Schnell und zart. Quick and delicate.
Schnell'walzer. A quick waltz.
Schnell wie zuerst. As quick as at first ; *tempo primo.*

Schnel'ler (*G.*). Quicker.

Nach und nach schnel'ler. Gradually quicker and quicker.
Schnel'leres Tem'po. (In) quicker time.
Schnell'er werd'end. Becoming quicker.

Schnel'ler (*G.*) } An inverted mordent.
Schnel'zer (*G.*) } (See **Mordent.**)

Schnell'igkeit (*G.*). Quickness, speed.

Nun wie'der auf die Schnell'igkeit des ers'ten Tempo zugeh'end. Now returning again to the speed of the first *Tempo.*

SCHNIT'GER, Arp. Noted organ builder ; *b.* Oldenburg, 1648 ; *d.* abt. 1720.

SCHNORR von CA'ROLSFELD, Ludwig. Noted tenor ; *b.* Munich, 1836 ; *d.* 1865. Leading tenor, Dresden, from 1860.

Created the part of "Tristan" in Wagner's opera of that name, Munich, 1865.

SCHNORR von CA'ROLSFELD, Malwine (*née* **Garrigues**). Wife of preceding ; *b.* 1832 ; *d.* Carlsruhe, 1904. One of the foremost of Wagnerian singers.

Created the part of "Isolde," Munich, 1865.

Schnur'ren (*G.*). To hum, buzz, rattle.

SCHNY'DER von WAR'TENSEE, Xaver. Noted teacher ; *b.* Lucerne, 1786 ; *d.* 1868. Settled in Frankfort, 1817.

Works : a fairy opera, an oratorio, Swiss songs for male voices, 2 symphonies, a "System der Rhythmik," &c.

SCHO'BERLECHNER, Franz. Pianist ; *b.* Vienna, 1797 ; *d.* Berlin, 1843. Played in public at 10 ; toured in Italy, Germany, Russia, &c.

Works : 5 operas, chamber music, pf. pieces, &c.

**SCHO'BERT, Pianist ; *b.* Strasburg, 1720 ; *d.* 1768. Chamber musician to the Prince de Conti, 1760.

Works : sonatas for clavecin and vn. ; clavecin concertos, sonatas, trios, &c. ; symphonies for clavecin, vn. and 2 horns,

SCHOE'NEFELD, Henry. Pianist and condr.;
b. Milwaukee, Wis., 1857. Studied Leipzig and Weimar ; settled in Chicago.
Has published numerous pf. pieces.

SCHŒLCHER, Victor. Paris, 1804-93.
Published a "Life of Handel," 1857.

SCHOLTZ, Hermann. Pianist and teacher ;
b. Breslau, 1845. "Royal Saxon
Chamber-virtuoso," Dresden, 1880.
Works : numerous attractive pf. pieces.

SCHOLZ, Bernard E. *B.* Mayence, 1835.
Court capellmeister, Hanover Theatre,
1859-65 ; condr. Breslau Orch. Soc.,
1871-83 ; Director, Hoch Cons., Frankfort, 1883.
Works : operas (*Ingo*, 1898, &c.), orchl. works,
chamber music, a Requiem, a pf. concerto,
sonatas for pf. and vn., pf. pieces, songs, &c.

SCHOLZ, Rd. Composer ; *b.* Berlin, 1866.

Schön (*G.*). Beautiful, handsome ; lofty,
noble.

SCHÖN, Dr. Ed. (See **Engelsberg.**)

SCHÖN, Moritz. Violinist ; pupil of Spohr ;
b. Krönau, Moravia, 1808 ; *d.* 1885.
Theatre capellmeister, Breslau, 1835-
1841. Made extensive tours.
Wrote a "Violin School," "12 Lessons for Beginners," vn. duets, vn. solos, &c.

SCHÖN'BERGER, Benno. Distinguished
pianist ; *b.* Vienna, 1863. *Début* at 11 ;
has toured with great success in Russia,
Germany, Austria, Sweden, England,
and America.
Works : pf. pieces, numerous songs, &c.

SCHON'DORF, Johann. Condr. and composer ; *b.* Röbel, 1833.

SCHÖN'FELD, Hermann. *B.* Breslau, 1829.
Cantor St. Maria Magdalenakirche.
Works : org. music, school songs, cantatas,
orchestral pieces, &c.

School. (1) Style, method, system ; as
Spohr's Violin School, the Ecclesiastical School, the Palestrina School,
the Wagner School, &c. (2) A group of
composers belonging to a particular
place or period ; as the Neapolitan
School, the Neo-German School, &c.

SCHÖRG, Franz. Violinist ; pupil of
Ysaye ; *b.* Munich, 1871.

SCHOTT, Anton. Famous Wagnerian tenor;
b. Schloss Staufeneck, 1846. First
appearance in London, 1879.

SCHOTT, Bernard. Founded the well-
known firm of B. Schott, Mayence,
1773. *B.* abt. 1748 ; *d.* 1817.
The firm's publications number abt. 30,000.
There are branches in London, Paris, and
Brussels.

Schottische (*E.* and *F.*)) A "Scottish" round
Schot'tisch (*G.*)) dance in 2-4 time.
It is a variety of the *Polka*, and differs from an
Ecossaise, which is a country dance.

SCHRA'DIECK, Henry. Violinist ; *b.*
Hamburg, 1846. Pupil of Léonard and
David. Teacher Moscow Cons. 1864-8 ;
leader, Hamburg Phil. Concerts, 1868-
1874 ; Gewandhaus, Leipzig, 1874-82 ;
&c. Chief vn. prof. New York National

Cons. ; afterwards Broad Street Cons.,
Philadelphia.
Works : numerous excellent studies, &c., for vn.

Schräg (*G.*). Oblique, slanting.
Schrä'ge Bewe'gung. Oblique motion.

SCHRECK, Gustav. *B.* Zeulenroda, 1849.
Teacher of theory and composition,
Leipzig Cons., 1885.
Works : an oratorio (*Christus*), cantatas, an oboe
concerto ; motets and other church music.

Schreib'art (*G.*). Style ; manner of writing.
No'ten schreiben. To copy music.

Schrei'end (*G.*). Screaming, shrieking.
Schrei'er-pfeife. A very acute mixture stop.

Schritt'mässig (*G.*). Slow(ly) ; *andante.*

SCHRÖDER, Alwin. 'Cellist ; *b.* Neuhal-
densleben, 1855. After holding important posts in Germany, joined the
"Kneisel Quartet," Boston (U.S.), 1886 ;
1st 'cellist Boston Sym. Orch.

SCHRÖDER, Carl. 'Cellist ; brother of
preceding ; *b.* Quedlinburg, 1848. 1st
'cello, Sondershausen Court Orch. at
14 ; 1st 'cello Brunswick Court Orch.
1873 ; solo 'cellist Gewandhaus Orch.
and Prof. at the Cons., Leipzig, 1874.
Court capellmeister, Sondershausen,
1881 ; founded a Cons. there. Conducted opera at Amsterdam, Berlin,
and Hamburg ; finally settled at
Sondershausen as Court conductor, &c.
Works : operas (*Aspasia*, 1892, &c.) ; a concerto,
a "Method," études, &c., for 'cello.

SCHRÖDER, Hermann. Brother of pre-
ceding ; violinist ; *b.* Quedlinburg, 1843.
Teacher Royal Inst. for Church Music,
Berlin, 1885.

SCHRÖDER, Konrad G. F. *B.* Marien-
werder, W. Prussia, 1850.
Works : opera, *Du dröggst de Pann weg* (1897,
the 1st "Low German" opera), songs, &c.

SCHRÖDER (**Schroe'der**) - **DEVRIENT,
Wilhelmine.** Famous soprano ; *b.*
Hamburg, 1804 ; *d.* Coburg, 1860.
" Triumphantly successful " *début,*
Vienna, 1821, in Mozart's *Magic Flute.*
Finest performance, " Leonore," in
Beethoven's *Fidelio*, 1822. Perma-
nently engaged Court Opera, Dresden,
1823. Married Carl Devrient, 1823.
She created the parts of "Adriano Colonna" in
Wagner's *Rienzi*, "Senta" in *The Flying Dutch-
man*, and "Venus" in *Tannhäuser.*

SCHRÖDER-HANF'STANGEL. (See **Hanf-
stängel.**)

SCHRÖTER, Christoph G. Noted organist.
B. Hohenstein, Saxony, 1699 ; *d.* 1782.
Works : 7 sets of church cantatas for the entire
year ; 5 Passions ; symphonies, sonatas, org.
pieces, secular cantatas ; works on pf. construction, harmony, &c. A claimant for the
invention of the pf.

SCHRÖTER, Corona E. W. Distinguished
soprano ; *b.* Guben, 1751 ; *d.* 1802.
Début, Leipzig, at 14. Her brother,
Joh. S. Schröter (1750-88), pianist to the
Prince of Wales and music-master to
the Queen, pub. 15 pf. concertos, &c.

SCHRO'TER, Leonard. Noted contrapuntist ; *b.* Torgau, abt. 1540 ; *d.* (?).
Works : motets, 55 "Protestant Songs," &c.

Schub (*G.*). "A shove." The slide of the bow (vn. playing).

SCHU'BART, C. F. Daniel. *B.* Swabia, 1739 ; *d.* 1791.
Works : operettas, cantatas, pf. pieces, &c.

SCHU'BERT, Ferdinand. Brother of Franz (below) ; *b.* Lichtenthal, 1794 ; *d.* 1859.
Wrote church music, part-songs, 2 children's operas, &c.

SCHU'BERT, Franz Peter. Great composer; *b.* Lichtenthal, nr. Vienna, Jan. 31, 1797 ; *d.* Vienna, Nov. 19, 1828. Son of a schoolmaster, who taught him the violin ; Holzer, the choirmaster, taught him the piano, organ, singing, and thorough-bass. 1st treble in the church choir at the age of 9, when he began to compose songs and "little instrumental pieces." Singer, Vienna Court Choir, 1808 ; in the "Convict" (the choir training school), he was taught composition by Salieri. His "earliest extant song," *Hagars Klage*, is dated Mar. 30, 1811 ; his 1st symphony was composed in 1813. Left the "Convict," 1813 ; wrote his 1st mass, 1814. To escape military service, became a teacher in his father's school, 1814-16. During this period he perfected the German *Lied* : in 1815 he wrote 144 songs—8 of them in one day (Oct. 13). "His usual method of composition was to jot down the melody with a sketch of the harmony ; " he then elaborated and re-wrote the piece (occasionally 3 or 4 times) until he was satisfied with it. In 1816 he settled in Vienna : and though he had occasional strokes of good fortune, and secured the recognition of numerous musicians, the rest of his life was a "continual battle for the daily means of subsistence." "He was wretchedly underpaid by his publishers, and his greatest works were almost totally neglected." For a song or pf. piece he sometimes received only a "Gulden" (less than a shilling !). Though numerous efforts were made on his behalf, he "could never obtain a salaried position."

As a song composer Schubert stands unrivalled ; and many of his other works only fall short of the "very highest rank" on account of the inexhaustible fertility which often prevented him from cutting his compositions down to due form and proportion. He was "a stupendous genius ;....in his music at its best there is a haunting and unutterable loveliness, an exquisite blending of tenderness, sweetness, and purity, with strength, nobility, and grandeur, to which....there is perhaps no other equivalent in the works of all the other masters put together."—*H. A. Scott.*
"There never has been one like him, and there never will be another."—*Grove.*
The inscription on his tombstone—he died at the early age of 31—reads as follows : "Music has

entombed here a rich Treasure, but still fairer Hopes."
A complete edition of his works has been published by Breitkopf & Härtel, and chronicled in Nottebohm's "Thematic Catalogue."
They include 18 dramatic works (*Alfonso und Estrella, Fierabras, Rosamunde*, &c.) ; 7 masses, an oratorio (*The Song of Miriam*), and other church music ; cantatas and part-songs ; 603 known songs (many others probably lost), 10 symphonies (the " Unfinished," No. 8, and the " C major," No. 10, being only second to those of Beethoven), 7 overtures, a vn. concerto in D ; the celebrated " Octet " for strings, horn, bassoon, and clar. ; 2 quintets, 20 string quartets, 2 pf. trios, 2 string trios, pieces for pf. and vn. ; 20 sonatas, 4 impromptus, 6 Moments Musicals, marches, waltzes, fantasias, variations, &c., for pf. solo ; 2 sonatas, divertissements, fantasias, rondos, waltzes, marches, &c., for pf. 4-hands ; &c. A fine biography is given in Grove's Dict.

SCHU'BERT, Franz. Violinist ; Dresden, 1808-78. Entered Dresden Royal Orch. 1823 ; 1st concertmeister, 1861-73.
Wrote études, fantasias, &c., for violin.

SCHU'BERT, Joh. Friedrich. Violinist ; *b.* Rudolstadt, 1770 ; *d.* 1811. Mus.-director of various theatres.
Works : an opera, a vn. concerto, a "Neue Singschule," &c.

SCHU'BERT, Joseph. *B.* Bohemia, 1757 ; *d.* Dresden, 1812.
Works : operas, 15 masses, instrumental music.

SCHU'BERT, Louis. Violinist and singing teacher ; *b.* Dessau, 1828 ; *d.* 1884.
Works : 4 operettas, a vn. method, songs, &c.

SCHU'BERT, Maschinka (*née* **Schneider**). Operatic soprano ; *b.* Reval, 1815 ; *d.* 1882. *Début*, London, 1832. Member Dresden Opera till 1860. Her daughter, **Georgine** (*b.* Dresden, 1840 ; *d.* 1878), was also a noted operatic singer. Sang in London, 1875.

SCHU'BERTH, Carl. Fine 'cellist ; *b.* Magdeburg, 1811 ; *d.* 1863. After long tours, apptd. soloist to the Czar of Russia, and (for 20 years) mus. director St. Petersburg Cons.
Works : 2 concertos and other music for 'cello ; an octet and other chamber music.

SCHU'BERTH, Julius F. G. *B.* Magdeburg, 1804 ; *d.* 1875.
Founded the music pub. firm of " J. Schuberth & Co.," Hamburg, 1826. Leipzig branch, 1832 ; New York, 1850.

SCHU'BIGER, Anselm. "Learned writer on the Music of the Middle Ages." *B.* Uznach, St. Gallen, 1815 ; *d.* 1888.

SCHUCH, Ernst. Violinist ; *b.* Graz, 1847.

SCHUCH, Frau E. ("**Clementine Prochàska**"). Soprano ; *b.* Vienna, 1853.

SCHUCHT, Jean F. Writer and critic ; *b.* Thuringia, 1832; *d.* 1894. Pupil of Spohr.
Works : a "Music Lexicon," a "Groundwork of Practical Harmony," a "Life of Chopin," &c.

Schuch'tern (*G.*). Modest, shy, retiring.

SCHU'ECKER, Edmund. Celebrated harpist ; *b.* Vienna, abt. 1856.
Harp teacher, Leipzig Cons., 1884. Harpist in the Chicago Orch., 1891.

Schuh (*G.*). A shoe.
Schuh'platttanz. A clog dance.

Schu′le (*G.*).   School ; method.
  Schul′gerecht. In regular "school" form ; correct.
Schü′ler (*G.*).   Pupil.
  Used in the opposite sense to the English
  "scholar" (one versed in scholarship).
  Schü′lerhaft. "Pupil-like"; clumsy; the opposite of
  "scholarly."

SCHUL′HOFF, Julius. Pianist ; *b.* Prague,
  1825 ; *d.* 1898. *Début*, Dresden, 1842.
  After extensive tours, settled in Berlin.
  Wrote good *salon* pf. music, études, &c.

Schul′ter (*G.*).   Shoulder.
  Schul′tergeige. The ordinary ("shoulder") violin as
  opposed to the old *Viola da gamba* ("leg-viol").

SCHULTZ, Edwin.   Baritone singer ; *b.*
  Dantzig, 1827. Settled in Berlin as
  teacher and conductor. *D.* 1907.
  Works : male choruses, songs, pf. pieces &c.

SCHUL′TZE, Adolf. Pianist ; *b.* Schwerin,
  1853. Court condr. and director of the
  Cons., Sondershausen, 1886-90.
  Works : orchestral pieces, a pf. concerto, pf.
  solos, &c.

SCHUL′TZE, Wm. Heinrich.   *B.* Celle,
  Hanover, 1827 ; *d.* 1888.
  For several years 1st violin Mendelssohn Quin-
  tette Club, Boston (U.S.).

SCHULZ. (See **Prätorius.**)

SCHULZ, August.   Violinist ; *b.* Brunswick,
  1837.
  Works : favourite male quartets.

SCHULZ, Ferdinand.   Singing teacher ; *b.*
  nr. Krossen, 1821 ; *d.* 1897. Condr.
  Cäcilienverein, Berlin, 1856.
  Wrote church music, male choruses, songs, &c.

SCHULZ, Johann A. P.   Song composer ;
  b. Lüneberg, 1747 ; *d.* 1800. Capellmeister, Rheinsberg, 1780-7 ; Court
  condr., Copenhagen, 1787-94.
  Works : numerous fine sacred and secular songs ;
  several operas and operettas ; an oratorio, a
  Passion cantata (*Christi Tod*) ; pf. music,
  treatises and articles on music, &c.

SCHULZ, Joh. P. C.   *B.* Thuringia, 1773 ;
  d. 1827. Condr. Gewandhaus Concerts,
  Leipzig, from 1810.
  Works : overtures, marches, songs, &c.

SCHULZ-BEUTHEN, Heinrich. *B* Beuthen,
  Upper Silesia, 1838. Studied Leipzig
  Cons. ; teacher in Zurich, 1867 ; pf.
  teacher Dresden Cons., 1881.
  Works : operas ; 6 symphonies ; overtures,
  cantatas, a Requiem, psalms, male choruses,
  pf. pieces, songs, &c.

SCHULZ-SCHWERIN, Carl.   Pianist ; *b.*
  Schwerin, 1845. Pupil of von Bulow.
  Works : orchestral music, church music, pf.
  pieces, &c.

SCHUL′ZE, Adolf.   Bass singer ; *b.* Mann-
  hagen, 1835. Head prof. of singing
  Royal Hochschule, Berlin.

SCHU′MACHER, P. Paul H.   Mayence,
  1848-91. Studied Leipzig Cons. ; served
  in the Franco-German war ; settled in
  Mayence as teacher, condr., and critic ;
  founded the Mayence Cons., 1881.
  Works : male choruses, songs, pf. music, orch.
  pieces, a cantata, an opera, a vn. concerto, &c.

SCHU′MANN, Clara Josephine (*née* **Wieck**).
  Celebrated pianist ; *b.* Leipzig, 1819 ;
  d. 1896. Trained by her father,
  Friedrich Wieck, from her 5th year ;
  1st public performance, 1828. Toured
  from 1832. Married to Robt. Schumann (below), 1840. After her
  husband's death she resumed concert
  playing and teaching ; pf. teacher Hoch
  Cons., Frankfort, 1878-92. She was an
  "authoritative interpreter" of her
  husband's pf. works, and did much to
  make them famous.
  She edited the Breitkopf & Härtel edition of
  Schumann's works, and published a number
  of pf. pieces and songs.

SCHU′MANN, Geo. Alfred.   Pianist and
  condr. ; *b.* Königstein, 1866. Studied
  Leipzig Cons.
  Works : choral works, orchestral music, chamber
  music, pf. pieces, songs.

SCHU′MANN, Frau P. ("Schumann-Heink").
  (See **Schumann-Heink.**)

SCHU′MANN, Robert Alexander.   Great
  composer ; *b.* Zwickau, Saxony, June 8,
  1810 ; *d.* Endenich, nr. Bonn, July 29,
  1856. Son of a bookseller ; attempted
  little compositions at the age of 6 ;
  wrote choral and orch. works at 10.
  Studied Zwickau Gymnasium, 1820-3 ;
  matriculated Leipzig Univ. as a law
  student, 1828. Relinquished law and
  devoted himself to music, 1830, living
  in Leipzig with Friedrich Wieck, and
  studying the pf. under him. An attempt
  to obtain independence of the fingers
  "by suspending the 4th finger of the
  right hand in a sling while he practised
  with the others" led to permanent
  disablement of the hand, and "fortunately for music," he had to abandon
  playing and give himself up to composition and literary work. Founded the
  Neue Zeitschrift für Musik, 1834 ; edited
  it 1835-44, contributing a remarkable
  series of articles (pub. in English as
  "Music and Musicians"). Married Clara
  Wieck (see **Clara Schumann**, above),
  1840. Wrote his first symphony, 1841 ;
  Paradise and the Peri, 1843 ; teacher
  Leipzig Cons., 1843 ; settled in Dresden
  1844-50. Wrote his C major symphony,
  1846, and the opera *Genoveva*, 1848.
  Town mus.-director, Düsseldorf, 1850-3.
  Insanity, which had previously given
  signs of its approach, reached a climax
  in Feb. 1854, and he threw himself into
  the Rhine. He was rescued from
  drowning, and conveyed to an asylum
  at Endenich, where he died.
  Schumann ranks high among the Great Composers ; he was the chief exponent of the
  German "romantic" school, and his influence as
  composer and writer was far reaching and
  permanent. He greatly developed the expressive resources of the pf., he "added something peculiarly his own to the Lied ;"

"concentrated passion and profound emotion," "subtle shadings and artistic refinements," are the "characteristics of his lyrical genius." Yet he could rarely adequately express what was within him.

A complete edition of his works, edited by his devoted wife and helpmate, is published by Breitkopf & Härtel.

Works : (1) Vocal—opera, *Genoveva*; music to *Manfred* and *Faust*; cantata, *Paradise and the Peri*; *Adventlied, Abschiedslied, Nachtlied*; Requiem (*Mignon*); cantatas and ballades (*The Pilgrimage of the Rose, The King's Son, The Luck of Edenhall*, &c.); several unaccompanied choruses for male voices, female voices, and mixed choirs; numerous fine songs with pf. accompt.; duets, part-songs, &c. (2) Instrumental—4 symphonies (in B♭, C, E♭, and D minor); "Ouvertüre, Scherzo und Finale;" 4 concert overtures; pf. concerto (Op. 54), Concertstück for pf. and orch., Concertstück for 4 horns, 'cello concerto (Op. 129); &c. Pf. quintet in E♭ (Op. 44), 3 string quartets, pf. quartet in E♭, 3 pf. trios, 4 Phantasiestücke (for pf., vn., and 'cello), 2 sonatas for pf. and vn., 5 Stücke for pf. and 'cello, and other chamber music; 6 studies, sketches, 6 fugues on B-A-C-H, for org. or pedal-piano; also a large number of pf. pieces for 2 and 4 hands.

SCHU'MANN - HEINK, Ernestine (*née* **Roessler**). Operatic contralto; *b.* nr. Prague, 1861. *Début*, Dresden, 1878. Specially good in Wagnerian *rôles*.

SCHUND, Joachim. One of the earliest known organ builders.
Built the organ, St. Thomas's, Leipzig, 1356.

SCHUN'KE, Carl. Pianist; *b.* Magdeburg, 1801; *d.* 1839.
Wrote brilliant pf. transcriptions.

SCHUN'KE, Ludwig. Pianist; *b.* Cassel, 1810; *d.* 1834. Intimate friend of Schumann; assisted him in founding the *Neue Zeitschrift für Musik*.

SCHUPPAN'ZIGH, Ignaz. Violinist; Vienna 1776-1830. Member Prince Rasumovski's private quartet ("interpreting Beethoven's quartets under the master's eye"). After long tours, Director German Opera, Vienna, 1828.
Works : vn. solos, 9 variations for 2 violins, &c.

SCHURÉ, Edouard. Noted writer on German music; *b.* Strasburg, 1841.
Works : "A Hist. of German Folk-song," "The Musical Drama," &c.

SCHU'RIG, V. Julius W. *B.* Saxony, 1802; *d.* 1889.
Works : fantasias and preludes for organ, motets, choruses, children's songs, a collection of "Pearls of German Song," &c.

SCHU'STER, Joseph. Conductor and composer; Dresden, 1748-1812.
Works : 24 operas (*Doctor Murner, Das Laternenfest*, &c.); a cantata, *Das Lob der Musik* (his best work); also oratorios, a mass, pf. pieces, &c.

Schu'sterfleck (*G.*). "Cobbler's patch." A rosalia (*q.v.*).

SCHÜTT, Eduard. Pianist; *b.* St. Petersburg, 1856. Studied Leipzig Cons. Condr. Wagnerverein, Vienna.
Works : an opera, a pf. concerto, pf. pieces, songs, &c.

SCHÜTZ (or **Sagitta'rius**), **Heinrich.** Distinguished composer; *b.* Köstritz, Saxony, 1585; *d.* Dresden, 1672. Studied Venice (under G. Gabrieli), 1609-12. Capellmeister, Dresden, 1617-1633, and again from 1645. He composed the first German opera, *Dafne*, 1627; as a composer he stands " at the parting of the ways between Palestrina and Bach."
Of his numerous works *The 7 words of Christ on the Cross* and 4 settings of the *Passion* are among the most notable. A complete edition of his works in 16 vols. is published by Breitkopf & Härtel.

SCHUY'LER, Wm. Song composer; *b.* St. Louis (U.S.), 1855.

Schwach (*G.*). Weak, feeble; delicate; *piano.*
Schwächen. To die away; *calando.*
Schwäch'er. Softer and slower.
Schwäch'er Takt'teil. Weak beat.
Schwäch'er wer'dend. Softer by degrees.

SCHWALM, Oskar. Composer and critic; *b.* Erfurt, 1856.

SCHWALM, Robert. Bro. of O. *B.* Erfurt, 1845. Studied Leipzig Cons.; condr. at Königsberg.
Works : an opera (*Frauenlob*), male choruses, an oratorio, orchestral pieces, &c.

SCHWAN'BERG, Joh. G. *B.* Wolfenbüttel, 1740; *d.* 1804. Court capellmeister, Brunswick.
Works : 12 operas; cantatas, concertos, pf. sonatas, &c.

Schwank'end (*G.*). Faltering; wavering.

Schwarm (*G.*). A swarm, flock, crowd.
Schwär'mer. A group of (4 or more) rapidly repeated notes.

SCHWARZ, Andreas G. *B.* Leipzig, 1743; *d.* 1804. Fine bassoonist; played in London and Berlin. His son, **Christoph G.** (*b.* 1768), also a noted bassoonist, was for some time chamber musician to the Prince of Wales.

SCHWARZ, Max. Pianist; *b.* Hanover, 1856. Pupil of Bülow and Liszt. Director Raff Cons., Frankfort, 1885.

Schwe'bung (*G.*). "Waving." (1) A beat caused by two sounds not quite identical in pitch. (See **Acoustics.**) (2) A tremulant (*q.v.*).

SCHWE'DLER, O. Maxmilian. Fine flautist; *b.* Silesia, 1853. 1st flute Gewandhaus Orch., Leipzig. Invented the "Schwedler flute."
Author of "The Flute and Flute-players."

Schwe'gel (*G.*). (1) Any wind inst. (2) A pipe; specially an organ flue pipe.
Schwe'gelpfeife. An organ stop with slightly tapering flue pipes.

Schweif (*G.*). A tail; a coda.

Schwei'ge (*G.*). A rest.
Schwei'gezeichen. A sign for a rest (▀ ▪, &c.).

Schweigt (*G.*). Same as **Tacet** (*q.v.*)

Schweins'kopf (*G.*). "Pig's head." An old name for a grand pf. (when viewed from the side).

SCHWEI'TZER, Anton. B. Coburg, 1737 ;
d. 1787. Capellmeister at Gotha.
Wrote 20 Singspiele (song-plays), &c.

SCHWEI'ZER, Otto. Pianist ; b. Zurich,
1846.
Works : suites, morceaux populaires, studies,
&c., for pf.

Schwei'zer (G.). A Swiss.
Schwei'zerflöte. (1) A flageolet or fife. (2) An 8 ft.
organ stop of flute-like tone.
Schweiz'erpfeife. A 4 ft. stop of similar tone quality.
Schweiz'er-flötenbass. A 16 ft. pedal stop of the same
class.
Schwei'zerpfeiff was the earliest German name of
the *flauto traverso.*

Schwel'len (G.). To increase in loudness ;
to swell.

Schwel'ler (G.). The swell of an organ.

Schwell'ton (G.). Messa di voce (q.v.).

Schwell'werk (G.). The swell organ.

SCHWEN'CKE, Christian F. G. B. Wachen-
hausen, 1767 ; d. 1822. Succeeded
C. P. E. Bach as town cantor, Hamburg.
Works : 2 oratorios, many cantatas ; organ
fugues, vn. sonatas, pf. pieces.

SCHWEN'CKE, Friedrich G. Son of J. F.
(below) ; Hamburg, 1823-96. Orgt.
Nikolaikirche, Hamburg, 1852.
Works : organ fantasias, sacred songs, &c.

SCHWEN'CKE, Johann Fr. Son of C. F. G.
Hamburg, 1792-1852. Orgt. Nikolaikirche, 1829-52.
Works : several cantatas ; over 500 org. preludes
and postludes ; a harmonized collection of
1,000 chorals ; 73 Russian folk-songs, the
"Hamburg Choralbuch," pf. arrangements of
classical works, &c.

SCHWEN'CKE, Karl. Brother of preceding;
b. Hamburg, 1797 ; d. (?). Noted
pianist. Wrote pf. music, &c.

Schwer (G.). Heavy, ponderous ; difficult.
Schwer'müthig.
Schwer'müt(h)svoll. } Sad, melancholy, dejected.
Schwer und kräf'tig, nicht zu schnell. Ponderous and
powerful, not too quick.
Schwer und zurück'haltend. Heavy and *rallentando.*

Schwie'gel (G.). (See **Schwegel.**)

Schwin'dend (G.). Dying away ; *morendo.*

Schwing'en (G.). To swing.
Schwing'ungen. Vibration.

Schwung'voll (G.). With swing, passion,
and enthusiasm ; sublime.

SCHYT'TE, Ludwig T. Pianist, teacher, and
composer ; b. Aarhus, Denmark, 1850.
Works : operas (*Hero*, 1898, &c.) ; abt. 60 songs,
and over 100 works for pf. (Swedish songs and
dances, Charakterstücke, Pantomimes for 4
hands, &c.).

Scia'lumo (I.). Chalumeau (q.v.).

Scintillan'te (I. and F.). Sparkling, brilliant.

Sciol'ta,-o (I.). (1) Free. (2) Distinct,
separate.
Contrapun'to sciol'to. Free counterpoint.
Fu'ga sciol'ta. A free fugue. (See *Fugue.*)
No'te sciol'ti. Notes (quavers, &c.) standing alone ;
♪♪♪ as opposed to— ♫♫
Scioltamen'te.
Con scioltez'za. } Freely, easily ; with agility.

Scivolan'do (I.). Same as **Glissando** (q.v.).

Sco'lia. Ancient Greek festive songs.

SCONTRI'NO, Antonio. B. Trapani, 1851.
Prof. of counterpoint, Florence Cons.,
1897.
Works : a " Sinfonia marinaresca," and severa
operas (*Gringoire*, 1890 ; *La Cortigiana*, 1896)

Scoop. To reach after a (vocal) tone by a
"rough *portamento* from a lower tone"
instead of attacking it justly and firmly.

Scorda'to (I.). Out of tune ; discordant.
Scordatu'ra. (1) The unstringing of an inst. (2) The
special tuning of an inst. (vn., &c.), for some particular purpose (or piece).

Score. (G., *Partitur' ;* F., *Partition ;* I.,
Partitu'ra, Partizio'ne.) An arrangement of all the "parts" (voices, insts.,
&c.), of a composition placed systematically one above the other on
separate staves.
The name is probably derived from the practice
of "scoring" the bar-lines with the pen through
all the staves from top to bottom.
OPEN SCORE. A score with each part on a
separate staff :—

Soprano.
Alto.
Tenor.
Bass.

N.B.—When there is only one part on a staff the
stems of low notes are turned " up," and those
of high notes turned " down."
SHORT SCORE. A score with two (or more) parts
to each staff :—

Soprano.
Alto.
Tenor.
Bass.

N.B.—In a short (vocal) score the stems of Treble
and Tenor notes are turned " up," those of
Alto and Bass " down," to show each part
distinctly.
FULL SCORE. A score showing all the parts of a
vocal work, an orchestral work, or a work for
voices and instruments combined (as an
oratorio, opera, or cantata).
The score of a classical symphony is generally
arranged with the insts. in the following order,
reading from the top downwards :—
I.—*The Wood-wind :* 2 flutes, 2 oboes, 2 clarinets,
2 bassoons.
II.—*The Brass and Percussion Insts.,* 2 (or 4)
horns, 2 (or 3) trumpets, 3 trombones, 2 (or 3)
kettledrums.
III.—*The Strings* (called in German scores "*The
Quartett*"). When additional insts. are used
they fall into their place according to the above
groups ; thus the piccolo is placed above the
flutes, the contra-fagotto below the bassoons,
&c. Voice parts are generally placed between
the viola and the 'cello ; if there is an organ
(or pf.) part it is either below the double-bass
staff (at the bottom of the score) or immediately
above it. (See also *Orchestra.*)

The following is the arrangement of the full score of Mendelssohn's "Thanks be to God" (*Elijah*).

2 Flauti.	Violino I.
2 Oboi.	Violino II.
2 Clarinetti in B.	Viola.
2 Fagotti.	Soprano
2 Corni in Es.	Alto
2 Corni in B.	Tenore }Chorus.
2 Trombe in Es.	Basso
Trombone Alto.	Organo
Trombone Tenore.	Organo }2 staves.
Trombone Basso.	Violoncello e Basso
Ophicleide.	(on same staff).
Timpani in Es, B.	

Compressed Score. (1) An arrangement of the essential parts of a score on two staves (for organ, pf., &c.). (2) An abridged score, or sketch.

Organ Score. (1) An organ accompt. compressed from a full score (on 2 or 3 staves). (2) Any music for organ (on 2 or 3 staves).

Pianoforte Score. (1) A compressed full score to serve as an accompt. (2) Any music for pf. (Some modern pf. scores consist of 3 or even 4 staves).

Vocal Score. A score containing the complete voice parts (with the accompts. usually added in compressed score for org. or pf.).

Supplementary Score. A score containing extra parts for which there is no room on the pages of the full score, or which have been subsequently added.

Scoring. Same as **Orchestration** (*q.v.*).

Scorren'do (*I.*). *Glissando :* gliding from one sound into another.

Scorre'vole. Flowing, gliding ; smooth.

Scotch scale. (See **Pentatonic Scale.**)

Scotch snap. A rhythmic figure which occurs in many modern Scotch tunes (especially *Strathspeys*).

SCOTCH SYMPHONY. Mendelssohn ; 1st performed, 1842.

SCOTT, Cyril M. Composer ; *b.* Oxton, Cheshire, 1879. "The English counterpart to Debussy."

SCOTTI, Signor. Vocalist ; *b.* 1867 ; *début*, 1890.

SCOTT-GATTY. (See **Gatty.**)

Scottish Music.

Scotland is peculiarly rich in national music and folk-song owing to the zealous labours of Allan Ramsay, Robt. Burns, James Hogg, and other enthusiastic collectors. The following are among the best representative collections :—

(1) ORPHEUS CALEDONIUS, W. Thomson ; Folio, London, 1725. Reprinted, 2 vols. 8vo, 1733.

(2) THE SCOTS MUSICAL MUSEUM, Jas. Johnson Edinburgh ; 6 vols. 8vo, 1787-1803.

(3) GEO. THOMSON'S COLLECTION, with symphonies and accts. for pf., vn., and 'cello, by Pleyel, Kozeluch, Haydn, Beethoven, Hummel, Weber, and H. R. Bishop ; 6 vols. folio, Edinburgh, 1793-1841. Burns contributed upwards of 100 new songs to this collection.

(4) THE SCOTTISH MINSTREL, R. A. Smith, 6 vols. 8vo, Edinburgh, 1821-4.

(5) THE SONGS OF SCOTLAND, G. F. Graham ; 3 vols. 8vo, Edinburgh, 1848-9. Known as "Wood's Songs of Scotland."

(6) THE VOCAL MELODIES OF SCOTLAND, Finlay Dun and Jn. Thomson ; 4 vols. folio, Edinburgh, 1836-40.

Messrs. Paterson, Edinburgh, issue numerous excellent collections and editions of Scottish songs.

Scozze'se (*I.*). Scotch.

Al'la scozze'se. In Scotch style.

Scraper. An awkward fiddler.

SCRIA'BINE, Alexander. Pianist and composer ; *b.* Moscow, 1872.
Works : interesting pf. pieces.

SCRIBE, Eugène. French dramatist ; Paris, 1791-1861.
Wrote the libretti of over 100 operas ; including Auber's *Fra Diavolo, Le Domino Noir,* and *Crown Diamonds ;* Meyerbeer's *Robert, Huguenots, Prophète,* and *l'Africaine ;* Boieldieu's *La Dame Blanche ;* and Halévy's *La Juive.*

Scri'va (*I.*). Written.
Si scri'va. As written ; without embellishment.

Scroll. (*G., Schneck'e ; F., Volute ; I., Volu'ta.*) The curve in the head of a violin, &c.

Scuci'to (*I.*). Disconnected.

SCUDE'RI, Salvatore. Popular song composer ; *b.* Terranova, Italy, 1845.

Scuo'la (*I.*). A school ; a course of study.

Sde'gno (*I.*). Scorn, disdain, indignation, anger, wrath.

Con sdegno	
Sdegnan'te	
Sdegnosamen'te	}Disdainfully, indignantly, scornfully.
Sdegno'so	

Sdrucciola're (*I.*). To play *glissando* (*q.v.*) ; to slide, to glide.

Sdrucciolan'do	
Sdrucciolamen'to	}Gliding, sliding ; *glissando.*
Sdrucciola'to	

Se (*I.*). If, as. Same as **Si** (*q.v.*).
Se biso'gno. If required ; if necessary.
Se pia'ce. If you please ; at will.

Se (*pron. See*). The leading-note of the minor scale (in Sol-fa).

SEARS, Edmund H. D.D. 1810-76. American Unitarian minister.
Wrote the hymn "It came upon the midnight clear."

SEASONS, The. Haydn's last oratorio ; first performance, 1801.

SEBASTIA'NI, Johann. *B.* Weimar, 1622. Capellmeister, Königsberg, 1661.
Works : The 1st Passion containing chorals (*Das Leiden Jesu Christi,* 1672), sacred songs, &c.

ŠEBOR, Karl. *B.* Brandeis, Bohemia, 1843. Operatic conductor and bandmaster.
Works : Czech operas (*The Templars in Moravia, The Frustrated Wedding,* &c.) ; orchl. works, cantatas, chamber music, pf. pieces, songs, &c.

Sec, Sèche (*F.*) } "Dry ;" plain, unadorned,
Sec'co (*I.*) } simple ; short, *staccato.*
A table sec (*F.*). Without accompaniment.
Recitati'vo sec'co (*I.*). Unaccompanied recitative. (See *Recitative.*)

Seccara'ra (*I.*). A Neapolitan dance.

Sechs (*G.*). Six.
Sechsach'teltakt. Six-eight time.
Sechs'er } A theme, section, &c., of 6 bars.
Sechs'taktiger Satz }
Sechs'saitig. Six stringed (of insts.).
Sechs'stimmig. For six voices or insts.
Sechs'te. A sixth.
Sechs'theilig. For six parts (voices, &c.).
Sechsvier'teltakt. Six-four time.
Sechs'zehn. Sixteen.
Sechs'zehnfüssig. Of 16 ft. tone (org. pipes, &c.).
Sech'zehntheilnote } A semiquaver.
Sechs'zehntelnote }
Sechs'zehntelpau'se. A semiquaver rest.

SECH'TER, Simon. "One of the foremost teachers of counterpoint of the 19th cent." *B.* Bohemia, 1788 ; *d.* 1867. Prof. of harmony and counterpoint Vienna Cons. from 1851. Among his pupils were Bruckner, Vieuxtemps, and Thalberg.
Pub. works : many organ pieces, contrapuntal pf. pieces, an opera, songs, a treatise on "The Groundwork of Musical Composition" (3 vols.), a "General-bass-Schule," &c.

Second. (*G., Sekun'de ; F., Seconde ; I., Secon'da.*) The interval from one degree to the next ; a step.
Seconds are minor, major, or augmented. (See *Interval.*)
Chord of the Second. The last inversion of chord of the seventh ; figured $\frac{6}{4}$, $\frac{4}{2}$, or merely 2.

Second, Seconds. Old name for Alto (or Contralto).

Secondaire (*F.*). Secondary.
Temps secondaire. A weak beat.

Secondan'do (*I.*). Following, supporting.
Secondan'do il can'to } Same as *Colla voce (q.v.).*
Secondan'do la vo'ce }

Secondary Chords. Distinct chords on the 2nd part of a pulse.—*Curwen.*

Secondary Chords or Triads. Other than those of the Tonic, Dominant, and Subdominant of any key.

Seconde dessus (*F.*). Second soprano.

Seconde fois (*F.*). The 2nd time.

Second Inversion. A chord with its 5th in the Bass ; a 6-4 chord, or "c" position.

Secon'do,-a (*I.*). (*G., Zweit'-er,-e,-es.*) Second.
Secon'da don'na. The chief female singer after the *pri'ma don'na.*
Secon'da par'te. The 2nd part.
Secon'da vol'ta. The second time (after a repeat).
Secon'da vol'ta mol'to crescen'do. Much louder the second time of playing.
Violi'no secon'do. The second violin.

Sec'tio cano'nis (*L.*). An aliquot division of a monochord (to produce a required harmonic).

Section. (See **Rhythmical Form.**)

Secun'de (*G.*). Second.
Secund'akkord. A chord of the second. (See *Second.*)

Secun'dum ar'tem (*L.*). According to art or rule.

Sede'cima (*I.*). Interval of a 16th.

SE'DIE. (See **Delle Sedie.**)

SEDL'MAIR, Sofia O. Soprano ; *b.* Hanover, 1863.

See'le (*G.*). (1) Soul, feeling. (2) Soundpost (of a vn.).
Mit See'le. } With feeling, soul, &c.
See'lenvoll. }

See'len-amt (*G.*) } A requiem.
See'len-mes'se (*G.*) }

SEE'LING, Hans (Hanuš). Distinguished pianist ; Prague, 1828-62.
Works : many brilliant pf. pieces and études.

Seer. A bard or rhapsodist.

26

SE'GER(T), Joseph. *B.* Repin, Bohemia, 1716 ; *d.* 1782. Orgt. Kreuzherren-kirche, Prague.
Works : masses, psalms, 8 toccatas and fugues for organ, &c.,

SEGHERS, Francois J. B. Violinist ; *b.* Brussels, 1801 ; *d.* 1881. Founded the Société Ste.-Cécile, Paris, 1848.

Se'gno (*I.*). The sign $\math8$
Al se'gno (or *Al S.*). "To the sign." Go back to the place marked .$\math8$:
Dal se'gno (or *Dal S.,* or *D.S.*). "From the sign." Repeat from the place marked :$\math8$:
Dal se'gno al se'gno. From (the 1st) sign to (the 2nd) sign.
D.S. al Fi'ne. Repeat from the :$\math8$: to the point marked *Fine.*

Se'gno d'aspet'to (*I.*). A rest, a pause.

SEGOND, L. A. Paris physician.
Wrote important works on voice production, &c. (1846-59).

Se'gue (*I.*). (1) Follows, succeeds. (2) In a similar manner.
E poi se'gue la coda. And then follows the coda.
Se'gue la fina'le. The finale follows.
Se'gue il co'ro. The chorus follows.
Se'gue sen'za interruzio'ne. Go on without stopping.
Se'gue sen'za rit. Go on without retarding the time.
Se'gue su'bito sen'za cambia're il tem'po. Proceed directly without changing the *tempo.*

Seguen'do (*I.*) }
Seguen'te (*I.*) } Following, succeeding.
Attac'ca su'bito il seguen'te. Attack the following at once.

Seguen'za (*I.*). A sequence (*q.v.*).

Seguidil'la (*S.*). A Spanish dance in triple time, usually rather slow, accompanied by the voice and castanets (or guitar).

SEGUIN, A. Edward S. Fine bass singer ; *b.* London, 1809 ; *d.* New York, 1852.

Segui'te (*I.*). Plur. of **Se'gue** (*q.v.*).

Segui'to (*I.*). (1) Followed, imitated. (2) A suite.

Sehn'en (*G.*). To long for, to desire passionately.
Sehn'lich. Longing(ly), ardent(ly).
Sehn'sucht. Desire, longing ; ardour, fervour.
Sehn'süchtig. Longingly, passionately.

Sehr (*G.*). Very, much ; greatly.
Sehr allmäh'lich im'mer et'was lang'samer. Becoming very gradually slower.
Sehr anwach'send. Greatly increasing ; *crescendo molto.*
Sehr auf'geregt. Very excited(ly) ; very quick.
Sehr aus'drucksvoll. Very full of expression.
Sehr bestimmt'. Very decided.
Sehr bewe'gt. Much moved ; very lively.
Sehr breit und schwer. Very broad and weighty.
Sehr frisch. Very lively.
Sehr gebund'en. Very smooth.
Sehr gehalt'en aber nicht gebund'en. Very sustained, but not slurred.
Sehr gemä'ssigt. Very *moderato* ; rather slow.
Sehr geschwind'. Very fast.
Sehr in'nig. Very heartfelt.
Sehr kraf'tig. Very energetic(ally).
Sehr lang'sam. Very slow.
Sehr leb'haft. Very lively.
Sehr lei'se. Very softly.
Sehr marki(e)rt'. Much marked ; *Ben marcato.*
Sehr mäs'sig. Very *moderato* ; rather slow.
Sehr rasch und in sich hinein'. Essentially very quick ; *presto.*

Sehr schnell und noch mehr beschleun'igend. Very fast and becoming still faster.
Sehr weich und klang'voll. Very soft and full (resonant).
Sehr zart. Very soft and delicate.

Se'i (*I.*). Six.

SEI'DEL, Friedrich L. *B.* Brandenburg, 1765; *d.* 1831. Orgt. Marienkirche, Berlin; Court capellmeister, 1822.
Works: an oratorio, operas (*Jery und Bätely*, &c.), church music, pf. pieces, songs.

SEI'DEL, Joh. J. Breslau, 1810-56.
Wrote a "clear and concise handbook" on "The Organ."

SEIDL, Anton. Noted Wagnerian conductor; *b.* Pesth, 1850; *d.* New York, 1898. Studied Leipzig Cons.; chorusmaster, Vienna Opera, 1872. Assisted Wagner to prepare the score and parts of the *Ring*, and conducted a great "Wagner tournée," 1879-83. Conducted in London, 1897, &c.

SEIDL, Dr. Arthur. Critic and writer; *b.* Munich, 1863. Author of a "Biog. of Rd. Strauss," &c.

SEI'FERT, Uso. Organist; pupil of Merkel; *b.* Thuringia, 1852. Teacher Dresden Cons.
Works: a pf. method, pf. pieces and études, songs, &c.

SEIF'FERT, Dr. Max. Critic and historian; *b.* Beeskow, 1868.

SEI'LER, Madame Emilia. Teacher of singing, and writer; *b.* abt. 1822; *d.* Philadelphia, 1887.

SEISS, Isidor W. Pianist; *b.* Dresden, 1860. Pf. teacher Cologne Cons., 1871.
Works: pf. pieces (preludes, studies, clavierstücke, sonatinas, &c.).

Seit'enbewe'gung (*G.*). Oblique motion. (See **Motion.**)

Seit'ensatz (*G.*) A "side-piece." An episode, secondary subject, &c.

Seizième (*F.*). Sixteenth.
Seizième de soupir. A hemidemisemiquaver rest.

SÉJAN, Nicolas. Famous organist; Paris, 1745-1819.
Wrote vn. sonatas, pf. sonatas, pieces for org. and pf., &c.

Sekun'de (*G.*). (See **Secun'de.**)

Se'lah. A term often used in the Psalms.
Its exact meaning is not known, but it was probably an instrumental interlude; perhaps "a pause for the priests to blow the trumpets."

SELBY, B. Luard. *B.* 1853. Orgt. Salisbury Cath., 1881-3; Rochester Cath., 1900.
Works: operettas, cantatas, church music, pf. pieces, songs, &c.

SELIGMANN, Hippolyte P. 'Cellist; *b.* Paris, 1817; *d.* 1882.
Works: études, divertisements, &c., for 'cello and pf.; songs.

SEL'LE, Thomas. Noted contrapuntist; *b.* Saxony, 1559; *d.* Hamburg, 1663. Mus.-dir., 5 chief Hamburg churches.
Works: church concertos, sacred songs, secular songs, &c.

SELL'NER, Jos. Oboe player; *b.* Bavaria,

1787; *d.* 1843. Oboe teacher, Vienna Cons., from 1821.
His "Theoretical and Practical Oboe School" is a standard work; he also wrote oboe concertos, solos, &c.

SEL'MER, Johann. Noted composer; *b.* Christiania, 1844. Studied Paris and Leipzig.
Works: orchestral pieces, ballads for voices and orch., *a cappella* choruses, female choruses, pf. pieces, songs, &c.

SEM'BRICH, Marcella. (Real name **P. Marcelline Kochanska.**) Celebrated soprano; *b.* Wisnewczyk, Galicia, 1858. *Début,* Athens, 1877; 1st appearance in London, 1880.

SEM'ELE. Secular oratorio, Handel, 1743.

Sem'i (*L.* and *I.*) Half.

Semibiscro'ma (*I.*). A 32nd note ( ).

Sem'ibreve. (*L.*, *Semibre'vis.*) The half breve, or whole note (𝄎).
Sem'ibreve rest. A rest equal (1) to a semibreve; or (2) to a whole bar in any time.

Sem'ichorus. A small (selected) chorus.

Semicro'ma (*I.*)   } A semiquaver, or 16th note ( ).
Sem'icrome

Sem'idemisemiquaver. A 64th note ( )

Sem'i-diapa'son (*L.*). A diminished octave.
Sem'i-diapen'te (*L.*). A diminished fifth.
Sem'i-diates'saron (*L.*). A diminished fourth.
Sem'i-dito'nus (*L.*). A minor third.
Sem'i-dito'nus cum diapen'te (*L.*). A minor 7th.

Semifredon (*F.*)   } A semiquaver, or 16th note ( ).
Semifu'sa (*L.*)

Semi-grand. A small grand pianoforte.
Semimin'ima (*L.*). A half minim, or crotchet (♩).
Semipau'sa (*L.* and *I.*). A semibreve rest.
Semiquaver. A 16th note ( ).
Semiquaver rest. A 16th rest (𝄿).
Semi-se'rio (*I.*). Serio-comic. A serious opera with comic scenes.
Semi-suspir'ium (*L.*). A quaver rest (𝄾).

Sem'itone. (*G.*, *Halb'ton*; *F.*, *Demiton*; *I.*, *Semituo'no.*) A half-tone; the smallest interval on the pf., &c.
N.B.—Intervals much smaller than a semitone are employed in practical music (as in the *portamento* of the voice or vn., the *celeste* stops of an org., &c.), but there is no recognized notation for these minute intervals.
Chromatic semitone. A semitone between notes on the same degree of the staff, as C to C♯.
Diatonic semitone. A semitone between notes on different degrees of the staff, as C to D♭.
Semi-tonique (*F.*). Chromatic.
Semito'nium (*L.*). A semitone.
Semito'nium fictum (*L.*). A chromatic semitone.
Semito'nium mo'di (*L.*). The leading-note.
Semi-tril'lo (*I.*). An inverted mordent.
Semituo'no (*I.*). A semitone.

Semi-vowels. The "liquids," **l**, **m**, **n**, **r**.

Sempli'ce (*I.*). Simple, plain, unadorned.
Con semplicità   } Simply, unaffectedly.
Semplicemen'te
Semplicis'simo. With the utmost simplicity, &c.

Sem'pre (*I.*). Always, throughout, continually.
Sem'pre con gran dolcez'za e gra'zia. Always with great sweetness and grace.
Sem'pre con ped. Using the loud pedal continuously; *i.e.,* pressing it down at each chord, and releasing it only *at the end* of each chord.
Sem'pre con peda'le e con sordi'no. Always with both pf. pedals.
Sem'pre for'te. Always loud.

Sem'pre lega'to. Legato throughout.
Sem'pre pia'no e dol'ce. Always soft and sweet.
Sem'pre più affrettan'do il tem'po. Continually hastening the time.
Sem'pre più di fuo'co. Always with more spirit.
Sem'pre più for'te. Continually *crescendo.*
Sem'pre più for'te all' ffmo. Louder and louder to the part marked *ff.*
Sem'pre più pres'to. Continually quicker.
Sem'pre pp e sen'za sordi'ni. Always *pp* and *sem'pre con ped.* (See above.)
Sem'pre rinforzan'do. Always emphasizing (the phrases).
Sem'pre ritardan'do. Continually slower.

SENESI'NO, Francesco Bernardi detto· Famous male mezzo-soprano ; *b.* Sienna abt. 1680 ; *d.* abt. 1750. Sang, London, for Bononcini, 1720 ; and in many of Handel's works from 1721 **to** 1733.

His voice was limited in compass, but according to many judges was superior in quality even to that of Farinelli.

SENFF, Bartholf. *B.* nr Coburg, 1815 ; *d.* 1900. Founded the Senff music publishing house, Leipzig, 1850.

SENFL (SENFFL, or SENFEL), Ludwig· Noted contrapuntist ; *b.* Basel-Augst, 1492 ; *d.* abt. 1555. Court conductor Munich.

Works : motets, salutations, settings of Horace's Odes, &c.

SEN'KRAH, Arma (Mad. Hoffman ; *née* **A. L. Harknes).** Violinist ; *b.* New York, 1864 ; suicide, Weimar, 1900.

Sen'net, Sig'net ⎫ (1) A trumpet flourish.
Sy'net, Syn'net ⎬ (2) "The sounding of a note seven times" in old plays, &c.

Sensi'bile (*I.*). Expressive, sensitive ; perceptible.
No'ta sensi'bile (I.) ⎫ The leading-note.
Note sensible (F.) ⎬
Sensibilità (I.). Feeling, sensibility.
Sensibilmen'te (I.). Expressively, feelingly, perceptibly.

Sensible (*F.*). (1) Sensitive, expressive. (2) The leading note.

Sentence. (1) A short anthem (or vocal interlude), as "Offertory Sentence," &c. (2) (See **Metrical Form.**)

Sentie (*F.*). Felt, expressed ; marked.
Mélodie bien sentie. The melody (to be) well accented.

Sentimen'to (*I.*). Sentiment, feeling.
Con sentimen'to ⎫ With feeling, &c.
Sentimenta'le ⎬

Senti'to (*I.*). " Felt ; " with (special) emphasis and expression.

Sen'za (*I.*). Without. Abbreviation *S.*
Sen'za accompagnamen'to. Without accompaniment.
Sen'za bas'si. Without the basses.
Sen'za battu'ta. "Without the beat." Not in strict time.
Sen'za fio'ri. Without ornaments ; as written.
Sen'za interruzio'ne. Go straight on (without interruption, or break).
Sen'za misu'ra. "Without measure ; " not in strict time.
Sen'za or'gano. Without organ.
Sen'za passio'ne, ma espressi'vo. Without passion, but with expression.
Sen'za piat'ti. Without cymbals ; *i.e.,* "drums alone" when the same performer plays drum and cymbals.
Sen'za peda'le. Without the pedals.
Sen'za repetizio'ne ⎫ Without repetition.
Sen'za re'plica ⎬

Sen'za rigo're. Not in rigorous or strict time.
Sen'za (di) ritarda're. Without retarding the time.
Sen'za sordi'ni. Without dampers (or mutes). In pf. playing, press down the right (loud) pedal at each change of chord, and keep it down until the next chord.
Sen'za sordi'no ⎫ "Take off the mute (mutes)" in
Sen'za sordi'ni ⎬ vn. playing.
Sen'za tem'po. Without (strict) time ; *ad lib.*

Separation. An old term for a passing-note between two notes forming a third.

Se pia'ce (*I.*). At pleasure.

Sep'tain. A section of 7 measures.—*Curwen.*

Septade'cima (*L.*) ⎫ A 17th.
Septde'zime (*G.*). ⎬

Sept'akkord (*G.*) ⎫ Chord of the 7th.
Sept-chord ⎬

Sep'tave. A scale of 7 notes (as from C to B).

Septet' (*E.*) ⎫ A composition for 7 voices
Septett' (*G.*) ⎬ or insts. The instru-
Septet'to (*I.*) ⎬ mental septet belongs to
Septuor (*F.*) ⎭ the domain of " chamber music," and is generally written in the form of a sonata (*q.v.*).

Septième (*F.*) ⎫ Interval of a 7th.
Sep'time (*G.*) ⎬
Septième diminuée (F.). Diminished 7th.
Sep'timenakkord (G.). A chord of the 7th.

Septimo'le (*G.*) ⎫ A group of 7 equal notes to
Septio'le ⎬ be played in the time
Septo'le (*G.*) ⎬ regularly allotted to 4
Sep'tuplet ⎭ or 6 :—

Septuor (*F.*). (See **Septet.**)

Sequence. (*L., Seguen'tia ; G., Sequenz'; F., Sequence ; I., Seguen'za ; from L. Sequor,* " I follow.") In general, any orderly progression or succession of notes or chords.

(1) In the Roman Catholic church, a kind **of** hymn founded on the jubilation of **the** Alleluia following the epistle. (Also called *Pro'sa* or *Prose.*)

This kind of sequence originated in the 9th century. The 5 sequences now used are *Lauda Sion, Stabat Mater, Dies Iræ, Victimi Paschali,* and *Veni Sancte Spiritus.*

(2) The repetition (*at least* 3 *times*) of a fragment of melody or harmony by regularly ascending or descending intervals.

The germ, or "motive" of the sequence may consist of any number of notes from 2 upwards.

Ascending Sequence.

Motive.

Descending Sequence.
Motive.   PINSUTI.

&c.

HARMONIC SEQUENCE. A sequence in each part of the harmony. A *melodic sequence* is limited to the chief melody.

MOZART.   *Sonata in A min.*

Descending Harmonic Sequence.

&c.

TONAL AND REAL SEQUENCES. A *Tonal* sequence is confined to the key in which it commences, the imitations being "not strict" as to interval. In a *Real* sequence, every interval and chord of the "motive" is exactly imitated. Thus real sequences lead to constant change of key :—

Real Sequences.

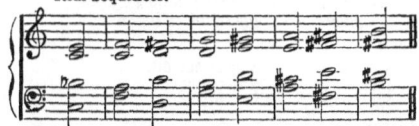

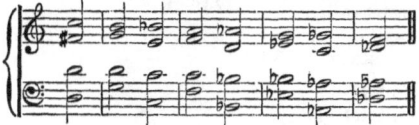

MIXED SEQUENCE. A sequence partly real and partly tonal (to avoid wandering too far into extraneous keys.)

BEETHOVEN. Sonata, Op. 106.

&c.

SEMITONIC SEQUENCE. A favourite device of modern composers in which each repetition is a semitone higher or lower.

Motive.

&c.

(See also *Sequence of Sevenths, Chromatic.*)

N.B.—A *Rosalia* (*q.v.*), may perhaps be defined as "a sequence based on an extended motive."

Sequence of Sevenths. A series of chords of the 7th in succession.

(*a*) Diatonic.

&c.

7   7   7   7   7   7   7   7

(*b*) Chromatic.

&c.

A similar sequence of chromatic 7ths may be used in ascending.

Sequence of Sixths, Thirds, &c. A succession of sixths, thirds, &c.

SERAFI'NO, Santo. Celebrated vn. maker ; Venice, 1730-45.

His nephew GREGORIO was also a noted vn. maker.

SERA'GLIO, Il. Opera by Mozart. (*G., Entführung aus dem Serail.*)

Ser'aphine. A precursor of the harmonium.

SERAS'SI. Family of Italian organ builders at Bergamo.

  (1) **Giuseppe** (the elder), 1694-1760.

  (2) **Andreas L.,** 1725-1799 ; built the Cath. organs at Crema, Parma, &c.

  (3) **Giuseppe** (the younger), 1750-1817. Built many fine insts., and pub. valuable works on organ construction.

Serba'no (*I.*). The serpent (*q.v.*).

Sere'na (*I.*). "Evening." An evening song of the troubadours.

Serenade (*E.*)
Sérénade (*F.*)
Serena'ta (*I.*)
Serena'de (*G.*)
Ständ'chen (*G.*)
"Evening music." (1) An open air concert of a quiet character performed "under the window of the person addressed." (2) An instrumental piece of similar character. (3) A pastoral cantata. (Handel's *Acis and Galatea* is a *Serenata*.) (4) A piece of chamber music in several movements ; a kind of *Suite*.

"Ständchen" is only used with meanings (1) and (2).

Serenatel'la (*I.*). A little serenade.

Sere'no (*I.*). Serene, calm, tranquil.
Con serenità. Calmly ; with serenity.

Se'ria (*I.*). Serious, tragic ; grave.
O'pera se'ria. A serious or tragic opera.
Con serietà. Seriously, gravely.

Se'rieux (*F.*)
Se'rieuse (*F.*)
Serious, grave.
Sérieusement. Seriously, gravely.

Serinette (*F.*). A small "bird organ," used in teaching birds to sing.

SE'RING, Friedh. W. *B.* nr. Frankfort-on-Oder, 1822 ; *d.* 1901. Head teacher, Strasburg Seminary, 1871.
Works : an oratorio, cantatas, male choruses, a vn. method, &c.

Se'rio,-a (*I.*). Serious, grave ; thoughtful.
Seriosamen'te
Serio'so
In a thoughtful, serious manner.

Serio-comic. "Combining the grave with the ridiculous."

SE'ROV (SJE'ROFF), Alexander N. Distinguished Russian dramatic composer (ranking "next to Glinka in popular estimation") ; St. Petersburg, 1820-71. Also a noted critic, and "an adherent of Wagner."
Chief operas : *Judith* (1863), *Rogneda* (1865), and *Wrazyia siela.*

Serpeggian'do (*I.*). Silently creeping onwards ; insinuatingly.

Serpent (*E.*)
Serpen'te (*I.*)
Serpento'no (*I.*)
An obsolete bass inst. with a cup mouthpiece, made of wood and leather, and curved like a serpent.
It gradually gave place to the *Serpentcleide* and *Ophicleide* (both of which are also now practically obsolete).

SERPETTE, H. C. A. Gaston. Operatic composer ; *b.* Nantes, 1846 ; *d.* 1904. *Grand Prix de Rome*, Paris Cons., 1871.
His numerous popular light operas include *Cendrillonette* (1890), *La dot de Brigitte* (1895), and *Le Carillon* (1896).

Serran'do (*I.*)
En serrant (*F.*)
Becoming faster.

SERRA'NO, Emilio. Pianist and composer ; *b.* Vittoria, Spain, 1850.

SERRA'O, Paolo. *B.* Filadelfia, Catanzaro, 1830 ; *d.* 1907. Studied Naples Cons. ; Prof. of composition, 1863.
Works : operas (*Pergolesi, La Duchessa di Guisa*, &c.) ; an oratorio, a Requiem, church music, pf. pieces, &c.

Serra'ta (*I.*). A concluding piece ; a *finale.*

Serra'to (*I.*)
Serré (*F.*)
Becoming faster.

Serrez (*F.*) Press on ; *accelerando.*
Serrez peu à peu le mouvement. Gradually quicken.

SERVAIS, Adrien François. Celebrated 'cellist ; *b.* Hal, nr. Brussels, 1807 ; *d.* 1866. *Début* as concert player, Paris, 1834. Professor Brussels Cons., 1848.
Works : concertos, études, &c., for 'cello.

SERVAIS, Joseph. 'Cellist ; son of A. F. ; *b.* Hal, 1850 ; *d.* 1885.

Service. Specially, a complete musical setting of the Canticles, &c., sung by the choir in an Anglican church service (morning or evening or both.)

Ses'qui (*L.*). (1) "One and a half." (2) Of intervals, the ratio of $x + 1$ to x (where x stands for the vibration number of the lower note).
Sesquial'tera. (1) A fifth ; ratio 3 to 2. (2) An organ mixture stop in which the 5th (or 12th) predominates. (Originally a 12th and 17th ; but now more usually a 17th, 19th, and 22nd.)
Sesquino'na. The minor tone ; ratio 10 : 9.
Sesquiocta'va. The major tone ; ratio 9 : 8.
Sesquiquar'ta. The major 3rd ; ratio 5 : 4.
Sesquiquin'ta. The minor 3rd ; ratio 6 : 5.
Sesquiter'tia. Perfect 4th ; ratio 4 : 3.
Ses'quitone. An interval of 1½ tones.

Ses'to,-a (*I.*). A sixth.
Ses'ta ecceden'te. Augmented 6th.
Ses'ta maggio're. Major 6th.
Ses'ta mino're. Minor 6th.

Sestet' (*E.*)
Sestet'to (*I.*)
A sextet (*q.v.*).

Sesti'na (*I.*). (1) A sextuplet (*q.v.*). (2) A stanza of 6 lines.

Ses'tole
Ses'tolet
A sextuplet (*q.v.*).

SE'THE, Irma. Violinist ; *b.* Brussels, 1876. Pupil of Wilhelmj and Ysäye. *Début*, London, 1895 ; Belgium, 1898. Married Dr. Sänger, Berlin, 1897.

Set'te (*I.*). Seven.
Set'timo,-a. The interval of a 7th.
Set'tima diminui'ta. Diminished 7th.
Settimi'no. A piece for 7 performers.

Setz'en (*G.*). To compose.
Setz'art. Style of composition.
Setz'kunst. Art of composition.

Seuf'zend (*G.*). Moaning, sighing.

Seul,-e (*F.*). Solo ; alone ; for a single performer.

Les Iers seulement. The 1st (violins) only.

Pas seul. A solo dance.

SĚV'CIK, Otakar J. Violinist and noted teacher ; *b.* Bohemia, 1852. Vn. prof. Prague Cons., 1892. Teacher of Kubelik and Marie Hall.

Several instructive books on violin technique, studies, dances, &c.

Seventeenth. The interval of 2 octaves and a third.

Seventh. (*G., Sep'time ; F., Septième ; I., Set'tima.*) An interval comprising 7 letter-names (or 7 degrees of the staff).

Chord of the 7th. A triad with a 7th added ; as— d m s t ; s₁ t₁ r f ; &c.
Diminished 7th. (See *Diminished.*)
Dominant 7th. (See *Dominant.*)
Leading 7th. Name sometimes given to the Leading-note 7th (in a major key) ; t, r, f, l.

Seve'ro (*I.*). Severe, strict, exact.

Con severità) Strictly, exactly ; with rigid obser-
Severamen'te) vance of *tempo*, &c.

SEWARD, Theodore F. Composer ; *b.* Florida (U.S.), 1835 ; *d.* 1902.

Sexquialtera. Same as **Sesquialtera.**

Sext, Sex'te (*G.*)) (1) A sixth (interval, &c.).
Sex'ta (*L.*)) (2) An org. mixture stop— 12th and 17th.

Sext'akkord (*G.*). A Chord of the 6th ; a 1st inversion of a triad.

Sex'tain. A section of 6 measures.—*Curwen.*

Sex'tenfolgen (*G.*). A sequence of 6ths.

Sextet. (*G., Sextett' ; F., Sextuor ; I., Sestet'to.*) A piece for 6 voices or insts.

The instrumental sextet is generally in sonata form. (See *Sonata.*)

Sex'tole, Sex'tolet) (1) A group of 6 equal
Sex'tuplet) notes to be performed in the time regularly allotted to 4 of the same kind :—

The accents are on the 1st, 3rd, and 5th notes.

(2) A double triplet —

Accents on the 1st and 4th ; also called a " false sextuplet."

Sextuor (*F.*). A sextet (*q.v.*).

Sex'tuple measure. Compound duple time ; 6-4, 6-8, &c.

Sex'tus (*L.*). A 6th part (or voice).

SEY'DEL, Oscar. Pen-name of **W. M. Hutchison** (*q.v.*).

SEY'DELMANN, Franz. Dresden, 1748-1806. Capellmeister, Dresden, 1787.

Works : operas (*Die Schöne Arsene*) ; masses, psalms, offertories, cantatas, pf. sonatas, fl, sonatas, vn. sonatas, songs, &c.

SEY'FFARTH, Ernest H. *B.* Krefeld, 1859. Condr. Neuer Singverein, Stuttgart, 1892.

Works : dramatic scene, *Thusnelda* ; orch. pieces, cantatas, pf. pieces, songs, &c.

SEY'FRIED, Ignaz X., Ritter **von.** Vienna, 1776-1841. Pf. pupil of Mozart. "Prolific, but not original, composer."

Works : numerous operas, symphonies, oratorios, masses, quartets, pf. pieces, &c. ; edited a "Complete edition of Albrechtsberger's Theoretical Works."

SEY'GARD, Camille. Soprano ; *b.* London, abt. 1868(?). *Début*, Covent Garden, 1888.

sf. Abbreviation of *Sforzando* or *Sforzato*.

sfp, or **fzp.** Suddenly loud, then soft ; *sforzando piano. sfpp, fzpp* are also used.

Sfoga'to (*I.*). " Exhaled ; " lightly sung (or played).

Soprano sfoga'to. A high light soprano.

Sfoggian'do (*I.*). Extravagant, pompous.

Sfor'za (*I.*). Force ; special emphasis.

Sforzan'do) " Forced ; " strongly accented ; marked.
Sforza'to) *sf, fz, ffz,* &c. (See *Rinforzando.*)
Sforzando piano. (See *sfp.*)
Sforza'r(e) la vo'ce. To force (overstrain) the voice.
Sforzatamen'te. With force ; energetically.

Sfor'zo (*I.*). Force, strain (of the voice, &c.).

Sfuggi'to,-a (*I.*). Avoided ; interrupted.

Caden'za sfuggi'ta. An avoided (or interrupted) cadence.

Sfuma'to (*I.*). Very lightly ; " like a vanishing smoke-wreath."

Sfumatu'ra. " A smoke-wreath ; " a light delicate piece.

Sgallinaccia're (*I.*). "To sing like a rooster." (*Gallinac'cio,* a turkey-cock.)

SGAMBA'TI, Giovanni. Distinguished pianist and conductor ; *b.* Rome, 1843. Played in public at 6 ; finished his pf. education under Liszt. After long tours apptd. head pf. teacher, Music School, Academy of St. Cecilia, Rome, 1877. Founded the "Nuova Società Musicale Romana," 1896. He is "an ardent admirer " and follower of Wagner.

Works : symphonies, overtures, a pf. concerto, an octet and other chamber music, a Requiem, numerous pf. pieces and études, &c.

Sgamba'to (*I.*). Tired, wearied(ly).

Sgriscia're (*I.*). To "quack" (on reed insts.).

Shade. Expression.

Shake, or **Trill.** (*G., Tril'ler ; F., Trille, Tremblement, Cadence ; I., Tril'lo.*) The rapid alternation of a principal note with an "auxiliary" a tone or semitone higher ; it usually ends with a turn (*q.v.*).

PLAIN (or UNPREPARED) SHAKE, commencing either with the auxiliary or principal note, at discretion.

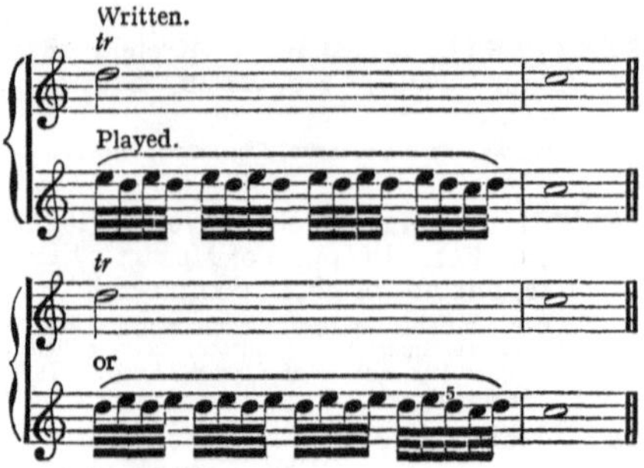

Written.
tr
Played.
tr
or
5

DOUBLE SHAKE.

Written.
tr
tr
Played.

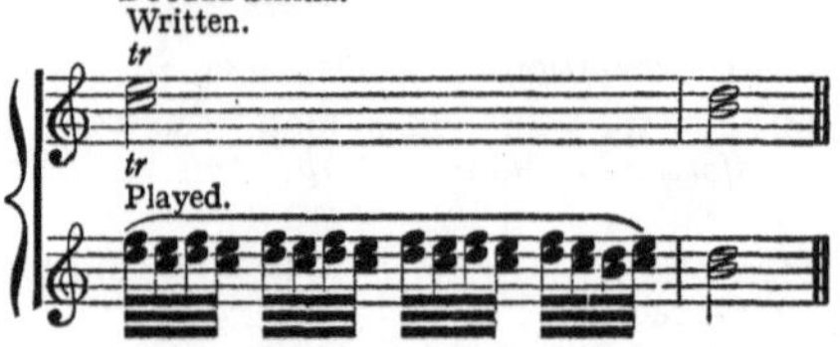

PREPARED SHAKE ; GRACED SHAKE.

Written.
tr (The initial turn is called a *Schleifer.*)
Played.
tr

tr

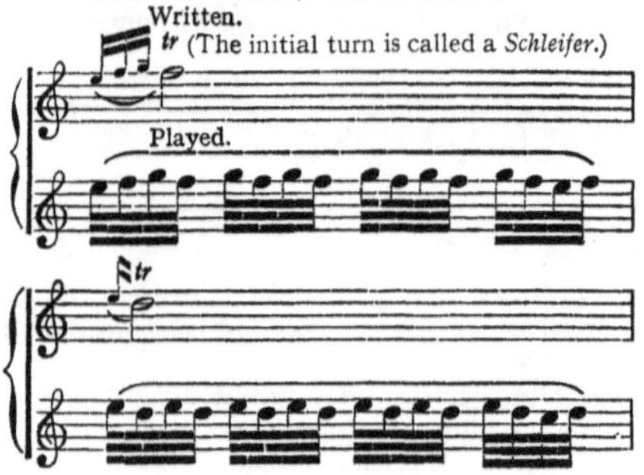

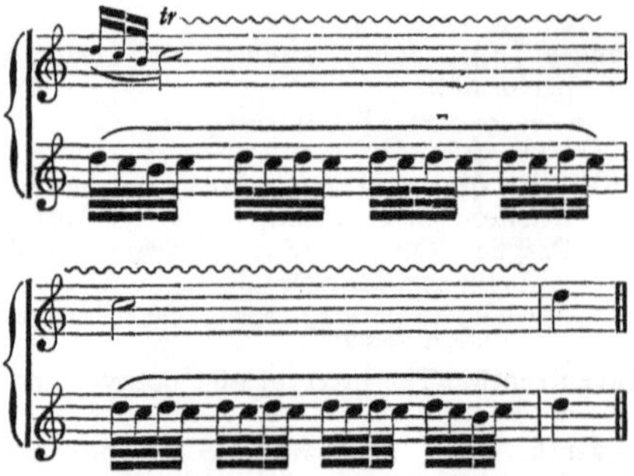

Modern composers generally indicate carefully how their shakes should begin and end. The intervening notes should be played as rapidly as possible, but there is no absolute rule as to the number of alternations. A shake or trill on a short note, especially in quick *tempo*, becomes merely an inverted mordent, or a turn. (See *Mordent* and *Turn.*)

The following illustrations (from Beethoven and Chopin) are worthy of attention:—

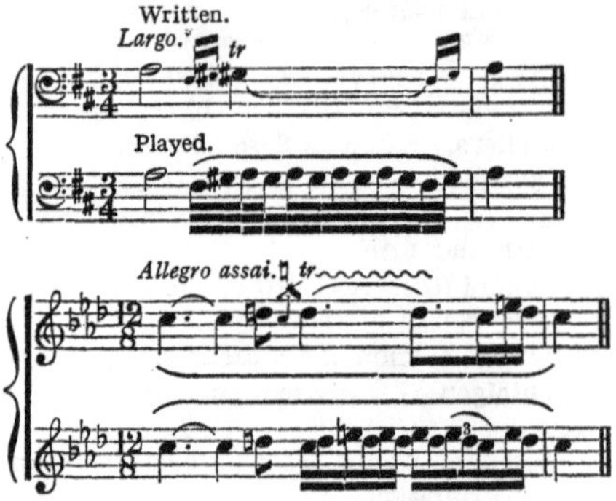

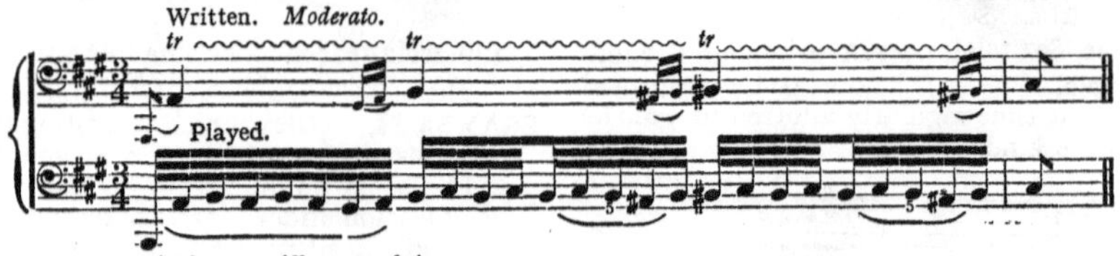

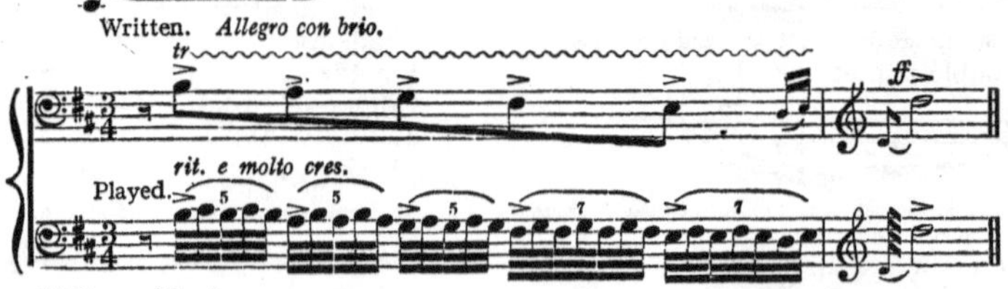

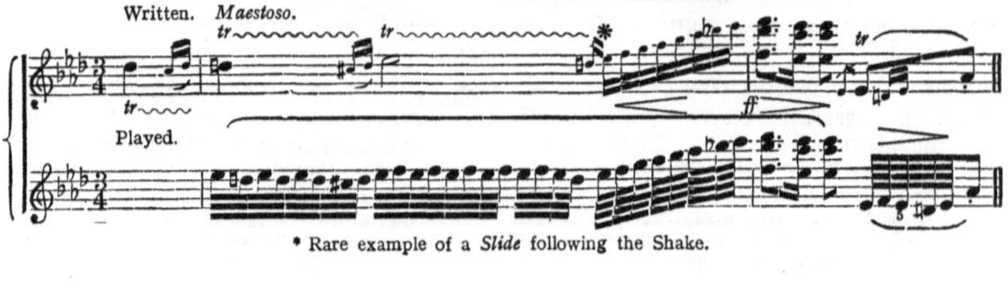

Written.
Largo.
tr
Played.
Allegro assai.
tr
3

Written. *Moderato.*
tr
tr
tr
Played.
5
5

Written. *Allegro con brio.*
tr
ff
rit. e molto cres.
Played.
5
5
5
7
7

Written. *Maestoso.*
tr
tr
*
tr
tr
ff
Played.
3

* Rare example of a *Slide* following the Shake.

The *Ribattu'ta*, a beautiful form of shake, commencing slowly and gradually accelerating, is employed by vocal and instrumental soloists in a cadenza, especially when the shaked note is marked with a pause :—

When it is very difficult to play a trill exactly as indicated (for the pf.), the *False Trill* may be employed :—

BEETHOVEN.

Major shake. A shake with the major 2nd above.
Minor shake. A shake with the minor 2nd above.
Close shake. Vibrato (*q.v.*).

SHAKESPEARE, William. 1564-1616.
The great dramatist mentions the word "music" 140 times in his plays, &c. Many of his references to its power and influence are unequalled in literature.

SHAKESPEARE, William. Tenor singer and vocal teacher ; *b.* Croydon, 1849. Won King's Scholarship, R.A.M., 1866 ; Mendelssohn scholar, 1871. Prof. of singing, R.A.M., 1878.

SHALIAPIN, Fedor I. Noted Russian bass; *b.* Kazan, 1873.

Shalm. Same as **Shawm** (*q.v.*).

Shank. Lengthening tube for a brass inst.

SHARMAN, Percy V. Violinist ; *b.* Norwood, 1870. Scholar, R.C.M. ; also studied under Joachim, Berlin. *Début*, 1887.

Sharp. (1) (*G., Scharf ; F., Aigu ; I., Acu'to,-a.*) Acute, shrill ; high.
(2) (*G., Kreuz ; F., Dièse ; I., Die'sis.*) The sign ♯ which raises a note a semitone above its "natural" sound in the scale of C major.
(3) Old name for augmented ; as *sharp 4th,* augmented 4th.
(4) (*G., Scharf.*). An organ mixture stop with shrill pipes.
Double sharp. The sign x (or ×) , raising a note 2 semitones.
Sharp intonation. Singing or playing slightly above the accurate pitch.
Sharp key. A key with one or more sharps in its signature. In Sol-fa, any key one or more removes to the *right* of any other on the modulator.
Sharp mixture. A mixture stop " composed of pipes of high pitch and acute tone." It should include the major 3rd (10th or 17th, &c.).
Sharp seventh. A leading-note.
Sharp sixth. The augmented 6th. (See *Extreme 6th.*)

SHARP, Cecil J. Collector of folk-songs, &c.; *b.* London, 1859.

SHARP, Edward. Vocalist and composer ; *b.* Acton, 1831.

SHARP, Mrs. William. Author of "Great Composers" (Camelot Classics), 1887.

SHARPE, Ethel. Pianist ; *b.* Dublin, 1872. Silver medal, Musicians Co., 1891. Married the violinist Alfred Hobday.

SHARPE, Herbert F. Pianist ; *b.* Halifax, 1861. Queen's Scholar, National Training School of Music ; Prof. R.C.M., 1884.
Works : songs, numerous pf. pieces, a "Pianoforte School," &c.

Sharpest Note, Theory of the.
If a "circle of fifths" (*q.v.*) be written down—commencing, say, at F♭♭—each successive note is regarded as sharper than its neighbour on the left.
F♭♭, C♭♭, G♭♭, D♭♭, A♭♭, E♭♭, B♭♭ : F♭, C♭, G♭, D♭, A♭, E♭, B♭ : F, C, G, D, A, E, B : F♯, C♯, G♯, D♯, A♯, E♯, B♯ : Fx, Cx, Gx, Dx, Ax, Ex, Bx.
In determining the key of a given passage " the sharpest diatonic note" present is always the leading-note.
N.B.—For a more complete exposition of this useful theory, see Greenish's "Tonality and Roots" (Vincent) or Dunstan's "A B C of Musical Theory" (Curwen).

SHAW, Mrs. Alfred (*née* **Mary Postans**). Contralto ; *b.* Lee, Kent, 1814 ; *d.* 1876.
Sang the contralto part in Mendelssohn's *St. Paul* on its first production in England, 1837.

SHAW, Geo. Bernard. Dramatic author and musical critic ; *b.* Dublin, 1856.

SHAW, Martin E. F. Composer ; *b.* London, 1875.

SHAW, Oliver. Noted American blind singer. 1778-1848.
Composed popular psalm tunes and ballads.

Shawm. (*G., Schalmei'.*) (1) An ancient double-reed inst., the precursor of the oboe.
(2) A reed stop on old organs.
" The chanter of the bagpipe is probably the sole surviving form of the ancient shawm." (See also *Chalumeau.*)

SHEDLOCK, John South. B. Reading, 1843. B.A., London, 1864. Musical critic, *Ncademy*, 1879 ; *Athenæum*, 1901.
Works : articles and treatises on mus. subjects (" Beethoven's Sketch-books," &c.) ; an Eng. translation of Riemann's " Lexikon," &c.

SHELLEY, Harry Rowe. Orgt. and composer ; *b.* New Haven, Conn., 1858. Teacher of theory and composition, New York Metropolitan Coll., 1899.
Works : orchl. music, church music, org. pieces, pf. pieces, songs, male choruses, &c.

SHEPARD, Frank H. *B.* Bethel, Conn., 1863. Est. the "Shepard School of Music," Orange, N.J., 1891.
Works : "Piano Touch and Scales," "How to Modulate," "Harmony Simplified," &c.

SHEPARD, Thos. G. Organist and conductor ; *b.* Madison, Conn., 1848. Mus. instructor Yale Glee Club, 1873.
Works : a comic opera, cantatas, anthems, sacred songs, &c.

SHEPHERD, Anne (*née* Houlditch). 1809-1857. Daughter of the rector of Speen. Wrote the children's hymn "Around the throne of God."

SHERIDAN, Caroline E. S. Maiden name of **Lady Stirling-Maxwell** (*q.v.*).

SHERIDAN, Mrs. (See Linley.)

SHER'RINGTON, Helen (Mad. **Lemmens-**). Eminent soprano ; *b.* Preston, 1834 ; *d.* 1906. London *début*, 1856 ; married **Lemmens,** the noted organist, 1857.
She was the first to sing the part of "Marguerite" (Gounod's *Faust*) in English.

SHERRINGTON, Jose. Sister of preceding ; soprano vocalist ; *b.* Rotterdam, 1850.

SHERWIN, Amy. Soprano ; *b.* Tasmania. London *début*, Drury Lane, 1883.

SHERWOOD, Edgar H. Pianist ; *b.* Lyons, N.Y., 1845.
Works : over 100 pf. pieces and songs.

SHERWOOD, Percy. Concert pianist ; *b.* Dresden, 1866 (of English parents). Teacher of pf. and score reading, Dresden Cons., 1890.
Works : pf. pieces (miniatures, waltzes, sketches).

SHERWOOD, William Hall. Noted pianist and teacher ; *b.* Lyons, N.Y., 1854. Studied under Kullak, Richter, and Liszt. Head of the pf. section, Chicago Cons., 1889 ; founded the "Sherwood Pf. School," 1897.
Works : numerous pf. pieces.

SHIELD, William. "Perhaps the most original English composer since Purcell."—*Grove.* B. Whickham, Durham, 1748 ; *d.* London, 1829. Studied thorough-bass under Avison. Violinist, Opera Orch., London, 1772 ; viola player, 1773 ; composer, Covent Garden, 1778-91, and 1792-7 ; Master of the Royal Music, 1817. Buried Westminster Abbey.
Works : about 40 Eng. operas (*A Flitch of Bacon*, &c.), vn. pieces, an "Introduction to Harmony," many fine songs ("The Wolf," "The Thorn," "The heaving of the lead," &c.).

Shift. A change of position of the left hand in playing a stringed inst. (vn., 'cello, &c.). (See **Position.**)
The "shifts" are now called "positions."
Half shift. The 2nd position.
Whole shift. The 3rd position.
Double shift. The 4th position.

SHINN, Frederick G. *B.* London, 1867. Mus.D. Dunelm, 1897.
Works : "Elementary Ear Training," "A method of teaching harmony," &c.

SHINNER, Emily. Violinist ; *b.* Cheltenham, 1862. Pupil of Joachim.

Shiv'aree. (An American corruption of *Charivari.*) A burlesque serenade to a married couple, or to any "object of general ridicule."
Piegnot says that the proper "orchestra" for such an occasion in a town of 15,000 or 20,000 inhabitants consists of "12 copper kettles, 10 saucepans, 4 big boilers, 3 dripping pans, 12 shovels, 12 tongs, 12 dish covers for cymbals, 6 frying pans,......4 warming pans, 8 basins, 6 watering pots, 10 hand bells,......2 tambourines, 1 gong, 1 or 2 empty casks, 3 cornets-à-bouquins, 3 big hunting horns, 3 little trumpets, 4 bad clarinets, 2 bad oboes, 2 whistles (these will be enough), 1 musette, 4 wretched violins to scrape, 2 hurdy-gurdies, 1 marine trumpet (if you can find one), 4 rattles, 10 screeching voices, 8 howling voices, 3 sucking pigs, 4 dogs to be well whipped.......I can assure you that when all this is vigorously set agoing at the same time, the ear will experience all desirable joy." (From Hughes' *Musical Guide.*) Mark Twain (in 1877) called Wagner's *Lohengrin* a "shivaree."

Sho'far, or Sho'phar. A Jewish trumpet.
Its tone was supposed " to frighten away Satan."

SHORE, John. Celebrated English trumpeter, and "reputed inventor of the tuning-fork." B. London, abt. 1662(?) *d.* 1752.

Short. Defective, deficient ; compressed.
Short Metre. A four-line Iambic stanza ; 6,6,8,6.
   Come, ye that love the Lord,
     And let your joys be known ;
   Join in a song with sweet accord,
     While ye surround His throne.
Short octaves. The lowest octaves in old organs, which generally had some of the pipes omitted to " save expense."
Short score. A compressed score. (See *Score.*)

SHRUBSOLE, Wm. *B.* Canterbury, 1760 ; *d.* 1806. Organist Clerkenwell, 1784.
Composed the hymn-tune "Miles Lane" (to "All hail the power of Jesu's Name ").

Si (pron. *See*). The name afterwards added to Guido's hexachord (see **Guido**) for the 7th note of the scale. (See **Tonic Sol-fa Syllables.**) In France and Italy it is the name of the note B♮.
Miss Glover altered it to Te for the 7th of the Major Scale.
Si bémol (F.) ⎫ The note B♭.
Si bemol'le (I.) ⎭
Si dièse (F.). The note B♯.
Si con'tra fa (L. and I.). The false relation of the tritone ; generally *mi contra fa.*

Si (*I.*). If, as ; one, it.
Si de've suona're tut'to que'sto pez'zo delicatissimamen'te e sen'za sordi'ni. It is necessary to play all this piece with the utmost delicacy, and using the loud pedal (to sustain the sounds) as much as possible.
N.B.—This direction from Beethoven's *Moonlight* sonata is often misunderstood. Many players keep down *both* pedals continuously ; but this is not necessary. (See also *Sempre con ped.*)
Si ha s'immaginar' la battu'ta di 6-8. "Imagine the time to be 6-8." (*Beethoven.*)
Si le'va il sordi'no. "One lifts the sordino ; " take off the mute.
Si pia'ce. " If (or as) one pleases ; " *ad lib.*

Si re'plica. Repeat ; D.C.

Si re'plica si pia'ce il Ritornel'lo. Repeat the *Ritornello* if you please.

Si scri'va. As written ; no embellishments, &c.

Si se'gue. " It follows ; " go straight on.

Si ta'ce. Be silent.

Si vol'ta. Turn over.

Si vol'ti su'bito. (Please) turn over quickly.

SIBE'LIUS, Jean. *B.* Tavastehus, Finland, 1865. Teacher of theory, Mus. Inst. and Orch. School, Helsingfors, 1893.

Works : *Tornissa olija impi* ("The Maid of the Tower"), the first Finnish opera (1896) ; orchl. works, pf. pieces, &c.

SIBO'NI, Erik A. W. Fine pianist ; Copenhagen, 1828-92. Orgt. and pf. prof., Royal Acad. of Mus., Sorö, 1864.

Works : opera (*The Flight of Chas. II*, 1862) ; 2 symphonies, a "tragic" overture, chamber music, notable choral works, &c.

Sib'ilants. Hissing letters ; as *s* and *z*.

Sib'ilate. . To speak or sing with a hissing sound.

Sib'ilus (*L.*). A little flute used to teach song-birds.

SICARD, Michel de. Violinist ; *b.* Odessa, 1868. *Début* at 9. Afterwards pupil of Joachim.

SICARD, Sigismund. Violinist.

" It is hard to refuse belief in
                 Eternal deities
Who rule the world with absolute decrees,
And write whatever time shall bring to pass
With pens of adamant on plates of brass
after reading the story of Sigismund Sicard, as lately told by the Liége journal, *La Meuse*. Sicard was the violin wonder-child of his day. He went everywhere ; played to crowned heads, gathered honours and cash galore, and was fortune's favourite in all that he risked. Returning from America in 1879, he visited Wieniawski at Brussels, and, with him, was overtaken by a storm when walking out. The friends sought shelter under a tree ; lightning fell, and Sicard was paralysed on one side, while Wieniawski experienced such a shock that, less than a year later, he died in Moscow. Sicard lived on, but ten years passed before he was well enough to take up his violin again. Then fell another stroke of relentless fate. His daughter, a singer of repute, died, a victim to cholera, at Hamburg, in 1892 ; his malady returned, with epilepsy in its grim company, insanity closely following. He partially recovered, but unable to follow his profession, and, having no other resource, he lived from day to day by casual earnings as a knife grinder."—*Daily Telegraph,* 1906.

Sich verlie'rend (*G.*). Vanishing, disappearing ; dying away.

Sicilia'na,-o (*I.*) ⎫ A graceful pastoral Sici-
Sicilienne (*F.*)   ⎬ lian peasant dance, in 6-8 or 12-8 time.

Al'la Sicilia'na. In the style of a *Siciliana.*

Side-drum. (See **Drum**.)

Sieb (*G.*). An organ sound-board.

Sie'ben (*G.*). Seven.

Sie'benklang. (1) A chord of the 7th. (2) A hepta-chord (or scale of 7 notes).

Sie'benpfei'fe des Pan. "The seven pipes of Pan." Pan pipes (*q.v.*).

Sie'benstimmig. For 7 voices.

Sie'bente. A seventh (fraction, not interval).

Sie'benzehn'te. A seventeenth.

SIE'BER, Ferdinand. Renowned singing teacher of the old Italian school ; *b.*

Vienna, 1822 ; *d.* 1895. Settled in Berlin, 1854.

Works : numerous valuable voice training studies, a "Catechism of the Art of Singing" (several editions), a "Catalogue of 10,000 German songs, duets, and trios," &c.

Sie'gesgesang (*G.*) ⎫ A song of victory.
Sie'geslied (*G.*)   ⎬

Sie'ges Marsch A triumphal march.

Sie'gue (*I.*) Same as **Segue** (*q.v.*).

SIEHR, Gustav. Operatic bass ; *b.* Arnsberg, 1837 ; *d.* Munich, 1896. Created the part of "Hagen" in Wagner's *Ring des Nibelungen*, Bayreuth, 1876.

SIE'MENS, Frieda. Pianist ;¦ *b.* Berlin, 1882.

SIE'VEKING, Martinus. Concert pianist ; *b.* Amsterdam, 1867. Successful tours in Europe and America.

SIFA'CE (real name **Grossi**), **Giovanni F.** Celebrated male soprano. Member Papal Chapel, Rome, abt. 1675. Sang later in London. Assassinated in Italy, abt. 1699.

Siffler (*F.*). To whistle.

Sifflet. A whistle.

Sifflet de Pan. Pan-pipes.

Sifflet diapason. A pitch-pipe.

Siffleur. A male whistler (with the lips).

Siffleuse. A female whistler.

Sif'flöt, Sif'flöte, Suf'flöt (*G.*). "Whistle-flute." An org. stop of 1 ft. or 2 ft. pitch.

SIGHICEL'LI. Noted family of violinists.

(1) **Filippo** ; *b.* nr. Modena, 1686 ; *d.* 1773. 1st vn. to the Prince of Este.

(2) **Giuseppe** ; son of F ; Modena, 1737-1826. Court violinist.

(3) **Carlo** ; son of G. ; Modena, 1772-1806. Court violinist.

(4) **Antonio** ; son of C. ; Modena, 1802-83. Fine player ; condr. Ducal Orch., 1835.

(5) **Vincenzo** ; son of A. ; *b.* Cento, 1830. Solo violinist and asst. condr. Modena Court, 1849 ; settled in Paris as teacher, 1855.

Sight-reading. Ability to sing or play music at first sight.

Sight-reading is largely a natural gift ; but it may be immensely improved by practice. Among the many methods advocated for singing at sight from the Staff notation, the following have been proved to be the most successful :—
(1) The use of Tonic Sol-fa syllables on the "Movable Doh" system.
(2) The use of figures on a "Tonic Basis ; " "1" for Tonic, "2" for Supertonic, &c.

SIGISMON'DI, Giuseppe. Singing teacher ; opera composer ; Naples, 1739-1826.

Signal'horn (*G.*). A bugle or trumpet.

Signal'ist. A bugle or trumpet player.

Sig'natur (*G.*) (plur. *Sig'naturen*.) ⎫

Sig'nature (*E.*). (Also *G., Vor'zeichnung ;* ⎬ *F., Signes accidentales.*) ⎭

(1) The collection of sharps or flats placed at the beginning of a piece to indicate the key.

(2) The figures (or other signs) following the key-signature to indicate the time.

KEY SIGNATURES. Each signature stands either for a major or a minor key.

C major,   G major,   D major,

or A minor.   or E minor.   or B minor.

A major,   E major,   B major,

or F♯ minor.   or C♯ minor.   or G♯ minor.

F♯ major,   C♯ major,   F major,

or D♯ minor.   or A♯ minor.   or D minor.

B♭ major,   E♭ major,   A♭ major,

or G minor.   or C minor.   or F minor.

D♭ major,   G♭ major,   C♭ major,

or B♭ minor.   or E♭ minor.   or A♭ minor.

ANCIENT SIGNATURES. These were written very erratically. Sometimes the same flat or sharp was marked twice; thus :—

Key G.   Key D.   Key E♭.

There was no regular arrangement of the signatures even as late as 1730.

From "Malcolm's Treatise of Music."

It was common in the time of Handel and Bach to omit the last flat in minor signatures; in the old full scores of the *Messiah*, for example, "And with His stripes" (in F minor) has a signature of 3 flats, the D♭ being marked by an accidental each time it occurs. Bach's major signatures are systematic, but not his minor.

TIME SIGNATURES. (See *Time*.)

Sign. (See **Segno**.)

Sign, Cancelling
Sign, Neutralizing } The natural (♮).

Signe (*F*.). (1) A sign or symbol. (2) The *Segno* (*q.v.*).

Allez au signe. Go to (return to) the sign.
Signe accidental. An accidental (♮, ♯, ♭, &c.).
Signe de silence. A rest.

Signed Clef. A clef "assigned" to some special line of the staff.

Signs and Symbols.

2′, 4′, 8′, &c. Two-foot, four-foot, eight-foot. (See **Acoustics** and **Pitch**.)

① ② &c. (See **Harmonium**.)

1-ma, 2-da, &c. Prima, Seconda, &c.
     1st time, 2nd time, &c., where a part is repeated with different ending.

1°, 2°, Primo, Secondo; as Violino 1°, "1st vn.," &c.

6, ¢, 5, ♯, &c. (See **Figured Bass**.)

I, II, VII°, &c. (See **Harmony Analysis**.)

O. (1) Open string. (2) Old sign for triple time.

o. (1) A harmonic mark (vn., &c.). (2) The heel in organ playing.

3, 5, 6, &c. Triplet, Quintuplet, Sextolet, &c.

(See **Staccato**.)

(1) *Forte-tenuto :* the note to be held *forte* for its full length. (2) Sometimes used for *mezzo staccato* of single notes ; *i.e.,* held about 3-4ths their length. (3) *Marcato.*

Mezzo staccato, but well accented.

Organ tone ; held evenly for its full length.

} | d :r :m   Line under notes ; a *slur* in Tonic Sol-fa notation.

⌒ (1) A hold, or *fermata.* (2) A cadenza mark. (See **Cadenza**.)

𝄋 𝄌 § (See **Segno**.)

+ or × The thumb (in pf. music).

, √ V // A breathing-place.

Mezzo legato : smooth, but not quite gliding one into the other.

⌒ ⌣ (1) Bind (tie), or slur. (2) The sign for *Legato* (*q.v.*). or *portamento* (*q.v.*).

> ∧ ∨ < Accent marks. (See **Dynamics**.)

∧ ∨ The toe in organ playing.

∪ O The heel in organ playing.

∧ ∧ Slide the toe to the next note.

∨ The up bow (vn., &c.).

∧ The down bow in 'cello playing.

⊔ or ⊓ The down bow in vn. playing.

tr ⌁ A trill, or shake (*q.v.*).

tr⌁⌁⌁ A continued trill or shake.

A Direct (*q.v.*).

⌁ Mordent ("stroked" mordent
⌁ Long or Double Mordent   } (See **Mordent**.)
⌁ Inverted Mordent

~ ⸨ Turn and inverted turn. (See **Turn**.)

⌁ Trill (or long mordent) beginning and ending with a turn.

⌁ Trill (or long mordent) beginning with an inverted turn.

* ⊕ + Release the loud (damper) pedal.

⊕ Go on from this sign to the Coda (after *Da Capo, Dal Segno,* &c.).

or ⟲ Thumb position on the 'cello·

Crescendo.
Dimuendo.
Swell.

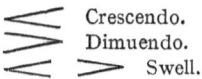

://: Repetition of a word (or words)—

Hal - le - lu- jah, *://:*

Bis. Bis.

Play the bar (or bars) twice.

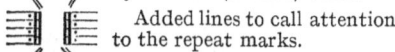

Added lines to call attention to the repeat marks.

(See also **Abbreviation, Notation, Ornaments, Rests, Shake, Signatures, Time, Trill,** &c.).

Sig'num (*L.*). A sign.

Siguidil'la (*I.*). A Seguidilla (*q.v.*).

SILAS, Eduard. Pianist ; *b.* Amsterdam, 1827 ; *d.* 1909. Settled in England, 1850. Prof. G.S.M. and L.C.M.
Works : an oratorio (*Joash*), a mass, cantatas, church music, organ pieces, orchestral works, chamber music, pf. pieces, songs, &c.

Sil'bendehnung. "Silvery extension ; " singing (slurring) more than one note to a syllable.

SIL'BERMANN. Celebrated family of organ builders and pf. makers.
(1) **Andreas** ; *b.* Klein-Bobritzsch, Saxony, 1678 ; *d.* 1734. Org. builder at Strasburg from abt. 1700.
(2) **Gottfried** ; brother of A. ; *b.* Klein-Bobritzsch, 1683 ; *d.* 1753. Settled in Freiberg as org. builder, 1712. Invented a hammer-action (similar to that of **Cristofori**) and became famous as "the first to manufacture pianofortes successfully." (Bach tried some of Silbermann's pianos on his memorable visit to Frederick the Great.)
Of his 47 organs, the chief is that of Freiberg Cath. (3 manuals, 45 stops; 1714).
(3) **Johann A.** ; eldest son of Andreas ; Strasburg, 1712-83. Organ builder.
(4) **Johann D.** ; brother of preceding ; 1717-66. Worked with his uncle (Gottfried), and afterwards on his own account as a pf. maker.
(5) **Johann H.** ; brother of preceding ; 1727-99. Pf. maker at Strasburg.
(6) **Johann F.** ; son of preceding ; 1762-1817. Organ builder ; orgt. Thomaskirche, Strasburg.

Sil'berton (*G.*). Silvery tone (*q.v.*).

SIL'CHER, Friedrich. Famous song composer ; *b.* Schnaith, Württemberg, 1789 ; *d.* 1860. Mus.-director Tübingen Univ., 1817.
Besides many songs, *Lorelei*, &c., he wrote a choralbuch, 3 books of hymns, male choruses, &c., and was an influential promoter of popular singing.

Silence (*F.*) **Silen'zio** (*I.*) A rest, a pause.
Lun'go silen'zio (*I.*). A long pause.

Silhouettes (*F.*). "Shadows ; " sketches, *souvenirs ;* recollections.

Sillet (*F.*). A nut.
Grand sillet. The nut at the tailpiece (of a vn., &c.).
Petit sillet. The nut at the neck.

SILO'TI, Alexander. Remarkable pianist ; *b.* Charkov, Russia, 1863. Pupil, Moscow Cons., of N. Rubinstein and Tschaikowsky ; won gold medal, 1881. *Début,* Moscow, 1880. Afterwards studied 3 years with Liszt. Prof. Moscow Cons., 1887-90. Has since toured extensively.

SIL'VA, David Poll da. Prolific composer ; *b.* nr. Bayonne, 1834 ; *d.* 1875. Soon after the age of 20 he became quite blind, and "his mother wrote out his compositions from dictation."
Works : 2 oratorios, 3 operas, cantatas, much chamber music, pf. pieces, part-songs, songs.

SIL'VER, Chas. *B.* Paris, 1868. *Grand Prix de Rome,* Paris Cons.
Works : operettas, fairy opera (*La Belle au bois dormant*), an oratorio, orchl. suites, ballets, songs, &c.

Silvery tone. Poetic name for a soft, clear, pure, sweet, and rich tone.

Sim. Abbn. of *Simile.*

SI'MANDL, Franz. Double-bass player ; *b.* Blatna, Bohemia, 1840. Prof. Vienna Cons., 1869.
Works : a fine "Contrabass School," &c.

Sim'icon (*Gk.*). A harp with 35 strings.

Similar motion. (See **Motion.**)

Si'mile (*I.*) }
Si'mili (*I.*) } Like ; in a similar manner
Simil'iter (*L.*) } (to the foregoing).
N.B.—*Simili,* though apparently incorrect, is often used.
Si'mile mark. The sign ═══ or ═══
(See *Abbreviations,* p. 4.)

SI'MON, Christian. Noted double-bass player ; *b.* Schernberg, 1809 ; *d.* 1872.

SIMON, Jean H. Violinist ; Antwerp, 1783-1861. Teacher of Vieuxtemps.
Works : 7 vn. concertos, an oratorio, cantatas.

SI'MON, Joh. Caspar. Cantor and organist at Nördlingen.
Pub. numerous fugues, preludes, chorals, &c., for organ (1750-4).

SIMONET'TI, Achille. Violinist and composer ; *b.* Turin, 1859.

SIMON-GIRARD (*née* **Girard**), **Julie J. C.** Noted operatic singer ; *b.* Paris, 1859. Created " Madame Favart," &c.

SIMONS - CANDEILLE. (See **Candeille, Amélie.**)

SIMPER, Caleb. Composer of simple popular anthems ; *b.* Barford-St.-Martin Wilts., 1856.

Sim'pla (*L.*). A *Semiminima* or crotchet (♩).

Simple. (1) Plain, unadorned ; as *Simple Counterpoint.*
(2) Of intervals, "not greater than an octave."
(3) Of a sound or tone, "without accompanying partials." (See **Acoustics.**)
The tone of a tuning-fork is practically " simple ;" that of a flute nearly so.
(4) Of time, "opposed to compound ;" as *Simple Triple Time,* &c.

Simplement (*F.*). Simply, unaffectedly.

SIMPSON (or **SYMPSON**), **Christopher.** *B.* abt. 1600 ; *d.* London, 1669.
Pub. "The Division-Violist," "The Principles of Practical Musick," &c.

SIMPSON, John. Pub. the "Delightful Pocket Companion for the German Flute," London, 1740.

SIM'ROCK, Nikolaus. *B.* Bonn, 1755 ; *d.* 1833. Founded the music publishing house of " Simrock," Berlin, 1790.

Sin' (*I.*). Abbn. of *Sino ;* to, unto, until.
Sin' al fi'ne. To the *Fi'ne.*
Sin' al se'gno. Up to the *Sign.*
Con fuo'co sin' al fi'ne. With spirit (fire) to the end.

SINCLAIR, George R. *B.* Croydon, 1863. Orgt. Hereford Cath., 1889 ; Mus.D. Cantuar, 1899.

SINCLAIR, John. Noted tenor singer ; *b.* nr. Edinburgh, 1790 ; *d.* 1857. *Début,* Haymarket Th., 1880. Rossini wrote for him the part of "Idreno" in *Semiramide.*

Sin'copa,-e (*I.*). Syncopation (*q.v.*).
Sincopa'to,-a. Syncopated.

SIN'DING, Christian. Organist, teacher, and gifted composer ; *b.* Kongberg, Norway, 1856. Pupil of Reinecke, Leipzig Cons., 1874-7 ; studied later at Dresden, Munich, and Berlin. Settled in Christiania.
Works : symphony in D minor ; a pf. concerto, chamber music, vn. sonatas, much characteristic pf. music, songs, &c.

Sinfoni'a (*I.*)   } (1) Symphony (*q.v.*).
Sinfonie' (*G.* and *F.*) } (2) A form of overture (*q.v.*).
Sinfonie'-canta'te (*G.*). A symphony with a cantata continuation. (Mendelssohn's *Hymn of Praise.*)
Sinfoni'a concertan'te (*I.*). A concerto for several insts.
Sinfoni'a da cam'era (*I.*). A chamber quartet or concerto.
Sinfoniet'ta (*I.*). A little symphony.

Sinfo'nico,-a (*I.*). Symphonic.
Poe'ma sinfo'nico. Symphonic poem.

SINGELÉE, Jean B. Violinist ; *b.* Brussels, 1812 ; *d.* 1875.
Pub. 144 works for vn. (solos, fantasias, arrangements, &c.).

Sing'akademie' (*G.*). The principal Musical Soc. of Berlin ; founded 1791.

Sing'en (*G.*). To sing ; to chant ; to warble.
Falsch sing'en. To sing out of tune.
Die'ser Säng'er kann noch das ho'he C sing'en. This singer may take the high C.
Sing'akademie' } A vocal society.
Sing'anstalt }
Sing'amt. An *a cappella* mass.

Sing'art. The art of singing.
Sing'bar. That may be sung ; pleasant to the ear ; singable.
Sing'bar im Vor'trag. In a singing manner.
Sing'chor. A choir.
Sing'gedicht. A poem to be set to music.
Sing'end. Singing(ly) ; *cantabile.*
Sing'(e)note. A note of music.
Sing'(e)tänz. A song-dance ; a ballad.
Sing'fuge. A vocal fugue.
Sing'kunst. The art of singing.
Sing'lehrer. A singing teacher.
Sing'märchen. A ballad.
Sing'mani(e)ren. Vocal embellishments.
Sing'oper. An opera without spoken dialogue.
Sing'schauspiel. A drama with songs.
Sing'schule. A vocal method or school.
Sing'spiel. "Song-play ;" the national form of German opera, including national or popular songs.
Sing'saite. The treble string (*chanterelle*) of a vn.
Sing'schlüssel. A clef.
Sing'stimme. The voice ; a vocal part ; good voice.
Sing'stück. An air ; melody ; a vocal piece.
Sing'verein. A singing society.
Sing'weise. (1) Same as *Sing'stück.*! (2) Manner or style of singing.

SIN'GER, Edmund. Celebrated violinist ; *b.* Totis, Hungary, 1831. Solo vn., Pesth Th., 1846 ; leader at Weimar, 1853 ; Prof. Stuttgart Cons., 1861.
Works : several vn. pieces (nocturnes, fantasias).

SING'ER, Otto. Pianist ; *b.* Sora, Saxony, 1833 ; *d.* 1894. Studied under Moscheles and Liszt. Settled in America as concert pianist, conductor, &c., 1867.
Works : cantatas, 2 pf. concertos, pf. pieces, &c.

SING'ER, Otto (Junr.). Son of preceding ; violinist ; *b.* Dresden, 1863. Teacher Cologne Cons., 1890 ; settled in Leipzig, 1892.
Works : a concertstück for vn. and orch. ; male choruses, &c.

SING'ER, Peter. Franciscan monk ; *b.* Lechthal, 1810 ; *d.* 1882.
Invented an orchestrion ; wrote 101 masses, 600 offertories, &c.

Singhiozza're (*I.*). To sob.
Singhioz'zo. A sob ; sobbing.
Singhiozzan'do. Sobbingly ; with a "catch" in the voice (or breath).

Singing. (See **Voice** and **Voice Production.**)

Single chant. (See **Chant.**)

Single fugue. A fugue on one subject. (See **Fugue.**)

Single relish. (See **Ornaments.**)

SINIGA'GLIA, Leone. Composer ; *b.* Turin, 1868.

Sini'stra (*I.*). Left.
Col'la sini'stra. With the left hand.
Ma'no sini'stra ; or *M.S.* The left hand.

Sink-a-pace. (Cinque-pace.) Old name for a *Galliard* (*q.v.*).

Si'no (*I.*). To, as far as, until, unto.
Si'no al'la fi'ne Until the end (*fine*).
Si'no al se'gno. As far as the sign (𝄋).

Si pia'ce. At pleasure ; "if you please." (See **Si.**)

SIPP, F. R. *B.* 1805 ; *d.* 1899. 1st vn. Leipzig Th. orchestra.
" Wagner is said to have been one of his *least promising* pupils ! "

Si'ren (*E.*) ⎫ (1) An acoustical inst. to calcu-
Sirène (*F.*) ⎬ late the number of vibrations
Sire'ne (*G.*) ⎭ of any sound. (2) A fog-horn.
Si re'plica (*I.*) Repeat.
Si re'plica u'na vol'ta. Repeat once only.

Sir ROGER de COVERLEY. A favourite old
English country dance in 9-8 time.

Si se'gue. Go on.

Siste'ma (*I.*). The staff.

Sis'ter (*G.*). An old German guitar with 7
strings.

SIS'TERMANNS, Anton. Operatic bass ; *b.*
Herzogenbusch, Holland, 1867.

SISTINE CHOIR. The Papal choir at Rome.

Sl'stro (*I.*). (1) A triangle. (2) A sistrum.

Sis'trum (*Gk.*). An ancient rattling inst.
used by the Egyptians, Greeks, and
Romans.
It consisted of a hoop-like iron frame hung with
movable rings or rods and held by a handle.

Si ta'ce (*I.*). Be silent.

Sit'ar. A Hindoo guitar.

Sito'le, Cito'le. A kind of zither.

SITT, Hans. Violinist ; *b.* Prague, 1850.
Vn. teacher Leipzig Cons., 1883 ; condr.
Bachverein, 1885.
Works : vn. concertos, a 'cello concerto, vn. pieces,
pf. pieces, songs, &c.

SITTARD, Josef. Teacher and writer ;
b. Aix-la-Chapelle, 1846 ; *d.* 1903.
Works : numerous essays and treatises on music,
a "History of the Stuttgart Court Opera," &c.

Sitz (*G.*). Position (in vn. playing, &c.).

SIVO'RI, Ernesto Camillo. Famous violinist;
Geneva, 1815-94. *Début* at 6 ; afterwards a favourite pupil of Paganini.
Made extensive tours ; was an admirable interpreter of Paganini's compositions and also a fine quartet leader.
Works : 2 vn. concertos, numerous vn. solos, &c.

SIVRAI, Jules de. Pen-name of **Mrs. J. L.
Roeckel** (*q.v.*).

Six-eight time. (See **Time.**)

Six-five chord. A 1st inversion of a chord of
the seventh.

Six-four chord. A second inversion, or *c*
position of a triad.

Six-three chord. (See **Sixth, Chord of the.**)

Sixième (*F.*) ⎫
Sixte (*F.*) ⎬ Interval of a sixth.

Six pour quatre (*F.*) A sextuplet (*q.v.*).

Sixteen feet. The length of the open pipe
which gives CCC (or C₃)
(See **Acoustics** and **Pitch.**)

8ve lower.

Sixteenth note. A semiquaver (♬).
Sixteenth rest. A semiquaver rest (𝄿).

Sixth. (*G., Sex'te ; F., Sixte ; I., Se'sta.*)
An interval comprising six degrees of
the staff. (See **Interval.**)
Sixths may be *augmented, major, minor,* or
(rarely) *diminished.*

Sixth, Chord of the. The first inversion of a
triad. (In Sol-fa theory, the *b* position
of a triad.)
Added sixth. (See *Added Sixth.*)
Augmented sixth ⎫
French sixth ⎬ (See *Extreme Sixth.*)
German sixth ⎪
Italian sixth ⎭
Neapolitan sixth. (See *Neapolitan Sixth.*)

Sixtine (*F.*) A sextuplet (*q.v.*).

Sixty-fourth note. A hemidemisemiquaver, 𝅘𝅥𝅱

Sixty-fourth rest. A hemidemisemiquaver rest, 𝄿

SJÖ'GREN, J. G. Emil. *B.* Stockholm, 1853.
Orgt. Johankirke, Stockholm, 1890.
Works : pf. pieces, sonatas for pf. and vn., &c.

Ska'la (*G.*). Scale, gamut.
Natur'skala. Natural scale ; scale of C major.

Skal'de (*G.*). (See **Scald.**)

SKENE Manuscript. A valuable collection
of Scottish vocal and dance music
supposed to have been collected by
John Skene of Halyards, 1614-20. He
died in 1644.

SKINNER, James C. Violinist ; *b.* Aber-
deenshire, 1843. "Reputed one of the
best players of Scottish dance music."
Works : reels, strathspeys, songs, &c.

Skip. (*G., Sprung ; F., Saut ; I., Sal'to.*)
A disjunct (or *discrete*) interval in
melody ; *i.e.,* any interval greater than
a minor or major 2nd.

Skip, To. (1) To overblow a wind inst. or
organ pipe so as to produce a harmonic
instead of the desired sound. (2) To
avoid the fundamental tone of a pipe
and intentionally produce a harmonic
(as in " harmonic " organ stops).

Skip, To. To overblow a wind inst. or organ
pipe so as to produce a harmonic
instead of the desired sound.

Skisma. (See **Schisma.**)

Skiz'ze (*G.*). (*I., Schiz'zo ; F., Esquisse.*) A
sketch ; a short piece in free form.

Skolien'. A Swedish drinking song.

SKROUP (or **SKRAUP), Franz.** First com-
poser of Bohemian operas ; *b.* Pardu-
bitz, Bohemia, 1801 ; *d.* 1862. Condr.
Bohemian Th., Prague, 1837 ; German
Opera, Rotterdam, 1860.
Works : operas, overtures, chamber music,
Bohemian songs, &c.

SKROUP, Jan Nepomuk. Brother of preceding ; *b.* Vositz, 1811 ; *d.* 1892.
2nd condr. Prague Th.
Works : Bohemian operas, a vocal method,
church music, &c.

SKU'HERSKÝ, Franz Z. *B.* Opocno,
Bohemia, 1830 ; *d.* 1892. Director
Prague Org. School, 1866 ; Hofka-
pelldirector, 1868.
Works : operas (*Vladimir, Lora,* &c.), masses,
several Bohemian text books on music, &c.

Slan'cio (*I.*). Vehemence, impetuosity.
  Con slan'cio. With vehemence. &c.
  Slancian'te ⎰ "Thrown off." (1) Deftly. (2)
  Slancia'to ⎱ Vehemently, with dash.

Slargan'do (*I.*) ⎰ "Enlarging."   *Rallen-*
Slargan'dosi (*I.*) ⎱ *tando ;* gradually slower (and broader in style). Often combined with *crescendo.*

Slarga'to (*I.*). Slower.

SLATER. (See **Barri.**)

SLAUGHTER, A. Walter. London, 1860-1908. Condr., successively, Royal Th., Olympic, Drury Lane, and St. James's.
  Operatic works : *Marjorie* (1889), *The Rose and the Ring* (1890), *The French Maid* (1897), &c.

SLA'VÍK, Joseph. Violinist ; *b.* Jince, Bohemia, 1806 ; *d.* 1833.
  Works : 2 vn. concertos, a concerto for 2 vns., chamber music, &c.

Slega'to (*I.*). Untied, disconnected. The opposite of *legato.*

Slentan'do (*I.*) ⎰ Gradually slower ; slacken-
Slentan'to (*I.*) ⎱ ing the time.

Slide. (1) A movable U-shaped tube in the trombone, slide-trumpet, &c.
  (2) A portamento (*q.v.*).
  (3) A slider (*q.v.*).

Slide. (*G., Schlei'fer ; F., Coulé.*) A group of two or more ascending or descending grace-notes gliding rapidly into the principal note.

Written.

Played.

Slider.
  A narrow flat strip of wood pierced with holes, which admits air into, or shuts it off from, the pipes of an organ. Each slider is controlled by a " stop."

Sliding Relish. An old harpsichord grace.

Slissa'to (*I.*). Slurred, gliding.

SLIVIN'SKI, Joseph von. Pianist ; *b.* Warsaw, 1865. Pupil of Leschetitzky and A. Rubinstein ; *début,* 1890 ; London *début,* 1893.

Slo'gan. A Highland rallying cry (war cry, &c.).

SLOPER, E. H. Lindsay. Pianist and teacher ; London, 1826-87. Pf. prof. G.S.M., 1880.
  Works : an orchl. suite, pf. pieces, songs, &c.

Slotted organ pipes. (See **Pierced organ pipes.**)

Slow movement. Term specially applied to the slow movement (generally the 2nd) of a piece in Sonata Form. (See **Sonata.**)

Slur. (*G., Lega'tobogen ; F., Liaison ; I., Legatu'ra.*) (1) A curved line above (or below) 2 or more notes to indicate that they are to be sung to one syllable.
  (2) A legato mark. (See **Legato.**)
  (3) A phrase mark. (See **Phrasing.**)
  (4) A portamento mark. (See **Portamento.**)
  The same sign is used for the **Tie** (*q.v.*).
  In Tonic Sol-fa a slur (1) is indicated by a straight line beneath the notes : |d :r :m ||

In vocal music, when two or more quavers (semiquavers, &c.), go to one syllable and have their stems connected, it is not necessary to add a slur mark (although it is sometimes done) :—

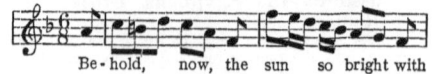

Be - hold,   now, the sun   so bright with
(a)

gleam - - ing, &c.
N.B.—The slur is advisable at (*a*), as the two groups of quavers belong to different halves of the measure.

Separate syllables should have separate notes :—

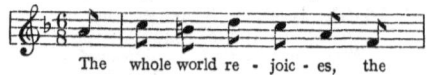

The   whole world re - joic - es,   the

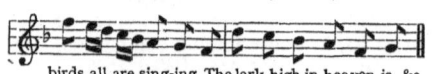

birds all are sing-ing, The lark high in heaven is, &c.
N.B.—A slur over *two notes set to different syllables* indicates a *portamento* (*q.v.*).

Slurs are generally omitted when a *long* passage is sung to one syllable :—

The hand that slaugh - - - - -

- - - - - - - - - - - ters.
N.B.—All *Ties* are, of course, carefully added in such cases.

Dotted slur : .... Placed over (or under) two or more notes which may be either sung to one syllable or to separate syllables, to suit the requirements of varying stanzas (or arrangement of words).

Slurred melody. Opposed to *syllabic* melody (in which there is but one note to each syllable).

Small octave. The octave from "Tenor C" to "Middle C."

Small register. Term sometimes employed for the highest tones of soprano voices.

SMALLWOOD, Wm. Kendal, 1831-97.
  Works : a "Pianoforte Tutor," *Salon* pf.-pieces, &c.

Sma'nia (*I.*) Fury, madness ; rage, frenzy.
  Smanian'te ⎫
  Smania're   ⎬ Frantically, wildly ; passionately.
  Smania'to   ⎮
  Smanio'so ⎭

Smanica're (*I.*). To shift the hand (in vn. playing, &c.).

SMARE'GLIA, Antonio. Opera composer ; *b.* Pola, Istria, 1854. Studied Vienna and Milan.
Chief operas : *Il Vassallo di Szigetti* (1889), *La Felena* (1897), &c.

SMART, Sir George T. London, 1776-1867. Knighted, 1811. Condr. Philharmonic Concerts, 1813-44 ; Lenten Oratorios, 1813-25. Conducted the music at the Coronation of William IV and Victoria.
Works : 2 vols. of sacred music, a collection of glees and canons, an edition of Gibbons' madrigals, &c.

SMART, Henry. Nephew of preceding ; London, 1813-79. Orgt. at several London churches.
Works : opera, *Bertha ;* cantatas, *The Bride of Dunkerron, King Rene's Daughter, The Fishermaidens,* &c. ; a Morning and Evening Service, anthems, part-songs, songs, fine organ pieces.

SME'TANA, Friedrich. One of the most noted of modern national Bohemian composers ; *b.* Leitomischl, Bohemia, 1824; *d.* insane, 1884. After a successful career as concert pianist, condr. Nat. Bohemian Th., Prague, 1866. Resigned on account of deafness, 1874.
Works : 8 Czech operas (*Prodana Nevesta*, 1866) ; a cycle of 6 symphonic poems, other symphonic poems and symphonies, chamber music, pf. pieces, part-songs, &c.

SMIETON, John More. *B.* Dundee, 1857 ; *d.* 1904.
Works : cantatas, orch. pieces, school music, &c.

Sminuen'do (*I.*). *Diminuendo ;* diminishing in force (and often in speed).

Sminul'to (*I.*). Softer.

SMIT, Johann. Violinist ; *b.* Utrecht, 1862.

SMITH, Alice Mary (Mrs. **Meadows White**). London, 1839-1884. Pupil of Sterndale Bennett and G. A. Macfarren. Married 1867.
Works : cantatas (*Ode to the North-East Wind*, 1878) ; orchl. and chamber music, part-songs, songs.

SMITH, A. Montem. Tenor vocalist ; *b.* Windsor, 1828 ; *d.* 1891. Gentleman Chapel Royal from 1858. Prof. R.A.M. and G.S.M. Sang at the principal English concerts and festivals.

SMITH, Bernard. (**Bernhardt Schmidt**). Noted org. builder ; known as " Father Smith." *B.* Germany, abt. 1630. Came to London with two nephews, 1660. Org.-builder in ordinary to the King ; afterwards court org.-builder to Queen Anne ; *d.* 1708.
His organs include : Chapel Royal, Whitehall, 1660 ; Westminster Abbey, 1671 ; St. Margaret's, Westminster, 1675 ; Durham Cath., 1683 ; the Temple, 1684 ; and St. Paul's, 1697.

SMITH, Boyton. Pianist ; *b.* Dorchester, 1837. Studied under S. S. Wesley.
Works : church music, songs, *salon* pf. pieces.

SMITH, Chas. Bass singer ; *b.* London, 1786 ; *d.* 1856.
Wrote dramatic works (*Yes or No, Hit or Miss*), songs, pf. pieces, &c.

SMITH, Chas. Wm. (" Chas. Fontaine "). Liverpool ; 1839-87.
Works : popular pf. pieces, songs, anthems, &c.

SMITH, David S. American organist and composer ; *b.* Toledo, Ohio, 1877.

SMITH, George Montague. Organist and composer ; *b.* Norwich, 1843.

SMITH, Geo. Townshend. *B.* Windsor, 1813 ; *d.* 1877. Orgt. Hereford Cath., 1843.

SMITH, Gerrit. Noted American concert organist ; *b.* Haggerstown, Maryland, 1859. Settled in New York, 1885.
Works : church music, cantatas, part-songs, numerous songs, &c.

SMITH, Hermann. Author of numerous articles on Acoustics, "The World's Earliest Music, &c."

SMITH, John. *B.* Cambridge, 1795 ; *d.* Dublin, 1861. Prof. of Music (and Mus.D.), Univ. of Dublin.
Wrote a "Treatise on Harmony and Composition," church music, &c.

SMITH, John Christopher. Handel's pupil and amanuensis ; *b.* Ansbach, 1712 ; *d.* Bath, 1795. When Handel's eyesight failed, Smith not only wrote his works from dictation, but acted as organist and cembalist for him at the oratorio performances. His fair copies of Handel's works are now in the Hamburg Library.
Handel bequeathed to him his MS. scores, his harpsichord, &c.
He wrote 10 operas and several oratorios of little permanent value.

SMITH, John Stafford. *B.* Gloucester, abt. 1750 ; *d.* 1836. Organist Chapel Royal, 1802. Aided Sir J. Hawkins with his "History of Music."
Works : a collection of glees, "Songs of Various Kinds for Different Voices," chants, anthems, &c. ; edited "Musica Antiqua."

SMITH, Joseph P. *B.* Dudley, 1856. Mus.D. Dublin, 1881 ; *d.* Jacksonville, 1907.
Works : masses, cantatas, anthems, part-songs, &c. Editor *Catholic Choir Music* (1891).

SMITH, Robt. Cambridge, 1689-1768. Master of Trinity Coll., 1742.
Pub. "Harmonics, or the Philosophy of Musical Sounds."

SMITH, Robt. Archibald. *B.* Reading, 1780 ; *d.* Edinburgh, 1829.
Edited and arranged several vols. of hymn-tunes, "The Scottish Minstrel," &c. ; composed several fine Scottish songs, including "Jessie, the Flower o' Dunblane." (See *Scottish Music.*)

SMITH, Sydney. Pianist ; *b.* Dorchester, 1839 ; *d.* 1889.
Wrote numerous showy *salon* pf. pieces.

SMITH, Wm. Braxton. Tenor singer ; *Début*, Crystal Palace, 1888.

SMITH, Wm. Seymour. *B.* Marlow, 1836; *d.* 1905. Prof. of singing R.C.M.
Works : cantatas, songs, pf. pieces, &c.

SMITH, Wilson G. American pianist ; *b.* Elyria, Ohio, 1855. Settled in Cleveland, 1882.
Works : numerous pf. pieces, 40 songs ; 200 miscellaneous arrangements, &c.

SMOLEN'SKY, Stephen V. *B.* Kazan, 1848. Authority on Russian Church music.

SMOLIAN, Arthur. Condr., composer,. and critic ; *b.* Riga, 1856.

Smoran'do (*I.*) ⎫ Dying away ; slower and
Smoren'do (*I.*) ⎭ softer by degrees.

Smorfio'so (*I.*). Affected ; coquettish.

Smorzan'do (*I.*) ⎫ Abbn. *Smorz*, Dying
Smorza'to (*I.*) ⎭ away ; becoming extinguished ; rather suddenly slower and softer.

SMYTH, Ethel M. Composer ; *b.* London. First important work a string quartet, Leipzig, 1884.
Works : orchl. pieces, a Solemn Mass, operas (*The Wreckers*, Leipzig, 1906), songs, &c.

Snap. (See **Scotch Snap.**)

Snare-drum. A side-drum. (See **Drum.**)

SNEDDON, James. *B.* Dalgety, 1833. Mus.B. Cantab., 1885.
Author of "The Musical Self-Instructor," articles in Grieg's "Musical Educator," &c.

SNEL, Joseph F. Violinist ; *b.* Brussels, 1793 ; *d.* 1861. Pupil of Baillot, Paris Cons. Director Training School for Military Bandmasters, Brussels, 1828 ; Chef de Musique, Civic Guard, 1837. Popularized music teaching through the methods of Galin and Wilhem.
Wrote operas, cantatas, military music, orchl. pieces, &c.

Snel'lo (*I.*). Nimble, quick, brisk.
Snellamen'te. Briskly, nimbly.

SNOW, Valentine. Trumpet player ; *d.* 1770. Played the trumpet parts in Handel's oratorios, &c.

So (*G.*). So, as, thus.
So rasch als mö'glich ⎫ As fast as possible.
So schnell wie mö'glich ⎭

SOARES, João. (See **Rebello.**)

Soa've (*I.*). Soft, sweet, suave, gentle.
Con soavità ⎫ Sweetly, suavely, gently.
Soavemen'te ⎭

SOBRI'NO, Mad. C. (*née* **Luisa Schmitz**). Soprano ; *b.* Düsseldorf, 18—.

Società del Quartet'to (*I.*). A quartet society.

Société chantante (*F.*). A singing society.

Society of British Musicians. Founded 1834.

SÖ'DERMANN, August J. Stockholm, 1832-1876. Studied Leipzig Cons. Th. condr., Stockholm, from 1862.
Works : Swedish operettas, a mass for voices and orch. (his finest work), orchl. pieces, &c.

Soffocan'do (*I.*) ⎫ Damping the strings of a
Soffogan'do (*I.*) ⎭ harp (with the hand).

27

SOFFREDI'NI, Alfredo. Editor *Gazzetta Musicale*, Milan, since 1896.
Works : operas (*Il piccolo Haydn*, 1893 ; *Salvatorello*, 1894 ; &c.).

Sofort' (*G.*). At once, immediately.

Sogget'to (*I.*). Subject, theme, motive.
Sogget'to invaria'to. A fixed (or invariable) subject.
Sogget'to varia'to. A variable subject.

Sogleich' (*G.*). Immediately.
Sogleich' das erst'e Zeit'mass. Immediately (resume) the 1st tempo.

Sognan'do (*I.*). Dreamy.

SOH. Tonic Sol-fa spelling of *Sol*, the 5th note (or Dominant) of the major scale.

SOKAL'SKY, Vladimir I. Composer ; *b.* Heidelberg, 1863.

SO'KOLOW, Nicholas. *B.* St. Petersburg, 1858. Harmony teacher to the Imperial Chapel.
Works : orchl. pieces, chamber music, pf. pieces, *a cappella* choruses, several songs.

Sol. The fifth of Guido's syllables. (See **Guido.**) In France and Italy the note G.
Sol bémol (*F.*). The note G♭.
Sol dièse (*F.*). The note G♯.

So'la (*I.*). Alone ; solo.
Vio'la so'la. Viola alone ; a viola solo.

SOLDAT, Marie (Soldat-Roger). Violinist ; pupil of Joachim ; *b.* Graz, 1864(3?).

Solem'nis (*L.*). Solemn.

Solen'ne (*I.*) Solemn, grave, splendid.
Solennemen'te. Solemnly.
Solennità. Solemnity, pomp.

Solennel (*F.*) ⎫ Solemn.
Solennelle (*F.*) ⎭
Solennellement. Solemnly.

Solen'nis (*L.*). Solemn.
Mis'sa solen'nis. A mass on a grand scale ; *e.g.*, Beethoven's *Missa solennis* in D.

Solfà (*I.*). (1) A gamut or scale. (2) A bâton. (3) Time.
Bat'tere la solfà. To beat time.

Solfa (*E.*). (1) Solmisation (*q.v.*). (2) Solfège (*q.v.*).

Sol-fa Notation. (See **Lancashire Sol-fa** and **Tonic Sol-fa.**)

Solfège (*F.*). ⎫ A vocal ex-
Solfeg'gio (*I.*). (Plur. *Solfeg'gi*). ⎭ ercise (on sol-fa syllables, or on any one syllable or vowel).
Solfeggia're (*I.*) ⎫
Solfeggi(e)'ren (*G.*) ⎬ To sing solfeggi.
Solfier (*F.*) ⎭

So'li (*I.*). Plural of Solo.
A passage marked *soli* is rendered with *one* performer to each part.
Vo'ci so'li. Voices alone.

Solid Chord. A chord with all its notes struck together, not *broken* (or *arpeggio*).

SOLIE (or SOULIER), Jean P. *B.* Nismes, 1755 ; *d.* 1812. *Début* as a tenor singer ; voice afterwards changed to a fine baritone. Sang Paris Opéra Comique, several composers writing parts specially for him.
Composed over 30 comic operas (1790-1811).

So'list. A soloist.

Soli'to (*I.*) Usual ; habitual.
Al soli'to. As usual.

SOL'LE, Friedrich. Thuringia, 1806-84.
Published a popular vn. method.

Solle'cito (*I.*). (1) Careful, precise, exact.
(2) Mournful, laboured, pressing on.
Sollecitan'do. Hastening, labouring.

Sol majeur (*F.*). The key of G major.

Sol mineur (*F.*). The key of G minor.

Solmisation. Sight-singing from staff nota-
tion by using syllables as names of notes.
For various methods of solmisation see *Tonic
Sol-fa Syllables.*
Solmisa're (*I.*)
Solmisi(e)'ren (*G.*) } To practise solmisation.
Solmiza're (*I.*)

So'lo (*I.*) (1) Alone. (2) A composition (or
a portion of one) for a single voice or
inst. (with or without accompaniment).
Violi'no solo. (1) Violin only. (2) The principal
1st violin.
Solo organ. The part of an organ containing the solo
stops ; or the manual connected with those stops.
Solo quartet. (1) A piece for 4 solo performers. (2) A
solo with 3 accompanying parts. (4) A group of
4 soloists.
Solo-gei'ger (*G.*). Solo violinist.
Solo-gesang' (*G.*). Solo (vocal).
Solo-säng'er (*G.*). A solo singer.
Solo-spie'ler (*G.*). A solo player.
Solo-stim'me (*G.*). A solo part.
Solo-tanz (*G.*). A *pas seul* (*q.v.*).

Solomanie'. A Turkish flute.

SOLOMON. Oratorio by Handel, 1748.

SOLOMON, Edward. 1855-95.
Works : operettas (*Billee Taylor, Nautch Girl*, &c.).

SO'LOVIEV (or **SOLOWIEW), Nicolai P.**
Distinguished Russian composer ; *b.*
Petrosavodsk, Olonetz, 1846. Prof. of
harmony, &c., St. Petersburg Cons.,
1874.
Works : cantata (*The Death of Samson*) ; operas
(*Vakula the Smith*, 1875 ; *Cordelia*, 1883) ;
orchl. pieces, characteristic pf. pieces, songs, &c.

Soltan'to (*I.*). Alone, only.
La trom'ba soltan'to. The trumpet alone.

Sombrer (*F.*). To produce a veiled sombre
tone.
Voix sombrée. A veiled voice.

SOMERSET, Lord Henry R. C. Amateur
composer ; *b.* 1849.
Works : pf. pieces, several songs, &c.

SOMERVELL, Arthur. *B.* Windermere,
1863. Studied Berlin and R.C.M.
London. Inspector of Music in Train-
ing Colleges, 1901 (succeeding Sir John
Stainer). Mus.Doc. Cantab., 1902.
Works : *The Forsaken Merman, The Power of
Sound, Ode to the Sea*, &c. ; orchl. pieces,
church music, pf. pieces, songs.

SOMERVILLE, Reginald. Song composer ;
b. Upton Cheyney, 1869.

SOMIS, Giovanni B. Eminent violinist ; *b.*
Piedmont, 1676 ; *d.* 1763. Pupil of
Corelli ; soloist and conductor, Turin.

Som'ma (*I.*). Greatest, highest, extreme.
Con som'ma passio'ne. Very impassioned.
Som'ma espressio'ne. With the utmost expression.

SOM'MER, Hans (H. F. A. Zincke). *B.*
Brunswick, 1837. Settled in Weimar,
1888.
Works : operas (*Lorelei*, 1891, very successful) ;
songs, &c.

Som'merlied (*G.*). A summer song.

Sommer'ophone. A kind of bombardon
invented by Sommer, Weimar, 1843.

Sommes'so,-a (*I.*). Subdued.
Con vo'ce sommes'sa. In a subdued voice.

Sommier (*F.*). A wind-chest.

Son (*F.*). Sound.
Son bouché. A closed note (on a horn).
Son cuivré. A "brassy" note.
Son doux. A sweet sound.
Son étouffé. A stifled, veiled, or muted sound.
Son harmonique. A harmonic.
Son naturel } An open note (on a horn, &c.).
Son ordinaire }
Son ouvert. An open or natural note on a brass inst.
Son plein. A full, round tone.
Sons pleins mais non stridents. The sounds to be full
but not strident.

Sona'bile (*I.*) } Sonorous, resounding ;
Sonan'te (*I.*) } resonant.

Sonaglia're (*I.*). To jingle (as a bell).

Sona're (*I.*). To sound, to play (upon).
Sona're al'la men'te. To improvise.
Sona're il violi'no. To play the violin.

Sona'ta } (From *I. Suona'ta*, a piece
Sona'te (*G.*) } to be " sounded," as op-
Sonate (*F.*) } posed to *Canta'ta*, a piece
to be " sung.")
(1) Originally, any instrumental piece ;
as *Sonata da Chiesa*, a piece to be played
in a church ; *Sonata da Camera*, a
(secular) piece to be played in a
"chamber" or concert-room.
(2) The most important form of classical
instrumental music.

Sonata Form. (1) The general plan of the
sonata as a whole.
N.B.—The classic symphony, duo, trio, quartet,
quintet, &c., are all designed on the same plan ;
while the concerto is the same with certain
modifications.
The smaller sonata comprises three movements ;
(1) The *Allegro* (with or without an introduction) ; (2) The *Slow Movement* ; (3) The
Finale. The larger or "Grand Sonata" comprises also a *Minuet* and *Trio* (or, in more
modern works, a *Scherzo*).
The plan of the 1st movement is sketched below.
The *Slow Movement* may be in any form ; the
Song-form (*q. v.*) is sometimes employed.
Beethoven's Slow Movements are often "great
Romances with many varied strophes, each
repetition of the theme being more and more
richly ornamented."—*Lavignac.*
The *Finale* may be a Rondo (*q.v.*), a *Theme with
Variations*, or an *Allegro* like the 1st movement
(but more animated and less formal).
The *Minuet* or *Scherzo* (when added) generally
comes as the 3rd movement.
The keys of the different movements are varied ;
but the 1st and last should be the same ;
the last may be the Tonic Major if the first
is Minor.
Examples : Beethoven, Pf. Sonata, Op. 79 :
Presto, G major ; *Andante*, G minor ; *Vivace*,
G major. Mozart, Symphony in G minor :
Allegro, G minor ; *Andante*, E♭ major ; *Minuet*,
G minor, G major, and G minor ; *Finale*,
G minor. Beethoven, Symphony, No. 5 :
Allegro, C minor ; *Andante*, A♭ major ; *Scherzo*,
C minor, C major, C minor ; *Finale*, C major.

(2) Specially, the plan of the "First Movement" of a work in sonata-form; called also "First Movement Form," "Haydn Form," "Sonata-Formula," "Sonatasatz" (*G.*), and "Binary Form" (because based on *two* principal themes).

This is the essential and distinctive feature of a sonata. It was foreshadowed by D. Scarlatti, Corelli, and others, and especially by C. P. E. Bach. Haydn was, however, the first "great" composer to see its vast capabilities and to mould it into clearly-defined and well-proportioned shape; hence the name "Haydn-form." Mozart and Beethoven brought the form to perfection. (See *Form*.)

(N.B.—The *Symphonic Overture* is a "First-movement" prefaced by a rather long Introduction; it does not repeat the first part, and usually has little of the "Free Fantasia" or *Development* portion.)

GENERAL CONSTRUCTION. — I, EXPOSITION; II, DEVELOPMENT; III, RECAPITULATION.

I. (*a*) Introduction (optional).
(*b*) The first principal subject (with or without auxiliary or subsidiary themes), in the principal key of the movement.
(*c*) Bridge; connective-matter leading to
(*d*) The second principal subject (with or without subsidiary themes), in some related key (usually that of the Dominant; or in Minor movements, that of the Rel. Major). It should be well contrasted with the first subject.
(*e*) Short codetta.
The end of this part is marked by a double bar with "repeats," but performers do not always play it a second time.

II. Free Fantasia or Development portion. Themes or parts of themes occurring in I are developed (see *Thematic Development*), repeated, interwoven, &c., at the composer's discretion and ability; or (occasionally) entirely new themes are introduced. This part is generally a little shorter than I, and the principal key of the piece should be avoided; it leads directly into

III. (*a*) The Repetition (or *Reprise*) of the first principal subject, either exactly as in I, or with modifications.
(*b*) Bridge, modified so as to lead to
(*c*) The second principal subject, this time in the principal key of the movement (or often in the Tonic Major if the principal key is minor).
(*d*) Coda.

A us'gewählte Sona'ten (*G.*). Selected sonatas.
Sona'ta di bravu'ra (*I.*). A brilliant, showy sonata.
Sona'ta per il cem'balo (*I.*). A sonata for the pf.
Sona'ta qua'si u'na fantasi'a (*I.*). A sonata in the style of a fantasia; not strictly formal.
Sona'ten für Klavier' allein' (*G.*). Sonatas for pf. solo.
Sonatil'la (*I.*) } A short work in sonata form; a little
Sonati'na (*I.*) } sonata.
Sonatine (*F.*) }

Sonato're (*I., Masc.*) } An instrumentalist.
Sonatri'ce (*I., Fem.*) }

Sone'vole (*I.*). Sonorous, resounding.

Song. (1) (*G., Gesang'; F., Chant; I., Can'to.*) Anything which may be sung, or uttered with musical modulations of the voice; a lay, a poem; poetry in general.
"Song is confined to human beings and birds."

(2) (*G., Lied; F., Chanson; I., Can-zo'ne.*) A musical composition for a solo voice, either with or without accompaniment.
Songs represent the most ancient and universal form of music. They range from the simple unaccompanied ballad to the highly-developed works of a Schubert or Schumann, and may be broadly divided into *Folk-songs* and *Art-songs*.

Art-song. (*G., Kunst'lied.*) An artistic song, as opposed to a folk-song.
Durchcomponi(e)'rt Lied (*G.*). A "through-composed" song (see below).
Erotic song. A love song.
Florid song. Opposed to plain song (*q.v.*).
Folk-song. (*G., Volks'lied.*) A song of the people; a popular song of which the origin is unknown or obscure; a traditional song.
Plain-song. (See under *P.*)
Sing-song. Monotonous modulation of the voice.
Song of the Three Holy Children. A chapter of 68 verses formerly included in the Book of Daniel; now in the Apocrypha.
Song-craft. The art of composing songs.
Song-men. Old name for vicars-choral in cathedrals.
Song without Words. (*G., Lied oh'ne Wort'e; F., Chant sans paroles.*) A melodious "song-like" piece for an inst.
Song-theme. Name sometimes given to the "second subject" in sonata form (*q.v.*).
Through-composed song. A song with different music for each verse (stanza).

Songeant (*F.*). Dreaming.

Song-form. (*G., Lied-form.*) A simple and effective form much employed for organ voluntaries, pf. pieces, "Songs without Words," &c.
I. First theme; a sentence, period, or strain. (See *Metrical Form*.)
II. Second theme; contrasted in style and in a different key.
III. Exact or varied repetition of First Theme.
IV. Short Coda.

Sonif'erous. Producing or conveying sound; sonorous.

Sonnante (*F.*). An inst. used in military bands, consisting of tuned steel bars struck with a hammer.

Sonner (*F.*). To sound.
Sonner le tambour. "To sound the drum." Used of a jarring G string on the 'cello.
Sonnerie. (1) A chime. (2) A military signal.

Son'net. A short poem of 14 lines (variously rhymed).
Sonnet to (*I.*). A sonnet set to music.

SONN'LEITNER, Joseph. Vienna, 1765-1835. Govt. councillor and patron of music. Discovered (1827) the famous "Antiphonary of St. Gallen," a 9th cent. MS. in Neume notation.

SONN'LEITNER, Leopold von. Nephew of J.; Vienna, 1797-1873. Staunch friend of Schubert; secured the publication of the *Erl King* (Schubert's 1st published work), and the performance of many of his other compositions.

So'no (*I.*). Sound, tone.
Sonneur (*F.*). A bell ringer.
Sonom'eter } "A sound measurer." (1) A monochord
Sonomètre (*F.*) } to aid pf. tuners. (2) A sounding board with two strings, for measuring vibrations.
Sonore (*F.*) }
Sono'ro (*I.*) } Sonorous(ly).
Sonoramen'te (*I.*) }
Sonoridad' (*S.*) }
Sonorità (*I.*) } Sonority, resonance.
Sonorité (*F.*) }
Sono'rophone. A kind of bombardon.
Sono'rous. Resounding, harmonious, resonant; rich-toned.

SONS, Maurice. Violinist; *b.* Amsterdam, 1857.

SON'TAG, Henriette G. W. (Countess **Rossi**). Famous dramatic soprano ; *b.* Coblenz, 1804 ; *d.* Mexico, 1854. *Début* at 16 ; created the part of "Euryanthe" in Weber's opera, 1823. Visited London, 1828 (where she married Count Rossi). Returned to the stage, 1848.
> Her brilliant singing aroused "an enthusiasm which was literally unbounded."

So'nus (*L.*). Sound, tone.

So'pra (*I.*). Above ; before ; upon, over.
Co'me so'pra }
Di so'pra } As above ; as before.
Nel'la par'te di so'pra. In the higher (highest) part.
So'pra u'na cor'da. On one string.
So'pra-dominan'te }
So'pra-quin'ta } The upper dominant.
So'pra-to'nica. The supertonic.

Sopral'to (*I.*). A high contralto (alto).

Sopran' (*G.*). (See **Soprano.**)

Soprani'no (*I.*). A high soprano (voice or inst.).

Sopra'no (*I.*). (Plur. *Sopra'ni ; G., Sopran'; F., Dessus.*) (1) The highest class of female (or boys') voices. (See **Voice.**)

Ordinary compass from about

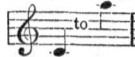

(2) The highest of a family of insts., as *Soprano Saxhorn, Soprano Cornet,* &c.
Mez'zo sopra'no. (See under *Mezzo.*)
Sopran'ista (*I.*). (1) A soprano singer. (2) A male soprano.
Sopra'no acu'to (*I.*). A high soprano.
Sopra'no concerta'to (*I.*). The solo soprano in a chorus.
Sopra'na cor'da (*I.*) }
Sopra'no string } The E string of the violin.
Sopra'no dramma'tico (*I.*). A dramatic soprano with a powerful voice.
Sopra'no leggie'ro (*I.*). A light soprano.
Sopra'no pri'mo (*I.*). First soprano.
Sopra'no secon'do (*I.*). Second soprano.
Sopra'no sfoga'to (*I.*). A very high soprano.
Sopran'schlüssel (*G.*). Soprano clef.
Sopran'stimme (*G.*). A soprano voice or part.

Soprano clef. The C clef on the 1st line of the staff. (See **Clef.**)

SOR (or **SORS**), **Fernando.** Noted guitar player ; *b.* Barcelona, 1778 ; *d.* 1839. Settled in Paris, 1828.
> Works : operas (*La foire de Smyrne,* London) ; ballets, symphonies, much guitar music, a "Guitar Method," &c.

Sordelli'na (*I.*). A small bagpipe.

Sordi'no (*I.*). (Plur. *Sordi'ni ; G.* plur. *Sordi'nen.*) (1) A mute (of a vn., &c.).
Con sordi'ni. With the mutes. (See *Mute.*)
Sen'za sord'ini }
Si leva'no i sordi'ni } Without the mutes ; take off
Sordi'ni leva'ti } the mutes.
(2) A pianoforte damper. (*G., Dämp'fer.*)
Senza sordini. Press the right (loud) pedal down (at each change of chord).
Con sordini. Used by Beethoven to mean "release the right pedal ; " *i.e.,* "let it rise."
(3) A kit (pocket violin).

Sor'do,-a (*I.*). Muffled, muted ; veiled.
Sordamen'te. Softly, gently, dully.
Trom'ba sor'da. The trumpet (to be) muted.

Sordo'no (*I.*). (*G., Sordun'; F., Sordone.*)
(1) An obsolete kind of bassoon.
(2) An old organ reed stop of muffled tone.

Sordun' (*G.*). (1) *Sordono.* (2) A mute for trumpet.

SOR'GE, George A. *B.* nr. Schwarzburg, 1703 ; *d.* 1778. Court orgt., Lobenstein, from his 19th year.
> Works : much organ and clavier music ; numerous theoretical treatises including "Musical Composition" (3 vols., his chief work).

Sorg'fältig (*G.*). Careful(ly), cautious(ly).

SORIA, Jules Diaz de. Baritone vocalist ; *b.* Bordeaux, 1843.

SORIA'NO. (See **Suriano.**)

SORIA'NO-FUER'TES, Don Mariano. Noted Spanish musician ; *b.* Murcia, 1817 ; *d.* 1880. Teacher Madrid Cons., 1843 ; director of the Lyceums, and opera condr., at Cordova, Seville, Cadiz, &c. Founded the *Gaceta Musical,* Barcelona, 1860.
> Works : Spanish *Zarzuelas* (operettas) ; a treatise on "Arabo-Spanish Music," a "History of Spanish Music to 1850" (4 vols.), &c.

SOR'MANN, Alfred R. G. Pianist ; *b.* Danzig, 1861. Studied under Liszt ; *début,* 1886. Court pianist, Mecklenburg-Strelitz, 1889.
> Works : a concerto, and other pf. music.

Sorri'so (*I.*). A smile.

Sortie (*F.*) } (1) A concluding voluntary.
Sorti'ta (*I.*) } (2) An entrance or exit aria in an opera.

Sospensio'ne (*I.*). Suspension ; suspense, doubt.
Sospensionamen'te. Doubtfully, irresolutely.

Sospiran'do (*I.*) } " Sighing, sobbing."
Sospiran'te (*I.*) } Catching the breath between the syllables of a word to express deep emotion.
Sospire'vole } " Sighing deeply." Plaintive, doleful,
Sospiro'so } subdued, yearning.

Sospi'ro (*I.*). " A sigh." A crotchet rest.

Sostenen'do (*I.*) } Abbn. *Sost.,* or *Sosten.*
Sostenen'te (*I.*) } (1) Sustained, prolonged ;
Sostenu'to (*I.*) } sometimes with a slight *rallentando.* (2) Rather slow ; *Andante.*
Andan'te sostenu'to. Rather slow, with the notes well held out.
Più sostenu'to. A little slower.
Sostenu'to lega'to. Sustained and slurred.
Sostenu'to mol'to. Notes very much sustained.

Sostinen'te pianoforte. A pf. with some mechanical device for sustaining the tones.

Sot'to (*I.*). Below, beneath, under.
Sot'to-dominan'te. The sub-dominant.
Sot'to il sogget'to. (Counterpoint) below the subject.
Sot'to vo'ce. In an undertone.

Soubasse (*F.*). Subbass. (See **Sub.**)

SOUBIES, Albert. Writer and critic ; *b.* Paris, 1846. Studied Paris Cons. Revived the "Almanach des Spectacles," 1874 (had pub. 26 vols. to 1898). Awarded the *Prix Voirac* by the Académie, 1893. Critic, *Le Soir,* 1876.
> His writings include a very complete "History of Music" (the English section founded on Henry Davey's work), "67 years at the Opéra, and 69 at the Opéra-Comique," essays on Wagner, &c.

SOUBRE, Etienne J. Liége, 1813-71. Director Liége Cons., 1862.
Works : an opera (*Isoline*), orchl. pieces, cantatas, church music, &c.

Soubrette (*F.*). A waiting-maid.
Applied to various light coquettish parts in comic opera, &c.

Soubret'tenrolle (*G.*). A soubrette's roll (or part).

Souchantre (*F.*). A succentor (*q.v.*).

Soudainement (*F.*). Suddenly.

Souffler (*F.*). To blow.
Soufflet. The swell, ⤝ ⤞
Soufflets. Bellows (of an organ, harmonium, &c.).
Soufflerie. The bellows action.
Souffleur. (1) An organ blower. (2) A prompter.
Souffleuse. A female prompter.

SOUHAITTY, Jean J. Monk at Paris. Said to have been "the first to employ figures in teaching sight-singing." His "Nouvelle Méthode" was published in 1665.

SOULIER. (See **Solié.**)

Soum. A Burmese harp.

Sound. (See **Acoustics.**)

Sound-board ⎫ (1) (*G., Resonanz'boden ;*
Sounding-board ⎭ *F., Table d'harmonie ; I., Ta'volo armo'nica.*) The board placed below (or behind) the strings of a pf. to increase its resonance. (See **Acoustics.**) The *belly* of a vn., &c.
(2) (*G., Pfei'fenstock ; F., Pied du tamis d'orgue ; I., Casso'ne.*) The flat cover of the wind-chest of an organ containing the holes in which the feet of the pipes are set.

Sound-body ⎫ The resonance chamber (or
Sound-box ⎭ cavity) of any inst. (See **Acoustics.**)
Sound-bow. The thick part of the rim of a bell where the clapper strikes.
Sound-hole. A hole cut in the belly of a stringed inst. to increase its resonance.
Soundpost. (*G., See'le, Stimm'stock; F., Âme; I., A'nima.*) The small piece of wood inside a vn., &c., connecting the back and belly; it keeps the body rigid and increases the resonance.
Sound waves. (See *Acoustics.*)

Soupape (*F.*). A valve (of a wind inst.).

Soupir (*F.*). "A sigh." A crotchet or quarter rest.
Demi-soupir ⎫ A quaver (or eighth) rest.
Soupir de croche ⎭
Huitième de soupir ⎫ A demisemiquaver (or 32nd)
Demi-quart de soupir ⎬ rest.
Soupir de triple croche ⎭
Quart de soupir ⎫ A semiquaver (or 16th)
Soupir de double croche ⎭ rest.
Seizième de double croche. A hemidemisemiquaver (or 64th) rest.

Sourdeline (*F.*). Same as **Sordellina.**

Sourdement (*F.*). Subdued.

Sourdine (*F.*). (1) A mute. (2) A device in the harmonium for cutting off some of the wind and producing soft tones. (3) The *pédale céleste,* a 3rd pedal found on some pianofortes. (4) An obsolete spinet (or lute) of muffled tone.

Sous (*F.*). Under, below, beneath.
Sous-dominante. Subdominant.
Sous-médiante. Submediant.
Sous-tonique. Leading-note.

SOU'SA, John Philip. Bandmaster ; *b.* Washington, U.S., 1854. Condr. of travelling theatre bands from 17 ; leader of the band of the U.S. Marine Corps, 1880 ; organized his own band, 1892.
Works : comic operas ; numerous military marches, waltzes, &c.

Soutenu (*F.*). Same as **Sostenuto** (*q.v.*).

SOUTH, Chas. F. *B.* London, 1853. Orgt. Salisbury Cath. since 1883.

SOUTHGATE, Thos. Lea. *B.* Highgate, 1836. Orgt. various London churches. Editor *Musical Standard,* 1871-91 ; joint editor *Musical News,* 1891-5 ; secretary Union of Graduates, 1893-1906. Hon. D.C.L., Durham, 1907.
His writings on music are of historic value.

Souvenir (*F.*). A reminiscence, a recollection.

SOWIN'SKY, Albert C. W. Pianist ; *b.* Ukraine, 1803(?) ; *d.* 1880. Settled in Paris as teacher, &c., 1830.
Works : a treatise on "Ancient and Modern Polish and Slav Musicians," 2 operas, church music, orchl. and chamber music, pf. pieces, &c.

SOYER, Berthe. Contralto ; *b.* Chalon-sur-Saône, 1877. *Début,* 1899.

Sp. Abbn. of *Spitz* (*q.v.*).

Space. (*G., Zwisch'enraum ; F., Espace ; I., Spaz'io.*) The interval between two adjacent staff lines (or leger lines).
Spaces are generally counted *upwards* :

Spagnole'sco (*I.*). In the Spanish style.

Spagnolet'ta (*I.*) ⎫ A Spanish minuet ; a
Spagnuo'la (*I.*) ⎭ serenade.
Spagnuola also means the guitar, or a Spaniard.

SPALDING, Albert. Violinist ; *b.* Chicago, 1888.

Spal'la (*I.*). Shoulder.
Vio'la da spal'la. A "shoulder viol ;" opposed to *Vio'la da gam'ba,* a "leg-viol."

Spanden'do (*I.*). Spreading, *crescendo.*

SPANG'ENBERG, Johann. *B.* nr. Göttingen, 1484 ; *d.* 1550.
Published Lutheran sacred songs, &c.
His son, CYRIAK (1528-1604), wrote a work on " The Musical Art of the Meistersingers."

Spanish Cross ⎫ The sign for a double
Spa'nischer Rei'ter (*G.*) ⎬ sharp (×).
Spa'nisches Kreuz (*G.*) ⎭

Spanish Guitar. (See **Guitar.**)

SPARK, Wm. *B.* Exeter, 1823 ; *d.* 1897. Articled pupil of Dr. S. S. Wesley. Orgt. St. George's, Leeds, 1850-80 ; Borough orgt., Leeds, 1860. Mus.Doc. Dublin, 1861. Editor " Organist's Quarterly Journal."
Works : an oratorio, cantatas, church music, organ pieces, songs ; a Memoir of Dr. S. S. Wesley, a biography of Henry Smart, &c.

SPARKES, Leonora. Soprano; *b.* Bristol. Sang Covent Garden, 1908.

Spart (*G.*) ⎫ Scattered, divided; distri-
Spar'to (*I.*) ⎭ buted. Hence, a *Score* (*q.v.*)·

Spar'ta, Sparti'ta, Sparti'to (*I.*) ⎫ A full score.
Spar'te (*G.*) ⎭

Sparti're (*I.*). ⎫ To score; to arrange old scores in
Sparti(e)'ren (*G.*). ⎭ modern notation.

Sparti'to can'to e pia'noforte (*I.*). A vocal score with pf. accompt.

Spassapensie'ro (*I.*). A Jew's harp.

Spass'haft (*G.*). Scherzando (*q.v.*).
Spass'haftigkeit. Playfulness.

Spa'tium (*L.*) ⎫ (1) A space (of the staff).
Spa'zio (*I.*) ⎭ (2) An interval.
The " void found between the lines whereon a piece of music is pricked or noted."—*Grassineau.*

SPAZIER', Johann G. K. *B.* Berlin, 1761; *d.* 1805. Prof. at Giessen; settled in Leipzig, 1800.
Works: several musical treatises and translations, and many popular songs.

Specification. (*G., Disposition'.*) The general plan of an organ, with the number and arrangement of the stops, &c.

Spedien'do (*I.*). Hastening, hurrying.

Speech; to speak. The sounding of a note on a wind inst., organ pipe, &c. Speech should be accurate and prompt.

SPEER, Charlton T. Composer and pianist; *b.* Cheltenham, 1859.

SPEER, Wm. Hy. Cousin of C. T. Orgt. and composer; *b.* London, 1863. Mus.D. Cantab., 1906.

SPEI'DEL, Wilhelm. Pianist and teacher; *b.* Ulm, 1826; *d.* 1899. Mus. director, Ulm, 1854; condr. Stuttgart Liederkranz, 1857. One of the founders of the Stuttgart Cons.; pf. prof. there until 1874, and again from 1884 (having in the interval carried on a "Klavier School" of his own.)
His numerous compositions include some interesting pf. pieces.

SPENCER, Chas. Child. London, 1797-1869. Author of "A concise explanation of the Church Modes" (1846), a useful work.

SPENG'EL, Julius H. *B.* Hamburg, 1853. Studied at Cologne and Berlin. Condr. Cäcilienverein, Hamburg, 1878; orgt. Gertrudenkirche, 1886.
Works: Orchl. pieces, chamber music, songs, &c.

SPENSER, Willard. *B.* Cooperstown, N.Y., 1856.
His comic operetta, *The Little Tycoon* (1886) is very popular in America.

Sperden'dosi (*I.*). Fading away.

Sperr'ventil (*G.*). An organ ventil acting on certain stops (or groups of stops).

Spezza'to (*I.*). Divided; broken.

Splana'ta,-o (*I.*). Smooth, level, even; tranquil; legato.
Spianar' la vo'ce. To make the voice smooth and even, to blend the registers, &c.

Spicca'to (*I.*). (*F., Piqué.*) Detached. (1) With the "springing-bow" (*q.v.*) and

"wrist-stroke" in violin playing. (2) With the point of the bow.
Spicca'to assa'i. Very detached.
Spiccatamen'te. Pointedly; brightly, brilliantly.

SPICK'ER, Max. *B.* Königsberg, 1858. Studied Leipzig Cons. Condr. "Beethoven Männerchor," New York, 1882; director Brooklyn Cons., 1888-95; teacher of harmony, National Cons., New York, 1895.
Works: orchl. pieces, male choruses, songs, &c.

Spiegan'do (*I.*). Extending; *crescendo.*

Spie'gelkanon (*G.*). A canon to be read backwards. (*Spie'gel,* a mirror.)

Spiel (*G.*). Playing; style of playing.
Spiel'art. (1) Style of playing; method of performance. (2) Touch.
Spiel'bar. Playable; suitable (handy) for playing.
Spiel'en. To play.
Spiel'end. (1) Playing. (2) Playful.
Spiel'en vom Blatt. To play at sight.
Spiel'er. Player.
Spiel'mani(e)'ren. Ornaments and graces in playing.
Spiel'mann. A musician.
Spiel'oper. A light or comic opera.
Spiel'tenor. A light tenor; comic tenor.
Vol'les Spiel. Full organ.

SPIER'ING, Theodor. Violinist; *b.* St. Louis, Missouri, 1871. Pupil of Joachim. Founder and leader of the "Spiering Quartet," Chicago.

SPIES, Hermine. Noted contralto. Fine interpreter of Brahms; *b.* nr. Weilburg, 1857; *d.* 1893. *Début*, 1882; married Dr. Hardtmuth, Wiesbaden, 1892.

SPIESS, Meinrad. *B.* Swabia, 1683; *d.* 1761. Published much church music with accompaniment for strings and organ.

Spigliatez'za (*I.*). Agility, sprightliness, swiftness.
Spigliatez'ze. Short lively pieces requiring dexterity.

Spill'flöte (*G.*). Same as **Spitzflöte** (*q.v.*).

Spi'na. (*L.,* a thorn.) The quill of a spinet or harpsichord.

Spin'delflöte (*G.*). Same as **Spitzflöte** (*q.v.*).

SPIN'DLER, Fritz. Pianist and noted teacher; *b.* nr. Lobenstein, 1817; *d.* 1906. Settled in Dresden 1841.
His works number about 400; including symphonies, concertos, chamber music, and numerous pf. pieces and studies.

SPINEL'LI, Nicola. Opera composer; *b.* Turin, 1865. Studied Naples Cons.
Chief opera: *A basso porto* (Rome, 1895).

Spin'et. (*G., Spinett'; F., Epinette; I., Spinet'ta.*) An obsolete small square form of harpsichord; so-called from its "spines" or quills.
Old names: *Virginal, Pair of Virginals, Couched Harp, Spinette.*

Spin'nen des Tons (*G.*). Drawing-out the tones. (See **Filar la voce.**)

SPINNEY, Walter S. Organist; *b.* Salisbury, 1852; *d.* 1894.
Works: church music, organ pieces, "The Organ Library," &c.

Spi'rant. (*L.*, *Spi'rans*, *Spiran'tis*, "*breathing.*") A consonant uttered with some perceptible escape of breath.
The English "Spirants" are *f*, *ph*, *v*, *th* ; *c*, *s*, *z* ; *g*, *j*, *ch*, *sh*, *zh* ; *h*, *wh*.

Spiran'te (*I.*). Expiring ; dying away.

SPIRI'DIO, Berthold. Monk and organist, St. Teodor, nr. Bamberg.
Published a "curious Instruction book for organ and clavier playing," 1668.

SPIRID'ION. (See **Xyndas.**)

Spi'rito (*I.*). Spirit, life ; soul ; energy.
Con spi'rito
Spiritosamen'te } With spirit and animation ; in
Spirito'so } spirited style.
Spirituo'so

Spiritua'le (*I.*). Sacred ; spiritual.

Spirituel (*F.*) } Ideal, ethereal ; witty.
Spirituelle (*F.*) }

SPIT'TA, Carl Joh. P. D.D. 1801-1859. Lutheran pastor.
Popular hymn writer ; " O how blest the hour" (Eng. by R. Massie), &c.

SPIT'TA, Friedrich. *B.* Wittengen, 1852. Prof. of theology, Strasburg Univ.
Works : "Handel and Bach," "H. Schütz," "The Passions of H. Schütz," &c.

SPIT'TA, Dr. J. A. Philipp. Brother of preceding ; learned writer ; *b.* nr. Hoya, Hanover, 1841 ; *d.* Berlin, 1894. Co-founder Bachverein, Leipzig, 1874. Prof. Mus. Hist., Berlin Univ., 1875.
His valuable historical works include the standard "Life of J. S. Bach" (Eng. edition, 3 vols., Novello), a critical edition of Buxtehude's Organ Works, 14 vols. of the complete edition of Schütz's works (completed by his brother), biographies of Schumann and Weber for Grove's Dict., &c.

Spitz (*G.*). Pointed ; tapering ; conical.
Spit'ze. (1) The point of the bow. (2) The toe in organ playing.
Spitz'flöte. An organ flue stop of pleasing tone, with conical pipes.
Spitz'harfe. (*Harfenett'*, *Flü'gelharfe*, *Zwit'schenharfe* ; *I.*, *Arpanet'ta.*) A small pointed (triangular) harp to be set on a table.
Spitz'quint. An organ stop similar to the *Spitzflöte*, tuned a 5th higher.

Spitz'ig (*G.*). Pointed, cutting, biting.

SPOFFORTH, Reginald. *B.* Southwell, Notts., 1770 ; *d.* 1827.
Works : glees ("Hail, smiling morn," &c.), songs.

SPOHR, Louis (or **Ludwig**). Celebrated violinist, composer, and teacher ; *b.* Brunswick, April 5, 1784 ; *d.* Cassel, Nov. 22, 1859. Son of a physician. Began to learn the vn. about 5 ; played a concerto of his own before the Brunswick Court at 14. Studied under Franz Eck, 1802-3 ; made his first tour, 1804 ; leader at Gotha, 1805. Married Dorette Scheidler, a harp player ; toured with her 1807 and 1809. Leader Vienna Th., 1812-15. After tours in Italy and Holland, opera condr. Frankfort, 1817; introduced conducting with a bâton against the wish of the singers. Visited London, 1820 ; conducted the Philharmonic Orch. with a bâton. (See

Bâton.) Court condr., Cassel, 1822-57. Spohr was one of the greatest conductors of his time, and conducted several of the chief German mus. festivals. His compositions rank high, but they are over-flavoured by " chromaticism."
Works (over 160) : 11 operas (*Faust*, 1818 ; *Zemire and Azore*, 1819 ; *Jessonda*, 1823 ; &c.); 4 oratorios (*Last Judgment*, 1826 ; *Calvary*, 1835 ; *Fall of Babylon*, 1841) ; a dramatic cantata, church music, part-songs, songs ; 9 symphonies (*The Power of Sound*, 1832) ; 8 overtures, 15 vn. concertos ; a "quartet-concerto" for 2 vns., viola, 'cello, and orch. ; 2 clar. concertos, much chamber music (including a nonet, an octet, 4 double quartets, a septet, 9 quintets, and 34 string quintets) ; an excellent " Violin School " (1831), &c.

Spon'dee (*L.*) } A metrical foot of two long
Spon'deo (*I.*) } syllables (— —).

SPONTI'NI, Gasparo L. P. Distinguished Italian composer ; *b.* Majolati, Ancona, 1774 ; *d.* 1851. Son of a poor peasant ; intended for the church, but afterwards allowed to follow his musical inclination. Studied Cons. della Pietà, Naples ; also received valuable advice from Piccinni. Condr. Neapolitan Court (where he produced 3 operas), 1800. Went to Paris, 1803 ; studied Mozart's works, and changed his style for one of greater depth and expression. Chamber composer to the Empress Josephine, 1804 ; director Italian opera 1810-12 ; Court composer to Louis XVIII, 1814. Court composer and musical director, Berlin, 1820-41.
Of his numerous operas the most important are *La Vestale* (1807), and *Fernando Cortez* (1809.)

Spött'isch (*G.*). Mocking(ly), Scoffing(ly).

Spott'lied (*G.*). A satirical song.

Spread Harmony. (See **Harmony.**)

Sprech'end (*G.*). Speaking.
Sprech'endgesang. Recitative.
Sprech'endmaschine. Talking-machine.
Sprech'endoper. An opera with spoken dialogue.

Spressio'ne (*I.*). Expression.

Spring. An ornament similar to the inverted mordent, but played more deliberately and distinctly.

Springing bow. (*G.*, *Spring'ender Bo'gen.*) Holding the bow from the wrist in vn. playing and letting it drop on the string and then rebound.
The *spicca'to* is one variety, used in staccato playing ; the *salta'to* has a higher fall and rebound.

Spruch'gesang (*G.*). An anthem.

Sprung (*G.*). A skip in melody.
Sprung'lauf. A rapid series of notes ; a *fusée* (*q.v.*).
Sprung'weise. Proceeding by skips.

Square pianoforte. (See **Pianoforte.**)

Square B. B natural (♮). (See **B quadratum.**)

Squil'la (*I.*). A little bell.
Squillan'te. Tinkling, ringing ; clear.

SQUIRE, Wm. Barclay. *B.* London, 1855. Writer of musical biographies for Grove's Dict., The Dict. of National Biography, &c. Edited with J. A. Fuller Maitland "The Fitzwilliam Virginal Book" (1894).

SQUIRE, William Hy. 'Cellist ; *b.* Ross, Herefordshire, 1871. Played in public at 7 ; afterwards won a scholarship at the R.C.M. London *début*, 1891.
Works : a concerto and other pieces for 'cello, pf. pieces, songs, &c.

SSAFFIEDDIN. (See Saffieddin.)

SSEROFF. (See Serov.)

SSOLOWIEW. (See Soloviev.)

Sta (*I.*). As it stands ; as written.

Stab'at Ma'ter Do'loro'sa (*L.*). "The Lamentation of the Blessed Virgin Mary." A famous hymn on the Crucifixion, by Jacoponus, 14th cent.
Settings of the Stabat Mater begin with Dunstable ; among the best are those of Palestrina, Astorga, Pergolesi, Haydn, Rossini, Verdi, Dvorak, and Stanford.

Sta'bile (*I.*). Firm, steady, stable.

STABI'LE, Annibale. Roman contrapuntist; pupil of Palestrina ; *d.* Rome, abt. 1595. Wrote motets, madrigals, litanies, &c.

Stac. \
Stacc. / Abbns. of *Staccato*.
Stacc. sem'pre. Always staccato.

Stacca're (*I.*). To make staccato ; to separate the notes.

Stacca'to (*I.*). (*G., Ab'gestossen.*) Detached, separated.
(1) Mezzo-staccato ; slur and dots :— Notes held about three-fourths their length.
(2) Staccato ; dots only :— Notes held about one-half their length, thus :—
(3) Staccatis'simo ; pointed dash :— Notes held about one-fourth their length.
Martelé (*F.*). Same as *Staccatissimo* in vn. playing.
Stacca'to touch. "A sudden lifting up of the fingers from the keys, giving to the music a light, detached, airy effect."—*Ellis.*

STA'DE, Dr. Friedrich W. *B.* Halle, 1817 ; *d.* 1902. Court orgt. and capellmeister, Altenburg, 1860-91.
Works : orchl. pieces, 7 books of organ pieces, pf. pieces, cantatas, arrangements of Bach's and Handel's sonatas, celebrated songs, &c.

STA'DEN, Johann. Organist ; Nuremberg, abt. 1579-1634.
Wrote motets, magnificats, dances, &c.

STA'DEN, Sigismund. Son of preceding.
"Wrote *Seelewig* (pub. 1644), the earliest known German opera."—*Riemann.*

STA'DLER, Abbé Maximilian. *B.* Melk, Lower Austria, 1748 ; *d.* 1833. Noted for upholding the genuineness of Mozart's *Requiem.*
Works : masses, psalms, org. fugues, pf. sonatas, songs, &c.

STA'DLMAYER, Johann. Contrapuntist ; *b.* Bavaria, 1560. Capellmeister at Innsbruck ; *d.* after 1646.
Works : masses and hymns in from 5 to 12 parts, sacred songs (up to 24 parts with instrumental accompaniment), Misereres, odes, cantatas, &c.

Stadt (*G.*). Town, city.
Stadt'musikanten \
Stadt'pfeifer } Town musicians.
Stadt'zinkenister /
Stadt'musikus. Leader of the town musicians.

STADT'FELDT, Alexander. *B.* Wiesbaden, 1826 ; *d.* 1853. *Grand Prix de Rome*, Brussels Cons., 1849.
Works : operas (*Hamlet*, 1857) ; 4 symphonies and other orchl. works ; chamber music, church music, &c.

Staff. (Plur., *Staves* ; *G., Li'niensystem, Funf'liniensystem, System'*; *F., Portée*; *I., Ri'go.*) The 5 parallel horizontal lines used in musical notation. (See Notation.)
Bass staff. A staff with the F or Bass Clef.
Treble staff. A staff with the G or Treble Clef.
Great staff. (See *Stave*.)
Gregorian staff. A staff of four lines.
Staff notation. Music written on the staff as opposed to Sol-fa, alphabetical, and figure notations.

STAFFORD, Wm. Cooke. *B.* York, 1793 ; *d.* 1876.
Author of a "Hist. of Music" (1830) "chiefly noted for its inaccuracy."

STÄ'GEMANN, Max. Baritone singer ; *b.* Freienwalde-on-Oder, 1843. Manager Leipzig City Th., 1882.

STAGGINS, Nicholas. Master of the Royal Music, and Mus.D. Cantab., 1682. First prof. of music, Cambridge Univ., 1684. *D.* 1705.

STAG'NO, Alberto. Operatic tenor ; *b.* Palermo, 1836 ; *d.* 1897. Sang in London, 1876.

Stahl'harmo'nika (*G.*) \ An inst. consisting
Stahl'spiel (*G.*) / of tuned steel bars played by means of a hammer.

STAI'NER (or STEINER), Jakob. Celebrated vn. maker ; *b.* Absam, Tyrol, 1621 ; *d.* insane, 1683. Attracted attention as a shepherd boy by his skilfully constructed fifes, &c. It is surmised that he learnt the art of vn. making at Cremona.
His brother, Markus, was celebrated as a viola maker.

STAINER, Sir John. *B.* London, 1840 ; *d.* 1901. Chorister, St. Paul's, 1847-56 ; Univ. orgt., Oxford, 1860 ; Mus.Doc., 1865. Orgt. St. Paul's (succeeding Sir John Goss), 1872-88. Prof. National Training School of Music, 1876 ; Principal, 1881. Inspector of Mus. in Training Colleges, 1882. Knighted, 1888.
Works : an oratorio (*Gideon*) ; cantatas (*Daughter of Jairus, St. Mary Magdalene, The Crucifixion*); 4 church services, several anthems, songs ; a "Treatise on Harmony," and (with W. A. Barrett), a "Dict. of Mus. Terms." Edited Novello's Music Primers (himself contributing "Harmony," "Composition," "The Organ"),

STAMATY, Camille M. Pianist; *b.* Rome, 1811; *d.* 1870. Settled in Paris as a teacher; Saint-Saëns and Gottschalk were his pupils.
Wrote pf. pieces and excellent pf. studies.

Stamen'tienpfeife (*G.*). Same as **Schwegel** (*q.v.*).

STA'MITZ, Anton. Violinist; son of J. K. (below).; *b.* Mannheim, 1753; *d.* (?). Settled in Paris, 1770.
Works: a vn. concerto; chamber music; 6 sonatas for vn., fl., and bass, &c.

STA'MITZ, Johann K. Renowned self-taught violinist; *b.* Bohemia, 1717; *d.* 1757. Concertmeister at Mannheim.
Works: 12 symphonies (written before Haydn's); sonatas for vn. and bass, for vn. and harpsichord, &c.; 6 vn. concertos, études for 2 vns., and other instrumental music.

STA'MITZ, Karl. Son of preceding; noted player on the vn. and viole d'amour; *b.* Mannheim, 1746; *d.* 1801.
Leader to the Duc de Noailles, Paris, 1770-85. Afterwards made long concert tours.
Works: 2 operas, 9 symphonies, 7 vn. concertos, a viola concerto, a pf. concerto, &c.
The Stamitz family, by cultivating orchestral expression, had very great influence on the development of music.

Stamm (*G.*). Stem, trunk; root.
Stamm'akkord. (1) A chord in its root (or *a*) position. (2) A fundamental chord.
Stamm'ton. A fundamental tone. (See *Acoustics.*)
Stamm'tonleiter. The scale of C major.

Stampi'ta (*I.*). A song, air, tune.

Stanchez'za (*I.*). Weariness, lassitude.
Con stanchez'za. As if weary; dragging the time.
Stan'co,-a. Weary, fatigued.

Standard scale of pitch. The scale of C as fixed by various standards. (See **A**, **Pitch**, &c.).

Ständ'chen (*G.*). A serenade (either morning or evening).

Stand'haft (*G.*). Firm, steady.
Stand'haftigkeit. Firmness, steadiness.

STANFORD, Sir Chas. Villiers. *B.* Dublin, 1852. Obtained an organ scholarship, Queen's Coll., Cambridge, 1870; orgt, Trinity Coll., 1873-92; condr. Cambridge Univ. Musical Soc., 1873-93; M.A., Cantab., 1878; Mus.Doc. Oxon, 1883; Cantab., 1888. Prof. of Composition and orchestral condr., R.C.M., 1883; condr. Bach Choir, 1885-1903; Prof. of Music, Cambridge Univ. (succeeding Macfarren), 1887. Condr. Leeds Philharmonic Soc., 1897; knighted, 1903. Condr. Leeds Festival since 1901.
Works: operas (*Savanorola*, 1884; *Shamus O'Brien*, 1896; &c.); incidental music to plays; oratorios (*The Resurrection*, 1875; *The Three Holy Children*, 1885; *Eden*, 1891); several odes and cantatas (*The Revenge*, 1886; *Voyage of Maeldune*, 1889; *Battle of the Baltic*, 1891; *Phaudrig Crohoore*, 1896; &c.); psalms, masses, 3 complete services, &c.; a fine *Stabat Mater*; 5 symphonies, overtures, a pf. concerto, a 'cello concerto, chamber music, pf. sonatas, songs, and song cycles, &c.

Stanghet'ta (*I.*). A bar-line.

STANLEY, Albert A. American musician; *b.* Manville, Rhode Island, 1851. Studied at Leipzig. Prof. of Music, Michigan Univ., 1888.
Works: orchl. and choral works, part-songs, songs, &c.

STANLEY, Arthur Penrhyn. D.D. 1815-81. Dean of Westminster, 1863.
Wrote the fine hymn "Lord, it is good for us to be."

STANLEY, C. John. Noted organist; blind from early youth; London, 1714-86. Pupil of Greene; esteemed by Handel. Orgt. successively of several London churches. Master Royal Band, 1779.
Possessed the most wonderful musical memory on record, repeating a new oratorio after once hearing it.
Works: 3 oratorios, a dramatic pastoral, songs, 6 concertos for org. or harpsichord, 6 concertos for strings and harpsichord, &c.

STANLEY, Samuel. Composer of hymn-tunes; Birmingham, 1767-1822.

Stan'za (*I.*). (*G., Stan'ze; F., Stance.*) A subdivision of a poem; a verse of a hymn; a strophe.
A stanza is what is commonly called a "verse" of poetry. The classic meaning of verse is "a *line* divided regularly into feet."

STARCK. (See **Bronsart**.)

Stark (*G.*). Loud, strong, vigorous.
Mit star'ken Stim'men. With loud stops.
Stark an'blasen. To blow strongly; with "brassy" tone.
Stär'ker. Louder.
Stark hervor'tretend. Well brought out, strongly prominent.
Stark und kräft'ig. Loud and vigorous.

STARK, Dr. Ludwig. Renowned pedagogue; *b.* Munich, 1831; *d.* 1884. Co-founder Stuttgart Cons., 1857; taught singing, harmony, and history there until 1873. Afterwards prof. of theory and history.
Works: edited (with Lebert) "Lebert and Stark's Great Pianoforte School," and (with Faiszt) a "Liederschule," &c.; also edited several collections of transcriptions for pf. He composed choral works, pf. pieces, songs, &c.

STAR'KE, Friedrich. Bandmaster; *b.* Elsterwerda, 1774; *d.* 1835.
Published much music for military bands.

STARMER, William Wooding. Well-known expert and authority on bells. *B.* Wellingborough, Nov. 4, 1866. Studied R.A.M.; A.R.A.M., 1889; F.R.A.M., 1906.
Works: church and org. music. Lectures: "Bells and Bell Tones," "Carillons and Bell Music," "Chimes and Chime Tunes," &c. Writer of articles in Grove's Dict., &c.

STASNY, Karl. Pianist; *b.* Mainz, 1855.

STASNY, Ludwig. *B.* Prague, 1823; *d.* 1883.
Works: 2 operas, popular dances, and skilful orchl. arrangements of Wagner's later operas.

STATHAM, H. Heathcote. *B.* Liverpool, 1839. Author of "Form and Design in Music," 1893.

STAU'DIGL, Josef. Celebrated bass singer; *b.* Wöllersdorf, Austria, 1807; *d.* insane, 1861. Court condr., Vienna, 1831.
His son, **Josef**, *b.* Vienna, 1850, is a fine baritone.

Stave. (1) Old name for staff. (2) A stanza ; a fragment of song, &c.

Grand Stave) A staff of 11 lines, comprising the
Great Stave ∫ treble staff, the bass staff, and the "Middle C" line between them.

The 5-lined staff for each of the various clefs is selected from the Grand Staff—the clefs never really changing their places :—

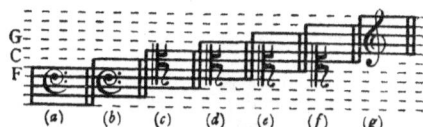

(*a*) Bass clef ; (*b*) Baritone ; (*c*) Tenor; (*d*) Alto ; (*e*) Mezzo-soprano; (*f*) Soprano ; (*g*) Treble.

STAVENHA'GEN, Bernhard. Distinguished pianist ; *b.* Greiz, Reuss, 1862.
Won "Mendelssohn Prize" for pf. playing, Berlin Hochschule, 1880. Studied with Liszt, 1885-6. Highly successful tours. Court condr., Weimar, 1895 ; Munich, 1898.

STCHERBAT'CHEFF, Nicolas de. Russian composer ; *b.* 1853.
Works : orchl. pieces, songs, numerous pf. pieces.

STEANE, Bruce H. D. Composer and orgt. ; *b.* Camberwell, 1866.

Stec'ca (*I.*). " A stick." A choked, strained voice.

Stech'er (*G.*). (1) An organ sticker. (2) An engraver.

STECK'ER, Karl. Orgt., writer, &c. ; *b.* Bohemia, 1861.

STEELE, Anne. 1716-78. Daughter of a Hampshire Baptist minister.
Wrote " Father of mercies," and other hymns.

STEFFA'NI, Abbate Agostino. *B.* Castelfranco, Venetia, 1655 ; *d.* 1730.
Choir-boy, St. Mark's, Venice. Court orgt., Munich, 1675 ; took Holy Orders, 1680. First opera, *Marco Aurelio*, 1681 ; chamber-music director to the Elector (abt. 1681-2). Court capellmeister, Hanover, 1688 (succeeded by Handel, 1710). He was also a Privy Councillor, a diplomatist, and a church dignitary.
Works : church music, and several operas (*Enrico detto il Leone*, 1869). His music is historically valuable for its (comparatively) rich orchestration and successful innovations.

Steg (*G.*). Bridge (of a vn., &c.).
Am Steg. Bow close to the bridge.

STEGGALL, Charles. *B.* London, 1826 ; *d.* 1905. Studied R.A.M. ; Prof. of organ and harmony, 1851. Mus.Doc. Cantab. Orgt. Lincoln's Inn, 1864.
Works : church music, an organ tutor, organ music, hymn tunes, &c.

STEGGALL, Reginald. Son of C. Orgt. and composer ; *b.* London, 1867.

STEG'MANN, Karl D. Tenor singer ; *b.* Dresden, 1751 ; *d.* 1826.
Début, Breslau, 1772. Capellmeister, Hamburg Opera, 1778 ; afterwards a director.
Works : 12 symphonies, 10 operas, ballets, pf. pieces, songs.

STEG'MAYER, Ferdinand. Vienna, 1803-63. Condr. successively of various theatres ; teacher of singing, Vienna Cons., 1835-7.
Works : male-voice pieces, pf. music, songs.

STEI'BELT, Daniel. Noted pianist ; *b.* Berlin, 1765 ; *d.* St. Petersburg, 1823. "Reigning pianist and favourite teacher," Paris, 1790-7. Toured (visiting London) for several years. Condr. St. Petersburg Court, 1810.
Works : 6 operas (*Roméo et Juliette*), ballets, chamber music, &c. ; and much showy and superficial pf. music. He will be probably longest remembered for his challenge to Beethoven (Vienna, 1799), which ended for him " in sad discomfiture."

Stei'gernd (*G.*). Intensifying, working up.

STEIN, Johann A. Noted organ builder and pf maker ; *b.* 1728 ; *d.* Augsburg, 1792. Invented what is called the "German" or "Viennese" pf. action.

STEIN, Theodor. Pianist ; *b.* Altona, 1819. *Début* at 12. Prof. of pf. playing, St. Petersburg Cons., 1872.

STEIN'BACH, Emil. *B.* Lengenrieden, Baden, 1849. Condr. Mayence Town Orch., 1877.
Works : orchl. music, chamber music, songs, &c.

STEIN'BACH, Fritz. Brother of E. ; *b.* Grünsfeld, Baden, 1855. Won Mozart scholarship, Leipzig Cons. Court condr. Meiningen, 1886.
Works : a septet, a 'cello sonata, songs, &c.

STEIN'DEL, Bruno (1). 'Cellist ; *b.* Zwickau, Saxony, 1864.

STEIN'DEL, Bruno (2). Pianist ; *b.* München-Gladbach, 1890. Played in public at 6.

STEI'NER, (See **Stainer.**)

STEIN'WAY & Sons. Renowned pf. manufacturers, New York and Hamburg.
The New York business was founded in 1853, by HEINRICH E. STEIN'WEG (b. Harz, 1797 ; d. 1871). It is said to be "now the largest establishment of its kind in the world."

Stel'lung (*G.*). Position, in vn. playing.

Stem. (*G., Hals ; F., Queue ; I., Gam'bo.*) The "tail" of a minim, crotchet, &c.

Double stem. Two stems to the
same note (up and down)
to show that it belongs to
two parts (or voices).

Stenden'do (*I.*). Holding back ; *rallentando.*

STEND'HAL. Assumed name of **Marie H. Beyle**, *b.* Grenoble, 1783 ; *d.* 1842. Military official.
Pub. a " Life of Rossini," and " Lives of Haydn, Mozart, and Metastasio."

STENGEL, Frau. (See **Sembrich.**)

STEN'HAMMER, Wilhelm. Noted composer ; *b.* Stockholm, 1871. Studied Stockholm Cons. ; 2nd capellmeister, Stockholm Royal Theatre.
Works : music dramas (*Tirfing*, 1898 ; *Das Fest auf Solhang*, 1899) ; a festival cantata, a pf. concerto, a Symphony in F and other orchl. music, several pf. pieces, songs, &c.

Stenta're (*I.*). (1) To delay. (2) To work hard.
Stentan'do. Delaying, retarding.
Stentamen'te. Slow ; laborious(ly).
Stenta'te) Forced, laboured ; held back and strongly
Stenta'to ∫ accented.

STEN'TOR. A herald in Homer with a very loud voice.

Stentor'ian. Very loud (in voice).

Sten'torphon. A loud-voiced org. stop; a kind of open diapason with a very wide mouth, and on a high pressure of wind.

Step. (*G., Schritt.*) A scale degree; the interval of a diatonic second.

Also used for the interval of a tone; *whole step,* a tone; *half step,* a semitone.

STEPHENS, Catherine ("Kitty"). Soprano; London, 1794-1882. A leading London singer in opera and concert, 1813-35; fine ballad singer. Countess of Essex, 1838.

STEPHENS, Charles E. Nephew of preceding; pianist and organist; London, 1821-92. F.R.C.O., 1865. Hon. Memb. R.A.M., 1870.

Works: 2 symphonies, chamber music, pf. pieces, organ pieces, glees, songs, &c.

Ster'bend (*G.*). Dying away; *morendo.*

Ster'begesang
Ster'belied } A death song; a funeral hymn.

STER'KEL, Abbé **Johann F. X.** Würzburg, 1750-1817. Capellmeister, Mayence, 1793. Founded a singing school, Ratisbon, 1807.

Works: 10 symphonies, 6 pf. concertos, chamber music, pf. sonatas, songs, &c.

STERLING, Antoinette. Eminent contralto; *b.* Sterlingville, N.Y., 1850; *d.* London, 1904. London *début,* 1873. Married **Mr. Mackinlay,** 1875 (*d.* 1893).

Her most striking successes were in ballad singing. Sullivan's "Lost Chord" and other favourite songs were specially composed for her.

Her son, **Sterling Mackinlay,** is a well-known vocalist and teacher.

STERN, Georg F. T. Strasburg, 1803-86.

Works: 7 series of organ pieces, sacred music, pf. pieces, songs.

STERN, Julius. *B.* Breslau, 1820; *d.* Berlin, 1883. With Kullak and Marx, founded the "Stern" Cons, Berlin, 1850. Condr. Berlin Symphony Orch., 1869-71; "Reichshalle" Concerts, 1873-4.

STERN, Leo ("Leopold Lawrence"). 'Cellist; *b.* Brighton, 1870; *d.* 1904. Pupil of Piatti. First concert tour, 1888.

Works: 'cello pieces, songs, &c.

STERN, Margarethe (*née* **Herr**). Pianist; pupil of Liszt and Madame Schumann; *b.* Dresden, 1857; *d.* 1899. Married Dr. Adolf Stern, 1881.

STERN'BERG, Constantin I. von. Pianist; *b.* St. Petersburg, 1852. Studied Leipzig and Berlin. Condr. at various German theatres; after long tours, director "Sternberg School of Mus.," Philadelphia, 1890.

Works: vn. pieces, a 'cello fantasia, pf. pieces, songs.

STERN'HOLD, Thomas. Issued (with J. Hopkins) the "Whole Booke of Psalmes," 1562 (known as the "Old Version.").

Ste'so (*I.*). Spread, stretched, diffused; slow.

Ste'so mo'to. Slow movement (speed).

Stes'so (*I.*). The same. (See **Istesso.**)

Lo stes'so tem'po. (At) the same *tempo.*

Stets (*G.*). Always.

Stets das glei'che Tem'po. Always at the same speed.

Stets pp. Always *pianissimo.*

STEVENS, Alfred Peck. Noted comic singer; known as the "**Great Vance** ; " London, 1840-88.

STEVENS, Richard J. S. Noted glee composer; London, 1757-1837. Gresham Professor, London, 1801.

His glees (over 40) include "Sigh no more, ladies," "Ye spotted snakes," "The cloud-capt Towers," "From Oberon," &c.

STEVENSON, Sir John A. *B.* Dublin, 1761(2?); *d.* 1833. Mus.Doc. Dublin, 1791. Knighted, 1803.

Works: stage pieces, church music, glees, songs, &c.; symphonies and accompts. to Moore's Irish Melodies" (1807-34).

STEVENSON, E. I. Noted American musical writer and critic. Mus. editor *New York Independent,* 1881; *Harper's Weekly,* 1895. His writings incline towards conservatism, but with a liberal appreciation of Wagner.

Works: 2 musical novels, numerous essays, &c.

STEWART, Sir Robt. P. Dublin, 1825-94. Orgt. Christ Ch. Cath., Dublin, at 18; condr. Univ. Choral Soc., 1846. Mus. Doc. Dublin, 1851. Knighted, 1872.

Works: odes, cantatas, church services, anthems, glees, songs.

Sthénochire (*F.*). A mechanical finger-strengthener.

STIAST'NY (ŠTAST'NÝ), Bernhard W. 'Cellist; Prague, 1760-1835.

Wrote a " 'Cello Method," 'cello duets, &c.

STIAST'NY, Franz J. 'Cellist; brother of B. W.; *b.* Prague, 1764; *d.* abt. 1820.

Published several 'cello solos and duets.

Stibbacchia'to (*I.*). *Rallentando.*

Sticca'do (*I.*) }
Sticca'to (*I.*) } A Xylophone (*q.v.*).

Stich (*G.*). A dot.

STICH, Jan V. (Italianized name **Giovanni Punto.**) Famous horn player; *b.* Bohemia, 1748; *d.* 1803. Beethoven wrote a horn sonata (Op. 17) for him, playing it with him at a concert, Vienna, 1800.

Works: 14 horn concertos, a sextet for horn and other insts., 24 quartets for horn and strings, 20 trios for 3 horns, a " Horn Method," &c.

Sticker. Part of the "tracker" action of an organ.

Stie'fel (*G.*). The boot of an organ reed-pipe.

STIEHL, Heinrich F. D. *B.* Lübeck, 1829; *d.* 1886. Orgt. St. Peter's and condr. Singakademie, St. Petersburg, 1853-66. Condr. Belfast St. Cecilia Soc., 1874-8; Condr. Singakademie, Reval, 1880.

Works: 2 operettas (*Jery und Bätely*); orch. pieces, chamber music, several vn. sonatas, pf. pieces, songs, &c.

STIEHL, Karl J. C. Brother of preceding; *b.* Lübeck, 1826. Condr. Lubeck Musikverein and Singakademie from 1878. Works: a " Hist. of Instl. Music in Lübeck," a " Musical Lexicon," &c.

STIEH'LE, Ludwig M. A. Violinist; *b.* Frankfort, 1850; *d.* 1896. Pupil of Vieuxtemps and Joachim. Noted quartet leader.

Stiel (*G.*). A stem or neck.

Stier'horn (*G.*). A cow-horn giving only one note. (Used by Wagner.)

Stift (*G.*). The "jack" of a harpsichord or spinet.

STIGĚL'LI, Giorgio (Georg Stie'gele). Celebrated tenor; *b.* Germany, abt. 1820; *d.* Italy, 1868. Made long concert tours. Wrote several songs ("Die schönsten Augen," &c.).

Stil (*G.*), **Sti'le** (*I.*), **Sti'lo** (*I.*), **Sti'lus** (*L.*). Style.

 Sti'le a cappel'la (*I.*) }
 Sti'le ecclesia'stico (*I.*) } The church style.
 Sti'lus ecclesias'ticus (*L.*) }
 Sti'le (or *Sti'lo*) *osserva'to* (*I.*) } The strict style.
 Sti'le (or *Sti'lo*) *rigoro'so* (*I.*) }
 Sti'le (or *Sti'lo*) *rappresentati'vo* (*I.*) } The modern or
 Sti'le (or *Sti'lo*) *dramma'tico* (*I.*) } dramatic style
 Sti'lus recitati'vus (*L.*) } introduced abt.
  1600 by Bardi, Peri, Caccini, &c.

Still (*G.*). Calm, quiet, still, hushed.
 Still'flöte. A soft flute-stop (org.).
 Still'geda(c)kt. A soft stopped diapason.

STILLIE, Thos. L. *B.* Maybole, 1832; *d.* 1883.
 Mus. critic *Glasgow Mus. Herald.* Left his valuable music library to Glasgow University.

Stim'me (*G.*). (1) Voice. (2) Sound. (3) A part. (4) An organ stop. (5) A sound-post (of a vn., &c.).
 Die Stim'men aus't(h)eilen. To distribute the parts.
 Mit der Stim'me. With the part or voice.
 Stimm'ansatz. Vocal attack.
 Stimm'bänder. The vocal cords.
 Stimm'bar. Tunable, singable.
 Stimm'bildung. Voice building; voice production.
 Stimm'führer. Chorus leader; choirmaster.
 Stimm'führung. Progression of parts.
 Stimm'gabel. A tuning-fork.
 Stimm'hammer } Tuning hammer; tuning key.
 Stimm'schlüssel }
 Stimm'horn. Tuning cone (for organ pipes).
 Stim'men. To tune. To voice organ pipes.
 Stim'menkreuzung. Crossing of parts.
 Stimm'los. Voiceless.
 Stimm'mittel. Vocal capacity.
 Stimm'pfeife } (1) A pitch-pipe. (2) A fife.
 Stimm'flöte }
 Stimm'stock } Sound-post (of a vn. or 'cello).
 Stimm'hölzchen }
 Stimm'umfang } Compass of a voice (or inst.).
 Stimm'weite }
 Stimm'wechsel. Breaking of the voice (in boys).
 Stimm'zug. A tuning slide.
 Zwei'te Stim'me. 2nd voice; alto, &c.

Stim'mung (*G.*). (1) Tune. (2) Accordatura (tuning). (3) Pitch. (4) Mood; key.
 Stim'munghalten. To keep in tune.
 Stim'mungbild. A tone picture.

STIMPSON, James. *B.* Lincoln, 1820; *d.* 1886. Orgt. Carlisle Cath., 1841; Town Hall, Birmingham, 1842. Founded Birmingham Festival Choral Soc., 1843; conducted it till 1855. Superintended the production of Mendelssohn's *Elijah*, Birmingham, 1846.
 Works : church music, organ pieces, a " Manual of Theory," &c.

Stinguen'do (*I.*). Dying away; *calando.*

Stiracchian'do }
Stiracchia'to } " Stretching." Retarding
Stiran'do } the time.
Stira'to }

Stiria'na (*I.*). (See **Styrienne.**)

STIRLING, Elizabeth. *B.* Greenwich, 1819; *d.* 1895. Orgt. All Saints', Poplar, 1839; St. Andrew's, Undershaft, 1858-80.
 Works : organ pieces, part-songs (" All among the barley," &c.).

STIRLING-MAXWELL, Lady. (See **Norton.**)

Sti'va (*L.*). A neume (*q.v.*).

STOBÄ'US, Johann. Early church composer; *b.* Graudenz, W. Prussia, 1580; *d.* 1646. Cantor, Cathedral School, Königsberg, 1602; Electoral capellmeister, 1627.
 Works : cantiones sacræ (5 to 10 voices), numerous songs for special occasions, sacred "Lieder" (5 to 8 voices), &c.

Stock (*G.*). Stick, stem, stalk; a bundle of 30 strings.
 Stock'fagott. An obsolete form of double bassoon.
 Stock'flöte. A combined walking stick and flute.
 Stock'pfeife. Old German flute.
 Stock'chen. The heel of a vn., &c.

STOCK, Friedrich W. A. Violinist, composer, and condr.; *b.* Yülich, 1872.

Stock'end (*G.*). Slackening, *rallentando.*

STOCK'HAUSEN, Franz. *B.* Gebweiler, Alsace, 1839. Studied Paris and Leipzig. Music-director, Strasburg Cath., 1868; director Strasburg Cons., 1871.

STOCK'HAUSEN, Julius. Elder bro. of F.; eminent baritone singer and teacher; *b.* Paris, 1826; *d.* 1906. Studied Paris Cons. and under Garcia (London). Condr. Hamburg Singakademie, 1862-7; condr. Stern Gesangverein, Berlin, 1874-8; Prof. of singing, Hoch Cons., Frankfort, 1878-9, and 1882-98. Author of a "Method of Singing."

STOCKLEY, Wm. Cole. *B.* Farningham, Kent, 1830. Chorus-master, Birmingham Festival Choir, 1858-94.

STOJOW'SKI, Sigismund. Pianist; *b.* Strelce, Poland, 1870. Won 1st prize for pf. playing and composition Paris Cons., 1889. Studied later under Paderewski.
 Works : a pf. concerto, orchl. pieces, a Romance for vn. and orch., graceful pf. music, &c.

STOKES, Walter. Composer; *b.* Shipton-on-Stour, Worcester, 1847. Mus.D. Cantab, 1882.

Stol'len (*G.*). (See **Strophe.**)

STOLTZ, Rosine. (Real name **Rosa Niva.**) Noted mezzo-soprano; *b.* Spain, 1813; *d.* 1903. Also sang as "Mme. Ternaux" and "Mlle. Héloise."

Stolz (*G.*). Proud(ly).

STÖL'ZEL (or **STÖL'ZL**), **Gottfried H.** Prolific composer ; *b.* Grünstädtl, 1690 ; *d.* 1749. Court condr. Gotha, 1719.
Works : 22 operas (*Narcissus*, 1711 ; *Venus and Adonis*, 1714 ; &c.) ; a pastoral, 14 oratorios, 8 double sets of cantatas and motets for the church year, masses, symphonies, &c.

STOL'ZENBERG, Benno. Operatic tenor ; *b.* Königsberg, 1829. *Début*, 1852. Director Danzig City Th., 1878-82 ; Prof. solo singing Cologne Cons., 1885. Head of a vocal school, Berlin, 1896.

Stonan'te (*I.*). Dissonant.

STONE, Alfred. Bristol, 1841-78. Organist; edited the "Bristol Tune Book" (1876 edn.). Did much for popular music in Bristol.

STONE, Samuel John. 1839-1901. Vicar St. Paul's, Haggerston.
Wrote "The Church's one Foundation," and other hymns.

STONE, Wm. Henry. Physician, and writer on acoustics; *b.* 1830; *d.* 1899(?). Double-bassoon player at various festivals.
Author of "The Scientific Basis of Music" (Novello), articles in Grove's Dict., &c.

Stone harmonica. A set of tuned stones struck with a hammer.

Stop. (1) (*G., Regis'terzug ; F., Registre ; I., Regi'stro.*) General name for the draw-stops, or stop-knobs, of an organ, harmonium, &c.

(2) (*G., Regis'ter ; F., Jeu d'orgue(s) ; I., Regis'tro.*) (*a*) A row or register of pipes of similar tone in an organ ; controlled by a draw-stop. (See **Organ.**) (*b*) A set of free reeds of similar tone-quality in a reed organ (harmonium, &c.).
Complete stop. One running through the whole compass of the inst., opposed to an *incomplete, partial,* or *half stop.*
Solo stop. A stop specially voiced for solo effects.

(3) (*G., Bund ; F., Touche ; I., Ta'sto.*) A fret on a mandoline, &c.
(4) (*a*) To press a finger on the string of a vn., &c., in order to vary its pitch. (*b*) To insert the hand in the bell of a horn for the same purpose. (*c*) To close · the hole of a flute, clarinet, &c.
Double stop. Two (or more) fingers "stopping" at the same time (vn., &c.).
Stopped notes. Notes obtained on any inst. by stopping ; opposed to "open" notes.
Stopped pipes. Organ pipes plugged or covered at the top. (See *Acoustics.*)

STÖ'PEL, Franz D. C. *B.* Saxony, 1794 ; *d.* 1836. Pf. teacher ; tried to introduce Logier's system (see **Logier**) at Berlin, Paris, &c.
Wrote several works on Logier's System.

Stop'fen (*G.*). To stop ; especially to "stop" the bell of a horn with the hand.
Stopf'horn. Hand-horn.
Stopf'töne. Hand-stopped notes on the horn, &c.

STOR, Karl. Violinist ; *b.* Stolberg, 1814 ; *d.* 1889. Court musician, Weimar, 1827 ; Court condr., 1857.
Works : an opera, orchl. pieces, ballets, male choruses, songs, &c.

STORA'CE, Anna Selina. Famous soprano ; London, 1766-1817. Pupil of Sacchini, Venice. London *début*, 1774 ; Italian *début*, 1780. A favourite opera singer in London, 1787-1808.

STORA'CE, Stephen. Brother of preceding ; London, 1763-96. Pupil of his father, a double bass player ; studied also at Naples. Composer to the principal London theatres.
Works : about 20 English operas (*No Song no Supper, Siege of Belgrade, The Iron Chest,* &c.) ; harpsichord pieces, songs, &c.

STORCH, M. Anton. Vienna, 1813-88. Capellmeister Carl and Josephstädter theatres.
Works : music to burlesques, favourite male-voice quartets, &c.

Stor'ta (*I.*). **Stor'to** (*I.*). A serpent (*q.v.*).

STORY, Mrs. J. (See **Eames.**)

Stoss (*G.*). A knock, a blow, a blast.
Gestoss'en. Detached, *staccato.*
Stoss'zeichen. A staccato mark.

Stot'tern (*G.*). To stutter, stammer.

STÖ'WE, Gustav. Potsdam, 1835-1891. Studied at Berlin ; founded the Potsdam School of Music, 1875.
Works : A "Thorough Analysis of the Elements of Pf. Touch" (1886), pf. pieces, songs, &c.

STOWELL, Hugh. 1799-1865. Rector, Christ Church, Salford,
Wrote "From every stormy wind that blows," and other hymns.

Str. Abbn. for *strings.*

Stracanta're (*I.*). To sing charmingly.

Straccican'do (*I.*). Babbling, prattling.

Straccina'to (*I.*). "Stretched ; " retarded.

STRACHAN, James K. Organist ; *b.* Errol, Perthsh., 1860. Studied under Guilmant.

Strad. Familiar name for a Stradivarius vn.
It is generally supposed that the tone of a violin continually improves by playing. But " a Strad is not immortal so far as its soul is concerned. A well-known authority, of great experience on violins, informed the writer that the 'life' of a Strad was a very great deal shorter than the life of a man if the instrument were used more or less casually as the every-day working bread-winner ; and it is stated that even so careful a protector of his violins as Dr. Joachim has exhausted the ' life ' for a time of two Strads. No doubt the ' life ' returns to the temporarily lifeless instrument with rest and care—Strads are intensely human—but each return is shorter than its predecessors, and the ' soul ' becomes less and less."—*Daily Telegraph,* 1907.

STRADEL'LA, Alessandro. Celebrated Italian composer. Supposed to have been born in Naples or Venice abt. 1645; and to have died at Genoa abt. 1681.
He is the hero of Flotow's *Stradella*, which is founded on the (probably legendary) story " that Stradella had fallen in love with the mistress of a Venetian nobleman, who hired

two of the most notorious assassins in Venice to assassinate him on the occasion of his conducting one of his oratorios at the Church of St. John Lateran, Rome. They were, however, so impressed with the beauty of his music, that they not only refrained from their cruel purpose, but revealed the plot to him and advised him to seek safety by leaving the city." Works: several oratorios and operas (*San Giovanni Battista*, pub. 1676); numerous cantatas, arias, and other church music. The Modena Library contains 148 of his MSS. (including 8 oratorios and 11 dramas), and numerous other works are in other libraries.

STRADIVA'RI (STRADIVA'RIUS), Antonio. The most famous of vn. and 'cello makers; *b.* Cremona, 1649(50?); *d.* there 1737. Probably worked under N. Amati, abt. 1667-79. His finest insts. date from 1700 to 1725.

He "marks the culminating point of the art of making stringed instruments.......No improvement has been made since his time."— *Grove's Dict.*

Of his 11 children, two sons, FRANCESCO (1671-1743), and OMOBONO (1679-1742), were co-workers with him. (See *Violin*.)

STRAE'TEN, Vander. (See **Vanderstraeten**.)

Straff (*G.*). Strict.
Straf'fer im Tem'po. In stricter time.

Strain. (1) A tune, melody, air, song. (2) (See **Metrical Form**.)
The term is often applied to the portions of a movement separated by double bars.

STRA'KOSCH, Mrs. C. (See **Kellogg**.)

STRA'KOSCH, Moritz. Pianist; *b.* Lemberg, Galicia, 1825 (30?); *d.* 1887. Pf. teacher, New York, 1845-60; also (from 1856) operatic *impresario.* Teacher (and brother-in-law) of Adelina Patti. Wrote an opera, pf. pieces, &c.

Strambot'to, Strambot'tolo (*I.*). A folk-song, a rustic love ditty.

Strappa're (*I.*). "To snatch off." To throw off a note (or chord) lightly by a rapid turn of the wrist.
Strappan'do \
Strappa'to / (*G., Geris'sen.*) Thrown off; torn off.

Strascican'do (*I.*) \ Dragging along; play-
Strascinan'do (*I.*) / ing slowly.
Strascinan'do l'ar'co. Drawing, dragging the bow; slurring the notes rather heavily.
Strascina're la vo'ce. Exaggerated portamento.
Strascina'to. Slow, dragged.
Strasci'no. A slur; a dragging slurring movement from note to note.

Strath'spey. A lively Scottish dance in 4-4 time.
The following rhythms are characteristic.

STRATTON, Stephen S. *B.* London, 1840; *d.* 1906. After various posts as orgt., &c., settled in Birmingham (1866), as teacher. Did useful work as musical critic of the *Birmingham Daily Post.*

STRAUS, Ludwig. Violinist; *b.* Pressburg, 1835; *d.* 1899. Soloist, Royal Band, London, 1864; leader, Philharmonic, Hallé's Orch., &c.; retired 1894.

STRAUSS, Johann (Senr.). "Father of the Waltz;" Vienna, 1804-49. Apprenticed to a bookbinder; ran away, and was afterwards allowed by his parents to study music. Orchestral violinist at 15. Joined the "Lanner Quartet," 1823. (See **Lanner**.) Started an independent orch. and wrote his first waltzes, 1826. After successful tours, condr. Vienna Court Balls, 1845.

Published 152 waltzes; also galops, polkas, quadrilles, &c.

STRAUSS, Johann (Junr.). "The Waltz King;" son of preceding; Vienna, 1825-99. Condr. of a Restaurant orch., Hietzing, 1844. His new waltzes became at once popular. At his father's death (1849) he united the two orchestras and commenced a series of highly successful tours. Engaged, 1855, for 10 years as condr. Summer Concerts, Petropaulovski Park, St. Petersburg; condr. Court Balls, 1863-70. Afterwards settled down at Vienna to the writing of popular operettas.

Works: some 500 dance pieces ("The beautiful Blue Danube," &c.) of real merit, and about 17 operettas (*Fürstin Ninetta*, 1893; *Waldmeister*, 1895).

STRAUSS, Joseph. Brother of preceding; *b.* Vienna, 1827; *d.* 1870.

Wrote 283 popular dances.

A third brother, **Eduard,** *b.* Vienna, 1835, succeeded Johann (Junr.) as condr., St. Petersburg, 1870.

STRAUSS, Joseph. Violinist; *b.* Brünn, 1793; *d.* 1866. Solo vn. Pesth Th., 1810. Capellmeister at Brünn, 1817; at Strasburg, 1822; at Mannheim, 1823. Court condr., Carlsruhe, 1824-63.

Works: an oratorio, 7 operas, orchl. pieces, songs, &c.

STRAUSS, Richard Georg. The most eminent of living German composers; *b.* Munich, 1864. Commenced studying the pf. at 4; began composing at 6. At 20 had composed a number of pieces on classical models; was then influenced by Brahms, and finally adopted the Berlioz-Liszt-Wagner style of orchestral program-music. Court capellmeister, Weimar, 1889; capellmeister Court Opera, Munich, 1894; Berlin Royal Opera, 1898. He is a master of orchestral colour; his later works (*e.g.*, *Salome* and *Elektra*) have caused almost as much controversy as did those of Wagner 50 years ago.

His most notable works are *Till Eulenspiegels lustige Streiche* ("Till Eulenspiegel's Merry Pranks"), *Also sprach Zarathustra* ("Thus spake Zoroaster"), *Ein Heldenleben* ("A Hero's Life"), *Don Quixote, Enoch Arden,* the *Domestic Symphony,* and 4 operas (*Guntram, Feuersnoth, Salome,* 1905, and *Elektra,* 1909). Also choral works, many songs, &c.

Stravagan'te (*I.*). Extravagant, fantastical, whimsical.
Stravagan'za. (1) An extravaganza (*q.v.*). (2)Eccentricity.

Straw-fiddle. (See **Strohfiedel.**)

Strazian'te (*I.*). Mockingly.

STREABBOG. Reversed name of **Gobbaerts.**

STREATFEILD, R. A. Author of "Masters of Italian Music" (1895), and "The Opera" (1896).

STREET, Georges E. *B.* Vienna, 1854. Studied Paris Cons. Notable musical critic (*Le Matin, L'Eclair*, 1898, &c.).
Works : several operettas, ballets, &c.

Street Cries. (See **Melody in Speech.**)

Strei'chen (*G.*). (1) To strike, to stretch, to touch in passing ; to draw a bow across (the strings). (2) To cut out (a portion of a work).
Strei'chend. Stringy (in tone).
Strei'chende Regis'ter. String-toned organ stops.
Strei'cher. (1) A player on a bowed inst. (2) String-toned organ stops.
Streich'instrumente. Bowed insts.
Streich'orchester. A string orchestra ; the "strings" of a full orchestra.
Streich'quartett, trio, &c. String quartet, trio, &c.
Streich'zither. A zither played with a bow.

STREI'CHER, J. A. *B.* Stuttgart, 1761 ; *d.* 1833.
Invented the pf. action which " drops the hammer from above," 1793.

STRELEZ'KI, Anton. Assumed name of Arthur B. Burnand ; *b.* Croydon, 1859 ; *d.* 1907. Studied Leipzig Cons. Also wrote as " Stepan Essipoff."
Works : songs, several popular pf. pieces, &c.

Strene. Old name for a breve.

Streng (*G.*). Strict, rigid ; severe.
Streng Fu'ge. A strict fugue. (See *Fugue.*)
Stren'ge gebun'den. Strictly *legato* ; very smooth.
Streng im Tem'po. ⎫ Strictly in time.
Streng im Zeitmass ⎭

Stre'pito (*I.*). Noise, bustle.
Strepitosamen'te ⎫ Noisily, impetuously, boisterously.
Strepito'so ⎭

STREPPO'NI, Giuseppina. Wife of Verdi (*q.v.*).

Stretta (*I.*) ⎫ (*G., Eng'führung ; F., Strette.*)
Stret'to (*I.*) ⎭ "Close, contracted, strait, pressed." (1) A coda or finale in quicker time than the rest of the piece. (2) The part of a fugue where subject and answer overlap. (See **Fugue.**) (3) Accelerando.
Al'la stret'ta,-o. Quicker ; *accelerando.*
Andan'te stret'to. Same as *Andante agitato.*
Più stret'to. Quicker.
Stret'to maestra'le (*I.*) ⎫
Stret'to majestra'le (*I.*) ⎬ A close masterly stretto.
Stretto magistrale (*F.*) ⎭

Striccian'do (*I.*). Strascicando (*q.v.*).

Strich (*G.*). (1) A stroke ; manner of bowing. (2) A line, dash, stroke.
Bo'genstrich. Bow-stroke.
Strich'art. The art of bowing ; the manner of bowing.
Strich'arten. Different styles of bowing.
Strich_ Stacca'to. The staccatissimo mark, ♭ ♩

Strict. According to strict rule ; exact ; opposed to " free."
Strict counterpoint. (See *Counterpoint.*)
Strict fugue. (See *Fugue.*)
Strict inversion. (See *Inversion.*)
Strict style. The ancient style of composition as opposed to the modern "free" style.

Stri'dent ⎫ Shrill, harsh, raucous,
Striden'te (*I.*) ⎬ noisy, blatant.
Stride'vole (*I.*) ⎭

STRIG'GIO, Alessandro. Lutenist ; *b.* Mantua, abt. 1535 ; *d.* (?).
Wrote *Intermezzi* in madrigal style (1565), and other festival music ; also madrigals, early attempts at program music, &c.

Striking reed. Opposed to a "free" reed. (See **Reed.**)

Strilla're (*I.*). To screech, scream, shriek.
Stril'lo. A loud, shrill cry, &c.

Strimpella'ta (*I.*). Strumming, scraping.

String. (*G., Sai'te ; F., Corde ; I., Cor'da.*) "Prepared wire or catgut, plain or covered, used for musical instruments." —*Stainer and Barrett.*
Open string. A free "unstopped" string. (See *Stop.*)
The Strings. The string group of an orchestra.
String band ⎫ (1) A band of bowed stringed
String orchestra ⎬ instruments. (2) The stringed insts. (collectively) of a full orchestra.
String gauge. A small gauge for measuring the thickness of strings.
String organ. A combination of the violin and harmonium.
String instruments. (*G., Sai'ten-instrumen'te ; F., Instruments à cordes ; I., Stromen'ti da cor'da.*) (1) (See *Instruments.*) (2) Specially, bowed stringed insts.
String quartet. (1) A quartet for 1st and 2nd vns., viola, and 'cello. (2) (*G., Quartett'* or *Quart.*) The string insts. (collectively) of an orchestra.
String quintet, trio, &c. A quintet, trio, &c., for stringed insts.

Stringen'do (*I.*). Hastening, drawing closer ; *accelerando* (and often *crescendo*).
Stringen'do con stre'pito. Hurried, and with impetuosity.
Stringen'do po'co a po'co. Gradually quickening.

Strin'gere (*I.*). To hasten.
Sen'za strin'gere. Without accelerating the speed.

Stringy. Having a "string-like" tone ; as the *viols* and *geigen* stops of modern organs.

Striscian'do (*I.*) ⎫ Slurring ; gliding
Striscia'to (*I.*) ⎬ smoothly from note to note.

Stro'fa (*I.*) ⎫ A strophe (*q.v.*).
Stro'fe (*I.*) ⎭

Stroh (*G.*). Straw.
Stroh'bass. The husky lower tones of some bass voices.
Stroh'fiedel. A Xylophone (*q.v.*).

Strombazza'ta (*I.*) ⎫ The sound of a trumpet.
Strombetta'ta (*I.*) ⎭
Strombetta're. To sound a trumpet.
Strombettie're. A trumpet player.

Stromen'to (*I.*). (Plur., *Stromen'ti.*) Instrument. (Also *Strumen'to,-i.*)
Stromenta'to. Instrumented ; scored (for an orch., &c.).
Strumentazio'ne. Scoring ; instrumental music.
Stromen'ti d'ar'co. Bowed instruments.

Stromen'ti da cor'da. Stringed instruments.
Stromen'ti da fia'to }
Stromen'ti di ven'to } Wind instruments.
Stromen'ti di rinfor'zo. Accessory, reinforcing insts.
Stromen'ti da ta'sto. Keyboard instruments.
Stromen'ti d'otto'ne. Brass instruments.
STRONG, David. Tenor ; *b.* London, 1852.
STRONG, George T. Composer ; *b.* New York, 1855. Studied Leipzig Cons. ; resides in Germany.
Works : orchl. pieces, cantatas, pf. pieces, &c.
STRONG, Susan. Vocalist ; *b.* 18—. *Début,* 1895.
Strong accent. The principal accent falling regularly on the 1st beat of any measure. (See **Accent.**)
Strong tones of the scale. The 1st, 3rd, and 5th (*d, m, s ;* in Minor, *l, d, m*).
Stro'phe. (1) The 1st part of a Greek Ode. (2) A group of metrically arranged lines forming a **stanza.**
The Greek *Stro'phe, Antis'trophe,* and *Ep'ode* closely correspond to the 2 *Stol'len* and the *Ab'gesang* of the poems of the Meistersingers.
STROZ'ZI, Pietro. Florentine musician ; one of the founders of the new *Stile rappresentativo.* (See **Bardi, Peri, Caccini, Cavaliere.**) Wrote music to Caccini's *La Mascarada degli accecati* (1595).
STRU'BE, Gustav. Violinist ; *b.* Ballenstedt, 1867. Studied Leipzig Cons. Joined the Symphony Orch., Boston, 1889.
His works include a symphony in C minor.
STRUCK, Johann B. (known as **Batistin Struck**). *B.* Florence, abt. 1680 ; *d.* Paris, 1755. Introduced (with Labbé) the 'cello into the orch. of the Paris Opéra.
Works : 3 operas, several ballets, 4 books of cantatas, &c.
Strumen'to (*I.*). Same as **Stromento** (*q.v.*).
STRUNGK (or **STRUNK**), **Nicolaus A·** Violinist and organist ; *b.* Celle, Hanover, 1640 ; *d.* Leipzig, 1700. Chamber orgt. to the Duke of Hanover ; vice-capellmeister, Dresden, abt. 1605 ; 1st capellmeister, 1694. Organized an Italian Opera, Leipzig, 1696.
Works : several operas for the 1st German Opera at Hamburg (1678-83), and 16 Italian operas for Leipzig (1693-1700).
STRUSS, Franz. Violinist ; *b.* Hamburg, 1847.
Stu'ben-or'gel (*G.*). A chamber organ.
Stück (*G.*) (plur. *Stück'e*(*n*)). "A piece ; " a composition.
Charak'terstück. A characteristic piece.
Concert'stück. A concert piece.
Clavier'stück }
Klavier'stück } A pf. piece.
Phantasie'stück. A Fantasia (*q.v.*) ; a fanciful piece.
Stück'chen. A little tune or air.
STUCKEN. (See **Van der Stucken.**)
Study. (*G., Stu'die,* plur. *Stu'dien ;* Etü'de, plur. *Etü'den ;* F., *Etude ;* I., *Stu'dio*.) An exercise ; a special exercise including some particular difficulty.

Stu'fe (*G.*). A step. A degree of the staff.
Stu'fe der Ton'leiter. A degree of the scale.
Stu'fen der Tö'ne. Musical intervals.
Stu'fenfolge }
Stu'fengang } A scale, a sequence.
Stu'fenweise ab'steigend. Descending by steps.
Stu'fenweise auf'steigend. Ascending by steps.
Stu'fenweise Fort'schreitung. Stepwise progression.
Stumm (*G.*). Dumb.
Stum'mes Klavier'. A dumb piano.
Stum'me Pfei'fe. A dummy pipe (on the organ).
STUMPF, Johann C. Bassoonist ; lived in Paris, abt. 1785 ; in Frankfort 1798.
Published 4 bassoon concertos, and numerous works for bassoon with other insts.
STUNTZ, Joseph H. *B.* nr. Basel, 1793 ; *d·* 1859. Court condr., Munich, 1826.
Works : operas, overtures, church music, male choruses, &c.
Stuonan'te (*I.*) }
Stuona'to (*I.*) } Dissonant, out of tune.
Stupo're (*I.*). Amazement, stupor.
Sturm (*G.*). Storm, tumult, fury.
Stürm'isch }
Stürm'end } Boisterous(ly), furious(ly).
Sturm und Drang. Storm and stress.
Stür'ze (*G.*). Bell (of a horn, &c.)
Stür'ze in der Höh'e. "Turn the bell upwards."
Stutt'gart pitch. Proposed at the Stuttgart Congress, 1834, reckoning the pitch of A at 400 vibrations per second.
Stutz'flügel (*G.*). A small grand pf. ; a "baby" grand.
Styl (*G.*). Style. Also **Stil** (*q.v.*).
Styrienne (*F.*). An air with *Jodelling* refrain. (See **Jodel.**)
Sù (*I.*). Above, upon ; up.
Ar'co in sù. The up bow (vn., &c.).
Suabe-flute. A sweet-toned org. flute-stop ; invented by W. Hill, London.
Sua've (*I.*) }
Suave (*F.*) } Sweet, soft ; suave.
Con suavità (*I.*). }
Suavemen'te (*I.*) } Sweetly, delicately ; pleasantly.
Sub (*L.*). Below, beneath, under.
Sub'bass (*G.*) }
Sub-bour'don } An organ pedal stop of 32 ft. tone.
Sub-bass. On Eng. organs, a Bourdon of 16 ft. tone.
Subcan'tor }
Subchanter } An assistant cantor ; a Succentor (*q.v.*).
Subdiapen'te }
Subdom'inant } The 5th note below the tonic.
Sub'flôte (*G.*). Same as *Siflôte* (*q.v.*).
Sub-harmonic. A difference tone. (See *Acoustics*.)
Subme'diant. The lower mediant, halfway between the tonic and subdominant ; the 3rd below the tonic.
Suboctave. (1) The octave below. (2) A coupler "bringing on" the octave below.
Subor'dinate. Secondary. The triads on the 2nd, 3rd, and 6th of the scale ; all diatonic 7ths except that of the dominant ; &c.
Subprincipal } A stop an octave below the *Prin-*
Subprinzipal' (*G.*) } *cipal.* On German organs, 16 ft. pitch on the manuals, 32 ft. pitch on the pedals.
Subsemifu'sa (*L.*). A demisemiquaver
Subsem'itone }
Subsemito'nium mo'di (*L.*) } The leading-note.
Subton'ic }

Su'bito (*I.*) Suddenly; without pause
Su'bitamen'te (*I.*) or break.
Vol'ti su'bito. Turn over (the page) at once.
Pia'no su'bito (or *p su'bito*). Soft immediately (after
a louder note or notes).

Subject. (*G., Sub'jekt ; F., Sujet ; I.,
Sogget'to.*) A theme ; a fugue subject,
&c.
Counter-subject. (See *Fugue.*)
Subsidiary subject. An auxiliary subject in a work in
sonata form. (See *Sonata.*)

Subjective Music.
Music of "individual" "reflective" character,
appealing rather to the intellect than to the
senses ; *e.g*, Bach's music. It is the opposite
of *Objective Music* (*q.v.*).

Substitu'tion. (1) Changing the fingers on a
key (pf., org., &c.). (2) Transferring a
dissonance from one part to another
before resolving it.

Substitutional Chords. The secondary chords
of a key.—*Curwen.*

Succen'tor. The deputy-precentor in a
cathedral choir.

Succès d'estime (*F.*). " A success due to the
sympathy of friends, &c., and not due
to those qualities which appeal to the
general (musical) public."—*Grove.*

Succes'sion. (1) A sequence. (2) Any
melodic or harmonic progression.

SUCH, Edwin Chas. *B.* London, 1840.
Works : Cantata (*Narcissus and Echo*), pf. pieces,
songs, &c.
His son, **Henry**, is a violinist ; pupil of
Joachim and Wilhelmj. *Début*, Berlin,
1893.
Another son, **Percy** (*b.* 1878), is a 'cellist.

SU'CHER, Joseph. Distinguished conductor ;
b. Hungary, 1844 ; *d.* 19)8. Choir-boy
Court Chapel, Vienna, 1854 ; condr.
Leipzig City Th., 1876. Married **Rosa
Hasselbeck,** 1877 ; both engaged Hamburg Th., 1878-88. Sucher was condr.
Royal Opera, Berlin (1888-99), his wife
(noted as a Wagnerian interpreter)
being *Prima Donna* (1888-98).

Sudden Modulation. Modulation to a
remote key without introducing intermediate modulating chords. Also called
an "Abrupt Transition." (See **Modulation.**)

SUDDS, Wm. F. *B.* London, 1843. Parents
settled in America, 1850.
He is chiefly self-taught, and has published over
100 pf. pieces, &c.

Suf'flöte (*G.*). Same as **Sifflöte** (*q.v.*).

Suffoca'to (*I.*). "Suffocated." Muffled,
choked, deadened.

Suffolamen'to (*I.*). A hiss, whistle, murmur.

Sugget'to (*I.*). Subject ; theme, melody.

Su'gli (*I.*) On the, upon the ; near the.
Su'i (*I.*)

28

Suite (*F.*, pron. *Sweet*) A set, cycle, or
Suite de pieces (*F.*) series of pieces
in the same key.
The suite was the precursor of the sonata and the
symphony. It was a succession of dance
movements, sometimes introduced by a prelude.
The chief dance forms employed were the
Allemande, Courante, Sarabande, and Gigue ;
to these might be added the Gavotte, Bourrée,
Minuet, Passepied, &c. Modern Orchestral
Suites do not necessarily keep to the same key
throughout. The Suites of Bach and Handel
are among the most important works of this
kind. Examples of construction :—
Bach : English Suite, No. 6, D minor ; Prelude,
Allemande, Courante, Sarabande and Double,
Gavotte and Musette, Gigue.
Bach : French Suite, No. 5, G major ; Allemande,
Courante, Sarabande, Gavotte, Bourrée, Loure,
Gigue.
Handel : Suite 11, B♭ major ; Allemande, Cour-
ante, Sarabande, Gigue.
Handel : Suite 3, D minor ; Prelude, Fuga,
Allemande, Courante, Air and 5 Doubles
(variations), Presto.
Handel : Suite 7, G minor ; Ouverture, Presto,
Andante, Allegro, Sarabande, Gigue, Passacaille.

Suivez (*F.*). "Follow." (1) Continue in the
same style. (2) Follow the soloist ;
same as **Col'la vo'ce** or **Col'la par'te.**
Suivez le chant. Follow the melody ; *colla parte.*

Sujet (*F.*). Subject ; theme, melody.

SUK, Josef. Violinist ; *b.* Křecovic, Bohemia, 1874. Studied Prague Cons.
under Dvorak and Bennewitz.
Works : overtures ; a pf. quintet, a pf. quartet,
2 books of pf. pieces, &c.

Sul, Sull', Sul'la, Sul'le (*I.*). On the, near
the, by the.
Sul A. On the A string (vn.), &c.
Sul'la mez'za cor'da. On the middle of the string.
Sul'la pedalie'ra. On the pedal-board.
Sul'la sopra'na cor'da. On the first string (vn., &c.).
Sul'la tastie'ra. (1) Bow on (or near) the finger-board.
(2) On the keyboard.
Sul mez'zo ma'nico. On the middle of the fingerboard.
Sul ponticel'lo. "Bow close to the bridge."

SULLIVAN, Sir Arthur Seymour. *B.* London,
1842 ; *d.* 1900. Chorister Chapel Royal,
1854 ; publ. his first work (a song, " O
Israel "), 1855. First "Mendelssohn
Scholar," R.A.M., 1856. Studied also
Leipzig Cons., 1858-61. His music to
Lalla Rookh was given at Leipzig, 1860 ;
that to *The Tempest*, Crystal Palace,
1862. Principal National Training
School for Music, 1876-81. Condr.
Philharmonic Soc., 1885-7 ; Leeds
Festivals from 1880. Mus.Doc.Cantab.
(*honoris causa*), 1876 ; Oxford, 1879.
Knighted, 1883. His light operas
(words chiefly by **W. S. Gilbert**) have
had an unprecedented success both
in England and America. For several
years he was the leading English
composer.
Works : oratorios and cantatas (*Kenilworth*,
1864 ; *The Prodigal Son*, 1869 ; *On Shore and
Sea*, 1871 ; *The Light of the World*, 1873 ; *The
Martyr of Antioch*, 1880 ; *The Golden Legend*,
1886) ; orchl. pieces, church music, and many
fine songs. His inimitable light operas include
Cox and Box (1867), *Trial by Jury* (1875), *The
Sorcerer* (1877), *H.M.S. Pinafore* (1878), *The*

Pirates of Penzance (1880), *Patience* (1881), *Iolanthe* (1882), *The Mikado* (1885), *Ruddigore* (1887), *The Yeoman of the Guard* (1888), *The Gondoliers* (1889), *Ivanhoe* (grand opera, 1891), *Utopia Limited* (1893), *The Rose of Persia* (1900) He also wrote 2 ballets, and incidental music to *The Tempest*, *The Merchant of Venice*, *Henry VIII*, *Macbeth*, &c.

Sulta'na. A kind of violin with wire strings in pairs.

SUL'ZER, Johann G. *B.* Winterthur, 1720 ; *d.* 1779. Prof. Joachimsthal Gymnasium and Ritterakademie, Berlin.
Works : "Reflections on the Origin of the Sciences and the Fine Arts," "A General Theory of the Fine Arts" (4 vols.), &c.

SUL'ZER, Salomon. *B.* Vorarlberg, 1804 ; *d.* 1890. Cantor chief synagogue, Vienna, from 1825. Set in order the Jewish musical service by adapting and arranging the old traditional melodies.
Published Hebrew hymns, psalms, &c.
His son **Julius** (Vienna, 1834-1891) was a fine violinist. Capellmeister Hofburgtheater, Vienna, 1875.
Wrote operas, orch. music, pf. pieces, and songs.

Suma'ra. A Turkish double-flute.
Sumer is icumen in. A celebrated Rota (or round) of great antiquity, said to have been written by John of Fornsete in the Abbey of Reading, about 1230.
Dr. Grattan Flood (*Hist. of Irish Music*, p. 66) claims that it is an ancient Irish melody—the original of Moore's "Rich and Rare"—and that John of Fornsete merely transcribed it.

Summational tone. (See **Acoustics.**)
Sum'men (*G.*). To hum. (Same as **Sumsen.**)
Sum'mend. Humming.
SUMMERS, Joseph. *B.* Somerset, 1843. Mus.D., Canterbury, 1890. Government Inspector of Music for Public Schools, Victoria, Australia.
Sum'sen (*G.*). To hum ; to buzz, to ring.
Ein Lied'chen sum'men (or *sum'sen*). To hum an air.
SUNDERLAND, Susan (*née* **Sykes**). Soprano; called the " Yorkshire Queen of Song ;" *b.* Brighouse, Yorks, 1819. *D.* 1905. *Début*, London, 1846. Sang at the chief Northern Festivals till 1864.
Sun'to (*I.*). An extract.
Su'o (*I.*). His, its.
Su'o lo'co. "In its own place : " as written. (See *Lo'co.*)
Suona're (*I.*). To sound ; to play on an instrument. Same as **Sonare.**
Suona'ta. "Sounded." A sonata (*q.v.*).
Suo'no. Sound, tone ; music.
Suo'ni altera'ti. Notes altered by flats or sharps.
Suo'ni armo'nici. Harmonics, overtones.
Suo'ni flauta'ti. "Flute-like sounds." (1) Sounds produced on the violin by bowing near the fingerboard. (2) Harmonics on the harp.
Su'per (*L.*). Above, over.
Superdominant. The note above the dominant ; the submediant.
Supe'rius (*L.*). Old name for the highest part.
Superoctave. (1) The octave above. (2) A 2 ft. organ stop. (3) A coupler which "brings on" the octave above.
Supertonic } The note above the Tonic ; the
Supertonique (*F.*) } 2nd degree of a scale.

Super'bo,-a (*I.*). Superb ; lofty, proud.
Superbamen'te. Loftily, proudly.
Super'fluous. Old name for augmented.
Superfluous fifth. Augmented fifth.
SUPPÉ, Franz von. *B.* Spalato, Dalmatia, 1820 ; *d.* Vienna, 1895. (Real name **Francesco E. E. C. Suppe-Demelli.**) Played the flute at 11 ; produced a Mass at 15. Studied at Padua and Vienna. Engaged at various Austrian theatres (Leopoldstädter Th., Vienna, from 1865).
His extremely popular comic operas, operettas, &c. (over 60 in all), include *Paragraph 3* (1858), *The Maiden and the Man* (1862), *Franz Schubert* (1864), *The Beautiful Galatea* (1865), *Fatinitza* (1876), *Boccaccio* (1879), and *Dichter und Bauer* ("The Poet and the Peasant"). He also wrote overtures, church music, songs, &c.

Supplican'do (*I.*) } Imploringly ; in a
Suppliche'vole (*I.*) } beseeching, sup-
Supplichevolmen'te (*I.*) } plicating manner.
Support. Accompaniment, reinforcement.
Supposed bass. The bass-note of an inversion of a chord, as opposed to the root or generator (called the *Real* Bass).
Sur (*F.*). On, upon, over, &c.
Sur la quatrième corde. On the 4th string (vn., &c.).
Sur la touche. On the fingerboard.
Sur le chevalet. On (near) the bridge.
Sur une corde. On one string.
Surabondant (*F.*). Superabundant ; more than usual.
Notes surabondantes. Triplets, quintuplets, septuplets, &c.
Suraigu,-ë (*F.*). Over-acute ; very sharp.
Surdelli'na (*I.*). Same as **Sordelli'na** (*q.v.*).
SURENNE, John T. *B.* London, 1814 ; *d.* 1878.
Published collections of Scottish dance music, songs of Scotland, songs of Ireland, &c.
SURETTE, Thos. W. Noted American composer ; *b.* Concord, Mass., 1862. Orgt. First Parish Church, Concord, 1883-93 ; Christchurch, Baltimore, 1895-1896 ; Lecturer on Music for the American Univ. Extension Soc. (Philadelphia).
Works : operetta, *Priscilla, or the Pilgrim's Proxy* (given over 500 times up to 1900), a romantic opera, orch. pieces, pf. pieces, numerous articles and lectures on music, &c.

SURIA'NO (or **SORIA'NO**), **Francesco.** Rome, 1549-1620. Pupil of Nanini and Palestrina. Maestro at various churches ; finally at St. Peter's, 1603.
Works : madrigals, masses, motets, psalms, &c., up to 16 parts ; also " 110 canons and cpts. on the melody of *Ave Maria Stella*."

Surprise Cadence. (See **Cadence.**)
SURPRISE SYMPHONY. Haydn's Symphony in G, commencing :—

The "surprise" occurs at the end of the 16th bar of the *Andante*, where a *pp* passage for strings is suddenly followed by a chord *ff* for full orchestra.

SUSA'TO. (See **Tylman Susato.**)

Sus-dominante (*F.*). The submediant.

Suspended Cadence. An interrupted cadence (See **Cadence.**)

Suspen'sion. (*G., Vor'halt ; F., Suspension ; I., Sospensio'ne.*) Holding or prolonging one (or more) of the notes of a chord into the chord which follows.

The notes most frequently suspended are those which become the 9th and 4th of the following chords ; but other intervals are suspended, and sometimes complete chords are suspended on other chords.

Suspended 9th.

Suspended 4th.

9   8

4   3
Complete Chord.

4th and 9th.

N.B.—The previous sounding of the suspended note, as at (*a*) is called its *preparation ;* the prolongation, as at (*b*) is called its suspension or *percussion ;* the progression to a consonance, as at (*c*) is called its *resolution.*

Double suspension. A suspension of two notes.

Triple suspension. A suspension of three notes.

Susp'irium (*L.*). A crotchet rest.

Süss (*G.*). Sweet(ly).

Süss'flöte. A soft flute stop on the organ.

SÜSS'MAYER, Franz X. *B.* Steyr, Upper Austria, 1766 ; *d.* 1803. Pupil and friend of Mozart. Capellmeister National Theatre, Vienna, 1792 ; 2nd capellmeister, Court Opera, 1794.

Works : an opera and several operettas. Assisted Mozart with his *Requiem.*

Sustained note. (1) Any note prolonged during several chords. (2) A pedal point (*q.v.*).

Sus-tonique (*F.*) ⎫ The Supertonic.
Sutonique (*F.*) ⎭

Susurran'do (*I.*) ⎫ Murmuring, whispering.
Susurran'te (*I.*) ⎭

SUTTON, Robt. Author of "Elements of the Theory of Music," 1870.

Sveglian'do (*I.*). Arousing, awakening.

Sveglia'to (*I.*). Brisk, lively, alert.

Svelte (*F.*) ⎫ Light, swift, easy, free.
Svel'to (*I.*) ⎭

SVEND'SEN, Johan S. Violinist ; *b.* Christiania, 1840. Studied Leipzig Cons., 1863-7. Toured extensively till 1883. Court condr., Copenhagen, 1883 ; condr. of the Royal Th., 1896.

Works : symphonies ; a string octet, a vn. concerto, a 'cello concerto ; overtures, legendes, rhapsodies, &c., for orch. ; chamber music, songs ; works for chorus and orch., &c.

SVEND'SEN, Oluf. Flautist ; *b.* Christiania, 1832 ; *d.* 1888. Settled in London, 1855 ; Prof. R.A.M., 1867.

Sviluppamen'to (*I.*) ⎫ Unfolding, develop-
Svilup'po (*I.*) ⎭ ment.

Sviz'zera, Al'la (*I.*). In Swiss style.

Sw. Abbn. of *Swell Organ.*

SWAN, Timothy. Composer of hymn-tunes ; *b.* Worcester, Mass., 1758 ; *d.* 1842.

SWEE'LINCK, Jan Pieter. Famous orgt. and teacher ; Amsterdam, 1562-1621. Organist, Old Church, Amsterdam. His organ works are of great historical interest. He was the first composer to develop a fugue systematically from a single subject (in the form afterwards perfected by Bach), and also the first "to employ the pedals in a real fugal part."

His complete works (12 vols., Breitkopf & Härtel), include organ and clavichord works, the 150 Psalms of David, Cantiones Sacræ, &c.

SWEETING, Ed. Thos. Orgt. and composer. Mus.D. Oxon, 1894 ; Orgt. St. John's Coll., Cambridge, 1897-1901 ; Music master, Winchester Coll., 1901.

Swell. (1) The swell-box of an organ. (2) A *crescendo* and *diminuendo* on a note ; marked ⟨⟩ (See **Dynamics** and **Messa di voce.**)

Venetian swell. A series of shutters forming the front of a swell box, constructed on the principle of a Venetian blind.

Swell organ. (*G., O'berwerk ; F., Clavier de récil ; I., Or'gano d'espressio'ne.*) The expressive part of an organ ; abbreviation, *Sw.*

SWEPSTONE, Edith. Composer ; studied G.S.M.

Works : a symphony (1887) ; *Elegiac Overture* (1897) ; cantatas, &c.

SWERT, Jules de. (See **De Swert.**)

SWINSTEAD, Felix. Pianist and composer ; *b.* London, 1880.

SYDENHAM, Edwin A. Composer ; *b.* Somerset, 1847 ; *d.* 1891.

Syl'be (*G.*). A syllable.

Syllab'ic melody. (*G., Silla'bischer Gesang' ; F., Chant syllabique.*) Melody with one note to each syllable of the words.

Syllabic melody is chiefly of interest in regard to church music (services and hymns). The ancient Latin hymns (from the 4th cent.) were almost purely syllabic. With the growth of counterpoint, composers had " more notes than they could find syllables for," and music became more and more florid until at the beginning of the 16th cent. whole motets were written (especially by Italian musicians) to a single word (as *Amen* or *Alleluia*), and much church music became " mere unmeaning vocalization."

Palestrina's *Missa Papæ Marcelli* (see *Palestrina*) " saved church music from this reproach."

The tunes of the Genevan Psalter (1542), and the Lutheran Chorals (from the 16th cent.), returned to the syllabic simplicity of the old Latin melodies, although occasional slurred notes were employed.

Early English church music, as exemplified in Tallis, was almost free from florid passages. Cranmer set the Litany (1544) to syllabic music only ; and the Injunctions of 1559 commanded "the best melody and music that may be devised, having respect that the sentence of the hymn may be understood and perceived " Elaborate florid passages are therefore rarely found in 16th cent. church music except in the " Amens " or " Glorias." (The *Anthems* of this period are rather less restricted.) The English Psalters were strictly syllabic. Este's Psalter (1592) does not contain a single example of slurred melody in the " tunes " (always set in the tenor part), while Ravenscroft's (1621) has only one or two examples. In both Psalters, however, occasional slurred passages occur in the accompanying parts. From the early 18th cent. to well on into the 19th cent. our hymn-tunes (Anglican as well as Nonconformist) became increasingly florid :—

Part of Tune " Bridgwater." Psalm 47.

Evison's Psalter (2nd edition, 1751).

Of God the u - ni -

Of God the u - ni - ver -

- ver - - - - - sal King

- - - - - - sal King.

The inevitable reaction against this kind of hymn-tune led to *Goss and Mercer's Psalter and Hymn-Book* (1857), *Hymns Ancient and Modern* (1861), *The Bristol Tune Book* (1863), &c. (See *Hymns*.)

N.B.—It should in justice be said that the florid hymn-tunes (as the well-known " Helmsley " to " Lo, He comes with clouds descending ") and " Set Pieces " (a peculiarly English growth) of 70 years ago were sung much more fervently and heartily than are most modern syllabic tunes ; and occasional revivals of them are still popular in many parts of England and Wales. In the recent new edition of *Hymns Ancient and Modern* there is a marked relaxation of the severe syllabic style : while the Salvation Army uses the older florid tunes very extensively.

Syllable names. *Doh, ray, me,* &c. ; opposed to *Letter names,* C, D, E, &c.

SYL′VA, Eloi. Tenor ; *b.* Belgium, 1847.
Sang for 7 years at the Paris Opéra.

Sympathetic vibration, or **Resonance.** (See **Acoustics.**)

Symphone′ta (*L.*). Polyphony (*q.v.*).

Sympho′nia. (*Gk., Sumpho′nia ; from Sun,* with, and *Pho′ne,* a sound.) (1) A consonance. (2) A symphony (*q.v.*). (3) Name given to various mediæval insts.

Symphon′ic. (*G., Sympho′nisch ; F., Symphonique ; I., Sinfo′nico.*) (1) Harmonious. (2) Pertaining to a symphony.
Symphonic Poem. (*G., Sympho′nische Dich′tung ; F., Poème symphonique.*) A work for orch. of the dimensions of a symphony, but in free form. It is based upon a *program* or *poem ;* Liszt has been

called the "Father of the Symphonic Poem." Rd. Strauss is at present (1909) its most famous exponent.

Symphonie. (*F.*). (1) A symphony. (2) Harmony, consonance. (3) An instrumental accompt. (4) An orchestra. (5) The "strings" of an orchestra.

Symphonie′-O′de (*G.*). (*F., Ode-symphonie.*) A symphonic work for chorus and orch.

Sympho′niker (*G.*). A composer for full orchestra ; a writer of symphonies.

Sympho′nion. (1) A pf. combined with an org. flute-stop. (2) A musical box.

Sympho′nious. Harmonious, sweet, consonant.

Symphoniste (*F.*). (1) A composer. (2) A writer of symphonies. (3) An orchestral player.

Sym′phony (*G., Symphonie′, Sinfonie′ ; F., Symphonie ; I., Sinfoni′a.*) (1) Consonance. (2) A form of overture (*q.v.*). (3) A *Ritornello* (*q.v.*). (4) Specially, since 1780, a work for an orchestra in the form of a Sonata (*q.v.*), but (generally) with fuller development and greater breadth of treatment. (See **Symphonia.**)
The symphony is the most important form of instrumental composition. Beethoven stands pre-eminent as a writer of symphonies, his "noble nine" still standing unequalled. Other great "Symphonists" are Haydn, Mozart, Mendelssohn, Schubert, Schumann, Spohr, Brahms, and Tschaikowsky.

SYMPSON. (See **Simpson.**)

Syncopa′ta,-e,-o (*I.*). Syncopated.

Syncopa′tion. (*L., Syncopa′tio ; G., Syn′kope ; F., Syncope ; I., Sin′copa.*) " A cutting-off." A temporary displacement of the regular metrical accent. (See **Accent.**)
It occurs (1) whenever a weak beat is prolonged through a stronger one, and (2) whenever a note begins after the commencement of any beat and is continued into the following beat.

The term is probably derived from the practice of "cutting through the notes" in early notation :—

&c.

Syncopi(e)′ren (*G.*).　}
Synkopi(e)′ren (*G.*).　} To syncopate.
Synkopi(e)rt′ (*G.*). Syncopated.

Synonyme (*F.*). Same as **Homophone** (*q.v.*).

SYNTAG'MA MU'SICUM. A rare work by M. Praetorius (*q.v.*), abt. 1615.
Exceedingly valuable for its early typography and illustrations of mediæval insts.

Syren. (See **Siren.**)

Syringe (*F.*)
Syr'inx } (See **Pan's Pipes.**)

Sys'tem. (*G.*, *Syste'ma*, "placing together.") Plan, method, arrangement, scheme ; as Greek System, Guido's (Hexachordal) System, Tonic Sol-fa System. Specially (1) the Staff ; (2) the arrangement of a score.
Li'niensystem (*G.*). The staff.

System of Keys. (See **Key.**)

Système (*F.*). (1) The whole range of musical tones. (2) The compass of an instrument.

Syzygi'a (*L.*). A chord ; a triad.

SZARVA'DY. (See **Clausz-Sarvady.**)

SZÉKELY, Imre. Pianist ; *b.* Malyfalva, Hungary, 1823 ; *d.* 1887. After concert tours, settled in Pesth (1852) as a teacher.
Works : Orchestral works, pf. pieces, (including numerous fantasias on Hungarian melodies), &c.

SZÉLL, George. Precocious composer and pianist ; *b.* Budapest, 1897.
First London appearance, 1908.

SZIGETI, Jóska. Precocious violinist ; *b.* Budapest, 1892. Trained by his father, a vn. teacher. *Début*, Budapest, 1900. Then trained by Hubay. German *début*, 1906 ; London, 1906.

Szopel'ka. A Russian oboe.

SZUMOW'SKA, Antoinette. Pianist ; *b.* Lublin, Poland, 1868. Pupil of Paderewski. Married **J. Adamowski.**

SZYMANOW'SKA, Maria (*née* **Wolow'ska**). Noted pianist ; *b.* Poland, 1790 ; *d.* 1831. Pupil of Field at Moscow. Lived in Warsaw, 1815-30 (with occasional brilliant European tours). Court pianist, St. Petersburg.
Works : 24 mazurkas, a nocturne, studies, &c., for pf. Her music was commended by Schumann.

T

T. Abbn. of *Talon*, of *Ta'sto*, of *Tem'po*, of *Tenor*, of *Toe*, of *Tre*, or of *Tutti*.

T.S. (or *t.s.*), Tasto solo (*q.v.*) ; *A T.* (or *a t.*), a tempo ; T.C., Tre corde. (See *Corda.*)

Ta. (Pron. *taw.*) The flat of **te** in Tonic Sol-fa.

Taatai ¦ **Names (taa, taatai, tafatefe, &c.)** (See **Time-names.**)

Tabal'lo (*I.*). A kettle-drum.

Tab'arde, Tab'arte (*Old E.*). A tabor (*q.v.*).

Tabl. An Egyptian drum.

Tab'lature. (*G., Tabulatur' ; F., Tablature ; I., Tablatu'ra ; Intavolatu'ra.*) (1) A general name for musical characters (notes, rests, &c.). (2) An obsolete system of letter-notation employed for the lute, viol, and organ. (See **Appendix.**)

Table, or **Table d'harmonie** (*F.*). (1) A table of chords, progressions, intervals, &c. (2) A sound-board.

Table d'instrument (*F.*). The sound-board (belly of a vn., &c.).
Table du fond (*F.*). The back (of a vn., &c.).

Table Entertainment. A mixture of song and narrative given by a single performer.

Among the most noted "table entertainments" were those of Dibdin (1789-1801). (See *Dibdin.*)

Table music. (1) Music to accompany a banquet, &c. (2) Music so printed that a number of performers seated round a table could sing or play from the same book.

Tableau (*F.*) (Plur. *Tableaux.*) (1) A representation of some scene by grouping a number of performers in appropriate postures. (2) A change of scenery.

Ta'bor, Ta'bour, Taboret' ⎫ A little drum
Tabouret (*F.*) ⎬ (like a tam-
Tabourin ⎭ bourine without jingles) generally beaten with the right hand.

The *tabor* and *pipe* were formerly favourite insts. in most parts of Europe, and were commonly both played by one performer, the pipe being held in the left hand.

TABOUROT, Jean. (See **Arbeau.**)

Ta'bret. A small tabor or tambourine.

Tab'ulature. (See **Tablature.**)

TACCHINAR'DI, Nicola. Noted operatic tenor and singing teacher ; Florence, 1772-1859.

His daughter, FANNY TACCHINARDI-PERSIANI, was a renowned soprano. (See *Persiani.*)

Ta'ce (*I.*) ⎫
Ta'cet (*L.*) ⎪ " Be silent." (*L. Plur.*,
Ta'ci (*I.*) ⎬ **Tacent ;** *I,* **Taccio'no.**)
Tacia'si (*I.*) ⎭

C. B. tacet. The double bass to be silent.
Fl. tacet. The flute to be silent.
Violi'ni taccio'no. The vns. are silent.

Tact (*G.*). Same as **Takt** (*q.v.*).

Tac'tus (*L.*). A beat ; a stroke with the hand (or bâton) in beating time.

TADOLI'NI, Giovanni. Bologna, 1793-1872. Accompanist and choirmaster, Th. des Italiens, Paris, under Spontini (1811-14), and again (1830-9). Lived in Italy as an opera composer, 1814-30.

Works : several operas ; romances, cantatas, canzonets, &c.

Ta'felklavier' (*G.*) ⎫ A table-shaped
Ta'felförmiges Klavier' (*G.*) ⎬ (square) piano-forte.

Ta'felmusik. Table music (*q.v.*).

TAFFANEL, Claude P. Flautist ; *b.* Bordeaux, 1844. Director of the concerts, Paris Cons., 1892 ; Prof. of flute playing, 1893.

TAG, Christian G. Saxon cantor and composer of church music ; 1735-1811.

Tag'(e)lied (*G.*). Morning song ; **Aubade** (*q.v.*).

TAGLIA'NA, Emilia. Operatic soprano ; *b.* Milan, 1854.

TÄ'GLICHSBECK, Thos. Violinist ; *b.* Ansbach, 1799 ; *d.* 1867. Made long tours, and conducted at various German theatres.

Works : an opera, a mass, 2 symphonies, a concerto and numerous other pieces for vn. and orch., part-songs, male choruses, songs, pieces for vn. and pf., &c.

Ta'glio (*I.*). A "cut" (to reduce the length of a work).

TAGLIO'NI, Ferdinando. Son of S. (below) ; *b.* Naples, 1810 ; Leader, conductor, and editor. Founded a series of "Historico-classical Concerts," 1856.

TAGLIO'NI, Salvatore. Famous ballet master ; 1790-1868.

Tail. The stem of a note.

Tail-piece. (*G., Sai'tenhalter ; F., Cordier, Queue.*) The piece of wood (generally ebony) to which the strings of a violin, &c., are attached.

Taille (*F.*). (1) A tenor voice or part. (2) The viola (or tenor violin).

Taille de basson. A tenor bassoon, or *Oboè da Cac'cia* (*q.v.*).
Taille de hautbois. A tenor oboe.

Takigo'ti, or **Takigo'to.** A Japanese dulcimer.

Takt (*G.*). (1) Time. (2) A beat. (3) A measure.

Im Takt. Same as *a tempo.*
Takt'accent. (1) Metrical accent. (2) The primary accent of a measure or group.
Takt'art. (1) The kind of time (duple, triple, &c.). (2) The style of rhythm.
Takt'bezeich'nung. Time signature.
Takt'erstickung. Syncopation.
Takt'fest. In steady time.
Takt'führer. Conductor ; leader.
Takt'glied. The " beat-note ; " *i.e.*, a crotchet in 3-4 time, a minim in 3-2 time, &c.
Takt'halten. To keep (correct) time.
Takti(e)'ren. To beat time,
Takt'mässig. In suitable time ; according to the time indicated ; measured ; well-timed.
Takt'messer. A metronome.
Takt'note. A whole note, or semibreve (○).

Takt'pause. A whole measure rest.
Takt'schlag. A beat.
Takt'schlagen. To beat time.
Takt'schritt. Measured step ; dance step.
Takt'stock. A *bâton.*
Takt'strich. A bar line.
Takt'teil
Takt'theil } A beat (or "count") of a measure.
Gu'ter or *schwe'rer Takt'teil.* Strong beat.
Schlech'ter or *leicht'er Takt'teil.* Weak beat.
Takt'vorzeichnung
Takt'zeichen } A time sign ; time signature.
Ein Takt wie vor'her zwei. Same as *Doppio movimento* (*q.v.*).
Vier takt'ig (4-*takt'ig*). 4-bar rhythm.

Talabalac'co. A Moorish drum.

Ta'lan. Hindu cymbals.

Talent and Genius.
Genius is the *soul* of art ; talent the educated use of its materials. Genius is inborn ; talent is developed by study and experience ; it is the necessary outfit for genius. "Genius," says Gounod, " is a tumultuous river always likely to overflow its banks ; *talent* builds quays for it." Talent helps to develop genius, but cannot create it. A man of genius *may* write a great work without much study ; but nearly all the great composers studied widely and deeply. "The man of genius *is in advance of his time ;* .... he is rarely understood at first ; he speaks a new language ; ....men follow this master, exploiting what he has discovered. Hence the great success of artists of second rank, while the true genius is most frequently misunderstood in his time."—*Lavignac, "Music and Musicians."*

TALE'XY, Adrien. Paris, 1820-81.
Wrote salon pf. pieces, studies, &c.

Talking machine. (See **Phonograph.**)

TALLIS (TALLYS or TALYS), Thomas. *B.* abt. 1510-15; *d.* London, 1585. Orgt. Waltham Abbey till 1540 ; Gentleman Chapel Royal under Henry VIII, Edward VI, Mary, and Elizabeth ; also joint orgt. with Byrd. Obtained (with Byrd) letters patent " for the exclusive privilege of printing music and ruled music paper for 21 years" (1575).
Works : 34 Cantiones Sacræ (with Byrd ; 16 by Tallis), a noted "Song of 40 Parts" (for 8 5-part choirs), much fine church music (including the well-known "Tallis's Responses"), &c. Tallis was one of the greatest composers of his time.

Talon (*F.*). (1) The heel (nut) of a bow. (2) The heel in pedal playing.

Tallo'ne (*I.*). Same as **Talon** (1).

TAMA'GNO, Francesco. Eminent operatic tenor ; *b.* Turin, 1851 ; *d.* 1905. Created the part of "Otello" in Verdi's opera of that name, La Scala, Milan, 1887.

TAM'BERLIK, Enrico. Celebrated tenor ; *b.* Rome, 1820 ; *d.* 1889. *Début*, Naples, 1840. Engaged Royal Italian Opera, London, during the season of 1850-64.

Tambour (*F.*). (1) A drum. (2) A drummer.
Tambour de Basque. A tambourine.
Tambour long. Tenor drum.
Tambour majeur. A drum major (*q.v.*).
Tambour militaire. Side drum.
Tambour roulante. A long drum. (See *Drum.*)

Tambou'ra
Tambu'ra } An Oriental inst. of the guitar kind.

Tambourin (*F.*). (1) A tambourine without jingles. (2) A French dance in lively 2-4 time.
"It ought to be well cadenced and bold."—*Rousseau.*

Tambourin' (*G.*). A tambourine.
Tambourin'schläger. Tambourine player.

Tambourine. (*G., Tamburin'; F., Tambour de Basque, Tambouret ; I., Tamburi'no.*) An ancient inst. of the drum species.
It consists of a hoop of wood or metal over which a piece of parchment or skin is stretched like the head of a drum. The hoop is fitted with "jingles" which rattle when the head is struck, or when the tambourine is shaken.
Tambourineur (*F.*). (1) A drummer. (2) A tambourine player.

Tamburel'lo (*I.*). A tabor (*q.v.*).

TAMBURI'NI, Antonio. Celebrated baritone; *b.* Faenza, 1800 ; *d.* 1876. *Début*, Cento, 1818.
Up to his retirement in 1859 he was one of the most noted of European singers ; " a conspicuous star in the brilliant constellation formed by Grisi, Persiani, Viardot, Rubini, Lablache, and himself."

Tambu'ro (*I.*). (1) A drum. (2) A side drum.
Tamburac'cio. A large drum.
Tamburi'no. (1) A drummer. (2) A tambourine.
Tambu'ro'ne
Cas'sa gran'de } A large drum ; the "big" drum of
Tambu'ro gran'de } a band or orchestra.
Tambu'ro gros'so }
Tambu'ro milita're. Side drum.
Tambu'ro rullan'te. Tenor drum.

TAMI'NI. Noted tenor ; *b.* Vienna, 18—. London *début*, 1909.

Tampon (*Old F.*). A bass-drumstick.

Tam-tam. (1) A gong. (2) A long Hindu drum.
Tamtamschlag (*G.*). A gong-stroke.

Tanbur' (*G.*). Same as **Tamburo** (*q.v.*).

TANCRE'DI. Opera by Rossini, 1813.

Tän'delnd (*G.*). Playfully ; banteringly.

TANE'IEFF, Sergei. Pianist and composer ; *b.* Russia, 1856.

Tan'gent. (*G., Tangen'te.*) The wedge-shaped hammer of a clavichord.
Tangen' tenflügel (*G.*). A clavichord of similar shape to a grand piano.

TANN'HÄUSER. Opera by Wagner ; produced Dresden, 1845.

TANS'UR, William. *B.* Dunchurch ; baptized 1706 ; *d.* 1783.
Pub. several musical treatises of antiquarian interest, including "A Musical Grammar and Dictionary, or a General Introduction to the Whole Art of Music, by William Tans'ur, Senior, MUSICO-THEORICO; Professor, Corrector, and Teacher of Church Music, above 50 years" (7th edition, 1829).

Tanti'no (*I.*). A little ; very little.

Tan'to (*I.*). So much; very; too much.
Ada'gio ma non tan'to. Slow, but not too slow.
Alle'gro non tan'to. Quick, but not too much so.
Cres. a tan'to possi'bile. Crescendo as much as possible.
Di tan'to in tan'to. By degrees; gradually.

Tanz (*G.*) (plur. *Tan'ze*). A dance.
Tanz'en. To dance.
Nach der Violi'ne tanz'en. To dance to the violin.
Tanz'künst. The art of dancing.
Tanz'lieder. Dance songs.
Tanz'musik. Dance music.
Tanz'schritt. Dance step.
Tanz'stücke. Dance pieces; dance tunes.

TAP'PERT, Wilhelm. Writer; *b.* Silesia, 1830. At first a schoolmaster. Formed a valuable collection of old tablatures. (See **Tablature.**)
> Works: a "Wagner-Lexikon" (list of abusive epithets against Wagner, 1877), a work on "Consecutive Fifths," arrangements of old German songs, "50 studies for the Left Hand," &c.

Tarantel'la (*I.*). **Tarantelle** (*F.*). (1) A lively Neapolitan dance in 6-8 time, the *tempo* gradually increasing. (2) A rapid instrumental piece in 3-8 or 6-8 time.
> Dancing the *Tarantella* until the dancer dropped from fatigue was supposed to be a cure for the bite of the *Tarantula* spider; hence its name.
Tarentelli'na. A short (little) tarantella.

Tarau Theyaou Thro } A Burmese fiddle with three silk strings.

TAR'CHI, Angelo. *B.* Naples, 1760; *d.* Paris, 1814.
> Works: several operas (*d'Auberge en auberge*, 1800, &c.).

Tar'da,-o (*I.*). Slow, dragging, lingering.
Tardamen'te Tardantemen'te } Slowly.
Tardan'do Tarda'to } Retarding the speed.

TARDI'TI, Orazio. Italian composer; maestro, Faenza Cath., 1648; *d.* after 1670.
> Works: masses, psalms, motets, litanies, madrigals, "Canzonette amorose," &c.

TARTI'NI, Giuseppe. Celebrated violinist; *b.* Pirano, 1692; *d.* Padua, 1770. Studied first for the Church, and afterwards for the legal profession; but after much opposition, and the entanglements caused by a secret marriage with a niece of Cardinal Carnaro, his passion for the violin finally triumphed. Discovered the "difference-tones" produced by two sounds (see **Acoustics**), about 1714 (hence called "Tartini's Tones"). He utilized them to secure pure intonation in double stopping, &c. Solo violinist and orchl. condr., St. Antonio, Padua, 1721; chamber musician, Prague, 1723; resumed his work at Padua, 1725; founded a vn. school there, 1728.
> Works: many concertos and sonatas for vn. (or for vn. and other insts.); "The Art of the Bow," the "Trillo del Diavolo;" several treatises on Harmony, &c.; a "Traité des Agrémens de la musique," &c.

Tartini's Tones. (See **Tartini.**)

Tasch'engeige (*G.*). A pocket fiddle or kit (*q.v.*).

TASKIN, E. Alexandre. Operatic baritone; grandson of H. J. (below); Paris, 1853-97. *Début*, 1875. Prof. of lyrical declamation, Paris Cons.

TASKIN, Henri J. Organist; son of P. (below); *b.* Versailles, 1779; *d.* 1852.
> Works: a pf. concerto, pf. trios, pf. solos, songs.

TASKIN, Pascal. *B.* Theux (Liége), 1723; *d.* Paris, 1795. Noted inst. maker. Invented leather tangents for the clavichord; introduced the pf. pedal worked by the foot (instead of the knee).

Taste. "Intellectual relish."
> "Taste is that which is most felt and least explained. Each man has his peculiar tastes, ...but let a concert be heard by ears sufficiently exercised and men sufficiently instructed, and the greatest number will generally agree on the judgment of the pieces.....Genius creates, but taste makes the choice; although the prejudices of custom or education often change, by arbitrary conventions, the order of natural beauties. We can do great things without taste, but it is that alone which makes them interesting. It is taste which makes the composer catch the ideas of the poet; it is taste which makes the executant catch the ideas of the composer."—*Rousseau.*

Tas'te (*G.*). Finger-key or foot-key (pedal).
O'bertasten Schwarz'e Tas'ten } The black keys.
Un'tertasten Weis'se Tas'ten } The white keys.

Ta'sto (*I.*). "The touch." (1) Key (of a pf., &c.). (2) A fret. (3) "Touch" in playing. (4) A fingerboard.
Tasta'me (I.) Tastatur' (G.) Tastatu'ra (I.) } (1) A keyboard; fingerboard.
Tas'tenbrett (G.) } (2) A hand-guide.
Tas'tenleiter (G.) Tastie'ra (I.)
Sul'la tastie'ra (I.) Sul ta'sto (I.) } "Bow near the fingerboard" (in vn. playing, &c.).
Tas'tenstäbchen (G.). A fret (of a mandoline, &c.).
Tas'tenwerk (G.). A keyed instrument.
Ta'sto so'lo (I.). Abbn. T. S. The bass to be played without accompanying chords, in unison or 8ves.

TATE, Nahum. *B.* Dublin, 1652; *d.* 1715. Poet laureate, 1692.
> Pub. (with Brady) the "New Version" of the Psalms, 1696. Wrote *Dido and Eneas* for Purcell.

Tat'to (*I.*). The touch; touch (in playing).

Tattoo'. The military drum-signal for retiring at night.

TAU'BERT, Ernst E. Composer; *b.* Regenswalde, 1838.

TAU'BERT, K. G. Wilhelm. Pianist; Berlin, 1811-91. Accompanist, Berlin Court concerts, 1831; condr. of the opera, 1842; Hofkapellmeister, 1845-70.
> Works: 6 operas, incidental music to plays, 4 symphonies, chamber music, pf. pieces, songs, &c.

TAU'BERT, Dr. Otto. *B.* Naumburg-on-Saale, 1833; *d.* 1903. Prof. Torgau Gymnasium, 1863.
> Works: church music, male choruses, songs, theoretical works, &c.

TAUDOU, Antoine A. B. Violinist ; *b.* Perpignan, 1846. Won *Grand Prix de Rome*, Paris Cons., 1869. Prof. of Harmony at the Cons., 1883.
Works : orch. pieces, a vn. concerto, chamber music, &c.

TAUSCH, Franz. Noted clarinettist ; *b.* Heidelberg, 1762 ; *d.* 1817. Member Electoral Orch., Mannheim, at 8. Played at Munich, 1777-89 ; afterwards in the Berlin Court Orchestra. Founded a School for Wind Insts., Berlin, 1805.
Works : 2 clar. concertos, 3 concertantes for 2 clars. ; clar. duos ; trios and quartets for wind insts., 6 military marches, &c.

TAUSCH, Julius. Pianist ; *b.* Dessau, 1827 ; *d.* 1895. Settled in Düsseldorf, 1846 ; Schumann's deputy (1853) and successor (1855) as condr. of the Musical Society, &c. Retired, 1890.
Works : orch. pieces, choral works, pf. pieces, male choruses, &c.

TAUSCH'ER, Frau. (See **Gadski.**)

TAU'SIG, Carl. Celebrated pianist ; *b.* Warsaw, 1841 ; *d.* Leipzig, 1871.
Pupil of Liszt from the age of 14 ; *début*, Berlin, 1858. Founded a School for advanced pf. playing, Berlin, 1865. Made extensive European tours.
Works : pf. pieces and transcriptions, a pf. score of Wagner's *Meistersinger*, &c. ; and "Tägliche Studien" (a set of highly valuable pf. exercises and studies).

Tautol'ogy. A tiresome repetition of the same passage (or passages).

TAU'WITZ, Eduard. *B.* Glatz, Silesia, 1812; *d.* 1894. Capellmeister at various theatres (Prague, 1846-63).
Works : over 1,000 compositions (including 3 operas).

TAVERNER, John (1). Distinguished composer of Henry VIII's reign. *B.* Boston. Called by Wolsey to Oxford.
Works : masses, motets, &c.

TAVERNER, John (2). 1584-1638. Gresham Professor, 1610.

TAYLER, Henry Lyell. Violinist ; *b.* London, 1872.

TAYLOR, H. J. Contemp. orgt. and composer ; resides at Dover.
Author of several musical booklets, &c.

TAYLOR, Ebenezer Wm. *B.* Stafford, 1851. Mus.D. Oxon, 1883.
Works : pedal scales, figured bass exercises, &c.

TAYLOR, Edward. Bass singer ; *b.* Norwich, 1784 ; *d.* 1863. Co-founder Norwich Musical Festivals, 1824 ; conductor, 1839 and 1842.
Settled in London, 1825 ; mus. critic to the *Spectator* ; Gresham Professor, 1837. Founder of the " Purcell Club."
Works : lectures, "The Art of Singing at Sight," &c. ; edited Purcell's *King Arthur* ; wrote English words to Mozart's *Requiem*, Spohr's *Last Judgment*, &c.

TAYLOR, Franklin. Pianist ; *b.* Birmingham, 1843. Settled in London, 1862. Prof. National Training School, 1876-1883 ; R.C.M., 1883.

Works : "Primer of Pf. Playing" (1877), a pf. tutor, "Technique and Expression in Pf. Playing" (1897), articles in Grove's Dict. ; translations of Richter's " Harmony," and " Counterpoint, Canon, and Fugue."

TAYLOR, John. *B.* abt. 1845 ; *d.* 1908. Orgt. Kensington Palace ; Prof. of sight-singing, G.S.M., 1897.
Author of "The Stave Modulator," works on sight-singing, &c. .

TAYLOR, Samuel Coleridge. (See **Coleridge-Taylor.**)

TAYLOR, Thos. R. 1807-35. Congregational minister.
Wrote the hymn " I'm but a stranger here."

TAYLOR, W. Sedley. Lecturer and writer ; *b.* Kingston-on-Thames, 1821.

TCHAIKOV'SKY (TSCHAIKOW'SKY), Peter Iljitch. The most distinguished of modern Russian composers ; *b.* Wotkinsk, 1840 ; *d.* St. Petersburg, Nov. 6, 1893. Intended for the legal profession. Entered St. Petersburg Cons. soon after its establishment by Rubinstein (1862) ; devoted himself to music, and became teacher of harmony at the Cons. (1866-1877) ; then gave up all his time to composition. Visited New York, 1891 ; Mus.Doc.Cantab. (*honoris causa*), 1893. His music is full of national spirit and colour ; he frequently utilized native folk-songs ; his works portray every shade of emotion ; and his orchestral compositions, in particular, are characterized by freshness, power, and originality.
Works : 10 Russian operas (*Vakula*, 1876; *Eugen Onégin*, 1879 ; *The Maid of Orleans*, 1881 ; *Mazeppa*, 1882) ; a lyric drama, *Snow-drop* ; 3 ballets, 2 masses, 6 symphonies, 7 symphonic poems, 4 orchl. suites ; overtures, marches, 3 pf. concertos, a pf. fantasia with orch., a vn. concerto, a sextet and other chamber music, many pf. pieces, Russian songs and duets, &c. ; a " Treatise on Harmony," a translation of Gevaert's "Instrumentation," &c.

Tche, or **Tchang.** A Chinese guitar.

Te (pron. *Tee*). The 7th note of the Major scale in Tonic Sol-fa.

Té (*F.*). C♯ ; *Ut dièse.*

Tea'tro (*I.*). A theatre.

TEBALDI'NI, Giovanni. *B.* Brescia, 1864(?). Maestro Padua Cath., 1894 ; Director Parma Cons., 1897. " A zealous reformer of church music in Italy."
Works : an opera, masses, organ pieces, an " Organ Method," &c.

Tech'nic ⎱ (*G., Tech'nik.*) The mechanical
Technique' ⎰ part of singing or playing (as opposed to the emotional or expressive part).
In pf. playing, some German writers distinguish between *Mecha'nik* (finger and wrist drill), and *Tech'nik* (skill and dexterity in performance).

Tech'nicon. An apparatus for training the hands and fingers.

Tech'niphone. An earlier name for the Virgil Clavier (*q.v.*).

Tech'nisch (*G.*).   Technical.

Tede'sco,-a (*I.*).   German.
Al'la tede'sca. In the German style.
Li'ra tede'sca. A hurdy-gurdy.
  "*Tede'sca* has special reference to waltz-rhythm,
  and invites changes of *tempo.*"—*Von Bülow.*

TEDES'CO, Ignaz A.   Pianist ; *b.* Prague,
  1817 ; *d.* 1882.   Called, from his
  technical facility, the "Hannibal of
  octaves."
  Wrote "light and brilliant" salon pf. music.

Te De'um Lauda'mus (*L.*).   "We praise
  Thee, O God." A hymn written by St.
  Niceta—not, as formerly supposed, by
  St. Ambrose and St. Augustine. It has
  been sung in the Catholic church since
  the 4th century.   (See **Niceta.**)
  "The oldest version is in a MS. of the 8th Cent.
  in a bold Irish hand, now in the British
  Museum."—*W. H. Grattan Flood.*

Teil (*G.*).   A part ; a portion.
Takt'teil. A beat (of a bar).
Teil'töne. Partials. (See *Acoustics.*)

Teil'ung (*G.*).   A division, subdivision, &c.

TE'LEMANN, Georg P.   Noted contemporary of J. S. Bach ; *b.* Magdeburg,
  1681 ; *d.* 1767. Wrote an opera at 12 ;
  condr. Catholic church, Hildesheim, at
  14. Orgt. and mus.-director, Neukirche,
  Leipzig, 1701. Capellmeister, Sorau,
  1704.   Concertmeister,   Eisenach,
  1708 ; Court condr., 1709.   Town
  mus.-director, Hamburg, from 1721.
  An amazingly prolific composer, "far
  better known in his day than Bach."
  Works : 12 series of cantatas and motets for the
  church year (about 3,000 numbers in all) ;
  44 Passions ; 112 cantatas, &c., for special
  occasions ; 300 overtures ; many oratorios,
  &c. ; and a vast amount of instrumental music.

Telemann's Curve.   A small curve above
  the figure 5 to indicate a diminished
  triad in figured bass ; 5̄ (01 ♭).
  It was introduced by Telemann, and is often
  found in old scores. It is not now used.

TEL'LE, Carl. *B.* 1826 ; *d.* Klosterneuburg,
  1895. Ballet master Vienna Hofopern-
  theater, 1858-88.   Wrote over 20
  ballets.

TEL'LEFSEN, Thos. D. A. *B.* Trondhjem,
  1823 ; *d.* 1874. Pianist ; pupil of
  Chopin ; settled in Paris as teacher.
  Works : 2 concertos, and other pf. music ; pieces
  for pf. and vn., &c.

Tell-tale.   A contrivance in an organ to
  indicate the amount of wind in the
  bellows.

Tem. Abbn. of *Tempo.*

Te'ma (*I.*). A theme, air, melody, or subject.
Te'ma con variazio'ni. A theme with variations.

Tem'perament. (*G., Temperatur'; F., Tem-
  pérament; I., Temperamen'to.*)   Tuning;
  especially the compromise between
  acoustically correct intervals and those
  required in practical music. (See also
  Tuning.)
  A reference to the article on Acoustics shows that
  the scientific steps of a major scale are of 3

kinds, major tones, minor tones, and semitones.
An attempt to make all the major scales
used in modern music scientifically accurate
on the pianoforte would require about 81 keys
to each octave ! Previous to the time of
Bach, when fewer scales were in use, com-
promises were effected by tuning the more
common scales fairly accurately and allowing
difficulties to accumulate in those with 4 (or
more) sharps or flats. Bach solved the
difficulty by boldly dividing the octave into 12
equal semitones, all scientifically wrong, but
sufficiently accurate to satisfy Bach's musical
ear. This *Equal Temperament* (suggested by
Willaert about 1550) is now universally adopted
on all keyboard instruments ; but though
theoretically simple, it must not be supposed
that each semitone is ever *exactly* one-twelfth
of an octave ; the "tuner seldom or never gives
precisely those intervals which theory lays
down."—*Dr. Ellis.*
Mean temperament } In this system, once largely
Mean-tone system } used, the major third was
tuned accurately and divided into two equal (or
mean) tones.

Temperan'do (*I.*).   Moderating (the speed).
Temperatamen'te. Moderately.
Temperi(e)'ren (*G.*). To temper, moderate, soften.

TEMPEST, The. Among the various settings
  of incidental music to Shakespeare's
  "Tempest," that of Sullivan is specially
  interesting, as it was his Op. 1 (1862).
  The original (1611) was by Robt. Johnson.

Tempe'sta (*I.*)   ⎫
Tempeste (*Old F.*)   ⎬ A tempest.
Tempête (*F.*)   ⎭
Tempestosamen'te (*I.*)   ⎫
Tempesto'so (*I.*)   ⎪ Impetuously, tempestuously,
Tempestueux (*F.*)   ⎬ furiously.
Tempestueuse (*F.*)   ⎪
Tempêtueux-se (*F.*)   ⎭

Tempête (*F.*).   A boisterous rapid dance
  in 2-4 time.

TEMPLE, Hope (**Mad. A. C. P. Messager**),
  Née **Dotie Davis.** Contemporary song
  writer ; *b.* Dublin. Pupil of J. F.
  Barnett and Messager (Paris).

TEMPLETON, John.   Tenor singer ; *b.* nr.
  Kilmarnock, 1802 ; *d.* 1886 ; Stage
  début, Worthing, 1828. Retired from
  the stage, 1840 ; afterwards gave
  lecture-recitals.

Tem'po (*I.*).   Time, measure, beat. Used
  especially of *speed*, or rate of movement.
A tem'po. In strict time (after *rall., accel.,* &c.).
A tem'po pri'mo } (Return to) the original *tempo.*
Tem'po pri'mo   }
Tem'po a cappel'la } In the time of church music ;
Tem'po al'la bre've } with a beat to each minim.
Tem'po al'la semibre've. With a beat to each crotchet.
Tem'po a piace're. Ad lib.; at pleasure ; not in
  strict time.
Tem'po bina'rio. Duple time.
Tem'po com'modo (or *co'modo*). At a convenient
  moderate speed.
Tem'po da ca'po. The same *tempo* as at the beginning.
Tem'po de'bole. A weakly accented beat.
Tem'po del pri'mo pez'zo. At the same speed as the
  first piece.
Tem'po di Bal'lo. In dance style ; light and spirited.
Tem'po di Bole'ro, Gavot'ta, Minuet'to, &c. In the
  time (style, speed) of a Bolero, Gavotte, Minuet, &c.
Tem'po di pri'mo par'te. At the same speed as the
  first part.
Tem'po dop'pio. Twice as fast.
Tem'po for'te. A strong beat.

Tem'po frette'vole (or *frettolo'so*). In hastened, hurried time.
Tem'po giu'sto. In just, steady time. With Handel, 4-4 time at moderate speed.
Tem'po maggio're. Same as *Tempo alla breve* (above).
Tem'po mino're. Same as *Tempo alla semibreve* (above).
Tem'po 1mo. Tempo primo (*q.v.*).
Tem'po 1 del Te'ma. The same speed as at the first appearance of the Theme.
Tem'po ordina'rio. Ordinary time. (1) 4-4 time at moderate speed. (2) Same as *Tempo primo* (*q.v.*).
Tem'po perdu'to. Unsteady, irregular time.
Tem'po pri'mo } At the same speed as at first;
Tem'po primie'ro } (resume) the strict *tempo*.
Tem'po reggia'to. Wait for the principal part; same as *Colla parte* (*q.v.*).
Tem'po ruba'to. (See *Rubato*.)
Tem'po terna'rio. Triple time.
L'istes'so tem'po } (See *Istesso*.)
Lo stes'so tem'po }
Sen'za tem'po. Without (strict) time; same as *ad lib.*, or *a piacere*.

Tempo-mark. (*G.*, *Tem'po-Bezeich'nung*.)
(1) A metronome mark (*q.v.*).
Towards the end of the 19th cent. metronome marks were added to almost every piece of music; there is now a reaction against them (except in studies and exercises) as they often tend to mechanical precision at the expense of expression.
(2) An abbn., word, or phrase indicating the approximate speed and general style of a piece (or movement)
Tempo marks fall into 3 classes: (1) a steady rate of speed, as *Largo, Adagio, Andante, Allegro*; (2) acceleration, as *Accelerando, Stringendo*; (3) retardation, as *Rallentando, Tardando, Calando, Morendo*.

Tempora'le (*I.*). (1) Time, season. (2) A storm, tempest.
Temporiser (*F.*). To accommodate the time of the accompt. to that of the soloist; to play *Colla parte*.
Tem'po wie vor'her (*G.*). The time (speed) as before.
Temps (*F.*). Time. Specially, a "beat" of a bar.
Temps faible } A weak beat.
Temps secondaire }
Temps fort } A strong beat.
Temps sensible }
Temps frappé. Down beat.
Temps levé. Up beat.
Tem'pus (*L.*). Time; time-division.
Tem'pus perfec'tum. The division of a breve into 3 semibreves in mensural music.
Tem'pus im'perfectum. The division of a breve into 2 semibreves in mensural music.
Tempus bina'rium. Duple time.
Tempus terna'rium. Triple time.
Ten. Abbn. of *Tenuto*.
TENA'GLIA, Anton F. Florentine composer. His opera *Cleano* (1661) is said to contain the first known example of an *Aria da Capo*.
Ten BRINK. (See **Brink**.)
Tendency Interval. The interval of the augmented 4th (or its inversion, the diminished 5th), so-called because each of its notes has a special tendency of progression (or resolution).
Tendrement (*F.*). Tenderly, delicately.
TENDUC'CI, G. Ferdinando. Noted male soprano; *b.* Siena, 1736; *d.* 18—(?). Great favourite in London; friendly with Mozart. Travelled in Scotland and Ireland with Dr. Arne.

Ten'ebræ. (*Lat.* plur. " gloom, darkness.") Lamentations sung on Good Friday in R.C. churches while the altar candles are extinguished one by one.
Tene're (*I.* and *L.*). To hold; to sustain.
Tenen'do il can'to (*I.*). (Well) sustaining the melody.
Tene'te (*I.*). Hold out, sustain.
Tene'te si'no al'la fi'ne del suo'no. Hold out the note to the very end.
Te'nero,-a (*I.*). Tender, soft, delicate.
Con teneres'za }
Teneramen'te } Tenderly, delicately.
Tenero'so }
Teneur (*F.*). The *canto fermo* of a hymn-tune or choral.
Tenir (*F.*). To hold, sustain.
Tenir la pédale. Hold on the pedal.
Ten KATE. (See **Kate**.)
TENNEY, John H. Composer; *b.* Rowley (U.S.), 1840.
Ten'or. (*G.*, *Tenor'*; *F.*, *Ténor*, or *Taille*; *I.*, *Teno're*.) Originally the " holding part" which sustained the chief melody (from *L. Tenere*, " to hold ").
In mediæval music the "tune" or "plain-song" was always in the tenor part, and the custom still survives in most churches where Gregorian music is used. Playford's Psalter was the first English work of its kind to allot the melody of psalm-tunes to the treble (or soprano) part. (See *Playford*.)
(1) The highest of natural male voices; compass from about—
(2) The part sung by such a voice, or played by any inst. of about the same compass or tone-quality.
First tenor. The higher tenor part in a chorus.
Second tenor. The lower tenor part in a chorus.
Hel'dentenor' (*G.*) } A full and powerful dramatic
Teno're robus'to (*I.*) } tenor, with voice-quality
Teno're di for'za (*I.*) } almost like that of a baritone; upward compass to A or B♭.
Ly'rischer Tenor' (*G.*) } A "lyric" or light tenor;
Teno're di gra'zia (*I.*) } upward compass to about
Teno're leggie'ro (*I.*) } C.
Tenor bell. The largest of a set of bells; the key-note of a peal (*q.v.*).
Tenor C. (1) The note [music notation] (2) The lowest string of the viola.
Tenor clef. The C clef on the 4th line of the staff. (See *Clef*.)
Teno're buf'fo (*I.*). A tenor who sings comic parts.
Teno're contralti'no (*I.*). A high tenor resembling a contralto.
Tenor drum. (See *Drum*.)
Teno're pri'mo (*I.*). First tenor.
Teno're secon'do (*I.*). Second tenor.
Teno're di mez'zo carat'tere. A robust tenor, almost baritone.
Tenor'jagott (*G.*). Tenoroon (*q.v.*).
Tenor'geige (*G.*). The viola.
Tenor horn. The sax-horn in E♭ of a brass band.
Tenori'no (*I.*). A falsetto tenor; a *castrato*.
Tenorist' (*G.*) } (1) A tenor singer. (2) A viola
Tenori'sta (*I.*) } player.
Tenoriste (*F.*) }
Tenoroon'. (1) A tenor oboe (or bassoon) with downward compass to tenor C. Also called a *Quint-bassoon* or *Oboè da cac'cia*. (2) An old organ stop, 16 ft. pitch, extending only to tenor C.
Tenor'posaune (*G.*). Tenor trombone.
Tenor'schlüssel (*G.*) } The tenor clef.
Tenor'zeichen (*G.*) }

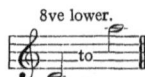

Tenor'stimme (G.). A tenor voice or part.
Tenor trombone. (See *Trombone.*)
Tenor violin, or simply *Tenor.* The viola (*q.v.*).

Tenth. (*G., De'zime ; F., Dixième ; I., De'cima.*) (1) The (compound) interval of an octave and a third. (See **Interval.**)

(2) An organ stop a tenth above unison pitch ; also called a *decima* or *double tierce.*

Tenu,-e (*F.*). Held, sustained.

Tenue (*F.*). A sustained note ; an organ-point.

Tenu'ta (*I.*). A holding-note ; a *Fermata.*

Tenu'ta lun'ga. A long holding-note.

Tenu'to,-a (*I.*). Abbn. *Ten.* Held out ; sustained for the full time. (See **Tenere.**)

For'te tenu'to, or *ften.* To be held *forte* throughout.
Tenu'te. Sustain the note (or notes) well.
Tenu'to mark. Same as "organ tone" mark. (See *Organ tone.*)
Tenu'to per il peda'le. Sustain by means of the pedal.
Tenu'to sem'pre (*I.*). In a sustained manner through-out (the piece or movement).

Téorbe (*F.*) ⎫
Teor'bo (*I.*) ⎬ A Theorbo (*q.v.*).

Teore'tico,-a (*I.*). Theoretical.

Teori'a (*I.*). Theory.

Teori'a del can'to. Theory of singing.
Teori'a d'armoni'a. Theory of harmony.

Teor'ico (*I.*). (1) Theoretical. (2) A teacher of theory.

Te'pido,-a (*I.*). Lukewarm.

Con tepidità ⎫ With lukewarmness, indifference ;
Tepidamen'te ⎬ in an even unimpassioned style.

Teponaz'tle. A drum used by the aborigines of Mexico and Central America.

It gives two different notes, and serves both to mark the rhythm and to supply a kind of rudimentary bass.

Ter (*L.*). Thrice.

Ter Sanc'tus. "Thrice holy ;" "Holy, holy, holy," in the Te Deum, &c.
Ter un'ca. "Thrice hooked." A demisemiquaver

(𝄽).

Tercet (*F.*). (1) A triplet. (2) A group of three rhyming lines in poetry.

Terminazio'ne (*I.*). The turn at the end of a shake (*q.v.*).

Ter'nary. (*F., Ternaire ; I., Terna'rio.*) Arranged in " threes ; " threefold.

Terna'rio tem'po (*I.*). Triple time.

Ternary Form. Name sometimes given to " Rondo Form," in which the chief theme appears three (or more) times. Also to the "First movement form" of a sonata, because in three main divisions.
Ternary measure. Triple time ; perfect time.

TERNI'NA, Milka. Soprano vocalist ; *b.* Croatia, 1864. Fine "Wagner" singer.

TERPAN'DER, Called the " Father of Greek music ; " *b.* Lesbos, 7th cent. B.C.

Terpo'dion. (1) An inst. resembling the pf. in appearance ; " the tone was pro-duced from blocks of wood struck with hammers." (2) An old org. stop (a kind of Gamba.).

TERPSICH'ORE. The Muse of dancing. (See **Muse.**)

Terpsichore'an. Relating to dancing.

TERRADE'LLAS (or **TERRADE'GLIAS**), **Domingo.** *B.* Barcelona, 1711 ; *d.* 1751. Pupil of Durante.

Wrote operas (*Astarte,* 1739 ; *Merope,* 1743 ; &c.)

TERRY, Mad. A. (See **Sybil Sanderson.**)

TER'SCHAK, Adolf. Flautist and com-poser ; Prague, 1832-1901.

Ter'tia (*L.*). A third (or tierce; 17th).

Ter'tia mo'di (*L.*). The 3rd note of a mode (or scale).
Ter'tian (*E.*) ⎫ An organ mixture-stop of
Tertian' Zwei'fach (G.) ⎬ 2 ranks (a major 17th and a 19th).

TERTIS, Lionel. Viola player ; *b.* W. Hartlepool, 1876.

Terz (*G.*) ⎫
Ter'za (*I.*) ⎬ (1) Third. (2) Interval of a third.

Gros'se Terz (G.). Major third.
Klei'ne Terz (G.). Minor third.
O'pera ter'za (*I.*). The third work (of a composer, or series of works).
Ter'za maggio're (*I.*). A major 3rd.
Ter'za mino're (*I.*). A minor 3rd.
Ter'za ma'no (*I.*). A " third hand ;" an octave coupler.
Ter'zade'cima (*I.*) ⎫ Interval of a 13th.
Terz'de'zime (G.) ⎬
Terz'dezimo'le (G.). A Tredecuplet (*q.v.*).
Terz'(en)lauf (G.). A succession of 3rds.
Terzett' (G.) ⎫ A trio (especially a vocal trio).
Terzet'to (*I.*) ⎬
Terzetti'no (*I.*). A short trio.
Terz'flöte (G.). (1) A "third" flute (a third higher than the ordinary flute). (2) An organ tierce. (See *Tierce.*)
Terzi'na (*I.*). (1) A triplet. (2) An E♭ or "Third" flute.
Ter'zo suo'no (*I.*). A difference tone. (See *Acoustics.*)
Terzquartsext'akkord (G.). A 6-4-3 chord.
Terzquintsext'akkord (G.). A 6-5-3 chord.
Terz'töne (G.). Tierce-tones. (See *Tierce.*)
Violi'no ter'zo (*I.*). Third violin.

TERZIA'NI, Eugenio. Rome, 1825-89. Pupil of Mercadente. Maestro, La Scala, Milan, 1867-71 ; prof. of com-position, Rome, 1877.

Works : an oratorio, a requiem, operas, &c.

TESCH'NER, Gustav W. Singing teacher ; *b.* Magdeburg, 1800 ; *d.* 1883.

Works : vocal exercises and solfeggi ; editions of vocalises, &c., by Italian masters ; editions of early church music.

TE'SI - TRAMONTI'NI, Vittoria. Noted singer ; *b.* Florence, about 1695 ; *d.* Vienna, 1775. Sang with great success at Venice, Naples, Madrid (with Farinelli), and Vienna.

Her voice was noted for its range ; she sang high and low parts equally well.

TES'SARIN, Francesco. Pianist ; friend of Wagner ; *b.* Venice, 1820.

Works : an opera, church music, pf. fantasias, &c.

TESSARI′NI, Carlo. Celebrated violinist of the Corelli school ; *b.* Rimini, 1690 ; *d.* (?). 1st vn. at Urbino Cath.

Works : sonatas for 2 vns. and bass ; 12 concertini for a vn. principal, 2 vns. ripieni, violetto, and 'cello, with a continued bass for organ or cembalo ; concerti grossi for strings and organ ; a Vn. Method, &c.

Tessitu′ra (*I.*) ⎫ " Texture ; web." The
Tess′iture (*E.*) ⎭ general range ("lie") or average pitch of a theme or song.

Thus the *tessitura* of " Hear ye, Israel" (*Elijah*) lies rather high ; that of "O thou that tellest" (*Messiah*) rather low.

Te′sta (*I.*). Head.

Di te′sta. Of or from the head.
Vo′ce di te′sta. The head voice.

Te′sto (*I.*). " Text." (1) Subject, theme, motive. (2) The words (of an opera, song, &c.).

TESTO′RI, Carlo G. ; Carlo A., and **Paolo A.** Father and two sons ; Vn. makers, Milan, about 1687-1754.

Testu′do. (*L.*, " A tortoise.") The lyre.

The resounding hollow part was formerly made of the shell of a sea-tortoise or turtle. An old Homeric hymn states that Mercury made the first lyre out of a dried-up tortoise.

Tête (*F.*). " Head." Head of a note ; scroll of a vn., &c.

Tête de registre. Initial notes of a theme, fugue-subject, &c.

Tet′ra. (*Gk.* prefix.) Four ; four-fold.

Tet′rachord (*Gk.*) ⎫ (1) An inst. of four strings. (2) A
Tetrachorde (*F.*) ⎬ scale of 4 diatonic notes.
Tetracor′do (*I.*) ⎭ N.B.—The modern major scale consists of two exactly similar tetrachords—
$$d \; r \; m \; f \quad \text{and} \quad s \; l \; t \; d'$$
Tet′rachordal System. A system of Sol-faing based on tetrachords.
Tetrachor′don. A small piano-like inst. with a resined rubber cylinder to set the strings in vibration.
Tetrato′non ⎫
Tet′ratone ⎬ An augmented 4th.
Tet′rad. A chord of 4 notes, as a 7th.
Tet′radiapa′son. An interval of 4 octaves.
Tetral′ogy. (*G.*, *Tetralogie′.*) A series of 4 oratorios or operas (as Wagner's *Ring*).
Tet′raphone. An augmented 4th.

TETRAZZI′NI, Madame. Distinguished high soprano. *B.* Florence, abt. 1875. Brilliant London *début*, 1907.

Text. The words of a composition.

Text′buch (*G.*). Libretto (*q.v.*).

TEY′BER (or **TAY′BER**), **Franz.** Pianist and conductor ; Vienna, 1756-1810.

Works : an oratorio, church music, songs, &c., and several operas and Singspiele.

THAL′BERG, Sigismund. Celebrated pianist ; *b.* Geneva, 1812 ; *d.* Naples, 1871. Had made a promising start at 14 ; pub. his first works, 1828. Started concert tours, 1830. Court pianist, Vienna, 1834. Toured with great success through Europe, Nth. America, and Brazil, till 1863.

His style was brilliant and dazzling ; but its "glittering superficiality has succumbed to modern romanticism" and to real musical depth of expression.

His numerous pf. pieces and transcriptions were widely celebrated in their day ; their popularity has now greatly waned.

THALLON, Robt. Orgt. and teacher ; *b.* Liverpool, 1852.

Settled in Brooklyn (U.S.) abt. 1876.

THAYER, Alexander W. *B.* South Natick, Mass., 1817 ; *d.* Trieste, 1897. Asst. librarian, Harvard Univ., 1843. Began to collect materials for a "complete and trustworthy biography of Beethoven." Spent two years in Germany (1849-51), and again from 1854 (except two years at Boston, 1856-8). Member of the American Embassy, Vienna, 1862 ; Consul at Trieste, 1865-97.

Works : " A Chronological Catalogue of Beethoven's Works," " Ludwig Beethoven's Life " (3 vols. completed), a work on " Beethoven Literature," &c.

THAYER, Arthur W. *B.* Dedham, Mass., 1857.

Works : church music, pf. pieces, part-songs, numerous songs.

THAYER, W. Eugene. Noted organist ; *b.* Mendon, Mass., 1838 ; *d.* 1889. Gave free organ recitals, Boston, from 1869 ; orgt. New York, 1881-8.

Composed org. pieces, part-songs, songs, &c.

Thea′ter-kapel′le (*G.*). Orchestra of a theatre.

Theil (*G.*). Part, portion, division. Same as **Teil.**

Erst′er Theil. Part I.
Zwei′ter Theil. Part II.

THEI′LE, Johann. Naumburg, 1646-1724. Pupil of Schütz. Capellmeister at various German courts. Called by his contemporaries " the father of counterpoint." Among his pupils were Buxtehude and Zachau.

Works : *Adam und Eva* (1678, the 1st German "Singspiel") ; a Christmas oratorio, 1681 ; a Passion, 20 masses ; instl. sonatas, preludes, courantes, &c., in double, triple, and quadruple counterpoint.

The′ma (*Gk.*, *L.*, and *G.*) ⎫ A subject, air,
Theme (*E.*) ⎪ melody ; a
Thème (*F.*) ⎬ *canto fermo*
Te′ma (*I.*) ⎭ (*q.v.*) ; a principal subject in a sonata (*q.v.*).

Thematic Catalogue ⎫ A list of
Thema′tisches Verzeich′niss (*G.*) ⎭ compositions, with a few bars of each principal theme.

Thematic Development. (*G.*, *Thema′tische Ar′beit.*) The varied repetition of a theme, motive, or figure, to bring out some of its infinite resources.

Thematic "transformation" roughly falls into 3 classes—Melodic, Rhythmic, and Harmonic—and these may be combined in countless ways.

The following, taking the first phrase of " God save the King " as a motive, are among the most usual methods :—

Motive

I.—Simple Melodic Changes—

(1) Melody removed to another part of the scale, or to another key :—

or

(2) Intervals contracted :—

(3) Intervals expanded :—

(4) Melody inverted :—

or

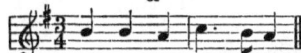

(5) Melody inverted and expanded (or contracted):

II.—Simple Rhythmic Changes.—
(6) Theme augmented :—

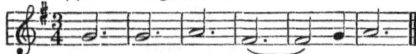

(7) Augmented and varied :—

(8) Notes diminished :—

(9) Time signature changed :—

(10) Lengthened by repeating a bar (or bars) :—

(11) Notes divided into shorter ones :—

(12) Varied by arpeggios, addition of passing-notes, &c. :—

(13) Varied by rests, syncopations, &c. :—

(14) Embellished by grace-notes :—

(15) Metamorphosed (see *Leit Motiv*).

Any of the above may also be contracted or extended in interval and the resulting themes may be inverted or transformed according to the composer's ability or discretion.

III.—Harmonic Changes.

The Theme, or any of its modifications, may be—
(1) Changed to the relative major or minor ;
(2) Harmonized in different ways ;
(3) Treated contrapuntally (in any of the 5 species), or freely ;
(4) Treated canonically, or in free Canonic Imitation. (See *Imitation*) ;
(5) Treated fugally. (See *Fugue*) ;
(6) Combined with other themes (in double, triple, or quadruple counterpoint) ;
(7) Supported by various forms of accompaniment. (See *Accompaniment*.)

The works of Haydn, Mozart, Beethoven, Schumann, Wagner, and Brahms exemplify every form of thematic development, and will amply repay the closest study.

The *Rondo* of Beethoven's pf. sonata in G (Op. 31, No. 1) may be particularly recommended to the attention of the beginner. The development of the theme is easy to follow, and the last 52 bars are specially characteristic and instructive ; also the Pastoral Sonata (Op. 28), 1st movement (after the repeat).

Theor'bo. (*G.*, *Theor'be* ; *F.*, *Théorbe* ; *I.*, *Tior'ba*, *Tuor'ba*.) A variety of double-necked bass lute popular in the 17th cent.

The bass strings, accompaniment strings, or diapasons, were attached to one neck, and the melody strings (with fingerboard) to the other. The *arch lute* or *chitlarone* was a variety of the theorbo. (See *Lute*.)

Theore'tiker (*G.*)
Théoricien (*F.*) } A theorist.

Theo'ria (*L.*)
Théorie (*F.*) } The *science*, as opposed to
The'ory (*E.*) the *art* of music.
Theo'rico (*I.*). A musical theorist.

THERN, Carl. *B.* Igló, Upper Hungary, 1817 ; *d.* 1886.

Works : 3 successful operas (*Pesth*), Hungarian songs, pf. pieces.

His sons **Willi** (*b.* 1847), and **Louis** (*b.* 1848) are noted for their fine ensemble playing on 2 pfs.

The'sis (*Gk.*). Strong beat.
Ar'sis (*Gk.*). Weak beat.
The Greeks marked the strong beat by an *upward* motion of the hand, and the weak beat by a *downward* motion.

Theur'gic hymns. Songs of incantation in ancient Egyptian and Greek mysteries.

THIBAUD, Jacques. Violinist ; *b.* Bordeaux, 1880. 1st prize, Paris Cons., 1896.

THIBAUD, Joseph. Pianist ; *b.* Bordeaux, 1875.

THIBAUT IV, King of Navarre. *B.* Troyes, 1201 ; *d.* 1253. Noted *Trouvère* (troubadour).

Sixty-three of his songs were published in 1742.

THIBAUT, Anton F. J. *B.* Hameln, 1774 ; *d.* 1840.

Published a work on " Purity in Musical Art."

THIE'LE, Karl L. Excellent organist ; *b.* nr. Bernburg, 1816 ; *d.* 1848.

Wrote variations, preludes, &c., for organ.

THIE'LE, Richard. Song composer ; Berlin, 1847-1903.

THIER'FELDER, Dr. Albert W. *B.* Mühlhausen, Thuringia, 1846. Mus.-director Rostock Univ., 1887.

Works : operas (*Der Heirathstein,* 1898) ; symphonies, choral works, pf. pieces, songs ; an essay on "Christian Psalms and Hymns from the time of Ambrose," a "Collection of Classic Songs," &c.

THIE'RIOT, Ferdinand. *B.* Hamburg, 1838.

Works : orch. pieces, choral works, a vn. concerto ; an octet and other chamber music, &c.

THILLON, Anna (*née* **Hunt**). Operatic soprano ; *b.* London, 1819. *Début,* Paris, 1838 ; London, 1844 (in Auber's *Crown Diamonds*).

Thin. (1) Of harmony ; scanty, lacking in sonority.

(2) Of a tone ; poor in quality, lacking fulness.

Thin Register. Name given especially to the upper (or head) register of male voices. Authorities differ as to the proper use of the term.

Thior'bo. Old spelling of *Theorbo* (*q.v.*).

Third. (*G., Terz ; F., Tierce ; I., Ter'za.*) (1) An interval comprising three degrees of the scale. (2) The mediant.

Augmented third. A third comprising 5 semitones, as F to A♯ (rarely used).
Diminished third. A third comprising 2 semitones, as C♯ to E♭.
Major third. A third comprising 4 semitones, as C to E.
Minor third. A third comprising 3 semitones, as C to E♭.
Third flute. (See *Terzflöte.*)
N.B.—The third of a common chord gives it its distinctive character of major or minor ; it also adds the element of "sweetness" to the harmony.

Third Inversion. A chord of a 7th (9th, 11th, &c.), with the 7th in the bass.

In Tonic Sol-fa theory it is called a "d" position.

THIRLWALL, John W. *B.* Shilbottle, Northumberland, 1809 ; *d.* 1876. Mus.-director successively at Drury Lane, Haymarket, Olympic, and Adelphi

theatres ; ballet condr., Royal Italian Opera, 1864.

Works : songs, ballads, violin solos, &c.

Thirteenth. The interval of an octave and a 6th (major or minor).

Chord of the 13th. A chord comprising a root with its major 3rd, perfect 5th, minor 7th, major or minor 9th, 11th, and major or minor 13th. The complete chord is rarely used. (See *Dominant 7th,* and *Fundamental Discords.*)

Thirty-second note. A demisemiquaver (𝅘𝅥𝅰)

Thirty-second rest. A demisemiquaver rest (𝄿).

THOINAN, Ernest (Antoine E. Roquet). *B.* Nantes, 1827 ; *d.* 1894. Collected a fine musical library.

Published several historical works on French music and musicians.

THOMA, Térese. (See **Vogl.**)

THOMAS, Arthur Goring. *B.* nr. Eastbourne, 1851 ; *d.* London, 1892. Won " Lucas Prize," R.A.M., 1879.

Works : operas (*Esmeralda,* 1883 ; *Nadeshda,* 1885) ; works for chorus and orch., fine songs.

THOMAS AQUINAS. (Thomas of Aquino.) *B.* nr. Aquino, 1225 (7?) ; *d.* 1274. Famous theologian ; wrote the sequence *Lauda Sion,* and several fine Latin hymns.

THOMAS, Ch. L. Ambroise. Eminent dramatic composer ; *b.* Metz, 1811 ; *d.* Paris, 1896. Entered Paris Cons., 1828 ; won the 1st prize for pf. playing (1829), and for harmony (1830) ; *Grand Prix de Rome,* 1832. Member of the Académie, 1851. Director Paris Cons., 1871.

Works : 22 operas and ballets (*Le Caïd,* 1849 ; *Le songe d'une nuit d'été,* 1850 ; *Mignon,* 1866, his best ; *Hamlet,* 1868) ; cantatas, church music, chamber music, canzonets, and several very fine male-voice choruses.

THOMAS, Florence A. (Mrs. J. Marshall). Composer and writer ; *b.* Rome, 1843.

THOMAS, Harold. Pianist ; *b.* Cheltenham, 1834 ; Pf. prof. R.A.M. and G.S.M.

Works : overtures, songs, pf. pieces, &c.

THOMAS, John. Harpist ; known as "Pencerdd Gwalia" (chief bard of Wales). *B.* Brigdend, Glam., 1826. Pupil R.A.M., 1840. Harpist, Royal Italian Opera, 1851 ; toured 1852-62. Harpist to the Queen, 1871.

Works : a dramatic cantata (*Llewelyn*), Welsh patriotic songs, 2 harp concertos ; duos for harp and pf. (or vn.) ; solos and transcriptions for harp, &c.

THOMAS, Lewis W. Bass vocalist ; *b.* Bath, 1826 ; *d.* 1896. London *début,* 1854. Gentleman, Chapel Royal, 1857-87.

Mus. critic *Musical World* and *Daily Telegraph ;* also editor of *The Lute* for some time.

His son, **W. Henry,** *b.* Bath, 1848, is a Prof. of Singing at the G.S.M. and R.A.M.

THOMAS of Celano. Franciscan Friar ; 13th century.
Reputed author of the *Dies Iræ*.

THOMAS, Theodore. Distinguished condr. ; *b.* Esens, East Friesland, 1835 ; *d.* 1905. Played the vn. in public at 6 ; went to New York, 1845 ; after concert tours, &c., organized orchestral " Symphony Soirées," New York (1864), and Summer Garden Concerts, 1866. His programs "attained European celebrity." President, Cincinnati Coll. of Music, 1878 ; condr. New York Philharmonic Orch., 1880; director Chicago, Cons., 1888.

THOMAS, Thos. (See **Aptommas.**)

THOMAS, Wm. Edwin. Orgt. and composer ; *b.* Oxford, 1867. Mus.D. Oxon, 1893. Prof. of Music, Univ. Coll., Auckland, 1900.

THOMÉ, Francis. (François-Luc-Joseph.) *B.* Port Louis, Mauritius, 1850. Studied Paris Cons., 1866-70.
Works : light stage pieces, a symphonic ode, songs, graceful pf. pieces (*Simple aveu*, &c.).

THOMPSON, General T. Perronet. *B.* Hull, 1783 ; *d.* 1869.
Writer on "Enharmonic Music;" constructed an "enharmonic organ" to illustrate just temperament.

THOMPSON, Lady H. (Kate F. Loder). Pianist and composer ; *b.* Bath, 1825 ; *d.* 1904.

THOMSON, César. Violinist ; *b.* Liége, 1857. Won the gold medal for vn., playing, Liége Cons., at 11. Prof. of vn., Brussels Cons., 1898. Has made successful tours.

THOMSON, George. *B.* Limekilns, Fife, 1757 ; *d.* 1851. His collections of national airs were harmonized by some of the best musicians of the time, including Haydn and Beethoven.
Works : "A Select Collection of Original Scottish Airs" (6 vols.); a "Collection of the Songs of Burns, Sir W. Scott, &c." (6 vols.); "Select Collection of Welsh Airs" (3 vols.), "Irish Airs" (2 vols.), &c. (See *Scottish Music.*)

THOMSON, John. *B.* nr. Roxburgh, 1805 ; *d.* 1841. Friend of Mendelssohn, Schumann, and Moscheles. First Reid Prof. of Music, Edinburgh Univ., 1839.
Works : operas, instl. music, songs, &c.

THOMSON, Wm. Son of Daniel Thomson, King's trumpeter. *B.* Edinburgh, abt. 1680(?). (See **Scottish Music.**)

THORNDIKE, Herbert E. Baritone vocalist; *b.* Liverpool, 1851.

THORNE, Edward Hy. *B.* Cranborne, Dorset, 1834. Orgt. Chichester Cath., 1853 ; afterwards at various churches ; and at St. Anne's, Soho, since 1891.
Works : church music, 2 pf. trios, sonatas for various insts, organ pieces, &c.

THORNE, John. *D.* 1573 ; mentioned by Morley and Hawkins. Buried York Minster, where he was probably orgt. " A musician most perfect in his art ; he set apart all vice, and he did moreover excel in the art of logic."

THORNTON, Edna. (Mrs. **F. Drake.**) Contralto vocalist ; *b.* Oakenshaw, Yorks, 18—.

Thorough-bass } (*G., General'bass ; F.,* **Continued bass** } *Basse chiffrée ; I., Continuo, Bas'so conti'nuo.*) Figured bass (*q.v.*).

Three Kings. Name given in the Roman Church to the Magi (Matt. ii. 1-12).

Three-quarter fiddle. (*I., Violi'no pic'colo.*) A small violin.

Three removes. (See **Removes of Key,** under **Key.**)

Three-step. (*F., Trois-temps.*) The ordinary Viennese waltz.

Three-time (3-time). Triple time.

Thren'ody. (*Gk., Threno'dia.*) A dirge ; a song of lamentation.

Thrice-accented octave. The octave starting with—
N.B.—It is the octave marked C², D², &c., in Tonic Sol-fa.

THRING, Godfrey. D.D. 1823-1903. Prebendary, Wells Cath., 1876.
Wrote " The radiant morn," and other hymns.

Through-composed. (*G., Durch'componi(e)rt.*) A song with different music for each stanza (as opposed to the *Ballad*).

THUDICHUM, Charlotte. Soprano vocalist ; *b.* Kensington. Won the Parepa-Rosa Scholarship, R.A.M., 1880.

Thumb-position. In 'cello playing a high position in which the thumb is used on the strings.

Thumb-string. The melody string of the banjo.

THUILLE, Ludwig W. A. M. *B.* Bozen, Tyrol, 1861 ; *d.* 1907. Teacher of pf. and theory, Munich Music School, 1883.
Works : operas (*Theuerdank*, 1897) ; org. pieces, pf. pieces, songs, male choruses, &c.

THUNDER, Henry G. Pianist ; pupil of Thalberg ; *b.* nr. Dublin, 1832 ; *d.* New York, 1891.

Thür'mer (*G.*). A watchman on a tower. Also used of a watchman (or wait) who formerly "called the hours" at night.

THUR'NER, Friedrich E. Oboist ; *b.* Montbéliard, 1785 ; *d.* 1827.
Works : 3 symphonies, 4 oboe concertos, several concerted works for oboe and other insts., pf. pieces, &c.

THURSBY, Emma. Distinguished soprano; daughter of an Englishman; *b.* Brooklyn, N.Y., 1857. *Début*, 1875.

Tib′ia (*L.*). "The shin-bone," used by the Greeks and Romans for "flutes" and pipes of all kinds; hence, specially, "a flute." (Plur., *Tibiæ*, flutes.)

Tib′ia clau′sa. A full-toned stopped diapason invented by Hope-Jones.
Tib′ia major. An organ flute stop of 16 ft. or 8 ft. pitch.
Tib′ia mol′lis. A soft-toned flute stop invented by Hope-Jones.
Tib′ia obli′qua (*L.*). The *flauto traverso,* or ordinary flute.
Tib′ia ple′na. A powerful org. flue stop invented by Hope-Jones.
Tib′ia utricula′ris (*L.*). An ancient bagpipe.
Tib′ia vas′ca (*L.*). Meaning obscure probably a *flauto traverso.*
Tibi′cen (*L.*). A flute player.
Tibici′na (*L.*). A female flute player.

TICH′ATSCHEK, Joseph A. Eminent operatic tenor; *b.* Ober-Weckelsdorf, Bohemia, 1807; *d.* 1886. Son of a poor weaver. After a varied career, engaged Dresden Court Opera, 1837-72.

Created the *rôle* of *Rienzi* (1842) and *Tannhäuser* (1845) in Wagner's operas.

Tie, or Bind. (*G., Bin′debogen; F., Liaison; I., Fa′scia.*) A curved line, like a *slur,* connecting two or more notes *of the same pitch.* (The slur connects notes of *different pitch.*)

The first note is sounded and continued for the full time indicated by the several notes. When more than two notes are "tied," a separate mark must be used to join each note to the next—not one curve over the whole: thus:—

Some editors mark the tie thus:—

N.B.—Printers give the name "tie" to the line joining the stems of 2 or more quavers, &c.,

Enharmonic Tie. Connecting two enharmonically equivalent notes:—

Tief (*G.*). Deep, low, grave (in pitch).
Hör′ner in tief C. Horns in low C. (Brahms' *Requiem*.)

Tief′er (*G.*). Lower, deeper.
Ein′e Okta′ve tief′er. An octave lower.
8va tief′er.
Tief′er stim′men. To lower the pitch of an inst.
Tief′stimmig. Deep-voiced.
Tief′tönend. Deep toned.

TIEFF′ENBRÜCKER. (See **Duiffopruggar.**)

TIEH′SEN, Otto. Song composer; *b.* Danzig, 1817; *d.* 1849.

Tiepidamen′te (*I.*) } Coldly; with in-
Con tiepiditá (*I.*) } difference.

29

Tier. A row, or *rank,* of organ pipes.

Tierce (*F.*). (1) The interval of a third. (2) An organ stop 2 octaves and a third above unison pitch (now rarely used except in *Mixtures.*) (3) The 5th note in the "Chord of Nature." (See **Acoustics.**)

Tierce coulée (*F.*). "A slurred third." (See *Slide.*)
Tierce maxime (*F.*). An augmented third.

Tierce de Picardie (or **Picardy**). A major third in the last chord of a piece in a minor key (formerly much used in Ecclesiastical music).

BACH.

Tier′cet. A triplet.

TIERSCH, Otto. Noted theorist; *b.* Kalbsreith, Thuringia, 1838; *d.* 1892. Teacher of singing, Stern Cons., Berlin.
Wrote works on Harmony, Modulation, Counterpoint, Rhythm, Phrasing, Accompaniment, &c.

TIERSOT, J. B. E. Julien. Since 1883, asst. librarian, Paris Cons.
Works: "Antique Music," "History of the *Chanson* in France," &c.

TIET′JENS (or **TITIENS**), **Therese J. A.** Famous operatic soprano; *b.* Hamburg, 1831; *d.* London, 1877. *Début*, Hamburg, 1849. Settled in London, 1858; for long a reigning favourite at Covent Garden, Drury Lane, &c.

Tige (*F.*). The stick of a bow.

TILKINS, Felix. ("Ivan Caryll.") Composer; *b.* Liége, 1861.

TILKINS, Mrs. F. (See **Ulmar.**)

TILMAN, Alfred. Pianist and composer; Brussels, 1848-95.

TILMANT, Théophile. Violinist and condr.; *b.* Valenciennes, 1799; *d.* 1878.

TI′MANOFF, Vera. Noted pianist; *b.* Ufa, Russia, 1855. Studied under A. Rubinstein, Tausig, and Liszt. Played in public at 8.

Timbal (*S.*) }
Timbale (*F.*) } A kettle drum.
Timbal′lo (*I.*) }

Timbalarion (*F.*) } A set of tuned drums on
Tambour chromatique (*F.*) } which scales and chords can be played.

Timbre (*F.*) } (1) Tone quality. (See
Tim′bro (*I.*) } **Acoustics.**) (2) A bell struck by a hammer—a clockbell. (3) The *snares* of a side-drum.
Jeux de timbres. Same as *Glockenspiel* (*q.v.*).

Timbrel. A tambourine (or a tabor).

Time. (1) The (absolute or relative) duration of notes.

TIME TABLE—

SHAPE.	ENGLISH NAME.	GERMAN.	FRENCH.	ITALIAN.
	Breve, or Double note.	Bre'vis.	Brève, Carrée.	Bre've.
	Semibreve, or Whole note.	Ganz'eno'te, Ganz'no'te, or Ganz'e Takt'note.	Semibrève, Ronde.	Se mibre've.
	Minim, or Half-note.	Hal'be No'te, or Halb'-no'te.	Blanche.	Min'ima, Bian'ca.
	Crotchet, or Quarter-note.	Vier'tel, or Vier'tel-no'te.	Noir.	Ne'ra.
	Quaver, or Eighth-note.	Ach'tel, or Ach'telno'te.	Croche.	Cro'ma.
	Semiquaver, or 16th note.	Sechzehn'tel, or Sech-zehn'telno'te.	Double-croche.	Semicro'ma.
	Demisemiquaver, or 32nd note.	Zwei'unddreissigs'tel (No'te).	Triple-croche.	Semibiscro'ma.
	Hemidemisemiquaver, or 64th note.	Vier'undsechzigs'tel (N'ote).	Quadruple-croche.	Quattricro'ma.

(See also *Mensural Music* and *Rests*.)

(2) The speed, or rate of movement, of a piece; now generally called its *Tempo* (as *Tempo moderato, Adagio, Presto,* &c.).

(3) (G., *Takt, Takt'art;* F., *Mesure;* I., *Tem'po*.) The metrical division of a piece into bars (or measures). The "kind of measure" is indicated by a *Time Signature.*

TIME SIGNATURES. (For the proper "measure accents" of each kind of Time, see *Accent.*)

	DUPLE	BEAT NOTE	TRIPLE	BEAT NOTE	QUADRUPLE	BEAT NOTE
SIMPLE TIMES.	2 or ¢ (Two minims).		3/2 (Three minims).		4/2 or ¢ (Four minims).	
	2/4 (Two crotchets).		3/4 (Three crotchets).		4/4 or C (Four crotchets).	
	2/8 (Two quavers).		3/8 (Three quavers).		4/8 (Four quavers).	
COMPOUND TIMES	6/4 (Two dotted minims).		9/4 (Three dotted minims).		12/4 (Four dotted minims).	
	6/8 (Two dotted crotchets).		9/8 (Three dotted crotchets).		12/8 (Four dotted crotchets).	
	6/16 (Two dotted quavers).		9/16 (Three dotted quavers).		12/16 (Four dotted quavers).	

(See also Appendix.)

Occasionally 12-32 time is used; it is a quadruple time of "4 dotted semiquavers" (beat note ♪) (Beethoven once used 12-32; Bach, 18-16). Octuple time is written as 4-4 (or 4-2). (See *Octuple Time.*)
Compound octuple time is sometimes employed, as 24-16.
In French music, Triple time is often shown by a large 3 :—

(4) Rhythm, or the varied contents of measures. (See **Rhythm.**)
N.B.—Formerly each beat of a measure was called a "time," *e.g.,* the "strong time" of a bar, the "weak time" of a bar, &c.
Cross Times } Two (or more) kinds of measure
Cross Rhythms } employed together.

MOZART'S *Don Giovanni.*

A very intricate example occurs in Elgar's *Apostles.* Chopin's *Grand Valse* (Op. 42) is a fine instance of "rhythmical" accentuation in 6-3 time combined with "metrical" accentuation in 3-4 time. (See *Accent.*)

&c.

Mixed Times } Old melodies (hymn-tunes,
Double Time Signatures } &c.) were very irregular in
rhythm, triple and duple rhythms following each
other almost at random. In arranging them in
modern notation a double signature is employed ;
3-2 ₵ if the melody is mostly triple, and **₵ 3-2**
if it is mostly duple.

"Ely" (English Tune). Psalm 20.
Ravenscroft's Psalter.

Melody in Tenor.

&c.

(Many instances occur in Lutheran Chorals.)

Time-beating. (See *Beating Time.*)

Irregular Times. Quintuple time—generally 5-4—**is**
sometimes employed ; as, for example, in Tschaikowsky's *Pathetic Symphony.*

Septuple Time—in alternate bars of 3-4 and 4-4—was
used by Berlioz in the "Incantation Music" of his
Childhood of Christ :—

&c.

A German philosopher has proved that "the
human mind cannot count beyond *three*," and
therefore these irregular times can only be
tolerated " very occasionally."

Time-names. The names of pulses, divided
pulses, &c., in Tonic Sol-fa.

EXAMPLES :—

Ti'mido (*I.*). Timid, fearful.

Timidamen'te } Timidly, fearfully, hesitatingly,
Con timidez'za } anxiously.

Ti'mist. One who keeps good time in singing
or playing.

TIMM, Henry C. Pianist and organist ; *b.*
Hamburg, 1811 ; *d.* 1892. Settled in
America, 1835 ; President New York
Phil. Soc., 1847-64.

Wrote part-songs, pf. pieces, transcriptions, &c.

TIMM'NER, Christian. Dutch violinist ;
b. 1860.

Timo're (*I.*). Fear, timidity.

Con timo're
Timorosamen'te } Hesitatingly, timidly.
Timoro'so

Tim'pano (*I.*). A kettle drum.

Tim'pani (*I.*). Kettle drums.

Tim'pano coper'to
Tim'pano sor'do } A covered (muffled) drum.

Timpani'sto. A kettle drummer.

**TINCTO'RIS, Johannes. (John Tinc'tor, or
Jean de Vaerwere.)** *B.* Poperinghe,
Belgium, abt. 1446 ; *d.* abt. 1511.
Maestro at Naples abt. 1475 ; Canon at
Nivelles from abt. 1487.

Chief works : " The Art of Counterpoint " (1477)
and " Terminorum Musicæ diffinitorium "
(about 1475), the earliest known Dict. of Music.
He also wrote church music, chansons, &c.
Tinctor's " Dictionary " remained long unknown :
Forkel discovered a copy (in the latter part of
the 18th cent.) in the Duke of Gotha's Library ;
Dr. Burney also discovered a copy (now in the
British Museum) in the Library of George III.
The whole dictionary—in Latin—is printed at
the end of Hamilton's Dictionary of Mus.
Terms, and would cover about 8 pages of the
present work. The following is a complete
chapter :—

Per H. Capitul. VIII.
HYMNUS est laus dei cum cantico.
HYMNISTA est ille qui hymnos canit.

TINEL, Edgar. Pianist and composer ; *b.*
Sinay, Belgium, 1854. Studied Brussels
Cons. ; 1st prize for pf. playing, 1873 ;
won *Grand Prix de Rome*, 1877 ; Prof.
of counterpoint and fugue, 1896 ;
Director (succeeding Gevaert), 1909.

Works : an oratorio (*Franciscus*, 1888) ; orchl.
music, cantatas, fine church music, songs, pf.
pieces, a work on " Gregorian Chant," &c.

Tinkle. To clink ; to jingle (as a small bell).

TINNEY, Chas. E. Bass vocalist ; *b.*
London, 1851.

Tint. Colour.

Clang-tint. Tone colour. Same as *Klang-farbe* (*q.v.*).

Tintamarre (*F.*). Hubbub, noise.

Tintement (*F.*). Tinkling (of a bell) ;
resonance.

Tintinnab'ulum (*L.*) } (1) A little bell.
Tintinna'bolo (*I.*) } (2) An ancient small
Tintinna'bulo (*I.*) } bell-rattle.

Tintinnabula'tion (*E.*). The jingling of (small) bells.

Tintinnamen'to (*I.*)
Tintinnan'do (*I.*)
Tintinni'o (*I.*) } Tinkling.
Tintin'no (*I.*)

Tin'to (*I.*). Shade, tint, colour (in expression or tone quality).

Con tin'to. With expression.

Tior'ba (*I.*). Same as **Theorbo** (*q.v.*).

Tipping. Double-tonguing (*q.v.*).

Tirade (*F.*). Slurring or sliding through an
interval ; a rapid run between two
melody notes.

Tiran'na (*S.*). A national air with guitar
accompaniment.

Tirant (*F.*). A stop-knob ; a button or
piston ; a drum-cord.

Tirant à accoupler. An organ coupler.

Tira're (*I.*). To draw, drag, pull.
Tira'ta. Same as *Tirade* (*F.*) (*q.v.*).
Tira'to. (1) The down bow (vn., &c.). (2) A pedal coupler. (3) A scale passage in equal notes.
Ti'ra tut'to. A pedal (or stop) to bring on the full organ. (*F.*, *Grand Jeu.*)
Trom'ba da tirar'si. A slide trumpet.

Tiré (*F.*). "Drawn, pulled, dragged." A down bow.
Tirasse. A pedal coupler.
Tirez. "Use the down bow."

TIRINDEL'LI, Pietro A. Violinist ; *b.* Conegliano, 1858. Studied Milan Cons. Vn. prof., Liceo Benedetto Marcello, Venice, 1887 ; afterwards director.
Works : operatic music, pf. pieces, pieces for pf. and vn., songs, &c.

Tirole'se (*I.*). Same as **Tyrolienne** (*q.v.*).

TISZA, Aladar. Pen-name of **V. Langer** (*q.v.*)

TI'TIENS. (See **Tietjens.**)

TI'TOFF, Nicolai A. Noted song composer ; St. Petersburg, 1801-76.

Tisch'harfe (*G.*). A "dish-harp ; " a kind of auto-harp (*q.v.*).

Tit'ty }
Tzi'ti } A Hindu bagpipe.

To'bend (*G.*). Blusteringly, violently.

Tocca'ta (*I.*, from *Tocca're*, "to touch," "to play "). A brilliant, showy piece in the nature of an improvisation.
Bach's organ toccatas are fine examples.
Toccati'na }
Toccatel'la } A short toccata.

Tocca'to (*I.*). In trumpet music, a 4th part for a bass-trumpet (instead of kettle-drums).

Tocca'to,-a (*I.*). Touched.
Tocca'to appe'na. Touched very lightly (as a gong &c.).

Toc'sin. An alarm bell.

Tod (*G.*). Death.

To(d)t (*G.*). Dead, lifeless, stagnant.
Tod(t)'enamt. Funeral service ; requiem.
To(d)t'englöckchen. Funeral bell.
To(d)t'enmarsch. A funeral march.
To(d)t'esgesang }
To(d)t'eslied } A funeral song ; a dirge.

TO'DI, Luiza Rosa de Aguiar. Famous mezzo-soprano ; *b.* Setubal, Portugal, 1753 ; *d.* 1833. Her rivalry with **Mara** (Paris, 1783), created "two bitterly hostile factions" known as the "Todistes" and the "Maratistes."

TOD JESU, Der. "The Death of Jesus ;" a Passion Cantata by Graun, 1755.
It is called the "Messiah" of Protestant Germany.

TOFFT, Alfred. Composer ; *b.* Copenhagen, 1865.
Works : an opera, songs, pf. pieces, &c.

To'gli (*I.*). Take away ; remove.
To'gli l'accoppiamen'to. Shut off the (organ) coupler.

Toile (*F.*). Curtain.
Derrière la toile. Behind the curtain.

TOLBECQUE. Name of four brothers ; Belgian musicians.
(1) **Isidore J.** *B.* Hanzinne, 1794 ; *d.* 1871.
Composed dance music.

(2) **Jean B. J.** 1797-1869. Violinist and conductor.
Composed a ballet and much favourite dance music.
(3) **Auguste J.** 1801-69. Violinist in Paris and London.
(4) **Charles J.** Paris, 1806-35. Violinist and conductor.

TOLBECQUE, Auguste. Eminent 'cellist ; son of A. J. (above) ; *b.* Paris, 1830. 1st prize Paris Cons., 1849 ; teacher Marseilles Cons., 1865-71.
Works : "The Gymnastics of the Violoncello" (excellent studies), a comic opera, &c.
His son, **Jean** (*b.* Niort, 1857), is also a fine 'cello player.

Tolerance of the Ear. (See **Acoustics,** p. 14.)

TOLHURST, Henry. Composer ; *b.* London, 1854.

TOM'ASCHEK (or TOMÁŠEK), Johann W. *B.* Skutsch, Bohemia, 1774 ; *d.* Prague, 1850. Largely self-taught ; admirable pianist and organist, and the most noted teacher in Prague. He was also a meritorious composer, but was overshadowed by his great contemporary, Beethoven.
Works : an opera (*Seraphine*), an orchl. mass, a symphony, a pf. concerto, cantatas, songs, chamber music, and many pf. pieces.

TOMASI'NI, Luigi. Violinist ; intimate friend of Haydn ; *b.* Pesaro, 1741 ; *d.* 1757. Director of the chamber music, Esterház, from 1757.
Published 2 vn. concertos, 12 string quartets, &c.

Tombeau (*F.*). "A tomb ;" an elegy.

TOMBELLE, Fernand de la. *B.* Paris, 1854. Studied Paris Cons.
Works : orchestral suites, chamber music, songs, numerous organ pieces, &c.

Tomb'estere (*Old E.*). A female dancer with a tambourine.

Tome (*F.*). A volume, a book.

TOMKINS, Thos. *B.* Pembroke, abt. 1586(?) ; *d.* 1656. Mus.Bac. Oxon, 1607. Orgt. Chapel Royal (1621), and later, Worcester Cath.
Wrote songs, madrigals, and sacred music.

TOMMA'SI, Cardinal G. M. Learned historical writer on church music. *B.* Alicante, Sicily, 1649 ; *d.* Rome, 1713.
An edition of his complete works was published in 7 vols., Rome, 1748-54.

Tom'-tom. A gong ; a Hindu drum.

Ton (*G.*). Tone, sound. (Plur., *Tö'ne.*)
Accessory meanings : *note, key, mode, timbre, tune, pitch, scale,* &c.
Den Ton an'geben. To give the pitch (for tuning).
Den Ton hal'ten. To sustain a note (in singing, &c.).
Ton'abstand. An interval.
Ton'art. Tonality (*q.v.*) ; key.
Ton'artverwandschaft. Key relationship.
Ton'ausweichung. Modulation, change of key.
Ton'bestimmung. The mathematical (acoustical) determination of sounds.

Ton'bild. Tone picture.
Ton'bildung. Voice production ; tone formation.
Ton'bühne. An orchestra.
Ton'dichter. A " tone-poet ; " a composer.
Ton'dichtung. A romantic or poetical mus. composition ; a tone-poem.
Tön'end. Sounding ; resounding.
Ton'fall. A cadence.
Ton'farbe. Tone colour ; *timbre*.
Ton'folge. A succession of sounds ; a melody.
Ton'führung. (1) A melodic succession. (2) Modulation. (3) Harmonic progression.
Ton'fülle. Volume ; melodiousness.
Ton'fuss. A metrical " foot ; " a rhythm, a measure.
Ton'gang. Same as *Tonführung.*
Ton'gebung. Intonation ; tone production ; tonality.
Ton'geschlecht. Mode ; the distinction between major and minor.
Ton'höhe. Pitch.
Ton'kunde. Science of music.
Ton'kunst. The art (knowledge) of music.
Ton'künstler. A musician.
Ton'lage. Pitch ; register ; compass.
Ton'lehre. Acoustics.
Ton'leiter. A scale.
Ton'malerei. Sound-painting, musical invention ; program music.
Ton'mass. Measure, time.
Ton'messer. A monochord.
Ton'messung. Tone-measuring. (See *Tonbestimmung.*)
Ton'reich. Rich and full in *timbre*.
Ton'reihe. A scale.
Ton'rein. True intonation of 5ths (on vn., &c.).
Ton'satz. A piece of music ; a phrase.
Ton'schluss. A cadence.
Ton'schlüssel. Key-note, key.
Ton'schrift. Written music, notes, rests, &c.
Ton'setzer. (1) A composer. (2) Ironically, a "music maker."
Ton'setzkunst. (Art of) musical composition.
Ton'spieler. A player ; a musical performer.
Ton'sprache. The language of tones ; music.
Ton'stück. A composition.
Ton'stufe. A step of the scale ; a degree.
Ton'system. (1) A scale. (2) A system of music. (See *System.*)
Ton'umfang. Compass (of a voice or inst.).
Ton'unterschied. An interval.
Ton'veränderung. Modulation, change of key.
Ton'verhalt. Rhythm.
Ton'verwandschaft. Key relationship ; affinity of sounds.
Ton'verziehung. Tempo rubato (*q.v.*).
Ton'weite. Compass (of a voice or inst.).
Ton'werk. A musical composition.
Ton'wissenschaft. Science of music.
Ton'zeichen. A note or other sign representing a musical sound.

Ton (*F.*). Tone, sound, pitch ; mode, scale, key ; crook (of a horn, &c.) ; interval of a whole tone ; old name for tuning-fork.

Donner le ton. To give the pitch (for tuning).
Ton bas. A deep, low sound.
Ton bouché. Stopped tone (of a horn).
Ton d'église. A church mode.
Ton de la trompette. Crook of a trumpet.
Ton de rechange }
Ton du cor } Crook of a horn.
Ton doux. A sweet soft tone.
Ton d'ut. The key of C.
Ton entier. A whole tone (2 semitones).
Ton feint. Old name for Bb (in ecclesiastical scales).
Ton générateur. (1) A fundamental tone. (See *Acoustics.*) (2) The principal key of a composition.
Ton haut. A high (acute) sound.
Ton majeur. A major key.
Ton mineur. A minor key.
Ton ouvert. An open note (on a horn, &c.).
Ton relatif. A related key.

Tona'da (*S.*). A tune, a melody, a song.
Tonadi'ca (*S.*) } A lively Spanish song
Tonadil'la (*S.*) } with guitar accompt.

To'nal. Relating to sounds ; specially, to the relationship of keys and modes.
Tonal fugue. (See *Fugue.*)
Tonal imitation. Imitation without changing the key.

Tonalità (*I.*) }
Tonal'ity } (*G., Tonalität'; F., Tonalité.*)
(1) Key structure. (2) Key relationship. (3) The whole scheme of scales, chords, chord progressions, and modulations employed in a composition.

The history of Tonality in European music may be roughly divided into three stages :—

(I) The *Vague Tonality* of the early modes ; gradually modified and made definite with the growth of harmony. (Examples of Vague Tonality may be found in the works of Purcell, Bach, and even Handel.)

(II) The *Fixed Classic Tonality* established by Haydn and Mozart, and perfected (and extended) by Beethoven.

(III) The *Reaction against Classic Tonality* (from Berlioz and Wagner to Rd. Strauss, Max Reger, and Claude Debussy).

N.B.—Whatever freedoms may now (or in the future) be allowed, as, for example, the simultaneous employment of two or three different keys, it is more than likely that the clear tonality of the classic masters (especially Beethoven) will long be regarded as the "standard" by which all modern developments will be judged.

Tonan'te (*I.*). Thunderous ; very loud.

Tona'rion }
Tona'rium } A Roman pitch-pipe.

Ton'do (*I.*). Round, full (in tone).

Tö'ne (*G.*). Plural of **Ton** (*q.v.*).
Getra'gene Tö'ne. Slurred notes.

Tone. (1) Sound. (2) Tone quality. (3) An interval of a major 2nd. (4) A Gregorian chant.

Accessory tones. Harmonics, upper partials, difference tones, &c. (See *Acoustics.*)
Explosive tone. A tone suddenly loud then soft. (See *Dynamics.*)
Gregorian Tones. The chants founded on the 8 Gregorian Modes. (See *Mode.*)
Major tone. Ratio 9 : 8. (See *Acoustics.*)
Minor tone. Ratio 10 : 9. (See *Acoustics.*)
Open tone. Produced on an open string, or on a wind inst. without " stopping."
Partial tone. (See *Acoustics.*)
Quarter-tone. (1) (See *Interval.*) (2) Name sometimes given to the small interval between D♯ and E♭, G♯ and A♭, &c., in Just Temperament.
Resultant tone }
Summational tone } (See *Acoustics.*)
Whole tone. A major 2nd (2 semitones).
Tone colour. Tone quality. (See *Acoustics.*)
Tone painting. Descriptive music ; program music.
Tone poem. "A poem in sounds ; " a piece of program music.

Tongue. (1) The vibrating part of an organ " reed." (2) To use the tongue in wind inst. playing.
Double tonguing } Methods of using the tongue to
Triple tonguing } produce rapid iteration of notes ; *e.g.*, *tootletootle ; tikka-takka*, &c.

Ton'ic. (*G., To'nika ; F., Tonique ; I., To'nica.*) The key-note (governing note) of a key or scale ; the note on which a scale is built up, and from which it takes its name; *e.g.*, C is the Tonic of the scales (keys) of C major and C minor.

In Tonic Sol-fa, *Doh* is the tonic of the Major scale, *Lah* the tonic of the ordinary minor scale.

Tonic basis. Any system of sight-singing, harmony, or theory, founded on the relationship of the various notes of the scale to the tonic.

Tonic cadence. A cadence ending on the Tonic chord.

Tonic chord } The diatonic triad built up on the key-
Tonic triad } note; as C E G in C major, C E♭ G in C minor (*d m s*, or *l, d m*).

Tonic pedal. (See *Pedal.*)

Tonic section. That part of a composition (especially one in sonata form) in which " the principal key reigns."

Tonic Sol-fa. The well-known letter-notation perfected by the Rev. John Curwen (*q.v.*).

It owes its origin to the disinterested labours of Miss Glover, daughter of a Norwich clergyman. In 1812 Miss Glover attempted to teach some Sunday school children to sing, but found so many difficulties in connection with the Staff Notation that she invented a new and simple notation for her own use. Nearly thirty years later (1841) the late Rev. John Curwen, then a young minister, was commissioned by a Sunday School Conference at Hull to find some easy way of teaching children to sing. His attention was directed to the system adopted by Miss Glover; he made some important improvements in the notation, and adopted it in his first " Grammar of Vocal Music," pub. 1842.

At first, the new method made but slow progress; but about 1851 a number of friends throughout the country, having tried the system, gave in their adhesion to it. Classes were formed, and considerable enthusiasm was aroused. In 1853 the first Tonic Sol-fa Association for the promotion of vocal music in congregations, schools, and families was formed. Under this Association the great choral gatherings at the Crystal Palace were commenced in 1857, when a choir of 3,000 children sang to an audience of more than 30,000. From this time the Tonic Sol-fa movement went forward by " leaps and bounds."

In 1863 the "Tonic Sol-fa School" was established to assist those who wished to go on to higher studies in music. From this came (in 1875) " The Tonic Sol-fa College " as it now exists. The examination of pupils has been an important part of the College work, and up to the close of the financial year ending March 31st, 1906, the total number of certificates issued was 805,619.—*From the Secretary's Report*, 1906. To March, 1908, the number was 847,852, of which 28,338 were for Staff notation.

Mr. J. S. Curwen's "Jubilee Souvenir" (1907) contains letters of appreciation from The Archbishop of Westminster, Dr. Adler (Chief Rabbi), Lord Avebury, Lord Monkswell, Lord Overtoun, Lord Reay, the Countess of Jersey, the late Sir August Manns, Sir F. Bridge, Sir Geo. Martin, Sir Walter Parratt, Sir John Kirk, Sir Edgar Speyer, Dr. Cowen, Dr. Coward, Dr. C. H. Lloyd, Dr. Kendrick Pyne, Dr. Emil Reich, Mr. Henry J. Wood, Mr. Ben Davies, Mr. Chas. Manners, Mr. Chas. Saunders, and many other distinguished contributors.

Tonic Sol-fa Modulator. (See *Modulator.*)

Tonic Sol-fa College. (See **Diplomas.**)

Tonic Sol-fa Syllables. The syllables developed from Guido's Hexachordal System. (See **Guido.**)

Guido used the syllables *Ut, Re, Mi, Fa, Sol, La.* About the end of the 16th cent. *Si* was suggested for the 7th note of the scale (either by Puteanus, a Netherlander, or Lemaire, a Frenchman). Mersennus mentions that *Za* was often used for B♭. *Do* was suggested in place of *Ut* in the 17th cent. and was soon adopted in almost every country of Europe except France (where *Ut* is still retained). The name *Do* is supposed to be either the first syllable of *Dominus* ("Lord"), or of *Doni* (a learned Italian theorist).

Miss Glover (see *Tonic Sol-fa* above) published in 1835 a Modulator with the names *Doh, Ray, Me, Fah, Sole, Lah,* and *Te* (*Te* being substituted for *Si*). The sharpened 4th was *Tu*; the flattened 6th, *Gah*; the flattened 7th, *Cole*; the melodic upper tetrachord of the minor scale, *Me, Bah, Ne, Lah.* Mr. Curwen altered *Sole* to *Soh,* and added a (modified) complete set of names for the sharps and flats.—(From Dr. McNaught's *History and Uses of the Sol-fa Syllables.*)

Toni′metro (*I.*). A tuning-fork or a pitch-pipe.

To′nisch (*G.*). Pertaining to the Tonic.

Tonitruone. (From *L., Tonitru,* thunder.) A piece of iron fastened to a wooden frame and shaken by hand.

It is used by Paderewski in his New Symphony (1909), to produce "a strange, thunderous sound, highly effective in furioso passages."

TONKING, Henry Ch. Organist; *b.* Camborne, 1863.

Tonnerre, Grosse caisse en (*F.*). " The big drum as thunder." A roll on the big drum. (Used in the overture to *Zampa.*)

To′no (*I.*). (1) Tone. (2) Key, mode.

Tonom′eter. An instrument for measuring the exact pitch of sounds.

To′nos (*Gk.*) } (1) A whole tone (major 2nd).
To′nus (*L.*) } (2) A mode.

To′nus peregri′nus (*L.*). A " foreign " or " alien " chant added to the 8 regular Gregorian tones. (See *Peregrine Tone.*)

Tons (*F.*). Plural of *Ton.*

Tons d'église. Church modes.
Tons de la trompette. Crooks of the trumpet.
Tons du cor. Crooks of the horn.

Toomour′ah. A Hindu tambourine.

Toorooree. A Brahmin trumpet.

TÖP′FER, Johann G. Famous organist and expert on organ construction. *B.* Niederrossla, Thuringia, 1791; *d.* 1870. Town orgt., Weimar, from 1830.

Works: a concertstück, sonatas, preludes, &c., for organ; several treatises on organ construction; 2 organ " schools," a comprehensive "Choralbuch" with organ interludes, &c.

Toph. A small Hebrew drum or timbrel.

TOPLADY, Augustus M. 1740-78. Vicar of Broadhembury.

Wrote the celebrated hymn " Rock of Ages."

Toquet (*F.*) } Same as **Toccato** (*q.v.*).
Touquet (*F.*) }

Torcel′lo (*I.*). Old name for organ.

TOR′CHI, Luigi. *B.* Mordano, Bologna, 1858. Prof. of Mus. Hist., Liceo Rossini, Pesaro, 1885; Bologna Cons., 1891.

Works: treatises on Wagner, a trans. of Hanslick's " Beautiful in Music," collections of Italian music of the 17th and 18th cents.; &c. He has also begun the publication of " Musical Art in Italy," to comprise 34 vols.

TOREL′LI, Giuseppe. Renowned violinist; *b.* Verona, abt. 1660; *d.* 1708. After tours, &c., Concertmeister, Brandenburg, 1703. He is said to have originated the " Concerto grosso" (*q.v.*).

Works: concerti, &c., for various groups of stringed insts., dating from 1686.

Tornan'do (*I.*). Returning.
Tornan'do al pri'mo tem'po) Returning to the original
Tornan'do co'me pri'mo ∫ speed.

TORRANCE, Rev. G. W. *B.* Rathmines,
Dublin, 1835. Went to Melbourne,
1869; Hon. Mus.Doc. Dublin, 1879.
Works : 3 oratorios, church services, anthems,
hymn-tunes, &c.

TOR'RI, Pietro. *B.* abt. 1665 ; *d.* Munich,
1737.
Works : an oratorio, 26 operas (Munich, 1690-
1737) ; &c.

TORRINGTON, Fredk. H. *B.* Dudley, 1837.
Orgt. Montreal, Canada, 1856-68 ;
orgt. and mus.-director, King's Chapel,
Boston, 1869-73 ; orgt. and conductor
of the Philharmonic Soc., Toronto,
1873. Founded the Toronto Coll. of
Music, 1888.

TÖ'SCHI, Johann B. Violinist ; *B.* of Italian
parents, Mannheim, before 1745 ; *d.*
Munich, 1800.
Wrote 18 symphonies which were "favourites in
Paris before Haydn's advent."

TOSEL'LI, Enrico. Pianist ; *b.* Florence,
1877.

TO'SI, Pier F. Male contralto ; *b.* Bologna,
1647 ; *d.* 1727. Settled in London,
1692, as concert giver and teacher.
His "Observations on Florid Song, &c." (1723),
is a notable work.

TO'STI, Francesco Paolo. Song composer
and singing teacher ; *b.* Ortona,
Abruzzi, 1846. Settled in London,
1875. Singing master to the Royal
Family, 1880 ; Prof. of Singing, R.A.M.,
1894. Knighted, 1908.

To'sto (*I.*). (1) Quick, nimble. (2) Sud-
denly, immediately.
Tostamen'te. Quickly, boldly.
Più to'sto. Almost, nearly ; rather.
Alle'gro mol'to, più to'sto pres'to. Very quick, almost
presto.
Tostissimamen'te) Very rapidly ; extremely quick.
Tostis'simo ∫

Totenmarsch, &c. (See under **To(d)t.**)

TOTT'MANN, Carl A. Composer and
writer ; *b.* Zittau, 1837.

Touch. (*G., An'schlag ; F., Toucher ; I.,
Ta'sto.*) (1) The method of striking
the keys (of a pf., &c.). (2) The
response of an inst. to the touch of the
fingers.
The two chief varieties of pf. touch are *legato*
and *staccato ;* but these allow of many intermediate distinctions, which some modern
teachers reduce to an elaborate system.

Touche (*F.*). (1) Touch. (2) A finger-key.
(3) A fret. (4) A finger-board.
Touche d'orgue. An organ key.
Toucher. As a *noun,* "touch ; as a *verb,* " to play,
to touch" (usually *jouer*).
Touchette. A fret.

Toujours (*F.*). Always. Same as **Sempre.**
Toujours plus animé. Continually more animated
(quicker).
Toujours unis. Always in unison.

TOULMOUCHE, Frédéric. *B.* Nantes, 1850.
Works: several light operas (*La veillée de noces,*
1888).

Touquet. (See **Toquet.**)

Tour de force (*F.*). A feat of strength or
skill ; a *bravura* passage, &c.

TOURJÉE, Dr. Eben. *B.* Warwick, Rhode
Island, 1834 ; *d* 1891.
Successful organizer and teacher ; introduced
the "class system" of mus. teaching in the
United States.

Tourmenté,-ée (*F.*). "Tormented ;" overloaded with eccentricities.

Tourne-boute (*F.*). A kind of flute.

TOURS, Berthold. Violinist ; *b.* Rotterdam,
1838 ; *d.* London, 1897. Musical
adviser to Novello & Co., from 1872.
Works : services, anthems, pf. pieces, songs, a
" Violin Primer," &c.

TOURTE, François. Famous maker of vn.
bows ; Paris, 1747-1835.
He introduced so many improvements in the
shape and construction of the bow that he is
called " the creator of the modern bow."

TOURVILLE, Chas. Pen - name of **J.
Williams** (*q.v.*).

Tous, Tout, Toute, Toutes (*F.*). All.
Tous les claviers accouplés. All the manuals (of an
organ) to be coupled.
Tout à coup. Suddenly ; at a stroke.
Tout à fait. Completely.
Toute la force. As loud as possible.

Touta'ri. A Hindu bagpipe.

Tout ensemble (*F.*). The general effect ;
the whole.

Toys. Old English name for light and
trifling pieces, dances, &c.

Toy Symphony. (*G., Kin'dersinfonie ; F.,
Foire des enfants.*)
Haydn's Toy Symphony—which has often been
imitated—contains parts for 6 toy instruments
(cuckoo, quail, whistle, triangle, trumpet,
drum), 2 vns., and a double bass.

TOZER, Augustus E. *B.* Sutton, Cheshire,
1857. Mus.D. Oxon, 1900.
Works : Catholic church music, "Catholic
Hymns," &c.

TOZER, John Ferris. *B.* Exeter, 1857.
Mus.D. Oxon, 1896.
Works : church music, cantatas, songs, " 50
Sailors' Songs or Chanties," &c.

Tpt. Abbn. of *trumpet.*

tr. Abbn. of *trumpet,* or *trill.*

Trabatte're (*I.*). To beat ; to strike (as a
reed, &c.).

Trache'a (*L.*). The wind-pipe.

Trackers. (*G., Abstrak'ten ; F., Abrégés.*)
(See **Organ.**)

Tract) A species of anthem in R.C.
Tractus (*L.*) ∫ and some other churches.

Tradol'ce (*I.*). Very sweet.

Tradot'to (*I.*)) Translated, arranged ; trans-
Traduit (*F.*) ∫ posed.

Traduzio'ne (*I.*). An arrangement (*q.v.*).

TRAET'TA (or TRAJETTA), Filippo. Son
of T. M. F. S. (below) ; *b.* Venice, 1777 ;
d. Philadelphia, 1854. While serving
as a soldier in Italy, he was captured

and imprisoned ; but managed to escape, and sailed to Boston, 1799. Founded the "American Conservatorio," Philadelphia, 1823.
Works : 2 oratorios, an opera, cantatas, " Vocal Exercises," songs, &c.

TRAET'TA (or TRAJETTA), Tommaso M. F. S. *B.* nr. Naples, 1727 ; *d.* 1779. Pupil of Durante. Maestro to the Duke of Parma, 1758 ; life pension from the King of Spain, 1765 ; director Cons. dell' Ospedaletto, Venice, 1765-8 ; Court composer, St. Petersburg, 1768-1775.
Works : 37 operas (*Farnace*, 1751.; *Ippolito ed Aricia*, 1759) ; an oratorio, a Passion, masses, motets, arias, &c.

Tra'gen der Stim'me (*G.*). " To carry the voice." Same as **Port de voix** (*q.v.*).

Trag'orgel (*G.*). A portable organ.

Traîné (*F.*). Slurred ; dragged.
Traînée. A slow German waltz.

Trait (*F.*). (1) A characteristic feature. (2) A tract (*q.v.*). (3) A run. (4) A passage (or short portion of melody or harmony).
Trait de chant. A melodic passage, figure, motive, &c.
Trait d'harmonie. A series of chord progressions ; a sequence.
Trait d'octave. Rule of the octave (*q.v.*).

Traité (*F.*). A treatise.
Traité d'harmonie. A treatise on harmony.
Traité d'instrumentation. A treatise on instrumentation.

Traktür' (*G.*). The mechanism (especially the "trackers") connecting the keys of an organ with the pallets.

Träll'ern (*G.*). To trill ; to hum.

Tranché,-ée (*F.*). Cut, crossed ; cut off.
C-tranché ⎱ The sign 𝄫
C-barré ⎰
Note tranchée. A note immediately damped (cut short).

Tranquil'lo (*I.*). Calm, tranquil ; *moderato.*
Con tranquillità ⎱ In a quiet tranquil style.
Tranquillamen'te ⎰
Tranquillez'za. Tranquillity.

Transcription. (1) An arrangement (*q.v.*). (2) A brilliant paraphrase, or showe piece, based on some standard theme or composition ; *e.g.*, Liszt's " Transcriptions" of Schubert's songs, &c.

Transcription (or **Transposition**) **of Time.** Halving, doubling (trebling, &c.) the lengths of notes.

Transcription uniforme (*F.*). A method originated in France, and now much used elsewhere, of writing the parts for all the instruments of a brass band in the G clef.

Transcrité (*F.*). Transcribed.

Transformation of Themes. (See **Leit-Motiv.**)

Transient. Passing, temporary ; brief, secondary.
Transient chord. An intermediate foreign chord introduced during the course of a modulation.
Transient modulation. A temporary modulation.

Transition. (*L.*, *Transi'tio* ; *F.*, *Transition;* *I.*, *Transizio'ne.*) (1) A sudden change of key. (2) A brief modulation. (3) In Tonic Sol-fa, a change of key without change of mode. (See **Modulation.**)
Note of transition. A passing-note (*q.v.*) ; specially an accented passing-note.
N.B.—The following refer to Tonic Sol-fa theory.
Cadence transition. One beginning "within two measures" of a cadence, and not extending beyond it.
Departing transition. Leaving the principal key.
Extended transition. Beyond the limits of a cadence transition.
Oscillating transition. From a sharp remove to a flat remove (or *vice versa*) " across the principal key."
Passing transition. Not in a cadence, and not extending beyond two or three pulses.
Returning transition. Coming back to the principal key.
Transition of 1, 2, 3, *&c., removes.* (See *Removes of Key,* under *Key.*)
Transitional Modulation. Change of key with change of mode.

Tran'situs (*L.*). A " passing through."
Tran'situs regula'ris. Progression by passing-notes.
Tran'situs irregula'ris. Progression by changing notes.

Transmutation chord. A chord common to the two keys at a change of key.

Transponi(e)'rende Instrumen'te Transposing insts. (See below.)

Transpose. (*G.*, *Transponi(e)'ren* ; *F.*, *Transposer ;* *I.*, *Variar' il tuo'no.*) To perform or write out a piece in a different key or mode.
(For the various methods of transposition, see the author's *A B C of Musical Theory*.)
Transposed Mode. A mediæval mode written higher or lower than usual. (See *Mode*.)

Transposing instruments. (*G.*, *Transponi(e)'-rende Instrumen'te.*) (1) Instruments which when playing from ordinary music give higher or lower sounds than the notes indicated. (See *Appendix*.)
The chief transposing insts. of an orchestra are clarinets, horns, and trumpets.
(2) Instruments which by shifting their keyboard (or by some other mechanical device) transpose the music into another key (as a transposing piano).

Transpositeur (*F.*). (1) One who transposes. (2) A transposing keyboard (see above). (3) A mechanism attached to a horn or trumpet to obviate the use of crooks (invented by Gautrot).

Transposition. (1) (See **Transpose.**) (2) Inverting the parts in double counterpoint.

Transverse flute. (See **Flute.**)

Traquenard (*F.*). A brisk French dance.

Trascinan'do (*I.*). Dragging ; *strascinando.*

Trascrizio'ne (*I.*). A transcription (*q.v.*).

Trasporta'to (*I.*) ⎱ Transposed.
Traspo'sto (*I.*) ⎰

Traspor'to, Con (*I.*). With ecstasy, transport, delight, passion.

Tratta'to (*I.*). A treatise.

Trattenu'to (*I*.). Abbn. *tratt.* (1) Held back, retarded ; *ritenuto.* (2) Sustained ; *sostenuto.*

Trat'to (*I*.). Dragged, retarded.

Trau'er (*G*.). Grief, affliction ; mourning.
Trau'ergesang. A dirge ; a funeral hymn.
Trau'ermarsch. A funeral march.
Trau'ermusik. Funeral music.
Trau'ervoll. Full of grief, &c.
Trau'rig. Sad, heavy, melancholy.
Trauer-Walzer. A mourning waltz.

Traum (*G*.). A dream, fancy, vision.
Träum'end. Dreaming.
Träum'erie. Dreaming ; day dream ; reverie.
Träum'erisch. Dreamy.

TRAUT'MANN, Marie. (See **Jaell.**)

Travailler (*F*.). To work ; to work hard. To lead (as a solo part).
Musique travaillée. Music abounding with difficulties.

TRAVERS, John. *B.* Windsor, abt. 1703 ; *d.* 1758. Orgt. Chapel Royal, 1737.
Works : "The Whole Book of Psalms," canzonets, anthems, org. pieces, &c.

Travers'flöte (*G*.). (1) A transverse flute. (See **Flute.**) (2) An organ flute stop of 4 ft. pitch.

Traversière (*F*.) ⎱ Transverse. (See **Flauto**
Traver'so (*I*.) ⎰ and **Flute.**)
Traver'so is sometimes found in old scores for *Flau'to traver'so.*

Travestie' (*G*.). A travesty ; a parody.

Tre (*I*.). Three.
A tre. For three voices or parts ; as *Canon a tre.*
A tre vo'ci. For three voices (or parts).
Tre cor'de. Release the "soft" pf. pedal ; " (used after *Una corda.*)
Tre vol'te. Three times.

TREBEL'LI, Zelia. (Real name **Zelia Guillebert.**) Brilliant mezzo-soprano ; *b.* Paris, 1838 ; *d.* 1892. *Début*, Madrid, 1859.
As "Madame Trebelli" she was for several years a great favourite in London.

Treb'le. (From *L.*, *Triplum*, "triple.") (1) Same as **Soprano** (*q.v.*). (2) The highest of a family of instruments. (3) The highest part in a composition. (See **Triplum.**) (4) The smallest bell of a peal (*q.v.*).

Treble C. The note

Treble clef. The G clef (See *Clef.*)

N.B.—A double G clef has been used for tenor parts to show that they are an octave lower

than written :—

(Also one treble clef with C added.)
Treble Viol. An old viol with 6 strings.

Tre'dec'uplet. A group of 13 equal notes.

Chopin ; Op. 48, No. 2.

&c.

Trede'zime (*G*.). Interval of a 13th.

Treff'übung (*G*.). An exercise for "attack" or "entry."

Trei'bend (*G*.). Hastening ; *accelerando.*

Treizième (*F*.). Interval of a 13th.

Trem. Abbn. of *Tremolo.*

Treman'do (*I*.) ⎫
Treman'te (*I*.) ⎬ With a tremolo (*q.v.*).
Tremolan'do (*I*.) ⎭ Trembling, tremulous.

Tremblant (*F*.). (1) Trembling. (2) A tremulant (*q.v.*).

Tremblement (*F*.). "A trembling." (1) A trill. (2) A tremolo.
Trembler. To perform a trill or a tremolo.
Tremblotant. Quivering.

Tremen'do (*I*.). Dreadful, terrible.
Tremendis'simo. Very dreadful, &c.

Tre'molo (*I*.) ⎱ A quivering or fluttering.
Tre'mulo (*I*.) ⎰ (1) In singing, same as **Vibrato** (*q.v.*). (2) On stringed insts., (*a*) a vibrato effect produced by the trembling of a finger ; or (*b*) a rapid reiteration of a note. (3) On the pf. the rapid alternation of the notes of a

chord ; &c. (4) On the organ or harmonium, a fluttering effect produced by a tremolo stop (or tremulant).
Tremolo'so. ⎫
Tremo're, Tremoro'so ⎬ Tremulous, fluttering.

Trem'ulant. A mechanical device (especially on the organ) for producing a tremolo effect.

Tremuli(e)'ren (*G*.). To trill, to tremolo ; *vibrato* (*q.v.*).
Nicht tremuli(e)'ren. Do not *tremolo.*

Trenchmore. An old English country dance in lively time.

Trénise (*F*.). The 4th figure in a quadrille.

Treno'dia (*I*.). Same as **Threnody** (*q.v.*).

TREN'TO, Vittoria. *B.* Venice, 1761 ; *d.* (?). Wrote 30 operas and about 15 ballets.

Trepak. A Russian dance.

Trepo'dion. Same as **Terpodion** (*q.v.*).

Très (*F*.). Very ; well.
Très accentué. Well accented.
Très animé. Very animated.
Très attaqué. Vigorously attacked.
Très déclamé. Well declaimed.
Très éclatant. Very brilliant.
Très élargi. With great breadth.
Très expressif. Very expressive.
Très fort. Very loud.
Très fortement accentué. Very strongly accented.
Très léger. Very light.
Très légèrement martelé dans un doux balancement. Very lightly accented, with a gentle *vibrato.*
Très lentement. Very slow.
Très marqué. Well marked.
Très piano. Very soft.
Très ralenti. Very much retarded.
Très saccadé. Very jerkily.
Très sec. Very abrupt, detached.
Très sonore. Very sonorous.
Très soutenu. Well sustained.
Très vif ⎱
Très vite ⎰ Very lively.

Tres'ca (*I.*)   } A country dance.
Tresco'ne (*I.*)   }

Tri (*Gk.* and *L.* prefix).   Three.

Tri'ad.   (*G., Drei'klang ; F., Triade ; I., Tria'de.*)   A chord of three notes, consisting of a note (called the "root") with its 3rd and 5th.

  Augmented triad. A root, 3rd, and augmented 5th ; as *d m se.*

  Diminished triad. A root, 3rd, and diminished 5th ; as *t₁ r f.*

  Harmonic triad. A major triad.

  Major triad. A root, major 3rd, and perfect 5th ; as *d m s.*

  Minor triad. A root, minor 3rd, and perfect 5th ; as *l₁ d m.*

  Secondary Triads. All the diatonic triads of a key except those of the Tonic, Dominant, and Subdominant (which are called "Primary" triads).

  Tonic triad. The triad of the key-note ; major in major keys, minor in minor keys.

Tri'ain.   A section of three measures.

TRIAL, Jean C. *B.* Avignon, 1732 ; *d.* Paris, 1771. Co-director (with Berton) Paris Opéra from 1767.
  Four of his operas were successfully produced.

Trial (*F.*).   A comic tenor ; *tenore buffo.*

Tri'angle.   (*L., Triang'ulus ; G., Triang'el ; F., Triangle ; I., Trian'golo.*)   A steel rod bent into a triangle, held by a string, and struck with a metal " beater."

Tri'as (*L.*).   A triad.
  Tri'as defic'iens. A diminished triad.
  Trias harmon'ica. A perfect triad, or common chord.

Tri'brach.   A metrical foot of 3 short syllables (∪ ∪ ∪).

Tri'chord.   An inst. of 3 strings (as the 3-stringed lyre).
  Trichord pianoforte. A pf. with 3 wires (tuned in unison) to each key (except in the lowest octaves).

Trich'ter (*G.*)   } (1) The tube of a reed
Shall'trichter (*G.*) }   pipe. (2) The bell of a brass inst.
  Trich'terförmiges Mund'stück. A conical mouthpiece (as that of the horn).

Trici'nium (*L.*).   A composition for 3 voices (unaccompanied).

Tricor'de (*I.*).   Three-stringed, trichord.

Tridiapa'son.   A triple octave ; the interval of 3 octaves.

TRIEBERT, Chas. L. Oboist ; b. Paris, 1810 ; *d.* 1867. Made many improvements in the oboe and bassoon.

Tri'gon, Trigo'num. A 3-stringed lyre-like inst.

TRIMNELL, Thos. Tallis. *B.* Bristol, 1850 ; *d.* 1897. Mus.Bac. Oxon, 1875 ; Orgt. Sheffield Parish Church, 1875-86.

Trill (*E.*)   } A shake (*q.v.*). Signs—*tr,*
Trille (*F.*) } *tr⌇⌇, ⌇⌇⌇, ⌇⌇⌇.* Also,
Trill'er (*G.*) } *⌇⌇, ⌇⌇⌇.* (See **Signs.**)
Tril'lo (*I.*) }

  Trillan'do (*I.*). Shaking ; a long trill.
  Cate'na di tril'li (*I.*) } A chain of trills.
  Tril'lerkette (*G.*) }
  Tril'lern (*G.*). To trill, to ornament with trills.
  Triller von o'ben (*G.*). Trill starting above the principal note.

  Tril'ler von un'ten (*G.*). Trill starting below the principal note.

  Trilletti'no. A short trill.

  Tril'lo capri'no (*I.*). Same as *Bockstriller* (*q.v.*).

  Tril'lo in maggio're (*I.*). A trill with the major 2nd above the principal note.

  Tril'lo in mino're (*I.*). A trill with the minor 2nd above.

  False trill. (See under *Shake.*)

  Imperfect trill. A trill (shake) without a turn at the close.

  Perfect trill. A trill ending with a turn.

Tri'logy (*E.*).   **Trilogie'** (*G.*).   A series of three operas or oratorios.

Trine.   Name given to a kind of triad formed by the tonic, its major 3rd above, and its major 3rd below ; as C with E and A♭.

Trinity College of Music. (See **Diplomas.**)

Trink'gesang (*G.*)   } A drinking song.
Trink'lied (*G.*) }

Tri'o (*I.*).   (1) A composition for 3 voices or insts. (2) The alternative minuet in the "Minuet and Trio" form ; probably so-called from being originally written in 3-part harmony.
  The term is now applied to many middle movements contrasting with other movements ; *e.g.*, the "Trio" of a march, scherzo, &c. Instrumental trios are generally in sonata form. (See *Sonata.*)

  Organ Trio. A 3-part org. piece for two manuals and pedal.

  Pianoforte Trio (*Pf. trio*). Generally for pf., vn., and 'cello.

  String Trio. Vn., viola, and 'cello ; or 2 vns. and 'cello.

  Vocal Trio. Usually in aria form, or song form, with or without accomp.

Trio'le (*G.*).   **Triolet** (*F.*).   A triplet (*q.v.*).
  Die Trio'len wohl markiert' (*G.*). The triplets (to be) well marked.

Triomphale (*F.*)   } Triumphal.
Trionfa'le (*I.*) }

  Triomphant (*F.*). } Triumphant.
  Trionfan'te (*I.*). }

Tripart'ite.   Divided (or divisible) into 3 parts.

Trip'el (*G.*).   Triple.
  Trip'elconcert'. (See *Tripelkonzert.*)
  Trip'elfuge. A fugue on three subjects.
  Trip'elkonzert'. A triple concerto (3 solo insts. with orch.).
  Trip'eltakt. Triple time.
  Trip'elzunge. Triple tonguing.

Tri'pla (*I.*).   (1) A triplet. (2) Triple time.
  Tri'pla di mi'nima. 3-2 time.

Triple Counterpoint. (See **Counterpoint.**)

Triple croche (*F.*) A demisemiquaver ($\mathbf{\clubsuit}$).

Triplet.   (*G., Trio'le ; F., Triolet ; I., Tri'pla, Terzi'na.*)   A group of 3 equal notes to be performed in the time allotted to 2 of the same kind:—

N.B.—In Bach and Handel (and many later composers) a passage marked—

is played

Triple time. (See **Time.**)

Trip'lum (*L.*). (1) In mediæval music a *third* part added to the *Canto Fermo ;* it was generally the highest part, hence the word *Treble* (*q.v.*). (2) A name given to old motets, &c., for 3 voices.

Tri'pola (*I.*). Same as **Tri'pla.**

Trisa'gion (*Gk.*) ⎱   "Thrice holy;" a
Ter Sanc'tus (*L.*) ⎰   Sanctus or Doxology commencing "Holy, holy, holy."

Trisemito'nium (*L.*). A minor 3rd.

TRIS'TAN UND ISOL'DE. Opera by Wagner, 1859. First performed 1865.

Tristesse (*F.*). Sadness, melancholy.

Tri'sto,-a (*I.*). Sad, melancholy ; afflicted.
Con tristez'za. Sadly, dejectedly.
Tri'ste e dol'ce. Sadly and sweetly.

Tri'tone. (*L., Trito'nus ; G., Tri'tonus ; F., Triton ; I., Trito'no.*) An interval of 3 whole tones ; an augmented 4th—

The tritone—formerly known as "Diabolus in Musica"—is the most characteristic interval in the Major scale. It is also the most distinctive portion of a Dominant 7th, and therefore one of the most important intervals in modulation. In old counterpoint there were numerous rules concerning its use and abuse.

Trito'nikon (*G.*). A double-bassoon made of metal.

TRITO'NIUS, Petrus. German musician ; pub. Augsburg, 1507, a curious work in which the music (for 4 parts) "conforms to the rules of prosody" without regard to musical rhythm.

Tritt (*G.*). Treadle ; pedal.
Tritt brett. Pedal board ; pedals.
Tritt'harfe. A pedal harp.

TRIT'TO, Giacomo. *B.* Altamura, 1735 ; *d.* 1824. Prof. of Counterpoint and Composition Cons. della Pietà, Naples, 1800 ; maestro Royal Chapel, 1816. Spontini was his pupil.
Works : about 50 operas ; 3 cantatas, a Mass for double-chorus and 2 orchestras, and much other church music.

Tri'tus (*L.*). The Lydian, or third authentic mode. (See **Mode.**)

Triumphi(e)'rend (*G.*). Triumphant.
Tri'umphlied. A song of triumph.
Tri'umphmarsch. Triumphal march.

Tro'chee. (*L., Trochae'us.*) A metrical foot of 2 syllables ; long, short (— ∪). (See **Metre.**)

Trois (*F.*). Three.
Mesure à trois-deux. 3-2 time.
Mesure à trois-huit. 3-8 time.
Mesure à trois-quatre. 3-4 time.

Troll. (1) A round or catch. (2) To take part in a round, or to sing in a jovial style.

Trom'ba (*I.*). (1) A trumpet (*q.v.*). (2) An organ reed stop.
Trom'ba a chia'vi. Keyed trumpet ; keyed bugle.
Trom'ba a pisto'ni. Trumpet with pistons.
Trom'ba bas'sa. Bass trumpet.
Trom'ba croma'tica. A trumpet with valves or pistons giving a complete chromatic scale.
Trom'ba da tirar'si. A slide trumpet, or soprano trombone.
Trom'ba Mari'na (*Marine Trumpet, Sea Trumpet, Nun's-fiddle ; G., Non'nengei'ge, Trum'scheit*). An ancient bowed inst. with a long body and a single gut string. Its tone was coarse, and so powerful that it was formerly used for naval signalling.
Trom'ba Rea'le. ("Royal Trumpet.") An 8 ft. organ trumpet stop.
Trom'ba sor'da. A muted trumpet.
Trom'ba spezza'ta. Old name for *trom'ba bas'sa.*
Trombet'ta ⎫
Trombettato're ⎬ A trumpeter.
Trombetti'no ⎭
Trombet'ta ⎫ A little trumpet.
Trombetti'na ⎭

Trom'be (*I.*). Plural of *Tromba.*

Trombone ("A large *Tromba.*") (*G., Posau'ne ; F., Trombone ; I., Trombo'ne,* plur. *Trombo'ni.*) A large deep-toned brass wind inst. of the trumpet kind provided with a "slide" by means of which the tube can be lengthened (and the pitch varied) at pleasure.

The trombone is a very ancient instrument, its present form dating from about the 15th cent. (See *Sackbut.*) It is made in 4 sizes : alto, tenor, bass, and contrabass, but the alto is nearly obsolete. The *tenor* trombone is the one most generally used. It has a complete chromatic range from—

Solo players can get a few higher notes, and there are also some deep "fundamental" or "pedal" notes from BB♭ downwards (first utilized by Berlioz).
The tone of the trombone is specially rich in "partials." (See *Acoustics.*)
Valve trombone. A trombone with valves or pistons instead of a slide.
N.B.—*Trombone* (*G., Posau'ne*) is also the name of a family of powerful reed stops on the organ.
Trombo'ne a cilin'dri (*I.*). Trombone with cylinders.
Trombone à coulisse (*F.*). Slide trombone.
Trombone à pistons (*F.*). Trombone with pistons.
Trombo'ne a ti'ro (*I.*) ⎫ Slide trombone.
Trombo'ne duttile (*I.*) ⎭

Trombo'ni (*I.*). Trombones.
Tromboni'no. Small trombone ; alto trombone.

TROM'LITZ, Johann G. Flute maker ; *b.* Cera, 1726 ; *d.* Leipzig, 1805.
Works : 3 concertos for fl. and strings, 2 books of sonatas for fl. and pf., &c. ; and several works on flute playing, &c.

Trom'mel (*G.*). A drum.
Trom'mel Bass. A bass part in repeated notes (like a drum part).
Trom'melklöppel ⎫ Drumsticks.
Trom'melstöcke ⎭
Trom'melruf. A drum-call.
Trom'melsaiten. Snare of a side-drum.
Trom'melschlägel. Drumstick.
Trom'melschläger. A drummer.
Trom'melwirbel. A roll on a drum.
Gros'se Trom'mel. A big drum ; bass drum.
Militär'trommel. Military drum ; side drum.
Roll'trommel. Tenor drum.
Wir'beltrommel. Side drum.

Trom′melstück (*G.*). A tambourine, or tabor.

Tromm′ler (*G.*). A drummer.

Trompe (*F.*). (1) A trumpet. (2) A hunting horn.

Trompe de Béarn } A Jew's harp.
Trompe à laquais }
Trompe de chasse. " Hunting horn ; " the immediate precursor of the orchestral " French horn."
Trompe des Alpes. An ancient Alpine horn made of the hollowed trunk (or branch) of a tree.

Trompe′te (*G.*). A trumpet.

Trompe′tenbläser. A trumpeter.
Trompe′tengeige. A " tromba marina " (*q.v.*).
Trompe′tenregis′ter, Trompe′tenwerk, Trompe′tenzug. Trumpet stop.
Trompe′tentusch. A trumpet flourish ; fanfare.
Trompe′ter. Trumpeter.

Trompette (*F.*). (1) A trumpet. (2) A trumpeter, or bugler. (3) A trumpet stop.

Trompette à clefs. Keyed trumpet ; keyed bugle.
Trompette à coulisse. Slide trumpet.
Trompette à pistons. Valve trumpet.
Trompette harmonieuse. Trombone.
Trompette d'harmonie. Orchestral trumpet.
Trompette marine. Tromba marina (*q.v.*).

Tron′co,-a (*I.*). Truncated ; cut off.

No′ta tron′ca. A note cut short ; suddenly damped.
Suo′ni tron′chi. Tones cut off abruptly ; *staccato.*

Troop. (1) A quick march. (2) The drum signal for marching.

Trop′po (*I.*). Too ; too much ; excessive(ly).

Alle′gro ma non trop′po. Quick, but not too much so.
Trop′po carica′to. Too much weighted (with accompt., ornaments, &c.).

TROTTER (TROTÈRE), Henry. Song composer ; *b.* London, 1855.

TROTTER, T. H. Yorke. *B.* Gt. Stainton, Durham, 1854. Mus.D. Oxon, 1892.

Troubadour (*F.*). (*S., Trovador'; I., Trova-to′re; F., Trouvère.*) A wandering minstrel—"poet musician"—11th to 13th centuries.

The troubadours probably originated in Provence.

Troublé (*F.*). Troubled, grieved.

TROUP, Josephine. Contemporary song composer.

Songs : " Spring flowers," " A faded violet," &c.

Troupe (*F.*). A company of musicians, players, &c.

TROUTBECK, Rev. John. *B.* Blencowe, Cumberland, 1832 ; *d.* 1899. M.A., Oxford, 1858 ; precentor, Manchester Cath., 1865 ; canon, Westminster Abbey, 1869.

Works : psalters, a hymn book, a music primer (with R. F. Dale), "Church Choir Training," Eng. translations of the words of standard oratorios, operas, &c.

Trovato′re (*I*) (See **Troubadour.**)

Trouvère (*F*) } A troubadour.
Trouveur (*F*) }

The *Trouvères* were found in Northern France, especially Picardy. They are said to have originated the " romances of chivalry."

TROYTE, Arthur H. D. *B.* nr Exeter, 1811 ; *d.* 1857.

Composed chants, hymn-tunes, &c,

Trüb′(e) (*G.*). Gloomy, sad, melancholy.

Trug′kadenz (*G.*)
Trug′schluss (*G.*) } A deceptive cadence.
Trug′schlüsse (*G.*) } (See **Cadence.**)

TRUHN, Friedrich H. *B.* Elbing, 1811 ; *d.* Berlin, 1886. Pupil of Mendelssohn. Capellmeister Danzig Th., 1835-7 ; writer for the *Neue Zeitschrift für Musik,* Leipzig ; director at Elbing, 1848-52.

Works : operas, choral works, songs, &c.

Trumb′scheit (*G.*). Tromba marina (*q.v.*).

Trum′mel (*G.*). Same as **Trommel** (*q.v.*).

Trump. Poetical name for trumpet.

Trumpet. (*G., Trompe′te ; F., Trompette ; I., Trom′ba.*) (1) A reed stop on the organ. (2) An orchestral brass wind inst.

The orchestral trumpet is an octave higher than the horn ; and like that instrument its pitch can be changed by means of crooks. The tube (which in the "C" trumpet is about 8 ft. in length) is of narrow scale, and the cupped mouth-piece is hemi-spherical (that of the horn being conical). Its tone, extremely rich in partials, is bright and penetrating, " a single trumpet note being easily heard above the whole orchestra."

The "natural" scale of the trumpet is—

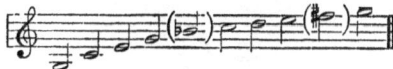

the notes in brackets being slightly out of tune.
The trumpet in C gives these sounds "exactly as written," trumpets in other keys being " transposing instruments."
The keys used range from the G below the C to the F above. The trumpets in B♭, C, and D give the best tone quality.
Bass trumpets of deeper pitch are also used.
Two trumpets were generally employed in the "classical" orchestra ; modern composers use any number they please. Bach and Handel used long high-pitched trumpets called *Clari′ni* (sing., *Clari′no*), recently revived.

Chromatic trumpet } A trumpet provided with
Trompette chromatique (*F.*) } valves or pistons, by
Valve trumpet } means of which the
Ventil trumpet } complete chromatic
scale is obtained.
Slide trumpet. A trumpet with a short slide similar to that of a trombone.
N.B.—On account of its greater ease of manipulation the chromatic trumpet is rapidly superseding the old natural trumpet ; but modern trumpet parts lack much of the "style" characteristic of earlier ones, and the change is " not all gain."

Trum′scheit (*G.*) }
Trun′scheit (*G.*) } Tromba marina (*q.v.*).

TRUST, Helen M. (*née* **Stark**). Soprano vocalist ; *b.* Norwich. Sang at the Monday and Saturday Popular Concerts, 1891-2 ; Leeds Festival, 1892 ; Norwich Festival, 1893; &c.

T. S. Tasto solo (*q.v.*).

TSCHAIKOWSKY. (See **Tchaikovsky.**)

Tscheng. (See **Cheng.**)

TSCHIRCH, Friedrich W. *B.* Lichtenau, Silesia, 1818 ; *d.* 1892. Court condr., Gera, 1852.

Works : an opera, several fine works for male-chorus and orch. (or wind band), salon pf. pieces, &c.

TSCHIRCH, Rudolf. Brother of preceding ; *b.* Lichtenau, 1825 ; *d.* 1872.

Works : pieces for wind band, a cantata (*Sans Souci*), &c.

Tschüng (*G.*). A Chinese gong.

TU'A, Teresina. Fine violinist ; *b.* Turin, 1867. Took 1st prize for vn. playing, Paris Cons., 1880. First English concert, 1883. Married Count Franchi-Verney della Valetta, abt. 1891.

Tu'ba (*L.*). (1) The straight trumpet of the Romans. (2) A powerful organ reed-stop on a high pressure of wind. (3) A deep bass sax-horn of the bombardon family. (See **Bombardon.**)

" Tuba " is also used for " Saxhorn " generally ;. *e.g.*, the " tenor " tubas in Wagner's *Ring.*

The tubas used in the orchestra are of various sizes ; the E♭ tuba (a 5th lower in pitch than the B♭ euphonium) is perhaps the most generally useful ; the contra-bass tuba in BB♭ is called in England a " monster bombardon."

Tuba clarion. A 4 ft. tuba.
Tuba cur'va. An old form of trumpet.
Tuba mira'bilis ⎫
Tuba major ⎬ (See *Tuba,* 2).
Tubasson (*F.*). A trombone on the pedal (org. stop.)
Tu'bicen. A trumpet player.

Tubalflöte. Corruption of **Jubalflöte** (*q.v.*).

TUCKERMAN, Samuel P. *B.* Boston, Mass., 1819 ; *d.* 1890. Studied in England.

Works : church services, anthems, hymns, collections ("Episcopal Harp", "National Lyre," &c.)

Tuck'et (*Old E.*). A trumpet flourish.

TU'CZEK, Franz. Tenor singer ; *b.* Prague, abt. 1755 ; *d.* 1820. Condr. Leopold-stadt Th., Vienna, 1802.

Works : several operas, 2 oratorios, cantatas, dance music, &c.

TUDWAY, Thomas. *B.* about 1650 ; *d.* Cambridge, 1726. Chorister, Chapel Royal, 1660 ; Lay-vicar, St. George's, Windsor, 1664 ; orgt., King's Coll., Cambridge, 1670 ; Prof. of Music, Cambridge Univ., 1704 ; Mus.Doc., 1705.

Works : services, anthems, &c., and a " Collection of services and anthems......from the Reformation to the Restoration " (6 vols. MS. in the Brit. Museum.)

TULOU, Jean L. Celebrated flautist ; *b.* Paris, 1786 ; *d* 1865. 2nd prize for fl. playing, Paris Cons., 1799 ; 1st prize, 1801. Played at the Italian Opera and Grand Opéra, Paris ; fl. prof. at the Cons. He favoured the old-fashioned flute, and "obstinately opposed" Böhm's improved inst.

Wrote 5 concertos and many other works for flute (flute with string quartet, duos, trios, &c.).

Tulau (*F.*). Same as **Tuyau** (*q.v.*).

Tumultuo'so (*I.*). Vehement, agitated, impetuous.

Tun. An ancient Yucatan drum.

TUN'DER, Franz. 1614-67. Orgt. Marien-kirche, Lübeck ; pupil of Frescobaldi ; predecessor of Buxtehude.

Tune. (1) An air, melody (with innate rhythm) ; specially a short composition (with or without harmony), as a "hymn-tune," &c. (2) Intonation (*q.v.*).

Tuner. (*G,* *Stim'mer ;* *F,* *Accordeur ;* *I.,* *Accordato're.*) One who tunes insts.

Tuney music. Name given in disparagement to " ear-catching " but trite and com-monplace music, without real originality or any truly artistic qualities.

Tuning. (1) The process of bringing an inst. into tune. (2) Temperament (*q.v.*). (3) The *accordatura* (*q.v.*) of a stringed inst.

Tuning-cone ⎫ A hollow metal cone used to tune the
Tuning-horn ⎬ metal flue-pipes of an organ. The point of the cone opens and sharpens the pipes ; the "hollow" slightly closes the ends and lowers the pitch.
Tuning-fork. A 2-pronged steel instrument tuned to a fixed pitch. Invented by John Shore, Royal trumpeter, 1711.
Tuning-hammer ⎫ The combined hammer and wrench
Tuning-key ⎬ used for tuning the pf.
Tuning-slide. A slide attached to many insts. to slightly lengthen the tube and adjust the pitch.
Tuning wire. A wire attached to the boot of an organ reed-pipe for tuning the tongue.

Tuning of Bells.

" In this country until recent times bells were tuned by chipping away either the inner surface of the sound-bow or the edge of the lip with a chisel-headed hammer—a crude and unsatisfactory process. Now, however, bells are tuned to the accuracy of a vibration by means of a specially constructed machine which is really a vertical lathe.

" The bell is inverted and gripped at different points by powerful vices to keep it firm and fixed to the face-plate. The steel cutter revolves—or the cutter is fixed and the bell revolves—paring out the metal from the inside of the bell for flattening and paring off the edge of the bell for sharpening. Bells may be flattened an eighth of a tone, or even more, but any sharpening is to be deprecated.

" The sound of a bell is a compound tone which presents to the ear five—and in many instances more—tones (partial tones).

" A good bell should have at least five of its tones in perfect tune, thus :—

The note of the bell...... Nominal. / Quint. / Tierce. / Fundamental. / (Strike or Tap-note.) / Hum note.

Approximate weight, 2 tons.

The following may be mentioned as examples of fine bells, both as to tone and tune :—

(1) OLD.		DATE.	WEIGHT.	NOTE.
Tenor	..Lavenham	1625	24 cwts.	D.
Seventh	..Exeter Cath.	1676	28 cwts.	E♭
Eighth	,,	1729	33½ cwts.	D
Ninth	,,	1676	40¼ cwts.	C⌡

(2) NEW.   DATE. WEIGHT. NOTE.
Tenor ..Exeter Cath.   1902   72½ cwts.   B♭
Tenor ..Beverley Minstr. 1901   41½ cwts.   C

" The perfection of the tuning in which England is now paramount is entirely due to the enterprise of Messrs. Taylor, the well-known Loughborough founders."—*W. W. Starmer.*

TUN′STEDE (TUNSTED, or DUNSTEDE), Simon. Minorite friar ; *b.* Norwich ; *d.* Bruisyard, Suffolk, 1369.

Reputed author of a historically valuable work on Mensural music.

Tuo′no (*I.*). (1) A tone or sound. (2) A mode (*q.v.*). (3) Thunder. (4) A whole tone.

Tuo′no ecclesias′tico. A church mode or tone.
Tuo′no maggio′re. A major key.
Tuo′no mez′zo. A semitone.

Tuo′ni (*I.*). Tones, sounds, modes.

Tuo ni aper′ti. Open notes (sounds).
Tuo′ni chiu′si. Closed notes (sounds).

Tuorbe (*F.*). Theorbo (*q.v.*).

Tur′bae (*L.*, " crowd "). The voice of the multitude in a Catholic setting of the Passion.

Turbinosamen′te (*I.*)   } In a furious, stormy manner.
Turbino′so (*I.*)

Turco,-a (*I.*). Turkish.

Al′la tur′ca (*I.*). In the Turkish style. (See *Janizary Music.*)

TURI′NI, Francesco. Brescia, abt. 1590-1656. Cathedral organist.

Works : masses, motets, madrigals, &c. Many of his madrigals have parts both for voices and insts.

TÜRK, Daniel G. Eminent organist and teacher ; *b.* Claussmitz, Saxony, 1750 ; *d.* 1813. Mus.-director, Halle Univ., 1779 ; orgt. Liebfrauenkirche, 1787.

Works : an important " Clavierschule," a work on " Figured bass playing," &c. ; an oratorio, pf. sonatas and sonatinas, 120 easy pf. pieces for 4 hands, church music, songs, &c.

Tür′kisch (*G.*). Turkish.

Tür′kisch-mu′sik. Turkish music.

Turkish music. (See **Janizary music.**)

TURLE, James. *B.* Somerton, Somerset, 1802 ; *d* London, 1882. Orgt. Westminster Abbey, 1831-75. Conducted the " Antient Concerts," 1840-3.

Works : services, anthems, chants, hymn-tunes ; edited collections of church music, &c.

Turn. (*G., Dop′pelschlag ; F., Groupe ; I., Gruppet′to, Groppet′to.*) A little group of grace notes "turning" round a principal note.

The grace-note above is called the "upper auxiliary ; " that below, the " lower auxiliary."

I.—DIRECT, COMMON, OR REGULAR TURN.

(*a*) Placed above a note.

(1) In slow time, or before a rest.

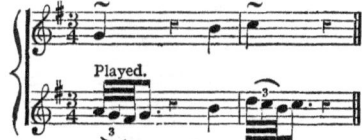

Played.

(2) In quick time ; or over a short note.

Played.

(*b*) Between two notes of different pitch.

(*c*) Above the first of two notes of the same pitch.

(*d*) An accidental above a turn refers to the upper auxiliary ; below, to the lower auxiliary.

(*e*) A turn on the first note of a phrase, or some other specially prominent note, is often played as a quintuplet.

II.—INVERTED OR BACK TURN.

Commences with the *lower* auxiliary; ' general rules of performance same as those for a direct turn.

Played.

III.—GRACED TURNS.

or

or

N.B.—Grace-notes are often written instead of the sign) or ~; and modern composers frequently write the turn in full *exactly as it should be played.*

DOUBLE TURN.
Two turns together :—

Played.

TRIPLE TURN.
Three turns together :—

Played

TURNER, Jas. Wm. Tenor vocalist; *b.* Sutton-in-Ashfield, Nottingham, 1845.

TURNER, J. Bradbury. *B.* Stockport, 1832; *d.* 1898. Entered R.A.M., 1852. Mus.B. Cantab., 1865. One of the founders of Trinity College, London.

TURNER, Wm. *B.* Oxford, 1651; *d.* 1739-1740. Mus.D. Cantab., 1696. Gentleman, Chapel Royal; Vicar-choral, St. Paul's; Lay-vicar, Westminster Abbey.
Works: operas, anthems, songs, &c.

TURN'HOUT, Gérard de. (Gheert Jacques.) Noted contrapuntist; *b.* Turnhout, Belgium, abt. 1520; *d.* Madrid, 1580. Maître de Musique, Antwerp Cath., 1563; maestro to Philip II, Madrid, 1572.
Wrote masses, motets, chansons, &c.

TURPIN, Edmund H. Organist; *b.* Nottingham, 1835; *d.* 1907. Settled in London, 1857. Mus.D. Cantuar, 1889. Editor *Musical Standard* for several years from 1880; joint editor *Musical News*, 1891. Sec. Royal Coll. of Organists from 1875.
Works: cantatas, church music, organ pieces, &c.

Turr. A 3-stringed Burmese violin.

TURTON, Right Rev. Thos. Bishop of Ely. *B.* Yorkshire, 1780; *d.* 1864.
Works: hymn-tunes and other church music.

TURTSHAN'INOFF, Peter I. St. Petersburg, 1779-1856. High Priest.
His MS. compositions (in the Imperial Chapel) are said to be important.

Tusch (*G.*). (1) A flourish. (2) A triple flourish of trumpets and drums.

Tu'te (*G.*). A cornet.

Tut'horn (*G.*). A cowherd's horn.

Tut'ta, Tut'to; *pl. Tut'te, Tut'ti* (*I.*). "All." The full chorus, the full band, &c.
Tut'ta for'za, or *Tut'ta la for'za.* With full power; as loud as possible.
Tut'ta for'za e prestez'za. As loud as possible and very quick.
Tut'te cor'de. "All the strings;" in pf. music, "Release the soft pedal."
Tut'ti uni'soni. All in unison.
Tut'to ar'co. With the whole bow.
Tut'to il cem'balo ma pia'no. Without the soft pedal, but *piano.*
Tut'to lega'to. The whole (to be) *legato.*

Tut'ti (*I.*). All. Used especially after *solo* passages.
Tut'ti passage. A passage for all the performers. Used particularly in concertos, where the orchestra alternates with the solo inst.

Tuyau (*F.*). A tube or pipe.
Tuyau à anche. An organ reed-pipe.
Tuyau à bouche. A flue-pipe.
Tuyau bouché. A closed pipe.
Tuyau d'orgue. An organ pipe.
Tuyau ouvert. An open pipe.

Twelfth. (1) An interval of an octave and a (perfect) 5th. (2) An organ stop a 12th above unison pitch.

TWELLS, Henry. 1823-1900. Hon. Canon, Peterboro' Cath., 1884.
Wrote the hymn "At even, ere the sun was set."

Twenty-second. A triple octave.

Twice-marked octave. The notes from—

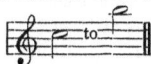

N.B.—*Once accented* in Tonic Sol-fa (C′ to B′).

Two removes. (See **Removes of Key,** under **Key.**)

Two-step. (*G., Zwei'tritt ; F., Deux-temps ; I., Val'zer a du'e pas'si.*) A quick waltz.

Two-time. Duple time.

TYE, Dr. Christopher. *B.* probably Cambridge, 1497; *d.* 1572. Orgt. Ely Cath., 1541-61. Mus.Doc. Cantab., 1545.
 Works : a service, anthems, &c. ; and the first 14 chapters of " The Actes of the Apostles ......with Notes to eche Chapter, to synge and also to play upon the Lute" (1553), now used as anthems.

Tym'bal. A kind of kettle-drum.

Tymb'estere. Same as **Tombestere** (*q.v.*).

Tym'pan. A timbrel, or drum.

Tym'pani. (Incorrect) spelling of *Timpani* (*q.v.*).

Tympanon (*F.*). (1) A dulcimer. (2) A kettle-drum.

Tym'panum (*L.*). (1) A drum. (2) The drum of the ear.

Ty'pophone. A kind of pf. with tuning-forks instead of strings.

Ty'ro. A beginner ; a learner.

Tyrolienne (*F.*). (1) A Tyrolese song or dance characterized by the *Jodel* (*q.v.*). (2) A round dance in 3-4 time in Tyrolese style.

Tzet'se. An Abyssinian guitar.

Tzi'ti. (**Tit'ty.**) A Hindu bagpipe.

U

U. Abbn. of *Und* (*q.v.*).

UBALD'US (UGBALDUS, UCHUBALDUS). (See **Hucbald.**)

Ü'bel (*G.*). Bad.
Ü'belklang } Discord ; " bad sound."
Ü'bellaut }

Ü'ben (*G.*). To practise.
Zu ü'ben. To be practised ; for practising.

Ü'ber (*G.*). Over, above.
Ü'berblasen. (1) To blow a horn, &c. (2) To overblow (a wind inst.).
Ü'bereilt. Over-hurried, precipitate.
Ü'bereinstimmung. Consonance, harmony.
Ü'bergang. " Going over ; " an intermediate passage ; change of key ; transition.
Ü'bergeführte Stim'men. Divided (organ) stops.
Ü'bergehend. Proceeding to.
Ü'bergreifen. (1) To cross hands (in pf. playing). (2) To lift the thumb from the neck (in 'cello playing).
Ü'berlaut " Over loud." Too loud, noisy.
Ü'berleitung. "Leading over." (1) Same as *Übergang.* (2) Specially, the "bridge" in sonata form (*q.v.*).
Ü'bermässig. Augmented ; excessive.
Ei'ne ü'bermässige Sekun'de. An augmented second.
Ü'bermässiger Sechst'akkord. Chord of the augmented sixth.
Ü'bermüt(h)ig. Over merry ; in wild spirits.
Ü'berschlagen. (1) To cross the hands. (2) To overblow. (3) To "break" the voice in singing.
Ü'bersetzen. (1) To translate, to transpose. (2) To pass a finger over the thumb (in pf. playing, &c.), or one foot over the other (in org. pedalling).
Ü'bersetzung. A translation.
Ü'bersteigen. To cross parts ; *e.g.*, for an under part to pass temporarily above a higher one.
Ü'berstimmen. To tune too sharp.
Ü'bertönend. "Over-sounding;" very prominent.
Ü'berstürst. Hurried.

U'BER, Christian B. Breslau, 1746-1812. Wrote vocal works, instl. divertimenti, pf. sonatas, &c.

U'BER, Friedrich C. H. Son of preceding ; *b.* Breslau, 1781 ; *d.* 1822. Cantor and mus.-director, Kreuzkirche, Dresden, 1818.
Works : an oratorio, a vn. concerto, stage works, songs, &c.

U'BER, Alexander, Brother of preceding ; *b.* Breslau, 1783 ; *d.* 1824. Fine 'cellist.
Works : a concerto, and other pieces for 'cello ; a septet, songs, &c.

UBER'TI (HUBERT), Antonio. Brilliant male soprano ; *b.* Verona, abt. 1697 ; *d.* 1783. He was one of Porpora's best pupils ; hence called " Il Porporino."

Ü'bung (*G.*). Practice ; exercise ; a study.
Ü'bungsabend. A pupil's concert.
Ü'bungsstück. A practice piece ; a study.

U. C. Abbn. of *Una corda* (*q.v.*).

UDBYE, M. A. Composer ; *b.* Trondhjem, 1820.

Udi'ta (*I.*) } (1) Heard. (2) The sense of
Udi'to (*I.*) } hearing.
Udito're. An auditor, listener.

Ue'bel (*G.*). Same as **Ubel** (*q.v.*).
Ue'ben (*G.*). Same as **Üben** (*q.v.*).
Ue'ber (*G.*). Same as **Über** (*q.v.*).
Ue'bung (*G.*). Same as **Übung** (*q.v.*).

U'gab (*Hebrew*). An " organ ; " probably a kind of flute.

UGALDE, Delphine (*née* **Beauce**). Operatic soprano ; *b.* Paris, 1829. Wrote an opera ; successful teacher.

UGOLI'NI, Biagio. Venetian monk.
Pub. a "Thesaurus of sacred antiquities" (34 vols., 1744-69) ; vol. 32 is on Hebrew music.

UGOLI'NI, Vincenzo. Noted contrapuntist ; *b.* Perugia, abt. 1570 ; *d.* 1638. Pupil of Nanini ; maestro, Vatican, Rome, 1620-6.
Works : masses, motets, psalms, madrigals, &c. (up to 8 and 12 parts).

Ugua'le (*I.*). Equal, like ; even.
Ugua'glianza } Equality, evenness, uniformity.
Ugualità }
Ugualmen'te. Evenly ; equally ; similarly.
Vo'ci ugua'li. Equal voices (*q.v.*).

UHL, Edmund. Pianist, organist, and critic ; *b.* Prague, 1853.
Works : pf. trios and other pf. pieces ; songs, &c.

UH'LIG, Theodor. Violinist ; *b.* Wurzen, Saxony, 1822 ; *d.* 1853.
Wrote symphonies, cantatas, theoretical works, &c. Supporter of Wagner's theories.

ULI'BISHEFF (OULIBISCHEFF), Alexander d'. *B.* Dresden, 1795 ; *d.* 1858.
His historical works ("Nouvelle Biographie de Mozart," &c.) are notable for his inability to understand Beethoven.

UL'MAR, Geraldine (Mrs. F. Tilkins), *née* **Annie Geraldine.** Soprano ; *b.* Boston (U.S.), 1862.

UL'RICH, Otto. *B.* Oppeln, Silesia, 1827 ; *d.* 1872. Teacher, Stern Cons., Berlin, 1859-63.
Works : 3 symphonies ; excellent arrangements of Beethoven's symphonies for pf. 4 hands ; &c

U'ltimo,-a (*I.*). The last.
U'ltima vol'ta. The last time.

Uma'no,-a (*I.*). Human.
Vo'ce uma'na. " Human voice." (1) A *Vox humana.* (2) A *Cor anglais.*

UM'BREIT, Karl G. *B.* nr. Gotha, 1763 ; *d.* 1829. Orgt. at Sonnenborn for 35 years.
Works : a " General Choralbook for the Protestant Church" (1811), church music, organ pieces, &c.

Um'fang (*G.*). Compass, extent.
Um'fang der Stim'me. Compass of the voice.

Um'gekehrt (*G.*). Reversed ; inverted.
Um'gekehrter Dop'pelschlag. An inverted turn.

Um'heim'lich (*G.*). Strange, uneasy, gloomy, sinister.

Um'kehrung (*G.*). Inversion of an interval, part, &c.
Ka'non in der Um'kehrung. A canon by inversion. (See *Canon.*)

UM'LAUF, Ignaz. *B.* Vienna, 1756 ; *d.* 1796. Mus.-director German Opera, Vienna.
Works : popular "Singspiele" (operettas), songs.

UM′LAUF, Michael. Son of I.; Vienna, 1781-1842. Capellmeister, German Opera, Vienna.
Works: an opera, ballets, sacred music, pf. pieces, &c.

UM′LAUFT, Paul. *B.* Meissen, 1853. "Mozart Scholar," Leipzig Cons., 1879-1883.
Works: opera (*Evanthia*, 1893), dramatic poems, pf. pieces, &c.

Um′laut (*G.*). The modification of a vowel in German words. It is indicated by two dots over the vowel, showing that a following vowel has been suppressed; ä = ae; ö = oe; ü = ue.

Umo′re (*I.*). Humour.
Umori′stico. Humorous.

Um′schlagen (*G.*). (1) Of the voice: to break, to crack. (2) Of a wind inst.: to overblow, to produce a "goose" note.
Um′schlagende Stim′me. Use of the voice near the "break;" the tone alternating between the higher and lower registers.

Um′setzen (*G.*). To compose.

Um′stellen (*G.*). To invert.
Um′stellung. Inversion.

Um′stimmung (*G.*). (1) Same as **Muta** (*q.v.*). (2) A special tuning (*Scordatura*) of a stringed inst.
F in E um′stimmen. Change the tuning (of the drum, &c.) from F to E.

Un (*L. prefix*). Not.
Unaccented note. A "weak" accent.
Unaccented octave. Same as *Ungestrichene Oktave* (*q.v.*).
Unacknowledged note. Name sometimes given to a passing-note (or other unessential note).
Uncoupled. (*G.*, *Kop′pel ab.*) Same as "coupler off," or " Gt. to Ped. off," &c., in organ playing.

Un, U′na, U′no (*I.*). One; a, an.
U′na cor′da. (With) one string; "use the soft pedal" (pf.).
Tre cor′de. (With) all the strings; "release the soft pedal."
Una cor′da col peda′le. Both pf. pedals together.
U′na vol′ta. Once. (Play, or sing, the passage once only.)

Un, Une (*F.*). One; a, an.
Une Harmonie. A military band.
Une mesure comme deux du mouvement précédent. One bar equal to two of the preceding movement.
Une musique militaire. Abbn. of *Une bande de musique militaire.* A military band.

Un′bedeckt (*G.*). Uncovered, open (as an organ pipe).

Un′ca. (*L.*, " Hooked.") A quaver (♪).
Bis un′ca. A semiquaver (♫).

Und (*G.*). Abbn. *u.* And.
Fl. u. Ob. Flute and Oboe.

Un′da ma′ris. (*L.*, "Wave of the sea.") An organ stop of a wavy undulating tone; a *Voix Celeste*.
The undulation is caused either by tuning the pipes slightly lower than those of some other stop to be drawn with the *Unda maris*, or by having two pipes to each note, one slightly lower than the other.

Unde′cima (*L.* and *I.*). Interval of an 11th (octave and 4th).

Undecimo′le (*I.*) ⎫ A group of 11 equal
Undec′uplet ⎭ notes —

Under. Below; secondary.
Undersong. A burden, a refrain.
Undertones ⎫ Difference tones. (See *Acoustics.*)
Un′tertöne (*G.*) ⎭

Unde′zime (*G.*). An eleventh.
Unde′zimo′le (*G.*). An undecuplet (*q.v.*).

Undulazio′ne (*I.*). " Undulation." The *Vibrato* on a stringed inst.

Unei′gentliche Fu′ge (*G.*). An irregular fugue.

Un′endlich (*G.*). Infinite.

Unequal Temperament. (See **Temperament.**)
Unequal counterpoint. Parts moving in unequal notes; *i.e.*, all species except the first.
Unequal voices. Mixed voices. The voices of an ordinary choir, as opposed to "equal" voices.

Unessential note. One not forming a part of a chord; a passing, auxiliary, or ornamental note.

Un′gar (*G.*)., **Ung′arisch** (*G.*). Hungarian.

Un′gebunden (*G.*). (1) Unconstrained. (2) Not tied or syncopated. (3) In the free style.

Un′geduldig (*G.*). Impatient.

Un′gefähr (*G.*). About; approximate(ly).
♩ = 60 *un′gefähr.* Crotchet = about M. 60.

UN′GER (UNGHER), Caroline. Noted soprano; *b.* Hungary, 1803; *d.* 1877. *Début*, Vienna, 1821.
At the 1st performance of the *Choral Symphony*, she turned Beethoven round " to show him the applause." (Beethoven, who conducted, was then stone-deaf.)

UN′GER, Georg. Fine dramatic tenor; Leipzig, 1837-87. *Début*, 1867.
Famous for his creation of the part of " Siegfried," in Wagner's *Ring*, Bayreuth, 1876.

UN′GER, Johann F. Brunswick, 1716-81. Said to have invented the first mechanical contrivance for recording pf. playing.

Un′g(e)rader Takt (or **Takt′art**). Uneven time. (Triple time.)

Un′gestrichene Okta′ve (*G.*). The unaccented octave;
In Sol-fa absolute pitch, C₁ to B₁

Un′gestüm (*G.*). Impetuous(ly), boisterous(ly), wild(ly).

Un′gezwung′en (*G.*). Easy, natural.

UNGHER-SABATIER. (See **Unger, Caroline.**)

Un′gleich (*G.*). Unlike; unequal.
Un′gleichschwebende Temperatur′. Unequal temperament.

Un′harmo′nisch (*G.*). Inharmonious.
Un′harmo′nischer Quer′stand. False relation.

Uni (*F.*). United.

U′nichord. (*L.*, *Unichor′dum.*) (1) A monochord. (2) A *Tromba Marina* (*q.v.*).

Union des registres (*F.*). Blending the registers of the voice.

Unio'ne (*I.*). A coupler (organ, &c.).
Unio'ne del G. Org. coll' Esp. Great coupled to Swell.

Unis } (*L., Uniso'nus ; G., Unison',*
U'nison } *Ein'klang ; F., Unisson ; I.,*
   Uni'sono.) (1) The sounding of the same tone by two or more voices, instruments, or "parts".
   N.B.—Unison notes on the same staff belonging to two (or more) parts are either "interlocked" or "double stemmed."

(2) Two or more parts moving together in unison ; and by extension, two or more parts moving together in unisons or octaves—

Unison Passage:—

or

&c.

N.B.—Unison or octave passages may be varied by syncopations, rests, appoggiaturas, figures, &c.

(1)

(2)

(3) VIOLINS.   HAYDN.

VOICES.

(4)

All' uni'sono (*I.*) } At the unison ; in unison.
A l'unisson (*F.*) }
'Cel'lo col bas'so all' uni'sono (*I.*) } The 'cello to play
'Cello c. B. all' uni'sono (*I.*) } from the double bass part.

Uni'sono (*I.*) } In unison (or octaves).
Unis'onous (*E.*) }
Uni'sono al flau'to pri'mo. In unison with the 1st flute.

Unison pitch. The pitch of notes as sounded on the pf. ; also called 8 ft. pitch, and non-transposing pitch. (See **Foot-pitch**, and **Pitch**.)
Unison stops. Stops on the org., harm., &c., which sound the notes as written ; opposed to 4-ft. stops, 16-ft. stops, quints, &c.

Uni'to,-a (*I.*). United, joined.
Unitamen'te. Unitedly ; together with.
Uni'ti. United ; in unison. Used after *divisi* (*q.v.*).

Un'merk'lich. By (almost) imperceptible degrees.
Un'merk'lich bele'bend } Very gradually acceler-
Un'merk'lich dräng'end } ating.
Un'merk'lich et'was beweg'ter }

U'no (*I.*). (See **Un.**)
U'no a uno (*I.*). One by one ; one after another.

Un peu (*F.*). A little ; rather.
Un peu élargi. A little broadened.
Un peu en dehors. Rather prominent.
Un peu largement. Rather broadly.
Un peu marqué. Rather marked (accented).
Un peu modéré. (Tempo) a little "moderated" (*i.e.*, slower).
Un peu moins lent. "A little less slow ;" rather quicker.
Un peu moins vite. "A little less quick ;" rather slower.
En peu plus lent } A little slower.
En peu retenu }
En peu plus vite. A little quicker.
Un peu vif et gaiment. Rather lively (quick) and gaily.

Un po'co (*I.*) } A little ; somewhat ; rather.
Un po' (*I.*) } (See also **Poco.**)
Un pochetti'no } A very little.
Un pochis'simo }
Un poco len'to. Somewhat slow.
Un po' largamen'te. Rather broadly.
Un po'co me'no pre'sto ma pochis'simo. A little less quick—but (only a) very little.

Un po'co me'no } (See under **Poco.**)
Un po'co più }

Un'rein' (*G.*). Imperfect ; out of tune, false.
Un'reiner Ton. A false (defective) note.

Unru'hig (*G.*). "Unrestful ;" restless(ly).

Unschul'dig (*G.*). Innocent(ly).

UN'SELD, Benjamin C. American composer ; *b.* 1843.

Unsing'bar (*G.*). Unmelodious ; not singable.

Un'ter (*G.*). Under, beneath, below.
Un'terbass. Low bass ; sub-bass ; a double bass.
Un'terbrochen. Interrupted (as a cadence).
Un'ter der Stim'me. Sotto voce (*q.v.*).
Un'terdominante. The subdominant.
Un'terhalbton. The leading-note.
Un'terleitton. The dominant 7th.
Un'termediante. The submediant.
Un'tersatz. Sub-bass ; a "supporting" part.
Un'terschlag. A *Backfall* (*q.v.*).
Un'tersetzen. To pass the thumb under a finger, or one foot under the other.
Un'terstim'me. (1) An under part. (2) The lowest part.
Un'tertaste. A white key (belonging to the lower or white row).
Un'tertöne } Difference tones. (See *Acoustics*.)
Un'tertonreihe }
Un'terwerk. The lowest manual of an organ.

Un'verziert (*G.*). Unadorned, unembellished.

Unvocal. Not suitable for singing ; containing awkward and unmelodious intervals, &c.

Un'vollkommen (*G.*). Imperfect, incomplete.
Un'vollkommene Kadenz'. An imperfect cadence.

Uo'mo (*I.*). Man.
Pri'mo uo'mo. The chief male singer (of an opera. &c.).

Up-beat. (*G., Auf'takt ; F., Levé ; I., Leva'ta.*) An unaccented beat ; specially, the *last beat* of a bar.

Up-bow. (*G., Hinauf'strich ; F., Poussé ; I., Ar'co in sù.*) The stroke of a bow in the direction " from point to nut ; " marked ∨ or ∧.

Upper partials. (See **Acoustics.**)

Upright piano. (See **Pianoforte.**)

UP'TON, Emily. Pianist ; *b.* London, 1864. *Début*, 1890.

UP'TON, George Putnam. Noted writer and critic ; *b.* Boston, Mass., 1835. On the editorial staff, *Chicago Tribune*, 1861-1885.
Writings ; " Woman in Music," " Standard Operas," " Standard Oratorios," " Standard Symphonies ; " translations of Nohl's " Life of Haydn," " Life of Liszt," " Life of Wagner," &c.

UR'BAN, Christian. *B.* Elbing, 1778 ; *d.* (?).
Wrote interesting works on musical theory.

UR'BAN, Friedrich J. *B.* Berlin, 1838. Singing teacher.
Works : a text-book (" The Art of Singing"), songs, &c.

UR'BAN, Heinrich. Brother of preceding ; Berlin, 1837-1901. Violinist and noted theorist.
Works : a symphony, overtures, a vn. concerto, &c.

URBA'NI, Valentino. (See **Valentini.**)

URFEY, Thos. d'. *B.* Exeter, abt. 1649 ; *d.* London, 1723. Playwright.
Wrote several stage pieces, with songs set by Purcell and other composers.
Pub. " Wit and Mirth ; or, Pills to purge Melancholy" (4 vols., abt. 1706 ; 6 vols., 1719-20).

URHAN, Chrétien. *B.* nr. Aix-la-Chapelle, 1790 ; *d.* Paris, 1845. Organist, violinist, and player on the Viole d'amour. Violinist at the Opéra, 1816.
Produced new effects by employing a 5-stringed *violon-alto*. Wrote string quintets, pf. pieces, songs, &c.

Urh-heen. A species of Chinese fiddle.

U'RIO, Francesco A. *B.* Milan ; Monk ; maestro Church of the Twelve Apostles, Rome, abt. 1690 ; afterwards at Venice.
Wrote motets, psalms, &c. ; and a *Te Deum* (from which Handel borrowed themes used in the *Dettingen Te Deum, Saul,* and *Israel.*)

URQUHART, Thos. London vn. maker in the reign of Chas. II.

URSIL'LO, Fabio. Known as **Fabio.** Player on the archlute, Rome, 18th cent.
Wrote trios for 2 vns. and 'cello, flute sonatas, concerti grossi for archlute (and other insts.), &c.

UR'SO, Camilla (Mad. F. Luères). Distinguished violinist ; *b.* Nantes, 1842 ; *d.* 1902. She toured with great success from 1852.

UR'SPRUCH, Anton. Pianist ; pupil ·of Raff and Liszt ; *b.* Frankfort-on-Main, 1850 ; *d.* 1907. Teacher, Raff Cons., Frankfort, 1887.
Works : operas, orchestral pieces, choral works, a pf. concerto, chamber music, several pf. pieces, songs, &c.

U'scir di tuo'no (*I.*). To get out of tune.

Use (*E.*)   ⎱ (1) Musical " use ; " *i.e.,* the
U'sus (*L.*)   ⎰ rules of music. (2) The special manner of rendering Gregorian melodies in any particular place ; as the Salisbury Use, the Hereford Use, the Roman Use, &c.

u. s. f. Abbn. of *Und so fort* (*G.*). And so on ; *simile.*

Ut. (1) The 1st of Guido's syllables. (See **Guido.**) (2) Name in France of the note " C."
Cors in Ut (*F.*). Horns in C.
Ut bémol (*F.*). The note C♭.
Ut bémol majeur (*F.*). Key of C♭ major.
Ut dièse (*F.*). The note C♯.
Ut dièse mineur (*F.*). The key of C♯ minor.
Ut majeur (*F.*). C major.
Ut mineur (*F.*). C minor.

Ut (*L.*). As ; like.
Ut su'pra. As above, as before.
Glo'ria ut su'pra. The *Gloria* as before.

U'TENDAL (UTENTHAL), Alexander. Flemish contrapuntist ; *d.* Innsbruck, 1581.
Works : psalms, masses, motets, &c., and a celebrated book of *Lieder* (1574).

Ut que'ant lax'is (*L.*). (See **Guido.**)

Utricula'riæ. (See **Tibia.**)

V

V. Abbn. for *Vide, Violino, Volti, Voce.*
Va. Viola.
Vc. Violoncello.
Vla. Viola.
VV or *Vv.* Violins (Violini).

Va (*I.*). Go on ; continue.
Va crescen'do. Go on increasing the volume of tone.
Va rallentan'do. Go on decreasing the rate of speed.

VACCA'I (VACCAJ), Niccolo. Operatic composer and singing teacher ; *b.* Papal States, 1790 ; *d.* 1848. Taught in Venice, Vienna, Paris, London, &c. Prof. of Compn., Milan Cons., 1838-44.
Works : 16 operas (*Giulietta e Romeo*, 1825) ; ballets, cantatas, church music, arias, duets, &c., and an excellent " Singing Method."

Vace'to (*I.*). Quick.

Vacillan'do (*I.*) ⎫ Vacillating ; wavering,
Vacillant (*F.*) ⎬ hesitating. On stringed
Vacillan'te (*I.*) ⎭ insts. same as **Balancement, Bebung,** or **Vibrato.**

VAET, Jacques. 16th cent. Flemish contrapuntist ; *d.* Vienna, 1567. Capellmeister to Maximilian II.
Wrote motets, chansons, " Modulationes," &c.

Va'gans (*L.*). Wandering.
Quin'tus va'gans. The "wandering" fifth part in mediæval compositions, which often "wandered about" from one voice to another.

Vaghez'za (*I.*). Grace, beauty, charm.

Va'go (*I.*). Vague, indefinite, dreamy.

Val'ce (*I.*). A waltz.

VALEN'TE, Antonio. Blind Neapolitan organist. Pub. works in score, 1580.

VAL'ENTINE, Thos. Composer and writer ; *b.* 1790 ; *d.* King's Heath, Birmingham, 1878.
Edited choruses from Handel ; wrote pf. pieces, songs, &c.

VALENTI'NI, Giovanni. Contrapuntist of the Roman School ; orgt. Court Chapel, Vienna, abt. 1615.
Works : motets, madrigals, &c. (up to 10 parts) ; also chamber music for voices and insts. (1611-22).

VALENTI'NI, Giovanni. Neapolitan operatic composer.
Produced 8 operas (1779-88).

VALENTI'NI, Giuseppe. Violinist ; *b.* Florence, abt. 1690 ; *d.* after 1735.
Works : numerous symphonies, sonatas, concertos, fantasias, &c., for various combinations of stringed insts. (vn., viola, 'cello, &c.).

VALENTI'NI, Pietro F. Eminent contrapuntist ; Rome, abt. 1570-1654. Pupil of Nanini.
Works : madrigals, motets, canzonets, &c., and a number of elaborate canons (including a canon on the "Salve Regina" with 2,000 possible solutions, and another for 96 voices).

VALENTI'NI (or Valentino Urba'ni). Noted male contralto ; afterwards a high tenor. *B.* Italy ; sang in London, 1707-14.

VALENTINO, Henri J. A. J. *B.* Lille, 1785 ; *d.* 1865. Condr. Paris Grand Opéra, 1824; Opéra-Comique,1831-7. Founded the first Parisian " popular concerts of classical music," 1837.

VALET'TA, Ippolito. Assumed name of Count **Franchi-Verney.**

Valeur (*F.*). **Va'lor** (*L.*). **Valo're** (*I.*). (*G., Werth.*) (1) Valour, bravery. (2) Value ; specially " time-value," duration.

VALLE DE PAZ, Edgardo del. Composer and writer ; *b.* Alexandria, 1861.

VALLERIA, Alwina. Mrs. R. H. P. Hutchinson (*q.v.*).

VALLOT'TI, Francesco A. Celebrated theorist and orgt. ; *b.* Vercelli, 1697 ; *d.* 1780. Maestro Church of S. Antonio, Padua, 1728. Teacher of Sabbatini and Vogler.
Works : masses, motets, &c., and a work on the " Theory and Practice of Modern Music."

Valse (*F.*). **Val'zer** (*I.*). A waltz.
Valse à deux temps. A quick waltz with two steps to each measure.
Valse chantée. A waltz-song.
Valse de salon. A salon pf. piece in waltz style.

Value. (*F., Valeur ; I., Valo're.*) The time-value, or relative duration, of a note or rest. (See **Valeur.)**

Valve. (*G., Ventil'; F., Piston ; I., Val'vola, Pisto'ne.*) A device for lengthening the tube of a brass wind-inst., and lowering its pitch.
By means of valves the " gaps " in the natural series of partials (see *Acoustics*) are filled up and a complete chromatic scale is obtained.
Brass insts. are ordinarily provided with three valves. The first valve lowers any "natural" tone by a major 2nd (two semitones), the second by a semitone, the third by three semitones.
The bass euphonium has a fourth valve (for the left hand) ; and many insts. are made with an additional " transposing valve." Sax invented insts. with six valves (for greater perfection of intonation), but they did not prove a success.
The piston-valve, working "up and down" in an air-tight cylinder, is the form commonly employed in England and France. In Germany and Italy a rotary-valve is more usual. " Its manipulation is lighter than that of the piston, but it is more liable to derangement."
The valve device was invented by Claggett, 1790.
Valve-horn, Valve-trumpet, Valve-trombone, &c. A horn, trumpet, trombone, &c., provided with valves.

Vamp. To improvise an accompaniment or prelude.

VAN BIE'NE, Auguste. Cellist ; *b.* Rotterdam, 1851. Notable in " A Broken Melody."

VAN BREE, Jean B. Condr. and composer ; Amsterdam, 1801-57.

VAN BRUYCK, Carl D. Composer and writer ; *b.* Brünn, 1828 ; *d.* 1901.

VAN CLEVE, John S. Pianist, teacher, and writer ; *b.* Maysville, Kentucky, 1851.

VAN DEN EEDEN. (See **Eeden.**)

VAN DEN GHEYN. (See Gheyn.)

VANDERLIN'DEN, Carl. ⁊Conductor ; b. Dordrecht, 1839.
Works : operas, overtures, choruses, songs.

VANDERSTRAE'TEN, Edmond. Musical historian and compiler ; Oudenarde, 1826-95. Studied under Fétis.
Of his numerous historical works " The music of the Netherlands before the 19th century " (7 vols.) is a "monumental work of reference."

VAN DER STUCKEN, Frank V. B. Fredericksburg, Texas, 1858. Studied under Benoît, Antwerp, and afterwards at Leipzig. Capellmeister Breslau City Th., 1881-2 ; mus.-director " Arion," New York, 1884 ; director Cincinnati Cons., 1895.
Works : an opera (Vlasda), orchestral music part-songs, pf. pieces, numerous songs, &c.

VAN DUY'ZE, Florimond. B. Ghent, 1853. Grand Prix de Rome, Ghent Cons., 1873.
Works : an ode-symphonie, several operas, &c.

VAN DYCK, Ernest M. H. Distinguished operatic tenor ; b. Antwerp, 1861. Became famous by his singing of the part of " Parsifal," Bayreuth, 1886. Member Vienna Court Opera, 1888.

VAN HAL. (See Wanhal.)

VAN OS, Albert. Earliest known organ builder. Called " Albert the Great " at Utrecht (abt. 1120).

VAN ROOY, Anton M. J. Noted dramatic baritone ; b. Rotterdam, 1870. First London appearance, 1898. Greatest rôle, " Wotan," in Wagner's Ring.

VAN WES'TERHOUT, Niccolo. Dramatic composer ; b. (of Dutch parents) Mola di Bari, 1862 ; d. 1898.
Works : operas (Cimbelino, 1892) ; 2 symphonies, a vln. concerto, pf. pieces, songs, &c.

VAN ZANDT, Marie. Soprano ; b. New York, 1861. Début, Turin, 1879.

VANNE'O, Stefano. Monk and writer ; b. Recanati, Ancona, 1493.
Wrote a treatise on " Plain Chant, Mensural Music, and Counterpoint " (Rome, 1553).

Vaporeux,-euse (F.). Light, delicate, " vapoury."

Variamen'te (I.). Differently, variously.
Varian'te (I.) ⎱ A variant. (1) Another reading.
Variante (F.) ⎰ (2) An optional reading. (See Ossia.)

Variamen'to (I.). (1) Varied ; full of changes and variations. (2) A variation.

Varia'tion. (G., Variation'; F., Variation ; I., Variazio'ne.) A modification or embellishment of a theme.
The original Doubles were merely variations of the melodic outline by means of increasingly elaborate figuration, embellishments, &c. (e.g., Byrd's ' Carman's Whistle," Buli's "Walsingham," &c.).
The more modern "Theme (or air) with Variations " (I., Te'ma con variazio'ni) of Bach, Haydn, and Beethoven, includes also harmonic and rhythmic transformations, and there is no limit to the devices which may be employed as long as it is felt that the theme is in some way the "text" of each variation.

Varia'to (I.). Varié (F.). Varied ; with variations.
Air varié ⎱ An air with variations.
Thème varié ⎰

Vari(e)'ren (G.). To vary.
Ein The'ma vari(e)'ren. To compose variations on a theme.

VARNEY, P. J. Alphonse. Paris, 1811-79. Conductor, and composer of operettas. His son, Louis, has composed over 30 operettas, &c., since 1876 (including Les Demoiselles des Saint-Cyriens, 1898).

Varsovia'na (I.) ⎱ " Warsaw dance." A
Varsovienne (F.) ⎰ dance in 3-4 time (and moderate tempo) with the down beat of every second measure strongly accented.
It was probably invented in France in imitation of the Polish Mazurka or Redowa.

VASCONCEL'LOS, Joaquim de. Contemporary Portuguese historian ; b. abt. 1830.
Chief work : a " Biographical Dict. of Portuguese Musicians " (1870).

VASSEUR, Léon F. A. J. B. Bapaume, 1844. Orgt. Versailles Cath., 1870 ; condr. Folies-Bergère and Concerts de Paris, 1882.
Works : church music, a method for organ and harmonium, several operettas (La timbale d'argent, 1872), &c.

Vat'erländisches Lied (G.). A patriotic song.

VAUCORBEIL, Auguste E. B. Rouen, 1821 ; d. 1884. Director Paris Opéra, 1880.
Works : string quartets, a comic opera, a lyric scene (La mort de Diane), pf. pieces, songs.

Vaudeville (F.). A light comedy with dialogue, pantomime, topical songs, &c.
It originated in popular convivial or topical street songs, &c.

VAUGHAN, Thos. Tenor vocalist ; b. Norwich, 1782 ; d. 1843.

Vaut (F.). Is equal to.
La ♩ vaut la ♪ de la mesure précédente. The ♩ equals (in duration) the ♪ of the preceding bar.

VAUXHALL GARDENS. A celebrated place of public entertainment, 1660-1859.
Handel, among others, wrote music for its popular open-air concerts, and most of the greatest English singers of the period sang there.

VA'VRINECZ, Mauritius. B. Czegled, Hungary, 1858. Cathedral condr., Pesth.
Works : operas (Rosamunda, 1895) ; an oratorio, masses, orchestral works, &c.

Vc., Vcllo. Abbn. of Violoncello.

VEC'CHI(I), Orazio. Noted composer ; b. Modena, abt. 1551 ; d. 1605. Maestro Modena Cath., 1596.
Works : much church music, exquisite madrigals and canzonets ; and Amfiparnasso, an interesting musical comedy in madrigal style produced in the same year (1594) as Peri's Dafne. The chorus sings throughout.

VEC'CHI(I), Orfeo. Maestro and composer ; Milan, abt. 1540-1613.

VEC'SEY, Franz Von. Gifted violinist ; studied under Hubay and Joachim. B. Budapesth, 1893. First English tour, 1903-4.

Veemen'te (*I.*). Passionate, vehement, forcible.
Con veemen'za. With vehemence; with force.

VEIT, Wenzel H. *B.* nr. Leitmeritz, Bohemia, 1806; *d.* 1864.
Works: church music, orchl. music, chamber music, male choruses, songs.

Veiled voice. (*I.*, *Vo'ce vela'ta*; *F.*, *Voix sombrée, Voix voilée.*) A voice sounding somewhat dull or obscure.
Often the "veil" is partial. Thus Jenny Lind's middle notes were slightly veiled while the upper notes were delightfully clear and pure.

Vela'to,-a (*I.*). Veiled (see above).

Velluta'to,-a (*I.*). Velvety, smooth.

VELLU'TI, Giovanni B. The last famous male soprano; *b.* Monterone, Ancona, 1781; *d.* 1861. Sang in London, 1829.

Velo'ce (*I.*). Swift, rapid; generally applied to a passage to be performed specially fast.
Con velocità ⎫ Swiftly.
Velocemen'te ⎭
Velocissimamen'te ⎫ With the utmost rapidity;
Velocis'simo ⎭ extremely fast.

Velouté (*F.*). Smooth, velvety.

VENABLES, Leonard Chas. Condr., teacher, and writer; *b.* St. John's Wood, London, 1847. Principal South London Institute of Music since 1880.

VENATORI'NI. (See **Mysliweczek.**)

Venezia'na (*I.*). Venetian; in the Venetian style.

VENI'TE. Name familiarly given to the 95th Psalm.

VENO'SA, Prince of. (See **Gesualdo.**)

Ventages (*G.*, *Ton'löcher*). Holes in wind instruments to be covered by the fingers or by keys.

Ven'til. (1) A valve (*q.v.*). (2) An arrangement on some organs by which a combination of stops can be "shut off" or "brought on."
Ventil'horn (G). A valve horn.
Ventil'hornett (G.). A *cornet à pistons* (the ordinary cornet of a brass band).
Ventil'posaune (G.). A valve trombone.

Venti'le (*I.*). A ventil.

VEN'TO, Ivo de. Spanish composer; orgt. Munich Court Chapel.
Works: motets, masses, lieder, &c. (1569-91).

VEN'TO, Mattia. *B.* Naples, 1739; *d.* London, 1777.
Works: 6 operas, 6 string trios, 36 pf. trios, 12 canzonets, &c.

VENTUREL'LI, Vincenzo. Mantua, 1851-1895.
Wrote 2 operas and several songs.

Venu'sto (*I.*). Elegant, graceful, beautiful.

VENZA'NO, Luigi. 'Cellist; *b.* Genoa, abt. 1814; *d.* 1878.
Works: stage pieces, solfeggi, pf. music, and many fine songs.

Vêpres (*F.*). Vespers (*q.v.*).

VERACI'NI, Antonio. Violinist at Florence.
Published sonatas for 2 vns. and bass (1692-6).

VERACI'NI, Francesco M. Noted violinist; nephew of A. *B.* Florence, abt. 1685; *d.* abt. 1750. Soloist Italian Opera, London, 1715-17; afterwards at Dresden and Prague.
Works: 24 violin-sonatas with bass, &c.

Verän'derungen (*G.*). Variations; modifications. (See **Variation.**)

Verbal Expression. The natural expression of the words of a piece. (See **Adaptation of Hymns and Tunes.**)
As a rule, the musical expression should suit the *general sentiment* rather than the *separate words* of the text. (See, however, *Word-painting.*)

Verbin'dung (*G.*). Connection, combination; slurring, binding.
Verbin'dungsakkord. A connecting chord.
Verbin'dungszeich'en. A *Tie* (*q.v.*); a slur.

Verdeckt' (*G.*). "Decked;" covered, concealed.
Verdeck'te Quint'en. Hidden fifths.

VERDELOT (or **VERDELOT'TO**), **Philippe.** Noted Belgian madrigal composer; singer, St. Mark's, Venice; resided in Florence 1530-40; *d.* before 1567.
Works: madrigals, motets, cantiones sacræ, &c. (1536-66).

VER'DI, F. Giuseppe F. One of the greatest of Italian opera composers; *b.* Le Roncole, nr. Busseto, Parma, Oct. 9, 1813; *d.* Milan, Jan. 27, 1901. Son of an innkeeper and grocer; trained by the village orgt., whom he succeeded at the age of 10. Refused admission to Milan Cons., 1831, "on the score of lack of musical talent." Studied under Lavigna, cembalist, La Scala Th., Milan. Condr. and orgt., Busseto, 1833. The operas, *Oberto* (performed at La Scala, 1839), *Nabucco* (or *Nebuchadnezzar*, 1842), and *I Lombardi* (1843), established his fame as a composer; and these were followed by a long series of successful works. Verdi was created "Marchese di Busseto," 1893, by the King of Italy. "He was the master and the moulder of Italian musical thought for half a century."
Works: abt. 30 operas (including *Ernani*, 1844; *Rigoletto*, 1851; *Il Trovatore*, 1853; *La Traviata*, 1853; *Un Ballo in Maschera*, 1859; *La Forza del Destino*, 1862; *Aida*, 1871; *Otello*, 1887; *Falstaff*, 1893); also a fine Requiem Mass, some church music, instrumental pieces, 2 books of romances, &c.

VER'DI, Giuseppina (*née* **Streppo'ni**). Operatic soprano; 2nd wife of Verdi (1840); *b.* Lodi, 1815; *d.* 1897. Début, Trieste, 1835.

VERDONCK', Cornelius. *B.* Turnhout, Belgium, 1564; *d.* 1625.
Works: a Magnificat, madrigals, French chansons, &c.

Verdop'pelt (*G.*). Doubled.
Verdop'pelung. Doubling.

Vereng'ung (*G.*). Diminution (of time-value, or interval).

Verein' (*G.*). Society, association.
Gesang'verein. Choral society.
Musik'verein. Musical society.

VERE-SA'PIO, Clémentine. Brilliant soprano; *b.* Paris. *Début*, Florence, at 16.
Has toured successfully in Italy, France, Spain, Berlin, London, United States, &c.

Vergel'len (*G.*). To diminish gradually.

Verget'te (*I.*)
Verghet'ta (*I.*) } The stem, or tail of a note.

Verglie'dern (*G.*). To articulate.

Vergnügt' (*G.*). Cheerful ; pleasant(ly).

Vergrös'serung (*G.*). Augmentation (of a fugue subject, &c.).

Verhal'len (*G.*). To die away.
Verhal'lend. Dying away ; *morendo.*

Verhält'niss (*G.*). Ratio, proportion (of intervals, &c.).

VERHULST, Johannes J. H. Condr. and organizer ; The Hague, 1816-91. Pupil of Mendelssohn, Leipzig, 1838 ; Royal Mus.-director, The Hague, 1842. Intimate friend of Schumann.
Works : orchl. music, 7 festival cantatas, church music, choruses, songs, &c.

Ver'ilay (*E.*). **Virelai** (*F.*). A vaudeville (*q.v.*).

Veris'mo (*I.*). Truth ; naturalism.
Veris'tisch (*G.*). Naturalistic.

Verkeh'rung (*G.*). Inverse imitation. (See **Imitation.**)

Verklei'nerung (*G.*). Diminution (of a theme).

Verkling'end (*G.*). Dying away.

Verkür'zung (*G.*). Drawing closer together ; *stretto.*

Verläng'erungs-zeich'en (*G.*). The dot of prolongation placed after a note.

Ver'lauf (*G.*). Progress.
Im Ver'lauf beweg'tes Tem'po. More animated *Tempo* during the course (of the piece).

Verliebt' (*G.*). Loving, tender.

Verlie'rend (*G.*). Dying away.

Verlö'schend (*G.*). Dying away ; extinguishing.

Vermin'dert (*G.*). Diminished.
Vermin'derter Drei'klang. A diminished triad.
Vermin'derte Quin'te. Diminished 5th.
Vermin'derte Terz. Diminished 3rd.

Vermit'telungssatz (*G.*). "A middle piece ; " an episode.

VERNE, Mathilde. (See **M. J. A. Wurm.**)

Vernehm'lich (*G.*). Clear, distinct.

VERNHAM, John Ed. Vocal teacher, writer, and composer ; *b.* Lewes, 1854.

VERNIER, Jean-Aimé. *B.* Paris, 1769 ; *d.* 1838(?). Harpist Opéra-Comique, 1795 ; Grand Opéra, 1813-38.
Works : sonatas, fantasias, &c., for harp ; and numerous pieces for harp with other insts.

VERNON, Jos. Male soprano, then tenor ; *b.* Coventry, abt. 1738 ; *d.* S. Lambeth, 1782.

VERO'VIO, Simone. First copper-plate mus. printer ; worked at Rome, abt. 1586-1604.

Vers (*G.*). Verse, couplet, stanza, strophe.

Verschal'len (*G.*). To cease to sound ; to die away.

Verschie'bung (*G.*). A "shifting pedal ; " the soft pedal of a Grand pf. ; hence the soft pedal generally.
Mit Verschie'bung. With the soft pedal ; *una corda.*
Oh'ne Verschie'bung. Without the soft pedal ; *tre corde.*

Verschie'den (*G.*). Various, several.
Die verschie'denen Stim'men ab'wechselnd. The various voices alternating.

Verschmel'zen (*G.*). To blend.
Die Tö'ne verschmel'zen. To blend the notes.

Verschwin'dend (*G.*). Vanishing ; dying away.

Verse. (1) Poetry. (2) Properly a "line" of poetry ; in hymns, &c., now applied to a "stanza." (3) In an anthem or service, any portion sung by solo voices.
Verse-anthem. One *beginning* with solo voices (verse).
Verse-service. A service for solo voices.

Verset (*E.* and *F.*)
Verset'te (*G.*)
Verset'to (*I.*) } (1) A versicle (*q.v.*). (2) A short prelude or interlude for the organ.

Verset'zen (*G.*). To transpose.
Verset'zung. Transposition.
Verset'zungs-zeich'en. A chromatic sign (♮, ♯, ♭, &c.).

Ver'sicle
Ver'sikel (*G.*) } "A little verse." A verse recited by the priest or minister, with a response for the congregation.
Versicle.—" O Lord, open Thou our lips."
Response.—"And our mouth shall show forth Thy praise."

Versila're (*L.*). To sing antiphonally.

Ver'si sciol'ti (*I.*). Blank verse(s).

Ver'so (*I.*). (1) A verse or stanza. (2) An air, tune, melody.
Ver'so ero'ico. Heroic verse.
Ver'so sciol'to. Blank verse.

Verspä'tung (*G.*). Retardation.

Verstär'ken (*G.*). To reinforce ; *rinforzando.*
Verstärkt'. Sforzando.

Verstim'men (*G.*). To put out of tune.
Verstimmt'. Depressed ; out of tune.
Verstimm'tes Klavier'. A pf. out of tune.

VERSTOV'SKI. (See **Werstowski.**)

Ver'te (*L.*)
Verta'tur (*L.*) } Turn (over). Same as **Volti.**
Ver'te su'bito. Turn (the leaf) immediately.

Vert(h)eilt' (*G.*). Divided, distributed.

Vertical slur. Name for the old arpeggio sign—

Verto'nen (*G.*). To compose.

Vertö'nen (*G.*). To die away.

Verträumt' (*G.*). Dreamy.

Verve (*F.*). Spirit, energy, animation, go.

Verwandt' (*G.*).   Related ; relative.
Verwand'te Ton'arten. Related keys.
Verwandt'schaft. Relationship ; affinity.

Verwech's(e)lung (*G.*).   Exchange;   interchange ; inversion.
Die enharmo'nische Verwech's(e)lung.   Enharmonic
change (of a note, chord, &c.). (See *Enharmonic*.)

Verwei'lend (*G.*).   Delaying, retarding.

Verwer'fung (*G.*).   Transposing.

Verzie'rende Vor'schlag (*G.*).   An ornamental
appoggiatura ; *i.e.*, an appoggiatura
with some additional grace note (or
notes).

BIZET, *Carmen.*

(a)

CHOPIN.

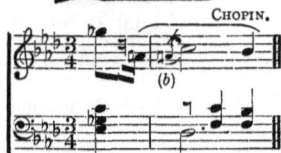

(b)

CHOPIN.

(c)

CHOPIN.

(d)

(a) Acciaccatura to the appoggiatura.
(b) Acciaccatura to principal note.
(c) Turn (inverted).
(d) Chordal note, written like an acciaccatura.

Verziert' (*G.*).   Ornamented, embellished.
Verzie'rung. Ornamentation.
Verzie'rungen. Embellishments.
Verzie'rungsnote. A grace-note.

Verzö'gerung (*G.*).   Retardation.

Verzwei'felt (*G.*).   Despairing,   broken-
hearted, despondent, desperate.
Verzwei'flungsvoll. Full of despair ; desperately.

Vesper(s).   (*G.*, *Ve'sper ; F., Vêpres ;
I., Ve'spro, Ve'spero.*) (1) Even-song.
(2) The 6th of the canonical hours.
Vesperti'ni Psal'mi (I.). Evening psalms.

VESQUE VON PUTT'LINGEN, Johann.
Pianist and operatic composer ; *b.*
Opole, Poland, 1803 ; *d.* Vienna, 1883.

VES'TRIS, Lucia E. Contralto singer and
actress ; *b.* London, 1797 ; *d.* 1856.
Noted (as MADAME VESTRIS) for her beauty and
her charming acting and singing.

Vezzo'so,-a (*I.*).   Graceful, elegant, sweet.
Vezzosamen'te. Gracefully, tenderly, softly.

Vi'a (*I.*).   Away, off.
Via sordi'ni. Take off the mutes.

VIADA'NA, Ludovico da.   (Real name
Ludovico Grossi.) Noted contrapuntist;
b. Viadana, nr. Mantua, 1564 ; *d.* 1645.
Maestro Mantua Cath., 1594-1609, and
again, 1644.
Works : canzonets, madrigals, masses, psalms,
vespers, " Falsi bordoni," motets, magnificats,
litanies, &c.
He is commonly credited with the invention of a
" continued bass," although Peri's *Euridice*
(1600) contains earlier examples. He was,
however, the first composer to write pieces for
one (or more) voices with an obbligato bass for
the organ (in his church concertos, 1602).
They are unfigured.

VIANE'SI, Auguste C. L. F.   *B.* Leghorn,
1837. Condr. Drury Lane, 1859 ;
afterwards for 12 years at Covent
Garden. *Chef d'orchestre* Paris Grand
Opéra, 1887 ; operatic condr. New
York, 1891-2.

VIAN'NA da MOT'TA, José.   Portuguese
pianist ; *b.* I. of St. Thomas, Africa,
1868.

VIARD-LOUIS (*née* **Martin**), **Jenny.** Pianist;
b. Carcassonne, 1831 ; *d.* 1903.

VIARDOT-GARCIA, M. F. Pauline. Famous
dramatic mezzo-soprano and wonderful
actress ; daughter of **Manuel del Popolo
Garcia** (*q.v.*) ; *b.* Paris, 1821 ; Concert
début, Brussels, 1837 ; operatic *début*,
London, 1839 ; married M. Viardot,
1841. After triumphant tours, retired
1863. Among her pupils were Desirée
Artot and Antoinette Sterling.
Works : 3 operas, 60 vocal melodies, a Vocal
Method, &c. Her voice was of extraordinary
compass—from

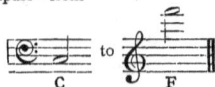

C   to   F

Four children are well-known musicians ;
(1) **Louise Héritte-Viardot.**   *B.* Paris,
1841. Singing teacher Hoch Cons.,
Frankfort, for some years (till 1886).
Est. a vocal school at Berlin.
(2) **Chamerot-Viardot** } Fine concert
(3) **Marianne-Viardot** } singers.
(4) **Paul Viardot.** *B.* Courtavent, 1857.
Violinist ; pupil of Léonard.

Vibran'te (*I.*).   Vibrating.   (1) Ringing,
resonant. (2) Agitated, tremulous.

Vibra'te (*I.*).   Vibrant, ringing, sonorous,
strong.

Vibra'tion   }
Vibration (*F.*)   } (*G., Schwing'ung.*) (See
Vibrazio'ne (*I.*)   }   **Acoustics.**)

Vibra'to (*I.*).   (1) On bowed insts., a wavering effect obtained by " trembling " the
finger on a string. (2) In singing, a

tremulous undulating effect expressive of extreme emotion.

N.B.—In singing, the vibrato, if used occasionally for special effect, is an admirable means of expression; used constantly on every note it is *detestable* from every point of view. In solo playing on bowed insts. it is nearly always of good effect on long notes.

(3) The term **Vibra′to,-a**, is also used to indicate **Sforzando** (*q.v.*).

N.B.—Elgar, *Sym. in A♭*, Op. 55, applies the term to trumpets, bass drum, and cymbals.

Vi′brator. A free reed (of a harmonium, &c.).

Vibrer (*F.*). **Vibri(e)′ren** (*G.*). To vibrate.

Mehr vibrie′ren las′sen als tremolie′ren (*G.*). Rather a *vibrato* than a *tremolo*.

Vicar choral. A lay vicar of a cathedral choir.

Vicen′da (*I.*). Change, alternation.

Vicende′vole. Changeable; vacillating; alternating.

VICENTI′NO, Nicola. *B.* Vicenza, 1511; *d.* abt. 1576. Pupil of Willaert; maestro at Ferrara and Rome.

Attempted to revive Greek music, and " paved the way for the monodic style." (See *Bardi.*)

Vici′no (*I.*). Near, neighbouring.

VICTORIA. (See **Vittoria.**)

VIDAL, Louis A. 'Cellist and writer; *b.* Rouen, 1820; *d.* 1891.

Published an interesting work on " Bowed Insts., their Makers and Players, and their European History; with a General Catalogue of Chamber Music " (3 vols., 120 illustrative plates).

VIDAL, Paul A. *B.* Toulouse, 1863. *Grand Prix de Rome,* Paris Cons., 1881. *Chef d'orchestre* Grand Opéra, 1896.

Works: ballets, operettas, pantomimes, orchl. pieces, choral works, &c.

Vide (*F.*) ⎫ ⎬ Open, empty.
Vi′do (*I.*) ⎭

Corde à vide. An open string (violin, &c.).
Corde à jouer. A string to be "stopped" (by the finger).

Vi′de (*L.*). See; as *Vi′de p.* 56—"see page 56."

Vi′de se′quens. " See the following " (passage, page, &c.).

Vi′del (*G.*). Fiddle.

Viel (*G.*). Much, great, strong.

Mit vie′lem Nach′druck. With great emphasis.
Viel beweg′ter. Much quicker.
Viel′chörig. For divided choirs; for several choruses.
Viel′facher Kon′trapunkt. Counterpoint in several parts.
Viel gemes′senere Bewe′gung als zu An′fang. Much more measured movement (slower) than at the beginning.
Viel lang′samer. Much slower.
Viel ruh′iger. Much more tranquil.
Viel′stimmig. Polyphonic (*q.v.*).
Viel Ton. " Much tone ; " vigorously, sonorously.

Vièle (*F.*) ⎫
Vielle (*F.*) ⎬ (1) A hurdy-gurdy. (2) A
Viel′la (*I.*) ⎭ viol.

Vielle à roue. A hurdy-gurdy.

Vier (*G.*). Four.

Vier′ach′teltakt. 4-8 time.
Vier′doppelter Kon′trapunkt. Quadruple counterpoint (*q.v.*).
Vier′fach. " Four-ranked " (See *Fach.*)
Vier′füssig. 4-foot (of stops or pitch).

Vier′gesang. A song for 4 voices (or parts).
Vier′gestrichen. Stroked, or accented, four times, as C″″.
Vier′händig. For 4 hands.
Vier′klang. A chord of 4 notes ; as a Dom. 7th, &c.
Vier′saitig. Four-stringed.
Vier′spiel. A 4-part piece ; a quartet.
Vier′stimmig. For 4 voices or insts ; in 4 parts.
Vier′stück. An instrumental quartet.
Vier′taktig. Four-bar rhythm.
Vier′tel ⎫
Vier′telnote ⎬ A quarter-note, or crotchet (♩).
Vier′telpause. A crotchet rest.
Vier′vier′teltakt. 4-4 time.
Vier′zwei′teltakt. 4-2 time.

VIER′DANK, Johann. Orgt. at Stralsund.

Published dance pieces, &c., for strings and basso-continuo (1641), and sacred concertos (1642-3).

VIER′LING, Georg. *B.* Frankenthal, Palatinate, 1820 ; *d.* 1901. Orgt. Frankfort - on - Oder, 1847 ; condr. Mayence " Liedertafel," 1852 ; settled in Berlin, 1853.

Works : oratorios, psalms, orchl. pieces, chamber music, fine *a cappella* choruses, organ pieces, pf. pieces, &c.

VIER′LING, Johann G. Organist ; *b.* nr. Meiningen, 1750 ; *d.* 1813. Studied under C. P. E. Bach and Kirnberger.

Works : numerous organ pieces ; a work on " Generalbass," a choralbuch, chamber music, pf. sonatas, &c.

Vier′te (*G.*). A fourth.

Vier′tel schlag′en (*G.*). Beat crotchets.

Vier′telton (*G.*). A quarter tone.

Durch Vier′teltöne fort′schreitend. Proceeding by quartertones : enharmonic.

Vier′zehn (*G.*). Fourteen.

Vier′zehnte. (Interval of) a fourteenth.

Vieta′to (*I.*). Forbidden, prohibited.

Interval′li vieta′ti. Forbidden intervals (in melody).

VIEUXTEMPS, Henri. Famous violinist ; *b.* Verviers, 1820 ; *d.* 1881. Taught by his father and Lecloux ; made a concert tour at 8. Studied under De Bériot, Brussels, 1829-30. Spent most of his life in touring : London (1834), Paris (1835), Vienna (1837), Russia (1838-9), Antwerp (1840), Paris and London (1841), America (1844-5), &c. Solo violinist to the Czar, and Prof. St. Petersburg Cons. 1846-52 ; Prof. Brussels Cons., 1871-3. " He stood with De Bériot at the head of the modern French school of vn. playing."

Works : 6 concertos, and several other works for violin and orchestra ; brilliant duos for vn. and pf., vn. solos (caprices, concert-studies, fantasias, &c.), 2'cello concertos, orchl. pieces.

VIEUXTEMPS, Jean J. L. Pianist ; brother of H. ; *b.* Verviers, 1828 ; *d.* 1901.

VIEUXTEMPS, Jules J. E. 'Cellist ; brother of H. ; *b.* Brussels, 1832 ; *d.* 1896.

For several years 'cellist at the Italian Opera, London, and in Hallé's orch., Manchester.

Vif (*F.*) ⎫ ⎬ Lively, brisk, animated.
Vive (*F.*) ⎭

VIGIER, Comtesse. ("Cruvelli.") (**Sophie C. Cruwell.**) Soprano ; *b.* Bielefeld, 1826; *d.* 1907.

Vigorosamen'te (*I.*) ⎫
Vigoro'so (*I.*)   ⎬ Energetically, vigor-
Con vigo're (*I.*)   ⎭ ously.

Vigue'la ⎱ Ancient form of the Spanish
Vihue'la ⎰ guitar.

Vigueur (*F.*). Vigour.
Avec vigueur. Vigorously.

VILBAC(K), A. C. Renaud de. *B.* Montpellier, 1829 ; *d.* 1884. Won *Grand Prix de Rome*, Paris Cons., 1844 ; orgt. St. Eugène, Paris, 1856.
Works : 2 comic operas, a pf. method, and numerous graceful pf. pieces.

VIL'DA, Maria. Stage name of **M. Wilt** (*q.v.*).

VILLAFIORI'TA, Giuseppe B. di. Operatic composer ; *b.* Palermo, 1845 ; *d.* 1902.

Villageois, Villageoise (*F.*). Rustic.

Villanci'co (*S.*) ⎱ A kind of anthem sung at
Villan'cio (*S.*)   ⎰ Spanish church festivals.

Villanel'la (*I.*) ⎱ A 16th century Italian
Villanelle (*F.*) ⎰ folk-song, allied to the madrigal, but in rustic or humorous style. Also a dance with song, of similar character.

Villanes'co (*I.*). Rustic, rural.

VILLA'NIS, Luigi A. Writer and critic ; *b.* nr. Turin, 1863. Prof. of Musical Æsthetics and History, Turin Univ., 1890.
His writings include " The Leit-motiv in Modern Music " (1891).

Villarec'cio (*I.*). Rustic, rural.

VILLARO'SA, C. de Rosa, Marchesi di. Naples, 1762-1847.
Works : a " Dictionary of the Musical Composers in the Kingdom of Naples," and a " Biography of Pergolesi."

VILLEBOIS, Constantin P. Song composer ; Warsaw, 1817-82.

VIL'LOING, Alexander. *B.* St. Petersburg ; *d.* there 1878. Pf. teacher of A. and N. Rubinstein.
Works : a " Practical Piano School," a pf. concerto, &c.

Villo'ta (*I.*). A Venetian folk-song.

VILLOTEAU, Guillaume A. *B.* Bellême, Orne, 1759 ; *d.* 1839.
Accompanied Napoleon to Egypt, and published 4 valuable " Dissertations " on ancient and modern Egyptian and Oriental music and musical insts.

Villot'te (*I.*). Old name for secular harmonized pieces.

Vi'na. An ancient Hindu viol.
The body consists of a section of bamboo, with a gourd at each end for resonance. There are 4 melody strings (with 18 movable frets), and 3 sympathetic strings.

Vina'ta, Vinet'ta (*I.*) ⎱ A vintage song, a
Vinet'te (*G.*)   ⎰ drinking song.

VINCENT, Alexandre J. H. Mathematician ; *B.* Hesdin, 1797 ; *d.* 1868.
Investigator of ancient Greek and Latin music ; held that the Greeks used chords.

VINCENT, Chas. John. *B.* Houghton-le-Spring, Durham, 1852. Chorister Durham Cath. ; Mus.Doc. Oxon, 1885 ; orgt. Christ Ch., Hampstead, 1883-91. Joint-editor *Organist and Choirmaster ;* managing director Vincent Mus. Pub. Company, Berners St., London.
Works : cantatas, organ pieces, songs, text-books.

VINCENT, Heinrich J. Tenor singer, condr., and composer ; *b.* nr. Würzburg, 1819 ; *d.* 1901.
Works : operas, operettas, songs, theoretical treatises, &c.

VIN'CI, Leonardo. *B.* Strongoli, Calabria, 1690 ; *d.* 1732. Maestro Royal Chapel, Naples.
Works : 25 operas (*Ifigenia in Tauride*, 1725 ; *Astianatte*, 1725) ; 2 oratorios ; cantatas, motets, masses, songs, &c.

VIN'CI, Pietro. *B.* Nicosia, Sicily, 1540 ; *d.* (?). Maestro Bergamo Cath.
Works : motets, masses, 10 vols. of madrigals, &c.

VINER, Wm. L. Orgt. and composer of hymn-tunes ; *b.* Bath, 1790 ; *d.* U.S., 1867.

Vinet'ten (*G.*). Vintage songs ; drinking songs.

VINING, Helen S. *B.* Brooklyn, N.Y., 1855. Author of a pf. primer, text-books, &c.

VINNING, Louisa. Soprano vocalist ; *b.* Kingsbridge, Devon, 1836.

VINNING, Rosetta (Mrs. O'Leary). Composer ; *b.* Newton Abbott, 18—.

Vi'ol. (*G.*, *Vio'le ; F.*, *Viole ; I.*, *Vio'la.*) A very ancient type of bowed instrument, the immediate precursor of the violin.
The viol had from 5 to 8 strings (the usual number being 6), and a fretted fingerboard. The belly was usually, and the back *always*, flat—thus essentially differing from the modern violin family.
The bridge was but slightly arched, and chord playing was therefore very easy. Viols and lutes were the principal stringed instruments of mediæval orchestras. The tuning of the 4 chief varieties was as follows :—
(1) Vio'la al'ta ; Treble viol :—

(2) Vio'la teno're ; alto or tenor viol :—

(3) Vio'la bas'sa ; bass viol :—

(4) Violo'ne ; contrabass viol. Tuned like the bass viol, but sounding an octave lower.

VIO'LA, Alfonso della. Maestro at Ferrara. Wrote some of the earliest-known " Pastorals " (1541-63). They were in madrigal style, with dialogue sung by the chorus.

VIO'LA, Francesco. Pupil of Willaert ; maestro at Ferrara.

Published 2 books of madrigals (1567, 1573).

Vio'la (*I.*). (1) The larger form of violin, called in England the *Tenor* and in France the *Alto.*

Music for the viola is generally written with the alto clef. It plays the 3rd part in the string quartet, and its 4 strings are tuned as follows, sounding exactly an octave higher than those of the violoncello :—

C   G   D   A

Vio'la (*I.*). (2) A viol (*q.v.*).

Vio'la al'ta. (1) (See *Viol.*) (2) A large form of orchestral viola.

Vio'la bastar'da. A larger form of *Viola da gamba.* (See below.)

Vio'la da brac'cio (*G., Bra'tsche*). "Arm-viol ; " practically the same as the present viola (1).

Vio'la da gam'ba. "Leg-viol." The bass-viol. (See *Viol.*)

Vio'la d'amo're (*F., Viole d'amour*). A tenor viol with 6 or 7 wire strings, and a tender sweet tone.

Vio'la da spal'la. "Shoulder-viol ; " an enlarged *Vio'la da brac'cio* (see above).

Vio'la di bordo'ne, or *Barytone.* A viol resembling the *viola da gamba,* with 6 or 7 gut strings, and a number of sympathetic metal strings. Haydn wrote many pieces for it.

Vio'la pompo'sa, or *Violoncel'lo pic'colo.* An inst. with 5 strings, midway between a tenor and a 'cello, invented by J. S. Bach.

VIO'LE, Rudolf. Pianist ; pupil of Liszt ; *b.* Schochwitz, 1815 ; *d.* 1867.

Works : 11 pf. sonatas, 100 pf. studies, characteristic pf. pieces, &c.

Vio'le (*G.*). Viol (*q.v.*).

Viole (*F.*). The ordinary viola. (Formerly, a viol.)

Viole d'amour. (See *Viola d'amo're.*)

Vio'len (*G.*). Modern plur. of (the ordinary) viola.

Violent (*F.*). Violent, impetuous.

Violentemen'te (*I.*). Violently, impetuously.

Violen'to. Violent.

Con violen'za. With violence.

Violet, or English violet. The Viola d'amore (*q.v.*).

Violet'ta (*I.*). A small viol.

Violet'ta mari'na. A form of viol invented by P. Castrucci. Handel wrote solos for it in *Orlando* and *Sosarme.*

Violette (*F.*). A small viola.

Violin'. (*G., Violi'ne ; F., Violon ; I., Violi'no.* "The King of the orchestra." The ordinary tuning of its 4 strings is as follows —

G   D   A   E

The most remote ancestor of the violin yet discovered is the Ravanastron, said to have been invented in Ceylon about 5,000 B.C., and still in use in India and China. Later developments of the Ravanastron were the Rebab of the Arabs and Persians (which became the European Rebeck of the Middle Ages), and the Breton Crwth (Crout, Rota, Lyra, &c.), and the various forms of Lute and Viol (*q.v.*).

The following are among the most noted makers of violins, those marked * being specially celebrated :—

Gasparo da Salo, Andrea Amati, *Nicolo Amati, Andrea Guarnerius, *Joseph Guarnerius, *A. Stradivarius, C. Begonzi, *G. Guadagnini, C. Landolfi, *Jacob Stainer, *Sebastian Klotz, Medard, Lupot, and Vuillaume.

The violin "bow" has been perfected through the efforts of Corelli, Vivaldi, Tartini, and Tourte.

French violin clef. The G clef on the first line.

Violin'bogen (*G.*). A violin bow.

Violin clef. The ordinary G (or treble) clef.

Violin diapason. An organ diapason of "stringy" tone.

Violin'concert (*G.*) } A violin concerto.
Violin'konzert (*G.*) }

Violin'schlüssel (*G.*). Treble clef.

Violin'stimme (*G.*). A violin part.

Violin'zeichen (*G.*). The treble clef.

Violi'na. A string-toned organ stop, generally of 4 ft. pitch.

Violina'ta (*I.*). (1) A piece for vn. (2) A piece imitating the vn.

Violincel'lo. An old spelling of Violoncello.

Violinette. (1) A kit (*q.v.*). (2) A violino piccolo (*q.v.*).

Violi'no (*I.*). A violin.

Violi'no di fer'ro. A nail-fiddle (*q.v.*).

Violi'no pic'colo. A small vn. tuned a 4th higher than the ordinary vn.

Violi'no pompo'so. (See *Viola pomposa.*)

Violi'no pri'mo. Vn. 1mo. First violin.

Violi'no principa'le. The principal vn. ; the leader of an orchestra, the solo violinist in a concerto.

Violi'no ripie'no. (See *Ripieno.*)

Violi'no secon'do. Vn. 2do. Second violin.

Violi'ni (*I.*). Violins.

Violi'ni uni'soni. The violins in unison.

Violin'schlüssel (*G.*). Violin clef ; *i.e.*, G clef—

Violi'sta (*I.*) }
Violiste (*F.*) } Player on a viol or viola.
Violier (*F.*) }

Violon (*F.*). (1) A violin. (2) A string-toned org. stop, generally of 8 ft. pitch.

Violon' (*G.*). A double-bass.

Violonar (*F.*). A double-bass.

Violona'ro. An octo-bass (*q.v.*).

Violoncel'lo (*I.*). (*G., Violoncell' ; F., Violoncelle.*) Abbns., *'Cello, 'cllo.* The bass of the ordinary string quartet.

The violoncello in its present form dates from the latter half of the 16th cent. Its 4 strings are tuned as follows, an octave below those of the viola :—

C   G   D   A

In modern scores the lowest string is sometimes tuned down to B, a semitone lower.

The tenor clef is often used for the higher notes, and sometimes (for very high notes) the treble clef.

Violoncelli'sta. A 'cellist.

Violoncello pic'colo. Same as *Viola pomposa* (*q.v.*).

Violo'ne (*I.*) ⎫ (1) (See **Viol.**) (2) An organ
Violo'no (*I.*) ⎭ stop of string-toned
quality, of 16 ft. (or 8 ft.) pitch, and
generally on the pedal.

Violoniste (*F.*). Violinist.

Viols, Chest of. (See **Chest of viols.**)

VIOT'TA, Henri. *B.* Amsterdam, 1848;
director The Hague Cons., 1896.
Editor *Maandblad voor Muziek.*

VIOT'TI, Giovanni Battista. Distinguished
violinist; *b.* Fontaneto da Pò, Italy,
May, 1753; *d.* Mar. 1824. Son of a
blacksmith; learned to play the vn.
without tuition; placed by the Prince
of Cisterna under the care of Pugnani,
Turin (where he soon joined the Court
orchestra). Started continental tours,
1780; visited London, 1782. After
operatic and other ventures in Paris,
resumed touring, 1791. Finally settled
in Paris; director of the Opéra, 1819-22.
Died in London "while on a pleasure
trip." He has been called the "father
of modern violin playing." His most
famous pupils were Rode and Baillot.
    Works : 29 vn. concertos, 21 string quartets, 21
    trios, 51 vn. duos, &c.

VIR'DUNG, Sebastian. Orgt. and priest at
Basle.
    Wrote an interesting work in Organ, Lute, and
    Flute tablature (1511).

Virelay (*F.*). A vaudeville (*q.v.*).

Vir'ga. One of the signs in Neum notation.
(See **Neum.**)

Virgil Practice Clavier. A "toneless" pf.,
invented by A. K. Virgil, New York,
1883.
    It is a superior kind of "dumb piano." By the
    help of audible "clicks" all kinds of touch are
    attainable (with mechanical precision) from
    staccatissimo to *legato*; and the "weight" of
    the touch can be regulated from 2 to 20 ounces.

Vir'ginal(s), or **Pair of Virginals.** A small
kind of harpsichord (*q.v.*).

Vir'gula. Same as **Virga** (*q.v.*).

Virtuos'. (*G.*; Fem., *Virtuo'sin.*) (1) A
virtuoso (*q.v.*). (2) Possessing the
qualities of virtuosity.
Violin'virtuos. A virtuoso on the violin.
Virtuo'senhaft ⎫ Virtuosity.
Virtuo'sität ⎭

Virtuose de pupitre (*F.*). "A virtuoso
of the (conductor's) desk;" a conductor
of unusual merit and fame.

Virtuo'so,-a (*I.*; Plur. *Virtuo'si,-e*). A
finished performer (player or singer).

Vis-à-vis (*F.*). A harpsichord or pf., with
2 keyboards opposite one another.

VISET'TI, Alberto A. *B.* Spalato, Dalmatia,
1846. Studied Milan Cons., 1855-65.
Afterwards settled in London as teacher
of singing.
    Works : "Hist. of the Art of Singing," &c.

Vi'sta (*I.*). Sight.
A vi'sta. At sight.
A pri'ma vi'sta. At first sight.

Vistamen'te (*I.*) ⎫ Briskly, with animation.
Vi'sto (*I.*) ⎭

VITA'LI, Filippo. Noted 17th cent. composer. *B.* Florence; singer Papal
Chapel, Rome, from 1631.
    Works : madrigals, hymns, motets, "Musiche,"
    psalms, &c.

VITA'LI, Giovanni B. *B.* Cremona, abt.
1644; *d.* 1690. Asst. maestro, Modena,
1674. One of the most noted of instl.
composers before Corelli.
    Works : dance music, sonatas for 2 vns. and bass,
    chamber-sonatas for 4 to 6 insts., and numerous
    other instrumental compositions.

Vitamen'te (*I.*). With life; rapidly.

Vite (*F.*). Quick, lively.
Vitement. With life, quickness, &c.
Vitesse. Swiftness, celerity, rapidity.

VITRY, Philippe de. (*Lat.* **Philippus di
Vitriaco.**) *B.* Vitry; *d.* as Bishop of
Meaux, 1316.
    Wrote an early work on "mensurable music."
    He is said to have introduced *red* notes, and to
    have invented the term "contrapunctus" (in
    place of the earlier "discantus"). (See *Counter-
    point* and *Discant.*)

VITTO'RI, Loreto. *B.* Spoleto, abt. 1588;
d. Rome, 1670. Member of the Papal
Chapel, 1622.
    Works : arias, a "dramma in musica" (*La Galatea*,
    1639), &c.

VITTO'RIA, Tomaso Ludovico da. (**Thomas
Luis de Victoria.**) Eminent contra-
puntist; friend of Palestrina; *b.*
Avila, Spain, abt. 1540; *d.* abt. 1608.
Vice-maestro, Royal Chapel, Madrid,
1589-1602.
    Works : masses, psalms, magnificats, motets, &c.,
    many of them in 8 and 12 parts. Also a famous
    6-part "Requiem for the Empress Maria," 1605.

Vitula (*L.*). A viol.

Viva'ce (*I.*). Animated, bright, lively.
(Generally, "quicker than *Allegro.*").
Con vivace'za ⎫
Con vivacità ⎪ Vivaciously, quickly; with life.
Vivacemen'te ⎪
Vivamen'te ⎭
Vivacissimamen'te. With the utmost life and rapidity.
Vivacis'simo. Very lively and quick.
Vivacet'to. Rather lively; quick, but not quite
    vivace.
Viva'ce scherzo'so. Quickly and playfully.

VIVAL'DI, Abbate Antonio. Noted violinist;
b. Venice, abt. 1675; *d.* 1743. Director
Cons. dell Pietà, Venice, from 1713.
    Works : 28 operas, 12 trios for 2 vns. and 'cello,
    18 vn. sonatas, and nearly 70 "concerti" for
    various insts. (chiefly strings), some of which
    are still prized.

Vive (*F.*) ⎫ Lively, brisk, animated.
Viven'te (*I.*) ⎭
Con vives'za (*I.*). With life; animated.
Vivement (*F.*). Same as *Vivace* (*q.v.*).

Vi'vido, Vi'vo (*I.*). Full of life; spirited,
quick, brisk.
Vivis'simo. Very spirited.

VIVIER, Eugene L. Remarkable horn-
player; *b.* Ajaccio, 1821; *d.* 1900.
    He is said to have been "able to produce three
    or four notes at once ;" but "always refused
    to tell how he produced them."
    Wrote some fine songs.

VLEES'HOUWER, Albert de. *B.* Antwerp, 1863. Pupil of Blockx.
Works : operas, symphonic pieces, &c.

Vn., Vnᵒ. Abbns. of *Violin, Violino.*

Vocal. Pertaining to the voice ; adapted for singing.
Vocal cords. The two ligaments in the larynx which, by their vibration, produce vocal tone. (See *Voice.*) N.B.—Sometimes spelt "Chords."
Vocal glottis. (*L., Ri'ma voca'lis.*) The slit between the vocal cords.
Vocal ligaments. The vocal cords (*q.v.*).
Vocal organs. The larynx with the vocal cords, &c. (See *Voice.*)
Vocal music. Music for a voice or voices.
Vocal register. (See *Voice.*)
Vocal score. (See *Score.*)

Voca'le (*I.***).** Vocal.
Vocalez'zo. A vocal exercise.

Voca'lion. A variety of the harmonium.

Vocalisation ⎱ Specially, the art of singing
Vocalization ⎰ prolonged vowel sounds. (Used also for singing in general.)
Vocaliser (F.). To sing on the vowel sounds.
Vocalises (F.). Vocal exercises ; especially exercises on vowel sounds, and solfeggi.

Vocalizza're (*I.***).** Same as **Vocaliser** (*q.v.*).

Vocaliz'zi (*I.***).** Same as **Vocalises** (*q.v.*).

Vo'ce (*I.***).** Voice ; part.

Vo'ces (*L.***).** Voices. Plural of **Vox** (*q.v.*).

Vo'ci (*I.***).** Voices ; parts .
Vo'ce ange'lica. (See *Vox angelica.*)
Vo'ce bian'ca. A "white" voice ; a child's or woman's voice, or the tone of an inst. of similar quality.
Vo'ce buo'na. A good voice (clear, sonorous, flexible, &c.).
Vo'ce catti'va. A bad voice (weak, throaty, nasal, &c.).
Vo'ce di ca'mera. A " chamber " voice of small volume, suitable for a chamber concert rather than a concert hall.
Vo'ce di go'la. A "throaty" or guttural voice.
Vo'ce di pet'to. The chest voice.
Vo'ce di ripie'no. (See *Ripieno.*)
Vo'ce di te'sta. Head voice.
Vo'ce grani'ta. A full, powerful voice.
Vo'ce pasto'sa. A soft, full, flexible voice.
Vo'ce principa'le. A leading voice or part.
Vo'ce so'la. The voice alone, unaccompanied.
Vo'ce spicca'ta. A clear, well-enunciated voice.
Vo'ce uma'na. (See *Vox humana.*)
Vociac'cia. A bad disagreeable voice.
A du'e vo'ci. For two voices or parts.
A tre vo'ci. For three voices or parts.
Co'lla vo'ce. With the voice. (See under *Colla.*)
Mes'sa di vo'ce. (See under *Messa.*)
Mez'za vo'ce. With half the power of the voice ; *mf* in singing (or playing).
Sot'to vo'ce. Beneath the voice ; in an undertone ; softly.

VOCK'ERODT, Gottfried. *B.* Thuringia, 1665 ; *d.* 1727. Rector Gotha Gymnasium.
Wrote several works intended to show that "excessive enjoyment of music injures the intellect."

VO'GEL, Dr. A. Bernhard. *B.* Plauen, Saxony, 1847 ; *d.* 1898.
Works : choruses, sacred songs, pf. pieces, and interesting monographs on Wagner, Brahms, Liszt, Schumann, &c.

VO'GEL, C. L. Adolphe. *B.* Lille, 1808 ; *d.* 1892. Studied Paris Cons.
Works : symphonies, church music, chamber music, pf. pieces, and several successful operas. (*La filleule du roi,* 1875).

VO'GEL, Dr. Emil. *B.* Wriezen-on-Oder, 1859. Librarian, Peters' Musical Library, Leipzig, 1893.
Works : useful musical catalogues, a monograph on Monteverde, &c.

VO'GEL, Friedrich W. F. Noted organist ; *b.* Havelburg, 1807.
Works : 2 operettas, a concertino for org. and trombones, choruses, orch. pieces, org. pieces.

VO'GEL, Johann C. *B.* Nuremberg, 1756 ; *d.* Paris, 1788.
Works : 2 operas, 3 symphonies, a bassoon concerto, 3 clar. concertos, much chamber music, &c.

VO'GEL, W. Moritz. Pianist, condr., and critic ; *b.* Sorgau, 1846. Studied Leipzig Cons.
Works : a pf. method (in 12 parts), instructive pf. pieces, songs, &c.

Vo'gel (*G.***).** A bird.
Vo'gelflöte ⎱ A " bird-flute," or bird-call. (A
Vo'gelpfeife ⎰ *Vogelflöte* is used in Mozart's opera *The Magic Flute.*)
Vo'gelgesang ⎱ (*L., Mer'ula.*) (1) A set of small pipes
Vo'gelsang ⎰ standing in water, producing a warbling bird-like tone when blown. (2) A "bird-stop" in an organ.

VO'GELSANG, Andreas. (See **Ornithoparcus.**)

VOG'GENHUBER, Wilma von. Operatic soprano ; *b.* Pesth, 1845 ; *d.* 1888. *Début*, Pesth, 1862. Married **F. Krolop,** 1868.

VOGL, Heinrich. Operatic tenor ; *b.* Au, Munich, 1845 ; *d.* 1900. *Début*, Munich, 1865. Member Munich Court Opera. Specially famous as a "Wagner" singer. Composed an opera, *Die Fremdlinge,* 1899.
His wife, **Therese** (*née* **Thoma**), is a fine operatic soprano ; *b.* Tutzing, 1845. Also a distinguished "Wagner" interpreter ; married H., 1868.

VOGL, Johann M. Tenor singer ; friend of Schubert ; *b.* Steyr, 1768 ; *d.* Vienna, 1840.
He "introduced Schubert's songs to the public."

VO'GLER, Georg Jos. (known as **Abbé** or **Abt Vogler**). Orgt. and theorist ; *b.* Würzburg, 1749 ; *d.* 1814. Pupil of Padre Martini and Vallotti. Took Holy Orders at Rome ; afterwards apptd. Court Chaplain and 2nd capellmeister at Mannheim ; founded the "Mannheimer Tonschule." Court condr., Stockholm, 1786-99. Obtained a 16 ft. organ-tone by combining an 8 ft. pipe with a " quint " (see **Acoustics**), and travelled extensively as an "improver of organs." Court capellmeister, Darmstadt, 1807 ; founded a " Tonschule" (in which Weber and Meyerbeer were pupils). His theories of harmony—founded largely on a semitonic scale—found little favour at the time (Mozart, in particular, opposing them), but they have been largely adopted in modern practice. He had gigantic hands, "stretching 2 octaves." Works: operas, ballets, much church music, orchl. pieces, a pf. concerto, an org. concerto, chamber music, &c., and numerous treatises exemplifying his special theories.

Vo′glia (*I.*). Ardour, longing, desire.

VO′GRICH, Max W. C. Pianist and "poet composer;" *b.* Transylvania, 1852. Played in public at 7; studied Leipzig Cons., 1866-9. After long tours, settled in New York, 1886.
Works: operas, an oratorio, cantatas, 2 symphonies, a vn. concerto (played by Wilhelmj), a pf. concerto, pf. pieces, songs, &c.

VOGT, A. G. Gustave. Noted oboe-player; *b.* Strasburg, 1781; *d.* Paris, 1879. Studied Paris Cons.; 1st oboist Opéra-Comique; Opéra, 1814-34; Cons. concerts, 1828-44. Prof. of oboe at the Cons.
Wrote 4 concertos and other music for oboe, &c.

VOGT, Johann. Pianist; *b.* nr. Liegnitz, 1823; *d.* 1888. Teacher of pf. St. Petersburg, 1850-5; after long tours, lived chiefly in Dresden and Berlin.
Works: an oratorio (*Lazarus*), chamber music, instructive pf. pieces.

Voice. (*L., Vox; G., Stim′me (Sing′-stim′me); F., Voix; I., Vo′ce.*) Sound produced in the larynx and shaped by the mouth, &c. (1) A voice-part in music. (2) By extension, any "part" in a musical score; thus, *Fugue for 3 voices*, a Fugue for 3 distinct parts (whether vocal or instrumental).
The voice is produced in the larynx (Adam's apple) by the vibration of two small ligaments called the "vocal cords." It is shaped into vowel sounds by the form of the mouth; the "checks" caused by tongue, teeth, lips, &c., give consonants. In singing, the sounds are maintained at a fixed pitch for definite periods of time; in ordinary speech the pitch is constantly changing by minute intervals or "inflections." Other vocal sounds, such as sneezing, clearing the throat, &c., fall under the category of "noises." The ordinary range of human voices is shown under *Compass of Voices* (*q.v.*). The extent of exceptional voices ranges from the low A♭ sung by Russian double-bass voices to the high C of Agujari (*q.v.*)—a total compass of over 5 octaves.

The names of the various "Registers" of the voice are a subject of dispute. Some teachers classify them as "chest notes," "head notes," and "falsetto;" others as "thick," "thin," "small," and "falsetto."
The voices of the greatest sopranos and contraltos all gave evidence of early development, *e.g.*—
ALBERTAZZI: *début* at 15.
ALBONI: greatest contralto of the 19th cent.; voice already formed at the age of 8.
ANNE CATLEY: sang from the age of 10; one of the "leading English singers" from 17.
BILLINGTON, Mrs.: *début* at 14.
BRENT, CATHERINE: *début* in Dublin at 15.
CATALANI: brilliant voice "up to G in altissimo" at 12.
COLBRAN: a highly-promising voice at 6.

CINTHIE-DAMOREAU: gave concerts at 14.
FODOR-MAINVILLE: *début* at 14.
C. GABRIELLI: voice well-formed at 14.
DORUS-GRAS: *début* at 14.
FAUSTINA HASSE: "a great singer at 16."
F. LEBRUN: *début* at 15.
LINLEY, Miss: soloist, Worcester Festival, at 16.
PAULINE LUCCA: sang in public "as a mere child."
MALIBRAN: sang in public at 5.
MARA: "a clear and resonant voice" at 10.
JENNY LIND: showed signs of an exceptional voice at 3.
CHRISTINE NILSSON: beautiful voice "from a child."
CLARA NOVELLO: established oratorio soloist at 15.
PAREPA-ROSA: *début* at 16.
PATTI: *prima donna* at 16.
PASTA: *début* at 15.
RONZI: an established favourite at 16.
SCHRODER-DEVRIENT: brilliant *début* at 16.
SONTAG: *prima donna* at 15.
ANN STORACE: oratorio *début* at 11.
TIETJENS: *début* about 15.
This overwhelming evidence disposes of the contention of some modern teachers that "all girls' voices are mezzo-soprano to the age of 15."

Voice-building ⎱ The training and de-
Voice-production ⎰ velopment of the voice.
"More humbug has been written about voice-production than any subject under heaven except patent medicines."—*American paper.*
There is no royal road to the acquisition of a beautiful voice, and no "secret method" of voice-training known only to "quacks." The broad lines of vocal development—subject to variation in special cases—are well-known to all reputable singing teachers. They may be briefly summarized as follows: (1) Control of breathing; (2) Pose of body; (3) Proper position of the head, mouth, tongue, lips, teeth, &c.; (4) Attack and production of long evenly-sustained tones on the various vowel sounds; (5) Proper practice of scales, slow and quick; (6) *Messa di voce* (*q.v.*); (7) Solfeggi, and similar exercises to promote flexibility of voice. To these should be added correct pronunciation and enunciation, expression, and style. Sometimes special exercises have to be practised for the control of the soft palate, the tongue, the avoidance of nasal tone, &c. "No system of training can make a bad voice into a good one; but every voice can be improved—some vastly—by diligent and well-directed practice."

Voice-part. (1) A vocal part. (2) Any part in a musical score. (See **Voice.**)

Voicing. Regulating the tone-quality and loudness of an organ pipe.

VOIGT, Carl. Hamburg, 1808-79.
Organized and conducted the Hamburg *Cäcilienverein.*

Voilé(e) (*F.*). Veiled.

Voix (*F.*). Voice; part.
Voix aigre. A harsh shrill voice.
Voix angélique. A Vox angelica (*q.v.*).
Voix céleste(s). An organ stop, with two rows of pipes, one slightly sharper than the other, producing an undulating effect.
Voix de poitrine. Chest voice.
Voix de tête. Head voice.
Voix éclatante. A loud piercing voice.
Voix glapissante. A shrill voice.
Voix grêle. A sharp, thin voice.
Voix humaine. (See *Vox humana.*)
Voix voilée. A veiled voice.
À deux voix. For 2 voices or parts.
À trois voix. For 3 voices or parts.
À quatre voix. For 4 voices or parts.

Vokal′ (*G.*). Vocal.
Vokal′musik. Vocal music.
Vokal′stil. In *a cappella* style. (See *A cappella.*)

Volan'te (*I.*). "Flying;" swift, light.

Vola'ta (*I.*) } (*G., Vola'te; F., Volatine.*)
Volati'na (*I.*) } A short run, trill, or other light and rapid series of notes.

VOL'BACH, Fritz. Condr. and composer; *b.* Wipperfürth, nr. Cologne, 1861.

VOLCK'MAR, Dr. Wilhelm V. Fine orgt.; *b.* nr. Cassel, 1812; *d.* 1887. Music teacher, Homberg Seminary, from 1835.
Works: several org. concertos, 20 org. sonatas, an org. symphony, an "Orgelschule," &c.

Volée (*F.*). A *Volata* (*q.v.*).

VOL'KERT, Franz. *B.* Heimersdorf, Bohemia, 1767; *d.* 1845. Capellmeister Leopoldstadt Th., Vienna, from 1821.
Works: over 100 singspiele, comic operas, &c.; church music, org. music, pf. pieces.

VOLK'LAND, Dr. Alfred. Pianist; *b.* Brunswick, 1841. Court capellmeister, Sondershausen, 1867; condr. Leipzig "Euterpe," 1869-75; condr., Basle, 1875.

VOLK'MANN, F. Robert. Noted composer; *b.* Lommatzsch, Saxony, 1815; *d.* Pesth, 1883. Greatly encouraged in his musical studies by Schumann. Lived chiefly in Pesth from 1842, in sad poverty.
Works: 2 symphonies, 2 overtures, 3 serenades for strings, a 'cello concerto, a concertstück for pf. and orch.; 6 string quartets, and much other chamber music; numerous pf. pieces (including transcriptions of songs by Mozart, Schubert, &c.); pf. pieces for 4 hands; masses and choruses for male voices; works for soli, chorus, and orch.; many songs, &c.

Volks'gesang (*G.*) }
Volks'lied (*G.*) } A folk-song; a people's
Volks'weise (*G.*) } song.
Im Volks'ton. In the style of a folk-song.
Volks'ausgabe. People's edition; popular edition.
Volks't(h)ümlich. In imitation of a folk-song; national, popular.
Volks't(h)ümliches Lied. An "art-song" in the style of a folk-song. Specially, a combination of a *Kunstlied* and a *Volkslied*; *i.e.*, an art song which becomes adopted as a folk-song.

Voll (*G.*). Full; complete.
Gedank'envoll. Full of thought; thoughtfully.
Stim'mungsvoll. Full of expression.
Vol'les Orches'ter. Full orchestra.
Vol'les Werk. Full organ.
Voll'gesang. With the full chorus.
Voll'griffig. In full chords.
Voll'kommen. Perfect, perfectly.
Voll'kommene Kadenz'. A perfect cadence.
Voll Rüh'rung. Full of emotion.
Voll Sehn'sucht. Full of yearning, longing.
Voll'stimmig. (1) In full chords. (2) For many parts. (3) Full-toned.
Voll'stimmigkeit. Fulness of tone.
Voll'tönend }
Voll'tönig } Sonorous, full-toned.

VOLL'HARDT, Emil R. Pianist and orgt.; *b.* Seifersdorf, Saxony, 1858. Condr. of singing societies, &c.

Völ'lig (*G.*). Perfect, complete; full.
In völl'iger Entrück'ung. With perfect rapture.

VOLL'WEILER, Carl. Pianist and teacher; *b.* Offenbach, 1813; *d.* 1848.
Works: pf. pieces and études, chamber music, &c.

Volonté (*F.*). Will, wish, pleasure.
A volonté. At pleasure; *ad lib.*

Vol'ta (*I.*). A turning round; a time.
Du'e vol'te. Twice.
Pri'ma vol'ta (1ma vol'ta, 1ma, 1a, or 1). The first time.
Secon'da vol'ta (IIda volta, 2da, &c.). The second time.
U'na vol'ta. Once.

Vol'ta (*I. and F.*). An old dance. (See **Lavolta.**)

Volteggian'do (*I.*). (1) Crossing hands (pf., &c.). (2) Nimbly, dexterously, "acrobatically."
Volteggia're. To cross hands; to be agile, &c.

Vol'ti (*I.*). "Turn over" (the leaf).
Vol'ti presto }
Vol'ti su'bito (or *V.S.*) } Turn over immediately.

Volubilmen'te (*I.*). Volubly, fluently; flippantly.

VOLUMIER, J. Baptiste. *B.* Spain, 1677; *d.* Dresden, 1728. Violinist and condr.

Vol'untary. An organ solo before, after, or during a religious service.
The term is occasionally used for an opening choral piece.

Volu'ta (*I.*), **Volute** (*F.*). Scroll (of a vn, &c.)

Vom (*G.*). From the.
Vom An'fang. From the beginning; *Da capo.*
Vom An'fang oh'ne Wie'derholung bis zum Schluss. From the beginning to the end without repetition.
Vom Blat'te. "From the page;" at sight.
Vom Zei'chen. From the sign; *Dal segno.*

Von (*G.*). From, by, of, &c.
Von An'fang. From the beginning.
Von hier ab im Zeit'mass. From here, in strict time.
Von hier an Al'la Bre've taktie'ren. From here beat two in a bar.
Von hier an nicht mehr schlep'pen. Do not slacken the time any more from here.

VON'DERHEI'DE, J. F. *B.* Cincinnati, 1857. Public singer and violinist at 10; Director, New York Cons., 1885-91.

VOOR'ZANGER, Haideé. Precocious violinist; pupil of Wilhelmj; *b.* Holland, 1896(?). London *début*, 1907.

VOPE'LIUS, Gottfried. *B.* nr. Zittau, 1645; *d.* 1715. Cantor Nicolaikirche, Leipzig.
Published a "Neues Leipziger Gesangbuch," 1682. Some of his chorals are still in use.

Vor (*G.*). Before, in front of; for; with; more than; above.
Vor'angehend. Foregoing, preceding.
Voraus'nahme. (1) Anticipation (*q.v.*). (2) Preparation (of a discord).
Vor'bereiten. To prepare.
Vor'bereitete Dissonanz'. A prepared discord.
Vor'bereitung. Preparation (of a discord, &c.).
Vor'dersatz. First subject or theme (of a sonata, &c.).
Vor'geiger. Leading violinist; leader.
Vor'greifung }
Vor'griff } Anticipation (*q.v.*).
Vor'her }
Vor'igen } Before, previous(ly); as before.
Tem'po wie vor'her. Tempo as before.
Vor'hergehend. Preceding, foregoing, previous.
𝅘𝅥=𝅘𝅥𝅭 *des Vor'hergehenden.* The crotchet equals the previous dotted minim.
Vor'heriges Zeit'mass. The preceding *tempo.*
Vor'sänger. Leading singer; precentor.
Vor'setzzeichen }
Vor setzungszeichen } A chromatic sign (before a note).
Vor'spiel. Overture, introduction, prelude; opening symphony of a song.
Vor'spieler. A principal performer (on any inst.).
Vor'tänzer. Leader of a dance.
Vor'zeichnung. (1) A signature. (2) The outline of a work.

VO'RETZSCH, J. Felix. Pianist and condr. ; *b.* Altkirchen, 1835.

Vor'halt (*G.*). A suspension (*q.v.*) ; a syncopation (*q.v.*).

Vor'haltslösung. The resolution of a suspension.

Vorhan'den (*G.*). Occuring, appearing.

Ist in der erst'en Aus'gabe nicht vorhan'den. This (note, passage, &c.) does not appear in the 1st setting (edition, arrangement).

Vor'her (*G.*). (See under **Vor.**)

Die ♩ *wie vor'her die* ♩ The crotchet to be equal to the preceding minim.

Vor'ig (*G.*). Previous, before, preceding.

Des vor'igen Zeit'mass ♩ = ♩ A crotchet equals a minim of the preceding *tempo.*
Vor'iges Zeit'mass. The original time ; *tempo primo.*

Vor'schlag (*G.*). " A fore-stroke." An appoggiatura (*q.v.*) ; a grace-note.

Lang'er Vor'schlag. Long appoggiatura.
Kur'zer Vor'schlag. Short appoggiatura.
Vor'schläge so schnell als mö'glich. The grace-notes as short as possible.

Vor'trag (*G.*). The "bringing forward" or presentation of a thing ; diction, delivery, interpretation, execution, rendering, style.

Vor'tragsbezeichnung) Expression mark, *tempo* mark,
Vor'tragszeichen ƒ or other musical sign.
Vor'tragsstück. A concert piece ; a show piece.

Vor'wärts (*G.*). Forward(s) ; *stringendo.*

Et'was vor'wärts ge'hend. Rather faster.

Vor'zutragen (*G.*). Brought out, made prominent.

Ton vor'zutragen. Bring out the tone.

VOSS, Charles. Pianist ; *b.* nr. Demmin, Pomerania, 1815 ; *d.* 1882. Studied Berlin ; lived chiefly in Paris from 1846.

Works : numerous brilliant salon pf. pieces, " together with other pf. music of a higher order."

VOSS, or **VOS'SIUS, Gerhard J.** *B.* Heidelberg, 1577 ; *d.* 1649.

Published a treatise on the " Art and Science of Music," 1650-8.

Vo'to (*I.*). Same as **Vuoto** (*q.v.*).

Vowels.

In singing, the vowels are of paramount importance ; they are "the bearers of the tone" which is formed on them. Consonants act as "checks" on the vowel sounds, "defining their attack and release."

Vox (*L.;* plur. *Vo'ces*). A voice.

Vox acu'ta. A high voice.
Vox ange'lica. " Angelic voice." A sweet-toned org. stop ; formerly a reed stop, now more usually a variety of the *Voix Célestes* (*q.v.*).
Vox antece'dens. The antecedent (of a canon, &c.).
Vox con'sequens. The consequent (of a canon, &c.).
Vox gra'vis. A deep voice.
Vox huma'na. " Human voice." An 8 ft. organ reed stop with short tubes, which has a fancied resemblance to a human voice.
Vox virgi'nea. " Girlish voice." Same as *Vox angelica.*
Vo'ces æqua'les. Equal voices.
Vo'ces Areti'næ. Guido's syllables. (See *Guido.*)
Tres vo'ces. Three voices ; three parts.

VROYE, Théodore J. de. *B.* Belgium, 1804 ; *d.* Liége, 1873.

Learned writer on Plain-song.

V. S. Abbn. of *Volti subito.*

Vue (*F.*). Sight, view.

A première vue. At first sight.

Vuide (*F.*). Open ; empty.

Corde vuide. An open string (vn., &c.).

VUILLAUME, Jean Baptiste. Eminent violin maker ; *b.* Mirecourt, Vosges, 1798 ; *d.* Paris, 1879. Learnt the trade from his father, **Claude Vuillaume** (*d.* 1834). Entered into partnership with Lété, Paris, 1825 ; worked alone after Lété's retirement, 1828. Became famous through his fine "imitations" of "Stradivarius" and "Duiffoprugger" violins and 'celli. Invented the octobasse, 1851. He also perfected the construction of the "Tourte" bow, and introduced many improvements in the manufacture of strings, &c.

VUL'PIUS, Melchior. *B.* Wasungen, abt. 1560 ; *d.* 1616. Cantor at Weimar.

Wrote much church music ("Cantiones sacræ," church "Lieder," &c.).

Vuo'to,-a (*I.*). Open ; empty.

Cor'da vuo'ta. An open string (vn., &c.).

W

W. Used occasionally for VV., *Violini.*

WACH, Karl G. W. Double-bass player ; *b.* Löbau, 1755 ; *d.* Leipzig, 1833.

WACHS, Paul. Pianist ; *b.* Paris 1851. Won 1st prize for org. playing, Paris Cons., 1872.
Works : popular salon pf. pieces.

Wach'send (*G.*). Crescendo (*q.v.*).

Wacht am Rhein, Die. "The Watch on the Rhine." A German national song. (See **National Songs.**)

Wach'tel (*G.*). (1) A quail. (2) A toy inst. imitating a quail.

WACH'TEL, Theodor. Eminent operatic tenor ; *b.* Hamburg, 1823 ; *d.* 1893. Son of a livery stable keeper. First London appearance, 1862. Member Berlin Royal Opera, 1865.

WACH'TER, Ernst. Wagnerian bass ; *b.* Mühlhausen, 1872.

WACK'ERNAGEL, Philipp. Historian ; *b.* Berlin, 1800 ; *d.* 1877.
Wrote works on German church melodies.

WADE, John A. Composer of stage pieces, songs, &c. ; *b.* Dublin, 1796(?) ; *d.* London, 1845.

WADE, James C. Orgt. and composer ; *b.* Coven (Staffs.), 1847.

WAELPUT, Hendrick. Condr. and composer ; Ghent, 1845-85. Won *Prix de Rome*, Brussels Cons.
Works : 4 symphonies, cantatas, songs, &c.

WAELRANT, Hubert. Distinguished contrapuntist ; *b.* Tongerloo, Brabant, abt. 1517 ; *d.* Antwerp, 1595. Pupil of Willaert ; founded a music school, Antwerp, 1547. Introduced a system of Solmisation on the syllables *bo ce di ga lo ma ni* (called "Bocedisation").
Works : motets, chansons, madrigals, &c.

WA'GENSEIL, Georg C. Vienna, 1715-77. Pupil of Fux.
Works : operas, harpsichord concertos, 18 divertimenti for cembalo ; several "symphonies" for 2 harps, 2 vns., and 'cello, &c.

WA'GENSEIL, Johann C. *B.* Nuremberg, 1633 ; *d.* 1708.
Wrote a work containing interesting information on the German Meistersingers (1697).

WAG'NER, Christian S., and **Johann G.** Brothers ; famous 18th cent. harpsichord makers at Dresden.
They made over 800 insts., including one with 3 pedals (1774), and another with 3 keyboards (1786).

WAG'NER, Ernst D. *B.* Pomerania, 1806 ; *d.* 1883. Pupil of A. W. Bach. Orgt. and music-director at Berlin.
Works :/ an oratorio, church music, org. pieces, pf. pieces, songs, &c.

WAG'NER, Gotthard. Benedictine monk ; *b.* Erding, 1697 ; *d.* 1739.
Published sacred solos with inst. accompt.

WAG'NER, Johann and **Michael.** Brothers ; 18th cent. organ builders.
Built the great organ at Arnheim (47 stops).

WAG'NER (or **JACH'MANN - WAG'NER), Johanna.** Niece of Wm. Richard (below) ; operatic soprano ; *b.* nr. Hanover, 1828 ; *d.* 1894. Leading soprano, Dresden, 1844 ; created the part of "Elizabeth" (*Tannhäuser*), 1845 ; member Court Opera, Berlin, 1850-62. Married Judge Jachmann, 1859.

WAG'NER, Karl J. Condr. and noted horn player ; Darmstadt, 1772-1822. Pupil of Abbé Vogler.
Works : 6 operas, 2 symphonies, overtures, cantatas, 40 horn duos, chamber music, &c.

WAG'NER, Wm. Richard. Great dramatic composer ; *b.* Leipzig, May 22, 1813 ; *d.* Venice, Feb. 13, 1883. (His father died when Rd. was 6 months old. His mother soon after married L. Geyer, ar actor, and the family removed t[Dresden.) Attended the Dresden Kreuzschule till 1827 ; good Greek scholar ; wrote a "grand tragedy in Shakesperian style" at 14 ; showed no special aptitude for music. Entered the Nikolai Gymnasium, Leipzig, 1827 ; studied Logier's "Thoroughbass ;" had a few lessons from Gottlieb Müller ; in 1830 studied composition under Theodor Weinlig, cantor of the Thomasschule. A thorough study of Beethoven's symphonies induced him to write a symphony in C major (prod. Gewandhaus, Leipzig, 1833). Began his professional musical career as chorusmaster, Würzburg Th., 1833. Condr. Magdeburg Th., 1834 ; Königsberg Th., 1836. Married the actress **Wilhelmine Planer,** 1836 (separated 1861). Condr. Riga Opera, 1837-9. While at Riga, wrote the libretto (and the music of the first two acts) of *Rienzi,* his first important work. Visited Paris (1839) with the hope of rivalling Meyerbeer. Unable to get a hearing for *Rienzi,* "he found himself in dire straits," and had to support himself by song-writing, arranging dance music, writing articles for musical journals, &c. In the meantime he made sketches for *Der fliegende Holländer* ("The Flying Dutchman"). Visited Dresden, 1842, and superintended the production of *Rienzi,* which was followed by the *Flying Dutchman,* 1843 ; condr. of the Dresden Opera, 1843-49. *Tannhäuser* (finished 1844, and prod. 1845) "aroused the most strenuous opposition," but gradually made its way to the chief German theatres. Among noted musicians who recognized Wagner's genius were Liszt—afterwards his foremost champion—Schumann, and Spohr. *Lohengrin* was finished in 1848, but only a portion of it was performed. An incautiously expressed sympathy with the revolutionary party led to his banishment, 1849, and, aided by Liszt, he fled to Paris, and thence to Zurich. Here he devoted himself to composition and the writing of elaborate treatises explaining his views of music and the drama and defending himself from the attacks of "prejudice, malice, and ignorance." Visited London and conducted 8 Philharmonic concerts, 1855. Afterwards visited Venice and Paris (where *Tannhäuser* was hissed, and completely failed, at the Grand Opéra, 1861). Amnestied, and returned to Germany, 1861. *Tristan,* after 57 rehearsals at the Vienna Court Opera, was "given up as impracticable." After "many failures and desperate efforts," King Ludwig II of Bavaria invited him to Munich, 1864. Retired to Lake Lucerne, 1865, and completed his later great "music-dramas." Through King Ludwig's patronage and the efforts of his friends (including the various German "Wagner Societies" which had gradually been established), the "dream of his life" was accomplished by the opening of the "ideal Wagner Theatre" at Bayreuth, Aug., 1876. The last years of his life were occupied with literary work and the composition of *Parsifal.* (In 1870 he married Cosima, daughter of Liszt, who had been divorced by Von Bülow.)

Although Wagner wrote orchestral and choral works, pf. pieces, arrangements, songs, &c. his claim to rank as a great musician rests on his operas and music-dramas. The following are the most important :—

Rienzi, composed 1838-40, produced Dresden, 1842; *Der Fliegende Holländer* ("The Flying Dutchman"), comp. 1841, prod. Dresden, 1843; *Tannhäuser,* comp. 1843-5, prod. Dresden, 1845; *Lohengrin,* comp. 1845-8, prod. Weimar, 1850; *Das Rheingold* (Part I of *Der Ring*) comp. 1848-53, prod. Munich, 1869; *Die Walküre* (Part II of *Der Ring*), comp. 1848-56, prod. Munich, 1870; *Tristan und Isolde,* comp. 1857-9, prod. Munich, 1865; *Siegfried* (Part III of *Der Ring*), comp. 1857-69, prod. Bayreuth, 1876; *Die Meistersinger,* comp. 1861-7, prod. Munich, 1868; *Götterdämmerung* (Part IV of *Der Ring*), comp. 1870-4, prod. Bayreuth, 1876; *Parsifal,* comp. 1876-82, prod. Bayreuth, 1882. Some arithmetical genius has discovered that the full score of the *Ring* contains 984,043 printed notes.

N.B.—*Die Feen,* his first opera (1833), was first performed in 1888, and is still occasionally given in Germany.

No composer has ever been the centre of such a storm of criticism and controversy as Richard Wagner. What was thought of him in England 50 years ago may be gathered from the article on **Criticism** (in this work). A Berlin critic asserted that if all the organ grinders in Berlin were shut in a circus and started grinding, each a different tune, the result would be less horrible than *Die Meistersinger.*

' Among the choice expressions applied to the *Ring* were ' musical slime,' 'seasick harmonies,' 'rancid music,' 'murderous harmonies,' 'paroxysms of musical nervousness,' ' delirium tremens in music,' 'hell noise,' 'pestiferous ranting in tone,' 'dog music,' 'tonal bleatings,' and 'epidemic of harmonic insanity.' Let us hope, at any rate, that none of these exquisite phrases were coined in London."—*Daily Telegraph.*

Wagner's theories, reduced to a sentence, were "that music, poetry, painting, sculpture, and architecture had run their course as separate arts, and that the art-work of the future was to be a combination of them," and all his great music-dramas are constructed on this basis. He made each personality characteristic by means of "leading motives" (see **Leit-motif**) "the very framework of his music-dramas ;" he wrote his own libretti; he largely discarded regular formal melodies for the voice in favour of "a melodious declamation or speech-song ;" in richness, variety, and novelty, his orchestration is unique; in the field of harmony and modulation he was "an innovator of unprecedented originality;" he fused and moulded all his dramatic work with the utmost genius and "an extraordinary abundance of ideas."

"Wagner is the most commanding figure in the modern music-world," and "has cast his spell on every succeeding writer for the stage."—*H. T. Finch.* Dr. Theo. Baker calls him "the grandest and most original dramatic composer of all times."

WAG′NER, Siegfried. Condr. and composer; son of preceding; b. Triebschen, 1869.

Wahn′sinnig (*G.*). Furious, frantic.

WAINWRIGHT, John. B. Stockport, abt. 1723; d. 1768. Orgt. Manchester Collegiate Ch., 1767.
Composed the well-known tune to "Christians, awake."

WAINWRIGHT, Richard. Son of J.; 1758-1825.
Wrote "Life's a bumper," and other glees, &c.

WAINWRIGHT, Robert. Son of J.; 1748-82. Orgt. Manchester Collegiate Ch., 1768; Mus.Doc. Oxon, 1774.
Wrote church music, hymn tunes, &c.

WAIS′SEL (or WAISSE′LIUS), Matthias. 16th cent. lutenist; b. Bartenstein, Prussia.
Published works in lute tablature.

Walts, Waytes, Wayghtes, &c. Originally street watchmen; later, town musicians, itinerant bands, &c.

"Christmas Waits" are still common in some parts of England. William Gibbons, father of Orlando Gibbons, was one of the Waits of Cambridge, a body of men of some importance centuries ago, who flourished particularly in the Eastern Counties. There is to this day a house in Norwich known as the "Waytes House," from which were taken to the Indies by Sir Walter Raleigh two or three performers, presumably to amuse him on board ship. The waits played upon hautboys during the night, and acted originally, as their name implies, as watchmen. John Ravenscroft and Thomas Farmer, Mus.Bac. Cantab. (1684) began their musical life as waits.

WAKEFIELD, Augusta M. *B.* Kendal, 1853. Promoted local festivals.
Composer of songs (" No, sir ; yes, sir," &c.).

WAL'CKER, Eberhard F. Noted organ builder ; *b.* Kannstadt, 1794 ; *d.* 1872.
The firm (now in the hands of his sons) has built more than 400 organs.

Wald (*G.*). A forest, a wood.
Wald'flöte (G.) ⎫ (*L.*, *Tib'ia silve'stris.*) An org. flute
Wald'flute (E.) ⎬ stop of full suave tone, generally
Wald'pfeife (G.) ⎭ of 4 ft. pitch.
Wald'horn (G.). (1) A hunting horn. (2) The " natural " French horn without valves.
Wald'quinte (G.) ⎫ An org. stop similar to the
Wald'flötenquinte (G.) ⎬ *Waldflöte*, but a 5th higher in pitch.

WALD'AUER, August. *B.* 1825 ; *d.* St. Louis, Missouri, 1900.
Founder and director, Beethoven Cons., St. Louis.

WALDECK, J. E. Pen-name of **J. Williams** (*q.v.*).

WAL'DERSEE, Paul, Count von. *B.* Potsdam, 1831.
Assisted in editing Breitkopf & Härtel's complete editions of Mozart and Beethoven.

Wald'stein sonata. Beethoven's pf. sonata in C, Op. 53, dedicated to Count Waldstein (1762-1823), one of Beethoven's earliest friends.

WALD'TEUFEL, Emil. Composer of popular waltzes, &c. ; *b.* Strasburg, 1837.

WALENN. Family of talented musicians.
(1) **Arthur.** Baritone vocalist ; *b.* London, abt. 1867 (?).
(2) **Charles.** Baritone vocalist ; *b.* 1869.
(3) **Herbert.** 'Cellist ; *b.* 1870.
(4) **Gerald.** Violinist ; *b.* 1872.
(5) **Dorothea.** Violinist and teacher ; *b.* London.

WALKER, Augustus H. Composer and teacher ; *b.* London, 1855. Mus.Doc. London, 1886.

WALKER, Edyth. Operatic soprano ; *b.* New York. Studied Dresden. Sang Vienna Court Opera (as contralto), 1899-1903 ; Covent Garden, 1908.

WALKER, Ernest. *B.* Bombay, 1870. Mus.Doc. Oxon, 1898. Orgt. Balliol Coll. Author of " A Hist. of Eng. Music," 1907.

WALKER, Frederick E. *B.* Marylebone, 1835. Vicar-choral, St. Paul's, 1858 ; master of the boys, 1867 ; Prof. of singing, R.A.M. and G.S.M.

WALKER, Joseph C. *B.* Dublin, 1760 ; *d.* 1810.
Wrote "Historical Memoirs of the Irish bards," &c.

WALKER, Thomas. Composer, alto vocalist, and teacher ; *b.* London, 1764 ; *d.* 1827.
Wrote anthems, hymn tunes, songs, &c.

WALKÜ'RE, Die. The 2nd part of Wagner's *Ring des Nibelungen ;* 1st performance, Munich, 1870.

WALLACE, Lady Maxwell (*née* **Grace Stein**). *B.* Edinburgh, abt. 1815 ; *d.* 1878.
Trans. the Letters of Mendelssohn, of Mozart, of Beethoven, &c. ; wrote " Reminiscences of Mendelssohn."

WALLACE, William. Composer; *b.* Greenock, 1860.

WALLACE, William Vincent. Composer ; *b.* Waterford, 1814; *d.* France, 1865. Toured most of his life from 1835 as concert giver in Australia, India, Sth America, Mexico, United States, &c. Produced his *Maritana* in London, 1845 ; from 1853 lived chiefly in London and Paris.
Works : 6 operas (*Maritana*, 1845 ; *Lurline*, 1860). Also numerous popular pf. pieces.

WALLASCHEK, Rd. Lecturer at Lemberg Univ.
Author of " Aesthetik der Tonkunst," 1886.

WAL'LENSTEIN, Martin. Pianist ; *b.* Frankfort-on-Main, 1843 ; *d.* 1896. Noted as a " master of phrasing."
Works : a pf. concerto ; pf. solos, études, &c.

WAL'LERSTEIN, Anton. Violinist and composer of dance music ; *b.* Dresden, 1813 ; *d.* 1892.
Works : abt. 300 dance pieces ; also songs, &c.

WALL'HOFEN, Madame. (See **Pauline Lucca.**)

WAL'LIS, John. Prof. of mathematics, Oxford Univ. ; *b.* Ashford, Kent, 1616 ; *d.* 1703.
Wrote treatises on ancient music, acoustics, &c.

WALLI'SER, Christoph T. Strasburg, 1568-1648.
Works : church music, dramatic music, a treatise on " Figured Music," &c.

WALL'NER, Leopold. Teacher and writer ; *b.* Kiev, Russia, 1847.

WALL'NOFER, Adolf. Baritone, afterwards tenor singer ; *b.* Vienna, 1854. Sang New York, 1897-8, &c.
Works : an opera (*Eddystone*, 1889) ; works for chorus and orch., songs, &c.

WALM'ISLEY, Thomas Attwood. Son of T. F. (below) ; *b.* London, 1814 ; *d.* 1856. Pupil of Attwood. Orgt. Trinity and St. John's, Cambridge, 1833 ; Prof. of music, Cambridge Univ., 1836 ; Mus.Doc., 1848.
Works : odes, anthems, chants, hymns, madrigals, &c.

WALM'ISLEY, Thomas F. Popular glee composer ; London, 1783-1866. Pupil of Attwood.

Walni'ka. A Russian peasant bagpipe.

Wals'(*Dutch*). A waltz.

WALSH, John. London music publisher ; commenced business abt. 1690 ; d. 1736.
Pub. many of Handel's operas.

WAL'TER, August. *B.* Stuttgart, 1821 ; d. 1896. Mus.-director, Basle, 1846. Promoter of church music.
Works : an octet, male choruses, songs, &c.

WALTER, Benno. Violinist ; brother of Joseph (below) ; b. Munich, 1847 ; d. 1901. Member of the Court Orch., 1863.

WALTER, Carl. Orgt., teacher, and writer ; b. Cransberg, Taunus, 1862.

WALTER, Dr. Friedrich Wm. Writer ; b. Mannheim, 1870.
Works : " The Theatres in Mannheim " (2 vols., 1899), &c.

WALTER, George Wm. Orgt. ; son of Wm. H. (below) ; b. New York, 1851. Played in public at 5. Has collected a fine musical library.

WALTER, Gustav. Tenor singer ; b. Bilin, Bohemia, 1836. Principal lyric tenor, Vienna Court Opera, 1856-87.

WALTER, Ignaz. Tenor singer ; b. Rado-witz, Bohemia, 1759 ; d. abt. 1830.
Works : several " Singspiele," cantatas, 6 masses, 6 motets, &c.

WALTER, Joseph. Violinist , pupil of De Bériot ; b. Neuberg-on-Danube, 1833 ; d. 1875. Vn. teacher Munich Cons.

WALTER, Wm. Henry. Organist and composer ; b. Newark, New Jersey, 1825. Orgt. New York, from 1842.
Works : masses, church services, anthems, collections of hymn-tunes, &c.

WAL'THER, Johann. *B.* Thuringia, 1496 ; d. 1570. Court capellmeister, Torgau, 1525-30 ; Dresden, 1548-55. Assisted Luther in composing and arranging the music for the Reformed Church.
Works : " Geystlich Gesangk Buchleyn," the first Protestant 4-part singing-book, Wittenberg, 1524 ; also magnificats, sacred Lieder, chorals, &c.

WAL'THER, Johann G. Noted organist ; b. Erfurt, 1684 ; d. 1748. Near relative and friend of J. S. Bach. Organist Thomaskirche, Erfurt, 1702 ; town orgt. Weimar, 1707 ; Court musician, Weimar, 1720. " He stands next to Bach as a master of choral variations for the organ."
Works : a "Musical Lexikon" (1732), the first dict. of biography, musical terms, and bibliography. Also preludes, fugues, toccatas, choral variations, &c., for organ.

WAL'THER, Johann J. Early instrumental composer ; b. nr. Erfurt, 1650.

WAL'THER von der VO'GELWEIDE. Greatest Minnesinger and lyric poet of mediæval Germany ; b. Tyrol (?), abt. 1160 ; d. Würzburg, after 1227.
He is introduced as an important character in Wagner's *Tannhäuser*, and is also referred to in *Die Meistersinger*.

WALTHEW, Richard H. Pianist and composer ; b. London, 1872.
Works : orchestral pieces, cantatas, songs, &c.

Waltz. (*G., Wal'zer ; F., Valse ; I., Val'zer.*)
(1) A popular dance in 3-4 time.
There are three distinct kinds of waltz : (a) The Slow German waltz, or *Ländler*. (b) The ordinary Vienna, or *Trois Temps* ; about $\cdot = 66$. (c) The Quick waltz, or *Deux Temps* ; about $\cdot = 88$.
(2) An instrumental piece in waltz style, but not meant for dancing
Waltz-song. (1) A song in waltz style. (2) A waltz combined with singing.

Wal'ze (*G.*). A rapid series of symmetrical ascending or descending melodic figures ; a roll ; a flight (of notes).

WAMBACH, Emile X. *B.* Arlon, Luxemburg, 1854. Studied Antwerp Cons.
Works : symphonic poems, 2 oratorios, cantatas, church music, choruses, songs, &c.

WANG'EMANN, Otto. Orgt. and singing teacher ; b. Loitz-on-the-Peene, 1848.
Works : school songs, pf. pieces, a " History of the Organ," &c.

WANHAL (or Van HAL), Johann B. *B.* Neu-Nechanitz, Bohemia, 1739 ; d. 1813. Prolific composer ; son of a peasant ; largely self-taught. Favourite composer of pf. music before Mozart and Beethoven.
Works : symphonies, chamber music, much pf. music (including " The Battle of Trafalgar," and other descriptive pieces) ; also 2 operas, church music, organ pieces, &c.

Wan'kend (*G.*). Hesitating, wavering ; uncertain.

WAN'SKI, Johann N. Violinist ; b. Poland, abt. 1800(?). Made extensive Continental tours.
Works : a vn. method, a viola method, numerous vn. pieces, a work on harmony, &c.

Warblers. The twirls, grace notes, flourishes, &c., with which pipers embellish their melodies.

WARD, Cornelius. *B.* Speen, Bucks, 1814 ; d. 1903.
Works : popular anthems, hymn-tunes, &c.

WARD, Francis M. Bass vocalist, orgt., and conductor ; b. Lincoln, 1830.

WARD, Frederick. Violinist ; b. Birmingham, 1845.

WARD, John Charles. *B.* Upper Clapton, 1835. Concertina soloist and orgt.
Works : org. music, cantatas, church music, concertina pieces, &c.

WARDLAW, Ralph. D.D. 1779-1853. Glasgow minister.
Wrote the hymn " Christ, of all my hopes the ground."

WARE, George. *B.* 1762 ; d. Liverpool, 1850.
Wrote " A Dict. of Musical Chords," glees, songs.

WAREHAM, Edwin J. Tenor vocalist and organist ; b. Wimborne, Dorset, 1862.

WAREING, Herbert W. *B.* Birmingham, 1857. Studied Leipzig Cons. Mus.Doc. Cantab., 1886.

WARING, Anna L. *B.* Neath, Glamorgan, 1820.
Author of the hymn "Father, I know that all my life."

WARLA'MOFF, Alex. J. *B.* Moscow, 1801 ; *d.* 1849. Singing teacher.
Wrote popular folk-songs.

WARMAN, John W. Orgt. and writer ; *b.* Canterbury, 1842.

Wär'me (*G.*). Warmth, fervour.
Mit gros'ser Wär'me. With great warmth, &c.

WARNOTS, Henri. Operatic lyric tenor ; Brussels, 1832-93. *Début,* Liége, 1856 ; singing teacher, Brussels Cons.
His daughter, **Elly,** *b.* Liége, 1857, is an operatic soprano. *Début,* Brussels, 1879 ; 1st London appearance, 1881.

WARREN, Geo. Wm. Self-taught organist ; *b.* Albany, N.Y., 1828. Orgt. St. Thomas's Ch., New York, 1870.
Works : church music, hymn-tunes, pf. pieces, &c.

WARREN, Samuel Prowse. Noted orgt. ; *b.* Montreal, Canada, 1841. Studied Berlin. Orgt. New York, from 1865.
Works : church music, org. transcriptions, songs.

WARREN, William. *B.* abt. 1770 ; *d.* Dublin, 1841. Mus.Doc. Dublin ; orgt. Christ Church Cath., Dublin, 1814. Wrote glees, &c.

WARRINER, John. *B.* Bourton, Shropshire, 1859. Mus.D. Dublin, 1892.
Works : church music, org. pieces, "National Portrait Gallery of Brit. Musicians," Primers on transposition, counterpoint, &c.

WARTEL, Pierre F. *B.* Versailles, 1806 ; *d.* 1862. Noted tenor and singing teacher ; Trebelli was his pupil.

WASIELEW'SKI, Joseph W. von. Violinist; *b.* nr. Dantzig, 1822 ; *d.* 1896. Pupil of David at Leipzig. Concertmeister, under Schumann, Düsseldorf, 1850-2 ; condr. at Bonn, 1852 ; settled in Dresden as writer, critic, &c., 1855 ; town mus.-director, Bonn, 1869-73.
His writings include a "Biography of Schumann," important works on the "History of the Violin," "Beethoven" (2 vols.), "Instrumental Music in the 16th century," &c.

Was'sail. "Good health." A convivial song ; a feast, &c.

Was'ser (*G.*). Water.
Was'serorgel. A water organ (hydraulic organ).

WAS'SERMAN, Heinrich J. Violinist ; pupil of Spohr ; *b.* nr. Fulda, 1791 ; *d.* 1838.
Wrote orchl. dances, guitar pieces, &c.

Watch on the Rhine. (See **National Music.**)

WATSON, Alfred R. Violinist, composer, and conductor ; *b.* Nottingham, 1845.

WATSON, Henry. *B.* Burnley, 1846. Mus.Doc. Cantab., 1887. Resides at Manchester. Collector of musical literature, &c. He has presented his fine musical library to the Manchester Corporation.

WATSON, Wm. Michael. Song composer ; *b.* Newcastle-on-Tyne, 1840 ; *d.* London, 1889.

WATTS, Isaac. D.D. *B.* Southampton, 1674 ; *d.* 1748. Pastor and hymn-writer.
His hymns are unequal in merit, but many of them are very fine. "O God, our help in ages past" (Psalm xc.) is one of the most solemn and sublime hymns in the English language.

WAUD, John H. 'Cellist and double-bass player ; *b.* London, 1848. Prof. G.S.M.
Author of a "Double Bass Tutor."

Waves, Sound. (See **Acoustics.**)

Waving tone. (See **Passing-notes.**)

Wayghtes, Waytes. (See **Waits.**)

WAYLETT, Mrs. Harriett (*née* **Cooke**). Soprano vocalist ; *b.* Bath, 1800 ; *d.* 1851.

Weak accent, Weak beat, Weak pulse. An unaccented accent, beat, pulse. (See **Accent,** &c.)

WEALE, William. *B.* abt. 1690 ; *d.* Bedford, 1727.
Composed the tune "Bedford."

WEATHERLY, Frederic E. Writer of song libretti, &c. ; *b.* Portishead, 1848.

WEBB, Daniel. *B.* Taunton, 1735 ; *d.* 1815.
Wrote on the "Correspondence between Poetry and Music" (1769).

WEBB, Frank R. *B.* Covington, Indiana, 1851. Organist and teacher.
Works : church music, pf. pieces, and abt. 200 pieces for military bands.

WEBB, George Jas. *B.* nr. Salisbury, 1803 ; *d.* 1887. Settled in Boston (U.S.), 1830; President Handel and Haydn Soc., 1840 ; taught in New York, 1876-85.
Co-editor of 2 mus. periodicals ; pub. "Vocal Technics," "Voice Culture," collections of class pieces, &c.

WEBB, Mrs. T. H. (See **Alice Gomez.**)

WEBBE, Samuel (senr.). *B.* Minorca, 1740 ; *d.* London, 1816. Chapel master, Portuguese Chapel, London, 1776.
Works : glees, catches, anthems, a "Cecilian Ode," &c.

WEBBE, Samuel (junr.). Son of preceding ; London, 1770-1843. Orgt. at various London churches.
Works : glees, duets, hymn-tunes, "Harmony Epitomised," &c.

WE'BER, Aloysia. (See **Mad. Lange.**)

WE'BER, Bernhard A. Pianist ; pupil of Abt Vogler ; *b.* Mannheim, 1766 ; *d.* 1821. Capellmeister Königstädt Th., Berlin, 1792.
Wrote operas, operettas, &c.

WE'BER, Carl Maria F. E. von. Eminent composer ; "founder of the German Romantic School;" *b.* Eutin, Holstein, Dec. 18, 1786 ; *d.* London, June 5, 1826. Son of an army officer who afterwards took up the profession of music. After some years of a "wandering life" with his father, Carl M. became chorister, Salzburg Cath., 1797. Taught composition (gratuitously) by Michael Haydn. Studied, Munich, 1798-1800, under Valesi and Kalcher, and appeared as concert pianist. Removed to Freiburg, Saxony, 1800, where his opera *Das Waldmädchen* was produced the same year. Returned to Salzburg, 1801, and studied further under M. Haydn. After visits to Hamburg and Augsburg, went to Vienna, 1803, and studied under Abt Vogler. Capellmeister Breslau City Th., 1804-6. After tours, &c., capellmeister National Th., Prague, 1813; organized and conducted here with such success that he was appointed condr. (with Morlacchi) Royal Opera, Dresden, 1817. Here he wrote his greatest operas, *Der Freischütz* and *Euryanthe*. His health had long been failing; and he died in London eight weeks after the performance of his *Oberon* at Covent Garden (1826). A statue to his memory was unveiled at Dresden. 1860.

Chief operas: *Der Freischütz* (1821), *Euryanthe* (1823), *Oberon* (1826); also *Peter Schmoll* (1803), *Silvana* (1810), *Abu Hassan* (1812), *Preciosa* (1820). Other works: 2 symphonies, a "Jubilee" overture, concertos, chamber music, much pf. music (including 2 concertos, and the well-known Concertstück for pf. and orch.), cantatas (*Kampf und Sieg*, 1815), masses, part-songs, scenas, songs, &c.
A complete thematic catalogue of Weber's works was published by Jähns, Berlin, 1871.

WE'BER, Edmund von. Step-brother of C. M.; *b.* Hildesheim, 1786; *d.* 1828. Condr. at Cassel. Lübeck, Dantzig, Cologne, &c.

WE'BER, Franz. Cologne, 1805-76. Orgt. Cologne Cath., 1838.
Works: Psalm 57, for male voices and orch.; numerous male choruses.

WE'BER, Friedrich A. Heilbronn, 1753-1806.
Wrote oratorios, cantatas, symphonies, pf. pieces.

WE'BER, F. Dionys. *B.* Welchau, Bohemia, 1766; *d.* 1842. Pupil of Abt Vogler. Co-founder and 1st director Prague Cons., 1811. Teacher of Moscheles.
Works: operas, 18 cantatas, military music, a sextet for 6 trombones, popular pf. quadrilles &c. Also a "General Theoretical School of Music," and a work on "Harmony and General-bass" (4 vols.).

WE'BER, Georg V. Expert on organ building and *a cappella* music; *b.* Upper Hesse, 1838. Capellmeister Mayence Cath., 1866.
Works: church music, treatises on organ-building, &c.

WE'BER, Gottfried. Lawyer and noted musical theorist; *b.* nr. Mannheim, 1779; *d.* 1839. State attorney, Darmstadt, 1832.
Chief work: "Theory of Musical Composition" (3 vols., 1817-21; Eng. edition, 1851). His

system of indicating chords by letters and figures is shown under Harmony Analysis (*q.v.*). He also wrote other treatises and numerous magazine articles, and composed masses, part-songs, &c.

WE'BER, Gustav. *B.* Münchenbuchsee, Switzerland, 1845; *d.* 1887. Orgt. St. Peter's, Zurich, from 1872.
Works: a symphonic poem, pf. pieces, choruses, arrangements of old German songs, &c.

WE'BER, Karl H. *B.* Frankenberg, 1834. Asst. teacher Moscow Cons., 1866-70; director Imperial Russian Mus. Soc., Saratov, 1877.
Works: a pf. method (in Russian), a sketch of "Music in Russia," &c.

WE'BER, Miroslav. Violinist; *b.* Prague, 1854. Concertmeister, Darmstadt, 1875; afterwards at Wiesbaden.
Works: stage music, orchl. pieces, chamber music, &c.

Weber's Last Waltz. A name erroneously given to a piece by Reissiger commencing thus—

WEBSTER, Joseph P. American musician; *b.* Manchester, N.H., 1819; *d.* 1875.
Wrote a cantata, many songs, a collection of Sunday school music, &c.

Wech'sel (*G.*). Change, variation; exchange.
Wech'selgesang. Antiphonal (or responsive) singing.
Wech'selnote. A changing-note (*q.v.*).
Wech'seln in G. Change the crook, tuning, &c., to G.
Wech'seln mit Klarinet'ten in B. Change to the clarinets in Bb.

WECKERLIN, Jean B. T. *B.* Gebweiler, Alsace, 1821. Studied Paris Cons.; asst. librarian, 1869; librarian, 1876.
Works: operas (*l'Organiste dans l'embarras,* 1853); operettas, an oratorio and other choral works, choruses, songs, a "History of Instrumentation from the 16th century;" collections of madrigals, Nöels, folk-songs, &c.

WE'DEKIND, Erica. Operatic soprano; *b.* Hanover. 1872. *Début* Dresden, 1894; married Herr Oschwald, Basle, 1898.

WEEKES, Samuel. Composer and writer; *b.* Plymouth, 1843. Mus. D. T.C.D., 1896.

WEELKES, Thomas. *B.* abt. 1578(?); *d.* 1623. Orgt. Winchester Cath., 1600; Mus.Bac. Oxon, 1602; orgt. Chichester Cath., 1608.
Works: madrigals in from 3 to 6 parts "apt for the Viols and Voyces" (1597-1614). Many of his madrigals are fine examples of original and scholarly work.

WE'GELER, Franz G. Physician; *b.* Bonn, 1765; *d.* 1848.
Wrote, with Ries, a "Biographical Notice of Beethoven."

WE'GELIUS, Martin. *B.* Helsingfors, 1846. Studied Vienna and Leipzig. Condr. Finnish Opera, Helsingfors, 1878.
Works: orchl. pieces, cantatas, pf. pieces, songs, a Swedish "Manual of Harmony," &c.

WEH'LE, Carl. Concert pianist , *b.* Prague, 1825 ; *d.* 1883. Studied under Moscheles and Kullak.
Wrote brilliant pf. pieces.

Weh'mut(h) (*G.*) } Melancholy, sad-
Weh'müt(h)igkeit (*G.*) } ness, sorrow.
Weh'müt(h)ig. Sad(ly), mournful(ly), doleful(ly).

Wei'berstimme (*G.*). A female voice.

Weich (*G.*). (1) Tender, soft, mellow. (2) Minor.
Weich'e Ton'art. Minor key.
Weich gestos'sen. Lightly detached.
Weich gestrich'en. Gently, lightly bowed.
Weich und getrag'en. Soft and sustained.
Weich'heit. Tenderness, kindness, &c.

WEIDT, Carl. *B.* Berne, 1857. Condr. Klagenfurt Männergesangverein, 1889. Has written fine male choruses.

Weight. Impressiveness, force ; dignity.

Weight of wind. The pressure of air supplied by organ bellows.
It is measured in "inches" by means of a *windgauge*. In large organs there are varied "weights" for different stops ; thus the diapasons are on about 3 or 4 inches of wind, the solo reeds on 6 to 10 inches, or more.

WEIGL, Joseph. *B.* Eisenstadt, Hungary, 1766 ; *d.* 1846. 2nd Court condr. Vienna, 1825. Wrote his first opera at the age of 16.
Works : over 30 operas (*Die Schweizerfamilie*, 1809, the most popular); also about 20 ballets, 2 oratorios, several cantatas, chamber music, songs, &c.

Weih'nachtslied (*G.*). A Christmas song ; a carol.

WEIN'BERGER, Carl. *B.* Vienna, 1861. Composer of successful operettas : *Pagenstreiche*, 1888 ; *Adam und Eva*, 1898 ; &c.

Wei'nend (*G.*). Whining, weeping, wailing.

WEIN'GARTNER, Paul Felix. Distinguished conductor ; *b.* Zara, Dalmatia, 1863. Won the "Mozart Prize," Leipzig Cons., 1883. Condr. successively at Königsberg, Dantzig, Hamburg, Mannheim, Berlin, Munich (1898), &c.
Works : operas (*Genesius*, 1892) ; orchl. pieces, pf. pieces, songs ; treatises on " Conducting," "Bayreuth," " The Musical Drama," &c.

WEIN'LIG (or WEIN'LICH), Christian E. Dresden, 1743-1813. Orgt. at Leipzig, 1767 ; Thorn, 1773 ; Dresden, 1780. Cantor Kreuzschule, Dresden, 1785.
Works : church music ; sonatas for pf., flute and 'cello ; &c.

WEIN'LIG, Ch. Theodor. Nephew of C. E. ; *b.* Dresden, 1780 ; *d.* 1842. Cantor Dresden Kreuzschule, 1814-17; Thomaskirche, Leipzig, 1823. Teacher of Wagner.
Works : a Magnificat, vocalises, a work on "Fugue," &c.

WEIN'WURM, Rudolf. *B.* Lower Austria, 1835. Founded the Gesangverein,

Vienna Univ., 1858 ; condr. Vienna Singakademie, 1864 ; condr. Männergesangverein, 1866 ; mus.-dir. of the Univ., 1880.
Works : male choruses, part-songs ; works on " Singing," " Theory," &c.

WEIN'ZIERL, Max von. *B.* Bergstadtl, Bohemia, 1841 ; *d.* 1898. Chorusmaster Vienna Männergesangverein, 1882.
Works : an oratorio (*Hiob*, 1870), operettas, choral works, songs.

Wei'se (*G.*). (1) A tune. (2) Manner, mood ; fashion, style.

WEIS'HEIMER, Wendelin. Operatic composer ; *b.* Osthofen, Alsace, 1836.
Wrote a valuable work on " Wagner and Liszt."

WEISS, Amalie. (See **Joachim.**)

WEISS, Carl. *B.* Mühlhausen, abt. 1738 ; *d.* London, 1795. Member private band of George III.
Works : 6 symphonies, 10 quartets for flute and strings, flute trios, &c.

WEISS, Carl. Son of preceding ; *b.* 1777. Settled in England.
Works : a concerto and other pieces for flute, a " Flute Method," &c.

WEISS, Franz. Viola player ; *b.* Silesia, 1778 ; *d.* 1830. Chamber musician to Prince Rasumovsky, Vienna ; member of the " Schuppanzigh Quartett."
Works : ballets, symphonies, concertos, chamber music, pf. sonatas, &c.

WEISS, Julius. Violinist ; *b.* Berlin, 1814.

WEISS, Willoughby H. Bass vocalist ; *b.* Liverpool, 1820 ; *d.* 1867.
Wrote " The Village Blacksmith," and other songs.

Weiss (*G.*). White.
Weis'se No'te. A "white" note ; as a minim, or semibreve.

WEISS'BECK, Johann M. *B.* Swabia, 1756; *d.* 1808. Cantor and organist at Nuremberg.
Wrote against Abbé Vogler's theories of composition, &c.

WEIST-HILL. (See **Hill.**)

Weit (*G.*). Broad, wide ; open, extended.
Wei'te Harmonie'. Dispersed or open harmony.

WEITZ'MANN, Carl F. Berlin, 1808-80. Violinist ; pupil of Spohr. Chorusmaster Riga Th., 1832 ; leader, Imperial Orch., St. Petersburg, 1836. Settled in Berlin as teacher of composition, 1848. Intimate friend of Liszt.
Works : 3 operas, pf. pieces (including " 1800 Preludes and Modulations"), songs, several historical treatises (including a valuable History of " Clavierspiels " and " Clavier-litteratur "), a " Harmonic system," &c.

WEL'CKER von GONTERSHAUSEN, Heinrich. 1811-73. Pf. maker to the Grand Duke of Hesse.
Pub. several works on pianoforte construction, &c.

WELDON, Georgina. Soprano vocalist and writer ; *b.* London, 1837.

WELDON, John. *B.* Chichester, 1676 ; *d.* London, 1736. Pupil of Purcell. Orgt. New Coll., Oxford, 1694 ; orgt. Chapel Royal, 1708.
Works : anthems, songs, a masque (*The Judgment of Paris*), &c.

Wel'le (*G.*). A roller (in organ mechanism). *Wel'lenbrett.* A roller-board.

WELLINGS, J. Milton. Song composer ; *b.* Handsworth, 1850.

WELLS, Wallace. Tenor vocalist ; *b.* Dilham, Norfolk, 1842.

Well-tempered. (*G., Wohl'temperirt.*) Tuned in equal temperament (*q.v.*). *Wohl'temperirtes Clavier'.* " Well-tempered Clavichord ; " Bach's 48 preludes and fugues.

WELS, Charles. Pianist ; *b.* Prague, 1825 ; *d.* 1906. Court pianist, Poland, 1847. Settled in New York, 1849.
Works : orchl. pieces, masses, pf. pieces, songs.

Welsh harp. (See **Harp.**)

Welsh music.
" There is no denying that Welsh music is more artistic than either that of the Scotch or the Irish."—(A Welshman's verdict in *Grove's Dict.*)
CHIEF COLLECTIONS :—
Ancient British Music, &c.; John Parry (3 vols., 1742-81).
Relicks of the Welsh Bards, &c.; Edward Jones (3 vols., 1794-1808?).
Welsh Melodies ; John Parry, "Bardd Alaw" (1809).
The Welsh Harper ; John Parry (2 vols 1839-48).
Original Welsh Airs, with accompts. by Haydn and Beethoven ; pub. by Thompson, Edinburgh (3 vols., 1809-14).
Welsh National Airs ; John Owen, "Owain Alaw" (4 series, 1860-64).
Welsh Melodies ; John Thomas, "Pencerdd Gwalia" (4 vols., 1862-74).

WELSH, Thomas. Bass singer and noted teacher of singing ; *b.* Wells, 1770 ; *d.* Brighton, 1848. Operatic *début*, London, 1792.
Works : a " Vocal Instructor," dramatic pieces, pf. sonatas, glees, &c.

His wife, **Mary Anne** (*née* **Wilson**), 1802-67, was a celebrated soprano singer, both in opera and concert. *Début*, in Arne's *Artaxerxes*, Drury Lane, 1821.

Welt'lich (*G.*). Secular. *Welt'liche Lied'er.* Secular songs.

WÉLY. (See **Lefébure-Wely.**)

WENCK, August H. Violinist. Invented a metronome, 1798.

WEN'DLING, Carl. Pianist ; *b.* Frankenthal, 1857.
Specialist on the Jankó keyboard (*q.v.*) ; teacher Leipzig Cons., 1887.

WENDT, Eduard. Violinist ; *b.* Berlin, 1807 ; *d.* 1890. Fine quartet player. Co-founder Tonkünstler-Verein, Magdeburg.

WENDT, Ernst A. Pianist ; *b.* Schwiebus, Prussia, 1806 ; *d.* 1850.
Works : a 4-hand sonata and other pf. pieces ; organ pieces, &c.

We'nig (*G.*). Little ; a little. *Ein klein we'nig lang'samer.* A very little slower. *Ein we'nig stark.* Rather loud.

We'niger (*G.*). Less. *We'niger ab'gemessen.* " Less measured," faster. *We'niger leb'haft.* Less lively. *We'niger stark.* Less loud.

WEN'NERBERG, Gunnar. Composer ; *b.* Lindköping, Sweden, 1817.

WEN'ZEL, Ernst Ferdinand. Pianist and noted pf. teacher ; *b.* nr. Löbau, 1808 ; *d.* 1880. Intimate friend of Schumann and Mendelssohn. Pf. teacher Leipzig Cons., 1843-80.

WEN'ZEL, Leopold. Violinist ; *b.* Naples, 1847. Settled in London, 1883 ; condr. Empire Th., 1889.
Works : operettas, ballets, songs, &c.

WERCK'MEISTER, Andreas. *B.* Beneckenstein, 1645 ; *d.* 1706. Orgt. Martinskirche, Halberstadt, 1696.
His numerous writings include the earliest treatise on "Equal Temperament" (1691).

Wer'den (*G.*). To become, to grow. *Et'was breit'er wer'den.* To become somewhat broader.

Werk (*G.*). Work ; mechanism. In the organ, (1) A stop ; (2) All the stops connected with one keyboard ; (3) The action.

WER'KENTHIN, Albert. Pianist ; *b.* Berlin, 1842. Pupil of Von Bülow.
Works : a pf. method (3 vols.), pf. pieces, songs.

WER'MANN, Friedrich O. *B.* nr. Trebsen, Saxony, 1840 ; *d.* 1906. Studied Leipzig Cons. Teacher Royal Seminary, Dresden, 1868 ; music.-director of the 3 chief churches, and cantor of the Kreuzschule, Dresden, 1876.
Works : a Reformation cantata, an 8-part Mass, motets, org. pieces, pf. pieces and studies, &c.

WER'NER, Gregor Jos. 1695- 1766. Haydn's predecessor as capellmeister to Prince Estaházy.
Works : masses, oratorios, instl. music for 2 vns. and bass, &c.

WER'NER, Johann G. *B.* Grossenhain, 1777 ; *d.* 1822. Orgt. and mus.-dir. Merseburg Cath.
Works : an Organ School, a " Musical A B C " for the pf., a work on Harmony, a " Choralbuch," numerous org. pieces, &c.

WER'NER, Josef. 'Cellist ; *b.* Würzburg, 1837. 'Cello teacher Munich School of Music.
Works : a 'cello method, a quartet for 4 'celli, 'cello solos, &c.

WERSTOW'SKI (VERSTOV'SKY), Alexei N. Moscow, 1799-1862. State councillor and theatre inspector, Moscow.
Works : 7 operas, including *Askold's Grave*, the first Russian opera based on folk-songs.

WERT, Jacob van. Noted Flemish contrapuntist ; *b.* 1536 ; *d.* Mantua, 1596. Maestro to the Duke of Mantua, abt 1566 ; maestro Santa Barbara Ch. Mantua, 1574. Prolific composer.
Extant works : 11 books of madrigals, canzonets, motets, &c.

Wert(h) (*G.*). Worth, value; especially *time-value* or duration.

WERY, Nicolas L. Violinist; *b.* nr. Liége, 1789; *d.* 1867. Solo violin Royal Orch., Brussels, 1823-60.

WESCHÉ, Walter. Pianist and composer; *b.* Colombo, Ceylon, 1857. Settled in London.

We'sentlich (*G.*). Essential (*q.v.*).
We'sentliche Dissonanz'. An essential dissonant component of a chord; as opposed to a passing-note, appoggiatura, &c.
We'sentliche Sep'time. An essential 7th (Dominant 7th, &c.).

WESLEY, Rev. John. M.A. 1703-91. Founder of Wesleyan Methodism.
Wrote and translated many hymns, issued books c. hymn-tunes, &c.

WESLEY, Rev. Charles. 1707-88. Brother of preceding; the first Oxford "Methodist;" wrote over 6,000 hymns. "Perhaps," says Canon Overton, "the great hymn-writer of all ages."
"Jesu, lover of my soul," "Love divine, all loves excelling," "Hark, the herald angels sing," &c.

WESLEY, Charles. Son of preceding; *b.* Bristol, 1757; *d.* 1834. Noted for his wonderful precocity. Orgt. St. George's, Hanover Square, London; orgt. in ordinary to Geo. IV.
Works: "A set of 8 songs," 6 concertos, for org. or harpsichord, anthems, hymn-tunes, &c.

WESLEY, Samuel. Brother and pupil of preceding; *b.* Bristol, 1766; *d.* 1837. "Foremost English organist of his time;" introduced Bach's organ works into this country. Deputy orgt. Bath Abbey; afterwards orgt. Camden Chapel, London (1834).
Works: Latin motets, org. pieces, services, anthems, hymn-tunes, pf. sonatas, &c.

WESLEY, Samuel Sebastian. Distinguished organist; third son of preceding; *b.* London, 1810; *d.* 1876. Orgt. in various London churches; then at Hereford Cath., 1832; Exeter Cath., 1835; Leeds Parish Church, 1842; Winchester Cath., 1849; Gloucester Cath., 1865. Mus.Doc. Oxon. 1839.
Works: 4 church services, many fine anthems, glees, part-songs, org. pieces, songs.

WES'SELY, Carl Bernhard. *B.* Berlin, 1768; *d.* 1826. Director Berlin National Th., 1788; capellmeister, Rheinsbeck, 1796; afterwards in Potsdam.
Works: 4 operas, ballets, cantatas, string quartets, songs, &c.

WES'SELÝ, Johann. Violinist; *b.* Frauenberg, Bohemia, 1762(8?); *d.* 1814.
Works: 2 comic operas, 14 string quartets, 3 quartets for clar. and strings, &c.

WEST, John E. *B.* South Hackney, 1863. Studied R.A.M. Orgt. St. Mary's, Berkeley Square, 1884; Sth. Hackney Parish Ch., 1891.
Works: cantatas, services, anthems, incidental stage music, org. pieces, songs, &c.

WESTBROOK, Wm. Jos. *B.* London, 1831; *d.* 1894. Mus.Doc. Cantab., 1878. Co-founder of the *Musical Standard*, 1862.
Works: cantatas, anthems, songs, numerous org. pieces and transcriptions; translations of the vn. methods of Alard, Dancla, and De Bériot.

WES'TERHOUT. (See **Van Westerhout**.)

WESTLAKE, Frederick. *B.* Romsey, Hampshire, 1840; *d.* 1898. Pf. prof. R.A.M., 1863.
Works: masses, pf. pieces, part-songs, songs, &c.

WEST'MEYER, Wilhelm. *B.* nr. Osnabrück, 1832; *d.* 1880. Studied Leipzig Cons.
Works: 2 successful operas, an overture, symphonies, an octet for wind and strings, songs, &c.

WESTMORELAND, John Fane, Earl of. *B.* London, 1784; *d.* 1859. British Minister, Berlin, 1841-51. Founded the R.A.M., 1822.
Works: 7 operas, 3 symphonies, church music, cantatas, glees, songs, pf. pieces, &c.

WEST'PHAL, Rudolf G. H. Philologian and writer; *b.* Operkirchen, 1826; *d.* 1892.
Wrote numerous works on rhythm and metre; "his exposition of Greek rhythms and metres is clear and systematic."

WESTROP, Henry J. Violinist and orgt.; *b.* Lavenham, Suffolk, 1812; *d.* London, 1879.

WESTROP, Thomas. Brother of preceding; composer and writer; *b.* Lavenham, 1816; *d.* 1881.
Works: a vn. tutor, an org. tutor, a collection of "120 short anthems," songs, hymn-tunes, pf. pieces, &c.

Wet'terharfe (*G.*). "Weather harp;" Æolian harp.

Wett'gesang (*G.*). A singing contest.

WETTON, Henry Davan. *B.* Brighton, 1862. Assist. orgt. Westminster Abbey, 1881-96; orgt. Foundling Hospital, 1892; Mus.Doc. Durham, 1903.

WETZ'LER, Hermann H. Pianist and orgt.; *b.* Frankfort-on-Main, 1870. Pupil of Madame Schumann. Settled in New York, 1892. Founded the "Wetzler Symphony Concerts," 1903.
Works: pf. pieces, ballads, &c.

WEY'SE, Christoph E. F. *B.* Altona, 1774; *d.* Copenhagen, 1842.
Works: several operas; orchl. pieces, cantatas, pf. pieces.

WHATELY, Richard. D.D. 1787-1863. Archbishop of Dublin, 1831.
Wrote the hymn "God, who madest earth and heaven."

WHEALL, Wm. (See **Weale**.)

Wheel. A refrain (of a ballad, &c.).

WHELPLEY, Benj. L. Pianist and orgt.; *b.* Eastport, Maine, 1864.

Whipping bow. (*G.*, *Gepeit'schte Srich'art*; *F.*, *Fouette*.) Striking the bow against the strings as if whipping them, for sharp emphasis of single tones in quick *tempo*.

WHISHAW, Fred. J. Tenor singer and song composer ; *b.* 1854.

Whistle. The primitive type of the flageolet, flûte-a-bec, organ flue-pipe, &c.

WHITAKER, John. Orgt. and composer ; *b.* 1776 ; *d.* London, 1847.
Wrote stage pieces, songs, glees ("Winds gently whisper"), &c.

WHITE, Adolphus C. Double-bass player ; *b.* Canterbury, 1830. Prof. R.A.M. and R.C.M. *D.* 190-(?).
Author of Novello's Primer for the Doublebass

WHITE, Mrs. F. M. (See **Alice M. Smith.**)

WHITE, John. *B.* W. Springfield, Mass., 1855 ; *d.* 1902. Orgt. Ch. of the Ascension, New York,. 1887-96 ; afterwards in Munich.
Works : Catholic church music, &c.

WHITE, Maude Valérie. *B.* of English parents, Dieppe, 1855. "Mendelssohn Scholar," R.A.M., 1879.
Works : a mass, pf. pieces, songs, &c.

WHITE, Robt. (See **Whyte.**)

WHITE, Robt. Thos. *B.* Marden, Kent, 1869. Mus.D. Oxon, 1898. Prof. of Mus. Goldsmith's Coll., New Cross, 1906.
Author of "Hints for Singers" "Training of Men's Voices," &c.

WHITEHOUSE, Henry. Bass vocalist ; *b.* Worcester, 1823.

WHITEHOUSE, Wm. Ed. Son of preceding; 'cellist ; *b.* London, 1859.

White keys.
The white keys (of a pf., &c.) are often called "naturals," as they all belong to the natural diatonic major scale of C.
White note. A note with an open head ($\bowtie$ $\downarrow$), as opposed to a black note ($\downarrow$ $\downarrow$ $\downarrow$ &c.).

WHITING, Arthur B. Pianist ; *b.* Cambridge, Mass., 1861. *Début*, Boston, 1880.
Works : pf. music, org. music, anthems, songs, &c.

WHITING, George E. Organist ; *b.* Holliston, Mass., 1842. Played in public at 13 ; orgt. and teacher at Boston, Cincinnati, &c.
Works : masses, cantatas, choral works with orch., a pf. concerto, org. pieces, pf. pieces, songs, "The First 6 Months at the Organ," &c.

WHITING, William. 1825-78. Master Choristers' School, Winchester.
Wrote the hymn "Eternal Father, strong to save."

WHITMORE, Chas. S. Composer of "Isle of Beauty, fare thee well ; " *b.* Colchester, 1805 ; *d.* 1877.

WHITNEY, Myron Wm. Bass vocalist ; *b.* Ashby, Mass., 1836. Retired 1900.

WHITNEY, Samuel B. Organist ; *b.* Woodstock, Vermont (U.S.), 1842. Orgt. Ch. of the Advent, Boston, 1871. Org. prof. Boston Univ.
Works : org. pieces, pf. pieces, songs, &c.

WHITTIER, John Greenleaf. 1807-92. American Quaker poet.
Wrote some fine hymns.

Whole. Complete, entire.
Whole note, A semibreve ($\bowtie$).
Whole shift. (See *Shift.*)
Whole rest. (1) A semibreve rest. (2) A bar's rest in any kind of time.
Whole step. A step (or interval) of a whole tone.
Whole tone. (G., *Ganz'ton ;* F., *Ton plein ;* I., *To'no inte'ro.*) A major 2nd. (See *Interval.*)

WHYTE, James. Tenor vocalist ; *b.* Fife, 1857.

WHYTE, Robert. Mus. Bac. *B.* abt. 1530(?) ; *d.* Westminster, 1574. Orgt. Ely Cath., 1562-7 ; Westminster Abbey, 1570.

WHYTOCK, Janet M. (See **Patey.**)

WI'BORG, Elisa. Contemp. operatic soprano ; *b.* Kragerö, Norway.

WICH'MANN, Hermann. Instrumental composer ; *b.* Berlin, 1824. Studied under Mendelssohn and Spohr.

WICHTL, Georg. Violinist ; *b.* Trostberg, Bavaria, 1805 ; *d.* 1877. 1st vn. (afterwards 2nd capellmeister) at Löwenberg, 1826-70.
Works : stage music, an oratorio, church music, orchl. pieces, vn. concertos, instructive vn. pieces, &c.

WICK'EDE, Friedrich von. Song composer ; *b.* Dömitz-on-Elbe, 1834 ; *d.* 1904.

WID'MANN, Benedict. *B.* nr. Donaueschingen, 1820. Rector at Frankfort.
Author of text-books on Form, Theory, Harmony, General-bass, &c.

WID'MANN, Erasmus. Capellmeister and poet laureate at Weikersheim.
Pub. church music, dance music, songs, &c., (1607-27).

WID'MANN, Joseph V. Distinguished poet and opera-librettist; *b.* Moravia, 1840. Literary Editor Bernese " Bund," 1880.
Author of "Reminiscences of Brahms" (1898).

WIDOR, Chas. M. Eminent organist; *b.* Lyons, 1845. Orgt. St. François, Lyons, 1860 ; St. Sulpice, Paris, 1869. Prof. of org.-playing, Paris Cons., 1890 ; Prof. of Counterpoint, Fugue, and Composition, 1896.
Works : stage pieces, church music, orchl. music, much fine organ music (including 10 Symphonies) ; a pf. concerto, a vn. concerto, a pf. quintet, chamber music, songs, &c.

Wie (*G.*). As ; as if.
Wie am An'fang. As at the beginning.
Wie aus der Fer'ne. As if from a distance.
Wie früh'er. As before.
Wie o'ben. As above.
Wie Or'geltöne. Like organ tones.
Wie träum'end. As if in a dream ; dreamily.
Wie vor'her
Wie vor'hin } As before.
Wie zuvor' }

WIECK, Friedrich. *B.* nr. Torgau, 1785; *d.* 1873. After trying theology, a pf. factory, and a circulating library, devoted himself to pf. teaching at Leipzig. Among his most distinguished pupils were his daughters Clara and Marie, Robert Schumann, von Bülow, A. Krause, and G. Merkel. Removed to Dresden (1840) and taught singing as well as pf. playing.

Works: pf. studies, "Clavier und Gesang" (1853), &c.

His daughter **Clara,** better known as **Madame Schumann** (*q.v.*) married Robt. Schumann, 1840.

Another daughter, **Marie,** *b.* Leipzig, 1835, played the pf. in public at 8; est. a school for pf. playing at Dresden.

His son **Alwin,** Leipzig, 1821-85, was a violinist (pupil of David). Member Italian Opera orch., St. Petersburg, 1849-59.

Wie'der (*G.*). Again, once more.

Wie'der-an'fangen. To begin again.
Wie'der bele'bend
Wie'der beschleun'igend }Again (becoming) animated.
Wie'der beweg'ter
Wie'der das vor'hergehen'de Haupt'zeitmass. Again the foregoing principal *tempo.*
Wie'der früh'eres Zeit'mass. Again the previous *tempo.*
Wie'dergabe. Interpretation, reading, manner of performance.
Wiederher'stellungszeichen. The natural sign (♮).
Wie'derho'lung. Repetition; recapitulation; *da capo.*
Wie'derholung vom Chor. Repeat with the Chorus (Choir).
Wie'derklang }
Wie'derschall } Echo.
Wie'derschlag. The *Ribattuta* (*q.v.*).
Wie'der schnell. Again fast.
Wie'der sehr leb'haft. Again very quick (lively).
Wie'derholungszei'chen. A repeat sign.

Wie'derkehr (*G.*). The re-entry of a part.

WIE'DERKEHR, Jacob C. M. 'Cellist, bassoonist, and trombone player; *b.* Strasburg, 1739; *d.* Paris, 1823. Singing teacher Paris Cons., 1795-1802.

Works: 12 concertantes for wind insts., 2 string quintets, 10 string quartets, &c.

Wie'derum (*G.*). Again.

Wie'derum kläg'lich. Again sadly, mournfully.

WIE'GAND, Jos. A. H. Operatic bass; *b.* Odenwald, 1842; *d.* 1899. Leading bass, Frankfort, 1873-7. Noted Wagnerian singer (London, 1882, Bayreuth, 1886, &c.).

Wie'genlied (*G.*). A cradle song, lullaby; *berceuse.*

WIEH'MAYER, J. Theodor. Pianist; *b.* Marienfeld, Westphalia, 1870. Pf. teacher, Leipzig Cons., 1902.

Works: Org. pieces, pf. pieces, studies, &c.

WIELHOR'SKI. (See **Wilhorski.**)

WIENIAW'SKI, Henri. Distinguished violinist; *b.* Lublin, Poland, 1835; *d.* Moscow, 1880. 1st prize for vn. playing Paris Cons., 1846. Gave a series of concert tours with his brother Joseph (see below) in Poland, Russia, Germany, Holland, England, &c. Solo violinist to the Czar, 1860. Lived in St. Petersburg until 1872. Violin prof. Brussels Cons., 1874-7.

Works: 2 concertos, fantasias, studies, &c., for violin.

WIENIAW'SKI, Joseph. Famous pianist; brother of preceding; *b.* Lublin, 1837. Studied Paris Cons., 1847-50. Toured with his brother (see above), 1850-5. Teacher Moscow Cons., 1866. Finally settled in Brussels (teacher at the Cons., &c.).

Works: orchl. pieces, a pf. concerto, chamber music, many pf. pieces (polonaises, waltzes, idylles, études, &c.).

WIE'PRECHT, Friedrich W. *B.* Aschersleben, 1802; *d.* 1872. Director-General of all the Prussian military bands.

Invented the bass tuba (1835), made many improvements in wood and brass insts., &c. He claimed to have invented saxhorns before Sax (*q.v.*), but his claim was not upheld in the Law Courts.

WIE'TROWITZ, Gabriele. Violinist; *b.* Laibach, 1866. Pupil of Joachim, Berlin Hochschule; won the Mendelssohn Prize, 1883. *Début* 1885. Now teacher at the Hochschule, "the first woman to hold such a position there."

WIGHT, Arthur N. Composer; *b.* Düsseldorf, 1858.

WIHAN, Hans. Noted 'cellist; *b.* nr. Braunau, 1855. Solo 'cellist Court Orch., Munich, 1880; 'cello prof. Prague Cons., 1888.

WIHTOL, Joseph. *B.* Wolmar, Livonia, 1863. Prof. of harmony St. Petersburg Cons., 1886.

Works: symphonic overtures, pf. pieces, songs.

WILBYE, John. The greatest of English madrigal composers; *b.* probably in Suffolk; but nothing certain is known of him.

Works: sets of madrigals "apt both for voyals and voyces" (1598-1609), &c.

Wild (*G.*). Furious, wild, ferocious.

Wild und lus'tig. Wild and gay.

WILD, Franz. Tenor singer; *b.* Lower Austria, 1792; *d.* 1860.

WIL'HELM, Carl. Schmalkalden, 1815-73. Composer of the German national song "The Watch on the Rhine" (1854). Director Crefeld Liedertafel, 1839-64. Wrote numerous male choruses.

WILHEL'MJ, August E. D. F. V. Eminent violinist; *b.* Usingen, Nassau, 1845. Played in public at 8; studied Leipzig Cons. under David, 1861-4. First concert tour, 1865. Leader, Bayreuth Orch. at the production of Wagner's *Ring,* 1876. Settled in London. Prof. of vn. playing G.S.M., 1894. *D.* 1908.

Works: a vn. concerto, vn. solos, songs, &c.

WILHEL′MJ, Maria W. (*née* **Gastell**). Sister-in-law of preceding ; concert soprano ; *b.* Mayence, 1856. Pupil of Viardot-Garcia.

WIL′HEM (real name **BOCQUILLON**), **Guillaume L.** Noted teacher of sight-singing in classes ; Paris, 1781-1842. Teacher of music Lycée Napoléon, Paris, 1810-42. Organized a system of musical instruction for the primary schools of Paris, 1819 ; Director-General of mus. instruction in all the primary schools, 1835. Also formed singing societies for adults (now popular under the name of " Orphéons ").

Works : songs, choruses, &c., and treatises on his method of teaching.

His method, commonly known as " Wilhem's Fixed-Do System," was introduced into England by John Hullah (*q.v.*).

WILHORSKI (or **WIELHORSKI**), **Count Matvei J.** Fine 'cellist ; *b.* Volhynia, 1787 ; *d.* 1863. Director Imperial Russian Mus. Soc., St. Petersburg.

WILLAERT (or **WIGLIAR′DUS, VIGLIAR, VUIGLIART**), **Adrian.** Known also as " **Adriano.**" Renowned contrapuntist ; *b.* Flanders, abt. 1480 ; *d.* Venice, 1562. Pupil of Mouton and Des Près. Maestro St. Mark's, Venice, 1527. Est. a music school at Venice ; among his pupils were Zarlino, De Rore, and A. Gabrieli ; he is called " the founder of the Venetian school of composition." He is also supposed to have been the first to write pieces for 2 choirs.

Works : masses, motets, madrigals, vespers, canzone, &c.

WILLEBY, Chas. Song composer ; *b.* Paris, 1865.

WILLENT-BORDOGNI, Jean B. J. *B.* Douay, 1809 ; *d.* 1852. Noted bassoonist ; bassoon teacher at Brussels Cons., and later at Paris Cons.

Works : 20 operas, a bassoon method, pieces for bassoon and orch., bassoon solos, &c.

WILLIAMS, Aaron. Composer of hymn-tunes, &c. ; *b.* 1731 ; *d.* London, 1776.

WILLIAMS, Albert E. *B.* Newport, Monmouth, 1864. Bandmaster Grenadier Guards, 1897. Mus.Doc. Oxon, 1906 (the first military conductor to obtain a Doctor's degree from a British Univ.).

WILLIAMS, Anna. Soprano vocalist ; *b.* London, abt. 1852 (?). First important public appearance Crystal Palace, 1872. Teacher R.C.M. and G.S.M., 1896.

WILLIAMS, C. F. Abdy. *B.* Dawlish, 1855. Mus.B. Cantab., 1891.

Works : church music, songs ; writings on Greek music, Plain-song, &c. ; music to " Alcestis," &c.

WILLIAMS, Chas. Lee. *B.* Winchester, 1852. Mus.B. Oxon, 1878 ; organist Gloucester Cath., 1882-97.

Works : church cantatas, services, songs, carols.

WILLIAMS, Joseph (" **Florian Pascal**," &c.). Composer and publisher ; *b.* London, 1850.

WILLIAMS, Mrs. R. S. (See **Marian Mackenzie.**)

WILLIAMS, Dr. Ralph Vaughan. Composer ; *b.* Down Ampney, Gloucester, 1872.

WILLIAMS, Wm. 1717-91. Welsh poet and preacher.

Wrote the hymn " Guide me, O Thou Great Jehovah."

WILLIAMS, Wm. Aubrey (" **Gwilym Gwent** "). Working miner and glee composer ; *b.* Tredegar, Wales, 1834 ; *d.* Plymouth (U.S.), 1891.

WILLIAMS, Wm. Warwick. Conductor ; *b.* London, 1846.

WILLING, C. E. C. Organist and condr. ; *b.* in Devon, 1830 ; *d.* 1904.

WIL′LING, Johann L. *B.* nr. Meiningen, 1755 ; *d.* 1805.

Wrote a 'cello concerto, a vn. concerto, 24 Eng. dances for pf., &c.

WILLIS, Henry. Celebrated org. builder. Known as " **Father Willis.**" *B.* 1821 ; *d.* London, 1901. Rebuilt the present organ at St. Paul's Cath.

WILLIS, Richard S. *B.* Boston, Mass., 1819 ; *d.* 1900. Studied in Germany. Editor of various New York musical journals.

Works : " Church Chorals," " Student Songs," patriotic songs, &c.

WILL′MERS, Heinrich R. Pianist ; *b.* Berlin, 1821 ; *d.* 1878. Was unrivalled in the performance of " chains of trills."

Works : a pf. quartet, and "brilliant" pf. solos (fantasias, études, &c.).

WILLY, John T. Violinist ; London, 1812-1885.

Led the 1st vns. at the 1st performance of Mendelssohn's *Elijah*, Birmingham, 1846.

WILM, Nicolai von. Pianist ; *b.* Riga, 1834. Studied Leipzig Cons. Prof. of pf. and theory Imperial "Nicolai" Inst., St. Petersburg, 1860-75.

Works : a string sextet, sonatas for pf. and vn., suites for 4 hands, pf. solos, male choruses, songs, harp pieces, &c.

WIL′SING, Daniel F. E. *B.* nr. Dortmund, 1809. Organist, Wesel, 1829-34 ; afterwards in Berlin. *D.* 190-(?).

Works : an oratorio, a De Profundis (for 16 voices), pf. sonatas, songs, &c.

WILSON, Archibald W. *B.* East Pinchbeck, Lincoln, 1869. Mus.D., 1897. Orgt. Ely Cath., since 1901.

WILSON, Grenville D. Composer of numerous popular songs and pf. pieces ; *b.* Plymouth (U.S.), 1833 ; *d.* 1897.

WILSON, Hilda M. E. Contralto vocalist; *b.* Monmouth, 1860. Studied R.A.M. *Début* Gloucester Festival, 1880.

WILSON, Hugh. Shoemaker and composer; *b.* Ayrshire, 1764; *d.* 1824. Composed the tune "Martyrdom."

WILSON, John. Tenor singer; *b.* Edinburgh, 1800; *d.* Quebec, 1849.

WILSON, John. Famous lutenist · *b.* Faversham, 1594; *d.* 1673. Mus.Doc. Oxon, 1644. Prof. of music, Oxford Univ., 1656-62. Chamber musician to Chas. II.
Works: "The Devotions of His Sacred Majestic in His solitudes and sufferings, Rendered in Verse, Set to Musick for 3 Voices, and an Organ or Theorbo" (1657); "Ayres or Ballads," glees, catches, &c.

WILSON, Mrs. W. Helen Hopekirk (*q.v.*).

WILT, Marie (*née* **Liebenthaler**). Distinguished operatic soprano. Vienna, 1833-91. *Début*, Graz, 1865. Sang in London, 1866-7 and 1874-5. She was especially fine in *bravura* singing.

WINCHESTER, Ernest C. Composer of anthems, &c. *B.* Osborne, 1854.

Wind. The wind insts. of an orchestra; generally called "The wind."

Wind-band. (1) A military band, or any band composed entirely (or chiefly) of wind insts. (2) The wind insts. of an orchestra taken collectively as opposed to the "strings."

Wind-chest. That portion of an organ in which the wind is collected and compressed ready for admission to the pipes.
In large organs each manual has a separate wind-chest; and single stops like the Tuba have separate wind-chests of their own according to the "weight of wind" required. (See *Weight of Wind.*)

Wind-instruments. (See **Instrument.**)

WIN'DERSTEIN, Hans W. G. Violinist and condr. *b.* Lüneberg, 1856. Organized the "Winderstein Orch.," Leipzig, 1896; condr. Leipzig Singakademie, 1898.
Works: orchl. pieces, vn. and pf. pieces, &c.

Wind'harfe (*G.*). Æolian harp.
Wind'kasten. Wind chest (of an organ, &c.).
Wind'lade. Sound-board of an organ.
Wind'wage. A wind-gauge.

WIN'DING, August H. Pianist; *b.* Denmark, 1825; *d.* 1900. Director and teacher Copenhagen Cons.
Works: a pf. concerto, a pf. quartet, 4-hand pf. pieces, a vn. concerto, numerous pf. solos and études, &c.

WINGHAM, Thomas. London, 1846-93. Orgt. St. Michael's, Southwark, at 10; pf. prof. R.A.M., 1871; orgt. All Saints', Paddington, from 1864.
Works: 2 masses, motets, and other church music; 4 symphonies, 6 overtures, chamber music, songs, &c.

WIN'KELMANN, Hermann. Operatic tenor; *b.* Brunswick, 1849. Took the *rôle* of "Parsifal," Bayreuth, 1882.

WINKWORTH, Catherine. 1829-1878. Translated many German chorals (*Lyra Germanica*), including "Now thank we all our God" (*Nun danket alle Gott*).

WINN, Rowland M. *B.* Birmingham, 1856. Mus.Doc. Oxon, 1883.

WINOGRAD'SKY, Alexander. Noted condr.; *b.* Kiev, 1854. President Imperial Soc. of Music, Kiev, since 1888.
Has conducted concerts in the chief Russian cities, also in Paris, &c.

Win'selig (*G.*). Plaintive.
Win'selstimme. A plaintive voice.

WINTER, Maud Agnes. Pianist; *b.* London, 18—.

WIN'TER, Peter von. Noted operatic composer; *b.* Mannheim, 1754; *d.* Munich, Oct., 1825. Pupil of Abbé Vogler; Court capellmeister, Munich, from 1788.
Works: 3 oratorios, 17 sacred cantatas, 26 masses, and much other church music; several secular cantatas; 9 symphonies, several concertos, chamber music, a popular "Singschule," &c. Also about 40 operas: *I fratelli rivali*, Venice, 1792; *Der Sturm*, Munich, 1793; *Das Labyrinth*, 1794; *Ogus*, Prague, 1795; *Das unterbrochene Opferfest* ("The Interrupted Sacrifice," his best opera), Vienna, 1796; *Marie von Montalban*, Munich, 1798; *Tamerlan*, Paris, 1802; *Calypso*, London, 1803.

WIN'TERBERGER, Alexander. Pianist; *b* Weimar, 1834. Pupil of Liszt. Pf. prof. St. Petersburg Cons., 1869; settled in Leipzig, 1872.
Works: interesting pf. pieces, songs, vocal duets.

WINTERBOTTOM, Frank. Bandmaster; *b.* London, 1861.

WIN'TERFELD, Carl G. A. V. von. Berlin, 1784-1852. Learned writer on musical history.
Works: treatises on Palestrina and J. Gabrieli, an important work on the Lutheran Church music of the 16th and 17th centuries, "Luther's German Sacred Songs," &c.

Wir'bel (*G.*). Rapid rotation; whirl. (1) A peg. (2) A roll (on a drum). (3) A drumstick, mallet, &c.
Wir'belkasten. Peg-box.
Wir'beltanz. A whirling or circular dance.
Wir'beltrommel. A tenor drum.

Wir'beln (*G.*). To "roll" on a drum.

WIRTH, Emanuel. Violinist; *b.* Luditz, Bohemia, 1842. Teacher Rotterdam Cons., 1864-77; vn. prof. Hochschule, Berlin, 1877.

WISE, Michael. Salisbury, 1648-87. Orgt., Salisbury Cath., 1668; Gentleman Chapel Royal, 1675.
Works: a Magnificat in E♭, anthems, &c.

WISKE, Mortimer. *B.* Troy (U.S.), 1853. Orgt. and condr. at Brooklyn.

WIT, Paul de. 'Cellist; *b.* Maestricht, 1852. Co-founder "Zeitschrift für Instrumentenbau," Leipzig, 1880.

WITA'SEK, Johann N. A. Pianist; *b.* Bohemia, 1771; *d.* 1839. Capellmeister Domkirche, Prague, 1814; diréctor of the org. school, 1826.

His rendering of Mozart's concertos was "warmly praised by the composer."

WITHERSPOON, Herbert. Basso cantante; *b.* Buffalo, New York, 1873.

WITT, Franz. Priest; *b.* Walderbach, Bavaria, 1834; *d.* 1888.

Founded a society for the improvement of Catholic church singing, and wrote several treatises on the subject.

WITT, Friedrich. Violinist; *b.* Halten-Bergstetten, 1771; *d.* 1837. Capellmeister, Würzburg, from 1802.

Works: 2 operas, oratorios, masses, cantatas, 9 symphonies, a flute concerto, a septet, &c.

WITT, Joseph von. Operatic tenor; *b.* Prague, 1843; *d.* 1887. Leading tenor at Schwerin from 1877.

WITT, Julius. *B.* Königsberg, 1819. Composer of favourite male choruses.

WITT, Theodor de. *B.* Wesel, 1823; *d.* 1855. Talented boy; aided by Liszt. "Laid the foundations" and edited some vols. of Breitkopf & Härtel's complete edition of Palestrina's works.

WIT'TE, Georg H. *B.* Utrecht, 1843. Condr. Essen Mus. Society, 1871.

Works: a pf. quartet, an elegy for vn. and orch., a 'cello concerto, songs, numerous pf. pieces (waltzes, impromptus, &c.).

WIT'TERKOPF, Rudolf. Dramatic singer; *b.* Berlin, 1863.

WIT'TICH, Marie. Soprano; *b.* Giessen, 1868.

WIXOM, Emma (Madame Nevada). Soprano vocalist; *b.* Austen, Nevada (U.S.), 1862.

Wo'gend (*G.*). Waving, undulating.

WOEFL, J. (See **Wölfl.**)

Wohl (*G.*). Well.

Wohl'gefällig. Agreeable, pleasing.
Wohl'klang } Concord, harmony.
Wohl'laut }
Wohl'klingend. Harmonious.
Wohl'temperirt. Well-tempered (*q.v.*).

WOHL'FART, Heinrich. *B.* nr. Apolda, 1797; *d.* 1883. Noted teacher.

Works: a "Child's Pianoforte School," 3 children's sonatas, and numerous other instructive works.

WOI'KÙ, Petresoù. Violinist; *b.* Roumania, 1885(?).

WOL'DEMAR, Michel. "Talented and eccentric violinist;" *b.* Orléans, 1750; *d.* 1816. Constructed a "violon-alto" by adding a 5th string to the violin.

Works: Methods for vn., viola, and clarinet; numerous vn. solos (including 3 concertos), a string quartet, string trios, &c.

Wolf. (1) A discord produced when playing in certain keys on an organ not tuned in equal temperament. (2) A jarring vibration occasionally produced by certain notes on bowed insts. owing to some defect in the string or in the construction of the inst.

WOLF, Ernst W. *B.* Grossheringen, 1735; *d.* 1792. Court capellmeister, Weimar.

Works: Passion oratorios, cantatas, 7 pf. concertos, 42 pf. sonatas, 6 string quartets, much orchl. music (in MS.), and several operas.

WOLF, Ferdinand. Vienna, 1796-1866. Librarian Vienna Imperial Library.

Wrote a valuable historical work on "Folk-songs Church-songs, and Art-songs."

WOLF, Georg F. *B.* Hainrode, 1762; *d.* 1814.

Works: a "Musical Lexicon," a "Course of pf. playing," &c.

WOLF, Hugo. *B.* Styria, 1860; *d.* 1903. Studied Vienna Cons.

Works: an unsuccessful 4-act opera, orchl. pieces, male choruses, over 500 songs, &c.

WOLF (or WOLFF), Ludwig. Pianist and violinist; *b.* Frankfort-on-Main, 1804; *d.* 1859.

Works: a pf. quartet, 3 string quartets, &c.

WOLF, Max. Composer of successful operettas; *b.* Moravia, 1840; *d.* 1886.

WOLFF, Auguste D. B. Pianist; Paris, 1821-87. Pupil, afterwards pf. teacher, Paris Cons. Partner in the firm of Pleyel, Wolff et Cie., 1852.

WOLFF, Edouard. Concert pianist; *b.* Warsaw, 1816; *d.* 1880. Settled in Paris, 1835, as composer and teacher.

Works: 38 duos for pf. and vn., abt. 350 pf. works (études, impromptus, valses, chansons, a concerto, &c.); also "The Art of Singing on the Piano," "The Art of Execution," and "The Art of Expression."

WOLFF, Johannes. Violinist; *b.* The Hague, 1862.

WOLF-FERRA'RI, Ermanno. Composer; *b.* Venice, 1876. Wrote his first opera at 19.

WÖLFL (or WÖLFFL, WOEFL), Joseph. Famous pianist; *b.* Salzburg, 1772; *d.* London, 1812. Pupil of L. Mozart and M. Haydn. After extensive tours, lived from 1801-5 in Paris, and from 1805-12 in London, being a great favourite in both cities. He had "enormous hands"—easily stretching an octave and a 5th—and as a pianist he even held his own in friendly rivalry with Beethoven. Teacher of Cipriani Potter (*q.v.*).

He was a prolific composer, and his pf. pieces were extremely fashionable at the time, though now almost forgotten. Of his works the following deserve mention: opera, *l'Amour romanesque* (1804); ballets, *La surprise de Diane* (1805), *Alzire* (1807); pf. pieces: Concerto "Militaire," concerto "Le Calme"; grand sonatas, "Non plus ultra," and "Le Diable à quatre."

WOL'FRAM, Joseph M. Amateur composer; *b.* Dobrzan, Bohemia, 1789; *d.* 1839. Mayor of Teplitz, 1824.

Wrote several operas, *Alfred* (Dresden, 1826) being specially successful.

WOL'FRUM, Dr. Philipp. *B.* Bavaria, 1855. Mus.-director Heidelberg Univ.

Works: choral works (*The Great Hallelujah*), pf. pieces, songs.

WOL'LANCK, Friedrich. Berlin, 1782-1831. City Counsellor.

Works: operas and operettas, 2 masses, a requiem, chamber music, part-songs, &c., and over 100 songs.

WOL'LENHAUPT, Heinrich A. Pianist; *b.* Schkeuditz, nr. Leipzig, 1827; *d.* New York, 1863. Made successful concert tours; teacher, &c., in New York, 1845-55.

Works: abt. 100 brilliant pf. pieces.

WOL'STENHOLME. Blind organist and composer; *b.* Blackburn, 1865. Mus.B. Oxon, 1887.

Works: Org. pieces, vocal works, pf. pieces, &c.

WOL'ZOGEN, C. A. Alfred von. *B.* Frankfort, 1833; *d.* 1883. Intendant Court Th., Schwerin, 1868.

Works: "The Theatre of Music," "Schröder-Devrient," a new German version of Mozart's *Don Giovanni*, &c.

WOL'ZOGEN, Hans P. von. Ardent Wagnerite, son of preceding; *b.* Potsdam, 1848. Apptd. by Wagner editor *Baireuther Blätter*, 1877.

Author of numerous valuable works on Wagner's music-dramas, aims, style, methods, &c.

WOOD, Charles. *B.* Armagh, 1866. Studied R.C.M., 1883; prof. of harmony, 1888; Mus.Doc. Cantab., 1894.

Works: choral works, madrigals, songs, &c.

WOOD, Daniel J. *B.* Brompton, nr. Chatham, 1849. Orgt. Exeter Cath., 1876; Mus.Doc. Cantuar., 1896.

WOOD, Henry J. Distinguished conductor; *b.* London, 1870. Studied R.A.M., winning 4 medals. Began his first series of Queen's Hall Promenade Concerts, 1895. His wife (*née* **Ourossov**), *b.* Odessa, is a concert soprano.

WOOD, Jn. Muir. *B.* Edinburgh, 1805; *d.* 1902.

Wrote articles on Scottish Music for *Grove's Dict.*

WOOD, Mrs. Mary Ann. (See **Paton.**)

WOOD, Mary Knight. Pianist; *b.* Easthampton, Mass., 1857.

Has published several songs.

WOOD, William G. Brother of Charles Wood (above); *b.* Armagh, 1859; *d.* 1895. Student, afterwards prof., R.A.M.

Wrote org. music, church music, an operetta, &c.

Wood } The wood insts. of the orch.
Wood-wind ʃ (fl., ob., clar., fag., &c.), or the players on these insts. (See **Orchestra.**)

WOODBURY, Isaac B. Composer of simple popular music; *b.* Beverley (U.S.), 1819; *d.* 1858.

WOODFORDE-FINDEN, Mrs. (*née* **Amy Ward**). *B.* Valparaiso, 18—.

Composer of songs ("Kashmiri Songs," &c.).

WOODMAN, Raymond H. Organist and musical editor; *b.* Brooklyn, N.Y., 1861. Head of the organ department New York Metropolitan Coll. of Music, 1889.

Works: pf. pieces, org. pieces, part-songs, songs, &c.

WOODS, F. Cunningham. Organist and composer; *b.* London, 1869. Mus.B. Oxon, 1891.

WOODWARD, Rev. H. H. *B.* nr. Liverpool, 1847. Mus.B. Oxon, 1866. Precentor Worcester Cath.

Works: Anthems ("The Radiant Morn," &c.), church services, &c.

WOODWARD, Richard. *B.* Dublin, abt. 1744; *d.* 1777. Mus.Doc. Dublin, 1768.

Wrote anthems, chants, &c.

WOOLF, Benjamin E. *B.* London, 1836; *d.* 1901. Taken to America by his father, 1839. Theatrical conductor, Boston, Philadelphia, &c.

Works: operas (*Westward Ho*, 1894), orchl. music, chamber music.

WOOLHOUSE, Wesley S. B. Writer on music; *b.* North Shields, 1809; *d.* London, 1893.

WOOLNOTH, Chas. H. Pianist and composer; *b.* Glasgow, 1860.

Word-painting. In music, the attempt to describe individual words in sounds.

In setting words to music it is a recognized principle that the "general verbal sentiment" should be depicted by the "general musical style" and expression. The following would evidently be absurd :—

Whisper thy love to me!

Praise ye the Lord with a loud voice.

It is equally ridiculous, in general, to try to "paint" each separate word or phrase (as in the following arrangement of the last part of the tune "Melcombe") :—

O when will all our wan - - d'rings cease,

Where all is love, and joy, and peace!

The painting of separate words is, however, often inevitable in descriptive or dramatic music, and the greatest composers have freely used "word-painting" whenever it suited their purpose. Haydn's *Creation* is full of word-painting; and while it is perhaps occasionally a little grotesque (as for example when at the words "By heavy beasts the ground is trod," the bassoons and double bassoon enter *ff* on the word "trod," as if the heavy feet would go through the earth's crust), yet on the whole it is charming and effective. Purcell has introduced a quaint example of word-painting in *King Arthur*, where the whole chorus have to depict their " quivering with cold " as follows :—

Tho' quiv - 'ring with cold,   &c.

Handel's works abound in fine examples of legitimate word-painting, as at "disdain" in the following :—

Samson.

So mean   a tri - umph I   dis-dain.

Beethoven's *Mass in D* also contains several striking illustrations (*Gloria*, &c.). When not carried to vulgar excess, word painting is a valuable means of expression. (See also *Descriptive Music, Imitative Music*, &c.)

WORGAN, George. *B.* England, 1802 ; *d.* New Zealand, 1888.
Composed hymn-tunes, &c.

WORGAN, John. London, 1724-90. Orgt. and composer to Vauxhall Gardens, 1751-74. Mus.Doc. Cantab., 1775.

WORDSWORTH, Christopher. D.D. 1807-1885. Nephew of the poet ; Bishop of Lincoln, 1869.
Wrote "See the Conqueror mounts in triumph," and other hymns.

WORK, Henry Clay. *B.* Middletown, Conn., 1832 ; *d.* 1884.
Self-taught composer of popular songs : "Grandfather's Clock," " Marching through Georgia," " Wake, Nicodemus," &c.

Working-out. Development (*q.v.*). (See also **Thematic development.**)

WORMSER, André A. T. *B.* Paris, 1851. 1st prize for pf. playing Paris Cons., 1872 ; *Grand Prix de Rome*, 1875.
Works : operas and pantomimes (*l'Enfant prodigue*, Paris, 1890 ; London, 1891), ballets, symphonic pieces, pf. pieces, &c.

Wort (*G.*). A word.
Wor'te. Words.
Oh'ne Wor'te. Without words.
Wör'terbuch. Dictionary.

Wort'klang (*G.*). Accent, tone of voice.

WOTTON, Tom S. Author of an excellent *Dict. of Foreign Mus. Terms* (Breitkopf & Härtel, 1907).

WOTTON, Wm. B. Bassoon player ; *b.* Torquay, 1832.

WOUTERS, F. Adolphe. *B.* Brussels, 1841. Pf. prof. Brussels Cons., 1871.
Works : masses and other church music, male choruses, pf. studies, &c.

WOY'CKE, Eugen A. Pianist ; *b.* Dantzig, 1843. Settled in Edinburgh as teacher.
Works : 7 sonatas, 6 characteristic pieces, &c., for pf.
His wife, **Emily D.** (*née* **Hamilton**), is a concert violinist.

WOY'CKE, Victor. Violinist ; son of preceding ; *b.* Edinburgh, 1872. Teacher New York National Cons., 1892.

WOYRSCH, Felix von. *B.* Troppau, Austrian Silesia, 1860. Condr. Altona Sing-akademie, 1895.
Works : operas (*Wikingerfahrt*, 1896), choral works, orchl. pieces, chamber music, settings of " German Folk-songs," &c.

WRANIT'SKY, Anton. Brother of Paul (below) ; violinist and teacher ; 1761-1819.
Wrote a vn. concerto, chamber music, a vn. method, &c.

WRANIT'SKY, Paul. *B.* Moravia, 1756 ; *d.* 1808. Violinist under Haydn at Esterházy ; capellmeister Imperial Opera, Vienna, 1785.
Works : numerous operas and ballets ; incidental dramatic music ; 27 symphonies ; 12 quintets, 45 quartets, and much other chamber music ; pf. pieces.

WRE'DE, Ferdinand. Pianist ; *b.* Hanover, 1827 ; *d.* 1899. Cantor Marienkirche, Frankfort.
Works : male choruses, pf. pieces, songs.

Wrest. A tuning hammer.

Wrestblock, Wrestplank. The part of a pf. in which the tuning-pins are fixed.

WRIGHTON, W. T. Song composer ; *b.* 1816 ; *d.* Tunbridge Wells, 1880.

WRIGLEY, James G. Orgt. and condr. ; *b.* Rochdale, 1849 ; *d.* 1905. Mus.B. Cantab., 1878.

Wrist-guide. (See **Chiroplast.**)

Wuch'tig (*G.*). Weighty, weightily ; ponderously, emphatically.
Wuch'tig, jedoch' nicht schlep'pend. Impressive(ly), but not dragging.

WÜ'ERST, Richard F. Berlin, 1824-81. Studied under Mendelssohn and David. Teacher of compn. Kullak's Academy, Berlin, 1846. Member of the Academy of Arts, 1877. Editor and esteemed critic of various musical journals.
Works : operas, 2 symphonies, overtures, a vn. concerto, string quartets, songs, &c.

WÜLL'NER, Franz. Pianist and distinguished condr. ; *b.* Münster, 1832 ; *d.* 1902. Pf. teacher Munich Cons., 1856 ; Town mus.-director, Aix-la-Chapelle, 1858. Court Chapel condr., Munich, 1864 ; Court condr., 1870-77. After various other appointments as condr., director Cologne Cons., 1884.
Works : choral works, church music, chamber pf. pieces, songs, &c.

WÜLL'NER, Dr. Ludwig. Son of preceding ; bass singer ; *b.* Münster, 1858. Studied at Münster, Berlin, Strasburg, and Cologne. Became an actor. Started as a singer in 1895.

WUN'DERLICH, Johann Georg. Distinguished flautist ; *b.* Bayreuth, 1755 ; *d.* 1819. 1st flute Paris Opéra and Royal Orch., 1787 ; flute prof. Paris Cons., 1794.
Works : a flute " Method ; " 6 flute duos, and numerous flute solos.

Wür'de (*G.*). Dignity.
Mit Ein'falt und Wür'de. With simplicity and dignity.
Mit Wür'de } With dignity.
Wür'devoll

WÜR'FEL, Wilhelm. Pianist ; *b.* Planian, Bohemia, 1791 ; *d.* 1852. Prof. Warsaw Cons., 1815 ; sub. condr. Kärnthnerthor Th., Vienna, 1826. Wrote operas, pf. pieces, &c.

WURM, Marie J. A. Pianist ; *b.* Southampton, 1860. Pupil of Madame Schumann. Won the "Mendelssohn Scholarship," R.A.M., 1884.
Works : a pf. concerto, pieces for pf. and vn., pf. pieces, &c.

WURM, Wilhelm. *B.* Brunswick, 1826 ; *d.* 1904. Settled in St. Petersburg, 1847 ; bandmaster - in - chief of the Russian Guards, 1869.

Wut(h) (*G.*). Rage, fury, madness.
Wü't(h)end } Furious(ly), frantic(ally).
Wü't(h)ig

WYLDE, Henry. *B.* Bushey, Herts., 1822 ; *d.* 1890. Studied R.A.M. Mus.Doc. Cantab., 1851. Founded the " New Philharmonic Soc.," 1852 ; conducted it, 1858-79. Gresham prof. of music, 1863. Est. the London Academy of Music, 1871.
Works : " Harmony and the Science of Music," " Modern Counterpoint," " Music as an Educator," &c.

WYMAN, Addison P. *B.* Cornish, N.H., 1832 ; *d.* 1872.
Wrote popular pf. pieces ("Silvery Waves," &c.).

WYNNE, S. Edith. Soprano vocalist ; "the Nightingale of Wales ; " *b.* Holywell, Flintsh., 1842 ; *d.* 1897. Sang in public at 9. Won the Westmoreland Scholarship, R.A.M. 1863. Married Mr. A. Agabeg, 1875.

WYNS, Charlotte F. (Mad. de Bruijn). Dramatic mezzo ; *b.* Paris, 1868.

WYRNAL, John. Orgt. York Minster abt. 1573 ; probably succeeding J. Thorne (*q.v.*).
" Musician and logician both,
John Wyrnal lieth here,
Who made the organs erst to speak,
As if, or as it were."
(*Trans. of Lat. Epitaph.*)

WYVILL, Zerubbabel. *B.* Maidenhead, 1763 ; *d.* 1837.
Composed glees, hymn-tunes, &c.

X

X. This letter is not used in Italian, *s* or *ss* taking its place. *Con express., con expressione, expressivo,* &c., are common errors for *con espress., con espressione, espressivo,* &c.

X. Ten. **Op.Xa.** Opus 10. (See **Opus.**)

Xänor'phika (*G.*). A kind of piano-violin, invented by Röllig, Vienna, 1797.

XAN'ROF (real name **Léon Fourneau**). *B.* Paris, 1867. Lawyer and composer.

Works : light stage pieces, songs, &c.

XAVIER, Anton M. Chamber violinist to Napoleon I ; *b.* Paris, 1769 ; *d.* (?).

Published violin pieces, songs, &c.

XERXES (*I. Serse*). Opera by Handel, produced 1737.

The first air, "Ombra mai fu," is very popular under the title of *Handel's Largo* (in G).

XY'LANDER (or **HOLTZ'MANN**), **Wilhelm.** *B.* Augsburg, 1532 ; *d.* 1576. Prof. of Greek at Heidelberg.

Translated a work on the "Quadrivium" (arithmetic, music, geometry, and astronomy).

Xylharmon'ica. (*G., Xylharmo'nikon.*) A keyboard inst. with tuned wooden bars struck by means of small hammers.

Xy'lophone ⎫ (*Gk., Xulon,* wood, and
Xylor'ganum ⎭ *phone,* sound ; *G., Xy'lophon, Stroh'fiedel, Holz'harmonika ; F., Claquebois ; I., Gigeli'ra, Sticca'do.*) A wooden dulcimer, with a compass of about 2 octaves.

The tuned wooden bars are sometimes laid on cords of twisted straw ; hence *Stroh'fiedel.* The inst. is of ancient origin, and has many names.

Xylosis'tron. An earlier form of Xylharmonica (*q.v.*).

XYN'DAS, Spiridion. *B.* Corfu, 1812 ; *d.* Athens, 1896.

Works : ballad operas, charming songs, &c.

Y

Y. There is no "y" in Italian. *Tympani* (or *Tympany*) is a wrong spelling of *Timpani* ("kettledrums").

Ya'bal (*Hebrew*). A trumpet blast.

Yang Kin. A Chinese dulcimer with brass strings.

YANIEWICZ, Felix. (See **Janiewicz.**)

Yankee Doodle. Favourite American air of obscure origin. It commences as follows —

&c.

From available evidence it seems to be conclusive that it is a Georgian tune adopted by the Americans.

YARWOOD, Joseph. Bass vocalist and composer ; *b.* Manchester, 1829.

YELLAND, Maria. Contralto ; *b.* St. Dennis, Cornwall, 1883. Won open scholarship, R.C.M., 1901. *Début*, Chappell Ballad Concerts, 1906. Operatic *début* in Wagner's *Ring*, Covent Garden, 1908.

Yo. A Hindoo flute.

Yo'del, Yo'dle, Yo'dler. (See **Jodel.**)

YOST, Michel. Noted clarinettist ; Paris, 1754-86.
Works : 14 clar. concertos, 30 quartets for clar. and strings, 8 books of clar. duos, &c.

YOUNG, Anthony. Organist and song-composer ; 17th and 18th cents. Has been claimed as the composer of "God save the King."

YOUNG, Isabella (Mrs. Lampe). Soprano vocalist ; married J. F. Lampe (*q.v.*).

YOUNG, John M. W. *B.* Durham, 1822 ; *d.* 1897. Orgt. Lincoln Cath., 1850-95.
Works : a sacred cantata, church services, anthems, &c.

YOUNG, Rev. Matthew. *B.* Roscommon, 1750 ; *d.* 1800. Bishop of Clonfert and Kilmacduagh.
Wrote "An Inquiry into the Principal Phenomena of Sounds and Musical Strings" (1784).

YORKSHIRE FEAST SONG, THE. An ode by Purcell, 1689.

YRAD'IER, Sebastian. Spanish song composer ; *d.* Vittoria, 1865.

YRIAR'TE, Don Thomas de. Spanish poet ; *b.* Teneriffe, abt. 1750 ; *d.* 1791.
Wrote a noted poem, " La Musica " (1779).

YRVID, Rd. *Nom de plume* (reversed name) of **d'Ivry** (*q.v.*).

YSAY'E, Eugène. Fine violinist ; *b.* Liége, 1858. Studied under Wieniawski and Vieuxtemps. Toured extensively from 1881. Prof. of vn. playing Brussels Cons., 1886.
Works : 6 vn. concertos, several vn. solos, &c.

His brother, **Theo. Ysaye,** is a pianist.

Yue Kin. The "moon guitar" of the Chinese.

YUS'SUPOFF, Prince Nicolai. Violinist ; *b.* St. Petersburg, 1827. Pupil of Vieuxtemps.
Works : a "program-symphony" with vn. obbligato, a "Concerto-symphonique" for vn., a " History of Music in Russia," &c.

YZAC. (See **Isaac.**)

Z

Za. A name for B♭ in old French solmization.

ZABAL'ZA y OLA'SO, Don Damaso. Concert pianist ; *b.* Navarra, 1833 ; *d.* 1894. Prof. of theory and declamation Madrid National Cons.
Works : numerous pf. pieces, studies, sonatinas &c.

ZACCO'NI, Ludovico. Augustinian monk ; *b.* Pesaro, 1540 ; *d.* abt. 1600.
Wrote " Prattica di Musica," a valuable work on mensural music, counterpoint, and mus. insts.

ZACHARI'Ä, Eduard. Pastor ; *b.* Nassau, 1828.
Invented a set of 4 pedals for pf. acting on various groups of strings.

ZACH'AU, Friedrich W. Teacher of Handel; *b.* Leipzig, 1663 ; *d.* 1712. Orgt. at Halle from 1684.
Wrote organ pieces, figured chorals, &c.

Zäh'len (*G.*). To count (time).

ZAHM. Author of " Sound and Music," Chicago, 1892.

ZAHN, Johannes. Noted writer on Lutheran church music ; *b.* Espenbach, Franconia, 1817 ; *d.* 1895.

ZA'JIČ, Florian. Noted violinist ; *b.* Unhoscht, Bohemia, 1853. Studied Prague Cons. Leader at Mannheim, 1881, and Hamburg, 1889 ; vn. teacher Stern Cons., Berlin, 1891.

Zale'o. A Spanish national dance. (See **Jaleo.**)

Zamacuca. The national dance of Chili.

ZAMPA. Opera by Hérold, 1831.

Zampo'gna (*I.*) ⎱ (1) A bagpipe. (2) A
Zampu'gna (*I.*) ⎰ shawm.

ZANARDI'NI, Angelo. Opera composer and librettist ; *b.* Venice, 1820 ; *d.* Milan, 1893.

ZANDT, Marie van. (See **Van Zandt.**)

Za'ner. An Egyptian inst. of the bassoon type.

ZANETTI'NI. (See **Gianettini.**)

ZANG, Johann H. Pianist and organist ; pupil of J. S. Bach ; *b.* nr. Gotha, 1733 ; *d.* 1811.

ZANG'E (*Lat.* **ZANGIUS**), **Nicolaus.** Capellmeister at Brandenburg.
Published numerous sacred and secular " Lieder," 1597 to 1630.

ZA'NI de FERRAN'TI, Marco A. Eminent guitar player and teacher ; *b.* Bologna, 1800 ; *d.* 1878. Made successful concert tours.

Zänk'isch (*G.*). Cantankerous, quarrelsome.

Zan'ze. An African drum.

Zapatea'do (*S.*). A Spanish dance characterized by stamping to mark the rhythm.

Zap'fenstreich (*G.*). A tattoo (*q.v.*).
Gros'ser Zap'fenstreich. A grand finale to a military review.

Zaraban'da (*S.*). A saraband (*q.v.*).

Zaramel'la (*I.*). An Italian rustic pipe with double reed ; a kind of musette.

ZARA'TE, Eleodoro Ortiz de. *B.* Valparaiso, 1865. Studied in Italy.
Produced the first Chilian opera, *La fioraia de Lugano*, Santiago, Chili, 1895.

ZAREM'BA, Nicolai I. de. *B.* 1824 ; *d.* St. Petersburg, 1879. Teacher St. Petersburg Cons., 1862 ; director, 1867-71.

ZAREMB'SKI, Jules de. Brilliant pianist ; *b.* Shitomir, Russian Poland, 1854 ; *d.* 1885. Pupil of Liszt ; pf. prof. Brussels Cons., 1879.
Wrote interesting pf. pieces and studies.

Zar'ge (*G.*). Border, rim, case.
Zar'gen. Ribs (of a vn., &c.).

ZARLI'NO, Gioseffo. Franciscan monk ; noted theorist ; *b.* Chioggia, 1517 ; *d.* Venice, 1590. Studied music under Willaert. Maestro St. Mark's, Venice, 1565.
Works : motets, " Modulationes," &c., and important treatises on " Harmony, Counterpoint, Canon, &c."

Zart (*G.*). Soft, tender, delicate ; slender.
Mit zar'ten Stim'men. With soft-toned (delicate) stops.
Mit Zart'heit. With delicacy, tenderness.
Sehr zart. Very soft and delicate.
Zart'flöte. An org. flute stop of delicate tone, generally of 4 ft. pitch ; *flauto dolce.*
Zart gestei'gert. Gently worked up.
Zart gesung'en. Delicately sung.
Zärt'lich. Softly, tenderly, caressingly.
Zärt'lich bewegt'. With gentle movement (animation).
Zart und lieb'evoll. Tender and affectionate.
Zart und sing'end. Tender and *cantabile* (in singing style).

Zarzue'la (*S.*). An operetta or short opera, generally in two acts.
Its name is derived from the Royal Castle of Zarzuela, where the first Spanish works of this kind were produced (17th cent.).

ZARZY'CKI, Alexander. Concert pianist ; *b.* Lemberg, Austrian Poland, 1831 ; *d.* 1895. Condr. Warsaw Musical Soc., 1870 ; director Warsaw Cons., 1879.
Wrote a pf. concerto and numerous effective pf. solos.

Zau'ber (*G.*). Magic.
Zau'berflöte. A magic flute. Also an org. stop consisting of stopped pipes overblown so as to produce their first upper partial (the 12th).
Zau'berlied. Magic song.

ZAU'BERFLÖTE, Die. Opera by Mozart, Vienna, 1791 (based on Freemasonry).
The overture is a fine example of fugue combined with sonata form.

ZAVERTAL, Joseph R. *B.* Bohemia, 1819 ; *d.* 1893. Bandmaster Royal Engineers, Chatham, 1867-90.

ZAVERTAL, L. J. P. P. Nephew of preceding ; *b.* Milan, 1849. Bandmaster Royal Artillery, Woolwich, 1881-1906.

ZAYTZ, Giovanni von. *B.* Fiume, 1834. Studied Milan Cons. Theatre condr., Agram, 1870.
Works: several operas and operettas (including *Nicola Subic Zrinjski*, the first Croatian opera), instrumental music, masses, songs, &c.

ZECK'WER, Richard. Pianist and orgt.; *b.* Stendal, Prussia, 1850. Orgt. in Philadelphia, 1870-80. Teacher Philadelphia Mus. Academy, 1870; director, 1876.

Zeffiro'so (*I.*). "Zephyr-like;" light, airy, delicate.

ZEGERT. (See **Seger(t).**)

Zehn (*G.*). Ten.
Zehn'te. Tenth; a tenth.

Zei'chen (*G.*). A sign, note, character, &c.
Alt'zeichen. The alto clef. (See *Clef.*)
Auf'lösungszeichen. The natural (♮).
Bass'zeichen. Bass clef.
Verset'zungszeichen. A chromatic sign (♯, 𝄪, ♭, &c.).
Wie'derholungszeichen. A repeat sign.

ZEIS'LER. (See **Bloomfield-Zeisler.**)

Zeit (*G.*). (1) Time. (2) A beat (of a measure, or bar).
Zeit las'sen. Do not hurry the time.
Zeit'messer. A metronome.
Zeit'wert(h). Time-value; duration.

Zeit'mass (*G.*, occasionally spelt *Zeit'maass*). Speed; rate of movement; *tempo.*
Das Zeit'mass sehr allmäh'lich beschleu'nigen. Quicken the time very gradually.
Im ers'ten Zeit'mass ⎱ In the original (first) time;
Im vor'igen Zeit'mass ⎰ *tempo primo.*
Zeit'mass des erst'en Stück'es. The *tempo* of the first piece.

Zei'tung (*G.*). Newspaper, periodical.
Musik'zeitung. Musical periodical.

Zelan'te (*I.*). Zealous, ardent, fervent.

ZEL'DENRUST, Eduard. Pianist; *b.* Amsterdam, 1865.

Zèle (*F.*). Zeal, energy, enthusiasm.

ZELEN'KA, Jan Dismas. *B.* Bohemia, 1679; *d.* 1745. Court condr. and composer at Dresden.
Works: 3 oratorios, 20 masses, 3 requiems, cantatas, arias, &c.

ZELEN'SKI, Ladislas. *B.* Galicia, 1837. Prof. of compn. Warsaw Cons.
Works: symphonic pieces for orch., cantatas, chamber music, pf. pieces, an opera (*Goplana*, 1896), &c.

ZEL'LER, Dr. Karl. *B.* Lower Austria, 1844; *d.* 1898. Councillor at Vienna.
Wrote several popular operettas (*Der Vogelhändler*, &c.).

ZELL'NER, Julius. *B.* Vienna, 1832; *d.* 1900.
Works: symphonies, choral works, chamber music, pf. pieces, songs.

ZELL'NER, Leopold A. *B.* Agram, 1823; *d.* 1894. Orgt. at 15; founded and edited the *Blätter für Musik*, Vienna, 1855-68; prof. of harmony Vienna Cons., 1868.
Works: a Method for harmonium, harmonium pieces, pf. pieces, choruses, &c.

Ze'lo (*I.*). Zeal, energy, fire, enthusiasm.
Con ze'lo
Zelosamen'te ⎱ With zeal, energy, &c.
Zelo'so ⎰

ZENATEL'LO. Noted contemp. operatic tenor; *b.* Verona.

ZEL'TER, Carl F. Berlin, 1758-1832. Condr. Berlin Singakademie, 1800; organized the Berlin Liedertafel, 1809. Also organized the Royal Inst. for Church Music. Great friend of Goethe, many of whose songs he set to music.
Works: about 100 male choruses, numerous songs, an oratorio, a Requiem, pf. pieces, &c.

ZEMLIN'SKY, Alexander von. *B.* of Polish parents, Vienna, 1877. Studied Vienna Cons. Capellmeister Carl Th., Vienna, 1900.
Works: a symphony in B♭, an opera (*Sarema* 1897), &c.

Zeng. Persian cymbals.

ZENG'ER, Dr. Max. *B.* Munich, 1837. Capellmeister, Ratisbon, 1860; Munich Court Opera, 1869. Court condr., Carlsruhe, 1872. Condr. Munich Oratorio Soc,. 1878-85.
Works: operas, cantatas, and ballets; an oratorio (*Kain*, 1867); symphonies, choruses, pf. pieces, songs, &c.

ZENTA, Hermann. *Nom de plume* of A. M. A. Holmès (*q.v.*).

ZEP'LER, Bogumil. *B.* Breslau, 1858.
Works: operettas, orchl. works, songs, &c.

ZERBI'NI, John B. Violinist; *b.* London, 1839; *d.* Melbourne, 1891.

ZERETELEV. (See **Lawrowskaja.**)

Zerflies'send (*G.*). Melting away.

Zerglie'derung (*G.*). Dissection; analysis. Reducing a theme to its component motives, figures, &c.

ZERRAHN', Carl. Noted conductor; *b.* Malchow, Mecklenburg, 1826. Conductor Handel and Haydn Society, Boston (U.S.), 1854-95. For several years prof. of harmony, &c., at the New England Cons., Boston, and conductor of the Harvard Symphony Concerts.

Zerstreut' (*G.*). Open, dispersed.
Zerstreut'e Harmonie'. Dispersed or open harmony.

ZEUG'HEER, Jacob. Violinist; *b.* Zurich, 1805; *d.* 1865. Condr. "Gentlemen's Concerts," Manchester, 1831; Liverpool Philharmonic Soc., 1838.

ZEU'NER, Carl Traugott. Pianist; *b.* Dresden, 1775; *d.* 1841.
Works: 2 pf. concertos, popular pf. pieces (polonaises, variations, &c.).

ZIA'NI, Marco A. Nephew of P. A. (below); *b.* Venice, 1653; *d.* 1715. Condr. at Vienna Court from about 1700.
Wrote abt. 40 operas and serenades, 9 oratorios, &c.

ZIA'NI, Pietro A. Opera composer; *b.* Venice, abt. 1630; *d.* 1711. 2nd orgt. St. Mark's, Venice, 1666; settled in Vienna, 1677.
Wrote 21 operas, an oratorio, sonatas for 3, 4, 5, or 6 insts., &c.

ZI'CHY, Geza, Count of. *B.* Sztára, Hungary, 1849. Lost his right arm at 17, but " by dint of unconquerable energy became a left-handed piano virtuoso of astonishing and brilliant attainments." Intendant National Theatre and Opera, Pesth, 1890-4.
Works: operas (*Meister Roland*, 1899), a colln., of pf. pieces and studies for L.H. alone, songs, &c.

Zieh'harmonika (*G.*). An accordeon.

Ziem'lich (*G.*). Somewhat, rather; suitable.
Ziem'lich bewegt' und frei im Vor'trag. Somewhat animated, and free (*ad lib.*) in style (delivery).
Ziem'lich geschwind' doch kräft'ig. Rather fast, but vigorously.
Ziem'lich lang'sam. Moderately slow.
Ziem'lich leben'dig
Ziem'lich leb'haft
Ziem'lich rasch }-Moderately fast.
Ziem'lich schnell

Ziera't(h)en (*G.*). Ornaments, embellishments.

Zier'lich (*G.*). Neat(ly), elegant(ly), graceful(ly).

Zif'fer (*G.*). A figure; numeral, cipher.
Bezif'ferbass. Figured bass.
Bezif'ferung. Figuring.
Zif'fern. To figure (as a bass).

Zigeu'ner (*G.*). A gypsy; a Bohemian.
Zigeun'erartig. Gypsy-like.
Zigeun'ermusik. Gypsy music.

Zim'balon. An improved dulcimer used in Hungarian music.

Zim'belstern. An obsolete org. stop, consisting of " a star hung with little bells" placed in front of the organ and made to jingle by a current of air.

Zi'lafone (*I.*). A xylophone.

Zil'lo (*I.*). A chirp; chirping.

ZIM'BALIST, M. E. Fine violinist; pupil of L. Auer; *b.* Russia, abt. 1893. 1st London appearance, Dec., 1907.

Zim'bel (*G.*). Cymbal.

ZIM'MERMAN, Pierre J. G. Famous pf. teacher; Paris, 1785-1853. Pf. prof. Paris Cons., 1816-48. Among his pupils were Alkan, Marmontel, Prudent, and Lefebvre.
Works: an opera, 2 pf. concertos; pf. études, fantasias, &c., 6 vols. of songs, and a valuable "Encyclopédie du Pianiste."

ZIM'MERMANN, Agnes. Renowned pianist; *b.* Cologne, 1847. Studied R.A.M., London, twice winning the " King's Scholarship," and also the silver medal. *Début*, Crystal Palace, 1863.
Works: sonatas for pf. and vn.; pf. solos, &c.; also careful editions of Mozart's sonatas, Beethoven's sonatas, &c.

ZIM'MERMANN, Anton. Pressburg, 1741-81. Orgt. Pressburg Cath.
Works: a Singspiel, 9 sonatas (and other pieces) for pf. and vn., a pf. concerto, 6 string quintets.

ZINCKE. (See **Hans Sommer.**)

Zi'ngano,-a (*I.*). A gypsy.
Zi'ngana. A gypsy song.

ZINGAREL'LI, Nicola Antonio. *B.* Naples, 1752; *d.* 1837. Prod. his first opera, 1768. *Alsinda* (La Scala, Milan, 1785) brought him fame, and commissions to write further works. Maestro Milan Cath., 1792; Santa Casa, Loreto, 1794; St. Peter's, Rome, 1804-11. Director Royal Collegio di Musica, Naples, 1813; maestro Naples Cath., 1816. Among his pupils were Bellini and Mercadante; his operas had at the time " immense vogue."
Works: abt. 30 operas (*Giulietta e Romeo*, 1796, being the best); also a vast amount of church music, including a series of masses for every day in the year, 80 Magnificats, 28 Stabat Maters, 21 Credos, 3 oratorios, &c.

Zingare'sca (*I.*). A gypsy song or dance.

Zi'ngaro,-a (*I.*). A gypsy.
Al'la zi'ngara }In gypsy style.
Al'la zingare'se }
Zingare'sco,-a. Gypsy-like.

Zink, Zin'ke, Zin'ken (*G.*). (*I., Cornet'to.*) An obsolete wind inst. with a straight or curved wooden tube and cupped mouthpiece. (See **Cornet.**)

ZINK'EISEN, Conrad L. D. *B.* Hanover, 1779; *d.* 1838. Chamber musician Brunswick Court Orch., 1819.
Works: 4 overtures, 6 vn. concertos, much chamber music, military music, male choruses.

ZINZENDORF, Count von. 1700-1760. Moravian bishop, 1737.
Wrote over 2,000 hymns, including " Jesu, Thy blood and righteousness." (Trans. by J. Wesley.)

ZIPO'LI, Domenico. Orgt. at Rome; *b.* abt. 1680 (?); *d.* after 1726.
Pub. " Table Sonatas " for org. or cembalo, 1726.

Zir'kel (*G.*). A circle.
Zir'kelkanon. An infinite canon. (See *Canon.*)

Zisch (*G.*). A hiss.
Zisch'laut. A hissing sound.

Zi'ther. An inst. consisting of a number of strings stretched over a resonance box.
There are numerous varieties of this instrument. (1) The modern *Schlag'zither*, or " plucked zither," has 32 or more strings—some metal, others gut or silk—plucked by the thumb (with a ring plectrum) and fingers of the right hand. It is made in 3 principal sizes: *Prim'-zither* (treble zither), *Conzert'-zither*, and *Elegie'-zither*.
(2) The older *Streich'zithern*, or " bowed zithers," are varieties of the *Viol* (*q.v.*).

Zi'therharfe (*G.*). A species of auto-harp (*q.v.*).

Zit'tera (*I.*). Zither.

Zit'ternd (*G.*). Trembling, shaking, undulating; *tremolando.*
Zit'tern der Stim'me. Faltering of the voice.

Zitti'no (*I.*). Silence.

ZOEL'LER, Carli. *B.* Berlin, 1849; *d.* London, 1889. Settled in London, 1873; bandmaster 7th Hussars, 1879.
Works: operettas, orchl. pieces, chamber music, songs, &c. Edited the "United Service Military Band Journal," and wrote a work on " The Viole d'amour."

Zö'gernd (*G.*).   Lingering, hesitating ; retarding.

Zolfà (*I.*).   Sol-fa.

ZÖLL'NER, Andreas. *B.* Arnstadt, 1804 ; *d.* 1862.
Wrote popular male choruses.

ZÖLL'NER, Heinrich. Son of K. F. (below); *b.* Leipzig, 1854. Mus.-director Dorpat Univ., 1878. Conductor Cologne Mannergesangverein, 1885 ; also teacher in the Cons., and condr. of the Singverein, the Wagner-verein, &c. Condr. New York " Deutscher Liederkranz," 1890 ; mus.-director Leipzig Univ., 1898.
Works : operas, choral works with orch., an oratorio, cantatas, male choruses, songs, &c.

ZÖLL'NER, Karl Friedrich. *B.* Thuringia, 1800 ; *d.* 1860. Vocal instructor " Rathsfreischule," Leipzig, 1820. Founded a male choral society (1833) which led to the formation of many similar societies.
He was a distinguished composer of male choruses ; wrote also motets, songs, &c.

ZÖLL'NER, Karl H. *B.* Oels, Silesia, 1792 ; *d.* 1836. Toured as organist till 1833 ; then settled in Hamburg.
Works : an opera, masses, motets, org. pieces, pf. pieces, &c.

Zopf (*G.*).   " Pigtail." " The German term for the old-fashioned obsolete style in music."—*Grove.*

ZOPFF, Dr. Hermann. *B.* Glogau, 1826 ; *d.* 1883. Co-editor *Neue Zeitschrift für Musik*, Leipzig, 1864 ; editor-in-chief, 1868.
Wrote choral works, a " Theorie der Oper," a " Gesangschule," &c.

Zop'po,-a (*I.*).   " Limping, halting."
Al'la zop'pa.   Syncopated.

Zor'nig (*G.*).   Angry, scorning(ly).

Zoulou. (*F.*, *Zulu.*) A form of small piano or pianette.

ZSCHIE'SCHE (pron. *Tshee'-shĕ*), **August.** Operatic bass ; Berlin, 1800-76. Sang Berlin Court Opera, 1829-61.

ZSCHOCH'ER, Johann. Pianist ; Leipzig, 1821-97. Noted teacher ; founded an Inst. of Music, Leipzig, 1846.

Zu (*G.*).   To, unto ; in addition to, along with ; at, in, on, by, for ; too.
Zu'klang.   Unison ; consonance, harmony.
Zu sehr.   Too much.
Zu vier Händ'en.   For 4 hands.
Zu 2.   Same as *A due*, *A.* 2. (*q.v.*).

Zuerst' (*G.*).   Firstly, at first.

Zu'fällige (*G.*).   Accidentals.
Zu'fälliges Verset'zungszeichen.   An accidental sign (♮, ♯, ♭, &c.).

Zuf'folo (*I.*) } A small whistle or flageolet
Zu'folo (*I.*) } used in training song-birds.
Zufolo'ne.   A large whistle.

Zug (*G.*).   A word of many applications, implying *drawing*, *pulling*, *progress*, *procession*, &c. (1) *Regis'terzug* ; a stop,

a stop-knob. (2) A pf. pedal. (3) Slide (of a flute, trombone, &c.).
Zug'posaune.   Slide trombone.
Zug'trompete.   Slide trumpet.
Zug'werk.   (1) Tracker-action of an organ. (2) Mechanical appliances (of an organ, &c.).

Zü'geglöck'chen (*G.*).   The passing-bell ; a knell.

Zu'kunftsmusik (*G.*).   " Music of the Future " (*q.v.*).
Also now used in the sense of " Music *with* a future."

Zum (*G.*).   To the, for the, &c.
Zum Beschluss'.   For the conclusion ; *finale.*

Zumma'rah. An Egyptian bassoon.

ZUM'PE, Hermann. *B.* Upper Lusatia, 1850 ; *d.* 1903. Worked with Wagner, Bayreuth, 1873-6 . Afterwards condr. at various theatres. Court capellmeister, Stuttgart, 1891 ; Munich, 1895.
Works : operas and operettas (*Farinelli*, 1888), orchl. pieces, songs, &c.

ZUMSTEEG', Johann R. 'Cellist ; *b.* Sachsenflur, 1760 ; *d.* 1802. Court capellmeister, Stuttgart, 1791.
Works : 8 operas, a 'cello concerto, church-cantatas, &c. ; and 20 "ballades" for solo voice with pf. accompt. As a song composer he is reckoned the precursor of Löwe and Schubert.

Zu'nehmend (*G.*).   Increasing, augmenting ; *crescendo.*
Zu'nehmende Bewe'gung.   With increasing movement ; quicker.

Zung'e (*G.*).   A tongue, a reed.
Auf'schlagende Zung'e.   A beating reed.
Dop'pelzunge.   (1) A double reed. (2) Double-tonguing.
Durch'schlagende Zung'e.   A free reed.
Zung'enpfeife.   A reed pipe.
Zung'enstimme.   A reed stop.
Zung'enwerk.   The "reed-work" of an organ.

Zung'enschlag (*G.*).   "Tonguing" (on wind insts.).

Zupf'end (*G.*).   Plucking ; *pizzicato.*

Zur (*G.*).   Contraction of *Zu den.* To the, with the, on the, by the, &c.
Zur Wie'derholung.   To be repeated.

Zur MÜH'LEN, Raimund von. Tenor singer ; *b.* Livonia, 1854. First London appearance, 1882.
Excels as a singer of German *Lieder.*

Zurna. A Turkish oboe.

Zur NIE'DEN, Albrecht. *B.* Emmerich-on-Rhine, 1819 ; *d.* 1872. Music-director Duisberg, 1850.
Wrote " Lyric Song-dramas " for soli, chorus, and orch. ; pf. pieces, songs, &c.

Zurück' (*G.*).   Back.
Zurück'-gehend.   Returning (to the original speed).

Zurück'halten (*G.*).   To retard, to hold back.
Zurück'halten.   Rallentando.
Zurück'haltung.   Retardation.
Zurück'kehrend.   Going back, returning.
Wie'der Zurück'kehrend in das Haupt'zeitmass.   Again returning to the principal *tempo.*
Zurück'schlag.   Ribattu'ta (*q.v.*).

Zusam'men (*G.*).   Together.   Abbn. *Zus.*
Bei'de Chö're zusam'men.   Both choirs (choruses) together.
Zusam'menklang.   Simultaneous sounding of 2 or more tones ; harmony, consonance.

Zusam'mengesetzt. Combined ; compound.
Zusam'mengesetzte Takt'art. Compound time.
Zusam'menlaut. Concord, harmony.
Zusam'menschlag. An *acciaccatura.*
Zusam'menspiel. Ensemble playing.
Zusam'menstreichung. Slurring.
Zusam'menziehend. Drawing together ; *stringendo.*

Zutrau'lich (*G.*). Confident(ly).

Zuvor' (*G.*). Before.
Wie zuvor'. As before.

ZVO'NAŘ, Joseph L. *B.* nr. Prague, 1824 ; *d.* 1865. Director Prague Organ School. Wrote numerous vocal works, and the " first treatise on Harmony in the Bohemian language."

Zwei (*G.*). Two.
Zwei Brat'schen allein'. For two solo violas.
Zwei'chörig. For two choirs (or divided choir).
Zwei ein'zelne Violi'nen. (For) two solo violins.
Zwei'fach. (1) Double ; two-fold. (2) In two ranks (of org. mixtures). (3) Compound (of intervals).
Zwei'fache Interval'le. Compound intervals.
Zwei'facher. A dance with alternative duple and triple time.
Zwei'füssig. Two-foot (as pitch, or org. pipes).
Zwei'gesang. A duet.
Zwei'gestrichen. Twice stroked, or accented. (See *Pitch.*)
Zwei'halbe Takt. 2-2 time.
Zwei'händig. For 2 hands.
Zwei'mal. Twice.
Zwei'spiel. A duet.
Zwei'stimmig. For 2 voices ; in 2 parts.
Zwei'tel
Zwei'tel-no'te } A half-note ( ).
Zwei'te La'ge. The 2nd position (vn. playing, &c.).
Zwei'te Mal. The 2nd time (after a repeat).
Das zwei'te Mal pp. The 2nd time *pianissimo.*

Zwei'tritt. A "two-step" (or quick waltz).
Zweiunddrie'ssigstel(-no'te). A 32nd note ( )
Zweivier'teltakt. 2-4 time.
Zwei'zähliger Takt. Duple time.
Zweizwei'teltakt. 2-2 time.

Zwerch (*G.*). Athwart, across.
Zwerch'flöte. The transverse flute ; *flauto traverso.*
Zwerch'pfeife. A piccolo, or fife.

ZWIN'TSCHER, Bruno. Pianist ; *b.* Ziegenhain, Saxony, 1838. Pf. teacher Leipzig Cons., 1875.
Works : pf. studies, a "School of Ornaments," &c.

Zwisch'en (*G.*). Among, between ; intermediate.
Zwisch'enakt. An *entr'acte* (*q.v.*).
Zwisch'enaktsmusik. Music between the acts.
Zwisch'engesang. An interpolated song ; an interlude.
Zwisch'enharmonie. An episode (*q.v.*).
Zwisch'enraum. A space of the staff.
Zwisch'ensatz. An episode (*q.v.*).
Zwisch'enschlag. The two small notes indicating a turn at the end of a trill (shake).
Zwisch'enspiel } An interlude between the verses of
Zwisch'enstück } hymns, &c. ; an *intermezzo.*
Zwisch'enstimme. A middle voice (or part).
Zwisch'enton. Intermediate sound, passing note, &c.

Zwit'scherharfe (*G.*). Same as **Spitz'harfe** (*q.v.*).

Zwit'schern (*G.*). To twitter, chirp, warble.
Ein Lied zwit'schern. To warble a song (air).

Zwölf (*G.*). Twelve.
Zwölf'ach'teltakt. 12-8 time.
Zwölf'saiter. A kind of guitar with 12 strings.

Zym'bel (*G.*). A cymbal.

SUPPLEMENTARY LIST

OF GERMAN TERMS AND PHRASES, REFERRING ESPECIALLY TO ORGAN AND
PIANOFORTE TECHNIQUE.

N.B.—Other terms and phrases are given in the body of the Dictionary.

Ab. Off.
   Kop'pel ab. Coupler off.

Ab'wärts. Descending (scale, &c.).
   Ab'wärts in De'cimen (De'zimen). Descending in 10ths.
   Ab'wärts in Okta'ven. Descending in 8ves.
   Ab'wärts in Sex'ten. Descending in sixths.
   Ab'wärts in Terz'en. Descending in thirds.

Ab'wechselnd. Alternating; changing manuals or fingers, &c.

An. On.
   Kop'pel an. Draw coupler.

Auch in an'dern Ton'arten. (Practise) also in other keys.

Auch so zu spiel'en ⎱ To be played (practised)
Auch so zu ü'ben ⎰ also in the following manner.

Auf das Un'tersetzen des Dau'mens zu ach'ten. Pay special attention to the passing under of the thumb(s).

Auf die Bäs'se zu ach'ten. Pay particular attention to the bass.

Auf'wärts. Ascending (scale, &c.).
   Auf'wärts in De'cimen (De'zimen). Ascending in 10ths.
   Auf'wärts in Okta'ven. Ascending in 8ves.
   Auf'wärts in Sex'ten. Ascending in sixths.
   Auf'wärts in Terz'en. Ascending in thirds.

Bei'de Peda'le. Both pf. pedals.

Bis zur gröss'ten Schnell'igkeit zu ü'ben. To be practised until it can be played with the greatest rapidity.

Brech'ung ein'es Akkor'des. Arpeggio.

Das Pedal' muss mit Vor'sicht an'gewendet werd'en. The pedal must be used with caution.

Dau'men. The thumb.

Deut'licher An'schlag mit dem 4ten Fing'er. Distinct stroke (touch) with the 4th finger.

Die Dop'pelschläge egal' zu spiel'en. The turns to be played evenly.

Die gehalt'enen No'ten stärk'er an'schlagen. The sustained notes to be struck firmly (loudly).

Die gehalt'enen Tö'ne sehr kling'en las'sen. The sustained tones to be very resonant and given their full time-value.

Die Hand'e leicht ü'berschlagen. The hands to be crossed lightly (deftly, gracefully).

Dunk'le Stim'men. Dull-toned stops.

Dur'tonleiter. Major scale.

Egal'ität. Equality, uniformity (of touch).

Ein'e gut'e Ton'leiter. A good (beautiful) scale.

Ein'er schö'nen Mecha'nik. A fine mechanical technique.

Ein'e schö'ne Aus'führung. A beautiful execution (technique).

Ein'greifen. To cross hands.

En'ger Fing'erzetzung. Close fingering.

Eng'mensurirte Stim'me 8 Fuss. A small scale 8 ft. stop.

Fing'erbildner. A "finger developer;" dumb piano, &c.

Fing'ersatz. Fingering.

Fing'erwechsel. Change of fingers on the same key.

Fort. Off.
   Flö'te fort. Flute off.

Für die link'e Hand. For the left hand.

Für die rech'te Hand. For the right hand.

Fuss. Foot (of pitch).
   Acht'-füssig, 8-füssig. 8 ft. pitch.
   Vier-füssig, 4-füssig. 4 ft. pitch.
   Sechs'zehnfüssig, 16 -füssig. 16 ft. pitch.
   Fuss'klavier. Organ pedals.

Gebroch'ene Akkor'de. Arpeggios.

Gebund'en. Legato.

Gedackt' 8 Fuss und Spitz'-flöte 4 Fuss. Stopped diapason 8 ft. and Spitzflöte 4 ft.

Gedehn'ter Fing'erzetzung. Wide fingering.

Gemisch'te Stim'men. Mixtures.

Gestos'sen. Staccato.

Grob. Wide scale (of organ pipes).

Hand'lage. Position of the hand.

Hand'stücke. Exercises for " forming " the hand.

Har'fenmässig. Harp-like; arpeggiando.

Haupt'manual. " Great " manual.

Haupt'prinzipal. 8 ft. diapason (on the manuals).

Haupt'werk. The " great " organ.

Hell'e und hoh'e Stim'men. Bright clear-toned stops.

Hervor'tretende Stim'me. (With) a reed stop.

In all'en Ton'arten zu spiel'en (ü'ben). Play (practise) in all keys.

In der Ge'genbewe'gung ⎱ In contrary
In Ge'genbewe'gung ⎰ motion.

In mehr'eren Dur- und Moll'tonarten zu spiel'en. To be played (practised) in several major and minor keys.

In spring'enden Octa'ven. In skipping octaves.

In viel'en Ton'arten zu spiel'en (ü'ben). Play (practise) in various keys.

Klavier'. (1) Pianoforte. (2) Keyboard.
   Klavier'mässig. In pf. style; suitable for pf.
   Klavier'satz. Pf. piece; pf. style.
   Klavier'stück. Pf. piece.
   Klavier' vier'handig. Pf. duet.

Klein, Klei'ne. Small.
   Klein'gedackt. Small scale stopped diapason.

Kop'pel. Coupler.
   Kop'pel ab. Coupler off.
   Kop'pler an. Coupler on.

Kurz in bei'den Händ'en. Short (detached, crisp, *staccato*) in both hands.

Labial'pfeife, Labial'stimme. Flue pipe, flue stop.
Labial'werk. Flue work.

Leicht ü'berschlagen. Cross over (the hands) lightly (deftly, easily).

Leicht und duft'ig zu spiel'en. Play lightly and crisply (airily).

Lingual'pfeife, Lingual'stimme. Reed pipe, reed stop.

Manual'. Manual, finger key.
Manual'iter. On the manuals alone.
Manual'koppel. Manual coupler.
Manual'taste. Finger key.

Mehr hoh'e und hel'le Stim'men. (More) clear and bright-toned stops.

Mehr tief'e und vol'le Stim'men. (More) deep and full-toned stops.

Mit dem 4ten (5ten) Fing'er deut'lich an'-schlagen. The 4th (5th) finger must strike (touch, press) distinctly.

Mit densel'ben vor'her an'gege'benen Nuan'-cen zu spiel'en. To be played with the same attention to the *nuances* (shades of expression) as before.

Mit Hinein'legen. Press down the keys gently and firmly, but do not strike them.—*F. Wieck.*

Mit leich'tem Hand'gelenk } With loose
Mit lock'erm Hand'gelenk } wrist.

Mit schnell'em Fing'erwechsel. With rapid change of fingers (on the same key).

Mit'telsanft. Moderately soft.

Mit'telstark. Moderately loud.

Mit'telstarken Stim'men. Moderately loud stops.

Mit wei'che Accent'uation. With gentle accentuation.

Moll'tonleiter. Minor scale.
Harmo'nische Moll'tonleiter. Harmonic minor scale.
Melo'dische Moll'tonleiter. Melodic minor scale.

Nach und nach mehr'ere Sai'ten. Gradually release the soft pedal.

Ne'benwerk. Choir organ.

O'bermanual, O'berwerk, &c. (See under **O.**)

Of'fen. Open.
Of'fenpfeife. Open pipe.

Oh'ne Pedal'. Without pedals.

Oktav'koppel. Octave coupler.

Or'gel, Or'gelbälge, Or'gelpfeife, &c. (See under **O.**)

Pedal'. Pedal.
Pedal' Cla'ves
Pedal' Claviatur' } Pedal keyboard.
Pedal' Klaviatur'
Peda'le dop'pelt. With both feet at once (org. or pf.).
Pedal'pfeife, Pedal'stim'me. Pedal pipe, pedal stop.

Per'lendes Spiel. "Pearly" playing ; tasteful finished execution.

Rech'te Hand. Right hand.

Ruh'ige Aus'dehnung der Hand. Gentle stretching (expansion) of the hand.

Ruh'iger Hand'haltung. Steady position of the hand.

Ruh'iger Un'tersatz des Dau'mens. Smooth passing-under of the thumbs.

Sanft'e, hell'e Flöte 8 Fuss. A soft, bright 8-ft. flute.

Sanft'e Stim'men. Soft stops.

Sca'len. Scales.

Scharf'e Stim'men. Bright shrill stops.

Schwell'werk. Swell organ.

Sechs'zehnfüssig. 16 ft. (of org. pipes).

Sehr lega'to in der rech'ten, und mit lock'erm Hand'gelenk in der link'en Hand. Very *legato* in the right hand, and with loose wrist in the left.

Stark auch pia'no zu spiel'en. To be played (practised) both *forte* and *piano.*

Stark'e Stim'men. Loud stops.

Stark und hoch. Loud and clear (stops).

Stark und tief. Loud and deep (stops).
Sehr stark'e, tief'e Stim'men. Very loud deep-toned stops.

Stum'me Pfei'fe. Dummy pipe.

Tas'te. Key (digital or pedal).
O'bertasten
Schwar'ze Tas'ten } Black keys.
Un'tertasten
Weis'se Tas'ten } White keys.
Tastatur'
Tas'tenbrett } Keyboard.

Tief'e Stim'men
Tief'ere Stim'men } Deep-toned stops.

Tief'tönend. Deep-toned.

Ton'arten. Keys.

Ü'bergreifen
Ü'berschlagen } To cross hands.

Ü'bersetzen. To pass a finger over the thumb in pf. playing ; to pass one foot over the other.

Ü'bung, Ü'bungsstück. A study, an exercise.

Un'tersatz des Dau'mens. Passing-under of the thumb(s).

Un'tersetzen. To pass the thumb under a finger, or one foot under the other.

Un'terwerk. The lowest manual of an organ.

Vier'fach. 4-ranked (of mixtures).

Vier'füssig. 4-feet (of stops).

Vol'les Werk. Full organ.

Weich ü'berschlagen. Cross over (the hands) smoothly (evenly).

Zuerst je'de Hand allein' zu ü'ben. First practise each hand separately.

Zug. A draw stop, pf. pedal, &c.
Crescendo Zug. Crescendo pedal.
Regis'terzug. A stop, a stop-knob.
Zug'werk. Mechanical appliances (of an organ, &c.)

Zu spiel'en. For playing ; to be played ; play.
Stark zu spiel'en. To be played loudly.

Zu vier Händ'en. For 4 hands.

Zwei'fach. 2-ranked (of mixtures).

Zwei'füssig. 2-feet (of stops).

Zwei'händig. For 2 hands.

Zu ü'ben. For practising ; to be practised ; practise.
In all'en Ton'arten zu ü'ben. Practice in all the keys

THE MODULATOR.

D♭	A♭	E♭	B♭	F	DOH=C		G	D	A	E	B
B♭	*F*	*C*	*G*	*D*	*LAH=A*		*E*	*B*	*F♯*	*C♯*	*G♯*
m¹	l	r¹	s	d¹	f¹				se	d¹	ba
	se		ba	t	m¹		l	r¹	s	t	f
r¹	s	d¹	f		re¹		se		ba		m
	ba	t	m	l	r¹		s	d¹	f	l	r
d¹	f		se	de¹			ba	t	m		
t	m	l	r	s	doh¹		f		r	se	d
	se	ba			te		m	l	r	s	t₁
l	r	s	d	f	ta — le		se		ba	ba	l₁
se	ba	t₁	m	lah			r	s	d	f	
s	d	f		la — se			ba	t₁	m		se₁
ba	t₁	m	l₁	r	soh		d	f		r	s₁
f		se₁		ba — fe			t₁	m	l₁		ba₁
m	l₁	r	s₁	d	fah			r	se₁	r	f₁
	se₁	ba₁	t₁	me			l₁	s₁	d	t₁	m₁
r	s₁	d	f₁	ma — re			se₁	ba₁		l₁	
ba₁		t₁	m₁	ray			s₁	r	ba₁		r¹
d	f₁	se₁		ra — de			ba₁	d	t₁	m₁	l₁
t₁	m₁	l₁	r₁	s₁	doh		f₁	t₁	m₁	l₁	se₁
	se₁	ba₁			t₁		m₁	l₁	r₁	s₁	d₁
l₁	r₁	s₁	d₁	f₁	ta₁		se₁		r₁	ba₁	t₂
se₁		ba₁	t₂	m₁	l₁		r¹	s₁	d₁	se₁	
s₁	d₁	f₁			se₁		s₁	ba₁	t₂	s₁	d₁
ba₁	t₂	m₁	l₂	r¹	s₁		d₁	f₁	m₁	ba₁	l₂

NOTE.—The capital letters at the top show the pitch of DOH in each key, and the italic letters the pitch of LAH.

N.B.—This "Chart for Teaching Tune" also shows pictorially the chief Acoustical theories relating to Scales, Intervals, Temperament, and Key-relationship.

TABLATURE.

(1) Lute Tablature: from Adrien Le Roy (1551)

(2) Lute Tablature · England, 16th Century

(3) Viol Tablature: England, 17th Century

HARMONIUM and ORGAN MANUAL.

* Some organs stop at F; others at G, A, or C.

SEVEN-OCTAVE PIANOFORTE.

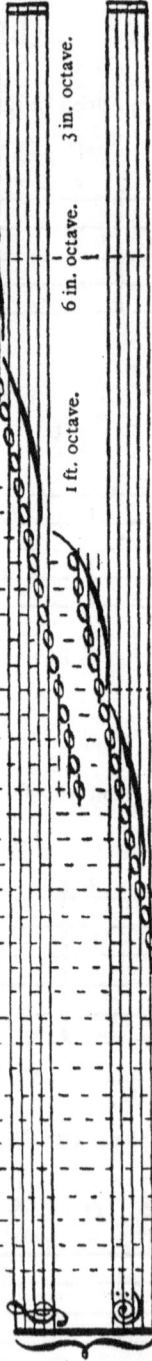

AMERICAN ORGAN.

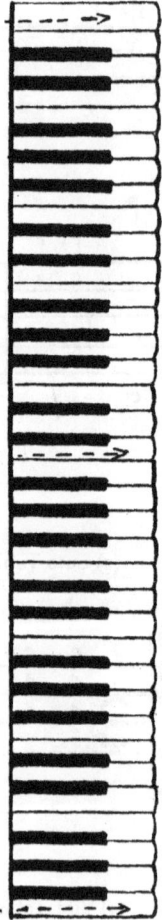

Middle C

32 ft. octave.

16 ft. octave.

8 ft. octave.

4 ft. octave.

2 ft. octave.

1 ft. octave.

6 in. octave.

3 in. octave.

CHARTS OF TIME-SIGNATURES, &c.

Time-Signatures.

		BEAT NOTE	ENGLISH	GERMAN	FRENCH	ITALIAN
SIMPLE. Duple.		$\frac{2}{2}$ or ¢	Two-two	Zweizwei'teltakt	Deux-deux ⊕	A cappel'la, or Alla bre've
		$\frac{2}{4}$	Two-four	Zweivier'teltakt	Deux-quatre	Du'e-quar'ti, or Quat'tro-du'e
		$\frac{2}{8}$	Two-eight	Zweiach'teltakt	Deux-huit	Du'e otta'vi, or Ot'to-du'e
Triple.		$\frac{3}{1}$ or 3	Three-one	Dreiein'teltakt	Trois-un	U'no-tre
		$\frac{3}{2}$	Three-two	Dreizwei'teltakt	Trois-deux	Tre-mez'zi, or Du'e tre
		$\frac{3}{4}$	Three-four	Dreivier'teltakt	Trois-quatre	Tre-quar'ti, or Quat'tro-tre
		$\frac{3}{8}$	Three-eight	Dreiach'teltakt	Trois-huit	Tre-otta'vi, or Ot'to tre
Quadruple.		$\frac{4}{2}$ or ¢	Four-two	Vierzwei'teltakt	Quatre-deux	Quat'tro-mezzi, or Du'e Quat'tro
		$\frac{4}{4}$ or ¢	Four-four	Viervier'teltakt	Quatre-quatre	Quat'tro quar'ti, or Quat'tro-quat'tro
		$\frac{4}{8}$	Four-eight	Vierach'teltakt	Quatre-huit	Quat'tro otta'vi, or Ot'to-quat'tro
		$\frac{4}{16}$	Four-sixteen	Viersechzehn'teltakt	Quatre-seize	Quat'tro-sedice'simi, or Sedi'ci-quat'tro
COMPOUND. Duple.		$\frac{6}{2}$	Six-two	Sechszwei'teltakt	Six-deux	Se'i-mez'zi, or Du'e-se'i
		$\frac{6}{4}$	Six-four	Sechsvier'teltakt	Six-quatre	Se'i-quar'ti, or Quat'tro-se'i
		$\frac{6}{8}$	Six-eight	Sechsach'teltakt	Six-huit	Se'i-otta'vi, or Ot'to-se'i
		$\frac{6}{16}$	Six-sixteen	Sechssechzehn'teltakt	Six-seize	Se'i-sedice'simi, or Sedi'ci-se'i
Triple.		$\frac{9}{4}$	Nine-four	Neunvier'teltakt	Neuf-quatre	No've-quar'ti, or Quat'tro-no've
		$\frac{9}{8}$	Nine-eight	Neunach'teltakt	Neuf-huit	No've-otta'vi, or Ot'to-no've
		$\frac{9}{16}$	Nine-sixteen	Neunsechzehn'teltakt	Neuf-seize	No've-sedice'simi, or Sedi'ci-no've
Quadruple.		$\frac{12}{4}$	Twelve-four	Zwölfvier'teltakt	Douze-quatre	Dodi'ci-quar'ti, or Quat'tro-dodi'ci
		$\frac{12}{8}$	Twelve-eight	Zwölfach'teltakt	Douze-huit	Dodi'ci-otta'vi, or Ot'to-dodi'ci
		$\frac{12}{16}$	Twelve-sixteen	Zwölfsechzehn'teltakt	Douze-seize	Dodi'ci-sedice'simi, or Sedi'ci-dodi'ci
Octuple.		$\frac{4}{4}$ (really $\frac{8}{8}$)	Eight-eight	Achtach'teltakt	Huit-huit	Ot'to-otta'vi, or Ot'to-ot'to
		$\frac{24}{16}$	Twenty-four-sixteen	Vier'undzwanz'ig-sechzehn'teltakt	Vingt-quatre-seize	Sedi'ce-ventiquat'tro
Quintuple.		$\frac{5}{4}$	Five-four	Fünfvier'teltakt	Cinq-quatre	Cin'que-quar'ti, or Quat'tro-cin'que
		$\frac{5}{8}$	Five-eight	Fünfach'teltakt	Cinq-huit	Cin'que-otta'vi, or Ot'to-cin'que
Septuple.		$\frac{7}{4}$	Seven-four	Siebenvier'teltakt	Sept-quatre	Set'te-quar'ti, or Quat'tro-set'te
		$\frac{7}{8}$	Seven-eight	Siebenach'teltakt	Sept-huit	Set'te-otta'vi, or Ot'to-set-te

⊕ Or *Mesure à deux-deux;* and similarly throughout.

Note-Names (Pitch).

English	Italian	French	German
C	Do	Ut	C
D	Re	Re	D
E	Mi	Mi	E
F	Fa	Fa	F
G	Sol	Sol	G
A	La	La	A
B flat	Si bemolle	Si bémol	B
B	Si	Si	H

For " flat," the Italian is *bemol'le* ; French, *bémol;*
German, *es* (*s* only after a vowel).
For " double flat," the Italian is *bemol'le dop'pia* ;
French, *double bémol* ; German, *eses* (*ses'* only
after a vowel).
For " sharp," the Italian is *die'sis* ; French, *dièse;*
German, *is*.
For " double sharp," the Italian is *die'sis dop'pio* ;
French, *double dièse* ; German, *isis*.
Thus :

	Italian	French	German
C♭♭	Do bemol'le dop'pia	Ut double bémol	Ceses
C♭	Do bemol'le	Ut bémol	Ces
C♯	Do die'sis	Ut dièse	Cis
Cx	Do die'sis dop'pio	Ut double dièse	Cisis

Key-Names.

Same as Note-Names (Pitch), with the additions
shewn below :—

English.	Italian.	French.	German.
Major	Maggio're	Majeur	Dur
Minor	Mino're	Mineur	Moll

Thus :—

English.	Italian.	French.	German.
C major	Do maggio're	Ut majeur	C dur
C♭ major	Do bemol'le maggio're	Ut bémol majeur	Ces dur
C♯ major	Do die'sis maggio're	Ut dièse majeur	Cis dur
C minor	Do mino're	Ut mineur	C moll
C♯ minor	Do die'sis mino're	Ut dièse mineur	Cis moll
A♭ minor	La bemol'le mino're	La bémol mineur	As moll
B♭ major	Si bemol'le maggio're	Si bémol majeur	B dur
B♭ minor	Si bemol'le mino're	Si bémol mineur	B moll

Note-Names (Duration).

Shape.	English Name.	German.	French.	Italian.
	Breve, or Double note.	Bre'vis.	Brève, Carrée.	Bre've.
	Semibreve, or Whole note.	Ganz'eno'te, Ganz'no'te, or Ganz'e Takt'note.	Semibrève, Ronde.	Semibre've.
	Minim, or Half-note.	Hal'be No'te, or Halb'no'te.	Blanche.	Min'ima, Bian'ca.
	Crotchet, or Quarter-note.	Vier'tel, or Vier'telno'te.	Noir.	Ne'ra.
	Quaver, or Eighth-note.	Ach'tel, or Ach'telno'te.	Croche.	Cro'ma.
	Semiquaver, or 16th note.	Sechzehn'tel, or Sechzehn'telno'te.	Double-croche.	Semicro'ma.
	Demisemiquaver, or 32nd note.	Zwei'unddreissigs'tel (No'te).	Triple-croche.	Semibiscro'ma.
	Hemidemisemiquaver, or 64th note.	Vier'undsechzigs'tel (N'ote).	Quadruple-croche.	Quattricro'ma.

Rest-Names.

English Name.	German.	French.	Italian.
Semibreve, or Whole rest	Takt'pause	Pause	Pa'usa del'la Semibre've
Minim, or Half rest	Hal'bepause, or Zwei'tel-pause	Demi-pause	„ „ Mi'nima
Crotchet, or Quarter rest	Vier'telpause	Soupir	„ „ Semiminima (or Quar'to)
Quaver, or Eighth rest	Acht'elpause	Demi-soupir	„ „ Cro'ma (or Mez'zo-quar'to)
Semiquaver, or 16th rest	Sech'zehntelpause	Quart de soupir	„ „ Semi-cro'ma (or Respi'ro)
Demisemiquaver, or 32nd rest	Zwei'unddrei'ssigstelpause	Demi-quart de soupir	„ „ Biscro'ma
Hemidemisemiquaver, or 64th rest	Vier'undsech'zigstelpause	Seizième de soupir	„ „ Semibiscroma

(For Shapes of Rests see p. 351).

33

AVERAGE COMPASS OF THE CHIEF MUSICAL INSTRUMENTS.

(See also each instrument in its proper place.)

N.B.—(1) Exceptional players can obtain higher notes than those given below. (2) Unless otherwise indicated the notes produced are of the same pitch as those written.

Piccolo in E♭
(Properly, Piccolo in D♭.)

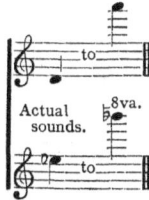

Actual sounds. 8va.

Piccolo in D.
(Ordinary Piccolo.)

All notes sound an octave higher.

Third Flute in F.
(Properly, Flute in E♭.)
All notes sound a minor 3rd higher.

Flute in D.
(Ordinary Orchestral Flute.)

8va.

Oboe.

Cor Anglais, Alto Oboe, or **English Horn.** Same range as Oboe. All notes sound a perfect 5th lower than written.

Clarinet in C, B♭, or **A.**
On the B♭ Clarinet the notes sound a major 2nd lower; on the A Clarinet, a minor 3rd lower.

Small Clarinet in E♭. About the same range as Clarinet in C. All notes sound a minor 3rd higher than written.

Alto Clarinet or Basset Horn. Same range as Clarinet in C. All notes sound a perfect 5th lower than written.

Bass Clarinet in B♭. Written with the G Clef. All notes sound a major 9th lower than written. Real pitch of lowest note generally—

Saxophone. The Soprano in C gives the notes as written; that in B♭ a major 2nd lower. The Alto in F sounds a perfect 5th lower than written; that in E♭ a major 6th lower. The Tenor in C sounds an octave lower; the Bass in C two octaves lower; the Bass in B♭ 2 octaves and a major 2nd lower. There are several other sizes.

Bassoon.
8va.

Contrafagotto or Double Bassoon. Sounds an octave lower than written.
or

Double-Bass Sarrusophone. From upwards. Sounds an octave lower. There are 6 principal varieties of the Sarrusophone, which is little used except in France.

Orchestral Horn in F. Sounds a perfect 5th lower than the written notes. (See **Horn.**)

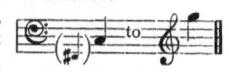

Trumpet in F. Sounds a perfect 4th higher than the written note. The Trumpet in E♭ sounds a minor 3rd higher than written; that in D a major 2nd higher, &c.

Soprano (Cornet) in E♭. Sounds a minor 3rd higher. Lower notes *very poor.*

Cornet in B♭. Lower notes *poor.* Sounds a major 2nd lower than written.

Tenor Horn in F. Same range as Cornet. Sounds a perfect 5th lower than the written notes.

Tenor Horn in E♭. Same range as Cornet. Sounds a major 6th lower than the written notes.
8va.

Baritone in B♭. Euphonium (3 valves) in B♭. Low notes of Baritone *poor.* All sounds are a major 2nd lower than written.

Bass Euphonium (4 valves). The B♭ instrument sounds a major 2nd lower than the written notes.
8va.
(Easy range.)

SAX-HORNS.

SAX-HORNS.

Bombardon. From upwards.

The E♭ Bombardon sounds a major 6th lower than the written notes; the F Bombardon a perfect 5th lower; the BB♭ Bombardon a major 9th lower.

N.B.—In much modern music for brass bands the G clef is used for *all* instruments.

Alto Trombone.

Tenor Trombone.

Bass Trombone in G.
(In Germany, in F, a tone lower.)

N.B.—In the modern orchestra 3 Tenor Trombones are mostly employed. The deep "pedal notes" of Trombones are sometimes utilized. (See *Trombone.*)

Violin.

Viola. From upwards.

Violoncello. From upwards.

Doublebass (Contrabass) 3 stringed.
From upwards.

4 stringed.
From upwards.

The tones of the Doublebass are an octave lower than the written notes.

Harp. From upwards; 6 to 7 octaves.

TRANSPOSING TABLE

Showing the Transpositions and Key-Signatures required in Writing for the chief Transposing Instruments so that they may be used with the Piano, Harmonium, or Organ.

(1) C Instruments.

Real pitch, with signatures of non-transposing instruments (as pf., organ, violin, voice, &c.)

(2) B♭ Instruments.

B♭ Clarinet, B♭ Cornet, B♭ Trumpet. Write all notes one degree higher. Signature two sharps more or two flats less than "C" instruments.

N.B.—The B♭ Baritone and Euphonium are similar, but the Bass Clef may be used.

Rarely used, the A instruments being better.

(3) A Instruments.

Clarinet in A, Cornet in A. Write all notes two degrees higher. Signature three sharps less or three flats more than "C" instruments.

Not used.

Rarely used, the B♭ instruments being better.

(4) F Instruments.

Tenor Horn in F, Orchestral Horn in F. Write all notes a 5th higher. Signatures one flat less or one sharp more than "C" instruments. For Trumpet in F write a 4th lower than for a "C" instrument; i.e., an octave lower than for Horns in F. For Bombardon in F the same signatures as here, but generally with Bass Clef.

(5) E♭ Instruments.

Tenor Horn in E♭, Orchestral Horn in E♭. Write all notes a 6th higher. (For Trumpet in E♭ and Soprano Cornet in E♭ a 3rd lower.) Signatures three flats less or three sharps more than "C" instruments. For Bombardon in E♭, the same transposition and signatures, but generally with Bass Clef.

NOTABLE QUOTATIONS, AND INTERESTING FACTS
IN MUSICAL HISTORY.

(See each name in its proper place. See also **Chronology of Music.**)

Author of the first musical dictionary—Tinctor.

Author of the oldest extant organ book—Paumann.

Bâton used in England abt. 1820. (See *Bâton*.)

"Belgian Orpheus"—Lasso (Lassus).

Birth of opera. (See *Bardi*.)

Birth of oratorio. (See *Neri*.)

Chief of the Meistersingers—Hans Sachs.

Chief promoter of "C" organs in England—Gauntlett.

Chief writer on orchestration—Gevaert.

"Christopher Columbus of brass instruments"—Adolphe Sax.

"Clown of the orchestra"—the bassoon.

Composer of "Rule Britannia"—Dr. Arne.

Composer of the first French opera—Abbé Mailly. (See also *Cambert* and *Lully*).

Composer of the first opera—Peri.

Creator of French burlesque opera—Offenbach.

Creator of French operetta—Hervé.

Creator of melodrama—Rousseau.

"Creator of the modern science of harmony"—Rameau.

"Creator of modern trombone playing"—Queisser.

"Creator of National Hungarian Opera"—F. Erkel.

"Creator of the modern Viennese Waltz"—Lanner.

Creator of the modern violin bow—Tourte.

"Diabolus in Musica"—the tritone.

Discoverer of difference-tones—Tartini.

Earliest composer in the "New Style"—Galilei.

Earliest known analytical programmes. (See *Ella*, and *Reichardt*.)

Earliest known attempts to show pitch by parallel lines. (See *Hucbald*.)

Earliest known organ-builder—Van Os.

Earliest known regular fugue. (See *P. Philipps*.)

Earliest work on conducting. (See *Pisa*.)

Earliest writer on mensurable music—Franco of Cologne.

"English Handel"—H. Purcell.

"English Mendelssohn"—Sterndale Bennett.

"English Palestrina"—O. Gibbons.

Famous left-hand pf. player—Zichy.

"Father of all such as handle the harp and organ"—Jubal (Gen. iv. 21.)

"Father of Christian Hymnology"—St. Ambrose.

"Father of English church music"—Tallis.

"Father of English counterpoint"—Dunstable.

"Father of German counterpoint"—Thiele.

"Father of Greek music"—Terpander.

"Father of the art of instrumentation"—Monteverde.

"Father of the German Lied"—Heinrich Albert.

"Father of modern French musical criticism"—Castil-Blaze.

"Father of modern instrumental music"—Haydn.

"Father of modern Norwegian music"—Nordraak.

"Father of modern pf. playing"—Clementi.

"Father of modern vn. playing"—Viotti. (See also *Corelli*.)

"Father of the New Style"—Caccini.

"Father of the nocturne"—Field.

"Father of the oratorio"—Animmuccia.

"Father of the Organ voluntary"—Frescobaldi.

"Father of the Roman school"—Goudimel.

"Father of the symphony"—Haydn.

"Father of the waltz"—Johann Strauss, senr.

"Father of ultra-modern orchestration"—Berlioz.

First Cambridge Prof. of Music—Staggins.

First composer of comic opera—Acciajuoli.

First composer of Polish opera—Kamienski.

First copper-plate music printer—Verovio.

First French opera. (See *Opera*.)

First German oratorio. (See *Oratorio*.)

First German organ. (See *Faber*.)

First German pf. maker—G. Silbermann.

First German Singspiel. (See *Opera*.)

First German to employ popular themes in opera—Keiser.

"First great composers for the harpsichord"—Byrd and Couperin.

First harpsichord sonata—Kuhnau, 1695.

First Hungarian national opera. (See *Opera*.)

First music printing by stereotype process —B. F. Reinhard.

First opera—Peri's *Euridice*, 1600.

First opera house—Venice, 1637.

First oratorio—Rome, 1600. (See *Oratorio*.)

First Protestant hymn-book—1524. (See *Walther*.)

First English Psalter with melody in the treble—Playford, 1654.

First published vocal score—Rore's chromatic madrigals, 1575.

First Russian national opera. (See *Opera*.)

First *tremolo* for strings—Monteverde.

First University musical degree on record— H. Abyngdon, 1463.

First use of *f, p, tr, < >* (See *Mazzocchi*.)

First use of the unprepared dominant 7th. (See *Mouton*.)

First use of three staves for pf. playing. (See *F. G. Pollini*.)

" Forerunner of Bach "—H. Schütz.

" Forerunner of Palestrina "—Gombert.

Founder of French grand opera—Lully. (See also *Cambert*.)

Founder of French Opera-bouffe—Duni.

Founder of German Romantic opera— Weber.

" Founder of modern pf. technique "— D. Scarlatti.

" Founder of modern violin technique "— Corelli.

Founder of the Neapolitan School—A. Scarlatti.

" Founder of the Scandinavian school "— Gade.

Founder of the Tonic Sol-fa system— Curwen (and Miss Glover).

Founder of the Venetian School—Willaert.

Founder of transcendental (or orchestral) pf. playing—Liszt.

" French Stradivarius "—Lupot.

" French Tartini "—Gaviniés.

" From Bach to Offenbach." (See *Offenbach*.)

Fugue in 64 parts. (See *P. Raimondi*.)

Greatest composer of the Netherland school —Lassus.

" Greatest contralto of the 19th century"— Alboni.

Greatest English composer—H. Purcell.

Greatest lyric poet of ancient Greece— Pindar.

Greatest oboist of the 18th century—L. A. Lebrun.

Greatest poet of the Greek church— Johannes Damascenus,

Greatest Portuguese composer—Portogallo.

Handel's chief rival—Bononcini.

" Hannibal of octaves "—Tedesco.

" Hercules of singing "—J. E. Lavigne.

Highest recorded voice—Agujari.

" Incarnation of the soul of the piano "— Chopin.

Inventor of an apparatus for tuning pianos —Delsarte.

Inventor of harmonic organ stops—Cavaillé-Coll.

Inventor of harp pedals—M. C. Oginski.

Inventor of movable types for music printing—Petrucci.

Inventor of the ballet-pantomime—Noverre.

Inventor of the Chiroplast—Logier.

Inventor of the claviharpe—Dietz (1814).

Inventor of the double-action harp—Erard.

Inventor of the first upright pianoforte— Del Mela (1730).

Inventor of the harmonium—Debain (1840).

Inventor of the hexachord system—Guido.

Inventor of the laryngoscope—M. Garcia.

Inventor of the melodeon—Dietz (1805).

Inventor of the (modern form of the) clarinet—J. C. Denner (abt. 1700).

Inventor of the organ wind-gauge—Förner.

Inventor of the pf. " hammer-action "— Cristofori.

Inventor of the pneumatic lever (organ)— C. S. Barker.

Inventor of the Serpentcleide—T. M. Glen.

Inventor of the symphonic poem—Liszt.

Inventor of valves for brass instruments— Claggett, 1790.

" Irish Handel "—O'Carolan.

" Italian Gluck "—Jommelli (or Sacchini).

" Italian Orpheus "—Crescentini.

" King of instruments "—the organ.

" King of Quadrilles "—Musard.

" King of the orchestra "—the violin.

" King of violin makers "—Stradivarius.

" l'Alexandre des violons "—Boucher.

" Last of the classic composers "—Brahms.

" Leader of the German Romanticists "— Schumann.

" Maid of Bath "—E. A. Linley.

" Moliere of Music "—Grétry.

Most wonderful musical memory on record —C. J. Stanley.

" Musical small-coal man "—Britton.

" Music personified "—Mozart.

" Northern Strauss "—Lumbye.

Oldest existing flute. (See *Egyptian Music*.)

Oldest known bowed string instrument—Ravanastron.

Oldest known free reed instrument—Chinese Cheng (or Tscheng).

" Orchestra of the home "—the pianoforte.

" Originator of modern pf. playing"—Clementi. (See also D. Scarlatti.)

Originator of the German Singspiel—J. A. Hüller.

" Paganini of the clarinet "—Cavallini.

" Paganini of the contra-basso "—Dragonetti.

" Paganini of the pianoforte"—A. Fumagalli.

" Palestrina of the 18th century"—Pisari.

Perfecter of the *Aria da capo*—A. Scarlatti.

Pioneer Russian national composer—Glinka.

" Precursor of Berlioz"—Lesueur.

Primitive type of the clarinet—Egyptian Arghool.

" Prince of composers "—Beethoven.

" Prince of counterpoint and fugue "—J. S. Bach.

" Prince of Italian conductors "—Mariani.

" Prince of song composers "—Schubert.

" Prince of violinists "—Paganini.

Probable composer of the " Old Hundredth" —Franc.

Probable inventor of the *Aria da capo*—B. Ferrari.

Propounder of fundamental bass theories—Rameau.

Reputed first Greek writer on musical theory—Lasus.

Reputed inventor of engraving on tin plates —J. Cluer.

Reputed inventor of organ pedals—Bernhard der Deutsche.

Reputed inventor of the tuning-fork—John Shore.

Root theories propounded by Rameau (*q.v.*).

" Saviour of church music "—Palestrina.

" Schubert of the North "—Lindblad.

" Shakespeare of music "—Mozart.

So-called " inventor of the staff "—Guido.

" Spanish Bach "—Cabezon.

" Swan of Pesaro "—Rossini.

" Swedish nightingale "—Jenny Lind.

"The *Messiah* of Germany " — Graun's *Der Tod Jesu.*

" The Tenth Muse"—Sappho.

" Waltz king "—Johann Strauss, junr.

" Welsh nightingale "—Edith Wynne.

Writer of the first recitative—Caccini.

" Zarlino of the East "—Safieddin.

THE ITALIAN LANGUAGE.

Although German and French composers freely use musical terms from their own languages, it must be understood that Italian is the musician's language *par excellence*. English composers may, of course, use English terms with perfect propriety, or they may use the universal Italian terms. They should also *understand* German and French terms and phrases; but it would be an absurd affectation to use them in their own musical compositions. It is fortunate for musicians who are not skilled linguists that Italian, both in structure and pronunciation, is perhaps the most simple and regular language in the world. The principal Italian words used for musical purposes are nouns, adjectives, adverbs, and prepositions.

Nouns.

All nouns are either masculine or feminine.

(1) Most masculine nouns end in *o*, *e*, or *a*. All these become plural by changing the final vowel into *i*; as *flauto*, *flauti*; *oboè*, *oboi*; *clarinetto*, *clarinetti*; *fagotto*, *fagotti*; *clarino*, *clarini*; *corno*, *corni*; *trombone*, *tromboni*; *timpano*, *timpani*; *violino*, *violini*; *violoncello*, *violoncelli* ('*cello*, '*celli*); *basso*, *bassi*; *sordino*, *sordini*.

(2) Most feminine nouns end in *a* or *e*. Those ending in *a* form their plurals in *e*; as *tromba*, *trombe*; *corda*, *corde*; *donna*, *donne*; *nota*, *note*; *viola*, *viole*. Those ending in *e* form their plurals in *i*; as *madre*, *madri*.

Adjectives.

(1) Most adjectives have two endings, the masculine in *o* and the feminine in *a*; the plurals being in *i* and *e*; as *bello*, *bella*, "beautiful;" plurals, *belli*, *belle*.

(2) Other adjectives end in *e* for both masculine and feminine singular; these end in *i* for both masculine and feminine plural; as *dolce* (masc. and fem.), plural, *dolci* (masc. and fem.); similarly, *soave*, *soavi*, &c.

(3) Adjectives agree with their nouns in number and gender; as *bello suono*, *bella nota*, *una corda*, *tre corde*, &c.; and the adjective is often placed after the noun; as *flauto solo*, *voci soli* (solo voices).

N.B.—*Mano* (the hand), though ending in *o*, is feminine, and therefore requires the feminine form of any adjective used with it; as *Mano destra*, right hand; *Mano sinistra*, left hand.

(4) Adjectives form their comparatives by adding the adverbs *più* for "more," and *meno* for "less;" as *più forte*, louder; *meno mosso*, slower.

(5) Superlatives are formed by changing the last vowel into *issimo* (masculine) or *issima* (feminine), with plurals *issimi* and *issime*; as *fortissimo*, very loud; *prestissimo*, very fast.

Also by repeating the word; as *presto presto*, very fast.

Adjectives and Adverbs.

(1) Most of the numerous adverbs used as musical terms are formed by adding the termination *mente* to the *feminine singular* form of an adjective (either positive or superlative).

Thus—*allegro*, quick, feminine *allegra*; *allegramente*, quickly; *allegrissima*, very quick (feminine); *allegrissimamente*, very quickly.

Similarly, *largo*, *largamente*; *timido*, *timidamente*; *dolce*, *dolcemente*; *forte*, *fortemente*.

N.B.—Adjectives ending in *le* generally drop the *e*, as *agilmente*, *facilmente*, *nobilmente*, *flebilmente*.

(2) Adjectives and the adverbs formed from them are used indiscriminately by composers with the same meaning. Thus— *vigoroso* (vigorous), *vigorosamente* (vigorously), and *con vigore* (with vigour), are merely three different ways of saying "In a vigorous manner."

Augmentatives and Diminutives.

(1) The only augmentative commonly used for musical purposes is *o'ne*, "large;" as *violo'ne*, a large *viol*; *fagotto'ne*, a double bassoon; *bombardon'e*, a large *bombard*.

(2) The chief diminutives are *ino*, *ina*, *etto*, *etta*, *ello*, and *ella*; as *clarino*, a small clarion (or trumpet); *andantino*, somewhat *andante*; *cantatina*, a short *cantata*; *arpanetta*, a small harp; *fughetta*, a short fugue; *larghetto*, rather slow; *cornetto*, a small horn; *violoncello*, a small *violone*; *pastorella*, a little (short) *pastoral*.

HINTS ON ITALIAN PRONUNCIATION.

General Rules.—(1) All letters (with the few exceptions mentioned below) are sounded. (2) The vowels are more round and open than in English, but generally pronounced more lightly and musically. (3) All consonants are softer and more delicate than in English. (4) Accents are, in general, not so strongly emphasized.

VOWELS.

(1) All Italian vowel sounds are longer (or more open) in accented syllables than in non-accented syllables.

(2) A vowel is generally long when it terminates a syllable, and short when it is followed by a consonant in the same syllable.

(3) Except in the cases mentioned below, if two vowels come together, each is pronounced separately.

N.B.—Every Italian word in this Dictionary has its chief accent marked with a "dash" after it, as *pia'no*, *anima'to*, *fuo'co*, &c.

A is always like *a* in *ah*, *far*, *father;* as *ca'po* (*kah'-pō*).

This vowel is much more open and full than the sound usually given to it in Wales and the West of England, but not so "cavernous" as is common in London (where it often becomes nearly *aw*). All the Italian vowels should be pronounced "well forward;" and if the mouth be shaped for *oo* or *aw*, and then the sound carried forward into *ah*—with the mouth freely opened—a good Italian *a* should be produced.

In unaccented syllables the vowel retains the same *quality*, but loses in *intensity*, becoming a shorter *ăh;* as *animato*, pron. *ăh-nĭ-mah'-to* (*o* as in *no*).

N.B.—It is never like *a* in *at*, or *a* in *fate*.

E varies, according to its position and the stress laid upon it, from the sound of *e* in *led* to that of *ay* in *pray;* as *lesto* (pron. *less'-tō*) ; *che* (pron. *kay*). When it is the last letter of an accented syllable, or marked *è* at the end of a word, it is like *ay* in *pray;* as *pieno* (*pĭ-ay'-nō*) ; *oboè* (*ō-bō-ay'*). Before *r*, or when not accented at the end of a word, it has an intermediate sound similar to that of *ai* in *pair;* as *Pergolesi* (*pair-go-lay'-se(e)*), *dol'ce*, *for'te*, &c., and all words ending in *men'te*. It is "long" before *gl* and *gn;* as *svegliato* (*svayl-yah'-tō*), *segno* (*sayn'-yō*.) It is generally "short" before a doubled consonant ; as *ecco* (*ĕk'-kō*), *ello* (*ĕl'-lō*), *ella* (*ĕl'-lah*).

N.B.—It has never the sound of *ee* (as in the English words *be*, *me*, *see*).

I varies, under almost precisely the same conditions, from the sound of *i* in *pin* to that of *ee* in *meet;* as *incalzando* (*ĭn-kahl-tzahn'-dō*) ; *fine* (*fee'-na(y)*).

Note also *Verdi* (*vair'-de(e)*), *liressa* (*lee-ress'-sah*), *sordini* (*sor-dee'-nee*), *inno* (*ĭn'-nō*), *di* (*dee*).

Especially after a liquid (*l*, *m*, *n*, *r*), *i* before another vowel in the same syllable has the effect of the English *y;* as *Pagliacci* (*pahl-yaht'-chee ;* *ch* as in *church*), *Masaniello* (*mah-sahn-yell'-lō*).

N.B.—The Italian *i* has never the sound of *i* in *light*.

I is practically silent before another vowel when it occurs after *c* or *g ;* as *acciaccatura* (*aht-chahk-kah-too'-rah*), *leggiero* (*led-jay'-rō*), *Giovanni* (*jō-vahn'-nee*), *accresciuto* (*ahk-krĕs-shoo'-tō*), *giusto* (*jooss'-tō*).

(Some authorities, however, allow a "very transient" sound of the *i* (as *ĭ* or *ee*) in such cases.)

O varies from the sound of *o* in *not*, *on*, *or*, to that in *note ;* as *ottava* (*ŏt-tah'-vah*), *obbligato* (*ŏb-blĭ-gah'-to*), *con* (*kŏn*), *col* (*kŏll*), *forte* (*fŏr'-ta(y)*) ; *solo* (*sō'-lō*), *piccolo* (*pĭk'-kō-lō*). When it terminates a syllable it is always like *o* in *note*.

N.B.—It is never like *o* in the English words *do*, *to*.

U varies from the sound of *u* in *bull*, to that of *oo* in *boot*, *stool*. When it terminates a syllable it is always like *oo ;* as *sù* (*soo*), *tuono* (*too-ō'-nō*), *strumento* (*stroo-men'-tō*). Before another vowel it is practically the same as *w* in English ; as *Guido* (*gwee'-dō*).

N.B.—It is never like *u* in *but*, or *ew* in *new*, *tune*.

J is used as a vowel. It has the sound of *ee* at the end of a syllable, and of *y* at the beginning of a syllable ; as *esercizj* (*ay-ser-chee'-tsee*), *gioja* (*jō'-yah*), *justo* (*yooss'-tō*).

"When a word, ending with any vowel, has such vowel accented (as *nobiltà*, *ilarità*, *intensità*), the voice makes no stop until it reaches that vowel."—*Barretti*.

CONSONANTS.

B, d, f, l, m, n, p, qu, t, v are pronounced as in English.

When a consonant is doubled it should be sounded twice ; thus, *batti* is *baht'-te(e) ;* not *baht'-ee ;* *nello* is *nell'-lō*, not *nell'-o ;* *freddo* is *fred'-dō*, not *fred'-ō ;* *commodo* is *com'-mō-dō*, not *com'-o-do ;* &c.

It must be said, however, that in England this rule is often "more honoured in the breach than in the observance"—especially in words that have become Anglicised ; thus one does not usually hear the *'cello* and *basso* called the *'chell'lō* and *bahss'-sō*, but rather the *chell'-ō* (or *sell'-ō*) and *bass'-ō*.

C is hard like *k*, except before *e* or *i ;* as *capo* (*kah'-pō*), *clarinetto* (*klah-rĭnet'-tō*), *corno* (*kor'-nō*), *croma* (*krō'-mah*), *cupo* (*koo'-pō*).

C is always soft, like *ch* in *church*, before *e* or *i ;* as *voce* (*vō'-chay*), *cembalo* (*chem'-bah-lō*), *voci* (*vō'-chee*), *citara* (*chee'-tah-rah*). But *h* after *c* hardens it into the sound of *k ;* as *che* (*kay*), *chiesa* (*kee-ay'-zah*).

When *c* is doubled, except before *e* or *i*, each *c* is pronounced hard ; as *ecco* (*ek'-ko*).

When doubled before *e* or *i*, the first *c* is pronounced as *t*, the second as *ch* in *church ;* thus : *accento* (*aht-chen'-tō*), *caccia* (*kaht'-chah*).

G is closely allied to *c*. It is "hard," like *g* in *get*, except before *e* or *i ;* as *gamba* (*gahm'-bah*), *largo* (*lahr'-gō*), &c.

It is "soft," like *g* in *ginger*, or *j* in *jam*, before *e* or *i ;* as *gentile* (*jĕn-tee'-la(y)*), *gioja* (*jo'-yah*), *giro* (*jee'-rō*).

An *h* after *g* makes it "hard ;" as *larghetto* (*lahr-get'-tō*), *larghissimo* (*lahrgĭss'-sĭ-mō ; g* as in *get*).

When doubled, except before *e* or *i*, each *g* is hard. Before *e* or *i* the first *g* is pronounced as *d*, the second as *j ;* as *leggenda* (*led-jen'-dah*), *leggiadro* (*ledjah'-drō*).

Gl, except at the beginning of a word, sounds like *ll* in *million ;* as *doglia* (*dōl'(l)yah*), *svegliato* (*svayl-yah'-tō*), *sugli* (*sool'-yee*)

Gn, except at the beginning of a word, is like the Spanish *n* in *cañon* (*han'-yon*) ; as *sdegno* (*sdayn'-yō*).

At the beginning of a word *gn* is practically *n ;* as *gnacchera* (*nahk-kay'-rah*).

H is silent ; it has a hardening effect after *c* and *g* (see above).

R is always pronounced, and should be usually trilled.

S has two sounds as in English ; "sharp" as in *sister*, "flat" as in *rose*. It is generally sharp at the beginning of a word or syllable and flat between two vowels ; but no hard and fast rules can be laid down.

Sc is like *sh* before *e* and *i ;* as *crescendo* (*krĕ-shen'-dō*), *scialumo* (*shahl'-oo-mō*), *sciolto* (*shol'-tō*).

Sch is like *sh ;* as *scherzo* (*skair'-tsō*).

Z is usually like *ts ; zz* like *ds* or *dz ;* as *sforzando* (*sfor-tsahn'-dō*), *mezzo* (*med'-sō*, or *med'-zō*).

PRONUNCIATION OF LATIN.

There are two ways of *speaking* Latin in England.

(1) THE ANGLICISED METHOD. Vowels and consonants as in English words ; thus : *Veni, Vidi, Vici ;* pron. *vee'nigh, vigh'-digh, vigh'-sigh* (*igh* as in *high*) ; *Crucem*, pron. *Kroo'-sem*.

(2) THE REFORMED METHOD. Vowels, and most consonants, as in Italian ; but *c* and *g* always hard (as in *cat, get*), *s* always sharp (as in *sister*), and *v* always like *w* (or *oo*). Thus *Veni, vidi, vici*, pron. *way'-ne(e)*, *wee'-de(e)*, *wee'-ke(e)* ; *Crucem*, pron. *kroo'-kem*.

In *singing* it is customary to pronounce Latin according to the Italian rules (as given above) ; *i.e.*, *c* and *g* are soft before *i* or *e ; s* has a flat and sharp sound (as in English) ; *v* is like English *v*. Thus *veni, vidi, vici*, pron. *vay'-ne(e)*, *vee'-dee(e)*, *vee'-che(e)—ch* as in *church ; Crucem*, pron. *kroo'-chem* (*ch* as in *church*).

ENGLISH-ITALIAN VOCABULARY.

N.B.—This vocabulary includes most of the common Italian terms, but does not pretend to be exhaustive.

Before finally selecting any of the following, the composer who is not well acquainted with Italian should consult the word (or phrase) in the Dictionary, so as to choose out of several almost synonymous terms the one which n.ost nearly coincides with his meaning and intention.

Accelerating (the speed). Accelerando, pressante, stringendo, ravvivando il tempo, con fretta, affrettando.

Accented. Accentato, enfatico, con enfasi, marcato, martellato, forzando, sforzando, rinforzando.

Affected(ly). Affettato, con affettazione, smorfioso.

Affectionate(ly). Affettuoso, affettuosamente, amorevole, amorevolmente.

Afflicted(ly). Con afflizione.

Agility. Agilità, velocità.

Agitated(ly). Agitato, con agitazione, tumultuoso, perturbato.

Agreeable, Agreeably. Gradevole, piacevole, leggiadro, grazioso.

All, Together. Tutti, unisoni.

Almost. Quasi.

Alternative note (or passage). Marked *ossia*, *oppure, ovvero,* or *facile.*

Always. Sempre.

And. E ; ed (before a vowel).

Angry, Angrily. Adirato, con ira, irato, iratamente.

Anguished. Angosciamente, con afflizione, affannosamente.

Animated(ly). Animato, con moto, più mosso, vivo, svegliato, risvegliato.

Anxious(ly). Ansioso, ansiosamente.

Ardent(ly). Ardente, fervido, appassionato, con fervore, con calore.

Artless(ly). Innocente, semplice, naturale, schietto.

As before. Come prima.

As if. Quasi.

At pleasure. A piacere, a bene placito, ad libitum (Lat.), senza tempo, a suo arbitrio, si piace.

At the former speed. A tempo, tempo primo, moto precedente.

Back to the beginning. D.C., Da Capo.

Back to the sign. D.S., Dal Segno.

Bitter(ly). Amarevole, con amarezza, crudelmente, acutamente.

Boisterous(ly). Strepitoso, strepitosamente, con strepito, impetuosamente, con violenza, tempestosamente.

Bold(ly). Ardito, animoso, fiero, fieramente, con bravura, intrepido, intrepidamente, francamente, tostamente, coraggiosamente, con abbandono.

Brilliant(ly). Brillante, con splendore, scintillante.

Brisk(ly). Vivo, vivamente, allegro, lesto, vigorosamente, con allegria, con gioja, con ilarità, con brio.

Broad(ly). Largo, largamente, ampiamente, con larghezza.

But. Ma.

By degrees. Poco a poco, poi a poi, di grado.

Calm(ly). Tranquillo, tranquillamente, con tranquillità, placido, placidamente, quieto, quietamente, calmato, sedatamente.
Becoming calmer. Calmando, calando, raddolcendo, raddolcente.

Carefully. Con osservanza, con precisione, con diligenza, accuratamente.

Careless(ly). Negligente, negligentemente.

Caressingly. Accarrezzevole, carrezzando, con amorevole.

Charming(ly). Vezzoso, vezzosamente, leggiadro, piacevolmente,

Cheerfully. Allegramente.

Clear(ly). Distinto, chiaro ; enfatico.

Coaxing(ly). Lusingando, lusinghevole.

Cold(ly). Freddo, freddamente, con fredezza.

Complaining. Lamentando, lamentoso, lagrimoso, lagrimando, doloroso.

Consoling(ly). Consolante, consolato.

Continually. Sempre.

Continue in the same style. Simile, segue, seguente.

Dashing(ly). Sbalzato, precipitato, precipitoso.

Decided(ly). Deciso, con fermezza, energico, risoluto.

In declamatory style. Declamando, narrante, parlando, declamatorio.

Decreasing in force. Decrescendo, diminuendo, raddolcendo, sminuito.

Decreasing in force and speed. (See **Dying away.**)

Decreasing in speed. Rallentando, ritardando, tardando, lentando, slentando, strascinando, rilasciando, meno mosso, ritenuto.

Deliberate(ly). Deliberato, deliberatamente, con deliberazione.

Delicate(ly). Delicato, tenero, delicatamente, teneramente, con tenerezza, con delizia, con delicatezza.

Despairingly } Desperate(ly) } Disperato, disperatamente, con disperazione.

Detached. Staccato, picchiettato.

Determined. Determinato, risoluto.

Devotional(ly). Devoto, con devozione, religioso, religiosamente, dedicato.

Distinct(ly). Distinto, chiaro, chiaramente, ben marcato, netto.

Disturbed. Inquieto.

Doleful(ly). Dolendo, dolente, con dolore, doloroso, mesto, lamentevole.

Dragging the time. Largando, allargando, strascinando, slentando.

Dwelling upon the notes. Tenuto, sostenuto.

Dying away. Dim. e rall., calando, deficiendo, estinto, diluendo, mancando, smorzando, morendo, smorendo, perdendosi, espirando, estinguendo, stinguendo, sminuendo.

Easy, Easily. Facile, commodo, agevole, disinvolto.

Elegant(ly). (See **Gracefully.**)

Emphatical(ly). (See **Accented.**)

Energetic(ally). Energico, con energia, risentito, risoluto, con brio, forte.

Enlivening the time. Ravvivando il tempo ; animando, &c. (See **Animated(ly).**)

Enthusiastic(ally). Con entusiasmo, con zelo, zeloso, fanatico.

Entreatingly. Supplichevole.

Even(ly). Eguale, equabile, uguale, ugualmente, tepido, spianato.

Exact(ly). Esatto, con esatezza, esattamente, giusto, proporzionato.

Exact time. Tempo giusto, a tempo.

Expiring. (See **Dying away.**)

Expressive(ly). Espressivo, con espressione (con espress.), sentito, risentito, sentimentale, con sensibilita.

Extravagant(ly). Stravagante.

Extremely. Molto, di molto ; -issimo (at the end of an adjective).

Fast. Allegro, vivace, vivo, presto.
Rather fast. Allegretto, allegro moderato, poco allegro, quasi allegro.
Very fast. Allegro assai, allegro molto, allegro vivo, vivacissimo, prestissimo. Allegrissimo, velocissimo.
Not too fast. Non troppo allegro.

Faster. Più mosso, più allegro, più animato, più stretto, più presto, più vivace, veloce.
Gradually faster. Accelerando, pressando, stringendo, incalzando, sempre accelerando, poco a poco più animato.

Fearful(ly). (See **Timidly.**)

Fervent(ly). Fervente, con fervore, ardente, con ardore.

Fierce(ly). Feroce, con ferocita, furioso, fieramente.

Firm(ly). Fermo, con fermezza, fermamente.

Flattering(ly). Lusingando, lusinghevole.

Flowing(ly). Scorrevole, sciolto, volubilmente, disinvolto. (See also **Smoothly.**)

Fond(ly). Appassionato, teneramente. (See also **Longingly.**)

Forcibly. Con forza, bruscamente, con violenza.
As forcibly as possible. Con tutta forza.

Forcing. Forzando, sforzato, sforzando.

Free as to time. Ad lib., a piacere.

Freely. (See **Flowingly.**)

With frenzy. Con delirio, con rabbia.

From the beginning. Da Capo ; D.C.

From the first sign to the second sign. Dal Segno al segno ; D.S. al S.

From the sign. Dal Segno ; D.S.

Full. Pieno, piena.

Funereal. Funebre, funerale.

Furious(ly). Furioso, furiosamente, con rabbia, con furia, furibondo, impetuosamente.

Gay, Gaily. Gajo, giojoso, gaiamente (gajamente).

Gentle, Gently. Piacevole, dolcemente, pian piano, con lenezza.

Gliding. Glissando, portamento, portando, scorrendo, strisciando.

Gloomily. Tristamente.

Graceful(ly). Grazioso, con grazia, graziosamente, leggiadramente, con garbo, disinvolto, elegante, con eleganza, vezzosamente.

Gradually. Poco a poco, poi a poi, di grado, passo a passo.
Gradually louder. Crescendo, cres. poco a poco.
Gradually softer. Diminuendo, dim. poco a poco, decrescendo.
Gradually faster. (See under *Faster.*)
Gradually slower. Rallentando, ritardando, poco a poco rall.
Gradually slower and softer. (See *Dying away.*)

Grand(ly). Grandioso, nobile, pomposo, maestoso.

Grieving(ly). Affan(n)osamente, afflitto, con dolore, doloroso.

In gypsy style. Alla zingara.

Half. Mezzo, mezza.
Half-loud. Mezzo forte, mf.
Half-soft. Mezzo piano, mp ; mezza voce.

Hammered. Martellato.

Harsh(ly). Stridente, duramente, aspramente, con asprezza, severamente.

Hastening. Accelerando, affrettando, calcando, incalzando, stringendo. (See **Accelerating** and **Faster.**)

Haughtily. Fieramente, altieramente.

Heartfelt. Intimo, affettuoso, imtimissimo.

Heavy, Heavily. Pesante, pesantemente, ponderoso, grave, gravemente.

Hesitating(ly). Timido, timidamente, vacillando, irresoluto.

Holding back (the time). Ritardando, ritenuto, ritenente, trattenuto, allargando, rimettendo.

Holding out the notes to their full length. Tenuto, sostenuto.

Humorously. Con umore, capriccioso, capricciosamente, fantasticamente.

Hurriedly. Affrettoso, frettoloso, precipitoso.

Hurrying. (See **Hastening.**)

Imitating. Imitando, simile, segue, seguente, seguendo.

Impassioned. Appassionato, appassionata, appassionamente, con passione,caloroso.

Impatient(ly). Impaziente, impazientemente.

Imperious(ly). Imperiosa,-o, imperiosamente, altieramente.

Impetuous(ly). Impetuoso, con impetuosità, impetuosamente, precipitoso, sbalzato, tempestoso, tempestosamente.

Imposingly. Imponente.

Increasing in force. Crescendo, accrescendo, rinforzando.

Increasing in speed. (See **Accelerating, Hastening,** &c.)

In devotional style. (See **Devotionally.**)

Indifferently. Indifferente, con indifferenza.

In haste. Con fretta, frettoloso. (See **Hastening.**)

Innocently. Con innocenza, innocentemente.

Insinuatingly. Con insinuazione. (See also **Flatteringly.**)

In the same time (speed). L'istesso tempo, lo stesso tempo, moto precedente.

In (strict) **time.** A tempo, tempo primo, tempo 1mo, misurato.

Ironically. Ironico, ironicamente.

Irregular time. Tempo rubato.

Irresolutely. Con irresoluzione, irresolutamente, irresoluto.

Jestingly, Jocosely. Scherzando, scherzevolmente, giocoso, giocosamente.

Jovial(ly). Con giovialità, giovale, piacevole.

Joyously. Giojoso, giojosamente, con allegrezza.

Jubilantly. Con giubilio, con giubilazione, giubiloso.

Judiciously. Con discrezione, discreto, prudente.

Lamenting. Lamentoso, lamentando, lamentabile, piangendo, deplorando.

Languishing(ly). Languendo, languente, languidamente, senza forza.

Left hand. Mano sinistra ; m.s.

Leisurely. (See **Rather fast,** under **Fast.**)

Less. Meno.
Less fast. Meno allegro, meno vivace, &c.
Less loud. Meno forte.

Light(ly). Leggiero, leggero, leggiermente, agilmente, svelto, facilmente, prestamente.

Lingering(ly). Tardo, tardamente, tardando.

Little by little. (See **By degrees.**)

Lively. Vivace, vivacemente, con vivo, vivo, vivamente, allegro, lesto, desto, &c. (See **Fast.**)

Lofty, Loftily. Nobile, nobilmente, pomposo. fastoso, elevato, con pompa, con nobilità, superbo.

Longingly. Con desiderio, aspiratamente.

Loud. Forte, con forza, *f.*
Very loud. Fortissimo, *ff*, con tutta forza, forte possibile.
Rather loud. Mezzo forte, *mf.*
Continually loud. Sempre forte.

Louder. Più forte, crescendo, rinforzando.

Lovingly. Amorevole, con amore, amoroso, amorosamente, amabile, affezionato, amabilmente.

Majestical(ly). Maestoso, maestosamente, maestevole, con maestà, pomposo, fastoso, fastosamente.

Major. Maggiore.

Marked. Marcato. (See **Accented.**)

Martial. Marziale, militare.

Measured (time). Misurata, a tempo giusto.

Melancholy. Malinconico, con malinconia, mesto.

Menacing(ly). Minaccevole, minacciando, minacciante.

Mildly. Dolce, dolcemente, piacevole, affabile. (See **Sweetly.**)

Minor. Minore.

Moderate speed. Moderato, moderatamente, a tempo moderato, tempo moderato, non troppo allegro. (See **Moderately fast,** and **Moderately slow.**)

More. Più.
More slowly. Più lento, più adagio, lentando. (See *slower.*)
More quickly. (See *Faster.*)

Mournful(ly). Mesto, mestoso, mestamente, lugubre, funebre, doloroso, dolente, flebile, piagnevole, tristo, tristamente, con afflizione.

Much. Molto, di molto.

Murmuring. Mormorando, susurrando.

Muted. Con sordino, con sordini.

Mysterious(ly). Misterioso, cupo, segreto, oscuro.

Natural(ly). Naturale, naturalmente. (See also **Simply.**)

Neat(ly). Netto, nettamente, leggiadro, destramente.

Nimble, Nimbly. Agile, agilmente, con agilità, svelto, lestamente, sciolto, scioltamente. (See also **Lightly.**)

Nobly. Nobilmente, con nobilità, splendidamente.

Noisily. Strepitoso, con fracasso. (See **Boisterously.**)

Not. Non.
Not so fast. Meno mosso.

Obligatory. Obbligato.

Obscure. Misterioso, cupo, oscuro.

Of. Di, del', della ; dei, de', delle.

One. Una, uno.

Or. O, od (before a vowel).

Or this. Ossia, oppure, ovvero.

Passionate(ly). Passionato, passionatamente, con passione, ardente, con ardore, fervente, con fervore ; furioso, furibondo, impetuoso. (See **Impassioned.**)

Pastoral. Pastorale, rustico.

Pathetic(ally). Patetico, pateticamente, doloroso, affettuoso.

Pedal. Pedale.
With pedal. Con pedale.
Without pedal. Senza pedale.
With soft pedal. Una corda.
Without soft pedal. Tre corde.

Pensive(ly). Pensieroso, pensoso, pensivo, pensierosamente.

Piquantly. Con piccanteria, piccante.

Placid(ly). Placido, placidamente. (See also **Tranquilly.**)

Plaintive(ly). (See **Mournfully.**)

Playful(ly). Giocoso, giocosamente, scherzando, giuchevole.

Pleading(ly). Supplicando, supplichevole.

Pleasing(ly). Piacevole, piacevolmente, compiacevole, gradevole.

Pompous(ly). Con pompa, pomposa, fastoso, fastosamente.

Ponderous(ly). Ponderoso, pesante.

Possible, As possible. Possibile.

Prattling. Straccicalando.

Precipitate(ly). Precipitato, precipitoso, precipitando, precipitatamente.

Precise(ly). Preciso, con precisione, distinto, esatto.

Pressing on. Stringendo. (See **Hastening.**)

Promptly. Pronto, con prontezza, prontamente, lestamente.

(Well) pronounced, enunciated. Pronunziato, ben pronunziato.

Proud(ly). Fiero, fieramente, altiero, altieramente, superbamente. (See **Haughtily.**)

Quiet(ly). Quieto, pacificamente, tranquillo, con lenezza. (See **Tranquilly.**)

Quick. (See **Fast.**)

Rapid(ly). Rapido, rapidamente, con rapidità, velocemente. (See also **Fast.**)

Rather. Quasi, poco.

Refined. (See **Noble.**)

Religious(ly). Religioso, religiosamente. (See also **Devotionally.**)

Repetition. Ripetizione, replica.

Reposeful(ly). Riposato, riposatamente.

Resonant(ly). Sonore, sonoramente, sonabile, sonante, con risonanza.

Restless(ly). Inquieto, senza riposo.

Right hand. Mano destra ; m.d.

Ringing(ly). (See **Resonantly.**)

Rough(ly). Aspro, aspramente, bruscamente, ruvido.

Rustic. (See **Pastoral.**)

Sad(ly). Mesto, mestamente, tristo, tristamente, languendo, dolente, doloroso, flebile, malinconico.

Same. Stesso, l'istesso.

Scorn. Sdegno.

Scornful(ly). Sdegnoso, sdegnosamente, altieramente.

Serious(ly). Serioso, con serietà, gravemente, seriamente.

Sighing(ly). Sospirando, sospirevole.

Similarly. Simile, simili, similiter, segue, seguente.

Simple, Simply. Semplice, semplicemente, con semplicità, innocente, schietto, schiettamente, naturale, naturalmente.

Singing(ly). Cantando, cantabile, melodico.

Sliding(ly). Sdrucciolando. (See also **Slurring.**)

Slow. Adagio, lento, lentamente, tardo.
Very slow. Adagio molto, lento molto, adagissimo, grave, gravissimo, largo, larghissimo.
Rather slow. Andante, andantino, adagietto, moderato.

Slower. Meno mosso, più adagio, più lento, più largo. (See also **Decreasing in speed.**)
Gradually slower. Rallentando, slargando, lentando, ritardando, poco a poco rallentando.
Gradually slower and softer. (See *Dying away.*)
Suddenly slower. Ritenuto.

Slurring. Legato, glissando, portamento, portando, slissando.

Smooth(ly). Legato, eguale, egualmente, soave, soavemente, strisciando, piacevole.

Sobbing(ly). Singhiozzo, singhiozzando, Singhiozzoso, singozzo.

Soft. Piano, *p*.
Softly. Pian piano, sotto voce.
Very soft. Pianissimo, *pp*, *ppp* ; estinto.
Rather soft. Mezzo piano, *mp*.

Softer. Meno forte.
Gradually softer. Diminuendo, decrescendo, poco a poco dim., sminuendo. (See also *Dying away.*)

Solemn(ly). Solenne, con solennità, solennemente.

Somewhat. Quasi.

Song-like. Cantabile.

Sonorous(ly). (See **Resonantly.**)

Sorrowfully. (See **Mournfully.**)

Sparkling. Scintillante, brillante.

Spirited(ly). Spiritoso, con brio, brioso, con spirito, spiritosamente.

Sprightly. Desto. (See **Nimble.**)

Stern(ly). Duro, duramente, severo, severamente.

Still, Yet. Ancora.
Still faster. Ancora più mosso.
Still slower. Ancora più moderato, ancora più lento.

Strict(ly). Giusto, severo, giustamente, severamente, esatto, esattamente.
In strict time. A tempo, a buttuta, misurato, tempo rigoroso, al rigore di tempo.

Suave(ly). Soave, soavemente, con dolce maniera. (See **Smoothly.**)

Suddenly. Subito, subitamente, di colpo.

Supplicating(ly). (See **Pleadingly.**)

Sustained, Sostenuto, tenuto, sostenente, sostenendo.

Sweet(ly). Dolce, affabile, amabile.
Very sweetly. Dolcissimo, &c.

Swift. (See **Fast.**)

Sympathetic(ally). Pietoso, con pietà, simpaticamente.

Tasteful(ly). Con gusto, gustoso.

Tearful(ly). Lagrimoso, lagrimando, piangendo, piangente, con pianto, flebile.

Tempestuous(ly). Tempestoso, tempestosamente.

Tender(ly). Tenero, teneramente, con tenerezza, dolce, dolcendo, dolcemente, affettuosamente. (See also **Lovingly.**)

Thoughtful. (See **Pensive.**)

Threatening(ly). (See **Menacingly.**)

Timid(ly). Timido, timidamente, con timore. (See **Hesitatingly.**)

Timorous(ly). Timoroso, timorosamente.

To. A, ad (before a vowel), al, alla, allo.

Together. Unisoni, tutti, insieme.

Too, Too much. Troppo.

Tranquil(ly). Tranquillo, tranquillamente, con tranquillità, placido, placidamente, con placidezza. spianato, quieto, quietamente, non agitato.

Trembling(ly). Tremolo, tremolando, tremoloso.

Triumphant(ly). Trionfante, trionfalmente, trionfale, con trionfo.

Troubled. Inquieto, afflitto, tumultuoso.

Turn over. Volti.

Turn over quickly. Volti subito.

Twice as fast. Doppio movimento.

Two. Due.

Unaccompanied voices. A cappella.

Undulating. Ondeggiante. (See also **Trembling.**)

Until } Fino, fin', sino, sin'.
Up to }

Urgent(ly). Insistendo, instantemente.

Vague(ly). Vago, vagante, incerto.

Vehement(ly). Veemente, veementemente, con veemenza, con ferocità, slancio, con islancio, smanioso, smaniante, con forza, impetuoso.

Very. Assai, molto, ben, bene.

Vibrant (ringing). Vibrante.

Violent(ly). Violentemente, violento, violente, con violenza.

Voice. Voce, canto, parte.
Follow, keep with, the voice. Colla voce, col canto.

Wailing(ly). (See **Mournfully.**)

Warlike. Bellicoso. (See also **Martial.**)

Warmly. Caloroso, con calore.

Wavering. Vacillando, tremolando.

Weak. Debole, debile.

Well. Bene, ben.

Whimsical(ly). (See **Capriciously.**)

Whispering. Susurrando, susurrante ; sotto voce.

Wild(ly). (See **Fiercely.**)

With. Con, col, colla, colle.

With abandon ; unrestrainedly. Con abbandono.
With accent. (See *Accented.*)
With affection (pathos). Con affetto. (See also *Affectionately.*)
With agility. Con agilità.
With anger. Con ira. (See also *Angry.*)
With anguish. (See *Anguished.*)
With animation. (See *Animatedly.*)
With ardour. Con ardore. (See also *Ardently.*)
With boldness. (See *Boldly.*)

With both pf. pedals. Una corda con pedale ; a due pedali.
With breadth. (See *Broadly.*)
With calmness. (See *Calmly.*)
With confidence. Con confidenza, con fiducia.
With dash. (See *Dashingly.*)
With decision. Deciso. (See also *Decidedly.*)
With deliberation. Con lentezza. (See also *Deliberately.*)
With delicacy. (See *Delicately.*)
With desperation. (See *Desperately.*)
With determination. (See *Determined.*)
With discretion. Con discrezione, discreto.
With distinctness. Distintamente, marcato. (See also *Distinctly.*)
With ease. Con agevolezza. (See also *Easily.*)
With emotion. Con affetto, affettuoso, con ardore, con agitazione.
With energy. Con energia. (See also *Energetically.*)

With expression. Con espressione, con espress. (See also **Expressively.**)
With facility. Con agevolezza. (See also *Easily.*)
With feeling. Sensibile, sentito.
With fervour. (See *Fervently.*)
With firmness. (See *Firmly.*)
With force. Con forza. (See *Forcibly.*)
With frenzy. Con rabbia, con delirio.
With fury. (See *Furiously.*)
With grace. (See *Gracefully.*)

With gradually increasing warmth, Sempre incalzando.
With grandeur. Con grandezza. (See also *Grandly.*)
With grief. Con duolo. (See also *Grievingly.*)

With growing animation. (See **Faster,** and **Gradually faster.**)
With harshness. (See *Harshly.*)
With haste. (See *Hastening.*)
With heartfelt emotion. (See *Heartfelt.*)
With heaviness (weight). (See *Heavily.*)

With hesitation. (See *Hesitatingly*.)
With humour. (See *Humorously*.)
With impetuosity. Con impeto. (See *Impetuously*.)
With intensity. Con intensità.

With life, soul. Con anima.

With lightness. Con leggerezza. (See *Lightly*.)
With longing. Con desiderio, aspiratamente.
With majesty. (See *Majestically*.)
With melancholy. (See *Melancholy*.)
With much passion. Con molto passione.
With nobility. Con nobilità. (See *Loftily*.)
With passion. (See *Passionately*.)
With promptness. (See *Promptly*.)
With rapidity. Con prestezza. (See also *Rapidly*.)
With resolution. Con risoluzione.
With resonance. Con sonorità. (See *Resonantly*.)
With sadness. Con tristezza. (See also *Sadly*.)
With scorn. (See *Scornfully*.)

With spirit. Con spirito, con brio.

With sweetness. Con soavità. (See *Suavely* and *Sweetly*.)
With taste. (See *Tastefully*.)
With tears. (See *Tearfully*.)
With tenderness. (See *Tenderly*.)

With the bow. Coll' arco ; arco, arcato.

With the fingers ; plucked. Pizzicato, pizz.

With the left hand. Colla mano sinistra, colla sinistra, sinistra ; m.s., or c.s.

With the loud (right) **pf. pedal.** Ped. ; tre corde ; senza sordini.

With loud pedal throughout. Sempre pedale, sempre con ped.

With the principal part. Colla parte.

With vehemence. (See *Vehemently*.)
With warmth. Con calore.
With wrath. Con ira, irato, iratamente.
With zeal. (See *Zealously*.)

With the right hand. Colla mano destra, colla destra, destra ; m.d., or c.d.

With the soft (left) **pf. pedal.** Una corda.

With (following) **the voice.** Colla voce, col canto.

Without. Senza.

Without getting faster. Senza accelerare.

Without getting slower. Senza rallentare.

Without interruption. Senza interruzione.

Without mutes. Senza sordini.

Without repeating. Senza ripetizione, senza replica.

Without retarding the time. Senza ritardare, senza di slentare, senza rall.

Wrathful(ly). Con ira, irato, iratamente, adirato.

Zealous(ly). Zeloso, con zelo, zelosamente.

HINTS ON GERMAN PRONUNCIATION.

Owing to the great geographical extent of Germany, there are several " varieties of German dialect ; " the purest form of the language is said to be spoken in Hanover. German pronunciation cannot be *mastered* without much patience and the constant help of a competent teacher ; but the following brief suggestions (together with the accent mark or marks added to each German word in this work), may be found useful.

A. Like *ah ;* as in Italian.

ä or ae. Nearly like *ay* in *pray ;* no exact English equivalent.

ai. Like *i* in *bite, light.*

au. Like *ow* in *cow, crown.*

äu or aeu. Almost like *oi* in *noise.*

B. Like English *b* at the beginning of a syllable ; like *p* at the end of a syllable.

C. Like *k* before *a, o,* and *u ;* like *ts* in *mats* before *e, i,* and *ü.*

  K is now generally used instead of hard *c,* and *z* instead of soft *c ;* as *Konzert* instead of *Concert.*

ch. Like *k* followed by a guttural *h ;* no English equivalent.

chs. Nearly like *ks ;* as *sechs (se'ks).*

D. Like English *d* in beginning a syllable ; like *t* (or *dt*) in ending a syllable.

E. Before a consonant in the same syllable, like *e* in *led ;* at the end of an accented syllable, like *ay* in *pray ;* as *Reger (ray'-gĕr).*

  E is always sounded when it is the last letter of a word ; it is then longer than *e* in *led,* but not so long as *ay* in *pray* (being much like the unaccented Italian *e* at the end of a word). It is " as if one started to say *ay* (as in *pray*) and cut the sound short in the middle."

ei. Always like *i* in *bite ;* as *leit (light).*

eu. Almost like *oi* in *noise.*

F. As in English.

G. (1) At the beginning of a syllable, like *g* in *get* (but rather softer). (2) At the end of a syllable, like a rather soft *k* followed by a guttural *h.*

ng. At the end of a word like *ng* followed by a transient *k ;* as *sang (sahng(k)).*

H. (1) At the beginning of a syllable, as in English. (2) After *t,* silent. (3) At the end of a syllable, guttural.

I. Usually short as in *pin* (with a tendency towards *ee* as in *meet*).

  It is like *ee* at the end of a syllable, or when a following *e* has been suppressed ; as in *moduli'ren,* also spelt *modulie'ren,* &c.

ie. Always like *ee* in *meet ;* as *lieder (lee'-der).*

J. Like *y* in *yet ;* as *ja (yah).*

K. As in English.

kh. Guttural.

L, M, N. As in English.

ng. (See **G.**)

O. Varies from *ŏ* as in *song* to *ō* as in *note.*

ö or oe. Between *e* in *bet* and *u* in *but ;* no exact English equivalent.

P. As in English.

Qu. Like *kv ;* as *quart (k'vahrt).*

R. Always strongly sounded.

S. (1) When commencing a syllable and preceding a vowel, like *z* in *zeal ;* as *so (zo).*

  (2) At the end of a syllable, like *ss ;* as *Das (dahss).*

sch. Like *sh ;* as *schnell (shnĕll).*

sp. Almost as *shp.*

st. Almost as *sht.*

T. As in English.

th. As *t ; h* silent.

  In modern German spelling the *h* is dropped thus, *mutig* instead of *muthig.*

U. Like *oo* in *boot.*

ü or ue. Almost like *i* in *brill ;* no exact English equivalent.

V. Like *f ;* as *vier (feer).*

W. Like English *v,* but " with a soft trace of *w* as in *was.*"

X. Like *x* in *six,* " even at the beginning of a syllable."

Y. Generally like *ee* in *meet.*

Z. Always like *ts* in *mats ;* as *zu (tsoo).*

N.B.—In German printing or writing, every noun commences with a capital letter.

FRENCH PRONUNCIATION.

As it is practically impossible to learn French pronunciation without a teacher, no hints are given in this work. As to accentuation, however, it may be said that there is no strongly emphasized (or accented) syllable in French words, but as a general rule the *last* syllable takes a very slight accent (or rising inflection).

Very many words have the same spelling in English and French : but the English accent is more often on the *first* syllable. Thus, for Paris, the Englishman usually says *Par'ris* (or *Parr'y*), the Frenchman more nearly *P'ree.*

34

MUSICAL CALIGRAPHY.

While preserving the same essential characteristics, written music differs in certain particulars from printed music.

A. POINTS COMMON TO WRITTEN AND PRINTED MUSIC—

(1) All notes struck together should be placed *exactly* underneath each other, thus—

&c.

In old books and manuscripts this rule was not observed, the notes appearing somewhat as follows :—

&c.

(2) In a short score for 4 voices the stems of treble and tenor notes should be turned *upwards*, those of alto and bass *downwards;* so as to keep each part distinct—

&c.

When two parts belonging to the same Staff have the same note (as at * *),and also in a unison passage, *double stems* are used :—

&c.

But if the alto and tenor have the same note it should *not* be written as one note with a double-stem ; nor should any tenor note, however high, be "carried up" into the treble staff, nor any alto note "carried down" into the bass staff (as in the following) :—

&c.

N.B.—Both these examples would, however, be quite correct for pf. or organ music.

(3) When only one part (vocal or instrumental) is written on a staff, high notes should have their stems turned *downwards*, and low notes their stems turned *upwards*, to keep the whole "well within the staff" and to preserve a symmetrical appearance, thus—

&c.

&c.

Not &c.

nor &c.

(4) Rests should as a rule be written in the 3rd space ; but when one part on a staff has a rest while the other has a note (or notes) the rest may be placed wherever convenient :—

(5) Dots after "notes in spaces" are placed immediately after the notes. A dot after a "note on a line" is frequently placed in the space above if the next note is higher, and in the space below if the next note is lower, but there is no invariable custom :—

&c.

(6) When there are two parts on a staff, slurs and ties are placed above the higher part and below the lower part—

If there is only one part, they are placed as near the heads of the notes as convenient—

(See also *Slur*, and *Tie*.)

The same rules apply in general to expression marks and other signs. Musical terms are, as a rule, placed above the music of vocal parts, and either above the right hand part or between the staves in pf. music.

(7) The arrangement of *three* separate parts on a staff, and any other features of notation not mentioned above, can be seen in any carefully printed edition of Bach's "48 Preludes and Fugues."

From Fugue No. 4 (1st book), Peters' Edn.

(8) The sharps or flats of key-signatures should be always arranged in their proper order and position. (*See* **Signature**.) The clef and key-signature should be placed at the beginning of each line of music; but the *time-signature* (unless there is a change of time during the course of the piece) is only used *at the beginning.*

The time-signature should be placed *after* the key-signature, thus—

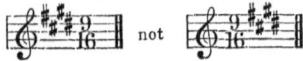

(9) All accidentals should be accurately set before the notes they qualify, and never placed *after* the notes, thus—

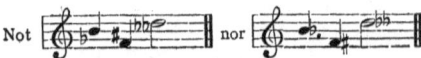

N.B.—In describing inflected notes (either on paper or orally) it is customary to use the accidentals *after* the letter-names; thus— Eb, G♯, B♭♭; called "E flat," "G sharp," "B double flat."

Sir G. A. Macfarren, however, always used the accidentals *before* the letter-names (to conform with the printed or written usage); thus— ♭E, ♯G, ♭♭B; called "flat E," "sharp G," "double-flat B."

B. POINTS PECULIAR TO WRITTEN MUSIC.

(1) The pen-nib should be broad-pointed and not too brittle ; or a flexible quill may be used.

A large "medium J" with rounded points is about the best for general purposes.

(2) The pen should not be held **as in** ordinary writing. The elbow and wrist should be kept well away from the body, and the pen should slope almost directly towards the right side of the paper.

(3) The heads of notes should all be made by pressure *from left to right.* White notes are most easily formed by two small curves, ⌣ and ⌢, one above the other, ◠; this is far better and quicker than trying " to draw a small circle." Heads of black notes (crotchets, quavers, &c.) can be easily made with *one pressure* of the pen. It is not necessary, as Sir John Stainer remarks, to form " little round pools of ink."

Each head should be placed accurately on its proper line or in its proper space so as to indicate clearly what note is intended.

(4) The stems should be thin, and drawn perpendicularly—not at all sorts of slopes.

Many composers make head and stem by one stroke of the pen; but beginners whose "musical hand" is not formed are advised to add the stems separately. It is not necessary to *rule* them.

(5) The crooks of quavers, semiquavers, &c., should be added on the *right* side of the stem, and should incline towards the stem.

The following examples are bad—or, at least, undesirable :—

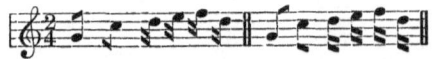

(6) When leger lines are used each note should have its own short lines ; leger lines continued from note to note are often very confusing, thus—

(7) When writing in short score composers generally "score" the bar-lines right through the two staves, thus—

Rather than

(8) The *size* of the notes depends on circumstances. In writing a song with pf. accompaniment, or any music which is to be played or sung from, the notes should be fairly large, very firm and distinct, and not crowded together. But in a full score, a harmony exercise, or a composer's "sketch," the notes may well be much smaller.

(9) In printed music stems turned upwards are always attached to the right hand side of the notes, those downwards to the left hand side—

&c.

These rules are not often observed in written music. The majority of distinguished composers fix all stems to the *right* of the notes; while others, as the following illustrations show, do not keep to any rule.

EXAMPLES OF COMPOSERS' MUSIC-WRITING.

(1) BACH—

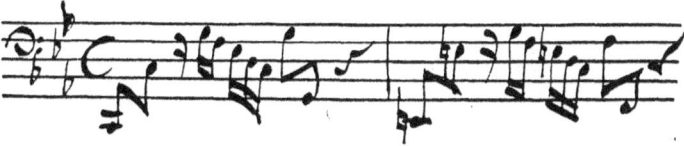

(2) HANDEL—

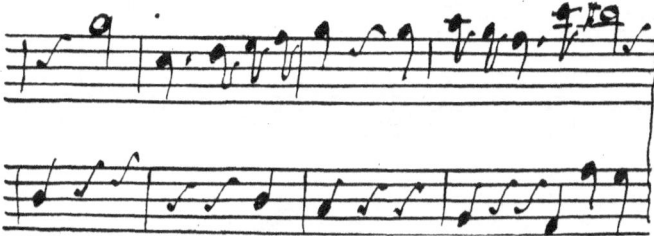

(3) HAYDN—

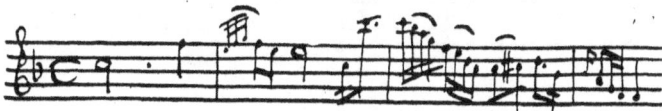

(4) MOZART—

(5) BEETHOVEN (variations on Handel's *See the conquering hero.*)—

(6) MENDELSSOHN—

(7) SCHUBERT—

(8) BERLIOZ—

(9) GOUNOD—

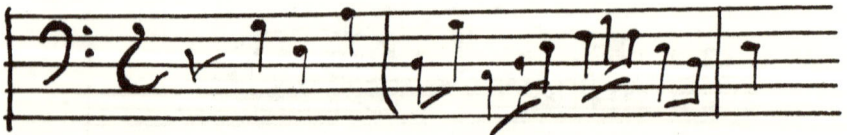

(10) Tschaikowsky—

(11) Grieg—

(12) Sir Hubert Parry—

CHART OF USEFUL MODULATIONS.

Every pianist and organist should know the following modulations "by heart."

(1) MODULATION UPWARDS BY STEP OF A SEMITONE THROUGH ALL THE MAJOR KEYS.

This formula is used in accompanying long sustained notes, and other vocal exercises, which have to be repeated higher and higher. The series may commence with any key, as required.

N.B.—Each successive change is equivalent to a "transition of 5 flat removes." The modulating chord is a Dominant 7th, the Tonic of the old key being re-struck as the Leading-note of the new key, while the bass falls a Major 3rd.

(2) MODULATION DOWNWARDS BY STEP OF A SEMITONE.

This is not so often required. It may be managed (a) by interpolation of the Dominant 7th of the new key:—

or (b), more smoothly, by the following formula:—

RUSSIAN MUSICAL TERMS.

The 35 Russian characters are modifications of an Alphabet derived from the ancient Greek letters by St. Cyril, of Constantinople, in the 9th Century.

The first Russian periodical was printed at Moscow in 1704.

Capital.	Small.	Italicized Small.	Equivalent.	Capital.	Small.	Italicized Small.	Equivalent.
А	а	*а*	a	Т	т	*m*	t
Б	б	*б*	b	У	у	*y*	ou (long *u*).
В	в	*в*	v (*or* w).	Ф	ф	*ф*	f (v)
Г	г	*г*	g *hard,* as in *get.* *	Х	х	*x*	ch (German).
Д	д	*д*	d	Ц	ц	*ц*	ts
Е	е	*е*	e (nearly *ye*).	Ч	ч	*ч*	tsch (*ch* as in *church*).
Ж	ж	*ж*	j *soft* (rather softer than in French *jamais*).	Ш	ш	*ш*	sh
З	з	*з*	z	Щ	щ	*щ*	sht (really *schtsch*).
И Ӥ	и ӥ	*и ӥ*	i	Ъ	ъ	*ъ*	{ silent; hardens or doubles preceding letter.
I	i	*i*	i (y)	Ы	ы	*ы*	i *close,* or *guttural.*
К	к	*к*	k	Ь	ь	*ь*	{ silent; softens preceding letter.
Л	л	*л*	l	Ѣ	ѣ	*ѣ*	e
М	м	*м*	m	Э	э	*э*	ĕ *short* (not *ye*).
Н	н	*н*	n	Ю	ю	*ю*	yu (iu, io).
О	о	*о*	o	Я	я	*я*	ya (ia).
П	п	*п*	p	Ѳ	ѳ	*ѳ*	f (th).
Р	р	*р*	r	Ѵ	ѵ	*ѵ*	u (in words borrowed from Greek).
С	с	*с*	c *soft;* s				

* This letter in Russian is also the substitute for H in foreign words, *e.g.,* Гендель=Handel, Гайднъ=Haydn.

N.B.—The Italicized Capitals are the ordinary capitals *sloped,* except Ѣ which becomes *ѣ.*

Russian Music is printed in the ordinary staff notation; and musical terms are usually Italian, (with occasional German or French).

In some Russian musical publications, only the Russian language is employed; but in most modern and popular editions, French or German is used (in addition to Russian, or solely) for titles and descriptions of pieces, while the musical terms are given in ordinary Italian, e.g., andante, allegro (or *andante, allegro*), etc.

In catalogues of Russian Music, it is common to find the three languages (Russian, French and German); and the titles and composers of pieces are frequently given in Russian Characters, even when no other Russian words occur.

It is obvious, therefore, that no extensive study of Russian Music is possible without a knowledge of the Russian Alphabet.

The following selected words and illustrations will also be found useful.

Alto. Альтъ (*Alt*).

Aria, Air. Арія (*Ari[y]a*).

Arioso. Аріозо (*Ariozo*).

Barcarolle. Баркарола (*Barkarola*).

Bass. Басъ (*Bass*).

Bassoon. Фаготъ (*Fagott*).

Choir. Хоры (*Chori*).

Chorus. Хоръ. (*Chor*).

Clarinet. Кларнетъ (*Klarnett*).

Concertina. Концертина (*Kontsertina*).

Cornet. Корнетъ (*Kornett*).

Crotchet. Чвартка (*Tschvartka*).

Counterpoint. Контрапунктъ (*Kontrapounkt*).

Double-bass. Контрабасъ (*Kontrabass*).

Drum. Барабанъ (*Barabann*).

Duet. Дуэтъ (*Douett*).

Dumka. Думка (*Doumka*).
Edition. Изданіе (*Izdanie*).
Eugène Onegin. Евгеній Онѣгинъ.
Flute. Флейта (*Fleita*).
Harmonium. Гармоніумъ (*Harmonioum*).
Harmony. Гармонія (*Harmoni[y]a*).
Harp. Арфа (*Arfa*).
Kettledrum. Литавра (*Litavra*).
Kündinger. Киндингеръ.
Liapounow. Ляпуновъ.
Libretto. Либретто (*Libretto*).
Mandoline. Мандолина (*Mandolina*).
Mazurka. Мазурка (*Mazourka*).
Minim. Полтакта (*Poltakta*).
Music. Музыка (*Mouzika*).
Oboe. Гобой (*Hoboi*).
Opera. Опера (*Opera*).
Oprit[s]chnik. Опричникъ.
Orchestra. Оркестра (*Orkestra*).
Organ. Органъ (*Organn*).
Pianoforte. Фортепіано (*Fortepiano*).
Piccolo, Fife. Флейточка (*Fleitot[s]chka*).
Quaver. Получвартка (*Polou[s]chvartka*).*
Recit. Речитъ (*Ret[s]chit*).†
Russian. Русскій (*Rousskii*); Русско (*Roussko*);
    Русская (*Rousskaya*).
Scena. Сцена (*Stsena*).
Scherzo. Скерцо. (*Skertso*).
Semibreve. Такта (*Takta*); Цѣлая нота (*Tselaya*
Snegourotschka. Снѣгурочка.   [*nota*).
Solo. Соло (*Solo*).
Sonata. Соната (*Sonata*).
Song, Canto. Пѣсня (*Pesnya*).
Soprano. Сопрано (*Soprano*)
Symphony. Симфонія (*Simfoni[y]a*).
Tenor. Теноръ (*Tenorr*).
Trombone. Тромбонъ (*Trombon*).
Trumpet. Труба (*Trouba*); Трубачъ (*Troubatch*).
Tuba. Туба (*Touba*).
Viola. Віола (*Viola*); Альтъ (*Alt*).
Violin. Скрипка (*Skripka*).
Violoncello. Віолончелъ (*Violont[s]chel*).
Waltz. Вальсъ (*Valss*).
Works (Compositions, etc.). Сочиненія (*Sotschi-*
Zither. Цитра (*Tsitra*).   [*nenia*).

---

* Literally, "half crotchet."
† The Russian, like the Italian, is the abbreviation
of the full word Речитативъ.

Specimens of Italicised Names.

Рубинштейнъ. *Rubins(h)tein.*
Направникъ. *Napravnik.*
Рихтеръ. *Richter.*
Ульрихъ. *Ulrich.*
Хваталъ. *Chwatal.*
Кризандеръ. *Chrysander.*
Чайковскій. *Tschaikowsky.*
Варламовъ. *Warlamoff.*

Extracts from a Musical Catalogue.

ДЛЯ АЛЬТА. (*For* VIOLA [ALTO]).

Брупи, Б. Школа (Shkola, School).

ДЛЯ ФЛЕЙТЫ. (*For* FLUTE).

Куммеръ. Практическая Школа (Practical
Waterstraat, F. 40 Etudes.   [School).

ДЛЯ КОРНЕТЪ-А-ПИСТОНА.
(*For* CORNET-À-PISTONS).

Сидоркинъ-Брошъ, М. 20 Этюдовъ (20 Studies).

ДЛЯ ГИТАРЫ. (*For* GUITAR).

Свинцовъ, В. Этюдъ безъ легато (Study without
Legato, *i.e.*, Staccato Study).

ДЛЯ ФОРТЕПІАНО ВЪ 4 РУКИ.
(*For* PF., 4 HANDS).

Berens, H. Melodische Uebungsstücke.
Bertini, H. 25 Etudes Musicales.
Кризандеръ, Н. Школа чтенія нотъ.

POUR 2 VIOLONCELLES AVEC ACCOMP.
DE PIANO.

Fréderiks, N. "Belle nuit étoilée" (Тихая,
звѣздная ночь) de Paufler.

Title-Page of an Arrangement from Tschaikowsky's "Opritchnik."

ARIOZO НАТАШИ
ИЗЪ ОПЕРЫ „ОПРИЧНИКЪ"
П. ЧАЙКОВСКАГО.

ARIOSO DE NATALIE
DE L'OPERA "OPRITCHNIK'
DE P. TSCHAIKOWSKY.

N.B.—In this piece, just published (Xmas, 1908) at St.
Petersburg, the Title-Page is in Russian and
French, with the words of the song in Russian
and German, and the musical terms in Italian.

SPANISH MUSICAL TERMS.

Spanish is closely allied to Italian, and a large number of musical terms are the same in both languages. The following list includes the chief exceptions; and some other Spanish terms have been given in the course of the work.

N.B.—The nearest equivalent of each ·word is given (either in English, French, or Italian), as defined in the body of this Dictionary.

Abertu'ra. Overture.
Acciden'te. Accidental.
Acen'to. Accent.
Ac'to. Act.
Afano'so. Affannoso.
Afe'cto. Affetto.
Agilidad'. Agility.
Agitacion'. Agitation.
Albar'das. Bards.
Albora'da. Aubade.
Ale'gro }
Ale'gre } Allegro.
Alegremen'te }
Alti'simo. Altissimo.
Amablemen'te. Amabile.
Anotacion'. Notation.
Apasiona'do,-a. Appassionato.
Apoyatu'ra. Appoggiatura.
Ardien'te }
Ardimien'to } Ardent.
Ar'duo. Difficile.
Ari'jo. Light; leggiero.
Arpe'gio. Arpeggio.
Articulacion'. Articulation.
Asonan'cia. Assonance.
Atabal'. Kettle-drum.
Ata'que. Attack.
A tiem'po. A tempo.
Audaz'. Audacious.
Aumentazio'ne. Augmentation.

Baje'te. Basso cantante.
Ba'jo. Bass; basso.
Bajon', Baxon'. Bassoon.
  Bajoni'sta. Bassoon player.
Bala'da }
Bala'ta } Ballad.
Barcaruo'la. Barcarolle.
Bastan'te. Assai.
Belle'za. Beauty.
Bien'. Well; ben, bene.
Bo'ca. Mouth.
  Boquil'la. Mouth piece.
Bue'no,-a. Good.
Bu'fo,-a. Buffo,-a.

Caden'cia. Cadence.
Calien'te. Warm, vehement.
Ca'mara. Camera.
Ca'ña. Reed.
Cancion'. Song; canzona.
  Cancion' de cu'na. Cradle song.
  Cancionci'ca }
  Cancioncil'la } Canzonet.
  Cancionci'ta }

Capil'la. Cappella.
Cantar'. To sing.
  Can'to lla'no. A chant; plain-song.
  Canturi'a. Vocal music; composition; vocal technique.
Ca'ños }
Caño'nes } Organ pipes.
Capri'cho. Capriccio.
  Caprichosamen'te }
  Capricho'so } Capriccioso.
Caramil'lo. Flageolet.
Cariciosamen'te }
Caricio'so,-a } Carezzando.
Caridad'. Charity; carita.
Celeridad'. Celerity.
Centellan'te. Scintillating.
Chan'za }
Chis'te } Joke, jest.
  Chanzone'ta. Canzonet.
Cim'balo. Cymbal.
Clarine'te. Clarinet.
Cla've. Clef; clavichord.
Compas'. Time, measure.
Compue'sta. Compound.
Concent'. Concord.
Concier'to. Concert, concerto.
Concor'de. Concordant.
Conjun'to. Conjunct.
Consonan'cia. Consonance.
Contraba'jo. Contrabasso.
Contrapun'to. Counterpoint.
Corche'a. Quaver.
Corne'ta. Cornet.
  Corne'te. Bugle.
Cre(s)cimien'to. Crescendo.
Cru'stico,-a. Beating; applied to percussion instruments.
Quad'riple }
Cuad'ruplo,-a } Quadruple.
Cuar'ta,-o. Fourth.
  Cuarte'te }
  Cuarte'to } Quartet.
Cua'si. Quasi.
Cuatril'lo. Quadrille.
Cua'tro. Four; quartet.

De ca'bo. Da capo.
De'cimo quin'to. Fifteenth.
Declamacion'. Declamation.
De'do. Finger.
Deleito'so. Delightful.
Deliberadamen'te. Deliberately.
Delicadamen'te }
Delica'do } Delicately.
Deliciosamen'te }
Delicio'so } Deliciously.
Descrecimien'to. Decrescendo.
Desden', Desde'ño. Sdegno.
Destre'za. Dexterity.
Die'si. Diesis.
Die'stra. Right hand.
  Diestramen'te. Dexterously.
Die'z. Ten.

Dicciona'rio. Dictionary.
Difi'cil } Difficult.
Difi'cilmen'te }
Discan'te. Discant ; treble.
Discor'de. Dissonant.
Do'ble. Double ; duple.
Do'ce. Twelve.
　Duode'cimo. 12th.
Dolien'te. Dolente.
Dos. Two.
Due'lo. Duolo.
Dul'ce. Dolce.
Du'plo. Double ; duple.

Eclo'ga. Eclogue.
Edicion'. Edition.
Efe'cto. Effect.
Ejecucion'. Execution.
• **Ejem'plo.** Example.
Ejerci'cio. Exercise ; practice.
El conjun'to. Ensemble.
Elevadamen'te } Elevated, sublime.
Eleva'do,-a }
Elo'gio. Eulogy.
El quin'to. A 5th.
Embellicimien'to. Embellishment.
Embocadu'ra. Mouthpiece ; imboccatura.
Entonacion'. Intonation.
　Entonamien'to. Tone, intoning, &c.
　Entonar'. To tune, intone, &c.
　Ento'no. Intoning, &c.
Entreac'to. Entr'acte.
Episo'dio. Episode.
Esceden'te } Augmented.
Exceden'te }
Escue'la. School.
Esca'la. Scale.
Esce'na. Scena.
Escritor'. Writer, composer.
Exac'to,-a. Exact ; true.
Expresion'. Expression.
　Expresivamen'te } Expressive(ly).
　Expresi'vo,-a }
Extin'to,-a. Estinto.
Extravagan'cia. Estravaganza.
Extremadamen'te }
Extrema'do,-a } Very, extremely.
Extremamen'te }

Fa'cil. Facile.
　Facilidad'. Facility.
False'te. Falsetto.
Feroz'. Feroce.
Fervien'te. Fervente.
Fie'sta. Feast, festival.
Fin. End ; *fine.*
　Final'. Finale.
Fir'me. Firm.
　Firmemen'te. Fermamente.
　Firme'za. Fermezza.
Flau'ta. Flute.
　Flau'ta delga'da } Flageolet ; piccolo.
　Flautil'lo }
　Flau'tas de or'gano. Organ pipes.
Flexibilidad'. Flexibility.
Flori'do,-a. Florid.
Forza'do,-a. Forced.
Fuer'te. Strong ; *forte.*
Fuer'za. Force.

Gai'ta. Bagpipe, flageolet, cornamusa.
Ga'ma. Gamut ; scale.
Gavo'ta. Gavotte.
Gentil'. Graceful, dignified.
Gita'no,-a. Gypsy.
Go'zo. Joy ; gioja.
　Gozosamen'te } Joyously.
　Gozo'so,-a }
Grace'jo. Joke, jest.
Gra'cil. Slender, graceful.
Graciosamen'te } Gracefully.
Gracio'so,-a }
Gradualmen'te Gradually.
Grande'za. Grandezza.
Gru'po. Gruppo.
Guitarre'ro,-a. Guitar player.

Hero'ico,-a. Heroic.
Him'no. Hymn.
　Coleccion' de him'nos. Hymn-book.
Hom'bre. Man.
　Hombru'no,-a. Man-like, virile.
Hosa'na. Hosanna.

Iden'tico. The same ; identical.
Igle'sia. Church.
Igual'. Equal, similar, even.
　Igualmen'te. Evenly, &c.
Imitacion'. Imitation.
Impacien'te. Impatient.
Imperfec'to,-a. Imperfect.
Inge'nio. Genius.
Ingles'. English.
Inocen'te } Innocently, naturally.
Inocentemen'te }
Instrumen'to de vien'to. Wind inst.
Instrumen'to de cuer'da. String inst.
Interrumpi'do,-a. Interrupted.
Interva'lo. Interval.
Introduccion'. Introduction.
Iracun'do,-a. Wrathful.

Jabe'ga. A kind of flute.
Jacare'ro. Ballad singer.
Jocosamen'te } Jocosely.
Joco'so }
Ju'bilo. Joy.
Jue'go. Jeu.
Ju'sto. Just ; giusto.

Lamentacion'. Lamentation.
Largue'za. Larghezza.
Lau'd. Lute.
Lega'do } Legato ; slur.
Liga'do }
　Legadu'ra } Ligature.
　Ligadu'ra }
Len'gua. Tongue.
Le'ño. Legno.
Leja'no. Lointain.
Leyen'da. Legend.
Libertadamen'te. Freely.
Li'bro. Book.
Licen'cia. License.
Ligeramen'te } Leggiero.
Lige'ro,-a }
　Ligere'za. Leggierezza.

Li'so,-a. Liscio.
Llama'da. Drum signal.
Lla've. Key, clef.
Lle'no,-a. Full.
Llevar' el compas'. To beat time.
Llevar' la voz. Portamento.
Llorosamen'te ⎫
Lloro'so,-a ⎭ Mournful(ly).

Magestad'. Majesty.
  Magestuosamen'te ⎫
  Magestuo'so,-a ⎭ Maestoso.
Maiti'nes. Matins.
Mane'jo. Technique.
Mane'ra. Maniera.
Ma'no. Hand.
  A dos ma'nos. With (for) both hands.
  Mañosamen'te ⎫
  Maño'so,-a ⎭ Dexterous(ly).
Marca'do,-a. Marqué.
Mar'cha. March.
Marcial'. Martial.
Martilla'do,-a. Martelé.
Mascara'da. Masquerade.
Mayor'. Major.
Medi'da. Measure.
  Me'dio,-a. Half.
  Me'dio. Middle ; mediant.
Medrosamen'te. Timorously.
Menor'. Minor.
Me'nos. Meno.
  Mu'cho me'nos. Much less.
Minue'te. Minuet.
Mi'sa. A Mass.
  Mi'sa de difunt'os. Requiem.
  Mi'sa mayor'. High Mass.
  Mi'sa menor'. Low Mass.
  Misal'. Mass-book.
Moderadamen'te ⎫
Modera'do,-a ⎭ Moderato.
Modulacion'. Modulation.
Moribun'do,-a. Morendo.
Mote'te. Motet.
Movimien'to. Movement.
Mu'cho,-a. Much, very.
Mutacion'. Mutation.

Na'da. Nothing.
Narrati'vo,-a. Narrente.
Nasar'do. Nasard.
Naturale'za. Nature.
Necesa'rio,-a. Necessario.
Ne'to,-a. Netto.
Noble'za. Nobility.
No'che. Night.
  No'che bue'na. Christmas eve.
No'no ⎫
Nove'no ⎭ Ninth.
No'ta ba'ja. Bass note, low note.
Nue've. Nine.

O'. Or.
Obli'cuo,-a. Oblique.
Obliga'do,-a. Obbligato.
Observan'cia. Osservanza.
Obstina'do,-a. Ostinato.

O'cho. Eight.
  Octa'va. Octave.
  Octavar'. To proceed in octaves.
  Octavin'. Piccolo.
  Octa'vo,-a. Eighth.
Oc'tuplo. Octuple.
O'da. Ode.
Oferto'rio. Offertorio.
Oi'do. Ear ; hearing.
  Buen oi'do. A good ear.
On'ce. Eleven.
  Once'no. Eleventh.
Oracional'. Prayer-book.
Ore'ja. Ear.
Orical'co. Brass (inst.).
Orque'sta ⎫
Orque'stra ⎭ Orchestra.
Oscilan'te. Vibrating.

Pacificamen'te. Peacefully.
Pajere'ro,-a. Gay, merry.
Pande'ro. Ancient timbrel.
Par. Equal.
Pa'ra. For.
Parale'lo,-a. Parallel.
Pasa'ge. Passage.
Pasion'. Passion.
Pa'so. Passo.
  Pa'so de gargan'ta. Trill, tremolo.
  Pa'so a pa'so. By degrees.
Paspi'e. Paspy.
Pastore'la. Pastorale.
Pausadamen'te ⎫
Pausa'do,-a ⎭ Deliberately.
Pe'cho. Breast ; petto.
Peda'zo ⎫
Pie'za ⎭ Piece.
Pe'na. Pain.
  Penosamen'te ⎫
  Peno'so,-a ⎭ Painful, laborious.
Pensati'vo,-a. Pensive.
Perfec'to,-a. Perfect.
Pian pia'no. Gently, softly.
Pi'e. Foot.
Pi'fano ⎫
Pi'faro ⎭ Piffaro.
Pi'to. Pipe, small flute.
Ple'no,-a ⎫
Lle'no,-a ⎭ Full ; pieno.
Poderosamen'te ⎫
Podero'so,-a ⎭ Ponderoso.
Po'lice. Thumb.
Por. For, by.
Posa'do,-a ⎫
Posan'te ⎭ Posa'to.
Posi'ble. Possible.
Posicion'. Position.
Precipitacion'. Precipitation.
  Precipitadamen'te ⎫
  Precipita'do,-a ⎭ Precipitate(ly).
Profe'sor. Professor.
Progresion'. Progression.
Prolongadamen'te. Prolongement.
Pronuncia'do,-a. Pronúnziato.
Prue'ba. Prova.
Pulgar'. Thumb.

Que'do. Quieto.
Querubin'. Cherubin.
Quie'bro. Trill ; vibrato.
Quin'ce. 15 ; 15th.
   Quince'na. 15th ; organ stop.
Quin'to. Fifth.
   Quin'tuplo. Quintuple.
Quirieleison'. Kyrie.
   Quirie's. Kyries.

Ra'bia. Rabbia.
Rai'z (*Plur.* **Rai'ces**). Root.
Ra'ya. Bar-line.
Recitati'vo } Recitative.
Recita'do }
Rec'to,-a. Retto.
Redo'ble. Reiteration (of a note, chord, etc.).
   Redoblamien'to. Reduplication.
Re'gla. Regola.
   Reglar'. Regular.
Regocija'do,-a. Merry, rejoicing.
Relacion'. Relation
Repeten'cia } Repetition.
Repeticion' }
Repo'so. Repose.
   Reposadamen'te } Reposefully.
   Reposa'do,-a }
Resbalan'te. Glissando.
Resolucion'. Resolution.
Resolutivamen'te }
Resolu'to,-a }
Resolutoriamen'te } Resolutely.
Resoluto'rio,-a }
Resonan'cia. Resonance.
Rigorosamen'te }
Rigurosamen'te } Rigoroso.
Riguro'so,-a }
Rimbomban'te. Resounding.
   Rimbom'be,-o. Echo ; repercussion.
Rodil'la. Knee.
Romance'ro. (1) Collection of romances.
   (2) Romanticist.
Ron'co,-a. Hoarse.
Rotun'do,-a. Rotondo.
Rui'do. Noise.
   Ruidosamen'te } Noisily.
   Ruido'so,-a }
Rumbo'so,-a. Pomposo.
Ruseñol'. Nightingale.

Sagra'do,-a. Sacred.
Sa'la. Hall ; concert-room.
Sali'da. Exit.
Saltan'te. Saltando.
Saltare'lo. Saltarello.
Saltarin' } Dancer.
Saltari'na }
Se'co. Secco.
Secuen'cia. Sequence.
Secunda'rio,-a. Secondary.
Segun'da. A second (interval).
Segun'do,-a. Second.
Segui'do,-a. Seguito.
Seis. Six, sixth.
   Seise'no,-a. Sixth.
   Seisil'lo. Sextuplet.
Semicorche'a. Semiquaver.

Semin'ima. Crotchet.
Semito'no. Semitone.
Seña, Señal'. Sign.
Sentidamen'te } Sentito.
Senti'do,-a }
Sentimien'to Sentimento.
Sep'timo,-a } 7th.
Sete'no,-a }
Serpien'te. Serpent.
Ses'ta. Sixth (interval).
Siem'pre. Sempre.
Sie'te. Seven, seventh.
Si'gno } Segno.
Siño }
Siguien'te. Seguente.
Silbar'. To whistle, hiss.
   Silba'to. A whistle.
   Silbi'do } Whistling.
   Sil'bo }
Simpati'a. Sympathy.
   Simpaticamen'te } Sympathetically.
   Simpa'tico,-a }
Simulta'neamen'te. Ensemble.
Sin. Senza.
Sinie'stra. Left hand.
Soberbiamen'te } Superb.
Sober'bio,-a }
So'bre. Sopra.
Sobreagu'do. High treble.
Sochan'tre. Sub-cantor.
Sociedad'. Society.
Solem'ne. Solemn.
   Solemnemen'te. Solemnly.
Solfeador'. Songster ; music-master.
   Solfe'o. Melody.
   Solfi'sta. Musician.
Sombri'o,-a. Sombre.
Son. Sound.
   Sona'ble. Sonorous.
   Sona'da. Sonata.
   Sona'ja. Timbrel.
   Sonecil'lo. A little tune.
   Soneti'co. A merry little song.
   Soni'do. Sound.
   Soni'do agu'do. Acute sound.
   Sonoridad'. Sonority.
Soñan'te. Dreaming.
Sordi'na. (1) A Kit. (2) A Mute.
Sosteni'do,-a. Sostenuto.
So'to. Sotto.
Suavidad'. Suavity.
Suel'to,-a. Svelto.
Suje'to. Subject.
Supera'no. Soprano.

Tabla'do. Stage.
Ta'cito,-a. Silent.
Tambor'. Drum.
   Baque'tas del tambor'. Drumsticks.
   Tambore'te. Timbrel.
   Tamboril'. Tabour.
Tarante'la. Tarantella.
Te'cla. Key (of an instrument).
   Tecla'do. Keyboard.
Temblo'so,-a. Tremulous.
Temerosamen'te } Timorous.
Temeroso,-a }
Templadu'ra. Temperament.
   Templador'. Tuner.

Tenu'do,-a. Tenuto.
Terce'ra. Third (interval).
Ter'cio,-a. Third.
Tetracor'dio. Tetrachord.
Tiem'po. Tempo.
Tie'rno,-a. Tenero.
Ti'ple. Treble (soprano).
  Tiplisonan'te. Acute.
Tocar'. To touch.
  Tocamien'to. (Act of) touch.
  Toca'ta. (1) Toccata. (2) A concert.
To'do,-a. All, tutti.
To'no de co'plas. Ballad-tune.
To'nos. Plur. of **Tono** (Tone, &c.).
Tranqui'lo,-a. Tranquillo.
Traspue'sto,-a. Transposed.
Travese'ro,-a. Transverse.
  Flau'ta travese'ra. Orchestral flute.
Trece'no. Thirteenth.
Tres. Three.
Trian'gulo. Triangle.
Tri'no ⎫
Trina'do ⎬ A trill.
Triun'fo. Triumph.
  Triunfal' ⎫
  Triunfalmen'te ⎬ Triumphal.
Trom'pa. Trumpet, horn.
  Trompe'ta. Trumpet.
  Trompeteri'a. Pipes of an org.

Undulacion'. Undulation.
Unidamen'te. Unitamente.

Variacion'. Variation.
  Varia'do,-a. Variato.
Vehemen'te. Vehement.
Velocidad'. Velocity.
  Velos' ⎫
  Velozmen'te ⎬ Veloce.
Versi'culo. Versicle.
Vien'to. Wind.
Vihue'la. Guitar.
Villa'no. A rustic dance.
Violine'te. Pocket-violin.
Violonce'lo ⎫
Violoncil'lo ⎬ Violoncello.
Vivaz'. Vivace.
Voz. (Plur. *Vo'ces*). Voice.
  En voz. In voice.
Vue'lta. Volta.

Xacare'ro. Ballad-singer.

Y. And.
Yam'bico,-a. Iambic.

Zampo'ña. Zampogna.
Zo'po,-a. Zoppo.
Zumbi'do ⎫
Zum'bo ⎬ Humming.

SPANISH ORGAN STOPS.

(From Hopkins and Rimbault's "The Organ," and other sources.)

N.B. "The figures 13, 26, 52, . . . seem to correspond with 8 ft., 16 ft., and 32 ft."

Baje'te. Bassette; 4 ft. pedal flue stop.
Bajon'. Bassoon.
  Bajoncil'lo ⎫ Lit. "small bassoon." Formerly, per-
  Baxoncil'lo ⎬ haps a diapason; now a reed stop.
Bombar'da. "A piece of ordnance." A heavy reed stop.
Chirimi'a. Clarion.
Clarin'. Clarion; trumpet.
  Clarin' cla'ro. Clear-toned clarion.
  Clarin' de campa'na. Hunting horn.
  Clarin' Rea'l. Royal (or Grand) Clarion.
  Clarin' sordi'na. Soft (muted) clarion.
Clarine'te. Clarinet.
Contraba'jo ⎫ Contrabasso; 16 ft. open
Contraba'xo ⎬ diapason.
Corne'ta. Cornet.
Die'zmonove'na. Larigot; 19th.
Docen' ⎫
Doce'na ⎬ Twelfth.
Fagot'. Bassoon, fagotto.
Flau'ta de 13. Flute, 8 ft.
  Flau'ta armo'nica. Harmonic flute.
  Flau'ta de 26. Flute (or double diapason), 16 ft.
  Flau'ta Euske'ria. Euskarian (or Basque) flute.
  Flau'ta travese'ra. Orchl. flute; transverse flute.
Flauta'do,-a. Large scale flute or diapason.
  Flauta'do principal'. Diapason.
  Flauta'do violon'. Gamba.
Flauton'ne. "Large flute." (1) Stopp^d. diapason. (2) Bass flute.
Kuerlofon'. (1) Basset horn. (2) Waldflöte.
Lle'no,-a. "Filling-up" stop; mixture.
Mu'do,-a. "Dummy;" accessory stop.

Nasar'do. Twelfth, nazard.
Octa'va. Octave; principal.
  Octa'va tapa'da. Stopped flute or principal.
Or'lo. Shawm.
Quince'na. Fifteenth.
Renglo'nes. Ranks (of mixtures).
Serpentin' ⎫ "Large serpent." A 16 ft reed
Serpenton' ⎬ stop.
Tapa'da. Stopped, covered.
Tapadil'lo. Stopped diapason.
Tolosa'no. A kind of diapason (perhaps named from "Toulouse").
Trom'pa de 13. Trumpet, 8 ft.
  Trom'pa campa'na. Hunting trumpet (bugle).
  Trom'pa de 26. Trumpet, 16 ft.
  Trom'pa de 52. Trumpet, 32 ft.
  Trom'pa de batal'la. Battle trumpet.
  Trom'pa bastar'da. Loud (double) trumpet.
  Trom'pa magna. Grand (loud, full) trumpet.
  Trom'pa Rea'l. Royal (regal) trumpet.
Varito'no. Baryton; reed stop akin to the *Cor Anglais.*
Vie'jos. "Eyebrows." A kind of stopped diapason with plug or cover of "eyebrow" shape.
Viola'ta. Small viol; gambette.
  Viola'ta sua've. Smooth-toned violata.
Violon' de 13. Gamba, 8 ft.
  Violon' de 26. Gamba, 16 ft.
  Violon' de 52. Gamba, 32 ft.
Voz Celes'te. *Voix céleste.*
  Voz de 13 ⎫
  Voz huma'ne ⎬ Vox humana, 8 ft.

MUSICAL BIBLIOGRAPHY.

A complete Musical Bibliography would fill a large volume. The following list does not, therefore, pretend to be exhaustive. It is an attempt, without prejudice, to supply the student with a Guide to historic and useful works (mostly published in English) on the chief musical topics. As far as possible the publisher (or English agent) of each work is given.

N.B.—Many other works are mentioned in connection with their authors in the body of the Dictionary.

Accompaniment. (See also **Organ Acct.**)
Glen : *How to Accompany* (Schirmer).
Reinecke-Baker : *Art of Song Accompt.* (Schirmer).

Accordion.
Cruikshank : *Accordion Teacher* (1851).
Instruction Book (Metzler).

Acoustics.
Airy : *Sound* (1868).
Baker : *How we Hear* (Vincent).
Blaserna : *Theory of Sound* (Kegan Paul).
Broadhouse : *The Student's Helmholtz* (Reeves).
Curwen : *Musical Statics* (Curwen).
Harris : *Handbook of Acoustics* (Curwen).
Helmholtz : *Sensations of Tone* (Longmans).
Mahillon : *Eléménts d'Acoustique* (Hachette).
Pole : *Philosophy of Music* (Trübner).
Radau : *l'Acoustique* (Hachette).
Sedley Taylor : *Sound and Music* (Macmillan).
Stone : *Scientific Basis of Music* (Novello).
Tyndall : *Sound* (Longmans).
Zahm : *Sound and Music* (McClurg, Chicago).

Æsthetics.
Ambros : *Boundaries of Music and Poetry* (Schirmer).
Banister : *Musical Ethics* (1884).
Baughan : *Music and Musicians* (Lane).
Combarieu : *Music, its Laws and Evolution* (Breitkopf).
Goddard : *Sources of Beauty and Expression in Music* (Reeves).
Gurney : *Power of Sound* (1880).
Hadow : *Studies in Modern Music*, 2 vols. (Seeley & Co.).
Hand : *Æsthetics of Musical Art* (Reeves).
Hanslick : *The Beautiful in Music* (Novello).
Huneker : *Mezzotints in Modern Music* (Reeves).
A. Kullak : *Æsthetics of Pf. Playing* (Schirmer).
Lavignac : *Music and Musicians*, Chap. IV (Putnam's).
Marx : *Music of the 19th century* (Eng. edition, 1885).
E. Newman : *Musical Studies* (Lane).
Parry : *Art of Music* (Novello).
Pauer : *The Beautiful in Music* (Novello).
Riemann : *Catechism of Æsthetics* (Augener).
Schumann : *Music and Musicians* (Reeves).
Stainer : *Music in its Relation to the Emotions, &c.* (Novello).
Thibaut : *Purity in Music* (Reeves).
Weingartner : *Post-Beethoven Symphonies* (Reeves).

Alt Horn and Baritone.
Kappey : *Alt Horn and Baritone Tutor* (Boosey).
Instruction Book for Baritone (Metzler).

American Organ. (See **Reed Organ.**)

Analysis. (See **Form** and **Harmony Analysis.**)

Ancient and Old Music. (See also **National Music** and **Plain Song.**)
De la Borde : *Musique Ancienne et Moderne*, 4 vols. (1780).
Dickinson : *Growth and Development of Music* (Reeves).
Donovan : *From Lyre to Muse* (Reeves).
Elson : *Curiosities of Music* (Schirmer).

Engel : *Music of the most Ancient Nations* (1864).
Gevaert : *History of the Music of Antiquity* (1875-81).
Gevaert : *Histoire de la Musique Grecque* (1881).
Goddard : *The Rise of Music* (Reeves).
Landowska : *Musique Ancienne* (Paris, 1909).
Monro : *Modes of Ancient Greek Music* (Schirmer).
Plainsong and Mediæval Society :
    Songs and Madrigals of the 15th cent. (Quaritch).
    Musical Notation of the Middle Ages (Quaritch).
    The Sarum Gradual (Quaritch).
    Early English Harmony (Quaritch).
Riano : *Early Spanish Music* (Quaritch).
Rowbotham : *Ancient and Mediæval Music.*
H. Smith : *The World's Earliest Music* (Reeves).
Stainer : *Early Bodleian Music* (Novello).
Wallaschek : *Primitive Music* (Breitkopf).
Williams : *Music of the Ancient Greeks* (Novello).

Anecdotes.
Burgh : *Musical Anecdotes*, 3 vols. (1814).
Crowest : *Musical Anecdotes* (Bentley).
Crowest : *Musicians' Wit and Humour* (W. Scott).
Gates : *Anecdotes of Musicians* (Weekes).
Musical Anecdotes (Geo. Gill).

Bagpipe.
Fraser : *The Bagpipe* (Hay, Edinburgh).
Glen : *Highland Bagpipe Music* (1876).
Mackay : *Tutor for Highland Bagpipe* (1840).

Banjo.
Instruction Book (Metzler).
    Also Methods by Briggs, Buckley, Dobson, Rice, Winner, &c.

Baritone. (See **Alt Horn.**)

Bassoon.
Kappey : *Bassoon Tutor* (Boosey).
Instruction Book (Metzler).
Bassoon Tutor (Williams).

Bells.
Ellacombe : *Belfries and their Ringers* (1871).
Fletcher : *Hand-bell Ringing* (Curwen).
Gatty : *The Bell* (1848).
Jones : *Art of Ringing.*
Lewis : *Bell Founding* (1878).
Lomax : *Bells and Bell-ringers* (1879).
Raven : *The Bells of England* (Methuen).
Starmer : *Bells and Bell Tones* (Novello).
Troyte : *Change Ringing* (1869).
Wigram : *Change Ringing* (1880).

Biography.
(1) GENERAL—
Histories of Music, p. 200, and below.
Biographical Dictionaries, p. 118.
Bourne : *Great Composers* (1884).
Charlton : *Sketches of Musicians* (1836).
Chorley : *Thirty years' Mus. Recollections* (1862).
Clayton : *Queens of Song*, 2 vols. (1863).
Crowest : *Great Tone Poets* (1874).
Dictionary of National Biography (Smith, Elder).
Elson : *Modern Composers of Europe* (Schirmer).
Ferris : *Great Singers*, 2 vols. (1880).
Ferris : *The Great Composers* (Walter Scott).
Hervey : *Masters of French Music* (Osgood, McIlvaine & Co.).
Maitland : *Masters of English Music* (Osgood & Co.).
Mason : *Grieg to Brahms* (Macmillan).
Mason : *Beethoven and His Forerunners* (Macmillan).
Mason : *The Romantic Composers* (Macmillan).
Parry : *Stories of Great Composers* (Routledge).
Rubinstein : *Music and its Masters* (Augener).
Hannah Smith : *Founders of Music* (Schirmer).
Stieler : *The Great German Composers* (Augener).
Streatfeild : *Masters of Italian Music* (Osgood, McIlvaine & Co.).
Willeby : *Masters of English Music* (Osgood, McIlvaine & Co.).

(2) INDIVIDUAL—
(A) IN SERIES—
Bell's *Miniature Series* (Bach, Handel, &c.).
Dent's *Half-crown Series of Lives.*
Dent's *Master Musicians,* ed. by Crowest.
John Lane's *Living Masters of Music.*
John Lane's *The Music of the Masters.*
Novello's *Primers of Mus. Biography,* ed. by Bennett,&c.
Sampson Low's *Great Musicians,* ed. by Hueffer, &c.
Beruhmte Musiker, edited by Riemann (Breitkopf & Härtel)
Les Maitres de la Musique (Breitkopf & Härtel).
Les Musiciens Célèbres (Breitkopf & Härtel).
(B) SEPARATE—
ARDITI : *Reminiscences* (Schirmer).
BACH : Forkel (1820) ; Spitta, 3 vols. (Novello) ;
    Wesley, *The Bach Letters* (Reeves) ; R. Boughton
    (Lane) ; Prout, *Notes of Bach's Church Cantatas*
    (Breitkopf) ; A. Pirro, *Bach the Organist*
    (Schirmer) ; E. Newman, *Bach le Musicien
    Poète* (Breitkopf & Härtel) ; Sedley Taylor,
    Life of Bach (Macmillan) ; Kay-Shuttleworth,
    Life (Houlston).
BALFE : W. A. Barrett (Reeves).
BEETHOVEN : Elterlein, *Beethoven's Symphonies*
    (Reeves) ; Elterlein, *Beethoven's Sonatas*
    (Reeves) ; Grove, *Beethoven's Nine Symphonies*
    (Novello) ; Nohl, *Beethoven* (1880) ; Schindler,
    Life, 2 vols. (1841) ; Teetgen, *Beethoven's
    Symphonies* (Reeves) ; Thayer, *Life,* 3 vols.
    (Eng. trans. by H. Deiters) ; Wagner, *Beethoven*
    (Reeves) ; E. Walker, *Life* (Lane) ; Kalischer-
    Shedlock, *Letters,* 2 vols. (Dent, 1909) ; Prod-
    homme, *Beethoven's Symphonies* (Delagrave,
    Paris) ; Kerst-Krehbiel, *Beethoven* (Gay & Bird).
STERNDALE BENNETT : J. F. R. Sterndale Bennett
    (Cambridge University Press).
BELLINI : Scherillo (Milan, 1885) ; Pougin (Paris,
    1868) ; Lloyd (Sisley, 1908).
BERLIOZ : H. M. Dunstan (Reeves) ; Bernard, 2 vols.,
    1882 ; Boult, *Memoirs* (Dent) ; Prodhomme,
    Life (Delagrave, Paris).
BIZET : Pigot (1886).
BOIELDIEU : Pougin (Paris, 1875) ; Hequet.
BORODIN AND LISZT : Habets (Reeves).
BRAHMS : Newmarch (Reeves) ; Colles (Lane) ;
    Florence May, 2 vols. (Ed. Arnold).
BRUCKNER : Brunner (Linz-on-Danube, 1895).
BRUNEAU : A. Hervey (Lane).
ZECHARIAH BUCK : Kitton (Jarrold).
OLE BULL : Sara Bull (Boston, 1883) ; Vlík (Bergen,
    1890).
BÜLOW : Mad. Bülow (Leipzig, 1895).
CALVÉ : Gallus (Schirmer).
CARRODUS : Ada Carrodus, *A Life Study.*
CHERUBINI : Bellasis (Reeves).
CHOPIN : Huneker, *Chopin, the Man and His Music*
    (Reeves) ; Jonson, *Handbook of Chopin's Works*
    (Reeves) ; Karasowski, *Frederic Chopin*
    (Reeves) ; Kleczynski, *How to play Chopin*
    (Reeves) ; Liszt, *Life of Chopin* (1877) ; Niecks,
    Chopin as Man and Musician (Novello) ;
    Tarnowski-Janotha, *Chopin* (Reeves).
CLEMENTI : Frojo (Milan, 1878) ; Chilesotti (Milan,
    1882).
CORNELIUS : Sandberger (Leipzig, 1887).
J. CURWEN : J. S. Curwen (Curwen).
FELICIEN DAVID : Azevedo (Paris, 1863).
FERD. DAVID : Eckardt (German).
DEBUSSY : Liebich (Lane) ; Daly (Simpson, Edinburgh).
DONIZETTI : Cicconetti (Rome, 1864).
DUFAY, &c. : Stainer (Novello).
DVORÁK : Zubaty (German).
DYKES, J. B. : Fowler (Murray, 1897).
ELGAR : E. Newman (Lane) ; Buckley (Lane).
FARINELLI : Sacchi (Venice, 1784).
CESAR FRANCK : Baldenspreger, Derepas, Destranges
    (all French). *A Study* by V. D'Indy (English
    edition, Lane).
FRANZ : Waldmann (Leipzig, 1895) ; Osterwald.
FUX : Köchel (Vienna, 1872).
GADE : D. Gade, *Life, &c.* (German).
GARCIA : Mackinlay, *Garcia the Centenarian* (Black-
    wood).
GLINKA : Fougue (French).
GOSSEC : Hellouin (French).

GLUCK AND THE OPERA : E. Newman (Dobell).
GOTTSCHALK : Peterson (Schirmer) ; Hensen (Schirmer).
GOUNOD : De Bovet (Sampson Low).
GREGORY THE GREAT : Dudden (Breitkopf).
GRÉTRY : A. J. Grétry (1815) ; Grégoir (1883) ;
    Brunet (1884).
GRIEG : Closson (Fischbacher, Paris) ; Finck (Lane).
SIR GEO. GROVE : Graves (Macmillan).
HALÉVY : Leon Halévy (1862).
SIR C. HALLÉ : *Life and Letters* (Breitkopf).
HANDEL : Chrysander (2 vols. completed) ; Main-
    waring (1760) ; Mattheson (1740) ; Rockstro
    (1883) ; Schoelcher (1857). Cusins, *The Messiah*
    (Augener) ; Chorley, *Handel Studies* (Augener) ;
    Cummings, *Life* (Bell) ; Sed. Taylor, *Indebted-
    ness of Handel to other Composers* (Camb. Univ.
    Press) ; Robinson, *Handel and his Orbit* (Sherratt
    & Hughes) ; Marshall, *Master of the Musicians*
    (Seeley).
HAYDN : Hadow, *A Croatian Composer* (1897) ;
    Ludwig, *Joseph Haydn* (1867) ; Mayr, *Life*
    (1809) ; Pohl and Mandyczewski, *Joseph Haydn*
    (3 vols.).
HELLER : Barbadette (1876).
HÉROLD : Jouvin (Paris, 1868).
J. A. HILLER : Peiser (Leipzig 1895).
E J. HOPKINS : Pearce, *Life and Works* (Vincent,
    1909).
AD. JENSEN : Niggli (Breitkopf).
JOACHIM : Fuller-Maitland (Lane).
KUHLAU : Thrane (German).
LESCHETIZKY : Annette Hullah (Lane).
JENNY LIND : Rockstro (Novello).
LISZT : Ramann (Reeves) ; Wohl (Reeves) ; C. Bache,
    Letters (H. Grevel) ; Martin (Reeves).
LORTZING : Kruse, Lortzing, Wittmann (all German).
MACDOWELL : Gilman (Lane).
G. A. MACFARREN : Banister (Bell) ; W. Macfarren,
    Memories (W. Scott).
W. MACFARREN : *Autobiography* (W. Scott).
MANNS : Saxe Wyndham (W. Scott).
MASSENET : Solenière (French).
MÉHUL : Vieillard (1859) ; Pougin (1889).
MENDELSSOHN : Eckardt (1884) ; Grove's Dict. ;
    Hiller (1874) ; Hensel (1879) ; K. Mendelssohn
    (1871). Edwards, *Hist. of Elijah* (Novello) ;
    Glehn, *Goethe and Mendelssohn* (Macmillan) ;
    Wallace, *Mendelssohn's Letters* (Longmans).
MERKEL : Janssen (German).
MEYERBEER : Lasalle (1864) ; Mendel (1868) ; Schucht
    (1869).
MOSCHELES : Mad. Moscheles (1872).
MOUSSORGSKY : Calvocoressi (Alcan, Paris).
MOZART : Clark and Hutchinson, *Mozart's "Don
    Giovanni"* (Reeves) ; Holmes, *Life of Mozart*
    (Novello) ; Jahn, *Life of Mozart,* 3 vols.
    (Novello) ; Nohl, *Life of Mozart,* 2 vols. (Long-
    mans) ; Pole, *Story of Mozart's Requiem*
    (Novello) ; Rau, *The Tone King* (Breitkopf) ;
    Wilder, *Mozart, Man and Artist* (Reeves).
NIKISCH : Pfohl (German).
NICOLAI : Mendel (Berlin, 1868) ; *Diary* (Leipzig,
    1893).
V. NOVELLO : Cowden-Clarke (Novello).
H. S. OAKELEY : E. M. Oakeley (Allen).
OFFENBACH : Wolff (French).
OUSELEY : Joyce.
PADEREWSKI : E. A. Baughan (Lane).
PAGANINI : Fétis (Paris, 1851 ; London, 1852) ;
    Niggli (1882).
PALESTRINA : Baini (Rome, 1828) ; Bartolini (Rome,
    1870) ; Bäumker (1877) ; Cametti (Milan, 1895).
PERGOLESI : Blasis (1817) ; Villarosa (1831).
PIATTI : M. Latham.
PUCCINI : Wakeling Dry (Lane).
PURCELL : Cummings (1882) ; Holmes (Novello).
RAMEAU : Du Charger (1761) ; Nisard (1867) ; Grique
    (1876).
SIMS REEVES : *Autobiography* (1888).
ROSSINI : Stendhal, Azvedo, Edwards (London, 1869),
    Zanolini, Kohut (Leipzig, 1892).
ROUSSEAU : Pougin (Paris).
A. RUBINSTEIN : *Memoirs* (St. Petersburg, 1889) ;
    MacArthur (London, 1889).
SAINT-SAËNS : Neitzel (German).
SANTLEY : *Reminiscences* (Pitman).

A. Scarlatti : Arnold (Dent).
Schubert : Barbadette (Paris, 1866) ; Grove's *Dict.* ; Von Hellborn (Vienna, 1861-65) ; Niggli (1880) ; Riemann (Berlin, 1873).
Schumann : Grove, *Letters* (Bell) ; Grove's Dict. ; Reissmann (Bell) ; Reimann (1887) ; Spitta ; (1882) ; Waldersee (1880) ; Wasielewski (1878). Writings 4 vols. (London, 1875).
Clara Schumann : *Life* (Breitkopf).
H. Schütz : Spitta (1886).
Sir Geo. Smart : Cox (Longmans).
Henry Smart : Spark (Reeves).
Spohr : *Autobiography* (Reeves) ; Malibran (Frankfort, 1860) ; Schletterer (1881).
Spontini : Loménie (1841) ; Montanari (1851) ; Raoul-Rochette (1882).
Sir Robert Stewart : Culwick (Chadfield, Derby).
A. Stradivarius : Fetis-Bishop (Reeves).
Rd. Strauss : E. Newmann (Lane) ; Dr. A. Siedl (Prague) ; Kalisch (Lane).
Sullivan : Findon (Sisleys Ltd.) ; Saxe Wyndham (Bell & Sons) ; Lawrence (James Bowden).
Tartini : Hiller (1784) ; Fayolle (1810).
Tschaikowski : Markham Lee (Lane) ; M. Tschaikowsky (Eng. trans., Lane).
Verdi : Monaldi (Leipzig, 1898) ; Checchi (1887) ; Roosevelt (London, 1887) ; Crowest ; Visetti (Bell).
Vieuxtemps : Randoux (1891).
Viotti : Fayolle (Paris, 1810) ; Baillot (1825).
Wagner : Barry, *Bayreuth*, &c. (Sonnenschein) ; Bennett, *Letters from Bayreuth* (Novello) ; H. C. Chamberlain, *Rd. Wagner* (Breitkopf) ; Dannreuther, *Wagner* (1873) ; Ashton Ellis, *Wagner's Letters*, &c. (H. Grevel) ; Finck, *Wagner*, &c. (H. Grevel) ; Glasenapp, *Biography* (1876) ; Glasenapp and Ellis, *Biography* (1900) ; Hall, *The Wagnerian Romances* (Lane) ; Heintz, *Parsifal* (Novello) ; Heintz, *The Meistersingers* (Novello) ; Heintz, *Tristan und Isolde* (Novello) : Hueffer, *Music of the Future* (Chapman & Hall) ; Hueffer, *Wagner* (1881) ; Kilburn, *Wagner's Life and Work* (Reeves) ; Kilburn, *Wagner's Parsifal* (Reeves) ; Kobbe, *How to understand Wagner's Ring* (Reeves) ; Krehbiel, *Wagnerian Drama* (Osgood & Co.) ; Lidgey, *Wagner* (Dent) ; E. Newman, *A Study of Wagner* (Dobell) ; E. Newman, *Wagner* (Lane) ; Pfordten, *Sixpenny Handbooks to Wagner's Works* (Breitkopf) ; Pohl, *Biography* (1883) ; Tappert, *Biography* (1883) ; Winworth, *The Epic of Sounds—Wagner's Ring* (Novello) ; Cleather and Crump, *Wagner's Music Dramas* (Methuen, 1909) ; Ellis, *Wagner* (Kegan Paul) ; Neumann-Livermore, *Personal Recollections* (Constable) ; Shaw, *The Perfect Wagnerite* (Constable).
Weber : Baron M. M. von Weber (3 vols., 1866-8).
Hugo Wolf : E. Newman (Methuen).
H. J. Wood : Rosa Newmarch (Lane).

Bombardon, Tuba, &c.

Instruction Book (Metzler).
Kappey : *Bombardon Tutor* (Boosey).

Brass Band.

Curwen : *Brass Band Book* (Curwen).
Kappey : *Brass Band Tutor* (Boosey).
Rose : *Talks with Bandsmen* (Rider).
Simpson : *Bandmaster's Guide* (Boosey).
Vincent : *Brass Band and How to Write for it* (Vincent). (See also *Instrumentation*.)

Breathing. (See Singing.)

Byzantine Music.

Hatherley : *Hymns of the Eastern Church* (1882).
Hatherley : *Treatise on Byzantine Music*.

Campanology. (See Bells.)

Canon. (See Double Counterpoint, &c.)

Carols.

Chope : *Carols* (1868-76).
Husk : *Songs of Nativity*.
Sandys : *Christmas Carols* (1833) ; *Christmas Tide* (1852).
Stainer : *Carols, &c.* (Novello).

Chamber Music.

Kilburn : *Story of* (W. Scott).

Choir Training. (See also Conducting.)

Class Singing for Schools (Stainer & Bell).
Curwen : *The Boy's Voice* (Curwen).
Hall : *Essentials of Choir Boy Training* (Novello).
Helmore : *Church Choirs* (1874).
Keeton : *Chorister's Singing Method* (Curwen, 1892).
Kidner : *How to Start a Men's Choir* (Curwen).
Kilburn : *How to manage a Choral Society* (Reeves).
Martin : *Art of Training Choir Boys* (Novello).
Nichol : *Choral Technics* (Curwen).
Mees : *Choirs and Choral Music* (Scribners).
M. Richardson : *Choir Training* (Novello).
M. Richardson : *Choir Training based on Voice Production* (Vincent).
Roberts : *Practical Method of Training Choristers* (Novello).
Simmons : *Practical Points for Choral Singers* (Vincent).
Stainer : *Choral Society Vocalization* (Novello).
Stubbs : *Practical Hints on the Training of Choir Boys* (Novello).
Troutbeck : *Church Choir Training* (Novello).
Venables : *Choral and Orchestral Societies* (Novello).
C. Vincent : *Choral Instruction for Treble Voices* (Vincent).
White : *Training of Men's Voices* (Vincent).
Wodell : *Choir and Chorus Conducting* (Presser).

Church Music—Collections.

Arnold : *Cathedral Music* (1790).
Ayrton : *Sacred Minstrelsy* (1835).
Barnard : *Church Music* (1641).
Bishop and Warren : *Repertorium Musicæ Antiquæ* (1848).
Boyce : *Cathedral Music*, 3 vols. (1760).
Jebb : *Choral Responses*, 2 vols. (1847-57).
Joule : *Directorium Chori Anglicanum* (1849).
Latrobe : *Sacred Music*, 6 vols. (1806-25).
Novello : *Various Collections*.
Novello : *Fitzwilliam Music* (Novello).
Ouseley : *Anthems*, 2 vols. (1861-66).
Ouseley : *Cathedral Services* (abt. 1853).
Page : *Harmonia Sacra*, 3 vols. (1800).
Rimbault : *Anthems* (1845).
Rimbault : *Services and Anthems*, 3 vols.
Also *The Church Music Society's Reprints* (H. Frowde)

Church Music—Literature.

Adcock : *The Choirmaster* (F. S. Turney).
Allon : *Church Song* (1862).
Barrett : *English Church Composers*.
Belcher : *Ecclesiastical Music* (1872).
Bumpus : *Hist. of Cath. Music in England*, 2 vols. (Laurie).
Burge : *On the Church Service, &c.* (1844).
Clément : *Histoire de la Mus. Religieuse* (1866).
J. S. Curwen : *Studies in Worship Music*, 1st and 2nd Series (Curwen).
Daniel : *Chapters on Church Music* (Elliot Stock).
Druitt : *Church Music* (1845).
Druitt : *Church Choral Music* (1853).
Edwards : *United Praise* (Curwen).
Edwards and Welsh : *Romance of Psalter and Hymnal* (Hodder).
Engel : *Reflections on Church Music* (1856).
Foster : *Anthems and Anthem Composers* (Novello).
Hackett : *Cathedral Choristers, &c. &c.* (1873).
Hicks : *Church Music* (1881).
Horder : *The Hymn Lover* (Curwen).
Jebb : *The Choral Service, &c.* (1843).
Jebb : *Cathedral Service, &c.* (1841).
Julian : *Hymnology* (2nd ed., 1904, Murray).
Latrobe : *Music of the Church* (1831).
Lightwood : *Hymn-tunes and their Story* (Kelly).
Pullen : *Real Work of a Cathedral, &c.* (1869).
Pullen : *Our Choral Services* (Simpkin).
M. Richardson : *The Psalms, their Structure, &c.* (Vincent).
M. Richardson : *Church Music* (Longmans).
Shuttleworth, Canon : *The Place of Music in Public Worship* (Elliot Stock).
Stubbs : *How to sing the Choral Service* (Novello).
Student : *Church Music and Congregational Singing* (Charles : Dublin).
Taylor : *English Cathedral Service, &c.* (1845).

35

Telford : *The Methodist Hymn Book* (Kelly).
Terry : *Catholic Church Music* (Greening).
Walcott : *Cathedralia* (Masters).
Wesley, S. S. : *Cathedral Music* ..*Reform* (Rivingtons).
Wesley, S. S. : *A Reply....relative to....Improvement of Cath. Music* (Simpkin Marshall).
West : *Cathedral Organists Past and Present* (Novello).
Whiston : *Cathedral Trusts, &c.* (Ollivier).

Clarinet.
Instruction Book for Clarinet (Metzler).
Kappey : *Bass and Alto Clar. Tutor* (Boosey).
Lazarus : *Clarinet Method.*
Williams : *Clarinet Tutor* (Boosey).
Also the French " Methods " of Beer, Klosé, Parès, and C. Baermann ; and the German " Method of Altenburg.

Colour and Music.
Allen : *Scales in Music and Colours.*
Hughes : *Harmonies of Tones and Colours* (1883).
Jameson : *Colour Music* (1844).
Macdonald : *Sound and Colour* (Longmans).

Composition. (See also Harmony, Counterpoint, and Form.)
Corder : *Modern Musical Composition* (Curwen).
Czerny : *School of Practical Composition,* 3 vols. (Augener).
Dunstan : *The Composer's Handbook* (Curwen).
E. Evans : *How to Compose, &c* (Reeves).
Goetschius : *Exercises in Melody Writing* (Schirmer)
Hamilton : *Musical Ideas* (1838).
Herbert : *How to write an Accompt.* (Schirmer).
Kollmann : *Musical Composition* (1799).
Marx : *Musical Composition* (Gordon, New York).
Stainer : *Composition* (Novello).
Wohlfahrt : *Guide to Musical Composition* (Schirmer).

Concertina.
Case : *Concertina Method* (Boosey).
Instruction Book, English Concertina (Metzler).
Instruction Book, German Concertina (Metzler).
Pietra : *Eng. Concertina Tutor* (Brewer).
Regondi : *Concertina Tutor.*

Congregational Music. (See Church Music.)

Conducting. (See also Choir Training.)
Croger : *Notes on Conducting* (Reeves).
Wagner-Dannreuther : *On Conducting* (Reeves).
Schroeder : *Handbook of Conducting* (Augener).
Weingartner : *On Conducting* (Breitkopf).
Wodell : *Choir and Chorus Conducting* (Presser).

Cor Anglais and Oboe d'Amore.
French " Methods," by Jancourt, Cokken, Beer, G. Parès, and C. Almenraeder.

Cornet.
Arban : *Method for Cornet à pistons* (Eng. trans.).
Brett : *Cornet Primer* (Novello).
Distin : *Cornet Tutor* (Boosey).
Instruction Book (Metzler).
Stanton Jones : *Cornet Method* (Boosey).
Levy : *Cornet Tutor.*

Counterpoint.
Bridge : *Counterpoint Primer* (Novello).
Cherubini : *Counterpoint and Fugue* (Novello).
Gladstone : *Counterpoint* (Novello).
A. Haupt : *Counterpoint, Fugue, and Double Counterpoint* (Schirmer).
Hiles : *Part Writing* (Novello).
Jadassohn : *Manual of Counterpoint* (Breitkopf).
Kitson : *Counterpoint, &c.* (Clarendon Press).
Macfarren : *Treatise on Counterpoint* (1879).
Macpherson : *Practical Counterpoint* (J. Williams).
Oakey : *Counterpoint* (Curwen).
Ouseley : *Treatise on Counterpoint* (Clarendon Press).
Pearce : *Student's Counterpoint* (Vincent).
Pearce : *Composer's Counterpoint* (Vincent).
Prout : *Counterpoint* (Augener).
Richter : *Counterpoint* (Cramer).
Riemann : *Counterpoint* (Breitkopf & Härtel).
Rockstro : *Counterpoint* (Augener).
Saunders : *Strict Counterpoint* (Novello).
Spalding : *Tonal Counterpoint* (Schirmer).
Wylde : *Counterpoint* (Cramer).

Dictation.
Ritter : *Musical Dictation* (Novello).

Dictionaries. (See page 118.)

Double Bass.
Bottesini : *Complete Method.*
Flockton : *Method.*
F. Simandl : *Method* (German).
Instruction Book (Metzler).
White : *Double Bass Primer* (Novello).

Double Counterpoint and Canon.
Ayres : *Counterpoint and Canon* (Schirmer).
Bridge : *Double Counterpoint and Canon* (Novello).
Jadassohn : *Manual of Counterpoint* (Breitkopf).
Prout : *Double Counterpoint and Canon* (Augener).
Richter : *Imitation, Canon, &c.*

Drum.
Instruction Book for Drums, Castanets, &c. (Metzler).
Keach : *Modern School.*
Also " Methods " by Kastner and De Sivry.

Ear Training.
Alchin : *Ear Training* (Schirmer).
Jadassohn : *Practical Course* (Breitkopf).
Johnstone : *Ear Tests, &c.* (Allan, Melbourne).
Oakey : *Text Book of Ear Training* (Curwen).
Sawyer : *Ear Training Primer* (Weekes).
Shinn : *Elementary Ear Training* (Vincent).

Education. (See also Psychology.)
Curwen : *The Standard Course* (Curwen).
Curwen : *Teacher's Manual* (Curwen).
J. S. Curwen : *Companion for Teachers* (Curwen).
Evans and McNaught : *School Music Teacher* (Curwen).
Fay : *Music Study in Germany* (1881).
Ingham : *Education in accordance with Natural Law* (Novello).
Mainzer : *Music and Education* (1848.)
Mason : *Pestalozzian Teacher.*
Warriner : *Art of Teaching as applied to Music* (Trinity College, London).

Elements. (See Principles of Music.)

Elocution, Enunciation, &c. (See also Singing.)
Mrs. Behnke : *The Speaking Voice* (Curwen).
Bell : *Standard Elocutionist* (Hodder).
Bell : *Visible Speech* (Simpkin).
Brennan : *Words in Singing* (Vincent).
Dunstan : *Enunciation Exercises* (Curwen).
Ellis : *Pronunciation for Singers* (Curwen).
Ellis : *Speech in Song* (Novello).
Harrison : *Primer of Elocution* (Curwen).
Sweet : *The Sounds of English* (Clarendon Press).

Euphonium.
Kappey : *Euphonium Tutor* (Boosey).
Instruction Book (Metzler).

Expression.
Curwen : *Musical Theory,* Part IV (Curwen).
Christiani : *Expression in Pianoforte Playing* (Reeves)
Johnstone : *Art of Expression* (Weekes).
Lussy : *Expression* (Novello).
F. Taylor : *Technique and Expression in Pf. Playing* (Novello).

Extemporization.
Sawyer : *Extemporization* (Novello).

Fife.
Instruction Book (Metzler).

Figured Bass. (See also Harmony.)
Dunstan : *Basses and Melodies* (Novello).
Oakey : *Figured Bass* (Curwen).

Flageolet.
Instruction Book (Metzler).

Flute.
Boehm : *Construction of the Flute* (1882).
Boehm : *The Flute and Flute Playing* (Rudall, Carte).
Clinton : *Flute Method* (Boosey).
Dipple : *Instructions for Flute* (Brewer).
James : *A Word or two on the Flute* (1826).
Instruction Book (Metzler).

Nicholson : *Instructions for Flute* (Brewer).
Rockstro : *Flute School.*
Skeffington : *The Flute* (1862).
Welch : *History of the Boehm Flute* (1883).
Wetzger : *Die Flöte* (Breitkopf).

Folk Music.   (See **National Music.**)

Form and Analysis.

Anger : *Form in Music* (Vincent).
Banister : *Musical Analysis* (Reeves).
Bertenshaw : *Rhythm, Analysis, and Form* (Longmans).
Boekelmann : 16 *Fugues from Bach analysed in Colours* (Novello).
Bussler-Cornell : *Musical Form* (Schirmer).
Curwen : *Musical Theory* Part III (Curwen).
M. H. Glyn : *Evolution of Musical Form* (Longmans).
Goetschius : *Counterpoint, &c., in Polyphonic Forms* (Schirmer).
Goetschius : *Homophonic Forms, &c.* (Schirmer).
Grove : *Beethoven's Symphonies* (Novello).
Hadow : *Sonata Form* (Novello).
Handbook of Mus. Form : Pianist's Handbook, Part II (Augener).
Harding : *Analysis of Beethoven's Sonatas* (Novello).
Iliffe : *Analysis of Bach's* 48 *Preludes and Fugues* (Novello).
Jadassohn : *Manual of Mus. Form* (Breitkopf).
Macfarren : *Structure of a Sonata* (Rudall, Carte)
Macpherson : *Form in Music* (J. Williams).
Ouseley : *Form* (1875).
Pauer : *Musical Forms* (Novello).
Prentice : *The Musician*, 6 grades (Curwen).
Prescott : *Form or Design in Music* (Ascherberg).
Prout : *Musical Form* (Augener).
Prout : *Applied Forms* (Augener).
Riemann : *Hist. of Mus. Forms* (Augener).
Riemann : *Analysis of Bach's* 48 *Preludes and Fugues* (Augener).
Sampson : *Analysis of Bach's* 48 *Fugues* (Vincent).
Statham : *Form and Design in Music* (1893).
Stainer : *Composition* (Novello).
Surette and Mason : *Appreciation of Music* (Novello).

French Horn.

Kappey : *French Horn Tutor* (Boosey).
Valve Horn, French Horn, and Trumpet (Metzler).

Fugue.

Cherubini : *Counterpoint and Fugue* (Novello).
Higgs : *Fugue* (Novello).
Jadassohn : *Canon and Fugue* (Breitkopf).
Marchant : 500 *Fugue Subjects and Answers* (Novello).
Prout : *Fugue* (Augener).
Prout : *Fugal Analysis* (Augener).
Richter : *Treatise on Fugue* (Breitkopf).
Röhner : *Fugue* (Metzler).

Glees.

Baptie : *Sketches of Eng. Glee Composers* (Reeves).
Barrett : *Eng. Glees and Part-songs* (Longmans).

Greek Music.   (See **Ancient and Old Music**).

Guitar.

Eulenstein : *Instructions* (Brewer).
Maldura : *Popular Method* (Ricordi).
Nava : *Tutor* (Ricordi).
Pratten : *Guitar Tutor* (Boosey).
Phipps : *Instructions* (Brewer).
Instruction Book (Metzler).
The Spanish Guitar (Metzler).

Harmonium.

Elliott : *Handy Book for the Harmonium* (Boosey).
Fisher : *Harmonium and American Organ Tutor* (Curwen).
King Hall : *Harmonium Primer* (Novello).
Hiles : *Catechism of the Harmonium and American Organ* (Reeves).
Mullen : *Harmonium Tutor.*
Rimbault : *The Harmonium* (1857).
Warren : *Catechism of the Harmonium* (Augener).
Instruction Book (Metzler).

Harmonizing Melodies.

Banister : *The Harmonizing of Melodies* (Reeves).
Duncan : *Melodies and How to Harmonize them* (Vincent).

Dunstan : *Basses and Melodies* (Novello).
Dunstan : *First Steps in Harmony, &c.* (Curwen).
Edwards : 200 *Melodies, &c.* (Weekes).
Harriss : *Harmonizing Melodies* (Novello).
Brook-Sampson : *Harmonizing of Melodies* (Modern).
Taylor : *Harmonizing Melodies* (Vincent).
Vernham : *Harmonization of Melodies* (Novello).
Rowland Winn : *Harmonizing Melodies* (Novello).

Harmony.

Albrechtsberger : *Collected Works* (Novello).
Anger : *Treatise on Harmony* (Vincent).
Bazin : *Cours d'harmonie* (Schott or Hachette).
Boise : *Harmony made Practical* (Schirmer).
Bridge and Sawyer : *A Course of Harmony* (Novello).
Bussler : *Elementary Harmony* (Schirmer).
Catel : *Treatise on Harmony* (Novello).
Chadwick : *Course of Study* (Schirmer).
Curwen : *How to Observe Harmony* (Curwen).
Dana : *Practical Harmony* (1884).
Day : *Treatise on Harmony* (1845).
Dunstan : *First Steps in Harmony* (Curwen).
Gadsby : *Harmony* (Novello).
Galli : *Teoria, &c.* (Nagas, Milan).
Gladstone : *Five-part Harmony* (Novello).
Goetschius : *A System of Harmony* (Schirmer).
Goss : *Introduction to Harmony* (1833).
Hauptmann : *Nature of Harmony and Metre* (Schirmer).
Hiles : *Harmony of Sounds* (Reeves).
Jadassohn : *Manual of Harmony* (Breitkopf).
Lavignac : *Recueil de leçons d'harmonie* (Schott or Hachette).
Macfarren : *Rudiments of Harmony* (Cramer).
Macfarren : *Six Lectures* (Longmans).
Macpherson : *Practical Harmony* (J. Williams).
Mansfield : *The Student's Harmony* (Weekes).
Oakey : *Harmony* (Curwen).
Ouseley · *Treatise on Harmony* (1868).
Oscar Paul : *Manual of Harmony* (Schirmer).
Pearce : *Trinity College Text Books*, Intermediate and Senior.
Prout : *Harmony* (Augener).
L. Prout : *Sidelights on Harmony* (Augener).
Stainer : *Harmony Primer* (Novello).
Stainer : *A Theory of Harmony* (Novello).
Tschaikowsky : *Guide to......Harmony* (Schirmer).
Reber : *Traité d'harmonie* (Schott or Hachette).
Riemann : *Harmony Simplified* (Augener).
Richter : *Manual of Harmony* (various publishers).
Sechter-Müller : *Fundamental Harmonies* (Schirmer).
C. Vincent : *Harmony, Diatonic and Chromatic* (Vincent).
Wylde : *Harmony and the Science of Music* (Hutchings and Romer).

Harmony Analysis.

Oakey : *Harmony Analysis* (Curwen).
L. Prout : *Harmonic Analysis* (Augener).

Harp.

Aptommas : *History of the Harp* (1859).
Bochsa : *First six weeks at the Harp* (Brewer).
Challoner : *Instruction for Harp* (Brewer).
Erard : *The Harp* (1821).
Flood : *Story of the Harp* (W. Scott).
Neilon : *Instructions for Harp* (Brewer).
Oberthür : *Method for Harp* (Schott).

History.

General : See Histories of Music, p. 200.
    AFRICA—
Villoteau : *De l'Etat actuel de l'art Musical en Egypte*, 1812.
    AMERICA—
Fletcher : *Nth. American Indian Story and Song* (Schirmer).
Ritter : *Music in America* (Schirmer).
Mathews : *A Hundred Years of Music in America* (Schirmer).
Elson : *History of American Music* (Macmillan).
    ARABIA—
F. S. Daniel : *La Musique Arabe*, 1879.
    BELGIUM AND BOHEMIA—
Soubies : *Histoire de la Musique.*
    CHINA—
Pere Amiot : *Mémories, &c.*, Vol. VI, 1781.

35a

Moule : *Musical Insts. of the Chinese* (Royal Asiatic Society).
Van Aalst : *Chinese Music*, 1884.

ENGLAND—
See Histories, p. 200.

FRANCE—
Bellaigue : *Un Siècle de Musique Française* (1887).
Chorley : *Music in France and Germany* (Longmans).
Coquard : *De la Musique en France* (1891).
A. Hervey : *Masters of French Music* (1894).
A. Hervey : *French Music in the 19th Cent.* (Grant Richards).

GERMANY—
Chorley : *Modern German Music*, 2 vols. (1854).
Reissmann : *Illus. Hist. of German Music* (1881).

HEBREW MUSIC—
Pfeiffer : *Ueber die Musik der alten Hebräer* (1779).
Stainer : *Music of the Bible* (1879).
Whitlock : *Hebrew and Early Christian Music* (Breitkopf).

HOLLAND—
(See *Belgium* and *Netherlands*.)

HUNGARY—
Liszt : *Die Zigeuner und der Musik in Ungarn* (1883).
Kaldy : *Hungarian Music* (Reeves).

INDIA—
W. Jones : *On the Musical Modes of the Hindoos* (1792).
Tagore : *Hindu Music* (1875-82).
Major Day : *Music and Mus. Insts. of Southern India, &c.* (Novello).

IRELAND—
Grattan Flood : *History of Irish Music* (Browne & Nolan, Dublin).
Walker : *Irish Bards* (1786).
See also Irish Music, p. 215.

ITALY—
Masutto : *Masters of Italian Music* (1880).
Naumann : *Die Italienischen Tondichter* (1874-6).
Streatfeild : *Masters of Italian Music* (1895).
Torchi : *L'Arte Musicale in Italia* (Ricordi).

JAPAN—
Piggott : *Music and Musical Insts. of Japan* (1893).

MEDIÆVAL MUSIC—
Hope : *Mediæval Music* (Elliot Stock).

NETHERLANDS—
Van der Straeten : *Histoire de la Musique aux Pays-Bas*, 5 vols. (1867-80).
Van der Straeten : *Les Musiciens Néerlandais en Italie* (1882).

PERSIA—
Ouseley : *Persian Miscellanies* (1791).
Ouseley : *Oriental Collections* (1797).

PORTUGAL—
Vasconcellos : *Os Musicos Portuguezes*, 2 vols. (1870).
Soubies : *Histoire de la Musique*.

RUSSIA—
Cui : *La Musique en Russe* (1880).
Jurgensen : *Russian edition of Riemann's Lexikon*.
Soubies : *Epitome of Russian Musical Hist.* (1893).

SCANDINAVIA—
Cristal : *L'Art Scandinave* (1874).
Soubies : *Histoire de la Musique*.

SCOTLAND—
See Scottish Music, p. 384.

SPAIN—
Soriano-Fuertes : *Historia de la Musica Espanola*, 4 vols. (1855-9).

SYMPHONY—
Brenet : *Histoire de la Symphonie* (1882).
Weingartner : *Symphony Writers since Beethoven* (Breitkopf).

SWITZERLAND—
Becker : *La Musique en Suisse* (1874).
Soubies : *Histoire de la Musique*.

WALES—
See Welsh Music, p. 473.

Horn. (See **French Horn.**)

Hymn. (See p. 205, and **Church Music.**)

Instrumentation.

Berlioz : *Instrumentation* (Novello).
Coerne : *Evolution of Modern Orchestration* (Macmillan).
Corder : *The Orchestra, and How to Write for it* (Curwen).
Daly : *The Orchestra and Orchestral Music* (Paterson, Edinburgh).
Gevaert : *Instrumentation* (Schott).
Gevaert : *Orchestration* (Schott).
Guiraud : *Traité d'instrumentation*.
Hamilton Clarke : *Manual of Orchestration* (Curwen).
Hoffmann-Legge : *Practical Instrumentation*, 7 Parts (Schirmer).
Jadassohn : *Course of Instrumentation* (Breitkopf).
Kastner : *Cours d'instrumentation*.
Kastner : *Traité d'instrumentation*.
Kling : *Modern Orchestration, &c.* (Chappell).
Lavoix Fils : *Histoire de l'instrumentation.*
Nikitits : *Das Orchester* (Augener).
Prout : *The Orchestra* (Augener).
Prout : *Instrumentation Primer* (Novello).
Riemann : *Catechism of Mus. Insts.* (Augener).
Riemann : *Catechism of Orchestration* (Augener).
Rosenkranz : *Manual of Orchestral Literature* (Novello).
Vincent : *Scoring for an Orchestra* (Vincent).
Widor : *Technique of the Modern Orch.* (J. Williams).

Lives of Musicians. (See **Biography.**)

Lute.

Brenet : *Hist. du Luth en France* (French).

Madrigals.

Barrett : *English Madrigal Writers* (1877).

Mandolin.

Bellenghi : *Complete Method* (Ricordi).
De Cristofaro : *Tutor*, Parts 1 and 2 (Ricordi).
Instruction Book (Metzler).
Also Pietrapertosa, Brunzoli, Gargiola.

Mass.

Dearmer : *Booklet of the Mass* (Breitkopf).
Devine : *Ordinary of the Mass* (Breitkopf).

Medicine and Music.

Brocklesby : *Application of Music to cure Diseases* (1749).
Browne : *Medicina Musica* (1729).
Lilley : *Therapeutics of Music* (1880).

Melodeon.

Instruction Book (Metzler).

Memory.

Clarke : *Memorizing Scales* (Vincent).
Goodrich : *Guide to Memorizing Music* (Breitkopf).
Kenyon : *How to Memorize Music* (Reeves).
Shinn : *Musical Memory* (Vincent).

Metre.

Omond : *Study of Metre* (Grant Richards).

Military Music.

Dana : *Mil. Band Instrumentation* (1876).
Farmer : *The Royal Artillery Band* (Boosey).
Griffiths : *The Military Band* (Rudall Carte).
Kappey : *Hist. of Wind Inst. Bands.*
Mandel : *Military Bands.*
Perrin : *Military Studies, Bands, &c.* (1863).
Simpson : *Instrumentation for Mil. Bands* (Boosey).

Modes. (See **Plain-song.**)

Modulation.

Banister : *Art of Modulating* (Reeves).
Cornell : *Easy Method of Modulation* (Schirmer).
Higgs : *Modulation* (Novello).
Shepard : *How to Modulate* (Schirmer).
Wigan : *Modulating Dictionary* (1852).
Zoeller : *Art of Modulation* (Reeves).

Musical Instruments. (See also **Pianoforte, Violin,** &c.)

Engel : *Musical Insts.* (Sth. Kensington Museum Handbook).
Henderson : *The Orchestra, &c.* (Schirmer).
Hipkins : *Musical Insts., Historic, Rare, and Unique* (Black).
Lynd : *Ancient Musical Insts.* (Breitkopf).
Schlesinger : *Modern Orchestral Insts.* (Reeves).
See also *Instrumentation*.

National and Folk Music.

Abbott : *Songs of Modern Greece* (Breitkopf).
Ashton : *A Century of Ballads* (1887).
Baring-Gould : *Songs of the West* (Methuen).
Lucy Broadwood : *English Traditional Songs and Carols* (Boosey).
Callcott : *Melodies of all Nations* (Brewer).
Champfleury : *Popular French Chansons* (1860).
Chappell-Macfarren : *Popular Music of the Olden Time* (Chappell).
Chorley : *Nat. Music of the World* (Reeves).
Dinaux : *Trouveres, Jongleurs, et Ménestrels* (1843).
E. Duncan : *Story of Minstrelsy* (W. Scott).
Eitner : *Das Deutsche Lied, &c.* (1876-80).
Engel : *Literature of Nat. Music* (Novello).
Elson : *Curiosities of Music* (Schirmer).
Emlyn Evans : *Treasury of Welsh Songs* (Curwen).
Foster : *Old Eng. Ballads* (Ward, Lock).
Joyce : *Old Irish Folk Music* (Longmans).
Kidson : *Old Eng. Country Dances* (1890).
Kidson : *Traditional Tunes of Yorkshire* (1891).
Liliencron : *Hist. of German Folk-Songs, 13th to 16th Cent.* (1865-9).
Lineff : *Peasant Songs of Great Russia* (David Nutt).
Moffat and Kidson : *Minstrelsy of England, Scotland, Ireland, Wales,* 4 vols. (Augener).
Nicholson : *Old German Love Songs* (Breitkopf).
Petrie : *The Complete Collection of Ancient Irish Music* (Boosey).
Ralston : *Songs of the Russian People* (1872).
Reay : *Songs, &c., of Northern England* (W. Scott).
Rhys : *Celtic Folk-Lore, &c.* (Breitkopf).
Riessman : *Hist. of the German Lied* (1874).
Cecil Sharp : *Folk-song Airs* (Novello).
Cecil Sharp : *Folk-dance Airs* (Novello).
Smith : *Stories of Great National Songs* (Schirmer).
Tiersot : *Hist. of the French Popular Chansons* (1860).
Weckerlin : *La Chansons Populaire en France.*
Also the Journal and publications of the Folk-Song Society.

Notation. (See also Plain Song.)

Corozzi : *Synthetic Notation* (Chicago).
Curwen : *Tonic Sol-fa* (Novello).
David and Lussy : *Histoire de la Notation Musicale* (Paris).
Riemann : *Musical Insts., Tone Systems, and Notations* (Augener).
Tardif : *Essai sur les Neumes* (Paris).
Watson : *Braille Notation for the Blind* (Novello).
Williams : *Story of Notation* (Walter Scott).
Joh. Wolf : *Geschichte der Mensural-Notation* (1 04).

Oboe.

Instruction Book (Metzler).
Kappey : *Oboe Tutor* (Boosey).
Also the French "Methods" by Brod, Verroust, and G. Parès.

Opera.

Annesley : *Standard Opera Glass* (Sampson Low).
Apthorp : *The Opera, Past and Present* (1901).
Arteaga : *La Rivoluzione del Teatro Musicale Italiano,* 3 vols. (1783-8).
Austin : *Opera for England* (1883).
Bunn : *The Stage* (1840).
Burgess : *Nights at the Opera* (each Opera separately : A. Moring).
Choquet : *Hist. de la Mus. Dramatique en France* (1873).
Chorley : *Recollections of the Opera,* 2 vols. (1862).
Chrysander : *Opera at Hamburg* (1878).
Dannreuther : *Wagner and the Opera* (Augener).
Davidson : *Stories from the Operas* (Werner Laurie).
Edwards : *History of the Opera,* 2 vols. (1862).
Edwards : *Lyric Drama,* 2 vols. (1881).
Elson : *History of Opera* (Breitkopf).
Gilman : *Aspects of Modern Opera* (Lane).
Gregoir : *Les Gloires de l'Opéra, &c.,* 3 vols. (1881).
Hadden : *The Great Operas* (separately, T. C. & E. C. Jack).
Hanslick : *Concerts in Vienna* (1869-70).
Lahee : *Grand Opera in America* (Schirmer).
Lumley : *Reminiscences of the Opera* (1864).
Maynard : *The Enterprising Impresario* (Bradbury, Evans).
Moskowa : *Hist. Sketch of Russian Opera* (1862).
Mount Edgcumbe : *Reminiscences* (1823).

E. Newman : *Gluck and the Opera* (Dobell).
Pougin : *Les Vrais Créateurs de l'Opéra Francais* (1881).
Schletterer : *Das Deutsche Singspiel* (1863).
Streatfeild : *The Opera* (1896-1902).
Upton : *Standard Operas* (Hutchinson & Co.).
Wagnalls : *Stars of the Operas* (Funk and Wagnalls).
Wyndham : *Annals of Covent Garden Theatre* (1906).

Oratorio.

Dr. Annie Patterson : *Story of Oratorio* (Walter Scott).
Upton : *Standard Oratorios* (Hutchinson & Co.).

Orchestration. (See Instrumentation.)

Organ.

Archer : *The Organ* (Novello).
Audsley : *Art of Organ Building* (Vincent).
Best : *Art of Organ Playing* (Novello).
Burgess : *The Organ Fifty Years Hence* (Reeves).
Dunstan : *The Organist's First Book* (Curwen).
Edwards : *Organs and Organ Building* (1881).
Elliston : *Organs and Tuning* (Weekes).
Hathaway : *Analysis of Mendelssohn's Organ Works* (Reeves).
Hiles : *Progressive Introduction to Organ Playing* (Novello).
Hinton : *Organ Construction* (Composers' and Authors' Press).
Hopkins and Rimbault : *The Organ* (1855).
Horner : *Organ Pedal Technique* (Novello).
Lewis : *Organ Building* (1878).
Matthews : *Handbook of the Organ* (Augener).
Merkel : *Organ School* (Novello).
Minshall : *Organs, Organists, and Choirs* (Curwen)
Page : *Organ Playing* (Vincent).
Pearce : *Mendelssohn's Organ Sonatas* (Vincent).
Pearce : *The Organist's Directory* (Vincent).
Pearce : *Old London Churches and their Organs* (Vincent).
Pearce : *Organ School—Three Books of Studies* (Hammond).
Pearce : *Organ Tutor* (Hammond).
Rimbault : *Early Eng. Organ Builders* (Reeves).
Rink : *Practical Organ School* (Novello).
Robertson : *Practical Treatise on Organ Building* (Reeves).
Schneider : *Practical Organ School* (Novello).
H. Smith : *Modern Organ Tuning* (Reeves).
Spark : *Handy Book for the Organ* (Boosey).
Stainer : *Organ Primer* (Novello).
Steggall : *Instruction Book for the Organ* (Novello).
Wedgwood : *Dictionary of Organ Stops* (Vincent).
Williams : *Story of the Organ* (Walter Scott).
Williams : *Story of Organ Music* (W. Scott).

Organ Accompaniment.

Bridge : *Organ Accompaniment* (Novello).
Niedermayer and Ortigue : *Gregorian Accompaniment* (Schirmer).
Pearce : *Organ Accompaniment to the Psalms* (Vincent).
Richardson : *Organ Accompaniment* (Longmans).

Ornamentation.

Dannreuther : *Musical Ornamentation* (Novello).
Fowles : *Studies in Musical Graces* (Vincent).
Germer : *Mus. Ornamentation* (Novello).
Harding : *Musical Ornaments* (Weekes).
Russell : *Embellishments of Music* (Schirmer).

Part Writing.

Hiles : *Part-Writing* (Novello).
Ivimey : *Part-Writing for Beginners* (Novello).

Periodicals. (See page 284.)

Phrasing.

Carpé : *Grouping, Articulation, and Phrasing* (Schirmer)
Marchant : *Phrasing in Pf. Playing*
Riemann and Fuchs : *Practical Guide to Phrasing* (Schirmer).

Pianoforte.

Berger : *First Steps at the Pianoforte* (Novello).
Beringer : *Daily Technical Studies* (Bosworth).
Bertini : *Modern Tutor* (Brewer).
Oscar Bie : *Hist. of the Pf. and Pf. Players* (Eng. edn., 1899).
Bonheur : *Standard Pf. Tutor* (W. Whittingham).
E. Brinsmead : *History of the Pf.* (Cassell).
Broadwood : *How the modern Pf. is made* (Broadwood).

Clementi : *Gradus ad Parnassum* (various).
Cramer : *Method*, 5 parts (1846).
Mrs. Curwen : *Teacher's Guide, and Child Pianist* (Curwen).
Czerny : 24 different works (Augener).
Ehrenfechter : *Technical Study* (Reeves).
Amy Fay : *Deppe Exercises* (Curwen).
Fillmore : *History of Pf. Music* (Reeves).
Fisher : *Construction, Tuning, and Care of the Pf.* (Curwen).
Fisher : *The Pianist's Mentor* (Curwen).
Germer : *Technics, Ornamentation, &c.* (Novello).
Amy Goodwin : *Technique and Touch* (Augener).
Hallé : *Practical School* (Forsyth).
Hemy : *Modern Pf. Tutor* (Metzler).
Hipkins : *History of the Pf.* (Novello).
Jos. Hofmann : *Pf. Playing* (Hodder & Stoughton).
Johnstone : *Touch, Phrasing, and Interpretation* (Reeves).
Jousse : *Complete Tutor* (Brewer).
Klauwell : *On Musical Execution* (Schirmer).
Köhler : *Practical Pf. Method* (Augener).
Krug : *Wrist Studies, &c.* (Novello).
Loeschhorn : *Technical Studies* (Augener).
Leeds : *My First Pf. Lesson* (Novello).
Lemoine : *Pf. Method* (Brewer).
Matthay : *The Act of Touch* (Longmans).
Matthay : *First Principles of Pf. Playing* (Longmans).
Midgley : *Scales and Arpeggios* (Vincent).
Méreaux : *Les Clavecinistes* (1867).
Myerscough : *School of Arpeggio Fingering* (Vincent).
O'Leary : *Diatonic and Chromatic Scales* (Novello).
Pauer : *Art of Pf. Playing* (Novello).
Pauer : *Dict. of Pianists and Pf. Composers* (Novello).
Pianist's Handbook (Augener).
Plaidy : *Technical Studies* (various publishers).
Prentice : *Touch and Technique* (Curwen).
Prentice : *Hand Gymnastics* (Novello).
Prentner : *Leschetizky Method* (Curwen).
Riemann : *Catechism of Pf. Playing* (Augener).
Rimbault : *The Pianoforte* (Augener).
Somervell : *Ten Minutes' Technique* (Curwen).
F. Taylor : *Scales, Studies, &c.* (Novello).
F. Taylor : *Technique and Expression* (Novello).
F. Taylor : *Double Scales* (Novello).
C. Vincent : *New Century Pf. Method* (Vincent).
Weitzmann : *Hist. of Pf. Playing and Pf. literature* (1863).
White : *Playing at Sight* (Curwen).
Wohlfahrt : *Young Pianist's Guide* (Novello).
Wohlfahrt : *Popular Pf. Method* (Augener).

Piano Tuning.
Babbington : *Tuning and Repairing Pianos*.
Fisher : *Pf. Construction, Tuning, &c.* (Curwen).
Hasluck : *Pf. Construction, Tuning, and Repair* (Cassell).

Piccolo.
Instruction Book (Metzler).

Plain Song. (See also **Ancient Music.**)
Von Arnold : *Die Alten Kirchenmodi* (1879).
Benedictines of Stanbrook : *Handbook of Rules for Plain Song*.
Briggs : *Elements of Plain Song* (Quaritch).
Burgess : *Plain Song and Gregorian Music* (Vincent).
Abbé Cartand : *Grammaire Élémentaire de Chant Grégorien* (Solesmes).
Croft : *The Solesmes System of Plain Song* (Croft).
Grammar of Plain Song (Stanbrook Benedictines).
Gregorian Chants (Burns, 1843).
Haberl : *Magister Choralis* (Pustet).
Helmore : *Plain Song Primer* (Novello).
Holly : *Rudiments of Plain Song*.
Jumilhac : *Art et Science du Plain Chant* (Paris).
Keinle : *Chant Grégorien* (Desclée : Tournai).
La Paléographie Musicale by the Benedictines of Solesmes (several vols., Appuldarcombe House, Wroxall, Isle of Wight).
Mocquereau : *Gregorian Rhythm* (Desclée : Tournai).
Pothier : *Les Mélodies Grégoriennes* (1880).
Richter : *Traité de Contrepoint* (Church tones specially studied).
Spencer : *Concise Explanation of the Church Modes* (1846).
Wagner : *Einführung in die Greg. Melodien* (3 parts, Eng. trans., pub. by the Plain-Song Society).

Playing from Score. (See also **Figured Bass.**)
Beck-Slinn : *100 Graded Exercises* (Weekes).
Daymond : *Score-reading Exercises* (Novello).
Fetis : *How to Play from Score* (Reeves).
Riemann : *Introduction to playing from Score* (Augener).
Sawyer : *Graded Score Reading* (Vincent).
Vincent : *Score Reading—Bach's Fugues* (Vincent).

Principles of Music.
Banister : *Music* (Bell).
Callcott : *Grammar of Music* (Boosey).
Catechism of Music (Augener).
Cummings : *Rudiments of Music* (Novello).
Curwen : *Musical Theory*, Parts 1 and 2 (Curwen).
Davenport : *Elements of Music*.
Dunstan : *A B C of Musical Theory* (Curwen).
Dunstan : *Manual of Music* (Curwen).
Fisher : *The Candidate in Music* (Curwen).
Johnstone : *Rudiments of Music* (Weekes).
Lobe : *Catechism of Music* (Augener).
Macpherson : *Rudiments of Music* (J. Williams).
Murby : *Musical Student's Manual* (Murby).
Oakey : *Musical Elements* (Curwen).
Pearce : *Rudiments of Musical Knowledge* (Vincent).
Peterson : *Elements of Music* (Augener).
Peterson : *Study of Theory* (Augener).
Sneddon : *Musical Self Instructor* (Curwen).
Trinity College Text Book of Musical Knowledge (Hammond).
Troutbeck and Dale : *Music Primer* (1873).

Psalmody. (See **Hymn,** p. 205 ; and **Church Music.**)

Psychology. (See also **Education.**)
Cox : *Music and Psychology* (Breitkopf).
Fisher : *Psychology for Music Teachers* (Curwen).
Meyer : *Psychological Theory of Music* (Breitkopf).

Reed Organ. (See also **Harmonium.**)
Archer : *Complete Method for American Organ*.
Instruction Book for American Organ (Metzler).
Stainer : *American Organ Tutor* (1883).

Rhythm.
Glyn : *Rhythmic Conception of Music* (Longmans).
Justis : *Studies in Rhythm* (Schirmer).
Mathys-Lussy : *Le Rhythm Musicale* (Paris).

Rudiments. (See **Principles of Music.**)

Saxhorn.
Instruction Book (Metzler).

Saxophone.
French " Methods " by Kokken, Klosé, Mayeur, and G. Parès.

Sarrusophone.
French " Method " by Coyon (Paris).

Scale.
Anger : *The Modern Enharmonic Scale* (1906).
Capes : *Growth of the Musical Scale, &c.* (Novello).
Ellis : *Musical Scales of all nations*.
Pole : *Diagrams of Scales, &c.* (1868).

Score Reading. (See **Playing from Score.**)

Scottish Music. (See p. 384.)

Shakespeare and Music.
Elson : *Shakespeare in Music* (David Nutt).
Naylor : *Shakespeare and Music*.

Shorthand Music.
Austin : *Stenographic Music*.
Hutchison : *Stenographic Music*.

Singers.
Chorley : *Mus. Recollections*, 2 vols. (1862).
Clayton : *Queens of Song*, 2 vols. (1863).
Ferris : *Great Singers*, 2 vols. (1880).

Singing and Voice Production.
Adcock : *The Singer's Guide* (Curwen).
Aprile : *Vocalises* (Augener).
Behnke : *Mechanism of the Human Voice* (Curwen).
Bates : *Voice Culture for Children* (Novello).
Birch : *The Voice Trainer* (Curwen).
Bordogni : *Exercises and Vocalises* (Novello).

Vocal Physiology.

Aikin : *The Voice, &c.* (Macmillan).
Browne : *Medical Hints on the Singing Voice* (Chappell).
Browne and Behnke : *Voice, Song, and Speech* (Sampson, Low)).
Castex : *Hygiene de la Voix* (Paris, 1894)
Hulbert : *Voice Training in Speech and Song* (Clive).
M. Mackenzie : *Hygiene of the Vocal Organs.*
Michael : *Formation of the Singing Registers* (Schirmer).
Wesley Mills : *Voice Production in Singing and Speaking* (Curwen).

Voice Production.   (See **Singing** and **Vocal Physiology.**

Zither.

German Methods by Arnold, Bennert, Edlinger, Jurik, Rudigièr, Thauer, &c.
Instruction Book (Metzler).

Miscellaneous.

Bennett, Joseph : *Forty years of Music* (Methuen).
Bridge : *Samuel Pepys, Lover of Music* (Smith Elder).
Bumpus : *Cathedrals of England and Wales* (Laurie).
Cummings : *History of God save the King* (Novello).
Donovan, J. : *From Lyre to Muse, a history of the Aboriginal Union of Music and Poetry* (Reeves).
Edwards : *Musical Haunts in London* (Curwen).

Estcourt : *Music the Voice of Harmony in Creation* (Longmans).
Gardner : *The Music of Nature* (1832).
Goodrich : *Music as a Language, &c.* (Schirmer).
Graves : *Diversions of a Music Lover* (Macmillan).
Greenish : *Tonality and Roots* (Vincent).
Hanchett : *Art of the Musician* (Macmillan).
Hatherley : *Hymns of the Eastern Church* (1882).
Hughes : *The Love affairs of Great Musicians* (2 vols., Eveleigh Nash).
Hume : *What Music is* (Vincent).
Huneker : *Dramatic Essays, &c.* (Constable).
Keeling : *Music of the Poets* (W. Scott).
Klein, Hermann : *Thirty years of Musical Life in London,* 1870-1900 (1903).
H. C. de Lafontaine : *The King's Music,* 1460-1700 (Novello, 1909).
La Mara : *Thoughts of Great Musicians* (Augener).
Lavignac : *Music and Musicians* (Putnam's).
A. C. Lunn : *Musings of a Musician* (Simpkin Marshall, 1846).
Matthews : *Wild Birds and their Music* (Putnam's).
Ritter : *Woman as a Musician* (Reeves).
Schumann : *Advice to Young Musicians* (Augener).
Sharp and Macilwaine : *Hist. of Morris Dancing* (Novello).
Stanford : *Studies and Memories* (Constable).
Turnbull : *Mus. Genius and Religion* (Elkin Mathews).
Wallace : *Threshold of Music* (Macmillan).
Weber : *Melody and Harmony in Speech* (Novello).

ADDENDA ET CORRIGENDA.

P. 22. Dr. H. P. Allen was born at Reading, 1869.
P. 33. Aschenbrenner, *b.* 1654, *not* 1645.
P. 36. *Aufspeilen* should be *Aufspielen.*
P. 62. Birthdays : June 26, Mercadente, *b.* 1795.
P. 65. Dr. J. Blow was born at Newark-on-Trent, Feb. 1649.
P. 172. Giovanelli, *d.* Rome, Jan., 1625.

N.B.—Some of the following terms and phrases have been given in the body of the Dictionary. They are included here in alphabetical order to facilitate reference.

Ab'fassen (*G.*). To compose.

Ab'flöten (*G.*). To play on the flute.

Ab'singen (*G.*). To sing, carol ; to fatigue oneself by singing.

Ab'spielen (*G.*). To play, finish playing, fatigue oneself by playing.

Ab'steigende To'narten (*G.*). Descending scales.

Accigliamen'to (*I.*). Melancholy, sadness.

Ad u'na cor'da (*I.*). Same as **Una corda** (*q.v.*).

Affiche de comédie (*F.*). A play-bill.

Air à boire (*F.*). Drinking song.

Airs des bateliers vénétiens (*F.*). Gondolier songs.

À la chasse (*F.*). In hunting style.

À l'improviste (*F.*). Extempore.

Al'la Tedes'ca (*I.*) ⎱ (See **Tedesco.**)
Al Tedes'co (*I.*) ⎰

Al'la uni'sono (*I.*). Same as **All' unisono** (*q.v.*).

Al'le neu ein'tretende Stim'men hervor'tretend (*G.*). Each new entry to be made prominent.

All' Espagnuo'la (*I.*). In Spanish style.

All' improvvi'so (*I.*) ⎱ Extempore ; impro-
All' improvvis'ta (*I.*) ⎰ vised.

Al più (*I.*). The most.

Al so'lito (*I.*). As usual ; in the usual manner.

Alt' otta'va (*I.*). An octave higher (than written).

Amarissimamen'te (*I.*) ⎱ Very sadly, de-
Amaris'simo (*I.*) ⎰ jectedly, bitterly.

A mez'za a'ria (*I.*). Same as **Aria parlante** (*q.v.*).

An'fangs-ritornel(l)' (*G.*). Introductory symphony (to an aria, &c.).

Animosamen'te (*I.*). Boldly, resolutely.

An'laufen (*G.*). Crescendo.

A quatre seuls (*F.*). For four solo voices (or insts.).

A su'o luo'go (*I.*). Same as **Loco** (*q.v.*).

Aus'füllung (*G.*). Middle parts, filling-up parts.

A vicen'da (*I.*). Alternately, by turns.

Be'bende Stim'me (*G.*). A quavering, tremulous voice.

Beck'en (*G.*). Cymbal.
Beck'enschläger. Cymbal player.

Beson'ders gebun'den (*G.*). Particularly *legato.*

Bestimmt'heit (*G.*). Precision, distinctness.

Bravis'sima,-o (*I.*). "Very well done ; " exceedingly good.

Bravour'-a'rie (*G.*). Aria di bravura (*q v.*).

Can (*Welsh*). A song.
Can y Prophwyd Davydd. The song of the Prophet David.

Canta'bile, ornamen'ti ad libitum, ma più to'sto po'chi e buo'ni (*I.*). In singing (flowing) style, with ornaments at pleasure, but few and well chosen.

Can'to lla'no (*S.*). Plain chant ; canto fermo.

Chapeau chinois (*F.*). "Chinese hat." Same as **Crescent** (*q.v.*).

Compiacimen'to (*I.*). Same as **Compiacevole** (*q.v.*).

Con intimis'simo sentimen'to (*I.*). With innermost (utmost) feeling.

Con som'ma espressio'ne (*I.*). With very great expression.

Contadines'co (*I.*). Rustic, rural, pastoral.

Con un di'to (*I.*). With one finger.

Cormorne. Same as **Cremona** (*q.v.*).

Crescen'do e incalcan'do po'co à po'co (*I.*). Gradually louder and quicker.

Crowder, Crowther. Old name for fiddler.

Da ca'po sin' al Fi'ne (*I.*). Same as *D.C. al Fine.*

Da ca'po sin' al Se'gno (*I.*). Same as *D.C. al Segno.*

Da que'sta par'te fi'no al Maggio're po'co à po'co più anima'to e più for'te (*I.*). (See under **Questa.**)

Di bel nuo'vo (*I.*). Again ; repeat.

Die letz'te No'te der Trio'len nicht ab'gestossen (*G.*). The last notes of the triplets not too staccato.

Die No'ten der link'en Hand durch'gängig gebun'den (*G.*). The notes for the left hand *legato* throughout.

Di net'to (*I.*). Neatly, cleverly.

Di pe'so (*I.*) ⎱ At once, immediately.
Di po'sta (*I.*) ⎰

Discio'lto (*I.*). Skilful, dexterous.

Donner du cor (*F.*). To blow a horn.

Dop'pio tem'po (*I.*). Twice as fast.

Drei'fach (*G.*). (See **Fach.**)

Drey (*G.*). Old spelling of **Drei.**

Emérilloné (*F.*). Merrily, briskly.

End'schluss (*G.*). Concluding piece ; *finale.*

Enjoué (*F.*). Gay, cheerful.

Entschlies'sung (*G.*). Resolution, determination.

Ermun'terung (*G.*). Animation, excitement.

Ernst, und mit stei'gender Leb'haftigkeit (*G.*). Earnestly (seriously) and with increasing animation.

Eröff'nungsstück (*G.*). Overture.

Erwach'en hei'terer Empfin'dungen bei der An'kunft auf dem Land'e (*G.*). The awakening of more cheerful sensations on arriving in the country (*Beethoven's Pastoral Sym.*).

Estrinien'da (*I.*). Very legato; *legatissimo.*

Estrincien'do (*I.*). With force and precision.

Et'was beweg'ter schnell (*G.*). A little quicker.

Expressif (*F.*). Expressive(ly).

Far fias'co (*I.*). To make a failure. (See **Fiasco.**)

Far furo're (*I.*). To procure enthusiastic admiration. (See **Furore.**)

Flying cadence. Old name for an interrupted cadence.

Frey (*G.*). Old spelling of **Frei.**

Froh'e und dank'bare Gefüh'le nach dem Sturm (*G.*). Joyful and thankful emotions (feelings) after the storm (*Beethoven's Pastoral Sym.*).

Für das gan'ze Werk (*G.*) } For full organ.
Für das vol'le Werk (*G.*) }

Ganz verhal'lend (*G.*). Completely dying away.

Gewit'ter (*G.*). Thunderstorm, tempest.

Grad'weise (*G.*). By degrees, gradually.

Hoch'horn (*G.*). Old name for *Hautboy.*

Hoch'mut(h) (*G.*). Dignity, loftiness.

Höch'sten (*G.*). Highest.
Die höch'sten und tief'sten No'ten mit Nach'druck ab'gestossen. The highest and lowest notes to be distinctly emphasised.

Hoh'en (*G.*). High.
Die hoh'en No'ten der rech'ten Hand mit ein'igem Nach'-druck. The high notes of the right hand with some emphasis.

Il ter'zo di'to à tut'te le no'te di bas'so (*I.*). The 3rd finger on all the notes of the bass.

Istes'so valo're, ma un po'co più len'to (*I.*). The same beat-note as before, but a little slower.

Lust'iges Zusam'mensein der Land'leute (*G.*). Merry gathering of the peasants (*Beethoven's Pastoral Sym.*).

Major semitone. A diatonic semitone.

Marca'to il pol'lice (*I.*). Emphasize strongly the thumb note(s).

Mel'ophare. "A lantern, inside of which music paper, previously soaked in oil, is placed, so that the notes can be read when a light is placed inside; used for serenades at night."—*Hiles.*

Mit ein'em Fing'er (*G.*). With one finger.

Mit ein'igem Aus'druck (*G.*). With some expression.

Mit ganz schwach'en Regis'tern (*G.*). With very soft stops.

Mit zar'ten Stim'men allein' (*G.*). With delicate (sweet-toned) stops only.

Nach'folge (*G.*). Imitation.

Partitur'-spiel (*G.*). Playing from score.

Pienamen'te (*I.*). Fully; in a sonorous majestic style.

Plus en plus (*F.*). More and more; gradually.

Po'co più len'to che andan'te (*I.*). A little slower than *Andante.*

Pol'iphant, Pol'yphant. A corruption of *Polyphone.* An inst. formerly in use somewhat resembling a lute, or zither, with a large number of wire strings. "Queen Elizabeth is said to have been a good performer on it."

Prim'ton (*G.*). A tonic, root, or generator.

Sans frappé (*F.*). "Without striking." Play the notes evenly, without striking forcibly.

S'attac'ca (*I.*). Same as **Attacca** (*q.v.*).

Sce'ne am Bach (*G.*). Scene by (or at) the Brook (*Beethoven's Pastoral Sym.*).

Schrei'werk (*G.*). "Shrill work;" mixtures, &c.

Silen'zio perfet'to (*I.*). A pause or rest for all the performers.

Si radop'pio il tem'po (*I.*). Twice as fast.

So'pra u'na cor'da (*I.*). On one string.

Sorg'fältig gebun'den (*G.*). Very smoothly.

Sot'to bo'ce (*I.*). Same as **Sotto voce.**

Tut'to ar'co (*I.*). With the whole length of the bow.

Un pochi'no più mos'so (*I.*). A very little quicker.

Völ'ler (*G.*). Fuller, louder.

Zö'gernder (*G.*). Slower and slower.

Zuzam'men-stim'mig (*G.*). Concordant, harmonious.

Zwey (*G.*). Old spelling of **Zwei.**